Affectionately S. L. Clemens

Sept 13/07.

Mark Twain's Library

Alan Gribben

Mark Twain's Library
A Reconstruction

Volume I

G.K.HALL &CO.
70 LINCOLN STREET, BOSTON, MASS.

Library of Congress Cataloging in Publication Data

Gribben, Alan.

    Mark Twain's Library
    Includes Finding List
      1. Clemens, Samuel Langhorne, 1835–1910—Library—
Catalogs.   2. Clemens, Samuel Langhorne, 1835–1910—
Books and reading. I. Title.
PS1342.B6G7   027'.2'7469   79-22518
ISBN 0–8161–8156–X

This publication is printed on permanent/durable acid-free paper
MANUFACTURED IN THE UNITED STATES OF AMERICA

A REQUEST
Additions and corrections for the annotated catalog can be addressed to the author at the Department of English, University of Texas, Austin, Texas 78712, or sent through the publisher, G. K. Hall & Co., 70 Lincoln Street, Boston, Mass. 02111.

Frontispiece courtesy of Mark Twain Papers, Bancroft Library, University of California, Berkeley.

For my parents

J. S. Gribben

Ruth Gribben

who appreciate reference books

Contents

Illustrations

Foreword

Anyone who reads these words will almost certainly be familiar with the substructure of reference tools and research skills of which Alan Gribben's annotated catalog forms a part. But we take this indispensable apparatus too easily for granted. Just as beneath the surface of a city street a material complex of pipes and valves and conduits and cables allows the circulation of the currents of electricity and gas and water that make possible the activities above ground, so the libraries of the world, with their dictionaries and encyclopedias, their catalogs and bibliographies, provide the fragile technical basis for the life of the mind in the contemporary world. A decade ago, when vandals were scattering trays of cards in university libraries, we suddenly became aware how quickly the ranges of books on the shelves would become inaccessible and the functioning of our society be paralyzed if these cards were destroyed or merely jumbled out of alphabetical order.

Alan Gribben's work contributes to the particular part of the collective enterprise of civilization called the writing of history. Thanks to his patient labor, we gain access to the intellectual life of a man who lived in the United States a hundred years ago. It is true that this man's thought had a special distinction, but information on such a level of detail concerning any human being of that era would be of great value because of its contribution to our understanding of our own life and thought. Such knowledge is not antiquarian but historical; it relates the past to the present. Only from the perspective of history can we become fully aware of our own thoughts, because only when we have entered into a different cultural world, especially one that is both as close to us and as far from us as was Mark Twain's, can we recognize fully the assumptions that control our own outlook on life.

It happens, however, that Samuel Clemens was a great writer. He repays our attention not only from the standpoint of history but even more abundantly from the standpoint of art. A knowledge of what books he read is as essential for an understanding of what he wrote as a knowledge of what pictures Cézanne saw is to an understanding of his painting. This fact—which may be generalized as the proposition that artists develop through imitation of or resistance to the work of other artists, their predecessors and contemporaries—is of course what gives Gribben's catalog its principal value. The point needs to be made about Mark Twain particularly because his persona, the mask that he invented for himself, represented him as a primitive, an innocent, a man of no education and no acquaintance with books. This pose was in a sense a collaboration between the writer and his readers: it corresponded to what they wanted him to be because the persona was a version of a major American myth, what we have come to call the myth of the American Adam. According to this powerful cultural image, the Europeans who crossed the Atlantic to settle the North American continent abandoned the complex culture of the Old World, summed up in its written records, in order to make a completely fresh beginning in the New World. "All the past we leave behind," chant the pioneers in Whitman's poem.

It is significant that throughout Mark Twain's life, his first book, *The Innocents Abroad,* which is by no means his best, continued to be by far his most widely read. The narrator of this work, shown a statue of Columbus or even an Egyptian mummy, can ask, "Is he dead?" The dead-pan joke is of course far from simple-minded but it presupposes an American cult of philistinism. To a considerable extent Mark Twain's charm for his countrymen still depends heavily on a tendency to identify him with his best-known character, Huckleberry Finn, the tousled son of the town drunkard hardly able to read who prefers sleeping in a sugar hogshead to being "sivilized" in the household of the wealthy Widow Douglas. (The pressure of this mythical conception is so great that it has generated an apparently impregnable mis-reading of *Adventures of Huckleberry Finn.* To this day, most readers of that masterpiece believe that at the end Huck "lights out" for the Indian territory, intending if possible to stay there permanently, because he is revolted by the corrupt slave-holding society of the Old South in which he has grown up.)

If solid, documented information can make a difference, Gribben's catalog of the thousands of books Samuel Clemens is known to have read should provide a corrective for the primitivist misconception. This work can be regarded as a major effort to rescue Mark Twain from the overpowering Norman Rockwell sentimentality in which he has been enveloped. It will have to make its impact indirectly, of course; it is not likely to reach the mass audience. But it can reach the journalists and writers and compilers of textbooks who control the images that make up American popular culture, including what is taught in the schools. Gribben has done his job, and done it well. Let us hope these intermediaries will now begin to do theirs.

HENRY NASH SMITH
Berkeley, California
January 1979

Acknowledgments

The scholar pursuing a topic that involves Mark Twain is blessed in the number of knowledgeable people across the nation who are eager to assist his efforts. Book collectors helped me more than I anticipated. Reference and rare book librarians devoted much time to aiding my research. Professors and graduate students shared information and ideas. Obviously the name "Mark Twain" inspires generosity across the United States, and while I have tried not to take undue advantage of this automatic cooperation, the scope and complexity of my task ensured that my debts would be many. Whenever feasible I have indicated the identity of my collaborators in author-title entries in the Annotated Catalog, each of which I hope will be taken as an expression of gratitude. But there are a few individuals whose contributions shaped and informed this entire project.

Frederick Anderson, Editor of the Mark Twain Papers at Berkeley until his death in January 1979, encouraged me to undertake the topic as a doctoral dissertation, critiqued drafts of the catalog, and proved himself an unstinting friend of the emerging book.

Henry Nash Smith, Professor Emeritus of English at the University of California, Berkeley, directed my work on "The Library and Reading of Samuel L. Clemens" (1974), one of the last doctoral dissertations conducted under his guidance. As a former Editor of the Mark Twain Papers, he was familiar with the resources that I should investigate; as an exemplary scholar and editor, he criticized my work with insight and charity.

Professor Thomas A. Tenney of Charleston, South Carolina, introduced me to my eventual publisher and instructed me in the methods of editing an unusually bulky manuscript.

Professors Gordon O. Taylor (Tulsa) and Robert Neill Megaw (Texas), together with Henry May, Professor of history at the University of California at Berkeley, read substantial portions of my manuscript and made valuable suggestions.

Professors Edgar M. Branch (Miami University), John S. Tuckey (Purdue, Calumet Campus), Larzer Ziff (Pennsylvania), Howard G. Baetzhold (Butler University), Hamlin Hill (New Mexico), Guy A. Cardwell (Cambridge, Massachusetts), Lewis Leary (North Carolina), Robert Regan (Pennsylvania), and Louis J. Budd (Duke), along with Ellen Moers of New York City, offered timely encouragement and advice.

Professor Robert H. Hirst of UCLA displayed enthusiastic interest in the progress of *Mark Twain's Library* at every stage in the development of this volume, influencing its concept and directions through countless discussions.

The staff of The Mark Twain Papers in the Bancroft Library at the University of California, Berkeley, supplied specific information to enrich the annotation of the catalog; especially generous were Dahlia Armon, Kenneth Sanderson, Michael Frank, Bruce Hamilton, Lin Salamo, Victor Fischer, Rob Browning, and Bernard Stein. Professor James D. Hart, Director of The Bancroft Library, was a learned consultant.

Earlier investigators of Mark Twain's reading were equally generous; among those offering ideas were Professors Harold Aspiz (Long Beach), Albert E. Stone (now at the University of Iowa, then of Emory University), and the late Norman Holmes Pearson (Yale).

Ralph Gregory, former curator of the Mark Twain Birthplace Memorial Shrine in Florida, Missouri; Ann Cameron Harvey, then of the University of Iowa in Iowa City; Robert and Katharine Antenne, Warren Leary, James and Mary Dorrance, and the late Mrs. Irene Leary Stinn of Rice Lake, Wisconsin; Chester L. Davis, Executive Secretary of the Mark Twain Research Foundation, Perry, Missouri; Henry Sweets, curator of the Mark Twain Boyhood Home and Museum, Hannibal, Missouri; and Estelle and the late John Winkler, of Hannibal, Missouri, gave me access to materials related to Mark Twain's library and warmed and enlivened my visits with Midwestern hospitality.

The late Henry Pochmann, Professor of English at the University of Wisconsin, Madison, offered me a series of excellent research reports written by graduate students Robert A. Rees, James C. Stalker, Lewis Lawson, and Ralph E. Sandler. Subsequently Professor Rees conferred with me when I visited Los Angeles in search of books from Clemens' library.

Mrs. Polly Peck, Library Chairman at the Mark Twain Memorial in Hartford, assisted me so frequently during my sojourns there that eventually she and her husband Dexter B. Peck, former Director of the Mark Twain Memorial, became my friends. Diana Royce, Librarian of the Stowe-Day Library in Hartford, proved to be an invaluable source of historical facts about Nook Farm, its residents, and the entire Hartford vicinity. Wilson H. Faude, former curator of the Mark Twain Memorial, advanced my project by every means at his disposal. I am also grateful for the cooperation of Joseph S. Van Why, director of the Stowe-Day Foundation.

Mrs. Peggy Sanford, former librarian of the Mark Twain Library at Redding, Connecticut, helped me in locating and examining the many books that Clemens and his daughter Clara donated, and this assistance continued with Mrs. Sanford's recent successor, Anne Cushman, wife of Professor Bigelow Paine Cushman, and the kindnesses of library sponsors Marge Webb and Dorothy Munro.

Among many cooperative book dealers, Howard S. Mott of Sheffield, Massachusetts, and Charles Sachs of Beverly Hills, California, became valued collaborators.

Mary Gayle, former librarian of the Carrie Estelle Doheny Collection in the Edward Laurence Doheny Memorial Library at St. John's Seminary, Camarillo, California, and her successor, Maureen Duffany, graciously introduced me to the holdings of that impressive collection. I benefited from the similar helpfulness of Carey Bliss, curator of rare books at the Huntington Library in San Marino, California; Sally Leach and Ellen Dunlap, librarians in the Humanities Research Center at the University of Texas in Austin; William Runge, curator of rare books for the Alderman Library at the University of Virginia, Charlottesville; C. Waller Barrett, the famed bibliophile and benefactor to the humanities, who chose the occasion of my visit to donate nearly two dozen books from Clemens' library to the University of Virginia collection; Richard J. Murdoch, rare book curator of the Z. Smith Reynolds Library at Wake Forest University; and Robert D. Armstrong, special collections librarian at the University of Nevada in Reno.

At different points in the progress of this study Sanford S. Elberg, Dean of the Graduate Division at the University of California, Berkeley, granted me funds to help defray my travel expenses. H. Eldon Sutton, Vice-President for Research at the University of Texas in Austin, awarded me funds from the University Research Institute to support my typing and photocopying costs; Professor Roger Abrahams, former chairman of the Department of English, was instrumental in obtaining this grant.

Jeanne Lewis Flattery of Berkeley, California prepared the typescript of the catalog, and I am thankful for her suggestions as well as her good-natured perseverance.

Paul M. Wright and Ara Salibian, my editors at G. K. Hall & Company, skillfully shepherded my manuscript through the tortuous mazes of publication.

Irene Wong married both Alan Gribben and his project.

My hope is that *Mark Twain's Library: A Reconstruction* will in some small part repay in pleasure all of those who have given so generously of their time and talents to help bring it to completion.

ALAN GRIBBEN
University of Texas
Austin

Howells' "Most Unliterary" Friend

"I don't know anything about anything, and never did," Clemens informed his designated biographer with pleasure in 1909.[1] This extreme statement about his lack of literary knowledge summarized a long series of similar disclaimers that commenced around 1890. "Personally I never care for fiction or story-books," he told Rudyard Kipling in that year. "What I like to read about are facts and statistics of any kind."[2] "With modern writers of fiction I confess I have no very extensive acquaintance," Clemens assured a newspaper interviewer in 1895. "I read little but the 'heaviest' sort of literature—history, biography, travels."[3] On other occasions he denied ever reading *Sartor Resartus* or *Gil Blas*,[4] although there is much evidence to the contrary. These repeated professions of ignorance are, no doubt, the ultimate source of the widely accepted representation of him as an unread man, an affected pose which several scholars have inveighed against with little success.[5]

Probably the most frequently cited expression of Clemens' views about literature occurs in a fragment that survives from a letter he wrote sometime between 1890 and 1893. There Mark Twain assured an inquisitive (unidentified) correspondent that he could as easily have written adult novels instead of boys' fiction if he had so chosen, for "I surely have the equipment, a wide culture; & all of it real, none of it artificial, for I don't know anything about books."[6] This declaration comes into clearer focus when it is juxtaposed with his assertion in "Is Shakespeare Dead?" (1909) that Shakespeare, like any other writer, was incapable of mastering the terminology of a profession merely from reading books about it. "He will not, and cannot, get the trade-phrasings precisely and exactly right," Mark Twain argued. For this reason in the same essay Twain lauded Richard Henry Dana's *Two Years Before the Mast,* since Dana "didn't learn his trade out of a book, he has *been* there!"[7] Those who quote Mark Twain's contention that he learned little from books should realize that he was simply trying, as a former steamboat pilot-printer-prospector-newspaper correspondent, to differentiate between actual and vicarious experience.[8]

Nearly two decades after the declaration appeared in *Mark Twain's Letters*

1. Albert Bigelow Paine, *Mark Twain: A Biography* (New York: Harper & Brothers, 1912), p. 1500.
2. "An Interview with Mark Twain," collected in *From Sea to Sea: Letters of Travel.* 2 vols. (New York: Doubleday and McClure, 1899), 2: 180.
3. "Visit of Mark Twain," Sydney [Australia] *Morning Herald,* 17 September 1895, pp. 5–6, reprinted by Louis J. Budd in "Mark Twain Talks Mostly about Humor and Humorists," *Studies in American Humor,* 1 (April 1974), 8.
4. Clemens to David A. Munro, 8 February 1905, ALS in the Henry W. and Albert A. Berg Collection, New York Public Library; Brander Matthews, *The Tocsin of Revolt and Other Essays* (New York: Charles Scribner's Sons, 1922), p. 267.
5. Beginning with Olin H. Moore's seminal essay in the June 1922 issue of *PMLA,* and including Friedrich Schönemann, Minnie M. Brashear, Harold Aspiz, Gladys Bellamy, Albert E. Stone, Edward Wagenknecht, and Walter Blair. (See the Critical Bibliography.)

in 1917, critics began to question the practice of accepting it as literal truth. Inasmuch as the dictum seemed to imply that Mark Twain disdained the kind of "culture" that may be absorbed by reading, Minnie M. Brashear proposed in 1934 that it should be construed as a "half-humorous" acknowledgment of "his sense of contrast between his equipment as a writer and that of Hawthorne, for instance, or his friend Brander Matthews." She perceived that Mark Twain's tendency to minimize his reading "was a part of the legend he deliberately created about himself, either because it pleased his vanity to believe that what he had read had been of small value in his development, or because he knew that he was more interesting to his American public in the rôle of an original, than as a man who had from boyhood extended his powers and his horizon by diligent reading."[9]

In 1962 Dewey Ganzel analyzed Mark Twain's pretense of having slight knowledge about literature with equal acuteness. Twain's "extravagant overstatement" of ignorance concerning books, Ganzel observed, "seems oddly incongruous with the novelist we know Clemens to have been, but it is characteristic of the persona which he fabricated: Mark Twain was the 'natural man' of the frontier, self-taught and full of savvy, possessing an imagination uncluttered with literary analogues. This persona, useful to Clemens, is delightful to us, but it can be misleading."[10]

Scholar-critics intent on looking behind the mask that Clemens constructed can find only a few contemporary comments on the scope of his reading. The most valuable of these is by Clemens' close friend Joseph H. Twichell, whose biographical sketch for the May 1896 issue of *Harper's Magazine* recounted the impediments Clemens faced in 1872 when he recognized that authorship would be his permanent career. "His qualification for it, in the ordinary reckoning, was small, as he perfectly well knew. He was not what is called an educated man. He had no formal literary culture. His acquaintance with books was limited" (p. 818). These remarks were meant to apply only to Mark Twain's handicaps in 1872. Twichell went on to explain that Twain's native talent and newspaper training accounted for his success, and alluded again to his "lack of educational furnishing at the outset of his literary career. That deficiency he has, during the thirty years that have since elapsed, applied himself with large diligence to repair." The Nook Farm clergyman took obvious pride in reporting: "All that time he has been an eager, industrious reader and student. He has acquired French and German. . . . He has widely acquainted himself with literature—modern literature especially—in various departments." Moreover, "he does not in the least share the slighting regard of the learning of the schools which so-called self-made men are prone to entertain." Rather, on many occasions he has expressed "his sense of disadvantage without remedy in having been denied the opportunity of a classical training in his youth" (p. 822). Twichell's depiction of

---

6. *Mark Twain's Letters,* ed. Albert Bigelow Paine (New York: Harper & Brothers, 1917), p. 543, corrected from ALS in the Mark Twain Papers, University of California, Berkeley (MTP).

7. *The Writings of Mark Twain,* Definitive Edition (New York: Gabriel Wells, 1922), 26: 304, 336.

8. Mark Twain made this distinction repeatedly. He once warned an aspiring writer: "The moment you venture outside your *own* experience, you are in peril. . . . What you have not lived you cannot write" (Clemens to Olivia Clemens, 11 January 1885, quoted in *The Love Letters of Mark Twain,* ed. Dixon Wecter [New York: Harper & Brothers, 1949], p. 228). In chapter 14 of *The American Claimant* (1892), Lord Berkeley is characterized as "a young fellow . . . who . . . hasn't any culture but the artificial culture of books, which adorns but doesn't really educate."

9. *Mark Twain: Son of Missouri* (Chapel Hill: University of North Carolina Press, 1934), p. 197.

10. "Samuel Clemens and Captain Marryat," *Anglia,* 80 (1962), 405.

Clemens as a man who was continually aware of, and striving to compensate for, his educational shortcomings seems suspiciously like the self-image that some Nook Farm residents might have preferred Clemens to entertain. It is unintentionally an anomalous description of the comic author who purported to be utterly ignorant of books. But this portrayal as self-educated intellectual evidently did not satisfy Clemens; he was already promulgating his poses as unsophisticated Westerner and disadvantaged student.

Conversations with associates were one means of achieving his desired public image. Carlyle Smythe, Clemens' companion during a portion of his global tour in 1895–96, first introduced in print the notion of Mark Twain as reader which has come down to the present. Inappropriately titled "The Real 'Mark Twain,'" Smythe's essay in the September 1898 issue of the *Pall Mall Magazine* paid careful attention to Twain's "curiously eccentric" yet "entirely serious" literary preferences. "He has a gluttonous appetite for books, but his taste is the despair of his family and friends," Smythe announced. "If he ever had a palate for poetry it has become atrophied, . . . and now the one poet whose works afford him any pleasure is Browning." As for fiction, "roughly speaking, I may say that he reads anything in prose that is clean and healthy, yet he has never been able to find a line in Thackeray which interested him. Addison and Goldsmith are thrown away upon him; and Meredith, perhaps not unnaturally, provokes him to laughter." Smythe repeated a remark by Clemens which indicates his willingness to sanction this picture of uncouth ignorance: "I asked Mr. Clemens one day how he explained this indifference to the acknowledged master-craftsmen in his own trade. The explanation candidly given was, 'I have no really literary taste, and never had.'" Smythe somewhat perceptively added, "Yet this is an explanation whose chief vice is that it fails to explain; for he is a thorough admirer of Stevenson, and reads Mr. Kipling . . . while I have heard him quote both Shakespeare and Tennyson." To Smythe's way of thinking there could be only one reason: his "devotion to newspapers is, I believe, the explanation why commonly he fails so hopelessly to appreciate the masters in literature" (pp. 30–31).

When Clemens died in 1910 his reading habits and tastes received an authoritative assessment that assured the survival of the developing fiction of their limited, eccentric nature. In *My Mark Twain* (1910) his friend William Dean Howells paused in his sketch of Mark Twain to recall the kinds of books he read. Curiously, Howells used himself as the standard for comparison, and matched his own literary knowledge against his friend's as though they had been rivals.

> If I mention my own greater bookishness, by which I mean his less quantitative reading, it is to give myself better occasion to note that he was always reading some vital book. It might be some out-of-the-way book, but it had the root of the human matter in it: a volume of great trials; one of the supreme autobiographies; a signal passage of history, a narrative of travel, a story of captivity, which gave him life at first-hand. As I remember, he did not care much for fiction, and in that sort he had certain distinct loathings. . . . His prime abhorrence was my dear and honored prime favorite, Jane Austen. . . . He seemed not to have any preferences among novelists; or at least I never heard him express any. He used to read the modern novels I praised, in or out of print; but I do not think he much liked reading fiction. As for plays, he detested the theatre, and said he would as lief do a sum as follow a plot on the stage. He could not, or did not, give any reasons for his literary abhorrences, and perhaps he really had none. But he could have said very distinctly, if he had needed, why he liked the books he did. . . .Generally, I fancy his pleasure in poetry was not great, and

I do not believe he cared much for the conventionally accepted masterpieces of literature. He liked to find out good things and great things for himself.[11]

Howells concluded his appraisal with the remark that was to become a mainstay of Mark Twain studies: "Of all the literary men I have known he was the most un-literary in his make and manner."

What Howells clearly intended to emphasize was the fact that Clemens' reading, though wide, was far less programmatic than that of a regular literary reviewer such as himself. But his many references to Clemens' literary dislikes had the effect of strengthening the image of Mark Twain as a writer very little influenced by his reading. Howells suggests that Clemens was comfortable only with biographies, vivid passages of history, and travel books, like a child curious about faraway places and notable people. The summary dismissal of fiction, drama, and poetry as of little interest to Clemens seems to imply that they are beyond his grasp, and Howells' phrase, "some *vital* book," damns with faint praise, connoting as it does the simple and overcolored. All in all, it is a remarkably condescending passage for a tribute written, as Howells claimed, "in a cloud of grief" in May 1910 shortly after the deaths of Clemens and of Elinor Howells.[12]

Had anyone other than Howells written of Clemens as an "unliterary" man, the label might soon have been recognized as ludicrous. But Howells' eminence in American letters and his intimate relationship with Clemens deterred anyone from challenging his judgment. In 1922, two years after Howells' own death, Olin H. Moore traced the doctrine of Mark Twain's supposed "ultra-originality" largely to Howells' comments about his reading.[13] And writing in 1934, Minnie M. Brashear found it odd that "even his friend Howells [should have] thought of him as an adventurer among literary men."[14] Yet the view that Clemens eschewed *belles-lettres* had also been affirmed by another leading American critic. In "Memories of Mark Twain," an essay of 1919, Brander Matthews remarked: "I was not at all surprised when Mark promptly assured me that he had never read 'Gil Blas'; I knew he was not a bookish man. He was intensely interested in all the manifestation of life, but had no special fondness for fiction,—an attitude not uncommon among men of letters. He was a constant reader of history and autobiography, not caring over-much for novels and getting far more enjoyment out of Suetonius or Carlyle than he did out of Scott or Thackeray."[15] Matthews thus applied the final touches to a portrait already sketched by Albert Bigelow Paine in his *Mark Twain: A Biography* (1912) and *Mark Twain's Letters* (1917).[16]

The annotated catalog which follows will reveal how inadequate is this prevailing notion of Samuel Clemens as an unlettered humorist (or rather, how cleverly he promoted this image). The evidence is drawn mainly from an inventory of the books in his personal library, but also documented are instances when he drew upon the resources of public and private libraries in Hartford and elsewhere. It might be supposed that with Clemens' affluence, the ample size of his own library, and his familiarity with the major American and English publishers, he would have found little occasion for using either lending libraries or private libraries, yet there

11. *My Mark Twain: Reminiscences and Criticisms,* ed. Marilyn Austin Baldwin (Baton Rouge: Louisiana State University Press, 1967), pp. 15–16.
12. *Mark Twain-Howells Letters,* ed. Henry Nash Smith and William M. Gibson (Cambridge: Harvard University Press, Belknap Press, 1960), p. 854.
13. "Mark Twain and Don Quixote," *PMLA,* 37 (June 1922), 324–325.
14. *Mark Twain: Son of Missouri,* p. 240.
15. *Tocsin of Revolt,* p. 267.
16. Paine's contribution is analyzed in my " 'I Detest Novels, Poetry & Theology': Origin of a Fiction Concerning Mark Twain's Reading," *Tennessee Studies in Literature,* 22 (1977), 154–161.

are indications that he borrowed books frequently from public and private collections to supplement his own holdings. His feeling of indebtedness, in fact, was great enough to move him, late in life, to make extensive book donations to a community library he established in Redding, Connecticut.

This attitude originated in Clemens' boyhood, and his father was partially responsible. John Marshall Clemens helped found the Hannibal Library Institute in 1844; before that decade ended the organization had seventy stockholders and 425 books. At the time of his death in 1847 the elder Clemens was its president and was authorized to call meetings of the stockholders. Twenty-eight-year-old Orion Clemens made efforts to revive its membership in 1853, shortly before his brother Sam left Hannibal permanently.[17] Although in the intervening years the Institute had fallen on hard times and had lost most of its members and books, young Clemens may have availed himself of his family's membership before the remnants of its collection were locked up for safekeeping until an attempt could be made at reorganization.

Clemens himself recalled that his first experience of libraries was in Sunday-school, where—provided that he could repeat by heart a specified number of verses from the New Testament—he was allowed to check out books for one week.[18] Immersion in those highly moral story-books left him with a shrewd understanding of the Sunday-school writers' motives and techniques, which he burlesqued in early sketches such as "Story of the Good Little Boy." Sunday-school books also contributed to the good boy/bad boy contrast he employed effectively in *Tom Sawyer* (1876), "Edward Mills and George Benton" (1880), and other works of fiction.

During his *Wanderjahr* in 1853–54 Clemens discovered the wealth of books available in urban libraries. On 31 August 1853 the seventeen-year-old typesetter wrote to his mother from New York to assuage her misgivings about his behavior in a large, unfamiliar city. In a postscript he added: "P.S. The printers have two libraries in town, entirely free to the craft; and in these I can spend my evenings most pleasantly. If books are not good company, where will I find it?"[19] Shortly thereafter he wrote to his sister Pamela: "You ask where I spend my evenings. Where would you suppose, with a free printer's library containing more than 4,000 volumes within a quarter of a mile of me, and nobody at home to talk to?"[20] He was referring to the Printer's Free Library and Reading Room of the New York Typographical Society, open nightly from six until ten p. m. for "all connected with the business."[21]

Most respectable hotels in the nineteenth century had libraries, and early in his travels Clemens developed a habit of looking into them. At nineteen, when family errands necessitated a one-night stopover in Paris, Missouri, in 1855, he disdainfully recorded in his first known notebook the two paltry volumes which constituted the contents of the library room in the local hotel.[22] His similar complaint about the

17. Minnie M. Brashear, *Mark Twain: Son of Missouri* pp. 95–96, 104, 200, citing the Hannibal *Weekly Journal*, 31 March 1853. See additionally the 22 June 1854 issue of the Hannibal *Missouri Courier*, which recapitulates the history of the Hannibal Library Institute.
18. *Mark Twain's Autobiography*, ed. Albert Bigelow Paine. 2 vols. (New York: Harper & Brothers, 1924), 2: 214–215.
19. *Mark Twain: Son of Missouri* p. 157.
20. Quoted in Paine's *Mark Twain: A Biography*, p. 95.
21. *Rode's New York City Directory* (New York: Charles R. Rode, 1853), Appendix, p. 36. Professor William Andrews of the University of Wisconsin helped to corroborate this fact.
22. *Mark Twain's Notebooks and Journals*, ed. Frederick Anderson, Michael B. Frank, and Kenneth M. Sanderson (Berkeley and Los Angeles: Univ. of California Press, 1975), 1: 37.

Plate 1: Sketch of Clemens in his library in 1891.
(Courtesy of Mark Twain Memorial, Hartford, Connecticut.)

quality of reading fare at the Deming House in Keokuk, Iowa, became a joke in his 19 April 1867 letter to the *Alta California,*[23] and later was developed further into an episode in chapter 57 of *Innocents Abroad* (1869). He noticed this detail throughout his life; a hotel's library was one of the criteria by which he judged it. On 21 September 1878, for instance, he observed in Notebook 16 that in Milan, Italy, "hotel libraries are only novels & hymn books."[24]

In addition to hotel libraries Clemens also took advantage of the ship libraries maintained by most oceangoing vessels. He scoffed at the anemic collection he found aboard the *Quaker City* in 1867, recalling that the passengers were instructed beforehand to bring along a specified assortment of books to make up the ship library. "It was the rarest library that ever was seen," he wrote in his letter from Jerusalem. "As we neared Gibraltar we could hardly find out from any book on board whether Gibraltar was a rock, or an island, or a statue, or a piece of poetry. . . . We were bound for France, England, Italy, Germany, Switzerland, Greece, Turkey, Africa, Syria, Palestine, Egypt, and many a noted island in the sea, and yet all our library, almost, was made up of Holy Land, Plymouth Collection and Salvation by Grace!"[25]

He derived more satisfaction from the books on board the ships that conveyed him about the Indian Ocean for his lecture tour in 1895 and 1896. On 8 January 1896 he noted that "on this voyage [from Sydney to Ceylon aboard the *Oceana*] I have read a number of novels," adding, "This is the best library I have seen in a ship yet" (Notebook 37, TS p. 3, MTP). A few months later, in April 1896, he commented again on how much reading added to his enjoyment of a voyage: "Seventeen days ago this ship sailed out of Calcutta; & ever since, barring a day or two in Ceylon, there has been nothing in sight but a tranquil blue sea & a cloudless blue sky. . . . Seventeen days of heaven. . . . One reads all day long in this delicious air, of course. To-day I have been storing up knowledge from Sir John Lubbock about the ant" (Notebook 37, TS p. 44, MTP).

Moreover, he always liked to browse in the private libraries of his relatives and friends. Rudyard Kipling discovered Clemens in his brother-in-law's library when Kipling went to Elmira in 1890. There Clemens was perusing the "Mathematics" essay in the Encyclopaedia Britannica.[26] Grace King visited Frederick Church's Moorish Victorian mansion "Olana" with the Warners and the Clemenses in 1886. She observed that following dinner Clemens composedly "shuffled in amongst us in slippers with a big pipe in his mouth. . . . I came through the library after a while to hunt up the others & found Clemens reading some antique book."[27] The superbly drawn descriptions of parlor libraries in Mark Twain's published writings give testimony to the care with which he noted the books in homes that he entered. From the ante-bellum "house beautiful" he meticulously catalogued in chapter thirty-eight of *Life on the Mississippi,* with its *Ivanhoe* and *Friendship's Offering,* to the volumes he recognized on parlor tables when he was a newspaper correspondent in Honolulu (Baxter's *Saint's Rest* and Tupper's *Proverbial Philosophy,* he recalled in chapter 3 of *Following the Equator*) Mark Twain shows how much he enjoyed the game of plucking from a few book titles the whole way of life of their owners.

23. *Mark Twain's Travels with Mr. Brown,* ed. Franklin Walker and G. Ezra Dane (New York: Alfred A Knopf, 1940), p. 153.
24. *Mark Twain's Notebooks and Journals,* ed. Frederick Anderson, Lin Salamo, and Bernard L. Stein (Berkeley and Los Angeles: University of California Press, 1975), 2: 193.
25. *Traveling with the Innocents Abroad,* ed. D. M. McKeithan (Norman: University of Oklahoma Press, 1958), pp. 303–304.
26. *From Sea to Sea,* 2: 180
27. Quoted by Robert Bush, "Grace King and Mark Twain," AL, 44 (March 1972), 34.

During his years of residence in Hartford, Clemens regularly supplemented his own book collection with material from the collection of the Hartford Library Association, which in 1884 contained 36,000 volumes.[28] On 13 October 1884 he wrote to Miss Caroline M. Hewins, who had become the librarian in 1875, to request that the young Hartford sculptor Karl Gerhardt be allowed to charge out books on Clemens' subscription—providing his quota had not yet been reached (ALS in Hartford Public Library). A receipt for Clemens' one-year fee is in the Mark Twain Papers, dated 9 June 1888. The "cash book" for the Hartford Library Association, now in the possession of its successor, the Hartford Public Library, reveals that Clemens paid a yearly $25 membership fee for the five members of his family routinely between 15 June 1881 and 12 June 1889.[29] Memberships entitled subscribers to withdraw ten books at a time. Unlike the carefully recorded borrowings by Nathaniel Hawthorne from the Salem Athenaeum,[30] Clemens' withdrawals are unknown to us.

Clemens also utilized metropolitan libraries in the United States and London. Sometimes he directed his publishers to undertake library searches on his behalf; in 1901, planning a book about American lynchings, he requested Frank Bliss to dispatch a research assistant to "the Hartford library or the Boston Public" to obtain a biography of Owen Lovejoy.[31] In a speech at the Savage Club in late September 1872 he had praised the great library of the British Museum; "I have read there hours together, and hardly made an impression on it," he quipped.[32] He included "London Library" in his budget of anticipated weekly expenses after moving to Tedworth Square in September 1896, and he was delighted to find another library with liberal lending policies: "Chelsea free library. Only one book allowed to one name. But if you really *want* to read, they are glad to make it easy for you. They give you a hint. You take out about 3 cards—I took out 3—as artist, poet, & scientist" (Notebook 39, TS pp. 4, 13, MTP).

The importance he attached to circulating libraries is evident in his defense of them as vital instruments of self-education for the masses. He spoke figuratively when addressing the ceremonial opening of a reading room in London on 27 September 1900: "A reading room is the proper introduction to a library, leading up through the newspapers and magazines to other literature."[33] In Clemens' view a city without libraries betrayed the mental indolence of its inhabitants; this was another thing for which he berated the French. "No circulating (public) libraries," he recalled disapprovingly (Notebook 34, TS p. 4, MTP). On the other hand he enthusiastically jotted down figures for the circulating collections of small libraries he passed on his lecture tour in 1895: Helena, Montana, had 13,000 volumes; Tacoma, Washington, reported 2,264 (Notebook 35, TS p. 27, MTP). In South Africa, too, he made a similar note: "*June 26* [1896], *Grahamstown*. Beautiful town. . . . Is cultured; has a library" (Notebook 38, TS p. 55, MTP). Therefore it is hardly surprising that in 1908 Clemens founded a lending library in Redding, Connecticut. For him the proliferation of public libraries was among mankind's signal achievements in the nineteenth century. Where this repository of learning

28. *The Memorial History of Hartford County Connecticut 1663–1884,* ed. J. Hammond Trumbull. 2 vols. (Boston: Edward L. Osgood, 1886), 1: 541–550.
29. Letter from Wilbur B. Crimmin, Acting Librarian of the Hartford Public Library, to Alan Gribben, 9 October 1973.
30. Marion L. Kesselring, *Hawthorne's Reading 1828–1850: A Transcription and Identification of Titles Recorded in the Charge-Books of the Salem Athenaeum* (New York: New York Public Library, 1949).
31. 26 August 1901, ALS, Humanities Research Center, University of Texas, Austin.
32. *Mark Twain Speaking,* ed. Paul Fatout (Iowa City: University of Iowa Press 1976), p. 71. Twain made the speech on or about 22 September.
33. *Mark Twain Speaking,* p. 341.

and the arts was lacking, the town seemed like his fictional Black Jack, Arkansas, in "The Second Advent" (1881): "There are no newspapers, no railways, no factories, no library; ignorance, sloth and drowsiness prevail."[34]

This affection for libraries is as impossible to reconcile with Clemens' public persona of an unbookish folk humorist as his bibliophilistic attention to his personal library. The passing of time and the surfacing of new materials have enabled scholars to strip away portions of the fallacy perpetuated by William Dean Howells, Albert Bigelow Paine, and other biographical commentators. From the earliest books we now know Clemens to have read, such as George Lippard's *Legends of the American Revolution* (1847) and J. L. Comstock's *Elements of Geology* (1851), down to the book in which Clemens pathetically sought cures for Jean Clemens' epilepsy, John Quackenbos' *Hypnotic Therapeutics* (1908), his appetite for factual, expository writing never abated. But probably the last book he annotated was William Lyon Phelps' *Essays on Modern Novelists* (presented to Clemens on 2 March 1910), and among the books he read shortly before his death was Thomas Hardy's *Jude the Obscure*. These and other titles in my Annotated Catalog of Clemens' library books and literary references reveal how much more widely Clemens read in *belles-lettres* than is generally realized.

Why Clemens instigated the ruse of literary ignorance is a question that involves his perceived relationship with his demotic audience. The author of *Innocents Abroad, Roughing It, Huckleberry Finn,* and other subscription books evidently doubted that his readers would identify with a well-read author.[35] In casting his persona as a common man, Twain was obliged to lower the admitted level of his sophistication about literature. It also gratified him that his public thought of his artistry as spontaneous and nonderivative. Eventually we will recognize Clemens as a writer who viewed reading as an essential daily occupation, who subscribed perennially to numerous newspapers and magazines, who inquisitively sifted a catholic range of reading materials. If his lifetime reading proves to be less purposeful than that of William Dean Howells, a professional literary reviewer, and if Clemens' investigations of various books were impulsive and arbitrary, the diversity and extent of his acquaintance with books nonetheless represented an astounding achievement, even for a prominent writer who resided in the stimulating atmosphere of Nook Farm. This self-education was part of Clemens' determination to conquer the odds against the likelihood that an author of world renown would emerge from early-day Hannibal, Missouri, and it constitutes an impressive victory for the human will in pursuit of intellectual quests.

34. *Mark Twain's Fables of Man,* ed. John S. Tuckey (Berkeley and Los Angeles: University of California Press, 1972), p. 53.
35. Hamlin Hill analyzes the subscription-book readers ("mechanics and farmers") and Twain's popular persona ("a groundling with some literary aspirations") in "Mark Twain: Audience and Artistry," *American Quarterly,* 15 (Spring 1963), 25–40.

Reconstructing
Mark Twain's Library

To reconstruct the library of Samuel L. Clemens and his family is also, in a sense, to evoke the atmosphere in which they lived. Encyclopedias, Bibles, etiquette books, collected correspondence, cookbooks, gardening manuals, fashion magazines, foreign-language grammars, novels, bird handbooks, poetry, songbooks, health-care guides, hymnals—scarcely any of the Clemenses' intellectual, social, and personal efforts, whether significant or quotidian, eludes representation in a catalog of their library volumes.[1] But whereas the libraries and reading of Emerson, Thoreau, Melville, Dickinson, Crane and other major American writers have been inferred or located and discussed by literary scholars, little has been written about Mark Twain's. His collection was dispersed by donations and by auctions in 1911 and 1951 that left few records of his interests.[2] Since 1970 I have been tracking down the more than 700 books once owned by Twain that still exist today, making three tours of the East Coast, several trips to the West Coast, and visits to Wisconsin, Missouri, Nevada, and other states to verify the authenticity of these volumes and transcribe marginal notations that Twain left behind.[3] In the course of this scholarly sleuthing I discovered half a dozen spurious books that forgers have attributed to Mark Twain's library and have sold to private and public archives across the nation.

My detective work paid off monumentally in May 1977 when, revisiting the public library in Redding, Connecticut, I learned from library volunteers Dorothy Munro and Marge Webb that the long-lost record of Mark Twain's book donations had finally turned up there. In the 152 ruled pages of this bound notebook a librarian had neatly inscribed the authors, titles, publishers, pages, numbers of illustrations, bindings, prices, dates of publication, and—most important of all—the donors of 2,315 books given to the Mark Twain Library shortly after its founding in 1908. Some of the books were the gifts of Dan Beard and other Redding residents, but the librarian had labeled 1,751 of them as the donations of "S. L. Clemens" and (beginning on page 118, accession number 1827) "Mrs. Gabrilowitsch." (Clara Clemens married Ossip Gabrilowitsch on 6 October 1909; they left for Germany soon thereafter.) Evidently Clemens donated books to the library in 1908 and 1909, to judge from their dates of publication. Since Clara's donations included a few volumes published in 1909, she presumably went through her father's library at the time of his death and added books to his previous gifts to the community library. The librarian apparently catalogued the books in the order of donation.

An article in the New York *Times* titled "Twain Books for Library" reported

1. Clemens' methods of assembling his collection of books are detailed in my "The Formation of Samuel L. Clemens' Library," *Studies in American Humor*, 2 (January 1976), 171–182.
2. Recounted in my "The Dispersal of Samuel L. Clemens' Library Books," *Resources for American Literary Study*, 5 (Autumn 1975), 147–165.
3. For generalizations about his marginalia, see my " 'Good Books & a Sleepy Conscience': Mark Twain's Reading Habits," *American Literary Realism*, 9 (Autumn 1976), 294–306.

from Redding on 10 July 1910 that "Mrs. Clara Clemens Gabrilowitsch . . . has formally notified the Director of the Mark Twain Free Library here that she will present to that institution practically the entire library of her father, now in the Redding residence, Stormfield. The gift includes nearly 2,500 volumes." As we know, Clara Clemens kept back enough books to furnish two lively auctions in 1911 and 1951, but she may nonetheless have given the 2,500 volumes she promised. The numbered book donations in the extant accession book of the Mark Twain Library end at the bottom of the last facing pages (150–151), as though the record were to be continued in another book. The final title in this column was assigned the number 2315. Various books survive from the Clemenses' donations to the Mark Twain Library which are not included in this list. Moreover, some of them display accession numbers subsequent to those recorded there—Isaac Hull Platt's *Bacon Cryptograms* (1905), for example, is labeled 3549—suggesting that Clara Clemens Gabrilowitsch made many additional contributions. But in the existing record we at last learn the titles and dates of novels by Walter Scott, Charles Dickens, Jane Austen, and many other books strangely absent from Clemens' library when he died in 1910. This list of 1,751 volumes constitutes a massive addition to Twain's known library, even though he may have donated a percentage of them without marking or even reading their pages. (Many donations published by Harper & Brothers after 1906, especially, seem to be duplicates of his previous favorites that he persuaded his publisher to contribute.)

Today the Mark Twain Library at Redding possesses only 240 volumes that can be identifed as books Clemens and his daughter donated. These are now assembled in special bookcases. When I first discovered how many hundreds of volumes had been destroyed during circulation as loan copies, I was appalled. Imagine treating the inscribed and annotated library volumes of a great American writer so cavalierly! Indeed, many current residents of Redding are truly repentant about the careless handling that Clemens' books received from the earlier librarians and their patrons (some volumes were even unwittingly sold to provide more shelf space for newer books). But after the accession record of the Mark Twain Library surfaced in 1977, documenting the donation of the 1,751 volumes by Clemens and his daughter Clara, and upon careful study of the list of donated books, I concluded that the people of Redding used Clemens' library volumes exactly as he intended. He did not bequeath the collection as a monument to his thought and writings, but rather as a core of books for the founding of a public library—a community institution which he always supported wherever he lived. Possibly it was Clemens himself or his secretary Isabel Lyon who defaced some of the volumes by ripping out flyleaves that (presumably) contained intimate family inscriptions. If he considered the presence of his marginalia in the donated books, it was hardly to reflect that future generations of Mark Twain students might lose the opportunity to see them; he most likely believed that the annotations would be instructive in showing library users how to interpret properly the texts that he had marked. Only in recent decades of this century have the cataloguing and describing of an author's library become important components of literary research.

Another cache of books from Clemens' library, ninety volumes given to Clemens' maid and housekeeper Katy Leary (1856–1934) after her employer died in 1910, eventually ended up in Rice Lake, Wisconsin. Now known as the Antenne-Dorrance Collection, these books belong to the descendants of Katy Leary, whose nephew Warren Leary, Sr. edited the Rice Lake *Chronotype*.[4]

4. A checklist of this collection appears in my article, "The Dispersal of Samuel L. Clemens' Library Books" (1975). Ann Cameron Harvey first notified me about the existence of these volumes.

Plate 2: Clemens' library in his Hartford house, where he conducted weekly readings of Robert Browning's verse in 1886–87. *(Courtesy of Mark Twain Memorial, Hartford, Connecticut.)*

The two auctions of 1911 and 1951 and the book donations by Clemens and his heirs widely disseminated his library collection across the United States. At present the following universities, libraries, and individuals own two or more of the approximately 700 books known to exist.

Henry E. Huntington Library, San Marino, California (5 volumes)

Charles Sachs, Beverly Hills, California (5-volume set of Woodrow Wilson's *History*)

University of California at Los Angeles, Research Library, North Campus, Special Collections (10-volume set of Casanova's *Mémoires*)

St. John's Seminary, Camarillo, California, Edward Laurence Doheny Memorial Library, Carrie Estelle Doheny Collection (60 volumes)

University of Nevada at Reno, Special Collections, University Library (6 books)

Mark Twain Papers, Bancroft Library, University of California, Berkeley (127 books)

University of Texas at Austin, Humanities Research Center (31 books)

Mark Twain Research Foundation, Perry, Missouri (12–15 books)

Ralph Gregory, Marthasville, Missouri (7 books that seemingly belonged to Clemens' relatives)

Antenne-Dorrance Collection, Rice Lake, Wisconsin (87 books, less 2 missing)

Newberry Library, Chicago, Illinois (Levi Bishop's *Poetical Works*)

University of Illinois at Urbana-Champaign (4 books, others possibly not yet catalogued)

Professor Bigelow Paine Cushman, Danbury, Connecticut (5 books)

Mark Twain Memorial, Hartford, Connecticut (60 books)

Yale University, Beinecke Rare Book and Manuscript Library (4 books)

New York Public Library, Henry W. and Albert A. Berg Collection, Astor, Lenox, and Tilden Foundations (11 books)

Mark Twain Library, Redding, Connecticut (240 books)

University of Virginia, Charlottesville, Alderman Library, C. Waller Barrett Collection (20 books)

Central Connecticut State College, Elihu Burritt Library, New Britain, Connecticut (7 books)

Wake Forest University, Winston-Salem, North Carolina (15 books)

Kevin B. Mac Donnell, Austin, Texas (5 books)

John F. Fleming, Inc., Rare Books and Manuscripts, New York City (15 books from the 1951 auction)

Elmira College, Elmira, New York, Gannett Tripp Learning Center, (sets of Dickens and Shakespeare)

Robert Daley, Burbank, California (7 books)

W. C. Attal, Jr., Austin, Texas (2 books)

Nick Karanovich, Fort Wayne, Indiana (2 books)

When I stumbled upon such exciting finds as the accession book in Redding, or when I casually ordered a copy of George Combe's *Notes on the United States* through Interlibrary Borrowing Service, and received Clemens' own copy, inscribed and annotated, inadvertently shelved among the loan-department volumes at UCLA many years ago, my investigation took on aspects of a literary detective's case. There were clues, informants, false leads, dull surveillance, dazzling breakthroughs. But if any wrongdoing were involved here, the guilty parties could never be prosecuted; they had merely dispersed for financial gain an author's personal library. And the

Plate 3: Hearth in Clemens' library, Hartford.
(*Courtesy of Mark Twain Memorial, Hartford, Connecticut.*)

only thing that required solving was the contents of this lost collection, now changing locations as ceaselessly as Clemens once did, and attracting forgeries that would have fascinated him. These spurious association copies were easy to recognize; Clemens virtually never signed his pseudonym to identify books belonging to his personal library, reserving "Mark Twain" as an autograph for his own literary writings. A few exceptions—Richard Grant White's *Words and Their Uses,* for example, signed "Mark Twain, 1873" in one place and "Saml. L. Clemens" in two others, and Dan Beard's *Moonblight,* evidently autographed by "Mark Twain" in 1905—appear to be authentic.

Inasmuch as Clemens esteemed the products of the printing press and employed custom-made notebooks, it seems odd that he never pasted any bookplates in his library volumes. (Occasionally people mistake the sale labels of the 1911 and 1951 auctions for bookplates.) But he was scrupulous about designating the ownership of books belonging to his household. Around 1877 Clemens began signing his library books with initials ("S. L. Clemens") rather than the "Saml. L. Clemens" form he previously preferred. During the last decade of his life he usually omitted the first period, linking the initials together with a single stroke of his pen. Pencil predominated in the signatures and inscriptions written in the 1870's and earlier; thereafter he generally used ink—violet, blue, brown, or black—until the post-1900 period, when he favored black ink. Knowing these habits can provide rough dates of probable acquisition for books Clemens signed.[5]

By locating and inspecting all surviving volumes and by reviewing auction catalogs; by examining all of Twain's published and unpublished letters, notebooks, and manuscripts; by exploring newspaper interviews with Twain, records of his household expenditures, family correspondence, and memoirs of his associates; and by reviewing scholarly books and articles that demonstrate literary influences in his writings, I have been able to establish that Clemens' library itself contained more than 2,500 volumes. These findings are presented under author or title headings in the following Annotated Catalog that lists and describes nearly 5,000 books, stories, essays, poems, plays, operas, songs, newspapers, and magazines with which Clemens was familiar. (Of the total entries, 4,135 refer to books that he and his family owned, read, or at least mentioned.) The catalog encompasses Mark Twain's *potential* literary sources, surveying items which were accessible for him to draw upon. The broad scope of this inventory requires the inclusion of many books that were not in his library at the time of his death. Clemens' reading tastes prove to be as variegated, shifting, and inquisitive as one might anticipate from what we know of this restless man's personality and career.

Information in the Annotated Catalog is arranged alphabetically under authors' names. Anonymous works are listed by title. Catalog entries for books give the basic bibliographic data—places of publication, publishers, dates—for the editions Clemens owned or borrowed. These facts were obtained from auction catalogs when the books themselves could not be examined. Where the auction catalog is not specific, I sometimes offer a conjecture as to which edition would most probably have been found in his library, based on information in the *National Union Catalog.* The reader is informed of flyleaf inscriptions, signatures, and marginalia; descriptions of the volumes in bookdealers' catalogs; provenance of the books, if determined; present locations of the volumes; and whether Clemens' original copies, photocopies, or duplicate editions were consulted for this study. Book auction prices derive from records in the Mark Twain Papers, Berkeley.

5. A more elaborate account of Clemens' signatures can be found in my "The Formation of Samuel L. Clemens' Library" (1976), pp. 177–178.

Commentaries on many entries assess the evidence for borrowings by Clemens or demonstrable influence on his works. Much research preceded mine, of course. Indeed, had Mark Twain foreseen the expanding multitude of source-studies devoted to his works, particularly *Huckleberry Finn,* he might have posted a prohibition in front of that novel against searching for sources as well as motives, morals, or plots. The abundance of scholarly studies that defy Bernard DeVoto's edict against source-hunting makes it necessary to refer readers to the list of Abbreviations and the Critical Bibliography for full citations to books and articles. Pertinent discussions by other scholars are frequently listed at the end of entries. One goal of this study is to reduce the mounting scholarship on Mark Twain's literary knowledge to a usable, nonrepetitive orderliness—collating facts about Clemens' library volumes, his reading, and the scholarly publications treating these topics.

While the catalog and its commentaries attempt to be comprehensive, they cannot be truly exhaustive concerning Clemens' reading or definitive in reviewing scholarship. A few boundaries had to be established. All of Mark Twain's own writings are excluded from this catalog. Nor is any attempt made here to record every mention of a writer by Clemens in his notebooks and correspondence; that he met or heard about other authors is no evidence of his reading their books. Business associations are also omitted. Perhaps it ought to be noted that the many chapter headings for *A Gilded Age* are not contained in the catalog; Clemens probably never knew—or cared to know—the esoteric sources from which they were culled by J. Hammond Trumbull. Music compositions are included only if they possess lyrics; they are listed by the lyricist rather than the composer of the melody. Traditional ballads appear under their titles.

It was impossible, of course, for me to duplicate the lifetime reading of someone like Clemens in the space of nine years. Nevertheless Clemens led me up many weed-choked alleyways of Victorian literature and thought, introducing me to odd ideas and characters I would never have encountered otherwise. Often I returned to my annotations of Clemens' library and commented on theoretical relationships between his writings and his reading. However, if timely publication of this volume were to occur, such explication was scarcely feasible for the large portion of his library that surfaced abruptly in May 1977 in the accession record of the Mark Twain Library at Redding, Connecticut.

All authorities advise that origin, overlapping, and borrowing among tales of the Old Southwest are virtually impossible to disentangle. Publications were generally ephemeral, and even the facilities of the best modern research libraries do not provide the comprehensive collections and adequate indexes necessary to understand the true nature of the humorists' interchanges. Consequently it seems futile to attempt to establish precisely the relationship of Mark Twain to writers such as Thomas Bangs Thorpe, Augustus Baldwin Longstreet, George Washington Harris, William Tappan Thompson, and others, though their work was undeniably present in Mark Twain's fund of memories. One may read the tentative calculations of Bernard DeVoto *(MTAm,* pp. 252–257) and Walter Blair *(NAH,* pp. 147–162) with profit, but even these experts remain exceedingly cautious about assigning "influence." Blair simply concludes that "whether his indebtedness was specific in any particular instance or not, there is no denying that in many passages of his works the subject matter and the attitudes of Mark Twain are definitely in the tradition of Southwestern humor" *(NAH,* pp. 155–156).

If tracing humor is like chasing will-o'-the-wisps in cypress swamps, the treatment of folklore in a study of "literary" sources is similarly impossible. While folklore was unquestionably one of his "sources," it was not an identifiable part of his reading. Moreover, several good studies of the folklore in Mark Twain's works already exist. The interested student might begin by consulting Ray W. Frantz, Jr.'s "The Role of Folklore in *Huckleberry Finn*," *AL*, 28 (November 1956), 314–327.

Wherever possible the catalog details the reading of members of Clemens' immediate family, since they often shared their books and magazines. Considering his creation of various child heroes, Clemens' knowledge of children's literature seems crucial to his development as a writer. He often read to his girls from their own books when they were young and he undoubtedly looked into their libraries from time to time out of curiosity as to what the younger audience (for whom, after all, he himself often wrote) was reading. His wife Livy's reading may have had a similar importance for his work; Albert Bigelow Paine claimed that Clemens and Charles Dudley Warner were spurred to attempt *The Gilded Age* as the result of a dinner-table argument with their wives about the inferior novels "in which their wives were finding entertainment" *(MTB,* p. 476). Whether or not Clemens approved of Livy's preferences in reading, he was constantly aware of her current favorites. That his entire family was conversant with the writings of authors venerated in the latter nineteenth century—Longfellow, Tennyson, Shakespeare, Eliot, Meredith, Browning, Kipling—has been generally assumed; but here is assembled a full listing of lesser-known books with which they were also familiar.

Mark Twain's unpublished and often unfinished stories, novels, plays, and essays furnished significant testimony for this study; frequently they contain literary allusions more explicit than those in his published works. But scholars who seek only information concerning his reading prior to 1890 will be dismayed at the relative scarcity of facts provided in this catalog about the periods when he was writing *Tom Sawyer, Huckleberry Finn,* and *A Connecticut Yankee* as compared to the far larger percentage of catalog entries that chart his post-1900 reading interests. The disproportionately greater amount of information about Clemens' later years, following the repayment of his financial debts and his return to the United States, is attributable to several factors. First of all, his immense popularity at that time brought him a deluge of presentation copies, many of which are recorded here. Most of the letters which accompanied these volumes still survive in the Mark Twain Papers at Berkeley, since Clemens traveled relatively little during his final decade and so retained more of his correspondence than was previously possible. Moreover, by then he was such a celebrity that newspaper and magazine interviewers regularly inquired into his literary opinions. Isabel V. Lyon's meticulous journals chronicle his daily activities after 1902, a resource available to us from no other period of his life. Albert Bigelow Paine's biography emphasizes the reading in which Clemens engaged during his four final years, merely sketching an impression of earlier periods. Finally, Clemens' retirement from business affairs left him with greater leisure to peruse the writings of other authors. In the last few years of his life, in fact, he found opportunities to sign the flyleaves of numerous volumes that (to judge from his marginalia and other signs of usage) he had purchased and read or even reread many years earlier. He signed the first volume of W. E. H. Lecky's *History of European Morals* "S. L. Clemens, 1906," even though he had read and annotated the book for many years. His copy of George Combe's *Notes on the United States of America* (1841), one of the books he consulted for *Life on the Mississippi,* bears an anachronistic signature in the first volume: "S. L. Clemens/1909." Students of his earlier major works can only remind themselves that his final library additions may help them understand his long-term intellectual preoccupations; even the titles of books he read in 1910 tell us something about the mind of Huck Finn's creator.

Anyone who might wish to extend the scope of this catalog can pursue the infinite by examining Mark Twain's "professional" reading. In this category are stories and articles in magazine issues that contain a piece by Mark Twain. Indeed, the earnest student should probably consider as potential reading all issues of those newspapers and magazines for which Mark Twain wrote with some regularity—especially the *Atlantic, Century,* and *Harper's.* He must have read many issues of newspapers and magazines that contained interviews with him or his family or accounts of his activities. He subscribed to at least one (and often two or three) newspapers throughout his life. Any of the selections in anthologies that reprinted one of his sketches might have attracted his interest. He undoubtedly read other volumes issued by his publishers, particularly those authors published in Tauchnitz' *Collection of British and American Authors* series, which he is known to have admired. All of these possibilities are omitted from the following catalog in favor of more tangible evidence. The books issued by Clemens' own publishing firm, Charles L. Webster & Company, are included, however, since Clemens oversaw its operations so closely for nearly a decade.

Even with these considerable restrictions, the scope of Clemens' reading as documented in the Annotated Catalog astonished many people who consulted the manuscript of my study before its publication. His curiosity about books, and his recorded responses to his reading, reflect an intellect more receptive to new influences and more critically mature than we have sometimes given him credit for possessing. Anxious to maintain his identity with the relatively unread audience for whom he profitably wrote subscription books, he was always self-conscious about his extensive literary knowledge. Unable to share the opinions of acclaimed critics like William Dean Howells and Brander Matthews, he disguised his own abilities as a critic, creating his "Library of Literary Hogwash"[6] and donning cap and bells for the Boston and New York literary establishments, just as he would eventually act the role of jester for Henry H. Rogers' financial and political cronies.[7]

Sufficient evidence survives, however, for us to gauge the hours of amusement and edification that Clemens privately gained from books—in armchairs and beds, at home and in hotels, on ships and trains, anytime he could indulge a vice he ranked with the pleasures of billiards and cigars and whiskey. Many admirers of Twain prize the rare photographs of him at work writing; we can now begin to value those other photographs that show him engaged in a complementary activity of the creative mind, reading.

6. Catalogued in my " 'I Kind of Love Small Game': Mark Twain's Library of Literary Hogwash," *American Literary Realism,* 9 (Winter 1976), 64–76.
7. See *Mark Twain's Correspondence with Henry Huttleston Rogers,* ed. Lewis Leary (Berkeley and Los Angeles: University of California Press, 1969), p. 5.

A Note on Citations

Authors of Mark Twain studies currently confront a dilemma in referring to literary texts. No authentic "complete edition" of Mark Twain's writings exists, and the numerous multi-volume collections of his works—few with identical pagination—contain serious textual errors, omissions, and major alterations. The solution to these problems is forthcoming: editors for the Iowa-California project, *The Works of Mark Twain,* are preparing a genuinely complete edition of his previously published works, returning to the original manuscript for textual authority wherever possible. At this point only a few volumes have been issued in the series, however.

Because of this prevailing state of transition toward a reliable, truly "complete" edition, I refer to literary passages by citing the one uniform phenomenon observable among the various editions commonly owned by university libraries—chapter numbers. Chapters in Mark Twain's books are usually short enough to make citation by chapter less inconvenient than citation by pages in one among many editions. (I except the Iowa-California editions of *Roughing It* and *What Is Man? and Other Philosophical Writings.*) Thus, my designation "HF (ch. 4)" refers the reader to chapter four of *Huckleberry Finn.*

A table explaining my abbreviations of book titles follows. Footnotes are seldom necessary in citing scholarly books and articles because the Critical Bibliography supplies full imprint information.

Abbreviations

Collections, Correspondents, and Documents

ABP	Albert Bigelow Paine
AD	Samuel L. Clemens' Autobiographical Dictations (typed manuscript in MTP)
Berg	Henry W. and Albert A. Berg Collection, New York Public Library, Astor, Lenox and Tilden Foundations
Columbia	Columbia University Library, New York City
CWB	Clifton Waller Barrett Collection, Alderman Library, University of Virginia, Charlottesville
DV	Prefix designating literary manuscripts in the Mark Twain Papers
IVL	Isabel V. Lyon (see entry in Critical Bibliography)
JHT	Joseph H. Twichell
MS	Manuscript
MT	Mark Twain
MTLAcc	Accession records, Mark Twain Library, Redding, Conn., a list of donations 1908–1910 (discovered in 1977)
MTM	Mark Twain Memorial (Stowe-Day Library), Hartford, Connecticut
MTP	Mark Twain Papers, The Bancroft Library, University of California, Berkeley
NB	Holograph notebook in the Mark Twain Papers, Berkeley
OLC	Olivia Langdon Clemens
Paine	Prefix designating literary manuscripts in the Mark Twain Papers
PH	Photocopy
Princeton	Mark Twain Collection, Princeton University Library
SLC	Samuel L. Clemens
TS	Typescript
WDH	William Dean Howells
Yale	American Literature Collections, Beinecke Rare Book and Manuscript Library, Yale University, New Haven, Conn.

Published Works Cited

(Consult the Critical Bibliography for evaluative descriptions.)

A1911	"The Library and Manuscripts of Samuel L. Clemens," Anderson Auction Company, Catalogue No. 892 (7–8 February 1911), New York City

AC	*The American Claimant*
AL	*American Literature* (scholarly journal)
AMT	Henry W. Fisher, *Abroad with Mark Twain and Eugene Field* (New York: Nicholas L. Brown, 1922)
C1951	"Mark Twain Library Auction," Hollywood, California, 10 April 1951
CG	*Contributions to "The Galaxy" 1868–1871 by Mark Twain,* ed. Bruce R. McElderry Jr. (Gainesville, Florida: Scholars' Facsimiles & Reprints, 1961)
CofC	*Clemens of the "Call": Mark Twain in San Francisco,* ed. Edgar M. Branch (Berkeley and Los Angeles: University of California Press, 1969)
CTMT	D. M. McKeithan, *Court Trials in Mark Twain and Other Essays* (The Hague: Martinus Nijhoff, 1958)
CY	*A Connecticut Yankee in King Arthur's Court*
DE	*The Writings of Mark Twain,* Definitive Edition (New York: Gabriel Wells, 1922)
FE	*Following the Equator*
FM	*Mark Twain's Fables of Man,* ed. John S. Tuckey (Berkeley and Los Angeles: University of California Press, 1972)
GA	*The Gilded Age*
HF	*Adventures of Huckleberry Finn*
HH&T	*Hannibal, Huck & Tom,* ed. Walter Blair (Berkeley and Los Angeles: University of California Press, 1969)
IA	*The Innocents Abroad*
IE	Albert E. Stone, *The Innocent Eye* (New Haven: Yale University Press, 1961)
L1912	Lexington Book Shop, Catalogue No. 19 (1912), New York City
LAMT	Edgar M. Branch, *The Literary Apprenticeship of Mark Twain* (Urbana: University of Illinois Press, 1950)
LE	*Letters from the Earth,* ed. Bernard DeVoto (New York: Harper & Row, 1962)
LH	*Letters from Honolulu* ed. John W. Vandercook (Honolulu: Thomas Nickerson, 1939)
LLMT	*The Love Letters of Mark Twain,* ed. Dixon Wecter (New York: Harper & Brothers, 1949)
LMT	Mary Lawton, *A Lifetime with Mark Twain: The Memoirs of Katy Leary* (New York: Harcourt, Brace and Co., 1925)
LonMiss	*Life on the Mississippi*
LSI	*Letters from the Sandwich Islands,* ed. G. Ezra Dane (Stanford: Stanford University Press, 1938)
MFMT	Clara Clemens, *My Father, Mark Twain* (New York: Harper & Brothers, 1931)
MMT	William Dean Howells, *My Mark Twain: Reminiscences and Criticisms,* ed. Marilyn Austin Baldwin (Baton Rouge: Louisiana State University Press, 1967)
MS	*The Mysterious Stranger*
MSM	*Mark Twain's Mysterious Stranger Manuscripts,* ed. William M. Gibson (Berkeley and Los Angeles: University of California Press, 1969)
MTA	*Mark Twain's Autobiography,* ed. Albert Bigelow Paine. 2 vols. (New York: Harper & Brothers, 1924)

MTAb	Dewey Ganzel, *Mark Twain Abroad* (Chicago: University of Chicago Press, 1968)
MTAL	Arthur L. Scott, *Mark Twain at Large* (Chicago: Henry Regnery Co., 1969).
MTAm	Bernard DeVoto, *Mark Twain's America* (Boston: Little, Brown, and Co., 1932)
MTB	Albert Bigelow Paine, *Mark Twain: A Biography* (New York: Harper & Brothers, 1912)
MTBP	Franklin R. Rogers, *Mark Twain's Burlesque Patterns* (Dallas: Southern Methodist University Press, 1960)
MTBus	*Mark Twain, Business Man,* ed. Samuel C. Webster (Boston: Little Brown, and Co., 1946)
MTC	Sydney J. Krause, *Mark Twain as Critic* (Baltimore: Johns Hopkins Press, 1967)
MTCor	*Mark Twain: San Francisco Correspondent,* ed. Henry Nash Smith and Frederick Anderson (San Francisco: Book Club of California, 1957)
MTDW	Henry Nash Smith, *Mark Twain: The Development of a Writer* (Cambridge: Harvard University Press, Belknap Press, 1962)
MTE	*Mark Twain in Eruption,* ed. Bernard DeVoto (New York: Harper & Brothers, 1940)
MT&EB	Hamlin Hill, *Mark Twain and Elisha Bliss* (Columbia: University of Missouri Press, 1964)
MTEnt	*Mark Twain of the "Enterprise,"* ed. Henry Nash Smith (Berkeley and Los Angeles: University of California Press, 1957)
MTFP	Henry Nash Smith, *Mark Twain's Fable of Progress* (New Brunswick: Rutgers University Press, 1964)
MTG	Edgar H. Hemminghaus, *Mark Twain's Germany* (New York: Columbia University Press, 1939)
MT&GA	Bryant Morey French, *Mark Twain and The Gilded Age* (Dallas: Southern Methodist University Press, 1965)
MTGF	Hamlin Hill, *Mark Twain: God's Fool* (New York: Harper & Row, 1973)
MT&GWC	Arlin Turner, *Mark Twain and G. W. Cable* (East Lansing: Michigan State University Press, 1960)
MTH	Walter Francis Frear, *Mark Twain and Hawaii* (Chicago: Lakeside Press, 1947)
MT&HF	Walter Blair, *Mark Twain & Huck Finn* (Berkeley and Los Angeles: University of California Press, 1960)
MTHHR	*Mark Twain's Correspondence with Henry Huttleston Rogers,* ed. Lewis Leary (Berkeley and Los Angeles: University of California Press, 1969)
MT&HI	Elizabeth Wallace, *Mark Twain and the Happy Island* (Chicago: A. C. McClurg & Co., 1913)
MTHL	*Mark Twain-Howells Letters,* ed. Henry Nash Smith and William M. Gibson (Cambridge: Harvard University Press, Belknap Press, 1960)
MT&JB	Howard G. Baetzhold, *Mark Twain and John Bull* (Bloomington: Indiana University Press, 1970)
MTL	*Mark Twain's Letters,* ed. Albert Bigelow Paine (New York: Harper & Brothers, 1917)

MTLA	Gladys C. Bellamy, *Mark Twain as a Literary Artist* (Norman: University of Oklahoma Press, 1950)
MTLBowen	*Mark Twain's Letters to Will Bowen* (Austin: University of Texas, 1941)
MTLC	Paul Fatout, *Mark Twain on the Lecture Circuit* (Bloomington: Indiana University Press, 1960)
MTLM	*Mark Twain's Letters to Mary,* ed. Lewis Leary (New York: Columbia University Press, 1961)
MTLMusc	*Mark Twain's Letters in the Muscatine Journal,* ed. Edgar M. Branch (Chicago: Mark Twain Association of America, 1942)
MTLP	*Mark Twain's Letters to His Publishers,* ed. Hamlin Hill (Berkeley and Los Angeles: University of California Press, 1967)
MTLW	*Mark Twain the Letter Writer,* ed. Cyril Clemens (Boston: Meador Publishing Co., 1932)
MTMF	*Mark Twain to Mrs. Fairbanks,* ed. Dixon Wecter (San Marino, California: Huntington Library, 1949)
MTM&L	DeLancey Ferguson, *Mark Twain: Man and Legend* (Indianapolis: Bobbs-Merrill, 1943)
MTMW	Edward P. Wagenknecht, *Mark Twain: The Man and His Work,* 3rd ed. (Norman: University of Oklahoma Press, 1967)
MTN	*Mark Twain's Notebook,* ed. Albert Bigelow Paine (New York: Harper & Brothers, 1935)
MTS (1910)	*Mark Twain's Speeches,* ed. Albert Bigelow Paine (New York: Harper & Brothers, 1910)
MTS (1923)	*Mark Twain's Speeches,* ed. Albert Bigelow Paine (New York: Harper & Brothers, 1923)
MTSatan	John S. Tuckey, *Mark Twain and Little Satan* (West Lafayette: Purdue University Studies, 1963)
MTSF	*Mark Twain's San Francisco,* ed. Bernard Taper (New York: McGraw-Hill Co., 1963)
MT&SH	Kenneth S. Lynn, *Mark Twain and Southwestern Humor* (Boston: Little, Brown, 1960)
MTSM	Minnie M. Brashear, *Mark Twain: Son of Missouri* (Chapel Hill: University of North Carolina Press, 1934)
MTSP	Louis J. Budd, *Mark Twain: Social Philosopher* (Bloomington: Indiana University Press, 1962)
MTSpk	*Mark Twain Speaking,* ed. Paul Fatout (Iowa City: University of Iowa Press, 1976)
MTTB	*Mark Twain's Travels with Mr. Brown,* ed. Franklin Walker and G. Ezra Dane (New York: Alfred A. Knopf, 1940)
MTW	Bernard DeVoto, *Mark Twain at Work* (Cambridge: Harvard University Press, 1942)
MTWY	Ivan Benson, *Mark Twain's Western Years* (Stanford: Stanford University Press, 1938)
NAH	Walter Blair, *Native American Humor* (New York: American Book Co., 1937; San Francisco: Chandler Publishing Co., 1960)
NF	Kenneth R. Andrews, *Nook Farm: Mark Twain's Hartford Circle* (Cambridge: Harvard University Press, 1950).
N&J, 1	*Mark Twain's Notebooks & Journals,* eds. Frederick Anderson, Michael B. Frank, and Kenneth M. Sanderson. Vol. 1 (Berkeley and Los Angeles: University of California Press, 1975)

N&J, 2	*Mark Twain's Notebooks & Journals,* eds. Frederick Anderson, Lin Salamo, and Bernard L. Stein. Vol. 2 (Berkeley and Los Angeles: University of California Press, 1975)
OMT1	Van Wyck Brooks, *The Ordeal of Mark Twain* (New York: E. P. Dutton & Co., 1920)
OMT2	Van Wyck Brooks, *The Ordeal of Mark Twain,* rev. ed. (New York: E. P. Dutton & Co., 1933)
OPMT	Arthur L. Scott, *On the Poetry of Mark Twain* (Urbana: University of Illinois Press, 1966)
Pen	*A Pen Warmed-up in Hell: Mark Twain in Protest,* ed. Frederick Anderson (New York: Harper & Row, 1972)
P&P	*The Prince and the Pauper*
PRI	*The Pattern for Mark Twain's "Roughing It,"* ed. Franklin R. Rogers (Berkeley and Los Angeles: University of California Press, 1961)
PW	*Pudd'nhead Wilson*
RL	*Republican Letters,* ed. Cyril Clemens (Webster Groves, Missouri: International Mark Twain Society, 1941)
RP	*Report from Paradise,* ed. Dixon Wecter (New York: Harper & Brothers, 1952)
RI	*Roughing It*
S&B	*Mark Twain's Satires & Burlesques,* ed. Franklin R. Rogers (Berkeley and Los Angeles: University of California Press, 1967)
SCH	Dixon Wecter, *Sam Clemens of Hannibal* (Boston: Houghton Mifflin Co., 1952)
S&MT	Edith Colgate Salsbury, *Susy and Mark Twain* (New York: Harper & Row, 1965)
SN&O	*Sketches New and Old*
SSix	*Sketches of the Sixties* (San Francisco: John Howell, 1927)
TA	*A Tramp Abroad*
TG	Guy A. Cardwell, *Twins of Genius* (East Lansing: Michigan State College Press, 1953)
TIA	*Traveling with the Innocents Abroad,* ed. D. M. McKeithan (Norman: University of Oklahoma Press, 1958)
TIH	Roger B. Salomon, *Twain and the Image of History* (New Haven: Yale University Press, 1961)
TJS	*The Adventures of Thomas Jefferson Snodgrass,* ed. Charles Honce (Chicago: Pascal Covici, 1928)
TS	*The Adventures of Tom Sawyer*
TSA	*Tom Sawyer Abroad*
UH	Robert Regan, *Unpromising Heroes* (Berkeley and Los Angeles: University of California Press, 1966)
W1868	*Washington in 1868,* ed. Cyril Clemens (Webster Groves, Missouri: International Mark Twain Society, 1943)
WG	*The Washoe Giant in San Francisco,* ed. Franklin Walker (San Francisco: George Fields, 1938)
WIM?	*What Is Man? and Other Philosophical Writings,* ed. Paul Baender (Berkeley and Los Angeles: University of California Press, 1973)
WWD?	*Mark Twain's Which Was the Dream? and Other Symbolic Writings of the Later Years,* ed. John S. Tuckey (Berkeley and Los Angeles: University of California Press, 1969)

Book Catalogs Listing Volumes from Clemens' Library
(Copies consulted in Mark Twain Papers, Berkeley)

A1911. "The Library and Manuscripts of Samuel L. Clemens," Anderson Auction Company, Catalogue No. 892. To be sold 7–8 February 1911 at the Anderson Auction Company, 12 East 46th Street, New York City.

Items #1–500 are mostly books from Clemens' library, with the exception of approximately twenty manuscripts and books by Clemens interspersed throughout. The 483 volumes generally contain manuscript fragments added by Albert Bigelow Paine to enhance their value as collectors' items.

American Art Association, Anderson Galleries, "The Mark Twain Collection of Irving S. Underhill," Sale No. 3911 (29 April 1931).

Item #116 is Clemens' copy of Anatole France's *The Crime of Sylvestre Bonnard;* the other items are letters and first editions.

The Bookman, "A Mark Twain Collection," Catalogue No. 25 (1970), 2243 San Felipe Road, Houston, Texas.

Items #328–331 are books from Clemens' library. The collection was formerly owned by William Hill of Houston. Its purchaser was Mrs. Nancy Susan Reynolds of Greenwich, Connecticut; she presented the collection to Wake Forest University in 1970.

C1951. "Mark Twain Library Auction," 10 April 1951, 2005 North LaBrea Avenue, Hollywood, California. E. F. Whitman, auction manager; Frank O'Connor, auctioneer.

The sale took place in two sessions—at 1 p.m. and 7:30 p.m.—at the home of Mrs. Clara (Clemens) Samossoud. Newspaper articles at the time referred to "the sale of 3,000 volumes from Twain's library," but the auction catalog listed only 310 books. Jacob Blanck described the unorthodox sale in the *Antiquarian Bookman* (5 May 1951; also 26 May 1951). Another account of the auction appeared in *American Book-Prices Current, 1950–51* (New York: R. R. Bowker, 1951), pp. 105–106, largely supplied by Glen Dawson of Dawson's Bookshop in Los Angeles.

Chicago Book and Art Auctions, Inc., Sale No. 30 (25 January 1933), 410 South Michigan Avenue.

Items #64 and #65 were books from Clemens' library. Franklin J. Meine was listed as the secretary and manager of this auction firm.

"Deficiencies of Lincoln Warehouse Inventory," 3 April 1947, prepared by the Henry E. Huntington Library and Art Gallery.

This list of items missing from the Mark Twain Papers when they reached the Huntington Library included two books from Clemens' library.

Fleming 1972. "List and Descriptive Material from the Personal Library of S. L. Clemens," John F. Fleming, Inc. (March 1972), 322 East 57th Street, New York City.

Includes fifteen volumes from Clemens' library, most of them originally sold at the 1951 auction in Hollywood.

Hunley 1958. "Mark Twain: A Collection of First Editions, Association Copies, Biographies and Books from His Library," Maxwell Hunley Rare Books

(June 1958), 9533 Santa Monica Boulevard, Beverly Hills, California.
Items #20–153 are books from Clemens' library.

Lew David Feldman, "House of El Dieff" Catalogue (1954), New York City.
Items #229r and #248 offer a total of four books from Clemens' library.

Lew David Feldman, "House of El Dieff" Catalogue, "American Books" (1955),
New York City.
Lists three books from Clemens' library originally sold at the 1951
auction in Hollywood.

Lew David Feldman, "House of El Dieff" Catalogue (1957), New York City.
Lists two books owned by Clemens.

L1912. Lexington Book Shop, Catalogue No. 19 (1912), 120 East 59th Street,
New York City. Christian Gerhardt and Maximillian Harzof, proprietors.
Items #1–29 are books purchased at the 1911 auction of Clemens'
library.

Mott 1952. "A Mark Twain Catalogue" (1952), Howard S. Mott, 8 West 40th
Street, New York City.
Items #21 and #35–97 are volumes from Clemens' library. The
catalog carries no date; Mr. Mott, now the proprietor of an antiquarian
bookshop in Sheffield, Massachusetts, believes that he issued it in 1952.

Parke-Bernet Galleries, Inc., "The Splendid Collection of Books, Autographs,
Manuscripts of Samuel L. Clemens Formed by the Late Alan N. Mendleson,
New York," Sale No. 1719 (11–12 December 1956), New York City.
Items #95 and #130 are from Clemens' library.

Parke-Bernet Galleries, Inc., "Mark Twain Items and Other Americana" (21–22
May 1957), New York City.
Includes three Clemens library books (items #122–124) from the
Harnsberger collection. Also one book (item #121) presented by Clemens
to Elsie Leslie Milliken.

"Retz Appraisal" (1944). "Inventory and Appraisal of the Estate of the Late Samuel
L. Clemens (Mark Twain) Contained in the Lincoln Warehouse Corp., 1195
Third Avenue, New York, New York." 17 January 1944. Charles Retz,
Inc. of New York City. 14 pp.
Pages 4–12 list and estimate the value of the books in the Mark Twain
Papers in 1944. Page 10 simply refers to one group of books as "a collection
of 19 volumes, miscellaneous in character," valued at $7.

Seven Gables Bookshop, Inc., "First and Other Editions of Samuel L. Clemens,"
List No. 3 (August 1972), 3 West 46th Street, New York City.
Items #139 and #140 are from Clemens' library.

Zeitlin 1951. "Books from the Library of Mark Twain . . . Purchased at the Sale
of the Library of His Daughter Clara Clemens Samossoud April 10–14,
1951," Zeitlin & Ver Brugge, Booksellers, List No. 132 (May 1951), 815
North La Cienega Boulevard, Los Angeles, California.
The six-page catalog contains 47 books from Clemens' library (items
#7–53). The proprietors explain: "We were fortunate enough to attend this
sale and obtain a number of books . . . which should be of great interest
to the future students of the mind and work of this great American."

Annotated Catalog
of Samuel L. Clemens'
Library and Reading

Annotated Catalog, A-M

Abbey, Edwin Austin (1852–1911), illus. and comp. *Old Songs, with Drawings by Edwin A. Abbey and Alfred Parsons.* New York: Harper & Brothers, 1889. 121 pp.
    Catalogs: *A1911,* #368, $2; *L1912,* #22, "small folio," $6.50.
    More than a hundred woodcuts by Abbey and Parsons (1847–1920) accompany a dozen English ballads and songs, including "With Jockey to the Fair," "The Leather Bottell," "Sally in Our Alley," and "Sweet Nelly."

Abbey, Henry (1842–1911). *Poems, by Henry Abbey.* New York: D. Appleton and Co., 1879. 149 pp.
    Source: MTLAcc, entry #2130, volume donated from Clemens' library by Clara Clemens Gabrilowitsch in 1910.

————. *The Poems of Henry Abbey.* New, enl. edition. Kingston, N.Y.: Henry Abbey, 1885. 256 pp.
    Source: MTLAcc, entry #2016, volume donated from Clemens' library by Clara Clemens Gabrilowitsch in 1910.

Abbott, Charles Conrad (1843–1919). *In Nature's Realm.* Illus. by Oliver Kemp. Trenton, N.J.: A. Brandt, 1900. 309 pp.
    Source: MTLAcc, entry #1938, volume donated from Clemens' library by Clara Clemens Gabrilowitsch in 1910.

Abbott, Jacob (1803–1879). *Agnes.* Franconia Stories Series. Illus. New York: Harper & Brothers, 1904. 224 pp.
    Source: MTLAcc, entry #1203, volume donated by Clemens.

————. *Ellen Linn.* Franconia Stories, vol. 7. New York: Harper & Brothers, [cop. 1852]. 215 pp.
    Source: MTLAcc, entry #1862, volume donated from Clemens' library by Clara Clemens Gabrilowitsch in 1910.
    Olivia Clemens read to her daughters from the stories about Beechnut, Rodolphus, Ellen Linn, and other children in March and April 1880 (*S&MT*, p. 118). In "A Cat Tale" (written in 1880), Mark Twain's Cattaraugus "had not failed to observe how harmoniously gigantic language and a microscopic topic go together" when he read "the able 'Franconia Series' " (*Concerning Cats,* ed. Frederick Anderson [San Francisco: Book Club of California, 1959], pp. xii, 15).
    IE, pp. 25–27.

————. *Ellen Linn.* Franconia Stories Series. Illus. New York: Harper & Brothers, 1904. 215 pp.
    Source: MTLAcc, entry #503, volume donated by Clemens.

————. *History of Mary, Queen of Scots.* Illus. New York: Harper & Brothers, 1904. 286 pp.
    Source: MTLAcc, entry #1204, volume donated by Clemens.

————. *History of Pyrrhus.* Illus. New York: Harper & Brothers, 1899. 304 pp.
   Source: MTLAcc, entry #1696, volume donated by Clemens.

————. *History of Queen Elizabeth.* Illus. New York: Harper & Brothers, 1876.
281 pp.
   Inscription: "S. L. Clemens, Hartford, 1877" on endpaper.
   Catalog: A1911, #1, $1.25.

————. *Jonas's Stories; Related to Rollo and Lucy* (1839). Original stories issued
separately in six volumes.
   No copies owned by Clemens have been discovered, but he obviously (see *The
Rollo Books* entry) read these often-reprinted stories that included "Jonas a Judge,"
"Jonas on a Farm in Winter," "Jonas on a Farm in Summer," and others. He
considered introducing Jonas and Rollo into *Tom Sawyer Abroad* in 1892 (NB 32,
TS p. 19, MTP).

————. *Learning to Think.* New York: Harper & Brothers, 1856. 192 pp.
   Source: MTLAcc, entry #1913, volume donated from Clemens' library by
Clara Clemens Gabrilowitsch in 1910.

————. *Malleville.* Franconia Stories Series. Illus. New York: Harper & Brothers,
1904. 219 pp.
   Source: MTLAcc, entry #436, volume donated by Clemens.

————. *Mary Erskine.* Franconia Stories Series. Illus. New York: Harper &
Brothers, 1904. 202 pp.
   Source: MTLAcc, entry #435, volume donated by Clemens.

————. *Mary, Queen of Scots.* Illus. New York: Harper & Brothers, 1900. 286 pp.
   Source: MTLAcc, entry #1912, volume donated from Clemens'
library by Clara Clemens Gabrilowitsch in 1910.

————. *Richard the Second of England.* Makers of History Series. Illus. New York:
Harper & Brothers, 1904. 347 pp.
   Source: MTLAcc, entry #429, volume donated by Clemens.

————. *Rodolphus.* Franconia Stories Series. Illus. New York: Harper & Brothers,
1904. 227 pp.
   Source: MTLAcc, entry #1196, volume donated by Clemens.

————. *The Rollo Books.* 24 vols.
   Catalog: C1951, 24 volumes belonging to Jean and Clara Clemens, no edition
specified, #J37.
   The Clemens girls evidently owned all of the books in the Rollo series, first
published between 1839 and 1855. These included the four volumes *(Air, Fire,
Sky, Water)* of *Rollo's Philosophy; Rollo's Museum; Rollo's Experiments,* an intro-
duction to physics for children; the most popular books in the series, *Rollo at
Work, Rollo at Play, Rollo at School;* all of the ten-volume set, *Rollo's Tour in
Europe;* and several additional volumes. Abbot assured parents about the "instruc-
tive" purposes of his books by their subtitles, such as *Rollo at Work; or, The Way
For a Boy to Learn To Be Industrious* (1839) and *Rollo at Play; or, Safe Amuse-
ments* (1838).
   The virtuous little Rollo was well known to the Clemens family. On 29 July 1877
Livy Clemens wrote to Clemens about her reading to Susy "that ever interesting
story in Rollo, 'Little Girl, *little girl,* you have left the gate open,' etc" *(LLMT,* pp.
202–204). This and other comments in her letter seem to take for granted Clemens'
familiarity with the outline of the story; probably he had read it to Susy previously.
He mentions Rollo's mother in "A Cat Tale" (written 1880). In December 1881 he

jotted down an idea for burlesquing Rollo's tour of Paris, Rome, Naples, and other cities and countries with his uncle in *Rollo's Travels:* "Rollo & his Uncle Visit the Hotels. Make a sketch of it," he wrote in Notebook 19 *(N&J,* 2:415). He had another inspiration in May 1887: "Write a Rollo with a Jonas in it who is sodden with piety & self-righteousness" (NB 26, TS p. 46). His references to Abbott's characters thereafter were less caustic: in August 1892 he thought of arranging for Tom and Huck to meet Rollo and Jonas in Africa in *Tom Sawyer Abroad* (NB 32, TS p. 19); in June 1893 he had the idea of portraying Rollo's visit to heaven (NB 33, TS p. 20); in June 1898 he wanted to assemble Rollo and Jonas among other young heroes of fiction (NB 40, TS p. 27); and he listed the *Rollo Books* under a notebook heading "For Cheap Books" (NB 40, TS p. 58) in July 1899, possibly contemplating another publishing venture. He alluded to Jonas and Rollo once again in 1900 (NB 43, TS p. 3).

————. *Stuyvesant.* Franconia Stories Series. Illus. New York: Harper & Brothers, 1904. 203 pp.
Source: MTLAcc, entry #1169, volume donated by Clemens.

————. *Wallace, A Franconia Story.* Franconia Stories, No. 2. Illus. New York: Harper & Brothers, [cop. 1878]. 203 pp.
Source: MTLAcc, entry #1861, volume donated from Clemens' library by Clara Clemens Gabrilowitsch in 1910.

————. *Wallace; A Franconia Story.* Illus. New York: Harper & Brothers, 1904. 203 pp.
Source: MTLAcc, entry #1582, volume donated by Clemens.

Abbott, John Stevens Cabot (1805–1877). *Daniel Boone, the Pioneer of Kentucky.* American Pioneers and Patriots Series. Illus. New York: Dodd & Mead, 1872. 331 pp.
Source: MTLAcc, entry #543, volume donated by Clemens. Subsequently sold to Dan Beard the artist, who lived in Redding, Conn.
The brother of Rollo's creator devoted himself to histories and biographies for adult readers. Clemens was not always pleased with Abbott's writing, however. On 8 June 1883 Clemens was amused by nine-year-old Clara's efforts to comprehend her father's penciled comment on the flyleaf of *Daniel Boone:* "A poor slovenly book; a mess of sappy drivel & bad grammar" ("A Record of the Small Foolishnesses of Susie & 'Bay' Clemens [Infants]," MS p. 101, CWB).

————. "Heroic Deeds of Heroic Men," *Harper's Magazine,* 30 (December 1864), 3–20; (January 1865), 150–166; (March 1865), 425–439; and other installments through vol. 34 (April 1867), 559–571.
Mark Twain intended to quote from these seventeen installments for historical details in *Life on the Mississippi,* but he eventually deleted the sections of the manuscript that relied on Abbott's accounts. At one time he had particularly wanted to use a clipping from the chapter that appeared in *Harper's Magazine,* 32 (February 1866), 302, for an Appendix that would describe the Battle of Memphis; but this portion also was dropped from the final version of *Life on the Mississippi.* Abbott's essays were based on Union war records; each of them described events in a different theater of conflict, ranging from Arkansas to Texas to Virginia to Florida. They display a pro-Union bias (Abbott requested that participants of the battles address corrections to him in New Haven, Connecticut), and tend to imbue the episodes of the recent war with glorification befitting the title of his series. If Clemens did not read all of the installments, he probably studied those that pertained to the Mississippi Valley engagements.

————. *History of Cyrus the Great*. Illus. New York: Harper & Brothers, 1904. 289 pp.
  Source: MTLAcc, entry #1152, volume donated by Clemens.

————. *History of Darius the Great*. Illus. New York: Harper & Brothers, 1899. 286 pp.
  Source: MTLAcc, entry #1156, volume donated by Clemens.

————. *History of Genghis Khan*. Illus. New York: Harper & Brothers, 1904. 335 pp.
  Source: MTLAcc, entry #1155, volume donated by Clemens.

————. *History of Henry the Fourth, King of France and Navarre*. Illus. New York: Harper & Brothers, 1904. 335 pp.
  Source: MTLAcc, entry #1158, volume donated by Clemens.

————. *History of Hernando Cortez*. Illus. New York: Harper & Brothers, 1900. 348 pp.
  Source: MTLAcc, entry #1157, volume donated by Clemens.

————. *The History of Hortense, the Daughter of Josephine, Queen of Holland, Mother of Napoleon III*. Illus. New York: Harper & Brothers, 1900. 379 pp.
  Source: MTLAcc, entry #1160, volume donated by Clemens.

————. *History of Joseph Bonaparte, King of Naples and of Italy*. Illus. New York: Harper & Brothers, 1904. 391 pp.
  Source: MTLAcc, entry #1161, volume donated by Clemens.

————. *History of Julius Caesar*. Illus. New York: Harper & Brothers, 1904. 278 pp.
  Source: MTLAcc, #1153, volume donated by Clemens.

————. *History of King Philip, Sovereign Chief of the Wampanoags*. Illus. New York: Harper & Brothers, 1904. 410 pp.
  Source: MTLAcc, entry #1151, volume donated by Clemens.

————. *History of Louis Philippe, King of the French*. Illus. New York: Harper & Brothers, [cop. 1871]. 405 pp.
  Source: MTLAcc, entry #1164, volume donated by Clemens.

————. *History of Madame Roland*. Illus. New York: Harper & Brothers, 1904. 304 pp.
  Source: MTLAcc, entry #1162, volume donated by Clemens.

————. *History of Margaret of Anjou*. Illus. New York: Harper & Brothers, 1904. 316 pp.
  Source: MTLAcc, entry #1159, volume donated by Clemens.

————. *History of Maria Antoinette*. Illus. New York: Harper & Brothers, 1904. 322 pp.
  Source: MTLAcc, entry #1163, volume donated by Clemens.

————. *The History of Napoleon Bonaparte*. 2 vols. New York: Harper & Brothers, [cop. 1883].
  Source: MTLAcc, entries #1497 and #1498, volumes donated by Clemens.

————. *History of Richard the Third*. Illus. New York: Harper & Brothers, 1904. 337 pp.
  Source: MTLAcc, entry #1166, volume donated by Clemens.

————. *History of Romulus.* Illus. New York: Harper & Brothers, 1904. 310 pp.
Source: MTLAcc, entry #1154, volume donated by Clemens.

————. *The History of the Civil War in America; Comprising a Full and Impartial Account of the Origin and Progress of the Rebellion.* 2 vols. New York: Henry Bill, 1863. (Only the first volume appeared with this imprint.)
Location: Mark Twain Library, Redding, Conn. (volume 1 only).
Copy examined: Clemens' copy.

————. *History of William the Conqueror.* New York: Harper & Brothers, 1904. 291 pp.
Source: MTLAcc, entry #1165, volume donated by Clemens.

Aberigh-Mackay, George Robert. *Serious Reflections and Other Contributions, Etc.* Bombay: Bombay Gazette Press, 1881.
In March 1896 Clemens consulted this "brilliant little book called 'Serious Reflections' by the late George Aberigh-Mackay—the best & delightfulest work in its line that I have seen in many a day" (NB 36, TS p. 55) for information concerning the rank and prerogatives of Indian royalty. Clemens was visiting Jeypore at the time.

Acklom, George Moreby (b. 1870). *Margaret, An Idyll.* Portland, Me: Smith & Sale, 1898. 106 pp.
Source: MTLAcc, entry #2133, volume donated from Clemens' library by Clara Clemens Gabrilowitsch in 1910.

Adams, Charles Abel (b. 1854). *Pete's Devils.* Illus. Chicago: Scroll Pub. Co., 1902. 239 pp.
Source: MTLAcc, entry #1914, volume donated from Clemens' library by Clara Clemens Gabrilowitsch in 1910.

Adams, Charles Follen (1842–1918). *Leedle Yawcob Strauss, and Other Poems.* Illus. by Morgan J. Sweeney. Boston: Lee and Shepard, 1878. 147 pp.
Source: MTLAcc, entry #2131, volume donated from Clemens' library by Clara Clemens Gabrilowitsch in 1910.

Adams, Charles Francis, Jr. (1835–1915). "Of Some Railroad Accidents," *Atlantic Monthly,* 36 (November 1875), 571–582.
Clemens' veneration for Charles Francis Adams' diplomatic achievements could not lead him to excuse the shortcomings of the son's prose. In 1875 Charles Francis Adams, Jr. (1835–1915), Henry's brother, was becoming a railroad expert; he would publish *Railroads: Their Origin and Problems* (1878), would serve as a state and federal railroad commissioner, and in 1884 would be named president of the Union Pacific Railroad. Soon after Clemens read Adams' essay in the November 1875 *Atlantic* he facetiously remarked to Howells that he was worried about "how awkwardly I do jumble words together; & how often I do use three words where one would answer." Alluding to Adams' recent article, he predicted: "I shall become as slovenly a writer as Charles Francis Adams if I don't look out," but then he added that he wrote this "in jest" because he would never "drop so far toward his & Bret Harte's level." He gave Howells an invented example of their type of verbose, cluttered sentence (23 November 1875, *MTHL,* p. 112).
Clemens probably felt that Adams' article did not merit its appearance in the same issue in which installments of Howells' *Private Theatricals* and Henry James' *Roderick Hudson* were published. Adams' piece merely related the details of six well-known rail accidents that resulted in deaths. His very first sentence would have prompted Clemens to reach for a pencil to mark revisions: "The assertion has a strange, at first, indeed, almost a harsh and brutal sound, and yet it is unquestion-

ably true, that, so far as the general welfare, the common good of mankind is concerned, few lives are so profitably expended as those of the unfortunate victims of
railroad accidents" (p. 571). Adams' optimism sprang from his belief that each
accident and its resultant investigation brought about new precautions and safety
inventions. Clemens—who rode railways regularly—might have shared Adams'
appreciation for this progress, but he was offended by such periphrastic sentences.

Adams, Edward Payson. *Story Sermons from Les Misérables*. Illus. by Sarah Taylor
Adams. Rochester, N.Y.: Western New York Institution for Deaf Mutes, 1895.
152 pp.
    Source: MTLAcc, entry #1863, volume donated from Clemens' library by
Clara Clemens Gabrilowitsch in 1910.

Adams, Henry (1838–1918). *Democracy, An American Novel*. New York: H. Holt
and Co., 1880. 374 pp. Reissued 1883.
    Clemens entered the title and publisher of this work in Notebook 22 (TS p. 36)
in 1884, apparently unaware of the identity of its author. *Democracy* had been
published anonymously, and was mistakenly assumed by many to be the work of
either John Hay or Clarence King.
    Critics have been baffled and displeased by the lack of evidence indicating that
Adams and Clemens knew each other. An illuminating study of thematic parallels
in the two men's writings is available in Tony Tanner's "The Lost America—The
Despair of Henry Adams and Mark Twain" (1961). Tanner thought it "strange
that Adams and Clemens never seem to have met," especially since they are "two
of the most notable alienated figures of their age" (p. 309). Tanner speculated that
Mark Twain's selecting the name Henry Adams to use in section 6 of "What Is
Man?" (written in 1905) resulted from his knowledge of the real Henry Adams.
But Paul Baender—*What Is Man? and Other Philosophical Writings*, Iowa-California Edition, p. 553—effectively refutes this hypothesis, showing that Adams and
another name employed in "What Is Man?" had been previously invented and
utilized in Twain's fiction.
    Charles Vandersee ("The Mutual Awareness of Mark Twain and Henry Adams,"
1968) discovered that, contrary to the widely shared supposition, Mark Twain and
Henry Adams did meet at least once—on 28 January 1886 in the home of John
Hay in Washington, D.C. Mark Twain was visiting the capital for a Senate committee hearing on copyright legislation. Unfortunately Vandersee then tries to depict
this single conversation as the basis for Twain's using a fictional Henry Adams to
represent an unhappy man in "What Is Man?" Vandersee also finds significance
in Mark Twain's naming a character Henry Adams in "The £1,000,000 Bank-
Note (1892)," though he concedes that this Adams is unlike the real man in
every respect. The fact is that Twain had a lifelong affinity for the name
"Adam," and the name of Henry Adams probably occurred to him simply as
a convenient designation for an Anglo-American. Not every literary character's
name is pregnant with hidden meanings. Mark Twain's reliance on the name in
1892 most likely proves nothing except that the actual Adams was only an ephemeral acquaintance: Twain invariably displayed a delicate reluctance to allude to
people in print whom he knew even slightly—especially in regard to using their
names for literary characters.

Adams, John (1735–1826). *Familiar Letters of John Adams and His Wife Abigail
    Adams, During the Revolution. With a Memoir of Mrs. Adams*. Ed. by Charles
    Francis Adams. New York: Hurd and Houghton, 1876. 424 pp.
    Inscription: on title page, black ink, probably Livy's hand: "S. L. Clemens/
Hartford".
    Marginalia: a few pencil markings.
    Location: Mark Twain Library, Redding, Connecticut.
    Copy examined: Clemens' copy.

On page 9 Clemens drew a heavy pencil bracket around the portion of the paragraph in John Adams' letter of 2 July 1774 in which Adams advised his wife to keep his letters in a safe and preserve them, since "they may exhibit to our posterity a kind of picture of the manners, opinions, and principles of these times of perplexity, danger, and distress." Clemens held the editor of their correspondence, Charles Francis Adams (1807–1886), in high regard; during a newspaper interview in 1876 he spoke of him as "a pure man, a proved statesman" ("Political Views of a Humorist," New York *Herald,* 28 August 1876).

Adams, (Sir) John (1857–1934). *The Herbartian Psychology Applied to Education, Being a Series of Essays Applying the Psychology of Johann Friedrich Herbart.* Boston: D. C. Heath & Co., 1897. 284 pp. English edition: London: Isbister, 1897. 284 pp.

Adams sent Clemens a copy of his book in 1898. On 5 December 1898 Clemens wrote from a Vienna hotel to praise the book and express agreement with its principles. Adams was then on the faculty of the Free Church Training College in Glasgow. Clemens' letter was published in part by Adams in his *Everyman's Psychology* (New York: Doubleday, Doran, 1929), pp. 202–203; more recently Lawrence Clark Powell published its entire text in "An Unpublished Mark Twain Letter," *AL,* 13 (January 1942), 405–407. Clemens informed Adams that he had taken the book to bed with him for a day and thus "was able to read to page 232 without a break—an uninterrupted view" (Powell, pp. 405–406). He mentioned a "mind-scheme" of his own he had written the previous summer, but claimed that "(shall I confess it?) I have never read Locke nor any other of the many philosophers quoted by you" (p. 406). Clemens seemed to assume that Adams would concur with his own theory that "man's proudest possession—his mind—is a mere machine."

John S. Tuckey has traced the influence of Adams' book on Mark Twain's "The Great Dark" (written 1898), which treats the dream psychology of the mind (*WWD?,* p. 17). Subsequently Clemens met Adams in London, on 2 June 1900 (NB 43, TS p. 14). But Clemens' copy of *Herbartian Psychology* has never been found. He mentioned in his letter that he was reading slowly in order to "make marginal notes" in the volume.

Despite Mark Twain's enthusiasm for Adams' treatise, in 1911 Adams would publish an extremely unsympathetic criticism of "What Is Man?" Adams dismissed Twain's entire dialogue in "Mark Twain as Psychologist," *The Bookman* (London) 39 (March 1911), 270–272: Twain's style was unsuited for "this class of composition" and he was obviously "working in an unfamiliar medium." Mark Twain's basic assumption of man's dual mental nature Adams rejected outright. He concluded by advising readers to avoid this "discouraging" book; "we can well believe that many temperaments will be greatly depressed by Twain's ingenious pages."

Adams, Joseph Henry (b. 1867). *Harper's Machinery Book for Boys.* Half-title: Harper's Practical Books for Boys. Illus. New York: Harper & Bothers, 1909. 373 pp.
Source: MTLAcc, entry #1181, volume donated by Clemens.

Adams, Myron (1841–1895). *The Continuous Creation; An Application of the Evolutionary Philosophy to the Christian Religion.* Boston: Houghton, Mifflin and Co., 1889. 259 pp.
Source: MTLAcc, entry #795, volume donated by Clemens.

Adams, Sarah (Flower) (1805–1848). "Nearer, my God, to thee" (hymn, 1841). The dying Helen in "Was It Heaven? or Hell?" (1902) hears the organ music from her daughter's funeral downstairs: "Why—it is a hymn! and the sacredest of all, the most touching, the most consoling. . . . 'Nearer, my God, to Thee,/Nearer to Thee,/E'en though it be a cross/That raiseth me.' " Mark Twain counted on this passage, occurring near the end of his story, to wring his readers' emotions. The hymn had gained enduring popularity in 1859, when Lowell Mason set it to music. By merely quoting its first stanza Mark Twain could evoke the melody and its associations with Christian faith and the pathos of bereavement.

Addison, Joseph (1672–1719). Minnie M. Brashear saw traces of the "character" essays from Addison and Richard Steele's *Spectator* in Mark Twain's earliest sketches, including his portrayal of Jim Smiley (*MTSM*, p. 228), though Twain seldom alluded to either writer. In "A Memorable Midnight Experience" (1874) he mentioned seeing Addison's monument in Westminster Abbey—a complimentary reference; but in chapter 36 of *A Tramp Abroad* (1880) he comically attributed the phrase "up a stump" to the English essayist. Carlyle Smythe believed that he was translating Mark Twain's genuine sentiments in 1898 when he observed that "Addison and Goldsmith are thrown away upon him" ("The Real 'Mark Twain,' " p. 31). This may be another instance where Clemens' early veneration gave way to a hostile re-estimate at a later period, but Addison hardly seems to have been a vital part of his literary development.

Ade, George (1866–1944). *Fables in Slang* (1899). Livy Clemens noted on 19 June 1902 that "Mr. George Ade (author of Fables in Slang)" joined Dr. Clarence Rice and Rodman Gilder for luncheon with the Clemenses at their Riverdale home (OLC's Diary, DV 161, MTP). The opening sketch in *Fables,* "The Fable of the Visitor Who Got a Lot for Three Dollars," describes a phrenologist who delivered invariably favorable opinions of his clients' skulls; Ade drew the characteristic moral that "A good Jolly is worth Whatever you Pay for it" (*Fables in Slang* [Chicago: Herbert S. Stone,1900], p. 7). Mark Twain depicted a strikingly similar phrenological charlatan in Book II (chapter 2) of his travesty of history textbooks, "The Secret History of Eddypus, the World-Empire," written in 1901 and 1902 (*FM*, pp. 349–353).

Gribben, "Mark Twain, Phrenology and the 'Temperaments': A Study of Pseudoscientific Influence" (1972).

————. *Forty Modern Fables.* New York: R. H. Russell, [cop. 1900]. 303 pp.
Source: MTLAcc, entry #1508, volume donated by Clemens.

————. *More Fables.* Illus. by Clyde J. Newman. New York: Duffield & Co., 1906.
Inscription: front free endpaper signed in pencil: "Gerald R. Maloney."
Marginalia: Mrs. Katharine Antenne reports that a pencil sketch on the front pastedown endpaper depicts a rakish young man wearing a Panama hat and smoking a cigarette. Someone has printed the name "Mr. Knight Byrd" beneath the picture.
Location: Antenne-Dorrance Collection, Rice Lake, Wisconsin.
Copy examined: none. Clemens' copy was temporarily lost in 1970 when I visited Rice Lake; subsequently the book was discovered in a school library in Eau Claire, Wisconsin and was restored to the Antenne-Dorrance Collection in 1971. Ann Cameron Harvey's checklist of the collection in 1966 stated that this volume contained no markings, so the penciled signature and drawing may have been added while the book was missing.

————. *People You Know*. Illus. by John T. McCutcheon and others. New York: R. H. Russell, 1903. 224 pp.
Source: MTLAcc, entry #1352, volume donated by Clemens.

————. *Pink Marsh. A Story of the Streets and Town*. Illus. by John T. McCutcheon. New York: Grosset & Dunlap, [cop. 1897]. 196 pp.
Inscription: signed "S. L. Clemens, 1905, Dec. 29. From Wm. Dean Howells" on front pastedown endpaper.
Catalog: C1951, #47c, sold for $12.50. Listed among books signed by Mark Twain.
Location: Franklin Meine Collection, University of Illinois at Urbana-Champaign.
Copy examined: none. Items in the Meine Collection were not available for inspection between 1970 and 1978, while they were being catalogued following their purchase.
Clemens may not have encountered this book until Howells sent him a copy in 1905. On 22 July 1908 he wrote to Howells from Redding: "Thank you once more for introducing me to the incomparable Pink Marsh. I have been reading him again after this long interval, & my admiration of the book has overflowed all limits, all frontiers. I have personally known each of the characters in the book & can testify that they are all true to the facts, & as exact as if they had been drawn to scale" *(MTHL*, p. 832). He also praised the illustrator, whom he declared to be "the peer of the writer." Ade based his novel about a Negro bootblack who becomes a railroad porter on a series of sketches he had written for the Chicago *Record,* and Mark Twain evidently welcomed a book in dialect that dealt with a Negro of the urban North. "Pink—oh, the shiftless, worthless, lovable black darling! Howells, he deserves to live forever," he declared *(MTHL,* p. 832). In his Autobiographical Dictation of 31 July 1906 Mark Twain mentioned Ade as a notable American humorist.

————. *True Bills*. Illus. New York: Harper & Brothers, 1904. 154 pp.
Source: MTLAcc, entry #1351, volume donated by Clemens.

Adventures at Sea, by F.[rank] H. Converse, John R. Coryell, Rear-Admiral T. H. Stevens, Maria Louise Pool, and Others. Illus. New York: Harper & Brothers, 1908. 198 pp.
Source: MTLAcc, entry #519, volume donated by Clemens.

Adventures in Field and Forest, by Frank H.[amilton] Spearman [1859–1937], Harold Martin, F. S. Palmer, William Drysdale, and Others. Illus. New York: Harper & Brothers, 1909. 212 pp.
Source: MTLAcc, entry #1200, volume donated by Clemens.

Adventures of Famous Travellers in Many Lands, with Descriptions of Manners, Customs, and Places. Thrilling Adventures on Land and Sea. Illus. New York: W. L. Allison Co., [18—]. 299 pp.
Source: MTLAcc, entry #1867, volume donated from Clemens' library by Clara Clemens Gabrilowitsch in 1910. Jean Clemens' copy.

Adventures with Indians, by Philip V. Mighels, W. O. Stoddard, Major G. B. Davis, U.S.A., Frances McElrath, and Others. Harper's Adventures Series. Illus. New York: Harper & Brothers, 1908. 234 pp.
Source: MTLAcc, entry #417, volume donated by Clemens.

Aesop. *Aesop's Fables. A New Edition, with Proverbs and Applications. With Over One-Hundred Illustrations*. London: Bliss, Sands & Co., 1897.
Location: formerly part of the Antenne-Dorrance Collection, Rice Lake, Wis-

consin, but now missing. The book was present when Ann Cameron Harvey compiled a checklist of the Antenne-Dorrance Collection in 1966; it was missing when I visited Rice Lake in 1970. Ms. Harvey's notes have furnished the information for this entry, supplemented by the *British Museum General Catalogue of Printed Books*, 2:309.

Minnie M. Brashear has commented on a puzzling incongruity: despite Mark Twain's experiments with fables such as "The Five Boons of Life" (and in spite of his ability to fashion anecdotes about animals, I might add), "no reference to Aesop or La Fontaine is to be found in his writings" *(MTSM*, p. 233). My research substantiates her finding.

—————. *Bewick's Select Fables of Aesop and Others. . . . I. Fables Extracted from Dodsley's (Select Fables of Aesop). II. Fables with Reflections [selected from S. Croxall's translation of Aesop]. . . . III. Fables in Verse. To Which Are Prefixed, the Life of Aesop, and an Essay upon Fable by Oliver Goldsmith. . . . Faithfully Reprinted from the Rare Newcastle Edition Published by T. Saint in 1784. With the Original Wood Engravings by Thomas Bewick [1753-1828], and an Illustrated Preface by Edwin Pearson.* London: Bickers & Son, [1871]. Reprinted in 1878 by Longman & Company of London. 312 pp.
  Catalog: A1911, #39, $2.50: "4to, half roan (binding broken). London, n.d."

—————. *The Fables of Aesop.* New York: Hurd & Houghton, [cop. 1865]. 311 pp.
  Source: MTLA, entry #2160, volume donated from Clemens' library by Clara Clemens Gabrilowitsch in 1910.
  On 14 July 1880 Estes & Lauriat of Boston billed Clemens the amount of $1.35 for "1 Aesop," very likely this book. Clemens paid for it on 20 July 1880 (MTP Receipts File).

Aflalo, Frederick George. *A Sketch of the Natural History of Australia, with Some Notes on Sport.* Illus. by F. Seth. London: Macmillan and Co., 1896. 307 pp.
  Mark Twain requested a copy of this book from Chatto & Windus on 13 November 1896, supplying the name of its author, title, and publisher (Berg Collection). He was engaged in writing *Following the Equator* at a London address.

Agassiz, (Mrs.) Elizabeth Cabot (Cary) (1822–1907), ed. *Louis Agassiz, His Life and Correspondence.* 2 vols. Boston: Houghton, Mifflin and Co., 1885. Reprinted 1886, 1887, 1888, 1890, etc.
  This book probably helped alter Mark Twain's attitude toward Louis Agassiz (1807–1873), the famous naturalist. In Twain's early writings he employed Agassiz' name for comic effect; in a letter to the *Alta California* on 6 June 1867 he claimed that he had mistaken Bladder-nose Jake in Harry Hill's saloon for Professor Agassiz of Harvard *(MTTMB*, pp. 270–274). He had similar fun with Agassiz' serious-minded pursuits in "Concerning a Rumor," a piece published in the January 1871 issue of *The Galaxy;* pretending to refute a rumor that Agassiz was losing his sanity, he explained that Agassiz' eccentric behavior merely resulted from his efforts to catch and identify the thousand varieties of flies. But after Mark Twain read the biography written and edited by Agassiz' wife, his tone became more respectful. He referred to the book in January 1898 while he was living in London: "You have an instance of this [X-ray vision] in the biography of Agassiz. In a dream he *saw through* the stone that contained a fossil shell, & woke up & drew a picture of that shell; & when he broke open the stone, his picture was correct" (NB40, *MTN*, p. 350). Livy Clemens wrote to Clara on 10 July 1903 about her admiration for Agassiz' fortitude in facing the prospect of blindness when he was a young man; he practiced the study of fossils by touch alone so that he would not be forced to give up his career (TS in MTP). In Notebook 48, probably in 1906, Clemens wrote regretfully, "I heard Phillips & Agassiz only once" (TS p. 10).

Aguilar, Grace (1816–1847). *The Days of Bruce; A Story from Scottish History* (1834). Often reprinted in the 1870's and 1880's.

This tale of the Scottish struggle for independence in the fourteenth century had great appeal for the Clemens girls, perhaps because its central charatcers included three dauntless women. Livy Clemens recorded in her diary on 12 July 1885 that she and her children "are reading together" this book at Quarry Farm, and that they are enjoying it "very much" (DV 161, MTP). Many years later Clara recalled *The Days of Bruce* as one of the girls' favorite books, and implied that her father sometimes read it to them (*MFMT*, p. 25). In the summer of 1885 the Clemens children named their Quarry Farm playhouse "Ellerslie" from this novel (*MTB*, p. 824; *S&MT*, p. 204).

Ahn, Franz (1796–1865). *Ahn's First German Book, Being the First Division of Ahn's Rudiments of the German Language.* Ed. by P. Henn. New York: E. Steiger & Co., [cop. 1873].

Inscription: signed on front pastedown endpaper, "S. L. Clemens, Hartford, Feb. 2, '76".

Marginalia: numerous notes by Clemens. On page 63 beside "Here they are" Clemens wrote "I say Hier sind sie."

Catalog: A1911, #233, $1.50.

————. *Ahn's First German Book.* Ed. by Peter Henn. New York: E. Steiger, 1873. 64 pp.

Source: MTLAcc, entry #368, volume donated by Clemens.

————. *Ahn's Second German Book.* Ed. by Peter Henn. New York: E. Steiger, 1873. 194 pp.

Source: MTLAcc, entry #369, volume donated by Clemens.

Aiken, George L. (1830–1876). *Uncle Tom's Cabin; or, Life Among the Lowly* (play, prod. New York, 1853).

Clemens probably was introduced to Harriet Beecher Stowe's novel through this crude adaptation for the stage written by Aiken, a dime-novelist. In his letter of 2 February 1867 to the *Alta California* Clemens recalled his first sojourn in New York City: "When I was here in '53, . . . 'Uncle Tom's Cabin' was in full blast . . . and had already run one hundred and fifty nights. Everybody went there in elegant toilettes and cried over Tom's griefs. But now. . . . Uncle Tom draws critical, self-possessed groups of negroes and children at Barnum's Museum" (*MTTMB*, p. 84).

Aikin, Lucy. *Memoirs of the Court of King James the First.* 2 vols. Boston: Wells & Lilly, 1822.

Catalog: A1911, #3, $4.50 ("2 vols, 8vo, calf").

————. *Memoirs of the Court of Queen Elizabeth.* Philadelphia: Abraham Small, 1823.

Roger Salomon's introduction to the forthcoming Iowa-California edition of *The Prince and the Pauper* identifies this as one of the background books to which Mark Twain referred in his working notes for the novel (DV115; Salomon's TS in MTP). Salomon points out that Mark Twain ultimately mentioned the young Elizabeth in the novel far less frequently than he originally intended.

Ainsworth, William Harrison (1805–1882). *Jack Sheppard; A Romance.* Illus. by George Cruikshank. [First ed. pub. in London, 1839; reprinted by various publishers in England and the United States.]

Inscription: flyleaf signed "S. L. Clemens, London, 1874."

Catalog: A1911, #4, $5 ("London, n.d."; "8vo, cloth").

Clemens was familiar with this idealized story of criminal life long before he purchased a copy in London; in an early character sketch entitled "Jul'us Caesar" (1856?) he ridiculed a possibly fictional boardinghouse lodger who "was decidedly literary, after a fashion of his own, and . . . such instructive and entertaining books as . . . 'Jack Sheppard,' &c., &c., were food and drink to his soul" (TS in MTP, DV400).

————. *The Lord Mayor of London; or, City Life in the Last Century.* Copyright Edition. 2 vols. Collection of British Authors Series. Leipzig: B. Tauchnitz, 1862. 314 pp.
   Source: MTLAcc, entries #1830 and #1831, volumes donated from Clemens' library by Clara Clemens Gabrilowitsch in 1910.

Alcott, Louisa May (1832–1888). *Little Men* (1871).
   Coleman O. Parsons concedes his "purely conjectural" basis for supposing that Clemens read this book to his daughters, yet produces a convincing demonstration of similarities between the burning of a toy village by the Plumfield children in chapter 8 of *Little Men* and the fire episode in "The Chronicle of Young Satan" (written 1897–1900), during which Philip Traum callously brushes the fleeing victims back into the flames ("Background of *The Mysterious Stranger,* p. 66). *MSM,* p. 22 n. 49.

————. *Little Women* (1868–1869).
   "Some of the Little Women" was how Mark Twain signed a poem entitled "The Last Word" that appeared in the 25 September 1869 issue of the Buffalo *Express* (*OPMT,* p. 70). The book would have been virtually a mandatory acquisition for any late-nineteenth-century household containing three young girls. On 1 January 1881 Clemens received a bill from Brown & Gross, Hartford booksellers, for the purchase of *Little Women* on 16 December 1880, probably as a Christmas gift (MTP).

————. *Little Women; or, Meg, Jo, Beth, and Amy.* Illus. by Frank T. Merrill. Boston: Little, Brown & Co., [cop. 1896]. 586 pp.
   Source: MTLAcc, entry #462, volume donated by Clemens.

————. *Little Women; or, Meg, Jo, Beth, and Amy.* Illus. by Frank T. Merrill. New York: Harper & Brothers, [cop. 1896]. 586 pp.
   Source: MTLAcc, entry #1182, volume donated by Clemens.

Alden, Henry Mills (1836–1919). *God in His World: An Interpretation.* New York: Harper & Brothers, 1890. 270 pp.
   Catalog: A1911, #187, $2.50.
   Clemens undoubtedly received a presentation copy of this theological treatise by the editor of *Harper's Weekly,* but it has not reappeared since the 1911 auction.

Alden, William Livingston (1837–1908). *The Adventures of Jimmy Brown, Written by Himself and Edited by W. L. Alden.* New York: Harper & Brothers, 1905. 236 pp.
   Source: MTLAcc, entry #1583, volume donated by Clemens.

————. *The Cruise of the "Ghost."* Illus. New York: Harper & Brothers, 1904. 210 pp.
   Source: MTLAcc, entry #432, volume donated by Clemens.

————. *Jimmy Brown Trying to Find Europe, Written by Himself and Edited by W. L. Alden.* Illus. New York: Harper & Brothers, 1905. 164 pp.
   Source: MTLAcc, entry #600, volume donated by Clemens.

————. *Shooting Stars as Observed from the "Sixth Column" of the Times.* New York: G. P. Putnam's Sons, 1878. 224 pp.

"N. Y. Times funy Man—little girl who got up drama of Robinson Crusoe," noted Mark Twain in 1880 while compiling a list of potential material for his projected anthology of American humor (NB 19, *N&J,* 2:366). Three sketches from Alden's collected columns from the New York *Times* eventually appeared in *Mark Twain's Library of Humor* (1888)—"Carrie's Comedy," a nonsensical dramatization of *Robinson Crusoe* purportedly written by a young girl; "The Belle of Vallejo"; and "Mr. Simpkin's Downfall."

Aldrich, Thomas Bailey (1836–1907). *Cloth of Gold and Other Poems.* Boston: James R. Osgood and Company, 1874.

Inscription: presentation inscription by Aldrich on verso of flyleaf, "Unalterably, T. B. A./Boston/Dec. 1874."

Catalog: C1951, #77c, $25; mistakenly listed in the category of books signed by Clemens.

Location: C. Waller Barrett Collection, University of Virginia, Charlottesville.

Copy examined: Clemens' copy.

Clemens complimented the author regarding these verses from Hartford on 18 December 1874: "I read the 'Cloth of Gold' through, coming down in the cars, and it is just *lightning* poetry. . . . 'Baby Bell' always seemed perfection, before, but now that I have children it has got even beyond *that*" *(MTL,* pp. 239–240). Modern readers must assume that Clemens made the latter declaration on the basis of friendship rather than literary criticism.

This was the first volume of poetry Aldrich gave Clemens, though several volumes of his fiction already formed part of Clemens' library. A quarter of a century later, after Aldrich's literary reputation had begun to decline, Clemens would still defend his poety in an Autobiographical Dictation of 3 July 1908: "Aldrich was never widely known; his books never attained to a wide circulation; his prose was diffuse, self-conscious, and barren of distinction in the matter of style; his fame as a writer of prose is not considerable; his fame as a writer of verse is also very limited, but such as it is it is a matter to be proud of. It is based not upon his output of poetry as a whole but upon half a dozen small poems which are not surpassed in our language for exquisite grace and beauty and finish. These gems are known and admired and loved by the one person in ten thousand who is capable of appreciating them at their just value" *(MTE,* p. 293). The thirteen books by Aldrich in Clemens' library constituted one of his largest collections of writings by a single author, aside from multi-volume sets.

————. *Flower and Thorn, Later Poems.* Boston: J. R. Osgood and Co., 1877. 148 pp.

Inscription: inscribed by Aldrich to Clemens and also signed by Clemens.

Catalog: C1951, #D78.

————. "The Friend of My Youth," *Atlantic Monthly,* 27 (February 1871), 169–177.

Mark Twain included this prose character sketch in *Mark Twain's Library of Humor* (1888). It recounts the career of a gifted sharper and gambler called Governor Dorr who periodically touched Aldrich for funds, always reminding him that he was "the friend of my youth."

————. *From Ponkapog to Pesth.* Boston: Houghton, Mifflin and Co., 1883. [Fourth edition, 1884; seventh edition, 1890.]

Catalog: C1951, #46c, $30, "given to Mark Twain by the author," edition unspecified. Listed among the books signed by Clemens.

————. *Judith of Bethulia, a Tragedy*. Boston: Houghton, Mifflin and Co., 1904. 98 pp. Reprinted in 1905.
>   *Catalog: C1951*, #54c, $20, "given to Mark Twain by the author," edition unspecified. Listed among the books signed by Clemens.
>   *Judith of Bethulia* was Aldrich's dramatization of his earlier narrative poem, *Judith and Holofernes* (1896). Clemens presumably referred to the verse drama when he wrote to Aldrich from Florence on 14 February 1904: "The publishers sent me your book three or four weeks ago, & it gave me a most stimulating & delicious time—& did also patly and timely justify & reinforce some laudations of you which I had dictated the day before (in my Autobiography)" (Houghton Library, Harvard). The play was produced in Boston in 1904. On 7 December 1904 Isabel Lyon made a pertinent entry in her journal: "And then Mr. Thomas Bailey Aldrich came in to ask Mr. Clemens and Jean to go tonight to see a tragedy that he has recently written" (1903–1906 Diary, TS p. 31, MTP).

————. *Marjorie Daw and Other People*. Boston: J. R. Osgood and Co., 1873. 272 pp. Reprinted 1874, 1875, 1878; issued by Houghton, Mifflin and Co. in 1882, 1884, 1885, etc.
>   *Catalog: C1951*, #45c, $30, "given to Mark Twain by the author," edition unspecified. Listed among the books signed by Clemens.
>   In a letter to Howells written on 14 September 1876 Clemens alluded to the "genius" possessed by "the man that wrote Marjorie Daw" *(MTHL, p. 153)*.
>   *SCH*, p. 232.

————. *An Old Town by the Sea*. Boston: Houghton, Mifflin and Co., 1893. 123 pp.
>   At a time when Clemens was being driven nearly to desperation by his financial plight, he wrote to Aldrich from New York City on 6 December 1893 to report that he had stayed up until 3 o'clock in the morning reading *An Old Town*. "Portsmouth [, New Hampshire] was become the town of my boyhood—with all which that implies & compels. . . . I enjoyed it all—every line of it; & I wish there had been more" (Houghton Library, Harvard).

————. *Ponkapog Papers*. Boston: Houghton, Mifflin and Co., 1903.
>   Clemens informed Howells from Florence on 17 January 1904 that he had stayed up late to read this book "night before last,"and then relied on whiskey to help him sleep *(MTHL, p. 779)*. Isabel Lyon related in her journal entry for 28 July 1904 that "this evening" Richard Watson Gilder "sauntered in" while she was playing euchre with Clemens and Jean in Lee, Massachusetts. "We kept on with our game, and Mr. Gilder read bits of 'Ponkapog Papers' and Kipling's 'Five Seas'. Mr. Clemens told of the day in Florence that he read Mr. Aldrich's comment upon Mark Twain's humor in the 'Ponkapog Papers', speaking of it as being deep rooted" (1903–1906 Journal, TS p. 25, MTP).

————. *Prudence Palfrey. A Novel*. Boston: James R. Osgood and Co., 1874. 311 pp.
>   *Inscription:* on front free endpaper, "Mark/from his friend/T. B. A."
>   *Marginalia:* computations in Clemens' hand in black ink on back flyleaf.
>   *Catalog: C1951*, #38c, presentation copy, mistakenly listed with books containing Clemens' signature.
>   *Location:* Carrie Estelle Doheny Collection, St. John's Seminary, Camarillo, California. Purchased by Mrs. Doheny from Maxwell Hunley, Beverly Hills rare book dealer, in 1951 for $39.50; donated to the library in 1952.
>   *Copy examined:* Clemens' copy.
>   Mark Twain urged Aldrich to publish an unnamed forthcoming book—probably *Prudence Palfrey*—by subscription, even offering to negotiate personally with Elisha Bliss of the American Publishing Company (SLC to Aldrich, 24 March 1874, Houghton Library, Harvard). Aldrich evidently neglected this offer, but he did ask Mark Twain for assistance in depicting the western mining scenes in the novel. Twain sent a lengthy list of proposed revisions concerning mining termin-

ology and lore, together with suggestions about miners' living habits; in an accompanying undated letter he diplomatically added: "I think it is ma[r]velous that you have made so few mistakes about mining, & that what you have written about it sounds so easy-going & natural" (Washington University, St. Louis, Missouri). The portion that involves mining begins with chapter 5, in which the hero John Dent resolves to earn a fortune in the California mines: "I mean to come back independent, or not at all" (p. 77). But the California regions with which Mark Twain was familiar are not Dent's ultimate destination; in chapter 6 he winds up in "the new gold regions" in Montana (p. 97). Nevertheless, Mark Twain's participation in the planning and writing of *Prudence Palfrey* insures that he knew this novel more thoroughly than through casual reading.

———. *The Queen of Sheba*. Boston: J. R. Osgood and Co., 1877. 270 pp.
Catalog: C1951, #67c, $50, "given to Mark Twain by the author," listed among the books signed by Clemens.
Clemens wrote an undated letter to Aldrich about *The Queen of Sheba*: "Your book came at 10 this morning. . . . So I ordered breakfast & a pipe to be brought up to the bed—which would give me a chance to glance at the book. Result: I have read every line of the bewitching thing & have lost my day's work & am not in the least sorry. . . . It is a delicious situation where that young fellow gets into the asylum" (Middlebury College). In chapter 4 of the novel, Edward Lynde inadvertently wanders into an asylum for the insane in northern New Hampshire, attempts to converse with the inmates (whom he believes to be local villagers), and is himself mistaken for a lunatic by the guards and incarcerated in a padded cell. One of the inmates of the asylum is a girl who believes herself to be the Queen of Sheba.

———. *The Sisters' Tragedy, with Other Poems, Lyrical and Dramatic*. Boston: Houghton, Mifflin and Co., 1891. 108 pp.
Inscription: "S. L. Clemens, from/his young/friend,/T. B. Aldrich/Feb. 1891."
Location: Mark Twain Library, Redding, Connecticut. Donated from Clemens' library by Clara Clemens Gabrilowitsch in 1910 (MTLAcc, entry #2132).
Copy examined: Clemens' copy.
On 21 February 1891 Clemens wrote to Aldrich from Hartford: "I thank you ever so much for the poems." He mentions the stanzas headed "Tennyson," in which (he claimed) he expected to find himself cited (Houghton Library, Harvard).

———. *The Stillwater Tragedy*. Boston: Houghton, Mifflin and Co., 1880. 324 pp. [Prose.]
Catalog: C1951, #70c, $27.50, presentation copy, listed among the books signed by Clemens.
On 15 September 1880 Clemens wrote to Aldrich from Elmira: "Thank you ever so much for the book—I had already finished it, & prodigiously enjoyed it, in the periodical of the notorious Howells, but it hits Mrs. Clemens just right" (Middlebury College, pub. in *MTL*, pp. 385–386).

———. *The Story of a Bad Boy*. Boston: Fields, Osgood & Co., 1869.
Critical interpretations of the Aldrich-Mark Twain literary relationship have centered almost exclusively on this quasi-autobiographical novel that Aldrich set in his boyhood home town of Portsmouth, New Hampshire. Strangely enough, however, Clemens' copy of this book—like so many others that might offer significant revelations about his reading—has utterly disappeared. The only opinion about it that he expressed in writing was unfavorable; shortly before his marriage he wrote to Livy Langdon from New Haven, where he was lecturing: "I have read several books, lately, but none worth marking, & so I have not marked any. I started to mark the Story of a Bad Boy, but for the life of me I could not admire the volume much" (27 December 1869, *LLMT*, p. 132). Perhaps he later altered this estimation; at any rate he extracted "How We Astonished the Rivermouthians"

for inclusion in *Mark Twain's Library of Humor* (1888). In June 1898 he scheduled Tom Bailey to be among the children he wanted to assemble in his projected "Creatures of Fiction" tale (NB 40, TS p. 26). Quite late in his life Mark Twain erroneously told Paine that Aldrich was writing *The Story of a Bad Boy* at the same time he himself was beginning *Tom Sawyer,* and that the two of them compared their works in progress *(MTB,* p. 1456)—an obvious mistake.

Walter Blair, "On the Structure of *Tom Sawyer*" (1939), p. 78; *MT&HF,* p. 64; *HH&T,* p. 158 n. 12; Albert E. Stone, *IE* (1961), pp. 27–31, 65; Jim Hunter, "Mark Twain and the Boy-Book" (1963), p. 433.

————. *Wyndam Towers.* Boston: Houghton, Mifflin and Co., 1890. 80 pp.

Catalog: C1951, #72c, $25, presentation copy, listed among books signed by Clemens.

Clemens must have received an advance copy of *Wyndam Towers,* for he wrote to Aldrich from Hartford on 19 November 1889: "It's a lovely book, & I thank you ever so much," and promised to send him a copy of *A Connecticut Yankee* (Houghton Library, Harvard). Aldrich published no other volumes during this period.

Alexander, (Mrs.) Cecil Frances (Humphreys) (1818?–1895). "The Burial of Moses" (poem).

Mrs. Alexander was the wife of an Irish Anglican prelate; she wrote tracts in the Oxford Movement, hymns, and verses whose subject was generally the Old Testament. Van Wyck Brooks was overstating the case when he asserted that "The Burial of Moses" became for Clemens a literary touchstone *(The Ordeal of Mark Twain,* rev. ed. [New York: E. P. Dutton & Co., 1933], p. 191), but he was only echoing Albert Bigelow Paine, who had cited this "noble and simple poem" as "a sort of literary touchstone" for Clemens *(MTB,* pp. 217, 338). There can be no doubt that Clemens was impressed with the poem, particularly the first stanza, in the 1860's and 1870's. Paine reported that he "often" recited its "stately lines" during his sojourn in Virginia City, Nevada *(MTB,* pp. 216–217). In 1867 Clemens copied the entire poem onto the first four pages of Notebook 9 *(N&J,* 1:380–382), seemingly from memory (to judge from discrepancies), and also noted its title farther on in the same notebook (p. 438). He quoted part of the poem in his *Alta California* letter of 12 September 1867, and he employed four lines from the first stanza in chapter 42 of *Innocents Abroad* (1869). Chapter 6 of *Roughing It* (1872) alludes to "The Mysterious Grave of Moses." A sentence in chapter 36 of *A Tramp Abroad*—"The secret of his sepulture, like that of Moses, must remain a mystery always"—originated from the last lines of the poem: "God hath his mysteries of grace,/Ways that we cannot tell,/He hides them deep, like the secret sleep/Of him he loved so well."

Alexander, William (1824–1911). *Primary Convictions; Being Discussions . . . Delivered . . . [at] Columbia College.* New York: Harper & Brothers, 1893. 322 pp.

Source: MTLAcc, entry #1392, volume donated by Clemens.

Alexander, William De Witt. *A Review of a Pastoral Address by the Right Rev. T. N. Staley, D.D., Reformed Catholic Bishop of Honolulu, Containing a Reply to Some of His Charges Against the American Protestant Mission to the Hawaiian Islands.* Honolulu: Printed by H. M. Whitney, 1865. 87 pp.

Mark Twain quoted from this book, citing its author and title, in his letter of 1 July 1866 published in the Sacramento *Weekly Union* issue for 4 August 1866 *(LSI,* p. 123). He sought to demonstrate the heartless attitude of Established Church clergymen toward funerals conducted by Dissenting ministers.

Alford, Henry (1810–1871). "Say, Wilt Thou Think of Me When I'm Away" (poem).
Alford, an English clergyman, poet, and scholar, was Dean of Canterbury from 1857 until 1871. On 9 March 1871 Livy Clemens copied a poem beginning with the above line into her commonplace book (DV161, MTP), attributing it to Alford.

Alger, Russell Alexander (1836–1907). *The Spanish-American War*. New York: Harper & Brothers, 1901. 466 pp.
Inscription: "S. L. Clemens, Riverdale-on-Hudson, Oct. 13, 1901." on flyleaf.
Catalog: A1911, #7, $4, "gilt top, uncut."
Alger was President McKinley's Secretary of War from 5 March 1897 until 1 August 1899, when he resigned at McKinley's request.

————. [Identical copy.]
Source: MTLAcc, entry #1708, volume donated by Clemens.

Allen, Alexander Viets Griswold (1841–1908). *Life and Letters of Phillips Brooks*. 2 vols. New York: E. P. Dutton and Co., 1900. Reprinted in 1901 in 3 vols.
That Clemens' reading tastes eventually differed markedly from those of his friend Twichell is apparent from their responses to this biography of the prominent American Episcopal bishop Phillips Brooks (1835–1893), who held the pastorate of Trinity Church in Boston for more than twenty years. Writing to Twichell from Ampersand, New York on 28 August 1901, Clemens labeled as "extravagant" Twichell's "suggestion that I read the biography of Phillips Brooks—the very dullest book that has been printed for a century." As depicted in this volume, Brooks "wearied me; *oh* how he wearied me!" The work was a "whole basketful of drowsy rubbish" *(MTL, p. 712).*

Allen, Chilion Brown and Mary A. Allen. *The Man Wonderful in the House Beautiful. An Allegory Teaching the Principles of Physiology and Hygiene, and the Effects of Stimulants and Narcotics*. New York: Fowler & Wells Co., [1883]. Sixth ed. 1888.
Clemens informed Charles L. Webster on 16 June 1887 from Hartford that "I shall keep 'The Man Wonderful' and read it" *(MTLP, p. 218).*

Allen, Elizabeth Ann (Chase) Akers (1832–1911). "Rock Me to Sleep, Mother" (poem, pub. 1860; song, cop. 1860, melody by Ernest Leslie).
Historians agree that Allen wrote this poem in May 1860 and published it under the pen name "Florence Percy" in the 9 June 1860 issue of the *Saturday Evening Post*. In the wake of its immediate and continued popularity its authorship was claimed by various writers, especially Alexander M. W. Ball. The first stanza contains the most famous lines: "Backward, turn backward, O Time, in your flight,/ Make me a child again just for to-night"; the refrain gives the title: "Rock me to sleep, mother—rock me to sleep!" The speaker in the poem expresses weariness with "toil" and "tears" and longs to relive her carefree childhood again.
Mark Twain first alluded to the poem in his letter to the *Alta California* from Capernaum in September 1867; he urged his readers to come to Galilee if they sought solitude. "If these things are not food for rock me to sleep mother, none exist, I think," he wrote *(TIA, p. 226).* In 1868 he burlesqued the dispute over its authorship by using its diction and meter in a satiric poem that ridiculed Ball, one of the chief claimants. Mark Twain's poem appeared in the Cincinnati *Evening Chronicle* for 4 March 1868 (see *OPMT*, pp. 10, 65; also *Twainian* 2 [February 1943], 2–3 and 2 [March 1943], 6).
Mark Twain alluded to the controversial status of this poem in chapter 31 of *Innocents Abroad;* he also used his earlier allusion to the Sea of Galilee region as "food for rock me to sleep, mother" in chapter 48. References to the heated dispute over its authorship recur throughout his lifetime. In "Mental Telegraphy" (published 1891, but written earlier) he recalled that "there was a war of this kind over . . . 'Rock Me to Sleep, Mother.' " No. 44 quotes several lines from the

poem—"Backward, turn backward, O Time, in thy flight—/ Make me a child
again, just for to-night!"—while he parades an Assembly of the Dead to show the
world's history in chapter 32 of "No. 44, The Mysterious Stranger," written between
1902 and 1908 *(MSM,* pp. 395, 397). Possibly to show his disdain for human
endeavors, 44 misquotes the lines in minor ways and ascribes them to "Beautiful
Snow," another poem that had numerous claimants. Clemens wrote to Howells
on 14 April 1903, stating his refusal to "regard as frauds the several claimants" to
tions of "mental telegraphy" *(MTHL,* p. 767). He quoted the poem once again
"Rock Me to Sleep, Mother"; he interpreted them instead as additional manifesta-
in Part 9 of "Is Shakespeare Dead?" (1909) to remind his readers about the phenomenal talents evinced in Shakespeare's canon: "Ordinarily when an unsigned
poem sweeps across the continent like a tidal wave whose roar and boom and
thunder are made up of admiration, delight, and applause, a dozen obscure people
rise up and claim the authorship. . . . Do you remember 'Rock Me to Sleep, Mother,
Rock Me to Sleep'? Do you remember 'Backward, turn backward, O Time, in thy
flight! Make me a child again just for to-night'? I remember them very well. Their
authorship was claimed by most of the grown-up people who were alive at the
time."

————. *The Triangular Society. Leaves from the Life of a Portland Family.* Portland, Me: Hoyt, Fogg & Donham, 1886. 381 pp.
    Source: MTLAcc, entry #461, volume donated by Clemens.

Allen, Horace Newton (1858–1932). *Things Korean; A Collection of Sketches and
Anecdotes, Missionary and Diplomatic.* New York: Fleming H. Revell Co., [cop.
1908]. 256 pp.
    Inscription: "To 'Mark Twain' with the profound-respect of the author, Horace
N. Allen."
    Location: Mark Twain Library, Redding, Connecticut.
    Copy examined: Clemens' copy.
    Clemens can hardly have valued this volume if he presented it to the library
in Redding the same year it was published. Allen wrote other books on Korean
literature, missions, and politics; most were published by the Methodist Publishing
House in Seoul, Korea.

Allen, James Lane (1849–1925). *Aftermath; Part Second of "A Kentucky Cardinal."* Illus. by Hugh Thomson. New York: Macmillan Co., 1906. 138 pp.
    Source: MTLAcc, entry #1860, volume donated from Clemens' library by
Clara Clemens Gabrilowitsch in 1910.

————. *The Choir Invisible.* New York: Macmillan Co., 1898. 361 pp.
    Source: MTLAcc, entry #1833, volume donated from Clemens' library by
Clara Clemens Gabrilowitsch in 1910.

————. *A Kentucky Cardinal; A Story.* New York: Macmillan Co., 1905. 138 pp.
    Source: MTLAcc, entry #1835, volume donated from Clemens' library by
Clara Clemens Gabrilowitsch in 1910.

————. *Summer in Arcady; A Tale of Nature.* New York: Macmillan Co., 1897.
170 pp.
    Source: MTLAcc, entry #1834, volume donated from Clemens' library by
Clara Clemens Gabrilowitsch in 1910.

Allen, Thomas G. *Letter from an Ex-Sailor and Ex-Tramp to Hon. Geo. S. Boutwell,
Ex-Governor and Ex-Secretary of Treasury.* St. Louis, 5 October 1900. 15 pp.
    Marginalia: a small amount on pages 11–12.
    Location: Mark Twain Papers, Berkeley (Paine 89aa).
    Copy examined: Clemens' copy.

Allen's paperbound political campaign pamphlet excoriates McKinley for "the prosecution of a death-dealing destructive war, in order to subjugate the Liberty-loving Filipinos) (pp. 10–11). Clemens annotated only the two pages that directly assailed McKinley's conduct. Since McKinley had originally decried the annexation of Cuba as "criminal aggression," Clemens wrote "Mr. Criminal Aggression McKinley" in pencil at the bottom of page 11. On page 12 he noted: "By their fruits ye shall know *Xnity*".

Allen, William Francis, Charles Pickard Ware, and Lucy McKim Garrison, compilers. *Slave Songs of the United States.* New York: A. Simpson & Co., 1867. 155 pp.

Clemens very likely meant this volume, believed to be the earliest published collection of Negro spirituals, when he wrote "The Slave Songs of the South—advertised in the South" in Notebook 19 *(N&J,* 2:394) in 1881. *Slave Songs* contained "Roll, Jordan, Roll" and many of his other favorite spirituals, but no evidence indicates that he owned the book.

[Allestree, Richard]. *The Whole Duty of Man, Laid Down in a Plain Familiar Way for the Use of All* (London, 1658).

A devotional work that was extremely popular for two centuries, *The Whole Duty of Man* was published anonymously but generally attributed to Richard Allestree (1619–1681), an English clergyman and scholar. It may have been one of Jane Lampton Clemens' reference books while rearing her family; at least Clemens teased his mother about her dependence on "that useful and highly entertaining volume" in a letter from Carson City written on 20 March 1862 *(PRI,* p. 35). He mentioned the book jokingly as "light reading" in Notebook 4 *(N&J,* 1:83) in 1865, and later recalled the ubiquity of *The Whole Duty of Man* on parlor tables in Honolulu in 1866 *(FE,* chapter 3). His *Alta California* readers were informed in his 5 April 1868 letter that the *Quaker City* passengers had brought this work along on the voyage *(TIA,* p. 303); an unfinished play he wrote about the trip in 1867 ("The *Quaker City* Holy Land Excursion") mentioned this title in the ship library (Act II, scene 1). In chapter 1 of "Those Extraordinary Twins" (1894) he contrasted the natures of his Siamese twins by specifying their choices in reading matter: Luigi sat down with Paine's *Age of Reason,* while Angelo chose Allestree's devotional tract.

Allibone, Samuel Austin (1816–1889). *A Critical Dictionary of English Literature and British and American Authors.* 3 vols. Philadelphia: J. B. Lippincott & Co., 1858–1871. Reprinted 1874 and numerous times.

On 5 November 1874 Mark Twain referred an unidentified correspondent who sought his biography to "Allibone's Dictionary of Authors; (although I am not sure, in the latter case, as I have not seen the work, but only *heard* it was in it)" (Hill Collection, PH in MTP). There *is* an entry for Clemens under "Twain, Mark" in Allibone's work. Twain intended to "examine Drake's & Allibone's Dictionaries of Authors to see who *have* been humorists" when he made preparations to edit *Mark Twain's Library of Humor* in 1880 (NB 19, *N&J,* 2:364).

Allingham, William (1824–1889). *William Allingham, A Diary.* Ed. by Mrs. Helen (Paterson) Allingham and Mrs. Dollie Radford. London: Macmillan and Co., 1907. 404 pp. Repr. 1908.

Catalog: C1951, #7a, $22.50, listed among books containing marginalia by Clemens, no edition specified.

Contains correspondence and reminiscences of various authors. Allingham was an Irish poet.

————. *Sixteen Poems by William Allingham. Selected by William Butler Yeats.* Dundrum, Ireland: Dun Emer Press, 1905. 34 pp.
>   *Inscription:* "S. L. Clemens/ 1908."
>   *Marginalia:* no markings; page 27 turned down at poem titled "Twilight Voices"; all leaves unopened.
>   *Catalog: A1911,* #144, $4.50, "uncut."
>   *Provenance:* W. Van R. Whitall bookplate is partially pasted over a W. T. H. Howe bookplate dated 1920.
>   *Location:* Henry W. and Albert A. Berg Collection, New York Public Library.
>   *Copy examined:* Clemens' copy.

Allmond, Marcus Blakey (1851–1909). *Estelle and Other Poems.* Louisville, Ky.: J. P. Morton & Co., [1884]. 79 pp.
>   *Source:* MTLAcc, entry #2005, volume donated from Clemens' library by Clara Clemens Gabrilowitsch in 1910.

Allyn, Eunice Gibbs. *The Cats' Convention.* Illus. by the author. New York: Cochrane Pub. Co., 1909. 255 pp.
>   *Inscription:* "For Samuel Clemmens [*sic*] (Mark Twain)/'He prayeth best who loveth best/ All things both great and small;/ For the dear God who loveth us/ He made and loveth all.' (Col.)/ Eunice Gibbs Allyn."
>   *Location:* Mark Twain Library, Redding. Donated in 1910 by Clara Clemens Gabrilowitsch (MTLAcc, entry #2159).
>   *Copy examined:* Clemens' copy.

Altrocchi, (Mrs.) Julia (Cooley) (b. 1893). *The Poems of a Child; Being Poems Written Between the Ages of Six and Ten.* Intro. by Richard Le Gallienne. New York: R. H. Russell, 1904. 151 pp.
>   *Source:* MTLAcc, entry #1692, volume donated by Clemens.

————. [An identical copy.]
>   *Inscription:* front pastedown endpaper inscribed in black ink: "SL. Clemens/ 1905/ A remarkable book."
>   *Location:* Antenne-Dorrance Collection, Rice Lake, Wis.
>   *Copy examined:* Clemens' copy.

Altsheler, Joseph Alexander (1862–1919). *The Candidate; A Political Romance.* New York: Harper & Brothers, 1905. 429 pp.
>   *Source:* MTLAcc, entry #1836, volume donated from Clemens' library by Clara Clemens Gabrilowitsch in 1910.

Am. Col.[?] *N. E. Society, Dec. 22, 1886.* N.p., [1886]. 93 pp. Paperbound.
>   Unidentified; possibly a publication of the American Colonization Society.
>   *Source:* MTLAcc, entry #341, volume donated by Clemens.

The American Architect and Building News (weekly periodical). Boston: J. R. Osgood & Co., first issue pub. 1 January 1876. [Moved to New York and changed title in 1904.]
>   Osgood & Co. billed Clemens $6.00 for the back numbers of 1876, purchased on 13 March 1877 (Scrapbook #10, p. 69, MTP).

The American Bookmaker (monthly periodical) Bristol, Conn.: Moore Pub. Co., first issue pub. July 1885. [Title changed in 1897.]
>   On 21 October 1889 Clemens mentioned in a letter that he had read the current issue of this printers' journal because of his interest in the Paige typesetter (SLC to Mr. Taylor, ALS in Mrs. Robin Craven Collection, PH in MTP).

The American Church Missionary Register (monthly periodical). New York: American Missionary Society.

In his 20 May 1867 letter to the *Alta California* Mark Twain reported on this journal: "Mr. Rising edits her, and she is a credit to him" *(MTTMB,* p. 210).

The American Cyclopaedia: A Popular Dictionary of General Knowledge. Ed. by George Ripley (1802–1880) and Charles Anderson Dana (1819–1897). 16 vols. New York: D. Appleton and Co., 1873–1876.

Source: MTLAcc, entries #694–709. Complete set donated by Clemens.

See entry for *Appletons' Annual Cyclopaedia.*

American Miscellany. A Magazine of Complete Stories (periodical). Boston: J. H. Brigham. Pub. 1865–1871[?].

Mark Twain may not have known that this magazine had suspended publication when he had Laura Hawkins refer to it in chapter 36 of *The Gilded Age* (1873) as "literary fatty degeneration of the heart."

The American Nation: A History from Original Sources by Associated Scholars. Ed. by Albert Bushnell Hart (1854–1943). 28 vols. New York: Harper & Brothers, 1906–1918.

Inscriptions: vol. 16 signed "S. L. Clemens, 1906"; vol. 21 signed "S. L. Clemens, 1907".

Catalogs: A1911, #8, 3 vols. only, $4.50; *Lexington 1912,* 3 vols. only, #13 ($3.50), #14 ($2.00), #17 ($3.50).

Clemens may once have owned more volumes in the set, but only three were offered at the 1911 auction: vol. 16, *Slavery and Abolition, 1831–1841,* by Albert Bushnell Hart (1906), inscribed; vol. 21, *Outcome of the Civil War, 1863–1865* by J. K. Hosmer (1907), inscribed; and vol. 28, *Analytic Index,* compiled by David Maydole Matteson (1908).

American Ornithology for the Home and School, 1901–1906. Ed. by Chester Albert Reed (1876–1912). 6 vols. Worcester, Mass.: Charles K. Reed, 1901–1906.

Source: MTLAcc, entry #1974, volume 1 only (pub. 1901, 246 pp.) donated from Clemens' library by Clara Clemens Gabrilowitsch in 1910.

Amicis, Edmondo de (1846–1908). *Holland and Its People.* [Trans. by Caroline Tilton.] The Zuyder-Zee Edition. Only 600 numbered copies printed. Illus. New York: G. P. Putnam's Sons, 1885. 397 pp.

Catalog: A1911, #10, $5.75, "royal 8vo . . . etchings by Joseph Pennell, Samuel Coleman, R. Swain Gifford, and others."

————. *Spain and the Spaniards.* [Trans. from the Italian by Wilhelmina W. Cady.] The Guadalquiver Edition. Only 600 numbered copies printed. Illus. New York: G. P. Putnam's Sons, 1885. 463 pp.

Catalog: A1911, #9, $12, small folio, gilt tooled cover design, uncut."

Spain and the Spaniards was first published as *Spagna* (Firenze, 1873); G. P. Putnam's Sons copyrighted the English translation in 1880. At first Clemens was unsure of its title: "An Italian in Spain—Putnam's Sons" he jotted in Notebook 25 in November or December 1885 (TS p. 32). He soon received the volume as a Christmas gift; he wrote to Jervis, Julie, and Ida Langdon from Hartford on 28 December 1885: "I thank you with enthusiasm; for that 'Spain' was a book which I more wanted than any other book that could be named. It gives me nightly peace, now, & I think of you when I read it" (MTP). The typography and paper pleased him especially, for he later proposed to Charles L. Webster that their publishing firm print a copy of Grant's *Memoirs* "on paper like that in De Amici's 'Spain'—ragged edges & 2 or 3-inch margins" for presentation to Pope Leo XIII (17 June 1886, *MTBus,* p. 361).

————. *Studies of Paris.* [Trans. from Italian by Wilhelmina W. Cady.] New York: G. P. Putnam's Sons, 1879.
>   Estes & Lauriat of Boston billed Clemens on 14 July 1880 for "1 Studies of Paris .65¢" (receipt in MTP). *Studies* contained descriptions of Paris and the Exposition as well as essays on Victor Hugo and Zola.

Amiel, Henri Frédéric (1821–1881). *Amiel's Journal; The Journal Intime.* Trans. with intro. and notes by (Mrs.) Mary Augustus (Arnold) Ward (1851–1920), "Mrs. Humphry Ward." London: Macmillan and Co., 1894. 318 pp.
>   *Inscription:* "Olivia L. Clemens/London/ <1896>1897".
>   *Marginalia:* notes and markings in pencil throughout.
>   *Provenance:* stamp, charge-card pocket, call number of Mark Twain Library, Redding. Donated by Clemens (MTLAcc, entry #1785).
>   *Catalog: Mott 1952,* #35, $15.
>   *Location:* Mark Twain Memorial, Hartford. Anonymous gift received in 1963.
>   *Copy examined:* Livy's copy. Notes appear to be in her hand. An unknown authority has identified these comments and a loose note in the book as Susy's writing, though Susy died on 18 August 1896.

Among the Daisies. Poems Old and New. Edited by E. B. Sold by Subscription Only. Hartford: American Publishing Co., 1884. 194 pp.
>   *Catalog: A1911,* #11, $2.50.
>   The publishers advertised this anthology of American and English poetry as "a book of rare beauty and merit; being a collection of all the poems that have ever been written about the daisy" *(MT&EB,* p. 183).

Andersen, Hans Christian (1805–1875). *Bilderbuch ohne Bilder.* Nach der 5 danischen Ausgabe, Deutsch von Edmund Lobedanz. Berlin: Grote'sche Verlagsbuchhandlung, 1874.
>   *Location:* Mark Twain Library, Redding, Conn.
>   *Copy examined:* Clemens' copy.
>   Apparently Clemens owned only this translation of *Billedbog uden billeder.* Colonel Sellers mistakenly refers to Andersen as a great painter in chapter 19 of *The American Claimant* (1892). In "Is He Living or Is He Dead?" (1893) the character named Smith relates "one of Hans Andersen's beautiful little stories."

Anderson, Rasmus Björn (1846–1936) and Jón Bjarnason, trans. *Viking Tales of the North. The Sagas of Thornstein, Viking's Son, and Fridthjof the Bold. Trans. from the Icelandic by R. B. Anderson and J. Bjarnason. Also Tegnér's Fridthjof's Saga, Trans. into English [in Verse] by G. Stephens.* Chicago: S. C. Griggs & Son, 1877. 370 pp.
>   Clemens purchased this book on 20 March 1877, according to a receipt from Osgood and Co. (Scrapbook #10, p. 69, MTP).

Anderson, Rufus. *The Hawaiian Islands: Their Progress and Condition Under Missionary Labors.* Boston: Gould and Lincoln, 1864. 3rd ed., 1865. 450 pp.
>   Mark Twain noted the author and title of this book on his copy of Jarves' *History of the Hawaiian or Sandwich Islands (N&J,* 1:105). The character called Mr. Brown, referring to Anderson by name, castigates such "books shoemakered up by them pious bushwhackers in America" in a letter Mark Twain wrote for the 25 August 1866 issue of the Sacramento *Weekly Union (LSI,* pp. 151–152).

Andrews, Lorrin (1795–1868). *A Dictionary of the Hawaiian Language, to Which Is Appended an English-Hawaiian Vocabulary and a Chronological Table of Remarkable Events.* Honolulu: Printed by H. M. Whitney, 1865. 559 pp.
>   Mentioned in Notebook 6 (1866), *N&J,* 1:206.

Andrews, Louis Robins (b. 1877). *The White Peril; or, How I Cured Myself of Consumption at Home*. Rev. edition. Danberry, Conn.: White Peril Co., 1909. 277 pp.
>   *Source:* MTLAcc, entry #1494, volume donated by Clemens.

Anecdote Library. Portraits and Views.
>   *Inscription:* "S. L. Clemens" on front pastedown endpaper.
>   *Catalog: A1911*, #12, $1.75, "16mo, calf (loose)," no publisher or date provided.

Anichkova, Anna Mitrofanovna (Avinova), pseud. "Ivan Strannik." *The Shadow of the House*. Trans. from French by Emma A. Clinton. New York: McClure, Phillips & Co., 1906. 307 pp.
>   *Inscription:* front pastedown endpaper signed in black ink "S. L. Clemens/1906."
>   *Marginalia:* grammatical correction on page 27 in black ink; at the bottom of the page Clemens comments: "It is a clumsy translation,—this book. (Sometimes.)" On page 85 Clemens wrote "armoué" beside the word "armoury." There are no other markings.
>   *Location:* Antenne-Dorrance Collection, Rice Lake, Wis.
>   *Copy examined:* Clemens' copy.

"Annie Laurie" (song, 1838).
>   Mentioned in Notebook 5 (1866), *N&J*, 1:121.

Anthon, Charles (1797–1867). *A Classical Dictionary, Containing an Account of the Principal Proper Names Mentioned in Ancient Authors*. New York: Harper & Brothers, 1880. 1,451 pp.
>   *Inscription:* "S. L. Clemens, Hartford, June, 1881" on flyleaf.
>   *Catalogs: A1911*, #14, $1.; *L1912*, #3, $5.
>   Treats Greek and Roman literature and history.

Appletons' Annual Cyclopaedia and Register of Important Events of the Year. 10 vols. New York: D. Appleton and Co., 1877, 1879, 1880, 1881, 1883, 1884 (three copies), 1885, 1886.
>   *Source:* MTLAcc, entries #711 through #720, volumes donated by Clemens.
>   In chapter 55 of *Roughing It* (1872) Mark Twain claimed that he "fell back" on this "steadfast friend of the editor, all over the land" when he was pressed by newspaper deadlines for editorials in Virginia City. (From 1862 until 1873 its title was *The American Annual Cyclopaedia and Register of Important Events of the Year*.) Twain referred to this resource numerous times thereafter. In 1882 he expressed pleasure that Whitelaw Reid's biography had not been sketched in *Appletons' Cyclopaedia* (NB 19, *N&J*, 2:423). In 1884 he received a statement for his "Amer. Encyclopedia" in the amount of $92.25 and another charge of $35 "for Annuals to Encyclopedia" (Charles L. Webster to SLC, 2 September 1884, MTP). Clemens gave this reference work as his source for his knowledge about early Irish history and the Pope's deceptive policies in an entry made in July 1885 in Notebook 24 (TS p. 32); he resolved to "look in supplements to Appleton" in July 1888 for information about the Franco-Prussian War (NB 28, TS p. 8); and he intended to credit *Appletons' Cyclopaedia* in a projected Appendix to *A Connecticut Yankee* as his source of knowledge about the process of excommunication and interdiction (NB 29 [1889], TS pp. 13, 15). All of his allusions to the *American Cyclopaedia* are implicitly complimentary; the series should be considered his central reference source for American history and biography (biographies of prominent men generally appeared in the first volume following their deaths). As a general reference tool he ranked it second only to the *Encyclopaedia Britannica*. See entry for *The American Cyclopaedia*.

[*Appletons' Annual Cyclopaedia and Register of Important Events*.] *A General and Analytical Index to Appletons' Annual Cyclopaedia*. Comp. by Thomas Jefferson Conant (1802–1891). New York: D. Appleton & Co., 1878. 810 pp.
>   *Source:* MTLAcc, entry #710, volume donated by Clemens.

[Arabian Nights.] *The Thousand and One Nights, Commonly Called, in England, The Arabian Nights' Entertainments. A New Translation from the Arabic, with Copious Notes. By Edward William Lane . . . Illustrated by . . . William Harvey.* 3 vols. London: Charles Knight & Co., 1839–1841.

Inscription: in pencil on flyleaf: "S. L. Clemens, Hartford, 1877. A rare and valuable copy."

Catalogs: C1951, #11c, "3 vols.," listed among books signed by Clemens; item #29 in Zeitlin & Ver Brugge Booksellers List No. 132 (May 1951), price $37.50.

In July 1877 Clemens made a memorandum to go to a secondhand bookstore in New York City and "get 2d hand Arabian Nights" along with other miscellaneous books (NB 13, *N&J,* 2:38). Apparently he required help in completing his set of volumes, for on 10 December 1877 he thanked Andrew Chatto of London "for the other half of the Arabian Nights" (Berg). It may also be relevant that Livy's ledger of expenses while the Clemenses visited Munich included a charge of "2.25" for "Arabian Nights" (NB 13a, 1878).

Clara Clemens recalled that her father occasionally related stories from *The Arabian Nights* while his family was dining *(MFMT,* p. 56). In 1924 Henry Pochmann wisely included the work among those dozen books he selected in "The Mind of Mark Twain" as Clemens' lifetime library classics. Harold Aspiz found "at least eight references to the *Arabian Nights,* establishing it as one of his favorite books" ("Mark Twain's Reading" [1949], p. 187). The following chronological list of Mark Twain's references to the book title or characters signifies the extent of his lifelong fondness for the collection. Next to the Bible and Shakespeare plays, it was the literary source from which he consciously and recurrently drew the most allusions.

He alluded to *The Arabian Nights* in his 10 September 1866 letter to the Sacramento *Weekly Union* (LH, p. 57), in 2 February and 2 March 1867 letters to the *Alta California* (MTTMB, pp. 86, 119), in *TIA,* p. 26, and in chapters 8, 13, 33, 34, 44 of *IA* (1869). A letter from SLC to an unknown addressee, n.d. (December 1869 or January 1870, Syracuse Univ.) alludes to "Open Sesame"; another from Clemens to Mr. Benton, [spring?] 1870, compares his new Buffalo house to "Aladdin's Palace" (Vassar). There is an allusion in chapter 49 of *TA* (1880); another in NB 19 (1880), *N&J,* 2:359. In "The Walt Whitman Controversy" (DV36, MTP), probably written around 1880, Mark Twain refers to it as one of the "old bad books" that he owns. He mentioned "The Old Man of the Sea," a figure in the tale of Sindbad the Sailor, in a letter to Howells written 8 January 1880 *(MTHL,* p. 287), then spoke of Aladdin and his lamp in "On Adam," a speech delivered on 23 May 1883 *(MTSpk,* p. 178). Another reference occurs in NB19 (1881), *N&J,* 2:428. Mark Twain wrote a burlesque of Scheherazade's tales in 1883, "1,002ᵈ Arabian Night" *(S&B,* pp. 91–133), but Howells objected to its prolixity. Twain alludes to Aladdin's lamp in chapter 55 of *LonMiss. The Arabian Nights* and *Don Quixote* inspire Tom Sawyer's raid on the Sunday-school picnickers in chapter 3 of *HF* (1885); Huck mentions Scheherazade in chapter 23 of *HF.* Clemens referred to *Nights* in a letter to Howells written on 15 February 1887 *(MTHL,* p. 586), as well as in "At the Shrine of St. Wagner" (1891); NB 30 (1891), TS p. 23; "Marienbad—A Health Factory" (1891); and "The £1,000,000 Bank-Note" (1893). Tom Sawyer relies on *The Arabian Nights* in chapters 7 (the missing camel), 9, 10 (the dervish and the camel-driver), 12 (the prince and the flying bronze horse), and 13 of *Tom Sawyer Abroad* (1894). Clemens cited *Nights* in NB 37 (1896), TS p. 37. In *FE* (1897), he used *Nights* metaphorically as he had previously in *IA* to describe strange sights and ancient cities in chapters 38 (three allusions), 39, and 43. There are references in NB40 (July 1899), TS p. 58; Clemens' letter to Henry H. Rogers, 9 April 1900 *(MTHHR,* p. 442); "To My Missionary Critics" (1901); "No. 44, The Mysterious Stranger," chapter 4, written 1902–1908 *(MSM,* p. 211); "What Is Man?" (1906), Part 5; 13 August 1906 Autobiographical Dictation *(MTE,* p. 310); and a letter from Clemens to Dorothy Sturgis, 27 October 1908 (Columbia Univ.). The magic carpet is mentioned in chapter 2 of "Extract from Captain Stormfield's Visit to Heaven" (1909).

[Arabian Nights.] *The Thousand and One Nights; or, The Arabian Nights' Enter-tainments. A New Edition.* "Alta Edition" lettered on cover. Philadelphia: Porter & Coates, [1881]. 543 pp.
> *Inscription:* "S. L. Clemens" in brown ink on front pastedown endpaper.
> *Catalog: C1951,* #D62, listed with books signed by Clemens.
> *Location:* collection of Chester Davis, Executive-Secretary, Mark Twain Research Foundation, Perry, Missouri.
> *Copy examined:* Clemens' copy.

Argyll, John George Edward Henry Douglas Sutherland Campbell, 9th Duke of. *Viscount Palmerston, K. G. By the Marquis of Lorne, K. T.* Ed. by S. J. Reid. New York: Harper & Brothers, 1892. 235 pp.
> *Catalog: A1911,* #299, $1.
> Henry John Temple Palmerston (1784–1865) was prime minister of England from 1855 until 1865.

Aristocracy: A Novel. New York: D. Appleton and Co., 1890. First pub. 1888. 257 pp.
> *Source:* MTLAcc, entry #955, volume donated by Clemens.

Aristotle.
> In the course of annotating Holmes' *Autocrat of the Breakfast-Table* in 1869 Clemens paused in chapter 11 where Holmes mentions Aristotle (p. 302) and asked, "Did you ever read a single paragraph of Aristotle, Livy—I never did" (Bradford A. Booth, "Mark Twain's Comments on Holmes' *Autocrat*" [1950], p. 463). But he would refer to Aristotle's extraordinary mind in chapter 21 of *The American Claimant* (1892) and in an Autobiographical Dictation of 30 May 1907 (*MTE,* pp. 22–23, 24).

The Armies of To-day; A Description of the Armies of the Leading Nations. Illus. New York: Harper & Brothers, [cop. 1892]. 438 pp.
> *Source:* MTLAcc, entry #1369, volume donated by Clemens.

Arndt, Ernest Moritz (1769–1860). "Das Lied vom Feldmarschall" (song, 1813).
> Clemens copied (in German) the last six stanzas of this nine-stanza song into Notebook 23 in late October 1884 (TS p. 8).

Arnold, (Sir) Edwin (1832–1904). *India Revisited.* "Author's Edition." Boston: Roberts Brothers, 1886. 324 pp.
> *Inscription:* in brown ink on flyleaf, Livy Clemens' handwriting: "Saml. L. Clemens/Nov. 30th 1886/Hartford/Livy".
> *Location:* Antenne-Dorrance Collection, Rice Lake, Wis.
> *Copy examined:* Clemens' copy.

————. *The Light of Asia; or, The Great Renunciation (Mahâbhinishkramana), Being the Life and Teachings of Gautama, Prince of India and Founder of Buddhism (As told in Verse by an Indian Buddhist).* Boston: Roberts Brothers, 1861. Repr. 1879, 1880, 1881, etc. by Roberts Brothers and other firms.
> *Catalog: C1951,* #J7, listed among the books owned by Jean and Clara Clemens.

————. *Pearls of the Faith; or, Islam's Rosary. Being the Ninety-nine Beautiful Names of Allah (Asmâ-el-husnâ). With Comments in Verse by Various Oriental Sources (as Made by an Indian Musulman).* Boston: Roberts Brothers, 1883. 319 pp.
> *Inscription:* "S. L. Clemens, 1883" on flyleaf.
> *Catalog: A1911,* #15, $3.

Arnold, Matthew. *Civilization in the United States: First and Last Impressions of America.* [First published in the April 1888 issue of *Nineteenth Century;* issued the same year in book form.]

"Matthew Arnold's civilization is *superficial* polish," Mark Twain observed in April 1888 (NB 27, TS p. 64). Yet in a letter written to Robert Louis Stevenson on 15–17 April 1888 Clemens blamed the "heedless" American press for misconstruing Arnold's "kind intent" (ALS in John Howell Papers, Silverado Museum, St. Helena, California). A few months later he castigated Arnold for preferring the worm-eaten & dilapidated social structure in England" (NB 28, TS p. 9). D. M. McKeithan has deduced that Mark Twain intended his speech "On Foreign Critics" *(MTS[1923],* pp. 150–153) as a retort to Arnold's criticisms, but Arnold's unexpected death in April 1888 compelled him to omit all personal references. McKeithan also demonstrates that Mark Twain's speech included a quotation of Sir Lepel Henry Griffin by way of Arnold, who modified it slightly in *Civilization* from Griffin's *The Great Republic* (1884) (see "The Occasion of Mark Twain's Speech 'On Foreign Critics' " in *CTMT,* pp. 144–147). Mark Twain's indignation still showed plainly in chapter 10 of *The American Claimant* (1892), in which Lord Berkeley listens to the assistant editor of the *Daily Democrat* read two passages from Arnold's book—both critical of the Americans' lack of awe and respect—and argue that Arnold overlooked the chief virtue of American journalism: "its frank and cheerful irreverence."

———. *Essays in Criticism. Second Series.* (London, 1888).
Arnold's essay on Shelley in this volume probably was the source of Arnold's opinions to which Mark Twain alluded in his "In Defence of Harriet Shelley" (1894).

———. *Poems.*
Catalog: C1951, #014, listed among the books which contained only Livy Clemens' signature.

Arnould, (Sir) Joseph (1814–1886). *Life of Thomas, First Lord Denman, Formerly Lord Chief Justice of England.* 2 vols. Boston: Estes & Lauriat, [1874].
Inscriptions: vols. 1 and 2 both signed in pencil on flyleaf: "Saml L. Clemens/ Hartford 1874".
Marginalia: respondent reports annotation in vol. 1; there are no markings in vol. 2.
Catalog: A1911, #64, vol. 1 only, sold with fourteen other volumes by various authors for $8.50 total; vol. 1 only offered for sale in 1963 by John Swingle of Alta California Rare Books, Berkeley, California.
Location: vol. 1 was given to the Mark Twain Memorial in Hartford by an anonymous donor in 1965; vol. 2 is in the Mark Twain Library, Redding.
Copy examined: Clemens' copy of vol. 2; his copy of vol. 1 was inspected by Diana Royce, Librarian of the Stowe-Day Library.

Arrhenius, Svante August (1859–1927). *The Life of the Universe as Conceived by Man from the Earliest Ages to the Present Time.* Trans. by Dr. H. Borns. 2 vols. London and New York: Harper & Brothers, 1909.
Catalog: C1951, #D16, listed among the books signed by Clemens.

———. *Worlds in the Making; The Evolution of the Universe.* Trans. by H. Borns. Illus. New York: Harper & Brothers, 1908. 230 pp.
Source: MTLAcc, entry #538, volume donated by Clemens.

Art and Letters. An Illustrated Review. Ed. by Frédéric Masson. (Monthly periodical). Published January 1888–December 1889. New York: Charles Scribner's Sons; London: Boussod, Valadin & Co. [English edition of *Les lettres et les arts.*]
Catalog: A1911, #16, $2.50, "January to December, 1888 (not consecutive) 11 parts. Small folio."

Arthur, Timothy Shay (1809–1885).

The little do-gooder heroine of "The Story of Mamie Grant, the Child-Missionary" (1868) hopes that she "may yet see my poor little name in a beautiful Sunday School book, & maybe T.S. Arthur may write it. Oh, joy!" *(S&B,* pp. 33–39). Laura Hawkins complains in chapter 36 of *The Gilded Age* (1873) that the peanut boys in railway cars always try to sell one a "Tupper or a dictionary or T. S. Arthur if you are fond of poetry." Arthur's most popular book was the temperance novel *Ten Nights in a Bar-Room, and What I Saw There* (1854).

Artistic Houses; Being a Series of Interior Views of a Number of the Most Beautiful and Celebrated Homes in the United States; with a Description of the Art Treasures Contained Therein. Illus. 2 vols. in 4. Limited edition of 500 copies. New York: Printed for subscribers by D. Appleton and Co., 1883–1884.

Catalog: A1911, #17, $8, "over 200 plates, . . . velvet-covered board portfolio, brass-tipped corners."

Clemens was furious when he received a bill for $300 for these books; calling it "a humiliating swindle," he vowed to order a like amount of other books from D. Appleton & Company and then make them repossess *Artistic Houses* as payment (Clemens to Charles L. Webster, 8 February 1885, *MTBus,* pp. 298–299). There is no evidence that he carried out this threat. Among the New York City mansions depicted in *Artistic Houses* were those of Louis C. Tiffany, Alexander T. Stewart, J. Pierpont Morgan, and William H. Vanderbilt; opulent homes in other American cities were also included.

The Art Journal (London periodical, pub. 1839–1912). London: Virtue & Co.

In May 1875 Clemens provided prizes for the contestants in a fund-raising spelling bee at the Asylum Hill Congregational Church of Hartford. The 13 May 1875 issue of the Hartford *Courant* published Clemens' preliminary remarks, in which he mentioned contributing the *London Art Journal for 1875,* "profusely illustrated with wood and steel" (Leah A. Strong, "Mark Twain on Spelling," *AL,* 23 [November 1951], 357–359).

Artman, (Mrs.) S. R. *Glimpses of the Sunny South.* Illus. New York: F. T. Neely & Co., 1903. 176 pp.

Source: MTLAcc, entry #802, volume donated by Clemens.

Asher, Georg Michael, ed. *Henry Hudson the Navigator. The Original Documents in Which His Career Is Recorded.* London: Printed for the Hakluyt Society, 1860. 292 pp.

In "Official Report to the I.I.A.S." (written 1909) Mark Twain cited Asher's opinion that the mermaid which Henry Hudson claimed to have seen was "probably a seal" *(LE,* p. 150). Asher brought out only this one book on Hudson's exploits.

Assollant, Alfred (1827–1886). *The Fantastic History of the Celebrated Pierrot.* Trans. by A. G. Munro. Illus. by Yan' Dargent. London: Sampson Low & Co., 1875. 262 pp.

Source: MTLAcc, entry #1864, volume donated from Clemens' library by Clara Clemens Gabrilowitsch in 1910.

Astor, William Waldorf, 1st Viscount Astor (1848–1919). *Sforza, A Story of Milan.* New York: Charles Scribner's Sons, 1889. 282 pp.

Source: MTLAcc, entry #11, volume donated by Clemens.

———. *Valentino. An Historical Romance of the Sixteenth Century in Italy.* New York: Charles Scribner's Sons, 1885. 325 pp.

"Valentino. Ch Scribner Sons" wrote Clemens in December 1885 (NB 25, TS p. 34).

Athenaeus. *The Deipnosophists; or, Banquet of the Learned, of Athenaeus.* Trans. by Charles Duke Yonge. 3 vols. London: H. G. Bohn, 1853–1854. Volumes #13–15 in Bohn's Classical Library series.
> *Inscription:* "Saml. L. Clemens,/Hartford, 1875" in each volume.
> *Marginalia:* none in vol. 3; other vols. unknown.
> *Catalog: A1911,* #19, $2.50, vols. 1 and 2 only.
> *Locations:* vols. 1 and 2, unknown; vol. 3 purchased by Carrie Estelle Doheny from Maxwell Hunley in 1940 for $12.20 and donated to St. John's Seminary, Camarillo, California.
> *Copy examined:* Clemens' copy of vol. 3.

Atherton. (Mrs.) Gertrude Franklin (Horn) (1857–1848). *Ancestors; A Novel.* New York: Harper & Brothers, 1907. 709 pp.
> *Source:* MTLAcc, entry #1837, volume donated from Clemens' library by Clara Clemens Gabrilowitsch in 1910.

————. *The Bell in the Fog, and Other Stories.* New York: Harper & Brothers, 1905. 301 pp.
> *Source:* MTLAcc, entry #1249, volume donated by Isabel V. Lyon, Clemens' secretary.

————. [Another identical copy.]
> *Source:* MTLAcc, entry #1250, volume donated by Clemens.

————. *Rulers of Kings; A Novel.* New York: Harper & Brothers, 1903. 413 pp.
> *Source:* MTLAcc, entry #954, volume donated by Clemens.

————. *The Traveling Thirds.* New York: Harper & Brothers, 1905. 295 pp.
> *Source:* MTLAcc, entry #1100, volume donated by Clemens.

Atkinson, Edward (1827–1905).
> In chapter 28 of *LonMiss* (1883), Mark Twain concludes his discussion of the Mississippi River Commission by deferring to Atkinson's view: "One thing will be easily granted by the reader: that an opinion from Mr. Edward Atkinson, upon any vast national commercial matter, comes as near ranking as authority as can the opinion of any individual in the Union." Appendix B to *LonMiss* publishes Atkinson's optimistic assessment of the river-control project, signed and dated in Boston on 14 April 1882. Mark Twain does not name the source for Atkinson's brief essay.

Atkinson, William Walker (1862–1932), pseud. "Yogi Ramacharaka." *Advanced Course in Yogi Philosophy and Oriental Occultism.* Chicago: The Yogi Publication Society, 1905. 337 pp.
> *Inscription:* front free endpaper signed in ink "Clara Clemens".
> *Location:* Mark Twain Library, Redding, Conn.
> *Copy examined:* Clara Clemens' unmarked copy.

Atlantic Monthly Magazine (Boston periodical). Began publication in 1857.
> Clemens read the *Atlantic* so steadily during Howells' tenure as its editor that virtually no issue between 1871 and 1881 should be ruled out of any list of his probable reading material. "I read the entire Atlantic this time. Wonderful number," he wrote to Howells on 4 July 1877 *(MTHL,* p. 187). The arrival of the journal at his hotel was a cheery event when he was abroad: in Heidelberg, he wrote to Howells on 26 May 1878, he spent one evening "tilted back . . . with a pipe & the last Atlantic" *(MTHL,* p. 230); in Baden-Baden he "went to bed early" on 10 August 1878, "with the new home magazines [*Harper's* and *Atlantic*], which I had saved all day & wouldn't cut a leaf" (NB 15, *N&J,* 2:134). It seems likely that Clemens continued to read the journal with some regularity between 1881 and

1890, the period when his friend Thomas Bailey Aldrich succeeded Howells to the editorship. Mark Twain also mentions the *Atlantic* in February 1879 (NB 17, *N&J,* 2:269–271); in "Mental Telegraphy," quoting an article in the June 1882 issue; in a letter to Charles L. Webster, 27 January 1885 *(MTBus,* p. 298); and in the tentative appendix to *A Connecticut Yankee* (NB 29, TS pp. 13, 15) set down in 1889. Roger Salomon *(TIH,* p. 111 n. 9) has traced the latter reference to an article entitled "The Old Bankers of Florence," *Atlantic Monthly,* 24 (1869), 629–637.

Auber, Daniel François Esprit (1782–1871). *The Crown Diamonds* (romantic comic opera).

Mark Twain reviewed a performance of this opera—"put upon the stage in creditable shape on Monday evening"—in the 15 October 1864 issue of *The Californian.* His review, titled "Still Further Concerning That Conundrum," concentrated upon a prop-man who moved furniture between scenes *(SSix,* pp. 131–135).

MTC, pp. 52–56.

Audubon, John James (1785–1851). *The Birds of America from Drawings Made in the United States and Their Territories.* Reissued by John Woodhouse Audubon. Plates engraved by J. Bien. 5 vols. New York: Roe, Lockwood & Son; also G. Lockwood, 1860–1870.

Catalog: A1911, #20, $85, "4 vols . . . of text . . . of 1870, & an elephant folio vol. of 106 plates (1860 edition)."

Audubon's original folio was published in London in 1827–1838; the text was first issued in Edinburgh in 1831–1839. The chromolithographic plates made by J. Bien in 1858–1859 for a reissue of the folio are not faithful reproductions, particularly in regard to the background in the pictures, and are considered vastly inferior to the original hand-colored engravings. But Audubon had charged $1,000 per set for his four volumes of engraved prints (of which 2,000 sets were issued), and these treasured books were unattainable for most buyers even in the nineteenth century.

Clemens may never have fully understood that the reissue he purchased was merely valuable and not rare or costly. Audubon's *Birds* was one of the very few antiquarian items which he showed a keen interest in possessing simply as a printed artifact. He noticed an advertisement for the set in an Estes & Lauriat catalog, and promptly requested Howells to investigate the offer for him in Boston. "I think the price is $150," he wrote. "It can't be in very good condition, I suppose, at that figure; but if it is, & is complete, & of Audubon's own issue . . . won't you please ask them to ship it" *(MTHL,* pp. 318–319). Surely Howells informed him that it was merely a reissue. On 25 August 1880 Estes & Lauriat of Boston billed Clemens for "Audubon's Birds of America. Plates in 1 vol folio. Text in 4 vols 8vo" that cost $150 and was sent by express to Hartford (MTP). On at least one occasion he put the illustrations to practical use; George Washington Cable reported from Hartford on 13 February 1884 about a day he passed with Clemens in Hartford: "Part of the time—I forgot to say—was spent in consulting Audubon to identify a strange & beautiful bird that we had seen at breakfast time from the window of the library" *(MT&GWC,* p. 32). The costly first folio continued to fascinate Mark Twain; his Autobiographical Dictation of 30 January 1907 contained an anecdote about one of Audubon's relatives who "possessed a copy, in perfect condition, of Audubon's great book," but was hoodwinked by a cunning university professor into selling it to him for one-tenth its true value *(MTE,* p. 96).

Auerbach, Berthold (1812–1882). *Auf der Höhe. Roman in acht büchern* (1864).

Mark Twain jotted down the author and title of this book in May 1885 (NB 24, TS p. 18).

————. [*Black Forest Village Stories*. Trans. by Charles Goepp. Illus. New York: Leypolt & Holt, 1869. 377 pp. Repr. by H. Holt and Co., 1874.]

Mark Twain seems to have read Auerbach's *Schwarzwälder Dorfgeschichten* (1843), which became available to American audiences in 1869, translated as *Black Forest Village Stories*. The English translation contained tales entitled "The Gawk," "The Pipe of War," "Manor-House Farmer's Vefela," "Nip-Cheeked Toney," "Ivo the Gentleman," "Florian and Crescence," and others. Its accessibility in an English translation argues against his using the German-language edition. In chapter 22 of *A Tramp Abroad* Mark Twain described a typical "heroine of one of Auerbach's novels," with her "Black Forest clothes, and her burned complexion, her plump figure, . . . and the plaited tails of hemp-colored hair hanging down her back." In the same chapter he also remarked that he "found the Black Forest houses and villages all that the Black Forest stories have pictured them."

————. *On the Heights; A Novel*. 3 vols. Authorized Edition. Trans. from German by Fanny E. Bunnett. Leipzig: B. Tauchnitz, 1867.

Source: MTLAcc, entry #1838, volume 3 only donated from Clemens' library by Clara Clemens Gabrilowitsch in 1910. All after page 432 is missing in vol. 3.

L'Aurore. Littéraire, artistique, social. (French periodical). Published 18 October 1897–29 May 1900[?].

In January 1898 Clemens "wrote Percy Mitchell (Paris) & asked him to try & get a copy of 'Aurore' for me (containing Zola's grand letter)" (NB40, TS p. 8). Mitchell sent the requested copy to Clemens in London. Presumably Zola's letter concerned the Dreyfus case.

Austen, Jane (1775–1817). *Pride and Prejudice* (1813).

Mark Twain did not mention Jane Austen in his correspondence, literary works, or notebooks before 1895, but during the last fifteen years of his life he displayed an unrelenting contempt for her novels that astonished and amused his friends. So great was his hatred for her mode of writing that the mere mention of her name could provoke him into a seething denunciation of Austen and her idolators. His hostility toward Austen seems especially strange because her critical champions in the United States, Howells and Brander Matthews, were men with whom Mark Twain generally tried to agree.

The first indication of the irritation she caused him is an entry he made in Notebook 36 while on Board the *Mararoa* in December 1895: "In past year have read Vicar of Wakefield & some of Jane Austin [*sic*]. Thoroughly artificial" (TS p. 3). On January 1896, still in the Indian Ocean, he perused the ship library and then resolved, "I must read that devilish Vicar of Wakefield again. Also Jane Austin [*sic*]" (NB 37, TS p. 3). This intention gave rise to his famous dismissal of her literary merit in chapter 62 of *Following the Equator* (1897), where he claimed that on the afternoon of 10 April 1896 he wrote in his diary: "Jane Austen's books, too, are absent from this [ship] library. Just that one omission alone would make a fairly good library out of a library that hadn't a book in it."

Austen would remain linked in his mind with Oliver Goldsmith (and James Fenimore Cooper) as examples of writers whose mannered fiction was vastly overpraised. When Joseph Twichell sided with Matthews in gently chastising Mark Twain for ridiculing Goldsmith and Cooper, Mark Twain admitted in a letter written to Twichell on 13 September 1898 that he knew he lacked Matthews' qualifications as a critic. Matthews could always distinguish the good points in any work he read, Mark Twain explained. Consequently "I haven't any right to criticise books, and I don't do it except when I hate them. I often want to criticise Jane Austen, but her books madden me so that I can't conceal my frenzy from the reader; and therefore I have to stop every time I begin" (*MTL*, 2: 667). Paine's edition of *Letters* indicates no ellipsis here, but in 1920 Brander Matthews quoted the full text of Mark Twains' remarks to Twichell, whom Matthews identified only as one of Mark Twain's close friends: ". . . and therefore, I have to stop every time I begin. Every time I read 'Pride and Prejudice' I want to dig her up and beat her over the skull with her own shin-bone" *(Essays on English,* p. 264).[1] Matthews hastened to assure his readers that Mark Twain "expressed his desire to desecrate her grave only in a letter to an intimate familiar with his imaginative exaggeration" (p. 265).

One of the abortive attempts to comment on Austen's novels that Mark Twain found he had "to stop every time" is now in the Mark Twain Papers (DV201), an undated and unfinished manuscript of seven and a half pages. Twain began this piece by remarking: "Whenever I take up 'Pride & Prejudice' or 'Sense & Sensibility,' I feel like a barkeeper entering the Kingdom of Heaven" (quoted in *MTB,* p. 1500; though quoting directly from the manuscript, Paine reports that Mark Twain uttered these remarks in June 1909 during a train ride from Baltimore to Redding—a misrepresentation of facts). Mark Twain's meaning becomes apparent in his succeeding comments in the essay: a barkeeper from the Bowery would probably try at first to hobnob with the "ultra-good Presbyterians" he would encounter in Heaven, but he simply would not enjoy their company. He himself feels a similar discouragement, Twain explains, after repeated efforts to recognize the "high art" acclaimed by respected critics. He has seldom been able to read through "to the other end" of Austen's books because of their common fault—"She makes me detest all her people, without reserve." Mark Twain avoids any further disparagement of Austen's artistry; he merely confesses that he is not to be classed among the Elect who can enjoy her novels and appreciate their elusive virtues.

Clemens very likely was less reserved in his discussions with friends. Howells needled him about their friendly dispute in a letter written on 1 May 1903 when Clemens was ill in Riverdale: "Now you're sick, I've a great mind to have it out with [you] about Jane Austen. If you say much more I'll come out and read 'Pride and Prejudice' to you" *(MTHL,* p. 769). Clemens did not restrict his arguments to Howells, Twichell, or Matthews, however; on 7 November 1906 Isabel Lyon noted that during dinner he and Kate Douglas (Wiggin) Riggs "had a friendly battle over Jane Austen, whose books the King abhors and Mrs. Riggs delights in" (IVL Journal, TS p. 201, MTP). Clemens obviously savored the set-to; the next day he wrote to Jean about the dinner party of the preceding evening at 21 Fifth Avenue: "A very pleasant party, & good talk. Some of it violent. Because Mrs. Riggs & I do not agree about Jane Austin [*sic*]. She respects Jane Austin [*sic*], whilst it is the one desire of my heart to dig her up" (Berg). No doubt Jean (like Twichell) could finish that sentence for herself.

The vehemence of Mark Twain's outbursts against Austen's fiction is phenomenal. He never slackened his fire on Howells' position, writing on 18 January 1909: "To me his [Poe's] prose is unreadable—like Jane Austin's [*sic*]. No, there is a difference. I could read his prose on salary, but not Jane's. Jane is entirely impossible. It seems a great pity to me that they allowed her to die a natural death" *(MTHL,* p. 841). Howells would recall sadly in *My Mark Twain* (1910): "His prime abhorrence was my dear and honored prime favorite, Jane Austen. He once said to me . . ., *'You* seem to think that woman could write,' and he forebore withering me with his scorn, apparently because we had been friends so long, and he more pitied than hated me for my bad taste" (p. 16). We may assume that this lapse in Mark Twain's critical judgment weighed heavily with Howells when he characterized his friend for posterity as "the most unliterary" of his author acquaintances.

Various interpreters have attempted to account for Mark Twain's animadversions on Austen. Van Wyck Brooks oversimplified the matter in 1920 in stating that "when he roars and rages against the novels of Jane Austen we can see that buried self taking vengeance upon Mr. Howells, with whom Jane Austen was a prime passion, who had even taken Jane Austen as a model" *(The Ordeal of Mark*

---

[1]Matthews first quoted Mark Twain's letter in "Mark Twain and the Art of Writing," *Harper's Magazine,* 141 (October 1920), 635–643, collected in *Essays on English* (1921).

Twain [New York: E. P. Dutton & Co., 1920], p. 183). But there is no question that Clemens' diatribes were directed at least in part against a nexus of literary standards with which he found himself in sharp disagreement. It is intriguing, in this regard, to remember Clara's testimony that Austen was one of the authors— along with George Meredith—from whose works Livy often read to the family at Quarry Farm, with Clemens sniping in the background *(MFMT*, p. 61).

Brander Matthews opened up a perhaps more profitable line of inquiry in his *Essays on English* (1921), speculating that Austen's artistic vision may have seemed restricted to Mark Twain; possibly "her little miracles of observation seemed to him only the carving of cherry-stones" (p. 264). Or conceivably Mark Twain felt a distaste for her "placid and complacent acceptance of a semi-feudal social organization, stratified like a chocolate layer-cake, with petty human fossils in its lower formations" (p. 265). Richard Poirier has more recently set himself the problem of accounting for Mark Twain's well-known dislike for Austen and has developed a valuable explanation along somewhat similar lines in *A World Elsewhere: The Place of Style in American Literature* (1966). According to Poirier, Mark Twain represents one facet of "a significant American dissatisfaction with the kind of social ordering of existence that takes place in her novels" (p. 145). Austen is confident that her audience "can be satisfied by social unions, especially by marriage" (p. 147); but Mark Twain, like Huck Finn, entertained "some larger distrust of social structures themselves" (p. 148). He and other American writers lack "her positive vision of social experience" and "the capacity to imagine society as including the threat of conformity and artificiality and [yet] as offering, nevertheless, beneficial opportunities for self-discovery" (p. 153). Poirier suggests that "Jane Austen's satire has behind it a confidence that English society gives everyone a chance, as the society in *Huckleberry Finn* does not, to find a place that can be called 'natural' " (p. 163). Even Poirier's illuminating insights by no means wholly account for the vitriol in Mark Twain's pronouncements, and more will surely be written about this topic.

————. *Mansfield Park. A Novel.* Collection of British Authors Series. Leipzig: Bernhard Tauchnitz, 1867. 442 pp.
   Source: MTLAcc, entry #1839, volume donated from Clemens' library by Clara Clemens Gabrilowitsch in 1910.

————. *Northanger Abbey.* London: George Routledge and Sons, n.d. 448 pp.
   Location: Mark Twain Library, Redding, Conn. Donated from Clemens' library by Clara Clemens Gabrilowitsch in 1910 (MTLAcc, entry #1840).
   Copy examined: Clemens' copy, unmarked. Rear pastedown endpaper displays the sticker of Brown & Gross Booksellers, Hartford, Conn.

————. *Sense and Sensibility* (1811).
   In the undated manuscript entitled "Jane Austen" (DV201, MTP) Mark Twain specified some of his objections to this novel. These remarks are especially important because of the generalized nature of his other statements about Austen's writings; they offer a key to understanding the grounds for his disagreement with her novelistic techniques. He claims to be rereading the first third of *Sense and Sensibility* at the moment, and he closes the essay with a catalogue of the characters and his criticisms of their portrayals. Elinor is a "harmless waxwork"; Edward "an unpleasant shadow"; Willoughby "criminal & filthy"; and the others strike him as being similarly offensive in various ways. His comments end abruptly at the top of a page after he noted these cavils. Evidently his critical standards required the creation of at least one character with whom he might identify and sympathize; finding none, he lost patience with Austen's novel of manners and its emphasis on dialogues from an earlier English society.

Austin, Alfred (1835–1913). *Flodden Field; A Tragedy*. New York: Harper & Brothers, 1903. 137 pp.
    Source: MTLAcc, entry #1456, volume donated by Clemens.

————. *A Tale of True Love, and Other Poems*. New York: Harper and Brothers, 1902. 139 pp.
    Source: MTLAcc, entry #643, volume donated by Clemens.
    Mark Twain poked fun at Tennyson's successor as poet laureate on several occasions. In 1896, the year that Victoria appointed Austin to the laureateship, Mark Twain read a silly poem of his own invention about an egg-laying mammal to a lecture audience in Benares, India, and then commented that "the present Laureate is just the same kind of poet as I am" (quoted in Coleman O. Parsons, "Mark Twain: Sightseer in India," p. 88). For chapter 36 of *Following the Equator* Mark Twain constructed a poem using sixty-six colorful names of Australian towns and then conceded, "Perhaps a poet laureate could do better, but a poet laureate gets wages, and that is different." He was more direct in belittling Austin in chapter 66, blaming him for over-hastiness in glorifying the actions of South Africans whose motives were not clear: "The new poet laureate lost no time. He came out with a rousing poem lauding Jameson's prompt and splendid heroism in flying to the rescue of the women and children." Disregarding the possible facts of the case, Austin "produced a poet-laureatic explosion of colored fireworks which filled the world's sky with giddy splendors."
    But perhaps Clemens eventually regarded with ambivalence the poems and verse dramas of Austin, who so often wrote of loneliness and death. Albert Bigelow Paine was present when Clemens, grieving over Jean's death in December 1909, "read aloud some lines by Alfred Austin, which Mrs. Crane had sent him—lines which he had remembered in the sorrow for Susy" (*MTB*, p. 1551). Paine quoted the lines: "When last came sorrow, around barn and byre/Wind-carven snow, the year's white sepulchre, lay./'Come in,' I said, 'and warm you by the fire':/And there she sits and never goes away."

Austin (Mrs.) Jane (Goodwin) (1831–1894). *Mrs. Beauchamp Brown*. No Name Series. Boston: Roberts Brothers, 1880. 319 pp.
    Source: MTLAcc, entry #13, volume donated by Clemens.
    In July 1880 J. R. Barlow, Hartford booksellers, billed Clemens for "1 Mrs. Brown (No Name Series) $1.00," a volume purchased on 10 May 1880; Clemens paid the bill on 5 July 1880 (receipt in MTP).

Austin, (Mrs.) Mary (Hunter) (1868–1934). *Lost Borders*. Illus. New York: Harper & Brothers, 1909. 209 pp.
    Source: MTLAcc, entry #1841, volume donated from Clemens' library by Clara Clemens Gabrilowitsch in 1910.

————. *Santa Lucia, A Common Story*. New York: Harper & Brothers, 1908. 345 pp.
    Source: MTLAcc, entry #10, volume donated by Clemens.

Austin, Maude Mason. *'Cension. A Sketch from Paso Del Norte*. Illus. New York: Harper & Brothers, 1896. 159 pp.
    Source: MTLAcc, entry #1322, volume donated by Clemens.

Babcock, (Mrs.) Winnifred (Eaton) (b. 1879), pseud. "Onoto Watanna." *A Japanese Blossom*. Illus. by L. W. Ziegler. New York: Harper & Brothers, 1906. 264 pp.
    Source: MTLAcc, entry #1314, volume donated by Clemens.

————. *A Japanese Nightingale*. Illus. by Genjiro Yeto. New York: Harper & Brothers, 1901. 225 pp. Repr. 1902.
    Catalog: C1951, #07, listed among volumes signed by Livy Clemens, edition unspecified.

————. *The Wooing of Wistaria.* New York: Harper & Brothers, 1902. 388 pp.
Inscription: front pastedown endpaper signed "S. L. Clemens, 1902."
Catalog: A1911, #477, $1.50.

Baby Days; A Selection of Songs, Stories and Pictures, for Very Little Folks. With an Introduction by the Editor of "St. Nicholas" [*Mary Mapes Dodge*]. New York: Scribner & Co., [cop. 1877]. 192 pp.
An undated letter from Clemens to Theodore Langdon's family, "Xmas Morning" [1877?], thanks the Langdons for *Baby Days* and other books given to Livy and the Clemens girls (MTP). *Baby Days* contained children's pieces selected from the *St. Nicholas Magazine,* which began publication in 1873.

Bacheller, Irving (1859–1950). *Darrel of the Blessed Isles.* Illus. by Arthur I. Keller. Boston: Lothrop Pub. Co., [cop. 1903]. 410 pp.
Source: MTLAcc, entry #1511, volume donated by Clemens.

————. *Eben Holden; A Tale of the North Country.* Fourth ed. Boston: Lothrop Publishing Co., [cop. 1900]. 432 pp.
Inscription: "My dear Mark Twain: Let me introduce my old friend Uncle Eb and credit me what you will on the great debt I owe you. Irving Bacheller/ 320 St. Nicholas Ave N.Y./ Dec. 5, 1900."
Location: Carrie Estelle Doheny Collection, St. John's Seminary, Camarillo, California. Purchased by Mrs. Doheny from Maxwell Hunley of Beverly Hills in 1940 for $12.20.
Copy examined: Clemens' copy.
Bacheller's novel was first published in July 1900; it sold so rapidly that copies issued in March 1901 were imprinted "250,000th." On 14 December 1900 Clemens wrote to Bacheller: "The book has this moment arrived. . . . A thousand thanks; have longed for the book. . . . I will . . . stretch out with a pipe and have a good time" (Irving Bacheller, *From Stores of Memory* [New York: Farrar & Rinehart, 1938], p. 62; date supplied from ALS in CWB).

————. *Eben Holden; A Tale of the North Country.* Illus. Boston: Lothrop Pub. Co., [cop. 1900]. 432 pp.
Source: MTLAcc, entry #885, volume donated by Clemens.

————. *Eben Holden's Last Day A-Fishing.* New York: Harper & Brothers, 1907. 60 pp.
Source: MTLAcc, entry #16, volume donated by Clemens.

————. [Another identical copy.]
Source: MTLAcc, entry #1510, volume donated by Clemens.

————. *The Hand-Made Gentleman; A Tale of the Battles of Peace.* New York: Harper & Brothers, 1909. 332 pp.
Source: MTLAcc, entry #1034, volume donated by Clemens.

————. [Another identical copy.]
Source: MTLAcc, entry #2180, volume donated by Clara Clemens Gabrilowitsch in 1910.

————. *The Master, Being in Part Copied from the Minutes of the School for Novelists, a Round Table of Good Fellows Who, Long Since, Dined Every Saturday at the Sign o'the Lanthorne, on Golden Hill in New York City.* New York: Doubleday, Page & Co., 1909. 302 pp.
Inscription: on front free endpaper: "Yours for peace/ Irving Bacheller/ Riverside Ct./ Dec. 3 '09"; also signed on front pastedown endpaper: "Catherine Leary/ Reading/ Conn."
Location: Antenne-Dorrance Collection, Rice Lake, Wis.
Copy examined: Clemens' copy, presumably. It seems doubtful that Bacheller himself would have inscribed a presentation copy to Clemens' housekeeper.

————. *The Master of Silence. A Romance.* New York: Charles L. Webster & Co., 1892. 176 pp.

Advertised in the *Publishers' Trade List Annual 1893* as "the first novel of Mr. Irving Bacheller, the head of the Bacheller newspaper syndicate. . . . A striking study of a mind-reader's experiences." Issued by Clemens' publishing firm in the "Fiction, Fact and Fancy" series edited by Arthur Stedman.

————. *Silas Strong, Emperor of the Woods.* New York: Harper & Brothers, 1906. 339 pp.

Inscription: "To Mark Twain/who, I hope, for/this little book/will credit me/something on my/great debt to him./Irving Bacheller/Riverside Conn./April 2 1906"; signed on front pastedown endpaper: "S L Clemens/1906/Apl./21 Fifth avenue."

Catalogs: C1951, #25c, listed among books signed by Clemens; Parke-Bernet Galleries, "English and American First Editions . . . Collected by Jean Hersholt, Beverly Hills, California," Sale No. 1503 (New York City), March 1954, item #175, p. 31; Lew David Feldman, "American Books" (1955), Catalogue of House of El Dieff, item #41, price $46.75.

Provenance: Bookplate of Jean Hersholt on rear pastedown endpaper.

Location: C. Waller Barrett Collection, University of Virginia, Charlottesville. Donated in 1970.

Copy examined: Clemens' copy.

————. [Another identical copy.]

Source: MTLAcc, entry #1449, volume donated by Clemens.

————. *Vergilius; A Tale of the Coming of Christ.* New York: Harper & Brothers. 1904. 279 pp.

Source: MTLAcc, entry #1512, volume donated by Clemens.

Bacon, Delia Salter. *The Philosophy of the Plays of Shakspere Unfolded.* Preface by Nathaniel Hawthorne. Boston: Ticknor and Fields, 1857. 582 pp.

Bacon (1811–1859) was an American writer who worked in England. She became violently insane soon after publishing this book, which originated the theory that the Shakespearean plays were written by a group directed by Francis Bacon. Mark Twain recalled the sensation Delia Bacon's book aroused in the first part of *Is Shakespeare Dead?* (1909), tracing his curiosity about the Baconian heresy back to his piloting days on the Mississippi River: "My fifty years' interest in that matter —asleep for the last three years—is excited once more. It is an interest which was born of Delia Bacon's book—away back in that ancient day—1857, or maybe 1856." According to these recollections, Clemens "discussed, and discussed, and discussed, and disputed and disputed and disputed" her book with a pilot named George Ealer, who "bought the literature of the dispute as fast as it appeared."

Bacon, Francis (1561–1626). *The Promus of Formularies and Elegancies (Being Private Notes, Circ. 1594, Hitherto Unpublished) by Francis Bacon. Illustrated and Elucidated by Passages from Shakespeare by Mrs. Henry Pott [Constance Mary (Fearon) Pott], with Preface by E[dwin] A[bbott] Abbott.* [London: Longmans, Green, and Co.?], 1883. 628 pp.

Catalog: A1911, #24, $5.50, "facsimile," place of publication listed as Boston but no such edition is recorded in the *National Union Catalog.*

Mrs. Pott attempts to demonstrate parallelisms of expression in Bacon's commonplace book and the works of Shakespeare.

Bacon, George Washington & Company, Ltd. *Bacon's Midget Map of London.* [London, first edition 1865].

Marginalia: "Charing Cross means 'dear Queen's Cross'".

Listed by Albert E. Stone in his catalog of Clemens' books in the Mark Twain Library at Redding in 1955.

Bacon, (Mrs.) Josephine Dodge (Daskam) (1876–1961). *The Madness of Philip, and Other Tales of Childhood.* Illus. by F. Y. Cory. New York: McClure, Phillips, & Co., 1902. 223 pp.
Source: MTLAcc, entry #459, volume donated by Clemens.

————. *The Memoirs of a Baby.* Illus. by F. Y. Cory. New York: Harper & Brothers, 1905. 272 pp.
Source: MTLAcc, entry #1455, volume donated by Clemens.

————. [Another identical copy].
Source: MTLAcc, entry #1695, volume donated by Clemens.

————. *Ten to Seventeen; A Boarding-School Diary.* Illus. New York: Harper & Brothers, 1908. 261 pp.
Source: MTLAcc, entry #1584, volume donated by Clemens.

Bacon, (Mrs.) Mary Schell (Hoke) (b. 1870), pseud. "Dolores M. Bacon," ed. *Songs That Every Child Should Know; A Selection of the Best Songs of All Nations.* New York: Doubleday, Page, & Co., 1907. 221 pp.
Source: MTLAcc, entry #479, volume donated by Clemens.

Badeau, Adam (1831–1895). *Grant in Peace. From Appomattox to Mount McGregor. A Personal Memoir.* Hartford: S. S. Scranton & Co., 1887. 591 pp.
Clemens instructed Charles L. Webster on 6 June 1886 to offer Badeau a ten-percent royalty because "it promises to be an interesting book—gossipy & entertaining to all kinds of readers" *(MTLP,* p. 198). After Badeau published with another firm Clemens wrote to Webster on 6 December 1886: "I have read 'Grant in Peace' up to the present time, and there hasn't been a dull chapter thus far. It is mighty well written" *(MTLP,* p. 209).

Badlam, Alexander. *The Wonders of Alaska.* Illus., maps. San Francisco: Bancroft Co., 1890. 152 pp.
Inscription: on flyleaf: "Samuel L. Clemens, Esq.,/Compliments of/Alex. Badlam".
Location: Mark Twain Library, Redding, Conn.
Copy examined: Clemens' copy.

Baedeker, Karl (1801–1859). *Austria, Including Hungary, Transylvania, Dalmatia, and Bosnia. Handbook for Travellers.*
In an undated note to Chatto & Windus, Clemens requested a copy of Baedeker's *Austria* (ALS in Berg).

————. *Italy. Handbook for Travellers.* Part 1, Northern Italy, 4th rev. ed. (1877); Part 2, Central Italy and Rome, 5th rev. ed. (1877); Part 3, Southern Italy and Sicily, 6th rev. ed. (1876). 3 vols. Leipsic: Karl Baedeker, 1876–1877. [First ed. pub. 1867.]
Praised for "curious & useful details" about Lake Como on 24 September 1878 (NB 16, *N&J,* 2: 193). Mentioned in May 1892 (NB 32, TS p. 5). Disparaged for its praise of the architecture and decorations of the Villa di Quarto near Florence in a January 1904 Autobiographical Dictation (MTP).

————. *London and Its Environs. Handbook for Travellers.* 10th rev. ed. Leipsic: Karl Baedeker, 1896. 424 pp. [Includes "Index of Streets."]
In 1896 Clemens could not find Tedworth Square listed in Baedeker's *London* (NB 39, TS p. 17).

————. *Paris and Its Environs. Handbook for Travellers.* 6th rev. ed. Leipsic: Karl Baedeker, 1878.
Reference in June 1879 (NB 18, *N&J*, 2: 314).

————. *The Rhine from Rotterdam to Constance. Handbook for Travellers.* 6th ed. Leipsic: Karl Baedeker, 1878. 341 pp.
Clemens presumably used this guidebook in July 1878; see Notebook 15 (*N&J*, 2: 116).

————. *Switzerland and the Adjacent Portions of Italy, Savoy, and the Tyrol. Handbook for Travellers.* 7th ed. Leipsic: Karl Baedeker, 1877. 470 pp.
References: Notebook 15 (1878, *N&J*, 2: 77); Notebook 16 (1878, *N&J*, 2: 161); *TA*, chapter 35. Mark Twain questioned Baedeker's estimates of distances on a few occasions, but the majority of his references to *Switzerland are* complimentary and a few are exceedingly favorable. In one of his notebooks for 1878, for instance, he praised "the iron integrity of Baedecker, who tells the petrified truth about hotels & everything. A wonderful guide book—a marvelous faithful & pains-taking work—you can go anywhere without a human guide, almost. And this book is absolutely correct & reliable" (NB 16, *N&J*, 2: 161). He repeated a version of these remarks in chapter 46 of *A Tramp Abroad* (1880): "Baedeker knows all about hotels, railway and diligence companies, and speaks his mind freely. He is a trustworthy friend of the traveler." Chapters 22, 28, 35, 36, 38, and 39 of *A Tramp Abroad* contain other generalized references to Baedeker's series of guidebooks.

Bagehot, Walter (1826–1877). *Biographical Studies.* London: Longmans, Green and Co., 1895. 398 pp.
Inscription: "S. L. Clemens from Mr. Skrine, Calcutta, April, 1896" in Clemens' hand.
Marginalia: several corrections and a few passages marked in pencil.
Catalogs: A1911, #25, $3.50; *L1912,* #5, $7.50.
Sketches of British statesmen, including Peel, Gladstone, Palmertston, and Disraeli.

Bagot, Richard (1860–1921). *The Passport.* New York: Harper & Brothers, 1905. 417 pp.
Source: MTLAcc, entry #1432, volume donated by Clemens.

Bahadur Rana, Mina. *Balabodhini.* Benares: Light Press, 1895.
Title page is reproduced in facsimile in chapter 53 of *Following the Equator* (1897).

Bailey, (Mrs.) Alice Ward (b. 1857). *Mark Heffron. A Novel.* New York: Harper & Brothers, 1896. 354 pp.
Source: MTLAcc, entry #1513, volume donated by Clemens.

Bailey, Henry Christopher (b. 1878). *Colonel Greatheart.* Illus. by Lester Ralph. Indianapolis, Ind.: Bobbs-Merrill Co., [cop. 1908]. 472 pp.
Source: MTLAcc, entry #876, volume donated by Mrs. Ralph W. Ashcroft (formerly Isabel Lyon), Clemens' secretary.

————. [Another identical copy.]
Source: MTLAcc, entry #964, volume donated by Mrs. Ralph W. Ashcroft (formerly Isabel Lyon), Clemens' secretary.

Bailey, James Montgomery (1841–1894), pseud. "Danbury News Man." *Life in Danbury: Being a Brief but Comprehensive Record . . . by . . . "The Danbury News Man"; and Carefully Compiled with a Pair of Eight-Dollar Shears.* Boston: Shepard and Gill, 1873. 303 pp.

Mark Twain's Library of Humor (1888) contains four sketches from this volume —"The Female Baseball Nine," "An Italian's View of a New England Writer," "After the Funeral," and "What He Wanted It For." Mark Twain alluded to Bailey by his pseudonym ("Danbury News") in Notebook 18 (1879, *N&J*, 2: 300); Notebook 19 (1880, *N&J*, 2: 362, 429); and in an Autobiographical Dictation on 31 July 1906 (*MTE*, p. 201).

Blair, "On the Structure of *Tom Sawyer*," pp. 78–79.

Bailey, Philip James (1816–1902). *Festus: A Poem.* New York: James Miller, n.d. 391 pp.

Source: MTLAcc, entry #656, volume donated by Clemens.

Bain, Francis William (1863–1940). *A Digit of the Moon; A Hindoo Love Story. Translated from the Original Manuscript.* 2nd ed. London: J. Parker and Co., 1901. 118 pp. [First ed. pub. 1899.]

Inscription: on front pastedown endpaper: "S. L. Clemens, 1903."

Catalog: A1911, #26.

Bainbridge, Oliver. *The Devil's Note Book.* Illus. by "Vet" Anderson. New York: Cochrane Publishing Co., 1908. 154 pp.

"I have sent you a copy of the 'Devil's Note Book' with hearty congratulations on your seventy-third birthday" (Bainbridge to Clemens, 1 December 1908, ALS in MTP).

Bainton, George, comp. and ed. *The Art of Authorship. Literary Reminiscences, Methods of Work, and Advice to Young Beginners, Personally Contributed by Leading Authors of the Day.* New York: D. Appleton and Co.; London: J. Clarke & Co., 1890. [First ed. pub. in London.]

Mark Twain contributed a letter on his "methods of composition" that Bainton published on pages 85–88, so Twain may have received a copy of this book.

Baker, Charles Hinckley (b. 1864). *Life and Character of William Taylor Baker, President of the World's Columbian Exposition and of the Chicago Board of Trade, by His Son.* New York: The Premier Press, 1908. 293 pp.

Inscription: on flyleaf: "To Mr. Samuel L. Clemens/'Mark Twain'/with the compliments and good/wishes of the author/Charles H. Baker/June 12th 1908".

Marginalia: in Clemens' hand with black ink on front pastedown endpaper: "A valuable book, & capably constructed. A tribute from a son to his father which does honor to both. SL C. June/08." No other annotation or markings.

Provenance: Contains stamps, charge-slip jacket, and call number of the Mark Twain Library, Redding, Conn. Donated by Clemens (MTLAcc, entry #1380).

Catalog: Mott 1952, item #36, $22.50.

Location: donated to the Mark Twain Memorial in Hartford, Connecticut as an anonymous gift in 1963.

Copy examined: Clemens' copy.

William Taylor Baker (1841–1903) was a Chicago business executive who constructed electric power plants in Seattle, Washington. All three hundred copies of this book were published for free distribution.

Baker, George Augustus (b. 1849). *Point-lace and Diamonds. Poems.* Illus. by Addie Ledyard. New York: F. B. Patterson, 1875. 153 pp.

Source: MTLAcc, entry #616, volume donated by Clemens.

Baker, (Sir) Richard (1568–1645). *A Chronicle of the Kings of England, from the Time of the Romans Government, to the Death of King James the First . . . with a Continuation to the Year 1660 by E. Phillips.* London: Printed for S. Ballard, 1733. 918 pp. [Last edition recorded in *British Museum Catalogue.*] First edition pub. London in 1660.

Mark Twain quotes from this "voluminous and very musty old book" (about the commission which tried Charles I) in a newspaper sketch for the San Francisco *Morning Call,* 16 September 1864 *(CofC,* pp. 111–112).

Baker, (Sir) Samuel White (1821–1893). *Cast Up By the Sea.* Illus. New York: Harper & Brothers, n.d. 419 pp.
Source: MTLAcc, entry #1585, volume donated by Clemens.

Baldwin, James (1841–1925). *The Horse Fair.* New York: Century Co., 1895. 418 pp.
Source: MTLAcc, entry #1873, volume donated from Clemens' library by Clara Clemens Gabrilowitsch in 1910.

————. *A Story of the Golden Age.* Illus. by Howard Pyle. New York: Charles Scribner's Sons, 1887. 268 pp.
Inscription: in Livy's hand on flyleaf: "Clara L. Clemens/Christmas 1887/Aunt Ida". Front free endpaper missing.
Marginalia: Clemens listed and added up in pencil a column of figures on the last page of Scribner's catalog of juvenile books at the back of the volume, presumably a computation for books he wished to order.
Location: Mark Twain Papers, Berkeley, California.
Copy examined: Clara's copy of Baldwin's popularized rendition of Greek myths.

Baldwin, James Mark (1861–1934). *The Story of the Mind.* New York: D. Appleton and Co., 1899. 236 pp.
Inscription: on half-title page: "Mark II/(Mr. Clemens)/from Mark I/(Mr. Baldwin)".
Marginalia: a few pencil markings in chapter one, "The Science of the Mind—Psychology"; heavy pencil markings and annotation throughout chapter two ("Introspective Psychology") and chapter three ("Comparative Psychology"). No notes or marks beyond page 38.
Location: Mark Twain Library, Redding, Connecticut.
Copy examined: Clemens' copy.

Baldwin visited Clemens on 2 June 1900 in London, accompanied by Sir John Adams. Clemens made a memo that "Prof. J. Mark Baldwin of Princeton" would arrive and that he "writes books on psychology" (NB 43, TS p. 14). Either then or shortly thereafter Baldwin presented Clemens with *The Story of the Mind,* first published in 1898. Clemens wrote to Baldwin on 5 June 1900: "Thank you very much for the book. So far—up to the middle—I find no attempts to deceive, and am gaining confidence" (quoted in Baldwin's *Between Two Wars 1861–1921* [Boston: Stratford, 1926], p. 111). Baldwin invited him to visit Oxford, but Clemens reluctantly declined for family reasons on 7 June 1900 (NB 43, TS p. 16; TS in MTP).

The Story of the Mind is a basic textbook designed to inform laymen about prevailing theories of psychology. In chapter 2 Baldwin describes how the mind *acts,* explaining the differences between the current concept of mental processes and the earlier view held by the Scottish School of "faculty" psychology. Clemens made several notes, including (p. 18) " 'Low bridge!' becomes instinct" and (p. 21) "it *is*"—the latter in opposition to Baldwin's assertion that "the mind is not a mere machine doing what the laws of its action prescribe."

Chapter three elicited the largest share of Clemens' marginalia in the book; there Baldwin describes "animal instinct" (using the housecat as an example) and gives theories of animal-play. The following comments are representative samples of his annotations:

p. 24 Written emphatically: "He [i.e., man] is wholly a machine."
p. 25 Regarding animal instinct: "It *was* thought—now it is instinct. Petrified thought."
Of the statement that a cat abhors water and is incapable of swimming: "She *can* swim".
p. 27 Written vertically in margin: "copulation—instinct, in man."
p. 28 Of different bird calls that resulted by isolating baby birds from hearing the notes of their species: "Xn & Mahometan".
p. 29 Concerning instinct operating in various situations: "Bee butts head against window all day—an ant would seek another way out. Or a dog." Regarding the origin of instinct: "Bird that became a meat-eater."
p. 30 In reference to Reflex Theory: "Horse shies at the same old place after the thing has been removed—memory & imagination. Putting on pants."
p. 33 Of Lapsed Intelligence: "Dog making his bed?"
p. 36 Concerning difficulty a chicken has in learning how to drink water: "Sandwich mountain mule afraid of water—then tried to bite it. Has no inherited instinct to drink it."
IE, pp. 237, 239–241.

Baldwin, Joseph Glover (1815–1864). *The Flush Times of Alabama and Mississippi. A Series of Sketches.* New York: D. Appleton and Co., 1853, Repr. 1872; also issued by other firms in various years.
Mark Twain used quotation marks in alluding to "our 'flush times' " in Virginia City in chapter 47 of *Roughing It* (1872), a possible echo (Iowa–California Edition, p. 297). He included the book title in his list of potential material for an anthology of humor in 1880 (NB 19, *N&J,* 2:361, 363), in 1882 (NB 20, *N&J,* 2:461), and in 1887 (NB 27, TS p. 23)—but nonetheless *Mark Twain's Library of Humor* (1888) failed to include any humorous sketches by Baldwin.
MT&SH, p. 117.

Baldwin, Samuel Davies. *Armageddon; or, the Overthrow of Romanism and Monarchy; the Existence of the United States Foretold in the Bible, Its Future Greatness; Invasion by Allied Europe; Annihilation of Monarchy; Expansion into the Millennial Republic, and Its Dominion Over the Whole World.* Cincinnati, Ohio: Applegate & Co., 1854. 480 pp. [Cop. 1845; first pub. by the Nashville Methodist Publishing House.]
Clemens wrote to his brother Orion on 26 April [1861]: "Orion, bring down 'Armageddon' with you if you have it. If not, *buy* it" (*MTBus,* p. 61). Baldwin's book of prophecy foretells the end of the world between 1860 and 1875, with Armageddon centering in the Mississippi Valley.

Balfour, Arthur James Balfour (1848–1930), First Earl. *A Defense of Philosophic Doubt; Being an Essay on the Foundation of Belief.* London: Macmillan and Co., 1879. 355 pp.
Inscription: presentation copy from George Wyndham to Knox Little, an English divine. Wyndham was the private secretary of its author, Balfour. Someone, possibly Canon Little, added a maxim by Mark Twain on the flyleaf: " 'There is something fascinating about Science,—one gets such wholesale returns of conjecture out of such a trifling investment of fact.'—Mark Twain."
Catalog: L1912, #6, $12.50, listed as belonging to Clemens' library, yet (unlike the other items) not originating from the 1911 Anderson Auction. Especially puzzling inasmuch as it apparently does not contain Clemens' signature. Possibly included in the 1912 catalog merely because it contained a maxim invented by Mark Twain. A dubious attribution to Clemens' library.

Ball, Charles. *Slavery in the United States: A Narrative of the Life and Adventures of Charles Ball, a Black Man, Who Lived Forty Years in Maryland, South Carolina and Georgia, as a Slave.* New York: J. S. Taylor, 1837. 517 pp. [Later published under title: *Fifty Years in Chains; or, the Life of an American Slave* (New York: H. Dayton, 1858). Prepared from Ball's oral narrative by an editor identified only as "Fisher."]
>   *Inscription:* on flyleaf: "S. L. Clemens, 1902".
>   *Catalog: A1911,* #435, $1.25, 1837 edition, "foxed and loose in binding."
>   Clemens wrote to Sue Crane on 29 August 1901: "You have a small book by a negro named Ball, which tells of terrible things in the Dismal Swamp in slavery times. Won't you send it to me—for use?" (MTP). Presumably he intended to employ it in writing his projected volume on lynchings in the American South. Previously (in 1889) Clemens had noted Ball's name as one of the sources for *A Connecticut Yankee* that he intended to acknowledge in an appendix to the novel (NB 29, TS p. 13). He twice credited Ball with supplying *"Prove that ye be free."* In "The Course of the Composition of *A Connecticut Yankee*" (1961) Howard G. Baetzhold revealed that Mark Twain wrote "Autobiography of Charles Ball" in the margin of a manuscript page ("Course," p. 211, n. 36).
>   *TIH* (1961), p. 109 n. 8; James D. Williams, "The Use of History" (1965), pp. 109–110; *MT&JB* (1970), pp. 151, 350 n. 33, 352 n. 39.

Ball, (Mrs.) Oona Howard (Butlin) (b. 1867), pseud. "Barbara Ball." *Barbara Goes to Oxford.* London: Methuen & Co., 1907. 294 pp.
>   *Source:* MTLAcc, entry #2171, volume donated from Clemens' library by Clara Clemens Gabrilowitsch in 1910.

Ballantyne, Robert Michael (1825–1894). *Erling the Bold, A Tale of the Norse Sea-Kings.* Illus. by the author. Philadelphia: J. B. Lippincott & Co., 1870. 437 pp.
>   *Source:* MTLAcc, entry #24, volume donated by Clemens.
>   "I have read & sent home . . . Erling the Bold" (Clemens to Livy Clemens, Steubenville, Ohio, 9 January [1872], *LLMT*, pp. 172–173). *Erling the Bold* was based on *The Heimskringla, or Chronicles of the Kings of Norway,* a poetic chronicle of Norse history and myth by Snorri Sturluson (1178–1241).

————. *Erling the Bold.* New York: J. W. Lovell Co., [cop. 1883]. 437 pp.
>   *Source:* MTLAcc, entry #2165, volume donated from Clemens' library by Clara Clemens Gabrilowitsch in 1910.

Ballou, Maturin Murray (1820–1895). *Under the Southern Cross; or, Travels in Australia, Tasmania, New Zealand, Samoa, and Other Pacific Islands.* Boston: Ticknor and Co., [1888]. 405 pp.
>   On 3 September 1895 Clemens noted: " 'Under the Southern Cross.' Get this mess of self-complacent twaddle" (NB 35, TS p. 41). At the time he was on board a ship off Hawaii.

Balzac, Honoré de (1799–1850). *Balzac's Contes Drolatiques; Droll Stories Collected from the Abbeys of Touraine, Translated into English [by George Robert Sims], Complete and Unabridged.* Illus. by Gustave Doré. London: Chatto & Windus, 1874. 650 pp.
>   *Edition:* this is probably the edition owned by Clemens, but other firms published similar volumes in 1874. No other editions were recorded until 1890.
>   In an undated manuscript entitled, "The Walt Whitman Controversy" (DV36, MTP), probably written around 1880, Mark Twain cites two tales and a picture by Doré on page 211 to support his contention that Whitman's offending lines are surpassed in vulgarity by the so-called classics found in many Victorian homes. Henry Fisher remembered hearing Mark Twain advise Bram Stoker that "the only satisfactory way to do a witchcraft story is to filch it bodily from Balzac. The Frenchman got the thing down to perfection in one of his Droll yarns" (*AMT,* p. 181).

————. *The Comedy of Human Life.* Translated by Katharine Prescott Wormeley. Introductions by George Frederick Parsons. 17 vols. Boston: Roberts Brothers, 1885–1893.

Edition: a surmise based on the fact that Roberts Brothers brought out the major American edition of Balzac's works in the later-nineteenth-century.

Catalog: C1951, #025, six volumes only, no edition indicated, listed with books signed by Livy Clemens: *Louis Lambert, The Magic Skin, Seraphita, Cousin Pons, Bureaucracy,* and *Ursula.*

Clara Clemens summarized the plot of *The Magic Skin* in her commonplace book (Paine 150, MTP), probably around 1888. Clemens mentioned Balzac favorably in 1867 (NB 8, *N&J,* 1:326), 1886 (NB 26, TS p. 9), and 1891 ("Aix, the Paradise of the Rheumatics"). Katy Leary, the family's housekeeper, believed that the French novel she found in the billiard room and enjoyed until Livy took it away from her was "maybe" an English translation of Balzac. "I used to hear Mr. Clemens talk about his [Balzac's] books," she recalled. "He thought they was wonderful" *(LMT,* p. 56). It seems likely that the Clemenses owned other novels in Balzac's grand series that have not survived.

————. *The Country Doctor* [*Le medecin de campagne*]. Trans. by Katharine Prescott Wormeley. Boston: Roberts Brothers, 1887. 304 pp. [First English-language edition published in the U.S.]

One of five book titles Clemens listed in September 1887 was "County Doctor—Balzac" (NB 27, TS p. 13).

————. *Une Fille d'Eve.* Paris, 1840.

Inscription: signed on flyleaf, "S. L. Clemens."

Catalog: A1911, #27, $1.25, "vol. 1 only," described only as "8vo, unbound, poor copy."

————. *Le Père Goriot* (1834).

"Description of the boarding house in 'Pere Goriot,' " wrote Clemens in 1888 (NB 27, TS p. 65).

Bancroft, Frederic (1860–1945). *The Life of William H. Seward.* 2 vols. New York: Harper & Brothers, 1900.

Source: MTLAcc, entries #861 and #862, volumes donated by Clemens.

Bancroft, Hubert Howe (1832–1918). *Literary Industries. A Memoir.* New York: Harper & Brothers, 1891. 446 pp.

Source: MTLAcc, entry #1792, volume donated by Clemens.

————. *The Native Races of the Pacific States of North America.* 5 vols. New York: D. Appleton and Co.; San Francisco: A. L. Bancroft & Co., 1874–1876.

Mark Twain was one of many notables who in 1876 received a presentation copy of *Native Races* during Bancroft's campaign for national recognition and endorsements. In *Literary Industries* (1890) Bancroft quoted a letter from his files that Charles Dudley Warner had written to him on 11 October 1876: "Mr Clemens was just in and was in an unusual state of enthusiasm over the first volume, especially its fine style. You may have a picture of his getting up at two o'clock this morning and, encased in a fur overcoat, reading it till daylight" (p. 363). Clemens remembered what he found in Bancroft's volumes. At the top of a page in Thomas Wright's *Early Travels in Palestine,* a volume Clemens signed in 1877, he wrote of the disfiguration of lips by enlargement: "This can be done by some Indians on our Northwest Coast. (See Bancroft.)" (p. 229). Mark Twain drew upon *Native Races* for a chapter of *A Tramp Abroad* that compared courtship and marriage customs of primitive tribes with those of contemporary French society (Box 6, #7, MTP), but he eventually discarded the essay.

Bangs, John Kendrick (1862–1922). *Bikey the Skicycle & Other Tales of Jimmieboy.* Illus. by Peter Newell. New York: Riggs Pub. Co., 1902. 321 pp.
    Source: MTLAcc, entry #1586, volume donated by Clemens.

————. *The Booming of Acre Hill, and Other Reminiscences of Urban and Suburban Life.* Illus. by C. Dana Gibson. New York: Harper & Brothers, 1900. 266 pp.
    Source: MTLAcc, entry #17, volume donated by Clemens.

————. *Cobwebs from a Library Corner.* New York: Harper & Brothers, 1899. 101 pp.
    Source: MTLAcc, entry #1340, volume donated by Clemens.

————. *Coffee and Repartee.* Illus. New York: Harper & Brothers, 1901. 123 pp.
    Source: MTLAcc, entry #1209, volume donated by Clemens.

————. *The Genial Idiot, His Views and Reviews.* New York: Harper & Brothers, 1908. 215 pp.
    Source: MTLAcc, entry #960, volume donated by Clemens.

————. *Ghosts I Have Met and Some Others.* Illus. by Newell, Frost, and Richards. New York: Harper & Brothers, 1899. 191 pp.
    Source: MTLAcc, entry #20, volume donated by Clemens.

————. *A House-Boat on the Styx.* Illus. New York: Harper & Brothers, 1902. 171 pp.
    Source: MTLAcc, entry #1514, volume donated by Clemens.

————. *The Inventions of the Idiot.* New York: Harper & Brothers, 1904. 185 pp.
    Source: MTLAcc, entry #959, volume donated by Clemens.

————. *Mrs. Raffles; Being the Adventures of an Amateur Crackswoman.* Illus. by Albert Levering. New York: Harper & Brothers, 1905. 180 pp.
    Source: MTLAcc, entry #961, volume donated by Clemens.

————. *Olympian Nights.* Illus. New York: Harper & Brothers, 1902. 224 pp.
    Source: MTLAcc, entry #962, volume donated by Clemens.

————. [Another identical copy.]
    Source: MTLAcc, entry #1274, volume donated by Clemens.

————. *Over the Plum-Pudding.* Illus. New York: Harper & Brothers, 1901. 244 pp. [Short stories.]
    Inscription: "S. L. Clemens, Riverdale, Oct. 1901."
    Catalog: A1911, #28, $8.

————. *Peeps at People; Being Certain Papers from the Writings of Anne Warrington Witherup* [pseud.] Illus. by Edward Penfield. New York: Harper & Brothers, 1899. 185 pp.
    Source: MTLAcc, entry #19, volume donated by Clemens.

————. *The Pursuit of the House-Boat.* Illus. by Peter Newell. New York: Harper & Brothers, 1900. 204 pp.
    Location: Mark Twain Library, Redding, Conn. Donated by Clemens (MTLAcc, entry #1105).
    Copy examined: Clemens' copy, unmarked.

————. *R. Holmes & Co.; Being the Remarkable Adventures of Raffles Holmes, Esq., Detective and Amateur Cracksman by Birth*. Illus. by Sydney Adamson. New York: Harper & Brothers, 1906. 231 pp.
Source: MTLAcc, entry #18, volume donated by Clemens.

————.[Another identical copy.]
Source: MTLAcc, entry #25, volume donated by Clemens.

————.[Another identical copy.]
Source: MTLAcc, entry #1248, volume donated by Clemens.

————. *Toppleton's Client; or, A Spirit in Exile*. New York: Charles L. Webster & Co., 1893. 269 pp.
Advertised by Clemens' publishing firm as a semi-humorous story of the supernatural about a barrister and his soul *(Publishers' Trade List Annual 1893)*.

————. *The Worsted Man; A Musical Play for Amateurs*. Illus. New York: Harper & Brothers, 1905. 86 pp.
Source: MTLAcc, entry #654, volume donated by Clemens.

————.[Another identical copy.]
Source: MTLAcc, entry #655, volume donated by Clemens.

Barclay, James Turner. *The City of the Great King; or, Jerusalem As It Was, As It Is, and As It Is To Be*. Philadelphia: J. Challen and Sons, 1858. 627 pp.
Mark Twain reported that this book was one of those recommended for *Quaker City* passengers to bring with them *(Daily Alta California*, 5 April 1868; *TIA*, p. 303).

Bardsley, Charles Wareing Endell (1843–1898). *Curiosities of Puritan Nomenclature*. London: Chatto & Windus, 1880; New York: R. Worthington, 1880.
See the following entry.

————. *Our English Surnames: Their Sources and Significances*. London: Chatto & Windus, 1873. Second ed. retitled: *English Surnames* (1875).
In the same purple ink in which Clemens made his declaration of reading preferences on a discarded envelope in 1909, he also listed among other titles "2 books by Rev. C. W. Bardsley" (MTP, Notebook fragments file). *Curiosities* and *English Surnames* seem the most likely references, since they were the best known of Bardsley's works on English nomenclature.
Gribben, " 'I Detest Novels, Poetry & Theology' " (1977).

Baring-Gould, Sabine (1834–1924). *In Exitu Israel; An Historical Novel*. New York: Macmillan & Co., 1870. 385 pp.
Source: MTLAcc, entry #2166, volume donated by Mrs. Gabrilowitsch in 1910.
The Reverend Joseph H. Twichell wrote to Clemens on 25 June 1877: "I send you by mail to-day Baring-Gould's novel 'In Exitu Israel,' which it has taken me longer than I thought to procure" (MTP). Clemens replied on 27 June from Elmira: "Exitu-Israel has just come—many thanks, Joe—I'll give you an opinion. Been reading a lot of French rot here & am glad to get this" (Yale). The opinion he may have delivered to Twichell is unknown, but his comments to Mollie Fairbanks on 6 August 1877 were complimentary. He mentioned to her that he had read " 'In Exitu Israel,' a very able novel by Baring-Gould, the purpose of which is to show the effect of some of the most odious of the privileges of the French nobles under *l'ancien regème*, & of the dischurching of the Catholic Church by the National Assembly in '92" *(MTMF*, p. 208).
Blair, "French Revolution," p. 23; *MT&HF*, p. 310; *MT&JB*, pp. 350 n. 34, 347–348 n. 21.

Barker, Mary Anne (Stewart), afterwards Lady Broome (1831–1911). *Station Amusements in New Zealand, by Lady Barker.* Copyright Edition. British Authors Series. Leipzig: B. Tauchnitz, 1874. 288 pp. [First edition 1873.]
   Catalog: C1951, #D1, $8, listed among the books signed by Clemens, Tauchnitz Edition specified.

———. *Station Life in New Zealand, by Lady Barker.* Copyright Edition. British Authors Series. Leipzig: B. Tauchnitz, 1874. 279 pp. [First ed. 1870.]
   Catalog: C1951, #D1, $8, listed among the books signed by Clemens, Tauchnitz Edition specified.
   Regarding New Zealand, Clemens wrote in December 1895: "At great intervals they have much snow & very hard winters in the Middle Island; Lady Barker tells of one" (NB36, TS p. 3).

Barnes, Albert (1798–1870). *Notes, Explanatory and Practical, on the New Testament. Acts of the Apostles.* Map. New York: Harper & Brothers, 1853. 356 pp.
   Source: MTLAcc, entry #950, volume donated by Clemens.

———. *Notes, Explanatory and Practical, on the New Testament. Book of Revelation.* Illus. New York: Harper & Brothers, 1852. 506 pp.
   Source: MTLAcc, entry #947, volume donated by Clemens.

———. *Notes, Explanatory and Practical, on the New Testament. Epistles of Paul to the Ephesians, Philippians, and Colossians.* Illus. New York: Harper & Brothers, 1850. 331 pp.
   Source: MTLAcc, entry #945, volume donated by Clemens.

———. *Notes, Explanatory and Practical, on the New Testament. Epistles of Paul to the Thessalonians, to Timothy, to Titus, and to Philemon.* New York: Harper & Brothers, 1853. 355 pp.
   Source: MTLAcc, entry #951, volume donated by Clemens.

———. *Notes, Explanatory and Practical, on the New Testament. Epistle to the Hebrews.* Illus. New York: Harper & Brothers, 1851. 335 pp.
   Source: MTLAcc, entry #946, volume donated by Clemens.

———. *Notes, Explanatory and Practical, on the New Testament. Epistle to the Romans.* New York: Harper & Brothers, 1853. 328 pp.
   Source: MTLAcc, entry #952, volume donated by Clemens.

———. *Notes, Explanatory and Practical, on the New Testament. First Epistle of Paul to the Corinthians.* New York: Harper & Brothers, 1848. 357 pp.
   Source: MTLAcc, entry #944, volume donated by Clemens.

———. *Notes, Explanatory and Practical, on the New Testament. General Epistles of James, Peter, John and Jude.* New York: Harper & Brothers, 1852. 459 pp.
   Source: MTLAcc, entry #948, volume donated by Clemens.

———. *Notes, Explanatory and Practical, on the New Testament. Second Epistle to the Corinthians and the Epistle to the Galatians.* New York: Harper & Brothers, 1852. 398 pp.
   Source: MTLAcc, entry #949, volume donated by Clemens.

———. *Notes, Explanatory and Practical, on the New Testament. The Gospels.* Illus. New York: Harper & Brothers, 1854. 413 pp.
   Source: MTLAcc, entry #953, volume donated by Clemens.

Barnes, James (1866–1936). *The Blockaders, and Other Stories*. New York: Harper & Brothers, 1905. 203 pp.
    Source: MTLAcc, entry #421, volume donated by Clemens.

―――. *For King or Country. A Story of the American Revolution.* Illus. New York: Harper & Brothers, 1905. 269 pp.
    Source: MTLAcc, entry #1311, volume donated by Clemens.

―――. *A Loyal Traitor; A Story of the War of 1812.* Illus. by A. J. Keller. New York: Harper & Brothers, 1905. 306 pp.
    Source: MTLAcc, entry #1305, volume donated by Clemens.

―――. *The Son of Light Horse Harry.* Illus. by W. E. Mears. New York: Harper & Brothers, 1904. 242 pp.
    Barnes' novel about Robert E. Lee was one of four "Harper's books" for which Clemens' business agent in Florence took receipt in 1904 (Sebastiano V. Cecchi to Clemens, 30 July 1904, MTP); later the business agent mentioned that Clemens left this book behind in Florence (Sebastiano V. Cecchi to Clemens, 4 November 1904, MTP).

Barney, Bill (b. 1855). *The Bright Side of Country Life.* Dallas, Texas: Farmers' Printing Co., 1906. 227 pp.
    Source: MTLAcc, entry #570, volume donated by Clemens.

Barnum, (Mrs.) Frances Courtenay (Baylor) (1848–1920). *Juan and Juanita.* Illus. by Henry Sandham. Boston: Ticknor and Co., 1888. 288 pp.
    Source: MTLAcc, entry #1875, volume donated from Clemens' library by Clara Clemens Gabrilowitsch in 1910.

Barnum, Phineas Taylor (1810–1891). *Dollars and Sense; or, How to Get On. The Whole Secret in a Nutshell.* Illus. by W. W. Denslow. New York: H. S. Allen, 1890. 488 pp.
    Inscription: "To Saml. L. Clemens, Esq. (Mark Twain) with kind regards of P. T. Barnum, Bridgeport, Conn., Oct. 16, 1890."
    Catalog: A1911, #29, $9.50.

―――. *Struggles and Triumphs; or, Forty Years' Recollections of P. T. Barnum. Written by Himself.* Hartford: J. B. Burr & Co., 1869. 780 pp.
    Catalog: C1951, #D77, presentation copy from Barnum, signed by Clemens, edition unspecified.
    Albert Bigelow Paine may have referred to this relatively early version of Barnum's memoirs (although Paine's title differs): "When the *Life of P. T. Barnum, Written by Himself,* appeared, . . . he [Clemens] sat up nights to absorb it, and woke early and lighted the lamp to follow the career of the great showman" (*MTB,* p. 410). Paine included Barnum's *Life* among Clemens' favorite books that "showed usage" (*MTB,* p. 1540).
    Hamlin Hill, "Barnum, Bridgeport and *The Connecticut Yankee,*" *AQ,* 16 (Winter 1964), 615–616; Harold Aspiz, "The Other Half of Pudd'nhead Wilson's Dog" (1975).

Barr, Robert (1850–1912). "How to Write a Short Story," *The Bookman,* 5 (March 1897), 42–44. [A symposium.]
    "I like your article ever so much," Clemens wrote from Vienna on 29 September 1897 (PH in MTP).

————. *A Prince of Good Fellows.* Illus. by Edmund J. Sullivan. New York: McClure, Phillips & Co., 1902. 340 pp.
    Source: MTLAcc, entry #2170, volume donated from Clemens' library by Clara Clemens Gabrilowitsch in 1910.

Barras, Charles M. (1826–1873). *The Black Crook; An Original Magical and Spectacular Drama in Four Acts* (perf. New York City, 1866).
    When Mark Twain gazed upon the chorus girls in the production of *The Black Crook* at Niblo's Gardens, he knew that he had encountered at last the evil allurements so often associated with the stage. For his California readers he criticized the extravaganza as "the wickedest show you can think of. . . . A shrewd invention of the devil" that displayed "all possible compromises between nakedness and decency" (2 February 1867 letter to *Alta California, MTTMB*, pp. 84–85). Mark Twain referred to *The Black Crook* again in a 23 February 1867 letter to the *Alta California (MTTMB*, p. 110) and in a 31 August 1867 letter published in the New York *Tribune* (25 October 1867 issue, *TIA*, p. 132). "Think of this insect [the Reverend Sabine] condemning the whole theatrical service as a disseminator of bad morals because it has Black Crooks in it," he wrote in "The Indignity Put Upon the Remains of George Holland by the Rev. Mr. Sabine" (1871). In 1873 he addressed the Monday Evening Club in Hartford on "License of the Press" and reminded the audience how "our newspapers—*all* of them, without exception—glorify the 'Black Crook' and make it an opulent success—they could have killed it dead with one broadside of contemptuous silence if they had wanted to" *(MTS [1923]*, p. 48).
    MTC, pp. 38–43.

Barras, Paul François Jean Nicholas (1755–1829). *Memoirs of Barras, Member of the Directorate.* Ed. by George Duruy. Trans. by Charles E. Roche. 4 vols. New York: Harper & Brothers, 1895–1896.
    Inscriptions: vol. 1 signed on flyleaf "S. L. Clemens/1895"; vol. 2 signed on flyleaf "S. L. Clemens./1895./From J. Henry Harper."
    Marginalia: Clemens wrote the word "French" in the margins of pages 6 and 12.
    Catalogs: C1951, #18c, $14, 2 vols. only; *Fleming 1972,* 2 vols. only.

Barrett, John (1866–1938). *Admiral Goerge Dewey; A Sketch of the Man.* Illus. New York: Harper & Brothers, 1899. 280 pp.
    Source: MTLAcc, entry #1202, volume donated by Clemens.

Barrie, (Sir) James Matthew (1860–1937). *The Little Minister* (London, 1891).
    Clemens spent the afternoon and evening of 3 July 1892 "absorbed in" *The Little Minister* in his bed at the Union League Club in New York City (NB 31, TS pp. 57–58).

————. *Peter Pan, or the Boy Who Wouldn't Grow Up* (play, prod. 1904).
    Ten days after Maude Adams opened in *Peter Pan,* Mark Twain assured Charles Frohman, the New York City theatrical manager, on 16 November 1905 that he had delivered "outspoken praises" of the play in a newspaper interview because "it hadn't a defect," and he thanked Frohman for the tickets (MTP).

————. *A Window in Thrums.* London: Hodder and Stoughton, 1889. 217 pp.
    On 4 July 1892—directly after finishing Barrie's *The Little Minister*—Clemens rose at the Union League Club in New York City, breakfasted, read the newspaper, "wrote a letter or two," and "began 'A Window in Thrums' " (NB 31, TS p. 58).

Barrili, Antonio Giulio (1836–1908). *The Eleventh Commandment; A Romance.* Trans. from Italian by Clara Bell. Rev. and corrected. New York: W. S. Gottsberger, 1882. 377 pp.
> *Source:* MTLAcc, entry #2184, volume donated from Clemens' library by Clara Clemens Gabrilowitsch in 1910.

Barritt, Leon. *How to Draw; A Practical Book of Instruction in the Art of Illustration.* Illus. New York: Harper & Brothers, 1904. 107 pp.
> *Source:* MTLAcc, entry #1225, volume donated by Clemens.

Barthélemy, Jean Jacques (1716–1795). *Travels of Anarcharsis the Younger in Greece, During the Middle of the Fourth Century Before the Christian Era. By the Abbé Barthelemi. Trans. from the French [by William Beaumont].* 4 vols. London: G. G. and J. Robinson, 1796.
> *Catalog: A1911,* #30, $1.50, "8vo, sheep."

Bartlett, John (1820–1905), comp. *The Shakespeare Phrase Book.* Boston: Little, Brown & Co., 1881. 1,034 pp.
> Title and publisher noted in February 1882 (NB 20, *N&J,* 2: 446).

Bartlett, William Henry. *Walks About the City and Environs of Jerusalem* (London, 1844).
> One of the "assortment of books" recommended to *Quaker City* passengers before they departed (*Daily Alta California,* 5 April 1868, *TIA,* p. 303).

Barzini, Luigi (1873–1947). *Pekin to Paris; An Account of Prince Borghese's Journey Across Two Continents in a Motor-Car.* Trans. by L. P. de Castelvecchio. Intro. by Prince Borghese. Illus. New York: M. Kennerley, 1908. 645 pp.
> *Source:* MTLAcc, entry #585, volume donated by Clemens.

Bashkirtseva, Mariiâ Konstantinovna (1860–1884). *Marie Bashkirtseff; The Journal of a Young Artist, 1860–1884.* Trans. by Mary J[ane] Serrano. New York: Cassell & Co., [1889]. 434 pp.
> *Catalog: C1951,* #75c, $10, listed among books signed by Clemens.
>
> In December 1889 Clemens jotted down the subtitle and publisher in Notebook 29: "The Journal of a Young Artist. Cassell" (TS p. 35). On 14 January 1906 Isabel Lyon noted that Mark Twain spoke of "Marie Bashkirtseff's enchanting and naively frank journal" as being "a perfect delight" (IVL Journal, TS p. 123, MTP).

Baskerville, Alfred, ed. and trans. *The Poetry of Germany; Consisting of Selections from Upwards of Seventy of the Most Celebrated Poets, Translated into English Verse, with the Original Text on the Opposite Page.* Fourth edition. Baden-Baden: Haendcke & Lehmkuhl, 1876. 332 pp.
> *Source:* MTLAcc, entry #624, volume donated by Clemens.
>
> Edgar H. Hemminghaus reported seeing Clemens' copy of this book on the shelves of the Mark Twain Library, Redding, Connecticut in 1945 ("Mark Twain's German Provenience," pp. 467–468), but it had vanished by the time Albert E. Stone compiled a catalog of the Clemens holdings in 1955 and I was similarly unable to locate it in 1970. Hemminghaus supplied the publisher and date in his article, but he did not mention inscriptions or marginalia.

Batt, John Herridge. *Dr. Barnardo, the Foster-Father of "Nobody's Children."* Illus. London: S. W. Partridge & Co., 1904. 196 pp.
> *Source:* MTLAcc, entry #835, volume donated by Albert Bigelow Paine, Clemens' designated biographer. Possibly Clemens saw this book, since the men exchanged reading materials.

Battle Abbey. *The Roll of Battle Abbey, Annotated. By John Bernard Burke.* Illus. London: Edward Churton, 1848.

Edition: conjectured because no others were issued for the general book trade until 1889.

Clemens wrote to Mrs. Fairbanks on 2 November 1872: "Now years ago it used to be a curious study to me, to follow the variations of a family name down through a Peerage or a biography from the Roll of Battle-Abbey to the present day—& manifold & queer were the changes, too" *(MTMF,* p. 167).

The Battle for the Pacific, and Other Adventures at Sea, by Rowan Stevens, Yates Sterling, Jr., William J. Henderson, G. E. Walsh, Kirk Munroe, F. H. Spearman, and Others. Illus. New York: Harper & Brothers, 1908. 238 pp.
Source: MTLAcc, entry #452, volume donated by Clemens.

————. [Another identical copy.]
Source: MTLAcc, entry #521, volume donated by Clemens.

————. [Another identical copy.]
Source: MTLAcc, entry #1071, volume donated by Clemens.

Baum, Lyman Frank (1856–1919). *Father Goose; His Book.* Illus. by William W. Denslow. Chicago: Geo. M. Hill Co., [cop. 1899]. 104 pp.
Source: MTLAcc, entry #1874, volume donated from Clemens' library by Clara Clemens Gabrilowitsch in 1910.

Bausman, Frederick (1861–1931), pseud. "Aix." *Adventures of a Nice Young Man; A Novel, by Aix.* New York: Duffield, 1908. 407 pp.
Inscription: on flyleaf "S. C. I've been reading your books long enough. Suppose you read the first chapter of mine. Aix."
Catalogs: A1911, #5, $3.50, "12mo, buckram"; *L1912,* #1, $6.50.

Baxter, Richard (1615–1691). *The Saint's Everlasting Rest; or, A Treatise on the Blessed State of the Saints, in Their Enjoyment of God in Heaven.* Abridged by Benjamin Fawcett. Philadelphia: Jonathan Pounder, 1817.
Inscription: on front pastedown endpaper: "Betsey Chichester's Book/Presented by a friend".
Location: Mark Twain Library, Redding, Connecticut.
Copy examined: very likely Clemens' copy, obtained second-hand, though there is no solid evidence that it was he who donated this book to the Redding Library at the time it was founded.

Mark Twain urged young people to read only "good" books such as *Saint's Rest* and *Innocents Abroad* in "Advice to Youth," a speech delivered on 15 April 1882 *(MTSpk,* p. 171); cited Baxter's faith in a dismal hell in Notebook 22 (1883), TS p. 22; listed *Saint's Rest* among the books on the parlor tables of Honolulu homes when he visited the Sandwich Islands in 1866 (chapter 3 of *Following the Equator* [1897]); in working notes for one version of *Mysterious Stranger* he referred to "Baxter looking over the balusters of heaven" at those writhing in agony below in hell (NB 40 [1898], TS p. 51). In a section of "What Is Man?" written in 1898 but eventually discarded, the Young Man concedes that the sight of their children burning in hell will not discountenance the parents but rather "will increase the joys of heaven for them—as Baxter of the 'Saint's Rest' has painted" *(WIM?,* Iowa-Calif. Ed., p. 482).

Baylis, Thomas Henry (1817–1908). *The Temple Church and Chapel of St. Ann, Etc.: An Historical Record and Guide.* Second ed. London: George Philip and Son, 1895. 152 pp.
Inscription: "CLEMENS" written in pencil on flyleaf; on half-title page in black

ink (not Clemens' hand) appears: "The Middle Temple Library/Author's Copy/13 May 1895/T Henry Baylis." Book also stamped on several pages: "MIDDLE TEMPLE".

Marginalia: no notes, but Clemens' pencil markings begin on page 56 at discussion of the two societies of inner and middle temple and continue on nearly every page thereafter (especially in the chapter concerning "The Knights Templars, Their History") up to page 113. Only one subsequent mark (p. 145) beside a reference to the sword with which Thomas of Canterbury was killed.

Catalogs: A1911, #31, $3.25; *The Bookman* (Houston, Texas), catalog no. 25 (1970), Hill Collection, item #328.

Location: Wake Forest University, Winston-Salem, N.C. Donated by Mrs. Nancy Susan Reynolds.

Copy examined: Clemens' copy.

Bayly, Thomas Haynes (1797–1839). "Gaily the Troubadour" (poem, song).

In 1881 Mark Twain constructed an atrocious doggerel parody of this song to commemorate James R. Osgood's departure for England in June 1881 (NB 19, *N&J,* 2: 386–387). In 1897 he recalled hearing the song in his youth in "Villagers of 1840–3" *(HH&T,* p. 34).

————. "The long ago" (song). Better known as "Long, long ago."

Favorably mentioned in Notebook 16 (1878, *N&J,* 2: 212); included among the music on the piano in "The House Beautiful" depicted in chapter 38 of *Life on the Mississippi* (1883). Brought to mind by Susy's death, its lines were quoted in Notebook 39 (January 1897), TS p. 57, and its title was mentioned in the same notebook (TS p. 58).

————. "The Mistletoe Bough" (poem).

Mark Twain reflected on Bayly's ballad while musing over plot possibilities for a manuscript he would never complete, "The Mysterious Chamber" (DV56, MTP), probably written in 1875. "We have a noble situation in the 'Mistletoe Bough,' " Mark Twain reminded himself in his working notes, "where the bride accidentally shuts herself into a chest and her fate is a mystery for 60 years. But the situation is too brief."

————. "The Pilot" (poem, song).

Two lines are quoted in "About All Kinds of Ships" (1893): "O pilot, 'tis a fearful night;/There's danger on the deep." Mark Twain's burlesque poem "The Aged Pilot Man" in chapter 51 of *Roughing It* (1872) very likely owes something to Bayly's "The Pilot."

————. "She wore a wreath of roses" (song).

Among the music on the piano in "The House Beautiful" in chapter 38 of *Life on the Mississippi* (1883).

Bayne, Samuel Gamble (1844–1924). *A Fantasy of Mediterranean Travel.* Illus. New York: Harper & Brothers, 1909. 104 pp.

Inscription: front free endpaper inscribed by the author: "To Sam'l. L. Clemens/With the author's compliments/New York/1909."

Provenance: donated by Clemens to the Mark Twain Library, Redding, Conn. (MTLAcc, entry #1488). Contains bookstamps of the Redding library.

Location: Elihu Burritt Library, Central Connecticut State College, New Britain, Conn.

Copy examined: photocopies of inscription and title page, supplied by Francis J. Gagliardi, Assistant Director, Library Services. The book is unmarked.

————. *The Pith of Astronomy (Without Mathematics): The Latest Facts and Figures as Developed by the Giant Telescopes.* Illus. New York: Harper & Brothers, 1907. 122 pp.

Inscription: signed in brown ink on front pastedown endpaper: "S L. Clemens/ 1909".

Marginalia: numerous notations in brown ink, black ink, and pencil between pages 12 and 92; none thereafter. A few of Clemens' comments ridicule Bayne's efforts to simplify his subject matter. On page 40, where Bayne mentions that "a web of cloth as long as from the earth to the moon" would still be insufficient to encircle Jupiter, Clemens penciled some advice: "A rope of the same length would serve just as well & would be cheaper, also easier to manage in windy weather. I recommend the rope." To Bayne's description of certain asteroids as being "no larger than rocks" (p. 66), Clemens objects in pencil: "This is inexact, because we do not know the precise size of a rock." Clemens asks whether Bayne means "the Rock of Gibraltar" or the "small kind" desired by the child in "Rock me to sleep, rock me to sleep." Other marginalia are serious, such as the note in black ink above Bayne's reference to the persecution of Bruno and Galileo (p. 83): "The Church has burned many other men besides Bruno for denying lies which it got out of the great central source of lies, the Bible." Frequently Clemens uses Bayne's figures to speculate about distances in the galaxy. An unidentified person has added a few notes in pencil (on pp. 24–25, for instance). Clemens made computations in brown ink on the back flyleaf and rear pastedown endpaper. Three newspaper clippings are inserted: an address by Professor Percival Lowell, "How the World Dies," Boston *Evening Transcript,* 2 April 1909, is pinned to the front free endpaper; an article about Jupiter from the New York *Sun,* 21 January [1910?], is pinned to page 39; and an article about Neptune clipped from the New York *Herald,* 20 November 1909, is pinned to page 55.

Catalogs: C1951, #32a, $20; *Bennett & Marshall Catalogue No. 9* (1970), Los Angeles, item #10, $200.

Location: Mark Twain Papers, Berkeley, California. Purchased from John Howell Books of San Francisco in 1970 for $250.

Copy examined: Clemens' copy.

Albert Bigelow Paine reported that when Clemens moved into the Hamilton Hotel in Bermuda in November 1909 he "brought along a small book called *The Pith of Astronomy*—a fascinating little volume—and he read from it about the great tempest of fire in the sun" (*MTB,* p. 1542).

The Bazar Book of Health. New York: Harper & Brothers, 1873. 280 pp.
   Source: MTLAcc, entry #1353, volume donated by Clemens.

Beach, Rex Ellingwood (1877–1949). *The Barrier.* Illus. by Denman Fink. New York: Harper & Brothers, 1908. 310 pp.
   Source: MTLAcc, entry #2161, volume donated from Clemens' library by Clara Clemens Gabrilowitsch in 1910.

————. *The Silver Horde; A Novel.* Illus. by Harvey T. Dunn. New York: Harper & Brothers, 1909. 390 pp.
   Source: MTLAcc, entry #1820, volume donated by Clemens.

Beard, Daniel Carter (1850–1941). *Moonblight and Six Feet of Romance.* Illus. by the author. New York: Charles L. Webster & Co., 1892. 221 pp.
   Advertised in *Publishers' Trade List Annual 1893* by Clemens' publishing firm.

————. *Moonblight and Six Feet of Romance.* Intro. by Louis F. Post. Trenton, N.J.: Albert Brandt, 1904. 238 pp.
   Inscription: signed "Mark Twain" on front pastedown endpaper, which is also inscribed to Mark Twain by the author in 1904.
   Location: Mark Twain Library, Redding, Connecticut.
   Copy examined: Clemens' copy.

Although Beard's inscription in this presentation copy is dated 1904, it was not until 9 August 1905 that Albert Brandt wrote to Clemens in Dublin, New Hampshire: "It affords me great pleasure to be able to unite with our mutual friend, Mr. Daniel Carter Beard, in sending you by to-day's mail, a special autographed copy of the new edition of 'Moonblight and Six Feet of Romance' " (MTP). The death of Livy Clemens in June 1904 may account for Brandt's delay in mailing the book.

Beattie, William (1793–1875). *Life and Letters of Thomas Campbell.* 2 vols. New York: Harper & Brothers, 1850.
    Source: MTLAcc, entry #1748, volume 2 only (521 pp.), donated by Clemens.

Beatty, Daniel F. *In Foreign Lands, from Original Notes.* Washington, New Jersey: Daniel F. Beatty, Publisher, 1878. 97 pp.
    Inscription: "Compliments of Daniel F. Beatty/Jany 8th 1878" written in ink on flyleaf.
    Marginalia: a few penciled notes by Clemens; numerous notes in pencil and ink by another hand, possibly Joseph H. Twichell's. One of the latter notes is dated 5 January 1884.
    Catalog: "Retz Appraisal" (1944), p. 4. Valued at $20.
    Location: Mark Twain Papers, Berkeley, California.
    Copy examined: Clemens' copy.
    Beatty issued this account of his European trip primarily to publicize the pianos and organs manufactured by his firm in Washington, New Jersey. Clemens shared the book with a friend, who also indulged in sarcastic commentary along its margins. The handwriting suggests that the Reverend Joseph H. Twichell might have been the unidentified fellow reader. In response to Beatty's glowing description of the "bright and glorious day" on which he departed (p. 1), Clemens quipped: "If *I* had been Nature, no matter how glad I was to see him go, I would have acted exactly as usual." Beatty claimed that his family, his employees, and his fellow townsmen all turned out at the railroad depot to watch his departure; Clemens noted, "Why *every*body's glad" (p. 2). During Beatty's account of his sojourn in Paris Clemens remarked: "Fact is, his English needs interpreting as well as his French" (p. 20). "The pious liar," Clemens wrote above Beatty's description of his "narrow escape" from Italian bandits (p. 43). "Gosh!" Clemens exclaimed of Beatty's less-than-breath-taking account of a glacier. "When this fellow isn't praying he is always lying," Clemens observed of Beatty's conduct while at sea en route home (p. 87). Concerning the absurdly elevated language Beatty attributed to the sailors on his ship ("this is a noble vessel, the best that ever rode the waves"), Clemens simply commented: "How like a sailor!" (p. 87). Arthur L. Scott errs in attributing two comments and a dated note to Clemens *(MTAL,* pp. 130, 319 n. 17); all three were written by the unidentified reader.

Beaumont, Francis (1584–1616) and John Fletcher (1579–1625). *A King and No King* (play, perf. 1611).
    Dr. James Ross Clemens remembered that "Mark never tired of poking fun" at Bessus, a cowardly braggart soldier in the tradition of Jonson's Captain Bobadill, "and likened him to several of our generals in the Civil War" ("Some Reminiscences of Mark Twain" [1929], p. 125).

Becke, Louis (1855–1913). *By Reef and Palm.* Third ed. London: T. Fisher Unwin, 1895. 220 pp.
    Inscription: title page autographed by Louis Becke; also inscribed on front free endleaf by Becke: "To S. L. Clemens/from Louis Becke/Sydney Sept. 1895".
    Marginalia: no markings, but pages 43–54 have been removed.
    Catalogs: C1951, #55c, erroneously listed with books containing Clemens' signature; Maxwell Hunley Rare Books Catalogue (June 1958), item #20, $5.
    Location: Humanities Research Center, University of Texas, Austin.
    Copy examined: Clemens' copy.

Mark Twain was at first uncertain about Becke's name. Reaching the Fiji Islands in September 1895, Twain resolved to "quote from X's (Beake?) two books about island life" (NB 35, TS p. 48). Soon thereafter he reminded himself to "read Philip Beake's delightful stories 'Palm—forget the name" (NB 35, TS p. 49). From Sydney Mark Twain wrote to Becke on 24 September 1895 "to thank you again for your book, which I find stands the sharp test of a third reading, whereas few are the books that can do that. Don't stop; search out *all* the Island tales & print them" (Public Library of New South Wales, Sydney, Australia).

Francis V. Madigan, Jr., "Mark Twain's Passage to India" (1974).

Becker, Karl Friedrich. *Erzählungen aus der alten Welt für die Jugend* (1810).
Clemens wrote the name of this book about Greek myths in Notebook 24 (May 1885), TS p. 18.

Beecher, Catherine Esther (1800–1878). *An Appeal to the People in Behalf of Their Rights as Authorized Interpreters of the Bible.* New York: Harper & Brothers, 1860. 380 pp.
Source: MTLAcc, entry #1815, volume donated by Clemens.

————. *Religious Training of Children in the School, the Family, and the Church.* New York: Harper & Brothers, 1864. 413 pp.
Source: MTLAcc, entry #943, volume donated by Clemens.

Beecher, Henry Ward (1813–1887). *The Life of Jesus, the Christ.* [One vol. only.] Illus. New York: J. B. Ford and Co., 1871. 387 pp. Part 1 only; no other parts of this edition were published.
Catalog: A1911, #33, $1, "one vol. only."
As Clemens remembered the events leading to the fall of his publishing house, Charles L. Webster "agreed to resurrect Henry Ward Beecher's *Life of Christ.* I suggested that he ought to have tried for Lazarus" (2 June 1906 Autobiographical Dictation, *MTE,* pp. 188–189). *The Life of Jesus* was brought out in two volumes by Bromfield and Co. of New York in 1891.

————, comp. *Plymouth Collection of Hymns and Tunes; for the Use of Christian Congregations.* New York: A. S. Barnes & Co., 1855. 484 pp. Reprinted 1856, 1857, 1858, 1859, 1860, and other years until 1872.
References: "the tunes are a shade too complicated for the excursionists" (Mark Twain's letter pub. in New York *Herald,* 20 November 1867, *TIA,* pp. 315–316); as soon as the passengers "get a settled stomach in them they get out their Plymouth Collections and start another storm" (unfinished play, "The *Quaker City* Holy Land Excursion," Act 2, Sc. 1, written 1867); passengers were expected to bring their copies along (5 April 1868 *Daily Alta California; TIA,* p. 303); cited as the source for hymns aboard the *Quaker City* in chapters 1, 4, and 55 of *The Innocents Abroad* (1869). Given as source of a hymn by Phoebe Hinsdale Brown in a letter to Howells, 8 November 1876 *(MTHL,* p. 162). Detective Bullet of New York City theorizes in "Cap'n Simon Wheeler, The Amateur Detective" (written 1877) that Millicent Griswold killed her sweetheart with a copy of the *Plymouth Collection* (*S&B,* pp. 252, 257).

————. *Plymouth Pulpit: A Weekly Publication of Sermons Preached by Henry Ward Beecher in Plymouth Church, Brooklyn.* New York: Fords, Howard, Hulbert, 1868–1884.
Clemens wrote to Livy from Davenport, Iowa on 14 January 1869 during a lecture tour: "Yes I lay abed till 1 P.M, . . . & re-read Beecher's sermon on the love of riches being the root of evil" (MTP)—accounting for his activities on 3 January 1869 in Fort Wayne, Indiana.

Beecher, Lyman (1775–1863). *Autobiography, Correspondence, Etc., of Lyman Beecher, D.D. Edited by Charles Beecher.* Illus. 2 vols. New York: Harper & Brothers, 1864–1865.

Mark Twain quoted from page 245 of the first volume of Beecher's *Autobiography* for a footnote to his manuscript of *Life on the Mississippi (1883)*, illustrating the coarse behavior that prevailed in early-day America. Eventually he decided to delete this note from the final version of his book. Beecher describes an ordination at Plymouth, Connecticut which he attended as a young pastor around 1810; he was embarrassed and angered to find that all of his fellow preachers at the assemblage drank liquor heavily, smoked pipes, and roared noisily at their stories. Beecher found the scene as offensive as "a very active grog-shop" and closed the description by assuring his readers that he attended no more ordinations "of that kind. . . . My heart kindles up at the thoughts of it now" (1: 245, 246).

Beecher, Thomas Kinnicut (1824–1900). *In Time With the Stars; Stories for Children.* Elmira, New York: H. H. Billings, 1901. 165 pp.
Source: MTLAcc, entry #1876, volume donated from Clemens' library by Clara Clemens Gabrilowitsch in 1910.

The Beecher Trial: A Review of the Evidence. Reprinted from the New York "Times" of July 3, 1875. With Some Revisions and Additions. Fourth edition. New York: n.p., 1875. 34 pp. 25¢ pamphlet.
Marginalia: none except for Clemens' penciled arithmetical computations on the back cover.
Location: Mark Twain Papers, Berkeley, California.
Copy examined: Clemens' copy.

Beerbohm, Julius (1854–1906). *Wanderings in Patagonia; or, Life Among the Ostrich-Hunters.* Illus. New York: Henry Holt & Co., 1879. 294 pp. [Another ed.: London: Chatto & Windus, 1879. 278 pp.]
Wanderings in Patagonia was one of the book titles Clemens listed in 1909 in connection with his declaration that he preferred to read "history, biography, travels, curious facts & strange happenings, & science" (MTP, Notebook Fragments file). See my essay, " 'I Detest Novels, Poetry & Theology': Origin of a Fiction Concerning Mark Twain's Reading" (1977). Beerbohm's narrative recounted his journey through a virtually unexplored region of South America in 1877.

Beers, Clifford Whittingham (1876–1943). *A Mind That Found Itself; An Autobiography.* New York and London: Longmans, Green, and Co., 1908. 363 pp.
Inscription: signed on front pastedown endpaper, "S. L. Clemens, 1908."
Catalogs: A1911, #34, $4; *Book Auction Records 1948–49* (London, 1950), 46: 45 reports Parke-Bernet Galleries sale, 29 November 1948 (item #89), $35.

Beeton, Samuel Orchart. *Beeton's Complete Letter-Writer for Ladies and Gentlemen; A Useful Compendium of Epistolary Materials Gathered from the Best Sources, and Adapted to Suit an Indefinite Number of Cases.* London: Ward, Locke & Co., [1873]. Another edition pub. 1895.
During Clemens' first sojourn in Bermuda in January 1908 he presented Elizabeth Wallace "with a precious volume which he had discovered in the island book store, entitled *Beeton's Complete Letter-Writer for Gentlemen.* . . . He had written this inscription on the blank page, 'To Young Lady desirous of perfecting Herself in the Epistolary Art [date in full]. Dear Miss ——————: Try Beeton, Trust Beeton, Beeton is your friend. Have no fear. Sincerely yours, S. L. Clemens.' " Miss Wallace remembered that "this choice book we carried with us and regaled ourselves, from time to time, with particularly rare specimens of the epistolary art" (*MT&HI*, p. 35).

Clemens had long been familiar with the formulas of *Beeton's Complete Letter-Writer* and its several dozen counterparts. Brown & Gross, Hartford booksellers, billed him on 1 January 1881 for "1 Letter Writer" purchased on 11 October 1880 (receipt in MTP). The slave Toby ludicrously misapplies model letters from *The People's Ready Letter-Writer* (Mark Twain's invented name) in chapter 4 of "Simon Wheeler, Detective," a novel Mark Twain worked on between 1877 and 1898 (*S&B*, pp. 354, 355–356, 385–386).

Behn, Mrs. Aphra (Amis) (1640–1689). *Love-Letters Between a Nobleman and His Sister; With the History of Their Adventures*. Sixth edition. 3 vols. London: Printed for D. Brown, J. Tonson, B. Tookes, G. Strahan, S. Ballard, W. Mears, and F. Clay, 1721.
   Catalog: A1911, #301, .75¢, "Part II" only.

Belcher, (Lady) Diana (Jolliffe) (1805?–1890). *The Mutineers of the "Bounty" and Their Descendants in Pitcairn and Norfolk Islands*. Illus. London: J. Murray, 1870. 420 pp.
   Catalog: C1951, #D60, listed with books signed by Clemens.
   Albert Bigelow Paine was told that *Mutineers* was one of the books Clemens and Theodore Crane favored during their leisure-hours reading in the summer of 1874 (*MTB*, p. 510).

Bell, John Joy (1871-1934). *Ethel*. New York: Harper & Brothers, 1903. 196 pp.
   Inscription: signed in black ink on front free endpaper: "SL. Clemens/ 1903."
   Location: Antenne-Dorrance Collection, Rice Lake, Wis.
   Copy examined: Clemens' copy.

————. *Later Adventures of Wee Macgreegor*. New York: Harper & Brothers, 1904. 214 pp.
   Source: MTLAcc, entry #1587, volume donated by Clemens.

————. [Another identical copy.]
   Source: MTLAcc, entry #1877, volume donated from Clemens' library by Clara Clemens Gabrilowitsch in 1910.

————. *Mr. Pennycook's Boy*. New York: Harper & Brothers, 1905. 272 pp.
   Source: MTLAcc, entry #1588, volume donated by Clemens.

————. *Oh! Christina!* New York: F. H. Revell Co., [cop. 1909]. 159 pp.
   Source: MTLAcc, entry #1916, volume donated from Clemens' library by Clara Clemens Gabrilowitsch in 1910.

Bell, Lilian Lida (1867–1929). *The Expatriates; A Novel*. New York: Harper & Brothers, 1902. 432 pp.
   Source: MTLAcc, entry #1435, volume donated by Clemens.

————. *The Instinct of Step-fatherhood*. New York: Harper & Brothers, 1898. 228 pp.
   Source: MTLAcc, entry #21, volume donated by Clemens.

————. *A Little Sister to the Wilderness; A Novel*. New York: Harper & Brothers, 1901. 267 pp.
   Source: MTLAcc, entry #1515, volume donated by Clemens.

————. *The Love Affairs of an Old Maid*. New York: Harper & Brothers, 1899. 188 pp.
   Source: MTLAcc, entry #673, volume donated by Clemens.

Bellamy, Edward (1850–1898). *Looking Backward, 2000-1887*. Boston: Ticknor and Co., 1888. 470 pp.

Despite obvious similarities between *Looking Backward (1888)* and *A Connecticut Yankee* (1889), no one has disputed the apparent order of occurrence which emerges from Mark Twain's notebooks and letters—that "when *A Connecticut Yankee* was ready for the printers, Twain found time to read Edward Bellamy's *Looking Backward,*" as Louis J. Budd has stated *(MTSP,* p. 145). Mark Twain finished revising his novel early in November 1889; his publishing firm issued the book on 10 December 1889. Almost as though determined to frustrate later scholars who might naturally speculate about an influence, Twain made a precise entry in Notebook 29: "Began 'Looking Backward' Nov. 5, 1889, on the train. A fascinating book" (TS p. 30).

Howells recalled correctly that Clemens "was fascinated with *Looking Backward* and had Bellamy to visit him" *(MMT,* p. 38). From Hartford on 1 December 1889 Mark Twain declined with regret an invitation from Sylvester Baxter of the Boston *Herald* to meet Bellamy, whom Twain called "the man who has made the accepted heaven paltry by inventing a better one on earth" (Berg, quoted in *MTHL,* p. 622). Mark Twain wrote Baxter on 19 December 1889 about his anticipation "to get acquainted with the maker of the latest & best of all the Bibles" (Berg, quoted in *MTHL,* p. 622). Twain entertained Bellamy and Baxter at his Hartford house on 3 January 1890 *(MTHL,* p. 622 n. 2), and later that year he listed Bellamy in Notebook 29 as the designated recipient of a complimentary copy of *A Connecticut Yankee* (TS p. 57).

TIH, p. 39.

Bellows, John (1831–1902). *Dictionary for the Pocket: French and English, English and French*. Rev. by Alexandre Beljame. Second ed. London: Trübner & Co., 1877. 605 pp. [First edition pub. 1873].

References: mentioned three times in Clemens' notebooks—its author and title (1878, *N&J,* 2: 158); its appearance resembles a pocket New Testament, and it is an "admirable dictionary" *(N&J,* 2: 314, 316). In "Paris Notes" (1882) Mark Twain claimed that the Protestant worshipers at a church in Paris actually hold "Mr. Bellows' admirable and exhaustive little French-English dictionary" instead of a "morocco-bound Testament" and surreptitiously study its lexicon. Bellows wrote to Mark Twain on 5 March, 24 April, and 6 June 1883 to thank him for this "kind and humorous notice" (MTP), and on the verso of Bellows' first letter Mark Twain wrote, "John Bellows author of the admirable little French-English Dictionary."

Bell's Life in London and Sporting Chronicle (periodical, pub. 1822–1886).

Mark Twain alluded to this magazine as his source for euphemistic boxing terminology in a column for the San Francisco *Golden Era,* 11 October 1863 *(WG,* p. 28).

Benham, William George. *The Laws of Scientific Hand Reading; A Practical Treatise on the Art Commonly Called Palmistry*. Illus. New York: G. P. Putnam's Sons, [1900]. 635 pp. Reprinted 1901, 1903, 1906.

Catalog: C1951, #J33, listed among the books belonging to Jean and Clara Clemens.

Benjamin Ben Jonah, of Tudela. *The Itinerary of Rabbi Benjamin of Tudela.*

Edition: Published under several titles and in various languages since the sixteenth century. Mark Twain read and marked passages (pp. 63–126) in the version included in Thomas Wright's *Early Travels in Palestine* (1848), a volume he signed in 1877.

Mark Twain mentioned the travels of this twelfth-century Jewish merchant in Notebook 28 (1888–1889), in the context of *A Connecticut Yankee* sources (TS p. 60).

Benkard, Johann Philipp. *Geschichte der Deutschen Kaiser und Könige. Zu den Bildern des Kaisersaals. 4e aufl.* Illus. Frankfort-a-M: H. Keller, 1869, 155 pp.
Inscription: signed on flyleaf: "S. L. Clemens, Frankfort-a-M./May 4, 1878."
Catalog: A1911, #35, $1.

Bennett, Emerson (1822–1905).
Mark Twain scoffed at the frontier adventure stories Bennett wrote for the dime-novel trade in chapter 19 of *Roughing It* (1872).
MTBP, p. 68; *RI* (Iowa-Calif. Ed.), p. 568; *MT&JB,* pp. 346–347 n. 10; *MT&GA,* p. 36.

Bennett, Sanford Fillmore. "The sweet by and by" (hymn, cop. 1868). Melody by Joseph Philbrick Webster.
Mark Twain first joked about the enduring popularity of this piece in a letter to D. F. Appleton on 5 December 1877: "There is a new song here [in Hartford] which you may not have heard, and if you care for music we shall be very glad indeed to sing it for you, by telephone. . . . I think it is called 'In the Sweet By-and-Bye' " *(The New England Society of the City of New York,* Seventy-second Anniversary Celebration [New York, 1877], p. 84). In the notebook he kept for 1878 he groused that this was a pretty and moving song—"at first" (NB 17, *N&J,* 2: 240). The idea of this tired tune's being sung over the telephone appealed to him so much that Rosannah Ethelton sings its "exquisitely soft and remote strains" several times on that instrument (flatting many notes in the effort) in "The Loves of Alonzo Fitz Clarence and Rosannah Ethelton" (1878). (Twain had sketched this antic in Notebook 14 [*N&J,* 2: 49] in 1877.) Hank Morgan hears a band salute the Queen in chapter 17 of *A Connecticut Yankee* "with what seemed to be the crude first-draft or original agony of the wail known to later centuries as 'In the Sweet Bye and Bye. . . . For some reason the queen had the composer hanged"; a few pages further on Hank himself gives the Queen permission to hang the entire band for their painful rendition of this song. Mark Twain referred to the piece again in Notebook 33 (October 1893), TS p. 35; and the Young Man in "What Is Man?" (written 1898–1906) alluded to it as an example of "the new popular song with the taking melody [that] sings thro' one's head day and night, asleep and awake, till one is a wreck" *(WIM?,* Iowa-California Ed., p. 178). Again in "Christian Science" (1907) Mark Twain used it as an illustration of "how wearisome the sweetest and touchingest things can become, through rep-rep-repetition" (Book 2, chapter 7, *WIM?,* Iowa-California ed., p. 323). Yet in spite of numerous gibes at the song, Clemens claimed in a letter to his sister-in-law following Livy's death that he had always associated the song with his wife, a surprising fact if true. He wrote to Susan Crane on 9 September 1904 that a street-organist playing "The Sweet By and By" outside his hotel reminded him that he initially heard the tune played in December 1867 at the time he first saw Livy, and that during the period of their engagement they often sang it in the evenings (MTP). Perhaps it *was* merely the repetitiveness to which Clemens objected, but the public and the private man seem strikingly at odds concerning this song.

Bennett, William Cox (1820–1895). "Baby May" (poem).
Clemens wrote to Mrs. Fairbanks on 6 July 1873 about his meeting the English poet in London: "W. C. Bennett (you remember his poem 'Baby May' in the Bryant Selections)" *(MTMF,* p. 173). The poem in Bryant's *Library of Poetry and Song* (1870) consists of a long catalogue of commonplace praises for his infant daughter (her "slumbers" are "sweet angel-seemings"), concluding, "Beauty all that beauty may be;—/That's May Bennett; that's my baby" (p. 76).

Benson, Edward Frederic (1867–1940). *The Book of Months.* New York: Harper & Brothers, 1903. 299 pp.
Source: MTLAcc, entry #847, volume donated by Clemens.

————. *Dodo: A Detail of the Day*. New York: F. M. Lupton Publishing Co., n.d. 213 pp. Paperbound. [First pub. 1893.]

Marginalia: on page 1 Clemens wrote, "Did you ever read it? It came out about 1897 I think. Very clever it was conceded and made him famous. He has written others since, but in a more serious vein."

Copy examined: none. Information for this entry derives from a letter of 13 November 1963 from Whitlock's, Inc. (New Haven, Conn.) to the Mark Twain Memorial in Hartford, Conn., offering the book for sale. There is no indication as to how the volume was identified as part of Clemens' personal library. "The pages are chipped and the title page torn." Although the price was only $10, the Mark Twain Memorial declined to purchase this volume because of their (since altered) policy of acquiring only those books which Clemens had in his library prior to 1891.

————. *The Judgment Books*. New York: Harper & Brothers, 1895. 176 pp.
Source: MTLAcc, entry# 1321, volume donated by Clemens.

Bent, James Theodore (1852–1897). *A Freak of Freedom; or, the Republic of San Marino*. Illus. London: Longmans, Green, and Co., 1879. 271 pp.
Inscription: signed on half-title page: "S. L. Clemens. London,/79."
Marginalia: "some notations," according to the auction catalog. One note criticizes the author's syntax in stating, "A small hamlet belonging to the Republic has grown up round a well, where the saint used to baptize his converts, springing from underneath a cliff." Clemens queried: "Did the converts spring, or was it the Saint?"
Catalog: A1911, #36, $9.

Bent, Samuel Arthur. *Short Sayings of Great Men. With Historical and Explanatory Notes*. Boston: J. R. Osgood & Co., 1882. 610 pp.
Marginalia: "some notations" by Clemens, according to the auction catalog.
Catalog: A1911, #37, $1.75.
Clemens requested this book in a postscript to a letter he wrote to James R. Osgood & Company on 6 January 1883 *(MTLP,* p. 162).

Benton, (Mrs.) Kate A. (d. 1899). *Geber; A Tale of the Reign of Harun al Raschid, Khalif of Baghdad*. New York: Frederick A. Stokes Co., [1900]. 487 pp.
Source: MTLAcc, entry #880, volume donated by Mrs. Ralph W. Ashcroft (formerly Isabel Lyon), Clemens' secretary.

————. [Another identical copy.]
Source: MTLAcc, entry #2162, volume donated from Clemens' library by Clara Clemens Gabrilowitsch in 1910.

Berard, Augusta Blanche (1824–1901). *Berard's History of the United States*. Rev. by Celeste E. Bush. Illus. Philadelphia: Cowperthwait & Co., [cop. 1878]. 358 pp.
Source: MTLAcc, entry #813, volume donated by Clemens. Title page missing.

Berger, Alfred, Freiherr von. *Habsburg. Marchenspiel in drei Acten*. Wien: Carl Konegen, 1898. 120 pp.
Berger is mentioned in Notebook 42 while Mark Twain was in Vienna in December 1897 (TS p. 52). Berger's verses are mentioned in September 1898 (NB 40, TS p. 40). Mark Twain translated fifteen lines of verse from *Habsburg* into English for Joseph H. Twichell on 28 September 1898 so that Twichell could sample Berger's "recent fairy-drama" (Yale). "The Memorable Assassination" (1898) closes with eight of these lines "to convey the spirit of the verses."

Berlichingen, Gotz von (1480–1562). [German feudal knight whose autobiography was pub. posthumously in 1731. It was used by Goethe as a source for the drama *Gotz von Berlichingen* (1773), which Sir Walter Scott translated in 1799.]
   Edition: unknown.
   Berlichingen's memoirs are mentioned in chapter 12 of *A Tramp Abroad* (1880); Berlichingen himself is referred to in chapters 11, 12, 14, and 15.

Bernard, A. Hermann. *Legends of the Rhine.* Trans. by Fr. Arnold. Mayence: Joseph Halenza, n. d. 316 pp. [First English edition pub. 1862.]
   Edgar H. Hemminghaus saw Clemens' copy on the shelves of the Mark Twain Library, Redding, Connecticut in 1945 ("Mark Twain's German Provenience," p. 473), but the volume has since disappeared.

Bernard, Frédéric. *Wonderful Escapes.* Trans. and ed. by Richard Whiteing (b. 1840). Illus. New York: Scribner, Armstrong & Co., 1872. 308 pp.
   Source: MTLAcc, entry #2001, volume donated from Clemens' library by Clara Clemens Gabrilowitsch in 1910.
   In chronological order Bernard relates more than forty supposedly true tales of escape from imprisonment in dungeons and towers; many of the wily prisoners manufacture useful implements in their cells, just as Tom Sawyer exhorts Jim to do in the later chapters of *HF* (1885). The fortunate escapees include Benvenuto Cellini, Baron Trenck, and Casanova de Seingalt.

Bernard, John (1756–1828). *Retrospections of America, 1797–1811.* Ed. by Mrs. Bernard. Intro., notes, and index by Laurence Hutton and Brander Matthews. New York: Harper & Brothers, 1887. 380 pp.
   Source: MTLAcc, entry #1711, volume donated by Clemens.

Bernard, Victor Ferdinand. *L'art d'intéresser en classe; nouveau manuel de lecture et de conversation. 3 éd.* Boston: Carl Schoenhof, 1885. 224 pp.
   Inscription: unknown (flyleaf torn out).
   Marginalia: some markings in ink.
   Location: Mark Twain Library, Redding, Conn.
   Copy examined: presumably Clemens' copy.

Bernardin de Saint-Pierre, Jacques Henri. *Paul et Virginie* (1788).
   Mauritius is the "scene of the sentimental adventure of Paul and Virginia"; their "romantic sojourn" was the only prominent event in the history of Mauritius, and it "didn't happen." A citizen informs Mark Twain that this book "is the greatest story that was ever written about Mauritius, and the only one" (ch. 62, *FE* [1897]).

Berriat-Saint-Prix (called Jacques Saint-Prix-Berriat) (1769–1845). *Jeanne d'Arc, ou Cou-d'oeil sur les révolutions de France au temps de Charles VI et de Charles VII, et sur-tout de la Pucelle d'Orléans.* Paris: Pillet, 1817. 368 pp.
   Listed among "authorities examined" for Mark Twain's *Joan of Arc* (1896) on the page preceding the "Translator's Preface."

Bertholet, Alfred (1868–1951). *The Transmigration of Souls.* Trans. by Henry John Chaytor. New York: Harper & Brothers, 1909. 133 pp.
   Source: MTLAcc, entry #1489, volume donated by Clemens.

Besant, (Sir) Walter (1836–1901). *All in a Garden Fair.* New York: J. W. Lowell Co., [cop. 1883]. 353 pp.
   Source: MTLAcc, entry #26, volume donated by Clemens.

————. *All Sorts and Conditions of Men; An Impossible Story.* A New Edition. London: Chatto & Windus, 1894. 331 pp.
   Source: MTLAcc, entry #2163, volume donated from Clemens' library by Clara Clemens Gabrilowitsch in 1910.

————. *All Sorts and Conditions of Men; An Impossible Story.* New York: Harper & Brothers, n.d. 412 pp.
  Source: MTLAcc, entry #2177, volume donated from Clemens' library by Clara Clemens Gabrilowitsch in 1910.

———— and James Rice (1843–1882). *The Chaplain of the Fleet.* New York: Dodd, Mead & Co., n.d. 447 pp.
  Source: MTLAcc, entry #2167, volume donated from Clemens' library by Clara Clemens Gabrilowitsch in 1910.

———— and James Rice. *The Chaplain of the Fleet.* London: Chatto & Windus, 1888. 447 pp.
  Source: MTLAcc, entry #2179, volume donated from Clemens' library by Clara Clemens Gabrilowitsch in 1910.

————. *Dorothy Forster; A Novel.* London: Chatto & Windus, 1895. 312 pp.
  Source: MTLAcc, entry #2172, volume donated from Clemens' library by Clara Clemens Gabrilowitsch in 1910.

————. *For Faith and Freedom.* London: Chatto & Windus, 1890. 334 pp.
  Source: MTLAcc, entry #2174, volume donated from Clemens' library by Clara Clemens Gabrilowitsch in 1910.

————. *London. A New Edition.* Illus. London: Chatto & Windus, 1894. 343 pp.
  Catalog: A1911, #38, $1.25.
  Clemens wrote to Andrew Chatto on 3 January 1895: "Many thousand thanks! The books arrived yesterday, & Besant's 'London' kept me most pleasantly awake the whole night, & lost me my day's work to-day" (ALS, Mark Twain Boyhood Home and Museum, Hannibal, Missouri).

————. *The Pen and the Book.* [With a chapter on "Copyright and Literary Property" by G. H. Thring.] London: Thomas Burleigh, 1899. 347 pp.
  Marginalia: extensive underscorings and marginal notes by Clemens on approximately thirty pages. His penciled marginalia occur mainly in passages discussing the costs and methods of book publishing and the financial relationships among authors, publishers, and booksellers. Clemens paused to compute Mary Baker Eddy's profits for *Science and Health* on pages 155–156. He liked Besant's attitude toward royalties: "His main point that those who hold that lit. men should not endeavor to make as much money as they can, talk nonsense. Those who say it 'are chiefly the unsuccessful writers' " (p. 134). Clemens also commented: "In our day it seems *indecent* to confess hunger for money—& yet if you have that you can add all other things to yourself" (p. 146). On page 177 he figured up his receipts for *Life on the Mississippi* ("robbery") and noted that he only "cleared about 65¢ on 40,000 copies." Commiserating with authors whom Besant describes as having been victimized by publishers, Clemens exclaimed on page 180: "Why, there are more fools than I." Further on he used the top margin of the page titled "Chapter VII. The Method of the Future" to advocate a system for book sales that would use the postal system to "offer the book *directly* to the man himself"; "selling books through booksellers is infinitely stupid," he asserted (p. 207). At the bottom of the same page he added: "I published Huck Finn—success. Pub'd 3 & paid pub a royalty—poor job." On page 265 he elaborated on his proposal "to abolish the *bookseller* & use the P.O.—make *it* the middleman & reduce the prices."
  Catalog: C1951, #27a, $20.
  Location: collection of Justin G. Turner, Los Angeles, Calif.
  Copy examined: photocopy of marginalia provided by Professor Howard G. Baetzhold, Butler University.

Mark Twain referred to Besant's review of *Joan of Arc* in a letter to Chatto & Windus written on 29 October 1896 (CWB). On 22 February 1898 Twain wrote from Vienna to thank Besant for his kind words about *Huckleberry Finn* in the February 1898 issue of *Munsey's Magazine* (vol. 18: 659–664) (ALS in Berg). Besant's recent column was probably responsible for Mark Twain's withdrawing from an agreement to review *The Pen and the Book* for *Harper's Monthly*. Mark Twain explained to John Kendrick Bangs on 2 March 1899 that he had to give up the attempt soon after the book arrived: "Besant is a friend of mine, and there was no way of doing a review that wouldn't cut into his feelings and wound his enthusiastic pride in his insane performance. . . . There isn't a rational page in it. Why, a person might as well undertake to review a lunatic asylum" (Francis Hyde Bangs, *John Kendrick Bangs* [New York: A. A. Knopf, 1941], p. 203). The preface to Besant's *The Pen and the Book* states that it was "written for the guidance and the instruction of those young persons who are thinking of the literary life."

————and James Rice. *The Seamy Side, a Story.* London: Chatto & Windus, 1880. [Published in the United States as: *The Seamy Side; A Novel.* New York: Dodd, Mead & Co., 1880.]

Lane Cooper, in "Mark Twain's Lilacs and Laburnums" (1932), recognized several unmistakable parallels between chapters 15 and 26 of *The Seamy Side* and chapter four of Mark Twain's "A Double-Barrelled Detective Story" (1902), in which Twain introduces a "solitary aesophagus" into a purple passage on October scenery.

Bethune, George Washington (1805–1862). *Memoirs of Mrs. Joanna Bethune, by Her Son.* New York: Harper & Brothers, 1863. 250 pp.
Source: MTLAcc, entry #1749, volume donated by Clemens.

Bettersworth, Alexander Pitts. *John Smith, Democrat: His Two Days' Canvass (Sunday Included) for the Office of Mayor of the City of Bunkumville.* Springfield, Ill.: H. W. Rokker, 1877. 249 pp.
Source: MTLAcc, entry #27, volume donated by Clemens.

Beveridge, Albert Jeremiah (1862–1927). *The Russian Advance.* New York: Harper & Brothers, 1904. 486 pp.
Source: MTLAcc, entry #1360, volume donated by Clemens.

Biart, Lucien (1828–1897). *Adventures of a Young Naturalist.* Ed. and adapted by Parker Gillmore. Illus. New York: Harper & Brothers, n.d. 491 pp.
Source: MTLAcc, entry #1589, volume donated by Clemens.

Bible.
Clemens and members of his family owned or referred to more than twenty-five copies of the Bible. In the course of reading Clemens' literary works, letters, and notebooks, I have identified more than 400 instances in which he alludes to specific biblical passages—excluding his references to Adam, Eve, Noah, or other familiar figures. He mentions or alludes to thirty-seven of the sixty-six books in the Bible; twenty-three of the thirty-nine Old Testament books and fourteen of the twenty-seven New Testament books figure in his writings. The majority of his allusions (sixty-eight) refer to the Book of Genesis; he alluded to passages in other books in the following descending order: Matthew (fifty-eight); Luke (forty-four); John, especially the raising of Lazarus (twenty-six); Exodus (twenty-five); Judges (sixteen); Isaiah (thirteen); Numbers (twelve); I Samuel (twelve); I Kings (twelve); Mark (eleven); the others ten or fewer.

Such computations reveal little about the manner in which Mark Twain approached the Bible as a literary source, but they do indicate the breadth of his familiarity with the book as well as his emphasis on the narratives in Genesis and those describing the life of Christ. Echoes of biblical passages are more prevalent in Mark

Twain's earlier works, and the largest concentration of allusions is to be found in *Innocents Abroad* (1869). These findings can be augmented by more thorough studies in the future, but as they stand they bear out Henry Pochmann's first study of the Bible as a source for Mark Twain's works (1924): "Of the one hundred and twenty-four Biblical allusions which I have found in Mark Twain's books, eighty-nine are in *Innocents Abroad*" ("Mind of Mark Twain," p. 7). From puns and simple allusions in Twain's early writings he moved to affectionate joshing about the Bible at mid-career, ending, in his last decade, with broadside blasts at the stories it related and the religion it propounded. His respect for the literary achievement of the book as a collection of writings central to European and American history and culture never varied, but he came to feel, as he wrote in 1891, that "the Christian's Bible is a drug-store. Its contents remain the same; but the medical practice changes" ("Bible Teaching and Religious Practice," *WIM?*, Iowa-California ed., p. 71).

Mark Twain's attitude toward the Bible is complex enough to have led several scholars to treat the topic in greater detail than is possible here. Alexander Jones paid attention to Mark Twain's use of the Bible in "Mark Twain and Religion" (doctoral diss., Univ. of Minnesota, 1950). Allison Ensor revised his own dissertation (1965) and published it as a brief book in 1969 (*Mark Twain and the Bible*). Ensor believes that "there is not much evidence that he read the Bible systematically; his citations of the Bible could more often than not have come from sermons, conversations, or memories of Sunday school teaching" (*MT&B*, p. 99). But this ignores Mark Twain's heavily annotated Bible now at the University of Texas in Austin, as well as his other surviving copies of the book. Ensor's succinct volume is worth reading nonetheless for its valuable section on Mark Twain's three major biblical images: the Prodigal Son, the Fall of Man (Adam and Eve), and Noah and the Flood (pp. 29–72).

Robert A. Rees produced a helpful doctoral dissertation in 1966, "Mark Twain and the Bible: Characters Who Use the Bible and Biblical Characters" (Univ. of Wisconsin), and Earl Reimer followed in 1970 with "Mark Twain and the Bible: An Inductive Study" (doctoral dissertation, Michigan State Univ.). Reimer's dissertation includes a useful concordance of biblical allusions in Mark Twain's writing. Other studies listed in the critical bibliography—especially those by Stanley Brodwin, Louis J. Budd, John Francis McDermott, and Betty L. Sloan—have commented on Mark Twain's uses of individual books of the Bible. See also the entry for "The Lord's Prayer."

Bible. English. N.d. *The Holy Bible, Containing the Old and New Testaments*. King James Version. Oxford: University of Oxford Press, n.d. Sold by Thomas Nelson and Sons, New York.
> *Inscription:* none; "O. L. S. Clemens" embossed in gold lettering on front cover.
> *Location:* Mark Twain Library, Redding, Conn.
> *Copy examined:* Livy's [?] copy.

Bible. English. N.d. *The Holy Bible*. Illus. Springfield, Mass.: W. J. Holland, n.d. 1494 pp.
> *Source:* MTLAcc, entry #1, volume donated by Clemens.

Bible. English. N.d. *Holy Bible*. N.p., n.d. 1061 pp. Lacks title page.
> *Source:* MTLAcc, entry #2309, volume donated from Clemens' library by Clara Clemens Gabrilowitsch in 1910.

Bible. English. 1817. *The Holy Bible: Containing the Old and New Testaments, Together with the Apocrypha*. King James Version. Philadelphia: M. Carey, 1817.
> *Marginalia:* contains handwritten Clemens-Lampton "Family Records" at pages 834–835. Loose fragmentary notes by Jane Lampton Clemens scattered throughout volume.

Catalog: 17 January 1944 Charles Retz, Inc. appraisal (p. 5). Valued at $10.
Location: Mark Twain Papers, Berkeley, California.
Copy examined: Jane Lampton Clemens' copy. When Mollie Clemens died in 1904 (Orion had died in 1897), Clemens requested only two specific books from her executor: John Marshall Clemens' encyclopedia "& my mother's old illustrated family Bible, if it still exists" (Clemens to Mr. Carpenter, Florence, 14 Feb. 1904, MTP).

Bible. English. 1827. *The Holy Bible.* Oxford: Clarendon Press by Samuel Collingwood and Co., 1827.
Provenance: explanatory card in book reports: "Mark Twain's Bible, found at the American Publishing Company, when the company went out of business." A dubious addition to Clemens' personal library.
Location: Mark Twain Memorial, Hartford, Connecticut. Donated by Mrs. John Helmer Johnson in 1957.
Copy examined: conceivably a copy Clemens once had an opportunity to see or use.

Bible. English. [1846]. *The Holy Bible. The Miniature Quarto Bible.* London: Samuel Bagster and Sons, n.d. [Editor's preface dated 1846.]
Location: Mark Twain Library, Redding, Conn.
Copy examined: copy believed by Mrs. Peggy Sanford, former librarian of the Mark Twain Library, Redding, Connecticut, to have once formed part of Clemens' personal library. Shown to me in 1970.

Bible. English. 1855. *Holy Bible.* New York: American Bible Society, 1855. 768 pp.
Source: MTLAcc, entry #2311, volume donated from Clemens' library by Clara Clemens Gabrilowitsch in 1910.

Bible. English. 1862. *The Holy Bible, Containing the Old and New Testaments, Translated Out of the Original Tongues; and with the Former Translations Diligently Compared and Revised.* New York: American Bible Society, 1862.
Inscription: "Mary E. Clemens,/Carson City,/December 25, 1863."
Marginalia: contains detailed Clemens family records compiled by Mollie (Mary) Clemens, Samuel Clemens' sister-in-law. On the flyleaf Mollie noted sadly: "Jennie commenced to read this through, and read as far as page 16 or 17." Mollie's daughter died in 1864.
Provenance: given by Mollie Clemens to Mrs. Joseph Montgomery Casey of Fort Madison, Iowa, shortly before Mollie died in 1904. Never actually in Samuel L. Clemens' possession. Description of book and photocopies of Mollie's genealogies sent to the Mark Twain Papers in 1968 by Rachel M. Varble, Fort Mitchell, Kentucky.
Location: presently unknown.

Bible. English. 1863. *The Holy Bible, Containing the Old and New Testaments.* King James Version. Oxford: Oxford University Press for the British and Foreign Bible Society, 1863. [Unpaged.]
Inscription: flyleaf inscribed in purple ink by Clemens: "Mrs. Jane Clemens/From Her Son—/Jerusalem, Sept. 24, 1867." Below that is illegible inscription in faded ink ending "by O. C." Wooden covers; front cover stamped: "Mrs. Jane Clemens from her son."
Catalog: 17 January 1944 Charles Retz, Inc. appraisal, p. 4; valued at $50.
Location: Mark Twain Papers, Berkeley, California.
Copy examined: Jane Lampton Clemens' copy.

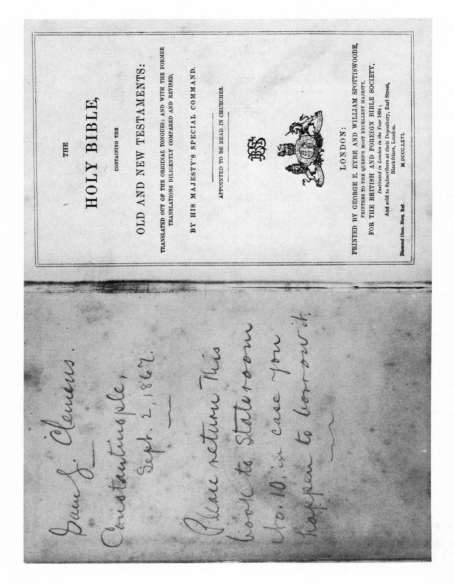

Plate 4: Penciled inscription and title page of Bible that Clemens took to the Holy Land in 1867.
(Courtesy of Humanities Research Center, University of Texas, Austin.)

Bible. English. 1866. *The Holy Bible, Containing the Old and New Testaments: Translated Out of the Original Tongues; and with the Former Translations Diligently Compared and Revised.* King James Version. London: George E. Eyre and William Spottiswoode for the British and Foreign Bible Society, 1866.

Inscription: signed in pencil on flyleaf opposite the title page: "Saml. Clemens./ Constantinople,/ Sept. 2, 1867./ Please return this book to stateroom No. 10, in case you happen to borrow it."

Marginalia: pervasive penciled markings, brackets, and underlinings (with a few additions in brown ink), concentrated most thickly in the New Testament—especially the Book of Saint Matthew. Further annotation in pencil and brown ink on the rear flyleaves. Examples: "At 27 goes to C— after temptation & begins his 4 yrs preaching. . . . Fame went abroad in Gal—touched the eyes of the blind—went healing & preaching through Gal. . . . Went to Naz—admired but suspected—They knew his family & his low estate. He wrought few miracles." Clemens chronicled numerous other events in the life of Christ on these rear flyleaves. They bear directly on chapters 46–56 of *The Innocents Abroad* (1869), where Mark Twain describes Gennesaret, Palestine, Galilee, Capernaum, Nazareth, Jerusalem, and the Garden of Gethsemane.

Catalogs: 17 January 1944 Charles Retz, Inc. appraisal (p. 5); valued at $30. Reported missing in "Deficiencies of Lincoln Warehouse Inventory," 3 April 1947, Henry E. Huntington Library and Art Gallery, p. 3, TS copy in MTP. Thus the Bible originally was part of the Mark Twain Papers, which Clara Clemens Samossoud eventually bequeathed to the University of California.

Location: Humanities Research Center, University of Texas, Austin. Purchased in 1962 as part of the Mark Twain Collection assembled by Frank C. Willson, Melrose, Massachusetts.

Copy examined: Clemens' copy, used during his tour of the Holy Land in 1867.

Bible. English 1867. *Holy Bible.* Glasgow: W. Collins, S. & Co., 1867. 977 pp.
Source: MTLAcc, entry #2312, volume donated from Clemens' library by Clara Clemens Gabrilowitsch in 1910.

Bible. English. 1872. *The Holy Bible Containing the Old and New Testaments According to the Authorized Version.* Illus. by Gustave Doré. 2 vols. London, New York: Cassell, Petter, and Galpin, [1872–1876].

Chief Inspector Blunt refers to the Bible illustrated by Doré ("the Doré costs a hundred dollars a copy, Russian leather, beveled") during an interrogation he conducts in chapter 1 of "The Stolen White Elephant" (1882).

Bible. English. 1874. *New Illustrated Bible for the Young.* Illus. Philadelphia, cop. 1874.

Inscription: gilt-stamped on front cover: "Susie and Clara". Gold lettering also reads: "Honor Thy Father and Thy Mother."

Catalog: Mott 1952, #72, $12.50.

Provenance: listed in the card catalog of the Mark Twain Library, Redding, Conn., but now missing.

Bible. English. 1885. *Holy Bible.* Revised Edition. New York: Harper & Brothers, 1885. 514 pp.
Source: MTLAcc, entry #1364, volume donated by Clemens.

Bible. German. 1874. *Die Bibel nach der deutschen uebersetzung von dr. Martin Luther.* Portrait. Leipzig, 1874.
Catalog: A1911, #41, $1.

Bible. Hawaiian. [Edition unknown.]
In 1866 Clemens returned from the Sandwich Islands with gifts for fifteen-year-old Annie Moffett, his niece. One present was a Hawaiian Bible, inscribed "from her venerable Uncle" (*MTBus*, p. 91).

Bible. New Testament. English. [Edition unknown].
John Marshall Clemens owned a copy of the New Testament, according to the appraisal of his personal property at the time of his death in 1847 (John Francis McDermott, "Mark Twain and the Bible," p. 198). One large Bible and two small ones also appear in the list of his estate.

Bible. New Testament. English. [Edition unknown]. *The New Testament.*
Catalog: C1951, #39C, $105, listed among books signed by Clemens.
Location: reportedly owned by Dr. Max Lewis Busch, Pasadena, California.

Bible. New Testament. English. 1859. *The New Testament of Our Lord and Saviour Jesus Christ.* New York: American Bible Society, 1859. 306 pp.
Inscription: two front flyleaves missing; signed in round, youthful hand on front pastedown endpaper: "Sam./Samuel/Clemens."
Marginalia: a few markings in ink in the Book of Saint Matthew.
Provenance: contains red-ink accession number of Mark Twain Library, Redding, Connecticut. Donated from Clemens' library by Clara Clemens Gabrilowitsch in 1910 (MTLAcc, entry #2313).
Catalog: Mott 1952, #73, $85.
Location: C. Waller Barrett Library, University of Virginia, Charlottesville.
Copy examined: Clemens' copy, probably used during his piloting days on the Mississippi River.

Bible. New Testament. English. 1863. *The New Testament and Psalms.* New York, 1863.
Marginalia: numerous notes on flyleaves.
Catalog: A1911, #362.

Bible: New Testament. English. *New Testament.* New York: American Bible Union, 1865. 979 pp.
Source: MTLAcc, entry #2310, volume donated from Clemens' library by Clara Clemens Gabrilowitsch in 1910.

Bible. New Testament. English. 1869. *New Testament.* London, 1869.
Inscription: title page inscribed: "The Clemens's. S. L. & O. L. Feby. 2d, 1870".
Catalog: A1911, #361, $5.

Bible. New Testament. English. *New Testament.* Oxford, Eng.: University Press, 1881. 332 pp.
Source: MTLAcc entry #910, volume donated by Clemens.

Bible. New Testament. English. *New Testament.* Revised Version. New York: Harper & Brothers, 1881. 442 pp.
Source: MTLAcc, entry #1471, volume donated by Clemens.

Bible. New Testament. English. *New Testament.* Revised Version. American Edition. New York: Harper & Brothers, 1881. 652 pp.
Source: MTLAcc, entry #1813, volume donated by Clemens.

Bible. New Testament. German. 1877. *Das Neue Testament unsers Herrn und Heilandes Jesu Christi* [, *nach dr. Martin Luther uebersetzung.*] New York: Amerikanische Bibel-Gesellschaft, 1877.

   Inscription: bookplate on front pastedown endpaper contains an inscription to Susy Clemens from a ship captain, dated 22 April 1878.

   Location: Mark Twain Library, Redding, Conn.

   Copy examined: Susy Clemens' copy.

Bible. New Testament. *The Apocrypha.* London: S. Bagster & Sons, n.d. 155 pp.

   Source: MTLAcc, entry #911, volume donated by Clemens.

   References: NB 8 (1867, *N&J,* 1: 321); NB 9 (1867, *N&J,* 1: 426); 2 June 1867 letter *(MTTMB,* pp. 251–254); chapter 51 of *Innocents Abroad;* "The Chronicle of Young Satan" (written 1897–1900, *MSM,* pp. 46–50). See entry for Henry Copley Greene (trans.), *The Gospel of the Childhood of Our Lord Jesus Christ* (1904).

   Gladys Bellamy *(MTLA,* pp. 352–353); Coleman O. Parsons ("Background," pp. 60–61); Albert E. Stone *(IE,* pp. 233–235, 241); William M. Gibson *(MSM,* p. 16 n. 31).

Bible. New Testament. *Apocryphal New Testament.* Boston: Colby & Rich, 1882. 291 pp.

   Source: MTLAcc, entry #925, volume donated by Clemens.

Bible. Old Testament. English. *Old Testament. Revised Version.* 4 vols. Cambridge: University Press, 1885.

   Source: MTLAcc, entries #1809–#1812, volumes donated by Clemens.

Bible. Polyglot. N. d. *The English Version of the Polyglot Bible.* London, n.d.

   Marginalia: three notes in the margins relate Susy Clemens' progress in learning the Bible in 1877 and 1878.

   Catalog: Mott 1952, #51, $45.

The Bible for the Young. [Ed. by George Alexander Crooke?]. Illus. Philadelphia: American Family Bible Publishing Co., [cop. 1874]. 500 pp.

   Source: MTLAcc, entry #1216, volume donated by Clemens.

Bible Stories in Bible Language. New York: D. Appleton & Co., 1869. 197 pp.

   Source: MTLAcc, entry #918, volume donated by Clemens.

Bibliothèque Morale de La Jeunesse (1858).

   Listed by Albert E. Stone in his catalog of Clemens' books at the Mark Twain Library, Redding, Connecticut in 1955, but I was unable to find the volume in 1970. Stone was not certain that it had belonged to Clemens or his family; it contained a "French schoolboy's bookmark."

Bickerstetk, Edward Henry (1825–1906). *Yesterday, To-day, and Forever; A Poem, in Twelve Books.* New York: R. Carter & Brothers, 1870. 441 pp.

   Source: MTLAcc, entry #634, volume donated by Clemens.

Bierce, Ambrose Gwinett (1842?–1912).

   Clemens' references to Bierce were invariably favorable: His "exquisite things" for *Fun* were "just delicious" (SLC to C. W. Stoddard, 1 February 1875, Buffalo Public Library). "Bierce is in San Francisco" (Clemens to Millet, 7 August 1877, Harvard). "Bierce's Fables" (NB 19, [July 1880], *N&J,* 2: 366); similar entry repeated in 1881 (p. 429). Six fables by Bierce were included in *Mark Twain's Library of Humor* (1888), including "The Dog and the Bees." Clemens mentioned Bierce as a West Coast ally in a letter to J. B. Pond, 24 May 1895 (Berg): "Still writing acceptably for the magazines today" (13 June 1906 Autobiographical Dictation, *MTE,* p. 262).

Bigelow, Edith Evelyn (Jaffray), "Mrs. Poultney Bigelow" (b. 1861). *Diplomatic Disenchantments, A Novel.* New York: Harper & Brothers, 1895. 235 pp.
   Source: MTLAcc, entry #1676, volume donated by Clemens.

Bigelow, John (1817–1911). *The Mystery of Sleep.* New York: Harper & Brothers, 1905. 226 pp.
   Source: MTLAcc, entry #1386, volume donated by Clemens.

Bigelow, Poultney (1855–1954). *The Children of the Nations; A Study of Colonization and Its Problems.* New York: McClure, Phillips & Co., 1901. 365 pp.
   Catalog: C1951, #J4, listed among books owned by Clara and Jean Clemens.

————. *The German Emperor and His Eastern Neighbors.* New York: Charles L. Webster & Co., 1892. 179 pp.
   Clemens very probably read this book issued by his own publishing firm. He mentioned Bigelow's name in NB 31 (April 1892), TS p. 38; also in NB 38 (May 1896), TS p. 20. He received a letter of condolence from Bigelow about Susy's death (Bigelow to Clemens, 24 August 1896, MTP); sent Bigelow a complimentary copy of *FE* (NB 42, TS p. 74); referred to Bigelow as "that old American friend of the German Emperor's & mine" (Clemens to Andrew Chatto, 24 September 1899, PH in MTP); and spoke at Bigelow's London house-opening on 11 May 1900 (London *Daily Express,* 17 May 1900, p. 2).

————. *History of the German Struggle for Liberty.* 4 vols. Illus. New York: Harper & Brothers, 1899–1905.
   Inscription: vol. 1 signed in pencil on front pastedown endpaper: "S L Clemens/ steamship 'Irene'/ '03" [Clemens added the word "steamship" in black ink]; vol. 3 signed in black ink on front pastedown endpaper: "S. L. Clemens/ 1903".
   Marginalia: a few pencil marks throughout vol. 1 only.
   Catalogs: C1951, #D30, $12; *Zeitlin 1951,* #7, $20.
   Location: Mark Twain Papers, Berkeley, California. Gift of Jake Zeitlin.
   Copies examined: Clemens' copies.
   Before sailing for Italy in 1903 Clemens wrote to Frederick A. Duneka of Harper & Brothers: "Won't you send vols. I & II of Poultney Bigelow's History on board the ship?" (21 October 1903, TS in MTP). He gave Duneka the location, stateroom, and sailing hour.

————. *History of the German Struggle for Liberty.* 3 vols. Illus. by R. Caton Woodville. New York: Harper & Brothers, 1903.
   Source: MTLAcc, entries #1709 and #1710, volumes donated by Clemens. Set lacks vol. 3.
   Edgar Hemminghaus noticed Clemens' copy of this set in the Mark Twain Library at Redding in 1945 ("Mark Twain's German Provenience," p. 475 n. 109), but neither Albert E. Stone (in 1955) nor I (in 1970) could find these volumes.

————. *Paddles and Politics Down the Danube.* Illus. New York: Charles L. Webster & Co., 1892. 253 pp.
   Could Clemens have resisted reading this journal of a canoe voyage down the "Mississippi of Europe" to the Black Sea, published by his own firm?

Birch, Samuel.
   In chapter 58 of *FE* (1897) Mark Twain quotes Captain Birch's account of military action during the Indian mutineers' siege of Lucknow, and his description of the rescue and evacuation of Inglis' forces inside the garrison. Francis Madigan ("Mark Twain's Passage to India," p. 360) discovered that Mark Twain quoted Birch's narrative from Lady Julia Inglis' *The Siege of Lucknow, A Diary.*

Bird, Robert Montgomery (1806–1854). *The Gladiator* (play, perf. 1831).
"I did not like parts of it much, but other portions were really splendid," Clemens wrote of a production that starred Edwin Forrest (Clemens to Pamela Moffett, New York City, October 1853, *MTL*, p. 24). He and Livy saw this play on 1 February 1884 (Clemens to Howells, Hartford, 2 February 1884, *MTHL*, p. 467).

————. *Nick of the Woods; or The Jibbenainosay* (novel, 1837).
In "The Mysterious Murders in Risse," a manuscript dated 1 August 1859, Clemens' narrator remarks that young Count Ritter von Muller would have been "a genial companion to our own 'Nick of the Woods,'" from whom "he probably borrowed an idea or so" (Jean Webster McKinney Family Papers, Randolph Rare Book Room, Vassar College Library). I am grateful to Professor Robert H. Hirst for noticing this allusion. Chapter 55 of *LonMiss* (1883) contains the story of a Hannibal carpenter who claimed to be "the Mysterious Avenger" (a sobriquet interestingly similar to the Mysterious Stranger) and supposedly terrorized young Sam Clemens by vowing to murder and mutilate all human beings named Lynch. "This ass had been reading the 'Jibbenainosay,' no doubt, . . . but as I had not yet seen the book then, I took his inventions for truth," explains Mark Twain. See also the entry for J. J. McCloskey (adapt.), *Nick of the Woods* (play, 1870).
Walter Blair, "French Revolution," p. 23; *MT&HF*, p. 117 n. 15; *HH&T*, pp. 139, 336–337.

"Bird waltz" (song).
Mentioned in chapter 38 of *LonMiss* (1883), "The House Beautiful."

Birkeland, Knut Bergesen (1857–1925). *Light in the Darkness; or, Christianity and Paganism. Reminiscences of a Journey Around the Globe.* Illus. Minneapolis, Minn.: Minnehaha Pub. Co., 1900. 669 pp.
Source: MTLAcc entry #577, volume donated by Clemens.

Birrell, Augustine (1850–1933). *Obiter Dicta.* London, 1896.
Inscription: "S. L. Clemens, 1907. London. June 21."
Catalog: A1911, #43, $4.75.

Bishop, Artemas (1795–1872). *Na Huaolelo a me na olelo kikeke ma ka Beritania a me ka olelo Hawaii, no na Haumana e ao ana i kela a me keia. A Manual of Conversations, Hawaiian and English. Hawaiian Phrase Book.* Honolulu: Henry M. Whitney, 1854.
Clemens referred to it as a "small phrase-book" (Notebook 6 [1866], *N&J*, 1: 196, 234–236).

Bishop, (Mrs.) Emily Montague (Mulkin) (1858–1916). *Seventy Years Young; or, the Unhabitual Way.* New York: B. W. Huebsch, 1907. 205 pp.
Source: MTLAcc, entry #843, volume donated by Isabel V. Lyon, Clemens' secretary.

Bishop, Levi. *The Poetical Works of Levi Bishop. Third Edition. With a Sketch of the Life of the Author.* Detroit: E. B. Smith & Co., 1876.
Inscription: on flyleaf: "This book belongs to/S. L. Clemens's/Library of Hogwash./Hartford, 1876."
Marginalia: Clemens underlined sentences in the biographical sketch of Bishop; at its conclusion he wrote: "The record of a respect-worthy & very valuable citizen, whose humble little distinctions & inconsequential achievements have been a great satisfaction to him & a hurt to no one; a nice well-meaning old man, whose only blemish was a penchant for constructing jingling twaddle & regarding it as poetry" (p. xvii). Other marginal notes include "Rot" scrawled at the head

of a poem titled "The Oyster" (p. 490). In the margin beside Bishop's definition of poetry (a prose essay, p. 504) Clemens wrote: "This is the ignoramus teaching the ignoramus."

    Catalog: C1951, #49a, $27.50.

    Location: The Newberry Library, Chicago, Illinois. Incorrectly cited by Arthur L. Scott *(OPMT,* p. 20) as the property of the Mark Twain Papers at Berkeley.

    Copy examined: I am grateful to Richard Colles Johnson, Bibliographer of the Newberry Library, for providing a photocopy of Clemens' notations for my use.

Bismarck, Otto Eduard Leopold von (1815–1898). *The Love Letters of Bismarck.* New York: Harper & Brothers, 1901.

    Marginalia: beside some verse quoted by Bismarck (p. 25): "I have never seen lines of poetry all of one length before." No other notes or markings.

    Location: Antenne-Dorrance Collection, Rice Lake, Wisconsin.

    Copy examined: the volume was temporarily on loan when I visited Rice Lake in 1970; this entry is based on the checklist of books in the Antenne-Dorrance collection compiled by Ann Cameron Harvey in 1966.

Bizet, Alexandre César Léopold, called Georges (1838–1875). *Carmen* (opera, 1875).

    Olivia Clemens wrote to her husband from Paris on 26 April 1894: "On Sunday I saw by the paper that on Monday there would be a representation of 'Carmen' at greatly reduced rates. I thought that was a good time for Susy and me to go" (ALS, MT Research Foundation, Perry, Mo.; quoted in *Twainian,* 37 [May–June 1978], 4).

Bjørnson, Bjørnstjerne (1832–1910). *A Happy Boy. A Tale of Norwegian Peasant Life.* Trans. from Norwegian by Helen R. A. Gade. Boston: Sever, Francis & Co., 1870. 120 pp.

    Source: MTLAcc, entry #1923, volume donated from Clemens' library by Clara Clemens Gabrilowitsch in 1910.

    "Bjornsen's books—Houghton," Clemens wrote in Notebook 22 (1883), TS p. 28.

Black, Clementina. *An Agitator; A Novel.* New York: Harper & Brothers, 1895. 177 pp.

    Source: MTLAcc, entry #1320, volume donated by Clemens.

Black, William (1841–1898). *A Daughter of Heth. A Novel.* New York: Harper & Brothers, n.d. 323 pp.

    Source: MTLAcc, entry #1430, volume donated by Clemens.

————. *Donald Ross of Heimra.* New York: Harper & Brothers, n.d. 355 pp.

    Source: MTLAcc, entry #1517, volume donated by Clemens.

————. *In Far Lochaber; A Novel.* New York: Harper & Brothers, n.d. 299 pp.

    Source: MTLAcc, entry #1516, volume donated by Clemens.

————. *Judith Shakespeare; Her Love Affairs and Other Adventures.* Illus. by E. A. Abbey. New York: Harper & Brothers, n.d. 391 pp.

    Source: MTLAcc, entry #1519, volume donated by Clemens.

————. *Kilmeny.* New York: Harper & Brothers, 1870. 136 pp.

    Source: MTLAcc, entry #967, volume donated by Clemens.

————. *Madcap Violet* (novel, 1876).

    Clemens mentioned this novel in Notebook 19 in January 1882 *(N&J,* 2: 422).

————. *The Maid of Killeena.* New York: Harper & Brothers, 1875. 151 pp.

    Source: MTLAcc, entry #968, volume donated by Clemens.

————. *Prince Fortunatus. A Novel.* Illus. New York: Harper & Brothers, 1905. 432 pp.
Source: MTLAcc, entry #1520, volume donated by Clemens.

————. *Stand Fast, Craig-Royston!* Illus. New York: Harper & Brothers, n.d. 429 pp.
Source: MTLAcc, entry #1145, volume donated by Clemens.

————. *The Strange Adventures of a House-Boat. A Novel.* Illus. New York: Harper & Brothers, 1892. 258 pp.
Source: MTLAcc, entry #1412, volume donated by Clemens.

————. *That Beautiful Wretch; A Brighton Story.* New York: Harper & Brothers, n.d. 240 pp.
Source: MTLAcc, entry #1518, volume donated by Clemens.

————. *White Wings* (yachting novel, 1880).
Clemens was aware that the character named Smethurst was modeled on George W. Smalley, a friend of Whitelaw Reid (Notebook 19 [January 1882], *N&J*, 2: 422).

————. *Wild Eelin: Her Escapades.* New York: Harper & Brothers, 1899. 512 pp.
Source: MTLAcc, entry #1522, volume donated by Clemens.

————. *Yolande. A Novel.* New York: Harper & Brothers, 1905. Illus. 462 pp.
Source: MTLAcc, entry #1521, volume donated by Clemens.

Blackmore, Richard Doddridge (1825–1899). *Lorna Doone: A Romance of Exmoor.* Illus. New York: Harper Brothers, n.d. 576 pp.
Source: MTLAcc, entry #1327, volume donated by Clemens.

————. *Lorna Doone, A Romance of Exmoor* (pub. 1869).
Catalog: C1951, #D4, $17.50, no edition specified.

————. *Perlycross; A Novel.* New York: Harper & Brothers, 1901. 493 pp.
Source: MTLAcc, entry #1523, volume donated by Clemens.

Blackstone's Commentaries.
John Marshall Clemens' personal property included "4 vols Blackstone's Commentaries," according to the appraisal filed on 21 May 1847 in Marion County Probate Court (McDermott, "Mark Twain and the Bible," p. 198). Samuel Clemens referred to *Blackstone* in Notebook 28 (September 1888). TS p. 24.

Blackwood, Mrs. Price. "The lament of the Irish emigrant" (song, 1843). Melody by William Richardson Dempster.
Mentioned favorably in October 1878 (NB 16, *N&J*, 2: 212).

Blackwood's Magazine (Edinburgh, founded 1817).
References: chapter 43 of *TA* (1880); January 1883 issue used in unpublished MS (Paine 91, MTP); 1871 bound issue mentioned (Clemens to Howells, Florence, 4 Dec. 1903, *MTHL,* p. 775); found "54 bound volumes . . . running backward from about 1870" in bookcase at Villa di Quarto in January 1904 (Autobiographical Dictation, TS p. 98, MTP).

Blaikie, William (1843–1904). *How to Get Strong and How to Stay So.* Rev. edition. New York: Harper & Brothers, 1902. 293 pp.
Source: MTLAcc, entry #398, volume donated by Clemens.

Blaine, (Mrs.) Harriet Bailey (Stanwood) (1828–1903). *Letters of Mrs. James G. Blaine*. Ed. by Harriet S. Blaine Beale. 2 vols. New York: Duffield and Co., 1908.
Inscriptions: both vols. signed "SL. Clemens/Xmas, 1908/from Clara".
Catalogs: C1951, #52c, $12; *Fleming 1972*, 2 vols.

Blanc, Charles (1813–1882). *The Grammar of Painting and Engraving. Translated from the French of Blanc's Grammaire des Arts du Dessin.* Trans. by Mrs. Kate (Newell) Doggett (1828–1884). Illus. New York: Hurd and Houghton, 1874.
Inscriptions: by Clemens in pencil on flyleaf: "Livy Clemens/1874." Clemens also wrote on the front pastedown endpaper: "Howells/37 Concord avenue/Cambridge".
Marginalia: a few pencil markings throughout, not Clemens'.
Location: Mark Twain Library, Redding, Connecticut.
Copy examined: Livy Clemens' copy.

Bland, (Mrs.) Edith (Nesbit) (1858–1924). *The Book of Dragons.* Illus. by H. R. Millar. New York: Harper & Brothers, 1901. 190 pp.
Source: MTLAcc, entry #510, volume donated by Clemens.

————. *The Red House; A Novel.* Illus. by A. I. Keller. New York: Harper & Brothers, 1903. 274 pp.
Source: MTLAcc, entry #1038, volume donated by Clemens.

————. *The Wouldbegoods.* Illus. by Reginald B. Birch. New York: Harper & Brothers, [cop. 1900]. 313 pp.
Source: MTLAcc, entry #1195, volume donated by Clemens.

Bland, Henry Meade (1863–1931). *A Song of Autumn, and Other Poems.* San Jose, Calif.: Pacific Short Story Club, [cop. 1907]. 96 pp.
Source: MTLAcc, entry #2012, volume donated from Clemens' library by Clara Clemens Gabrilowitsch in 1910.

Bland, James A. (1854–1911). "Oh! Dem golden slippers" (Negro spiritual, copyrighted by Bland in 1879).
Clemens heard two Negro cabin hands sing this to banjo accompaniment on Horace Bixby's *City of Baton Rouge* in 1882 (NB 21, *N&J*, 2: 562). In August 1889 he listed it with his favorite spirituals and songs (NB 29, TS p. 21).

"Blau ist das Blumelein" (song).
Listed with Clemens' favorite songs (NB 29 [August 1889], TS p. 21).

Blicher, Steen Steenson (1782–1848). *The Minister of Veilby* (novel, 1829).
Mark Twain's footnote at the beginning of *Tom Sawyer, Detective* (1896), cites "an old-time Swedish [sic] criminal trial" as the source for his story. J. Christian Bay's concise and authoritative essay—"*Tom Sawyer, Detective:* Origin of the Plot" (1929)—first explained how Mark Twain borrowed from a Danish (not Swedish) murder mystery novel in constructing *TSD.* Although *The Minister of Veilby* was apparently his literary source, Mark Twain never read the book himself; he apparently learned about its plot from the wife of the Ambassador of Denmark to the United States. See also the entry for Samuel M. Phillipps, *Famous Cases.*
Adolf B. Benson, "Mark Twain's Contacts with Scandinavia" (1937); D. M. McKeithan, *CTMT* (1958).

Bliss, Edgar Janes. *The Peril of Oliver Sargent.* New York: Charles L. Webster & Company, 1891. 177 pp.
Clemens' publishing firm advertised Bliss' book as being reminiscent of *Dr. Jekyll and Mr. Hyde,* a study of "the dual character of man" (*Publishers' Trade List Annual 1893*).

Bliss, Philip Paul (1838–1876), Ira David Sankey (1840–1908), James McGranahan (1840–1907), and George Coles Stebbins (1846–1945), joint eds. *Gospel Hymns Consolidated, Embracing Volumes No. 1, 2, 3, and 4, without Duplicates, for Use In Gospel Meetings and Other Religious Services.* New York, Chicago: Biglow & Main; Cincinnati, New York: J. Church & Co., 1883. 400 pp.
 Inscription: "S. L. Clemens, 1887" on flyleaf.
 Catalog: A1911, #194, $1.

————. "Only an armour-bearer" (hymn).
 A calm Sabbath in Bermuda was "profaned" by Mark Twain's neighbors' singing this hymn to the accompaniment of a metallic piano (NB 13 [May 1877], *N&J,* 2: 19).

Bliss, William Root. *Paradise in the Pacific; A Book of Travel, Adventure, and Facts in the Sandwich Islands.* New York: Sheldon and Co., 1873.
 Title noted on back cover of Clemens' copy of James Jackson Jarves' *History of the Hawaiian or Sandwich Islands (N&J,* 1: 104–105).

Blix, Ragnvald. *Le Voile Tombe: Caricatures par Blix.* Paris: Librairie Nilsson [imprimerie Bröderna Lagerström, Stockholm], 1908. [Collection of color prints.]
 Inscription: "Mark Twain/le maître des hautes-oeuvres/de Blix/le [traître?] des chefs-d'oeuvres."
 Catalog: 17 January 1944 Charles Retz appraisal (p. 5). Valued at $10.
 Location: Mark Twain Papers, Berkeley, California.
 An accompanying letter from Blix, 8 December 1908, thanks Clemens for a letter of praise and offers to send him the original of any caricature he especially likes. Blix's prints mimic the master painters of Western Europe.

Bloomfield-Moore, (Mrs.) Clara Sophia (Jessup) (1824–1899), pseud. "Mrs. H. O. Ward." *Sensible Etiquette of the Best Society, Customs, Manners, Morals, and Home Culture.* Philadelphia: Porter and Coates, 1878. 567 pp.
 Source: MTLAcc, entry #2144, volume donated from Clemens' library by Clara Clemens Gabrilowitsch in 1910.
 Intent on writing a burlesque book of etiquette, Clemens wrote to James R. Osgood on 7 March 1881: *"Yes,* send me a collection of etiquette books" (Harvard Univ., TS in MTP).

Blouet, Paul (1848–1903), pseud. "Max O'Rell." *A Frenchman in America.* [Pub. originally in 1891 as *Un Français en Amérique.*]
 Catalog: C1951, #57a, $22.50, listed among the books containing Clemens' marginal notes.

————. "Mark Twain and Paul Bourget," *North American Review,* 160 (March 1895), 302–310.
 Blouet contends that by reading a wretched translation in a New York paper, Mark Twain missed the nuances of Paul Bourget's *Outre-Mer.* Mark Twain's ridicule of *Outre-Mer* was "unkind, unfair, bitter, hasty." Blouet charges that morals in America are actually lower than those in Paris. Bourget's book "has passed over Mark Twain's head." From *Outre-Mer* Mark Twain might at least have learned "a lesson in politeness and good manners" (p. 310). Twain wrote "A Little Note to M. Paul Bourget" in response to Blouet's defense; referred to O'Rell unfavorably in a letter to General Bryce, 9 March [1895] (CWB); and brought up his literary quarrel with O'Rell in an interview published in the Melbourne, Australia *Argus,* 16 September 1895.

————. *Woman and Artist.* New York: Harper & Brothers, 1900. 228 pp.
 Source: MTLAcc, entry #1638, volume donated by Clemens.

Blowitz, Henri Georges Stephane Adolphe Opper de (1825–1903). *Memoirs of M. de Blowitz.* New York: Doubleday, Page and Co., 1903. 321 pp.
> *Catalog: C1951,* #99c, $7.50, listed among books signed by Clemens.
> Clemens thanked Frank N. Doubleday on 12 October 1903 for sending some books, then added in a postscript: "I've dipped into Blowitz and find him quaintly and curiously interesting. I think he tells the straight truth, too. I knew him a little, 23 years ago" *(MTL,* p. 746).

Boccaccio, Giovanni (1313–1375). *The Decameron or Ten Days' Entertainment of Boccaccio. A Revised Translation by W. K. Kelly.* Bohn's Standard Library Series. London: H. G. Bohn, 1869. 545 pp.
> *Inscription:* signed twice ("S. L Clemens") on first pages of advertisements, and signed on verso of frontispiece portrait: "S. L. Clemens, 1872".
> *Catalogs: C1951,* #73c, $25; *Zeitlin 1951,* #8, $$35.
> Mark Twain envied Boccaccio's freedom in expressing things "unprintable (in our day)" (NB 14 [May 1878], *N&J,* 2: 87). In "The Walt Whitman Controversy" (DV36, MTP), written about 1880, Mark Twain states that he owns "an English copy, but [I] have mislaid it" and has borrowed a French edition from a neighboring clergyman—presumably a joke intended to emphasize the ubiquity of the book. He mentions the *Decameron* in a letter to Baroness Alexandra Gripenberg, 27 December 1888, PH in MTP; also in NB 32 [May 1892], TS p. 8; in a letter to Susan Crane, 30 September 1892 from Florence *(MTL,* p. 571); and in "Private History of the 'Jumping Frog' Story" (1894). He refers to Boccaccio as a great Italian writer in "Three Thousand Years among the Microbes" (written 1905, *WWD?,* p. 529).

––––––. *Stories of Boccaccio (The Decameron) Translated from the Italian into English with Eleven Original Etchings by Léopold Flameng.* [Trans. by Walter Keating Kelly.] Philadelphia: G. Barrie, [1881]. 493 pp.
> *Inscription:* uncharacteristic signature on flyleaf: "This is authorized/Mark Twain".
> *Location:* C. Waller Barrett Collection, Alderman Library, University of Virginia, Charlottesville. Obtained from Jennings Wise, a Virginia collector.
> *Copy examined:* very possibly Clemens' copy, though its provenance is not firmly traceable to Clemens' library and the signature is curious. Several illustrations in the book portray nude women.

Bôcher, Ferdinand (1832–1902), ed. *College Series of French Plays; With English Notes, by Ferdinand Bôcher.* New edition. 2 vols. New York: Henry Holt and Co., [1870].
> *Inscription:* "Livy L. Clemens/1873".
> *Location:* unknown; I could not locate this volume when I visited Redding in 1970, but it appears in the catalog of Clemens' books in the Mark Twain Library at Redding that was compiled by Albert E. Stone in 1955.
> Its contents include works by Girardin, Scribe, Sandeau, Labiche, Vacquerie.

Boggs, (Mrs.) Sara Elizabeth (Siegrist) (b. 1843). *Sandpeep.* Illus. by May Bartlett. Boston: Little, Brown, and Co., 1906. 421 pp.
> *Source:* MTLAcc, entry #2178, volume donated from Clemens' library by Clara Clemens Gabrilowitsch in 1910.

Bohny, Nikaus. *Neues Bilderbuch. Anleitung zum Anschauen. Denken, Rechnen, und Sprechen fur Kinder.* Esslingen: I. F. Schreiber, 187?.
> Title, author, publisher noted in NB 22 (1883), TS p. 28.

Boieldieu, François Adrien (1775–1834). *La Dame Blanche* (light opera, perf. 1825).
> "Not noise, but music," Clemens noted after attending a performance in Munich on 14 January 1879 *(N&J,* 2: 261).

Boileau-Despréaux, Nicolas (1636–1711). *Épîtres.*
Clemens quoted (and altered slightly) a sardonic couplet on materialism from Épître V (lines 85–86) in Notebook 1 (1855), *N&J*, 1: 38. He may have copied it from a French grammar book.

Bond, Alvan (1793–1882), ed. *Young People's Illustrated Bible History. With an Introduction by the Reverend Alvan Bond, D.D.* Norwich, Conn.: Henry Bill Pub. Co., 1878.
Inscription: "Olivia Susan Clemens/From her grandmother/Olivia Langdon/ Dec. 25th 1879."
Location: Mark Twain Library, Redding, Conn.
Copy examined: Susy Clemens' copy.

————, ed. *Young People's Illustrated Bible History.* Illus. Norwich, Conn.: Henry Bill Publishing Co., 1908. 584 pp.
Source: MTLAcc, entry #1215, volume donated by Isabel V. Lyon, Clemens' secretary.

Bonner, John (1828–1899). *A Child's History of the United States.* 3 vols. New York: Harper & Brothers, 1899.
Source: MTLAcc, entries #1148–#1150, volumes donated by Clemens.

Bonsal, Stephen (1865–1951). *Morocco As It Is.* New York: Harper & Brothers, 1893. Illus. 349 pp.
Source: MTLAcc, entry #1712, volume donated by Clemens.

Bonwick, James, F. R. G. S. *The Lost Tasmanian Race.* London: Sampson Low, Marston, Searle and Rivington, 1884.
References: author and title (NB 35 [September 1895], TS p. 53); passages deleted from final version of *FE* (MS in Berg); chapter 26 of *FE* (1897).
Dennis Welland, "Mark Twain's Last Travel Book," p. 46; Howard G. Baetzhold, *MT&JB*, pp. 183, 357 n. 10; Francis Madigan, "Mark Twain's Passage to India," p. 355.

The Book of Pleasures. 1. The Pleasures of Hope, by Thomas Campbell. 2. The Pleasures of Memory, by Samuel Rogers. 3. The Pleasures of Imagination, by Mark Akenside. Philadelphia: Key & Biddle, 1836. 187 pp.
Source: MTLAcc, entry #2048, volume donated from Clemens' library by Clara Clemens Gabrilowitsch.
See also the entry for Thomas Campbell.

Boone, Henry Burnham and Kenneth Brown. *The Redfields Succession; A Novel.* New York: Harper & Brothers, 1903. 318 pp.
Source: MTLAcc, entry #1524, volume donated by Clemens.

Booth, Josiah (1852–1930). *Everybody's Guide to Music, with Illustrated Chapters on Singing and Cultivation of the Voice.* New York: Harper & Brothers, [cop. 1893]. 176 pp.
Source: MTLAcc, entry #1684, volume donated by Clemens.

Booth, William Stone (1864–1926). *Some Acrostic Signatures of Francis Bacon, Baron Verulam of Verulam, Viscount St. Alban, Together with Some Others, All of Which Are Now for the First Time Deciphered and Published.* Boston: Houghton Mifflin Co., 1909. 631 pp.
John Macy brought Mark Twain galleys of Booth's book on 8 January 1909 (notes by IVL, Berg, TS in MTP), and Mark Twain promptly produced the first pages of "Is Shakespeare Dead?" Paine reported that Booth's *Acrostic Signatures* established Bacon's authorship of the Shakespeare canon as far as Mark Twain was concerned (*MTB*, pp. 1479, 1485–86).

Boothby, Guy Newell (1867–1905). *My Strangest Case.* Illus. Boston: L. C. Page & Co., 1901. 300 pp.
  Source: MTLAcc, entry #30, volume donated by Clemens.

Borrowings; A Compilation of Helpful Thoughts from Great Authors. San Francisco, Calif.: C. A. Murdock & Co., 1889. 78 pp.
  Source: MTLAcc, entry #647, volume donated by Isabel V. Lyon, Clemens' secretary.

Boscawen, William St. Chad (1854–1913). *The First of Empires, "Babylon of the Bible" in the Light of Latest Research.* New York: Harper & Brothers, 1903. 356 pp.
  Source: MTLAcc, entry #1294, volume donated by Clemens.

Bosguerard, Marie de. *Scenes Enfantines.* Paris, n.d.
  Provenance: unknown; very possibly not from Clemens' library. Shelved with his books in 1970, however.
  Location: Mark Twain Library, Redding, Connecticut.

Boston *Evening Transcript.*
  Mark Twain refers to the February 1903 issue in *Christian Science,* Book 2, chapter 7 (1907). A clipping from 2 April 1909 issue is pinned inside Clemens' copy of Bayne's *Pith of Astronomy.*

Boston *True Flag* (periodical).
  Mentioned in "Jul'us Caesar," an unpublished manuscript written around 1856 (DV400, MTP).

Boswell, James (1740–1795). *The Life of Samuel Johnson, LL.D. New Edition, with Notes and Additions by J. W. Croker.* 2 vols. New York: Harper & Brothers, 1875.
  Edition: One of the twenty-one books for which Estes & Lauriat of Boston billed Clemens on 14 July 1880 was "1 Johnson $2.50"; since many of the books were listed by title rather than author, Boswell's *Johnson* may have recently joined Clemens' library (MTP). With the standard cloth binding this Harper & Brothers edition sold for $4 at retail prices; but Clemens generally received a substantial author's discount from bookdealers. In "English as She Is Taught" (1880) Mark Twain begins by quoting an anecdote from "Croker's Boswell's Johnson."
  Sam and Orion Clemens occasionally turned to Boswell's biography when they required filler for columns in the Hannibal *Journal* in 1852–1853 (Brashear, *MTSM,* p. 143). Clemens mentioned Boswell in NB 12 (July 1873, *N&J,* 1: 563). "Every great personage must be shadowed by a parasite who is infinitely little— Johnson had his Boswell," Clemens wrote on the flyleaf of A. S. Evans' *Our Sister Republic (A1911,* #159). He alluded to Boswell's *Johnson* in "Mental Telegraphy"; referred to Johnson as "that great man and his imposing diction" ("Which Was It?" written 1899–1903, *WWD?,* p. 278); and mentioned Johnson in a letter to Howells, 14 April 1903 *(MTHL,* p. 767). Henry Fisher recalled Clemens' saying that he had never read Johnson's writings, but from Boswell had gained the impression that Johnson was anti-American in the Revolution, anti-Catholic, pro-monarchy, and a zealous Protestant *(AMT,* pp. 71, 150–153).

Bothmer, (Countess) Marie von (1845–1921). *German Home Life.* New edition. London: Longmans, Green & Co., 1878.
  Inscription: signed in pencil on front free endpaper: "Olivia L. Clemens/Paris 1879."
  Marginalia: notes and markings in pencil by Clemens. On page 216, where Bothmer tells how Prussian princes often join their peasants on the battlefields, Clemens notes: "You never saw Victoria's tribe at it."
  Catalog: Mott 1952, #57, $15.
  Location: Mark Twain Papers, Berkeley, California.
  Copy examined: copy shared by Samuel and Livy Clemens. Contains bookstamps of the Mark Twain Library at Redding.

Boucicault, Dion (1820–1890). *Arrah-na-Pogue* (play, perf. 1864).

References: " 'Mark Twain' on the Ballad Infliction," San Francisco *Californian*, 4 November 1865 (*MTWY*, p. 195); "It was [Edward H.] House & Dion Boucicault that wrote Arrah-na-Pogue in partnership" (Clemens to Elisha Bliss, 9 June 1870, MTM); "House didn't write Arrah na Pogue" (NB 29 [March 1890], TS p. 42); House lied in claiming this work (28 August 1907 Autobiographical Dictation, MTP).

————, adapt. *Rip Van Winkle* (play, dramatized from the tale by Washington Irving, prod. 1865).

Clemens and Livy attended one of Joseph Jefferson's many performances "last night" (SLC to Charles Dudley Warner, Elmira, 5 May [1874], TS in MTP). Mark Twain hoped that *Colonel Sellers* might "run twenty years . . . like Jo Jefferson's 'Rip Van Winkle' " (SLC to Mr. Watt, 26 January 1875). On 27 November 1887 Livy took Susy and Clara to see Jefferson in the play and "they enjoyed it all immensely" (OLC's Diary, DV161, MTP).

————. The *Shaughraun* (play, prod. 1874).

References: "when the 'Shaughran' was played at Wallack's" (chapter 10 of *TA* [1880]). "Con [Conn] the Shaughran" (Clemens to Howells, 18 February 1884, *MTHL*, p. 474).

Bourdillon, Francis William (1852–1921). "Light" (poem, 1878). Better known as "The Night Has a Thousand Eyes."

Livy copied and sent the poem to Clemens while she was waiting for him in Paris, 31 July 1894 (TS in MTP).

Bourget, Charles Joseph Paul (1852–1935), known as "Paul Bourget." *Cosmopolis*. New York: Amblard & Meyer, 1893.

"To call together several thousand nice people & dissect & ransack a putrid body before them—what business has one to do that? Where is the *raison d'être* of Cosmopolis?" (NB 34 [1895], TS p. 2).

————. *Outre-Mer: Impressions of America* (1895).

Outre-Mer provoked two rebuttals by Mark Twain, "What Paul Bourget Thinks of Us" (1895) and "A Little Note to M. Paul Bourget" (1895). "I am translating a French article which I wish to abuse" (SLC to HHR, Étretat, 30 September 1894, *MTHHR*, p. 79); "M. Paul Bourget and his idiotic 'Outre Mer' " (SLC to HHR, Rouen, 11 October 1894, *MTHHR*, p. 85); "he is too small game to go after elaborately" (SLC to HHR, Rouen, 13 October 1894, *MTHHR*, p. 85); "wretchedly small game, . . . but I kind of love small game" (SLC to Gen. Bryce, Rouen, 13 October 1894, Yale); mentioned in a derogatory fashion on 8 April 1896 (NB 37, TS p. 29). It is interesting also that Clara Clemens attributed one of the quotations in her commonplace book to Paul Bourget (ca. 1888?, Paine 150, MTP).

Louis J. Budd, *MTSP*, p. 160; Sydney J. Krause, *MTC*, p. 282 n. 19; Arthur L. Scott, *MTAL*, pp. 183–184.

Bourke, (Captain) John G. *On the Border with [Gen. George] Crook*. New York: Scribner, 1891.

Clemens made efforts to obtain this book for his publishing firm (Clemens to Howells, 10 February 1891, *MTHL*, pp. 634–635). Colonel Sellers' scheme for materializing cavalry seems to satirize Crook's plan for pacifying Indians, as William M. Gibson and Henry Nash Smith point out (*MTHL*, p. 635 n. 1).

Bourrienne, Louis Antoine Fauvelet de (1769–1834). *Memoirs of Napoleon Bonaparte. By . . . His Private Secretary*. London: Lockwood, 1888. [First pub. 1829 in Paris.]

The title, place of publication, and date of this edition were listed in Clara Clemens' commonplace book, probably around 1888 (Paine 150, MTP).

Boutet de Monvel, Louis Maurice (1851–1913). *Joan of Arc*. Illus. New York: The Century Co., 1907. [Oblong volume of large color illustrations, accompanied by a brief narrative.]
  Inscription: "To Dorothy Quick/with the love of/S L. Clemens/1907./21 Fifth Ave."
  Location: Mark Twain Papers, Berkeley, California.
  Copy examined: copy intended for Dorothy Quick, retained by Clemens.
  "The pictures he liked best were one of Joan in her prison talking to her 'Saints,' and the one of the battle scenes," recalled Dorothy Quick (Mrs. James Adams Mayer) in *Enchantment: A Little Girl's Friendship with MT* (Norman: Univ of Oklahoma Press, 1961), p. 145.

Bowman, Elmer. "Go way back and sit down" (song, 1901). Melody by Al Johns.
  Mark Twain refers to the song in Book II, chapter 8 of "Christian Science" (1907), pub. in *WIM?*, pp. 341, 574.

Boyesen, Hjalmar Hjorth (1848–1895). *Gunnar; A Tale of Norse Life*. Boston: J. R. Osgood & Co., 1874. 292 pp.
  Source: MTLAcc, entry #1917, volume donated from Clemens' library by Clara Clemens Gabrilowitsch in 1910.

————. *Ilka on the Hill-top, and Other Stories*. New York: C. Scribner's Sons, 1881. 240 pp.
  Source: MTLAcc, entry #1918, volume donated from Clemens' library by Clara Clemens Gabrilowitsch in 1910.

————. *Literary and Social Silhouettes*. New York: Harper & Brothers, 1894. 218 pp.
  Catalog: C1951, #J29, listed among books belonging to Jean and Clara Clemens.

————. *Queen Titania*. New York: Charles Scribner's Sons, 1881. 254 pp.
  Source: MTLAcc, entry #1921, volume donated from Clemens' library by Clara Clemens Gabrilowitsch in 1910.
  A letter from Clemens to Boyesen, 26 October 1881, thanks Boyesen for a copy of *Queen Titania* and promises to send the next book he himself publishes in return (Anderson Galleries, Sale No. 411 [10 May 1934], item #133).
  Per Seyersted, "The Drooping Lily: H. H. Boyesen as an Early American Misogynist" (1971); Louis Budd, *MTSP*, p. 115.

Boylan, (Mrs.) Grace (Duffie). *The Kiss of Glory*. Illus. by J. C. Leyendecker. New York: G. W. Dillingham, [cop. 1902]. 298 pp.
  Source: MTLAcc, entry #1103, volume donated by Clemens.

Boyle, (Mrs.) Virginia (Frazer) (1863–1938). *Devil Tales*. Illus. by A. B. Frost. New York: Harper & Brothers, 1900. 211 pp.
  Source: MTLAcc, entry #29, volume donated by Clemens.

————. [Another identical copy.]
  Source: MTLAcc, entry #1509, volume donated by Clemens.

————. *Serena, A Novel*. New York: A. S. Barnes & Co., 1905. 378 pp.
  Source: MTLAcc, entry #4, volume donated by Clemens.
  Inscribed to Mark Twain by the author.

Boys on the Railroad, by Molly Elliot Seawell [1860–1916], James Barnes, Ellen Douglas Deland, John R. Coryell, E. Carruth, and Others. Illus. New York: Harper & Brothers, 1909. 213 pp.
  Source: MTLAcc, entry #1452, volume donated by Clemens.

Boyton, Paul. *The Story of Paul Boyton. Voyages on All the Great Rivers of the World. . . . A Rare Tale of Travel and Adventure. . . . A Book for Boys, Old and Young.* Milwaukee: Riverside Printing Co., 1892. 358 pp.
    References: "no terms till we see the MS" (NB 27 [October 1887], TS p. 32). "Captain Boyton's ten-cent adventures" for a "juvenile level" (SLC to Fred J. Hall, Hartford, 7 May 1888, *MTLP*, p. 245).

Brace, Charles Loring (1826–1890). *Gesta Christi; or, A History of Humane Progress Under Christianity* (London, 1880).
    Howells recommended this book to Mark Twain on 17 October 1889 to help him appreciate the medieval monastic life satirized in *A Connecticut Yankee* (*MTHL*, p. 614).

Brachet, Auguste (1844–1898) and J. Dussouchet. *Petite Grammaire Française.* Paris: Librairie Hachette et Cie, 1884.
    Inscription: "Clemens" written in ink on outer front cover.
    Location: Mark Twain Library, Redding, Conn.
    Copy examined: copy belonging to the Clemens family.

Bradbury, W. B. "Rally round the flag, boys" (song)
    Reference: chapter 13 of "A Horse's Tale" (1906).

Bradley, Edward (1827–1889), pseud. "Cuthbert Bede." *The Adventures of Mr. Verden Green.* Illus. by the author. Ninetieth thousand. New York: Carleton, 1878.
    Inscription: "S. L. Clemens, Hartford, 1878."
    Catalog: A1911, #32, $4.50.

Bradley, (William M.) and Co., Philadelphia. *Atlas of the World for Commercial and Library Reference.* Philadelphia: L. D. Maltby & Co., William M. Bradley & Bros., 1886. 139 pp. 75 col. maps.
    Source: MTLAcc, entry #2, volume donated by Clemens.

Brady, Cyrus Townsend (1861–1920). *The Bishop; Being Some Account of His Strange Adventures on the Plains.* Illus. New York: Harper & Brothers, 1903. 304 pp.
    Source: MTLAcc, entry #984, volume donated by Clemens.

——. *For Love of Country: A Story of Land and Sea in the Days of the Revolution.* Illus. New York: Charles Scribner's Sons, 1904. 354 pp.
    Source: MTLAcc, entry #36, volume donated by Clemens.

——. *The Grip of Honor: A Story of Paul Jones and the American Revolution.* Illus. New York: Charles Scribner's Sons, 1904. 246 pp.
    Source: MTLAcc, entry #32, volume donated by Clemens.

Brassey, (Lady) Anna (Annie) Allnutt (1839–1887). *A Voyage in the Sunbeam, Our Home in the Ocean for Eleven Months.* Copyright Edition. 2 vols. Leipzig: Bernhard Tauchnitz, 1879.
    Catalog: C1951, #D1, $8., 2 vols.

Bray, (Mrs.) Anna Eliza (Kempe) Stothard (1790–1883). *Joan of Arc and the Times of Charles the Seventh, King of France.* London: Griffith and Farran, 1874. 360 pp.
    Headed a bibliography of six books about Joan of Arc that Chatto & Windus prepared for Clemens at his request in 1892 (Clemens to Chatto & Windus, Florence, 13 October 1892, PH of list and letter in MTP).

Breck, Samuel (1771–1862). *Recollections of Samuel Breck, with Passages from His Notebooks.* Ed. by Horace Elisha Scudder (1838–1902). Philadelphia: Porter & Coates, 1877. 310 pp.

In November 1877 James R. Osgood & Company of Boston billed Clemens for a book purchased on 4 June 1877: "Recollections of Saml Breck." The price of $2 was discounted to $1.60 (Scrapbook #10, p. 69, MTP). Breck described his life in Boston and Philadelphia.

Brée, (Mme.) Malwine. *The Groundwork of the Leschetizky Method; Issued with His Approval by His Assistant, Malwine Brée, with Forty-Seven Illustrative Cuts of Leschetizsky's Hand. Translated from the German by Dr. Th[eodor] Baker.* New York: G. Schirmer, 1902.
  Catalog: A1911, #386, $1.
  Includes both elementary and advanced exercises employed by Theodor Leschetizky (1830–1915).

Breen, Henry H. *Modern English Literature: Its Blemishes & Defects.* London: Longman, Brown, Green, & Longmans, 1857. 307 pp.
  Inscription: inscribed across title-page by Clemens in pencil: "Saml. L. Clemens/ Hartford 1876/Use with care, for it is a scarce book—England had to be ransacked in order to get this copy—or the bookseller speaketh falsely."
  Marginalia: marked and annotated in blue-black ink, particularly in the section entitled "Plagiarism."
  Catalog: "Retz Appraisal,'" p. 5, valued at $40.
  Location: Mark Twain Papers, Berkeley.
  Copy examined: Clemens' copy.
  In a manuscript probably written soon after he obtained Breen's *Modern English Literature,* "Comments on English Diction," Mark Twain observed that "one is sleepily unconscious of the blemishes that disfigure our best literature until he inspects a page of it through Mr. Breen's disenchanting magnifier" (quoted by Jervis Langdon in *Some Reminiscences* [1938], p. 20). Mark Twain favored books which exposed fallacies in common assumptions, so the thesis that supposedly impeccable "masterpieces" of English literature are in reality riddled with grammatical flaws predictably had a certain appeal for him. He turned to Breen's book for the names of twenty-four famous writers, including Carlyle, Macaulay, and Scott, who employed "bad grammar and slovenly English" sufficiently to exonerate General Grant from Matthew Arnold's strictures on his ungrammatical constructions (speech to the Army and Navy Club of Connecticut, 27 April 1887, *MTSpk,* pp. 225–227). Paine considered *Modern English Literature* to have been among Mark Twain's favorite books, and he reported that on one occasion Mark Twain used the volume as a text for a paper on slipshod English which he prepared for the Saturday Morning Club *(MTB,* p. 1539).
  MTC, p. 113; *MT&HF,* pp. 59–60.

Brennan, George Hugh (b. 1865). *Bill Truetell, A Story of Theatrical Life.* Illus. by James Montgomery Flagg. Chicago: A. C. McClurg & Co., 1909. 282 pp.
  Source: MTLAcc, entry #2175, volume donated from Clemens' library by Clara Clemens Gabrilowitsch in 1910.

Brewer, Ebenezer Cobham (1810–1897). *A Dictionary of Miracles: Imitative, Realistic, and Dogmatic, with Illustrations.* London: Chatto and Windus, 1884. 582 pp.
  Inscription: on flyleaf in purple ink, by Livy Clemens: "S L. Clemens/Rue de L'Universite 169/Paris 1895".
  Marginalia: Clemens marked with black ink the entry for "Imposture: Richard Mainy" (pp. 188–191), drawing a series of marginal brackets. Under the entry for "Celibacy" he used black ink to insert a question mark beside the word "celibacy," which he underlined on page 496 near the words "when the marriage was consummated."
  Location: Mark Twain Library, Redding, Conn.
  Copy examined: Clemens' copy.

————. *A Dictionary of Phrase and Fable, Giving the Derivation, Source, or Origin of Common Phrases, Allusions, and Words* (1871).
> On 14 July 1880 Estes & Lauriat of Boston billed Clemens for "1 Phrase & Fable $2.50"; Clemens paid on 20 July 1880 (receipt in MTP).

————. *The Reader's Handbook of Allusions, References, Plots and Stories. Thirteenth thousand.* London: Chatto & Windus, 1892. 1,399 pp.
> *Inscription:* "S. L. Clemens. 1895 Paris."
> *Catalog: Mott 1952,* #37, $12.50.

Brewster, (Sir) David (1781–1868). *The Martyrs of Science; or, The Lives of Galileo, Tycho Brahe, and Kepler* (pub. London, 1841).
> In the same purple ink with which he made his well-known declaration of his predilections as a reader, Clemens listed at the top of the same discarded envelope: "The Agony Column./2 books by Rev. C. W. Bardsley/Wanderings in Patagonia./ The Martyrs of Science (Brewster)" (MTP). The first title refers to a novel published in 1909.
> Gribben, " 'I Detest Novels, Poetry & Theology' " (1977).

Briggs, Charles Augustus. "Criticism and Dogma," *North American Review, 182* (June 1906), 861–874.
> Mark Twain scoffed at this article by (in his words) "the most daringly broadminded religious person now occupying an American pulpit" in his 20 June 1906 Autobiographical Dictation.

Briggs, T. F. "Jordan am a hard road to trabbel" (plantation song).
> Clemens merely noted the title in Notebook 9 *(N&J,* 1: 421, 437) during his own arduous journey through the Holy Land in 1867.

Bright Things from Everywhere. Albany, N.Y.: J. B. Lyon, 1888. 167 pp.
> *Source:* MTLAcc, entry #366, volume donated by Clemens.

Brine, (Mrs.) Mary Dow (Northam). *Grandma's Attic Treasures. A Story of Old-Time Memories.* New York: E. P. Dutton and Co., [1881]. 94 pp. [Poetry.]
> Annie Moffett Webster wrote to her brother Samuel E. Moffett on 19 December 1881 about her Christmas gift-buying excursion in downtown New York City: "We meant to go to Leggat's but I was thankful to stop at Dutton's on Broadway and buy all the books we wanted there. We bought 'Grandma's Attic treasures' for Aunt Livy" (MTP).

————. *My Boy and I; or, On the Road to Slumberland.* Illus. New York, 1881.
> *Catalog: A1911,* #48, $2.

Brinkley, Frank (1841–1912), ed. *Japan; Described and Illustrated by the Japanese; Written by Eminent Japanese Authorities and Scholars.* 5 vols. Boston: J. B. Millet Co., [cop. 1904].
> *Inscription:* in vol. 1 only, on flyleaf: "S L Clemens/(Mark Twain)".
> *Location:* C. Waller Barrett Collection, Alderman Library, University of Virginia, Charlottesville.
> *Copy examined:* Clemens' copy.

Brisbin, James Sanks (1837–1892). *Trees and Tree-Planting.* New York: Harper & Brothers, 1888. 258 pp.
> *Source:* MTLAcc, entry #1802, volume donated by Clemens.

Bristed, Charles Astor. *Five Years in an English University*. Third edition, rev. New
    York: G. P. Putnam & Sons, 1873.
    Inscription: in pencil on front free endpaper: "S. L. Clemens/1873".
    Marginalia: penciled brackets on pages 61, 65, 66, 77; page 95 folded over.
    Catalogs: A1911, #49, $2.25; *L1912,* #7, $5.
    Provenance: bookplate of Frederick W. Skiff, Westhaven, Connecticut.
    Location: Carrie Estelle Doheny Collection, St. John's Seminary, Camarillo,
California. Purchased from Maxwell Hunley Rare Books of Beverly Hills by Mrs.
Doheny for $35 and donated to St. John's Seminary in 1945.
    Copy examined: Clemens' copy.

Brodhead, (Mrs.) Eva Wilder (McGlasson) (1870–1915). *Bound in Shallows; A Novel.*
    Illus. New York: Harper & Brothers, 1897. 271 pp.
    Source: MTLAcc, entry #1526, volume donated by Clemens.

————. *Diana's Livery.* New York: Harper & Brothers, 1891. 286 pp.
    Source: MTLAcc, entry #1439, volume donated by Clemens.

————. *An Earthly Paragon; A Novel.* Illus. by Frank V. DuMond. New York:
    Harper & Brothers, 1892. 207 pp.
    Source: MTLAcc, entry #1624, volume donated by Clemens.

Brontë, Charlotte (1816–1855), pseud. "Currer Bell." *Jane Eyre.* Illus. New York:
    T. Y. Crowell & Co., [cop. 1890]. 313 pp.
    Source: MTLAcc, entry #1044, volume donated by Isabel V. Lyon, Clemens'
secretary. Title page loose.

————. *Jane Eyre* (pub. 1847).
    Catalog: Livy Clemens owned a copy bound with Brontë's *Villette* (1862 ed.),
according to *Mott 1952,* #38.
    Livy gave this novel to Katy Leary as part of her attempt to advance her maid's
meager education *(LMT,* p. 59). Clemens mentioned Brontë in some ruminations
in June 1891 about changes introduced into the publishing field by the typewriter:
"If Jane Eyre was written in that woman's customary hand—500 words to the
square inch & a microscope required—no wonder no publisher accepted it" (NB
30, TS p. 49).

————. *Life and Works of Charlotte Brontë and Her Sisters.* Illus. 7 vols. London:
    Elder & Co., 1872–1873. Reprinted seven times between 1872 and 1903. [Contains
all novels written by the Brontës.]
    Catalog: C1951, #76c, $13, edition unspecified, listed among the books signed
by Clemens.

————. *Shirley. A Tale.* New York: Derby & Jackson, 1856. 572 pp.
    Source: MTLAcc, entry #966, volume donated by Clemens.

————. *Shirley.* Illus. Philadelphia: Porter & Coates, n.d. 587 pp.
    Source: MTLAcc, entry #2173, volume donated from Clemens' library by
Clara Clemens Gabrilowitsch in 1910.

————. *Shirley.*
    Livy Clemens owned a copy bound with Brontë's *Villette* (1862 edition), accord-
ing to *Mott 1952,* item #38.

————. *Villette.* New York, 1862.
    Inscription: "Olivia L. Langdon. Spuyten Duyvil. June 1863."
    Catalog: Mott 1952, #38, $5, bound with Brontë's *Shirley* and *Jane Eyre.*
    Clara Clemens listed the title of this novel in her commonplace book (1888?–
1904, Paine 150, MTP).

Brontë, Emily (1818–1848), pseud. "Ellis Bell" and Anne Brontë (1820–1849), pseud. "Acton Bell." *Wuthering Heights and Agnes Grey, by Ellis and Acton Bell.* New edition, rev. Preface by Charlotte Brontë. 2 vols. Leipzig: B. Tauchnitz, 1851.
> *Source:* MTLAcc, entry #2183, vol. 1 only (336 pp.), donated from Clemens' library by Clara Clemens Gabrilowitsch in 1910.
> While summering at Kaltenleutgeben, Austria in 1898 Mark Twain wrote a fragmentary sketch about a maid whom he called "Wuthering Heights" (DV236, MTP). He never makes clear how she reminds him of the novel, but since she "talks all the time" perhaps he thought she resembled the major narrator in *Wuthering Heights,* the housekeeper Nelly Dean. The fragment is not successfully humorous. Clemens wrote to Jean in July 1906 from Henry H. Rogers' sumptuous home in Fairhaven, Massachusetts: "I got up at 5 in the morning yesterday at Wuthering Heights" (MTP).

Brooks, Arthur (1845–1895). *Phillips Brooks.* New York: Harper & Brothers, 1893. 50 pp.
> *Source:* MTLAcc, entry #1205, volume donated by Clemens.

Brooks, Elbridge Streeter (1846–1902). *Chivalric Days, and the Boys and Girls Who Helped to Make Them.* Illus. New York: G. P. Putnam's Sons, 1886. 308 pp .
> *Source:* MTLAcc, entry #1924, volume donated from Clemens' library by Clara Clemens Gabrilowitsch in 1910.

Brooks, Henry S. *A Catastrophe in Bohemia, and Other Stories.* New York: Charles L. Webster & Co., 1893. 372 pp.
> Clemens' publishing firm advertised this as a volume of short stories set in mining towns in localities of Lower California and Mexico (*Publishers' Trade List Annual 1893*).

Brooks, John Graham (1846–1938). *The Social Unrest: Studies in Labor and Socialist Movements.* New York: Macmillan Co., 1903. 394 pp.
> *Source:* MTLAcc, entry #548, volume donated by Clemens.

Brooks, Noah. "Personal Reminiscences of Lincoln," *Scribner's Monthly,* 15 (March 1878), 673–681.
> In "About Magnanimous-Incident Literature" (1878) Mark Twain quotes Brooks' anecdote about Abraham Lincoln's praising the acting of J. H. Hackett, who afterward became an annoying office-seeker. The story appears on page 675 of Brooks' essay.

————and Isaac Bromley. "Punch, Brothers, Punch" (newspaper jingle).
> Mark Twain included the "author of Punch Brothers Punch (now on Tribune)" in his lengthy list of humorists compiled in 1881 (NB 19, *N&J,* 2: 429). Brooks is also mentioned in Notebook 22 (1884), TS p. 43. The jingle itself served as a source for Mark Twain's own sketch, "Punch, Brothers, Punch!" (1876).

Brooks, Walter (1856–1933), trans. *Retold in English. Stories from Four Languages.* New York: Brentano's, [cop. 1905]. 335 pp.
> *Source:* MTLAcc, entry #2168, volume donated from Clemens' library by Clara Clemens Gabrilowitsch in 1910.

Brough, William. *The Field of the Cloth of Gold* (extravaganza, prod. 1868).
> Hawley, Goodrich & Company of Hartford charged Clemens on 24 May 1880 for "one ticket to 'The Field of the Cloth of Gold' $1.00" (receipt in MTP).

Brougham, John (1810–1880). *The Christian Martyrs under Constantine and Maxentius* (spectacle, prod. 1867).

Mark Twain poked fun at the production performed at Barnum's Museum, in which a menagerie of wild animals was marched across the stage (2 March 1867 letter to *Alta California; MTTMB*, pp. 118–119).

————. *David Copperfield. A Drama in Two Acts. Adapted from Dickens' Popular Work*. New York: S. French & Son, n.d. 24 pp.

Source: MTLAcc, entry #2126a, volume donated from Clemens' library by Clara Clemens Gabrilowitsch in 1910.

———— (adapt.). *Dombey and Son* (dramatization of Dickens' novel).

Mark Twain lauded Dan Setchell's characterization of Captain Cuttle ("that old sea monster") in "A Voice for Setchell" (*Californian*, 27 [May 1865], 9; quoted by Edgar M. Branch in " 'My Voice is Still for Setchell': A Background Study of 'Jim Smiley and His Jumping Frog,' " *PMLA*, 82 [December 1967], 598). Subsequently in Notebook 6 (1866) he used "Sea Monster" and "Captain Cuttle" as nicknames for passengers he met aboard the *Ajax* (*N&J*, 1: 188). He alluded to Setchell's role as Captain Cuttle as late as 15 January 1903 (NB 46, TS pp. 5, 6).

————. *The Lottery of Life* (play).

Grace King attended Augustin Daly's production of this comedy with the Clemenses on 20 November 1888. "We had Daly's own stage box—and Daly's company, most of the time," she reported. "Oh, it was all great fun!" (King to May King McDowell, 22 November 1888; quoted by Robert Bush, "Grace King and MT," *AL*, 44 [March 1972], 44).

———— and John Elderkin, eds. *Lotos Leaves*. Boston: William F. Gill & Co., 1875.

Inscription: in blue-purple ink: "To My Beloved Wife/Xmas—'74." (Evidently Mark Twain obtained a copy in advance of the publication date because he was a contributor to the volume.)

Location: collection of Charles F. Cornman, Redwood City, California.

Copy examined: apparently Clemens' copy, though its provenance is unestablished.

Meditating revenge in January 1881 against Whitelaw Reid, Mark Twain wrote "W. Reid—'Lotos Leaves' " (NB 19, *N&J*, 2: 417). Reid was another contributor to the volume.

Brown, Alexander. *The Genesis of the United States*. Portraits, Illus., Maps. 2 vols. Boston: Houghton, Mifflin and Co., 1890.

Inscription: on flyleaves of both volumes: "S. L. Clemens, Hartford, December, ["Dec." in vol. 1] 1890".

Catalogs: A1911, #50, $1.50, vol. 2 only; *C1951*, #D28, $2.50, presumably vol. 1 only; *Zeitlin 1951*, #9, $25, vol. 1 only.

Clemens must have objected initially to receiving Brown's book, for on 10 December 1890 Houghton, Mifflin and Company wrote: "We beg to enclose herewith the slip of paper which seemed to warrant us in sending you a copy of Alexander Brown's work on the 'Genesis of the United States.' " On the envelope of their letter Clemens wrote in pencil: "Pay it. SLC" (MTP).

Brown, Alice (1857–1948). *Judgment, A Novel*. Illus. by W. T. Smedley. New York: Harper & Brothers, 1903. 195 pp.

Source: MTLAcc, entry #2169, volume donated from Clemens' library by Clara Clemens Gabrilowitsch in 1910.

Brown, Emma Elizabeth. *The Life of Oliver Wendell Holmes*. Boston: D. Lothrop & Co., 1884. 332 pp.

Catalog: C1951, #D19, $15, listed among books signed by Clemens.

Brown, Horatio Robert Forbes (1854–1926). *Studies in the History of Venice.* 2 vols. New York: E. P. Dutton and Company, 1907.
  Inscriptions: vol. 1 signed: "Feb. 1908./S L. Clemens"; vol. 2 signed: "S L. Clemens/Feb. 1908."
  Marginalia: lengthy note on front free endpaper of vol. 1 describes Clemens' meeting with Brown in Venice thirty years earlier, signed "S. L. C." and dated 21 February 1908. Correction in black ink in preface of vol. 1, p. ix. Pages 35 and 179 folded over in vol. 1; page 177 (at subject of Othello) folded over in vol. 2.
  Catalog: C1951, #37a, $60.
  Location: Carrie Estelle Doheny Collection, St. John's Seminary, Camarillo, California. Donated by Mrs. Doheny in 1951 after she purchased the volumes for $95 from Zeitlin & Ver Brugge, Booksellers, Los Angeles.
  Copies examined: Clemens' copies.

Brown, James Moore (1799–1862). *The Captives of Abb's Valley, A Legend of Frontier Life.* Philadelphia: Presbyterian Board of Publication, [cop. 1854]. 168 pp.
  Source: MTLAcc, entry #546, volume donated by Clemens.

Brown, John, M.D. (1810–1882). *Letters of Dr. John Brown, Edited by His Son and D. W. Forrest. With Letters from Ruskin, Thackeray, and Others. . . . With Biographical Introductions by Elizabeth T. McLaren.* London: A. and C. Black, 1907. 367 pp.
  Catalog: C1951, #45a, 85, listed among the books containing Clemens' marginal notes.

————. *Marjorie Fleming, A Sketch; Being the Paper Entitled "Pet Marjorie": A Story of Child-Life Fifty Years Ago* (first pub. 1863).
  Edition: unidentified.
  Location: unknown.
  In 1904 Clemens inscribed a note to Clara Clemens inside the front cover of his copy of L. Macbean's *The Story of Pet Marjorie* (1904): "This enlargement will properly go with the first 'Marjorie Fleming' which Dr. John Brown gave to your mother in Edinburgh in 1873. S. L. C." (Carrie Estelle Doheny Collection, St. John's Seminary). He repeated this allusion in "Marjorie Fleming, the Wonder-Child" (1909): Dr. Brown "gave my wife his little biography of Marjorie, and I have it yet." But in writing this sketch Mark Twain actually relied on Macbean's book, which contained a reprint of Brown's sketch; Twain heavily annotated this portion of the Macbean volume. On 14 February 1906 Clemens wrote to Gertrude Natkins (whom he often called "Marjorie") from New York City to explain that he had purchased a copy of Dr. John Brown's *Marjorie Fleming* for her, but "fell to reading it, & became fascinated as always before"; he promised to send it along soon (PH in MTP). He wrote to Gertrude Natkins again on 24 March 1906 about Brown's "little comrade of his musings & his dreams" in terms which invite comparisons with Mark Twain's "My Platonic Sweetheart" (written in 1898). On 2 February 1906 Mark Twain dictated a tribute to "Dr. John Brown, that noble and beautiful soul—rescuer of marvelous Marjorie from oblivion" (MTP).

————. *Rab and His Friends* (first pub. 1859).
  Clemens complimented Brown on 27 April 1874 for the many friends *Rab* had made since its first publication, assuring him that "Rab's friends are your friends" (*MTL*, p. 218). Mark Twain pointedly specified that an edition of *Rab* was visible in the "richly furnished apartment" of Aunt Susan, "a refined and sensible lady, if signs and symbols may go for anything," in "The Loves of Alonzo Fitz Clarence and Rosannah Ethelton" (1878). He drew on autobiographical recollections when he caused Alice Edwards to remind Henry in "The Great Dark" (written 1898) that "Doctor John Brown, of *Rab and His Friends,*" had visited them in Edinburgh (*WWD?*, p. 128). Mark Twain mentioned Brown's book again in an Autobiographical Dictation on 2 February 1906 and referred to it as "that pathetic and beautiful masterpiece" in another dictation on 5 February 1906 (MTP).

————. *Spare Hours.* Boston: Ticknor and Fields, 1862. [Contains "Rab and His Friends" on pp. 21–40.]
> *Inscription:* none, but binding is loose and some flyleaves might be missing.
> *Marginalia:* pencil mark on page 149 (which is turned down) at the story entitled "My Other's Memoir."
> *Location:* Mark Twain Library, Redding, Connecticut.
> *Copy examined:* Clemens' copy.

Brown, Katharine Holland (d. 1931). *Diane; A Romance of the Icarian Settlement on the Mississippi River.* Illus. by S. J. Dudley. New York: Doubleday, Page & Co., 1904. 440 pp.
> *Source:* MTLAcc, entry #957, volume donated by Isabel V. Lyon, Clemens' secretary.

Brown, Mary Irene (1872–1895). *Poems.* Cambridge, Mass.: Riverside Press, 1906. 82 pp.
> *Source:* MTLAcc, entry #2014, volume donated from Clemens' library by Clara Clemens Gabrilowitsch in 1910.

Brown, Phoebe (Hinsdale) (1783–1861). ["Autobiography." Unpub. MS.]
> On 16 December 1881 Clemens wrote to Howells from Hartford about Joseph H. Twichell's bringing over Brown's "MS autobiography (written in 1848,)" with the result that "by George I came near not getting to bed at all, last night, on account of the lurid fascinations of it. Why in the nation it has never got into print, I can't understand" (*MTHL,* p. 381).

————. "I love to steal a while away" (hymn).
> Burlesqued in 8 November 1876 letter to Howells (*MTHL,* p. 162); mentioned in 16 December 1881 letter to Howells (*MTHL,* p. 381).

Browne, Charles Farrar (1834–1867), pseud. "Artemus Ward."
> Clemens became friends with Browne in Virginia City in 1863, but not before he wrote a newspaper piece which mimicked Artemus Ward's cacography (Branch, *LAMT,* pp. 103–104). Browne was the subject of "First Interview with Artemus Ward" (1871). In 1879 Clemens mentioned "2 or 3 yarns of Artemus Ward" (NB 18, *N&J,* 2: 303). Artemus Ward was included in two lists of humorists to be considered for an anthology of American humor (NB 19 [1880], *N&J,* 2: 363 and [1881], *N&J,* 2: 429). Nine pieces by Artemus Ward, including "Artemus Ward and the Prince of Wales," appear in *Mark Twain's Library of Humor* (1888). Artemus Ward is mentioned in chapter 9 of *CY* (1889) and is praised at length in a newspaper interview (Winnepeg, Canada *Nor'-Wester,* 27 July 1895, p. 1; reported by Louis J. Budd). Clemens wrote "Babes in the Wood," a Ward lecture, in Notebook 40 (June 1898), TS p. 27. Ward was "beloved in England" (NB 46 [15 January 1903], TS p. 6); his name was noted in Notebook 48 (1906?) TS p. 10 and mentioned in a 31 July 1906 Autobiographical Dictation (*MTE,* p. 202).
> In 1932 Bernard DeVoto simply listed "fifty words" which represented Mark Twain's verbal indebtedness to Artemus Ward, including the "Is He Dead?" joke from *Innocents Abroad.* "Their minds were disparate, their intentions antagonistic, their methods incommensurable," DeVoto declared. "They were humorists and in the production of humor Artemus Ward was chronologically the first. That is all" (*MTAm,* pp. 219–221). Edgar M. Branch noted certain similarities, however: affectations of naiveté, logical confusions, comic lists of words, anti-climax, understatement" (*LAMT* [1950], p. 104). Yet Branch concluded that Mark Twain learned far more from Ward about the art of lecturing (story-telling) than literature—a valid point. Walter Blair also noted a few parallels in *Native American Humor* (1937), but followed DeVoto's lead in stating that "it is probable . . . that neither author particularly influenced the writings of the other. Both were following a well-established tradition in American humor" (p. 150).

Dissenting opinions have been expressed vigorously. Harold Aspiz protested DeVoto's slighting of Ward as a model for Mark Twain's literary style and mounted a counter-argument that is full-scale but largely based on circumstantial evidence ("Mark Twain's Reading" [1949], pp. 99–104). Aspiz incidentally nominates Ward's "The Loss of the Good Ship Polly Anne: A Pathetical Nautical Ballad" as a possibly influential precursor of Mark Twain's "The Aged Pilot Man" in *Roughing It*. The Norton Critical Edition of *Huckleberry Finn* (1961), edited by Bradley, Beatty, and Long, reprints Ward's "Artemus Ward and the Prince of Wales" sketch and recommends its comparison with Huck's discourse on kings and royal pretensions. One of Ward's most popular lectures, "Babes in the Wood," has been put forward by James C. Austin as Mark Twain's source for "The Invalid's Tale" ("Artemus Ward, Mark Twain, and the Limburger Cheese" [1963]). A recent dissent from DeVoto's opinion has been raised by Robert Rowlette in "Mark Ward on Artemus Twain" (1973), which disputes DeVoto's "pontifical" opinion that Mark Twain owed almost nothing to Ward. Rowlette convincingly lines up parallel treatments of the Mormons from Ward's writings and Mark Twain's *Roughing It* and locates other striking examples of borrowing in Mark Twain's *Innocents Abroad* and *Sketches New and Old*. It seems from Rowlette's findings that Mark Twain used Ward's jokes, anecdotes, catch-phrases, snappers, and one-liners, but ceased the practice around 1872. Possibly he disliked the growing public recognition that he was imitating Ward. In 1973 Paul C. Rodgers, Jr. ("Artemus Ward and Mark Twain's 'Jumping Frog' ") traced Ward's influence on the deadpan narration of, and his role as audience for, Twain's famous story. Edgar M. Branch—" 'The Babes in the Wood': Artemus Ward's 'Double Health' to Mark Twain" (1978)—develops other fascinating similarities in their techniques and topics.

————. *Artemus Ward, His Travels*. Illus. New York: Carleton; London: S. Low, Son & Co., 1870.

Inscription: front flyleaf inscribed by Dan Beard in black ink: "This book is from/Mark Twain's private/library. Stormfield./Redding, Conn./Dan Beard/Vice President/Mark Twain Library." Beard was a resident of Redding during the years Clemens lived there, and the artist donated several books from his own library collection to Clemens' community library.

Marginalia: Clemens made the following pencil notes on the front free endpaper, writing sideways: "Wendell P[hillips] 95/sewing s[oc]iety 95/Built fire 99/Onions do/flap jax 101." These notations refer to passages and page numbers in the text. Clemens drew marginal brackets on pages 14, 17, 18, 19, 21, 22, 24, 26, 36, 37, 38, 39, 63, 67, 70, 72, 95, 99, 100, 101.

Provenance: red ink accession number ("3097") of the Mark Twain Library, Redding, Connecticut on the rear endpaper, upper center. At the lower inner corner of the rear pastedown endpaper is the ticket of Maxwell Hunley, rare book dealer, Beverly Hills, California.

Location: private library of Kevin B. Mac Donnell, Austin, Texas. Purchased from Maxwell Hunley in January 1973. I am grateful to Mr. Mac Donnell for supplying the information reported here.

Browne, John Ross (1821–1875). *Crusoe's Island: A Ramble in the Steps of Alexander Selkirk. With Sketches of Adventure in California and Washoe*. New York: Harper & Brothers, 1864.

Harold Aspiz feels that Mark Twain used the book in preparing *Roughing It* ("Mark Twain's Reading," p. 311). Franklin R. Rogers concentrates on the portion of *Crusoe's Island* composed of "A Dangerous Journey" (first published as two articles in *Harper's Monthly* for May and June 1862); Rogers cannot prove that Mark Twain read this section, but "he was personally acquainted with Browne and, therefore, probably knew of his narrative" *(MTBP,* pp. 69–70).

————. "A Peep at Washoe," *Harper's New Monthly Magazine*, 22 (December 1860–February 1861).

Clemens repeatedly recommended this series to his family as a forthright introduction to the Far West region in which he was then living. On 10 May 1862 he mentioned the series in a letter he wrote jointly with Orion to the Keokuk *Gate City (PRI,* p. 45). See also *MTL,* p. 65. Actually Browne's articles are broad burlesques, not factual—so Clemens was jesting *(PRI,* p. 41).

NAH, pp. 158–159; Diane R. DeNyse, "J. Ross Browne and Mark Twain: The Question of Literary Influence" (Master's thesis, Univ. of Wyoming, 1965).

Browne, Junius Henry (1833–1902). *Sights and Sensations in Europe: Sketches of Travel and Adventure.* Illus. Hartford, Conn.: American Publishing Co., 1871. 591 pp. Repr. 1872.

Jane Lampton Clemens wrote to her son and Livy on 11 April 1874, asking if Clemens and Charles Dudley Warner would donate books to the reading room opened by the Women's Christian Temperance Union in Fredonia, New York. According to the 9 December 1874 issue of the Fredonia *Censor,* Clemens gave his mother sixteen volumes to present to the newly opened reading room. Accession records in the Darwin R. Barker Library, which succeeded the WCTU reading room and acquired its book collection, indicate that a copy of Browne's *Sights and Sensations* was one of Clemens' gifts. Most of the books were publications of the American Publishing Company.

Browne, (Sir) Thomas (1605–1682).

References: one of the "world's master-minds" ("Which Was It?" written 1898–1903, *WWD?,* p. 306); "that wise old philosopher" (SLC to William Lyon Phelps, 24 April 1901, *MTL,* p. 707–708); "old Sir Thomas Browne" (SLC to Joseph H. Twichell, 24 April 1904, Yale).

Browne, Thomas Alexander (1826–1915), pseud. "Rolf Boldrewood." *Old Melbourne Memories.* London: Macmillan and Co., 1896.

Ralph [*sic*] Boldrewood" and other Australian writers have built out of their native materials "a brilliant and vigorous literature, and one which must endure" (chapter 22 of *FE* [1897]).

Francis Madigan, "Mark Twain's Passage to India," p. 355.

Brownell, Henry Howard (1820–1872).

"Brownell (funny poems.)," Mark Twain noted in his jottings for an anthology of humorists in July 1880 (NB 19, *N&J,* 2: 361). Brownell published light newspaper verse in addition to the serious Civil War poetry upon which his reputation rests.

Browning, Elizabeth Barrett (1806–1861). *Aurora Leigh* (pub. 1856).

Clemens found *Aurora Leigh* obscure and turned to Livy Langdon for explanations in an unpublished letter written around 1868–1869, according to Dixon Wecter *(LLMT,* p. 34). On 30 September 1896 he wished to obtain the works of Mrs. Browning—but *"not* Aurora Leigh" (NB 39, TS p. 6).

————. *Casa Guidi Windows* (pub. 1851).

Listed in Clara Clemens' commonplace book sometime between 1888 and 1904 (Paine 150, MTP).

————. *The Poems of Elizabeth Barrett Browning.*

Inscription: Livy Clemens' signature.

Catalog: C1951, #016, edition not supplied.

Clemens once referred to "some dark & bloody mystery out of the Widow Browning" (Clemens to Livy Langdon, 17 May 1869, *LLMT,* p. 96). In the second week of their marriage Livy appended a teasing note to a letter Clemens wrote to

Mrs. Fairbanks on 13 February 1870: "We [Livy, Pamela, Annie Moffett] will make Mr Clemens read aloud to us in Mrs Browning—Felicity to us—but what to him?" (MTM, Hartford). There is a complimentary reference to Mrs. Browning in a letter from Clemens to Charles F. Wingate, 31 March 1870, Anthony Collection, NYPL). "If they were to set *me* to review Mrs. Browning," Clemens wrote to Livy around 1872, "it would be like asking you to deliver judgment upon the merits of a box of cigars" *(MFMT, p. 47).*

Browning, Robert (1812–1889).

I have outlined Clemens' infatuation with Browning's poetry in " 'It Is Unsatisfactory to Read to One's Self': Mark Twain's Informal Readings," *Quarterly Journal of Speech,* 62 (February 1976), 49–56, and have discussed the topic more fully in " 'A Splendor of Stars & Suns': Twain as a Reader of Browning's Poems," *Browning Institute Studies,* 6 (1978), 87–103. In addition to Clemens' comments about Browning which appear in these articles, Clemens assured William Dean Howells on 22 August 1887 that he had succeeded in getting Browning "in focus" *(MTHL,* p. 848). He read Browning to a group on 12 September 1888, but the women's "unresponsiveness" made it a "failure" (NB 28, TS p. 22). He planned to quote Browning in *A Connecticut Yankee* (NB 28 [September 1888], TS p. 22), and listed several Browning poems in December 1888 (NB 28, TS pp. 35–36). Livy Clemens wrote to her mother on 15 September 1890 about Clemens' entertaining fellow vacationers in the Catskill Mountains with Browning readings (ALS in MTM).

In January 1897 Clemens recalled wistfully that Susy "was fond of Browning" (NB 39, TS p. 48). Arthur Scott finds Mark Twain's elegies to Susy—"Broken Idols" (written 1898) and "In Dim & Fitful Visions They Flit Across the Distances" (written 1902) to be "perhaps influenced by Browning" in their dramatic monologue form *(OPMT,* p. 31). Katy Leary told Mary Lawton that on a typical evening "Mr. Clemens would have Browning or Dickens and would read aloud to his family" before the fireplace *(LMT,* p. 8). Howard G. Baetzhold correctly concluded that "Clemens knew Browning's works better than those of any other poet except Kipling" *(MT&JB,* p. 289).

————. *Agamemnon, La Saisiaz, Dramatic Idyls, and Jocoseria.* Boston: Houghton, Mifflin and Co., 1885. 547 pp.

Inscription: front flyleaf inscribed by Clemens in black ink, "Livy L. Clemens/ 1886".

Marginalia: profusely annotated by Clemens in pencil. Several poems are marked with especial thoroughness, including "Muléykeh" (pp. 377–386), in which Clemens wrote the instruction " 'sh!" beside the stanza describing the theft of of Hóseyn's steed (p. 383). Clemens marked "Iván Ivànovitch" extensively. In another poem which reflects Clemens' careful attention, "Clive," he jotted "I said," "he said," "he retorted," and other explanatory insertions that would assist listeners at an oral reading.

Catalog: C1951, #48a, one of "8 vols." of Browning, $72 total.

Location: Mark Twain Papers, Univ. of California, Berkeley. Donated in July 1978 by Robert Dawson Wallace of Ft. Myers, Florida. Mr. Wallace purchased this and six other Browning volumes in 1952 from Dawson's Bookshop in Los Angeles.

Copy examined: Livy Clemens' copy, annotated by Clemens.

————. "Andrea del Sarto" (poem).

Mark Twain read this meditative, self-revealing monologue at Smith College on 21 January 1889 (NB 28, TS p. 40).

————. *Asolando; Fancies and Facts.* Eighth edition. London: Smith, Elder & Co., 1890. 157 pp.

Inscription: "for Mr. Clemens/with Mrs. Browning/affectionate regards/Venice 1892.

Location: Mark Twain Library, Redding, Conn. Donated from Clemens' library by Clara Clemens Gabrilowitsch in 1910 (MTLAcc, entry #2018).

Copy examined: Clemens' unmarked copy, presumably a gift from Robert Browning's daughter-in-law.

————. *Asolando; Fancies and Facts.* Author's Edition. Boston: Houghton, Mifflin & Co., 1890. 114 pp.

Source: MTLAcc, entry #2013, volume donated from Clemens' library by Clara Clemens Gabrilowitsch in 1910.

————. *Balaustion's Adventure, Aristophanes' Apology, Pacchiarotto and Other Poems.* Boston: Houghton, Mifflin and Co., 1885. 644 pp.

Inscription: front flyleaf inscribed by Clemens in black ink, "Livy L. Clemens/ 1886."

Marginalia: a few pencil markings in the table of contents. Clemens also marked one poem for reading aloud—"A Forgiveness," the confession of a Spanish nobleman guilty of murder.

Location: Mark Twain Papers, Univ. of California, Berkeley. Donated in July 1978 by Robert Dawson Wallace of Ft. Myers, Florida. Mr. Wallace purchased this and six other Browning volumes in 1952 from Dawson's Bookshop in Los Angeles.

Catalog: C1951, #48a, one of "8 vols." of Browning, $72 total.

Copy examined: Livy Clemens' copy, annotated by Clemens.

————. "Clive" (poem).

Mark Twain included "Clive" in his program of readings for Bryn Mawr in 1891 (NB 30 [February 1891], TS pp. 23, 25); mentioned the poem in June 1891 (NB 30, TS p. 49); and planned to quote the entire poem in *Following the Equator*, according to a note he made at sea on 11 April 1896 (NB 37, TS p. 36). Clara Clemens wrote of her father's rendition of "After": "Never shall I forget the ring of awe in his voice as he read the last words of Clive [*sic*], 'Cover the face'" (*MFMT*, p. 66). The poem, an old man's reminiscences about Robert Clive's words, deeds, and death, has the dramatic monologue form that Clemens favored.

————. *Dramas by Robert Browning.* Two vols. in one. Boston: Houghton, Mifflin and Co., 1885.

Inscription: front flyleaf inscribed by Clemens in black ink, "Livy L. Clemens/ 1886."

Marginalia: Clemens used pencil in marking *King Victor and King Charles* for reading aloud.

Catalog: C1951, #48a, one of "8 vols." of Browning, $72 total.

Location: Mark Twain Papers, Univ. of California, Berkeley. Donated in July 1978 by Robert Dawson Wallace of Ft. Myers, Florida. Mr. Wallace purchased this and six other identically bound Browning volumes in 1952 from Dawson's Bookshop in Los Angeles.

Copy examined: Livy Clemens' copy, annotated by Clemens.

————. *Dramatic Lyrics, Romances, Etc.* Vol. 2 of *The Poetic and Dramatic Works of Robert Browning.* Riverside Edition. 6 vols. Boston: Houghton, Mifflin and Co., 1887.

Catalog: A1911, #52, sold with two other volumes, $2.25 total price.

————. *Dramatis Personae.*

Edition: unknown.

Marginalia: on the flyleaf Clemens wrote in pencil: "One's glimpses & confusions, as one reads Browning, remind me of looking through a telescope (the small sort which you must move with your hand, not clock-work): You toil across dark spaces which are (to *your* lens) empty; but every now & then a splendor of stars & suns bursts upon you and fills the whole field with flame. Feb. 23, 1887" (quoted in *MTB*, p. 847; also quoted in William Lyon Phelps' *Autobiography* [1939], p. 65. Phelps, who examined the volume independently, reports that Clemens noted he was making the observation after reading "Easter-Day" aloud). Albert Bigelow Paine reported that "in another note he speaks of the 'vague dim flash of splendid humming-birds through a fog' " *(MTB*, p. 847). Paine notes that Clemens "indicated with pencil every shade of emphasis which would help to reveal the poet's purpose" *(MTB*, p. 846).

Location: unknown.

————. *Dramatis Personae, Dramatic Romances and Lyrics, Strafford, Etc.* Boston: Houghton, Mifflin and Co., 1884. 612 pp.

Marginalia: on the second flyleaf of this worn and much-marked volume, Clemens explained: "The pencilings in this book are inexplicable, except by this explanation, which is the true one: they were made in order to give the eye instant help in placing & shading emphases—a very necessary precaution when one reads Browning aloud. SLC". Robert Dawson Wallace transcribed this comment and other marginalia in "An Analytical-Historical Study of the Factors Contributing to the Success of Mark Twain as an Oral Interpreter," doctoral dissertation (Univ. of Southern California, 1962), pp. 291–346. Among the poems which Clemens marked most meticulously were "Easter-Day," "Abt Vogler," and "Rabbi Ben Ezra."

Catalog: C1951, #48a, one of "8 vols." of Browning, $72 total.

Location: Mark Twain Papers, Univ. of California, Berkeley. Donated in July 1978 by Robert Dawson Wallace of Ft. Myers, Florida. Mr. Wallace purchased this and six other identically bound Browning volumes in 1952 from Dawson's Bookshop in Los Angeles.

Copy examined: Clemens' copy.

————. *Ferishtah's Fancies.* Boston: Houghton, Mifflin and Co., 1886.

Inscription: "Livy L. Clemens/1887".

Location: Mark Twain Library, Redding, Conn.

Copy examined: Livy Clemens' copy.

Clara Clemens described this poem and "Caliban Upon Setebos" in her commonplace book (ca. 1888?, Paine 150, MTP).

————. *Fifine at the Fair, Red Cotton Night-Cap Country, and the Inn Album.* Boston: Houghton, Mifflin and Co., 1883. 663 pp.

Inscription: front flyleaf inscribed by Clemens in black ink, "Livy L. Clemens/1886."

Catalog: C1951, #48a, one of "8 vols." of Browning, $72 total.

Location: Mark Twain Papers, Univ. of California, Berkeley. Donated in July 1978 by Robert Dawson Wallace of Ft. Myers, Florida. Mr. Wallace purchased this and six other Browning volumes in 1952 from Dawson's Bookshop in Los Angeles.

Copy examined: Livy Clemens' copy, unmarked.

————. *The Letters of Robert Browning and Elizabeth Barrett Browning 1845–1846.* Third impression. 2 vols. London: Smith, Elder & Co., 1899.

Marginalia: a few pencil markings in both volumes.

Location: Mark Twain Library, Redding, Conn.

Copies examined: possibly Clemens' copies. I found these volumes on the circulating shelves in 1970.

————. *"Memorabilia"* (poem).
Mark Twain read "Memorabilia" and Shelley's "Skylark" at a Shelley-Keats memorial program on 14 February 1907 (IVL Journal, TS p. 225).

————. *Men and Women.* Boston: Ticknor and Fields, 1856.
Inscription: in brown ink on the flyleaf: "Livie L. Langdon/1864/New York."
Marginalia: on the front free endpaper Clemens noted in pencil the name of a dramatic monologue inside, "Saul." Clemens marked most of the poems for reading aloud, indicating stresses, connecting stanzas, and glossing terms. He also penciled a number of marginal notes, of which those surrounding "Old Pictures in Florence" (pp. 206–216) are the most extensive and significant.
Catalog: "Retz Appraisal," p. 5, valued at $15.
Location: Mark Twain Papers, Berkeley, California.
Copy examined: Clemens' copy.

————. *Men and Women and Sordello.* Two vols. in one. Boston: Houghton, Mifflin and Co., 1884 .
Inscription: front flyleaf inscribed by Clemens in black ink, "Livy L. Clemens/1886."
Marginalia: a few pencil marks.
Catalog: C1951, #48a, one of "8 vols." of Browning, $72 total.
Location: Mark Twain Papers, Univ. of California, Berkeley. Donated in July 1978 by Robert Dawson Wallace of Ft. Myers, Florida. Mr. Wallace purchased this and six other Browning volumes in 1952 from Dawson's Bookshop in Los Angeles.
Copy examined: Livy Clemens' copy, marked by Clemens.

————. *"Muléykeh"* (poem).
Mark Twain planned to read Browning's "Horse-race" to a Smith College audience on 21 January 1889, along with another Browning poem, Uncle Remus' tales, and some of Twain's own stories (NB 28, TS p. 35). In "Muléykeh," included in *Dramatic Idyls* (Second Series, 1880), Hóseyn races against a thief riding Hóseyn's own horse, Muléykeh the Pearl. Twain used this poem in a reading he gave on 13 April 1889 (NB 28, TS pp. 55–56).

————. *Parleyings with Certain People of Importance in Their Day.* Boston: Houghton, Mifflin and Co., 1887.
Marginalia: most poems marked densely in pencil by Clemens. Only two are entirely ignored—"With Gerard de Lairesse" (pp. 115–133) and "Fust and His Friends: An Epilogue" (the final poem in the volume). Extremely profuse markings in "With Bernard de Mandeville" (pp. 23–36). "With Daniel Bartoli" (pp. 39–53) contains numerous speculations about possible interpretations; some were canceled as new meanings emerged and were recorded. At the bottom of page 49, for example, Clemens wondered: "(Is this to say our girl found a lion (a King) about to <destroy> diminish a dukedom, using the duke's love for *her* as a means, & she nobly checkmated his little game by renouncing her big chance & backing out from the marriage?)" Clemens' penciled markings underscore lines, add stress marks to denote intonations, and offer explanatory notes—all in preparation for public readings, no doubt.
Catalog: C1951, #56a, $75.
Location: Carrie Estelle Doheny Collection, St. John's Seminary, Camarillo, California. Donated by Mrs. Doheny in 1951 after she purchased it from Maxwell Hunley Rare Books for $82.
Albert Bigelow Paine reported that during the winter of 1886–1887 Mark Twain entertained his Browning class with "rich, sympathetic and luminous" readings from *Parleyings (MTB,* p. 846).
Gribben, " 'A Splendor of Stars & Suns' " (1978), p. 98.

MULÉYKEH.

IF a stranger passed the tent of Hóseyn, he cried "A
 churl's!"

Or haply "God help the man who has neither salt nor
 bread!"

— "Nay," would a friend exclaim, "he needs nor
 pity nor scorn

More than who spends small thought on the shore-
 sand picking pearls

Holds but in light esteem the seed-sort, bears instead

On his breast a moon-like prize, some orb which of
 night makes morn.

"What if no flocks and herds enrich the son of Sinán?

They went when his tribe was mulct, ten thousand
 camels the due,

Blood-value paid perforce for a murder done of old.

'God gave them, let them go! But never since time
 began,

Plates 5 A-J: Penciled marginalia in Clemens' copy of Browning's *Dramatic Idyls* (1885 edition). Clemens referred to this poem as the "horse race"; at its climax Hóseyn races against a thief riding Hóseyn's horse, Muléykeh the Pearl. In this same volume Clemens also made extensive preparations for reading aloud "Clive" and "Ivan Ivanovitch."
Courtesy of Mark Twain Papers, University of California, Berkeley. Photographed by Robert Dawson Wallace.)

Muléykeh, peerless mare, owned master the match of
     you,
And you are my prize, my Pearl : I laugh at men's
     land and gold ! '

" So in the pride of his soul laughs Hóseyn — and
     right, I say. *For instance —*
Do the ten steeds run a race of glory ? Outstripping
     all
Ever Muléykeh stands first steed at the victor's
     staff.
Who started the owner's hope, gets shamed and
     named, that day
' Silence,' or, last but one, is ' The Cuffed,' as we use
     to call
Whom the paddock's lord thrusts forth. Right,
     Hóseyn, I say, to laugh."

Surprise. " Boasts he Muléykeh the Pearl ? " the stranger re-
     plies : " Be sure
On him I waste nor scorn nor pity, but lavish both
On Duhl the son of Sheybán, who withers away in
     heart
For envy of Hóseyn's luck. Such sickness admits no
     cure.
A certain poet has sung, and sealed the same with an
     oath,

Plate 5B

'For the vulgar ~~and~~ flocks and herds! The Pearl is a
　　prize apart.'"

Lo, Duhl the son of Sheybán comes riding to Hóseyn's
　　tent,

And he casts his saddle down, and enters and
　　"Peace" bids he. *+ goes on:*

"You are poor, I know the cause: my plenty shall
　　mend the wrong.

'T is said of your Pearl ~~#~~ the price of a hundred cam-
　　els spent

In her purchase were scarce ill paid: such prudence
　　is far from me

Who proffer a thousand. Speak! Long parley may
　　last too long."

Said Hóseyn "You feed young beasts a many, of fa-
　　mous breed,

Slit-eared, unblemished, fat, true offspring of Múzen-
　　nem:

There stumbles no weak-eyed she in the line as it
　　climbs the hill.

But I love Muléykeh's face: her forefront whitens in-
　　deed

Like a yellowish wave's cream-crest. Your camels —
　　go gaze on them!

Her fetlock is foam-splashed too. Myself am the
　　richer still."

Plate 5C

A year goes by : lo, back to the tent again rides Duhl. *says*

"You are open-hearted, ay — moist-handed, a very
     prince.

Why should I speak of sale ? Be the mare your sim-
     ple gift !

My son is pined to death for her beauty : my wife
     prompts 'Fool,

Beg for his sake the Pearl ! Be God the rewarder,
     since

God pays debts seven for one : who squanders on
     Him shows thrift.' "

fröhlich

Said Hóseyn "God gives each man one life, like a
     lamp, then gives

That lamp due measure of oil : lamp lighted — hold
     high, wave wide

Its comfort for others to share ! once quench it, what
     help is left ?

The oil of your lamp is your son : I shine while Mu-
     léykeh lives.

Would I beg your son to cheer my dark if Muléykeh
     died ?

It is life against life : what good avails to the life-
     bereft ? "

st

3 picture

Another year, and — hist ! What craft is it Duhl de-
     signs ?

Plate 5D

He alights not at the door of the tent as he did last
    time;

But creeping behind, he gropes his stealthy way by
    the trench

Half-round till he finds the flap in the folding, (for
    night combines

With the robber — and such is he :) Duhl, covetous
    up to crime,

Must wring from Hóseyn's grasp the Pearl, by what-
    ever the wrench.

Soliloquy of Duhl:

" He was hunger-bitten, I heard : I tempted with half
    my store,

And a gibe was all my thanks. Is he generous like
    Spring dew ?

Account the fault to me who chaffered with such an
    one ! *Why!*

He has killed, to feast chance comers, the creature he
    rode : nay, more

For a couple of singing-girls his robe has he torn in
    two : ! *So —*

I will beg ! Yet I nowise gained by the tale of my
    wife and son.

" I swear by the Holy House, my head will I never
    wash

Till I filch his Pearl away. Fair dealing I tried, then
    guile,

Plate 5E

And now I resort to force.   He said we must live or
    die :
Let him die, then, — let me live ! Be bold — but not
    too rash !
I have found me a peeping-place : breast, bury your
    breathing while
I explore for myself ! Now, breathe ! He deceived
    me not, the spy !

" As he said — there lies in peace Hóseyn — how
    happy ! Beside
Stands tethered the Pearl : thrice winds her headstall
    about his wrist :
'T is therefore he sleeps so sound — the moon through
    the roof reveals.
And, loose on his left, stands too that other, known
    far and wide,
Buhéyseh, her sister born : fleet is she yet ever missed
The winning tail's fire-flash a-stream past the thunder-
    ous heels.

" No less she stands saddled and bridled, this second,
    in case some thief
Should enter and seize and fly with the first, as I
    mean to do.
What then ? The Pearl is the Pearl : once mount her
    we both escape."

Plate 5F

Through the skirt-fold in glides Duhl, — so a serpent
    disturbs no leaf
In a bush as he parts the twigs entwining a nest :
    clean through,
He is noiselessly at his work : as he planned, he per-
    forms the rape.

He has set the tent-door wide, has buckled the girth,
    has clipped
The headstall away from the wrist he leaves thrice
    bound as before,
He springs on the Pearl, is launched on the desert
    like bolt from bow.
Up starts our plundered man : from his breast though
    the heart be ripped,
Yet his mind has the mastery : behold, in a minute
    more,
He is out and off and away on Buhéyseh, whose worth
    we know !

And Hóseyn — his blood turns flame, he has learned
    long since to ride,
And Buhéyseh does her part, — they gain — they are
    gaining fast
On the fugitive pair, and Duhl has Ed-Dárraj to cross
    and quit,
And to reach the ridge El-Sabán, — no safety till that
    be spied !

Plate 5G

384   MULÉYKEH.

And Buhéyseh is, bound by bound, but a horse-length
    off at last,
For the Pearl has missed the tap of the heel, the touch
    of the bit.

She shortens her stride, she chafes at her rider the
    strange and queer :
Buhéyseh is mad with hope — beat sister she shall and
    must,
Though Duhl of the hand and heel so clumsy, she
    has to thank.
She is near now, nose by tail — they are neck by
    croup — joy ! fear !
What folly makes Hóseyn shout "Dog Duhl, Damned
    son of the Dust,
Touch the right ear and press with your foot my Pearl's
    left flank ! "

And Duhl was wise at the word, and Muléykeh as
    prompt perceived
Who was urging redoubled pace, and to hear him was
    to obey,
And a leap indeed gave she, and evanished for ever
    more.
And Hóseyn looked one long last look as who, all be-
    reaved,

Plate 5H

Looks, fain to follow the dead so far as the living
    may:
Then he turned Buhéyseh's neck slow homeward,
    weeping sore.

And, lo, in the sunrise, still sat Hóseyn upon the
    ground
Weeping: and neighbors came, the tribesmen of
    Bénu-Asád
In the vale of green Er-Rass, and they questioned him
    of his grief;
And he told from first to last how, serpent-like, Duhl
    had wound
His way to the nest, and how Duhl rode like an ape,—
    so bad!
And how Buhéyseh did wonders, yet Pearl remained
    with the thief.

And they jeered him, one and all: " Poor Hóseyn is
    crazed past hope!
How else had he wrought himself his ruin, in fortune's
    spite?
To have simply held the tongue were a task for a boy
    or girl,
And here were Muléykeh again, the eyed like an ante-
    telope,

25

Plate 5I

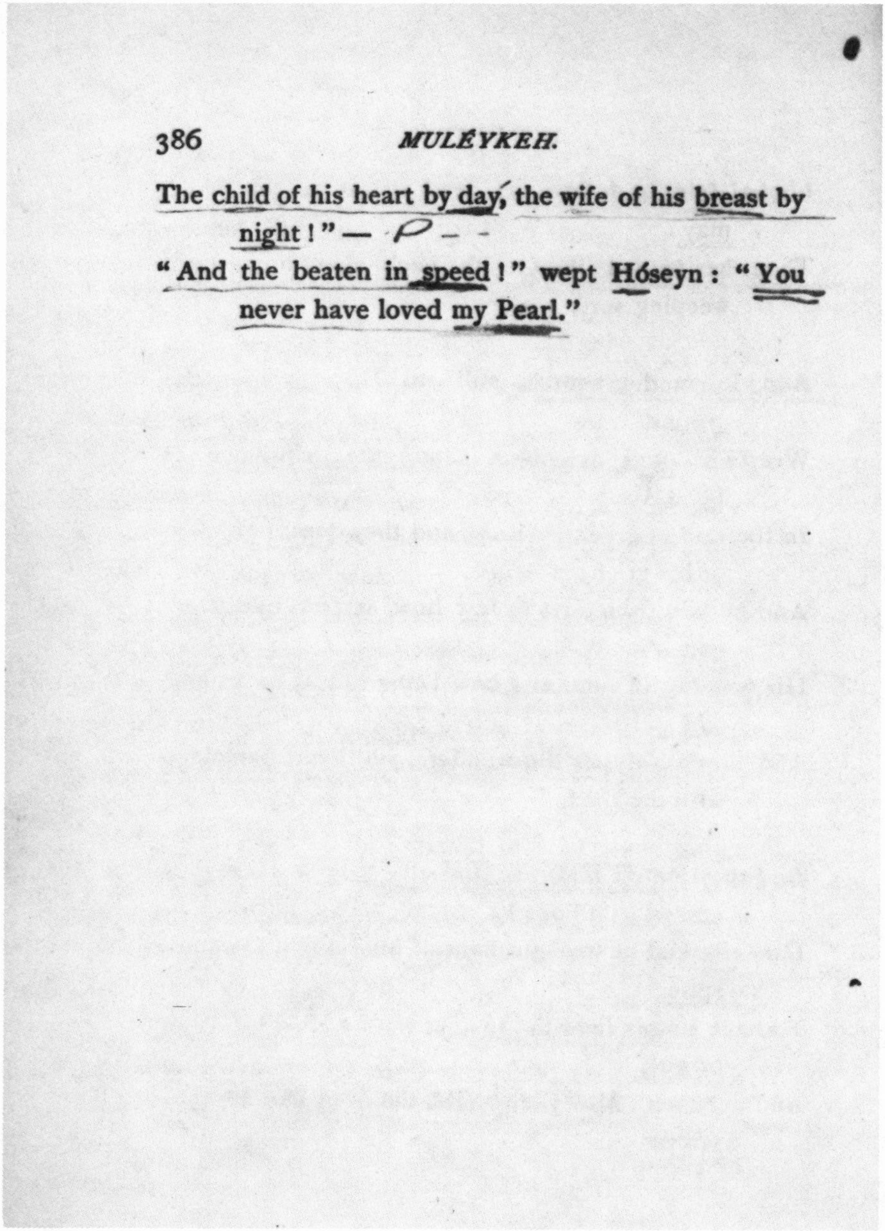

386 *MULÉYKEH.*

The child of his heart by day, the wife of his breast by night!" — ρ - -

"And the beaten in speed!" wept Hóseyn: "You never have loved my Pearl."

Plate 5J

————. *Parleyings with Certain People of Importance in Their Day*. London: Smith, Elder & Co., 1887. 268 pp.

Marginalia: none by Clemens, but someone else—probably Livy—copied notes from the New York *Tribune* on the flyleaves and throughout the book in black ink. Some pages remain unopened.

Location: Mark Twain Library, Redding, Conn. Donated from Clemens' library by Clara Clemens Gabrilowitsch in 1910 (MTLAcc, entry #2019).

Copy examined: presumably Livy Clemens' copy.

————. *Pauline; Paracelsus; Strafford: A Tragedy; Sordello; Pippa Passes: A Drama; King Victor and King Charles: A Tragedy*. Vol. 1, *The Poetic and Dramatic Works of Robert Browning*. Riverside Edition. 6 vols. Boston: Houghton, Mifflin and Co., 1887.

Inscription: flyleaf missing.

Marginalia: heavily marked and annotated in pencil; marginalia confined to *Paracelsus* and *Sordello* (pp. 68–261), however. Clemens recorded his progress in reading along the margins: "Finished here March 20/89. I *declare!* What *time* it is!" (p. 81); "stopped here Mch 27" (p. 101); "Stopped here Apl. 4/89" (p. 196); "Begin *here* Apl. 24/89" (p. 207); "Begin here May 1/89" (p. 225); "Begin here May 15 '89" (p. 249); "Begin here May 22/89" (p. 261). A plethora of other notes edit the material for reading aloud, adding marks for emphasis, syllable stress, and comprehension.

Location: Mark Twain Library, Redding, Conn.

Copy examined: Clemens' copy.

————. *The Poetical Works of Robert Browning*. Copyright Edition. 2 vols. Leipzig: Bernhard Tauchnitz, 1872.

Inscription: on flyleaf of first volume in black ink: "To Susie Clemens,/These volumes, (in place of a promised mud turtle,) are presented, with the love of Papa./May 25, 1882/N.B. The turtle was to have been brought from New Orleans, but I gave up the idea because it seemed cruel. S.L.C." Volume 2 also inscribed in black ink: "To Susie Clemens from Papa."

Catalog: does not appear in *C1951*.

Location: Carrie Estelle Doheny Collection, St. John's Seminary, Camarillo, California. Donated by Mrs. Doheny in 1951 after she purchased the volumes from Maxwell Hunley Rare Books (Beverly Hills) for $100.

Copies examined: Susy Clemens' copies.

————. *Rabbi Ben Ezra*. Second edition. Portland, Maine: Thomas B. Mosher, 1909.

Location: Antenne-Dorrance Collection, Rice Lake, Wisconsin. Information in this entry is taken from Ann Cameron Harvey's checklist, compiled in 1966. The book was temporarily on loan when I catalogued the collection in 1970.

"I suppose I have read Rabbi Ben Ezra . . . a couple of dozen times" [to the Browning class] (SLC to Mrs. Fairbanks, 22 March 1887, *MTMF*, pp. 260–261). Mark Twain planned to include the poem in his program for a reading on 2 April 1889 (NB 28, TS p. 52). After luncheon on 8 March 1907 "Mrs. Whitmore asked him to read Rabbi Ben Ezra to us—which he did" (IVL Journal, TS p. 229, MTP).

————. *Red Cotton Night-Cap Country; Aristophanes' Apology; The Inn Album; Pacchiarotto and How He Worked in Distemper; and Other Poems*. Vol. 5 of *The Poetic and Dramatic Works of Robert Browning*. Riverside Edition. 6 vols. Boston: Houghton, Mifflin and Co., 1887.

Catalog: A1911, #52, sold with two other volumes; total price $2.25.

————. *The Ring and the Book*. Two vols. in one. Boston: Houghton, Mifflin and Co., 1885.

Inscription: front flyleaf inscribed by Clemens in black ink, "Livy L. Clemens/ 1886."

Marginalia: a few notes and markings in pencil, including (at the top of page 265) the reminder "Next (Nov. 16)" written above Giuseppe Caponsacchi's speech.

Catalog: C1951, 48a, one of "8 vols." of Browning, $72 total.

Location: Mark Twain Papers, Univ. of California, Berkeley. Donated in July 1978 by Robert Dawson Wallace of Ft. Myers, Florida. Mr. Wallace purchased this and six other Browning volumes in 1952 from Dawson's Bookshop in Los Angeles.

Copy examined: Livy Clemens' copy, annotated by Clemens.

————. *The Ring and the Book*. Vol. 3 of *The Poetic and Dramatic Works of Robert Browning*. Riverside Edition. 6 vols. Boston: Houghton, Mifflin and Co., 1887.

Catalog: A1911, #52, sold with two other volumes; total price $2.25.

Mary Bushnell Cheney attended one of the Browning study sessions at Clemens' Hartford home and heard him resume reading *The Ring and the Book* where he left off previously ("Mark Twain as a Reader" [1911], p. 6). Grace King too happened to visit the Clemenses during the summer of 1887 when Clemens was reading *The Ring and the Book* to his class: "To him there were no obscure passages to be argued over, no guesses at meaning. . . . He understood Browning as did no one else I ever knew" *(Memories,* p. 84).

————. *Sordello* (pub. 1840).

When Mary Bushnell Cheney visited Clemens' Browning class in 1887 she observed that "in *Sordello* only we saw him confused and perplexed, and after two readings the book was abandoned" ("Mark Twain as a Reader" [1911], p. 6). Clemens joked about the obscurity of *Sordello* in Notebook 38 [June 1896], TS p. 32, doubting whether Browning himself knew the meaning of certain passages. (Clemens attributes the joke to Carlyle Smythe.)

————. *Strafford* (pub. 1837).

As Mary Bushnell Cheney listened to Clemens' reading of *Strafford,* "the grand character of that man and the nation-wide canvas of the drama were brought out conspicuously and to our intense delight" ("Mark Twain as a Reader" [1911], p. 6).

————. "Up at a Villa—Down in the City" (poem).

"I suppose I have read [to the Browning class] . . . Up in the Villa a couple of dozen times & Abt Vogler, Caliban in Setebos, & some others nearly as often. Ben Ezra & Abt Vogler are called for the oftenest—yes, & Up in a Villa. We should read Easter Day just as often, but for its length" (SLC to Mrs. Fairbanks, 22 March 1887, *MTMF*, pp. 260–61). The title "Up at a Villa" was entered in Notebook 28 (November 1888), TS p. 33. The Reverend Joseph H. Twichell declared in an essay on Mark Twain in 1896 that "whoever may have had the good fortune to hear his rendering of anything from Browning—for instance, 'Up at a Villa—Down in the City,' which is one of his favorites—will not be likely to forget the pleasure of it" (p. 822).

Browning Society. London. *Illustrations to Browning's Poems. Photographs . . . with a Notice of the Artists and the Pictures by E[rnest] Radford.* London: Published for the Browning Society by N. Trübner and Co., 1882. Repr. 1883.

Clemens jotted the title and publisher of this book on the flyleaf of his copy of Edgar Watson Howe's *The Story of a Country Town,* inscribed to Clemens by Howe in 1884 *(The Twainian,* 27 [March–April 1968], 1).

Bruce, Robert, of Wallelberdina, South Australia. *Re-Echoes from Coondambo.* Adelaide, Australia: W. K. Thomas & Co., 1902. 437 pp.

Source: MTLAcc, entry #1691, volume donated by Clemens.

Brücke, Professor Ernst Wilhelm Ritter von (1819–1892). *Vorlesungen über Physiologie* (pub. 1873–1874).

Mark Twain specifically referred to this work in his article on vivisection, dated 26 May 1899 and addressed to Sidney G. Trust from Vienna (Hemminghaus, "Mark Twain's German Provenience," p. 476). Brücke was a professor of physiology and microscopic anatomy in Vienna.

Brueys, Abbé David Augustin de (1640–1723). *L'Avocat Patelin: A Comedy in Three Acts. Adapted by the Abbé Brueys from the Famous Farce of the Fifteenth Century and First Performed Théâtre Français in 1706. Translated by Samuel F. G. Whitaker.* London: T. Fisher Unwin, 1905.

Inscription: "To Mark Twain, this slight attempt at a presentation of 15th–18th century humour, with the Translator's profound yet affectionate respect. Independence Day, 1907."

Marginalia: Clemens wrote a brief essay in brown ink on the rear endpaper concerning "interviewer vulgarities" and the stupidity of using the third-person form in British Parliamentary debate. No notes or markings in text.

Catalog: A1911, #481.

Location: Carrie Estelle Doheny Collection, St. John's Seminary, Camarillo, California. Mrs. Doheny donated the volume in 1953 after obtaining it from Maxwell Hunley Rare Books, Beverly Hills.

Copy examined: Clemens' copy.

Bruner, Jane W. *Free Prisoners: A Story of California Life.* Philadelphia: Claxton, Remsen & Haffelfinger, 1877.

James R. Osgood & Company of Boston billed Clemens for Bruner's *Free Prisoners* in 1877 (Scrapbook #10, p. 69, MTP). He made the purchase on 19 July 1877.

Clemens knew Mrs. Bruner in California before she divorced her husband and became an author and aspiring playwright. He mentions her "book" in late 1882 (NB 20, *N&J,* 2: 508), presumably an allusion to *Free Prisoners,* a romantic novel set in the Sierra Nevada foothills.

—————. *A Mad World* (play, 1882).

Bruner levied on her prior acquaintanceship with Mark Twain in California to obtain a reading of her play. After he missed its New Haven preview she sent a copy to him on 7 April 1882, seeking his opinion "even if it is unfavorable—I want to know my fate" (MTP). In Notebook 20 (April 1882) Mark Twain noted: "[William] Gillette ask Chas W Butler [an actor] about Mrs. Bruner's play—'A Mad World' " *(N&J,* 2: 461).

Brush, (Mrs.) Christine (Chaplin) (1842–1892). *The Colonel's Opera Cloak.* Boston: Roberts Brothers, 1879. 228 pp.

Clemens noted the title in Notebook 19 early in the summer of 1881 *(N&J,* 2: 397).

Bryant, William Cullen (1794–1878). "The Battle-Field" (poem, 1839).

Mark Twain attributes "the lie of virtuous ecstasy" to Bryant for writing that "truth crushed to earth will [*sic*] rise again" ("My First Lie, and How I Got Out of It" [1899]).

————, comp. *The Family Library of Poetry and Song. Being Choice Selections from the Best Poets, English, Scottish, Irish, and American.* New York: J. B. Ford and Co., 1870. 950 pp.

When Mark Twain met William Cox Bennett in London in 1873, he reminded Mrs. Fairbanks: "You remember his poem 'Baby May' in the <Whittier> Bryant Selections" (6 July 1873, *MTMF*, p. 173); Bennett's rhapsodic tribute to his infant daughter appears on page 76 of Bryant's anthology. To a correspondent seeking Bryant's autograph, Clemens explained on 31 July 1873: "There is a volume (issued by Scribner I think, some 3 or 4 years ago) of selections from the whole world's poets which contains Bryant's autograph—the collection *is compiled by Bryant* but I forget its title" (SLC to "Dear Sir," Massachusetts Historical Society). Clemens recalled correctly: below the frontispiece portrait of Bryant in *The Family Library* appears his autograph; facsimile autographs of other poets are scattered through the volume.

Clemens' familiarity with this anthology opens up the possibility that he knew a few pieces by many poets whose books he never owned or mentioned, for Bryant's *Library* remains one of the most (perhaps *the* most) comprehensive one-volume collections of poetry published in the United States. His selections run the gamut from established masterpieces by Coleridge and Wordsworth to the near-doggerel of contemporary versifiers for American newspapers and magazines. All periods are represented, commencing with that of Chaucer.

————— and Sydney Howard Gay. *A Popular History of the United States, from the First Discovery of the Western Hemisphere by the Northmen, to the End of the Civil War.* 4 vols. New York: Scribner, Armstrong and Co., 1876–1881. [Also issued by Charles Scribner's Sons, 1878–1882.]

Clemens notified Charles L. Webster on 20 March 1884 that "the Bryant History has arrived" (*MTBus*, p. 242); on 2 September 1884 Webster sent Clemens a statement of his personal expenses charged against Charles L. Webster & Company which included a charge of $31.80 for the purchase on 22 March 1884 of "1 Set of Bryants U.S. Histy" (MTP).

————. "Thanatopsis" (poem).

A character named "Holmes" claimed the authorship of this poem in Mark Twain's ill-fated Whittier Birthday Dinner speech on 17 December 1877 (*MTB*, p. 1646).

Bryce, Lloyd Stephens (1851–1917). *Friends in Exile. A Tale of Diplomacy, Coronets, and Hearts.* New York: Harper & Brothers, 1900. 270 pp.
   Source: MTLAcc, entry #1438, volume donated by Clemens.

Buchanan, Thompson (1877–1937). *The Castle Comedy.* Illus. by Elizabeth Shippen Green. New York: Harper & Brothers, 1904. 236 pp.
   Source: MTLAcc, entry #986, volume donated by Clemens.

————. *Judith Triumphant.* New York: Harper & Brothers, 1905. 255 pp.
   Source: MTLAcc, entry #33, volume donated by Clemens.

Buchheim, Karl Adolf (1828–1900). *Materials for German Prose Composition; or, Selections from Modern English Writers.* Ninth edition. New York: G. P. Putnam's Sons, 1885. 252 pp.
   Source: MTLAcc, entry #382, volume donated by Clemens.

Buck, Charles (1771–1815), comp. *Anecdotes; Religious, Moral and Entertaining, . . . with a Preface by Ashbel Green.* Two vols. in one. New York: J. C. Riker, 1831.
   Inscription: "J. Langdon [Clemens' father-in-law], Salina, June 1, 1833."
   Marginalia: a few passages marked in the margin by Clemens.
   Catalog: A1911, #53, $6.

[Buck, Sir Edward.] *Indo-Anglican Literature.* Second Issue. For Private Circulation Only. Calcutta: Thacker, Spink and Co., 1887. [First edition pub. 1883. Preface signed merely "B. A." Certified by a friend of the compiler to be the work of Sir Edward Buck, Secretary to the Governor of India (James Kennedy, W. A. Smith, and A. F. Johnson, *Dictionary of Anonymous and Pseudonymous English Literature* [Edinburgh: Oliver and Boyd: 1928–1932], 3: 149; 6: 282).]

Inscription: on the front cover of this paperbound volume Clemens wrote in pencil, "Lt Gov of Bengal".

Marginalia: Clemens made notes in pencil throughout the book and cut out certain sections for use in *Following the Equator.* Keshav Mutalik quotes various annotations (including Clemens' quip on page 67, "A very heavy day for a child") in *Mark Twain in India.*

Catalog: "Retz Appraisal" (1944), p. 9, valued at $15.

Location: Mark Twain Papers, Berkeley, California.

Copy examined: Clemens' copy.

The book consists of supposedly humorous examples of English prose culled from letters and essays written by Indians. In chapter 61 of *Following the Equator* (1897) Mark Twain mentions his receiving *Indo-Anglican Literature* in the mail; he finds it "well stocked with 'baboo' English—clerky English, booky English, acquired in the schools," but adds that "strange as some of these wailing and supplicating letters are, humble and even groveling as some of them are, and quaintly funny and confused as a goodly number of them are, there is still a pathos about them, as a rule, that checks the rising laugh and reproaches it." Nevertheless he proceeds to quote a number of extracts that he finds especially amusing.

Mutalik, *MT in India* (1978), pp. 112–113.

Buckingham, James Silk (1786–1855). *America, Historical, Statistic, and Descriptive.* 7 vols. New York, 1841.

Dewey Ganzel concedes that "Buckingham is not mentioned by Twain in his list of travelers [cited in *Life on the Mississippi*] . . . , but Twain wrote that there were other authorities which he consulted but did not list" ("Twain, Travel Books, and *Life on the Mississippi*" [1962], p. 47 n. 14). Ganzel suspects that Twain used Buckingham's *America* as a source in referring to anti-abolitionist mobs in Philadelphia, a passage he later dropped from the final version of *LonMiss* ("Twain, Travel Books," pp. 43–44).

Buckland, Francis Trevelyan (1826–1880). *Curiosities of Natural History.* Third Series. Second edition. 2 vols. London: Richard Bentley, 1868. [Descriptions of giants, dwarfs, etc.]

Inscription: on verso of front free endpaper in vol. 2: "To Saml L. Clemens/ with the sincere regard of his friend/the Editor/Henry Lee/Sept. 17th 1872".

Location: Mark Twain Library, Redding, Conn. (vol. 2 only).

Copy examined: Clemens' copy of vol. 2, unmarked.

Buckle, Henry Thomas (1821–1862). *History of Civilization in England.* 2 vols. (First volume pub. 1857; second volume pub. 1861.)

One of Mark Twain's sources for *A Connecticut Yankee* was listed in a version of his projected appendix: "King's evil. Hist Civilization" (NB 29 [1889], TS p. 15). On 4 January 1896 Twain noted that "Buckle says the bulk of population of India is the Sudras—the workers, the farmers, the creators of wealth. Their name—laborer—is a term of contempt" (NB 36, TS p. 16); comparing Australasia with India, he reminded himself on 5 January 1896 to "see previous quotation from Buckle" (NB 36, TS p. 18). In chapter 39 of *Following the Equator* (1897) Mark Twain quotes from Buckle's description of the *Sudra* (laborer) and his humble station in Indian society. This definition comes from chapter 2 of the first volume of Buckle's *History,* part of his "General Introduction" which was all he lived to complete. Buckle termed the condition of *Sudras* "slavery, abject, eternal slavery" (*History of Civilization in England,* 2 vols. [New York: D. Appleton and Co., 1866]. 2: 56–58).

Buckley, James Monroe (1836–1920). *A History of Methodism in the United States.* 2 vols. New York: Harper & Brothers, 1898.
   Source: MTLAcc, entries #1817 and #1818, volumes donated by Clemens.

Bué, Henri. *Early French Lessons.* Twenty-first edition. London: Dulau & Co., Hachette & Co., 1900. 57 pp.
   Marginalia: none by Clemens. Heavy pencil markings—possibly by Jean or Clara Clemens—on pages 1, 32–33.
   Provenance: sticker on rear pastedown endpaper: Brentano's Booksellers & Stationers, Union Square, New York.
   Location: Mark Twain Papers, Berkeley, California.
   Copy examined: copy belonging to a member of Clemens' family.

"Buffalo gals" (minstrel song).
   While navigating dangerous snags, the river pilot named Stephen calmly whistled "Buffalo gals, can't you come out to-night, can't you come out to-night, can't you come out to-night" (ch. 14, *LonMiss* [1883], pub. previously in "Old Times on the Mississippi" [1875]). In chapter 2 of *TS* (1876) "Jim came skipping out at the gate with a tin pail, and singing "Buffalo gals." "Buffalo Gals" was one of the songs sung by a South Carolina Negro for the boys in chapter 26 of "No. 44, The Mysterious Stranger" (written 1902–1908, *MSM*, pp. 354–355). Since "microbes like sentimental music best," he sang "Buffalo Gals Can't You Come Out To-night" for ten years in "Three Thousand Years Among the Microbes" (written 1905, *WWD?*, p. 462). Mark Twain remembered it as one of the "rudely comic" songs introduced by minstrel troupes of the 1840's (30 November 1906 AD, *MTE,* p. 114).

Buffum, Edward Gould (1820–1867). *Sights and Sensations in France, Germany, and Switzerland.* New York: Harper & Brothers, 1869. 310 pp.
   Source: MTLAcc, entry #1713, volume donated by Clemens.

Bulfinch, Thomas (1796–1867). *The Age of Fable; or, Beauties of Mythology.* Boston: Tilton, 1863. 485 pp.
   Inscription: on flyleaf: "Livia L. Langdon, Jan. 1864," to which Clemens added: "Her father's hand. Noe [?]. Livy was 19 then. She would be 63 now. S. L. C. (1908, Nov. 1)" *(Zeitlin 1951,* p. 2).
   Catalogs: C1951, #D79, erroneously listed as part of a two-volume set; *Zeitlin 1951,* #10, $25, "worn, spine torn, loose."

————. *The Age of Fable.* Boston: Tilton, 1865. 488 pp.
   Marginalia: Clemens noted on the flyleaf: "The feet of the avenging deities are shod with wood. Justice is lame—slow but sure" *(Zeitlin 1951,* p. 6).
   Catalogs: C1951, #D79, erroneously listed as part of a two-volume set; *Zeitlin 1951,* #53, $10, "worn, spine torn."
   On 3 January 1869, Clemens reported later to Livy Langdon, "I lay abed [in Fort Wayne, Indiana] till 1 P.M., & read . . . a most entertaining volume containing the Grecian & other Mythologies in a condensed form—& smoked thousands of cigars, & was excessively happy" (14 January 1869, ALS in MTP).

Bullen, Frank Thomas (1857–1915). *The Cruise of the Cachalot Round the World after Sperm Whales* (pub. London, 1898).
   At a dinner in London on 29 March 1900 Mark Twain was aware he was to meet "Bullen, author of the 'Cruise of the Cachelot' " (NB 43, TS p. 6a). Bullen wrote to Mark Twain on 5 April 1900 (MTP).
   WWD?, p. 100.

————. *The Log of a Sea-Waif: Being Recollections of the First Four Years of My Sea Life*. Second Impression. Illus. London: Smith, Elder & Co., 1899.
Inscription: "To Mark Twain/as the tiniest mark of/grateful recognition of sorrow/lightened, care driven away,/and even health restored by/the sweet and genial influences/of his incomparable books/with the undying love/and gratitude of the/Author/F T Bullen/London March 30/1900."
Location: Mark Twain Library, Redding, Connecticut.
Copy examined: presentation copy to Clemens.

Bunner, Henry Cuyler (1855–1896). *The Midge*. New York: Charles Scribner's Sons, 1886. 235 pp.
"Get 'The Midge' by H C Bunner" (NB 26 [June? 1886], TS p. 9a). In December 1893 Clemens wished to "write Bunner" (NB 33, TS p. 42).

————. *Three Operettas. Music by Oscar Weil. Illustrations by C. D. Weldon and C. J. Taylor*. New York, 1897.
Catalog: A1911, #55, $5.

Bunyan, John (1628–1688) *The Pilgrim's Progress*. London, 1862.
Marginalia: contains a marginal note supposedly in Samuel Clemens' hand: "The natural argument of the sinner" *(Mott 1952)*.
Provenance: Orion Clemens' bookplate, inserted while he was territorial secretary of Nevada.
Catalog: Mott 1952, #39, $30.

————. *The Pilgrim's Progress as Originally Published by John Bunyan, Being a Fac-Simile Reproduction of the First Edition*. London: Elliot Stock, 1875. [Reproduces 1678 edition (part 1) and 1684 edition (part 2).]
Inscription: signed in brown ink on flyleaf: "Saml. L. Clemens/Hartford, 1875."
Marginalia: pencil mark on page 64; pencil marks on pages 70–71; blue ink marks on pages 260–265; no marks in second part (1684 edition). On page 6 of the 1678 text Clemens wrote: "Correct picture of selfishness & baseness." (Howard G. Baetzhold explains that in this passage Pliable leaves Christian alone in the Slough of Despond [*MT&JB*, p. 374].) See Chester L. Davis, "Mark Twain's Personal Marked Copy of John Bunyan's 'Pilgrim's Progress,'" *The Twainian*, 18 (May–June 1959), 1–2.
Catalogs: C1951, #42c; *Hunley 1958,* #24, $15.
Location: Mark Twain Research Foundation, Perry, Missouri.
Copy examined: Clemens' copy.
Alluded to in "The *Quaker City* Holy Land Excursion," II, i (play written 1867). Mentioned among books the *Quaker City* passengers were advised to bring on their journey *(Daily Alta California,* 5 April 1868; *TIA,* p. 303). Mark Twain eventually gave his first book—*Innocents Abroad, or The New Pilgrim's Progress* (1869)—the subtitle he originally considered (in variant form) as his main title; in the text of *Innocents Abroad*, however, he merely alludes to the Slough of Despond in the first part of the book and drops any conscious effort to construct parallels between the two books. He envied Bunyan because "solitary imprisonment" offered him "the *best* of opportunities" for writing (SLC to Mollie Fairbanks, 6 August 1877, *MTMF,* pp. 206–207). In handwriting that closely resembles his script of the 1880's, Mark Twain copied passages from *Pilgrim's Progress* onto eight manuscript pages, which he headed "From The Pilgrim's Progress, by John Bunyan" (DV117, MTP). All of these excerpts describe heaven according to the narrator's vision, replete with white robes, wings, crowns of gold, golden harps, reunions with departed friends, ringing bells, and streets of gold. At the end of these extracts Mark Twain resolved to write an account depicting "Mr. J. G. Elliott's Visit to the New Jerusalem," which presumably evolved into *Captain Stormfield's Visit to Heaven* (1909). Huckleberry Finn's thumbnail summary of *Pilgrim's Progress* has become celebrated: on the Grangerfords' parlor table he discovered the story of "a

man that left his family it didn't say why. . . . The statements was interesting, but tough" (ch. 17, *HF* [1885]). Mark Twain told Howells he "would rather be damned to John Bunyan's heaven" than read James' *The Bostonians* (21 July 1885, *MTHL*, p. 534). Twain showed a close knowledge of Bunyan's work and familiarity with his life (he cites Southey's biography of Bunyan) in a burlesque "cipher" argument that John Milton actually wrote *Pilgrim's Progress;* in the course of his deliberately specious reasoning he suggests an interpretation that seems serious—"The Dream must be read between the lines—then it becomes a grisly & almost Hudibrastic satyre" (NB 27 [September 1887], TS pp. 19–22). Mark Twain had a brainstorm early in October 1887 about promoting a "stereopticon panorama of Bunyan's Pilgrim's Progress" that would provide a travelogue of "twenty interesting cities" and "would clear a fortune" (NB 27, TS pp. 27–28). He listed the title in March 1888 (NB 27, TS p. 61); halfheartedly tried to make a joke about Bunyan in 1892 (NB 32, TS p. 47); wrote a satire on the Brahmin faith suggested by Bunyan in its capitalized landmarks ("Well of Long Life") and its progressive "Great Pilgrimage" (ch. 51, *FE* [1897]); and likened the Hindu gods to Bunyan's Christian, who "went wandering away" (ch. 53, *FE*). In working notes about 44 for "Schoolhouse Hill," probably written in 1898, Mark Twain's character revealed that Bunyan was mistaken in details about heaven ("not so small; & Presbyterians are not so plenty") (*MSM*, p. 440). Twain joked again about Bunyan's advantages as a writer in being shut up in a cell ("Mark Twain Home, an Anti-Imperialist," interview in New York *Herald,* 16 October 1900). He seemed briefly sincere in "About Cities in the Sun" (written 1901[?], DV357, MTP) where he acknowledges what a "wonderful experience" it would be to stand in the New Jerusalem "& hear Shakspeare & Milton & Bunyan read from their noble works" (MS p. 19).
   MT&JB, pp. 264–265.

————. *The Pilgrim's Progress. With a Life of the Author and Bibliographical Notes by Robert Southey [1774–1843].* Illus. by W. Harvey. London: John Hogg, 1881. 402 pp. [Earlier editions by Southey pub. 1830, 1847.]
   Clemens cited *"Southey's Bunyan"* as a source in September 1887 (NB 27, TS p. 22).

————. [*The Pilgrim's Progress.* Chinese.] *The Pilgrim's Progress (in the Canton Vernacular).* Illus. 2 vols. Canton, China, 1870–1871.
   Inscription: on the cover of vol. 1 in Clemens' hand: "Bunyan's Pilgrim's Progress, Part I. Sent from Bangkok Siam by H. R. H. the Rajah of Ambong and Morocco in the Island of Borneo. This prince is a full-blooded Yankee, and was born in Boston. Hartford, March, 1882."
   Catalog: A1911, #56.

————. [*The Pilgrim's Progress.* French and English.]
   Source: in November 1877 James R. Osgood & Company billed Clemens $1.08 for "1 Fr. & Eng. Pilgrim's Progress" purchased on 12 February 1877 (receipt in Scrapbook #10, p. 69, MTP).

————. [*The Pilgrim's Progress.* Hawaiian.] *Ka Hele Malihini Ana mai Keia ao aku a Hikî i kela Ao.* [Trans. by Artemas Bishop (1795–1872).] Honolulu: Mea Paipalapala A Na Misionari, 1842. 418 pp.
   Inscription: in pencil by Clemens on flyleaf: "Sam. L. Clemens/From Rev. S. C. Damon/Honolulu, Hawaii,/March 22/1866." Opposite, on verso of front free endpaper, Clemens wrote in pencil: "Bunyan's Pilgrim's/Progress./To Sammy Moffett,/St Louis,/From his aged Uncle/Sam Clemens".
   Provenance: bookplate of Clifton Waller Barrett.
   Location: Clifton Waller Barrett Collection, Alderman Library, University of Virginia, Charlottesville.
   Copy examined: Clemens' copy.

Burdette Robert Jones (1844–1914). *The Rise and Fall of the Mustache and Other "Hawk-Eyetems."* Burlington, Iowa: Burlington Publishing Co., 1877. 328 pp.

In Notebook 20 (March 1882) Mark Twain noted "Teaching boy about Wash[n] (Reader)—an allusion to a sketch by Burdette entitled "The Artless Prattle of Childhood" *(N&J,* 2: 450). Twain took Burdette's story from pages 102–107 of *Rise and Fall,* shortened it, changed the title to "The Simple Story of G. Washington," and included it in *Mark Twain's Library of Humor* (1888). The narrator of the sketch attempts unsuccessfully to instruct a five-year-old boy about George Washington's tree-chopping incident, but each detail supplied by the adult only adds to the boy's confusion.

Burdette is mentioned in Notebook 18 (1879, *N&J,* 2: 300). His name appeared in 1880 in Mark Twain's list of humorists to be considered for an anthology (NB 19); in 1881 Mark Twain included his name again in a long list of humorists (NB 19, *N&J,* 2: 362, 429). Twain made a note to send a complimentary copy of *The Prince and the Pauper* to " 'Hawkeye' R. J. Burdette" (NB 19, *N&J,* 2: 384); he inscribed and sent a copy of his book to Burdette from Hartford on 20 December 1881 (book now in MTM). He planned to "refer to & quote from" Burdette in a projected "Essay on Humor" (NB 24 [August 1885], TS p. 36). He decreed that *Mark Twain's Library of Humor* "must have . . . Burdette's very latest & best. *Lots* of Burdette," and reminded himself to "get a book fm B'dette" (NB 27 [September 1887, TS p. 16). He sketched a brief compliment to Burdette for inclusion in the proposed preface to *Library of Humor* (NB 27 [1887], TS p. 11). The published version of *Library of Humor* (1888) contained eleven pieces by Burdette—surpassed only by Mark Twain's twenty. Burdette was designated to receive a complimentary copy of *A Connecticut Yankee* (NB 29 [1889], TS p. 13). Twain mentioned Burdette among the "seventy-eight other American humorists" whose vogue passed within forty years (31 July 1906 AD, *MTE,* p. 201).

Walter Blair, "On the Structure of *Tom Sawyer,*" p. 79.

Burgess, Gelett (1866–1951). *Are You a Bromide? or, The Sulphitic Theory Expounded and Exemplified According to the Most Recent Researches into the Psychology of Boredom, Including Many Well-Known Bromidioms Now in Use.* New York: B. W. Huebsch, 1906. 63 pp. Repr. 1907, 1908, 1910.

Catalog: C1951, #J8, edition unspecified, "presented by the author to Jean," listed among the books of Jean and Clara Clemens.

Burgess, W. Starling. *The Eternal Laughter, and Other Poems.* Intro by Julian Hawthorne. Illus. by Edward Lyne and Edmund H. Garrett. Boston: W. B. Clarke Co., 1903. 60 pp.

Source: MTLAcc, entry #632, volume donated by Clemens.

Burgin, George Brown (b. 1856). *Tomalyn's Quest, A Novel.* New York: Harper & Brothers, 1897. 279 pp.

Source: MTLAcc, entry #1527, volume donated by Clemens.

Burke, Edmund (1729–1797). *Articles of Charge of High Crimes and Misdemeanors Against Warren Hastings* (pub. 1786).

Burke, "regarded by many as the greatest orator of all times," is quoted in "Edmund Burke on Croker and Tammany," a speech to the Order of the Acorns, 17 October 1901, later published in *Harper's Weekly,* 19 October 1901 (Box 3, No. 1, MTP). In the speech (reprinted in a shortened version in *MTS [1910]* and more fully in *MTSpk* [pp. 404–413]), Mark Twain refers to "the unsmirched great name of Edmund Burke" and "the mighty shade of Edmund Burke." (See also *MTB,* p. 1145.)

Burke's Peerage. A Genealogical and Heraldic History of the Peerage and Baronetage of the United King. [First compiled in 1826 by John Burke (1787–1848), Irish genealogist.]

"See legend in the Peerage," Clemens wrote beside an account of repartée between Lord Darnley and Lord Henry in Peter Cunningham's edition of *The Letters of Horace Walpole* (vol. 9, page 401, 1866 ed.). "I've been glancing through Burke," says Colonel Sellers (ch. 5, *AC* [1892]).

Burlin, Natalie (Curtis) (1875–1921), ed. *The Indians' Book; An Offering by the American Indians of Indian Lore, Musical and Narrative, to Form a Record of the Songs and Legends of Their Race, Recorded and Edited by Natalie Curtis; Illustrations from Photographs and from Original Drawings by Indians.* New York: Harper and Brothers, 1907. 572 pp.

Catalog: C1951, #10c, $20, signed by Clemens, merely listed as *The Indians Book—made and illustrated by Indians* [*sic*].

Burnand, (Sir) Francis Cowley (1836–1917).

Mark Twain alluded to the satires of "your Mr. Burnand" in "Concerning the American Language" (1882). Burnand edited *Punch* between 1880–1906; he also wrote many burlesques and farces for English audiences.

Burnett, (Mrs.) Frances (Hodgson) (1849–1924). *A Fair Barbarian.* Boston: James R. Osgood and Co., 1881. 258 pp.

Osgood reported sending a copy of this book to Clemens on 2 April 1881, after receiving Clemens' request of 30 March: "Please send me the enclosed dam book. Got the others. Much obliged" *(MTLP,* p. 136).

————. *Little Lord Fauntleroy.* Illus. New York: Charles Scribner's Sons, 1886. 209 pp.

Inscription: in brown ink on flyleaf: "Clara Clemens/Christmas 1886./From Papa."

Location: Mark Twain Library, Redding, Conn. Donated from Clemens' library by Clara Clemens Gabrilowitsch in 1910 (MTLAcc, entry #1925).

Copy examined: Clara Clemens' copy, which perhaps also served as the household copy.

Early in 1881 Mark Twain made a memorandum to send Mrs. Burnett a complimentary copy of *The Prince and the Pauper* (NB 19, *N&J,* 2: 385). In a letter to the Reverend F. V. Christ written on 27 August 1908 he claimed credit for thus providing her with the model for *Little Lord Fauntleroy* (pub. serially 1885–1886 in *St. Nicholas) (MTL,* p. 814). He also alluded to her in Notebook 27 (January 1888) as an author enjoying a fortunate arrangement with her publisher (TS p. 49).

————. *Louisiana.* New York: Charles Scribner's Sons, 1880. 163 pp.

Inscription: on flyleaf: "S. L. Clemens, Hartford, 1880."

Catalog: A1911, #57, $3.75.

————. [Another identical copy.]

Source: MTLAcc, entry #2181, volume donated from Clemens' library by Clara Clemens Gabrilowitsch in 1910.

————. *That Lass O'Lowrie's.* New York: C. Scribner's Sons, 1888. 269 pp.

Source: MTLAcc, entry #2164, volume donated from Clemens' library by Clara Clemens Gabrilowitsch in 1910.

Burney, Frances (Fanny) (1752–1840), later Frances d'Arblay. *Evelina; or, The History of a Young Lady's Entrance into the World*. Collection of British Authors Series. Leipzig: Bernhard Tauchnitz, 1850. 444 pp. [First pub. in 1778.]
    Catalog: C1951, #D1, $8, listed among volumes signed by Clemens.
    Fanny Burney would have been quoted ("where printable") in Mark Twain's proposed appendix to *A Connecticut Yankee* in 1889 (Howard G. Baetzhold, "Course of Composition" [1961], p. 200). Mark Twain later desired to review her works and other "old-time literary mud idols" (NB 33 [1894], TS p. 61).

Burnham, (Mrs.) Clara Louise (Root) (1854–1927). *Next Door*. Boston: Houghton Mifflin Co., 1886. 371 pp.
    Title and author noted in September 1887 (NB 27, TS p. 13).

Burns, Robert (1759–1796).
    General references: a literary critic is a person who assumes "all the genial, warm-hearted jolly Scotch poetry" to be by Burns, quipped Clemens (17 June 1865 *Californian;* quoted in *LAMT*, p. 141). In chapter 37 of *IA* (1869) Mark Twain quotes a bitter remark attributed to Burns' mother ("Ye asked them for bread and they hae gi'en ye a stane"). Mark Twain listed Burns' poetry as one of the "old bad books" on his library bookshelves ("The Walt Whitman Controversy," DV36, MTP, 1880[?]). Twain amused himself in 1895 by inventing rhyming couplets in Burns' Scottish dialect (NB 35, TS pp. 49, 63). In chapter 5 of *FE* (1897) he told of fooling some ship passengers with an invented "Burns" quotation. *MT&JB*, p. 275.

———. "Auld lang syne" (song, pub. 1799).
    Mentioned in Thomas Jefferson Snodgrass' letter of 18 October 1856 *(TJS*, p. 6). Used as the basis for a burlesque in January 1867 (NB 7, *N&J*, 1: 274). Mark Twain composed two burlesque songs—"Miss Slimmens" *(MTTMB*, pp. 63–64) in 1867 and "Ye Equinoctial Storm" *(OPMT*, pp. 8–9) in 1868—that were to be sung to the tune of "Auld Lang Syne." He mentioned the song favorably in 1878 (NB 16, *N&J*, 2: 212) and included it among a list of (presumably) favorite songs in August 1889 (NB 29, TS p. 21).

———. "Ye banks and braes o' Bonnie Doon" (song, 1792).
    "Tunes are good remembrancers," Clemens explained to Livy Langdon on 19 December [1869]. "Almost every one I am familiar with, summons instantly a face when I hear it. It is so with the Marseillaise, with Bonny Doon and a score of others" *(MFMT*, p. 23). He mentioned it favorably in 1878 (NB 16, *N&J*, 2: 212). Clemens remembered this as one of the songs that "tended to regrets for bygone days and vanished joys" ("Villagers of 1840–3," written in 1897, *HH&T*, p. 34). Forty-four repeats the song title in chapter one of "Schoolhouse Hill" (written 1898, *MSM*, p. 179). In "Three Thousand Years Among the Microbes" (written 1905) the cholera germ amused the microbes by singing "Bonny Doon" and "Buffalo Gals" for ten years *(WWD?*, p. 462); after he was married, however, the narrator became sentimental about the song: "Always in the dream I hear distant music—distant and faint, but always sweet, always moving: 'Bonny Doon.' It was Margaret's favorite, therefore it was mine too" *(WWD?*, p. 464). "Bonnie Doon" was one of the airs Clemens requested Isabel Lyon to play on the orchestrelle on 6 and 14 February 1906 (IVL Journal, TS p. 135, MTP; IVL Journal, Humanities Research Center, Univ. of Texas at Austin). Undoubtedly it was one of the "three little Scotch songs" Clemens requested Clara to sing to him on his death bed *(MFMT* p. 290). Albert Bigelow Paine listed it among the songs Clemens liked especially well *(MTB*, p. 1555).

———. "The Campbells are comin' " (Scottish national song).
    One of the tunes Clemens requested Isabel Lyon to play for him on 6 and 14 February 1906 (IVL Journal, TS pp. 132, 135, MTP). He enjoyed this Scotch air in December 1909, Albert Bigelow Paine reported *(MTB*, p. 1555).

————. "Comin' thro' the rye" (song).
"Just as the soprano was in the midst of that touching ballad" (ch. 31 [a chapter written by Charles Dudley Warner], *GA* [1873]).

————. "Flow gently, sweet Afton" (Scottish air).
Clara sang this to Clemens as he lay dying (Holmes, "Mark Twain and Music").

————. "Man Was Made to Mourn" (poem).
Mark Twain informed A. H. H. Dawson on 24 January 1880: "I have the highest appreciation of Burns's genius, & the greatest respect for his memory," even though Mark Twain himself feels that "Man was *not* made to Mourn" (MTP). In Letter #7 Satan quote two lines (*"Man's* inhumanity to man/Makes countless thousands mourn!"*) ("Letters to the Earth," written October-November 1909, *LE*, p. 36; also *WIM?*, p. 434). In 1898 and again in 1904 Clemens mused: "God's inhumanity to man/Makes countless thousands mourn" (NB 42, TS p. 61; NB 47, TS p. 18).

————. *Merry Muses* (collection of bawdy Scottish songs privately printed about 1800 and again in 1827).
Author and title noted in 1879 (NB 18, *N&J*, 2: 335).

————. "My heart is in the highlands" (song).
"That passenger's heart is in the highlands, so to speak," when his mule trods a mountain path (chapter 35 of *TA* [1880]).

————. "Scots, wha hae wi' Wallace bled" (song).
No. 44 mentions this song title in chapter one of "Schoolhouse Hill" (written 1898, *MSM*, p. 179). Mark Twain disparages Mary Baker Eddy's remarks about her descendant's relationship to this Scottish air ("Christian Science" [1907], Book II, chapter 1, *WIM?*, p. 268).

————. "Tam O'Shanter's Ride" (poem).
"The dance that Tam O'Shanter witnessed was slow in comparison to it" (letter from Carson City, 3 February 1863, *MTEnt*, p. 56). "Nothing like it [the French *can-can*] had ever been seen on earth since trembling Tam O'Shanter saw the devil and the witches at their orgies that stormy night in 'Alloways auld haunted kirk' " (ch. 14, *IA* [1869]).

————. "To a Mouse" (poem).
Misquoted humorously in a letter from Clemens to Thomas Bailey Aldrich, 24 March 1874 (Houghton Library, Harvard).

————. *The Works of Robert Burns.* Biographical essay by John Gibson Lockhart (1794–1854). New York: Leavitt & Allen, n.d. 438 pp.
Source: MTLAcc, entry #2122, volume donated from Clemens' library by Clara Clemens Gabrilowitsch in 1910.

Burr, Enoch Fitch (1818–1907). *Ecce Coelum; or, Parish Astronomy. In Six Lectures.* Boston: Noyes, Holmes & Co., [cop. 1867]. 198 pp.
Source: MTLAcc, entry #540, volume donated by Clemens.

Burroughs, John (1837–1921). *Bird and Bough.* Boston: Houghton, Mifflin & Co., 1906. 70 pp.
Source: MTLAcc, entry #2011, volume donated from Clemens' library by Clara Clemens Gabrilowitsch in 1910.

————. *Birds and Bees: Essays.* Intro. by Mary E. Burt. Boston: Houghton, Mifflin & Co., 1887. 88 pp.
  Source: MTLAcc, entry #1940, volume donated from Clemens' library by Clara Clemens Gabrilowitsch in 1910.

————. [Another identical copy.]
  Source: MTLAcc, entry #1941, volume donated from Clemens' library by Clara Clemens Gabrilowitsch in 1910.

————. "Hard Fare," essay collected in *Signs and Seasons* (1886).
  Identified by Sherwood Cummings in "Science" as the article by Burroughs to which Mark Twain alluded in his 1907 Autobiographical Dictation published in *MTE*, pp. 336–337.

————, ed. *Songs of Nature.* New York: McClure, Phillips & Co., 1901. 359 pp.
  Inscription: on front pastedown endpaper: "S. L. Clemens, Riverdale, Jan. 1902."
  Catalog: A1911, #58, $3.50.
  Burroughs is "a heavyweight" who intimates that "he knows more about an animal than the animal knows about itself" (29 May 1907 AD, *MTE*, p. 19); he backs up his assertions merely by his "say-so" (30 May 1907 AD, *MTE*, p. 24).

Burrows, S. M. *The Buried Cities of Ceylon: A Guide Book to Anuradhapura and Polonnarua. With Chapters on Dambulla, Lalawewa, Mihintale, and Sigiri.* Second edition. Colombo [, Ceylon]: A. M. & J. Ferguson, 1894.
  Marginalia: annotation scattered throughout. On page 59 Mark Twain noted in pencil along the margin: "This guide-book is about as mouldy an antiquity as the temples it treats of." On page 62 he adds: "A nobly-padded guide-book. Puts in all the *a & b & c,* with nothing to refer to."
  Catalog: "Retz Appraisal" (1944), p. 5, valued at $10.
  Location: Mark Twain Papers, Berkeley, California.
  Copy examined: Clemens' copy.

Bürstenbinder, Elisabeth (1838–1918), pseud. "E. Werner." *Glück auf! Roman von E. Werner.* Zweite Auflage. 2 vols. Leipzig: Ernst Keil, 1877.
  Catalog: Zeitlin 1951, #49, $3.
  Location: Mark Twain Papers, Berkeley, California. Gift of Jake Zeitlin.
  Copy examined: Clemens' unmarked copies.

————. *Vineta Roman von E. Werner.* 1. Band. Zweite Auflage. Leipzig: Ernst Keil, 1877.
  Catalog: Zeitlin 1951, #50, $2.
  Location: vol. 1 only, Mark Twain Papers, Berkeley, California. Gift of Jake Zeitlin.
  Copy examined: Clemens' unmarked copy of vol. 1.

Burt, Mary Elizabeth (1850–1918). *Literary Landmarks: A Guide to Good Reading for Young People, and Teachers' Assistant.* Illus. Boston: Houghton, Mifflin & Co., 1889. 152 pp.
  Source: MTLAcc, entry #449a, volume donated by Clemens.

————. *Poems That Every Child Should Know; A Selection.* Illus. by Blanche Ostertag. New York: Doubleday, Page, & Co., 1907. 355 pp.
  Source: MTLAcc, entry #481, volume donated by Clemens.

Burton, Nathaniel Judson, comp. *The Christian Hymnal. A Selection of Psalms and Hymns, with Music, for Use in Public Worship*. Hartford, Conn.: Hamersley & Co., 1877 [Jointly compiled by Burton, Joseph Hopkins Twichell, and Edwin Pond Parker.]
> *Inscription:* "S. L. Clemens. From Rev. J. H. Twichell, Munich, Bavaria, Feb. 1879."
> *Catalog: A1911,* #78, $1.25.

————. *Yale Lectures on Preaching and Other Writings*. Ed. by Richard E. Burton. New York: Charles L. Webster & Company, 1888. [Includes a memorial address by the Reverend Joseph H. Twichell.]
> Clemens voted "yes," Charles L. Webster "no" on the idea of publishing Burton's sermons "at half-profits" (SLC to Webster, 30 October 1887, TS in MTP). The book figures prominently in Clemens' notebook of the period (NB 27, TS pp. 31–48).

Burton, Richard Eugene (1861–1940). *Message and Melody; A Book of Verse*. Boston: Lothrop Pub. Co., [cop. 1903]. 186 pp.
> *Inscription:* presented to Mark Twain by the author in April 1903.
> *Provenance:* Mark Twain Library, Redding, Conn. Donated from Clemens' personal library by Clara Clemens Gabrilowitsch in 1910 (MTLAcc, entry #2020).
> *Catalog: Mott 1952,* #40, $4.

Burton, (Sir) Richard Francis. *Mecca and Medina*. 2 vols. Tauchnitz edition.
> *Catalog: C1951,* #D1, $8 ea., listed among the books signed by Clemens.

Burton, William Evans, (1802–1860), comp. *The Cyclopaedia of Wit and Humor; Containing Choice and Characteristic Selections from the Writings of the Most Eminent Humorists of America, Ireland, Scotland, and England*. 2 vols. New York: D. Appleton and Co., 1858. Repr. 1859, 1864, 1866, 1867, 1870 (one vol., 1136 pp.), 1875.
> This became Mark Twain's model for his own *Library of Humor* (1888) after George Gebbie, a Philadelphia subscription publisher, proposed that he assemble an anthology of humorists "similar to Burtons Encyclopaedia" (Gebbie to SLC, 14 July 1880, MTP). Mark Twain wrote "Burton's Cyclopédia D. Appleton, 1858" in Notebook 19 *(N&J,* 2: 361, 364) and followed the entry with a series of suggestions for possible writers who might be included. Eventually he would publish the volume himself. In 1874 Clemens donated a volume titled *Wit and Humor* to the reading room sponsored by the Women's Christian Temperance Union in Fredonia, New York; no record of its author or publisher survives (Jane L. Clemens to SLC, 11 April 1874, ALS in MTP; Fredonia *Censor,* 9 December 1874; records of Darwin R. Barker Library, Fredonia, N.Y.).

[Bury, (Lady) Charlotte Campbell (1775–1861), "Lady Colin Campbell," pseud. "Baroness Staffe."] *The Lady's Dressing-Room (Le cabinet de toilette)*. [Purportedly] trans. from French by Lady Charlotte Campbell. London: Cassell & Co., 1893. 361 pp.
> *Location:* Mark Twain Library, Redding, Conn. Donated by Clemens (MTLAcc, entry #399).
> *Copy examined:* unmarked copy belonging to a member of the Clemens family.

Bury, John Bagnell (1861–1927). *The Student's Roman Empire. A History of the Roman Empire from Its Foundation to the Death of Marcus Aurelius (27 B.C.– 180 A.D.)* Illus. New York: American Book Co., [190?]. 638 pp.
   Inscription: front pastedown endpaper signed in black ink "SL. Clemens/1908". Signature of Tilghman H. Sharp in rear of volume.
   Catalog: A1911, #59, $2.
   Location: collection of Connie Gibbes, Westport, Conn. The volume came into her possession "after the death of a neighbor in Baltimore, Tilghman H. Sharp, a Virginian in his eighties" (Gibbes to Gribben, 25 May 1978).
   Copy examined: photocopy of Clemens' signature.

Busbecq, Ogier Ghislain de (1522–1592). *The Life and Letters of Ogier Ghiselin de Busbecq.* Ed. by Charles Thornton Forster and Francis Henry Blackburne Daniell. 2 vols. London: C. K. Paul & Co., 1881.
   Inscription: one volume is signed "S. L. Clemens, 1888."
   Catalog: A1911, #170, $3.50.

Busch, Moritz (1821–1899). *Bismarck in the Franco-German War 1870–1871.* "Authorized Edition." Two vols. in one. New York: Charles Scribner's Sons, n.d.
   Inscription: in Clemens' hand: "SL. Clemens/Dec. Xmas, 1879./From S. <L.> E. Moffett."
   Marginalia: approximately twenty-five penciled vertical lines and brackets in vol. 1, beginning on page 25; only five markings in vol. 2 between pages 21 and 31. No markings thereafter. Clemens made a few comments in the margins. On page 325 of vol. 1, where Bismarck complains of ill-treatment by the French press and asks, "What can the public be, on whose belief in such stories people can confidently reckon?", Clemens drew a bracket and wrote: "This is a good point."
   Location: Antenne-Dorrance Collection, Rice Lake, Wis.
   Copy examined: Clemens' copy.
   The book is mentioned in a letter from Samuel E. Moffett to Pamela Moffett, 24 December 1879 (MTP). Mark Twain referred to Bismarck in chapter 7 and "Appendix C" of *TA* (1880).

———. *Unser Reichskanzler: Studien zu einem Charakterbilde.* 2 vols. Leipzig: F. W. Grunow, 1884.
   Catalog: A1911, #60, $1.50.

Busch, Wilhelm (1832–1908). *Max und Moritz; eine bubengeschichte in sieben streichen.* München: Verlag von Braun und Schneider, n.d.
   Inscription: front pastedown endpaper: "Jean L. Clemens/Berlin/Jan 2, 1909".
   Location: Mark Twain Library, Redding, Conn.
   Copy examined: Jean Clemens' copy.

———. *Schnunrrdiburr; oder, Die Bienen.*
   Catalog: C1951, #J13, listed among books of Jean and Clara Clemens.

Bushnell, Frances Louisa. *Poems.* New York: Privately printed [at the De Vinne Press], 1900. 81 pp.
   Source: MTLAcc, entry #2015, volume donated from Clemens' library by Clara Clemens Gabrilowitsch in 1910.

Butler, Ellis Parker (1869–1937). *Pigs Is Pigs.* Illus. by Will Crawford. New York: McClure, Phillips & Co., 1906.
   Inscription: presented to Mark Twain by the author, dated April 1906 in Flushing, New York.
   Location: Antenne-Dorrance Collection, Rice Lake, Wis.
   Copy examined: Clemens' unmarked copy.

————. *Pigs Is Pigs*. [Another copy.]
   Catalog: C1951, #78c, presentation copy to Mark Twain from the author, listed among books signed by Mark Twain.

————. "The Reformation of Uncle Billy," *Century Magazine,* 57 (February 1899), 538–541.
   "Say—that fish-liar tale in the Century which arrived this morning is *mighty* well done," Clemens wrote to Richard Watson Gilder from Vienna on 2 February 1899 (PH in MTP). In Butler's story the members of the First Church of a small village who gather in front of a grocery store every day resolve to break seventy-eight-year-old Billy Matison's habit of lying about the fish he never catches. Led by the "deacon," they confront Billy when he returns from fishing and gradually compel him to reduce the weight of the fish he allegedly hooked until he finally agrees that he didn't catch one at all. But (little did they know!) he really did have a bass that weighed "four pound, two ounces" (p. 541). He doesn't tell them about it since they seem intent on "reforming" him, but simply weighs it after they leave. Today Butler's dialect sketch of rural characters seems clumsy and silly.

Butler, Samuel (1612–1680). *Hudibras. With Notes by Rev. Treadway Russel Nash.* Illus. 2 vols. London, 1847.
   Catalog: A1911, #61, $1.50.
   Mark Twain noted that "Butler who wrote 'Hudibras' " is buried in Westminster Abbey in "A Memorable Midnight Experience" (written 1872, *MTB,* p. 469). "Ida—Hudibras," Clemens wrote and canceled in Notebook 28 (December 1888), TS p. 37; a few entries farther on he added: "Send 2ᵈ Vol to Ida" (also canceled).

Butler, Samuel (1835–1902). *Life and Habit* (London, 1877).
   Clemens noted the title and author (" 'Life & Habit' by Butler") of this rebuttal of the Darwinian theory (NB 17 [November 1878], *N&J,* 2: 247).

Butler, William Allen (1825–1902). *Nothing to Wear.* Boston: Houghton, Mifflin & Company.
   Mark Twain included "Nothing to Wear" in *Mark Twain's Library of Humor* (1888), and credited the Houghton, Mifflin edition. In "Mental Telegraphy" (pub. 1891) Mark Twain mentioned the dispute over the authorship of "Nothing to Wear," published anonymously in 1857.

Byers, Samuel Hawkins Marshall (1838–1933). *The Happy Isles and Other Poems.* New York: Charles L. Webster & Co., 1891.
   Issued by Clemens' publishing firm.

Bynner, [Harold] Witter (b. 1881). *An Ode to Harvard* (pub. 1907).
   On 25 February 1906 Bynner visited Clemens and "recited a little poem of his own which is to appear shortly in McClure's (IVL Journal, TS p. 138, MTP). Clemens wrote to Bynner on 5 October 1906 from Dublin, New Hampshire to support Bynner's decision to devote himself to poetry: "With your reputation you can have your freedom and yet earn your living" *(MTL,* p. 798). After Isabel Lyon read *An Ode to Harvard,* Clemens "chatted for a few minutes with me about Walter [*sic*] Bynner's verses" on 25 August 1907 (IVL Journal, TS p. 272, MTP). Bynner "sent Clara [Clemens] a copy of my first book, 'An Ode to Harvard,' " and then was chided by Clemens for not addressing it to him (Bynner to Rodman Gilder, December 1938, MTP).

Byron, George Gordon Noël Byron (1788–1824). *Childe Harold's Pilgrimage; A Romaunt.* London: John Murray, 1860. 192 pp.
   Source: MTLAcc, entry #2047, volume donated from Clemens' library by Clara Clemens Gabrilowitsch in 1910.

————. *Childe Harold's Pilgrimage; A Romaunt.* New York: Cassell & Co., 1886. 192 pp.

Source: MTLAcc, entry #973, volume donated by Clemens.

Mark Twain called attention to the fact that he was "the only free white man of mature age" who had written about the Coliseum and its gladiators without alluding to Byron's famous line, "butchered to make a Roman holiday" (*IA* [1869], ch. 27). "All went merry as a marriage bell" ("The Facts in the Case of the Great Beef Contract" [May 1870], *CG*, p. 39). Mark Twain joked about the celebrated phrase regarding the Coliseum (from Canto IV, stanza 141) in March 1892 (NB 31, TS p. 35).

————. "The Destruction of Sennacherib" (poem).

This was one of Clemens' favorite poems; he protested mightily in the columns of the *Californian* in 1865 when he was accused of not knowing the piece (Branch, *LAMT*, p. 142). The misunderstanding arose over a spoof entitled "Answers to Correspondents" (written ca. 1865, collected in *SN&O*), which attributed the poem to Melton Mowbray of Dutch Flat. In a letter published in the Sacramento *Weekly Union* (27 October 1866) Mark Twain alternated lines from "Destruction" and Wolfe's "Burial of Sir John Moore" to create a composite that burlesques both (*LSI*, pp. 199–200; repr. in *OPMT*, p. 54). Mark Twain quoted from "Destruction" and listed its title in Notebook 9 (1867, *N&J*, 1: 424, 438). In an *Alta California* letter (26 January 1868) he wrote that this was the only poem he ever memorized: "I never knew but one poem by heart in my life—it was impressed upon my mind at school by the usual process, a trifle emphasized" (*TIA*, p. 235); but he omitted this passage on the reflections of stars shining on the Sea of Galilee when he revised his *Alta* letters for *Innocents Abroad* (1869). In chapter 21 of *Tom Sawyer* (1876) the Examination Evening recitations at the schoolhouse include the poem beginning "The Assyrian came down like the wolf on the fold,/ And his cohorts were gleaming in purple and gold"; schoolmaster Dobbins listens distractedly to this same declamatory gem in Act III of "Tom Sawyer: A Play" (written 1875–1884, mainly 1884, *HH&T*, p. 303). In November or December 1895 Mark Twain burlesqued the poem by substituting New Zealand names for various words (NB 35, TS p. 63). Clemens used the first verse of "Destruction" for a shorthand exercise that interrupts "Advice to Paine" in 1910 (Washington Univ., Paine 278, PH in MTP).

————. *Don Juan* (pub. 1819–1824).

"Get Don Juan," Clemens noted in Germany in November 1891 (NB 31, TS p. 13).

————. *Poems of Lord Byron, Tastefully Selected.* 2 vols. London, n.d.

Inscription: "Susy Clemens with the love of her Papa. Florence, Xmas, 1892."

Catalog: Lew David Feldman, "American Books" (1955), #173, $50, described as a tiny pocket reprint, vol. 1 only.

————. "The Prisoner of Chillon" (pub. 1816).

"Whose story Byron has told in such moving verse" (ch. 42, *TA* [1880]).

————. *The Select Poetical Works of Lord Byron . . . with a Memoir of the Author.* Boston: Phillips, Sampson, & Co., 1851.

Inscription: in pencil: "A Gift from Henry Clemens/To his Sister M. E. C./ March 1855." Also contains the bookplate of Orion Clemens on front pastedown endpaper.

Location: Humanities Research Center, University of Texas, Austin. Obtained from the Frank C. Willson Collection in 1962.

Copy examined: volume belonging to Mollie Clemens, whom Orion married on 19 December 1854.

Byron's verse contributed to "sentimentality and romance among young folk" during Clemens' childhood in Hannibal ("Villagers of 1840–3," written 1897, *HH&T*, pp. 34–35). "Ardent love poetry, tricked out in affluent imagery" *(Californian,* 17 June 1865; quoted in *LAMT,* p. 141). "The loose but gifted Byron" and his "misspent life" with its "lucid and unintoxicated intervals" ("Political Economy," written ca. 1870, collected in *SN&O).* The crew on the boat in "The Aged Pilot Man" threw overboard "a violin, Lord Byron's works,/a rip-saw and a sow" in an effort to save the vessel (ch. 51, *RI* [1872]). In "The Walt Whitman Controversy" (written 1880?) Mark Twain noted that Byron's works might well be considered indecent, yet he owns them (DV36, MTP). Byron's was one of the spirits conjured up at the Hotchkiss house in "Schoolhouse Hill" (written 1898), but his poetry was "rhymy and jingly . . . for his mind had decayed since he died" *(MSM,* p. 206).
Paul Baender, "Mark Twain and the Byron Scandal," *AL,* 30 (January 1959), 478–482; Baetzhold, *MT&JB,* pp. 280–283.

———. "To Tom Moore" (poem).
Quoted in "About All Kinds of Ships" (1893).

———. *The Two Foscari: An Historical Tragedy* (pub. 1821).
Allusion in chapter 23 of *IA* (1869).

———. "The Vision of Judgment" (satirical poem, pub. 1822).
Described in a burlesque letter from Byron in the Under-World to Mark Twain (Paine 260, MTP).

———. *The Works of Lord Byron, in Verse and Prose. Including His Letters, Journals, Etc.* New York: Leavitt & Allen, 1863. 627 pp.
Source: MTLAcc, entry #2123, volume donated from Clemens' library by Clara Clemens Gabrilowitsch in 1910.

———. "Written After Swimming from Sestos to Abydos" (poem).
Allusion in chapter 33 of *IA* (1869).

Byron, Henry James (1834–1884). *Jack the Giant Killer; or, Harlequin King Arthur and Ye Knights of Ye Round Table* (extravaganza, prod. London, 1859).
Clemens probably saw R. G. Marsh's Juvenile Comedians perform this nursery-tale burlesque in Carson City in January 1864 (Franklin R. Rogers, *MTBP,* p. 105).

———. *Mazeppa! A Burlesque Extravaganza in One Act* (prod. London, 1859).
In San Francisco Mark Twain went to see Adah Isaacs Menken ("that manly young female") in this role, and wrote a lengthy, sarcastic review (13 September 1863 letter, *MTEnt,* pp. 78–80).

Cabell, James Branch. *Chivalry* (pub. 1909).
Paine noted that Clemens read *Chivalry* in November 1909 "with great enjoyment"; he admired "the subtle poetic art with which Cabell has flung the light of romance about dark and sordid chapters of history" *(MTB,* p. 1535).

———. *Gallantry.* New York: Harper & Brothers, 1907.
Location: Antenne-Dorrance Collection, Rice Lake, Wis.
Copy examined: almost certainly Clemens' copy, unmarked.

————. *The Line of Love.* New York: Harper & Brothers, 1905.
Inscription: on the front pastedown endpaper: "S. L. Clemens, Oct. 1905."
Location: collection of Professor Bigelow Paine Cushman, Department of English, Western Connecticut State College, Danbury, Conn.
Copy examined: none; information supplied by Professor Cushman.

Clemens praised *The Line of Love* in a letter to Frederick A. Duneka of Harper & Brothers on 9 October 1905. It was "the charmingest book I have read in a long time"; even the archaic speech, to which he often objected, "allures & bewitches, the art of it is so perfect" (Harper & Row).

Cable, George Washington (1844–1925). *The Cavalier* (pub. 1901).
"Your book came three days ago. . . . I finished reading the story night before last. From start to finish it kept me electrically a-tingle with its rush & go, & charmed with its brilliances of phrasing & its other manifold fascinations" (SLC to Cable, Riverdale, 15 October 1901, *TG,* p. 111).

————. *Dr. Sevier* (pub. 1884).
Mark Twain heard Cable read selections from this book—generally "Mary's Night Ride"—on their 1884-1885 lecture tour (NB 23, TS pp. 15, 40; Cardwell, *TG,* p. 12). Cable also read the parts called "Kate and Ristofolo," "Narcisse in Mourning," and "Richling's Visit to Kate." Twain praised Cable's reading of French dialects on this tour in chapter 47 of *Life on the Mississippi* (1883).

————. *The Grandissimes. A Story of Creole Life.* New York: Charles Scribner's Sons, 1882.
Inscription: on half-title page: "To S. L. Clemens. Yours truly, G. W. Cable. Hartford, Apl 4, 1883".
Marginalia: on page 111 in margin, written in black ink: "Same old device." No other markings.
Location: Carrie Estelle Doheny Collection, St. John's Seminary, Camarillo. Donated by Mrs. Doheny in 1940 after its purchase from Maxwell Hunley in 1940 for $12.20.
Copy examined: Clemens' copy.

————. *The Grandissimes. A Story of Creole Life.*
Catalog: C1951, #98c, $35, edition not supplied, listed among books signed by Clemens.

Howells wrote to Cable that he and Clemens were so impressed with *The Grandissimes* that they "went about talking Creole all day" (Kjell Ekström, "The Cable-Howells Correspondence," *Studia Neophilologica,* 22 [1949–1950], 53, cited in *TG,* p. 123 n. 125). On 2 May 1882 Clemens informed Livy from New Orleans that Cable had read to neighborhood children "from the Grandissimes & sketches" (*LLMT,* p. 212); in chapter 44 of *LonMiss* (1883) Mark Twain referred to "the South's finest literary genius, the author of 'The Grandissimes.'" *Mark Twain's Library of Humor* (1888) contained "Frowenfeld's Clerk" from *The Grandissimes.*

————. *Madame Delphine.* New York: Charles Scribner's Sons, 1881.
Inscription: on half-title page: "To S. L. Clemens/Yours truly G. W. Cable, Hartford, April 4, 1883."
Catalogs: "The Fine Library of the Late Ingle Barr," Parke-Bernet, Los Angeles, Sale No. 68, 18–19 February 1973, item #82; purchased by Seven Gables Bookshop, New York City, for $190.
Location: Mark Twain Memorial, Hartford, Connecticut. Given by an anonymous donor in 1973 (*Mark Twain Memorial Newsletter,* 7 [August 1973], 5).
Copy examined: none; information supplied by auction catalogs and the report of Warren Howell of San Francisco at the time the volume was sold in 1973.

Clemens may have received another copy of *Madame Delphine* from Cable in 1881, or Cable may have autographed a volume he sent earlier when he visited the Clemens household in April 1883. At any rate, Clemens seems to refer to *Madame Delphine* in a letter of 17 July 1881 to Cable: "The book has come; I read it last night, & the charm of it, & the pain of it, & the deep music of it are still pulsing through me" (*TG,* p. 81).

————. *Old Creole Days.* New York: Charles Scribner's Sons, [cop. 1879].
Inscription: on half-title page: "To S. L. Clemens from G. W. Cable/Apl 4, 1883—Hartford."
Location: Carrie Estelle Doheny Collection, St. John's Seminary, Camarillo, California. Donated by Mrs. Doheny in 1940 following its purchase from Maxwell Hunley Rare Books of Beverly Hills for $12.20.
Copy examined: Clemens' copy.
References: William Dean Howells wrote: "I remember especially his raptures with Mr. Cable's *Old Creole Days,* and the thrilling force with which he gave the forbidding of the leper's brother . . . 'Strit must not pass!' " *(MMT* [1910], pp. 99–100). Clemens referred to " 'Posson Jone,' " one of the stories collected in *Old Creole Days,* when he wrote about a lecture-reading Cable gave in 1883: "He got out his Parson Jones, & by George he just simply carried the house by storm" (SLC to "My Dear Waring," 6 April 1883, CWB; same compliment repeated in another letter of same date to Frances A. Cox, TS in MTP).

————. *Old Creole Days. Part I. Madame Delphine. Café des Exiles. Belles Demoiselles Plantation.* New York: Charles Scribner's Sons, 1883.
Inscription: on half-title page: "To Mrs. Saml. L. Clemens from G. W. Cable/ Hartford, Nov. 20, 1883."
Location: Carrie Estelle Doheny Collection, St. John's Seminary, Camarillo, California. Donated in 1940 after its purchase from Maxwell Hunley Rare Books of Beverly Hills for $12.20.
Copy examined: Livy Clemens' copy.

————. *Old Creole Days, Pt. II.* New York: C. Scribner's Sons, 1883. 155 pp.
Source: MTLAcc, entry #2192, volume donated by Clara Clemens Gabrilowitsch in 1910.

————. *Strange True Stories of Louisiana* (pub. 1889).
Cable wrote to Clemens from Northampton, Massachusetts on 6 January 1890: "I have asked my publishers . . . to send you a copy of my Strange True Stories of Louisiana" *(TG,* p. 110).

Cabot, James Elliot. *A Memoir of Ralph Waldo Emerson.* 2 vols. Boston: Houghton, Mifflin & Co., 1887.
Livy Clemens informed Grace King on 7 August 1888: "I am just now reading the new Life of Emerson by Cabot. . . . I enjoy it exceedingly, but I don't think I like Emerson as well as I did before reading it. He seems so very cold, so removed from the passions and struggles of other men" (Louisiana State Univ., Baton Rouge).

Caddy, (Mr.) F. *Footsteps of Joan of Arc.* London: Hurst.
Included in a six-book bibliography on Joan of Arc prepared for Mark Twain in 1892 by Chatto & Windus (Box 36, no. 6, PH in MTP).

Caesar, Gaius Julius. *Caesar's Commentaries on the Gallic and Civil Wars. Literally Translated.* New York, 1885.
Inscription: on flyleaf: "S. L. Clemens, Hartford, 1885. Presented by President Smith, of Trinity College." The Reverend George Williamson Smith was president of Trinity College, according to *Geer's Hartford City Directory, 1886.*
Catalog: A1911, #62, $6.
U. S. Grant's *Memoirs* had only one equal, in Clemens' opinion: "Caesar's Commentaries (on the Gallic War & the Civil War)" (NB 24 [June 1885], TS p. 25). "By chance, I had been comparing the [Grant] memoirs with Ceasar's 'Commentaries.' . . . The same high merits distinguished both books—clarity of statement, directness, simplicity, unpretentiousness, manifest truthfulness, fairness and justice toward friend and foe alike, soldierly candor and frankness, and soldierly avoidance of flowery speech" (1 June 1906 AD, *MTE,* p. 183).

Caine, Hall. *The Eternal City*. New York: D. Appleton and Co., 1901.
Inscription: on front free endpaper: "George Melville Lincoln/January 28th 1902".
Location: Mark Twain Library, Redding, Connecticut.
Copy examined: possibly Clemens' copy; in 1970 it was shelved beside his books in the Mark Twain Library. A doubtful item.

————. *The Manxman, A Novel*. New York: D. Appleton and Co., 1895.
Inscriptions: library bookplate of James B. Pond on front pastedown endpaper; inscribed on flyleaf: "To/Major James B. Pond,/With the author's/very cordial greetings, Hall Caine/New York/New York/7 Nov/95." Pond explained on the second flyleaf: "This volume was the traveling companion of The Mark Twain Troup which left Cleveland July 16, 1895—& sailed on board the S. S. Warrimoo, at Victoria, B.C. Aug. 23, 1895 where the party separated. . . . This book was read on that journey by Mr. & Mrs. Clemens, Miss Clara Clemens, & Mrs. J. B. Pond,—& later by Major Pond himself—about the time it was submitted for the author's signature. J. B. Pond."
Marginalia: on back flyleaf are memorandums of food expenses on the trip, penciled by Livy Clemens; these are dated 17–23 July 1895.
Location: Mark Twain Memorial, Hartford, Connecticut. Gift of Professor Norman Holmes Pearson of Yale in 1965.
Copy examined: James B. Pond's copy, read by Clemens.

Cairnes, John Elliott (1823–1875). *The Character and Logical Method of Political Economy*. [Second ed.] New York: Harper & Brothers, n.d. 235 pp. [Preface dated 1875.]
Source: MTLAcc, entry #669, volume donated by Clemens.

Caldwell, George W. *Oriental Rambles*. Poughkeepsie, New York: George W. Caldwell, [cop. 1906].
Inscription: on front free endpaper: "To the Genial philosopher 'Mark Twain'/ with the compliments of the constructor/George W. Caldwell/Nov. 20, 1906."
Location: Mark Twain Library, Redding, Conn.
Copy examined: Clemens" unmarked copy. Some leaves unopened.

Cameron, Margaret (1867–1947). *The Cat and the Canary*. Illus. by W. D. Stevens. New York: Harper & Brothers, 1908. 62 pp.
Source: MTLAcc, entry #454, volume donated by Clemens.

————. *The Involuntary Chaperon*. Illus. New York: Harper & Brothers, 1909. 348 pp.
Source: MTLAcc, entry #1480, volume donated by Clemens.

Cameron, Verney Lovett. *Across Africa*. 2 vols. Tauchnitz Edition. [Originally pub. 1877.]
Catalog: C1951, #D1, $8 ea. vol., listed among books signed by Clemens.

Campan, Jeanne Louise Henriette (Genet).
Mémoires sur la Vie Privée de Marie Antoinette (pub. 1822).
Mark Twain intended to mention this book (or the English translation) in his proposed appendix to *CY* (1889) "in support of the assertion that there were not real ladies and gentlemen before our century" (Howard G. Baetzhold, "Course of Composition" [1961], p. 200). The one-page MS of Mark Twain's appendix is now in the Berg Collection, NYPL.

Campbell, (Sir) John Logan. *Poenamo; Sketches of the Early Days of New Zealand. Romance and Reality of Antipodean Life in the Infancy of a New Colony.* London: Williams & Norgate, 1881.

Inscription: "To Mrs Clemens/POENAMO is presented by the author/Eugene [*sic*] Campbell./Kilbeyee, Auckland 25–11–95".

Marginalia: note by Campbell requesting Livy Clemens to invite Clemens to visit his verandah for a smoke; on the last page is a brief note, presumably by Livy Clemens, about Ragitoto, a mountain near Auckland (p. 360).

Catalog: C1951, #011, erroneously listed with books containing Livy Clemens' signature.

Location: Mark Twain Memorial, Hartford, Conn. Obtained from Maxwell Hunley Rare Books of Beverly Hills; Mr. Hunley purchased it at the 1951 auction and offered it for sale in 1970 at $87.50.

Copy examined: Livy Clemens' copy.

Francis Madigan, "Mark Twain's Passage to India," pp. 355–356.

Campbell, John (1779–1861), First Baron Campbell. *Lives of the Chief Justices of England.* 4 vols. Boston: Estes & Lauriat, 1873.

Inscription: in vol. 2, black ink, on flyleaf: "S. L. Clemens/Hartford/Conn./ Apparently the proof-reader was drunk, all the way through." Vol. 1 signed in black ink, on flyleaf: "S. L. Clemens/1874."

Marginalia: typographical corrections and grammatical notes in Clemens' hand, in black ink, on page 143 of vol. 1 and throughout the four vols.

Catalogs: A1911, #64, sold with eleven other volumes for a total of $8.50; offered for sale in 1963 by John Swingle of Alta California Rare Books, Berkeley, California.

Location: Mark Twain Memorial, Hartford, Conn. Gift of anonymous donor in 1965.

Copies examined: Clemens' copies were not available for inspection in 1970. Information in this entry is compiled from *A1911,* photocopies of Clemens' inscription and marginalia on file in MTP, and a report prepared by Diana Royce, Librarian of the Stowe-Day Library.

————. *Lives of the Lord Chancellors and Keepers of the Great Seal. . . . Edited by John Allan Mallory.* 10 vols. Boston: Estes & Lauriat, 1874.

Inscription: signed on title page of vol. 6: "Saml. L. Clemens Hartford 1874". Vols. 1–5 and 8–10 signed and dated in pencil on flyleaf: "Saml L. Clemens/ Hartford, Oct. 1874."

Marginalia: annotation on pages 148, 163, 165, 183, 200, and 232 of vol. 1, and various pages of the other vols. Mainly these brief notes in pencil and black ink criticize the grammar and overall prose style. "Sad grammar," Clemens penciled on p. 232 of vol. 1, the most extensively corrected volume.

Catalogs: A1911, #64, nine vols. (lacking vol. 6) sold with six other vols. for $8.50 total; nine vols. offered for sale in 1963 by John Swingle of Alta California Rare Books, Berkeley, California. Vol. 6 only listed in *Mott 1952,* #41, $10.

Provenance: vol. 6 contains book stamps of the Mark Twain Library, Redding, Connecticut.

Location: all ten volumes now in Mark Twain Memorial, Hartford, Connecticut. Vol. 6 was the gift of an anonymous donor in 1963; the other nine volumes were donated anonymously in 1965.

Copies examined: Clemens' copies were not available for inspection in 1970; information for this entry was compiled from *A1911, Mott 1952,* a card catalog in MTM, photocopies of marginalia in MTP, and a report prepared by Diana Royce, Librarian of the Stowe-Day Library.

Campbell, Thomas (1777–1844). "Battle of Hohenlinden" (poem, song lyrics).

Four men attempt to recite this poem while drinking aboard a Sacramento steamboat in "On Linden, Etc." (*The Californian,* 7 April 1866; *SSix,* pp. 208–209).

————. "Ye Mariners of England" (war lyric).
Mark Twain quotes from the third stanza in "About All Kinds of Ships" (1893); these booming verses are "the stateliest lines in the literature of the sea."

————. *The Pleasures of Hope* (pub. 1799).
Two lines (339–340) are quoted in *TA* (Author's National Edition, 5:70), reports Henry Pochmann, "The Mind of Mark Twain," p. 149.

Campbell, William Wilfred. "Love Came at Dawn" (poem), collected in *Beyond the Hills of Dream* (pub. 1899).
Reference in 22 January 1907 AD, MTP.

Canfield, (Mrs.) Flavia A. (Camp) (b. 1844). *The Kidnapped Campers; A Story of Out-of-Doors.* Illus. New York: Harper & Brothers, 1908. 312 pp.
Source: MTLAcc, entry #1409, volume donated by Clemens.

Cape Town, South Africa. *Photographic Views of Cape Town, South Africa.* Cape Town, 1896.
Inscription: presented to Mark Twain by the Members of the Owl Club as a memento of his visit to South Africa, dated 13 July 1896.
Catalog: A1911, #18, $6.

"Captain Kidd" (ballad).
"Captain Kydd . . . 'when he sailed, when he sailed' " ("Christian Science" [1970], Book II, chapter 15, *WIM?,* pp. 356, 574).

Cardelli, Cesare. *Nouvelle Methode Pratique de Langue Italienne.* Paris, 1882.
Inscription: Jean Clemens, 169 rue de l'université, Paris, 16 November 1894.
Catalog: Mott 1952, #42, $2.50.

Carleton, Will (1845–1912). *City-Ballads.* New ed. Illus. New York: Harper & Brothers, 1906. 164 pp.
Source: MTLAcc, entry #652, volume donated by Clemens.

————. *City Festivals.* Illus. New York: Harper & Brothers, 1893. 161 pp.
Source: MTLAcc, entry #1686, volume donated by Clemens.

————. *Songs of Two Centuries.* Illus. New York: Harper & Brothers, 1902. 157 pp.
Source: MTLAcc, entry #801, volume donated by Clemens.

————. [Another identical copy.]
Source: MTLAcc, entry #1687, volume donated by Clemens.

Carlisle, George Lister (b. 1852). *Around the World in a Year.* Illus. New York: R. G. Cooke, 1908. 310 pp.
Source: MTLAcc, entry #582, volume donated by Clemens.

Carlyle, (Mrs.) Jane Baillie (Welsh) (1801–1866). *Letters and Memorials of Jane Welsh Carlyle, Prepared for Publication by Thomas Carlyle.* Ed. by James Anthony Froude. 3 vols. London, 1883.
Clemens' letter of 3 November 1884 to a cousin of William Dean Howells (PH in MTP) indicates that he read the *Letters* when they were issued in 1883.

Carlyle, Thomas. *The Correspondence of Thomas Carlyle and Ralph Waldo Emerson 1834–1872.* [Ed. by Charles Eliot Norton.] 2 vols. Boston: James R. Osgood and Co., 1883.
Inscription: flyleaves of both volumes torn out.

Marginalia: a note in pencil at the top of page 61 resembles Clemens' hand: a line is drawn to the name of Andrews Norton in the text and the query posed: "Father of the editor of this book?" [He was.] Pencil marks characteristic of Clemens' marginalia on pages 207, 217–218, 222 of first volume. No marks evident in second volume.

Location: Mark Twain Library, Redding, Connecticut.

Copy examined: I discovered these volumes on the shelves of the circulating collection on 11 September 1970. The marginalia, the publisher, the date of publication, and the fact that their flyleaves have been ripped out convince me that these volumes originally belonged to Clemens.

————. *Critical and Miscellaneous Essays* (pub. 1838).

"Get Carlyle's 'Essays' " (NB 24 [June 1885], TS p. 26).

————. *The French Revolution: A History.* 2 vols. New York: Harper & Brothers, 1856.

Inscriptions: front free endpaper of vol. 1 inscribed in pencil: "Livy Langdon/ Elmira, N. Y." Half-title page of vol. 1 inscribed in black ink "Mrs. SL. Clemens/1870." Both inscriptions are in Clemens' hand; the latter one resembles his signature of the post-1900 period (he added "Mrs." after signing the book).

Marginalia: annotated by Clemens in purple pencil, blue ink, and black ink. On page 13, at "Ye are heard in Heaven," Clemens rejoined: "Yes, after a thousand years. Let us sing praises, for wonderful promptness, O Providential Show-Coach!"

Catalog: C1951, #22a, $25, edition not specified, listed among the books containing notations by Clemens.

Location: vol. 1 only, Mark Twain Memorial, Hartford, Conn. Donated by Mrs. John L. Martin of Darien, Conn.

Copy examined: Olivia Clemens' copy, read by Clemens.

Albert Bigelow Paine reported that Clemens' *French Revolution* was "among the volumes he read oftenest" although "there were not many notes" in his copy. Mark Twain attacked Carlyle for anti-democratic sympathies in a 27 August 1869 Buffalo *Express* column (Baetzhold, *MT&JB,* p. 327 n. 33); believed that he first began reading *French Revolution* in 1871 *(MTL,* 2:490); called it "one of the greatest creations that ever flowed from a pen" (SLC to Mollie Fairbanks, 6 August 1877, *MTMF,* p. 207); catalogued French barbarities from the volume in Paris in 1879 (NB 18, *N&J,* 2: 321–322); read the book in Paris in 1879 because "The Reign of Terror interested him," Paine explained *(MTB,* p. 644); and intended for the book to comprise part of his projected "Royalty & Nobility Exposed" series (NB 26 [May 1887], TS p. 49). "Every time I have read it since [1871], I have read it differently—being influenced . . . by . . . Taine & St. Simon," Clemens wrote to Howells on 22 August 1887 *(MTHL,* p. 595). The Revolution itself was "that immortal benefaction. . . . It was the noblest & the holiest thing & the most precious that ever happened in this earth" (22 September 1889, *MTHL,* p. 613). Mark Twain mentioned the book title in July 1893 (NB 33, TS p. 22); visited Carlyle's home in November 1896 and saw the "one small scrap of the 1st vol of French Revolution left" (NB 39, TS p. 21); and mentioned the French Revolution, depicted mobs, and employed passwords, secret grips, and oaths in "Tom Sawyer's Conspiracy" (written 1897–1900) that suggest Carlyle's book (Walter Blair, *HH&T,* pp. 158, 167). "I have a reverent affection for Carlyle's books, and have read his *Revolution* eight times," Mark Twain wrote seriously in "My First Lie, and How I Got Out of It" (1899). Charlotte Teller recalled that when she was writing her play entitled *Mirabeau* Clemens lent her his own copy of *French Revolution* (1905[?], Teller's preface to privately printed pamphlet, Berg, TS in 1906 Letters file in MTP). On 3 November 1909 Clemens "finished the evening by reading . . . a fine pyrotechnic passage—the gathering at Versailles," Paine reported *(MTB,* p. 1535). Shortly before Clemens died, he supposedly turned again to his copy of *French Revolution* (Hartford *Courant,* 22 April 1910, cited by Baetzhold, *MT&JB,* p. 87); Henry M. Alden repeated the story that when Clemens "was about to die, [he] turned to Carlyle's *French Revolution" (Bookman* [1910], p. 366).

Walter Blair, "French Revolution" (1957), pp. 21–35; *MT&HF,* pp. 117, 310–311; Hamlin Hill and Walter Blair, eds., *The Art of Huckleberry Finn* (1962), pp. 429–444; James D. Williams, "Use of History" (1965), p. 106; *MT&JB,* (1970), pp. 128–160 (esp. pp. 143–148), 343 n. 39.

———. *History of Friedrich II of Prussia, Called Frederick the Great.* Illus. 10 vols. London: Chapman & Hall, [1871].
   Inscription: in vol. 1: "S. L. Clemens, Hartford, Conn."
   Catalog: A1911, #65, $26.
   Edition: A1911 does not supply the date of publication for Clemens' copies, but one citation in Notebook 20 (1882) is correct for the thirty-volume Chapman & Hall edition of Carlyle's works (1871), of which *Frederick the Great* was a part.
   Clemens requested *Frederick the Great* from his own publisher in 1882; W. Rowland of James R. Osgood & Co. replied on 22 July 1882, describing the three editions available—The Library Edition and The People's Edition issued by Chapman & Hall, or the Harper & Brother's edition (MTP); in early autumn Clemens noted that "Fred the Great was a bad speller—& Carlyle can't account for it!" (NB 20, *N&J,* 2: 503). In the Swiss Alps Mark Twain fumed at "Frederick the Great Scoundrel" (NB 31 [September 1891], TS p. 4); in chapter 21 of *AC* (1892) Lord Berkeley reflects that once he himself "was a very Frederick the Great for resolution and staying capacity."

———. *Letters.* [Full title and edition unknown.]
   Isabel Lyon noted that in assisting with Clemens' packing for his departure from Dublin, New Hampshire on 17 October 1905, she "sent back to Library" a one-volume edition of Carlyle's *Letters* (IVL Daily Reminder, Antenne-Dorrance Collection, Rice Lake, Wis.)

———. *Life of John Sterling* (pub. 1851).
   Clemens requested this book from James R. Osgood & Company in 1882; on 22 July 1882 W. Rowland replied in behalf of the firm, describing the three editions of Carlyle's works then available (MTP).

———, ed. *Oliver Cromwell's Letters and Speeches, with Elucidations.* Illus. 5 vols. London: Chapman & Hall, n.d.
   Inscription: in vol. 2: "S. L. Clemens, Hartford, 1883."
   Catalog: A1911, #66, $7.50.
   On 22 July 1882 an employee of James R. Osgood & Company, responding to Clemens' request, described three editions of Carlyle's works which included *Cromwell* (W. Rowland to SLC, MTP). Mark Twain set down the germ for "The Death Disk" (1901) in Notebook 22 (1883) after reading Carlyle's commentary on Letter 90, dated 8 March 1648 (1870 Chapman & Hall ed., 2: 106, 122–123); he also sent a dramatic scene based on the episode to Howells on 20 December 1883, suggesting that they collaborate in writing "a tragedy" *(MTHL,* p. 459 n. 1; the precise source originally discovered by Howard G. Baetzhold). Cromwell's career is recalled by Tom in "Tom Sawyer's Conspiracy," written 1897–1900 *(HH&T,* p. 168). Mark Twain affixed an introductory footnote to "The Death Disk" (1901), acknowledging his source as Carlyle's *Cromwell.* "It takes a Cromwell . . . ten years to raise the standards of English official and commercial morals to a respect-worthy altitude" (30 January 1907 AD, *MTE,* p. 81).

————. *On Heroes, Hero-Worship, and the Heroic in History.* [Collected in Clemens' copy of *Sartor Resartus.*]
In a 1909 Autobiographical Dictation Mark Twain spoke of Henry H. Rogers in terms which evoke Carlyle's book: "Hero worship consists in just that. Our heroes are the men who do things which we recognize with regret and sometimes with a secret shame that we cannot do" (*MTA*, 2: 263–264). A passage in Lecture I, "The Hero as Divinity," proposes a "life is a dream" explanation similar to the one that 44 delivers in "No. 44, The Mysterious Stranger," written 1902–1908 (*MSM*, pp. 403–405): "This World is after all but a show,—a phenomenon or appearance, no real thing. All deep souls see into that,—the Hindoo Mythologist, the German Philosopher,—the Shakespeare, the earnest Thinker wherever he may be: 'We are such stuff as Dreams are made of!' "
UH, pp. 66–67.

————. *Past and Present.* [Collected in Clemens' copy of *Sartor Resartus.*]

————. *Sartor Resartus, Heroes and Hero-Worship, and Past and Present . . . Complete in One Volume.* London: Ward, Locke, and Co., n.d.
Inscription: in light black ink on front free endpaper: "S L Clemens/1888".
Catalogs: A1911, #6, $4.50, place of publication erroneously reported as New York; Lew David Feldman, "House of El Dieff, Inc." (1957), item #987, $17.50.
Location: Humanities Research Center, University of Texas at Austin. Contains *A1911* sale label on front pastedown endpaper.
Copy examined: Clemens' copy.
Henry W. Fisher claimed that Mark Twain coined the imaginary name "Castle Teufelsdröckh" for a noble's residence in Berlin in 1891 (*AMT*, p. 202). In chapter 37 of *FE* (1897) Mark Twain inveighed against European clothes—"a sign of insecurity," he called them, adding that "our clothes are a lie"; later he declared that "the skin of every human being contains a slave. It is the clothes that make the man" (NB 47 [1904], TS pp. 18–19). Despite the fact that he had signed his own copy in 1888, on 8 February 1905 Mark Twain assured David A. Munro, associate editor of the *North American Review,* "I have never read Sartor Resartus," but he then consented to make certain changes in the clothes-philosophy expressed in "The Czar's Soliloquy" (1905) (Berg Collection); Howard G. Baetzhold properly termed Clemens' assertion "inconceivable" (*MT&JB*, p. 234). When "The Czar's Soliloquy" appeared in the March 1905 *NAR,* Twain acknowledged the precedent of Teufelsdröckh near its beginning. Henry W. Fisher claimed that once in London Clemens made up a doggerel poem which went in part: "Life's . . ./A Drama by Teufelsdroeckh [*sic*] (*AMT*, p. 160).
James D. Williams, "Use of History" (1965), p. 106; Howard G. Baetzhold, "Course of Composition" (1961), p. 202.

————. *Sartor Resartus & Lectures on Heroes.* London: Chapman and Hall, 1858.
Inscription: on flyleaf: "Clara Langdon Clemens/Sydney Australia/Sept. 1895".
Marginalia: a few pencil marks, seemingly Clara's.
Location: Mark Twain Library, Redding, Conn.
Copy examined: Clara Clemens' copy.

Carnan d'Ache, Emmanuel Poiré (1859–1909). *Bric à Brac; album par Carnan d'Ache.* Paris: E. Plon, n.d. 52 pp.
Chiefly illustrations—caricatures and cartoons by a French wit and comic artist. Title, author, and publisher noted in December 1893 when Clemens was in New York City (NB 33, TS p. 40).

Carey, Henry. "Sally in our alley" (song, 1715?). Words and melody by Carey. Also known as "Of all the girls that are so smart."
Reference in "Ten Thousand Years Among the Microbes" (written 1905), *WWD?*, p. 462.

Carnegie, Andrew. *James Watt.* New York: Doubleday, Page & Co., 1905. 241 pp.
 Inscription: in pencil on half-title page: "To one I am proud to/call friend/
Mr. Clemen<t>s/Andrew Carnegie/Dec 16th 1905".
 Location: Mark Twain Library, Redding, Conn.
 Copy examined: Clemens' copy.

————. *Triumphant Democracy; or Fifty Years' March of the Republic.* New
York: Charles Scribner's Sons, 1888. 509 pp.
 Inscription: on dedicatory page: "S. L. Clemens, Esq. with regards of his
fellow Republican/Andrew Carnegie."
 Catalog: A1911, #68, $11.
 Location: Humanities Research Center, University of Texas at Austin.
 Copy examined: Clemens' copy.
 On 17 March 1890 Clemens thanked Carnegie for "the books," and added that
Triumphant Democracy was a "favorite" volume that "helped to fire me up" for
writing *CY* (1889). He was rereading the anti-monarchical *Triumphant Democracy* again just then, he said (NYPL).
 James D. Williams, "Use of History" (1965), pp. 106–107; *MT&JB,* pp. 341 n.
19, 342, n. 27.

Cartoons from "Punch." Illus. 4 vols. London: Bradbury, Agnew & Co., 1906.
 Inscriptions: front pastedown endpaper of each volume signed "S. L. Clemens/
1906". Bookplate of William Harris Arnold.
 Catalogs: A1911, #393, $5.50; *Literature List No. 126,* Pt. 2 (1971), Strand
Book Store, New York City, item #4611, $200.
 Location: Mark Twain Memorial, Hartford, Conn. Four vols., donated
anonymously in 1975 through Black Sun Books, New York City. Valued at
$400. (Mrs. Dexter B. Peck supplied this information.)

Cartwright, Peter. *Autobiography of Peter Cartwright, the Backwoods Preacher.*
Ed. by W. P. Strickland. New York, 1857.
 Catalog: A1911, #70, $1.50.

Casanova de Seingalt, Giovanni Jacopo (1725–1798). *Mémoires de Jacques
Casanova de Seingalt, Écrits par lui-même.* 10 vols. Paris: Paulin, Librarie-
Éditeur, 1833–37. [Rebound.]
 Inscriptions: vol. 1 signed in pencil on front free endpaper: "S. L. Clemens/
Paris, July 1879"; vol. 2 signed: "S. L. Clemens/Paris, 1879." Other vols. not
inscribed.
 Marginalia: pencil markings are scattered throughout the volumes: vol. 1
contains vertical lines on pages 98, 282, 284, 380, heavy underlining in first
paragraph of page 107, and notes and markings on pages 255 and 358; vol. 2
has no markings except for Clemens' signature; vol. 3 contains neither a signature nor any marks; vol. 4 has vertical pencil lines on pages 307, 308, 315,
316, 355, 363, 364, 365, 427, 445, and (at the conclusion of the first paragraph
on page 200) a note, "Horrible!"; penciled diagrams are on the recto and verso
of the front free endpaper in vol. 6, together with vertical marks on pages 8
and 15; no markings in volumes 6, 7, or 8; pencil marks on pages 32 and 42
of vol. 9; no markings in vol. 10, but the front free endpaper contains small
holes where Clemens once pinned his pamphlet copy of *The Case of C. O.
Godfrey* (now in MTP).
 Catalog: C1951, #D5, $40.
 Location: University Research Library, University of California at Los Angeles.
 Copies examined: Clemens' copies.
 On 26 February 1880 Clemens explained to his brother Orion that Casanova's
Mémoires "are not printed in English. . . . He frankly, flowingly, & felicitously
tells the dirtiest & vilest & most contemptible things on himself, without ever

suspecting that they are other than things which the reader will admire & applaud" *(MTBus,* pp. 143–144). In "The Walt Whitman Controversy" (1880?) Mark Twain listed the *Mémoires* among the "old bad books" he owns, and quotes a comically expurgated passage from chapter 5 of "that richest of all rich mines" of obscenity (DV36, MTP). Clemens listed "the fifth volume of Casanova" in French among his recent reading in a letter to Edward H. House on 14 January 1884 (CWB). In chapter 35 of *HF* (1885) Tom Sawyer models himself on the "heroes" of this and other books. Hank Morgan referred to the torture of "Louis XV.'s poor awkward enemy" in chapter 18 of *CY* (1889), and cited "the pleasant Casanova" as his source for this allusion to the French fanatic Robert François Damiens, who attempted to assassinate the king in 1757.

Henry Pochmann, "The Mind of Mark Twain," pp. 16, 151.

Case, Frances Powell, pseud. "Frances Powell." *The Prisoner of Ornith Farm.* New York: Charles Scribner's Sons, 1906. 315 pp.

Inscription: " 'He didn't ever have to tell anybody to mind their manners— everybody was always good-mannered where he was. Everybody loved to have him around, too; he was sunshine—'/Mr. Samuel L. Clemens/with sincere admiration—and respect/Frances Powell Case/Flotsam/Wainscott, Long Island/ August, 1906".

Location: Mark Twain Library, Redding, Conn.

Copy examined: Clemens' copy, unmarked.

Casement, [(Sir) Roger David.] *Treatment of Women and Children in the Congo State; What Mr. Casement Saw in 1903.*

King Leopold quotes extensively from this pamphlet, excoriating "that spy, that busy-body" in "King Leopold's Soliloquy" (1905).

The Case of C. O. Godfrey. [Hannibal, Missouri? 1880?]. 11 pp. Tiny, unbound pamphlet.

Inscription: in pencil on front of first leaf: "Both of these 'ladies' are wealthy, & move in the first society of their city. I knew them as little girls. SLC." Below this he added: "The guilt of neither of them is doubted" *(HH&T,* p. 26 n. 4).

Location: Mark Twain Papers, Berkeley, California. Pinholes penetrate all of the leaves where the pamphlet was once attached to the first flyleaf of vol. 10 of *Mémoires de Jacques Casanova de Seingalt.*

Copy examined: Clemens' copy.

The pamphlet presents the proceedings of a trial held by the Congregational church of Hannibal to judge the personal morals of a parishioner, C. O. Godfrey, charged with adultery. His admissions are extremely detailed, though he denied actually having sexual intercourse with the woman, Mrs. M. E. Cruikshank. Mrs. Cruikshank's husband, John, was suspected of an adulterous affair with Mrs. C. P. Heywood.

Caster, Andrew. *Pearl Island.* Illus. by Florence Scovel Shinn. New York: Harper & Brothers, 1903. 267 pp.

Marginalia: Clemens penciled comments and markings throughout the book. On the front free endpaper, vertically: "The conversations in this book are incomparably idiotic." Across top of title page: "Containing many interesting facts plundered from the cyclopedia." Many similarly sneering comments in the margins, for example (bottom of page 63): "Son of a bitch, why don't you pray— —& *say* you are thankful?" On verso of illustration opposite page 259, written vertically: "This person has even stolen material from the French fraud who was exposed in London in 1900." Beside a hint in the concluding paragraph (p. 267) that Caster might relate other adventures in another volume: "If you do, you ought to be flayed & then hanged."

Location: Antenne-Dorrance Collection, Rice Lake, Wis.

Copy examined: Clemens' copy.

————. *Pearl Island*. Illus. by Florence Scovel Shinn. New York: Harper & Brothers, 1903. 267 pp.
>   *Source:* MTLAcc, entry #448, volume donated by Clemens.

Catalogue of Oil Paintings. Illus. Melbourne: Ferguson & Mitchell, 1904. 37 pp. (36 illus.)
>   *Source:* MTLAcc, entry #402, volume donated by Isabel V. Lyon, Clemens' secretary.

Catelin, Camille de (pseud. "Stéphen d'Arve"). *Histoire du Mont Blanc et de la vallée de Chamonix. Ascensions catastrophes célèbres, depuis les premières explorations*. Preface by Francis Wey. 2 vols. in one. Paris: Delagrave, [1878].
>   In chapter 40 of *TA* (1880) Mark Twain quotes from D'Arve's grisly account of the discovery in 1861 of the remains of three mountaineers lost in 1820; they had been frozen in a glacier. Twain mentions Stéphen d'Arve's book by its title in chapter 44, and quotes directly from it in chapter 45 concerning eleven mountain climbers frozen to death in 1870 while descending Mont Blanc.

Cather, Willa Sibert. "The Palatine" (poem), *McClure's Magazine*, 33 (June 1909), 158–159.
>   Clemens praised "The Palatine" in a conversation with Albert Bigelow Paine: "Here is a fine poem, a great poem, I think" *(MTB*, p. 1501). Franklin L. Jensen—"MT's Comments on Books" (1964)—supplies the citation (Paine had reported that the poem appeared in the *Saturday Times Review*).

————. *The Troll Garden*. New York: McClure, Phillips & Co., 1905. [A collection of short stories.]
>   "We sent you a little while ago a copy of 'The Troll Garden' by Miss Willa Sibert Cather. . . . We are venturing to call it to the attention of a few people, like yourself, of discernment and appreciation of the better sort of thing" (John S. Phillips, McClure, Phillips & Co., to SLC, 14 April 1905, MTP).

Catlin, George (1796–1872).
>   Mark Twain's quotes Catlin's *Indian Tribes*, vol. 1, p. 86 in a discarded chapter of *A Tramp Abroad* (1880) which describes courtship and marriage practices among primitive tribes (verso of MS p. 70, Box 6, no. 7, MTP).

Catullus, Gaius Valerius. *The Poems of Catullus and Tibullus, and the Vigil of Venus. A Literal Prose Translation, with Notes, by Walter K. Kelly*. Bohn's Classical Library Series. London: Bohn, 1854.
>   *Inscription:* on title page: "Saml. L. Clemens, Hartford, 1875."
>   *Catalog: A1911*, #71, $4.50.
>   "Catullus" is the name of a cat in a "A Cat-Tale" (written 1880).

Causes célèbres de tous les peuples. Illus. Paris, n.d. [No author or title on first page.]
>   *Marginalia:* list of contents in Clemens' hand.
>   *Catalog: A1911*, #72, $1.25.

Cawood, John. "Hark!" what mean those holy voices" (hymn, 1816). Melody composed by George Jarvis Geer (his only published composition).
>   "We play euchre every night," Clemens wrote to Susan Crane on 31 March 1869 from Hartford, "& sing 'Geer,' which is Livy's favorite, & . . . a dozen other hymns" (MTP). The first verse of Geer's popular hymn is: "Hark! what mean those holy voices,/Sweetly sounding thro' the skies?/Lo, th' angelic host rejoices,/Heav'nly alleluias rise" *(Franklin Square Song Collection, No. 6.*, ed. and comp., J. P. McCaskey [New York: Harper & Brothers, 1889], p. 25).

Cazin, Achille Auguste (1832–1877). *The Phenomena and Laws of Heat.* Trans. and ed. by Elihu Rich. Illus. New York: Scribner, Armstrong & Co., 1872. 265 pp.

 Source: MTLAcc, entry #1987, volume donated from Clemens' library by Clara Clemens Gabrilowitsch in 1910.

Cellini, Benvenuto (1500–1571). *The Life of Benvenuto Cellini, Newly Translated into English.* Trans. by John Addington Symonds (1840–1893). Illus. by F. Laguillermie. 2 vols. London: J. C. Nimmo, 1888.

 In July 1892, aboard the S. S. *Lahn,* Clemens noted: "Symod's [*sic*] Life of Cellini. Nimmo" (NB 32, TS p. 11).

 "Autobiog's? I didn't know there *were* any but old Franklin's & Benvenuto Cellini's" (SLC to WDH, 6 June 1877, *MTHL,* p. 180). "Benvenuto Cellini (what an interesting autobiography is his!)" (NB 17 [October 1878], *N&J,* 2: 227). References in Notebook 17 (1878) duplicate language from explanatory notes in *Memoirs of Benvenuto Cellini,* trans. Thomas Roscoe (London: Henry G. Bohn, 1850), but (later) in October 1878 Clemens made a memorandum to "send to Chatto for . . . Benvenuto" (NB 17, *N&J,* 2: 234). He alluded to "that most entertaining of books, Benvenuto's. It will last as long as his beautiful Perseus" (NB 17 [October 1878], *N&J,* 2: 229), and mentioned Cellini in Notebook 18 (1879), *N&J,* 2: 298. The royal furniture in Tom Canty's new room "is beautiful by designs which wellnigh made it priceless, since they were the work of Benvenuto" (chapter 7 of *P&P* [1882]). Tom Sawyer is astounded that Huck Finn has never read "Benvenuto Chelleeny . . . nor none of them heroes" (chapter 35 of *HF* [1885]). "One believes St. S[imon] & Benvenuto," Clemens observed (NB 26 [1886], TS p. 9). Cellini would have been cited in Mark Twain's proposed appendix to *CY* (Howard G. Baetzhold, "Course of Composition" [1961], p. 200); "Benvenuto Cellini, that rough-hewn saint" (chapter 17 of *CY* [1889]). Cellini's account of Florentine Renaissance life influenced "A Whisper to the Reader," the preface to *PW* (1894), which mentions Giotto's campanile, Dante's awaiting Beatrice, and a Ghibelline outbreak. Cellini was to appear in Mark Twain's projected "Back Number" magazine (NB 33 [January 1894], TS p. 46). In an essay now known as "Memories of a Missouri Farm" (DV274[2], MTP), an early section of Mark Twain's autobiography probably written in 1897, he remarked: "The incident of Benvenuto Cellini and the salamander must be accepted as authentic and trustworthy" *(MTA,* 1: 95). Subsequently he would say: "If Benvenuto Cellini's salamander had been in that place [the Whittier Birthday dinner] he would not have survived to be put into Cellini's autobiography" (11 January 1906 AD, MTP). The salamander incident occurs in chapter one of Cellini's *Autobiography:* when Cellini was five years old, his father, spying a rarely seen salamander emerge from logs in the hearth and seem to enjoy the warmth of the flames, boxed his son's ear so that he would remember the event.

 Henry Pochmann, "Mind of MT," p. 15; Olin H. Moore, "MT and Don Quixote" (1922), pp. 333–335.

Centennial Ode. Illus. [Unidentified. Evidently not Rebecca S. Pollard's *Centennial and Other Poems* (1876), since Clemens signed his copy of her book in 1876.]

 James R. Osgood & Company of Boston billed Clemens $3.20 ($4.20 before his author's discount) for "*Centennial Ode* Ill^d," purchased on 21 January 1877; Clemens paid the bill on 13 November 1877 (Scrapbook #10, p. 69, MTP). See entry for Bayard Taylor's *The National Ode* (1877).

Les Cent Nouvelles Nouvelles (collection of French tales, pub. 1462).

 In "The Walt Whitman Controversy" (1880?) Mark Twain states that he owns a copy of these tales, although their licentiousness surpasses that allowed modern works (DV36, MTP).

The Century Cyclopedia of Names. A Pronouncing and Etymological Dictionary of Names in Geography, Biography, Mythology, History, Etc. Ed. by Benjamin Eli Smith (1857–1913) *et al.* New York: Century Co., 1900. 1085 pp.
   Catalog: A1911, #128, $8.

Century Magazine (pub. 1881–1930).
   Clemens wished to "scrap-book" a story from the April 1891 issue—"Adoration" (NB 30 [April 1891], TS p. 33). Issues were supposed to be mailed to him in Europe (NB 30 [May 1891], TS p. 40). He was disgruntled with an article about a portrait of Columbus (SLC to Mr. Hogue, 14 October 1892, CWB); mentioned an article about Nikola Tesla "in Jan. or Feb. Century" (SLC to OLC, 7 Feb. 1894, partially pub. in *MTL,* p. 609); recommended an article in the February 1894 issue to Susy and Clara Clemens (SLC to OLC, 9 Feb. 1894, *LLMT,* p. 294); complained to F. G. Whitmore that it has been *"many months"* since a *Century* issue has arrived (7 October 1894, CWB); complained to F. G. Whitmore on 6 November 1894 from Paris that the last three numbers of *Century* arrived all at once (MTP); received a subscription by mail while residing in Kaltenleutgeben, Austria (SLC to JHT, 13 Sept. 1898, *MTL,* p. 666); praised several pieces "in the Century which arrived this morning" (SLC to Richard Watson Gilder, Vienna, 2 Feb. 1899, PH in MTP); consulted "the bound Century" at the offices of the Century Company (SLC to R. U. Johnson, postcard, 31 March 1901?, CWB).

Cervantes Saavedra, Miguel de. *Don Quixote.* Illus.
   Catalog: C1951, #4c, $25, edition not indicated, listed among books signed by Clemens.
   On 18 March 1860, in St. Louis, Clemens called *Don Quixote* one of his *"beau ideals"* of fine writing" (SLC to Orion Clemens, *MTL,* p. 45). On 24 October 1867 the countryside in the southern provinces of Spain seemed "precisely as it was when Don Quixote and Sancho Panza were possible characters" (SLC to Jane Lampton Clemens and family, *MTL,* p. 138). On 1 March 1869 from Rochester, New York he seriously advised Livy Langdon not to finish the book until he could censor it for her: "Don Quixote is one of the most exquisite books that was ever written, & to lose it from the world's literature would be as the wresting of a constellation from the symmetry & perfection of the firmament," but "neither it nor Shakespeare are proper books for virgins to read until some hand has culled them of their grossness" *(LLMT,* p. 76). On 6 January 1870 Clemens informed Livy from New York City that he would entrust his copy of *Don Quixote* to Susan Crane's safekeeping until his return: "I hold her strictly responsible for it. And she might as well abuse Livy as abuse that book" (MTP). *Don Quixote* is mentioned in "A Royal Compliment" (September 1870 *Galaxy, CG,* p. 73). Cervantes' writings formed one of the topics of discourse in *1601* (written 1876).
   Cervantes, Clemens noted, had the *"best* of opportunities" for writing a masterpiece—"solitary imprisonment, by compulsion" (SLC to Mollie Fairbanks, 6 August 1877, *MTMF,* pp. 206–207). Simon Wheeler "was another Don Quixotte [sic], and his library of illustrious shams [was] as honored, as valued, and as faithfully studied and believed in as was the Don's" ("Simon Wheeler, Detective," written 1877–1898?, *S&B,* p. 439). Clemens mentioned Don Quixote in 1880 (NB 19, *N&J,* 2: 359). "When DeSoto stood on the banks of the Mississippi . . . 'Don Quixote' was not yet written" (chapter 1, *LonMiss* [1883]); *Don Quixote* "swept the world's admiration for the mediaeval chivalry-silliness out of existence," but Scott's *Ivanhoe* restored it (chapter 46, *LonMiss).* Mark Twain resolved in November 1893 to "speak to Howells" about dramatizing *Don Quixote* (NB 33, TS p. 38). The devil in "Conversation with Satan" (fragment, written 1898) bears the "features of 'Don Quixotte' " (Paine 255, MTP, quoted in *MSM,* p. 17). "We should not have the pleasure of reading 'Don Quixote' if Cervantes had not spent several years in prison," Mark Twain told the Jameson raiders who were incar-

cerated at Pretoria ("MT Home, an Anti-Imperialist," New York *Herald*, 16 October 1900). The cholera germ in "Three Thousand Years among the Microbes" (written 1905) names two of the microbes "Don Quixotte" and "Sancho Panza" (*WWD?*, p. 472). In working notes for "No. 44, The Mysterious Stranger" (written 1902–1908), 44 was supposed to summon "St George from the past, Don Quixotte from the future & *try* to interest a tournament" (*MSM*, p. 464).

Olin H. Moore, "MT and Don Quixote" (1922), pp. 337–339 esp.; Henry Pochmann, "Mind of MT" (1924), pp. 17 n. 3, 152; *MTM&L* (1943), p. 26; *MTMW*, p. 62; *MTC*, p. 118 n. 7; *MT&HF*, p. 349; *UH*, p. 133; *HH&T*, p. 109; Gilman, "Cervantes" (1947); Serrano-Plaja, *"Magic" Realism* (1970).

————. *The Exemplary Novels of Miguel de Cervantes Saavedra: To Which Are Added El Buscapié, or, The Serpent; and La Tia Finginda, or, The Pretended Aunt.* Trans. from Spanish by Walter K. Kelly. London: Henry G. Bohn, 1855.
  Inscription: on half-title page: "Saml. L. Clemens/Hartford, 1875."
  Location: Carrie Estelle Doheny Collection, St. John's Seminary, Camarillo, California. Donated by Mrs. Doheny in 1940 after its purchase from Maxwell Hunley Rare Books, Beverly Hills, for $12.20.
  Copy examined: Clemens' copy.

————. *Galatea, A Pastoral Romance by Miguel de Cervantes Saavedra. Literally Translated by G. W. J. Gyll.* London, 1867.
  Inscription: on title page: "Saml. L. Clemens, Hartford, 1875."
  Catalog: *A1911*, #74, $3.

Chabannes, (Mme. La Comtesse) Armand de. *La Vierge Lorraine, Jeanne d' Arc: son histoire au point de vue de l'héroisme, de la sainteté et du martyre.* Nouvelle Edition. Paris: E. Plon, Nourrit et Cie, 1890. Paperbound volume.
  Marginalia: heavily annotated by Clemens in pencil and brown ink. Excerpts quoted in *TIH*, pp. 175, 178, 178 n. 4 and *IE*, pp. 216–217, 224 n. 2.
  Catalog: "Retz Appraisal" (1944), p. 8, valued at $20.
  Location: Mark Twain Papers, Berkeley, California.
  Copy examined: Clemens' copy.
  Mark Twain listed this book among his "authorities examined" in writing *JA* (1896) on the page preceding the "Translator's Preface."

Chadwick, John White (1840–1904). *George William Curtis, an Address.* Illus. New York: Harper & Brothers, 1893. 76 pp.
  Source: MTLAcc, entry #1208, volume donated by Clemens.

Chaffers, William. *Handbook of Marks and Monograms on Pottery and Porcelain.* [London: Bickers & Son, 1874.]
  Catalog: *C1951*, #012, listed among books containing Livy Clemens' signature.

Chaillé-Long, Charles (1842–1917). *Central Africa: Naked Truths of Naked People. An Account of Expeditions.* Illus. from sketches by the author. New York: Harper & Brothers, 1877. 330 pp.
  Source: MTLAcc, entry #1724, volume donated by Clemens.

Chamber's Journal of Popular Literature, Science, and Arts (periodical, Edinburgh).
  Hamlin Hill ("MT's 'Brace of Brief Lectures on Science' " [1961]) pinpointed the source for paleontological information in Mark Twain's "A Brace of Brief Lectures on Science" (*American Publisher*, September, October 1871). He drew on an anonymous review article of Louis Figuier's *Primitive Man* (1870) entitled "Our Earliest Ancestors" that appeared in *Chamber's Journal*, 7 (13 August 1870), 521–524. Mark Twain's essays satirize the tendency of scientists to

hypothesize from meager evidence about the dates, conditions, and customs of prehistoric man. On 7 July 1871 Clemens wrote to Orion Clemens from Elmira: "Look in the library—any late work on paleontology will furnish the facts. I got mine from an article in Chamber's Edinburgh Journal (have lost it long since)" (TS in MTP).

Chambers, Julius (1850–1920). *The Destiny of Doris; A Travel-Story of Three Continents.* New York: Continental Pub. Co., 1901. 336 pp.
  Source: MTLAcc, entry #2193, volume donated from Clemens' library by Clara Clemens Gabrilowitsch in 1910.

Chambers, Robert (1802–1871). *Vestiges of the Natural History of Creation.* Intro. by Henry Morley. Morley's Universal Library Series. London: George Routledge and Sons, 1887. 286 pp.
  Location: Special Collections, Elihu Burritt Library, Central Connecticut State College, New Britain, Conn.
  Copy examined: photocopy of title page. A card laid in the volume attests: "This is from M.T.'s Lib—flyleaf (probably inscribed) torn out. Some markings & underlining by S.L.C. No marginal notations. HLM". An accession notation on the title page accords with those found in other books that Clemens donated to the Mark Twain Library in Redding, Conn.
  Mark Twain joshingly alludes to *Vestiges of Creation* as the work of T. H. Huxley in his satirical "review" of a non-existent book ("A Book Review," February 1871, *CG*, pp. 122, 156).

Chambers, Robert William (1865–1933). *Cardigan; A Novel.* Illus. New York: Harper & Brothers, 1902. 513 pp.
  Source: MTLAcc, entry #1312, volume donated by Clemens.

————. *The Conspirators, A Romance.* Illus. New York: Harper & Brothers, 1905. 226 pp. Damaged copy.
  Source: MTLAcc, entry #1495, volume donated by Clemens.

————. *The Makers of Moons.* New York: G. P. Putnam's Sons, 1896. 401 pp.
  Source: MTLAcc, entry #1046, volume donated by Clemens.

————. *River-Land, A Story for Children.* Illus. by Elizabeth Shippen Green. New York: Harper & Brothers, 1904. 92 pp.
  Source: MTLAcc, entry #507, volume donated by Clemens.

————. *A Young Man in a Hurry, and Other Short Stories.* Illus. New York: Harper & Brothers, 1904. 284 pp.
  Source: MTLAcc, entry #81, volume donated by Clemens.

————. [Another identical copy.]
  Source: MTLAcc, entry #1272, volume donated by Clemens.

Chamisso, Adelbert von (1781–1838). *Peter Schlemihl's wundersame geschichte.* Nürnberg: J. L. Schrog, 1835.
  Marginalia: underlinings and translations in Clemens' hand.
  Location: unknown. Edgar H. Hemminghaus saw Clemens' copy in the Mark Twain Library at Redding in 1945 ("MT's German Provenience," p. 470); Albert E. Stone included it in his catalog of Clemens' books at the Mark Twain Library, Redding in 1955; but the Mark Twain Library has since listed the volume as "not found," and I was unable to locate it there in 1970. Information for this entry is taken from records in the Mark Twain Library, Redding.

————. *Peter Schlemihl's wundersame geschichte.* Leipzig: Philipp Reclam, n.d. 72 pp.
   Source: MTLAcc, entry #379, volume donated by Clemens.

————. *Peter Schlemihl's wundersame geschichte. Nach des Dichters Tode neu hrsg. von Julius Eduard Hitzig. Mit Anmerkungen und Vocabulair zum Uebersetzen in's Englische von F. Schröer.* Elfte Auflage. Hamburg: J. F. Richter, 1879.
   Inscription: signed in pencil on front free endpaper: "S. L. Clemens/Hartford, Conn."
   Provenance: C1951 auction label on front pastedown endpaper.
   Catalog: Zeitlin 1951, #44, $35.
   Location: Mark Twain Papers, Berkeley, California.
   Copy examined: Clemens' copy, bound with Karl Gustav Nieritz' *Die Wunderpfeife.*

————. *The Shadowless Man; or, The Wonderful History of Peter Schlemihl.* Illus. London, n.d.
   Inscriptions: "S. L. Clemens, Venice, Oct. 1878." Also signed "Olivia L. Clemens."
   Catalog: A1911, #75, $4.75.

Champlin, John D., Jr. *Young Folks' Cyclopaedia of Common Things.* Illus. New York: Henry Holt & Co., 1879.
   Clemens purchased "1 Cyclo. Common Things" at author's discount on 20 December 1880, according to a bill from Brown & Gross, Hartford booksellers (receipt dated 1 January 1881, MTP).

————. *Young Folks' Cyclopaedia of Persons and Places.* Illus. New York: Henry Holt & Co., [1880].
   A bill from Brown & Gross, Hartford booksellers, records Clemens' purchase at author's discount of "1 Cyclo. Persons & Places" on 20 December 1880 (receipt dated 1 January 1881, MTP).

Champney, (Mrs.) Elizabeth (Williams) (1850–1922). *All Around a Palette.* Illus. by J. Wells Champney. Boston: Lockwood, Brooks, and Co., 1878. 314 pp.
   Source: MTLAcc, entry #449b, volume donated by Clemens.

————. *In the Sky-Garden.* Illus. by J. Wells Champney. Boston: Lockwood, Brooks, & Co., 1887. 211 pp.
   Source: MTLAcc, entry #1919, volume donated from Clemens' library by Clara Clemens Gabrilowitsch in 1910.

Chaney, George Leonard. *"Alo'ha": A Hawaiian Salutation.* Boston: Roberts Brothers, 1880 [cop. 1879].
   Reference: Clemens listed the author, title, publisher, and (illegible) publication date on the back of his copy of Jarves' *History of the Hawaiian or Sandwich Islands (N&J,* 1: 105).

Channing, W[illiam] E[llery]. *Letter on Slavery to J. G. Birney.* Boston, 1837.
   [Bound with five other anti-slavery pamphlets of 1830's by various authors.]
   Marginalia: "writing on title [page]" *(A1911).*
   Catalog: A1911, #76, $2 total.

Chapin, Anna Alice (1880–1920). *Wotan, Siegfried, and Brünnhilde.* New York: Harper & Brothers, 1899. 133 pp.
   Source: MTLAcc, entry #1683, volume donated by Clemens.

Chapin, Willis O. *The Masters and Masterpieces of Engraving.* Sixty engravings and
heliogravures. New York, 1894.
    Catalog: A1911, #157, $8.

Chapman, Edwin O., ed. *Home Book of Poetry.* New York: Worthington Co.,
1890. 399 pp.
    Source: MTLAcc, entry #617, volume donated by Albert Bigelow Paine,
Clemens' designated biographer. Possibly Clemens saw this book, since the men
exchanged reading materials.

Chapman, Frank Michler (1864–1945). *Handbook of Birds of Eastern North
America.* Illus. New York: D. Appleton & Co., 1903. 431 pp.
    Inscription: in Clemens' hand on front pastedown endpaper: "To Jean Clemens/
with her Father's love/Sept. 1903". Someone (possibly Clemens himself) traced
a photograph (ca. 1902) of Clemens onto onionskin paper with black ink and
glued it to the first flyleaf of the book.
    Location: Mark Twain Library, Redding, Connecticut.
    Copy examined: Jean Clemens' copy. Donated from Clemens' library by
Clara Clemens Gabrilowitsch in 1910 (MTLAcc, entry #1943).

————. *The Warblers of North America.* New York: D. Appleton & Co., 1907.
306 pp.
    Inscription: on front free endpaper in Jean Clemens' hand: "Jean L. Clemens/
August 1907".
    Location: Mark Twain Library, Redding, Conn. Donated from Clemens'
library by Clara Clemens Gabrilowitsch in 1910 (MTLAcc, entry #1942).
    Copy examined: Jean Clemens' copy.

[Chapple, Joseph Mitchell (b. 1867), comp.] *Heart Throbs in Prose and Verse Dear
to the American People.* 2 vols. Boston: Chapple Publishing Co., [cop. 1905,
1911].
    Source: MTLAcc, entry #630, volume 1 only (published 1905, 416 pages)
donated by Clemens.

Charles, (Mrs.) Elizabeth (Rundle) (1828–1896). *Diary of Mrs. Kitty Trevylyan;
A Story of the Times of Whitefield and the Wesleys.* New York: M. W. Dodd,
1864. 436 pp.
    Source: MTLAcc, entry #1851, volume donated from Clemens' library by
Clara Clemens Gabrilowitsch in 1910.

————. *Schönberg-Cotta Family.* New York: M. W. Dodd, 1864. 552 pp.
    Source: MTLAcc, entry #1857, volume donated from Clemens' library by
Clara Clemens Gabrilowitsch in 1910.

Chaucer, Geoffrey (d. 1400). *The Canterbury Tales by Geoffrey Chaucer from the
Text and with Notes and Glossary of Thomas Tyrwhitt.* New edition. Illus. by
Edward Corbould. Boston: Lee and Shepard, 1874. 586 pp. [Obsolete letters
are modernized in this edition (the "thorn" is rendered as "th," for example), but
the archaic diction and syntax are not altered.]
    Inscription: Clemens wrote in black ink on the front flyleaf: "For/Livy
Clemens/Dec. 1874,/S.L.C."
    Marginalia: pencil marks and a few notes. Page 33 in "The Knight's Tale" is
turned down; pencil notes in "The Wife of Bath's Prologue" at page 166, with
notes on word meanings; a line in the "Frere's Tale" ("But if it be to hevy or to
hote") on page 193 underlined in pencil and note added by Clemens: "500 yrs
old"; line drawn by Clemens in pencil on page 282 to word *"heronçeaux"* in

textual note, with "I can tell a hawk from a heronshaw—(heronceaux?)—*Hamlet*" added in margin; penciled bracket around lines 916–917 of "The Squire's Tale" on p. 296 ("Therefore behoveth him . . . herd I say"); a few other pencil markings and notes.

  Catalog: C1951, #44c, $25.
  Location: Humanities Research Center, University of Texas at Austin.
  Copy examined: Livy Clemens' copy, annotated by Clemens.
  Chaucer is mainly distinguished by his "broken-English poetry" (*Californian*, 17 June 1865, *LAMT*, p. 142). "Tabard Inn in Southwark" is one of Mark Twain's entries in "Middle Age phrases for a historical story" (DV114, MTP). "Chaucer for Children/Chatto & Windus," Livy Clemens wrote in her notebook for 1878 (MTP); Clemens entered the same title in NB 18 (1879, *N&J*, 2: 335). In chapter 21 of *CY* Hank Morgan and Sandy join a "company of pilgrims [which] resembled Chaucer's in this: that it had in it a sample of about all the upper occupations and professions the country could show, and a corresponding variety of costume"; enroute to the Valley of Holiness these pilgrims told merry tales that would have embarrassed "the best English society twelve centuries later." On 6 and 7 January 1897 Mark Twain amused himself with working notes "for a farce or sketch" (or perhaps "an Operetta") which would employ "pilgrims to Canterbury" accompanied by Chaucer himself (NB39, TS p. 43; NB 40, TS p. 1). "Chaucer's rotten spelling" ("A Simplified Alphabet," written 1899). "Chaucer . . . and a lot of other people who did not know how to spell anyway" (speech at Associated Press dinner, 19 September 1906, *MTSpk*, p. 526). Sandy McWilliams attempts unsuccessfully to communicate "with one Langland and a man by the name of Chaucer" in "Captain Stormfield's Visit to Heaven" (1909) (*RP*, p. 78).

————. *Chaucer for Children; a Golden Key.* Ed. by Mary Eliza (Joy) Haweis (1852–1898). Illus. London: Chatto & Windus, 1877. 112 pp.
  Source: MTLAcc, entry #1219, volume donated by Clemens.

Cheever, Henry Theodore (1814–1897). *The Island World of the Pacific; Being the Personal Narrative and Results of Travel Through the Sandwich or Hawaiian Islands, and Other Parts of Polynesia.* New York: Harper & Brothers, 1851. Reissued 1855, 1856, 1871.
  Mr. Brown excoriates "these mush-and-milk preacher travels," naming "Mr. Cheever's book" (Sacramento *Weekly Union*, 25 August 1866; *LSI*, pp. 151–152).

Cheney (Mrs.) Mary (Bushnell), ed. *Life and Letters of Horace Bushnell.* New York: Harper & Brothers, 1880. 579 pp.
  "Ten pages of Mrs. Cheney's masterly biography of her father—no, five pages of it—contain more meat, more sense, more literature, more brilliancy," than the entire volume of A. V. G. Allen's *Life and Letters of Phillips Brooks* (SLC to Joseph H. Twichell, 28 August 1901, *MTL*, p. 712). Horace Bushnell was the "greatest clergyman that the last century produced" (speech to the Art Students' Association, St. Louis, Missouri, 7 June 1902, *MTLW*, TS in MTP).

Chesebrough, Robert Augustus. *A Reverie and Other Poems.* New York: J. J. Little & Co., 1889.
  "I reckon even Cheseborough's [*sic*] poetry failed to kill him" (SLC to Henry H. Rogers, Paris, 11 November 1894, *MTHHR*, p. 94).

Chesterton, Gilbert Keith (1874–1936). *The Club of Queer Trades.* Illus. New York: Harper & Brothers, 1905. 270 pp.
  Source: MTLAcc, entry #2194, volume donated from Clemens' library by Clara Clemens Gabrilowitsch in 1910.

————. *Orthodoxy.* New York: John Lane Co., 1909. 299 pp.
Source: MTLAcc, entry #2195, volume donated from Clemens' library by Clara Clemens Gabrilowitsch in 1910.

Child, (Mrs.) Lydia Maria. *Anti-slavery Catechism.* Newburyport, 1836. [Bound as a volume with W. E. Channing's *Letter on Slavery,* along with five other pamphlets.]
Catalog: A1911, #76, $2 total.

Child, Theodore (1846–1892). *Delicate Feasting.* New York: Harper & Brothers, n.d. 214 pp. [First pub. 1890.]
Source: MTLAcc, entry #1801, volume donated by Clemens.

————. *Wimples and Crisping-Pins; Being Studies in the Coiffure and Ornaments of Women.* Illus. New York: Harper & Brothers, 1895. 209 pp.
Source: MTLAcc, entry #1358, volume donated by Clemens.

Childs, George William (1829–1894). *Recollections.* Philadelphia: J. B. Lippincott Co., 1890. 404 pp.
Source: MTLAcc, entry #829, volume donated by Clemens.

Chittenden, Hiram Martin (1858–1917). *History of Early Steamboat Navigation on the Missouri River: Life and Adventures of Joseph LaBarge, Pioneer Navigator and Indian Trader, for Fifty Years Identified with the Commerce of the Missouri Valley.* 2 vols. New York: Francis P. Harper, 1903.
Inscription: "To Saml L. Clemens/from/Frederic Remington/1906" on front free endpapers of both volumes (not in Clemens' hand).
Location: Mark Twain Library, Redding, Conn.
Copies examined: Clemens' copies, unmarked.

Chorley, Henry Fothergill (1808–1872). "God, the all-terrible" (hymn). Also called "God, the omnipotent."
In "The War Prayer" (1904–1905) the church congregation "poured out that tremendous invocation—'God, the all-terrible! Thou who ordainest,/Thunder thy clarion and lightning thy sword!' "

Chrestomanos, Konstantinos A. *Tagebuchblätter. I. Folge. II. Auflage, etc.* Wien: Verlag von Moritz Perles, 1889. 285 pp.
Inscription: by Jean Clemens on flyleaf: "To The Black Spider/with the wishes for as peaceful a Christmas as is possible under/the existing circumstances of/her most affectionate/Jean Clemens/Vienna 1898."
Location: Mark Twain Library, Redding, Conn.
Copy examined: Clara Clemens' gift copy.

Christian, Eugene and Mollie (Griswold). *Uncooked Foods and How to Use Them.* New York: Health-Culture Co., [cop. 1904]. 246 pp.
Source: MTLAcc, entry #400a, volume donated by Clemens.

[Christian Science?]. *"C. S. Tracts."* London: George Morrish, n.d. 206 pp.
Source: MTLAcc, entry #926, volume donated by Clemens.

Christian Science Hymnal.
Discussed in Book 2, chapter 7 of "Christian Science" (1907).

The Christian Science Journal. Vol. 13, April 1895–March 1896, nos. 2–12. Septimus J. Hanna, ed. Boston: J. Armstrong. 542 pp. [Bound volume.]
Inscriptions: on front pastedown endpaper in black ink: "SL. Clemens/1903"; on paper cover of first issue, in Isabel Lyon's hand: "Isabel Lyon/from/Mr. Clemens."

Marginalia: profusely annotated in black ink and (predominantly) pencil. Several notes on pages 428–429 establish the fact that Clemens read the volume in 1902 as well as 1903. The front pastedown endpaper is filled with Clemens' record of approximately sixty pages that he has annotated. There are numerous computations of the sales for Mrs. Eddy's *Science and Health* and the growth of her churches and their membership. Clemens' comments on Mrs. Eddy are as caustic as one might expect. A few notes touch upon other topics: above the assertion that while Christian Science occasionally is fatal to its practitioners, "medicine also fails," Clemens penciled: "What Dr. Rice [Clarence C. Rice, Clemens' physician-friend] says/A concession at last—doctors kill, too" (p. 254). At the top of the following page, where Emerson is quoted concerning the "severe morality" of women, Clemens notes: "It may achieve woman's rights".

Location: Henry W. and Albert A. Berg Collection, New York Public Library.

Copy examined: Clemens' copy.

Mark Twain alludes to later issues of *The Christian Science Journal* in "Christian Science" (pub. 1907): in Book 1, chapter 6 he quotes from the October 1898 issue as a chapter epigraph; in chapter 7 he mentions the *Journal;* in Book 2, chapter 2 he quotes from the January 1899 issue *(WIM?,* p. 272); in chapter 5 of Book 2 he quotes from the January 1901 issue *(WIM?,* p. 286); in chapter 7 he quotes from an article in the February 1898 issue *(WIM?,* p. 328); and he quotes a paragraph from the "Editor's Table" of the March 1902 number in chapter 8 of Book 2 *(WIM?,* p. 341).

Robert Peel, *Mary Baker Eddy,* pp. 194–206.

Christian Science. *List of Members of the Mother Church.* 10 February 1903. Boston. [Paperbound volume.]

Inscription: signed on cover: "S. L. Clemens, March 1903."

Catalog: A1911, #79, $1.50.

————. *Official Report of the National Christian Science Association.* Boston: National Christian Science Association, 1890.

Mark Twain quotes from the *Official Report*—citing page numbers—in "Christian Science," Book 2, "Mrs. Eddy in Error."

Christian Union (periodical).

Clemens joked about the propriety of this religious weekly, sending Howells in September or October 1879 a ribald manuscript which he purportedly contemplated submitting to this journal *(MTHL,* p. 271). The Clemenses subscribed to the publication *(MTB,* p. 820); in the mid-June 1885 issue Mark Twain read a letter republished from *Babyhood* entitled "What Ought He to Have Done?" and replied with a letter published in the 16 July 1885 issue of *Christian Union.* See *MTB,* pp. 819–820, 1409; see also *The Twainian* (May 1944), 1–4.

Chronicles of the Crusades; Contemporary Narratives of the Crusade of Richard, Coeur de Lion, by Richard of Devizes [trans. by Dr. John Allen Giles] and Geoffrey de Vinsauf, and of the Crusade of Saint Louis, by Lord John de Joinville [trans. by Col. Johnes Thomas]. [Ed. by Henry G. Bohn.] London: G. Bell and Sons, 1876. 562 pp. [Orig. published in 1848 in Bohn's Antiquarian Library series.]

Inscription: on verso of frontispiece: "S. L. Clemens, Hartford, 1877."

Catalogs: A1911, #80, $2; *L1912,* #8, $5.

James R. Osgood & Company of Boston billed Clemens in November 1877 for "1 Chronicles of Crusaders" [sic] purchased on 24 October 1877 (Scrapbook #10, p. 69, MTP). In December 1884 Mark Twain thought of describing a battle between "Prince de Joinville's Middle Age Crusaders" and "a modern army" equipped with new weaponry (NB 23, TS p. 17). Twain requested De Joinville's *Memoirs of the Crusades* from Chatto & Windus in 1891 while he was in France (NB 31, TS p. 6).

Church, Alfred John (1829–1912). *Two Thousand Years Ago; or, the Adventures of a Roman Boy.* Illus. by Adrian Marie. London: Blackie & Son, 1886. 384 pp.
    Source: MTLAcc, entry #1920, volume donated from Clemens' library by Clara Clemens Gabrilowitsch in 1910.

————. *With the King at Oxford; A Tale of the Great Rebellion.* Illus. New York: Dodd, Mead & Co., n.d. 298 pp.
    Source: MTLAcc, entry #2198, volume donated from Clemens' library by Clara Clemens Gabrilowitsch in 1910.

Church, Daniel Webster. *The Enigma of Life.* (See following entry.)

————. *The Records of a Journey. A Prologue.* Greenfield, Iowa: Berlin Carey Co., (cop. 1888]. 80 pp.
    Source: MTLAcc, entry #641, volume donated by Clemens.
    Church, an attorney in Greenfield, Iowa, wrote to Clemens on 7 May 1892: "When my former book 'The Records of a Journey' was published I sent you a copy of it. And although it probably did not attract your attention I have concluded to try again, and hence send you the succeeding volume 'The Enigma of Life' " (MTP).

Church, Richard William (1815–1890). *Bacon.* English Men of Letters Series. New York: Harper & Brothers, 1902. 214 pp.
    Source: MTLAcc, entry #1750, volume donated by Clemens.

Church, S. H. *Horatio Plodgers; A Story of To-Day.* New York: W. B. Smith & Co., [cop. 1881]. 136 pp.
    Source: MTLAcc, entry #73, volume donated by Clemens.

————. [Another identical copy.]
    Source: MTLAcc, entry #987, volume donated by Clemens.

Churchill, Winston (1871–1947). *Mr. Crewe's Career.* Illus. by Arthur I. Keller. New York: Macmillan Co., 1908. 498 pp.
    Source: MTLAcc, entry #2199, volume donated from Clemens' library by Clara Clemens Gabrilowitsch in 1910.

————. *A Modern Chronicle.* Illus. by J. H. Gardner Soper. New York: Macmillan Co., 1910. 524 pp.
    Source: MTLAcc, entry #2200, volume donated from Clemens' library by Clara Clemens Gabrilowitsch in 1910.

Cicero, Marcus Tillius. *Select Orations.* Trans. C. D. Yonge. New York, 1888.
    Inscription: signed by Clemens.
    Marginalia: a few markings and notes, including: "8:15 'till bedtime read German."
    Catalog: A1911, #81, $1.75.
    De Legibus, 3:15; *Philippics,* 4:4; and *Paradoxa,* 6:3, 49 are literary sources for Mark Twain's "Political Economy" (1870), according to a research paper prepared for Professor Henry Pochmann by Lewis Lawson. In the early 1900's Mark Twain listed Cicero among the "intellectual giants" in "Proposal for Renewal of the Adam Monument Petition" *(FM,* p. 452).

[*The Cid.*] *The Chronicle of the Cid.* Ed. with an intro. and appendix by Richard Markham. Trans. by Robert Southey (1774–1843). Illus. by H. W. McVickar and Alfred Brennan. New York: Dodd, Mead & Co., 1883. 313 pp.
    Catalog: C1951, #84c, specifies Richard Markham's edition, listed among volumes signed by Clemens, $16.

Clark, Charles Heber (1841–1915), pseud. "Max Adeler." *The Fortunate Island and Other Stories.* Boston: Lee & Shepard, 1882. 333 pp.
  Source: MTLAcc, entry #3, volume donated by Clemens.
  "Max Adler" [*sic*] was included in a list of humorists for a projected anthology in July 1880 (NB 19, *N&J,* 2: 361). Mark Twain discussed whether *CY* (1889) borrows from Adeler in the New York *World,* 12 January 1890 (information supplied by Louis J. Budd).
  Walter Blair, "On the Structure of *TS,*" pp. 77–78.

Clark, Francis Edward (1851–1927). *The Mossback Correspondence, Together with Mr. Mossback's Views.* Boston: D. Lothrop & Co., [cop. 1889]. 194 pp.
  Source: MTLAcc, entry #798, volume donated by Clemens.

————. *A New Way Around an Old World.* Illus. New York: Harper & Brothers, 1902. 213 pp.
  Source: MTLAcc, entry #512, volume donated by Clemens.

Clark, Frederick Thickstun (b. 1858). *The Mistress of the Ranch; A Novel.* New York: Harper & Brothers, 1897. 357 pp.
  Source: MTLAcc, entry #1528, volume donated by Clemens.

Clark, Gordon. *The Church of St. Bunco; A Drastic Treatment of a Copyrighted Religion—Un-Christian Non-Science.* New York: The Abbey Press, [1901]. 251 pp.
  Inscription: on flyleaf in pencil by Clemens: "X^n Science/—formerly Quimby Science."
  Catalog: C1951, #62a, $25.
  Marginalia: numerous penciled notes in the first hundred pages, concentrated especially in the passages detailing Mary Baker Eddy's unacknowledged indebtedness to Phineas Parkhurst Quimby. Clemens wrote vertically in the margin of page 96 concerning the genesis of Christian Science religion: "1866 is the date of the theft, not the publication of it. That seems to have happened in 1875."
  Location: Mark Twain Papers, Berkeley, California. Purchased from Maxwell Hunley Rare Books of Beverly Hills for $35 in 1956.
  Copy examined: Clemens' copy.
  In Book II, chapter 15 of "Christian Science" (1907) Mark Twain tried to link Mrs. Eddy's doctrines of mental healing to those advanced earlier by the American healer Phineas Parkhurst Quimby (1802–1866): "If she borrowed the Great Idea, did she carry it away in her head, or in manuscript?" Later he boldly wrote to J. Wylie Smith that Mrs. Eddy's getting hold of Quimby's healing principle "was a tramp stealing a ride on the lightning express" (7 August 1909, MTP). Mark Twain asserted in "The International Lightning Trust" (written 1909) that she merely devised a new name and religion for Quimby's ideas (*FM,* p. 99).

Clark, Imogen. *We Four and Two More.* Illus. New York: T. Y. Crowell & Co., [cop. 1909]. 274 pp.
  Source: MTLAcc, entry #1487, volume donated by Clemens.

Clarke, Albert Gallatin, Jr. *The Arickaree Treasure, and Other Brief Tales of Adventurous Montanicans.* New York: Abbey Press, [cop. 1901]. 232 pp.
  Source: MTLAcc, entry #74, volume donated by Clemens.

Clarke, Edward H. *Sex in Education; or, A Fair Chance for Girls.* Boston, 1873.
  Catalog: A1911, #83, $1.

Clarke, James Freeman (1810–1888). *Memorial and Biographical Sketches.* Boston: Houghton, Osgood and Co., 1878.

Estes & Lauriat of Boston charged Clemens on 14 July 1880 for "1 Memo Sketches $1.25" (receipt in MTP). The book sold for $2 in retail bookstores, but Clemens generally received an author's discount. Subjects: John Albion Andrew, James Freeman, Charles Sumner, Theodore Parker, Samuel Gridley Howe, William Ellery Channing, Walter Channing, Ezra Stiles Gannett, Samuel Joseph May, Susan Dimock, George Keats, Robert J. Breckinridge, George Denison Prentice, Junius Brutus Booth the elder, George Washington, Shakespeare, Jean Jacques Rousseau, William Hull, and others.

————. *Selections from Sermons Preached to the Church of the Disciples.* Boston: J. A. Lowell, n.d. [Small unbound pamphlet of twenty leaves, tied together with purple ribbon. Arranged by seasons, such as: "Spring: Seed Time—Resurrection—Immortality."]

Location: Mark Twain Papers, Berkeley, California. Gathered with other Olivia Clemens association items in DV162.

Copy examined: Livy Clemens' copy.

Clarke, Marcus Andrew Hislop (1846–1881). *For the Term of His Natural Life.* London: Richard Bentley and Son, 1893.

Inscription: by Clara Clemens in black ink at top of "Preface" (page iii): "To/ Kathleen with love/from/Clara L. Clemens/*July 1896.*"

Location: Antenne-Dorrance Collection, Rice Lake, Wis.

Copy examined: gift volume from Clara Clemens, presumably to Katy Leary, the Clemenses' housekeeper.

Clara Clemens recalled attending a play based on Clarke's novel in Melbourne; she and her parents found it "gruesome," but "did not . . . regret" having seen it *(MFMT,* p. 145). Clemens' own notes reveal that they saw the performance in Sydney: "Even when the chain-gang were humorous they were still a most pathetic sight. . . . That old convict life . . . [was] invented in hell & carried out by Xtian devils" (NB 36 [December 1895], TS p. 5). In the original manuscript of *FE* (1897) Mark Twain called *Term* "the book that stands at the head of Australian literature. . . . It reads like a dream of hell," and he quoted at length the scene in which Troke and Burgess, prison officers, flog young Kirkland to death and flog Rus Dawes, another convict, into insane ravings. But the final text of *FE* omitted these passages (Francis Madigan, "MT's Passage to India," pp. 349–351, 356). Mark Twain did mention Clarke passingly but approvingly in a list of Australian writers that appears in chapter 22 of the published version of *FE.*

————. "Introduction" in Adam Lindsay Gordon's *Poems.*

Mark Twain originally quoted a lengthy portion from Clarke's introduction for chapter 9 of *FE* (1897), but later canceled the passage.

Madigan, "MT's Passage to India," pp. 351–353, 358.

————. *Selected Works, Together with a Biography and Monograph of the Deceased Author, Compiled and Edited by Hamilton Mackinnon.* The Austral Edition. Melbourne: Fergusson & Mitchell, 1890. 504 pp.

Marginalia: notes and editorial revisions by Clemens in black ink and pencil throughout Part I, "Australia of the Past." No markings beyond page 169. Clemens edited "The Seizure of the 'Cyprus'" (pp. 112–117) for inclusion in a projected "APPENDIX" to *FE* (1897). "Reads like romance," he observed on page 16 about some details of the story. He also marked for quotation certain passages in "Buckley, the Escaped Convict" (pp. 131–140), and heavily annotated "The South Australian Land Bubble" (pp. 141–148).

Provenance: sold at *C1951* sale, but not listed in catalog.

Location: Mark Twain Papers, Berkeley, California. Gift of the General Library, U.C.L.A.

Copy examined: Clemens' copy.

Mark Twain mentioned Clarke's works repeatedly in newspaper interviews during his global tour: see the Melbourne *Age,* 27 September 1895, p. 6, for instance (information provided by Louis J. Budd). In September 1895 Clemens noted "Collected Works of Marcus Clark" [*sic*] (NB 35, TS p. 53); regarding the penal colonies in early Australia, Mark Twain wrote on 2 November 1895: "Gentleman said Marcus Clark exaggerated. . . . But that won't do" (NB 34, TS p. 25); on 11 January 1896 he apparently referred to an edition of Clarke's *Works:* "See that trial in Vol III 300 lashes one day, *500* the next. The man died" (NB 37, TS p. 8).

Dennis Welland, "MT's Last Travel Book," pp. 45–46.

Clarke, (Mrs.) Mary Victoria Cowden-(1809–1898). *The Complete Concordance to Shakespeare.* Boston, 1875.
Inscription: on flyleaf in pencil: "S. L. Clemens, Hartford 1876."
Catalog: Mott 1952, #43, $12.50.

Clarke, Rebecca Sophia (1833–1906) (pseud. "Sophie May"). *Janet, A Poor Heiress.* Boston, 1882.
Inscription: "From Mamma. Xmas 1890."
Catalog: Mott 1952, #44, $2.50.

————. *Quinnebasset Girls.* Illus. Boston: Lee and Shepard, 1877. 336 pp.
Inscription: (on flyleaf) "From Aunt Carrie/Xmas 1889."
Location: Mark Twain Library, Redding, Conn.
Copy examined: copy belonging to one of Clemens' daughters.

Clarke, Samuel (1599–1863). *A Mirror or Looking-Glass Both for Saints & Sinners.* London: R. Gaywood, 1671.
Marginalia: Clemens marked certain passages and made a number of notes. On page 82, in reference to Saturus, who said he was resolved to forsake wife, children, house, and possessions for the love of Christ, Clemens wrote "Atrocious Scoundrel." He agreed with the opinion of Laelius Socinus that a man may be saved without the knowledge of the Scriptures: "Sensible, again" (p. 276). At a description of the power in prayer demonstrated by Fulgentius, who was able to keep his own city in safety when the rest of the province was captured by the Moors, Clemens commented: "They ought to have hired him to travel around" (p. 462). Farther down the same page, to an assertion concerning the ability of the Church, by fervent and frequent prayer, to restore a prominent person to health, Clemens noted: "It failed in Gen. Garfield's case." (President Garfield died on 19 September 1881.)
Catalog: A1911, #84, $10; Scribner's, New York City (1956), $85.
Location: collection of D. M. McKeithan, Austin, Texas.
Copy examined: Clemens' copy.
Paul Baender, *WIM?,* p. 3 n. 7.

Clarke, Samuel (1684–1750). *Promises of Scripture.* New York: American Tract Society, n.d. 348 pp.
Source: MTLAcc, entry #2315, volume donated from Clemens' library by Clara Clemens Gabrilowitsch in 1910.

Clay, Henry (1777–1852). *Speeches.*
Reference: Huck Finn noted that Henry Clay's *Speeches* was one of the volumes on the parlor table at the Grangerford house *(HF* [1885], chapter 17).

Cleland, John (1709–1789). *Fanny Hill: Memoirs of a Woman of Pleasure* (pub. in 2 vols. 1748–1749).

"I have labored hard to get a copy of 'Fannie Hill' [*sic*] for him [unidentified "old man"] to read, but I have failed sadly" (SLC to William H. Clagget, Carson City, 8 March 1862, CWB). "The Earl's [Jesse Leathers'] literary excrement charmed me like Fanny Hill. I just wallowed in it" (SLC to James R. Osgood, Hartford, 30 March 1881, *MTLP*, p. 136).

Clemens, Will M. *Mark Twain, His Life and Work* (pub. 1892).

On 11 June 1900 Mark Twain warned the Bowen-Merrill Company of New York not to issue another volume by Will M. Clemens, *The Mark Twain Story Book* (NB 43, TS p. 16). On 13 June 1900 Mark Twain grumbled to Henry H. Rogers from London: "Here is this troublesome cuss, Will M. Clemens, turning up again. . . . Clemens can't write books—he is a mere maggot who tries to feed on people while they are still alive" (*MTHHR*, p. 447).

Clement, (Mrs.) Clara Erskine. *Painters, Sculptors, Architects, Engravers, and Their Works: A Handbook.* Illus. [pub. 1874, reissued frequently by several publishers; James R. Osgood & Company of Boston published the seventh ed. in 1882].

Catalog: C1951, #06, edition not supplied.

Cleveland, Cecilia. *Story of a Summer* (pub. 1874).

"I have written a rather lengthy review of that unfortunate & sadly ridiculous book of Miss Cleveland's about Chappaqua" (SLC to Stillson of the New York *World*, 23 March 1874, CWB, quoted in *MTMF*, pp. 185–186 n. 2). In answer to a request to puff *Story of a Summer*, Clemens informed Mrs. Fairbanks on 24 March 1874: "I ain't going to write that lady, because it isn't pleasant to say no to a stranger" (*MTMF*, p. 185).

Cleveland, Grover (1837–1908). *What Shall We Do With It?* New York: Harper & Brothers, 1888. 68 pp.

Source: MTLAcc, entry #1736, volume donated by Clemens.

Clevenger, Shobal Vail (1843–1920). *The Evolution of Man and His Mind. A History and Discussion of the Evolution and Relation of the Mind and Body of Man and Animals.* Chicago: Evolution Publishing Co., 1903. 615 pp.

Inscription: in black ink on front pastedown endpaper: "SL. Clemens/1903".

Marginalia: numerous markings and notes in pencil up to page 113; none thereafter. Clemens' comments indicate mild divergences from Clevenger's view; on page 26 Clevenger states that, though mankind "has still his brutish instincts," nonetheless "Evolution shows that he advances." Clemens extended this sentence to read "—toward altar & halter." At the bottom of page 49 Clemens' inclinations toward cynicism again came to the fore; he noted: "But then the modern human race is frankly devoted to the game of grab, just as the race was earlier devoted to piety & hypocrisy" (quoted in *TIH*, p. 132).

Location: Mark Twain Papers, Berkeley, California. Purchased from Maxwell Hunley Rare Books of Beverly Hills in 1953 for $20.

Copy examined: Clemens' copy.

WIM?, p. 102.

————. *Fun in a Doctor's Life, Being the Adventures of an American Don Quixote in Helping to Make the World a Better Place.* Atlantic City, N.J.: Evolution Publishing Co., 1909. 291 pp.

Inscription: on front free endpaper: "To Sam L. Clemens/from his old towns-man/of St. Louis in the 50's/S. V. Clevenger/Park Ridge, Ill/Christmas 1909".

Marginalia: notes and markings in ink and pencil up to page 93. Beside a reference to Lord Bacon's many activities, Clemens added in black ink, "And writing Shakspeare, which he certainly did" (p. 13). Heavy ink markings alongside a quoted Wells Fargo express receipt that stated: "This company will not be responsible for the acts of God, Indians or other public enemies of the government" (p. 18). Clemens did not mark the passage about river boats on page 90 that mentions his name.

Location: Mark Twain Library, Redding, Conn.

Copy examined: Clemens' copy.

Clifford, (Mrs.) Lucy (Lane) (d. 1929), "Mrs. W. K. Clifford." *Margaret Vincent, A Novel.* New York: Harper & Brothers, 1902, 356 pp.

Source: MTLAcc, entry #75, volume donated by Clemens.

————. [Another identical copy.]

Source: MTLAcc, entry #1270, volume donated by Clemens.

————. *Mrs. Keith's Crime; A Record.* New York: Harper & Brothers, 1901. 234 pp.

Source: MTLAcc, entry #1529, volume donated by Clemens.

Clifford, William Kingdon (1845–1879). *Lectures and Essays by the Late William Kingdon Clifford.* Ed. by Leslie Stephen and Frederick Pollock, with intro. by F. Pollock. 2 vols. London: Macmillan and Co., 1879.

Marginalia: contains a handwritten note by Clemens.

Catalogs: A1911, #101, $1.50, vol. 1 only; L1912, #9, $3, vol. 1 only.

Location: Franklin Meine Collection, University of Illinois at Urbana-Champaign (both volumes, according to the library card).

Copy examined: none. Information compiled from photocopies of library card supplied by respondent, Mrs. Mary Ceibert. The book(s?) were not available for inspection in 1974.

Clifton, William. "The last link is broken" (song, ca. 1840).

References: among the music on the piano in chapter 38 of *LonMiss* (1883); the young ladies in the Grangerford household sing this song in chapter 17 of *HF* (1885); Tom Sawyer suggests that Jim play "The Last Link" to his rats in chapter 38 of *HF;* Clemens remembered it as one of the "songs that tended to regrets for bygone days and vanished joys" in "Villagers of 1840–3," written 1897 (*HH&T,* p. 34).

Clodd, Edward. *The Story of Creation: A Plain Account of Evolution.* A New and Revised Edition. London: Longmans, Green, and Co., 1894. [Pro-Darwin thesis.]

Inscription: "To Miss Clara Clemens, with every good wish from Carlyle Smythe".

Provenance: bookseller's sticker on rear endpaper: Wildman & Lyell, Auckland, New Zealand.

Location: Carrie Estelle Doheny Collection, St. John's Seminary, Camarillo, California.

Copy examined: Clara Clemens' unmarked copy.

Clodd describes (with illustrations) on pages 126–127 the duck-billed platypus, an animal species that amused Mark Twain immensely in *FE* (1897) and his notebooks.

Clouston, Joseph Storer (1870–1944). *The Adventures of M. D'Haricot.* Illus. by Albert Levering. New York: Harper & Brothers, 1902. 365 pp.

Source: MTLAcc, entry #76, volume donated by Clemens.

————. *The Lunatic at Large; A Novel.* Illus. by Latimer J. Wilson. New York: F. M. Buckles & Co., [cop. 1905]. 312 pp.
Source: MTLAcc, entry #1095, volume donated by Clemens.

————. *Our Lady's Inn; A Novel.* New York: Harper & Brothers, 1903. 324 pp.
Source: MTLAcc, entry #989, volume donated by Clemens.

Coan, Titus Munson (1836–1921). *Ounces of Prevention.* New York: Harper & Brothers, 1888. 188 pp.
Source: MTLAcc, entry#1383, volume donated by Clemens.

Cobb, Augustus G. "Earth-Burial and Cremation," *North American Review,* 135 (1882), 266–282.
Mark Twain introduced clippings from this article into his discussion of cremation in *LonMiss* (1883), but he deleted the section before publication.

Cobb, Sylvanus.
Mentioned as a popular novelist in "A General Reply" in the November 1870 *Galaxy.*

Cobbe, Frances Power (1822–1904). *Life of Frances Power Cobbe as Told by Herself.* Illus. London, 1904.
Inscription: "S. L. Clemens, London July 1907."
Marginalia: many marked paragraphs and notes. On a flyleaf Clemens observed: "To the pure all things are impure. S.L.C." Where the text refers to Charles Kingsley's salutation to Miss Cobbe as "At *last,* Miss Cobbe, at *last* we meet," Clemens quipped: "What he really said was 'at l-l-ast we m-m-meet'—for he was a delightful stammerer."
Catalog: A1911, #102, $9.50.

————. *The Peak in Darien, with Some Other Inquiries Touching Concerns of the Soul and the Body.* Boston: G. H. Ellis, 1882. 266 pp.
Source: MTLAcc, entry #914, volume donated by Clemens.

Cobbett, William. *A Year's Residence in the United States of America . . . in Three Parts.* New York, 1819.
Marginalia: a few notations in pencil by Clemens.
Catalog: A1911, #103, $1, Part 3 only.
Dewey Ganzel, "Twain, Travel Books," p. 41 n. 4.

Cobden, Richard. *The Life of Richard Cobden.* 2 vols. London, 1905.
Inscriptions: "To S. L. Clemens, D. Lit., with grateful memories of his noble work for the downtrodden natives of the Congo. Jane Cobden Unwin." Both vols. signed: "S. L. Clemens, London, July/07."
Catalog: A1911, #104, $6.75.

Cody, William Frederick (1846–1917). *The Adventures of Buffalo Bill.* New York: Harper & Brothers, [cop. 1904]. 156 pp.
Source: MTLAcc, entry #438, volume donated by Clemens.

————. [Another identical copy.]
Source: MTLAcc, entry #1172, volume donated by Clemens.

————. *The Adventures of Buffalo Bill, by Col. William F. Cody . . . To Which Is Appended a Short Sketch of His Life.* New York: Harper & Brothers, 1905. 155 pp.
Inscription: on front pastedown endpaper: "SL. Clemens/Sept. 1905".

Marginalia: pencil line on page 126 beside figures for pony-express riders' speed. No other markings.

Location: Antenne-Dorrance Collection, Rice Lake, Wis.

Copy examined: Clemens' copy.

The horse named "Soldier Boy" in "A Horse's Tale" (1907) was once Buffalo Bill's "favorite horse, out of dozens." The description of Cody in chapter one is specific enough to have been influenced by Cody's *Adventures.*

————. *The Life of the Hon. William F. Cody, Known as Buffalo Bill, the Famous Hunter, Scout and Guide. An Autobiography.* Illus. Hartford, Conn.: F. E. Bliss, [1879]. 365 pp.

At the time Mark Twain was collecting Far West materials to use in "Huck Finn and Tom Sawyer among the Indians" (written 1884), Charles L. Webster wrote him from New York City on 9 July 1884: "I sent you Buffalo Bill's, also an old frontier book" (MTP). Clemens replied on 10 July: "Package has arrived—Buffalo Bill's book, I hope" (*MTBus,* p. 267).

HH&T, pp. 85–86, 336.

Coffin, Charles Carleton (1823–1896). *Abraham Lincoln.* Illus. New York: Harper & Brothers, [cop. 1892]. 542 pp.

Source: MTLAcc, entry #867, volume donated by Clemens.

————. *The Boys of '76. A History of the Battles of the Revolution.* Illus. New York: Harper & Brothers, 1904. 398 pp.

Source: MTLAcc, entry #1183, volume donated by Clemens.

————. *Drum-Beat of the Nation: The First Period of the War of the Rebellion.* Illus. New York: Harper & Brothers, [cop. 1887]. 478 pp.

Source: MTLAcc, entry #864, volume donated by Clemens.

————. *Marching to Victory: The Second Period of the War of Rebellion.* Illus. New York: Harper & Brothers, [cop. 1888]. 491 pp.

Source: MTLAcc, entry #865, volume donated by Clemens.

————. *Old Times in the Colonies.*

Catalog: C1951, #13c, $27.50, listed with books signed by Clemens.

According to a bill from Brown & Gross, Hartford booksellers, Clemens purchased "1 Old Times Colonies $2.40" on 22 November 1880, but the same statement also *credits* him with $2.40 on 7 December 1880 for "1 Old Times Colonies" (MTP). Perhaps the bookkeeper made an error in the latter entry, meaning to charge Clemens for a second copy.

————. *Old Times in the Colonies.* New York: Harper & Brothers, [cop. 1880]. 460 pp.

Source: MTLAcc, entry #863, volume donated by Clemens.

————. *Redeeming the Republic: The Third Period of the War of the Rebellion.* Illus. New York: Harper & Brothers, [1889]. 478 pp.

Source: MTLAcc, entry #866, volume donated by Clemens.

————. *The Story of Liberty.* Illus. New York: Harper & Brothers, [cop. 1878]. [A children's book about European history.]

Inscription: in Clemens' hand on flyleaf in blue ink: "Merry Christmas/ to/ Margaret Warner/ from Susie & Clara Clemens/ 1883."

Location: Mark Twain Memorial, Hartford, Connecticut. Given by an anonymous donor in 1963.

Copy examined: gift copy from Clemens' children.

Probably Clemens meant Coffin's book when he noted in May 1888: "Get Jean a 'Liberty' " (NB 27, TS p. 68).

Coggins, Paschal H. "Old Sile's Clem," *Harper's Monthly*, 96 (May 1898), 922–928.
Coggins' sentimental dialect sketch describes the experiences of a homeless, wandering boy, Clement Smedley, who seeks a home for himself and his horse Nap in a backwoods region after his employer Sile Farley dies. Young Clem is eventually adopted by a kindly farmer, Uncle Billy Churchman.
Clemens wrote to an unidentified Hartford correspondent, probably Joseph H. Twichell: "Have you read 'Old Sile's Clem?' (May 'Harper.') I feel sure that it must be the best back-settlement study that was ever printed. O, the art of it! How well Coggins knows his ground, and what a sure and reserved and delicate touch he has. . . . Coggins must have heard them uttered. There are things which the finest genius cannot counterfeit with exactness, cannot perfectly imitate, and back-settlement wit is one of these, I think. . . . Watch out for Paschal H. Coggins; he is valuable and entitled to a grateful welcome" (undated, unidentified newspaper clipping in May 1898 letter files, MTP). Clemens would pay similar tribute to a sketch by Ellis Parker Butler in the February 1899 *Century Magazine* that also combined pathos, American humor, and regional dialect. (See entry for Butler.)

Coke, E. T. *A Subaltern's Furlough; Descriptive of Scenes in Various Parts of the United States, Upper and Lower Canada, New-Brunswick, and Nova Scotia, During the Summer and Autumn of 1832.* 2 vols. New York: J. & J. Harper, 1833. [Only vol. 1 of Clemens' copy has been found.]
Marginalia: marked and annotated in pencil by Clemens on pages 78, 101, 148, 153, 154, 155, 164 of vol. 1. In the margin of page 101 Clemens penciled: "Any foreign scrub can familiarly visit the President—whereas with us it is held a high honor"; at the bottom of the page he noted about the White House: "These people usually strain their politeness, & try to compliment it, as they do the steamboats." Along the bottom margin of page 155 Clemens penciled: "English efforts to write as Americans talk—I guess, calc'late, reckon, &c". At the top of page 164, which contains a description of the untidy appearance of rutted, dank East Hartford, Clemens noted *"Old* Hartford." There are a few other notes.
Location: Carrie Estelle Doheny Collection, St. John's Seminary, Camarillo, California. Donated by Mrs. Doheny in November 1940 after its purchase from Maxwell Hunley Rare Books of Beverly Hills.
Copy examined: Clemens' copy.

Colby, Frank Moore (1865–1925). *Imaginary Obligations.* New York: Dodd, Mead & Co., 1906. 335 pp.
Marginalia: notes in black ink by Clemens on pages 62, 63, and 110; passages marked on pages 120 and 121. Note on page 62 concerns Colby's reference to "a schoolboy mind" that edits a paper; Clemens observed: "It fits another living public man—also Mr. McKinley." A note on page 63 makes the same assertion about those who display a "taint of commonness." Regarding a discussion of hazing practices at West Point, Clemens wrote: "They made the place unsatisfactory to Whistler & to Edgar A. Poe."
Provenance: sticker of Brentano's Booksellers of New York City on rear pastedown endpaper.
Catalogs: A1911, #105, $4.50, "also letter of presentation of the book by Eleanor Jay Chapman to Mr. Clemens"; Dawson's Bookshop Catalog No. 70 (1930), p. 8, "laid in . . . Autographed Letter Signed, from Eleanor Jay Chapman to Mr. Clemens, 4 pp. 12mo, no place or date, relative to sending the above work to Clemens"; Chicago Book & Art Auction, Inc., Sale No. 30 (25 January 1933), E. W. Evans Collection, p. 12, "also an ALS laid in from Eleanor Jay Chapman to Clemens."
Location: Henry W. and Albert A. Berg Collection, New York Public Library.
Copy examined: Clemens' copy, containing *A1911* sale label.

Cole, T. "Notes by T. Cole on the 'Adoration,' " *Century Magazine,* 41 (April 1891), 842–843.

Treats Leonardo da Vinci's unfinished painting, "The Adoration of the Magi." Cole's engraving of a detail from the painting, which he copied in the Uffizi Gallery at Florence, is reproduced on page 843. Cole describes the work meticulously, gives its measurements, and specifies exactly where it hangs. He even records the colors of each section. He concludes by asserting that "Adoration" in his opinion "far surpasses anything else of its kind" (p. 842). Cole's brief note and his engraving accompany W. J. Stillman's "Leonardo da Vinci, 1452–1519" (pp. 838–842), an essay that was part of the Italian Old Masters series in the *Century.*

Clemens wished to "scrap-book the 'Adoration' 842–3 April Century, 1891," he wrote in April (NB 30, TS p. 33).

Coleman, F. M. *Typical Pictures of Indian Natives, Being Reproductions from . . . Photographs.* Illus. Bombay: "Times of India" Office, 1898. 50 pp.
   Source: MTLAcc, entry #1221, volume donated by Clemens.

Coleridge, Samuel Taylor (1772–1834). *The Complete Works of Samuel Taylor Coleridge.* Ed. by William Greenough Thayer Sledd (1820–1894). 7 vols. New York: Harper & Brothers, 1884.
   Source: MTLAcc, entries #1751–1756, 2771, complete set donated by Clemens.

————. *The Poems of Samuel Taylor Coleridge.* Ed. by Derwent and Sara Coleridge. Copyright Edition. Collection of British Authors Series. Leipzig: B. Tauchnitz, 1860. 344 pp.
   Source: MTLAcc, entry #2050, volume donated from Clemens' library by Clara Clemens Gabrilowitsch in 1910.

————. *The Rime of the Ancient Mariner.* Illus. by Gustave Doré. New York: Harper & Brothers, 1876. [Folio-size book.]
   Inscription: front flyleaf inscribed by Clemens in violet ink "To Livy L. Clemens/Nov. 27, 1876./From S. L. Clemens".
   Catalog: A1911, #135, $37; resold at *C1951* auction, #D74.
   Location: Mark Twain Memorial, Hartford, Conn. Donated by Mrs. John L. Martin of Darien, Conn.
   Copy examined: Olivia Clemens' copy.

————. *The Rime of the Ancient Mariner.* Illus. by J. Noel Paton. New York: 1875.
   Inscription: on flyleaf: "Saml. L. Clemens, Hartford, 1875."
   Catalog: A1911, #106, $4.
   In 1866 Clemens referred to Captain James Smith of the *Ajax* as "Ye Ancient Mariner" (NB 6, *N&J,* 1: 188). He jocularly addressed Miss Emma Beach as "Ancient Mariner" in a letter from Washington, D.C. on 10 February 1868 (Doheny Collection, St. John's Seminary). The "waiter . . . kept his ancient-mariner eye steadily & accusingly on us while our breakfast cooked" (NB 13 [May 1877], *N&J,* 2: 15). During a snow-storm Riley backed his hapless victim "against an iron fence, buttonholed him, fastened him with his eye, like the ancient mariner, and proceeded to unfold his narrative" in chapter 26 of *TA* (1880), a miniature burlesque of Coleridge's mariner lecturing the Wedding Guest. "A poor old broken-down, superannuated fellow" is referred to as "the ancient mariner" in chapter 30 of *LonMiss* (1883). The hero and heroine of Mark Twain's abortive "Burlesque Sea Story" (written 1895) hear "a burst of mocking laughter" that sounds like "ship-wrecked mariners gone mad with hunger and thirst and misery," and discover that "the hush of death lay upon ship and sea" (DV331, MTP). Mark Twain's "The Enchanted Sea-Wilderness" (written 1896) also resembles the dismal shipboard scenes in Coleridge's fantastic

poem. Twain told a reporter in 1900 that when he finally repaid his enormous business debts he "felt like the Ancient Mariner when the dead albatross fell into the sea. I became a new man" ("MT Home, An Anti-Imperialist," New York *Herald,* 16 October 1900). Andrew Carnegie, said Mark Twain, has "the deadliest affliction I know of. He is the Ancient Mariner over again; it is not possible to divert him from his subject" (2 December 1907 AD, *MTE,* pp. 37–38).

    MT&JB, p. 277; S. B. Liljegren, "Revolt," p. 24; Roger L. Brooks, "A Second Possible Source"; *OPMT,* p. 5.

Coleridge, Sara (Coleridge) (1802–1852). *Memoir and Letters of Sara Coleridge.* Ed. by Edith Coleridge. New York: Harper & Brothers, 1874. 528 pp. [First edition pub. in London, 1873].

    "How I do love our babies and how I do desire to have wisdom given me for their guidance," Livy Clemens wrote to her husband in June 1874 or 1875. "There is much in this life of Sara Coleridge that is suggestive on this subject." In another undated letter, written on "Monday afternoon" during the same period, Livy Clemens amplified: "Sara Coleridge says in writing to her husband of one of their children 'Don't fancy that children will listen to lectures either in learning or morality.' . . . And more that I would like to quote but will wait and read it to you" (ALS in Chester Davis' collection, Mark Twain Research Foundation, Perry, Mo.; pub. in *The Twainian,* 37 [November–December 1978], 3–4).

————. *Phantasmion, A Fairy Tale . . . With an Introductory Preface by Lord Coleridge.* Boston: Roberts Brothers, 1874. 348 pp. [Orig. pub. in London, 1837, as *Phantasmion: Prince of Palmland.*]

    Estes & Lauriat of Boston billed Clemens on 14 July 1880 for "1 Phantasmion .75¢" and he paid the bill on 20 July (receipt in MTP). No other titles in this period are sufficiently similar to cause doubt that Clemens or Livy Clemens bought a copy of Coleridge's book.

"Colin, Lady M." (pseud. of Gertrude Elizabeth [Blood] Campbell, "Lady Colin Campbell" [d. 1911]?) and Mary (French) Sheldon. *Everybody's Book of Correct Conduct; Being Hints for Everyday Life.* New York: Harper & Brothers, 1893. 182 pp.

    Source: MTLAcc, entry #1332, volume donated by Clemens.

[Collier, William Francis. *History of the British Empire.*] Originally pub. in London, 1861. Revised editions published in Nelson's School Series issued by T. Nelson and Sons of London in 1891, 1894, etc.

    Edition: unknown (title page missing).

    Inscription: in pencil at top of table of contents: "Clara Langdon Clemens/ Ballarat October 1895,/Australia."

    Marginalia: a few notes in pencil, seemingly by either Clara or Livy Clemens.

    Provenance: contains book stamps of Mark Twain Library, Redding, Connecticut.

    Catalog: Mott 1952, #45, $2.50.

    Location: Mark Twain Memorial, Hartford, Connecticut. Anonymous gift in 1963.

    Copy examined: presumably Clara Clemens' book, but it lacks all leaves up to the table of contents. Merely the author's last name—Collier—is recoverable; since the book narrates English history from its beginnings, the author and title can be supplied with some certainty.

Collier's Weekly (periodical, pub. 1888–1957).

A photograph of Clemens that Albert Bigelow Paine took in 1906 (now in MTP) shows him reading an unidentifiable issue of *Collier's Weekly* in bed. To its editors on 6 July 1908 Clemens expressed approval of the installments of Will Irwin's *Japanese Schoolboy* that were appearing in *Collier's* (Yale). He ridiculed Norman Hapgood's editorial comment in the 11 July 1908 issue (14 July 1908 AD, *MTE*, pp. 24–32). Clemens' nephew Samuel E. Moffett joined the staff of *Collier's* in 1908; when Moffett died in 1908 Clemens quoted from the obituary published by the magazine in a piece entitled "Samuel Erasmus Moffett" that Clemens wrote on 16 August 1908.

Collin, Grace Lathrop. *Putnam Place*. New York: Harper & Brothers, 1903. 262 pp.
Source: MTLAcc, entry #1440, volume donated by Clemens.

"Putnam Place did not much interest me; so I knew it was high literature. I have never been able to get up high enough to be at home with high literature" (SLC to WDH, Riverdale, 29 April 1903, *MTHL*, p. 769). Howells continued the argument in a jesting spirit from New York City on 1 May 1903: "But you'd better take a brace, and try to get up as high as 'Putnam Place' " *(MTHL,* p. 769). Such remarks by Clemens encouraged his friend to think of him as essentially "unliterary."

Collins, Wilkie (1824–1889). *Armadale; A Novel*. New York: Harper & Brothers, 1905. 658 pp.
Source: MTLAcc, entry #1675, volume donated by Clemens.

————. *Basil*. Illus. New York: Harper & Brothers, 1904. 336 pp.
Source: MTLAcc, entry #1142, volume donated by Clemens.

————. *The New Magdalen. A Novel*. Illus. New York: Harper & Brothers, [cop. 1873]. 325 pp.
Source: MTLAcc, entry #1141, volume donated by Clemens.

Mark Twain attended a dinner for Wilkie Collins in Boston on February 1874 (SLC to James Redpath, 13 February 1874, Yale). He mentioned the "Longfellow-Whittier-Trowbridge-Wilkie-Collins dinner" in 1897 (NB 42, TS p. 22). Twain quoted Collins' statement that "Cooper is the greatest artist in the domain of romantic fiction yet produced by America" as an epigraph to "Fenimore Cooper's Literary Offences" (1895), citing no specific book by Collins.

————. *The Two Destinies; A Novel*. Illus. New York: Harper & Brothers, 1905. 312 pp.
Source: MTLAcc, entry #1530, volume donated by Clemens.

Collins, William (1721–1759). "Ode Written in 1746" (pub. 1747). Better known as "How Sleep the Brave."

Clemens began a letter to his mother written in Carson City on 30 January 1862 with lines from this poem intermixed with lines from other poets' works. "Bully, isn't it?" he asked *(PRI*, p. 29).

Collyer, Robert (1823–1912). *Nature and Life: Sermons*. Boston: Horace B. Fuller, 1867. 313 pp. [Unitarian church sermons.]
Source: MTLAcc, entry #904, volume donated by Clemens.

On 16 January 1869 Clemens wrote to Olivia Langdon from Chicago: "In the cars, the other day I bought a volume of remarkable sermons—they are from the pen & pulpit of Rev. Geo. [sic] Collyer, of Chicago: I like them very much. . . . They are more polished, more poetical, more elegant, more rhetorical, & more dainty & felicitous in wording" than Henry Ward Beecher's sermons *(LLMT,* p. 53). Robert Collyer was pastor of the First Unity Church on the North Side of Chicago.

Colombo, Cristoforo (1446?–1506). *Writings of Christopher Columbus, Descriptive of the Discovery and Occupation of the New World.* Ed. by Paul Leicester Ford. New York: Charles L. Webster & Co., 1892. 255 pp.

Clemens' publishing firm issued this book, so he may have examined it in manuscript or book form.

Colquhoun, Archibald Ross (1848–1914). *Greater America.* Maps. New York: Harper & Brothers, 1904. 436 pp.

Source: MTLAcc, entry #1714, volume donated by Clemens.

Colton, Arthur Willis. *"The Debatable Land."* A Novel. New York: Harper & Brothers, 1901. 312 pp.

Inscription: "S. L. Clemens, Riverdale, Dec. 1901."

Catalog: A1911, #108, $2.75.

Colvin, Verplanck (1847–1920). *The Adirondack Region.* Illus. Albany, N. Y.: Weed, Parsons & Co., 1880. 536 pp.

Source: MTLAcc, entry #578, volume donated by Clemens.

Combe, George (1788–1858). *Notes on the United States of North America. During a Phrenological Visit in 1838–9–40.* 2 vols. Philadelphia: Carey & Hart, 1841. [Only vol. 1 of Clemens' copy has been located.]

Inscription: in ink on front pastedown endpaper of vol. 1: "SL. Clemens/1909."

Marginalia: vol. 1 contains a few markings and notes in brown ink and pencil. The fullest comment appears on page 94, where Combe quotes a "highly intelligent friend" who prophesied the fall of the Church of England within five years; Combe himself predicts that this will occur in fifty years. Clemens wrote vertically in brown ink along the margin: "The one highly intelligent prophet missed it by 5 years, & the other by 70—& still no prospect."

Catalog: A1911, #109, $1, vol. 1 only.

Location: Mark Twain Papers, Berkeley, California. Acquired from UCLA in 1971 after I discovered it in the Circulation Department of the UCLA general library.

Copy examined: Clemens' copy of vol. 1.

Mark Twain referred to this book in the manuscript of *LonMiss* (1883) as his authority for the severity of laws regulating morality in early-day Hartford. He added in his footnote that "this Scot always praised us when he could; and found fault with us reluctantly"—but the entire passage was dropped from the final version of Mark Twain's book. Here is a clear instance of his signing a volume many years after he originally purchased and read it.

Dewey Ganzel, "Twain, Travel Books," p. 41 n. 4.

Combe, William. *The History and Antiquities of the City of York, from Its Origin to the Present Times.* Illus. 3 vols. York, England, 1785.

Inscription: each volume signed: "Saml. L. Clemens, York, July 19, '73."

Marginalia: numerous notes in vol. 1. Regarding the expulsion of Jews in the time of Edward I, Clemens commented: "The question is, when did savagery cease in England?" He also observed: "Edward's son was the first nobleman that was ever beheaded in England—started the fashion." *A1911* quotes a few other minor notes.

Catalog: A1911, #242, $10 for 3 vols.

WIM?, p. 83.

Comines, Philippe de (1447?–1511). *The Memoirs of Philip de Commines, Lord of Argenton: Containing the Histories of Louis XI. and Charles VIII., Kings of France, and of Charles the Bold, Duke of Burgundy. To Which Is Added, the Scandalous Chronicle, or Secret History of Louis XI., by Jean de Troyes.* Ed. by Andrew R. Scoble. 2 vols. London: Henry G. Bohn, 1856. [Only vol. 2 of Clemens' copy has been located.]

> *Marginalia:* vol. 2 contains Clemens' pencil markings and one comment at the top of page 35 in dark brown or black ink (near the underscored word "nobility"): "Nowhere in this book, as far as I can remember, are the common people ever thought of." Page 34 folded down; pencil marks at pages 37, 40, 94, 145, 153; page 168 turned down; leaves not opened between pages 177 and 296; leaves opened beginning with the "Scandalous Chronicles" of Louis of Valois; page 352 folded down; index leaves unopened.

> *Location:* Carrie Estelle Doheny Collection, St. John's Seminary, Camarillo, California. Donated by Mrs. Doheny in 1940 after its purchase from Maxwell Hunley Rare Books of Beverly Hills for $5.

> *Copy examined:* Clemens' copy.

Common Prayer. New York: D. Appleton & Co., 1870. 564 pp.

> *Source:* MTLAcc, entry #2314, volume donated from Clemens' library by Clara Clemens Gabrilowitsch in 1910.

Comstock, J. L. *Elements of Geology; Including Fossil Botany and Palaeontology. A Popular Treatise. . . Designed for the Use of Schools and General Readers.* New York: Pratt, Woodford, and Co., 1851.

> *Inscription:* signed on front free endpaper in pencil with a youthful flourish below the name: "Samuel L. Clemens/1856./June 25th, 1856." On flyleaf, vertically, in pencil: "Jennie N. Curtis/1915."

> *Marginalia:* pencil mark around Charles Lyell's works in list of "Authorities" at front of book. A few money figures on rear pastedown endpaper do not appear to be Clemens'. Several stray pencil marks on first pages of volume.

> *Provenance:* bookplate on front pastedown endpaper identifies volume #583 from library of Charles L. Webster, New York City. Priced at $15 in corner of front free endpaper. Yale University bookplate dated 1946 on rear pastedown endpaper.

> *Location:* Beinecke Library, Yale University.

> *Copy examined:* Clemens' copy, very possibly the earliest-acquired book from his library to have survived. Presumably Clemens' mother or sister brought the volume East when they moved to Fredonia, New York to live with Annie (Moffett) Webster and her husband; the Charles L. Websters later moved to New York City in 1882, when Jane Lampton Clemens returned to Keokuk, Iowa, and Pamela (Clemens) Moffett left for California to live with her son. Evidently this book remained in Webster's library.

Conant, Charles Arthur (1861–1915). *The Principles of Banking.* New York: Harper & Brothers, 1908. 487 pp.

> *Source:* MTLAcc, entry #536, volume donated by Clemens.

———. *The Principles of Money and Banking.* 2 vols. New York: Harper & Brothers, 1905.

> *Source:* MTLAcc, entries #534 and #535, volumes donated by Clemens.

———. *The Principles of Money and Banking.* 2 vols. New York: Harper & Brothers, [cop. 1905].

> *Source:* MTLAcc, entries #1698 and #1699b, volumes donated by Clemens.

Condition of the Blind. Illus. Albany, N. Y.: J. B. Lyon Co., 1906. 586 pp.

> *Source:* MTLAcc, entry #889, volume donated by Clemens.

Conkling, Alfred Ronald. *The Life and Letters of Roscoe Conkling, Orator, Statesman, Advocate*. New York: Charles L. Webster & Company, 1889. 709 pp. Issued by Clemens' publishing firm.

Conn, R. D. *Life of the Germ*. (New York, 1897).
    Henry J. Lindborg—"A Cosmic Tramp," p. 654 n. 9—identifies Conn's book as the source for Mark Twain's point in "Three Thousand Years among the Microbes" (1905) that most bacteria are actually beneficial. Lindborg calls attention to page 128 of Conn's work, which contains a statement about the harmlessness, even the usefulness, of most bacteria. Twain's narrator alludes to a prior existence "when I was studying micrology under Prof. H. W. Conn [*sic*]" (*WWD?*, p. 523); Conn, the narrator says, comprehended the vital part played by microbes in the life cycle on earth.

Conrad, Joseph (1857–1924). *The Mirror of the Sea*. New York: Harper & Brothers, 1906. 329 pp.
    Source: MTLAcc, entry #1175, volume donated by Clemens.

———. *Nostromo; A Tale of the Seaboard*. New York: Harper & Brothers, 1904. 631 pp.
    Location: Mark Twain Library, Redding, Conn. Donated by Clemens (MTLAcc, entry #1326).
    Copy examined: Clemens' copy, unmarked.

———. *The Secret Agent; A Simple Tale*. New York: Harper & Brothers, 1907. 373 pp.
    Source: MTLAcc, entry #77, volume donated by Clemens.

———. [Another identical copy.]
    Source: MTLAcc, entry #1423, volume donated by Clemens.

Conway, Moncure Daniel. *Autobiography: Memories and Experiences of Moncure Daniel Conway*. 2 vols. Boston: Houghton Mifflin and Co., 1904.
    Inscription: on front pastedown endpapers of both volumes in black ink: "SL. Clemens/Oct. 1905."
    Marginalia: profuse markings and notes in pencil throughout both volumes. Conway's recollections repeatedly stirred Clemens' autobiographical tendencies. On page 277 Clemens noted in pencil: "I seem to have met the most of the people mentioned in this book." After a list of his childhood acquaintances in Hannibal at the top of page 147, Clemens wrote: "They are all gone; why were they created?" Many other revealing reminiscences occupy the margins of various pages, including the passage (2:146) in which Conway recalls showing the Clemenses around Paris in 1879.
    Catalog: C1951, #35a, $50, 2 vols.
    Location: Mark Twain Research Foundation, Perry, Missouri (in Chester L. Davis' home).
    Copy examined: Clemens' copy, one of the most autobiographically revealing of all Clemens' annotated books.
    Isabel Lyon noted on 30 November 1904 at 21 Fifth Avenue in New York City: "Tonight at dinner Mr. Clemens was talking of Moncure D. Conway. He is reading Conway's autobiography just published, and it made him hark back to the days in London 25 years ago" (1903–1906 Journal, TS p. 28, MTP). Albert Bigelow Paine reported that Conway's autobiography "gave him [Clemens] enjoyment" (*MTB*, p. 1540). Conway's book obviously must have influenced Mark Twain's eventual choice of a narrative mode for his own autobiography, which he would launch in earnest (following earlier, sporadic attempts) in 1906. Conway soon discarded the strictly chronological organization of his first chapters in favor of a thematic approach that allowed him to discuss fully the individuals, literary groups, and social sets with which he had become acquainted at various phases of his life.

―――. *Demonology and Devil Lore* (pub. 1878).
   Reference: on 19 January [1880] Clemens wrote to Conway from Elmira upon receiving an unspecified book: "If I enjoy it as much as I have enjoyed your devil-lore I shall know it is a happy success" (Columbia Univ.).
   Coleman O. Parsons, "Background," p. 60.

―――. *The Sacred Anthology* (pub. 1874).
   Marginalia: Albert Bigelow Paine quotes from Clemens' annotation concerning religion written on a flyleaf (*MTB*, p. 1584): "RELIGION/The easy confidence with which I know another man's religion is folly teaches me to suspect that my own is also. MARK TWAIN, 19th Cent., A. D." In another note he observed: "I would not interfere with any one's religion, either to strengthen it or to weaken it. I am not able to believe one's religion can affect his hereafter one way or the other, no matter what that religion may be. But it may easily be a great comfort to him in this life—hence it is a valuable possession to him."
   Catalog: C1951, #38a, $47.50, listed among books annotated by Clemens.

Cook, Clarence Chatham. *The House Beautiful: Essays on Beds and Tables, Stools and Candlesticks.* Illus. New York: Scribner, Armstrong and Co., 1878. 336 pp. [Pub. serially in *Scribner's Monthly*.]
   In an updated letter to Theodore and Susan Crane written on "Xmas Morning," Clemens wisecracked: "I have taken Ida's House Beautiful & Baby Days & Ik Marvel's book & shall give Livy & the children copies of my works in place of them" (MTP).
   MT&HF, p. 291.

Cook, Theodore Andrea. *Old Touraine: The Life and History of the Famous Chateâux of France.* 2 vols. New York: J. Pott & Co., 1900.
   Clemens noted the title and number of volumes on a flyleaf of Notebook 44 in 1901 (MTP).

Cooke, Edmund Vance. *Chronicles of the Little Tot.* Illus. by Clyde O. De Land. New York: Dodge Publishing Co., 1905. [Verses on children resembling those of James Whitcomb Riley.]
   Inscription: on the front free endpaper Cooke inscribed a poem of two stanzas headed "To Samuel Langhorne Clemens at Seventy/To Mark Twain at the same age" and dated at "Cleveland, Nov. 30th, 1905."
   Provenance: curiously, the volume contains the book stamps and red-ink accession number of the Mark Twain Library at Redding, yet it was also catalogued in the "Retz Appraisal" of items belonging to the Mark Twain Estate in 1944 (p. 7), when it was valued at $5. Perhaps Clemens or Clara had a change of heart about donating the volume to the Redding library.
   Location: Mark Twain Papers, Berkeley, California.
   Copy examined: Clemens' copy.
   "Under another cover I send you a memento, with inscription," wrote Cooke from Cleveland, Ohio on 26 November 1905. He signed his letter "with my warmest esteem and deepest admiration" (MTP).

Cooke, (Mrs.) Grace (McGowan) (b. 1863). *Their First Formal Call.* Illus. by Peter Newell. New York: Harper & Brothers, 1906. 55 pp.
   Source: MTLAcc, entry #453, volume donated by Clemens.

Cooke, (Mrs.) Rose (Terry) (1827–1892). "Freedom Wheeler's Controversy with Providence: A Story of Old New England" (short story), *Atlantic Monthly*, 40 (July 1877), 65–84.
   "I read the entire Atlantic this time," Clemens informed Howells on 4 July 1877 from Elmira. "Mrs. Rose Terry Cooke's story was a ten-strike. I wish she would write 12 old-time New England tales a year" (*MTHL*, p. 187). Early in 1881 Clemens reminded himself to send a complimentary copy of *P&P* to this local-colorist who was born in West Hartford and lived in Winsted, Connecticut. In February 1889 he noted, "Rose Terry Cooke,/Pittsfield, Mass./Read there March 6" (NB 28, TS p. 43).

————. *Somebody's Neighbors*. Boston: J. R. Osgood and Co., 1881. 421 pp.
   Source: MTLAcc, entry #2201, volume donated from Clemens' library by
Clara Clemens Gabrilowitsch in 1910.

————. *Steadfast: The Story of a Saint and a Sinner*. Boston: Ticknor and Co.,
1889. 426 pp.
   Inscription: inscribed to Clemens by the author.
   Source: offered for sale in June 1976 by Seven Gables Bookshop, New York
City. Price $125.

Cooper, James Fenimore (1789–1851). *Leather-Stocking Tales: The Pathfinder;
The Deerslayer; The Last of the Mohicans.*
   Edition: unknown.
   Catalog: C1951, #023, listed among books belonging to Livy Clemens.

————. *Leather-Stocking Tales.*
   Edition: unknown.
   Catalog: C1951, #J33, listed among books belonging to Jean and Clara
Clemens.
   Cooper became synonymous for Mark Twain with wholly unwarranted,
sentimental, idealized notions of American Indian tribes. Clemens' experiences
in the Far West disabused him of youthful suppositions, and the poverty and
squalor he found endemic to the Nevada and California aborigines made him
disgusted with the "romances" he had once enjoyed. In 1897 he recalled that
Cooper was one of the Hannibal idols during his childhood, when "any young
person would have been proud of a 'strain' of Indian blood" ("Villagers of
1840–3," *HH&T*, p. 34). He wrote to Jane Lampton Clemens from Carson City
on 20 March 1862 to ridicule Cooper's "lordly sons of the forest" and to provide
instead "a full and correct account of these lovely Indians—not gleaned from
Cooper's novels, Madam" (quoted in *PRI*, p. 37). In his letter of 5 June 1867 to
the *Alta California* he wrote about marauding natives: "I suppose the humani-
tarians want somebody to fight the Indians that J. Fenimore Cooper made. There
is just where the mistake is. The Cooper Indians are dead—died with their creator" (*MTTMB*, p. 266).
   "Recall their mighty deeds! Remember Uncas!" Mark Twain admonished the
putative "Indians" he encountered in "Day at Niagara" (1869). Cooper's Indians
"are an extinct tribe that never existed," he argued in chapter 20 of *IA* (1869),
and in chapter 50 he quipped: "Commend me to Fenimore Cooper to find beauty
in the Indians, and to Grimes [William C. Prime] to find it in the Arabs." In
chapter 19 of *RI* (1872) Mark Twain derided "the scholarly savages of the 'Last
of the Mohicans' " (Iowa-Calif. Ed., p. 146). Twain planned to make "a vicious
and entertaining book" by reviewing Cooper and other novelists whom "the last
two generations of Englishmen and Americans admired" (SLC to Henry H.
Rogers, 16 May 1894, *MTHHR*, pp. 53–54). To Livy Clemens he revealed: "I am
writing a review of Fenimore Cooper's Deerslayer—the most idiotic book I ever
saw" (London, 16 May 1894, ALS in Mark Twain Research Foundation, Perry,
Mo.; quoted in *The Twainian*, 37 [July-Aug. 1978]. 1). He published "Fenimore
Cooper's Literary Offences" in July 1895, concentrating on *Deerslayer* and
Pathfinder and scoffing at the Leather-Stocking books as the "Broken Twig Series";
he took issue in this essay with Brander Matthews and other critics, and semi-
facetiously sought to prove that Cooper violated eighteen specific literary rules. In
another sally against Cooper's over-estimators, "Fenimore Cooper's Further Literary Offences" (published by Bernard De Voto as "Cooper's Prose Style" in *LE*,
pp. 137–145), written in 1894 or 1895, Mark Twain also berated *The Last of
the Mohicans.* Twain was consequently taken to task by Brander Matthews in an
introduction to an edition of the *Leather-Stocking Tales* published by G. P.
Putnam's Sons, and (more vigorously) by D. L. Maulsby in an essay that

appeared in *The Dial* in 1897. Mark Twain countered in chapter 22 of *FE* (1897), remarking that "Fenimore Cooper lost his chance. . . . He wouldn't have traded the dullest of them [Australian aborigines] for the brightest Mohawk he ever invented".

S. B. Liljegren, "Revolt," pp. 35, 43–49; *MTC*, p. 134.

Coppée, François (1842–1908). *The Rivals*. New York: Harper & Brothers, 1893. 99 pp.
> *Source:* MTLAcc, entry #2202, volume donated from Clemens' library by Clara Clemens Gabrilowitsch in 1910.

Cornaro, Luigi (1475–1566). *The Art of Living Long. A New and Improved English Version . . . with Essays by Joseph Addison, Lord Bacon, and Sir William Temple.* Illus. Milwaukee: W. F. Butler, 1903. 214 pp. [*Translation of Discorsi della vita sobria.*]
> *Catalog: A1911*, #112, $2.50.

Corson, Hiram (1828–1911). *An Introduction to the Study of Robert Browning's Poetry* (pub. 1886).
> Clemens' study group on Browning heard this Cornell professor lecture: "Prof. Corson is coming to give us a reading," Clemens wrote proudly to Mrs. Fairbanks on 22 March 1887 (*MTMF*, p. 261). He may have read Corson's recently published book.

Cory, Vivian, pseud. "Victoria Cross." *Life's Shop Window*. New York: M. Kennerley, [cop. 1907]. 371 pp.
> *Source:* MTLAcc, entry #2207, volume donated from Clemens' library by Clara Clemens Gabrilowitsch in 1910. Subsequently withdrawn from circulation by the librarian.

Cosmopolitan (periodical, pub. 1886–   ).
> Clemens disliked David Ker's travel essays but praised "that charming Chinese story" in an issue he read in March 1889 (NB 28, TS p. 49). In December 1893 he reminded himself to send Livy a copy of the "story by Miss Van Etten" in the *Cosmopolitan* (NB 33, TS p. 42).

Cotes, Sara Jeannette (Duncan) (1862?–1922). *An American Girl in London*. Illus. by F. H. Townsend. London: Chatto & Windus, 1891. 321 pp.
> *Source:* MTLAcc, entry #995, volume donated by Clemens.

Cottler, G. *Cours Complet de Langue Allemande*. Paris: Berlin Frère. Librairie Classique Eugene Belin, 1893.
> *Inscription:* in purple ink on front free endpaper: "Jean Clemens/le 2 Fevrier 1894/Paris". Bookplate torn off front pastedown endpaper.
> *Location:* Mark Twain Library, Redding, Connecticut.
> *Copy examined:* Jean Clemens' copy.

Cotton, A. J. *Cotton's Sketch Book. (Autobiographical Sketches of the Life, Labors and Extensive Home Travels of the Reverend A. J. Cotton)*. Portland, Maine: B. Thurston & Co., 1874.
> *Location:* Mark Twain Library, Redding, Connecticut.
> *Copy examined:* presumably Clemens' unmarked copy, since it was grouped with Clemens' personal books when Albert E. Stone visited Redding in 1955 (and also when I saw it in 1970).

Coulton, George Gordon (1858–1947). *From St. Francis to Dante: Translations from the Chronicle of the Franciscan Salimbene (1221–1288); with Notes and Illustrations from Other Medieval Sources.* Second rev. edition. London: David Nutt, 1907. 446 pp.

Inscription: signed on front pastedown endpaper: "SL. Clemens/June, 1909./ Stormfield. From James M. Beck." Inscribed to Clemens by Beck in June 1909 on half-title page.

Marginalia: markings and notes in pencil and black ink throughout. Above a passage on page 81 that attributes earthquakes to wind trapped in cavernous mountains, Clemens wrote in ink: "Theological 'science,' you see, was as 'ansome a product 600 years ago as it is in Gladstone's & Canon Lightfoot's day." At page 318, in reference to St. Dominic's pulling apart a shrieking sparrow which had interrupted his studies and therefore seemed to him the Devil incarnate, Clemens noted in ink: "Another heroic hunter, like Roosevelt."

Location: Carrie Estelle Doheny Collection, St. John's Seminary, Camarillo, California. Donated by Mrs. Doheny in 1940 after its purchase from Maxwell Hunley Rare Books of Beverly Hills for $12.20.

Copy examined: Clemens' copy.

Courthope, William John (1842–1917). *Addison.* English Men of Letters Series. New York: Harper & Brothers, 1902. 182 pp.

Source: MTLAcc, entry #1287, volume donated by Clemens.

Cow-Boys Ballads. N.p., n.d. 81 pp.

Source: MTLAcc, entry #2008, volume donated from Clemens' library by Clara Clemens Gabrilowitsch in 1910.

Cowie, William. *Latter-Day Poems.* Syracuse, N.Y.: Wolcott's Bookshop, 1904. 251 pp.

Source: MTLAcc, entry #646, volume donated by Clemens.

[Cowles, Alfred Abernethy (1845–1916)]. *The Poet in Embryo; Being the Meditations of Algernon Byron Stripling.* Illus. by Maud Sherman Cowles. New York: E. P. Dutton and Co., 1905. 18 pp.

Source: MTLAcc, entry #1903, volume donated from Clemens' library by Clara Clemens Gabrilowitsch in 1910.

Cowley, Abraham (1618–1667). *Essays.* [Intro. by Henry Morley.] New York: Cassell & Co., 1886. 192 pp.

Source: MTLAcc, entry #975, volume donated by Clemens.

Cowper, William (1731–1800). "Verses Supposed to be Written by Alexander Selkirk" (poem).

Cowper and Dryden and Shelley produced "all the poetry that everybody admires and appreciates, but nobody ever reads or quotes from" (*Californian,* 17 June 1865; *LAMT,* p. 142); "Oh, Solitude, where are the charms which sages have seen in thy face?" quotes Mark Twain in chapter 9 of *IA* (1869).

Cox, Samuel Sullivan (1824–1889), known as "Sunset Cox." *The Diversions of a Diplomat in Turkey.* New York: Charles L. Webster & Co., 1887. 685 pp.

Clemens discussed the manuscript of Cox's book (but stated that he hadn't read it) in a letter to the Ohio lawyer on 9 July 1887 (PH in MTP). Clemens' publishing firm issued Cox's *Diversions of a Diplomat* in 1887 and 1893; four sketches from the book appeared in *Mark Twain's Library of Humor* (1888).

———. *The Isles of the Princes; or, The Pleasures of Prinkipo.* Illus. New York: G. P. Putnam's Sons, 1887. 381 pp.

Source: MTLAcc, entry #573, volume donated by Clemens.

Cozzens, Frederick Swartwout (1818–1869). *Acadia; or, A Month with the Blue Noses*. New York: J. C. Derby, 1859.
   Catalog: Catalog 75 (January 1977), In Our Time Bookshop, Cambridge, Mass., item #65, $100. The catalog reports that this volume contains an *A1911* sale label, is unmarked, and is in fine condition. The Anderson Auction Company did not list this book for the auction in 1911.

———. *The Sparrowgrass Papers*. Philadelphia: T. B. Peterson & Brothers, n.d. (originally pub. 1856).
   Mark Twain's Library of Humor (1888) credited two pieces to this volume.

Craik (Mrs.) Dinah Maria (Muloch) (1826–1887). *Christian's Mistake*. New York: Harper & Brothers, 1871. 260 pp.
   Source: MTLAcc, entry #1634, volume donated by Clemens.

———. *The Cousin from India*. New York: Harper & Brothers, 1904. 229 pp.
   Source: MTLAcc, entry #414, volume donated by Clemens.

———. *Hannah*. New York: Harper & Brothers, 1904. 310 pp.
   Source: MTLAcc, entry #1139, volume donated by Clemens.

———. *The Head of the Family; A Novel*. Illus. New York: Harper & Brothers, 1905. 528 pp.
   Source: MTLAcc, entry #1328, volume donated by Clemens.

———. *A Hero, Bread Upon the Waters, Alice Learmont*. New York: Harper & Brothers, n.d. 269 pp.
   Source: MTLAcc, entry #1138, volume donated by Clemens.

———. *His Little Mother, and Other Tales and Sketches*. New York: Harper & Brothers, 1881. 269 pp.
   Source: MTLAcc, entry #1635, volume donated by Clemens.

———. *Is It True? Tales, Curious and Wonderful*. New York: Harper & Brothers, 1904. 208 pp.
   Source: MTLAcc, entry #1611, volume donated by Clemens.

———. *John Halifax, Gentleman*. New York: Harper & Brothers, 1903. 485 pp.
   Source: MTLAcc, entry #1632, volume donated by Clemens.
   References: "reading that high-flown batch of contradictions and inconsistencies, 'John Halifax, Gentelman' " (San Francisco *Daily Morning Call*, 30 August 1863, letter written from Steamboat Springs Hotel, photocopy supplied by Edgar M. Branch). "A novel by the author of John Halifax" (SLC to OLC, Steubenville, Ohio, 9 January 1872, MTP). Katy Leary claimed that Livy Clemens was forever trying to upgrade the reading tastes of her maid by giving her copies of "Dickens or *John Halifax,* or something dull and good like that" (*LMT,* p. 56).

———. *A Life for a Life, A Novel*. New York: Harper & Brothers, n.d. 396 pp.
   Source: MTLAcc, entry #1630, volume donated by Clemens.
   Clemens' letter to Olivia Langdon on 5 December 1868 from New York City mentions his reading *Life for a Life* at her recommendation (*LLMT,* p. 356). On 17 February 1869 Clemens wrote to her from Titusville, Pennsylvania: "I read & marked 'A Life for a Life' in the cars yesterday—I like it right well" (MTP).

----------. *The Little Lame Prince*. Illus. New York: Harper & Brothers, n.d. 194 pp.
Source: MTLAcc, entry #1188, volume donated by Clemens.

----------. *Little Sunshine's Holiday: A Picture from Life*. New York: Harper & Brothers, 1904. 210 pp.
Source: MTLAcc, entry #422, volume donated by Clemens.

----------. *Miss Moore*. Illus. New York: Harper & Brothers, 1904. 235 pp.
Source: MTLAcc, entry #418, volume donated by Clemens.

----------. *Mistress and Maid, A Household Story*. New York: Harper & Brothers, 1904. 327 pp.
Source: MTLAcc, entry #1629, volume donated by Clemens.

----------. *A Noble Life*. New York: Harper & Brothers, n.d. 302 pp.
Source: MTLAcc, entry #1631, volume donated by Clemens.

----------. *The Ogilvies. A Novel*. New York: Harper & Brothers, n.d. 421 pp.
Source: MTLAcc, entry #1633, volume donated by Clemens.

----------. *Olive. A Novel*. Illus. New York, 1905.
Cataog: A1911, #349, $1.

----------. *Plain Speaking*. New York: Harper & Brothers, 1882. 249 pp.
Source: MTLAcc, entry #1329, volume donated by Clemens.

----------. *Songs of Our Youth. Set to Music by Various Composers*. New York, 1875.
Catalog: A1911, #348, $1.50.

----------. *Studies from Life*. New York: Harper & Brothers, 1861. 290 pp.
Source: MTLAcc, entry #1140, volume donated by Clemens.

----------. "Too Late" (poem collected in *Poems* [Boston: Ticknor and Fields, 1866], pp. 186–187).
Clemens employed the refrain—"Douglas, Douglas, tender and true"—to satirize the advertising techniques employed by Harper & Brothers to promote Charles Dudley Warner's *Library of the World's Best Literature* (SLC to WDH, Kaltenleütgeben, 16 August 1898, *MTHL*, p. 676). Around 1865 Olivia Langdon copied another poem, "Philip, My King," into her commonplace book; sometime thereabouts she also inserted a handwritten copy of "Outward Bound" in the same book, crediting it to Miss Mulock (DV161, MTP).

----------. *Twenty Years Ago. From the Journal of a Girl in Her Teens*. New York: Harper & Brothers, 1904. 354 pp.
Source: MTLAcc, entry #1167, volume donated by Clemens.

----------. *A Woman's Thoughts about Women, by the Author of "John Halifax, Gentleman."* New York: Rudd & Carleton, 1858.
Inscription: "Livi L. Langdon June 1864".
Source: library card in Mark Twain Library at Redding. I could not locate the book in 1970.

----------. *A Woman's Thoughts about Women*. New York: Tollet, Foster & Co., 1864.
Inscription: "Livi L. Langdon—Jan [June?] 1864".
Location: Mark Twain Library, Redding, Connecticut.
Copy examined: Livy (Langdon) Clemens' copy.

Craik, George Lillie (1798–1866). *A Manual of English Literature and of the History of the English Language*. Tenth edition. London: Charles Griffin and Co., n.d. [Preface signed 1883.]
> *Inscription:* by Clemens in black ink: "Olivia L. Clemens/Hartford/1888".
> *Location:* Mark Twain Library, Redding, Connecticut.
> *Copy examined:* Clemens' gift copy to his wife.

Crane, Stephen (1871–1900). *The Monster and Other Stories*. Illus. New York: Harper & Brothers, 1899. 189 pp.
> *Source:* MTLAcc, entry #1531, volume donated by Clemens.

Crane, Thomas (b. 1843?) and Ellen E. Houghton. *Abroad*. London: Marcus Ward & Co., [1882]. 56 pp. [Illustrated verses by various authors.]
> *Source:* MTLAcc, entry #1879, volume donated from Clemens' library by Clara Clemens Gabrilowitsch in 1910.

Crawford, Francis Marion (1854–1909). *A Roman Singer*. Boston: Houghton, Mifflin & Co., 1884. 378 pp.
> *Source:* MTLAcc, entry #78, volume donated by Clemens.
> Clemens nominated Crawford for membership in the American Academy of Arts and Letters in 1905 (SLC to Robert Underwood Johnson, 28 April 1905, American Academy of Arts and Letters).

Crawford, (Mrs.) Louisa (Macartney) (1790–1858). "Kathleen Mavourneen" (song, 1840). Melody by Frederick Nicholls Crouch. [Lyrics sometimes ascribed to Mrs. Annie (Barry) Crawford or Mrs. Julia Crawford.]
> Annie (Moffett) Webster recalled that Clemens sang a parody of this poem during the period when he resided in St. Louis (1857–1861), substituting "Samuel Clemens" throughout for "Kathleen Mavourneen" (*MTBus*, pp. 39–40). "Called me . . . Aileen Mavourneen. She got it out of a song") "A Dog's Tale" [1903]).

Crawford, Samuel Wylie. *The Genesis of the Civil War: The Story of Sumter, 1860–61*. New York: Charles L. Webster & Co., 1887.
> *Catalog:* A1911, #113, $4.25.
> Clemens mentioned the title of this eye-witness account early in 1887 (NB 26, TS p. 36); his publishing firm had accepted the manuscript in 1886 (*MTB*, p. 831).

Crim, (Miss) Matt. *Adventures of a Fair Rebel*. Frontispiece by Dan Beard. New York: Charles L. Webster & Co., 1891. 323 pp.
> A young girl travels from North Carolina to Georgia during the Civil War. Issued by Clemens' publishing firm.

————. *Elizabeth, Christian Scientist*. New York: Charles L. Webster & Co., 1893. 350 pp.
> Clemens' publishing firm advertised this as "a novel of a girl who leaves her Georgia mountain home to convert the world to Christian Science." Her destiny, however, "is to be loved and wedded" (*Publishers' Trade List Annual 1893*).

————. *In Beaver Cove and Elsewhere*. New York: Charles L. Webster & Co., 1892. 346 pp.
> Short stories about life in the Georgia mountains. Published by Clemens' firm.

The Crisis in China, by George B. Smyth, Rev. Gilbert Reid, Charles Johnston [and Others], Reprinted . . . from the North American Review. Maps. New York: Harper & Brothers, 1900. 271 pp.
> *Source:* MTLAcc, entry #1742, volume donated by Clemens.

The Critic (periodical, pub. 1881–1906).
"Please have 'The Critic' sent regularly and permanently to Mrs. Clemens, Care Drexel Harjes & Co.," (SLC to Frank G. Whitmore, n.d. [1893?], MTP).

Crockett, Samuel Rutherford (1860–1914). *Bog-Myrtle and Peat: Tales, Chiefly of Galloway*. London: Bliss, Sands and Foster, 1895. 426 pp.
Source: MTLAcc, entry #2205, volume donated from Clemens' library by Clara Clemens Gabrilowitsch in 1910.

————. *Cleg Kelley, Arab of the City: His Progress and Adventures* (pub. 1895).
The Scottish novelist wrote Clemens on 23 August 1897: "I've got some boys I'd like to send you, if I might. I think Tom and Huck would like to know them. One of them is called 'Cleg Kelly.' Hully Gee, what a scrap there'd a been if Tom and Cleg had met" (MTP).

————. *The Dark o' the Moon. A Novel*. Illus. New York, 1902.
Inscription: signed on flyleaf: "S. L. Clemens, 1902."
Catalog: A1911, #114, $2.25.

————. *The Men of the Mountain*. Illus. New York: Harper & Brothers, 1909. 316 pp.
Source: MTLAcc, entry #1446, volume donated by Clemens.

————. *The Play-Actress*. New York: G. P. Putnam's Sons, 1894. 194 pp.
Source: MTLAcc, entry #2185, volume donated from Clemens' library by Clara Clemens Gabrilowitsch in 1910.

————. *The Raiders; Being Some Passages in the Life of John Faa, Lord and Earl of Little Egypt*. 2 vols. Collection of British Authors Series. Leipzig: B. Tauchnitz, 1894.
Source: MTLAcc, entries #2186 and #2206, volumes donated from Clemens' library by Clara Clemens Gabrilowitsch in 1910.

————. *The Red Axe*. Illus. by Frank Richards. New York: Harper & Brothers, 1902. 370 pp.
Source: MTLAcc, entry #1532, volume donated by Clemens.

————. *The Stickit Minister* (pub. 1893).
Catalog: C1951, #D65, listed with books signed by Clemens.

————. *Tales of Our Coast*. Illus. London: Chatto & Windus, 1896. 171 pp.
Source: MTLAcc, entry #2204, volume donated from Clemens' library by Clara Clemens Gabrilowitsch in 1910.

Croker, Bithia Mary (Sheppard) (d. 1920). *The Cat's-Paw*. Lippincott's Select Novels Series. Philadelphia: J. B. Lippincott Co., 1903. 374 pp. Paperbound.
Source: MTLAcc, entry #71, volume donated by Clemens.

————. *Mr. Jervis*. Lippincott's Select Novels Series. Philadelphia: J. B. Lippincott Co., 1903. 397 pp. Paperbound.
Source: MTLAcc, entry #70, volume donated by Clemens.

Croly, George (1780–1860). *Tarry Thou Till I Come; or, Salathiel, the Wandering Jew*. Illus. by T. de Thulstrup. New York: Funk & Wagnalls Co., 1901. 588 pp.
Source: MTLAcc, entry #1277, volume donated by Clemens.

Cronise, Titus Fey. *The Natural Wealth of California.* . . . *with a Detailed Description of Each County.* San Francisco: H. H. Bancroft & Co., 1868. 696 pp.
   Source: MTLAcc, entry #747, volume donated by Clemens.

Crookes, William. *Diamonds.* Illus. London: Harper & Brothers, 1909.
   Inscription: signed on front pastedown endpaper in black ink: "SL. Clemens/ 1909".
   Location: Antenne-Dorrance Collection, Rice Lake, Wis.
   Copy examined: Clemens' copy.
   In 1907 Mark Twain said that he was skeptical of Crookes' scientific renown because of his credulity about Archdeacon Wilberforce's Holy Grail (August? 1907 AD, *MTE,* p. 345).

Crooks, George Richard (1822–1897). *The Life of Bishop Matthew Simpson, of the Methodist Episcopal Church.* Illus. New York: Harper & Brothers, 1891. 524 pp.
   Source: MTLAcc, entry #1757, volume donated by Clemens.

Crosby, Ernest Howard (1856–1907). *Swords and Ploughshares.* New York: Funk & Wagnalls Co., 1902. 126 pp.
   Source: MTLAcc, entry #613, volume donated by Clemens.

Crothers, Samuel McChord (1857–1927). *The Gentle Reader.* Boston: Houghton, Mifflin and Co., 1904. 321 pp.
   Source: MTLAcc, entry #797, volume donated by Clemens.

Crouch, Archer Philip. *Señorita Montenar.* Illus. New York: Harper & Brothers, 1898. 300 pp.
   Source: MTLAcc, entry #1533, volume donated by Clemens.

"C. S." Tracts. London: Geo. Morrish, n.d. 206 pp.
   Source: MTLAcc, entry #926, volume donated by Clemens.

Cumming, (Rev.) John (1807–1881). *The Great Consummation. The Millennial Rest; or, The World As It Will Be.* New York: G. W. Carleton, 1863.
   Mark Twain wrote to the *Alta California* on 19 April 1867 to report that the porter at the Heming House in Keokuk (actually he stayed at the Deming House) had brought him a copy of *The Great Consummation* for his reading pleasure (*MTTMB,* p. 153). In chapter 57 of *IA* (1869) he told the same story, altering the hotel name to "Benton House." Cumming was a minister of the Scottish National Church who wrote evangelistic sermons.

Cundall, Joseph (1818–1895), pseud. "Stephen Percy." *Robin Hood and His Merry Foresters* (London, 1841; New York and Boston, 1842).
   Alan Gribben—"How Tom Sawyer Played Robin Hood 'by the Book,' " *English Language Notes,* 13 (March 1976), 201–204—describes Mark Twain's use of this literary source.

Cunliffe-Owen, Marguerite (de Godart) (1859–1927). *The Cradle of the Rose.* Illus. by the author. New York: Harper & Brothers, 1908. 320 pp.
   Source: MTLAcc, entry #1853, volume donated from Clemens' library by Clara Clemens Gabrilowitsch in 1910.

———. *A Doffed Coronet, A True Story.* Illus. New York: Harper & Brothers, 1902. 545 pp.
   Source: MTLAcc, entry #7, volume donated by Clemens.

———. [Another identical copy.]
   Source: MTLAcc, entry #1346, volume donated by Clemens.

————. *Emerald and Ermine; A Tale of the Argoät.* Illus. by the author. New York: Harper & Brothers, 1907. 329 pp.
Inscription: "To Doctor Clemens/With the compliments/of the Author./25th May 08."
Marginalia: nine pages turned down, but no marks or notes.
Catalog: "Retz Appraisal" (1944), p. 4, valued at $5.
Location: Mark Twain Papers, Berkeley, California.
Copy examined: Clemens' copy.

————. [Another identical copy.]
Source: MTLAcc, entry #1856, volume donated from Clemens' library by Clara Clemens Gabrilowitsch in 1910.

————. *Gray Mist; A Novel.* Illus. by the author. New York: Harper & Brothers, 1906. 282 pp.
Source: MTLAcc, entry #1507, volume donated by Clemens.

————. [Another identical copy.]
Source: MTLAcc, entry #1854, volume donated from Clemens' library by Clara Clemens Gabrilowitsch in 1910.

————. *Imperator et Rex, William II of Germany.* Illus. New York: Harper & Brothers, 1905. 282 pp.
Source: MTLAcc, entry #1298, volume donated by Clemens.

————. *A Keystone of Empire, Francis Joseph of Austria.* Illus. New York: Harper & Brothers, 1903. 322 pp.
Source: MTLAcc, entry #1297, volume donated by Clemens.

————. [Another identical copy.]
Catalog: A1911, #21, $2.

————. *The Martyrdom of an Empress.*
Catalog: C1951, #68c, $10, listed among the books signed by Clemens.

————. *The Tribulations of a Princess.* Portraits from photographs. New York: Harper & Brothers, [cop. 1901]. 378 pp.
Source: MTLAcc, entry #1506, volume donated by Clemens.

————. *The Tribulations of a Princess.* Portraits from photographs. New York: Harper & Brothers, 1901. 379 pp.
Source: MTLAcc, entry #1855, volume donated from Clemens' library by Clara Clemens Gabrilowitsch in 1910.

————. *The Trident and the Net; A Novel.* Illus. by the author. New York: Harper & Brothers, 1905. 550 pp.
Source: MTLAcc, entry #1317, volume donated by Clemens.

————. [Another identical copy.]
Inscription: on inner cover: "S. L. Clemens, 1906."
Catalog: A1911, #460, $2.25.

Cunningham, Alan (1784–1842). "A Wet Sheet and a Flowing Sea" (poem, song, pub. 1825).
In February 1882 Mark Twain declared that the title of this poem and song "has always been meaningless to me," owing to his ignorance of nautical terminology (NB 20, *N&J,* 2: 448). He quoted from the song in "About All Kinds of Ships" (1893). Cunningham's poem depicts the life of robust sailors whose ship "like the eagle free,/ . . . leaves/Old England on the lee."

Cupples, George (1822–1891). *The "Green Hand." A "Short" Yarn.* No. 68, Franklin Square Library Series. New York: Harper & Brothers, 1879. 83 pp.
> Clemens wrote "Green Hand 68 (No.)" in Notebook 19 (1881, *N&J,* 2: 395). On 23 May 1881 he requested of James R. Osgood: "Please send me No's 68 and 142 of Harper's Franklin Square Library (Green Hand and Sailor's Sweetheart.)" (*MTLP,* p. 136). See entry for W. C. Russell.
> *IE,* p. 161; *HH&T,* p. 145.

Curie, Marie. "Radium and Radioactivity," *Century Magazine,* 67 (January 1904), 461–466.
> Quoted by Satan ("what Madame Curie says about radium") in "Sold to Satan" (first pub. 1923).
> Sherwood Cummings, "Science" (unpub. doctoral dissertation, 1961).

Current Literature: A Magazine of Record and Review (New York), 6 (April 1891), 481–640. [A single issue with paper covers.]
> *Inscription:* Clemens penciled across the top of the front cover: "Contains Copyright bill." (Pages 484–489 reprint the full text of the International Copyright Bill.)
> *Marginalia:* Clemens annotated the main points of the Copyright Bill in pencil, for example (p. 485): "2 copies to Lib. Cong." He also made corrections on page 546 to a selection from M. Quad's "The Demon and the Fury" from the Detroit *Free Press.* Portions of page 546 and the following one have been cut out; pages 630–631 are also missing several cut-out sections.
> *Catalog:* "Retz Appraisal" (1944), p. 7, valued at $20.
> *Location:* Mark Twain Papers, Berkeley, California.
> *Copy examined:* Clemens' copy.

Curtis, Charles Albert (1835–1907). *Captured by the Navajos.* Illus. New York: Harper & Brothers, 1904. 291 pp.
> *Source:* MTLAcc, entry #1591, volume donated by Clemens.

Curtis, David A. (1846–1923). *Stand Pat; or, Poker Stories from the Mississippi.* Illus. by Henry Roth. New York: L. C. Page & Co., 1906. 269 pp.
> *Source:* MTLAcc, entry #2208, volume donated from Clemens' library by Clara Clemens Gabrilowitsch in 1910.

Curtis, George William (1824–1892). *Early Letters of George Wm. Curtis to John S. Dwight; Brook Farm and Concord.* Ed. by George Willis Cooke (1848–1923). New York: Harper & Brothers, 1898. 294 pp.
> *Source:* MTLAcc, entry #1463, volume donated by Clemens.

————. *The Howadji in Syria.* New York: Harper & Brothers, 1852.
> Clemens wrote to Emeline Beach on 10 February 1868 from Washington, D.C.: "You know very well that I am particularly fond of a happy expression, & that I never tired of reading that Howajji in Syria, simply because it could furnish that charm in such profusion" (quoted in Bradford A. Booth's "Mark Twain's Friendship with Emeline Beach," *AL,* 19 [November 1947], 219–230). Leon Dickinson's explanatory notes for the forthcoming Iowa-California edition of *IA* mention Mark Twain's drawing on Curtis' book for the account of a Turkish bath in chapter 34 of *IA* (1869).

————. *Potiphar Papers* (pub. 1853).
> Two pieces from this collection appeared in *Mark Twain's Library of Humor* (1888).

————. *Prue and I.* Illus. New York: Harper & Brothers, 1899. 223 pp.
> *Source:* MTLAcc, entry #1534, volume donated by Clemens.

Curtis, Lillian E. *Forget-Me-Not. Poems.* Albany, New York: Weed, Parsons and Co., 1872.

> *Inscription:* "To Mark Twain/from his sincere friend/and admirer/Edwin F. Schirely." At top of title page is signature: "E. F. Schirely/7/12/89."
>
> *Marginalia:* Clemens read the volume thoroughly in search of humorous passages, commenting in pencil, correcting syntax and rhymes, and occasionally making outright gibes such as the one on page 56 ("Letter to My Cousin, J. W. H., On His Birthday"): "Did he have to stand this every year?" On page 58, at the penultimate stanza of the same poem, Clemens urged: "Hit him again next year."
>
> *Location:* Antenne-Dorrance Collection, Rice Lake, Wis.
>
> *Copy examined:* Clemens' copy.

Curtis, William Eleroy (1850–1911). *The Capitals of Spanish America.* Illus. New York: Harper & Brothers, [cop. 1888]. 715 pp.

> *Source:* MTLAcc, entry #1378, volume donated by Clemens.

Cusack, Mary Francis (1830–1899) (pen name, "Sister Mary Francis Clare"). *Three Visits to Knock. With the Medical Certificates of Cures and Authentic Accounts of Different Apparitions.* New York: P. J. Kenedy, 1898. 135 pp. [Bound with John MacPhilpin's *The Apparitions and Miracles at Knock.* New York: P. J. Kenedy, 1898.]

> *Inscription:* signed on front pastedown endpaper in black ink: "Clemens".
>
> *Marginalia:* Clemens marked the volume in pencil up to page 86; he also commented on page 98 about the eviction of Irish tenants around Knock because of poor harvests.
>
> *Location:* Antenne-Dorrance Collection, Rice Lake, Wis.
>
> *Copy examined:* Clemens' copy.

Three visions—of the Virgin Mary and Saints Joseph and John—were allegedly seen in the parish chapel at Knock, a tiny village in County Mayo, Ireland. Pilgrims to the site soon reported miraculous cures. While heading northward from New Orleans on a steamboat in 1882 Clemens noted the title of MacPhilpin's book and resolved to "compare one of these with a miracle from the Bible" (*N&J*, 2: 475–476). He may have been aware then of Cusack's writings on the visions, since she was the chief proponent of their authenticity. Cusack's *Three Visits* was first published in London and Dublin in 1882.

Custer, Elizabeth B. *"Boots and Saddles"; or, Life in Dakota with General Custer.* New York: Harper & Brothers, 1885. 312 pp.

Clemens noted "Boots & Saddles E. B. Custer" in NB 24 (May 1885), TS p. 18.

————. *Tenting on the Plains; or, General Custer in Kansas and Texas.* New York: Charles L. Webster & Co., 1887. 403 pp.

> *Inscription:* "Clara L. Clemens/Elmira/July 1888".
>
> *Location:* Mark Twain Library, Redding, Connecticut.
>
> *Copy examined:* Clara's copy, published by her father's firm.

Custer, (Gen.) George A. *My Life on the Plains.* New York: Sheldon and Co., 1874. 256 pp.

On the verso of Clemens' letter of 24 July 1884 to Charles L. Webster (containing a request for Col. Dodge's Indian book), Webster wrote: "My Life on the Plains/Gen. G. A. Custer USA/Sheldon & Co" (TS in MTP).

> *HH&T*, p. 86.

Cutter, Bloodgood Haviland (1817–1906). *The Long-Island Farmer's Poems, Lines Written on the "Quaker City" Excursion to Palestine, and Other Poems*. New York: N. Tibbals & Sons, 1886.

Mark Twain preserved this poetaster's place in American letters by calling him the "Poet Lariat" and chuckling over his verse in *Innocents Abroad* (1869); thereafter Mark Twain took pleasure in encouraging Cutter's publication of his effusions. Notebooks 8 (1867) and 46 (1903) contain references to Cutter. Bradley, Beatty, and Long's edition of *Huckleberry Finn* (1962) reprints an example of Cutter's "lugubrious, sentimental, and semi-literate verse" (p. 252).

Dagless, Thomas. *The Light in Dends Wood, and Other Stories*. London: Greening & Co., 1903. 116 pp.
Source: MTLAcc, entry #112, volume donated by Clemens.

Dahlgren, (Mrs.) Madeleine Vinton (1825–1898). *Memoir of John A. Dahlgren, Rear-Admiral United States Navy*. New York: Charles L. Webster & Co., 1891. 660 pp.
Published by Clemens' firm.

Dallas, J. A. "Up the Mississippi," *Emerson's United States Magazine*. [Date and pages unknown; *Emerson's* periodical was published in New York between 1854 and 1858.]

W. Rowlands of James R. Osgood & Company responded on 22 July 1882 to Clemens' undated request for books relating to the Mississippi River. Rowlands assured him that they were sending "a number of 'Emerson's Magazine,' with 'Up the Miss.' by J. A. Dallas in it" (MTP).

Daly, Augustin (1838–1899). *Divorce* (play, perf. 1871).

Grace King remembered seeing this play with the Clemenses at Daly's Fifth Avenue Theatre, probably in 1887 when she visited Hartford and took a side-trip to New York City to meet William Dean Howells. Ada Rehan and Mrs. John Drew had the leading female roles in *Divorce;* Daly provided the Clemenses and Miss King with a proscenium box (King, *Memoirs*, p. 87).

———— (adapt.). *The Lottery of Love* (perf. 1888). [An adaptation of *Les surprises du divorce* by Alexandre Bisson and Antony Mars.]

In the autumn of 1888 Clemens promised to take his family to see the one-act curtain-raiser that preceded Daly's play, Justin Huntly McCarthy's *The Wife of Socrates* (SLC to Daly, undated ALS. Houghton Library, Harvard).

Daly, Thomas Augustine (1871–1948). *Canzoni*. Illus. by John Sloan. Philadelphia: Catholic Standard and Times Publishing Co., 1906. 172 pp. [Collection of brief poems.]
Inscription: on first flyleaf: "To/Samuel L. Clemens,/Master Craftsman,/with the admiring regards/of his humble servant,/T. A. Daly/Oct. 13/'06".
Location: Mark Twain Library, Redding, Connecticut. Donated from Clemens' library by Clara Clemens Gabrilowitsch in 1910 (MTLAcc, entry #2023).
Copy examined: Clemens' copy.

Dana, Charles Anderson (1819–1897), comp. *The Household Book of Poetry. Collected and Edited by Charles A. Dana*. Eleventh edition. Revised and enlarged. New York: D. Appleton and Co., 1869. 816 pp.
Inscription: on flyleaf: "Merry Christmas to Livie L. Langdon from her Brother Dec. 25th 1868".
Catalog: C1951, #027; *Zeitlin 1951,* #13, $6.50.
Location: Mark Twain Papers, Berkeley, California.
Copy examined: Livy Clemens' copy.

Dana, James Dwight (1813–1895). *Manual of Mineralogy, including Observations on Mines.* New ed., rev. and enl. Philadelphia: T. Bliss & Co., 1864. 456 pp.
  Source: MTLAcc, entry #816, volume donated by Clemens.

Dana, Richard Henry (1815–1882). *To Cuba and Back. A Vacation Voyage.* Boston: James R. Osgood & Company, 1875. 288 pp.
  Inscription: signed in pencil on flyleaf: "Saml L. Clemens/Hartford 1876".
  Location: Humanities Research Center, University of Texas at Austin.
  Copy examined: Clemens' copy, unmarked. Page 170 folded down.

————. *Two Years Before the Mast: A Personal Narrative. New Edition, with Subsequent Matter by the Author.* Boston: Houghton, Mifflin and Co., 1876.
  Inscription: "S. L. Clemens, Hartford, 1876."
  Marginalia: various passages marked.
  Catalog: A1911, #116, $6.
  Albert Bigelow Paine reported that Dana's book was one of the "reliable favorites" enjoyed by Clemens and Theodore Crane on the lawn of Quarry Farm during the summer of 1874 *(MTB,* p. 511). Mrs. James T. Fields recorded in her diary that on 27 April 1876 Clemens, her host in Hartford, had awakened early and "had been re-reading Dana's *Two Years before the Mast* in bed . . . and revolving subjects for his Autobiography," an interesting linking ("Bret Harte and MT in the 'Seventies': Passages from the Diaries of Mrs. James T. Fields," *Atlantic Monthly,* 130 [September 1922], 346). In April 1878 Clemens expressed his preference for the narratives of Dana or Franchère, which show "that a common sailor's life is often a hell," over the "lying story-books which make boys fall in love with the sea" (NB 14, *N&J,* 2: 69). Paine remembered that *Two Years* was a book "he loved, and never tired of" during his adult lifetime *(MTB,* p. 1540); this assertion is borne out by Mark Twain's quoting from the work in Part 7 of "Is Shakespeare Dead?" (1909) to show that "Richard H. Dana served two years before the mast, and had every experience that falls to the lot of the sailor. . . . His sailor-talk flows from his pen with the sure touch and the ease and confidence of a person who has *lived* what he is talking about, not gathered it from books and random listenings."
  A brief vignette that Dana relates in chapter 35 of his book eventually became Clemens' favorite passage in the book and served him as a reliable literary source on several occasions. In Dana's version, the narrator on board the *Alert* recounts at second-hand how "a man named Sam, on board the Pilgrim, used to tell a story of a mean little captain in a mean little brig, in which he sailed from Liverpool to New York." This captain "insisted on speaking a great, homeward-bound Indiaman, with her studding-sails out on both sides, sunburnt men in wide-brimmed hats on her decks, and a monkey and paroquet in her rigging. . . . There was no need of his stopping her to speak her, but his vanity led him to do it and then his meanness made him so awestruck that he seemed to quail. He called out, in a small, lisping voice, 'What ship is that, pray?' A deep-toned voice roared through the trumpet, 'The Bashaw, from Canton, bound to Boston. Hundred and ten days out! Where are you from?' '*Only* from Liverpool, *sir,*' he lisped, in the most apologetic and subservient voice" (pp. 413–414). Dana very nearly spoils the story by explaining it: "But the humor will be felt by those only who know the ritual of hailing at sea. No one says 'sir,' and the 'only' was wonderfully expressive."
  Mark Twain's repetitious notebook entries reveal that he was practicing its delivery for many years. In March 1888 he copied into Notebook 27 the key lines he would later use to great effect: "The Bashaw of Bengal [Dana's *Bashaw* from Canton lacked this alliteration], 260 days out [Dana's ship was only 110 days away from port] from Calcutta [another addition by Mark Twain],—homeward bound!—the Mary Ann, 3 days out from Boston—only goin to Liverpool" (TS p. 60). Two years later Mark Twain entered another variation of the same elements in Notebook 30: " 'The <Bashaw> Begum of Bengal 116

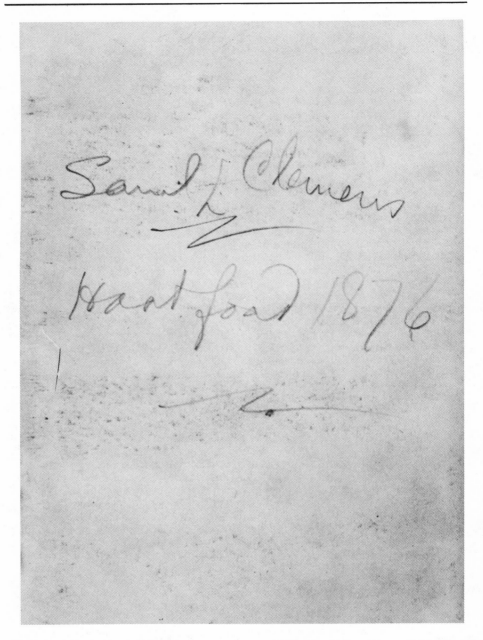

Plate 6: Flyleaf in Richard Henry Dana's *To Cuba and Back* (1875). This form of Clemens' penciled signature identifies many volumes he acquired in the early and mid-1870's. Eventually he adopted "S. L. Clemens" as the customary inscription for his library books.
(Courtesy of Humanities Research Center, University of Texas, Austin.)

days out from <Hong *Kong*> Canton, homeward *bound*. What vessel's that?' " (TS p. 4). Again in 1904 Mark Twain jotted down a mental rehearsal of the sketch: " 'The Begum of Bengal!' " (NB 46, TS p. 34). Finally on 10 July 1907 Mark Twain introduced the story into his address at the Town Hall banquet in Liverpool, the occasion of what Hamlin Hill has called "the most poignant speech of his entire career" (*MTGF*, p. 175). In this ultimate recital of the borrowed anecdote, Mark Twain credited Dana's book but altered the details: "Came the answer back through a speaking trumpet, 'The *Begum of Bengal*, a hundred and twenty-three days out from Canton—homeward bound! What ship is that?' The little captain's vanity was all crushed out of him, and most humbly he squeaked back: 'Only the *Mary Ann*, fourteen hours out from Boston, bound for Kittery Point with—with nothing to speak of!' " (*MTSpk*, p. 582). Shortly thereafter Mark Twain retold the story as the climax to his final Lotos Club speech on 11 January 1908, crediting the *Begum* with 148 days out from Canton and saying it was an incident he gathered "many, many years ago . . . from Mr. Dana's *Two Years Before the Mast*" (*MTSpk*, p. 609).

Dante, Alighieri (1265–1321). *The Divine Comedy of Dante Alighieri*. Trans. by Henry Wadsworth Longfellow (1807–1882). Authorized Edition. 3 vols. Leipzig: Bernhard Tauchnitz, 1867.
Source: MTLAcc, entries #2043–2045, volumes donated from Clemens' library by Clara Clemens Gabrilowitsch in 1910.
References: chapter 24 of *IA* (1869); one of the "names familiar to every school-boy" (NB 17 [1878], *N&J*, 2: 227); "Dante's Francesco di Rimina [*sic*] & that romantic tragedy" (NB 32 [May 1892], TS p. 8); mentioned twice in letter from Clemens to Susan Crane from Florence, 30 September 1892 (*MTL*, pp. 570–571). In June 1893 Clemens passed the "window in Monastery where Dante wrote part of the Divine Comedy" (NB 33, TS p. 18). Dante is mentioned in the preface to *PW* (1894), "A Whisper to the Reader"; referred to in "Instructions in Art" (1903); and mentioned reverently in "Three Thousand Years among the Microbes" (written 1905).

——. *The Divine Comedy of Dante Alighieri*. Trans. by Henry Wadsworth Longfellow (1807–1882). 3 vols. Boston: Houghton, Mifflin and Co., 1895.
Source: MTLAcc, entries #1768 and #1769, volumes 2 (*Purgatorio*) and 3 (*Paradiso*) only, donated by Clemens.

——. *The Vision; or, Hell, Purgatory and Paradise of Dante Alighieri*. Trans. by Henry Francis Cary (1772–1844). With biography, notes and index. Illus. by John Flaxman. New York: D. Appleton & Co., 1864. 587 pp.
Source: MTLAcc, entry #2022, volume donated from Clemens' library by Clara Clemens Gabrilowitsch in 1910.

Darby, (Mrs.) Sarah. *That Affair in Philadelphia*. New York: Broadway Publishing Co., 1909. 75 pp.
Source: MTLAcc, entry #2209, volume donated from Clemens' library by Clara Clemens Gabrilowitsch in 1910.

Darley, Felix Octavius Carr (1822–1888). *Compositions in Outline by Felix O. C. Darley, from Hawthorne's Scarlet Letter*. 12 plates. Boston: Houghton, Mifflin & Co., [cop. 1879].
Catalog: A1911, #118, $2.25.

————. *Compositions in Outline by Felix O. C. Darley, from [Sylvester] Judd's Margaret* [novel, pub. 1845]. Engraved by Konrad Huber. Middleton, N. Y., 1856.

> *Catalog: A1911,* #117, $2.50.
> Clemens notified Dr. John Brown on 28 February 1874 that he had shipped him a copy of this American illustrator's book of drawings inspired by *Margaret.* "We in America think a deal of Darley's work," Clemens wrote (*MTL,* p. 215).

[Darrow, Allen R. (b. 1826)]. *Iphigenia: A Legend of the Iliad, and Other Poems.* Buffalo, N. Y.: C. L. Sherrill Co., 1888. 98 pp. Paperbound, ribbon-tied.

> *Source:* MTLAcc, entry #2009, volume donated from Clemens' library by Clara Clemens Gabrilowitsch in 1910.

Darwin, Charles Robert (1809–1882). *The Descent of Man, and Selection in Relation to Sex.* 2 vols. New York: D. Appleton and Co., 1871. [Only Clemens' copy of vol. 1 has been located.]

> *Inscription:* front flyleaf missing.
> *Marginalia:* plentiful annotation, of which samples are quoted by Sherwood Cummings in "MT's Acceptance of Science" (1962).
> *Location:* vol. 1 only in Mark Twain Papers, Berkeley, California.
> *Copy examined:* Clemens' copy.
> Sometime around 1871 Clemens wrote in July to Jim [Gillis?] from Elmira, offering to buy any of Darwin's books and forward them (ALS in St. John's Seminary, Camarillo). Albert Bigelow Paine reported that *The Descent of Man* belonged to Clemens' "earlier reading, . . . a book whose influence was always present, though I believe he did not read it any more in later years" (*MTB,* p. 1540). Clemens "talked with the great Darwin" at Grasmere in the English Lake District in August 1879 (NB 18, *N&J,* 2: 339). He referred jokingly to Darwin's concept of "rudimentary" forms in NB 18 (1879, *N&J,* 2: 349) and in chapter 35 of *TA* (1880). "Mr. Darwin was grieved to feel obliged to give up his theory that the monkey was the connecting link between man and the lower animals" ("Some Thoughts on the Science of Onanism," written 1879, DV200, no. 3, MTP). "Mr. Darwin's *Descent of Man* had been in print five or six years, and the storm of indignation raised by it was still raging in pulpits and periodicals," recalled Mark Twain in "A Monument to Adam." Clemens' invectives against Whitelaw Reid recorded in Notebook 20 (1882) included the allegation that Reid was "<the Remote Darwinian> The Missing link" (*N&J,* 2: 442). "It obliges me to renounce my allegiance to the Darwinian theory of the Ascent [*sic*] of Man from the Lower Animals" ("The Lowest Animal," probably written 1897, *LE,* p. 223). Twain mentioned *The Descent of Man* in his 29 March 1906 AD (MTP).
> Waggoner, "Science," pp. 365–366; Cummings, *"WIM?:* Scientific Sources," pp. 111–113; Cummings, "MT's Acceptance of Science"; *MT&JB,* p. 56; *WIM?,* pp. 83, 542.

————. *The Descent of Man, and Selection in Relation to Sex.* New ed., rev. New York: D. Appleton and Co., 1887. 688 pp. [Part of Clemens' 12-vol. set of Darwin's writings.]

> *Location:* Wake Forest University, Winston-Salem, N. C. Donated by Mrs. Nancy Susan Reynolds.
> *Copy examined:* Clemens' unmarked copy.

————. *The Different Forms of Flowers on Plants of the Same Species.* Illus. New York: D. Appleton and Co., 1884. [Part of Clemens' set of Darwin's works.]

> *Catalog:* "MT Collection," *The Bookman,* No. 25 (1970), #329.
> *Location:* Wake Forest University, Winston-Salem, N. C. Donated by Mrs. Nancy Susan Reynolds.
> *Copy examined:* Clemens' unmarked copy.

————. *The Effects of Cross and Self-Fertilisation in the Vegetable Kingdom*. New York: D. Appleton and Co., 1883. [Part of Clemens' set of Darwin's works.]
> *Catalog:* "MT Collection," *The Bookman*, No. 25 (1970), #329.
> *Location:* Wake Forest University, Winston-Salem, N. C. Donated by Mrs. Nancy Susan Reynolds.
> *Copy examined:* Clemens' unmarked copy.

————. *The Expression of the Emotions in Man and Animals*. New York: D. Appleton and Co., 1886. [Part of Clemens' set of Darwin's works.]
> *Inscription:* signed on second flyleaf in black ink: "SL. Clemens/Hartford, 1887."
> *Marginalia:* numerous pencil marks by Clemens on page 31 (the powerful force of habit—caterpillars will die rather than eat the leaves of an unfamiliar tree), pp. 36, 38 (reflex actions), pp. 76–77 (joy and terror indicated in animals), p. 87 (an ape known to sing), 91 (dog barking), 94 (bird courtship sounds), 135, 138–139, 145, 167, and others.
> *Catalog:* "MT Collection," *The Bookman*, No. 25 (1970), #329.
> *Location:* Wake Forest University, Winston-Salem, N. C. Donated by Mrs. Nancy Susan Reynolds.
> *Copy examined:* Clemens' copy.

Clemens noted in February or March 1891 that he wished to "examine Darwin again" to see what he stated about the correlation of a lunatic's hair condition and his prognosis; Clemens thought Darwin found that dry, harsh hair means "not curable" (NB 30, TS p. 24). In chapter 12 of *Expression* Darwin does claim correlations exist between hair condition and mental states, and he specifically alludes to the "dryness and harshness" of hair that accompanies insanity; one mental institution, Darwin reports, has noticed that its patients show marked improvement "whenever their hair ceases to be rough and unmanageable" (p. 296). In Notebook 30 Clemens also wrote in connection with Darwin's research: "Monkey's emit a low chuckling laugh when you tickle them under the armpits." In chapter 5 of *Expression* Darwin notes, regarding expressions of pleasure by monkeys: "If a young chimpanzee be tickled—and the armpits are particularly sensitive to tickling, as in the case of our children, —a more decided chuckling or laughing sound is uttered" (p. 131). Clemens memorized the fact, for in Paris during April or May 1895, formulating his attacks on man's supposed superiority among living creatures, he noted: "Man has been called the laughing animal to distinguish him from the others—but the monkey laughs" (NB 34, TS p. 9). Later he observed that monkeys, like man, are capable of laughter, "as Mr. Darwin pointed out" ("The Lowest Animal," written about 1897, LE, p. 225). Mark Twain also probably owes the inspiration for one of his most celebrated maxims—"Man is the Only Animal that Blushes. Or needs to" (chapter 27, FE [1897])—to chapter 13 of Darwin's *Expression of the Emotions*, which begins: "Blushing is the most peculiar and the most human of all expressions. Monkeys redden from passion, but it would require an overwhelming amount of evidence to make us believe that any animal could blush" (p. 309).

————. *The Formation of Vegetable Mould, Through the Action of Worms, with Observations on Their Habits*. Illus. New York: D. Appleton and Co., 1885. [Part of 12-vol. set.]
> *Marginalia:* no annotation except for brown ink mark at the top of page 17 (structure of worms).
> *Catalog:* "MT Collection," *The Bookman*, No. 25 (1970), #329.
> *Location:* Wake Forest University, Winston-Salem, N.C. Gift of Mrs. Nancy Susan Reynolds.
> *Copy examined:* Clemens' copy.

————. *Insectivorous Plants*. New York: D. Appleton and Co., 1886. [Part of 12-vol. set.]
 Catalog: "MT Collection," *The Bookman*, No. 25 (1970), #329.
 Location: Wake Forest University, Winston-Salem, N.C. Gift of Mrs. Nancy Susan Reynolds.
 Copy examined: Clemens' unmarked copy.

————. *Journal of Researches into the Natural History and Geology of the Countries Visited During the Voyage of H.M.S. Beagle Round the World*. New ed. New York: D. Appleton and Co., 1887. [Part of 12-vol. set.]
 Inscription: signed on second flyleaf in black ink: "SL. Clemens/Hartford, 1887."
 Catalog: C1951, #56c, $25, listed among books signed by Clemens; "MT Collection," *The Bookman*, No. 25 (1970), #329.
 Location: Wake Forest University, Winston-Salem, N.C. Given by Mrs. Nancy Susan Reynolds.
 Copy examined: Clemens' copy.
 WIM?, p. 181.

————. *The Life and Letters of Charles Darwin*. Ed. by Francis Darwin. 2 vols. New York: D. Appleton and Co., 1887.
 Isabel Lyon noted in her Daily Reminder on 17 October 1905—while preparing to leave Dublin, New Hampshire—that she "sent back to Library" two volumes of Darwin's letters, presumably borrowed by Clemens (MTP). In a speech at the Pilgrims Luncheon in London on 25 June 1907 Mark Twain recalled that Joseph H. Twichell procured an early copy of Darwin's *Life and Letters* and joshed Mark Twain about Darwin's fondness for Twain's books *(MTSpk*, p. 559).

————. *The Movements and Habits of Climbing Plants*. Second ed., rev. Illus. New York: D. Appleton and Co., 1884. [Part of 12-vol. set.]
 Catalog: "MT Collection," *The Bookman*, No. 25 (1970), #329.
 Location: Wake Forest University, Winston-Salem, N.C. Gift of Mrs. Nancy Susan Reynolds.
 Copy examined: Clemens' unmarked copy.

————. *On the Origin of Species by Means of Natural Selection, or the Preservation of Favored Races in the Struggle for Life*. New York: D. Appleton and Co., 1884. [Part of 12-vol. set.]
 Marginalia: small ink dot in margin of page 106 at summary of chapter 5. No other markings.
 Catalog: "MT Collection," *The Bookman*, No. 25 (1970), #329.
 Location: Wake Forest University, Winston-Salem, N.C. Donated by Mrs. Nancy Susan Reynolds.
 Copy examined: Clemens' copy.
References: In September 1872 Clemens visited London, and his account of the trip mentioned Darwin facetiously: "We entered the great Zoological Gardens with Mr. Henry Lee. . . . I wanted to find Mr. Darwin's baboon that plays mother to a cat but did not succeed. So Mr. Darwin invented that. In the house of monkeys there was one long, lean active fellow that made me a convert to the theory of Natural Selection. He made a natural selection of monkeys smaller than himself to sling around by the tail" *(The Twainian*, 36 [March-April 1977], 3). "This is what Mr. Darwin might call a 'rudimentary' sign" ("Concerning the American Language" [1882]). Mark Twain's concept of natural law as he articulated it on 6 November 1895 appears to have been influenced by Darwin's *Origin of Species* (1859): "There is nothing kindly, nothing benificent, nothing friendly in Nature toward *any* creature, except by capricious fits & starts; that Nature's attitude toward all life is

profoundly vicious, treacherous & malignant" (NB 34, TS p. 31). In chapter 8 of *FE* (1897) Mark Twain called the duck-billed platypus "a survival—a survival of the fittest. Mr. Darwin invented the theory that goes by that name," attributing the remark to an English naturalist in New Zealand. In "Three Thousand Years among the Microbes" (1905) a man-turned-cholera germ observes that "evolution is the law of policies: Darwin said it," but erroneously recalls that "Cuvier proved it and established it for all time in his paper on 'The Survival of the Fittest,' " another of Mark Twain's late attempts to achieve humor through mangled "histories" *(WWD?,* p. 467).
Cummings, "MT's Social Darwinism," p. 165; *MT&JB,* p. 56.

————, assisted by Francis Darwin. *The Power of Movement in Plants.* Illus. New York: D. Appleton and Co., 1885. |Part of 12-vol. set.]
Catalog: "MT Collection," *The Bookman,* No. 25 (1970), #329.
Location: Wake Forest University, Winston-Salem, N.C. Donated by Mrs. Nancy Susan Reynolds.
Copy examined: Clemens' unmarked copy.

————. *The Variation of Animals and Plants Under Domestication.* Second ed., rev. 2 vols. New York: D. Appleton and Co., 1884. [Part of 12-vol. set.]
Catalog: "MT Collection," *The Bookman,* No. 25 (1970), #329.
Location: Wake Forest University, Winston-Salem, N.C. Gift of Mrs. Nancy Susan Reynolds.
Copy examined: Clemens' copy.
Sherwood Cummings, "MT's Social Darwinism" (1957), p. 165.

————. *The Various Contrivances by Which Orchids Are Fertilised by Insects.* Second ed., rev. Illus. New York: D. Appleton and Co., 1886. [Part of 12-vol. set.]
Catalog: "MT Collection," *The Bookman,* No. 25 (1970), #329.
Location: Wake Forest University, Winston-Salem, N.C. Gift of Mrs. Nancy Susan Reynolds.
Copy examined: Clemens' unmarked copy.

Dasent, George Webbe (1817–1896), ed. and trans. *The Story of Burnt Njal; or, Life in Iceland at the End of the Tenth Century.* 2 vols. Edinburgh, 1861.
Catalog: Mott 1952, #47, $2.50, vol. 2 only, inscribed to Jean Clemens from "G. D."

Daudet, Alphonse (1840–1897). *Fromont jeune et Risler aîné.* Boston, 1877.
Inscription: signed on flyleaf: "S. L. Clemens, Hartford, 1877."
Marginalia: a few notes.
Catalog: A1911, #119, $2.

————. *The Immortal; or, One of the "Forty."* Trans. from French by Arthur Woollgar Verrall and Margaret de G. Verrall. Illus. Chicago: Rand, McNally & Co., 1889. 307 pp.
Source: MTLAcc, entry #2210, volume donated from Clemens' library by Clara Clemens Gabrilowitsch in 1910.

————. *Le siège de Berlin, et d'autres contes, par Alphonse Daudet.* New York: W. R. Jenkins, 1885. 73 pp. [Reissued by the same firm in 1886, 1887, 1888. No English edition pub. until 1903.]
"Examine 'The Siege of Berlin,' & perhaps publish it in the Century," wrote Mark Twain in March 1889 (NB 28, TS p. 52).

Davie, Oliver. *Nests and Eggs of North American Birds*. Fifth ed., rev.
Illus. Columbus, Ohio: Landon Press, 1898. 545 pp.
 Inscription: on second flyleaf, not SLC's hand: "Jean Lampton Clemens,/
Riverdale on the Hudson/New York/1903".
 Provenance: bookseller's sticker of G. P. Putnam's Sons of New York City
on the front pastedown endpaper.
 Location: Mark Twain Library, Redding, Connecticut. Donated from
Clemens' library by Clara Clemens Gabrilowitsch in 1910 (MTLAcc,
entry #1944).
 Copy examined: Jean Clemens' copy.

Davies, Hubert Henry (1876-1917). *Cousin Kate* (play, prod. 1903).
 In April 1904 Mark Twain gave a curtain-raiser speech for a benefit
performance of *Cousin Kate* in Florence (Hamlin Hill, *MTGF*, p. 82).

Davis, George Breckenridge (1847-1914). *The Elements of International
Law*. New York: Harper & Brothers, [cop. 1900]. 612 pp.
 Source: MTLAcc, entry #1363, volume donated by Clemens.

Davis, L. Clarke, ed. *The Story of the Memorial Fountain to Shakespeare at
Stratford-upon-Avon*. Cambridge: Riverside Press, 1890.
 Inscription: on the first flyleaf: "Mrs. Samuel L. Clemens/with cordial
regard of/L. Clarke Davis/June 3, 1890". Frontispiece inscribed by the
donor of the fountain, George W. Childs: "To his friend/Mrs. S. L.
Clemens/1890". No markings in volume.
 Location: Mark Twain Library, Redding, Connecticut.
 Copy examined: Livy Clemens' copy.

Davis, Mary Evelyn (Moore) (1852-1909). *An Elephant's Track, and Other
Stories*. Illus. New York: Harper & Brothers, 1897. 276 pp.
 Source: MTLAcc, entry #1535, volume donated by Clemens.

Davis, Norah (b. 1878). *Wallace Rhodes, A Novel*. New York: Harper &
Brothers, 1909. 335 pp.
 Source: MTLAcc, entry #1109, volume donated by Clemens.

Davis, Richard Harding (1864-1916). *The Bar Sinister*. Illus. by E. M. Ashe.
New York: C. Scribner's Sons, 1903. 108 pp.
 Source: MTLAcc, entry #1880, volume donated from Clemens' library
by Clara Clemens Gabrilowitsch in 1910.

————. *Gallegher, and Other Stories*. Illus. by Charles Dana Gibson. New
York: Charles Scribner's Sons, 1903. 236 pp.
 Source: MTLAcc, entry #113, volume donated by Clemens.

————. *Her First Appearance*. Illus. by Charles Dana Gibson and E. M. Ashe.
New York, 1901.
 Inscription: signed "S. L. Clemens, Riverdale-on-Hudson, Nov. 1901."
 Catalogs: A1911, #120, $5; item #208 sold from Library of Charles E.
Feinberg, 21 May 1968, $130 (*American Book-Prices Current* [New York:
Columbia Univ. Press, 1971], p. 214).

————. *Soldiers of Fortune*. Illus. by Charles Dana Gibson. London: W.
Heinemann. 1897. 288 pp.
 Source: MTLAcc, entry #2211, volume donated from Clemens' library
by Clara Clemens Gabrilowitsch in 1910,

————. *Vera, the Medium*. Illus. by Frederic Dorr Steele. New York: Charles Scribner's Sons, 1908. 216 pp.
   Source: MTLAcc, entry #121, volume donated by Clemens.

Davis, Robert G. *Reports of a Portion of the Decisions Rendered by the Supreme Court of the Hawaiian Islands, In Law, Equity, Admiralty and Probate, 1857-1865*. Honolulu: Government Press, 1866.
   Clemens examined this volume with the critical eye of a former typesetter in 1866, pronouncing it "elegantly printed & bound—800 pages—in a shape do honor to any printers" (NB 6, *N&J*, 1: 204).

Davis, Samuel Post (1850-1918). *Short Stories*. San Francisco: Golden Era Co., 1886. 189 pp.
   "The First Piano in Camp" from this volume appeared in *Mark Twain's Library of Humor* (1888).

Davis, Varina Anne Jefferson (1864-1898). *A Romance of Summer Seas; A Novel*. New York: Harper & Brothers, 1898. 278 pp.
   Source: MTLAcc, entry #1099, volume donated by Clemens.

Davitt, Michael (1846–1906). *The Fall of Feudalism in Ireland; or, the Story of the Land League Revolution*. New York: Harper & Brothers, 1904. 751 pp.
   Source: MTLAcc, entry #593, volume donated by Clemens.
   On 13 December 1896, in London, Clemens noted: "Met Michael Davitt to-day" (NB 39, TS p. 33). In chapter 30 of *FE* (1897) he observed of Dunedin, New Zealand: "This town justifies Michael Davitt's praises." Clemens' business agent listed Davitt's *Fall of Feudalism* as one of "four Harper's books" from Messrs. French, Lemon & Co. that arrived in Florence after Clemens departed following Livy's death in June 1904 (S. V. Cecchi to SLC, 30 July 1904, Haskard & Co., Bankers, Florence). On 4 November 1904 the parcel had still not been forwarded from Florence (Cecchi to SLC, Haskard & Co., Bankers).

Dawson, A. J. (1872-1951). *The Genteel A. B.* Illus. London, 1907.
   Inscription: on the flyleaf Dawson quotes three stanzas from Mark Twain's doggerel poem, "The Aged Pilot Man" (chapter 51 of *RI* [1872]), attributing them to "Gems of Classic Thought, c.f. The World's Poetical Masterpieces, Twain's Reliques." An ALS from Dawson is pasted on the front pastedown endpaper, dated 3 May 1908 from Tigh-Na-Rosan, Nairn, N. B., Scotland, inviting Clemens to return.
   Catalog: A1911, #121, $10.

Dawson, William James (1854–1928) and Coningsby William Dawson (1883–1959), eds. *The Great English Essayists. Introductions and Notes*. New York, 1909.
   Inscription: signed on front pastedown endpaper: "S. L. Clemens, 1909. See de Quincy."
   Catalog: A1911, #158, $2.50.

————, ed. *The Great English Letter Writers, with Introductory Essays and Notes*. 2 vols. New York: Harper & Brothers, 1909. [Only vol. 1 located.]
   Inscription: signed in brown ink on front pastedown endpaper of vol. 1: "SL. Clemens/1909."
   Marginalia: lengthy comment in brown ink at bottom of page 93, where Robert Louis Stevenson explains his religion of kindness; Clemens wrote in part: "To him, all his listeners are alike, & the same sermon will fit them all. He is evidently as ignorant as a priest or a Bible—or a god." Another note in brown ink in the margin of page 114 expresses disgust at Benjamin Robert Haydon's

paean to Shakespeare's Stratford birthplace ("you hear the very breezing of the trees he himself heard, and listen to the very humming watery ripple of the river he must often have enjoyed"): "Now where *is* the use in spewing up all these raptures over that third-rate actor, who never wrote a line in his life?" Clemens made grammatical corrections in a letter from David Hume (p. 138) and a letter from John Keats (p. 266), eliminating wordy constructions. On page 143, at Coleridge's describing his employment as that of "writing MS. sermons for lazy clergymen," Clemens underlined four lines and wrote above them: "Oh, grotesque trade!" To Southey's assertion that "literature cannot be the business of a woman's life, and it ought not to be" (p. 197), Clemens noted at the bottom of the page: "That settles it!" No additional markings or notes.
  Location: vol. 1 only in Antenne-Dorrance Collection, Rice Lake, Wis.
  Copy examined: Clemens' copy.

Day, Holman Francis (1865–1935). *The Eagle Badge; or, the Skokums of the Allagash.* Illus. New York: Harper & Brothers, 1908. 290 pp.
  Source: MTLAcc, entry #1319, volume donated by Clemens.

————. *King Spruce; A Novel.* Illus. by E. Roscoe Shrader. New York: Harper & Brothers, 1908. 372 pp.
  Source: MTLAcc, entry #415, volume donated by Clemens.

Day, Thomas (1748–1789). *History of Sandford and Merton* (juvenile story, pub. 1783–1789).
  Mark Twain thought of introducing the good Harry Sandford and the bad Thomas Merton into *TSA* (1893–1894); in June 1898 he considered having "Sanford & Merton" [*sic*] join other children's "Creatures of Fiction" in a projected but never realized tale (NB 40, TS p. 27); and he jotted down and then canceled "<Sandford & Merton>" in January 1910 (NB 49, TS p. 1).

Deeping, George Warwick (1877–1950). *Bertrand of Brittany.* New York, 1908.
  Inscription: signed on front pastedown endpaper: "S. L. Clemens."
  Catalog: A1911, #123, $1.25.

————. *Bess of the Woods.* New York: Harper & Brothers, 1906. 406 pp.
  Source: MTLAcc, entry #1538, volume donated by Clemens.

————. *The Slanderers.* New York: Harper & Brothers, 1905. 384 pp.
  Source: MTLAcc, entry #1539, volume donated by Clemens.

————. *A Woman's War; A Novel.* New York: Harper & Brothers, 1907. 354 pp.
  Source: MTLAcc, entry #1540, volume donated by Clemens.

De Flers, Robert and Gaston Caillavet. *Love Watches.* [Comedy in four acts, adapted by Gladys Unger. Produced by Charles Frohman at the Lyceum Theatre in New York City on 27 August 1908, with Billie Burke as Jacqueline.]
  Isabel Lyon recorded on 26 September 1908, a Saturday: "In the afternoon the King had a box at the Lyceum to see Billie Burke in her new play 'Love Watches'" (IVL Journal, TS p. 332, MTP). Dorothy Sturgis Harding recalled that during her visit to Stormfield in 1908, "one day Mr. Clemens took us all into New York to see Billie Burke in *Love Watches.* He took us back stage to meet her in the 'green room'" ("MT Lands an Angel-fish," *Columbia Library Columns,* 16 [February 1967], 9).

Defoe, Daniel (1661–1731). *The Journal of the Plague Year* (pub. 1721).
  In remarks to an interviewing reporter in New Zealand, Mark Twain indicated that he was familiar with this book (Coleman O. Parsons, "MT in New Zealand," *SAQ,* 61 [Winter 1962], 74).

————. *Life and Strange Surprising Adventures of Robinson Crusoe* [vol. 1]. *The Further Adventures of Robinson Crusoe, Being the Second and Last Part of His Life* [vol. 2]. 2 vols. Plates and map. London, 1747.

Inscriptions: both volumes inscribed: "S. L. Clemens from Edward S. Gudeisk, Wyndham."

Catalog: A1911, #124, $7.50 for 2 vols.

Clemens' fascination with Defoe's fictional castaway began early in his writing career and continued unabated throughout his lifetime. During his visit to the Sandwich Islands in 1866 Clemens imagined how "dark savages come from some mysterious locality as they did with Crusoe, & have great battles & then eat up the prisoners" (NB 6, *N&J*, 1: 184). Clemens wrote to Olivia Langdon on 6 January 1870 from New York City about his recent experiences in a railroad car: "I read 3 pages of Robinson Crusoe, lost & found the book some twelve or fifteen times, & finally lost it for good a couple of hours ago" (MTP). In a letter to the unfortunate James Henry Riley on 2 December 1870, Clemens enthusiastically compared his dispatching Riley to investigate the South African diamond fields to Defoe's sending "the ingenious Robinson W. Crusoe" to test life on a deserted island (Berg). Mark Twain began a never-actualized fragment in 1875, "The Mysterious Chamber," for which his working notes (DV56, MTP) specified a number of parallels between his bridegroom's confinement in a dungeon and Robinson Crusoe's artful uses of his time and materials at hand.

In 1879 Mark Twain joked about Robinson Crusoe's reliance on masturbation in "Some Thoughts on the Science of Onanism" (DV200, no. 3, MTP). Clara Clemens listed *Robinson Crusoe* among the favorite books from which Clemens often read to his daughters (*MFMT*, p. 25). Joliet and Marquette "one day came upon the footprints of men in the mud of the western bank [of the Mississippi River]—a Robinson Crusoe experience which carries an electric shiver with it yet, when one stumbles on it in print" (chapter 2, *LonMiss* [1883]). "Robinson Crusoe leaves the bag of doubloons in the wreck, a fine literary point, but untrue," wrote Clemens in August 1885. "No man would have done that" (NB 24, TS p. 37). When Clemens listed the chief characteristics of various authors in March 1888, he approvingly set down "tone" beside Defoe's name (NB 27, TS p. 61). On 16 March 1888 Clemens wrote to Livy from the Murray Hill Hotel in New York City, lamenting: "Here I have been, Crusoing on a desert hotel—out of wife, out of children, out of linen, out of cigars" (*LLMT,* p. 250). Hank Morgan recognizes the similarities of his situation in chapter 7 of *CY* (1889): "I saw that I was just another Robinson Crusoe cast away on an uninhabited island, with no society but some more or less tame animals, and if I wanted to make life bearable I must do as he did—invent, contrive, create, reorganize things; set brain and hand to work, and keep them busy."

Beset by financial difficulties, Clemens fell back on a favorite book in February 1891, planning for his publishing house to issue *Robinson Crusoe* in twenty-five-cent installments (NB 30, TS p. 23). Clemens thought of "Buckley" as the "first Crusoe" of Australia and "Murrell" as the "second Crusoe" (NB 35 [September 1895], TS p. 53). Clemens displayed an informed view of Defoe's works in a newspaper interview published in the Wellington *New Zealand Mail,* 12 December 1895, p. 51 (Louis J. Budd supplied this citation). "Like Crusoe upon the footprint & is aghast," wrote Mark Twain on 1 June 1896 (NB 38, TS p. 28). "Breed a new Buckley-Crusoe," he wrote to Chatto & Windus from Kaltenleutgeben on 26 September 1898, in reference to the Australian explorer (Berg). Clemens listed Defoe's book title in Notebook 40 (July 1899), TS p. 58, under a heading, *"For Cheap Books".* On 9 September 1905 Isabel Lyon heard Clemens, in speaking about journal-keeping, allude to "the splendid Robinson Crusoe narrative and how interested you are in everything he took away from the ship" (IVL Journal, TS p. 96, MTP).

————. *The Life and Surprising Adventures of Robinson Crusoe.* Illus. New
York: A. L. Burt Co., n.d. 452 pp.
Source: MTLAcc, entry #599, volume donated by Clemens.

————. *Moll Flanders* (pub. 1721).
In "The Walt Whitman Controversy," possibly written in 1880, Mark Twain
testified that his personal library contained this book despite its coarseness and
obscenity (DV36, MTP).

————. *Robinson Crusoe in Words of One Syllable.* Ed. by Lucy Aikin (1781–
1864), pseud. "Mary Godolphin." New York: McLoughlin Brothers, 1869.
93 pp.
Source: MTLAcc, entry #1934, volume donated from Clemens' library by
Clara Clemens Gabrilowitsch in 1910.

————. *Roxana, or The Fortunate Mistress* (pub. 1724).
William Dean Howells urged Clemens to read this novel for "the deepest
insights" into the human soul and "the best and most natural English that a book
was ever written in. You will find it in the Bohn library" (9 August 1885, *MTHL*,
p. 536). Henry Nash Smith and William M. Gibson report that "there is no
conclusive evidence that Mark Twain read *Roxana*," but point out the likelihood
that the slave woman Roxana in *PW* (1894) may owe her name to Defoe's
novel *(MTHL,* p. 537 n. 2).

De Forest, John William (1826–1906). *Kate Beaumont* (pub. 1872).
When De Forest wrote to Clemens on 31 July 1874 suggesting work on a joint
volume of sketches, Clemens noted on the envelope of his letter: "J. W. De
Forest, Novelist." Clemens jotted down the title of De Forest's novel in March
1882, shortly before departing for New Orleans (NB 20, *N&J*, 2: 452).
MT&HF, pp. 218–219, 318; Frank Bergmann, "MT and John William De
Forest."

De Forest, Julia B. *A Short History of Art.* Illus. New York: Dodd, Mead, and Co.,
[cop. 1881].
Inscription: erased inscription in brown ink on third flyleaf is still partly
legible: "Mrs. Orion Clemens/Keokuk/1887," it appears to read. A later
inscription in black ink at the top of the title page reads: "Dec. 15, 1892
[*sic*]/I. V. Lyon from —.—.—. [three illegible initials]. Miss Lyon was not
yet affiliated with Clemens' family in 1892, so the latter inscription, which appears
to be in her handwriting, is puzzling.
Marginalia: a penciled note by Isabel Lyon at the top of page 13 refers to
an article in the August 1916 issue of the *Century Magazine.*
Location: Mark Twain Memorial, Hartford, Connecticut. Purchased in 1962
for $15.
Copy examined: volume once belonging to Mollie Clemens, later acquired by
SLC, and afterward in the possession of Isabel V. Lyon (1868–1958).

De Forest, Lockwood, ed. *Indian Domestic Architecture.* Boston: Heliotype
Printing Co., [cop. 1885]. [Twenty-five photographic plates; no text.]
Inscription: flyleaf inscribed by Clemens: "Livy L. Clemens/Christmas/
1885./From SLC".
Catalog: "Retz Appraisal" (1944), p. 9, valued at $15.
Location: Mark Twain Papers, Berkeley, California.
Copy examined: gift copy from Clemens to his wife.
The photographs in this large volume record impressive examples of Hindu
and Mohammedan houses in India. De Forest states in his brief introduction
that such artistry in wood and stone carving, "with all the advantages of the
caste‚ system," is currently in danger of expiring unless European and American

patronage is increased. Inserted in the volume is a photographic copy of the "Lotto Portrait of Columbus" by Lorenzo Lotto (1476–1554), accompanied by a description written by Frank H. Mason of Frankfort, Germany. (See the entry for John C. Van Dyke, "The Lotto Portrait.")

De Graff, Esmond Vedder (1835–1885). *The School-Room Guide . . . Intended to Assist Public School Teachers*. Syracuse, N. Y.: C. W. Bardeen, 1882. 444 pp.
  Source: MTLAcc, entry #814, volume donated by Clemens.

"De Hurst, C." (pseud.). *How Women Should Ride*. Illus. New York: Harper & Brothers, 1892. 248 pp.
  Source: MTLAcc, entry #844, volume donated by Clemens.

De Lancey, Magdalene (Hall). *A Week at Waterloo in 1815. Lady De Lancey's Narrative; Being an Account of How She Nursed Her Husband, Colonel Sir William Howe De Lancey*. Ed. by Major B. R. Ward. Illus. London: J. Murray, 1906.
  Inscription: presentation copy inscribed: "Mark Twain, with the compliments of the editor, August, 1906." Signed on front pastedown endpaper: "Mark Twain, December, 1906."
  Catalog: A1911, #280, $6.

Deland, Ellen Douglas (1860–1923). *Alan Ransford, A Story*. Illus. by Harry C. Edwards. New York: Harper & Brothers, [cop. 1897]. 281 pp.
  Source: MTLAcc, entry #1413, volume donated by Clemens.

————. *In the Old Herrick House, and Other Stories*. Illus. New York: Harper & Brothers, [cop. 1896]. 282 pp.
  Source: MTLAcc, entry #1304, volume donated by Clemens.

————. *Josephine*. Illus. by W. E. Mears. New York: Harper & Brothers, 1904. 273 pp.
  Source: MTLAcc, entry #446, volume donated by Clemens.

————. *A Little Son of Sunshine; A Story for Boys and Girls*. Illus. by W. E. Mears. New York: Harper & Brothers, 1906. 284 pp.
  Source: MTLAcc, entry #1592, volume donated by Clemens.

————. *Miss Betty of New York*. Illus. by Rachael Robinson. New York: Harper & Brothers, 1908. 285 pp.
  Source: MTLAcc, entry #1102, volume donated by Clemens.

————. *Oakleigh*. Illus. New York: Harper & Brothers, [cop. 1895]. 233 pp.
  Source: MTLAcc, entry #1536, volume donated by Clemens.

Deland, (Mrs.) Margaret Wade (Campbell) (1857–1945). *The Awakening of Helena Richie*. New York: Harper & Brothers, n.d. 357 pp.
  Source: MTLAcc, entry #1821, volume donated by Clemens.

————. *Dr. Lavendar's People*. Illus. by Lucius Hitchcock. New York: Harper & Brothers, 1903. 370 pp.
  Source: MTLAcc, entry #1537, volume donated by Clemens.

————. *Good for the Soul*. New York: Harper & Brothers, 1899. 86 pp.
  Source: MTLAcc, entry #116, volume donated by Clemens.

————. [Another identical copy.]
  Source: MTLAcc, entry #660, volume donated by Clemens.

————. *John Ward, Preacher* (1888).

"Surely the test of a novel's characters is that you feel a strong interest in them & their affairs—the good to be successful, the bad to suffer failure," reasoned Clemens in February 1889. "Well in John Ward, you feel *no* divided interest, no discriminating interest—you want them all to land in hell together, & right away" (NB 28, TS p. 41). This cavil is strikingly similar to Clemens' objections to Jane Austen's characters.

————. *Where the Laborers Are Few*. Illus. by Alice Barber Stephens. New York: Harper & Brothers, 1909. 85 pp.

Source: MTLAcc, entry #2212, volume donated from Clemens' library by Clara Clemens Gabrilowitsch in 1910.

De La Pasture, (Mrs.) Elizabeth (Bonham) (1866–1945). *The Man from America, a Sentimental Comedy*. New York: E. P. Dutton & Co., 1907. 417 pp.

Source: MTLAcc, entry #1313, volume donated by Clemens.

————. *Peter's Mother*. New York: E. P. Dutton & Co., 1905. 354 pp. [New edition, with intro., pub. 1906. 354 pp.]

Isabel V. Lyon wrote to Mrs. Franklin G. Whitmore on 17 August 1908, thanking her for some books and reporting that Clemens "found Peter's Mother a 'perfect Godsend' " (MTM).

De la Ramée, Marie Louise (1839–1908), pseud. "Ouida." *Bimbi. Stories for Children* (pub. 1882).

Catalog: C1951, #J12, no information about edition supplied, listed with the books belonging to Jean and Clara Clemens.

Mark Twain mentioned "Miss De La Ramé (Ouida)" in "A Petition to the Queen of England" (1887) concerning international copyright.

————. *Under Two Flags*. Philadelphia: J. B. Lippincott Co., 1887. 652 pp.

Source: MTLAcc, entry #983, volume donated by Albert Bigelow Paine, Clemens' designated biographer. Possibly Clemens saw this book, since the men exchanged reading materials. The pages after 448 are missing.

Del Mar, Alexander (1836–1926). *The Worship of Augustus Caesar, Derived from a Study of Coins, Monuments, Calendars, Aeras, and Astronomical and Astrological Cycles, the Whole Establishing a New Chronology and Survey of History and Religion*. New York: Cambridge Encyclopedia Co., 1900. 346 pp.

Inscription: signed "S. L. Clemens, 1909."

Catalog: A1911, #125, $2.

Clemens received a bill from The Truth Seeker Company, Publishers, Booksellers, and Importers of Freethought Works, New York City, on 20 April 1909 for "1 Worship of Caesar $3.00" (MTP). Clemens paid the bill on 3 May 1909.

Demarest, Mary Augusta (Lee). "My ain countrie" (song).

Clemens listed this air—also known as "I am far frae my hame"—among his favorite songs in August 1889 (NB 29, TS p. 21).

De Mille, James (1837–1880). *Cord and Creese; A Novel*. Harper's Franklin Square Library Series, No. 746. New York: Harper & Brothers, [cop. 1897]. 305 pp.

Source: MTLAcc, entry #1035, volume donated by Clemens.

————. *A Strange Manuscript Found in a Copper Cylinder, with Illustrations by Gilbert Gaul*. New York: Harper & Brothers, [cop. 1888]. 291 pp.

Source: MTLAcc, entry #1843, volume donated from Clemens' library by Clara Clemens Gabrilowitsch in 1910.

————. [Another identical copy.]
Source: MTLAcc, entry #1859, volume donated from Clemens' library by Clara Clemens Gabrilowitsch in 1910.

De Morgan, William Frend (1839–1917). *Alice-for-Short: A Dichronism.* New York: H. Holt & Co., 1907. 563 pp.
Source: MTLAcc, entry #2213, volume donated from Clemens' library by Clara Clemens Gabrilowitsch in 1910.

Denslow, William Wallace (1856–1915), ed. and illus. *Denslow's Mother Goose; Being the Old Familiar Rhymes and Jingles of Mother Goose.* New York: McClure, Phillips & Co., 1901.
Inscription: autographed presentation copy from Denslow. Also signed: "S. L. Clemens, Riverdale, Nov. 1901."
Catalog: A1911, #126, $4.25.

Depping, Guillaume (1829-1901). *Wonders of Bodily Strength and Skill, in All Ages and All Countries.* Trans. from French by Charles Russell. Illus. New York: Scribner, Armstrong & Co., 1873. 338 pp.
Source: MTLAcc, entry #1998, volume donated from Clemens' library by Clara Clemens Gabrilowitsch in 1910.

De Quincey, Thomas (1785-1859).
Clemens signed his name in 1909 and wrote "See de Quincy" [*sic*] on the inner front cover of his copy of *The Great Essayists* (1909), edited by William James Dawson and Coningsby William Dawson (*A1911*, #158).

Derby, George Horatio (1823-1861), pseud. "John Phoenix." *Phoenixiana* (pub. 1855).
"Made *me* feel like John Phenix [*sic*] in Boston," Mark Twain wrote in Notebook 5 (1866, *N&J*, 1: 153). He hints at a feeling of rivalry in a letter of 14 December 1866 to the Clemens family from San Francisco: "I sail tomorrow . . . leaving more friends behind me than any newspaper man that ever sailed out of the Golden Gate, Phoenix not excepted" (*MTBus*, p. 89). Mark Twain mentioned Phoenix in connection with a Fort Yuma anecdote in chapter 56 of *RI* (1872) and Notebook 18 (1879, *N&J*, 2: 347). He repeatedly included Phoenix in the lists of American humorists he compiled for a planned anthology (NB 19 [1880], p. 363; three times in NB 19 [1881], p. 429; NB 24 [August 1885], TS p. 36; NB 27 [March 1888], TS p. 61); when *Mark Twain's Library of Humor* was finally issued in 1888 it contained eight sketches from *Phoenixiana*. Mark Twain referred to John Phoenix in his 31 July 1906 AD (*MTE*, p. 201) and in "Dress Reform and Copyright" (1908).
MTAm, pp. 165–166; Bellamy, "MT's Indebtedness to John Phoenix" (1941).

Desbordes-Valmore, (Mms.) Marceline Félicité Josèphe (1785–1859). *Memoires.*
Catalog: C1951, #D52, signed by Clemens.

De Vinne, Theodore Low (1828-1914). *The Invention of Printing* (pub. 1876).
"Get Devinney's [*sic*] History of Printing," Clemens jotted in October 1887 (NB 27, TS p. 30).

Devotional Hymns. Selected from Various Authors. New York: Anson D. F. Randolph, 1866. 116 pp. (76 hymns).
Source: MTLAcc, entry #661, volume donated by Clemens.

Dewing, (Mrs.) Maria Richards (Oakey) (1855-1927), "Mrs. T. W. Dewing." *Beauty in Dress.* New York: Harper & Brothers, 1881. 196 pp.
Source: MTLAcc, entry #400, volume donated by Clemens.

————. *Beauty in the Household.* Illus. New York: Harper & Brothers, 1882.
183 pp.
    Source: MTLAcc, entry #796, volume donated by Clemens.

Diaz, (Mrs.) Abby (Morton) (1821-1904). *The Jimmyjohns, and Other Stories.*
Illus. Boston: J. R. Osgood and Co., 1878. 262 pp.
    Source: MTLAcc, entry #490, volume donated by Clemens.

Dick, Thomas. *The Practical Astronomer, Comprising . . . Practical
Descriptions of All Kinds of Telescopes . . . A Particular Account of the
Earl of Rosse's Large Telescopes, and Other Topics Associated with Astronomy.*
New York: Harper & Brothers, 1846. 437 pp.
    Inscription: signed in pencil on first flyleaf: "Henry Clemens/Hannibal/Mo."
Two bookplates on inner front cover, crudely printed by letterpress. The top
one reads: "The Property of/Henry Clemens/No. 2." The other says: "THE
PROPERTY OF/HENRY CLEMENS/HANNIBAL MO." [the latter book-
plate is partially effaced].
    Location: collection of Ralph Gregory, former curator of the Mark Twain
Birthplace Memorial Shrine in Florida, Mo. Mr. Gregory currently lives
in Marthasville, Mo.; he received the volume in 1965 from Mrs. Gertrude
Shotwell of Greybull, Wyoming. Mrs. Shotwell was born Mary Gertrude
Stotts in 1882, the daughter of Joseph Patterson Stotts (d. 1893). She lived
with Orion and Mollie (Stotts) Clemens in Keokuk from the age of nine onward.
    Copy examined: a volume owned by SLC's younger brother, who was
killed in a steamboat explosion in 1858.

Dickens, Charles [John Huffam] (1812–1870).
    Clemens' attitudes toward Dickens resemble the pattern noticeable in his
opinions about Scott and Cooper: early admiration, even emulation, followed
by increasing disenchantment until finally, in his late years, Clemens
completely disavows any interest in, or influence by, the great English
novelist's works. Clemens recalled in "Villagers of 1840-3" that Scott, Cooper,
Dickens, Byron, and Marryat were the favorite writers in Hannibal during
his own boyhood (*HH&T*, p. 34). He also remembered with gratitude that one
of his fellow lodgers at a St. Louis boarding house in 1853 "was fond of
Dickens, Thackeray, Scott & Disraeli, & was the only reading-man in the
establishment . . . equipped with fine literary appreciations" (SLC to Frank
E. Burrough, 15 December 1900, Southeast Missouri State College, Cape
Girardeau). Albert Bigelow Paine reportedly found that Keokuk residents
recalled young Clemens' carrying "a volume of Dickens" under his arm in
1856 and 1857 (*MTB*, p. 106).
    During his days as a newspaper writer in California in the 1860s, however,
Clemens decided that certain fellow authors were unfairly seeking immediate
literary renown by "ambitiously and undisguisedly imitating Dickens," particularly
Bret Harte, whose "pathetics" came straight out of Dickens' novels (14 June
1906 AD, *MTE*, p. 265). Thereafter Harte and Dickens seemed inextricably
linked in Clemens' mind, and his professed aversion for Dickens' writings grew
more pronounced decade by decade. Conceivably this disaffection was
furthered initially by envy of Dickens as an artist on the lecture platform, for
at the time that Clemens was beginning his own lecture circuits Dickens was
carrying the nation by storm with readings from his novels. Shortly before
Clemens saw Dickens perform in New York City, Clemens wrote to his family
on 19 November 1867: "You bet you when Charles Dickens sleeps in this
room next week it will be a gratification to him to know that I have slept
in it also" (*MTBus*, p. 94).
    By 1876 Clemens complained almost routinely in "Comments on English
Diction" that "Sir Walter Scott and Mr. Dickens were distressingly given to
using too many words" (quoted by Jervis Langdon in *Some Reminiscences,*

p. 20). Clemens' friend Joseph H. Twichell observed in 1896 that "his literary tastes are in instances surprising; e.g., he does not relish Dickens" ("Mark Twain," p. 822). And in June 1909 Clemens affected the pose of unlettered genius by claiming: "I don't know anything about anything, and never did. My brother used to try to get me to read Dickens, long ago. I couldn't do it—I was ashamed; but I couldn't do it" *(MTB,* pp. 1500–01). This avowal is contradicted by Clemens' multitudinous references to Dickens' books, of course, leading various Mark Twain scholars to speculate about his motives. Minnie M. Brashear thought that Clemens' disclaimer of an early knowledge of Dickens either resulted from a lapse of memory or (which seems more likely) "boredom at the critics' insistence upon a Dickens influence and his own belief that his knowledge of Dickens was too slight to justify any such critical assumption" *(MTSM,* p. 212). Howard G. Baetzhold presumes that Clemens "was merely giving way to his mood of the moment," but adds that such a rejection of Dickens probably stemmed from his unconscious efforts to diminish his literary models, to appear to be an "original" *(MT&JB,* pp. 304, 317). Albert E. Stone observes that "what put Twain off was the very aspect of Dickens' fiction that made him so successful and invited imitation—his pathos" *(IE,* pp. 15, 17).

Harold Aspiz states that "most of Mark Twain's reading of Dickens took place during the years before 1870" ("Mark Twain's Reading," p. 209), but this assumption can now be modified by evidence introduced in the following entries. Howard G. Baetzhold provides a convenient review of Mark Twain's allusions to Dickens' characters in *MT&JB* (pp. 304–317). The most comprehensive treatment of Clemens' knowledge of Dickens' novels is Joseph Gardner's "Mark Twain and Dickens" (1969), in which Gardner observes that "for over fifty years Clemens was a constant and careful reader of Dickens. . . . But his distaste for anything that suggested Dickens idolatry remained constant and unambiguous" (p. 101). Perhaps the best gauge of the extent of this distaste is obvious in the annotated catalog: despite Clemens' lifelong preoccupation with Dickens' characters and narrative mode, relatively few books by Dickens have been identified as part of the library belonging to Clemens and his family.

————. *American Notes for General Circulation* (pub. 1842).

Mark Twain resolved to "see Dickens for a note on Cairo" while he was returning from his Mississippi River excursion in May 1882 (NB 20, *N&J,* 2: 482). Obviously he was aware that in chapter 12 of *American Notes* Dickens had dismissed Cairo, Illinois as "a hotbed of disease, an ugly sepulchre, a grave uncheered by any gleam of promise: a place without one single quality, in earth or air or water, to commend it." But in chapter 25 of *LonMiss* Mark Twain prudently forbore quoting Dickens' description, merely noting that "Cairo is a brisk town now; and is substantially built, and has a city look about it which is in noticeable contrast to its former estate, as per Mr. Dickens's portrait of it." In chapter 38 of *LonMiss* Mark Twain referred to Dickens' disapproval of the habit of Mississippi Valley residents in alluding to their river steamboats as "floating palaces."

Dewey Ganzel, "Twain, Travel Books," p. 41 n. 4.

————. *Barnaby Rudge* (pub. 1841).

Presumably it was Clemens himself who extracted a paragraph from a magazine article about unavailing efforts by some American tourists to visit the Maypole Inn and pinned the clipping to a leaf in Notebook 14 (1878, *N&J,* 2: 91). The essay was James Payn's "An Adventure in a Forest; or, Dickens's Maypole Inn," *Harper's Magazine* (July 1878), 298–302. Clara Clemens once recorded in her commonplace book the opinion that " 'Barnaby Rudge' has no less power to interest me today than it had when I was thirteen years old" (Clara was thirteen in 1887) and she set down a long synopsis of, and commentary on, the novel (Paine 150, MTP). Mark Twain implied that he read *Barnaby Rudge* as a young man in a newspaper interview he gave in 1895: "How I used to laugh at Simon Tapperwit" [*sic*], he said then (Sydney [Australia] *Morning Herald*, 17 September 1895, quoted by Joseph Gardner, "MT and Dickens," p. 91).

————. *The Battle of Life; A Love Story*. London: G. Routledge & Sons, 1889. 255 pp.
   Source: MTLAcc, entry #2216, volume donated from Clemens' library by Clara Clemens Gabrilowitsch in 1910.

————. *Bleak House* (pub. 1852–1853).
   Dixon Wecter anachronistically reported that Orion Clemens published excerpts from *Bleak House* in his Hannibal *Journal* in 1851–1852 *(SCH*, p. 240); and Joseph Gardner cites Wecter's biography in conjecturing that these installments "may have been the first Dickens [Sam] Clemens read" ("MT and Dickens," p. 92). Gardner misconstrued an entry in Clemens' notebook for January 1882, hypothesizing that Clemens shopped in Montreal bookstores to buy a copy of *Bleak House* for Anna Dickinson when in actuality Clemens wrote "Courting Anna Dickinson—going to educate her—buy Bleak House" (NB 19, *N&J*, 2: 420) among a long list of Whitelaw Reid's foibles. Clara Clemens set down lengthy character analyses and discussions of *Bleak House* in her commonplace book (Paine 150, MTP), so at least one copy of the novel entered the Clemens household.

————. *A Child's History of England* (pub. 1853).
   Livy Clemens wrote to her husband on 28 November 1871 to relate that she was reading this book but finding it "almost too condensed" (MTP; quoted by Joseph Gardner, "MT and Dickens," p. 91).

————. *A Christmas Carol* (pub. 1843).
   Clemens closed a letter of 17 December 1870 to Mrs. Fairbanks with the quotation (in quotation marks), " 'God bless us, every one' " *(MTMF*, p. 144).

————. *David Copperfield* (pub. 1849–1850).
   One definite reference occurs in a letter Clemens wrote on 30 June 1866: "that long native word means—well, it means Uriah Heep boiled down—it means the soul and spirit of obsequiousness" Sacramento *Weekly Union*, 4 August 1866; *LSI*, p. 111). On 31 December 1867 Clemens heard Dickens read from *David Copperfield* at Steinway Hall in New York (date established by Howard G. Baetzhold, "MT's 'First Date' with Olivia Langdon," *Bulletin of the Missouri Historical Society*, 11 [1955], 155–157); Clemens later recalled that Dickens "did not merely read, but also acted. His reading of the storm scene in which Steerforth lost his life was so vivid, and so full of energetic action, that the house was carried off its feet, so to speak" (12 October 1907 AD, *MTE*, p. 213). Franklin R. Rogers advanced the theory that Billy's courtship of Amy in "The Boy's Manuscript," written around 1870, began as a literary burlesque of David Copperfield's doting courtship of Dora *(MTBP* [1960], pp. 102-104), a suggestion with which Howard G. Baetzhold concurs; Baetzhold contributes additional parallel details *(MT&JB*, pp. 312–314). Clemens notified Henry H. Rogers on 17 November 1898 that he had been approached by several London dramatists about their possibly adapting one of his recent stories for the stage; "Barkis is willing," quipped Clemens, quoting Peggotty's suitor *(MTHHR*, p. 378). Mark Twain's most explicit tribute to the novel occurs in his fragmentary "Three Thousand Years among the Microbes" (written 1905); in chapter 10 "Huck," a cholera germ, renames his microbe chums after his favorite literary characters—Don Quixote, Gulliver, Rip Van Winkle, and David Copperfield *(WWD?*, p. 472).

————. *Dombey and Son* (pub. 1846–1848).

Clemens wrote to his mother from Carson City, Nevada on 30 January 1862 to describe a wagon-ride to Humbolt; he and his three companions took along a few luxuries, he reported—"two dogs, Watt's hyms [*sic*], fourteen decks of cards, 'Dombey and Son' " (quoted in *PRI*, p. 30). In a letter to William H. Clagget from Carson City on 28 February 1862 he rehearsed the tag-lines and characteristics associated with the major characters of the novel: Susan Nipper, Captain Cuttle, Mr. Toots, Biler, Florence, Major Bagstock, and Captain Jack Bunsby; then (to make sure that Clagget knew he was quoting from memory) he ended by wishing that he had the book at hand so he could continue the list (CWB). "As Captain Cuttle would say," Mark Twain remarked in a piece on spirit mediums that appeared in the 11 February 1866 issue of the *Golden Era* (*WG*, p. 126); aboard the *Ajax* in 1866 Clemens was amused by a boy "leaning to roll of ship like Capt. Cuttle," the name Clemens gave Captain James Smith of the *Ajax* (NB 6, *N&J*, 2: 181). Meanwhile in 1865 or 1866 Olivia Langdon copied two purple passages from *Dombey and Son* into her commonplace book (DV161, MTP). In August 1885 Clemens jotted down his opinion that as a humorous character "Captain Cuttle is good any where," whether on the stage or in a novel (NB 24, TS p. 36). Clemens was fond of John Brougham's dramatization of *Dombey and Son* (see Brougham entry). On 15 January 1903 Clemens mentioned Captain Cuttle in his appointment book (NB 46, TS pp. 5, 6).

————. *Great Expectations*. London: Chapman & Hall, n.d. 462 pp.

Source: MTLAcc, entry #2217, volume donated from Clemens' library by Clara Clemens Gabrilowitsch in 1910.

J. M. Ridland—"Huck, Pip, and Plot," *Nineteenth-Century Fiction*, 20 (1965), 286–290—"cannot prove" that Mark Twain read *Great Expectations*, but argues convincingly that the "conscience" episode in chapter 21 of *HF* (1885) owes something to Pip's helping the convict Magwitch, all the time believing that he is only showing cowardice. Ridland also points out that a German steamer on the Thames runs over a rowboat and a galley at the conclusion of *Great Expectations*, frustrating Pip's efforts to help Magwitch escape, much as the collision of the steamboat and the raft in chapter 16 of *HF* sets back Jim's plans for obtaining his freedom.

————. *Little Dorrit*. Copyright Edition. Illus. by H. K. Browne. Collection of British Authors Series. 4 vols. Leipzig: B. Tauchnitz, 1856-1857.

Source: MTLAcc, entries #979, #2222–2224. Volume 1 donated by Clemens; volumes 2, 3, and 4 donated from Clemens' library by Clara Clemens Gabrilowitsch in 1910. Possibly Clemens signed volume 1 in 1892, since the accession book erroneously listed this as the publication date for the 240-page book.

On 18 October 1856 Clemens quoted "Mr. Clennam at the Circumlocution Office" in his third letter from Thomas Jefferson Snodgrass to the Keokuk *Saturday Post* (*TJS*, p. 12). Joseph Gardner ("MT and Dickens," p. 92) cites another allusion in "The Mint Defalcation," *Territorial Enterprise*, 8 January 1866. In his May 1870 *Galaxy* column Mark Twain declared: "I only know that if a man lives long enough, he can trace a thing through the Circumlocution Office of Washington" ("The Facts in the Case of the Great Beef Contract," *CG*, pp. 40-41).

————. *Little Dorrit*. 2 vols. New York: J. W. Lovell Co., 1883.

Source: MTLAcc, entry #2221, volume one only, donated from Clemens' library by Clara Clemens Gabrilowitsch in 1910.

————. *Martin Chuzzlewit* (pub. 1843–1844).

Clemens had read the novel closely by 20 November 1860, when he wrote to his brother Orion from St. Louis, comparing the nurse who was attending Pamela Moffett after the birth of her child with Sarah Gamp and quoting Sairey's lenient views on alcoholic refreshments (ALS in MTP). Clemens referred to *Martin Chuzzlewit* in a letter of 6 February 1861 to his brother Orion, predicting a day in the future when Laura Wright "and I (like one of Dickens' characters,) are Another's" *(MTBus,* p. 57): his allusion (as Howard G. Baetzhold explained in *MT&JB,* p. 305) is to Augustus Moddle's hyperbolic letter to Charity Pecksniff—"I love another. She is Another's"—in the final, fifty-fourth chapter of the novel (obviously, therefore, Clemens had found time to read *Martin Chuzzlewit* during his stint as a Mississippi River pilot). He alluded to Mark Tapley in a letter to William Claggett written on 18 April 1862 (TS in MTP). He may have meant *Martin Chuzzlewit* in criticizing Dickens' attempt "to produce a Yankee dialect. . . . He made his Yankee talk as no Yankee" (NB 12 [1873], *N&J,* 1: 552–553). In a speech at the Scottish Corporation in London" (1873) he included the nurse "Sairey Gamp" among a list of "sublime women" *(MTSpk,* p. 80). There are notable parallels between Martin Chuzzlewit's hopeful trip to America and Lord Berkeley's idealistic pilgrimage to the home of his plebian kin in chapter 1 of *AC* (1892).

————. *Master Humphrey's Clock.* Copyright Edition. Collection of British Authors Series. 3 vols. Leipzig: B. Tauchnitz, 1846.

Source: MTLAcc, entries #2219 and #2220, volumes 2 and 3 only, donated from Clemens' library by Clara Clemens Gabrilowitsch in 1910.

————. *Nicholas Nickleby* (pub. 1838–1839).

In assigning names of his favorite literary characters to his twelve microbe friends, "Huck" the cholera germ of "Three Thousand Years among the Microbes" (written 1905) at first calls one of them Nicholas Nickleby. But Mark Twain—probably realizing that he already had included David Copperfield and had not yet listed Don Quixote, dropped this penultimate name from the list *(WWD?,* p. 472).

————. *The Old Curiosity Shop.* 2 vols. London: Chapman & Hall, 1858.

Source: MTLAcc, entry #2214, volume 1 only (435 pp.), donated from Clemens' library by Clara Clemens Gabrilowitsch in 1910.

————. *The Old Curiosity Shop.* 2 vols. Boston: Ticknor & Fields, 1858.

Source: MTLAcc, entry #1267, volume 2 only (435 pp.), donated by Clemens.

Both Joseph Gardner ("MT and Dickens," p. 91) and Howard G. Baetzhold *(MT&JB,* p. 307) speculate plausibly that a newspaper sketch titled "Mark Twain Overpowered" in the 2 December 1865 *Californian (SSix,* pp. 191–193) may be a literary burlesque of Nelly's devotion to her grandfather. Twain's piece concerns eight-year-old "Addie" and her drunken Uncle Lige.

————. *Oliver Twist* (pub. 1837-1839).

In February 1868 Mark Twain declared, while criticizing the successes of Vinnie Ream in obtaining government contracts for her sculpture, that "it would take but little to turn my sympathies in favor of the Artful Dodger" *(W1868,* p. 36).

————. *Our Mutual Friend.* London: Chapman & Hall, n.d. 523 pp.

Source: MTLAcc, entry #2215, volume donated from Clemens' library by Clara Clemens Gabrilowitsch in 1910.

————. *Our Mutual Friend.* New York: D. Appleton & Co., 1878. 340 pp.

Source: MTLAcc, entry #1266, volume donated by Clemens.

In a letter to Mrs. Fairbanks from Chicago on 7 January 1867 Clemens claimed that the odor of cigars "makes you 'drop into poetry' like Silas Wegg" (*MTMF*, p. 65); Howard G. Baetzhold discovered two other instances where Clemens employed this locution (*MT&JB*, p. 306)—*MTH*, p. 367 and *W1868*, p. 11. In a perceptive note ("Gaffer Hexam and Pap Finn" [1968]), Joseph H. Gardner shows that Pap Finn's diatribe against Huck's newly acquired literacy in *HF* (1885) might well have its source in chapter 6 of Book I of Dickens' novel, in which the unsavory Hexam assaults his son Charley for learning how to read and write. Gardner also spots other similar elements, including a description of drunkenness and threats with a knife.

―――. *Pickwick Papers* (pub. 1836–1837).
In a letter of 5 December 1863 from Carson City, Clemens knowledgeably reviewed and praised James Stark's "recital of the speech of Sergeant Buzfuz, in the great breach of promise case of Bardell vs. Pickwick. . . . Heretofore I had looked upon that as the tamest of Mr. Dickens' performances" (*MTEnt*, p. 92). Mark Twain presumably had Mr. Pickwick's sumptuous feasts in mind when he complained, in a mock review of Homer's *Odyssey*, that Homer "exhibits as animal a relish in describing" food, "& its preparation & annihilation, as does Mr. Dickens" (Paine 8, MTP). In a series of notes to himself set down in June, July, and August 1885 for an essay on humor, Clemens stated that he detected no humor in *Pickwick Papers* "except the kind the clown makes in the circus. . . . Every line in the book says: 'Look at me—ain't I funny!' "; "if there is a humorous passage in the Pickwick Papers, I have never been able to find it"; only the characters "in Pickw Papers, & the body-snatcher in Tale of 2 Cities" did not strike Clemens as amusing (NB 24, TS pp. 28, 33, 36). But Joseph H. Gardner quotes an interview Mark Twain gave in 1895 in Australia in which he confessed that he "used to laugh" at Samuel Weller and his father, "but I can't do it now somehow" (Sydney *Morning Herald*, 17 September 1895; "MT and Dickens," p. 100).

―――. *Pictures from Italy* (pub. 1846).
Joseph H. Gardner ("MT and Dickens," p. 91) suggests that Mark Twain's description of the tomb of St. Carlo Borromeo in chapter 18 of *IA* (1869) may owe something to Dickens' account. Howard G. Baetzhold demonstrates that Mark Twain's description of Leonardo's "The Last Supper" in chapter 19 of *IA* bears a strong resemblance to Dickens' reactions (Dickens criticizes those who praise excellences which are no longer present).

―――. *The Poems and Verses of Charles Dickens*. Ed. by Frederick George Kitton (1856-1904). New York: Harper & Brothers, 1903. 206 pp.
Source: MTLAcc, entry #1147, volume donated by Clemens.

―――. *Sketches by Boz* (pub. 1836).
Clemens listed "Boz" among the authors esteemed by residents of ante-bellum Hannibal, Missouri. Along with Scott, Cooper, and other such writers, this literary diet induced "sentimentality and romance among young folk" which was "soft, sappy, melancholy" ("Villagers of 1840–3" [1897], *HH&T*, p. 35).

―――. *A Tale of Two Cities*. New York: J. W. Lovell Co., 1882. 352 pp.
Source: MTLAcc, entry #2218, volume donated from Clemens' library by Clara Clemens Gabrilowitsch in 1910.
"It is uncertain when Clemens first read *A Tale of Two Cities*, but it was by far his favorite" among Dickens' novels, states Joseph H. Gardner in "Mark Twain and Dickens" (1969), p. 92. Howard G. Baetzhold (*MT&JB*, p. 349 n. 29) believes that Mark Twain must have read the novel before he wrote "Open Letter to Commodore Vanderbilt" (1869), which describes Vanderbilt's careless mode of driving his carriage past pedestrians. Walter Blair developed

the idea that Mark Twain might have gained an inspiration for the graveyard scene in chapter 9 of *TS* (1876) from Book 2, chapter 14 of *Tale,* in which a frightened boy watches three body-snatchers at work in a graveyard ("French Revolution" [1957], p. 22; *MT&HF* [1960], p. 61). Howard G. Baetzhold agrees that the scene in which the junior Jerry Cruncher observes his father and two companions robbing graves must have contributed to the episode at Hoss Williams' grave in *TS,* especially since Clemens evidently had no personal recollection of graverobbers in Hannibal, Missouri *(MT&JB* [1970], pp. 315–316); but Albert E. Stone argues that "the superior skill with which Twain mixes humor and the atmosphere of terror cannot simply be attributed to . . . an unconscious debt to *A Tale of Two Cities.* . . . Any specific literary source has been kept firmly in the background" *(IE* [1961], p. 67).

All members of Clemens' family read the novel while they sojourned in Paris in 1879 *(MTB,* p. 644); even Katy Leary, who had resisted Livy Clemens' urging to read *A Tale of Two Cities,* finally read the book along with Mrs. Susan Crane when the family visited France *(LMT,* pp. 56–57). Walter Blair focuses on the probable influence of this novel on *HF* (1885) in "French Revolution" (1957), pp. 21–35 and *MT&HF* (1960), pp. 128, 311–312; some of the passages from *Tale* cited by Blair are reproduced in facsimile in Hill and Blair's *The Art of Huckleberry Finn* (1962), pp. 417–427. Howard G. Baetzhold supplies additional intricate parallels in *MT&JB* [1970], pp. 149–151. Clemens cited "the body-snatcher [Jerry Cruncher] in Tale of 2 Cities" as one of Dickens' humorous creations which failed to amuse (NB 24 [August 1885], TS p. 36). (See also the entry for Dickens' *Works.)* In Vienna in the late 1890's Clemens told Henry W. Fisher that on his last visit to Paris, Dickens' *Tale* was one of the guides his family used in visiting "the places of horror" *(AMT,* p. 59). On another unspecified later occasion Clemens supposedly said: "I have always been a great admirer of Dickens, and his 'Tale of Two Cities' I read at least every two years. . . . I have finished 'The Two Cities' for the 'steenth time" *(AMT,* p. 60). In June 1909 Clemens reportedly told Albert Bigelow Paine: "Yes, I have read *The Tale of Two Cities,* and could do it again. I have read it a good many times" *(MTB,* pp. 1500–01).

————. *Works of Charles Dickens.* Household Edition. 55 vols. New York: Hurd and Houghton, 1866–1870.

Inscriptions: Theodore W. Crane signed the forty-two extant volumes. In many volumes Crane added the date 23 December 1870.

Marginalia: four of the vols. contain a total of eighteen notes in pencil by Clemens. In vol. 1 of *A Tale of Two Cities* (1866) Clemens jotted a disparaging comment about Dickens' sense of humor (p. 76) and criticized the character Jerry Cruncher (p. 216). *Nicholas Nickleby* (vol. 2 of four vols., pub. in 1867) has six notes, mostly favorable, including the comment (on page 46), "Curious old system—& very natural." The volume containing *Master Humphrey's Clock* and *New Christmas Stories* (1869) displays six short remarks; several object to Dickens' sense of humor, another on page 32 observes a type of error that proofreaders tend to overlook. *The Old Curiosity Shop* (1870) has four marginal notes in vol. 1, including (on page 10): "The yearning after tranquil islands in lonely seas . . . a yearning whose desire is *Heaven,* really, though the soul does not know it." These and others of the forty-two surviving vols. also contain markings in pencil.

Location: Gannett Tripp Learning Center, Elmira College, Elmira, New York. Forty-two volumes donated by Mr. and Mrs. Jervis Langdon in 1977. Clemens and his brother-in-law Theodore Crane (1831–1889) often shared reading materials during Clemens' summer sojourns at Quarry Farm. See also the entry for Crane's set of Shakespeare's *Works.* (John W. Berry, Public Services Coordinator for the Gannett Tripp Learning Center, supplied the information for this entry.)

Dickerson, Mary Cynthia (1866–1923). *The Frog Book: North American Toads and Frogs.* Illus. with photographs by the author. New York: Doubleday, Page & Co., 1906. 253 pp.

Source: MTLAcc, entry #745, volume donated by Clemens.

Dickinson, Anna Elizabeth (1842–1932). *A Crown of Thorns, or Ann Boleyn* (play, prod. 1876).

Clemens saw Anna Dickinson's performance in the Boston production of the play she wrote and in which she played the title role, on 8 May 1876; the play had opened on 4 April 1876 (*MTHL*, pp. 117, 133–134).

Dickinson, Emily Elizabeth (1830–1886).

Clemens at least knew of the reclusive poet, for he quoted Thomas W. Higginson's description of her father's house in Notebook 31 (October 1891), TS pp. 8–9. In a letter to Clemens on 23 October 1898 William Dean Howells quoted the second stanza from Dickinson's poem about death, "The bustle in a house," identifying its source and asking Clemens rhetorically whether he was familiar with the lines (*MTHL*, p. 681).

[Dickinson, Goldsworthy Lowes (1862–1932)] *Letters from a Chinese Official; Being an Eastern View of Western Civilization.* New York: McClure, Phillips & Co., 1904.

Marginalia: many penciled notes and markings in Clemens' hand; the comments are favorable toward Dickinson's point of view, but criticize the American government, newspapers, and missionaries (particularly Ament). In pencil on the front pastedown endpaper Clemens wrote: "The first & foremost—shall we say the only?—function & mission of our civilization is to hunt up ways to multiply wants. And—consequently—to propagate hardship & worry." Clemens' annotations are characterized by his sarcastic remark on page 23: "Brother Ament, D.D., missionary pirate, is out there ameliorating this barbarism the best he can." Arthur L. Scott quotes from Clemens' notes in *MTAL*, p. 265. A newspaper clipping of Lionel Strachey's satirical poem, "Progressional" (a parody of "Onward, Christian Soldiers") is pinned to the front free endpaper.

Catalog: "Retz Appraisal" (1944), p. 9, date of publication erroneously listed as 1914, valued at $15.

Location: Mark Twain Papers, Berkeley, California.

Copy examined: Clemens' copy; possibly he was initially curious about *Letters from a Chinese Official* because of the similarities to his own early pieces, "Goldsmith's Friend Abroad Again" (1870–1871).

Dilke, Charles Wentworth (1843–1911). *Greater Britain: A Record of Travel in English-Speaking Countries During 1866 and 1867* (pub. 1868).

Clemens attended Dilke's dinner parties in the summer of 1873 and dictated "Sir Chas Wentworth Dilke's Greater Britain" into his stenographic journal (NB 12, *N&J*, 1: 529).

Dill, (Sir) Samuel (1844–1924). *Roman Society from Nero to Marcus Aurelius.* London: Macmillan and Co., 1905. 639 pp.

Catalog: A1911, #129, $1.75.

———. *Roman Society in the Last Century of the Western Empire.* Second ed., rev. London: Macmillan and Co., 1905. 459 pp.

Inscription: front pastedown endpaper signed "SL. Clemens/October 1905."

Marginalia: notations by Clemens on three pages.

Catalog: C1951, #9a, $30.

Location: collection of Robert Daley, Burbank, Calif. Mr. Daley, a film producer, provided the facts reported here.

Dimsdale, Thomas J. *The Vigilantes of Montana; or, Popular Justice in the Rocky Mountains. Being a Correct and Impartial Narrative of the Chase, Trial, Capture, and Execution of Henry Plummer's Road Agent Band.* Virginia City, Montana Territory: D. W. Tilton & Co., 1866.

Mark Twain provides the author and title in a footnote to quotations from Dimsdale's "bloodthirsty little Montana book" in chapters 10 and 11 of *RI* (1872). He recommended the chapter on the Western outlaw Slade in "the thrilling little book" as "well worth reading" (Iowa-Calif. ed., pp. 94, 98–103). Mark Twain quotes far more lengthily than was his wont to do in the 1870's. Franklin R. Rogers corrects the version of the full title given by Mark Twain and observes that he made numerous stylistic revisions in the quoted text *(RI,* Iowa-Calif. ed., pp. 557–559).

Dircks, Henry. *The Life, Times and Scientific Labours of the Second Marquis of Worcester. To Which is Added, A Reprint of His Century of Inventions, 1663, with a Commentary Thereon.* London: Quaritch, 1865.
Inscription: signed on flyleaf: "S. L. Clemens. Hartford, 1886."
Catalogs: C1951, #D39; *Zeitlin 1951,* #14, $35.
Paul Baender deduced that Mark Twain got from this book the idea that Worcester (1601–1667) preceded James Watt in developing a steam-engine. In a footnote to Part 5 of "WIM?" (pub. 1906), Mark Twain stated that "the Marquess of Worcester had done all of this more than a century earlier" *(WIM?,* p. 183).

Disraeli, Benjamin (1804–1881), first earl of Beaconsfield. *Alroy. A Romance.* Copyright Edition. Collection of British Authors Series. Leipzig: B. Tauchnitz, 1846. 286 pp.
Source: MTLAcc, entry #2225, volume donated from Clemens' library by Clara Clemens Gabrilowitsch in 1910.

———. *Coningsby.* Collection of British Authors Series. Leipzig: B. Tauchnitz, 1844. 442 pp.
Source: MTLAcc, entry #2226, volume donated from Clemens' library by Clara Clemens Gabrilowitsch in 1910.
Clemens once recalled that a friend he made in 1853 while living in a St. Louis boarding house "was fond of Dickens, Thackeray, Scott, & Disraeli, & was the only reading-man in the establishment" (SLC to Frank E. Burrough, 15 December 1900, Southeast Missouri State College, Cape Girardeau). In 1879 he noted the name "Disraeli" in NB 17 *(N&J,* 2: 270). Clara Clemens listed the title of Disraeli's *Tancred* (pub. 1847) in her commonplace book (Paine 150, MTP).

D'Israeli, Isaac (1766–1848). *Curiosities of Literature* (6 vols., pub. 1791–1834).
Catalog: C1951, #D31, $16, 4 vols. only, no edition supplied, listed among books signed by Clemens.

Disturnell, John. *Sailing on the Great Lakes and Rivers of America.* Philadelphia: J. Disturnell, 1874.
Franklin R. Rogers discovered that Mark Twain used this guidebook in constructing the section of *LonMiss* (1883) that describes the Upper Mississippi River. For chapter 59 of *LonMiss* he "borrowed with only four minor changes the passage concerning the 'sublime Maiden's Rock,'" and larded the old panoramist's long-winded speech with parodies of Disturnell's phrases *(MTBP,* pp. 91–93, 171 n. 63).

Ditmars, Raymond Lee (1876–1942). *The Reptile Book: A Comprehensive Popularized Work.* Illus. with photographs. New York: Doubleday, Page, & Co., 1907. 472 pp.
  Source: MTLAcc, entry #744, volume donated by Clemens.

Dix, Beulah Marie (b. 1876) and Carrie A. Harper, *The Beau's Comedy.* New York: Harper & Brothers, 1902. 320 pp.
  Source: MTLAcc, entry #1541, volume donated by Clemens.

Dix, Morgan (1827–1908). *Memoirs of John Adams Dix [1798–1879], Compiled by His Son.* 2 vols. New York: Harper & Brothers, 1883.
  Source: MTLAcc, entries #1760 and #1761, volumes donated by Clemens.

Dixon, Thomas (1864–1946). *The Leopard's Spots: A Romance of the White Man's Burden—1865–1900.* Illus. by C. D. Williams. New York: Doubleday, Page & Co., 1902. 465 pp. [A novel set in North Carolina, Boston, and New York.]
  Inscription: signed on first flyleaf in black ink: "SL. Clemens/Riverdale, March 1902". No markings.
  Catalogs: C1951, #D49; "MT Collection," *The Bookman,* No. 25 (1970), #330.
  Location: Wake Forest University, Winston-Salem, N.C. Donated by Mrs. Nancy Susan Reynolds.
  Copy examined: Clemens' copy.

Dixon, William Hepworth (1821–1879). *History of Two Queens: Catherine of Aragon and Anne Boleyn.* London: Hurst & Blackett, 1873.
  Clemens entered the author, title, and publisher in NB 12 (July 1873, *N&J,* 1: 559), presumably intending to purchase the book.

Doane, T. W. *Bible Myths and Their Parallels in Other Religions.* Fourth ed. New York: The Commonwealth Co., [cop. 1882].
  Inscription: signed on front pastedown endpaper in black ink: "SL Clemens/Innocence at Home/1908."
  Marginalia: profuse pencil markings and some notes begin on page 128 in chapter 12, "The Miraculous Birth of Christ Jesus." Pencil marks are numerous in pages 128–135. (In the margin of page 125 Clemens inserted a comment vertically in black ink: "Apparently Jupiter was a formidably active co-respondent.") On page 249 Clemens changed "Narduk" to "Marduk" with black ink. He penciled a grammatical correction on page 251 in a quotation from an ancient medal. In pencil Clemens wrote vertically in the margin of page 267: "The human spirit of superiority—inherited from the monkey"; on the opposite side of the same page he noted: "The Cheneys often saw Home [presumably Daniel Dunglas Home (1833–1886), the Scottish spiritualist medium who grew up in the United States from the age of nine] rise & fly at his ease when they were all boys together. Later, Dickens, Huxley & others saw Home do this." At page 269 Clemens altered "earlier" to "later" with a pencil; on page 271 he wrote the German language equivalent of "well said" ("gut gesazt") in pencil beside a quotation from Celsus; on page 272 he wrote in pencil at the top of a quotation: "They still say it"; also in pencil he noted: "An early 'seance.'"
  Location: Mark Twain Library, Redding, Connecticut.
  Copy examined: Clemens' copy. It may be significant that Clemens noted the author, title, and publisher of Doane's book on page 389 of his copy of Philip Vivian's *The Churches and Modern Thought* (1907), which Clemens signed in London in July 1907.

Dobson, [Henry] Austin (1840–1921), ed. *The Quiet Life. Verses by Various Hands.* Prologue and Epilogue by Austin Dobson. Illus. by Edwin A. Abbey and Alfred Parsons. New York, 1899.
> *Catalog: A1911,* #130, $2.25.

————. *Vignettes in Rhyme* (pub. 1873).
> Ida Langdon related how the Langdon family celebrated her grandmother's birthday one August when the Clemens girls were young: "My sister had written a little romantic comedy, really no more than a dramatic dialogue in the manner of Austin Dobson's *Vignettes in Rhyme.* Jean Clemens and I were to play its two parts, she as a fairy-tale prince, I as a milkmaid. My uncle [Clemens], who was very fond of amateur theatricals, was to coach us!" *(Mark Twain in Elmira,* ed. Robert D. Jerome and Herbert A. Wisbey, Jr. [Elmira, N. Y.: Mark Twain Society, 1977], p. 59).

Dodd, Anna Bowman. *Cathedral Days: A Tour in Southern England.* Boston: Little, Brown, and Co., 1901.
> *Inscription:* on first flyleaf: "Mrs. Clemens/Happy/New Year!/Marie Van Vorst/1902."
> *Location:* Mark Twain Library, Redding, Connecticut.
> *Copy examined:* Livy Clemens' copy, unmarked.

Dodd, Lee Wilson (1879–1933). *A Modern Alchemist, and Other Poems.* Boston: R. G. Badger, 1906. 135 pp.
> *Source:* MTLAcc, entry #640, volume donated by Isabel V. Lyon, Clemens' secretary.

Dodge, Mary Abigail (1833–1896), pseud. "Gail Hamilton." *Skirmishes and Sketches.* Boston: Ticknor and Fields, 1865. 447 pp.
> *Source:* MTLAcc, entry #912, volume donated by Clemens.

————. *Stumbling Blocks.* Boston: Ticknor and Fields, 1864. 435 pp.
> *Source:* MTLAcc, entry #913, volume donated by Clemens.

Dodge, Mary Elizabeth (Mapes) (1831–1905). *Hans Brinker; or, the Silver Skates. A Story of Life in Holland.* Illus. New York: Scribner, Armstrong & Co., 1874. 347 pp.
> *Source:* MTLAcc, entry #1881, volume donated from Clemens' library by Clara Clemens Gabrilowitsch in 1910.
> Hans Brinker was one of the child figures Mark Twain wished to put into a story with many other "Creatures of Fiction" (NB 40 [June 1898], TS p. 26); but the nearest he came to employing the name was the paralyzed, deaf and dumb Johann Brinker of "No. 44, The Mysterious Stranger."

————. "Miss Molony on the Chinese Question" (story).
> *Mark Twain's Library of Humor* contained this piece, taken from the pages of *St. Nicholas Magazine.*

————. *Rhymes and Jingles.* Illus. New York: Scribner, Armstrong & Co., 1875. 271 pp. Last page missing.
> *Source:* MTLAcc, entry #1694, volume donated by Clemens.

Dodge, Richard Irving. *Our Wild Indians: Thirty-Three Years' Personal Experience among the Red Men of the Great West . . . With Introduction by General Sherman.* Illus. Hartford, Conn.: American Publishing Co., 1883.
> *Marginalia:* contains numerous notes by Clemens, which include: on page 62 a reference to the American Indian as being "volatile as a Frenchman, and yet patient"; on page 75, "Success succeeds"; among the Indians, he notes on page 81,

"killing a husband and child is no impairment of respectability." He compares the Indian's Great Spirit with the Christian deity on page 112: "Our illogical God is all-powerful in name, but impotent in fact; the Great Spirit is not all-powerful, but does the very best he can for his injun and does it free of charge"; and on page 108 he commented: "We have to keep our God placated with prayers, and even then we are never sure of him—how much higher and finer is the Indian's God." Albert E. Stone quotes from these annotations in *IE* (1961), p. 177.

    Catalog: A1911, #132, $25, representative marginalia quoted.

    "Send to me, right away, a book by *Lieut. Col. Dodge, USA,* called '25 Years on the Frontier'—or some such title—I don't remember just what. . . . I think he has written only the one book; & so any librarian can tell you the title of it," Clemens wrote to his business agent Charles L. Webster on 6 July 1884; he went on to explain that he planned to "take Huck Finn out there" to the plains and mountains *(MTBus,* pp. 264–265). "I sent you Dodge's book yesterday," Webster notified Clemens on 9 July 1884 from New York (MTP). But on 24 July 1884 Clemens wrote to Webster impatiently after receiving what Webster assumed to be the volume he desired: " 'Our Wild Indians' is Col. Dodge's *second* book. The title of his *first* one contains the words 'twenty-five-years,' & you will find it in the catalogue of any big library, no doubt. The present one is useful to me, but I want *that* one also" (MTP). The bill for personal expenses that Webster eventually sent to Clemens on 2 September 1884 (items charged against Charles L. Webster & Co. in Clemens' name) included two of Dodge's books—*Our Wild Indians* and *Life on the Plains* [*sic*]—at a total cost of $3.84; both volumes were listed as having been purchased on 14 July 1884 (MTP). Walter Blair synopsizes Mark Twain's acquisition, use, and disposal of these books in *HH&T,* p. 85; Mark Twain "chiefly depended upon Dodge's book" for information about Indian depravity in writing "Huck Finn and Tom Sawyer Among the Indians" in 1884. He also borrowed information about Indian religious beliefs, the Germaine massacre, prairie fog, the waterspout phenomenon, and the Indians' custom of not harming travelers believed to be insane *(HH&T,* pp. 87, 329–337). Albert E. Stone notes that Mark Twain undoubtedly approved of Dodge's comment on page 529 about Indian barbarity toward white female captives: "Cooper, and some other novelists, knew nothing of Indian character and customs when they placed their heroines prisoners in their hands" *(IE,* p. 179). Dodge claimed that gang-rape generally followed such captures. See also the entry for Jacob P. Dunn, *Massacres of the Mountains.*

————. *The Plains of the Great West and Their Inhabitants, Being a Description of the Plains, Game, Indians, &c. of the Great North American Desert.* Intro. by William Blackmore. Illus. New York: G. P. Putnam's Sons, 1877. 448 pp.

    Inscription: signed "S. L. Clemens, Hartford, 1877."

    Catalog: A1911, #131, $14, "passages marked."

    Clemens purchased a copy of Dodge's *Plains* on 21 January 1877, according to a bill he received from James R. Osgood & Co. in November 1877 (Scrapbook #10, p. 69, MTP). On 22 February 1877, when Rutherford Hayes' election seemed confirmed, Clemens wrote to Howells from Hartford that he hoped the new president "will put Lt. Col. Richard Irwin [*sic*] Dodge (Author of 'The Great Plains & their Inhabitants') at the head of the Indian Department. There's a man who knows all about Indians, & yet has some humanity in him" *(MTHL,* p. 172).

————. *The Plains of the Great West and Their Inhabitants, Being a Description of the Plains, Game, Indians, &c. of the Great North American Desert.* Illus. New York: G. P. Putnam's Sons, 1877. 448 pp.

    Marginalia: undated, unsigned by Clemens (penciled dates of 1877 on first flyleaf are not in his hand). Contains a pencil mark at description of a flood on page 84; penciled annotation on pages 432–434 resembles Clemens' handwriting and his sentiments.

    Location: Mark Twain Library, Redding, Connecticut.

Copy examined: presumably Clemens' copy; very likely obtained in 1884. On the verso of Clemens' letter of 24 July 1884 urging Charles L. Webster to send him a copy of Dodge's *"first"* book, Webster wrote: "The Plains of the Great West, and Their Inhabitants/G P Putnam & Son" (TS in MTP). A statement of account that Webster sent Clemens on 2 September 1884 included charges for two "Indian Books" purchased on 14 July 1884, one of them "Life on the Plains" (MTP).

HH&T, pp. 329–337; *WIM?,* pp. 452, 580; McNutt, "MT and the American Indian."

Dodgson, Charles Lutwidge (1832–1898), pseud. "Lewis Carroll." *Alice's Adventures in Wonderland.* Illus. by Peter Newell. New York: Harper & Brothers, [cop. 1901]. 187 pp.

Source: MTLAcc, entry #439, volume donated by Clemens.

Clemens recalled that in 1879 he found Dodgson, whom he met in England, to be "the stillest and shyest full-grown man I have ever met except 'Uncle Remus' " (*MTA,* 2: 232). Livy wrote to Clemens in March 1880 that she and the children "are almost half through 'Alice in Wonderland' " (ALS in MTM, quoted in *S&MT,* p. 118). In 1895 Mark Twain told an Australian reporter that he had always regarded Lewis Carroll as "a true and subtle humorist" (Sydney *Morning Herald,* 17 September 1895, quoted in *MT&JB,* p. 36). In October 1908 Mark Twain referred to "the immortal Alice" (a phrase that also appears in *MTA,* 2: 232) in a letter to Francis Wilson praising L. M. Montgomery's *Anne of Green Gables* (quoted in advertising for the book in the back pages of its later editions). Mark Twain enjoyed the Cheshire Cat, but (like most of us) had difficulty remembering which of Dodgson's books this character appeared in: he saw a young woman pianist in London in November 1896 who, following her performance, mustered "a machine-made smile, & it could have sat for the portrait of the Cheshire Cat in Alice in the Looking Glass. Wonderland?" (NB 39, TS p. 20). He alludes again to the grinning feline from chapter 6 of *Alice in Wonderland* in chapter 30 of "No. 44, The Mysterious Stranger" (written 1902–1908): "she smiled quite Cheshirely (my dream-brother's word, he knew it was foreign and thought it was future, he couldn't be sure)" (*MSM,* p. 381).

————. *The Hunting of the Snark, and Other Poems and Verses.* Illus. by Peter Newell. New York: Harper & Brothers, [cop. 1903]. 248 pp.

Source: MTLAcc, entry #412, volume donated by Clemens.

————. [Another identical copy.]

Source: MTLAcc, entry #2051, volume donated from Clemens' library by Clara Clemens Gabrilowitsch in 1910.

————. *Through the Looking-Glass, and What Alice Found There.* Illus. by John Tenniel. 39th Thousand. New York: Macmillan & Co., 1875.

Inscription: in Livy Clemens' handwriting: "Daisy Warner—/from Mrs. Clemens/Christmas, 1876."

Location: Mark Twain Memorial, Hartford, Connecticut.

Copy examined: unmarked gift volume from Livy Clemens, indicative of the esteem in which Lewis Carroll's books were evidently held by the Clemenses. In May 1881 the "Jabberwocky" poem as expounded by Humpty Dumpty occurred to Clemens when he saw the figures created from tree and shrub roots by Mrs. Thomas K. Beecher: "They are real creatures out of Wonderland," he wrote to Mrs. Beecher, "secretly alive, natural, proper, and ungrotesque to eyes used to them in the world they came from—and so they take the fiction all out of the Jabberwock and I recognize and accept him as a fact" (*S&MT,* p. 119). Susy Clemens longed for *Through the Looking-Glass* while passing idle hours (*"read, sew, read, sew"*) in Venice, she wrote to Clara on 29 April 1893 (TS in Harnsberger Collection, *S&MT,* p. 331).

————. *Through the Looking-Glass and What Alice Found There.* Illus. by Peter Newell. New York: Harper & Brothers, 1902.
Inscription: signed on front pastedown endpaper in black ink: "SL Clemens/ 1902".
Location: Antenne-Dorrance Collection, Rice Lake, Wis.
Copy examined: Clemens' copy, unmarked.

————. *Through the Looking-Glass and What Alice Found There.* Illus. by Peter Newell. New York: Harper & Brothers, [cop. 1902]. 211 pp.
Source: MTLAcc, entry #419, volume donated by Clemens.

Dods, John Bovee. *Spirit Manifestations Examined and Explained. Judge Edmonds Refuted; or, an Exposition of the Involuntary Powers and Instincts of the Human Mind.* New York: De Witt & Davenport, [cop. 1854].
Inscription: signed in pencil on front pastedown endpaper: "Orion Clemens."
Location: collection owned by Ralph Gregory, former curator, Mark Twain Birthplace Memorial Shrine, Florida, Mo. Mr. Gregory now lives in Marthasville, Mo.; he was given the book by Mrs. Mary Gertrude (Stotts) Shotwell of Greybull, Wyoming in 1965. (See entry for Thomas Dick's *The Practical Astronomer* for explanation of provenance.)
Copy examined: Orion Clemens' copy, conceivably read by his brother but never in Samuel Clemens' possession.

Dole, Nathan Haskell (1852–1935). *Peace and Progress; Two Symphonic Poems; The Building of the Organ; Onward.* Limited and numbered edition. Boston, 1904.
Inscription: "S. L. Clemens, 1905."
Catalog: A1911, #133, $3.25.

[Döllinger, Johann Joseph Ignaz von (1799–1890), pseud. "Janus."] *The Pope and the Council. By Janus.* [Written in collaboration with Johannes Huber (1830–1879).] Boston: Roberts Brothers, 1870. 346 pp.
Catalog: A1911, #252, .50¢.

Donnell, Annie Hamilton (b. 1862). *Rebecca Mary.* Illus. New York, 1905.
Inscription: signed on front pastedown endpaper: "S. L. Clemens, 1905."
Catalog: A1911, #134, $3.

————. *The Very Small Person.* Illus. by Elizabeth Shippen Green. New York: Harper & Brothers, 1906. 193 pp.
Source: MTLAcc, entry #1593, volume donated by Clemens.

Donnelly, Ignatius (1831–1901). *Atlantis: The Antediluvian World.* New York: Harper & Brothers, [cop. 1882]. 490 pp.
Source: MTLAcc, entry #1715, volume donated by Clemens.

————. *Caesar's Column. A Story of the Twentieth Century.* Chicago: F. J. Schulte & Co., [cop. 1890]. 367 pp.
Source: MTLAcc, entry #122, volume donated by Clemens.

————. *The Great Cryptogram: Francis Bacon's Cipher in the So-Called Shakespeare Plays.* Chicago: R. S. Peale & Co., 1888. 998 pp.
In a letter written to Fred J. Hall on 9 July 1887 from Elmira, Clemens deleted a sentence which mentioned the forthcoming book: "<Couldn't we get Ignatius Donnelly's [*sic*] Shakspeare-cipher book? . . .> No—we don't want it" (*MTBus*, p. 384); but later Clemens decided that he very much had wanted to publish the work, and in a letter to Orion Clemens on 7 September 1887 he blamed Charles L. Webster ("probably never heard of Bacon & didn't know there was a controversy") for losing this opportunity (MTP). An entry in Notebook 27 in November

1887 reiterates Webster's failure in this regard (TS p. 37). Clemens was interested in Donnelly's theories even aside from their publishing prospects, however; he had probably read *The Great Cryptogram* by the time he jotted down Donnelly's name and the phrase "Bacon-Shakspere" in Notebook 27 in September 1887 (TS p. 7), since he soon began to make notes for a burlesque that would prove Milton actually wrote *Pilgrim's Progress* (TS pp. 19–22). In 1909 Clemens testified that he both "published" and "read" Donnelly's book when it first appeared; he found it then "an ingenious piece of work," but nearly everyone scoffed at it. Though Donnelly's acrostics did not entirely convince Clemens, he was enormously impressed by the point Donnelly made about Shakespeare's never having used any Stratford scenes in his plays and poems (11 January 1909 AD, MTP).

Donworth, Grace. *The Letters of Jennie Allen to Her Friend Miss Musgrove.* Illus. by Frederick R. Gruger. Boston: Small, Maynard and Co., 1908. 291 pp.
  Source: MTLAcc, entry #2227, volume donated from Clemens' library by Clara Clemens Gabrilowitsch in 1910.

Doré, [Paul] Gustave (1833–1883) and Blanchard Jerrold, illus. *London.*
  Catalog: C1951, #D73, signed by Clemens.
  Clemens mentions a "Doré book" he ordered for Livy in letters to her on 6 and 10 January 1870 (MTP), but he fails to supply the title. He mentions Doré's illustrations in chapters 34 and 50 of *TA* (1880), chapter one of *SWE* (1882), and in Notebook 39 (26 September 1896), TS p. 3. (See the Finding List for other books owned by Clemens that contain illustrations by Doré.)

Doubleday, (Mrs.) Nellie Blanchan (De Graff), pseud. "Neltje Blanchan." *Bird Neighbors. An Introductory Acquaintance with One Hundred and Fifty Birds.* Intro. by John Burroughs. New York: Doubleday, Page & Co., 1908. 234 pp.
  Source: MTLAcc, entry #746, volume donated by Clemens.

———. *Birds That Every Child Should Know.* Illus. with photographs. New York: Doubleday, Page & Co., 1907. 281 pp.
  Source: MTLAcc, entry #480, volume donated by Clemens.

———. *Nature's Garden; An Aid to Knowledge of Our Wild Flowers and Their Insect Visitors.* Illus. New York: Doubleday, Page, & Co., 1907. 415 pp.
  Source: MTLAcc, entry #739, volume donated by Clemens.

Dowden, Edward (1843–1913). *The Life of Percy Bysshe Shelley* (pub. 1886).
  Mark Twain's "In Defence of Harriet Shelley" (1894) castigated Dowden's biography as "a literary cake-walk" and a "fat diet spread for the righteous."
  Paul Baender, "MT and the Byron Scandal" (1959), p. 478; Sydney J. Krause (*MTC* [1967], pp. 99–105).

———. *Shakspere: A Critical Study of His Mind and Art.* New York: Harper & Brothers, n.d. 386 pp.
  Source: MTLAcc, entry #1396, volume donated by Clemens.

Downes, Alfred Michael (1862–1907). *Fire Fighters and their Pets.* Illus. New York: Harper & Brothers, 1907. 185 pp.
  Source: MTLAcc, entry #517, volume donated by Clemens.

———. *Fire Fighters and Their Pets.* Illus. New York: Harper & Brothers, 1908. 185 pp.
  Source: MTLAcc, entry #1184, volume donated by Clemens.

Doyle, (Sir) Arthur Conan (1859–1930).

That Mark Twain derived satisfaction from burlesquing Doyle's Sherlock Holmes detective stories is well known. Walter Blair believes that Twain "had an ambivalent attitude toward detectives and detective stories. He admired brilliant deductions," yet "he was irked by pretentious and arrogant detectives in life and in books" *(HH&T* [1969], p. 155). Howard G. Baetzhold agrees that "what especially irked him . . . was Doyle's insistence on the almost supernatural intellectuality of his detective" *(MT&JB* [1970], p. 299). As true as these observations may be, however, it cannot be denied that Mark Twain mainly objected to other people's detectives—those of Pinkerton and Doyle, particularly—and gave indications in *Pudd'nhead Wilson* (1894) and other stories that he wished his own characters to master the complex art of reasoning by deductions. Moreover, Mark Twain was always on the lookout for burlesque materials (a holdover from his days as a West Coast journalist), and for him literary burlesque did not necessarily signify intense disrespect; often it was merely his instinctive method of paying literary homage.

All the same, apparently not a single copy of Doyle's detective books has survived from Clemens' personal library. Consequently Howard G. Baetzhold *(MT&JB*, pp. 299, 300–304, 381 n. 15) and other scholars have performed a fair amount of their own detective-sleuthing in efforts to determine which of Sherlock Holmes' feats has parallels in each of Mark Twain's burlesques. Cases have been made for adding Doyle's principal earlier books to Clemens' reading log: *A Study in Scarlet* (1887), *The Sign of the Four* (1890), *The Adventures of Sherlock Holmes* (1892), *The Memoirs of Sherlock Holmes* (1894), and *The Hound of the Baskervilles* (1902).

Most of Mark Twain's references to Holmes are too general in nature to allow exact identification of parallel passages, however. Certainly he seemed to have Holmes in mind when he described "Simon Wheeler, Detective" (written 1877–1898?) as "a born detective," unlike "the 'booky' one, that brilliant, sagacious, all-seeing, all-divining creation of the great modern novelists" *(S&B*, p. 438). Perhaps Twain got from Sherlock Holmes his notion to have the wise man deduce from the camel's footprints that it is lame in chapter 7 of *Tom Sawyer Abroad* (1893–1894). The sleuthing procedures in *PW* (1894) probably owe something—however immeasurable—to Holmes' exploits. In *Tom Sawyer, Detective* (1896) Huck Finn is the Dr. Watson-chronicler of the mystery's solution. The Australian aborigine, claims Mark Twain in chapter 17 of *FE* (1897), can detect minute differences "not detectible by you or me, or by the late Sherlock Holmes." Walter Blair traces influences of Doyle's "Silver Blaze" (collected in *The Memoirs of Sherlock Holmes)* and "The Boscombe Valley Mystery," as well as *The Sign of the Four,* that are evident in "Tom Sawyer's Conspiracy," written 1897–1900 *(HH&T,* pp. 158–159). Mark Twain wrote to Henry H. Rogers about his inspiration for writing "A Double-Barrelled Detective Story": "I happened upon a text for a story. . . . It is a burlesque of Sherlock Holmes" (6 September 1901, *MTHHR,* p. 469). Howard G. Baetzhold presumes that Clemens was referring to the first installment of *The Hound of the Baskervilles,* which had appeared in the August 1901 issue of *Strand Magazine (MT&JB,* p. 299); this conjecture seems likely, for on 8 September 1901 Clemens alluded to "the recent resurrection" of Sherlock Holmes in a letter to Joseph H. Twichell, telling Twichell that "the seed" for "A Double-Barrelled Detective Story" (pub. 1902) "was planted in your house many years ago when you sent me to bed with the book of a new author, not heard of by me until then—Sherlock Holmes. I planned to make fun of that pompous sentimental 'extraordinary man' with his cheap & ineffectual ingenuities—but the plan wouldn't sprout. . . . But this time I've pulled it off" (ALS in Yale, quoted in *MTB,* p. 1139). Howard G. Baetzhold argues that the "seed-book" Twichell pressed upon Mark Twain was Doyle's *A Study in Scarlet* (1887), which has much of its setting in Utah, concerns a "human bloodhound," and is also some-what "double-barrelled" in its structure, like Mark Twain's story *(MT&JB,* pp. 300–304). Sherlock Holmes is introduced as a character in chapter 6 of "A

Double-Barrelled Detective Story" (1902), yet his nephew Fetlock Jones asserts that Holmes "can't detect a crime except where he plans it all out beforehand and arranges the clews"; the miners in Hope Canyon yearn for a look at "the great scientific detective," but Holmes proves adept only in arranging theatrical effects and he is thoroughly humiliated in chapter 8. Twain evidently intended to mention Sherlock Holmes in "The Secret History of Eddypus" (written 1901–1902), because he wrote his name among his B–2 working notes (*FM*, p. 469). In 1905 he entered A. Conan Doyle's name in Notebook 48 (TS p. 1); and in 1905 or 1906 he recalled hearing a joke about Sherlock Holmes' reaching heaven and identifying Adam and Eve, because they had no navels (NB 48, TS p. 11).

————. *The Crime of the Congo* (pub. 1909).
   Doyle mentioned sending a copy of this book in a letter to Clemens on 9 October 1909, and Clemens began a reply on [15] October 1909 ("I have received your book, 'The Crime of the Congo' "), but only half-completed his letter, which assails King Leopold's atrocities (MTP). On 29 October 1909 Albert Bigelow Paine wrote to Doyle to explain that because of Clemens' heart disease he "does not permit himself to read any matter pertaining to the cruelties practiced there. . . . Mr. Clemens thanks you most sincerely for the booklet you sent, and for your cordial letter (*Sir Arthur Conan Doyle: Centenary 1859–1959* [London: John Murray, 1959], p. 73).

————. *The Great Shadow; A Novel.* New York: Harper & Brothers, 1893. 218 pp.
   Source: MTLAcc, entry #2228, volume donated from Clemens' library by Clara Clemens Gabrilowitsch in 1910.

————. *A Study in Scarlet, and the Sign of the Four.* New York: Harper & Brothers, 1904. 287 pp.
   Source: MTLAcc, entry #1543, volume donated by Clemens.

————. *The War in South Africa: Its Cause and Conduct.* New York, 1902.
   Inscription: signed on cover: "S. L. Clemens."
   Catalog: *A1911,* #137, $1.

Drake, Francis Samuel (1828–1885). *Dictionary of American Biography* (pub. 1872).
   "Examine Drake's & Allibone's Dictionaries of Authors to see who *have* been humorists," Mark Twain wrote in 1880 when he began contemplating an anthology of humor (NB 19, *N&J*, 2: 364).

————. *Indian History for Young Folks.* Illus. New York: Harper & Brothers, [cop. 1884]. 479 pp.
   Source: MTLAcc, entry #1186, volume donated by Clemens.

Drake, Joseph Rodman. "The American Flag" (poem).
   Mark Twain copied the last four lines from this poem, which begins "Forever float that standard sheet," into Notebook 5 (*N&J*, 1: 146).

Drake, Samuel Adams (1833–1905). *The Heart of the White Mountains, Their Legend and Scenery.* Illus. by W. Hamilton Green. New York: Harper & Brothers, 1882. 318 pp.
   Source: MTLAcc, entry #1227, volume donated by Clemens.

Dramatists of the Restoration. [Ed. by James Maidment and William Hugh Logan.] 14 vols. Limited edition of 450 copies. Edinburgh: W. Paterson, 1872–1879. [Contains dramatic works of A. Cokain, J. Crowne, W. D'Avenant, J. Lacy, S. Marmion, J. Tatham, J. Wilson.]

    Catalogs: A1911, #138, $10 total, 13 vols. only; *Lexington 1912,* #10, $20, 13 vols. only.

Draper, John William (1811–1882). *Human Physiology, Statical and Dynamical; or, The Conditions and Course of the Life of Man.* Illus. New York: Harper & Brothers, 1856.

    Catalog: C1951, #D3, $7.50, listed as signed by Clemens.

    Draper's book contains many curious "facts," such as the assertion that the "total weight" of all Americans is "two thousand six hundred and thirteen millions of pounds" (p. 541). His remarks on women must have seemed old-fashioned even by the 1880's: their personalities, he wrote, illustrate "phrenological predominance of the moral over the intellectual regions of the brain" (p. 546). But Clemens found a flattering description to send to an ill Livy on 31 March (1903?): "Hear Dr. Draper writing about you prophetically, thirty years ago [*sic*], in his great work on 'physiology,' chapter on Woman" (MTP). Clemens then quotes a passage about the "beautiful qualities" of women, who remain devoted to their husbands until, "at the close of a long life checkered with pleasures and misfortunes," the aged man finds that "her affection alone is unchanged, true to him in sickness as in health, in adversity as in prosperity, true to the hour of death."

Dressel, C. M. F. *The Cuban Spanish American War, Sketched by C. M. F. Dressel.* New York: Dressel Co., 1898. 12 pp.

    Inscription: on title page: "To Mark Twain (S. L. Clemens)/C. M. F. Dressel. Nov. 16/98."

    Marginalia: Clemens scrawled on the cover in pencil: "Keep it," and under-lined in pencil several lines in the footnotes.

    Location: Mark Twain Papers, Berkeley, California.

    Copy examined: Clemens' copy.

Dresser, Amos. *Narrative of Amos Dresser.* New York, 1836. [One of six pamphlets bound as a volume with W. E. Channing's *Letter on Slavery* (1837).]

    Catalog: A1911, #76, $2 total.

Dresser, Horatio Willis (b. 1866). *The Heart of It. A Series of Extracts from "The Power of Silence" and "The Perfect Whole."* Ed. by Helen Campbell and Katharine Westendorf. New York: G. P. Putnam's Sons, 1901. 145 pp.

    Source: MTLAcc, entry #670, volume donated by Clemens.

Dreyfus, (Mrs.) Lilian Gertrude (Shuman). *From Me to You.* Boston: Lee and Shepard, 1898. 92 pp.

    Source: MTLAcc, entry #873, volume donated by Mrs. Ralph W. Ashcroft (formerly Isabel Lyon), Clemens' secretary.

Drummond, Hamilton (1857–1935). *A Man of His Age.* Illus. by J. Ambrose Walton. New York: Harper & Brothers, 1900. 303 pp.

    Source: MTLAcc, entry #1544, volume donated by Clemens.

Drummond, Henry (1851–1897). *"Beautiful Thoughts" from Henry Drummond.* Comp. by Elizabeth Cureton. New York: James Pott & Co., 1892. 280 pp.

    Source: MTLAcc, entry #930, volume donated by Clemens.

————. *The Greatest Thing in the World. An Address.* London: Hodder and Stoughton, 1890.

Albert Bigelow Paine reported that the Scottish evangelical writer and lecturer Drummond visited Clemens in 1879 in Hartford *(MTB,* p. 661). Perhaps the newspaper publicity attendant upon Drummond's death on 11 March 1897 aroused Clemens' interest in the efforts of Drummond to reconcile science and theology: in London in April 1897 Clemens listed four of Drummond's books in his notebook: "Natural Law in the Sp. Θ/Ascent of Man/Pax Vobiscum/ Greatest Thing in the World" (NB 41, TS p. 21). Clemens requested copies of these same books in an undated postcard to Andrew Chatto of Chatto & Windus (Berg).

————. *The Lowell Lectures on the Ascent of Man.* London: Hodder and Stoughton, 1894.

Catalog: C1951, #03, listed as containing Livy Clemens' signature.

Clemens noted the title in Notebook 41 (April 1897) and requested a copy of the book in an undated postcard to Andrew Chatto of Chatto & Windus in London (Berg).

————. *Natural Law in the Spiritual World.* London: Hodder and Stoughton, 1883.

Clemens recorded the title in his notebook in April 1897 (NB 41, TS p. 21) and requested the work in an undated postcard to Andrew Chatto (Berg).

————. *Pax Vobiscum. An Address.* London: Hodder and Stoughton, 1890.

Clemens made note of the title in April 1897 (NB 41, TS p. 21) and requested Andrew Chatto to send him a copy of the book (undated postcard, Berg).

Drummond, William Henry (1854–1907). *The Great Flight. Poems and Sketches.* Illus. by Frederick Simpson Coburn. New York: G. P. Putnam's Sons, [cop. 1908].

Inscription: in pencil on front flyleaf: "Clara Clemens/from J. B. Learmont."
Location: Antenne-Dorrance Collection, Rice Lake, Wis.
Copy examined: Clara Clemens' copy, unmarked.

————. *The Habitant, and Other French-Canadian Poems.* Illus. New York, 1902.
Inscription: signed "S. L. Clemens, Riverdale, Jan. 1903."
Catalog: A1911, #139, $7.50.

Dryden, John (1631–1700).

Mark Twain named Dryden in 1865 as one of those responsible for "all the poetry that everybody admires and appreciates, but nobody ever reads or quotes from" *(Californian,* 17 June 1865, quoted in *LAMT,* p. 142).

Drysdale, William (1852–1901). *The Mystery of Abel Forefinger.* Illus. New York: Harper & Brothers, 1894. 208 pp.

Source: MTLAcc, entry #1451, volume donated by Clemens.

DuBarry, Marie Jeanne Bécu (1746?–1793). *Memoirs of Madame DuBarri.* Trans from the French [of Baron E. L. de la Mothe Langon] by the translator of "Vidocq" [H. T. Riley]. 4 vols. New York: Merrill and Baker, n.d.

William Dean Howells sent Clemens the first three volumes of an unspecified edition on 21 December 1877, promising to send the fourth as soon as he regained it from a borrower *(MTHL,* p. 211). The Mark Twain Papers contain thirteen pages of extracts from DuBarry's *Memoirs* (DV416), formerly inserted in a family scrapbook dated 1878–1879 (Scrapbook #21, MTP) and written in purple ink by Orion Clemens on the Crystal-Lake Mills writing paper that Mark Twain used between 1876 and 1880. Presumably Orion copied the passages at his brother's direction. One quotation from vol. 1 tells of the discovery of the putrefied bodies of Madame de Mellamière's lovers; the second passage from the same volume describes more commonplace events in the French court. The citations (except for one mistake by the copyist in citing page 43 instead of page 41 for the first-named passage) accord with the pagination of the edition listed for this entry. DuBarry's *Memoirs* may be the book Clemens meant when he wrote Edward H. House on 14 January 1884 that he had recently diverted himself by reading "in English, . . . the second volume of The Autobiography of a Whore" (CWB). Mark Twain planned to credit DuBarry in his projected appendix to *CY* for "Lettres de cachet" forms and "Castle d'If" (NB 29 [1889], TS p. 15). Henry W. Fisher mentioned hearing Clemens refer once to DuBarry's *Memoirs (AMT,* p. 64).

Du Chaillu, Paul Belloni (1831–1903). *The Country of the Dwarfs* (pub. 1871). *Catalog: C1951,* #50a, $40, listed among books containing marginalia by Clemens.

An account of African explorations.

————. *Wild Life Under the Equator. Narrated for Young People.* Illus. New York: Harper & Brothers, [cop. 1866]. 363 pp. *Source:* MTLAcc, entry #1174, volume donated by Clemens.

Dugmore, Arthur Radclyffe (1870–1955). *Bird Homes. The Nests, Eggs, and Breeding Habits of the Land Birds.* Illus. New York: Doubleday, Page & Co., 1902. 183 pp. *Inscription:* signed "Jean Langdon Clemens/Riverdale on the Hudson/ November 18th 1902." *Location:* Mark Twain Library, Redding, Connecticut. Donated from Clemens' library by Clara Clemens Gabrilowitsch in 1910 (MTLAcc, entry #1946). *Copy examined:* Jean Clemens' copy, unmarked.

————. *Nature and the Camera. How to Photograph Live Birds and Their Nests, Animals, Wild Game.* Illus. New York: Doubleday, Page & Co., 1902. 126 pp. *Inscription:* front pastedown endpaper: "To Jean Clemens/from me,/her Father,/Sept. '03." *Location:* Mark Twain Library, Redding, Conn. Donated from Clemens' library by Clara Clemens Gabrilowitsch in 1910 (MTLAcc, entry #1945). *Copy examined:* Jean Clemens' copy, unmarked.

Dumas, Alexandre (1802–1870), known as Dumas *père. Novels.* Illus. 14 vols. London: Routledge, n.d. [Includes *The Count of Monte Cristo; The Three Musketeers: Twenty Years After; The Viscount of Bragelonne* (2 vols.); *Marguerite de Valois; Chicot the Jester; The Forty-Five Guardsmen; The Conspirators; The Regent's Daughter; Memoirs of a Physician; The Queen's Necklace; The Taking of the Bastille; The Countess de Charny.*] *Catalog: A1911,* #140, $4 total.

Dumas' works furnished Clemens with escapist reading on numerous occasions. In a letter purportedly written to his infant daughter Susy on 9 May 1872, Clemens informed her that "many's the night I've lain awake till 2 oclock in the morning reading Dumas & drinking beer, listening for the slightest sound you might make" (ALS in MTM, quoted in *LLMT,* p. 174). On 23 April 1877 Clemens wrote to Livy from the St. James Hotel in New York City: "I had a delightful afternoon. I left behind me those 2 men who have not been absent from my thoughts (& my hate) for months—[John T.] Raymond & [Bret] Harte—so I read Dumas & was serene & content" (*LLMT,* p. 194). This reading seems reflected in a fragmentary novel that Clemens possibly began in 1875, "The Mysterious Chamber" (DV56, MTP). Although set in eighteenth-century Italy rather than France, this tale of "jealousy and revenge" with its haunted castle, ancient sword, dark corridors, dusty cobwebs, iron doors, treasure chests, interrupted betrothal, and a prisoner confined in dungeon conditions who writes with home-made ink, would have been reminiscent of Dumas as well as various Gothic novels. Clemens continued to show an interest in Dumas' writings beyond the 1870's. "Get the rest of Dumas at the German Buchhandlung," he reminded himself in 1885 (NB 24, TS p. 15). Henry W. Fisher remembered that in the late 1890's Clemens told him Dumas was one of the guides the Clemenses used to look up "the places of horror" in Paris (*AMT*, p. 59).

———. *The Count of Monte-Cristo*. 2 vols. London: G. Routledge and Sons, n.d. 754 pp.
   Source: MTLAcc, entry #2229, vol. 2 only, donated from Clemens' library by Clara Clemens Gabrilowitsch in 1910.
   Before leaving on the *Quaker City* in 1867 Mark Twain reminded himself to purchase an unspecified book by Dumas (NB 8, *N&J*, 1: 326). In chapter 11 of *IA* (1869) he mentions visiting the Castle d'If in which the "heroes of 'Monte Cristo' " whiled away their confinement in "damp, dismal cells"; there he also catalogues some of the prisoner's implements—pen, lamp, chisel, blood-ink— that would plague the hapless Jim in *HF* (1885).
   Olin H. Moore, "Mark Twain and Don Quixote" (1922), pp. 333–335; Henry Pochmann, "The Mind of MT" (1924), pp. 15, 158–159; Walter Blair, "French Revolution" (1957), p. 25; Franklin Rogers, *MTBP* (1960), p. 149.

———. *Taking the Bastille, or Six Years Later*. London: George Routledge and Sons, n.d.
   Inscription: signed in pencil on flyleaf: "SL Clemens/Hartford 1877."
   Location: Antenne-Dorrance Collection, Rice Lake, Wis.
   Copy examined: Clemens' copy, unmarked. Apparently he owned two copies of the same edition of this book; see the entry above for Dumas' *Novels* listed in *A1911*, #140. On 6 August 1877 Clemens mentioned reading "one of Dumas' novels, 'The Taking of the Bastille,' " in a letter to Mollie Fairbanks (*MTMF*, p. 208).

———. *The Viscount of Bragelonne* (parts of which are often published separately as *Louise de la Vallière* and *The Man in the Iron Mask*).
   Mark Twain called Dumas "the great Mulatto in the Iron Mask" in 1867 (*Alta California*, 17 May 1867; *MTTMB*, p. 170). In Mark Twain's "The Wild Man Interviewed" (1869) his Wild Man claims that he "moped in a French dungeon for fifteen years, and wore a ridiculous Iron Mask." In chapter 11 of *IA* (1869) Mark Twain mentions seeing "the noisome cell where the celebrated 'Iron Mask'—that ill-starred brother of a hard-hearted king of France—was confined. . . . These dank walls had known the man whose dolorous story is a sealed book forever!" Walter Blair warns that this reference "does not prove that he was familiar with the book" by 1869 ("French Revolution," p. 27 n. 31). On 14 July 1880 Estes & Lauriat of Boston sent Clemens a bill for twenty-one books, including "1 Iron Mask $1"; Clemens paid the bill on 20 July 1880 (receipt in MTP). Walter Blair proposes that the *Iron Mask* taught Mark Twain about its legendary figure and suggested the ideas of scratching messages on tin plates (chapter 36 of *HF* [1885]) and smuggling notes in a loaf of bread (the witch pie) (Blair, "French Revolution," p. 27 n. 31). Clemens noted "Villeneuve (iron Mask 8 days)" in Notebook 31 (TS p. 8) in October 1891. Tom Sawyer and Huck Finn "hunted out the old chain and padlock and two keys that we used to play out the Prisoner of the Basteel with" in chapter 3 of "Tom Sawyer's Conspiracy," written 1897–1900 (*HH&T*, p. 178).

Dumas, Alexandre (1824–1895), known as Dumas *fils. Camille* (play, perf. 1852 as *La Dame aux camélias*).

On 20 December 1905 Isabel Lyon recorded: "Ah, we saw [Sarah] Bernhardt in Camille today. . . . She goes beyond [Eleonora] Duse's art in that play, in all but the gambling scene" (IVL Journal, TS p. 115, MTP).

————. *Le Demi-Monde* (play, prod. 1855).

Clemens received a bill from James R. Osgood & Company of Boston in November 1877 for "1 Les Demi Monde [*sic*], 2 v.," purchased on 9 August 1877 (Scrapbook #10, p. 69, MTP).

Du Maurier, George Louis Palmella Busson (1834–1896). *A Legend of Camelot, Pictures and Poems.* Illus. New York, 1898.
   Catalog: A1911, #141, $3.

————. *The Martian* (novel, pub. 1896, illus. by the author).

In October 1907 Clemens told Isabel Lyon to make a note of the fact that "Harper paid Du Maurier 50 000 for the Martian" (Isabel Lyon Notebook #3, MTP).

————. *Peter Ibbetson.* Illus. by the author. New York: Harper & Brothers, 1904. 418 pp.
   Source: MTLAcc, entry #1545, volume donated by Clemens.

————. *Social Pictorial Satire.* Illus. New York: Harper & Brothers, 1893. 100 pp.
   Source: MTLAcc, entry #1357, volume donated by Clemens.

————. *Trilby* (novel, pub. 1894).

In an undated statement Clemens mentioned the lucrative publishing terms that Harper & Brothers voluntarily gave Du Maurier when *Trilby* turned out to be a gigantic success (*MTHHR*, pp. 533–534). Clemens referred to *Trilby* in a newspaper interview published in the Durban [South Africa] *Natal Mercury Weekly,* 8 May 1896; reprinted in the *Natal Witness,* 9 May 1896, and the Pretoria *Press,* 15 May 1896 (information supplied by Louis J. Budd).

Du Maurier, Guy Louis Busson (1865–1915). *An Englishman's Home; A Play in Three Acts.* New York: Harper & Brothers, 1909. 131 pp.
   Source: MTLAcc, entry #1101, volume donated by Clemens.

Dunbar, Paul Lawrence (1872–1906). *Majors and Minors: Poems.* Toledo, Ohio: Hadley & Hadley, [cop. 1895]. 148 pp.
   Inscription: on second flyleaf: "To S. L. C./fm/J. B. Pond/Sept. 10 '96."
   Marginalia: on page 47 Clemens altered "foot" to "span" in the second poem.
   Location: Mark Twain Library, Redding, Conn. Donated from Clemens' library by Clara Clemens Gabrilowitsch in 1910 (MTLAcc, entry #2054).
   Copy examined: Clemens' copy, a gift from James B. Pond after Clemens' lecture tour around the world.

Duncan, Norman (1871–1916). *The Cruise of the Shining Light.* New York: Harper & Brothers, 1907. 344 pp.
   Source: MTLAcc, entry #120, volume donated by Clemens.

————. *Every Man for Himself.* Illus. New York, 1908.
   Inscription: signed on front pastedown endpaper "S. L. Clemens, 1909."
   Catalog: A1911, #142, $2.25.

Duncan, Robert Kennedy (1868–1914). *The Chemistry of Commerce: A Simple Interpretation of Some New Chemistry.* Illus. New York: Harper & Brothers, 1907. 263 pp.
    Source: MTLAcc, entry #1799, volume donated by Clemens.

Dunkley, Henry (1823–1896). *Lord Melbourne.* New York: Harper & Brothers, 1890. 248 pp.
    Source: MTLAcc, entry #1759, volume donated by Clemens.

Dunn, Jacob Piatt (1855–1924). *Massacres of the Mountains: A History of the Indian Wars of the Far West.* Illus. New York: Harper & Brothers, 1886. 784 pp.
    Source: MTLAcc, entry #1716, volume donated by Clemens.

    Dunn graphically documents more than twenty slaughters by American Indians, white settlers, and the U. S. Cavalry, including the Mountain Meadows massacre and the Little Big Horn. His narratives teem with bloody details of Indian raids and tortures; on pages 489–490, for example, he describes how the Sioux tribes would torture a prisoner by building a fire on the man's stomach while he was outstretched and staked to the ground. Dunn's preface urges the standard nineteenth-century solution to the "Indian problem": Christian conversion and "civilization."
    Walter Blair demonstrated that in "Huck Finn and Tom Sawyer Among the Indians" Mark Twain borrowed the majority of his details about Indian customs from several books written by Richard Dodge *(HH&T,* pp. 84–88, 328–337). If Twain by any chance sought corroboration of Dodge's reports, or if he wrote part of the uncompleted manuscript later than the date Blair conjectures for its composition (1884), then Dunn's book—copyrighted and published in 1886—reinforced the authority of Dodge's assertions about Indian depravity. For instance, Dunn states that "the treatment of women, by any Indians, is usually bad, but by the plains Indians especially so. When a woman is captured by a war-party she is the common property of all of them, each night, till they reach their village, when she becomes the special property of her individual captor. . . . If she resists she is 'staked out,' that is to say, four pegs are driven into the ground and a hand or foot tied to each, to prevent struggling. She is also beaten, mutilated, or even killed, for resistance" (p. 427). In fact, there is an entry in Dunn's index for "Women, white, treatment by Plains Indians." The discovery of four stakes signalling the gang-rape of Peggy Mills (at the site where Huck secretly notices a torn and bloody piece of her dress) sickened Brace Johnson and apparently prevented Twain from taking the story beyond this grisly development. But Blair points out that Dodge's *Plains of the Great West* (1877) mentions the use of stakes in the rape of women prisoners *(HH&T,* p. 336).

Dunne, Finley Peter (1867–1936), pseud. "Mr. Dooley." *Dissertations by Mr. Dooley.* New York, 1906.
    Catalogs: C1951, #D51; *Zeitlin 1951,* #15, $30.
    Inscription: signed in ink on front pastedown endpaper, "S. L. Clemens, 1906".
    Norman Hapgood recalled Dunne as the only younger person "whom I ever heard address Mr. Clemens as Mark to his face. . . . It was a pleasant relation between these two humorists, and many an hour spent in billiards" *(Changing Years* [1930], p. 211). Isabel Lyon's journal contains an entry for 7 December 1904: "This has been a day of events—for this morning Mr. Dunne (Mr. Dooley) came for a closeting with Mr. Clemens" (1903–1906 Diary, TS p. 31, MTP); Miss Lyon also recorded on 20 October 1905 Clemens' analysis of a sentence by Dunne in which "one or two non-essential words are left out: 'Why do people marry Lillian Russell?' " (IVL Journal, TS p. 109, MTP). Clemens wanted Dunne in the literary group that Clemens tried to organize in New York City in 1906 for the purpose of entertaining visiting foreign authors (SLC to WDH, 10 April 1906, *MTHL,* p. 804). Clemens mentioned Dunne as a

familiar name in American humor in his 31 July 1906 Autobiographical Dictation
(*MTE,* p. 201). In a subsequent dictation, Clemens said that Dunne "is brilliant;
he is an expert with his pen, and he easily stands at the head of all the satirists of
this generation" (22 January 1907 AD, MTP). He joked in "Christian Science"
(1907) that "style" at least would differentiate "Mr. Dooley's books" from those
by "the late Jonathan Edwards" (Book 1, chapter 3). Clemens wrote to Jean
Clemens from Fifth Avenue on 26 January 1906: "Dooley came & played
billiards yesterday & won a dollar" (TS in MTP); the next month he chatted
with Dunne at a party until shortly after midnight (19 February 1908 AD, MTP).
Letters from Dunne were among the only sort of mail ("friendly letters & letters
from friends, of an unirritating sort") that Clemens allowed Jean to send him
in Bermuda in 1909 (SLC to Jean Clemens, 6 December 1909, MTP).

Dunphy, Thomas, and Thomas J. Cummins. *Remarkable Trials of All Countries,*
Particularly of the United States, Great Britain, Ireland, and France. New York,
1878.
> *Inscription:* signed on front pastedown endpaper, "S. L. Clemens, 21 5th
Avenue, 1907."
> *Catalog: A1911,* #145, $3.25.

Dunster, H. P. *Historical Tales of Lancastrian Times.* London: Griffith and Farran,
1864.
> *Inscription:* Livy Clemens wrote on the flyleaf in pencil: "S. L. Clemens/1873".
> *Location:* Mark Twain Library, Redding, Connecticut.
> *Copy examined:* Clemens' copy.

Duoir, Paul. "My Kingdom" (poem, pub. 1865).
> Mark Twain quotes, parodies, and berates this poem in his "Real Estate Versus
Imaginary Possession, Poetically Considered," *Californian,* 28 October 1865
(*SSix,* pp. 188–190). Duoir's "Kingdom" turns out to be "One True Woman's
Heart."

Duplessis, Georges (1834–1899). *The Wonders of Engraving.* Illus. New York:
Charles Scribner & Co., 1871. 338 pp.
> *Source:* MTLAcc, entry #2000, volume donated from Clemens' library by
Clara Clemens Gabrilowitsch in 1910.

Durst, Simon (pseud.) *Bub and Sis; A 20th Century New England Story.* Illus.
Woonsocket, Rhode Island: Woonsocket Publishing Co., 1903. 144 pp.
> *Source:* MTLAcc, entry #633, volume donated by Clemens.

Dussouchet, J. *Petite Grammaire Française.* Paris: Librairie Hachette et C., 1883.
> *Inscription:* signed on front free endpaper, "Clara L. Clemens/Jan. 4th 1887."
> *Marginalia:* annotation by a child throughout the first twenty pages. Some
pages missing from front section.
> *Location:* Mark Twain Library, Redding, Connecticut.
> *Copy examined:* Clara Clemens' copy.

Dwight, James (1852–1917). *Practical Lawn Tennis.* Illus. New York: Harper &
Brothers, 1893. 168 pp.
> *Source:* MTLAcc, entry #808, volume donated by Clemens.

Dyar, Muriel Campbell. *Davie and Elisabeth, Wonderful Adventures.* New York:
Harper & Brothers, 1908. 131 pp.
> *Source:* MTLAcc, entry #1198, volume donated by Clemens.

Dziewicki, Michael Henry. *Entombed in Flesh*. London: W. Blackwood & Sons, 1897. 282 pp.

    Source: MTLAcc, entry #996, volume donated by Clemens.

    Clemens mentioned this book title in computing costs of book publishing on the front free endpaper of Émile Zola's *Rome* (1896).

Eadie, John (1810–1876), ed. *A New and Complete Concordance to the Holy Scriptures, on the Basis of [Alexander] Cruden*. Ed. by John Eadie. Intro. by David King. New York: American Tract Society, n.d. [Eadie's "Note to the Fourteenth Edition" is dated 1850.] 561 pp.

    Inscription: in purple ink, possibly Clemens' hand: "Livie L. Langdon/Feb 2^d 1870" (the date of her wedding).

    Marginalia: pencil marks throughout at the following entries: Ass (every entry); Blind, Adjective; Error and Errors; Fowl and Fowls; Low (Deuteronomy 28:43, "shalt come down very low"); Run, Runnest, Runneth, Running (one penciled word in Clemens' hand beside Lev. 15:2, 22:4: "dispute"); Safe; Second; Seventh Month, Seventh Year; Stole and Stolen; Stop; Struck; Swift; Third; Threw, Throw, Throwing, Thrown.

    Provenance: contains bookstamps and trace of charge-slip jacket from Mark Twain Library, Redding.

    Catalog: Mott 1952, #48, $3.

    Location: Mark Twain Memorial, Hartford, Conn. Gift of anonymous donor in 1963.

    Copy examined: Livy Clemens' copy, apparently consulted frequently by her husband.

Earle, Maria Theresa (Villiers) (1836–1925). *Pot-pourri from a Surrey Garden* (pub. 1897).

    Clemens jotted down the title (erroneously writing "summer Garden") and the author's name in 1900 (NB 43, TS p. 2a).

Eastlake, Charles Lock (1793–1865). *Hints on Household Taste in Furniture, Upholstery, and Other Details*. Ed., with notes, by Charles C. Perkins. First American, from rev. London edition. Boston: James R. Osgood & Co., 1872.

    Inscription: signed on second flyleaf, "Livy L. Clemens/1872".

    Catalogs: A1911, #147, $2.75 (sold to the Mark Twain Company); *C1951,* #015; *Hunley 1958,* #38, $6.50, contains *A1911* auction label.

    Location: Mark Twain Memorial, Hartford, Conn. Contains *A1911* auction label on front pastedown endpaper.

    Copy examined: Livy Clemens' copy, unmarked but appears well-used. The volume contains colored samples of wallpaper design and colored plates of parquetry floor patterns.

Eastman, Annis F. "A Dose of Paradise" (short short story, pub. in *The Independent*, 24 June 1897).

    Livy Clemens clipped and preserved this piece in her diary (MTP). Evidently she showed it to Clemens, for several markings and corrections in brown ink appear to be his ("she felt sick" is changed to "she fell ill"). The writer's residence is given as Elmira, New York, so possibly Livy was acquainted with the author of this didactic tale, which concerns an ill and exhausted woman who imagines a visit to heaven during her sickness. Returning to "her dingy rooms, homely table, troublesome children, monotonous work," she decides that "Paradise is good, but home is better." A final paragraph urges women to recognize their own paradises here on earth.

Ebers, Georg Moritz (1837–1898). *Eine Aegyptische Königstochter. Historischer roman.* 3 vols. Leipzig: Carl Reigner, 1885.
> *Source:* MTLAcc, entry #387, volume 3 only, donated by Clemens.

Ebner von Eschenbach, Marie Freifrau (1830–1916). *Margarete.* Stuttgart: J. G. Cotta, 1895. 144 pp.
> *Source:* MTLAcc, entry #373, volume donated by Clemens.

Ebsworth, J[oseph] Woodfall (1824–1908), ed. *Choyce Drollery: Songs and Sonnets.* Boston: R. Roberts, 1876.
> *Inscription:* signed in pencil on flyleaf, "S. L. Clemens, Hartford, 1876."
> *Catalogs: C1951,* #28c; *Zeitlin 1951,* #16, $30.

————. *Westminster Drolleries, Both Parts, of 1671, 1672; Being a Choice Collection of Songs and Poems, Sung at Court and Theatres. . . . Now First Reprinted from the Original Editions.* Boston: R. Roberts, 1875.
> *Inscription:* signed on flyleaf, "Saml L. Clemens, Hartford, 1875".
> *Catalogs: C1951,* #D58; *Zeitlin 1951,* #17, $20.
> A facsimile edition of songs and poems that treat romantic love in a Metaphysical tone. Ebsworth supplies a lengthy and defensive introduction and notes.

Eckstorm, (Mrs.) Fannie (Hardy) (1865–1946). *The Penobscot Man.* Boston: Houghton, Mifflin and Co., 1904. 326 pp.
> *Catalog: A1911,* #148, $1.
> Houghton, Mifflin and Company wrote to Clemens on 8 August 1904: "At the suggestion of the author, we take pleasure in sending you . . . a complimentary copy of 'The Penobscot Man' by Fannie Hardy Eckstorm. We believe that years ago you took a trip up Katahdin and down the West Branch with the same Lewey Ketchum who figures in two of the stories." Isabel Lyon recorded a reply at the bottom of the letter: "Away indefinitely or would send thanks himself" (MTP).

————. *The Woodpeckers.* Illus. Boston: Houghton, Mifflin and Co., 1901. 131 pp.
> *Inscription:* inscribed from Clemens to Jean in September 1903.
> *Catalog: Mott 1952,* #49, $30.

————. [An identical copy.]
> *Source:* MTLAcc, entry #1947, volume donated by Clemens' library by Clara Clemens Gabrilowitsch in 1910.

The Eclectic Magazine. For 1860. 3 vols. New York, 1860.
> *Catalog: A1911,* #149, $2.
> In January 1888 Clemens wrote "The Eclectic—annually" in Notebook 27, TS p. 56.

Eddy, (Mrs.) Mary (Baker) (1821–1910). *Manual of the Mother Church, the First Church of Christ, Scientist, in Boston, Massachusetts.* 28th ed. Boston: The Christian Science Publishing Society, 1903. 111 pp.
> *Inscription:* signed on inside front cover, "S. L. Clemens/March 1903." Contains *C1951* sale label.
> *Marginalia:* heavily annotated in pencil throughout by Clemens.
> *Catalogs:* sold at *C1951* sale, though not listed in catalog; purchased by Jean Hersholt; listed in "American Books," Lew David Feldman Catalogue (1955), #243, $143.
> *Location:* formerly in the Mark Twain Papers, Berkeley, Calif. Missing since at least 1964, and presumed stolen.
> Clemens wrote an undated letter to Frederick W. Peabody from Riverdale: "I shall take good care of the Church Manual, & return it to you. I never knew

until now, who sent it to me. I do not remember asking for it. . . . But I find it useful. I thought it was my own, so I have marginal-noted it, & am very sorry" (ALS quoted in Parke-Bernet Galleries Catalogue, Sale No. 223 [October 30–November 1, 1940], item #186). To Frank Bliss he wrote on 4 March 1903, requesting a copy of the 1902 edition of Mrs. Eddy's *Manual* ("I have an *old* copy," he added). He wanted Bliss to borrow the book from his Hartford or Boston friends (PH in MTP). Paul Baender has determined that Mark Twain used a copy of the eleventh (1899) edition in writing "Christian Science" (1907), but this volume has evidently been lost *(WIM?,* p. 561). In the section of "Christian Science" entitled "Mrs. Eddy in Error," Mark Twain roundly assailed her *Manual:* "Her governance is all there; all in that deceptively innocent-looking little book, that cunning little devilish book, that slumbering little brown volcano, with hell in its bowels. In that book she has planned out her system, and classified and defined its purposes and powers."

————. *Miscellaneous Writings 1883–1896.* Boston: J. Armstrong, 1897.
Mark Twain criticized "the divinity-circuit style" of *Miscellaneous Writings* in chapter 7 of Book 1, "Christian Science." In chapter 3 of Book 2 he quoted from the preface of this "fat volume."

————. "O'er waiting harpstrings of the mind" (hymn).
"Pretty good, quite fair to middling" ("Christian Science" [1907], Book 1, chapter 7).

————. *Retrospection and Introspection.* Twentieth thousand. Boston: Joseph Armstrong, 1902. 130 pp.
Marginalia: annotated by Clemens in both pencil and ink.
Catalog: "Retz Appraisal" (1944), p. 8, valued at $40.
Location: Mark Twain Papers, Berkeley, California.
Copy examined: Clemens' copy.
Clemens wrote to W. D. McCrackan from Riverdale on 5 December 1902 to request a copy of Mrs. Eddy's autobiography, *Restrospection* (MTP). When the book had not arrived by 1 January 1903 he wrote again, asking McCrackan to "inquire why" (PH in MTP), and made a memorandum in Notebook 46 on 2 January 1903 about reminding McCrackan (TS p. 4). He treated Mrs. Eddy's autobiography extensively in Book 2 of "Christian Science" (1907), ridiculing her supposed statements of fact and her mode of writing.

————. "Saw ye my Saviour" (hymn).
Mark Twain mentions this hymn in "Christian Science" (1907), Book 1, chapter 7.

————. *Science and Health; A Key to the Scriptures.* Tenth ed. 2 vols. Boston: published by the author, 1884. [Only Clemens' copy of vol. 2 is known to exist.]
Inscription: vol. 2 signed in black ink on front pastedown endpaper, "SL. Clemens/Riverdale, New York City, 1902."
Marginalia: vol. 2 contains annotation by Clemens.
Catalog: "Retz Appraisal" (1944), p. 8, vol. 2 only, valued at $25.
Location: vol. 2 only in Mark Twain Papers, Berkeley, California.
Copy examined: Clemens' copy of vol. 2.
Science and Health antagonized Mark Twain far more than any of Mrs. Eddy's other writings, and became, it may be said, a true obsession for him during his final decade. He objected to the immense power that it seemed to wield over large numbers of people, he insisted that Mrs. Eddy had purloined its chief ideas from Phineas Parkhurst Quimby, and he was convinced that because she had hired ghost-writers to produce or at least edit much of the text, she deserved no credit for the book that bore her name. In 1901 and 1902 Mark Twain labored doggedly at a manuscript he never could finish—"The Secret History of Eddypus,

the World-Empire"—that was largely prompted by growing public faith in Mrs. Eddy's *Science and Health*. John S. Tuckey has termed "Eddypus" a fictional presentation of Mark Twain's anxieties about her doctrines, "a nightmare vision of a future in which the religion of Mrs. Eddy has become all-powerful as a world empire whose leader is both pope and monarch" (*FM*, p. 316). Previously Mark Twain had included (but canceled) a paragraph from *Science and Health* in the working notes for "The Chronicle of Young Satan," written 1897–1900 (*MSM*, p. 417). He cast aspersions on Mrs. Eddy's "cloudy & complacent romance" which purported to be "a Substitute for the Scriptures" in an undated, unpublished criticism of G. W. Warder's *The Cities of the Sun* (DV357, MTP). In chapter 13 of "Three Thousand Years among the Microbes" (written 1905) Mark Twain launched into a punning onslaught against the "Giddyites" sect whose chief text is "Science and Wealth, with Key to the Fixtures" (*WWD?*, pp. 491–494). The fad-prone Stanchfield Garvey in "The Refuge of the Derelicts" (written 1905–1906) is infatuated with principles "drawn from 'Science and Health' " (*FM*, p. 240).

In 1906 Mark Twain marveled at the multitude of Americans prepared to believe in *Science and Health* "although they can't understand a line of it" who also "worship the sordid and ignorant old purloiner of that gospel—Mrs. Mary Baker G. Eddy" (22 June 1906 AD, MTP). He again leveled an attack on the book in another Autobiographical Dictation of 5 October 1906, claiming that Quimby was its true author and ruminating upon how easy, "today, it is to humbug the human race" (MTP). In "Papers of the Adam Family" Mark Twain predicted by the Law of Periodical Repetition that Mrs. Eddy's book, "its orgies of style and construction tamed by an educated disciple," would be inflicted upon the human race again and again (*LE*, p. 101). At the beginning of "Is Shakespeare Dead?" (1909) Twain remarked upon Mrs. Eddy's "flimsy" claim "that she wrote *Science and Health* from the direct dictation of the Deity."

Mark Twain's full-length review of *Science and Health*, however, occurs in his scathing but heavy-handed assault upon Mrs. Eddy's empire, "Christian Science" (pub. 1907). Paul Baender's annotated edition of this lengthy diatribe turns up the somewhat surprising fact that at various junctures in the work Mark Twain used no fewer than *five* different editions of *Science and Health*—those of 1881 (*WIM?*, p. 575); 1883 (*WIM?*, p. 271); 1884 (vol. 2 of which survives in MTP; *WIM?*, p. 293); 1898 (*WIM?*, pp. 554–555); and 1899 (*WIM?*, p. 339).

Robert Peel, *Mary Baker Eddy*, pp. 198–209, 447–452.

Edgeworth, Maria (1767–1849). *Classic Tales, . . . with a Biographical Sketch by Grace A. Oliver*. Boston: Roberts Bros., 1883. 332 pp.
Source: MTLAcc, entry #1926, volume donated from Clemens' library by Clara Clemens Gabrilowitsch in 1910.

————. *The Parent's Assistant; or, Stories for Children*. Illus. Philadelphia: J. B. Lippincott & Co., 1883. 535 pp.
Source: MTLAcc, entry #807, volume donated by Clemens.

Edler, Karl Erdmann (1844–1931). *Der Kampf um die Kunst. Drei Novellen*. Wien: Wilhelm Frick, 1895. 196 pp.
Source: MTLAcc, entry #375, volume donated by Clemens.

Edmundson, Sarah Emma. *Nurse and Spy in the Union Army: Comprising the Adventures and Experiences of a Woman in Hospitals, Camps and Battlefields*. Hartford, 1865.
Clemens recollected that "Nurse & Spy" sold 200,000 copies when he computed the possibilities for U. S. Grant's *Memoirs* in June 1885 (NB 24, TS p. 25).

Edwards, Amelia Ann Blanford (1831–1892). *Barbara's History*.
    Susy Clemens praised this novel to Clara from Venice on 10 April 1893: "It resembles 'Jane Eyre' a good deal . . . and it isn't grand and stunning like 'Wages' " *(S&MT,* p. 329).

―――――. "Give Me Three Grains of Corn, Mother" (poem, song). Sometimes subtitled: "The Irish Famine."
    This seven-stanza exercise in pathos was the third title listed in the program of "Country School Exhibition," a shipboard program of amateur talent that Clemens helped organize on the *Montana* on 10 July 1868 *(Alta California,* 6 September 1868; reprinted in *The Twainian,* 7 [November-December 1948], 5). It was to be a "Duett" performed by "Messrs. L. & H." Perhaps the sentiment in the piece was too strong for its inclusion in the similar schoolhouse declamations in chapter 21 of *Tom Sawyer;* the fifth stanza begins: "What has poor Ireland done, mother,—/What has poor Ireland done,/That the world looks on, and sees us starve,/Perishing one by one?" Clemens wrote "Give me 3 grains of corn" on the cover of his copy of F. B. Ogilvie's *Two Hundred Old-Time Songs* (1896).

―――――. *Untrodden Peaks and Unfrequented Valleys. A Mid-Summer Ramble in the Dolomites.* Illus. London, 1890.
    Inscription: by the author on the half-title page: "I wish that Mr. and Mrs. Clemens had been with L. and the writer on this journey,—but if so, Mr. Clemens would have written a book so much better than 'Untrodden Peaks and Unfrequented Valleys' that the present volume would never have been committed by Amelia B. Edwards, Jan. 27/90."
    Catalog: A1911, #150, $5.25.

Edwards, (Mrs.) Annie (d. 1896). *Ought We To Visit Her? A Novel.* New York: Sheldon and Co., n.d. 194 pp.
    Source: MTLAcc, entry #2230, volume donated from Clemens' library by Clara Clemens Gabrilowitsch in 1910.

Edwards, Jonathan (1703–1758). *Freedom of Will* (pub. 1754).
    Early in 1902 Joseph Twichell lent Clemens a copy of *Freedom of Will* for perusal on his way back from Hartford to Riverdale *(MTL,* pp. 719–720). Clemens wrote a lengthy analysis of the book, which he read "from Bridgeport to New York, thence to home, & continuously until near midnight" *(MTB,* pp. 1156–57). The reading experience was searing, he informed Twichell: "I wallowed & reeked with Jonathan in his insane debauch"; it left him with "a strange & haunting sense of having been on a three days' tear with a drunken lunatic" *(MTB,* p. 1157). The work is, he wrote, lit by "the glare of a resplendent intellect gone mad—a marvelous spectacle." Clemens found himself agreeing with Edwards' assumptions that man never creates an impulse by his own will, and that "in his natural state" he is universally dominated by selfish motives. These views concur with Clemens' notions of Necessity and Motive. But "then he suddenly flies the logical track & (to all seeming) makes the man & not those exterior forces responsible to God for the man's thoughts, words, & acts. It is frank insanity" *(MTB,* p. 1157). All this comes about, unfortunately, when Edwards "was pointed straight for the only rational & possible next station on *that* piece of road—the irresponsibility of man to God" *(MTB,* p. 1157).
    The copy of *Freedom of Will* that Twichell loaned Clemens in 1902 was not his first introduction to Edwards' doctrines, however. In June 1882 Clemens had noted the title of an early biographical sketch of Edwards that he subsequently obtained (see entry for Samuel Hopkins), and this book included excerpts from Edwards' diary and sermons. The following year Clemens alluded to Edwards' faith in a tormenting Hell (NB 22 [1883], TS p. 22). In 1889 or 1890 he reminded Andrew Lang that the Salvation Army is more effective than Jonathan Edwards in converting the poor to Christianity *(MTL,* p. 527). A passage Clemens read

in Meredith Townsend's *Asia and Europe* (1901) reminded him of Edwards' thought, and he wrote Edwards' name in the margin of page 14 at Townsend's explanation of the Mohammedan philosophy "that God acts because He wills, and not because He is bound by His own nature. 'These to hell and I care not, these to heaven and I reck not.' It seems to the European an abominable explanation," wrote Townsend. Mark Twain thought of joking about Edwards in a speech at Princeton University for which he made notes on 14 October 1902 (NB 45, TS p. 31). Shortly after Livy's death Clemens wrote to Twichell on 28 July 1904 to vent his opinion that the human race can muster no more evidence of its intelligence than can "Jonathan Edwards in his wildest moments" (Yale). He mentioned Edwards once again in Book 2, chapter 3 of "Christian Science" (1907).
MTGF, p. 48.

Eggleston, Edward (1837–1902). *A First Book in American History.* New York: D. Appleton & Co., 1889. 203 pp.
Source: MTLAcc, entry #1594, volume donated by Clemens.

————. *The Mystery of Metropolisville.* New York: Orange Judd and Co., 1873.
Clemens defended Eggleston's novel (which he mistakenly calls "Mystery of Mechanicsville") somewhat lefthandedly in a notebook that he kept in Paris during 1879. Comparing the book to those by Rabelais, Fielding, and Smollett, he argues that evidently "it depends on who writes a thing whether it is coarse or not" (NB 18, *N&J,* 2: 303). Actually, however, Eggleston's novel is highly moralistic, sentimental, and professedly Christian in outlook. Perhaps Clemens meant the rude, unrefined prairie-town society that Eggleston depicted during the period of rampant land speculation in Minnesota in 1856. In this respect, with its emphasis on colorful local characters and the motive of revenge, *The Mystery of Metropolisville* prefigures another novel set in a similarly bleak, indifferent landscape—Edgar Watson Howe's *The Story of a Country Town* (1883), of which Clemens would heartily approve. Mark Twain mentioned Eggleston twice in his notebooks—in January 1888 (NB 27, TS p. 49) and December 1889 (NB 29, TS p. 35).
MT&GA, pp. 229, 231–232.

Eickemeyer, Rudolf (1862–1932). *Winter, Pictured by Rudolf Eickemeyer, Jr.* Intro. by Sadakichi Hartmann. Illus. New York: R. H. Russill, 1903. 55 pp.
Source: MTLAcc, entry #1366, volume donated by Clemens.

Elder, Samuel J. "Duration of Copyright" (pub. in *Yale Law Journal,* 1905).
On 12 June 1905 Elder, a Boston attorney, wrote to Clemens: "I have taken the liberty to have the publishers send you a copy of the Yale Law Journal containing my article on 'Duration of Copyright.'" He added: "You will notice that my article . . . takes up your suggestion in the North American" (MTP). (A letter by Clemens on copyright legislation had appeared in the January 1905 issue of the *North American Review.*) On 21 June 1905 Clemens replied to Elder: "I have read your article with great interest—& also with great profit. I am glad to have it & I thank you" (TS in MTP).

Elderkin, John. *A Brief History of the Lotos Club.* New York: [Press of Macgowan & Slipper, 1895]. 166 pp.
Inscription: presentation copy inscribed by Elderkin, dated 15 April 1895.
Catalog: Hunley 1958.

Eldridge, George Dyre (b. 1848). *In the Potter's House.* New York: Doubleday, Page & Co., 1908. 338 pp.
Source: MTLAcc, entry #125, volume donated by Clemens.

Elgin, James Bruce (1811–1863). *Letters and Journals of James, Eighth Earl of Elgin*. Ed. by Theodore Walrond. Preface by Arthur Penrhyn Stanley. London: J. Murray, 1872. 467 pp.

"Lord Elgin's Diary & Letters," Clemens noted late in April 1888 (NB 27, TS p. 64).

Eliot, Charles William. *John Gilley*. True American Types Series. Boston: American Unitarian Association, 1905.

C. L. Stebbins of the American Unitarian Association wrote to Clemens on 6 April 1905 to inform him that he would soon receive the first volume in the "True American Types" series, written by the president of Harvard. Stebbins asked Clemens to contribute a volume to these sketches of "sterling American manhood." They sought a biography of "some plodder in some quiet walk of life," an obscure individual. "We wish to have represented a typical character of the middle West and we can think of no better one than a Mississippi deck-hand." On the back of the second page of Stebbins' letter Isabel Lyon noted Clemens' refusal (MTP).

Eliot, George, pseud. of Marian (Evans) Cross (1819–1880). *Adam Bede*. 2 vols. New York: J. W. Lovell Co., 1883. 484 pp.

Source: MTLAcc, entries #980 and #1261, volumes donated by Clemens.

Susy Clemens wrote from Bryn Mawr in 1890 to report, "I am reading 'Daniel Deronda' and enjoying it, endlessly; much more than I did Adam Bede" *(S&MT,* p. 279).

————. *Adam Bede*. New York: Worthington Co., 1887. 377 pp.

Source: MTLAcc, entry #1260, volume donated by Clemens.

————. *Adam Bede*. 2 vols. Illus. New York: Harper & Brothers, 1899.

Source: MTLAcc, entries #1132 and #1262, volumes donated by Clemens.

————. *Daniel Deronda*. 2 vols. New York: Harper & Brothers, [cop. 1876].

Source: MTLAcc, entries #2232 and #2233, volumes donated from Clemens' library by Clara Clemens Gabrilowitsch in 1910.

Clemens told Howells in a letter from Elmira on 12 July 1885 that he had recently attempted to read this novel: "I dragged through three chapters, losing flesh all the time, & then was honest enough to quit, & confess to myself that I haven't *any* romance-literature appetite, as far as I can see" *(MTHL,* p. 533); but Clemens' opinion obviously was not shared by members of his household: Clara Clemens' commonplace book (1888?) quotes and discusses *Daniel Deronda* and refers frequently to Eliot's life and her writing in general (Paine 150, MTP); indeed, George Eliot seems to have provided Clara's major reading experiences during her adolescence. Susy mentioned "reading 'Daniel Deronda' and enjoying it, endlessly" at Bryn Mawr in 1890 *(S&MT,* p. 279, ALS in MTM); and on 2 January 1908 Isabel Lyon, a brevet member of Clemens' family, noted that she herself was "reading 'Daniel Deronda' with greater delight than ever" (IVL Journal, TS p. 290, MTP).

————. *Daniel Deronda*. 4[?] vols. Copyright Edition. Collection of British Authors Series. Leipzig: Bernhard Tauchnitz, 1876.

Source: MTLAcc, entry #2234, volume 1 only (296 pp.), donated from Clemens' library by Clara Clemens Gabrilowitsch in 1910.

————. *Daniel Deronda*. New York: Geo. Munro, [1883?]. 553 pp.

Source: MTLAcc, entry #1265, volume donated by Clemens.

————. *Daniel Deronda*. 2 vols. New York: Harper & Brothers, 1905. 427 pp.

Source: MTLAcc, entry #1134, vol. 2 only (427 pp.), donated by Clemens.

————. [Another identical copy, vol. 2 only].
Source: MTLAcc, entry #1264. volume donated by Clemens.

————. *Felix Holt, the Radical.* Illus. New York: Harper & Brothers, 1906. 529 pp.
Source: MTLAcc, entry #1548, volume donated by Clemens.

[————.] *The George Eliot Birthday Book.* Boston, 1882.
Inscriptions: signed by members of the Clemens family.
Catalog: A1911, #6, $3.25.

————. *George Eliot's Life as Related in Her Letters and Journals. Arranged and Edited by Her Husband, J[ohn] W[alter] Cross.* 3 vols. New York: Harper & Brothers, 1885.
On 7 June 1885 Livy Clemens began a new diary by noting: "I am reading with great interest 'George Elliott's Life' [*sic*] by her husband J. W. Cross. It is most delightful. . . . The only thing in the book that annoys me is her constant mentions of her ill health" (DV161, MTP). Very probably Clemens read or at least discussed this work with Livy, for in late October 1885 he thought of writing an article about "Carlyle's whines & complaints," especially regarding his chronic stomach trouble, and "George Elliott's [*sic*] ditto" (NB 25, TS p. 25). Clara Clemens expressed fervent admiration for George Eliot in her commonplace book (1888?) and quoted devotedly from Cross' biography in its pages (Paine 150, MTP).

————. *George Eliot's Life as Related in Her Letters and Journals.* Ed. by John Walter Cross (1840–1924). 3 vols. New York: Harper & Brothers, 1899.
Source: MTLAcc, entries #1135, #1136, and #1758, volumes donated by Clemens.

————. *Impressions of Theophrastus Such.* New York: Harper & Brothers, [188–]. 234 pp.
Source: MTLAcc, entry #1546, volume donated by Clemens.

————. *Middlemarch: A Study of Provincial Life.* 2 vols. [Only Clemens' copy of vol. 2 has been discovered.] Harper's Library Edition of the Novels of George Eliot. New York: Harper & Brothers, n.d.
Inscription: on first flyleaf in pencil, possibly a signature: "Clemens".
Marginalia: pencil marks on pages 15, 99, 156, 185, 209, 269, 387, 395, 396, 403. No other markings.
Location: Antenne-Dorrance Collection, Rice Lake, Wis.
Copy examined: copy belonging to a member of Clemens' family, very possibly Livy.
Clemens praised Howells' *Indian Summer* by relating how he himself "bored through Middlemarch during the past week, with its labored & tedious analyses of feelings & motives, its paltry & tiresome people, its unexciting & uninteresting story, & its frequent blinding flashes of single-sentence poetry, philosophy, wit, & what-not, & nearly died from the over-work. I wouldn't read another of those books for a farm." Clemens concluded with a compliment to his friend Howells: "You make all the motives & feelings perfectly clear without analyzing the guts out of them, the way George Eliot does. I can't stand George Eliot, & Hawthorne & those people; I see what they are at, a hundred years before they get to it, & they just tire me to death" *(MTHL, pp. 533–534).* Nevertheless Clemens couldn't tolerate utter ignorance of Eliot's identity or stature: he castigated Charles L. Webster's personality because "once in a drawing-room company some talk sprang up about George Eliot and her literature. I saw Webster getting ready to contribute. . . . He filled that vacancy with this remark, uttered with tranquil complacency: 'I've never read any of his books, on account of prejudice' "

(29 May 1906 AD, pub. in *MTE,* pp. 180–181). Webster's son, Samuel C. Webster, doubted the veracity of this anecdote and noted in his own copy of *Mark Twain in Eruption* that his father "had a set of G. E." (marginalia on p. 180, book in MTP).

————. *Middlemarch; A Study in Provincial Life.* New York: T. Y. Crowell & Co., n.d. 776 pp.
Source: MTLAcc, entry #2231, volume donated from Clemens' library by Clara Clemens Gabrilowitsch in 1910.

————. *The Mill on the Floss.* Illus. New York: Harper & Brothers, 1902. 464 pp.
Source: MTLAcc, entry #1547, volume donated by Clemens.

————. *Poems, Together with Brother Jacob and The Lifted Veil.* New York: Harper & Brothers, 1885. 380 pp.
Source: MTLAcc, entry #1133, volume donated by Clemens.

————. [Another identical copy.]
Source: MTLAcc, entry #1263, volume donated by Clemens.

————. *Romola.* 2 vols. Copyright Edition. Collection of British Authors Series. Leipzig: B. Tauchnitz, 1863.
Source: MTLAcc, entries #2235 and #2236, volumes donated from Clemens' library by Clara Clemens Gabrilowitsch in 1910.
On Sunday, 11 August 1878, Clemens recorded in Notebook 15: "Been reading Romola yesterday afternoon, last night & this morning; at last I came upon the only passage which has thus far *hit me with force*—Tito compromising with his conscience & resolving to do, not a bad thing, but not the *best* thing." Clemens had purchased the volume "24 hours ago in Heidelberg," yet "nothing in the book had taken hold of me till I came to that one passage on page 112 Tauchnitz edition" *(N&J,* 2: 135).
Perhaps from this historical novel set in fifteenth-century Florence Clemens gained his interest in the celebrated monk of Ferrara, Girolamo Savonarola (1452–1498): he mentioned Savonarola among historical personages and events in "How to Make History Dates Stick" (unpub. until 1914); "George, old Savvana-rola—gee! they only just *burnt* him," wisecracks Dug Hapgood upon taking some medicine in chapter 12 of "Which Was It?" (written 1899–1903, *WWD?,* p. 291). In 1901 Mark Twain wrote: "a Savonarola can quell and scatter a mob of lynchers with a mere glance of his eye" ("The United States of Lyncherdom," *Pen,* p. 156). The other source from which Clemens might have learned about Savonarola is Margaret Oliphant's *The Makers of Florence* (1888), chapters 9 through 13.

————. *Romola.* New York, 1869.
Catalog: *A1911,* #151, $1, "8vo, unbound."

————. *Romola.* Illus. The Florentine Edition. 2 vols. Philadelphia, 1890.
Catalog: *A1911,* #152, $3.25.

————. *The Spanish Gypsy. A Poem.* Boston: Ticknor & Fields, 1868. 287 pp.
Source: MTLAcc, entry #2024, volume donated from Clemens' library by Clara Clemens Gabrilowitsch in 1910.

[Elizabeth, Queen of Rumania (1843–1916), pseud. "Carmen Sylva."] *A Real Queen's Fairy Tales. By Carmen Sylva.* Trans. by Edith Hopkirk. Illus. by H. Nelson and A. G. Jones. Chicago, 1901.
Inscription: signed, "S. L. Clemens, Riverdale-on-Hudson, Feb. 22, 1902."
Catalog: *A1911,* #445, $4.25.

In "Does the Race of Man Love a Lord?" (1902) Mark Twain referred to "that charming and lovable German princess and poet, Carmen Sylva, Queen of Roumania," who "remembers yet that the flowers of the woods and fields 'talked to her' when she was a girl, and she sets it down in her latest book." Mark Twain quotes passages from her account of the homage shown to her by squirrels, birds, wasps, bees, and dogs.

Elliot, Charles S., ed. *Songs of Yale: A New Collection of College Songs*. Ed. by Charles S. Elliot. Rev. and enl. by Elmer P. Howe. Fifth ed. New York: Taintor Brothers, Merrill & Co., 1880.
    Catalog: A1911, #497, withdrawn from sale.
    Location: Mark Twain Memorial, Hartford, Connecticut. Donated in 1965 by Olivia Loomis Lada-Mocarski.
    Copy examined: Clemens' copy, containing *A1911* sale label on front paste-down endpaper. No inscription or markings, but the book appears used.

Elliot, Daniel Giraud (1835–1915). *The Life and Habits of Wild Animals*. Illus. by Joseph Wolf. London, 1874.
    Inscription: signed on front endpaper: "Saml. L. Clemens. London, Dec. 21, 1873."
    Catalog: Mott 1952, #50, $12.50.

Elliot, (Mrs.) Frances Minto (Dickinson) (1820–1898). *Diary of an Idle Woman in Italy*. 2 vols. Collection of British Authors Series. Leipzig: Bernhard Tauchnitz, 1872.
    Catalog: C1951, #D1, $8, listed among books signed by Clemens.

Elliott, Charles Wyllys. *Remarkable Characters and Places of the Holy Land*. Hartford, Conn.: J. B. Burr & Co., 1867.
    Dewey Ganzel established the identity of this work, which Mark Twain referred to only as "C. W. E.'s 'Life in the Holy Land' " in chapter 48 of *IA* (1869), where he quotes with scorn its description of the Sea of Gallilee ("Guidebooks" [1965], p. 88 n. 18). Leon Dickinson's explanatory notes for the forthcoming Iowa-California edition of *IA* point out that "Life in the Holy Land" was the short title stamped on the cover of Elliott's volume and that Mark Twain quoted Elliott more approvingly in chapter 56.
    Hirst, "Making of *IA*" (1975).

Elliott, Charlotte (1789–1871). "Just as I am" (hymn).
    "You hear him [Robert Wicklow] sing 'Just as I am—poor, wretched, blind'— just you hear him sing that once, and see if you don't melt all up and the water come into your eyes!" ("A Curious Experience" [1881]).

Elliott, James W. *Mother Goose Set to Music* (pub. 1870).
    There may have been an edition of Elliott's collection of nursery rhymes published earlier than 1870; at any rate, Mark Twain listed *Mother Goose's Melodies* as one of the few secular works available in the *Quaker City* ship library ("The *Quaker City* Holy Land Excursion," uncompleted play written 1867, Act 2, scene i, MTP). In November or December 1880 the Clemenses gave a Mother Goose party modeled on the one they attended in November 1879 in Hartford; Clemens listed the characters and those who acted the parts in Notebook 19 (*N&J*, 2: 378–379). Clemens seems to refer to Elliott's musical collection in Notebook 19 (1881): "Mother Goose—W A Elliott" (p. 394). In June 1898 Mark Twain decided to "introduce Mother Goose & her people" into his planned piece on childhood "Creatures of Fiction" (NB 40, TS p. 27).

Ellis, William (1794–1872). *Three Visits to Madagascar During the Years 1853–1854–1856.* Illus. New York: Harper & Brothers, 1859. 514 pp.
   Source: MTLAcc, entry #1717, volume donated by Clemens.

Elmore, James B. *Love Among the Mistletoe and Poems.* Alamo, Indiana: published by the author, 1899. 233 pp.
   Inscription: in brown ink on front pastedown endpaper: "S. L. Clemens/1902/ Hogwash, but not atrocious enough to be first-rate."
   Marginalia: ink markings on pages 48, 69, 70, 72, 213, 214.
   Location: Antenne-Dorrance Collection, Rice Lake, Wis.
   Copy examined: Clemens' copy, another addition to his "Library of Literary Hogwash."

Ely, Richard Theodore (1854–1943). *French and German Socialism in Modern Times.* New York: Harper & Brothers, [cop. 1883]. 274 pp.
   Source: MTLAcc, entry #691, volume donated by Clemens.

Emanuel, Walter Lewis (1869–1915). *A Dog Day; or, The Angel in the House.* Illus. by Cecil Charles Windsor Aldin (1870–1935). New York: E. P. Dutton, [1907].
   Inscription: on front flyleaf, "The Major/with much love/from Annie an Louise". Second flyleaf inscribed: "To S. L. Clemens BECAUSE HE LIKED IT? Personally & with great affection to the Major:—"
   Marginalia: someone has laboriously printed captions in ink for all of the illustrations, naming members of Clemens' Stormfield circle—Isabel Lyon, Clemens, "the Major," and cats called Sinbad, Omar Kayam, and Tammany.
   Location: Mark Twain Memorial, Hartford, Connecticut. Donated by Eugene Grummond in 1958.
   Copy examined: Clemens' copy, a gift from Dorothy Sturgis (see catalog entry for Rudyard Kipling's *The Brushwood Boy*).

————. *The Dogs of War.* Illus. by Cecil Charles Windsor Aldin (1870–1935). London: Bradbury, Agnew, & Co., [cop. 1906]. 237 pp.
   Inscription: presentation copy to Clemens inscribed by Emanuel at 17 Holland Park Avenue, London.
   Provenance: Mark Twain Library, Redding, Conn. Donated by Clemens (MTLAcc, entry #506).
   Catalog: Mott 1952, #52, $12.50.

Emerson, Ralph Waldo (1803–1882). "Brahma" (poem).
   Mark Twain burlesqued this poem ("I pass and deal *again!*") in his 17 December 1877 Whittier Birthday dinner speech (quoted in *MTB,* p. 1645).
   Henry Pochmann, "The Mind of MT" (1924), p. 42; Henry Nash Smith, "That Hideous Mistake" (1955).

————. "Concord Hymn" (poem).
   Mark Twain alluded to the famous last line from the first stanza in "To the Person Sitting in Darkness" (1901): "in that utterance he [McKinley] fired another 'shot heard round the world.' "

————. "Domestic Life" (essay).
   Clemens had a quotation from this essay—"The ornament of a house is the friends who frequent it"—engraved in brass over the fireplace in his library of the Hartford house. "Mind you, it is from Emerson," he wrote to an unidentified correspondent on 19 September 1881 (Yale). Howells reported this fact in *My Mark Twain* (1910), p. 32.

————. *Essays.* Boston, n.d.
Inscription: signed on cover, "S. L. Clemens, Hartford, Conn."
Marginalia: several paragraphs marked.
Catalog: A1911, #154, $1.25.

Clemens' acquaintance with Emerson's writings may have begun in Hannibal; in 1906 Clemens recalled with amusement that Emerson turned down Orion Clemens' offer for publication of one of his works in the Hannibal *Journal* in 1853 (10 September 1906 AD, *MTE,* p. 236). Mark Twain defined a literary "connoisseur" in 1865 as one who is secure if he attributes "all the poetry that you can't understand, to Emerson" *(California,* 17 June 1865; *LAMT,* p. 142). In 1878 Joseph H. Twichell wrote to Clemens excitedly about extracts from FitzGerald's *Omar Khayyám* that had appeared in the Hartford *Courant:* "Read it, and we'll talk it over. There is something in it very like the passage of Emerson you read me last night, in fact identical with it in thought" (quoted in *MTB,* p. 615 n. 1). Clemens visited Emerson in Concord with Howells in April 1882; Emerson died shortly thereafter on 27 April, while Clemens was on the Mississippi River. "So glad I visited him," Clemens wrote in June 1882 (NB 20, *N&J,* 2: 486). He intended to "say a word about that visit" in *LonMiss* (1883), but wanted mainly to describe "our going in the evening to reverently look at his *house*" (p. 486). Henry W. Fisher remembered that around 1891 Clemens called Emerson a man "who valued impressions and ideas above everything—in his way as great a man as Virchow and certainly a great benefactor of his countrymen," but also spoke of Emerson's losing his memory in the late 1870's *(AMT,* p. 103). In "The German Chicago" (1892) Mark Twain described Theodor Mommsen, the German classical scholar and historian, as having an "Emersonian face." He alluded to Emerson in a speech on copyright reform on 7 December 1906 *(MTS [1923],* p. 327).
MTG, pp. 115–117; *IE,* pp. 11–12.

————. *Essays.* New York: Worthington Co., 1886. 320 pp.
Source: MTLAcc, entry #682, volume donated by Clemens.

————. "Mithridates" (poem).
Henry Pochmann identified this poem as Mark Twain's allusion in the 17 December 1877 Whittier Birthday dinner speech *(MTB,* p. 1644): "Give me agates for my meat."
"The Mind of MT" (1924), pp. 41, 161; Henry Nash Smith, "That Hideous Mistake" (1955).

————. "Monadnoc" (poem).
Henry Pochmann cited this poem as the source for Mark Twain's quoted lines— "Is yonder squalid peasant all/That this proud nursery could breed?" *(MTB,* p. 1646)—in Twain's Whittier Birthday dinner speech on 17 December 1877 ("The Mind of MT" [1924], pp. 41, 161). In Dublin, New Hampshire on 16 May 1906 Isabel Lyon reported in her journal: "Just before dinner I went onto the porch and Mr. Clemens sat there with Emerson's poems. He read Monadnock. There we sat under its mighty shadows and he read the stately poem as no one else in the world can read. After dinner he read much more of Emerson" (TS p. 159, MTP).
Henry Nash Smith, "That Hideous Mistake" (1955).

————. "The Over-Soul" (essay).
The last entry in Livy Clemens' commonplace book, probably written about 1871, is a quotation from Emerson's essay: "In sickness, in languor, give us a strain of poetry or a profound sentence, and we are refreshed; or produce a volume of Plato or Shakespeare or remind us of their names and instantly we come into a feeling of longevity" (MS p. 108, MTP).

————, ed. *Parnassus.* Boston: Houghton, Mifflin & Co., 1882. 534 pp.
　　Source: MTLAcc, entry #2025, volume donated from Clemens' library by
Clara Clemens Gabrilowitsch in 1910.

————. *Selections from the Writings of Ralph Waldo Emerson, Arranged Under
the Days of the Year.* Boston: Houghton, Mifflin & Co., 1889.
　　Source: MTLAcc, entry #2128, volume donated from Clemens' library by
Clara Clemens Gabrilowitsch in 1910.

————. "Song of Nature" (poem).
　　Mark Twain burlesqued several lines from this poem—"I tire of globes and
aces,/Too long the game is played!" *(MTB,* p. 1645)—in his speech at the 17
December 1877 Whittier Birthday dinner, as Henry Pochmann pointed out in
"The Mind of Mark Twain" (1924), pp. 41, 161.
　　Henry Nash Smith, "That Hideous Mistake" (1955).

Emmett, Daniel Decatur (1815–1904). "Dixie's land (I wish I was in Dixie's land)"
(song, 1860).
　　"If a Democrat were elected, Hereford was to carry the flour to the tune of
'Dixie' " (16 May 1864 letter from Virginia City, *MTEnt,* p. 187). Mentioned in
1885 as a song sung by Confederate troops that antagonized nearby Federal
soldiers (NB 25, TS p. 22). "That antidote for melancholy, merriest and gladdest
of all military music on any side of the ocean" (chapter 13 of "A Horse's Tale"
[1906]).

————. "Old Dan Tucker" (song, 1843).
　　This was one of the "rudely comic" songs of the early minstrel shows, Mark
Twain recalled (30 November 1906 AD, *MTE,* p. 114).

Encyclopaedia Britannica. A Dictionary of Arts, Sciences, and General Literature.
　　Ninth ed. Illus. 24 vols. New York, 1878.
　　Inscriptions: each volume signed by Orion Clemens.
　　Catalog: A1911, #156, $2.50 total.

Encyclopaedia Britannica. A Dictionary of Arts, Sciences, and General Literature.
　　Ninth ed. Illus. 24 vols. With 4 vols. of the American Supplement (1883–1889)
and 1-vol. Index. Together, 29 vols. Boston, 1875–1889.
　　Catalog: A1911, #155, $5.50 total.
　　Clemens wrote to his mother-in-law, Mrs. Jervis Langdon, on 22 December
[1875?] "to tell you how thoroughly delighted I am with the Cyclopedia & how
much the book transcends even *its* splendid reputation. You could not have given
me a thing I should prize more highly" (MTM); very likely he had received the
first volumes of the new ninth edition, with the rest promised as they were issued.
In 1876 he solemnly assured Mrs. James T. Fields that his early deprivation of
reading materials left him able to read only the encyclopedia. ("Which is not
true—he reads everything," added Mrs. Fields in her diary, later published as
Memories of a Hostess, p. 245.) Clemens referred to "Cyclo. Britan." in July 1885
as his source for a bit of English history (NB 24, TS p. 32). On 6 December 1888
he paid fulsome tribute to this reference work in a letter (once again) to Mrs.
Jervis Langdon: "Yes, indeed, mother dear, the Supplementary volumes & Index
will be a vastly valuable addition to what is already the most valuable book in
the house. The Brittanica [*sic*] grows upon one, all the time; & I have long ago
arrived at the opinion that the other Cyclopedias are of small consequence as
compared to it. Livy & I couldn't choose a better Christmas present than these
additional volumes" (MTM).
　　He would never learn the proper spelling of its title, but there is evidence to
corroborate his dependence on "the most valuable book in the house." Intending
to sketch the absurdities of Prussian monarchies and wars, Clemens first noted

in July 1888: "Look in Cyclo. Britan—for Franco-Prus'n war" (NB 28, TS p. 8). When Rudyard Kipling dropped in upon Clemens at his brother-in-law's home in Elmira in 1890, Clemens promptly assumed the pose of untutored genius that he had tried out previously on Mrs. Fields—and even gave the same example of his reading habits. "Personally I never care for fiction or story-books," he told Kipling. " 'What I like to read about are facts and statistics of any kind. . . . Just now, for instance, before you came in'—he pointed to an encyclopaedia on the shelves—'I was reading an article about "Mathematics" ' " ("Rudyard Kipling on Mark Twain," New York *Herald,* 17 August 1890, collected in *From Sea to Sea* [1899]). Whether or not Clemens truly preferred facts over fiction, the *Britannica* was often his initial source of information when he tackled a new project. On 13 October 1892, for example, he wrote to Chatto & Windus from the Villa Viviani at Florence, where he lacked reference books: "Won't you please look at the bottom of the article on Joan of Arc in the Encyclopedia Brittanica [*sic*] & send me a list of the books one is referred to for information on the subject?" (PH in MTP). Henry W. Fisher reported that in Paris in May 1894 Clemens looked up the entry for Queen Elizabeth of England to search for any hints that perhaps she was really a man (*AMT,* pp. 52–53). In "Concerning the Jews" (1899) Mark Twain quotes population figures, then modestly avows: "I take them from memory; I read them in the Encyclopaedia Britannica about ten years ago."

English, Thomas Dunn (1819–1902). "Ben Bolt, or, oh! don't you remember" (song, 1848). Melody composed by Nelson Kneass.
Clemens mentioned this sentimental ballad in a letter of 25 November 1867 to Charles Webb (Berg). He told Albert Bigelow Paine that he was "thrilled" when he met the author, a New Jersey physician, in the 1890's, for he had sung "Ben Bolt" in his childhood (*MTB,* p. 1555). Under a 1 June 1903 heading in his appointment book Clemens remarked: "Sweet Alice, Ben Bolt. I met the author once at the Author's Club in his age. He looked it." Then Clemens added: "Alice was a poor thing, & Ben was a cad" (NB 46, TS p. 18). (A line in the song asks, "Don't you remember sweet Alice, Ben Bolt?")

————. *The Boy's Book of Battle-Lyrics: A Collection of Verses.* Illus. New York: Harper & Brothers, 1885. 168 pp.
Source: MTLAcc, entry #1190, volume donated by Clemens.

Epictetus. *A Selection from the Discourses of Epictetus, with the Encheiridion.* Trans. by George Long (1800–1879). New York and London: G. P. Putnam's Sons, [1892]. 260 pp.
Inscription: in Clemens' hand, "Samuel L. Clemens/& Clara Clemens/Paris 1894."
Location: Mark Twain Library, Redding, Connecticut.
Copy examined: Clemens' copy, unmarked, shared with his daughter.

Erckmann, Émile (1822–1899) and Alexandre Chatrian (1826–1890). *Waterloo; A Sequel of the Conscript of 1813.* Trans. from the French. New York: Charles Scribner and Co., 1869.
From Geneva, New York on 4 December 1871 Clemens wrote to Livy about his meeting "Rev. Mr. Foster, Episcopal City Missionary of Syracuse—a Twich-ell." Foster so impressed Clemens with his "whole-hearted cordiality" that upon parting from him "I gave him 'Waterloo,' & told him to read it & then mail it to you, as I had marked it somewhat" (MTP). Clemens' subsequent letters indicate apprehension that Foster neglected his promise to send the historical novel along to Livy.

The Ethical World (periodical, pub. 1898–1900).

In Notebook 43 Clemens wrote in 1900: "The Ethical World for '99. Cloth, 12.6/17 Johnson Court/Fleet st (Pub. Co.)" (TS p. 2).

Eucken, Rudolf Christof (1846–1926). *Christianity and the New Idealism: A Study in the Religious Philosophy of To-day.* Trans. from German by Lucy Judge (Peacock) Gibson and William Ralph Boyce Gibson. New York: Harper & Brothers, 1909. 163 pp.

Source: MTLAcc, entry #1490, volume donated by Clemens.

Evans, (Col.) Albert S. *Our Sister Republic: A Gala Trip Through Tropical Mexico in 1869–70.* Illus. Published by Subscription Only. Hartford, Conn.: Columbian Book Co., 1870. 518 pp.

Marginalia: in pencil Clemens wrote on the third flyleaf: "Every great man Λ personage Λ must be shadowed by a parasite who is infinitely little.—Johnson had his Boswell, Seward his Evans, Victoria her 'John' " (quoted in *A1911*). On page 192 Clemens vertically penciled the comment "delicious" beside Evans' account of his haggling with a Mexican vendor over the price of a pair of boots, even though (by Evans' own admission) "they were cheap at twice or three times the money, according to our American ideas." Clemens penciled the word "coarse" on page 225 at Evans' story about an American who bought a rancho and unsuccessfully tried to breed mules. Clemens drew a pencil mark on page 378 alongside a paragraph about Emperor Norton of San Francisco; another pencil mark on page 385 at a description of the pity felt by Mexicans, especially women, for prisoners convicted of being revolutionaries; and two pencil marks on page 386 by the story of Evans' conversation in Spanish about a foreigner, in his presence. Clemens also commented unfavorably on Evans' mentioning that "I wore a [military] uniform which I felt bound to honor while in a foreign land" (p. 387).

Catalog: A1911, #159, $10.

Location: Henry W. and Albert A. Berg Collection, New York Public Library.

Copy examined: Clemens' copy, containing *A1911* auction label and bookplate of William F. Gable, both on the front pastedown endpaper.

Clemens wrote to Elisha Bliss from Buffalo on 29 October 1870, ridiculing Evans' military title ("who made him a *Colonel?*"), belittling his writing abilities ("a one-horse newspaper reporter who has been trying all his life to make a joke"), and requesting a copy of Evans' *Our Sister Republic,* which he is "suffering" to read (TS in MTP). See *MTCor* for an explanation of Clemens' antagonism toward Evans.

Evans, Howard (1839–1915), pseud. "Noblesse Oblige." *Our Old Nobility.* London: Political Tract Society, 1879. [Orig. pub. as a series of articles in the *Echo.*]

Clemens jotted " 'Our Old Nobility' (from Echo)" in Notebook 18 while he was in England in August 1879 (*N&J*, 2: 339). Evidently he had learned that Evans' book attacked the hereditary aristocracy and traced the genealogy of various noble families; it also contained a chapter criticizing the Church of England. A decade later Clemens would gain ammunition for *CY* (1889) from a similar work by George Standring (see Standring entry).

Evelyn, John (1620–1706). *Diary and Correspondence of John Evelyn.* Ed. by William Bray. Portraits and illus. 4 vols. London, 1872.

Marginalia: numerous marked paragraphs and marginal notes by Clemens.

Catalog: A1911, #160, $10.

At a time when Clemens was rereading Pepys' *Diary,* he mentioned to Edward H. House on 14 January 1884 that he had also just finished reading "the fourth volume of Evelyn" (CWB).

Everett, David (1770–1813). "You'd Scarce Expect One of My Age" (poem for declamation by children). Also called "The Boy Reciter" and "My First Speech."

It seems likely that Mark Twain organized the "Country School Exhibition" presented on 10 July 1868 aboard the *Montana* which he described in a letter to the *Alta California* (pub. 6 September 1868; reprinted in *The Twainian,* 7 [November-December 1948], 5). The first selection on the program was "Oration— You'd Scarce expect one of my age—Mr. G. W." In chapter 21 of *TS* (1876), at the Examination Evening in the village schoolhouse, "a very little boy stood up and sheepishly recited, 'You'd scarce expect one of my age to speak in public on the stage, etc'—accompanying himself with the painfully exact and spasmodic gestures which a machine might have used—supposing the machine to be a trifle out of order." This is also one of the pieces dutifully recited "with stilted elocution and cast-iron gestures" by Old Dobbins' pupils in Act 3 of "Tom Sawyer: A Play," written 1875–1884 *(HH&T,* p. 303).

Everett, (Mrs.) H. D., pseud. "Theo. Douglas." *Iras: A Mystery.* New York: Harper & Brothers, 1896. 251 pp.
Source: MTLAcc, entry #1542, volume donated by Clemens.

Ewing, (Mrs.) Juliana Horatia (Gatty) (1841–1885). *Daddy Darwin's Dovecote.* 2 vols.
Catalog: C1951, #J15, listed among the books of Jean and Clara Clemens.

———. *The Doll's Wash.* N.p., n.d.
Source: MTLAcc, entry #1882, volume donated from Clemens' library by Clara Clemens Gabrilowitsch in 1910.

———. *Lob Lie-by-the-Fire; or, The Luck of Lingborough.* Illus. by Randolph Caledcott. London: Society for Promoting Christian Knowledge, n.d.
Inscription: on flyleaf in Livy Clemens' handwriting, "Clara L. Clemens/June 8th, 1886. (From Mamma.)"
Location: Carrie Estelle Doheny Collection, St. John's Seminary, Camarillo, California. Donated by Mrs. Doheny in 1940 after its purchase from Maxwell Hunley Rare Books of Beverly Hills.
Copy examined: Clara Clemens' copy, unmarked.

———. *Parables from Nature.* Illus. by Paul de Longpré. New York, 1893.
Catalogs: A1911, #179, $1.50; sold for $75 at Auction No. 24 (25 January 1968) by Charles Hamilton Autographs, according to *American Book-Prices Current* [New York: Columbia Univ., 1971], p. 214.

Eyre, Edward John (1815–1901). *Journals of Expeditions of Discovery into Central Australia, and Overland from Adelaide to King George's Sound, in 1840–1, Including an Account of the Manners and Customs of the Aborigines, and the State of Their Relations with Europeans.* 2 vols. London, 1845.
"Sir George Grey and Mr. Eyre testify that the natives dug wells fourteen or fifteen feet deep" (chapter 22 of *FE* [1897]).

Fabbri, Cora Randall (1871–1892). *Lyrics.* New York: Harper & Brothers, [cop. 1892]. 162 pp.
Source: MTLAcc, entry #1689, volume donated by Clemens.

Fabre, Joseph-Amant. *Procès de condamnation de Jeanne d'Arc, d'apres les textes authentiques, . . . traduction avec éclaircissements, par Joseph Fabre.* Paris: C. Delagrave, 1884. Repr. 1895.
Mark Twain listed this book among his "authorities examined" for *Joan of Arc* (page preceding "Translator's Preface").

"Fading, still fading, the last beam is shining" (hymn). Also known as "The last beam."

Clemens considered this hymn for one of the ten tunes he selected for the four-hundred-dollar music box that he purchased in Geneva in 1878 (NB 16, *N&J*, 2: 211)—though he referred to it by its second line: "Father in Heaven, the day is declining." In chapter 6 of *LonMiss* (1883), first published in "Old Times" (1875), he wrote about one of his hair-raising experiences as a cub pilot: on a dark night "Mr. Bixby made for the shore and soon was scraping it, just the same as if it had been daylight. And not only that, but singing: 'Father in heaven, the day is declining,' etc." Clemens may have learned the anonymous hymn from Henry Ward Beecher's *Plymouth Collection of Hymns* (1855), where it appeared as No. 1353; he owned a copy of this hymnal. The first stanza is: "Fading, still fading, the last beam is shining,/Father in heaven! the day is declining,/Safety and innocence fly with the light,/Temptation and danger walk forth with the night;/From the fall of the shade till the morning bells chime,/Shield me from danger, save me from crime./Father, have mercy, through Jesus Christ our Lord, Amen." Arthur M. Kompass—"Twain's Use of Music: A Note on *Life on the Mississippi*" (1964)—shows how aptly the lyrics suit the situation.

[Fargus, Frederick John (1847–1885), pseud. "Hugh Conway."] *Circumstantial Evidence, [and Other Stories]*. New York: N. L. Munro, 1884. 123 pp.
   Source: MTLAcc, entry #1847, volume donated from Clemens' library by Clara Clemens Gabrilowitsch in 1910.

Farrar, Charles Samuel. *History of Sculpture, Painting, and Architecture. Topical Lessons, with Special References to Valuable Books*. Chicago: Townsend MacCoun, 1881.
   Clemens entered the author and title of this book in Notebook 22 while he was thinking up suitable prizes for a children's contest to memorize historical dates in 1883 (TS p. 16).

Farrar, Frederic William (1831–1903). *Westminster Abbey*. Illus. by Herbert Railton. London: Isbister & Co., 1897.
   Inscription: "Clara Clemens/A souvenir of a visit to the loveliest/and most loveable thing in Christendom./KE)/London 11th: III: 97".
   Marginalia: pencil markings on pages 49 and 50.
   Location: Mark Twain Library, Redding, Connecticut.
   Copy examined: Clara Clemens' copy.

Farrington, Margaret Vere. *Tales of King Arthur and His Knights of the Round Table*. Illus. by Alfred Frederic and others. New York: G. P. Putnam's Sons, 1888.
   Inscription: signed on second flyleaf, "Jean Clemens".
   Location: Mark Twain Library, Redding, Connecticut.
   Copy examined: Jean Clemens' unmarked copy, acquired long after Mark Twain conceived the plot for *CY*.

Faversham, Julie (Opp) (1871–1921). *The Squaw Man. A Novel*. Adapted from the play by Edwin M. Royle [prod. 1905]. Illus. New York, 1906.
   Inscription: signed on inner front cover, "S. L. Clemens, 1906".
   Catalog: A1911, #162, $3.25.

Favorite Album of Fun and Fancy. Illus. by Ernest Griset and others. London, Paris, and New York: Cassell, Petter, Galpin & Co., [1880]. 192 pp.
   Source: MTLAcc, entry #1871, volume donated from Clemens' library by Clara Clemens Gabrilowitsch in 1910.

Favorite Fairy Tales; The Childhood Choice of Representative Men and Women. Illus. by Peter Newell. New York: Harper & Brothers, 1907.

> *Inscription:* signed on inner cover, "S. L. Clemens, 21 Fifth Avenue, Dec./07."
> *Catalog: A1911,* #169, $3.50.

Clemens was one of the prominent authors asked to nominate these standard tales, which include "Jack the Giant-Killer" and "The Ugly Duckling."

Fawcett, John (1740?–1817). "Lord, dismiss us with Thy blessing" (hymn, pub. 1773).

On 19 December 1868 Clemens wrote to Livy that "the melody of an old familiar hymn is sounding in my ear. It comes like a remembered voice—like the phantom of a form that is gone, a face that is no more. You know the hymn—it is 'Oh, refresh us.' " He remembered the hymn, he explained, because he sang it frequently during the return voyage from the Sandwich Islands in 1866, since it was the "only *one* hymn that I knew." He refers to it as "that simple old hymn . . . freighted with *infinite* pathos" *(MFMT,* p. 23). Michael B. Frank informed me in 1974 that the phrase "O refresh us" occurs in the first stanza of the hymn (which is generally attributed to Fawcett): "Lord, dismiss us with thy blessing,/ Fill our hearts with joy and peace,/ Let us each thy love possessing/ Triumph in redeeming grace./ O refresh us,/ Traveling through this wilderness."

Fearon, Henry Bradshaw. *Sketches of America. A Narrative of a Journey of Five Thousand Miles Through the Eastern and Western States of America.* Third ed. London: Longman, Hurst, Rees, Orme, and Brown [printed by Straham and Spottiswoode], 1819.

> *Marginalia:* pencil marks throughout; notes in pencil on pages 251–358. On page 251, beside an allusion to swearing heard in Kentucky, Clemens wrote "yet"; on page 269 he noted that whites, Negroes and American Indians all seemed equally savage in Fearon's day; at the top of page 295 he jotted "To-day, Jap indemnity"; at the top of page 324 he alluded to Thomas Moore's visit to the United States in 1803; at the bottom of page 324 he characterized Englishmen; and he again noted Moore's name beside the first paragraph of page 358.
> *Catalogs: A1911,* #163, $1.25; its resale on 27 October 1965 was recorded in *American Book-Prices Current Index 1960–1965* (New York, 1968), p. 368, $200.
> *Provenance:* bookplate on inner cover reads: "PRESENTED BY/Mr. John Mayle/Librarian".
> *Location:* Mark Twain Memorial, Hartford, Connecticut. Donated anonymously in 1965.
> *Copy examined:* Clemens' copy.

Mark Twain cited this book in a passage eventually deleted from the *LonMiss* manuscript that emphasized the necessity of joining a church in early-day America (see Dewey Ganzel, "Twain, Travel Books," p. 41 n. 4).

"Der Feldmarschall" ("Song of the Fieldmarshal") a German folk song.

Clemens placed this title on a list of his favorite songs in August 1889 (NB 29, TS p. 21).

Felsen, H. V. *Getraumt und erlebt.* Wien: J. N. Vernay, 1891. 126 pp. Paperbound.

> *Source:* MTLAcc, entry #385, volume donated by Clemens.

Fénelon, François de Salignac de La Mothe- (1651–1715). *Les aventures de Télémaque, fils d'Ulysse.* Ed. by Louis Fasquelle. New York: Ivison, Phinney, Blakeman, 1867.

Presumably Clemens referred to this edition when he made a memorandum in Notebook 8 in 1867 to "get Telemaque" *(N&J,* 1: 326).

Fenn, Frederick (1868–1924) and Richard Pryce. *'Op-o'-me-Thumb. A Play in One Act* (cop. 1904).

Clemens spoke at a performance of this play on behalf of the Educational Alliance on 23 April 1908 (IVL Journal, TS p. 319, MTP).

Fenn, George Manville (1831–1909). *The Chaplain's Craze; Being the Mystery of Findon Friars.* New York: Harper & Brothers, 1886. 206 pp.
Inscription: signed on title page, "Clemens."
Catalog: A1911, #164, $1.25.

Fenollosa, (Mrs.) Mary (McNeill), pseud. "Sidney McCall." *The Breath of the Gods.* Boston: Little, Brown and Co., 1905. 431 pp.
Source: MTLAcc, entry #1021, volume donated by Clemens.

————. [Another identical copy.]
Source: MTLAcc, entry #1051, volume donated by Clemens.

Ferguson, V. Munro. *Music Hath Charms.* New York: Harper & Brothers, 1894. 300 pp.
Source: MTLAcc, entry #1549, volume donated by Clemens.

Fergusson, James (1808–1886). *A History of Architecture in All Countries from the Earliest Times.* Illus. 2 vols. Boston, 1883.
Catalog: A1911, #165, $4.

Ferrero, Guglielmo (1871–1942). *The Greatness and Decline of Rome.* Trans. by A. E. Zimmern. 5 vols. New York, 1909.
Inscription: each volume signed "S. L. Clemens, 1909".
Catalog: A1911, #166, $14.50.

Ferris, George Titus (b. 1840). *Gems of the Centennial Exhibition; Consisting of Illustrated Descriptions of Objects of an Artistic Order . . . at the Philadelphia International Exhibition of 1876.* Illus. New York: D. Appleton & Co., 1877. 164 pp.
Source: MTLAcc, entry #1228, volume donated by Clemens.

Fetridge, William Pembroke. *Harper's Handbook for Travelers in Europe and the East.* New York: Harper and Brothers, 1862.

Leon Dickinson's forthcoming Iowa-California edition of *IA* (first pub. 1869) reveals that in chapter 44 Mark Twain used a quotation from page 347 of Fetridge's book: "Though old as history itself, thou art fresh as the breath of spring, blooming as thine own rose-bud, and fragrant as thine own orange-flower, O Damascus, pearl of the East!"

Field, Eugene (1850–1895). *Culture's Garland: Being Memoranda of the Gradual Rise of Literature, Art, Music and Society in Chicago, and Other Western Ganglia.* Intro. by Julian Hawthorne. Boston: Ticknor and Co., 1887. 325 pp.

Clemens included two pieces by Field—"His First Day at Editing" and "Oon Criteek De Bernhardt"—in *Mark Twain's Library of Humor* (1888), naming this book as their source. When Clemens visited St. Louis in June 1902 he participated in dedication ceremonies for a memorial tablet at Field's birthplace. In a brief speech Clemens paid tribute to "a man who, by his life, made bright the lives of all who knew him, and by his literary efforts cheered the thoughts of thousands who never knew him" *(MTB,* pp. 1174–75).

Field, Joseph M. (1810–1856). *The Drama in Pokerville* (pub. 1847).

DeVoto offered a sketch in Field's collection of newspaper anecdotes—"A Resurrectionist and His Freight"—as the model for Mark Twain's "grotesquely awful story about smells, 'The Invalid's Story,' " written in 1879 but held back until its inclusion in *Merry Tales* (1892) (*MTAm*, pp. 252–254). Walter Blair (*NAH*, p. 154) noted that "Kicking a Yankee" developed the same theme that Clemens employed in his first-published tale, "Dandy Frightening the Squatter" (1852). Subsequently Blair found other parallels: from this volume (pp. 177–183) Mark Twain might have become familiar with Field's version of "The Death of Mike Fink," to which Clemens seems to refer in working notes for *HF* ("about Carpenter & Mike Fink") and in Notebook 20 in April 1882: "Mike Fink shooting tin cup off Carpenter's head." Blair also pointed out parallels between the Duke's playbills for Bricksville in *HF* (1885) and those posted by Mr. T. Fitzgerald in the title story of Field's *Drama in Pokerville* (*MT&HF*, pp. 303–304).

Fielding, Henry (1707–1754). *Joseph Andrews* (pub. 1742).

Around 1880 Clemens mentioned that he owned a copy of this book ("The Walt Whitman Controversy," DV36, MTP). In 1894 he laid down plans to write honest reviews of "Joseph Adams" [*sic*], and other literary classics (NB 33, TS p. 61).

————. *Tom Jones* (pub. 1749).

Clemens' attitude toward Fielding's works was simultaneously negative and envious. He was repelled by the social mores he found reflected in the pages of *Tom Jones,* yet he professed an admiration for the fidelity with which Fielding's books mirrored his society and for the prevailing moral tolerance that allowed their publication. Clemens expressed his feelings about *Tom Jones* and his creator in the late winter (possibly in March) of 1879, while he was living in Paris. Evidently the licentiousness he thought he saw rampant there left him in no mood for encountering hedonism in an eighteenth-century English novel. "Been reading that disgusting Tom Jones," he wrote in Notebook 18. "The same old paltry stuff & poverty of invention— . . . gambling & whoring & beggary & enlisting & fighting, & finally his magnificent father turns up—Roderick Random over again." Squire Western alone suited Clemens' notions of characterization: "he is the only man whose violent death one does not hunger for" (*N&J*, 2: 294). He made additional comments about *Tom Jones* in the succeeding pages of Notebook 18: "no drearier reading," he declared in defiance of the usual critical opinions (p. 298). He was indignant that "people praise Tom Jones & Rod. Random" (p. 303).

These cavils were curiously altered, however, when Mark Twain first alluded to *Tom Jones* in print in chapter 50 of *TA* (1880). There he commented that "Fielding and Smollett could portray the beastliness of their day in the beastliest language; we have plenty of foul subjects to deal with in our day, but we are not allowed to approach them very near, even with nice and guarded forms of speech." In "The Walt Whitman Controversy," perhaps written in 1880, Mark Twain hinted similarly that he found the parlor-table standard of decorum both hypocritical and inconsistent, and that he chafed under its strictures; *Tom Jones* was one of the "old bad books" on his and everyone's library shelves, he pointed out (DV 36, MTP). Twain seemed to accept the novel as a sociological survey of English society during a prior period. He intended to quote from Fielding ("where printable") in a proposed appendix to *CY* (see Howard G. Baetzhold, "Course of Composition," p. 200), and in chapter 4 of *CY* (1889) Hank Morgan reports that "many of the terms used . . . by this great assemblage of the first ladies and gentlemen in the land would have made a Comanche blush. . . . However, I had read 'Tom Jones,' and 'Roderick Random,' and other books of that kind, and I knew that the highest and first ladies and gentlemen in England had remained little or no cleaner in their talk, and in the morals and conduct which such talk implies, clear up to a hundred years ago." On 27 April 1890 Mark Twain made a speech, "On Foreign Critics," in which he reminded his audience sarcastically that when the American Revolution took place, "Tom Jones and Squire Western were gentlemen" in England (*MTSpk*, p. 259). As late as 1894 Clemens listed *Tom Jones* among the English classics for which he planned to "write a really honest review" (NB 33, TS p. 61).

Fielding-Hall, Harold (1859–1917), pseud. "H. Fielding." *Thibaw's Queen.* Illus. New York: Harper & Brothers, 1899. 294 pp.
Source: MTLAcc, entry #1042, volume donated by Clemens.

Fields, (Mrs.) Annie (Adams) (1834–1915). *Whittier; Notes of His Life and of His Friendships.* New York: Harper & Brothers, [cop. 1893]. 103 pp.
Source: MTLAcc, entry #653, volume donated by Clemens.

————. [Another identical copy.]
Source: MTLAcc, entry #838, volume donated by Clemens.

Fields, James Thomas (1817–1881). *Ballads and Other Verses.* Boston: Houghton, Mifflin and Co., 1881. 133 pp.
In July 1880 Clemens wrote "The Alarmèd Skipper, by James T. Fields" in a list of humorists and their works to be considered for an anthology (NB 19, *N&J*, 2: 361). When *Mark Twain's Library of Humor* appeared in 1888 it contained two poems by Fields—"The Alarmed Skipper" (sometimes called "The Nantucket Skipper") and "The Owl-Critic," both taken from Fields' *Ballads and Other Verses.*

————. *Barry Cornwall and Some of His Friends.* Boston: James R. Osgood and Co., 1876.
Inscription: on first flyleaf in purple ink: "For Mrs. Clemens/with the cordial regards of/James T. Fields/May 1876."
Location: Antenne-Dorrance Collection, Rice Lake, Wis.
Copy examined: unmarked gift copy belonging to Livy Clemens.

————. *Hawthorne.* Boston: James R. Osgood and Co., 1876.
Inscription: at top of title page: "With the author's regards."
Location: Antenne-Dorrance Collection, Rice Lake, Wis.
Copy examined: unmarked copy belonging to member of the Clemens family.

Figuier, Louis. *Primitive Man.* Rev. trans. New York: D. Appleton & Co., 1871.
Inscriptions: signed in pencil on flyleaf, "Saml. L. Clemens/July, 1871." As a small joke the half-title page is also inscribed in pencil so as to read: "Saml. L. Clemens,/The" [*Primitive Man*].
Marginalia: numerous notations in pencil, beginning on page 1 and ending on page 133. Pages 154–158 have been cut open, however, so Clemens probably read the entire book. Notes occur on pages 14, 15, 45, 46, 65, 71, 91, 94, 95, 108. Clemens' comment on page 71 resembles the skeptical view he would express about paleontology in "A Brace of Brief Lectures" (pub. September and October 1871): at Figuier's identification of bones "gnawed by hyaenas" Clemens objected, "(?—or merely *supposed?* can any man classify the teeth-marks on a bone 50,000 years old?" Similarly he labeled as "absurd" the assertions on page 91 that human teeth marks were detected on various bones.
Location: Carrie Estelle Doheny Collection, St. John's Seminary, Camarillo, California. Donated by Mrs. Doheny in 1940 following its purchase from Maxwell Hunley Rare Books of Beverly Hills.
Copy examined: Clemens' copy, containing a book-seller's sticker from Hall Brothers, Elmira, New York on the rear endpaper.
Hamlin Hill explained in "Mark Twain's 'Brace of Brief Lectures on Science' " that Mark Twain based his essays on an anonymous review of Figuier's *Primitive Man* that appeared in the 13 August 1870 issue of *Chamber's Journal.* Although

Mark Twain's first installment of "Lectures" in *The American Publisher* (September 1871) was accompanied by an extended passage from *Primitive Man*, Hill was not certain whether he actually possessed first-hand knowledge of Figuier's book. As Hill makes clear, Mark Twain's articles display both scorn for the far-fetched theories of scientists and (farther on) a sympathy for their trial-and-error inductive procedures and for geological theory as a whole.

Filippini, Alexander. *Handy Volume Culinary Series.* 7 vols. New York: Charles L. Webster & Co., 1892.

Clemens' publishing firm advertised this series as the recipes of Delmonico's chef of twenty-five years. There are one hundred recipes for each of seven categories of dishes—soups, fish, eggs, poultry and game, salads and entrees, sauces, desserts.

————. *The Table: How to Buy Food, How to Cook It, and How to Serve It.* New York: Charles L. Webster & Co., 1889. 507 pp. Repr. 1890, 1891, with supplements.

Clemens' publishing firm boasted that this volume contained 1,550 recipes. Some of its dishes evidently pleased the Clemenses' palates; on 7 October 1891 Clemens wrote from Germany to request that Chatto & Windus send a copy of *The Table* "(cookbook issued by Webster & Co., New York)" to his next address in Berlin (CWB). In an undated note on letterhead stationery of The Players Club, Clemens also requested of Fred J. Hall: "Please send Mrs. Clemens 2 copies of the cook book—new edition" (Berg). In 1900 he made a cryptic memorandum in Notebook 43: "Delmonico (?) Cookbook" (TS p. 32).

Fillebrown, Rebekah Huddell (Miller) (1842–1917). *Rhymes of Happy Childhood.* Illus. by Edwin John Prittie. Philadelphia: J. C. Winston Co., 1908. 119 pp.
Source: MTLAcc, entry #2028, volume donated from Clemens' library by Clara Clemens Gabrilowitsch in 1910.

Fillmore, John Comfort. "A Study of Indian Music," *Century Magazine*, 47 (February 1894), 616–623.

Clemens recommended this article to his daughters ("I think it will interest them") in a letter written to Livy Clemens on [9] February 1894 *(LLMT*, p. 294). Fillmore's essay describes native American Indian songs in technical terms. The final paragraph concludes: "Those whom we are accustomed to despise as an inferior and barbarous race reveal, in the glimpse this music affords into their inner life, a noble religious feeling" (p. 623).

Finch, Francis Miles (1827–1907). "Smoking Song" (poem).

Clemens borrowed passages from this piece in constructing a limerick, "Sparkling & Bright," in 1866 (NB 5, *N&J*, 1: 157). See also C. F. Hoffman.

A First German Course, Containing Grammar, Delectus, and Exercise-Book, with Vocabularies, and Materials for German Conversation. On the Plan of Dr. William Smith's [1813–1893] "Principia Latina." Third ed. Rev. New York: Harper, 1856. 237 pp. Repr. by Harper & Brothers in 1876. 158 pp. [At head of title: "The German Principia, Part I."]

In March 1878 Clemens noted "The First German Principia—A First [German] Course. Harper" in Notebook 14 *(N&J*, 2: 54). Later he considered using it in *TA:* "Begin chapter with Ollendorff & First German Reader" (NB 14, p. 60).

Fischer, Henry William Hubert (1856–1932), pseud. "Ursula, Countess von Eppinghoven." *Private Lives of William II [1859–1941] and His Consort [Empress Auguste Viktoria, 1858–1921] and Secret History of the Court of Berlin, from the Papers and Diaries Extending Over a Period, Beginning June, 1888, to the Spring of 1898, of Ursula, Countess von Eppinghoven.* 2 vols. New York:

Fischer's Foreign Letters, [1904].
Catalog: C1951, #57c, $5, listed among the books signed by Clemens.
Fischer, identifying himself as president of Fischer's Foreign Letters and News, wrote Clemens on 12 April 1904: "Will you do me the honor to accept, with my best wishes, the set of 'PRIVATE LIVES OF WILLIAM II' coming herewith. You once told me of your great and lasting fondness for the Margravine of Bayreuth, well, here is a continuation of the story of Voltaire's friend" (MTP).

Fish, Williston (1858–1939). *Short Rations.* Illus. by C. J. Taylor. New York: Harper & Brothers, 1899. 189 pp.
Source: MTLAcc, entry #1550, volume donated by Clemens.

Fisher, (Mrs.) Arabella Burton (Buckley) (1840–1929). *The Fairyland of Science.* New York: H. M. Caldwell Co., n.d. 266 pp.
Source: MTLAcc, entry #1590, volume donated by Clemens.

————. *Life and Her Children: Glimpses of Animal Life from the Amoeba to the Insects.* Illus. New York: D. Appleton & Co., 1885. 312 pp.
Source: MTLAcc, entry #1939, volume donated from Clemens' library by Clara Clemens Gabrilowitsch in 1910.
At Quarry Farm on 2 July 1885 Livy Clemens noted: "Tonight I was reading to Susy and Clara from a book 'Life and her Children' a very interesting book on the lower forms of Animal Life" (OLC Diary, DV161, MTP). She also recorded on 12 July that "we are reading together 'Life and her Children.' "

Fisher, George Park (1827–1909). *Essays on the Supernatural Origin of Christianity, with Special Reference to the Theories of Renan, Strauss, and the Tübingen School.* New ed. New York: Charles Scribner's Sons, 1887.
Inscription: signed on first flyleaf, "S. L. Clemens/1887."
Catalog: A1911, #167, $3.
Location: Carrie Estelle Doheny Collection, St. John's Seminary, Camarillo, California. Donated by Mrs. Doheny in 1945 following its acquisition from Maxwell Hunley Rare Books of Beverly Hills for $35.
Copy examined: Clemens' copy.

Fisher, L. H. *Figures and Flowers.* Buffalo, N.Y.: Moulton, Wenburne & Co., [cop. 1888]. 160 pp.
Source: MTLAcc, entry #642, volume donated by Isabel V. Lyon, Clemens' secretary.

Fisk, May Isabel. *Monologues.* New York: Harper & Brothers, 1903. 190 pp.
Source: MTLAcc, entry #360, volume donated by Clemens.

————. [Another identical copy.]
Source: MTLAcc, entry #1551, volume donated by Clemens.

————. *The Talking Woman (Monologues).* Illus. New York: Harper & Brothers, 1907. 169 pp.
Source: MTLAcc, entry #359, volume donated by Clemens.

Fiske, John (1842–1901). *The Beginnings of New England; or, The Puritan Theocracy.* Boston: Houghton, Mifflin and Co., 1889. 296 pp.
In preparing for his departure for Elmira in June 1889 Clemens noted " 'Beginnings of New England.' Fisk" [*sic*], apparently intending to obtain the book (NB 29, TS p. 9).

————. *A Century of Science and Other Essays.* Boston: Houghton, Mifflin and Co., 1900. 466 pp.
　Inscription: "SL. Clemens/Riverdale-on-Hudson/Feb. 1902."
　Marginalia: pencil markings and notes (primarily scientists' names) throughout the first essay, "A Century of Science" (pp. 1–38); pencil markings in the chapter titled "The Arbitration Treaty" (pp. 166–193). No other marks. Page 55 is turned down in the essay on "Sir Harry Vane."
　Catalog: C1951, #69c, $12.50.
　Location: Mark Twain Papers, Berkeley, California. Donated in 1973 by Professor Blake Nevius of the Department of English, University of California at Los Angeles. Professor Nevius purchased the volume at the 1951 auction.
　Copy examined: Clemens' copy.

————. "Charles Darwin," *Atlantic Monthly,* 49 (June 1882), 835–845.
　Mark Twain quotes extensively from Fiske's article in the postscript section of "Mental Telegraphy" (pub. 1891), which discusses the Darwin–Wallace coincidence of theories in 1858.

————. *The Discovery of America, with Some Account of Ancient America and the Spanish Conquest.* 2 vols. Boston: Houghton, Mifflin and Co., 1892.
　At Riverdale on 13 April 1902 Mark Twain made notes for a love story set in the "Quarternary Epoch," two million years ago. He immediately thought of the solution to one problem: "For the early scenery & animals, see John Fiske's Discovery of America, vol. I" (NB 45, TS p. 10). In a speech at Carnegie Hall on 22 January 1906, Mark Twain joked: "The historian, John Fiske, whom I knew well and loved, was a spotless and most noble and upright Christian gentleman, and yet he swore once" *(MTSpk,* p. 481).

Fitchett, William Henry (1845–1928). *The Tale of the Great Mutiny.* Illus. New York: Charles Scribner's Sons, 1901. 384 pp. Repr. in succeeding years.
　Catalog: C1951, #50c, $10, listed among books signed by Clemens.

Fitzball, Edward (1792–1873). *Maritana* (opera, prod. 1845). Libretto by Fitzball; Vincent Wallace, composer. [Based on the play *Don César de Bazan* by D'Ennery and Dumanoir.]
　Clemens made a favorable reference to "Maritana. Alas those chimes so sweetly singing" in 1878 (NB 16, *N&J,* 2: 213). Act II of *Maritana* opens with an aria by Lazarillo, beginning: "Alas! those chimes, so sweetly pealing,/Gently dulcet to the ear,/Sound like Pity's voice, revealing,/To the dying, 'death is near!' "

Fitzgerald, Percy Hetherington (1834–1925). *The Life of George the Fourth, Including His Letters and Opinions.* New York: Harper & Brothers, 1881. 921 pp.
　Source: MTLAcc, entry #1765, volume donated by Clemens.

Flagg, John Henry (1843–1911). *Lyrics of New England, and Other Poems.* Cedar Rapids, Ia: Torch Press, 1909. 142 pp.
　Inscription: "Saml L. Clemens,/with affectionate/Regards of the/Author".
　Location: Mark Twain Library, Redding, Connecticut. Donated from Clemens' library by Clara Clemens Gabrilowitsch in 1910 (MTLAcc, entry #2026).
　Copy examined: Clemens' unmarked copy, with many leaves still unopened.

————. *The Monarch and Other Poems.* New York: Privately printed, 1902. 102 pp.
　Inscription: on first flyleaf, "To S L Clemens/with unfailing regards of/The Author/Oct 18, 1904."
　Location: Mark Twain Library, Redding, Connecticut.
　Copy examined: Clemens' unmarked copy.

————. [Another identical copy.]
 Marginalia: Clemens marked pages 5–6 and 8 with a pencil, and commented
at the bottom of page 5: "Those two [stanzas]—never mind about details—
successfully give you the atmosphere."
 Location: Antenne-Dorrance Collection, Rice Lake, Wis.
 Copy examined: Clemens' copy.

Flamini, Francesco (1868–1922), ed. *Compendio di Storia della Letteratura Italiana
ad Uso Delle Scuole Secondarie.* Quarta edizione. Livorno: Raffaello Giusti,
Editore. Libraio-Tipografo, 1904.
 Inscription: signed in black ink on first flyleaf: "Jean L. Clemens/Villa di
Quarto/Firenze./Febbraro 1904."
 Marginalia: unmarked except for the name "flamini" written in brown ink on
the verso of the title page.
 Catalog: Mott 1952, #53, $2.
 Location: Mark Twain Memorial, Hartford, Connecticut. Gift of an anonymous
donor in 1963.
 Copy examined: Jean Clemens' copy.

Flamma, Ario. *Dramas.* New York: Ario Flamma, 1909.
 Location: formerly in the Mark Twain Library, Redding, Connecticut. Recorded by Albert E. Stone in 1955, but listed as missing in 1963. I was unable
to find the volume in 1970.
 The first play is dedicated to Mark Twain.

Flammarion, Camille (1842–1925). *L'inconnu. The Unknown.* New York: Harper
& Brothers, 1905. 488 pp.
 Source: MTLAcc, entry #1806, volume donated by Clemens.

Flaubert, Gustave. *Madame Bovary* (pub. 1857).
 In March 1888 Clemens made note of "Mme. Bovary—translated by Mrs.
Marx Aveling—English edition" (NB 27, TS p. 60). When he was preparing to
board the *Princess Irene* for a voyage to Italy in 1903, he requested Frederick A.
Duneka of Harper & Brothers to send a copy of *Madame Bovary* to his stateroom
(21 October 1903, TS in MTP).

————. *Salammbô* (pub. 1862).
 On 5 August 1909 Albert Bigelow Paine noticed that Clemens had been reading
a copy of *Salammbô,* which Paine lent him. When Paine asked Clemens his
opinion of the book, Clemens told him that he "read every line of it," but found
only "a continuous procession of blood and slaughter and stench. . . . It has great
art—I can see that. That scene of the crucified lions and the death cañon and
the tent scene are marvelous, but I wouldn't read that book again without a
salary" *(MTB,* p. 1516).

Fleming, Thomas (1853–1931). *Around the "Pan" with Uncle Hank. His Trip
Through the Pan-American Exposition.* New York: Nut Shell Pub. Co., 1901.
262 pp.
 Source: MTLAcc, entry #365, volume donated by Clemens.

Fletcher, C. R. L. *An Introductory History of England, from the Earliest Times to
the Close of the Middle Ages.* Maps. New York, 1904.
 Inscription: signed on inner cover, "S. L. Clemens, 21 Fifth Avenue, 1905."
 Catalog: A1911, #168, $2.

Fletcher, E. A. *The Woman Beautiful.* 1901.
> *Source:* Albert E. Stone recorded this book in his checklist of Clemens' volumes in the Mark Twain Library at Redding, Connecticut in 1955. Stone reported that the flyleaf was missing. I was unable to locate the book in 1970.

Fletcher, John (1579–1625) and Francis Beaumont (1584–1616). *A King and No King* (play).
> Dr. James Ross Clemens remembered that "in one of Ford's [*sic*] plays a Roman general named Bessus specialized in making strategic movements to rear [in the tradition of Captain Bobadill]. At this cautious gentleman Mark never tired of poking fun and likened him to several of our generals in the Civil War" ("Reminiscences of MT" [1929], p. 125).

Fogazzaro, Antonio (1842–1911). *Il Mistero del Poeta.* Romanzo, Milano, 1900.
> *Inscription:* "To Jean Clemens on a Birthday, July 26th 1903."
> *Catalog: Mott 1952,* #54, $3.50.

[Fonseca, José da (1792?–1866] and Pedro Carolino. *The New Guide of the Conversation in Portuguese and English.* Intro. by Mark Twain. Boston: James R. Osgood & Co., 1883. 182 pp.
> *Source:* MTLAcc, entry #817, volume donated by Clemens.
> Mark Twain's introduction ridiculed the writer as "an honest and upright idiot who believed he knew something of the English language."

Fontaine, Camille (1855–1923). *Livre de lecture et de conversation.* Boston: D. C. Heath & Co., [cop. 1893]. 249 pp.
> "I want to bother you once more about a French book," Livy Clemens wrote to her husband from Paris on 26 April 1894. "There was a new book come out in New York pub. by D. C. Heath & Co. called Prof. C. Fontaine's 'Livre de Lecture et de Conversation.' It is spoken very well of by the Critic & I should like it if you could get it & bring it to me when you come" (ALS, Mark Twain Research Foundation, Perry, Mo.; quoted in *The Twainian,* 37 [May–June 1978], 4).

Fonvielle, Wilfrid de (1826–1914). *Thunder and Lightning.* Trans. from French, and ed. by, Thomas Lamb Phipson. Illus. N. Y.: Scribner, Armstrong & Co., 1872. 285 pp.
> *Source:* MTLAcc, entry #1985, volume donated from Clemens' library by Clara Clemens Gabrilowitsch in 1910.

Foote, Mary (Hallock) (1847–1938). *John Bodewin's Testimony.* Boston: Ticknor and Co., 1886. 344 pp.
> In September 1886 Clemens noted the author and title of this novel, along with the instructions: "(if they've *got* it.)—Don't send for it" (NB 26, TS p. 20). Three decades later he referred to Clara Clemens' "dear & valued & level-headed friend & mine, Mary Foote," who was "a fine human being, of full age" (29[?] August 1906, *MTHL,* p. 819).

Forbes, Arthur Litton Armitage. *Two Years in Fiji.* London: Longmans, Green and Co., 1875.
> At the end of a list of books that Clemens read in London in November 1896 appears "2 Years in F.—Lytton Forbes" (NB 39, TS p. 26). Subsequently he quoted from Forbes' book (merely citing "Forbes's 'Two Years in Fiji' ") in chapter 8 of *FE* (1897), where he presented Forbes' account of two foreigners who mysteriously appeared in Fiji and whose homeland could never be determined.

Forbes, Frank. *How to Be Happy—Through Living*. London: Neville & Co., [1902]. 112 pp.
> *Source:* MTLAcc, entry #396, volume donated by Clemens.

Forbes–Mitchell, William. *Reminiscences of the Great Mutiny, 1857–59*. London: Macmillan and Co., 1893.
> *Catalog: C1951,* #29c, presentation copy, $10.
> Clemens entered the name of the author and the title in Notebook 35 while he was visiting New Zealand in October–November 1895 (TS p. 64). In chapter 54 of *FE* (1897) he stated that he had read about military marches with the temperatures at 138° "in Sergeant-Major Forbes–Mitchell's account of his military experiences in the Mutiny . . . and in Calcutta I asked him if it was true, and he said it was."

Forbush, Edward Howe (1858–1929). *Useful Birds and Their Protection*. Pub. under direction of the Massachusetts State Board of Agriculture. Boston: Wright & Potter Printing Co., n.d. 437 pp.
> *Inscription:* presentation copy from the author, inscribed on second flyleaf: "Mr. Samuel L. Clemens/with the compliments/and kind regards/of E. H. Forbush/Boston/May 24, 1909."
> *Location:* Mark Twain Library, Redding, Connecticut. Donated from Clemens' library by Clara Clemens Gabrilowitsch in 1910 (MTLAcc, entry #1948).
> *Copy examined:* Clemens' copy, unmarked.

Ford, Harriet. *A Gentleman of France* (play, prod. 1901).
> Clemens and his wife attended a performance on 1 February 1902 in New York City—a matinée (SLC to Miss Marbury, 10 February 1902, CWB).

Ford, Paul Leicester (1865–1902), ed. *A House Party*. Boston: Small, Maynard & Co., 1901.
> The advertising for Ford's book infuriated Clemens, since it implied that he and other prominent American authors had contributed pieces to the collection. On 9 January 1902 Clemens mailed form letters to the twenty-three authors, seeking to determine whether twelve of them actually *had* written stories for *A House Party,* or whether the publishers had perpetrated a fraud. Evidently the responses he received from Cable, Bangs, Jewett, Stockton, Tarkington, Wister, and others satisfied him that no legal action was warranted.

"For he's a jolly good fellow" (college song).
> Clemens referred to this song in *"A Champagne Cocktail and a Catastrophe": Two Acting Charades* (privately printed, 1930); in chapter 11 of *PW* (1894); and in his 28 January 1907 AD *(MTE,* p. 76).

Forman, Justus Miles (1875–1915). *Buchanan's Wife; A Novel*. Illus. by Will Grefé. New York: Harper & Brothers, 1906. 262 pp.
> *Source:* MTLAcc, entry #131, volume donated by Clemens.

————. *The Island of Enchantment*. Illus. by Howard Pyle. New York: Harper & Brothers, 1905. 106 pp.
> *Inscription:* signed in black ink on inside front cover, "SL. Clemens/1905".
> *Location:* Antenne–Dorrance Collection, Rice Lake, Wis. The matching cardboard box for the volume is in the Mark Twain Papers, Berkeley, California; it bears Clemens' note: "Family miniatures (early)". Evidently Katy Leary neglected to take the box when she chose Forman's volume as a keepsake after Clemens' death in 1910.
> *Copy examined:* Clemens' copy, unmarked. Apparently he used its box to keep photographs in.

————. [Another identical copy.]
Source: MTLAcc, entry #1048, volume donated by Clemens.

————. *Jason, A Romance.* Illus. by W. Hatherell. New York: Harper & Brothers, 1909. 357 pp.
Source: MTLAcc, entry #2238, volume donated from Clemens' library by Clara Clemens Gabrilowitsch in 1910.

————. *A Stumbling Block.* New York: Harper & Brothers, 1907. 310 pp.
Source: MTLAcc, entry #1552, volume donated by Clemens.

Forneron, Henri (1834–1886). *Louise de Kéroualle, Duchess of Portsmouth, 1649–1734; or, How the Duke of Richmond Gained His Pension.* Preface by the translator, Mrs. G. M. Crawford. London: Swann Sonnenschein & Co., 1887. 346 pp. [Fifth ed. issued by the same publisher in 1897 as *The Court of Charles II, 1649–1734.*]

Perhaps Clemens was looking for more racy narratives of court affairs and intrigues like those of Saint-Simon when he wrote in November 1887: "Book about Chas II & Kerouaille, translated by Mrs. M. G. Crawford, pub by Scribner & Welford" (NB 27, TS p. 40). Another entry in the same notebook adds: "Louise de Keroualle/Scribner & Welford" (December 1887, TS p. 45). Forneron's book provided a surprisingly frank (for its time) account of the days "when Louise de Keroualle was above the crowned Queen at Whitehall" (p. xi), describing her strategems as an agent of Louis XIV while "consciously trying to bring England into subjection to France" (p. xiv). In 1907 Clemens would mention Charles II disparagingly as one who pulled down English standards of "official and commercial morals" that were raised by Cromwell (30 January 1907 AD, *MTE*, p. 81).

Forney, John Wien (1817–1881). *Anecdotes of Public Men.* Vol. 1. New York: Harper & Brothers, [cop. 1873]. 444 pp. A continuation was issued in 1881 as vol 2.
Source: MTLAcc, entry #1464, volume 1 only, donated by Clemens.

Forster, John (1812–1876). *The Life of Jonathan Swift. Volume the First, 1667–1711.* New York: Harper & Brothers, 1876. 487 pp.
Source: MTLAcc, entry #1766, volume donated by Clemens.

Forsyth, George Alexander (1837–1915). *Thrilling Days in Army Life.* Illus. by Rufus F. Zogbaum. New York: Harper & Brothers, 1902. 197 pp.
Source: MTLAcc, entry #501, volume donated by Clemens.

Forsyth, W. *The Novels and Novelists of the Eighteenth Century, in Illustration of the Manners and Morals of the Age.* New York: D. Appleton and Co., 1871. 339 pp.

On 14 July 1880 Estes & Lauriat of Boston billed Clemens for "1 Novels & Novelists," and Clemens paid on 20 July (receipt in MTP). Forsyth's book was the only one published with this title between 1870 and 1880.

Foster, Mary Louise (b. 1865), pseud. "Louise Forsslund." *The Ship of Dreams; A Novel.* New York: Harper & Brothers, 1902. 307 pp.
Source: MTLAcc, entry #130, volume donated by Clemens.

Foster, Stephen Collins (1826–1864). "De camptown races (Gwine to run all night)" (song, 1850).

Nicodemus Dodge plays "Camptown Races" with a comb and paper in chapter 23 of *TA* (1880). Jasper and Martha, slaves in the kitchen, sing this "gay song" to banjo accompaniment in "Which Was It?," written 1899–1903 (*WWD?*, p. 420). Clemens recalled "Camptown Races" as one of the "rudely comic" songs in early minstrel shows (30 November 1906 AD, *MTE*, p. 114).

———. "Ellen Bayne" (song, 1854).

Outside the ice cream parlor in Indiantown, prior to the Civil War, young people were "plaintively singing 'Sweet Ellen Bayne' " in "Which Was It?," written 1899–1903 (*WWD?*, p. 302); Clemens remembered it as one of the "sentimental songs" worked into the later minstrel shows (30 November 1906 AD, *MTE*, p. 114).

———. "Massa's in de cold, cold ground" (song, 1852).

Clemens recalled that early-day residents of Hannibal enjoyed this and other "Negro Melodies" that tended toward "regrets for bygone days and vanished joys" ("Villagers of 1840–3," written in 1897, *HH&T*, p. 34). Evidently Clemens was remembering his last few years in Hannibal.

———. "My old Kentucky home, good night" (song, 1853).

Hannibal residents liked this song when he was a youth, Clemens recalled in 1897 ("Villagers of 1840–3," *HH&T*, p. 34).

———. "Nelly Bly" (song, 1849).

This was one of the "sentimental songs" that Clemens remembered from the later minstrel shows (30 November 1906 AD, *MTE*, p. 114).

———. "Old Black Joe" (song, 1860).

In 1882 Clemens heard two Negro cabin hands sing this song to banjo accompaniment on Horace Bixby's *City of Baton Rouge* (NB 21, *N&J*, 2: 562).

———. "Old Dog Tray" (song, 1853).

In "On Linden, Etc." (pub. 7 April 1866) Mark Twain blunders out a line from "Old Dog Tray," mistakenly believing that he is quoting Thomas Campbell's "Hohenlinden." In 1866 Mark Twain heard the ship's choir on the *America* sing this and other "d-dest, oldest, vilest songs"; "D--n Dog Tray," he groused in Notebook 7 (*N&J*, 1: 262–263). He reported to his *Alta California* audience on 23 December 1866 that the ship's choir sang this and other "venerable melodies" (*MTTMB*, p. 28); in his 1 January 1867 letter he lost patience at continually hearing these "wretchedest old songs in the world" while amidst natural scenic beauty at sea. "Confound Dog Tray!" he snapped (*MTTMB*, p. 59). Much later, in 1897, he recollected hearing the song in ante-bellum Hannibal, one of those whose lyrics "tended to regrets for bygone days and vanished joys" (Villagers of 1840–3," *HH&T*, p. 34).

———. "Old folks at home" (song, 1851). Also called "Swanee River."

Clemens included this among his favorite songs in August 1889 (NB 21, TS p. 21). In 1897 he listed "Swanee River" among the "Negro Melodies" favored by Hannibal townspeople during his boyhood ("Villagers of 1840–3," *HH&T*, p. 34). The South Carolina slave in chapter 26 of "No. 44, The Mysterious Stranger" (written 1902–1908) sings this minstrel song, "and there was never anything so beautiful, never anything so heart-breaking, oh, never any music like it below the skies!" (*MSM*, pp. 355–356).

————. "Willie, we have missed you" (song, 1854).

Clemens mentioned this as a song generally seen on music stands in parlors in Honolulu when he visited the port in 1866 (chapter 3, *FE* [1897]).

Fothergill, Jessie (1851–1891). *Healey*. New York: George Munro, [cop. 1885]. 233 pp.

Source: MTLAcc, entry #2237, volume donated from Clemens' library by Clara Clemens Gabrilowitsch in 1910.

Fowler, Montague. *Some Notable Archbishops of Canterbury*. London: Society for Promoting Christian Knowledge, 1895.

Inscription: on verso of first flyleaf: "To 'Mark Twain'/from the author/ Montague Fowler/a tribute to a giant from a pigmy/June 22, 1899." Part of second flyleaf torn out.

Location: Mark Twain Library, Redding, Connecticut.

Copy examined: Clemens' copy, unmarked.

Fowler, Orson Squire (1809–1887). *Love and Parentage, Applied to the Improvement of Offspring, Including Important Directions and Suggestions to Lovers and the Married Concerning the Strongest Ties and the Most Momentous Relations of Life*. Fortieth ed. New York: Fowler & Wells, [cop. 1844].

Inscription: contains bookplate and signature of "J. H. Hatch/August 26/1861".

Marginalia: markings on pages 53 and 54.

Location: owned by Ralph Gregory, former curator, Mark Twain Birthplace Memorial Shrine, Florida, Mo. Mr. Gregory now lives in Marthasville, Mo.

Copy examined: a copy which reportedly belonged to Orion Clemens. Given to Mr. Gregory in 1965 by Mrs. Mary Gertrude (Stotts) Shotwell, who lived in Orion and Mollie Clemens' home. See entry for Thomas Dick's *Practical Astronomer* for explanation of provenance.

———— and Lorenzo Niles Fowler (1811–1896). *New Illustrated Self-Instructor in Phrenology and Physiology*. New York: Fowler & Wells, n.d. [Rev. ed. cop. 1859; reprinted in 1877, 1890, and probably in other years as well.]

Inscription: signed on endpaper, "Clemens, 1901," a date that accords with Clemens' appointment with Jessie Allen Fowler (of the Fowler & Wells firm) for a phrenological character reading on 7 March 1901; she probably presented him with this volume when he underwent analysis at her office in New York City (Notebook 44, TS p. 7).

Marginalia: in the chart of phrenological faculties at the front of the book, marks are placed beside "Self-Esteem," "Veneration," and "Calculation." These are three of the organs found to be predominant in "Bishop" Mark Twain in Book 2 (chapter 2) of "The Secret History of Eddypus, the World-Empire," written 1901–1902.

Catalog: *A1911*, #385, $3.50.

I have explained in "Mark Twain, Phrenology and the 'Temperaments' " (1972) how Mark Twain inserted a satire on the Fowler & Wells method of examination into "The Secret History of Eddypus" (*FM*, pp. 348–353). He took a portion of his phrenologist's "lecture" practically verbatim from the preface (p. viii) of the Fowler brothers' *Self-Instructor in Phrenology and Physiology*. See pp. 61–64 of my article for a fuller discussion of his borrowings.

Fowler, Samuel Page (1800–1888), ed. *Salem Witchcraft: Comprising More Wonders of the Invisible World, Collected by Robert Calef; and Wonders of the Invisible World, by Cotton Mather; Together with Notes and Explanations by Samuel P. Fowler*. Boston: W. Veazie, 1865. 450 pp.

Marginalia: Clemens rollicks through Mather's *Wonders*, adding sarcastic notes to many of the putative "proofs" of witchcraft and occasionally suggesting that the accusers were drunk when they imagined their visions. His knowledge of

European history restrains him from wholly denouncing the government of the American colonies, however. He notes on page 341: "Well, their infamies covered but one year, & were heartily confessed & repented of; whereas Europe's iniquities in the same line covered eight centuries. Nothing so fantastic, & ignorant, & barbarous, as these Salem Witch-trials can be found, outside of the Scriptures." On the last page of the book Clemens wrote: "Calef really deserves a monument." All of Clemens' marginalia are in bluish-black ink.

    Catalogs: C1951, #3a, $35; *Zeitlin 1951*, #11, $75.
    Location: Mark Twain Papers, Berkeley, California.
    Copy examined: Clemens' heavily underlined and annotated copy.

Fowler, Thomas (1832–1904). *Locke*. English Men of Letters Series. New York: Harper & Brothers, 1899. 200 pp.
    Source: MTLAcc, entry #1283, volume donated by Clemens.

Fox, Caroline (1819–1871). *Memories of Old Friends, Being Extracts from the Journals and Letters of Caroline Fox, of Penjerrick, Cornwall, from 1835–1871*. Ed. by Horace N. Pym. Philadelphia: J. B. Lippincott & Co., 1882.
    In April 1882 Clemens wrote "Caroline Fox's Memories" in Notebook 20 (*N&J*, 2: 460) shortly before he made trips to Boston and New York City. He might have been interested in her vivid portraits of the prominent English authors —Carlyle, Wordsworth, Mill, Coleridge, Macaulay, and others—with whom she associated.

Fox, John (1863–1919). *The Little Shepherd of Kingdom Come*. Illus. by F. C. Yohn. New York: C. Scribner's Sons, 1903. 404 pp.
    Source: MTLAcc, entry #998, volume donated by Clemens.

————. *A Mountain Europa*. New York: Harper & Brothers, 1899. 192 pp.
    Source: MTLAcc, entry #1553, volume donated by Clemens.

————. *The Trail of the Lonesome Pine*. Illus. by F. C. Yohn. New York: C. Scribner's Sons, 1909. 422 pp.
    Source: MTLAcc, entry #999, volume donated by Clemens.

————. [Another identical copy.] Leaves loose.
    Source: MTLAcc, entry #878, volume donated by Mrs. Ralph W. Ashcroft (formerly Isabel Lyon), Clemens' secretary.

Foxe, John (1516–1587). *The Book of Martyrs* (pub. 1563).
    Mark Twain recalled that a copy of "Fox's Martyrs" generally lay on the parlor table of the snow-white wooden cottages he visited in Honolulu in 1866 (*FE* [1897], chapter 3).

Fränkel, Ranudo. *Erstes Lesebuch. Leichte Erzählungen fur ganz kleine artige kinder von drei bis sechs Jahren*. Illus. Leipzig: Verlag von Emil Berndt, 1877. 18 pp.
    Inscription: Jean Clemens traced over Livy's brown ink handwriting with a heavy lead pencil: "Jean Clemens, from Mamma/April 26th 1888./Hartford, Conn."
    Location: Mark Twain Papers, Berkeley, California.
    Copy examined: Jean Clemens' copy, unmarked, with bookstore sticker of "F. W. Christern/37 West 23d Street/New York" on front pastedown endpaper.

Fraipont, Gustave. *The Art of Sketching*. Trans. from French by Clara Bell. Preface by Edwin Bale. Fifty illustrations by the author. New York: Charles L. Webster & Co., 1893. 100 pp.
    Published by Clemens' firm.

France, Anatole (1844–1924). *The Crime of Sylvestre Bonnard (Member of the Institute).* Trans. and intro. by Lafcadio Hearn (1850–1904). New York: Harper & Brothers, 1906. 281 pp.

Inscription: Clemens wrote in black ink on the front pastedown endpaper: "The world has said that the French have wit, but not humor: (meaning humor 'on the American plan,' no doubt.) The humor in this book is either that, or it is better than that./SL. Clemens/1906."

Marginalia: numerous markings, grammatical corrections, and notes—generally charitable.

Catalogs: A1911, #229, $21; "Irving S. Underhill Collection," American Art Association, Anderson Galleries, Sale No. 3911 (29 April 1936), #116, $100.

Location: Henry W. and Albert A. Berg Collection, New York Public Library.

Copy examined: Clemens' copy.

See Alan Gribben's "Anatole France and Mark Twain's Satan," *AL,* 47 (January 1976), 634–635.

————. [An identical copy.]

Source: MTLAcc, entry #1554, volume donated by Clemens.

————. *L'Île des Pingouins* (pub. 1908).

Elizabeth Wallace wrote Clemens about this witty satire in 1909 and ordered a copy to be sent to him. On 13 November 1909 Clemens reported from Redding: "No, I haven't read it, but you make me *want* to read it—hungry to read it, in fact. I am all ready for it" *(MT&HI,* p. 134).

Francis, Philip W. *The Remarkable Adventures of Little Boy Pip.* Illus. by Merle Johnson. San Francisco and New York: Paul Elder & Co., [cop. 1907]. 60 pp.

Source: MTLAcc, entry #497, volume donated by Isabel V. Lyon, Clemens' secretary.

François, Luise von (1817–1893). *Die Letzte Reckenbürgerin.* Berlin: Janke, 1888.

Catalog: C1951, #64c, $5, listed among books signed by Clemens.

Franklin, Benjamin (1706–1790). *The Life of Benjamin Franklin, Written by Himself. Now First Edited from Original Manuscripts and From His Printed Correspondence and Other Writings, by John Bigelow [1817–1911].* 3 vols. Philadelphia: J. B. Lippincott & Co., 1875.

Inscription: signed in each volume, "Saml. L. Clemens, Hartford, 1875".

Marginalia: a few passages marked by Clemens.

Catalog: A1911, #172, $11.50.

Clemens forever associated Franklin with Orion Clemens' short-lived regimens for exercise, diet, and sleep, but occasionally Clemens showed that he himself venerated Franklin's achievements. Dixon Wecter learned that Orion scattered Franklin's maxims through the Hannibal newspapers he edited in the early 1850's *(SCH,* p. 235); and when Sam Clemens reached Philadelphia in 1853 he lost little time before informing Orion that he had viewed Franklin's grave (26 October 1853, *MTL,* p. 27). Later (in 1856 and 1857) Sam Clemens worked in Orion's printing shop in Keokuk, Iowa, which Orion chose to name the Ben Franklin Book and Job Office. Clemens would remember Franklin's maxims, but always remained skeptical about their universal applicability. He headed his column in the 3 July 1864 issue of the San Francisco *Golden Era* with Franklin's "early to bed and early to rise" maxim, urging (with tongue in cheek) his readers to heed such advice *(WG,* p. 83). He ironically characterized Franklin's optimistic philosophy in a letter from San Francisco on 23 December 1865: when the newspaperman gets up in the morning he can do as old Franklin did, and say, "This day, and all days, shall be unselfishly devoted to the good of my fellow-creatures—to the amelioration of their condition" (quoted in *LAMT,* p. 154). In the comic sketch, "Private Habits of Horace Greeley" (1868), Mark Twain reported that Greeley arises at

3 o'clock in the morning and quotes Franklin's lines to his assembled family: "Early to bed and early to rise/Makes a man healthy, wealthy, and wise"— another gibe at the maxim that appeared in *Poor Richard's Almanack*. Mark Twain discussed Franklin's maxims in "Last Words of Great Men" (1869), where he asserted that Josh Billings' "proverbial originality" transcends the efforts of "Franklin, the author of Poor Richard's quaint sayings; Franklin, the immortal axiom-builder, who used to sit up at nights reducing the rankest old threadbare platitudes to crisp and snappy maxims that had a nice, varnished, original look in their regimentals." He continued this bantering in "The Late Benjamin Franklin" (1870), in which he quoted maxims by Franklin and claimed they are "full of animosity toward boys." Yet he mentioned Franklin approvingly as a historical figure ("a Benjamin Franklin or other laboring man") in "About Smells" (May 1870).

The origins of Clemens' malice became clear when he began to write a humorous biography of his brother in 1877, "Autobiography of a Damned Fool." Franklin's *Autobiography* figures prominently in this piece, and some fragmentary notes that Clemens made after reading Franklin's work (Box 37, MTP) may date from this period and may derive from John Bigelow's edition of 1875. In chapter 3 of "Damned Fool" the fool relates: "I presently got hold of a copy of Benjamin Franklin's autobiography, and was charmed with it. I saw that here was a man after my own heart" *(S&B,* p. 144). The tributes to Franklin seem sincere on Clemens' part as well as the fool's: "Franklin had the welfare of his fellow beings far more at heart than his own" (p. 144); "Franklin was broad, liberal, catholic" (p. 145); "The moving impulse of Franklin's every act was a principle," except that "Franklin had a disposition to accumulate money for his own selfish uses" (p. 145). The problem is the fool's ludicrous attempts to emulate him. "I read Franklin with avidity, and took him for a model," the fool explains (p. 145). These efforts include self-education at the hearthside, noondays without lunch to work overtime, private practice in oratory, and cold baths. But the fool's idolatry abates after he falls ill from a chilly plunge in an ice-covered creek, his interpretation of Franklin's advice about cold baths. Clemens reveals a considerable knowledge of Franklin's *Autobiography* in writing "Autobiography of a Damned Fool" (perhaps he read or reread the work at this time in order to discover his brother Orion's motives for behavior that had seemed puzzling in the 1850's), but he is intent upon poking fun at those, like the fool, who idealize human existence and strive after "noble," altruistic ends. Nevertheless, when Howells queried him about suitable autobiographies for a forthcoming series of "Choice Autobiographies," Clemens replied without hesitation on 6 June 1877: "Autobiog's? I didn't know there *were* any but old Franklin's & Benvenuto Cellini's" *(MTHL,* p. 180)—linking Franklin's work with one of his favorite books.

Franklin remained a constant presence in Mark Twain's writings: he referred to him in 1878 while criticizing a manuscript by Orion (DV415, MTP); he claimed that "the immortal Franklin" endorsed masturbation in "Some Thoughts on the Science of Onanism" in 1879 (DV200, no. 3, MTP); he ridiculed the adages espoused by Franklin ("Go to bed, get up early") in "Advice to Youth," a speech he made on 15 April 1882 *(MTSpk,* p. 169). In "Affeland (Snivelization)," which exists only as a fragment probably written in 1892, Clemens again created in young Albert a character who resembles Orion: "At twelve he read the life of Franklin, and at once set about making a Franklin of himself. For a month he lived scantly on bread and vegetables, did his studying at night by the light of a single candle, rose before dawn, bathed in deadly cold water, practiced gymnastic exercises in his room, took stated walks, framed a set of austere rules of conduct, listened sharply to the sermon, Sundays, and from memory bored the family with it at dinner. . . . Then at the end of the month he retired . . . and plunged into some new ambition or other" *(S&B,* pp. 170–171). But here again the onus is placed upon a silly imitator, and not on Franklin's original principles. Indeed, "Franklin's Autobiography" promptly occurred to Clemens in January 1894 as ideal material for his projected "Back Number" magazine (NB 33, TS p. 46).

Always, however, Clemens was drawn back to Orion's preoccupation with Franklin. In "Villagers of 1840–3," sketches of early Hannibal residents that Clemens wrote in 1897, Orion Clemens is thinly disguised as Oscar Carpenter, who, "at 18, wrote home to his mother, that he was studying the life of Franklin and closely imitating him; that in his boarding house he was confining himself to bread and water; and was" [the MS breaks off here, possibly destroyed by Clemens after he learned of Orion's death on 11 December 1897] (*HH&T*, p. 40). Likewise in the third chapter of the uncompleted "Hellfire Hotchkiss," also written in 1897, a character called Oscar Carpenter models himself on Franklin, arising at four in the morning "because that was Franklin's way," and dividing his day "on the Franklin plan—eight hours for labor, eight for sleep, eight for study, meditation and exercise" (*S&B*, p. 202). In 1898 Clemens thought up an addition to Franklin's "healthy, wealthy, and wise" maxim: "too wise to do it again," Clemens appended (NB 42, TS p. 68).

Mark Twain's "What Is Man?" (part 6, 1906) relates an experiment with ants and sugar that Sir John Lubbock credited Franklin with performing, but Paul Baender has noted that Mark Twain apparently altered the details in order to endow the ants with even more intelligence than Franklin reported (*WIM?*, pp. 196–197). In "Which Was It?" (written 1899–1903) Mark Twain described General Landry of Indiantown as "the very image of Benjamin Franklin, broad benignant face and all" (*WWD?*, 275). He mentioned Franklin's ambassadorial duties in "Diplomatic Pay and Clothes" (1899), and Franklin's name is mixed up among the "wonderful men" of the *nineteenth* century in "The Secret History of Eddypus," written 1901–1902—but the reference is complimentary (*FM*, p. 357). The cholera germ in "Three Thousand Years among the Microbes" (written 1905) names his yellow-fever-germ friend "Benjamin Franklin," but he respects this "renowned specialist" who instructs him about the true nature of life forces (*WWD?*, p. 449). Twain linked himself with Franklin, Edison, and others who, like Adam, lacked a college education in a speech of 1906, "Introducing Doctor Van Dyke" (*MTSpk*, p. 488). In "The Refuge of the Derelicts" (written 1905–1906), however, Clemens returned a final time to Orion's follies: Stanchfield Garvey, like Orion (and Sam Clemens), began working as a printer's apprentice; "he had a burning ambition to be a Franklin; so he lived strictly on bread and water, studied by the firelight instead of using candles, and practised swimming on the floor. Then he discarded Franklin, and imitated somebody else a while" (*FM*, p. 240).

Franklin, Samuel Rhoades (1825–1909). *Memories of a Rear-Admiral . . . in the Navy of the United States.* New York: Harper & Brothers, 1898. 398 pp.
 Source: MTLAcc, entry #1764, volume donated by Clemens.

Franzos, Karl Emil (1848–1904). *The Jews of Barnow. Stories.* Trans. from German by M. W. Macdowall. New York: D. Appleton and Co., 1883. 334 pp.
 Source: MTLAcc, entry #554, volume donated by Clemens.

————. *Namens Studien.*
 In describing the systems by which Jews were renamed ("in a way to make the angels weep"), Mark Twain culls ridiculous examples such as "Abraham Bellyache" from Franzos' book, citing the author and title in a footnote ("Concerning the Jews" [1899]).

Fraser, William Alexander (1859–1933). *The Lone Furrow.* New York: D. Appleton and Co., 1907. 354 pp.
 Source: MTLAcc, entry #133, volume donated by Isabel V. Lyon, Clemens' secretary.

Frazer, James George (1854–1941), comp. *Passages of the Bible, Chosen for Their Literary Beauty and Interest.* London, 1895.
  Catalog: A1911, #40, $5.50.

Frederic, Harold (1856–1898).
  Clemens delicately defended Frederic's moral reputation in a speech at the Savage Club Dinner on 6 July 1907; informed by a previous speaker that Frederic listened to readings from Clemens' books during his fatal illness, Clemens told the audience: "I did not know Harold Frederic personally, but I have heard a great deal about him, and nothing that was not pleasant, and nothing except such things as lead a man to honor another man and to love him. I consider that it is a misfortune of mine that I have never had the luck to meet him, and if any book of mine read to him in his last hours made those hours easier for him and more comfortable, I am very glad and proud of that" *(MTSpk,* p. 572). As many in Clemens' audience must have known, Frederic maintained separate households with two women.

Freeland, Isabelle M. *Thoughts in Verse.* Columbus, Ohio: New Franklin Printing Co., [cop. 1909]. 45 pp.
  Source: MTLAcc, entry #2027, volume donated from Clemens' library by Clara Clemens Gabrilowitsch in '1910.

Freeman, Edward Augustus (1823–1892). *The Historical Geography of Europe.* Second ed. 2 vols. London: Longmans, Green, and Co., 1882. [Only Livy Clemens' copy of vol. 1 has been located.]
  Inscription: vol. 1 inscribed by Clemens in black ink on half-title page: "Livy L. Clemens/1886."
  Catalog: Mott 1952, #55, $3, vol. 1 only.
  Location: vol. 1 only in Mark Twain Memorial, Hartford, Connecticut.
  Copy examined: Livy Clemens' unmarked copy of vol. 1. Contains stamps, traces of chargeslip jacket, and call number of Mark Twain Library, Redding, Connecticut.

Freeman, (Mrs.) Mary Eleanor (Wilkins) (1852–1930). *By the Light of the Soul; A Novel.* Illus. by Harold M. Brett. New York: Harper & Brothers, 1907. 497 pp.
  Source: MTLAcc, entry #1000, volume donated by Clemens.

———. *Evelina's Garden.* New York: Harper & Brothers, 1904. 120 pp.
  Source: MTLAcc, entry #1339, volume donated by Clemens.

———. *The Fair Lavinia, and Others.* Illus. New York: Harper & Brothers, 1907. 308 pp.
  Source: MTLAcc, entry #1555, volume donated by Clemens.

———. [An identical copy.]
  Inscription: signed on front pastedown endpaper, "S. L. Clemens, 1907".
  Catalog: A1911, #173, $1.50.

———. *Giles Corey, Yeoman; A Play.* Illus. New York: Harper & Brothers, 1893. 108 pp.
  Source: MTLAcc, entry #1201, volume donated by Clemens.

———. *The Givers; Short Stories.* Illus. New York: Harper & Brothers, 1904. 296 pp.
  Source: MTLAcc, entry #1001, volume donated by Clemens.

————. *A Humble Romance, and Other Stories.* New York: Harper & Brothers, 1887. 436 pp.

Inscriptions: front free endpaper signed (crudely) in black ink, "Olivia L. Clemens"; the ink did not adhere to the paper and the signature is barely legible. On the front pastedown endpaper Clemens noted in black ink: "Dec. 4, 1905. She has been in her grave a year & a half to-morrow. She probably made that attempt with that annoying pen eighteen years ago when she was 42 & looked ten years younger. I know she did not lose her temper, but kept it & her sweet dignity unimpaired. If I was present I probably laughed, for we had no cares then—I could easier cry, now. It is many years since I have seen this book. Susy was 15 then; she is gone, these nine years & more. I have just closed my seventieth year." Sticker of Brown & Gross, Hartford booksellers, on rear pastedown endpaper.

Catalog: "Retz Appraisal" (1944), p. 12. Valued at $50.
Location: Mark Twain Papers, Berkeley, Calif.
Copy examined: Livy Clemens' unmarked copy.

————. *Jane Field; A Novel.* Illus. New York: Harper & Brothers, 1905. 267 pp.
Source: MTLAcc, entry #1080, volume donated by Clemens.

————. *The Love of Parson Lord, and Other Stories.* Illus. New York: Harper & Brothers, 1901. 233 pp.
Source: MTLAcc, entry #232, volume donated by Clemens.

————. *Madelon; A Novel.* New York: Harper & Brothers, 1904. 376 pp.
Source: MTLAcc, entry #1079, volume donated by Clemens.

————. *A New England Nun, and Other Stories.* New York: Harper & Brothers, [cop. 1891]. 468 pp.
Source: MTLAcc, entry #1107, volume donated by Clemens.

————. "The Old-Maid Aunt," chapter two of *The Whole Family* (a composite novel by twelve authors), *Harper's Bazar,* 42 (January 1908), 16–26.

Invited to contribute to *The Whole Family,* a novel narrated by a dozen different characters who would be created by twelve eminent authors, Mark Twain read the first two chapters sent by the editor of *Harper's Bazar.* He liked William Dean Howells' depiction of the father ("well done"), but he had reservations about the second chapter, written by Mrs. Freeman. Explaining in an autobiographical dictation of 29 August 1906 why he declined to supply the boy's chapter ("the imagined boy would have to tell his story *himself* and let me act merely as his amanuensis"), Twain commented on Mrs. Freeman's writings without naming her. "A lady followed Howells and furnished the old-maid sister's chapter. This lady is of high literary distinction, she is nobly gifted, she has the ear of the nation and her novels and stories are among the best that the country has produced, but *she* did not tell those tales, she merely held the pen and they told themselves. . . . But [she] wrote the old-maid sister's chapter out of her own head, without any help from the old maid. The result is a failure. It is a piece of pure literary manufacture and has the shopmarks all over it" (*MTE,* p. 244).

Faithful readers of *Harper's Bazar* would not have concurred with Twain's assessment, and even today his appraisal seems to ignore the amusing ironies Mrs. Freeman achieved in taking on the assignment. In her chapter, spinster aunt Elizabeth Talbert returns to visit her brother and his family in Eastridge, where she formerly had several beaus. Her relatives underestimate Aunt Elizabeth's sophistication and attractiveness; they are astonished when Ned Temple's wife storms into their house to complain that Elizabeth took a stroll with her husband, who once courted Elizabeth. " 'If you can't get a husband for yourself,' said she, 'you might at least let other women's husbands alone!' " The aunt calms the irate wife ("I cannot imagine myself making such a spectacle over any mortal man," Elizabeth muses), and assures her of Ned Temple's faithfulness. "It was all highly ridiculous, but it actually ended up in my going into the Temple house and showing Ned's wife how to do up her hair like mine. . . . Then I taught her how to put on her corset and pin her shirt-waist taut in front and her skirt behind. . . . It ended in her fairly purring around me" (pp. 24–25). The Talbert family is flabbergasted by the effects produced by "old" aunt Elizabeth. Ned Temple avers that she "had not changed at all." Twain may have been annoyed by the talky, stilted monologue form.

See also an entry for *The Whole Family* (1908).

————. *Pembroke; A Novel*. Illus. New York: Harper & Brothers, [cop. 1894]. 330 pp.
   Source: MTLAcc, entry #1082, volume donated by Clemens.

————. *Pembroke*. New York: Harper & Brothers, 1903. 330 pp.
   Source: MTLAcc, entry #1670, volume donated by Clemens.

————. *The Portion of Labor*. Illus. New York: Harper & Brothers, 1901. 563 pp.
   Inscription: flyleaf signed "S. L. Clemens/Riverdale, Nov. 1901."
   Catalog: A1911, #485, $2.75.
   Location: collection of Robert Daley, Burbank, Calif. Mr. Daley supplied information for this entry.

————. *The Shoulders of Atlas; A Novel*. New York: Harper & Brothers, 1908. 294 pp.
   Source: MTLAcc, entry #879, volume donated by Mrs. Ralph W. Ashcroft (formerly Isabel Lyon), Clemens' secretary.

————. [Another identical copy.]
   Source: MTLAcc, entry #1003, volume donated by Mrs. Ralph W. Ashcroft (formerly Isabel Lyon), Clemens' secretary.

————. *Six Trees; Short Stories*. Illus. New York: Harper & Brothers, 1903. 207 pp.
   Source: MTLAcc, entry #1002, volume donated by Clemens.

————. *Young Lucretia, and Other Stories*. Illus. New York: Harper & Brothers, 1905. 258 pp.
   Source: MTLAcc, entry #1081, volume donated by Clemens.

French, Alice (1850–1934), pseud. "Octave Thanet." *The Missionary Sheriff; Being Incidents in the Life of a Plain Man Who Tried to Do His Duty*. Illus. by A. B. Frost and Clifford Carleton. New York: Harper & Brothers, 1897. 248 pp.
   Source: MTLAcc, entry #303, volume donated by Clemens.

————. [Another identical copy.]
   Source: MTLAcc, entry #1078, volume donated by Clemens.

Frénilly, Auguste François Fauveau de. *Recollections of Baron de Frénilly, Peer of France (1768–1828)*. Ed. with intro. and notes by Arthur Chuquet. Trans. by Frederic Lees. London: William Heinemann, 1909.
   Catalog: C1951, #16c, listed among books signed by Clemens.

Friendship's Offering; A Christmas, New Year, and Birthday Present. Issued yearly, 15 vols. pub. 1841–1855. Philadelphia: Marshall, Williams and Butler.
   Mark Twain's catalog of books in "The House Beautiful" along the Mississippi before the Civil War includes " 'Friendship's Offering,' and 'Affection's Wreath,'

with their sappy inanities illustrated in die-away mezzotints" (chapter 38, *LonMiss* [1883]). These names neatly combined the actual titles of two gift annuals— *Affection's Gift* (issued 1832, 1838, 1855, and other years by various American publishers) and *Friendship's Offering*, published in 1843–1844 as *Friendship's Offering, and Winter's Wreath*. Whether purposeful or not, this nice stroke of naming illustrates Mark Twain's close familiarity with such parlor-table fixtures in American homes. His main objection to them was his conviction that nobody ever really read through these gift-book concoctions. Among the books stacked on the corners of the Grangerford's parlor table, Huck Finn finds that "another was *Friendship's Offering*, full of beautiful stuff and poetry; but I didn't read the poetry" (chapter 17, *HF* [1885]).

Mark Twain associated the volumes with excessively elegant phrasing as well; he claimed as one of the rules that James Fenimore Cooper habitually violates: "When a personage talks like an illustrated gilt-edged, tree-calf, hand-tooled, seven-dollar Friendship's Offering" at one point, he ought not to "sound like a negro minstrel" farther on ("Fenimore Cooper's Literary Offences" [1895]). As late as 1907 Mark Twain derided Mrs. Eddy's reference to "the heart of a moonbeam" as "a pretty enough Friendship's-Album expression—let it pass, though I do think the figure a little strained" ("Christian Science," Book 2, chapter 2).

Frisbie, Alvah Lillie (1830–1917). *The Siege of Calais and Other Poems*. Des Moines, Iowa: Mills & Co., 1880. 166 pp.
    Source: MTLAcc, entry #625, volume donated by Clemens.

————. *Songs of Sorrow and Miscellaneous Poems*. Des Moines, Iowa: Mills & Co., 1873. 63 pp.
    Source: MTLAcc, entry #638, volume donated by Clemens.

Frith, William Powell (1819–1909). *My Autobiography and Reminiscences*. 2 vols. New York: Harper & Brothers, 1888.
    Source: MTLAcc, entries #1762 and #1763, volumes donated by Clemens.

Froissart, Jean (1338?–1410?). *Chronicles of England, France, Spain, and the Adjoining Countries*. Trans. from French by Thomas Johnes. Illus. New York: Leavitt & Allen, 1853.
    Catalog: A1911, #174, $1.50.
    Mark Twain alluded to "old dead Froissart's poor witticism" in "A Burlesque Autobiography" (DV409, MTP). "Quote Shaks & Froissart," Mark Twain reminded himself in working notes for *P&P* jotted down in 1879 (DV115, MTP).

Froude, James Anthony (1818–1894). *Caesar; A Sketch* (pub. London, 1879).
    Intent upon comparing the dying U. S. Grant with Caesar in June 1885, Clemens wrote "Froude's Caesar" in Notebook 24 (TS p. 26).

————. *History of England from the Fall of Wolsey to the Defeat of the Spanish Armada*. 12 vols. New York: Charles Scribner and Co., 1870.
    Catalog: C1951, #D76, incomplete, 10 vols. only, signed by Clemens.
    Clemens was already making plans in July 1877 to assemble material from his home library to study for writing *The Prince and the Pauper*. On his way home to Hartford from New York City he made a memorandum to "get Froude & notes" (NB 13, *N&J*, 2: 39). In his working notes for *P&P* he referred to "Froude, iv" and also cited incidents in chapters 17 and 18 of vol. 5 (DV115, MTP).

————. *Short Studies on Great Subjects*. New York: Charles Scribner and Co., 1868. 534 pp.

Inscriptions: signed, "Livy L. Langdon, Elmira, N. Y., 1869"; also signed, "S. L. Clemens, Buffalo, 1870."

Marginalia: a few notes, of which one in the chapter on Homer reads: "Let us change the form & say: The repudiation of religion is the beginning of wisdom" *(Hunley 1958)*.

Catalogs: C1951, #63c, $12.50, signed by Clemens; *Hunley 1958,* #50, $27.50.

Howard Baetzhold reports that Mark Twain referred to Froude's collection of essays in a marginal note to his manuscript of *CY* (1889) *(MT&JB,* p. 343 n. 39).

————. *Thomas Carlyle: A History of the First Forty Years of His Life, 1795–1835.* 4 vols. New York: Scribner's, 1882.

Inscriptions: vols. 1 and 2 inscribed by Clemens: "Livy L. Clemens/1882"; vols. 3 and 4 signed "Olivia L. Clemens/1885".

Marginalia: markings on pages 23, 134, 174 of vol. 3.

Catalog: C1951, #D32, $20, listed carelessly as "Thomas Carlyle. 4 vols.," signed by Clemens; *Fleming 1972,* 4 vols.

————. *Thomas Carlyle: A History of His Life in London, 1834–1881.* 2 vols. (pub. London, 1884).

Catalog: C1951, #D12, listed among the books signed by Clemens.

Fuller, Anna (1853–1916). *A Venetian June.* Illus. by George Sloane. New York: G. P. Putnam's Sons, [cop. 1896]. 315 pp.

Source: MTLAcc, entry #129, volume donated by Clemens.

Fuller, Henry Blake (1857–1929). *The Chevalier of Pensieri-Vani* (pub. 1890).

Clemens entered the title, Fuller's name, and the subject "(Italy)" on the rear flyleaf of Notebook 44 in 1901. Fuller's Chevalier, or Cavaliere, as he is called by the narrator, is a bachelor with no permanent home, although he favors Florence. The American viewpoint is represented in Fuller's first novel by a young, bright, prepossessing "barbarian," George W. Occident of Shelby County, who "really had no more business among the monuments that fill the valley of the Po or of the Arno than a deaf man has at a symphony concert, or a paralytic among the diamond-fields of Africa" (chapter 7). In the end Occident returns to America and marries, but the Chevalier remains, "still sufficient unto himself . . . and enamored only of that delightful land" (chapter 13).

Fuller, Horace Williams. *Noted French Trials. Impostors and Adventurers.* Boston: Soule & Bugbee, 1882.

Inscription: "S. L. Clemens/Hartford, June 1882."

Catalogs: A1911, #175, $3; *L1912,* #11, $6.

Location: Franklin Meine's Mark Twain Collection, University of Illinois at Urbana-Champaign.

Copy examined: photocopy of flyleaf inscription.

Soule & Bugbee announced the issue of this book in *Publishers' Weekly* on 10 June 1882; Clemens made a memorandum to look up the volume in his 1882 notebook, although he garbled its publisher and title: "Bugbee & Soule—300 Celebrated Cases. Just published" (Notebook 20, *N&J,* 2: 484). Fuller chronicles the findings of eight court trials—not three hundred, as Clemens had been informed—which resulted from mistaken identification or deliberate imposture. Paraphrasing his judicial sources, Fuller briskly narrates the careers of Collet, Cartouche, Mandrin, and other French scoundrels from four centuries who relied upon multiple disguises. Walter Blair believes that Fuller's account of the brazen claimants to the title of Louis XVII ("The False Dauphins") possibly influenced Mark Twain's depiction of the king in *Huckleberry Finn,* and that Fuller's first chapter, "The False Martin Guerre," was germinal to the Wilks episode *(MT&HF,*

pp. 327–328). In a previous article, "The French Revolution and Huckleberry Finn" (1957), Blair analyzed the possible effects of Fuller's book more extensively, emphasizing Fuller's astonishment at the gullibility encountered by all seven "Dauphins" and discussing the final ludicrous claimant to the French throne, Eleazar the Iroquois.

Fuller's opening sentences in his chapter about the "False Dauphins" undoubtedly impressed Clemens: whenever a great historical figure suddenly vanishes, Fuller observes, "there appear on every side counterparts, sometimes dangerous, but more often ridiculous,—doubles of heroes and of kings, whose grotesque courts are composed of fools, always ready to adore an impostor." The author of *The Prince and the Pauper* and the gestating *Huckleberry Finn* must have concurred with Fuller's opinion that these "celebrated impostors" are "at the same time diverting to the curious and sorrowful to the moralist" *(Noted French Trials,* p. 100).

Fuller, Thomas (1608–1661).
Mollie Fairbanks received a letter from Clemens written on 9 February 1876 which recommended "an old book by Thomas Fuller—I have forgotten its name, but I think Charles Lamb devotes a chapter to it. . . . Just read it—or part of it . . . for the pleasure of searching out what I call 'pemmican sentences.' . . . Old Fuller, who wrote in Charles I's time, boils an elaborate thought down & compresses it into a crisp & meaty sentence. It is a wonderful faculty. When I had the book I purposed searching out & jotting down a lot of these pemmican sentences, . . . but I neglected it, of course" *(MTMF,* pp. 195–196).

Funk, Isaac Kauffman (1839–1912). *The Psychic Riddle.* New York: Funk & Wagnalls, 1907. 243 pp.
Inscription: "With Compliments/to Samuel L. Clemens/Believing him to be one of the men on earth today who dare to look a fact squarely in the face—however unpopular it may be, holding judgment in abeyance until the fact is duly classified and interpreted—understanding that the personal experience of the humblest of men is entitled to the most careful attention, while the ignorance of the ablest is not worth a moment's thought./Author/March 4, 1907."
Location: Mark Twain Library, Redding, Connecticut.
Copy examined: Clemens' unmarked copy.
Clemens was already familiar with Funk's research, for in 1902 or 1903 he wrote Livy a sick-room note about Funk's "furnishing some spiritualism of a most unaccountable & interesting character" (MTP). *The Psychic Riddle* discusses typical psychic phenomena, admits fraud in many cases, neither accepts nor rejects spiritualism as a truth, and urges systematic scientific investigation of psychic phenomena.

Furth, Emanuel (1857–1931). *The Tourist; Outward and Homeward Bound.* Second ed. Illus. by H. Moeller. Philadelphia: Gilliam's Sons Co., 1909. 183 pp.
Source: MTLAcc, entry #1375, volume donated by Clemens.

Fyffe, Charles Alan (1845–1892). *History of Modern Europe.* New York: Holt & Co., 1881.
Edgar Hemminghaus reported seeing Clemens' copy of this edition of Fyffe's book in the Mark Twain Library at Redding ("Mark Twain's German Provenience" [1945], p. 475 n. 109), but Albert E. Stone did not list the volume in his checklist in 1955 and I was unable to locate it when I visited Redding in 1970.

Gagneur, (Mme.) Louise (Mignerot) (d. 1902). *A Nihilist Princess.* Chicago: Jansen, McClurg & Co., 1881. 366 pp.
Source: MTLAcc, entry #2239, volume donated from Clemens' library by Clara Clemens Gabrilowitsch in 1910.

The Galaxy, An Illustrated Magazine of Entertaining Reading.
    Catalog: C1951, #89c, $12.50, listed among volumes signed by Clemens; no volume numbers or dates provided.

Galignani's Messenger (daily English-language periodical, pub. in Paris).
    In an 1878 letter to Sue Crane surviving only as a fragment, Clemens described his daily regime: "After breakfast I lie slippered & comfortable on the sofa, with a pipe, & read the meagre telegrams in the German paper & the general news in Galignani's Messenger" (MTP). During another sojourn on the Continent, Clemens made a memorandum on 26 September 1892: "order Galignani & l'Italy" (NB 32, TS p. 26). In Paris in 1894 Livy Clemens first saw a published report of the bankruptcy of Charles L. Webster & Company in *Galignani's Messenger;* she experienced "heart-sickness" at reading the "squib" containing this "hideous news," she wrote *(MTB,* pp. 986–987).

Galignani's New Paris Guide for 1867.
    Dewey Ganzel found this volume to be Mark Twain's "chief source in rewriting the Paris section of *IA"* *(MTAb,* p. 110; see also p. 117). Ganzel quotes parallel passages from the *Paris Guide* and *IA* (1869) concerning Notre Dame ("Guidebooks," pp. 83–85).

Gallick Reports; or, An Historical Collection of Criminal Cases, Adjudged in the Supreme Courts of Judicature in France. To Which Is Prefixed a Copious Preface in Relation to the Laws and Constitution of France. London: Printed by J. Applebee for J. Hazard, 1737. 306 pp.
    Inscription: signed on inner cover, "S. L. Clemens".
    Catalog: A1911, #176, $3.25.

Gallup, Elizabeth (Wells) (b. 1846). *The Bi-Literal Cypher of Sir Francis Bacon Discovered in His Works.* Detroit, Mich.: Howard Pub. Co., [cop. 1901]. 383 pp.
    Source: MTLAcc, entry #1397, volume donated by Clemens.

————. *The Bi-Literal Cypher of Sir Francis Bacon Discovered in His Works.* Detroit, Mich.: Howard Pub. Co., 1908. 8 pp.
    Source: MTLAcc, entry #1400, volume donated by Clemens.

————. *The Bi-Literal Cypher of Sir Francis Bacon Discovered in His Works.* Detroit, Mich.: Howard Pub. Co., n.d. 229 pp.
    Source: MTLAcc, entry #1399, volume donated by Clemens.

————. *The Bi-Literal Cypher of Sir Francis Bacon Discovered in His Works.* Detroit, Mich.: Howard Publishing Co., n.d. 40 pp.
    Source: MTLAcc, entry #1401, volume donated by Clemens.

————. *The Bi-Literal Cypher of Sir Francis Bacon Discovered in His Works.* Detroit, Mich.: Howard Publishing Co., n.d.
    Source: MTLAcc, entry #1402, volume donated by Clemens.

————. *The Tragedy of Anne Boleyn. A Drama in Cipher Found in the Works of Sir Francis Bacon. Deciphered by Elizabeth Wells Gallup.* Detroit, Mich.: Howard Publishing Co.; London: Gay & Bird, [cop. 1901]. 169 pp.
    Location: Mark Twain Library, Redding, Connecticut. Donated by Clemens (MTLAcc, entry #1398).
    Copy examined: Clemens' unmarked copy.

Galton, Francis (1822–1911). *Finger Prints.* London: Macmillan and Co., 1892. 216 pp.

On 10 November 1892 Clemens wrote to Chatto & Windus from Florence: "The Finger-Prints has just arrived, & I don't know how you could have done me a greater favor. I shall devour it" (Berg). Anne P. Wigger—"The Source of Fingerprint Material" (1957)—demonstrates Mark Twain's reliance upon Galton's book while writing *Pudd'nhead Wilson* in 1892. In a letter to Chatto & Windus on 30 July 1893 he acknowledged that the book which they sent had furnished him with an idea for plot (Wigger, p. 520). A few years later, however, Clemens could not even recall the author's name. He informed an unidentified correspondent on 25 June 1895: "My dim impression is that it was called 'Finger Prints.' . . . Mr. Chatto sent it to me when I was writing Pudd'nhead Wilson; & that accident changed the whole plot & plan of my book" (Humanities Research Center, Univ. of Texas at Austin). On 23 February 1897 he wrote to a Miss Darrall from London: "The finger-mark system of identification. . . . has been quite thoroughly & scientifically examined by Mr. Galt [*sic*], & I kept myself within the bounds of his ascertained facts" (ALS owned by Robert H. Daley, Universal City, California).

Gane, Douglas M. *New South Wales and Victoria in 1885.* London: Sampson Low, Marston, Searle and Rivington, 1886.
Inscription: "To Samuel L. Clemens, Esq., with compliments, from Douglas M. Gane, 24, 2, 99" (*A1911;* year given seems questionable).
Catalog: A1911, #177, $1.
Mark Twain quotes Gane's description of an Australian dust-storm in chapter 9 of *FE* (1897); in chapter 11 he juxtaposes Gane's contradicting accounts of hospitality in Sydney.

Ganz, Hugo (b. 1862). *The Land of Riddles (Russia of To-day).* Trans. from German and ed. by Herman Rosenthal. New York: Harper & Brothers, 1904. 331 pp.
Source: MTLAcc, entry #1718, volume donated by Clemens.

Gardenhire, Samuel Major (1855–1923). *The Long Arm.* Illus. New York: Harper & Brothers, 1906. 344 pp.
Inscription: signed on inner cover, "S. L. Clemens, 1906".
Catalog: A1911, #178, $1.25.

————. *Purple and Homespun; A Novel.* New York: Harper & Brothers, 1908. 371 pp.
Source: MTLAcc, entry #138, volume donated by Clemens.

————. *The Silence of Mrs. Harrold.* New York: Harper & Brothers, [cop. 1905]. 462 pp.
Source: MTLAcc, entry #1092, volume donated Clemens.

Garibaldi, Giuseppe (1807–1882).
Clemens negotiated cautiously for the publishing rights to Garibaldi's autobiography in 1887, but informed Charles L. Webster on 28 May 1887: "Garibaldi is stale enough already; so we shouldn't want to contract for his book for 1892, but for next year—before he gets *too* stale" (*MTBus*, p. 383). Charles L. Webster & Company never published Garibaldi's life.

Garland, Hamlin (1860–1940). *The Captain of the Gray-Horse Troop; A Novel.* New York: Harper & Brothers, 1902. 415 pp.
Inscription: signed on third flyleaf, "S. L. Clemens/1902".
Location: Mark Twain Library, Redding, Connecticut. Donated by Isabel V. Lyon, Clemens' secretary (MTLAcc, entry #1004).
Copy examined: Clemens' unmarked copy.

————. *The Captain of the Gray-Horse Troop.* New York: Harper & Brothers, 1906. 415 pp.
  Source: MTLAcc, entry #1557, volume donated by Clemens.

————. *Diverse Affections.* London: Century Press, 1906. 230 pp.
  Source: MTLAcc, entry #1005, volume donated by Clemens.
This title is not listed in the *National Union Catalog* or other standard bibliographic reference works.

————. *Hesper; A Novel.* New York: Harper & Brothers, 1903. 445 pp.
  Source: MTLAcc, entry #1556, volume donated by Clemens.

————. *The Light of the Star; A Novel.* New York: Harper & Brothers, 1904. 278 pp.
  Source: MTLAcc, entry #2240, volume donated from Clemens' library by Clara Clemens Gabrilowitsch in 1910.
After Clemens' departure from Florence in June 1904 his business agent received a package from French, Lemon & Company that contained this and other "Harpers' books"; the book remained in Florence at least until 4 November 1904 (Sebastiano Cecchi to SLC, 30 July, 4 November 1904, Haskard & Co., Bankers, Florence).

————. *The Moccasin Ranch; A Story of Dakota.* New York: Harper & Brothers, 1909. 137 pp.
  Source: MTLAcc, entry #1426, volume donated by Clemens.

————. *Money Magic; A Novel.* Illus. by J. N. Marchand. New York: Harper & Brothers, 1907. 355 pp.
  Source: MTLAcc, entry #2241, volume donated from Clemens' library by Clara Clemens Gabrilowitsch. in 1910.

————. *The Shadow World.* New York: Harper & Brothers, 1908. 295 pp.
  Source: MTLAcc, entry #1445, volume donated by Clemens.

————. *The Tyranny of the Dark.* New York: Harper & Brothers, 1905. 439 pp.
  Source: MTLAcc, entry #2242, volume donated from Clemens' library by Clara Clemens Gabrilowitsch in 1910.
On 30 June 1905 Clemens wrote to Garland from Dublin, New Hampshire: "I put in yesterday's holiday [from writing] & up to 2 this morning reading your book—criminal dissipations for a laboring man & slow reader, . . . but I was caught with the last third unread, & had to go on to the end, it was so enthralling. I like that book exceedingly" (American Academy of Arts and Letters). Isabel Lyon wrote in her diary on Sunday, 2 July 1905: "Reading Hamlin Garland's 'Tyranny of the Dark'. Mr. Clemens has just finished it. Yesterday he said it was 'good done'" (TS p. 72, MTP). Garland replied to Clemens' letter on 7 July 1905, discussing the treatment of spiritualism in his book (MTP).

————. *The Tyranny of the Dark.* Illus. New York: Harper & Brothers, 1906. 439 pp.
  Source: MTLAcc, entry #1087, volume donated by Clemens.

————. *Ulysses S. Grant, His Life and Character*. New York: Doubleday & McClure Co., 1898. 524 pp.

Inscription: on second flyleaf: "To Samuel M [*sic*] Clemens./Who aided 'The Old Warrior' when he needed it most./From the author/Hamlin Garland/London, June 14, 99".

Location: Clifton Waller Barrett Collection, Alderman Library, University of Virginia, Charlottesville.

Copy examined: Clemens' unmarked copy. Contains bookstamps and accession number of the Mark Twain Library, Redding, Connecticut.

Garner, Richard Lynch (1848–1920). *The Speech of Monkeys*. New York: Charles L. Webster & Co., 1892. 217 pp.

Issued by Clemens' publishing firm.

Garrett, [Fydell] Edmund and E. T. Edwards. *The Story of an African Crisis. Being the Truth About the Jameson Raid and Johannesburg Revolt of 1896, Told with the Assistance of the Leading Actors in the Drama*. Westminister: Archibald Constable & Co., 1897. 308 pp.

Marginalia: Clemens annotated the book rather thoroughly in pencil in the introduction and text up to page 122; he also made notes in ink on pages 104–122. No marks or notes thereafter except for pencil marks in appendices, especially in "The National Union Manifesto," pp. 275, 277, 284. Some of Clemens' notes occur on pp. xxx, xxxi, 4 ("But the preparations for force had all been made," he wrote vertically in margin), 5 ("But the 'populace' wanted to rush out & bring Jim in in triumph," he wrote at the top of the page), 41, 51, 60, 61, 69, 80, 88, 104–105 120; but there are even more notes than these.

Location: Clifton Waller Barrett Collection, University of Virginia, Charlottesville.

Copy examined: Clemens' copy. Contains bookstamps, accession number, and traces of charge-slip jacket of the Mark Twain Library, Redding, Connecticut.

On an undated card sent to Chatto & Windus of London early in 1897, Clemens requested a copy of this book, which he had seen "reviewed this morning" (Berg). He mentions Garrett's *Story of an African Crisis* in chapter 65 of *FE* (1897), characterizing Garrett as "a brilliant writer partial to Rhodes." In chapter 67 he quotes Garrett's analysis of Jameson's comparatively meager forces and those of the Boers, remarking, "Mr. Garrett's account of the Raid is much the best one I have met with, and my impressions of the Raid are drawn from that."

Gaskell, (Mrs.) Elizabeth Cleghorn (Stevenson) (1810–1865). *Cranford*. New York: Harper & Brothers, n.d. 329 pp.

Source: MTLAcc, entry #1845, volume donated from Clemens' library by Clara Clemens Gabrilowitsch in 1910.

In 1893 Clemens suffered the symptoms of a severe cold during a visit to Chicago, and while he was convalescing Eugene Field came to see him. Clemens wrote to Livy on 18 April 1893: "Eugene Field brought me 'Cranford' —I never could read it before; but this time I blasted my determined way through the obstructing granite, slate & clay walls, not giving up till I reached the vein—since then I have been taking out pay ore right along" (*LLMT*, p. 264). Sometime between 1888 and 1904 Clara Clemens listed the titles of Gaskell's *Ruth* (pub. 1853) and *Life of Charlotte Brontë* (pub. 1857) in her commonplace book (Paine 150, MTP).

————. *Cranford*. New York: A. L. Burt, n.d. 278 pp.

Source: MTLAcc, entry #2248, volume donated from Clemens' library by Clara Clemens Gabrilowitsch in 1910.

Gatty, (Mrs.) Margaret (Scott) (1809–1873). *Parables from Nature*. Illus. by Paul
de Longpré. New York: G. P. Putnam's Sons, 1893. 280 pp.
   Source: MTLAcc, entry #544, volume donated by Clemens.

Gaullieur, Henri. *The Paternal State in France and Germany*. New York: Harper
& Brothers, 1898. 225 pp.
   Source: MTLAcc, entry #677, volume donated by Clemens.

Gay, Mary Ann Harris (1827–1918). *Prose and Poetry, by a Georgia Lady*. Nashville, Tenn.: Privately printed, 1858. 199 pp.
   Hamlin Hill, in "The Composition and the Structure of *Tom Sawyer*" (1961),
identifies Gay's book as the one from which Mark Twain extracted two essays
and a poem for graduation elocutions in chapter 21 of *TS* (1876). In a footnote
at the end of the chapter Mark Twain acknowledges that the "compositions"
of Tom's female classmates "are taken without alteration from a volume entitled
'Prose and Poetry, by a Western [*sic*] Lady'—but they are exactly and precisely
after the school-girl pattern, and hence are much happier than any mere
imitations could be." Hill proves that the pieces "were not then, as Dixon
Wecter suggested, Twain's own satiric efforts. On the contrary, the humorist
pasted actual pages torn from Mary Ann Gay's book in his manuscript"
("Composition and Structure," pp. 383–384). In *Mark Twain as Critic* (1967)
Sydney J. Krause examined the style of Gay's volume ("Miltonic ornamentation
in a country version of the prose of sensibility"). According to Kristina Simms,
"Mark Twain and the Lady from Decatur" (1972), eleven editions of Gay's
book were issued between 1858 and 1881.

Geer's Hartford City Directory.
   On 11 October 1880 Clemens purchased "1 City Directory" from Brown &
Gross of Hartford (bill and receipt in MTP). He later bought "1 Copy of Geer's
No. 51, July, 1888, Hartford City Directory, $3.00" (receipt dated 7 September
1888 in MTP).

Geikie, John Cunningham (1824–1906). *Hours with the Bible; or, The Scriptures
in the Light of Modern Discovery and Knowledge*. 6 vols. Illus. New York:
James Pott, 1882–1883.
   Source: MTLAcc, entries #938–#942, volumes 1–5 only, donated by
Clemens.
   On 14 January 1884 Clemens listed his recent reading for Edward H. House;
it included "the third volume of Geike's [*sic*] Hours with the Bible" (CWB).

Gellibrand, Emma. *J. Cole*. New York: Thomas Y. Crowell & Co., [189–?]. 86 pp.
   Source: MTLAcc, entry #871, volume donated by Mrs. Ralph W. Ashcroft
(formerly Isabel Lyon), Clemens' secretary.

Genlis, Comtesse de (*nee* Stéphanie Félicité du Crest de Saint-Aubin) (1746–1830).
   Clemens informed Mollie Fairbanks on 6 August 1877 that he recently read
"a story by Madame de Genlis . . . in French . . . which [failed to] cast much
light upon my subject [the French Revolution] or amounted to much. I would
have done well to stop with Carlyle & Dumas" (*MTMF*, p. 208).

Genung, John Franklin (1850–1919). *The Practical Elements of Rhetoric, with
Illustrative Examples*. Boston: Ginn & Co., 1887. 488 pp.
   Source: MTLAcc, entry #803, volume donated by Clemens.

George, Henry, (1839–1897). *The Condition of Labor. An Open Letter to Pope
Leo XIII*. New York: Charles L. Webster & Co., 1893. 157 pp.
   Issued by Clemens' publishing firm.

————. *The Land Question.* New York: Charles L. Webster & Co., 1893. 157 pp. Issued by Clemens' publishing firm.

————. *A Perplexed Philosopher, Being an Examination of Mr. Herbert Spencer's Various Utterances on the Land Question, with Some Incidental References to His Synthetic Philosophy.* New York: Charles L. Webster & Co., 1892. 319 pp. Issued by Clemens' publishing firm.

————. *Progress and Poverty.* New York: Charles L. Webster & Co., 1892. 512 pp. Issued by Clemens' publishing firm. There appear to be traces of its influence in the essays read at the Mechanics' Debating Club in chapters 10 and 14 of *AC* (1892) and in Lord Berkeley's reflections in chapter 13 and elsewhere in the novel.

————. *Property in Land.* New York: Charles L. Webster & Co., [1892]. Issued by Clemens' publishing firm.

————. *Protection or Free Trade.* New York: Charles L. Webster & Co., 189?. Issued by Clemens' publishing firm, according to *Publishers' Trade List Annual 1893*—but no edition by CLW & Co. is listed in the *National Union Catalog.*

————. *Social Problems.* New York: Charles L. Webster & Co., 1893. 342 pp. Issued by Clemens' publishing firm.

Gerard, Emily (1849–1905). *The Extermination of Love; A Fragmentary Study in Erotics.* Edinburgh: William Blackwood & Sons, 1901. 313 pp.
    Source: MTLAcc, entry #136, volume donated by Clemens.

————. *A Foreigner; An Anglo-German Study.* Edinburgh: William Blackwood & Sons, 1896. 526 pp.
    Inscription: presented by the author to Clara Clemens, Vienna, 28 January 1898.
    Provenance: MTLAcc, entry #2250, volume donated from Clemens' library by Clara Clemens Gabrilowitsch in 1910.
    Catalog: Mott 1952, #56, $8.50.

————. *The Land Beyond the Forest.* Illus. 2 vols. Edinburgh: W. Blackwood & Sons, 1888.
    Inscription: in vol. 1, "To Mark Twain with sincerest regards from a humbler worker on the same field so brilliantly occupied by his 'Tramps' and 'Innocents'. Emily Laszowska-Gerard. Vienna, December 19th, 1897."
    Catalogs: A1911, #180, $1.50, vol. 1 only; *C1951,* #24c, presumably vol. 2, listed among books signed by Clemens.

————. *A Secret Mission, A Novel.* Copyright Edition. Collection of British Authors Series. Leipzig: B. Tauchnitz, 1893. 294 pp.
    Source: MTLAcc, entry #2249, volume donated from Clemens' library by Clara Clemens Gabrilowitsch in 1910.

————. *The Tragedy of a Nose. (A Brief Delirium).* London: Digby, Long & Co., 1898. 194 pp.
    Source: MTLAcc, entry #137, volume donated by Clemens.

————. *The Waters of Hercules.* Edinburgh: William Blackwood & Sons, n.d. 396 pp.
    Source: MTLAcc, entry #2251, volume donated from Clemens' library by Clara Clemens Gabrilowitsch in 1910.

Gerard, John (Jesuit, of Stonyhurst). *What Was the Gunpowder Plot? The Traditional Story Tested by Original Evidence.* London: Osgood & McIlvaine, 1897 [cop. 1896]. 288 pp.

Gerard re-evaluates the evidence against Guy Fawkes (1570–1606), conspirator against James I. Clemens apparently heard about Gerard's controversial book while it was still in press; in London in November 1896 he was aware that "a book is just out by a Cath priest which shows (proves) that history has done some large but awkward & unscientific lying in the G. F. matter" (NB 39, TS p. 20). It may be coincidental that Tom Sawyer mentions Guy Fawkes in "Tom Sawyer's Conspiracy," written 1897–1902 (*HH&T*, p. 173).

Gerrard, Ernest A. *France and the Maid. A Drama in Three Acts.* Limited and numbered edition. Privately printed, 1904.

Inscription: "To Samuel L. Clemens: In admiration of your story woven about 'The Maid,' and with many thanks for happy hours spent on the Mississippi, in the West, and abroad through 'Mark Twain.' Ernest A. Gerrard."

Catalog: A1911, #182, $1.50.

Gettke, Ernst and Georg Engel. *In Purgatory* (play).

Clemens wrote to Henry H. Rogers from Vienna on 15 March 1898: "Meantime I have arranged to translate a couple of plays—a melancholy one ('Bartel Turaser') and a funny one ('In Purgatory')" (*MTHHR,* p. 326).

Gibbon, Edward (1737–1794). *The History of the Decline and Fall of the Roman Empire* (pub. 1776–1788).

In an undated letter possibly written in 1871, Clemens attributes the authorship of *The Decline and Fall* to "the lamented Josephus" (TS in MTP); Clemens again joshed about the book in an undated letter of 1873 or 1874 to Charles Warren Stoddard, facetiously informing Stoddard that he had "tried and rejected" the idea of contributing an essay of this title to an album Stoddard was editing (Huntington Library). He showed renewed interest in the work many years later: when Isabel Lyon entered Clemens' room in his New York City home on 2 January 1906 she found him reading "the first volume of Gibbon's Rome," with "wreaths of smoke" hovering over his head. That night "at dinner he warmed to the subject of Gibbon and his Rome, and Gibbon, the man, whose followings of many creeds made him finally an unbeliever." Clemens then told the story of a "pretty Geneva girl" whom Gibbon spurned, but who later became surprisingly prominent despite his low opinion of her (IVL Journal, TS p. 118, MTP). On 3 November 1909 Clemens told Albert Bigelow Paine: "I have been reading Gibbon's celebrated Fifteenth Chapter . . . and I don't see what Christians found against it. It is so mild—so gentle in its sarcasm" (*MTB,* p. 1535).

Gibbs, George Fort (1870–1942). *The Love of Monsieur; A Novel.* New York: Harper & Brothers, 1903. 297 pp.

Source: MTLAcc, entry #1558, volume donated by Clemens.

Gibson, Eva Katherine (Clapp) (1857–1916). *Zauberlinda, the Wise Witch.* Illus. by Mabel Tibbitts. Chicago: R. Smith Ptg. Co., [cop. 1901]. 256 pp.

Source: MTLAcc, entry #455, volume donated by Clemens.

Gibson, William Hamilton (1850–1896). *Camp Life in the Woods and the Tricks of Trapping.* Illus. by the author. New York: Harper & Brothers, [cop. 1881]. 300 pp.

Source: MTLAcc, entry #792, volume donated by Clemens.

————. *Highways and By-ways; or Saunterings in New England.* Illus. by the author. New York: Harper & Brothers, 1883. 157 pp.
Catalog: A1911, #184, $5.50.
Location: Mark Twain Memorial, Hartford, Conn. Donated in 1976 by Aileen Harlow, according to Mrs. Dexter B. Peck, Library Chairman. Mrs. Peck reports that the book has no inscriptions or marginalia.

————. *Pastoral Days; or, Memories of a New England Year.* Illus. by author. New York: Harper & Brothers, 1881. 153 pp.
Catalog: A1911, #183, $7.25.
The Clemenses ordered two copies of *Pastoral Days* on 20 December 1880, according to a bill they received on 1 January 1881 from Brown & Gross, Hartford booksellers. They paid for the volumes on 17 January 1881 (receipt in MTP).

————. *Pastoral Days; or, Memories of a New England Year.* Illus. by author. New York: Harper & Brothers, 1886. 153 pp.
Catalog: A1911, #185, $2.

————. *Sharp Eyes; A Rambler's Calendar of Fifty-Two Weeks Among Insects, Birds, and Flowers.* Illus. by the author. New York: Harper & Brothers, 1904. 322 pp.
Source: MTLAcc, entry #1180, volume donated by Clemens.

Gibson, Willis. "Arkansas Fashion," *Century Magazine,* 70 (June 1905), 276–292. [Illus. by Walter Jack Duncan.]
Isabel Lyon wrote to Richard Watson Gilder of the *Century* on 1 June 1905 from Dublin, New Hampshire: "Mr. Clemens wishes me to ask you if you will be good enough to send him the address of the author of the delightful story 'Arkansas Fashion,' if you have it" (PH in MTP). Clemens' pleasure in the short story is easily explained: not only does it employ regional dialects and feature a hero from the state of Arkansas, familiar to Clemens from his years as a river pilot, but Gibson repeatedly alludes to the works of Mark Twain in the most flattering manner possible.
The story takes place at Saint's Rest, Minnesota—a railroad depot that gathered no town around it. Humdrum duties at the isolated depot disgust the first telegraph operator, who transfers to Powderly, Iowa. Then Kirby Harbin, a former resident of Arkansas, takes the job at Saint's Rest and is contented. He plays his banjo, smokes a pipe, and savors *Huckleberry Finn.* Harbin's cat—named Tom Sawyer—snoozes complacently in the sun beside him. But the I & I Railroad engineers and workers go on strike and Harbin's tiny station becomes a battleground over a load of refrigerated peaches bound for Chicago. Scab laborers attempt to deliver the peaches; strikers gather at Saint's Rest to stop them. A fight ensues, the strikers win out, and the peaches are temporarily returned north to Selby. Kirby Harbin resumes his pipe, his banjo-playing, and his copy of *Huckleberry Finn.* But the battle over the peaches occurs again at Saint's Rest, with the same results. Once more Kirby Harbin repairs the damage to his depot and takes up his reading. But when yet another set-to shapes up over the peaches, the disgusted Arkansan couples the two opposing trains together and uses one locomotive to move the cause of the argument away from his placid domain. The strikers and scabs join forces in an effort to retake the engine from the angry station agent; Harbin retaliates by opening the throttle fully. He refuses to stop the train until he has delivered the peaches south to Division headquarters, quite a feat for someone who has never himself operated a locomotive, but has only observed the engineers. The taciturn young hero brushes aside the superintendent's thanks and simply asks to borrow a copy of *Huckleberry Finn* until he can return to his haven at Saint's Rest.

Gifford, Evelyn. *Provenzano the Proud*. London: Smith, Elder & Co., 1904. 331 pp.
> *Source:* MTLAcc, entry #2252, volume donated from Clemens' library by Clara Clemens Gabrilowitsch in 1910.

Gifford, Franklin Kent (b. 1861), pseud. "Richard Brinsley Gifford." *The Belle Islers; A Novel*. Illus. by Wallace Goldsmith. Boston: Lothrop, Lee & Shepard Co., 1908. 423 pp.
> *Source:* MTLAcc, entry #868, volume presented by an unknown donor, possibly Clemens.

Gilbert, James Stanley (1855–1906). *Panama Patchwork; Poems, by James Stanley Gilbert*. Intro. by Tracy Robinson. Second ed., rev. and enl. Panama: Star & Herald Co., 1905. 172 pp.
> *Inscriptions:* on flyleaf, " 'Mark Twain'/A reminder of the 'Ends of the Earth', from one of the 'Ends' where he is admired and esteemed by a 'Band of Brothers'./With the lasting regard of/J. S. Gilbert/Colon 1906". On inside front cover is another inscription: "And its me as put Gilbert up to sending this— & its me as put some paper clips to mark some things that did me good & its me that is glad I'm leaving for Home—this 8th of April, 1906/Yours ever/ Poultney Bigelow/Colon".
> *Marginalia:* a clipping inside the volume reports Gilbert's death on 15 August 1906; Clemens wrote on the clipping: "Enclosed by Tracy Robinson". The obituary article is clipped from the Colón, Panama *Independent*, 17 August 1906. Clemens made markings in black ink throughout the poems. On page 128 ("The Prayer of a Timid Man") below the lines "Reply to my unspoken questions—/The questions I dare not repeat!," Clemens wrote: "An old, old prayer—& was never yet answered."
> *Location:* Mark Twain Library, Redding, Connecticut. Donated by Clemens (MTLAcc, entry #1690).
> *Copy examined:* Clemens' copy.

Gilbert, L. Wolfe. "Lily of the valley" (song). Melody composed by Anatole Friedland.
> Clemens listed "Lily of the Valley" among his favorite songs in August 1889 (NB 29, TS p. 21).

Gilbert, William Schwenck (1836–1911). *Iolanthe* (operetta, prod. 1882). Music composed by Arthur S. Sullivan.
> Susy Clemens appeared as Phyllis in the Bryn Mawr production which Livy watched in February 1891, but men were not invited (*S&MT*, p. 286).
> *MT&JB*, p. 127.

———. *The Mikado* (operetta, prod. 1885). Music composed by Arthur S. Sullivan.
> On 18 April 1886 Susy Clemens recorded in her diary that "mama and papa Clara and Daisy [Margaret Warner] have gone to New York to see the 'Mikado' " (quoted in 28 March 1907 AD, MTP). "Mikado Music," Clemens noted in May 1886 (NB 26, TS p. 6). In "The Man That Corrupted Hadleyburg" (1899, Part 3), "Somebody wailed in, and began to sing this rhyme . . . to the lovely 'Mikado' tune of 'When a man's afraid of a beautiful maid'; the audience joined in, with joy"; they sing this "Mikado travesty" repeatedly throughout the town meeting. The lines are actually "When a man's afraid,/A beautiful maid/Is a cheering sight to see."
> *MT&JB*, pp. 228–229.

————. *Patience; or, Bunthorne's Bride*. No. 15 of 100 copies. New York: Doubleday, Page & Company, 1902. 92 pp.

Inscriptions: front pastedown endpaper signed in black ink, "S. L. Clemens/ Dec. 1902." Front free endpaper inscribed: "To Paul and Florence with an awful lot of love—*Cause* I know you will appreciate Gilbert—Mark Twain and ME. D[add?]ly. July 6, 1936."

Catalog: A1911, #186, $3.75.

Location: collection of Kevin Mac Donnell, Austin, Texas. He acquired the volume in October 1977 and sent me a detailed description of his purchase.

Clemens' household had been familiar with this operetta (produced in 1881) for two decades. Young Susy Clemens wrote to her father during his Mississippi River tour in 1882 about her hearing a visitor to the Hartford home play "some pieces from Patience" *(LLMT,* p. 209).

————. *H. M. S. Pinafore* (operetta, prod. 1878). Music composed by Arthur S. Sullivan.

"One day I was there at dinner, and remarked, in a general way, that we are all liars. She was amazed, and said, 'Not *all?*' It was before 'Pinafore's' time, so I did not make the response which would naturally follow in our day, but frankly said, 'Yes, *all*—we are all liars; there are no exceptions" ("On the Decay of the Art of Lying," pub. 1882). Howard G. Baetzhold points out an instance of Mark Twain's borrowing (chapter 8 of *CY* [1889]) from one of Little Buttercup's songs: "Jackdaws strut in peacock's feathers" *(MT&JB,* p. 116).

————. *The Yeoman of the Guard* (operetta, prod. 1888). Music composed by Arthur S. Sullivan.

In 1895 Mark Twain praised Gilbert and Sullivan in a newspaper interview for "saying not only the wittiest of things," but for "saying them in verse." He spoke of the "grinning skull" behind Gilbert's humor, and alluded to the jester in *Yeoman,* Jack Point (Sydney, Australia *Morning Herald,* 17 September 1895; quoted in *MT&JB,* pp. 116, 228, 341 n. 26).

Gilchrist, Alexander (1828–1861). *Life of William Blake, "Pictor Ignotus."* 2 vols. Illus. London: Macmillan and Co., 1863.

In November 1878 Clemens noted, "Wm Blake, poet & painter" (NB 17, *N&J,* 2: 244); a memorandum on the back flyleaf of the same notebook reminds him to "Return . . . 'Life of Blake'" (p. 281).

Gilder, Jeannette Leonard. *The Tomboy at Work.* Illus. by Florence Scovel Shinn. New York: Doubleday, Page & Co., 1904.

Inscription: front pastedown endpaper signed in black ink, "SL. Clemens/ 1908/From the Author."

Location: Antenne-Dorrance Collection, Rice Lake, Wis.

Copy examined: Clemens' unmarked copy.

Gilder, Joseph Benson. "The Parting of the Ways" (poem), *Harper's Weekly,* 44 (17 March 1900), 251.

Quoted by Mark Twain in "The Secret History of Eddypus," written 1901–1902 *(FM,* p. 349).

Gilder, Richard Watson (1844–1909).

In Mark Twain's "King Leopold's Soliloquy" (March 1905) King Leopold remarks that the poet Gilder and his *Century Magazine* led the crusade against the Russian Czar. On 7 December 1905 Isabel Lyon recorded: "This morning Mr. Clemens read me a very great poem by Mr. Gilder in the Times. It is a poem on this terrible massacring of Jews and peasants in Russia. Mr. Clemens said it was difficult to decide—you couldn't decide—if it was satire or not, unless you know your man" (IVL Journal, TS p. 112, MTP).

Giles, Chauncey (1813–1893). *Our Children in the Other Life.* London: James
Speirs, 1874. 75 pp.
   Source: MTLAcc, entry #927, volume donated by Clemens.

Gillespie, G. Curtis, comp. *Rumford Fireplaces and How They Are Made . . .
Containing [Sir Benjamin Thompson Rumford's] . . . Essay on "Proper Fireplace Construction."* Illus. New York: W. T. Comstock, 1906. 199 pp.
   Source: MTLAcc, entry #688, volume donated by Isabel V. Lyon, Clemens'
secretary.

Gillette, William (1855–1937). *The Professor* (play, prod. 1881).
   Gillette wrote and produced this drama, and played the title role of Professor
Hopkins. Since Clemens lent financial backing to its production, he presumably
saw it or at least read it. On 17 June 1876 he wrote to Susie and Lilly Warner
that "it surely ought to succeed" in Madison Square Garden (MTP); he
mentioned the play in Notebook 24 (1885), TS p. 7; and Gillette wrote him
about it on 29 July 1886 (MTP).

————. *Secret Service* (play, prod. 1895).
   In June or July 1897 Cleméns asked Dr. James Ross Clemens to join him
"and help me see Gillette's play, *Secret Service,*" which had begun a run at the
Adelphi Theatre in London on 15 May 1897 (*MTLW,* p. 81); James Ross
Clemens would mistakenly recall their attending this performance at the Strand
Theatre, but he adds the interesting detail that the two men sat in a stage box
as guests ("Reminiscences of MT" [1929]). In the top margin of a manuscript
page of the unfinished novel "Simon Wheeler, Detective" (written 1877–1898?)
Mark Twain noted "Gillette's S S speech," probably referring to Gillette's role
as Captain Thorne (*S&B,* pp. 310–311, 424 n. 47). Gillette was second on Mark
Twain's list of ten nominees for election into the American Academy of Arts
and Letters in 1905 (SLC to Robert Underwood Johnson, 28 April 1905,
American Academy of Arts and Letters).

Gilliam, E. W. "Chinese Immigration," *North American Review,* 143 (July 1886),
26–34.
   "I've read that fellow's article in the North American. With what delicious
unconsciousness he gives himself away in his last sentence" concerning racial
stereotypes of superiority (SLC to WDH, Elmira, 15 July 1886, *MTHL,* p. 572).

Gilliat, Edward (1841–1915). *Forest Outlaws; or, Saint Hugh and the King.* Illus.
New York: G. P. Putnam's Sons, 1887. 404 pp.
   Inscription: second flyleaf inscribed "Clara Clemens/with love of/Chas.
Dudley Warner/Dec. 25, 1886".
   Location: Mark Twain Library, Redding, Conn. Donated from Clemens'
library by Clara Clemens Gabrilowitsch in 1910 (MTLAcc, entry #2253).
   Copy examined: Clara Clemens' unmarked copy.

Gillmore, Inez (Haynes). "The Story That Took," *McClure's Magazine,* 25 (June
1905), 214–224.
   On 3 June 1905 Mrs. Gillmore wrote to Clemens from Scituate, Massachusetts: "Mr. S. S. McClure has just sent me a letter quoting the charming and
exciting and unforgettable thing that you wrote him about one of my first
attempts at fiction, 'The Story That Took' in the June McClure. . . . I am still
young enough not to be able to sleep through most of the night that followed
that event" (MTP).

[Gilman, (Mrs.) Stella (Scott) (b. 1844).] *Mothers in Council*. New York: Harper & Brothers, 1884. 194 pp.
 Source: MTLAcc, entry #395, volume donated by Clemens.

Gilmore, Patrick Sarsfield (1829–1892), pseud. "Louis Lambert." "When Johnny comes marching home" (song, 1863).
 In "Answers to Correspondents" (June 1865) Mark Twain recommends poetry that is "spirited—something like 'Johnny Comes Marching Home' "; in " 'Mark Twain' on the Ballad Infliction," however, he complained that "a year ago. . . . that song was sung by everybody, in every key, in every locality, at all hours of the day and night, always out of tune" (San Francisco *Californian,* 4 November 1865; *MTWY,* p. 194). The pianist in "The Scriptural Panoramist" (November 1865) strikes up, "Oh, we'll all get blind drunk/When Johnny comes marching home!" Mark Twain mentioned "When Johnny Comes Marching Home" as part of "the popular-song nuisance" (Sacramento *Weekly Union,* 28 April 1866; *LSI,* p. 51). On 1 January 1867 he grumbled about the ship choir's singing these "wretchedest old songs" while afloat among scenic splendors (*MTTMB,* p. 59). In Mark Twain's lamented Whittier Birthday Dinner speech on 17 December 1877, the three literary impostors compelled the narrator to sing this song repeatedly—"till I dropped" (*MTB,* p. 1646). The residents of Hope Canyon sing "When Johnny Comes Marching Home" in chapter 5 of "A Double-Barrelled Detective Story" (1902), and Mark Twain alludes to "that rollicking frenzy of a tune" in chapter 13 of "A Horse's Tale" (1906).

Gilson, Roy Rolfe (b. 1875). *In the Morning Glow; Short Stories*. Illus. New York: Harper & Brothers, 1904. 187 pp.
 Source: MTLAcc, entry #1496, volume donated by Clemens.

————. *Miss Primrose. A Novel*. New York: Harper & Brothers, 1906. 295 pp.
 Source: MTLAcc, entry #142, volume donated by Clemens.

————. *When Love Is Young. A Novel*. New York: Harper & Brothers, 1901. 283 pp.
 Source: MTLAcc, entry #141, volume donated by Clemens.

Gindely, Anton (1829–1892). *Geschichte des dreissigjährigen Krieges*. 4 vols. Prag, 1869–1880. [*History of the Thirty Years' War*.]
 When Clemens listed his current reading to Edward H. House on 14 January 1884, he included "in German . . . the third volume of The Thirty-Years' War" (CWB). Shortly thereafter the work became available in translation: *History of the Thirty Years' War*. Trans. by A. Ten Broek. 2 vols. (New York: G. P. Putnam's Sons, 1884).

Girardin, Delphine (Gay) de (1804–1855), pseud. "Mme. Émile de Girardin." *La joie fait pèur; comédie en un acte, par Mme. Émile de Girardin*. English notes by Ferdinand Bôcher. College Series of Modern French Plays, No. 1. New York: Leypoldt & Holt, 1870. 46 pp.
 Inscription: signed on second flyleaf, "Livy L Clemens/1873".
 Location: Mark Twain Library, Redding, Connecticut.
 Copy examined: Livy Clemens' unmarked copy.
 Clara Clemens listed this author and title in her commonplace book sometime between 1888 and 1904 (Paine 150, MTP).

Girdlestone, Arthur Gilbert. *The High Alps Without Guides: Being a Narrative of Adventures in Switzerland*. London: Longmans, Green & Co., 1870.

On 28 August 1878 Clemens noted the title of Girdlestone's book and reminded himself to acquire a copy; he had just seen Girdlestone himself ("a long, wiry, whiskered man"), who was "starting up some new break-neck place with a friend" (NB 16, *N&J*, 2: 164–165). While Clemens was working on the Swiss Alps section of *A Tramp Abroad* on 25 April 1879, he wrote to remind Andrew Chatto that he was awaiting his copy of Girdlestone's *High Alps* (TS in MTP). In chapter 36 of *TA* (1880) he referred to Girdlestone as "the famous Englishman who hunts his way to the most formidable Alpine summits without a guide."

Gizen-no-Teki. *Colorphobia. An Exposure of the "White Australia" Fallacy*. Sydney: R. T. Kelley, 1903. 236 pp.
    Inscription: on verso of first flyleaf: "To Samuel L. Clemens (Mark Twain)/ with compliments/of/"Gizen no Teki"/E. W. Foxall/Sydney/Australia/14 July 1903."
    Location: Mark Twain Library, Redding, Connecticut.
    Copy examined: Clemens' unmarked copy.

Glasgow, Ellen Anderson Gholson (1873–1945). *The Ancient Law*. New York: Doubleday, Page & Co., 1908. 485 pp.
    Source: MTLAcc, entry #1006, volume donated by Clemens.

————. *The Voice of the People*. New York: Doubleday, Page & Co., 1900. 444 pp.
    Source: MTLAcc, entry #2254, volume donated from Clemens' library by Clara Clemens Gabrilowitsch in 1910.

Glyn, Elinor (Sutherland) (1864–1943). *Three Weeks* (pub. 1907).
    Glyn visited Clemens at the end of 1907 in the hope of gaining a prominent champion for her recently published novel. In his Autobiographical Dictation of 13 January 1908 Clemens gave a lengthy account of their interview and a synopsis of her novel, conceded that "its literary workmanship was excellent," but explained why he disappointed her by refusing to defend her views publicly. Although his notions about the innate laws of Nature accorded with hers, and he spoke to her "with daring frankness" about adultery ("one of the damnedest conversations I have ever had with a beautiful stranger of her sex"), nevertheless "her book was an assault upon certain old and well-established and wise conventions, and . . . it would not find many friends, and indeed would not deserve many" (*MTE*, pp. 314–316). Elinor Glyn gives her account of this interview in *Romantic Adventure* (1936), p. 144.

"Go, chain the lion down" (Negro spiritual).
    Clemens included this spiritual in a list of what appear to be his favorite songs in August 1889 (NB 29, TS p. 21). Clara Clemens recalled it as one of the songs her father frequently "rendered in a truly impressive way, despite the fact that musically certain lacks were noticeable" (*MFMT*, p. 188). "Go, chain the lion down" was published by J. B. T. Marsh in *The Story of the Jubilee Singers; with Their Songs*. Rev. ed. (Boston: Houghton, Mifflin and Co., 1880), p. 174. Its first stanza repeats the title three times and ends, "Before the heav'n doors close."

[Goddard, (Mrs.) Martha (Le Baron) (1829–1888) and Harriet Waters Preston (1843–1911), comps.] *Sea and Shore: A Collection of Poems*. Boston: Roberts Brothers, 1874. [Published anonymously.]
    Inscription: on verso of front flyleaf, "With the regards of/M. LeB. Goddard". Clemens wrote on title page: "SL. Clemens/from/Thomas Bailey Aldrich./Oct. 31, 1905."

Marginalia: the name "Kingsley" [?] appears on page 77, not in Clemens' hand. There are pencil marks in the index of first lines at the back of the book.
Location: Antenne-Dorrance Collection, Rice Lake, Wis.
Copy examined: Clemens' copy.

The poems in *Sea and Shore* all have the sea or sailing as their theme; the poets range from Homer, Pindar, and Euripides to Longfellow, Bayard Taylor, and Elizabeth Stuart Phelps.

Godey's Lady's Book (monthly periodical, Philadelphia, pub. 1830–1898).

Clemens browsed through the February 1834 issue while he lodged in a boarding house in Hamilton, Bermuda with Joseph H. Twichell in May 1877 (NB 13, *N&J,* 2: 21). "The House Beautiful" in chapter 38 of *Life on the Mississippi* (1883) contains the "current number of the chaste and innocuous 'Godey's Lady's Book,' with painted fashion-plate of wax-figure women with mouths all alike—lips and eyelids the same size—each five-foot woman with a two-inch wedge sticking from under her dress and letting-on to be half of her foot." The narrator of "Which Was the Dream?" (written 1897), imaginatively reliving his life, awakens in the 1850's in a California mining cabin whose walls were graced by "a number of steel engravings from Godey's Lady's Book" (*WWD?,* p. 68).

"God save the King" (British national anthem, sometimes attributed to Henry Carey, [d. 1743]).

Clemens noted in Victoria, British Columbia that when nobility entered the hall, "several bars of God Save the Queen played" (NB 35 [August 1895], TS pp. 31–32). Clemens was present in 1907 when Senator Clark of Montana "rose to the tune of . . . 'God Save the King,' frantically sawed and thumped by the fiddlers and the piano" during speeches at the Union League Club (28 January 1907 AD, *MTE,* p. 76).

Goethe, Johann Wolfgang von (1749–1832). "Der Erlkönig" (poem, ballad).

Clemens quoted from the poem while he was in Munich in December 1878 (NB 17, *N&J,* 2: 255).

———. *Faust.* Paris: A. Quantin & Cie., 1869. 60 pp. Paperbound.
Source: MTLAcc, entry #390, volume donated by Clemens.

———. *Faust; A Tragedy.* Trans. by Thomas James Arnold [1804–1877]. Illus. by Alexander Liezen Mayer [1839–1898] with ornaments by Rudolf Seitz. Munich: T. Stroefer, 1877.
Catalog: A1911, #191, $3.50.

At the end of December 1878 Clemens wrote from Munich to his mother-in-law: "I want to thank you very sincerely for the magnificent 'Faust' which you sent me Xmas. It is of an edition which has made the most of a stir of any that has ever appeared except for the one with Kaulbach's illustrations. The man who drew the fine pictures for this book . . . is an Austrian with an American wife, & lives in Munich. . . . There are two or three pictures of Margaret in this new Faust which beat Kaulbach to pieces" (MTM). Very likely Livy Clemens purchased the volume in Munich at Mrs. Langdon's behest: Livy's account book for 1878 contains an entry for " 'Faust' illustrated for Mr Clemens" under the heading of "Mother's account" (MTP).

———. *Faust. A Tragedy.* Trans. by Bayard Taylor. 2 vols. Boston: Riverside Press, 1879.
Catalog: A1911, #190, $2.75.

The fact that Taylor received only a pittance for his translation never ceased to amaze Clemens. "Bayard Taylor's noble translation of Faust filled the English-speaking world with his fame," Clemens reminded Mrs. Fairbanks on

31 October 1877, "but he told me his copyright has only yielded him five dollars thus far" *(MTMF,* p. 211). Taylor was Clemens' fellow passenger in 1878 on the *Holsatia* enroute to Germany, where Taylor was to begin his duties as the United States ambassador; Clemens later told Henry W. Fisher that he heard Taylor "recite whole acts of his metric translation of Faust" on the ship *(AMT,* p. 139). After Taylor's sudden death, Clemens recalled ruefully in Munich in January 1879 that despite the popularity of his *Faust* Taylor earned only "$5 for 2 yrs work" on the project (NB 17, *N&J,* 2: 268).

On 20 March 1884 Clemens wrote to his business agent in New York City, Charles L. Webster: "I wish you would buy & send to me an *unbound* copy of Bayard Taylor's translation of Goethe's 'Faust.' I mean to divide it up into 100-page parts and bind each part in a flexible cover—to read in bed" *(MTBus,* p. 242). Accordingly, the statement of Clemens' personal expenses that he received from Webster on 2 September 1884 charged him for the purchase on 10 April 1884 of "1 Taylor's Faust" for $5.80 (MTP). In September 1887 Clemens noted that Taylor's "royalties in Goethe's Faust were $1,000" (NB 27, TS p. 16). Toward the end of his life Clemens referred to Taylor as the poet who "made the best of all English translations of Goethe's 'Faust' " (7 July 1908 AD, MTP).

Yet Clemens' references to *Faust* were relatively infrequent. He mentioned the work in July 1897 (NB 42, TS p. 22), and made up a comic English slang translation of a few lines from *Faust* for the amusement of Henry W. Fisher in Vienna *(AMT,* p. 192). In Mark Twain's "Conversations with Satan," written in Vienna in 1898, the devil has the features of "Don Quixotte," Richelieu, or Sir Henry Irving playing Mephistopheles (Paine 155, MTP). In "Which Was It?" (written 1899–1903) Mark Twain describes Deathshead Phillips as "clothed from skull-cap to stockings in dead and lustreless black. . . . The cut of the raiment was not modern, but ancient and mephistophelian" *(WWD?,* p. 268). Goethe is mentioned in "The Secret History of Eddypus" (written 1901–1902) as one of the "extraordinary men" of the nineteenth century *(FM,* p. 357). In 1904 Mark Twain constructed a spoof of *Faust,* "Sold to Satan," in which the soul-seller is surprised that Satan arrives noiselessly without any thunderclap or stench of brimstone—though he is wearing "the well-known and high-bred Mephistophelian smile." The narrator takes it for granted that Goethe ended up in Satan's province, and offers Satan some cigars to take back to the creator of *Faust.*

Frederick A. G. Cowper, "The Hermit Story" (1928), p. 336; Coleman O. Parsons, "Background," p. 62; William M. Gibson, *MSM,* p. 2 n. 4, 17.

————. [*Faust.*] *Illustrations to Goethe's Faust; Twenty-six Etchings by Moritz Retzsch [1779–1857], with Illustrative Selections from the Text of Bayard Taylor's Translation.* Boston: Estes and Lauriat, 1877.
Inscription: inscribed as a gift to Clemens from his daughters.
Catalog: A1911, #161, $7.

————. *Gedichte.* Halle a. d. S.: Otto Hendel, 1888. 375 pp.
Edgar Hemminghaus reported seeing Clemens' copy of this volume in the Mark Twain Library at Redding in 1945, but neither Albert E. Stone (in 1955) nor I (in 1970) was able to relocate it there ("Mark Twain's German Provenience," p. 471).

————. *Aus meinem Leben: Dichtung, und Wahrheit.* Illus. 2 vols. Berlin, 1873.
Catalog: A1911, #188, $4.

————. *Reineke Fuchs.* Illus. by Wilhelm von Kaulbach [1805–1874].

Clemens wrote to Mrs. Jervis Langdon from Munich at the end of December 1878: "Take it by & large, it was a very happy & abundant sort of Christmas which we had here. Livy gave me a noble great copy of the 'Reinicke Fuchs' [*sic*], nearly as big as the Faust [the illustrated *Faust* that Mrs. Langdon had given him], & containing the original Kaulbach illustrations" (MTM). Livy Clemens had written "Kaulbach's illustrations of Reynard the Fox" in her personal notebook for 1878; later in Munich she recorded an expense of $12.50 for the volume (NB 13a, MTP).

————. "Über allen Gipfeln ist Ruh' " (poem).

Edgar Hemminghaus identifies this as the poem which Mark Twain quotes in "Marienbad" (1891). Twain explains that the passage he quotes impresses him with Goethe's idea of *Waldeinsamkeit* ("Mark Twain's German Provenience," p. 471).

————. *Werke.* 4 vols. Stuttgart, 1887.
Catalog: A1911, #189, $2.75.

Goff, George Paul. *Nick Baba's Last Drink, and Other Sketches.* Illus. Lancaster, Pennsylvania: Enquirer Printing and Pub. Co., 1879. 84 pp.
Source: MTLAcc, entry #143, volume donated by Clemens.

Goldsmith, Jay C. (pseud. "The P. I. Man").

Mark Twain included "Herald P. I. man" in his list of American humorists compiled in 1881 (NB 19, *N&J,* 2: 429).

Goldsmith, Oliver (1728–1774). *The Citizen of the World* (pub. 1762).

Clemens wrote to Orion from St. Louis on 18 March 1860 to commend the "quiet style" of a portion of Orion's recent letter; the passage, he stated, "resembles Goldsmith's 'Citizen of the World' and 'Don Quixote,'—which are my *beau ideals* of fine writing" (*MTL,* p. 45). Possibly Clemens absorbed this opinion from a senior river pilot with whom he sometimes served, George Ealer. In chapter 19 of *Life on the Mississippi* (1883) he recalled of his piloting days that "while we lay at landings I listened to George Ealer's flute, or to his readings from his two Bibles—that is to say, Goldsmith and Shakespeare." Mark Twain imitated Goldsmith's "Chinese Letters" with a series of his own, "Goldsmith's Friend Abroad Again" (October 1870–January 1871), purportedly written by a Chinese immigrant to California named Ah Song Hi who describes his mistreatment in America.

MTG, pp. 113–114; *MTC,* pp. 118–120; Edward H. Weatherly, "Beau Tibbs and Colonel Sellers" (1968), 310–313; *MT&JB,* pp. 271–272.

————. *The Deserted Village.* Illus.

Catalog: C1951, #026, listed among books containing Livy Clemens' signature.

Clemens noted "Deserted Villages" among a series of observations and ideas about Hawaii in 1866 (NB 6, *N&J,* 1: 215). In "To Raise Poultry" (1870) he claimed to be such an unusual poultry-raiser that "old roosters that came to crow, 'remained to pray,' when I passed by"—a play on line 180 of Goldsmith's poem, which describes the Auburn pastor's powers of persuasion as so great that "fools who came to scoff, remained to pray." In chapter 36 of *FE* (1897) Mark Twain likens Goldsmith's "deathless story" to Julia A. Moore's *The Sentimental Song Book.*

————. *The Good-Natured Man* (play).

Catalog: C1951, #J34, listed among the books belonging to Jean and Clara Clemens.

———— and Richard Brinsley Sheridan. *Dramatic Works of Sheridan and Goldsmith. With Goldsmith's Poems.* [See Sheridan entry.]

————. *She Stoops to Conquer* (play).
    Catalog: C1951, #J16, listed among the books belonging to Jean and Clara Clemens.
    Clemens noted the title on 10 April 1900 (NB 43, TS p. 7); conceivably he saw a performance of it around that time in London.

————. *The Vicar of Wakefield, A Tale.* New York: John W. Lovell Co., 1882. 156 pp.
    Source: MTLAcc, entry #2255, volume donated from Clemens' library by Clara Clemens Gabrilowitsch in 1910.
    Clemens' contemptuous opinions of *The Vicar* are well known. William Dean Howells recalled that "there were certain authors whose names he seemed not so much to pronounce as to spew out of his mouth. Goldsmith was one of these" *(MMT,* p. 15). This must have been a fairly late critical heresy, however, for Jervis Langdon testified that *The Vicar of Wakefield* was one of Clemens' favorite sources of pictures with which he amused the children at Quarry Farm in 1883. "Fancy the possibilities lying in scenes devised by sedate old Goldsmith and interpreted to small children by Mark Twain's fantasy," wrote Langdon *(Some Reminiscences,* pp. 15–16). Clemens listed Goldsmith's novel among the sources he wished to quote for his proposed appendix to *A Connecticut Yankee* (Howard G. Baetzhold, "Course of Composition," p. 200).
    Sometime between February and June in 1894 Clemens registered the first inkling of profound hostility toward the work: "Now that our second-hand opinions, inherited from our fathers, are fading," he wrote, "perhaps it may be forgivable to write a really honest review of the Vicar of Wakefield & try to find out what our fathers found in it to admire, & what not to scoff at" (NB 33, TS p. 61). In December 1895 (aboard the *Mararoa*) Clemens noted: "In past year have read Vicar of Wakefield & some of Jane Austin [*sic*]. Thoroughly artificial" (NB 36, TS p. 3). On 8 January 1896, having boarded a ship with a superb library, he resolved: "I must read that devilish Vicar of Wakefield again. Also Jane Austin [*sic*]" (NB 37, TS p. 3). His forthcoming *Following the Equator* (1897) provided Clemens the opportunity to vent his disgruntlement with prevailing critical estimates of *The Vicar.* In chapter 36 of *FE* he compares it to Julia A. Moore's *The Sentimental Song Book:* "I find in it the same subtle touch —the touch that makes an intentionally humorous episode pathetic and an intentionally pathetic one funny." He heaps additional insults on the novel in chapter 62: "To be fair, there is another word of praise due to this ship's library: it contains no copy of the Vicar of Wakefield, that strange menagerie of complacent hypocrites and idiots, of theatrical cheap-john heroes and heroines, who are always showing off, of bad people who are not interesting, and good people who are fatiguing. A singular book. Not a sincere line in it, and not a character that invites respect; a book which is one long waste-pipe discharge of goody-goody puerilities and dreary moralities; a book which is full of pathos which revolts, and humor which grieves the heart. There are few things in literature that are more piteous, more pathetic, than the celebrated 'humorous' incident of Moses and the spectacles." He purports to be quoting from an entry he made in his diary on 10 April [1896], but no such comment appears in his surviving notebooks.
    MT&HF, pp. 330–331; *MTC,* pp. 109, 120–127, 297.

Goldthwaite, Vere. *The Philosophy of Ingersoll*. San Francisco: Paul Elder & Co., n.d. [cop. 1906].
   Inscription: "To Mark Twain,/with special reference to the following lines, 'I believe in the medicine of mirth and in what I might call the longevity of laughter. Every man who has caused real, true, honest mirth, has been a benefactor of the human race'/and with the kind regards of/Vere Goldthwaite/Dec. 1906."
   Location: Mark Twain Library, Redding, Connecticut.
   Copy examined: Clemens' unmarked copy.

Gomez, Madeleine Angèlique (Poisson) de (1684–1770). *La Belle Assemblée: Being a Curious Collection of Some Very Remarkable Incidents Which Happened to Persons of the First Quality in France*. [Trans. by (Mrs.) Eliza Haywood.] 4 vols. London, 1754.
   Catalog: A1911, #192, vols. 2–4 only.

Goodale, (Mrs.) Frances Abigail (Rockwell), ed. *The Literature of Philanthropy*. New York: Harper & Brothers, 1893. 210 pp.
   Source: MTLAcc, entry #1342, volume donated by Clemens.

Good Literature (New York periodical).
   Clemens wrote to Joseph G. Hickman of Florida, Missouri on 24 July 1881 about this "weekly journal published in New York City at 50 cts. per year, devoted to advertising some astonishingly cheap books. . . . The books are worth much more than the price asked for them" (Monroe [County, Missouri] *Appeal*, 12 August 1881).

Goodman, Joseph T. (1838–1917). *The Archaic Maya Inscriptions*. London, 1902.
   Clemens' friend from the Virginia City *Territorial Enterprise* later operated a grape ranch in California, but Clemens always considered Goodman one of the mute inglorious Miltons such as Captain Stormfield would see recognized with acclaim in heaven. In a letter written to Livy Langdon on 10 January 1870 Clemens lamented that "a born poet" like Goodman had been unfortunate in his choice of a wife: "he *could* have been so honored of men, & so loved by all for whom poetry has a charm, but for the dead weight & clog upon his winged genius of a wife whose soul could have no companionship save with the things of the dull earth" (MTP).
   Consequently he was delighted to receive a letter from Goodman many years later, written on 24 May 1902 from Alameda, California, promising to send "as a curiosity" a copy of his forthcoming book—a translation of "the inscriptions on the ruins of Central America and Yucatan" to be issued in London. "There is no hope of profit in it," Goodman added. "Not a thousand persons care anything about the study. The only compensation is that I found out what nobody else could, and that my name will always be associated with the unraveling of the Maya glyphs, as Champollion's is with the Egyptian. But that is poor pay for what will be twenty years' hard work" (MTP). After Clemens got the copy he wrote on 13 June 1902 from Riverdale: "Yesterday I read as much as half of the book, not understanding a word but enchanted nevertheless—partly by the wonder of it all, the study, the erudition, the incredible labor, the modesty . . . and partly by the grace and beauty and limpidity of the book's unsurpassable English" (*MTL*, p. 721). In the first Autobiographical Dictation that commenced Clemens' long series in 1906, he praised Goodman's "most unpromising and difficult study" that had produced "a great <big> book" and had established Goodman's status as an expert among European scholars (9 January 1906 AD, MTP).

Goodrich, C. F. *Report of the British Naval and Military Operations in Egypt, 1882*. Maps and illus. Washington, D. C. 1885.
   Catalog: A1911, #193, $1.25.

Goodrich, S. G. *History of All Nations from the Earliest Periods to the Present Time*. Rev. edition. Illus. 2 vols. New York: Miller, Orton & Co., 1857.
  Inscriptions: presented to Clemens' brother Orion by William Stotts. Book-plates of Orion Clemens pasted in.
  Source: card catalog of Mark Twain Library, Redding, Conn. The volumes were missing in 1979.

Gordon, Adam Lindsay (1833–1870). *Poems*. [Preface by Marcus Clarke.] Melbourne, Australia: A. H. Massina & Co., 1894. 354 pp.
  Source: MTLAcc, entry #2031, volume donated from Clemens' library by Clara Clemens Gabrilowitsch in 1910.
  Mark Twain quoted Marcus Clarke's introduction to this volume at considerable length in chapter 9 of the manuscript for *Following the Equator*, but he deleted this portion before publishing the book in 1897 (Francis Madigan, "MT's Passage to India," pp. 351–353, 358). The final version of *FE* did include Gordon among the Australian authors listed approvingly in chapter 22.

————. *Poems*. Preface by Marcus Clarke. London: S. Mullen, n.d. 325 pp.
  Source: MTLAcc, entry #2030, volume donated from Clemens' library by Clara Clemens Gabrilowitsch in 1910.

Gordon, (Gen.) George Henry (1823–1886). *A War Diary of Events in the War of the Great Rebellion, 1863–1865*. Boston: J. R. Osgood and Co., 1882.
  "War Diary of Gen. Geo. H. Gordon," Clemens wrote down in April 1882 before he left for New Orleans and the Mississippi River (NB 20). He had seen Osgood recently in Boston, so Osgood may have told him about this book, which recounts Gordon's part in Union military operations in Virginia, South Carolina, Florida, and (pp. 306–331) along the Mississippi River. Gordon's narrative emphasizes the open corruption and collusion with the enemy that he saw practiced by Federal ship officers and their crews, particularly with regard to lucrative cotton shipments.

Gordon-Cumming, Constance Frederica (1837–1924). *In the Himalayas and on the Indian Plains*. Illus. London: Chatto & Windus, 1886.
  Inscription: signed on half-title page, "S. L. Clemens, Bombay, 1896."
  Marginalia: contains "hundreds" of notes, corrections, and markings in Clemens' hand, according to *A1911*. One note reads: "We must take the position that burial is stuck to merely in the interest of the undertaker (who has his family cremated to save expense)." Sections of several pages have been cut out.
  Catalog: A1911, #115, $35.
  In chapter 49 of *Following the Equator* (1897) Mark Twain states that the Indian native in a loincloth "answers properly to Miss Gordon Cumming's flash-light picture of him—as a person who is dressed in 'a turban and a pocket handkerchief' "; he repeats her remark—"turban and pocket-handkerchief"—in chapter 50 also. Subsequently he uses her statistics (*Himalayas*, chapter 3, p. 63) to document the number of people killed by dangerous wild animals in India (*FE*, chapter 57).
  Madigan, "MT's Passage to India," p. 358.

Gordon-Cumming, Roualeyn George (1820–1866). *The Lion Hunter in South Africa: Five Years of a Hunter's Life . . . with Anecdotes of the Chase and Notices of the Native Tribes*. 2 vols. London, 1850. [Title varies in later editions.]
  In a footnote to chapter 47 of *FE* Mark Twain quotes Gordon-Cumming's account of his deliberate cruelty to an elephant he had wounded; after leisurely brewing himself some coffee, he experimented with the elephant's vulnerability to bullets by firing his rifles at various parts of its body, during all of which the animal cried tears of pain and explored the wounds with the tip of its trunk. The worst of the Indian Thuggee chieftains, comments Mark Twain, was only "the

Gordon Cumming of his day." Twain's excerpt is enclosed within quotation marks but varies considerably from the version that appears in *The Lion Hunter* (London: John Murray, 1855), 2:8–10 (chapter 17); though Mark Twain added no details to make the episode appear more heartless (which could hardly have been possible, anyway), he compressed the account.

Madigan, "MT's Passage to India," pp. 358–359.

Gorky, Maxim (1868–1936). *Orlóff and His Wife. Tales of the Barefoot Brigade.* Trans. by Isabel F. Hapgood. New York: Charles Scribner's Sons, 1905.

Inscription: signed inside front cover in black ink, "SL. Clemens/1906".

Location: Antenne-Dorrance Collection, Rice Lake, Wis.

Copy examined: Clemens' unmarked copy.

On 26 August 1906 Isabel Lyon recorded the fact that Clemens defended to Jane Addams his action in dropping his sponsorship of Gorky's visit to the United States after Gorky's marital impropriety came to light (IVL Journals, TS p. 182, MTP).

Gorst, Harold Edward (1868–1950). *The Philosophy of Making Love.* London: Cassell & Co., 1908. 180 pp.

Source: MTLAcc, entry #1467, volume donated by Clemens.

"The gospel train" (Negro spiritual). Also known as "Get on board."

Clemens included "Gospel Train" in what appears to be a list of his favorite songs in August 1889 NB 29, TS p. 21).

Gosse, Edmund William (1849–1928). *Thomas Gray.* English Men of Letters Series. Ed. by John Morley. New York, 1882.

Inscription: signed, "S. L. Clemens, Hartford, 1884."

Catalog: A1911, #201, $1.50.

Clemens wrote "Life of Gray (Morley's English Men of Letters)" in Notebook 22 (TS p. 36) in 1884. The statement of his personal expenses charged against Charles L. Webster & Company for 1884 included "1 English Men of Letters .50¢" that was purchased on 28 April 1884 (Charles L. Webster to SLC, 2 September 1884, MTP).

—————. *Thomas Gray.* New York: Harper & Brothers, n.d. 223 pp.

Source: MTLAcc, entry #1285, volume donated by Clemens.

Gouin, François. *The Art of Teaching and Studying Languages.* Trans. by Howard Swan and Victor Bétis. London: George Philip & Son, 1892.

Clemens noted the title and publisher in July 1892 (NB 32, TS p. 12).

Gowen, Herbert Henry. *The Paradise of the Pacific. Sketches of Hawaiian Scenery and Life.* London: Skeffington & Son, 1892.

In chapter 3 of *FE* (1897) Mark Twain quotes Gowen's account of the plight of Hawaiian lepers and cites his book by title.

Madigan, "MT's Passage to India," p. 359.

Gower, Ronald. *Joan of Arc.* Illus. London: John C. Nimmo, 1883.

Marginalia: Clemens marked and annotated both Gower's text and his list of sources with pencil as well as brown and black ink.

Catalog: "Retz Appraisal" (1944), p. 8, valued at $20.

Location: Mark Twain Papers, Berkeley, California.

Copy examined: Clemens' copy.

Mark Twain listed Gower's book among his "authorities examined" for *Joan of Arc* (see the page preceding the "Translator's Preface"). He told Albert Bigelow Paine that he remembered the book as one of his three main sources (*MTB*, p. 958).

Graham, Clementina Stirling (1782–1877). *Mystifications, by Clementina Stirling Grahame*. Ed by John Brown, M.D. Edinburgh: Edmonston and Douglas, 1865. 100 pp.

On 16 June 1896 Clemens noted " 'Mystifications' (Edmonston & Douglas, Edinboro)—1865—ask Chatto to get it for me" (NB 38, TS p. 47). He was aboard the *Norham Castle* off East London, South Africa at the time. *Mystifications* is a book of prose and verse about social customs in Edinburgh.

Grahame, Kenneth (1859–1932). *Dream Days*. London: John Lane, 1899. 291 pp.
Source: MTLAcc, entry #500, volume donated by Clemens.

Grand, Sarah (pseud. of [Mrs.] Frances Elizabeth [Clark] MacFall) (1862–1943). *Babs, the Impossible*. Illus. by Arthur I. Keller. New York: Harper & Brothers, 1901. 462 pp.
Source: MTLAcc, entry #2243, volume donated from Clemens' library by Clara Clemens Gabrilowitsch in 1910.

————. *The Heavenly Twins*. New York: Cassell Publishing Co., [cop. 1893]. 679 pp.
Marginalia: Clemens made scores of notations on the pages of this novel during a trans-Atlantic voyage in March 1894. He sailed from New York City on 7 March 1894 aboard the *S. S. New York*, bound for Southampton and scheduled to arrive on the 14th (see *MTHHR*, p. 41). Much of his marginalia is quoted in *A1911*. A note on page 345, dated 9 or 10 March (Clemens is uncertain which day it is) explains why he has so much time to devote to reading and annotating the novel: he has been at sea several days in heavy rain ("How it does pour!") and there is "not a soul on deck," the purser informs him. Clemens penciled another note at the top of pages 556–557 while reading in bed at midnight on 10 March, extolling "the gentle rolling of a ship in a moderate sea," and wishing that he might always remain at sea.

Clemens' comments about Sarah Grand's novel initially disparage its characters and dialogue, then reveal a grudging admiration for certain aspects of the work, and finally become openly complimentary. By the time he had progressed to page 74 his cavils were beginning: "Thus far, the twins are valueless lumber, & an impertinent & offensive intrusion." At page 149 he recommends that a "blank page in the place of these twins would be a large advantage to the book"; "Are these tiresome creatures supposed to be funny?" he wonders on page 150; "Good-bye, dears. God bless you. Don't come any more," is the adieu he bids them on page 154. He complains: "These disgusting creatures talk like Dr. Samuel Johnson & act like idiots. The authoress thinks that this silly performance of theirs is humorous" (p. 270). His criticisms are sharpest on page 274 ("The art of all this is intolerably bad. It is literary 'prentice-work") and page 275: "This is wretchedly done. A cat could do better literature than this."

Thereafter his tone grows more charitable: "This writer preserves her dignity & her sanity except when she is talking about her putrid twins—then she is vulgar & idiotic." Of chapter 6 he remarks: "A difficult chapter to write well— but she did it" (p. 283). When slightly more than halfway through the novel he opined: "With the twins left out, this book is more than good, it is great; and packed full of hideous truths powerfully stated. I will not sit in judgment upon the ENGLISH woman who disapproves of this book—she has done that herself. While it is true that the American woman is & always has been a coward & a slave, like her sex everywhere, she has escaped some of the [Clemens turns page, writes on verso] degradations of her English sister—degradations whose source is rank & caste, the sacredness of property, & the tyranny of a heartless political Church" (pp. 340–342). He recognizes that his attitude toward Grand's novel is changing: "It is very curious. There is nothing but labored & lubberly & unsuccessful attempts at humor concerning the twins up to Chap 7, Book III—but all this about the Boy in this Book IV is very good fun indeed" (p. 417). And,

"I can't understand it. The boy *is* humorous now, but as a child he was only disgusting. I think that this part of the book must have been written a long time after the first part—& after severe training" (p. 419). Thereafter his numerous notes generally make grammatical revisions. "Darn the subjunctive—it is always a snare," he observes on page 555, altering a word. Before closing the volume he wrote in pencil on the fourth flyleaf, opposite the copyright notice at the front: *"After reading the book:* the grammar is often dreadful—even hideous—but never mind that, it is a strong, good book." The volume contains a great many other notes, including (on the rear pastedown endpaper) several maxims—one of them denigrates the French national character; the other would head chapter 3 of *FE* (1897): "It is more trouble to make a maxim than it is to do right." On the rear flyleaf Clemens began a comment he never completed: *"There's* a curious thing: I am an aristocrat (in the aristocracy of the mind & of achievement) & from my Viscountship look reverently up at all earls, marquises and dukes above me, & superciliously down upon the barons, baronets and Knights below me but I can't find anything endurable in the aristocracy of birth and privilege—*it* turns my stomach. I feel in this way although I. . . ." (the latter note quoted in *MT&JB,* pp. 172–173).
    Catalogs: A1911, #195, $55; George A. Van Nosdall, New York City, List No. 109 (20 November 1923), item #1, $100.
    Location: Henry W. and Albert A. Berg Collection, New York Public Library.
    Copy examined: Clemens' copy, one of the most exhaustively annotated volumes in his library. Contains bookstamps of the Mark Twain Library of Redding inside the front cover; evidently Albert Bigelow Paine retrieved it from that collection for the auction in 1911. It was donated from Clemens' library by Clara Clemens Gabrilowitsch in 1910 (MTLAcc, entry #2244).
    On 27 February 1902 Livy Clemens included Mme. Sarah Grand in the list of guests she had entertained at Riverdale-on-Hudson since October 1901 (OLC's Diary, DV161, MTP). Clemens wrote down the following dialogue between a librarian and a patron in Notebook 48, whose entries span the years 1905–1908 and largely consist of risqué jokes: " 'Got the Indiscretions of a Duchess?' 'It's out,—but we have the sequel, "The Heavenly Twins" ' " (TS p. 19).

Grandgent, Charles Hall (1862–1939). *Italian Grammar.* Boston, 1902.
    Catalog: A1911, #196, $1.

Grant, Alan. *Love in Letters, Illustrated in the Correspondence of Eminent Persons; with Biographical Sketches of the Writers.* New York: G. W. Carleton & Co., 1867.
    Inscription: on front flyleaf in Clemens' handwriting: "Livy Langdon"; (below, in larger script) "Livy Clemens/1872".
    Location: Antenne-Dorrance Collection, Rice Lake, Wis.
    Copy examined: Livy Clemens' unmarked copy.

Grant, Percy Stickney (1860–1927). *Ad Matrem and Other Poems.* New York: Ingalls Kimball, 1905.
    Inscription: on second flyleaf, "Samuel L. Clemens/from a neighbor and admirer,/Percy S. Grant."
    Location: Mark Twain Library, Redding, Connecticut.
    Copy examined: Clemens' unmarked copy.

————. *The Search of Belisarius, a Byzantine Legend.* New York: Brentano's, 1907. 114 pp.
    Source: MTLAcc, entry #2029, volume donated from Clemens' library by Clara Clemens Gabrilowitsch in 1910.

Grant's Farm. Illus. [Author, publisher, date not supplied.]
    Source: MTLAcc, entry #1224, volume donated by Clemens.

Grant, Ulysses Simpson (1822–1885). *Personal Memoirs of U. S. Grant.* 2 vols. New York: Charles L. Webster & Co., 1885.
    Catalog: A1911, #197, vol. 1 only, .75¢.

————. [Another identical copy.]
    Catalog: A1911, #198, vol. 1 only, $1.

————. [Another identical copy.]
    Catalog: A1911, #199, vol. 1 only, $1.

————. [Another identical copy.]
    Inscription: presented to Clemens by Mrs. Grant in 1885 and signed by Clemens.
    Catalog: C1951, #1a, $110, listed among books containing Clemens' marginal notes.

————. [Another identical copy.]
    Inscription: "To/'Brer Whitmo' '/(otherwise F. G. Whitmore)/from his friend/S. L. Clemens/(Chief of the firm of C. L. Webster & Co.)/Hartford, Apl. 2, 1887."
    Location: Mark Twain Memorial, Hartford, Connecticut.
    Copy examined: presentation copy from Clemens to his friend and business agent, Franklin G. Whitmore.

————. [Another identical copy.]
    Location: Mark Twain Papers, Berkeley, California.
    Copy examined: another copy owned by Clemens, unmarked.
    U. S. Grant's military exploits and stature as a public hero perennially fascinated Clemens, and his references to Grant are numerous. Consequently when he became Grant's sole publisher Clemens felt that he was truly participating in history—insuring the financial security of Grant's family, recording the dying general's view of the events he had shaped, answering reporters' queries concerning Grant's physical condition, waiting with the nation for the "simultaneous voice" of the bells that would announce Grant's momentarily expected death (NB 23, TS p. 40). Clemens wrote to Howells on 5 May 1885 from Hartford: "In two days General Grant has dictated 50 pages of foolscap, & thus the Wilderness & Appomattox stand for all time in his own words. This makes the Second volume of his book as valuable as the first" *(MTHL,* p. 528). On 11 December 1885 Clemens joyfully copied Howells' praise for Grant's work into his notebook: "The book merits its enormous success, simply as literature" (NB 25, TS p. 34). Clemens heatedly defended Grant's prose style in "General Grant's Grammar" (1886). (See entry for Caesar's *Commentaries.)*

Grau, Robert. *Forty Years Observation of Music and the Drama.* New York: Broadway Publishing Co., 1909.
    Marginalia: no signature or markings, but a piece of manuscript approximately six inches square is interleaved, containing penciled calculations of the number of words in a two-volume book of 600 pages.
    Location: Antenne-Dorrance Collection, Rice Lake, Wis.
    Copy examined: Clemens' copy.
    Grau's book contains a photograph of Clara Clemens preceding its first page; underneath the portrait is the caption: "Clara Clemens/Contralto (daughter of 'Mark Twain')."

Gravert, W. *Drittes Deutsches Lesebuck.* New York: E. Steiger, 1872. 236 pp.
    Source: MTLAcc, entry #370, volume donated by Clemens.

————. [Another identical copy.]
  Source: MTLAcc, entry #371, volume donated by Clemens.

Gray, Asa (1810–1888). *Botany for Young People. Part II. How Plants Behave.*
  Illus. New York: Ivison, Blakeman, Taylor and Co., 1875. 46 pp.
  Source: MTLAcc, entry #514, volume donated by Clemens.

————. *Botany for Young People and Common Schools. How Plants Grow.* New
  York: Ivison, Blakeman, Taylor & Co., 1876. 233 pp.
  Source: MTLAcc, entry #1949, volume donated from Clemens' library by
  Clara Clemens Gabrilowitsch in 1910.

————. *Gray's School and Field Book of Botany.* New York: Ivison, Phinney,
  Blakeman & Co., 1869. 386 pp.
  Source: MTLAcc, entry #1950, volume donated from Clemens' library by
  Clara Clemens Gabrilowitsch in 1910.

Gray, David. *Letters, Poems and Selected Prose Writings.* Ed. with a Biographical
  Memoir by Josephus Nelson Larned (1836–1913). Buffalo, N. Y., 1888.
  Inscription: signed "S. L. Clemens, 1888."
  Catalog: A1911, #200, $3.
  Clemens knew Gray as a newspaperman-poet in Buffalo in the early 1870's. In
  1885 he noted Gray's name for a complimentary copy of *Huckleberry Finn* (NB
  23, TS p. 38). In an Autobiographical Dictation on 31 July 1906 he spoke of
  Gray's praise for *1601* in 1876 *(MTE,* p. 209).

Gray, Thomas (1716–1771). "Elegy Written in a Country Churchyard" (poem,
  pub. 1751).
  Clemens quoted from stanza 32 in an early unpublished sketch, "Jul'us
  Caesar" (TS in DV400, MTP), probably written around 1856. He traced "all the
  grave-yard poetry to Elegy Gray or Wolfe, indiscriminately" in a humorous piece
  for the *Californian,* 17 June 1865 *(LAMT,* p. 142). In a sketch for the 7 April
  1866 issue of the *Californian,* a man who has been drinking on a steamboat
  quotes from "Elegy" while attempting to remember "Hohenlinden" *(SSix,* p.
  209). In 1872 Clemens mentioned "Gray who wrote the *Elegy"* in his English-
  notebook description of the tombs in Westminster Abbey *(MTB,* p. 469); he
  repeated this same reference in "A Memorable Midnight Experience" (1874).
  Many years later he quoted from the poem once again ("Homeward the bandit
  [*sic*] plods her weary way/And leaves the world to darkness and to me") in a
  letter to Dorothy Quick written from Tuxedo Park on 12 September 1907
  (Enchantment, p. 90). Clemens owned a copy of Edmund Gosse's biography of
  Gray. See also *RP,* p. xvii.

————. *The Poems of Thomas Gray.* New York: White, Stokes, and Allen, 1883.
  167 pp.
  Source: MTLAcc, entry #2032, volume donated from Clemens' library by
  Clara Clemens Gabrilowitsch in 1910.

Gray, Zenas J. *Driftwood.* Harrisburg, Pa.: Patriot Publishing Co., 1884. 86 pp.
  Source: MTLAcc, entry #610, volume donated by Clemens.

————. [Another identical copy.]
  Source: MTLAcc, entry #628, volume donated by Clemens.

Great Religions of the World, by Herbert A[llen] Giles [1845–1935], T. W. Rhys
Davids, Oskar Mann, A. C. Lyall, D. Menant, Lepel Griffin, Frederic Harrison,
E. Denison Ross, M. Gaster, Washington Gladden, and Cardinal Gibbons. New
York: Harper & Brothers, 1901. 301 pp.
  Inscription: front free endpaper inscribed in pencil, "S. L. Clemens/Amper-
sand/Saranac Lake, N. Y./Sept. 15, 1901."
  Marginalia: considerable annotation by Clemens. See *The Twainian,* 38
(January-February 1979), 1–4; March-April 1979), 1–3.
  Provenance: C1951 sale label.
  Location: collection of Chester Davis, Executive-Secretary, Mark Twain
Research Foundation, Perry, Missouri.
  Copy examined: Clemens' copy.

Greeley, Horace (1811–1872). *What I Know of Farming.* New York, 1871.
  Inscription: presentation copy inscribed by Greeley: "To Mark Twain, Esq.,
Ed. Buffalo Express, who knows even less of MY farming than does Horace
Greeley. N. York."
  Catalog: A1911, #204, $22.
  Clemens ridiculed Greeley's notions in "Private Habits of Horace Greeley"
(1868), but conceded that he was "an upright and an honest man—a practical,
great-brained man—a useful man to his nation and his generation." In 1869
Clemens alluded to Greeley's interest in political economy in "Last Words of
Great Men"; about the same time Olivia Langdon copied a quotation attributed to
Greeley into her commonplace book in Elmira (DV161, MTP). Mark Twain
poked cruel fun at Greeley's outlandish costume and countenance in "The Tone-
Imparting Committee" (February 1871). Much later Clemens would recall that
he met Greeley only once ("by accident") in 1871 (undated AD, *MTE,* pp. 347–
348). In chapter 20 of *Roughing It* (1872) he told and retold the story of Greeley
and Hank Monk. He mentioned Greeley as "a man . . . whose memory I still
revere" in a letter to the editor of *Harper's Weekly* published in the 21 October
1905 issue.

Green, John Richard (1837–1883). *History of the English People.* 4 vols. [New
York: Harper & Brothers, 1878–1880.] Edition conjectured; the publisher of
Clemens' copy is not known.
  Catalog: C1951, #D7, $48, listed among books signed by Clemens.

————. *A Short History of the English People.* With maps and tables. New York,
1875.
  Inscription: signed on flyleaf, "Saml. L. Clemens, Hartford 1875."
  Marginalia: A1911 reports numerous emendations in Clemens' hand through-
out chapter one, correcting grammatical errors, mixed metaphors, and convoluted
sentence structures. On page 55, where Green states that "The great fabric of the
Roman law, indeed, never took root in England," Clemens jeered: "Does a fabric
EVER take root?" Further down the same page the historian recounts that "the
King, however, recovered from his wound, to march on the West-Saxons";
Clemens queried, "Did he recover from his wound MERELY for the purpose
of marching upon the West Saxons?" On page 56 Green writes that the king
"slew and subdued all who had conspired against him"; Clemens summarizes this
sequence as: "He made corpses of the conspirators and then subdued the corpses."
  Catalog: A1911, #205, $16.
  Clemens wrote to Brown & Gross, Hartford booksellers, on 15 January 1887,
requesting a one-volume edition of Green's *Short History of the English People*
(ALS sold by Alta California Bookstore, April 1976; purchased by C. A. Valverde,
Wahrenbrock's Book House, San Diego, Calif.). On 20 January 1887 Clemens
replied to "friend Gross": "As I understand it, you already have Green in ½
calf, & can get a ½ calf Macaulay. . . . That'll do—send 'em along" (CWB).
  Stone, "MT's Joan of Arc," p. 4; Baetzhold, *MT&JB,* p. 343 n. 39).

Green, Mary Anne Everett (1818–1895). *Lives of the Princesses of England from the Norman Conquest.* 6 vols. 1850–1855.
    Catalog: A1911, #441, sold as part of the uniformly bound set of Agnes Strickland's *Queens* (26 vols.). See entry for Strickland.

Green, Mason A. *Springfield* [, *Massachusetts*], *1636–1886; History of Town and City.* Portraits, plans, illus. Springfield, Mass., 1888.
    Catalog: A1911, #206, $3.50.

Greene, Belle C. *A New England Conscience.* New York: G. P. Putnam's Sons, 1885. 196 pp.
    Source: MTLAcc, entry #2247, volume donated from Clemens' library by Clara Clemens Gabrilowitsch in 1910.

Greene, Henry Copley, trans. *The Gospel of the Childhood of Our Lord Jesus Christ; Translated from the Latin by Henry Copley Greene, with Original Text of the Manuscript at the Monastery of Saint Wolfgang.* Intro. by Alice Meynell. Illus. by Carlos Schwabe. New York: Scott-Thaw Co., London: Burns and Oates, 1904. 272 pp.
    On 1 January 1906 Isabel Lyon noted in her journal: "Tonight I took a little book down to Mr. Clemens, a little book sent me by Belle Greene, 'The Childhood of Christ', translated from the Latin of an old monkish manuscript found in a monastery in the Saly Kammergut. Translation by Harry Greene. . . . I . . . read it to its finishing page with delight. Mr. Clemens read a part of it too, and found it delightful, but he was 'afraid it was a lie' " (TS p. 118, MTP). Greene's book was a translation of the Gospel of the Infant According to St. Peter, from the New Testament Apocryphal Books.

Greene, (Mrs.) Sarah Pratt (McLean) (1856–1935). *Cape Cod Folks, A Novel.* Boston: A. Williams & Co., 1881. 327 pp.
    Source: MTLAcc, entry #214, volume donated by Clemens.
    Miss McLean sent Clemens a complimentary copy of *Cape Cod Folks* (McLean to SLC, 30 November 1881, ALS in MTP). "I hope that you will read it sometime," she added. He praised the book in a letter written to her from Hartford on 12 December 1881 (ALS in MTP), declaring "I have *already* read it—months ago—& vastly enjoyed & admired it, too; as did also the rest of this family" (ALS in Humanities Research Center, Univ. of Texas at Austin).

————. [Another identical copy.]
    Source: MTLAcc, entry #1259, volume donated by Clemens.

————. *Flood-tide.* New York: Harper & Brothers, 1901. 350 pp.
    Inscription: flyleaf signed "S. L. Clemens, Riverdale, October, 1901."
    Catalog: A1911, #207, $2.
    Clemens informed William Dean Howells on 29 April 1903 that he had written to Bliss Perry, editor of the *Atlantic Monthly*, "praising [George S.] Wasson's book & Miss McLean's 'Flood Tide,' " and recommending that the two works "be read together, chapter-about." In Clemens' opinion, "Wasson's delightful worldly people & Miss McL's delightful unworldly people belonged together & should mix together on the same stage" (*MTHL*, p. 769). On 26 May 1903 Henry H. Rogers wrote to Clemens from Fairhaven, Massachusetts: "Much obliged for 'Flood tide' [;] I have enjoyed it" (*MTHHR*, p. 529).

————. *Stuart and Bamboo; A Novel.* New York: Harper & Brothers, 1897. 276 pp.
    Source: MTLAcc, entry #1595, volume donated by Clemens.

————. *Vesty of the Basins; A Novel.* Illus. by Otto H. Bacher. New York: Harper & Brothers, 1902. 271 pp.
    Source: MTLAcc, entry #1427, volume donated by Clemens.

————. *Winslow Plain.* New York: Harper & Brothers, 1902. 290 pp.
    Source: MTLAcc, entry #1007, volume donated by Clemens.

Greenough, James Bradstreet (1833–1901). *The Queen of Hearts. A Dramatic Fantasia. For Private Theatricals.* Cambridge, Mass., 1875.
    On 28 April 1876, two days after Clemens appeared in a performance of James R. Planché's *The Loan of a Lover,* William Dean Howells inquired: "Did you get the Queen of Hearts?" *(MTHL,* p. 134).

Greenslet, Ferris. *The Life of Thomas Bailey Aldrich.* Boston: Houghton Mifflin Company, 1908. 259 pp.
    Catalog: C1951, #87c, $7.50, listed among books signed by Clemens.
    Aldrich died in 1907. At Greenslet's request William Dean Howells turned over his letters from Aldrich at about the same time that Albert Bigelow Paine asked Howells for Clemens' letters.

Greenwood, Granville George (1850–1928). *The Shakespeare Problem Restated.* London and New York: John Lane Co., 1908. 523 pp.
    Marginalia: prolific annotation in both pencil and black ink. Clemens' notes argue against Shakespeare's authorship. On the verso of the third flyleaf Clemens calls Shakespeare "The Arthur Orton of literary 'Claimants' "; on the front of the flyleaf he writes in the same black ink: "Predecessors of Mr. Greenwood have in the course of half a century trimmed <a good deal> several hatfuls of tissue from Arthur Orton's Shakespeare, & now—as it seems to me—this book reduces him to a skeleton & scrapes the bones" *(Zeitlin 1951).* The marginalia reveal (e.g., p. 56) that Clemens is particularly impressed that Shakespeare seems not to have written about his own experiences, but only what he discovered in books. On page 75, beside a description of Ben Jonson's lounging around London, Clemens penciled Huck Finn's name. A few notes are in someone else's handwriting. One of these on page 130 advises skipping the following chapter, which "is not biography but literary argument of the kind that scholars use"; another on pp. 366–367 quotes Francis Bacon's reference to himself as a "concealed poet." A typed and signed note by Clara Clemens Samossoud is tipped in to authenticate the marginalia as her father's.
    Catalogs: C1951, #17a, $155; Zeitlin 1951, #18, $350.
    Location: Henry W. and Albert A. Berg Collection, New York Public Library.
    Copy examined: Clemens' copy, one of the most heavily annotated volumes in his library.
    Albert Bigelow Paine reports that Greenwood's book and a work by William S. Booth "added the last touch of conviction that Francis Bacon . . . had written the Shakespearean dramas" *(MTB,* p. 1479). Isabel Lyon's records show that John Macy sent Greenwood's book to Clemens; the volume arrived on 5 February 1909, following Macy's visit to Stormfield on 8 January 1909 (Berg, TS in MTP). Clemens talked excitedly of the forthcoming book in an Autobiographical Dictation of 11 January 1909; from what John Macy had told him of its arguments, and from the examples Macy related from its text, Clemens had concluded that this book by an English clergyman would prove to be the "bombshell" that would "unhorse" Shakespeare and elevate Bacon into his rightful place. Macy had promised to send Clemens proofsheets of the volume as they were printed up (AD, MTP).
    Clemens' marginalia in his copy of the book (p. 57) indicate his agreement with the thesis that Bacon would not have wished to be known in court as a playwright, a vocation then associated with vagrant actors. Isabel Lyon noted

on 8 March 1909 that Clemens wished to write Greenwood a letter commending the book (Berg, TS in MTP). Mark Twain opened Part One of "Is Shakespeare Dead?" (1909) by remarking: "A friend has sent me a new book, from England —*The Shakespeare Problem Restated*—well restated and closely reasoned." In Part Eight he quoted nine pages of extracts from Greenwood's volume to demonstrate the inadequacy of Shakespeare's background in law for the writing of certain scenes in the plays. But Mark Twain skirted the issue of Bacon's authorship in *Is Shakespeare Dead?*, merely pointing out in Parts Nine and Ten that Bacon possessed suitable training for the task and that Bacon's contemporaries praised his abilities highly.

Greenwood, James. *The Wilds of London.* Illus. London, 1874.
> *Inscription:* signed on flyleaf "Saml. L. Clemens, Hartford, 1875."
> *Catalog: A1911,* #208, $7.

Greey, Edward (1835–1888). *The Bear-Worshippers of Yezo and the Island of Karafuto.* Illus. Boston: Lee & Shepard, 1884. 304 pp.
> *Inscription:* presented by its author to Jean Clemens.
> *Provenance:* MTLAcc, entry #1887, volume donated from Clemens' library by Clara Clemens Gabrilowitsch in 1910.
> *Catalog: Mott 1952,* #59, $4.

————. *A Captive of Love, Founded Upon Bakin's Japanese Romance.* Illus. Boston: Lee & Shepard, 1886. 280 pp.
> *Source:* MTLAcc, entry #2256, volume donated from Clemens' library by Clara Clemens Gabrilowitsch in 1910.

————. *Japanese Romance. The Loyal Ronins of Tamenaga Shunsui. By Shiui-chiro Saito and Edward Greey.* Illus. by Kei-Sai Yei-Sen. New York, 1880.
> *Marginalia:* on one page Clemens wrote: "Mitford's translation of the Ronin story is better literature than this one. S.L.C."
> *Catalog: A1911,* #268, $5.

————. *The Wonderful City of Tokio.* Boston: Lee & Shepard, 1883. 301 pp.
> *Provenance:* MTLAcc, entry #1888, volume donated from Clemens' library by Clara Clemens Gabrilowitsch in 1910.
> *Inscription:* presented by its author to Clara Clemens.
> *Catalog: Mott 1952,* #60, $4.

————. *Young Americans in Japan.* Illus. Boston: Lee & Shepard, 1882. 372 pp.
> *Source:* MTLAcc, entry #1886, volume donated from Clemens' library by Clara Clemens Gabrilowitsch in 1910.

Gregg, Mary (Kirby) (1817–1893) and Elizabeth Kirby (1823–1873). *Stories About Birds of Land and Water.* London and New York: Cassell, Petter & Galpin, [18–?]. 256 pp.
> *Source:* MTLAcc, entry #1961, volume donated from Clemens' library by Clara Clemens Gabrilowitsch in 1910.

Gregory, (Lady) Augusta (1852–1932). *Cuchulain of Muirthemne: The Story of the Men of the Red Branch of Ulster.* Preface by William Butler Yeats. London: John Murray, 1902. 360 pp.
> *Inscription:* front free endpaper inscribed in black ink: "To Mark Twain—/ With kind remembrances/from Augusta Gregory—/Apr 1907." A letter from Lady Gregory is tipped in.
> *Marginalia:* Clemens made favorable pencil notes and markings throughout.
> *Catalog: C1951,* #12a, $35, listed among the volumes containing annotation by Clemens.

Location: Mark Twain Memorial, Hartford, Conn. Donated by Mrs. John L. Martin of Darien, Conn.

Copy examined: Clemens' copy.

————. *Fate of the Children of Uisneach . . . with Translation, Notes, and a Complete Vocabulary.* Society for the Preservation of the Irish Language. Dublin: M. H. Gill & Son, 1898. [Title supplied from *British Museum Catalogue of Printed Books,* 56:296.]

Clemens praised this book in an undated letter to Lady Gregory: "I wanted to say it again & thank you again—& Mrs. Clemens said go on & do it" (Howard S. Mott Books, Catalogue No. 183, item #152). In a letter to Lady Gregory written in March 1903, apparently thanking her for a copy of *Poets and Dreamers,* Clemens wrote: "We should always be grateful, even if you had given us [readers] the Fate of the Children of Usnech [*sic*] alone, that moving and beautiful tale, that masterpiece!" (quoted in Lady Gregory's autobiography, *Seventy Years* [London: Colin Smythe, 1973], pp. 400–401).

————. *Gods and Fighting Men: The Story of the Tuatha De Danaan and of the Fianna of Ireland. Arranged and Put into English by Lady Gregory.* Preface by William Butler Yeats. London: John Murray, 1904. 476 pp.

Inscription: front pastedown endpaper signed in black ink: "SL. Clemens."

Catalogs: A1911, #209, $4.50; *Lexington 1912,* #12, $7.50.

Location: Mark Twain Memorial, Hartford, Conn. Donated anonymously in 1974, according to Mrs. Dexter B. Peck, Library Chairman.

Copy examined: none; I am thankful to Diana Royce and Mrs. Dexter B. Peck for confirming the present location of this volume.

On 21 February 1904 Lady Gregory wrote to Clemens in concern about Livy Clemens' health. Lady Gregory mentioned that *Gods and Fighting Men* was meeting a favorable reception, for which she was thankful. "It gave me harder work than Cuchulain . . . but it was love's labour" (MTP).

————. *Poets and Dreamers: Studies and Translations from the Irish by Lady Gregory.* Dublin: Hodges, Figgis, and Company, 1903.

Inscription: "To 'Mark Twain' with very kind regards from Augusta Gregory, March 1903."

Marginalia: one stray pencil mark at the bottom of page 240. No other markings. Leaves opened.

Catalogs: C1951, #61c, $17.50; "The Fine Library of the Late Ingle Barr," Sotheby Parke-Bernet, Los Angeles, Sale No. 68 (18–19 February 1973), item #107, $150; placed on sale by John Howell Books, San Francisco, 24 February 1973, $180.

Copy examined: Clemens' copy (at John Howell Books).

In her autobiography Lady Gregory quotes a letter from Mark Twain written to her from Riverdale-on-the-Hudson in March 1903: "I have been marvelling along through your wonderful book again, and trying to understand how those people could produce such a literature in that old day, and they so remote (apparently) from the well-springs and inspirations of such things. . . . But we've got the stories and that is the important thing, and we are grateful to you for that" (*Seventy Years* [London: Colin Smythe, 1973], pp. 400–401).

Grendel, M. R. *Contrasts*[*: A Story*]. New York: G. P. Putnam's Sons, 1881. 392 pp.

Source: MTLAcc, entry #2245, volume donated from Clemens' library by Clara Clemens Gabrilowitsch in 1910.

Greville, Charles Cavendish Fulke (1794–1865). *The Greville Memoirs; A Journal of the Reigns of King George IV. and King William IV., by the Late Charles C. F. Greville.* Ed. by Henry Reeve. Second ed. 3 vols. London: Longmans, Green, and Co., 1874.

Inscriptions: vol. 1 signed in pencil on half-title page: "Saml. L. Clemens/ Hartford 1875"; front pastedown endpapers of vols. 2 and 3 signed "S. L. Clemens" (vol. 2 signed in two places).

Marginalia: vol. 1 annotated in brown ink and pencil; portions of Clemens' marginalia are quoted in *MTB*, pp. 1539–40, and *TIH*, p. 31. One of Clemens' notes occurs beside Greville's criticism of Byron: "What a man sees in the human race is merely himself in the deep and honest privacy of his own heart" (*MTB*, pp. 1539–40); Paine also quotes other comments. All of Clemens' scattered notes appear to have been made after 1900. The handwriting itself indicates a late period of his life. A penciled remark on page 158 refers to the Spanish-American War; a note in brown ink on page 386 alludes to an event that Clemens dates as having occurred in 1904. Many pages are folded over. On the half-title page of vol. 3 Clemens wrote: "He overworks the word 'that.' Sometimes when he gets to that-ing he does not seem to know where to stop" (*A1911*). The amount of annotation in vols. 2 and 3 is unknown.

Catalogs: A1911, #210, vols. 2 and 3 only, $1.50 total; *C1951,* #5a, vol. 1 only, $27.50; Mail Auction, Pennsauken, N.J. (October 1977), vol. 3 only, $175 bid recommended.

Location: vol. 1 only in Mark Twain Papers, Berkeley.

Copy examined: Clemens' copy of vol. 1.

On 26 January 1875 Clemens wrote to William Dean Howells from Hartford: "I've been sick abed several days. . . . How little confirmed invalids appreciate their advantages. I was able to read the English edition of the Greville Memoirs through without interruption . . . & smoke 18 cigars a day" (*MTHL*, p. 62).

————. *The Greville Memoirs.* Ed. by Richard Henry Stoddard. New York: Scribner, Armstrong & Co., 1875.

Possibly Clemens owned two editions of Greville's *Memoirs;* at any rate he referred to a page number from Stoddard's abridgment in reminding himself of a humorous story (Leslie's disrespectful remarks in 1880 about the North Pole and the Equator) for his projected anthology of humor: "Sydney Smith (Dn the Equator)/ (Greville, page 265" (NB 19, *N&J,* 2: 364).

Grey, (Sir) George. *Journals of Two Expeditions of Discovery in North West and Western Australia, During the Years 1837, 38, and 39. With Observations on the Moral and Physical Character of the Aboriginal Inhabitants.* 2 vols. London, 1841.

"Sir George Grey and Mr. Eyre testify that the natives dug wells fourteen or fifteen feet deep" (*FE* [1897], chapter 22).

Grieb, Christoph Friedrich. *Dictionary of the English and German Languages.* Two vols. in one. Stuttgart: P. Neff, 1884.

Catalog: A1911, #181, $1.50.

Griffin, Lepel Henry. *The Great Republic.* London and New York, 1884.

Mark Twain quoted Griffin in a speech Twain made on 27 April 1890, "On Foreign Critics" (*MTSpk,* pp. 257–258); he mentioned Griffin in April 1889 (NB 28, TS p. 54), February 1890 (NB 29, TS p. 39), and December 1895 (NB 36, TS p. 4). Evidence that Clemens knew Griffin's book at first-hand is hazy; see *MTHL,* pp. 600–601 n. 1 and D. M. McKeithan, "The Occasion of Mark Twain's Speech 'On Foreign Critics' " (*CTMT,* pp. 144–145).

Griffis, William Elliot (1843–1928) and others. *Bible Stories for Young People.* Illus. New York: Harper & Brothers, [cop. 1894]. 178 pp.

Source: MTLAcc, entry #1390, volume donated by Clemens.

Grinnell, George Bird (1849–1938). *The Punishment of the Stingy, and Other Indian Stories*. Illus. New York, 1901.
>   *Inscription:* flyleaf signed "S. L. Clemens, Riverdale, October, 1901."
>   *Catalog: A1911*, #211, $4.75.

Griswold, Stephen M. *Sixty Years with Plymouth Church*. New York: Fleming H. Revell Co., 1907.
>   *Inscriptions:* flyleaf inscribed "Samuel L. Clemens/'Mark Twain'/With kind regards of Stephen M. Griswold." Signed in black ink on front pastedown endpaper: "SL. Clemens/1907."
>   *Marginalia:* above and below Griswold's frontispiece portrait Clemens wrote in black ink: "Here is the real old familiar Plymouth-Church self-complacency of 40 years ago. It is the way God looks when He has had a successful season. This is the Griswold that was out in the Quaker City Excursion with us. He was a Beecher-idolater" *(MTMF,* p. xii, n. 1). Clemens turned down the corner of page 73 and drew a line in black ink beside Griswold's account of Henry Ward Beecher's dramatic purchase of a young slave girl during church services he was conducting. (Beecher asked members of his congregation to pledge money to buy the girl from her master and set her free.) The only other notes or markings occur in "The Beecher Trial" chapter (pp. 90–100); there Clemens blames Henry Ward Beecher for maintaining his silence when the charges of adultery were first made, instead of telling "that honorable lie" at once.
>   *Catalog:* "Retz Appraisal" (1944), p. 8, valued at $20.
>   *Provenance:* contains bookstamps of Mark Twain Library, Redding; apparently it was returned to the Mark Twain Estate after its donation to that library.
>   *Location:* Mark Twain Papers, Berkeley, California.
>   *Copy examined:* Clemens' copy.

Grose, Francis (1731?–1791). *A Classical Dictionary of the Vulgar Tongue*. London: Printed for S. Hooper, 1785.
>   *Inscription:* half-title page signed in black ink "Saml. L. Clemens/Hartford, 1875."
>   *Marginalia:* prolific notes and markings by Clemens on virtually every page. All are in pencil. He adds current usages of certain terms and lists modern replacements for others. "Bilk," he notes, is a "Californian" word. "Blarney" has "changed to flattery." Is "Canterbury Story," he wonders, "from the 'Pilgrims'? " The life and death of Jack of Legs, Clemens observes, was the "same as the legend of Robin Hood." He associates the definition of "Willow" with "Ophelia's song in Hamlet." A transcript of a dozen examples of Clemens' annotations is now in MTP.
>   *Catalogs: C1951*, #30a, $55; sold by The Scriptorium, Beverly Hills, 18 December 1967, $135; purchased by Frank Greenagel, Pacific Palisades, Calif.
>   *Location:* collection of Justin G. Turner, Los Angeles, Calif. in 1970.
>   *Copy examined:* photocopy of complete marginalia provided by Professor Howard G. Baetzhold, Butler University.
>   *MT&JB,* pp. 52, 331 n. 14.

Grube, August Wilhelm. *Charakterbilder aus der Geschichte und Sage*. Three vols. in one. Portraits. Leipzig: Friedrich Brandstetter, 1882.
>   *Catalog: A1911*, #212, $1.
>   Hemminghaus, "Mark Twain's German Provenience," p. 474.

Grumman, William Edgar. *The Revolutionary Soldiers of Redding, Connecticut, and the Record of Their Services; with Mention of Others Who Rendered Services or Suffered Loss at the Hands of the Enemy During the Struggle for Independence 1775–1783; Together with Some Account of the Loyalists of the Town and Vicinity, Their Organization, Their Efforts, and Sacrifices in Behalf of Their King, and Their Ultimate Fate.* Hartford, Conn.: Hartford Press; Case, Lockwood & Brainard Co., 1904. 208 pp.
> *Inscription:* presented to Mark Twain by its author.
> *Location:* Mark Twain Library, Redding, Conn.
> *Source:* described in "Books from Stormfield and Their Annotations," Redding, Connecticut *Pilot,* 15 June 1972, p. 6 (in section titled "New Mark Twain Library").

Gualdo Priorato, Galeazzo (1606–1678). *The History of the Managements of Cardinal Julio Mazarine, Chief Minister of State of the Crown of France, Translated According to the Original.* 3 vols. London, 1691. [Only vols. 1 and 3 of Clemens' set are known to exist.]
> *Catalog: A1911,* #243, vols. 1 and 3 only, .75¢; *Lexington 1912,* #20, $4.
> *Provenance:* the arms and name of Robert Harley, Earl of Oxford, are on the front and back covers.

Guillemin, Amédée Victor (1826–1893). *The Heavens: An Illustrated Handbook of Popular Astronomy.* Ed. by Norman Lockyer. Rev. by Richard A. Proctor. London: Richard Bentley & Son, 1878. 436 pp.
> *Inscription:* signed in pencil on first flyleaf: "S. L. Clemens/Munich, Dec. 1878".
> *Marginalia:* Clemens made penciled notes on pp. 144–145 for a story about Captain Ned Wakeman's visiting the moon, where he would encounter naked "Moonites" who eat lava dust. A similar note projecting Wakeman's solar travels appears on p. 234. The volume contains a few other notes and numerous pencil markings. Computations in brown ink, blue ink, and pencil cover the rear flyleaves and rear pastedown endpaper. The volume was evidently rebound after Clemens made his notes.
> *Catalog: C1951,* #16a, $20.
> *Location:* Mark Twain Papers, Berkeley, Calif. Given by the University of California at Los Angeles, which purchased the book at the *C1951* auction.
> *Copy examined:* Clemens' copy.

———. *The Sun.* Trans. from French by Thomas Lamb Phipson. Illus. New York: Scribner, Armstrong & Co., 1872. 297 pp.
> *Source:* MTLAcc, entry #1992, volume donated from Clemens' library by Clara Clemens Gabrilowitsch in 1910.

Guizot, François Pierre Guillaume (1787–1874). *Concise History of France.* Trans. by Gustave Masson.
> *Catalog: C1951,* #024, listed as containing the signature of Olivia Clemens.

———. *History of France.* 6 vols.
> *Catalog: C1951,* #1c, listed among volumes signed by Clemens.

———. *History of France.* Illus. by De Neuvill. 5 vols.
> Clemens supplied this five-volume set as one of the prizes for a spelling bee held at the Asylum Hill Congregational Church in May 1875. He described the prizes in the course of his preliminary speech at the event, published in the 13 May 1875 issue of the Hartford *Courant.* Leah A. Strong reprinted Clemens' remarks in "Mark Twain on Spelling," *AL,* 23 (November 1951), 357–359.

————. *A Popular History of England.* Trans. by M. M. Ripley. Illus. 5 vols. Boston, 1876.
> *Inscription:* each vol. signed "S. L. Clemens."
> *Catalog: A1911,* #214, $6.75 total.

————. *A Popular History of France.*
> A receipt from Estes & Lauriat of Boston, dated 16 May 1874, credits Clemens' account for payments on a serial publication: "2 Each 1st 8 Parts France 8.00" sent on 4 April 1874; and "2 Each Parts 9 & 10 France 2.00" sent on 13 April 1874, a total of $10. This receipt presumably refers to Guizot's *History,* for the envelope in which the receipt was mailed on 16 May 1874 advertises: "Agents Wanted for/GUIZOT'S/POPULAR HISTORY OF FRANCE,/One of the finest Serial Works ever issued in America" (MTP).

Gümpel, Carl Godfrey. *Common Salt: Its Use and Necessity for the Maintenance of Health and the Prevention of Disease.* London: Swan Sonnenschein & Co., 1898. 380 pp.
> *Source:* MTLAcc, entry #545, volume donated by Clemens.

Gunn, John C. *Gunn's Domestic Medicine, or Poor Man's Friend, in the Hours of Affliction, Pain, and Sickness. This Book Points Out, in Plain Language, Free from Doctor's Terms, the Diseases of Men, Women, and Children, and Expressly Intended for the Benefit of Families.* Knoxville, Tenn.: James C. Gunn, 1830. 440 pp.
> Huck Finn notes the presence of this book on a corner of the Grangerford's parlor table: "another was Dr. Gunn's *Family Medicine,* which told you all about what to do if a body was sick or dead" (chapter 17, *HF).* Gunn's book was often reprinted, usually in Kentucky or Tennessee, between 1830 and 1842, then in New York between 1843 and 1870. A revised edition was published between 1870 and 1872. A similar but distinct work was also brought out during the years between 1857 and 1888, *Gunn's New Domestic Physician; or Home Book of Health.*
> Aspiz, "Mark Twain's Reading," p. 327; *MT&HF,* p. 230.

Gurney, Edmund (1847–1888), Frederic William Henry Myers (1843–1901), and Frank Podmore (1855–1910). *Phantasms of the Living.* 2 vols. London: Trubner, 1886.
> *Phantasms* collected the proceedings of the Society for Psychical Research in London. The book reported upon cases of apparitions, materializations, dematerializations, clairvoyance, telepathy, precognition, and dream experiences. Around Christmas time in 1896 Clemens noted in London: "Been reading Apparitions [*sic*] of the Living—Gladstone suddenly appears—is *solid*—talks, & disappears. Emperor William, Barnum, P. of Wales, &c." (NB 39, TS p. 36). John S. Tuckey identifies *Phantasms* as the work Clemens was reading (*MTSatan,* p. 26).

Guthrie, Thomas Anstey (1856–1934), pseud. "F. Anstey." *Vice Versâ; or, A Lesson to Fathers.* New York: D. Appleton and Co., 1882. 349 pp.
> *Inscription:* flyleaf signed "S. L. Clemens/Hartford, 1882".
> *Catalogs: A1911,* #13, $2.50; *Lexington 1912,* #2, $5.

Habberton, John (1842–1921). *Helen's Babies. With Some Account of Their Ways, Innocent, Crafty, Angelic, Impish, Witching and Repulsive. Also, a Partial Record of Their Actions During Ten Days of Their Existence. By Their Latest Victim.* Boston: Loring, 1876. 206 pp.

In Habberton's novel two mischievous little boys, Budge (age five) and Toddie (age three) try the patience of their uncle Harry Burton, a bachelor. But all turns out well, for Harry's troublesome nephews bring him together with Miss Alice Mayton, a courtship ensues, and their blissful marriage is arranged. Neither the romantic plot nor Habberton's attempts to reproduce the prattle of children probably appealed to Clemens. He apparently offered a vitriolic review of the novel to the *Atlantic Monthly,* for on 30 November 1876 William Dean Howells urged him "to write something better than that about Helen's Babbies [*sic*]. You use expressions there that would lose us all our book-club circulation. Do attack the folly systematically and analytically—write what you said at dinner the other day about it" (*MTHL,* p. 165). In an anonymous review of E. P. Hammond's *Sketches of Palestine* (*Atlantic Monthly,* June 1877), Clemens noted that he had refrained from saying that Hammond's book of absurd poetry "is worse than Helen's Babies . . . ; I never went to that length" (quoted by Philip B. Eppard, "MT Dissects an Overrated Book" [1977], p. 440). Clemens mentioned Habberton's "nauseous & idiotic" novel to Mrs. Fairbanks on 31 October 1877 (*MTMF,* p. 211). In a letter to Howells on 1 November 1877 he complained that if any story is written "wretchedly & nastily & witlessly" one may expect that "the whole nation of Helen's Baby's admirers will welcome it as a very inspiration of humor & read & copy it everywhere" (*MTHL,* p. 208). While making notes for his projected anthology of humor in 1881 Clemens noted: "Helen's Babies & The Worst Boy in Town—by the ass Habberton" (NB 19, *N&J,* 2: 428). Twice Mark Twain made a joke about the possibility of converting the expletive "Hell" into the socially acceptable book title "—en's Babies": on the margin of the manuscript for "Simon Wheeler, Detective" (written 1877–1898?) and in the text of "1,002d Arabian Night" (written 1883) (*S&B,* pp. 342, 109). On 14 February 1884 William L. Hughes, seeking Mark Twain's permission to translate into French *Tom Sawyer* and the forthcoming *Huckleberry Finn,* sent him a copy of a work Hughes had recently translated—*Les Bébés d'Hélène* (ALS in CWB). Clemens noted receipt of Hughes' work in Notebook 22 (1884), TS p. 33.

The financial success of Habberton's novel amazed Clemens. On 17 January 1887 he expressed bewilderment at the continuing sales of "the very worst & most witless book the great & good God Almighty ever permitted to go to press" (SLC to Belle C. Greene, MTP). He mentioned Habberton's mistake in not copyrighting the novel in England to prevent its piracy there ("American Authors and British Pirates" [1888]). As late as 1895 Clemens manifested disgust that "when you travel on the Continent . . . the one book which has been translated as the best type of American literature is *Helen's Babies* ("Mark Twain in Sydney," Sydney, Australia *Argus,* 17 September 1895, clipping in Scrapbook #26, MTP).

————. *The Jericho Road; A Story of Western Life.* Chicago: Jansen, McClurg & Co., 1877. 222 pp.

Inscription: flyleaf inscribed "With the Author's Compliments."

Marginalia: Clemens made scores of notes and markings in pencil through the first three chapters (pp. 7–37), but only a few comments appear in the margins of the remaining pages. In the first chapter he quibbles about the terminology and details Habberton uses in depicting life aboard a river steamboat. Clemens began with the belief that he was reading "a diligent & determined imitation of Bret Harte" (p. 7); but on the last page he admitted to finding it "a right down good book—with the exception of the first two chapters, which are execrable" (p. 222). The Mark Twain Papers at Berkeley contain a photocopy of Clemens' marginalia.

Location: Carrie Estelle Doheny Collection, St. John's Seminary, Camarillo, California. Donated by Mrs. Doheny in 1940 after its purchase from Maxwell Hunley Rare Books of Beverly Hills for $12.20.

Copy examined: Clemens' copy.

The title *Jericho Road* is taken from the biblical story of the Good Samaritan who assisted the man beaten and robbed by thieves on the road from Jerusalem to Jericho. Habberton's novel opens with a "wooding" operation by roustabouts for the steamboat *Helen Douglas* somewhere near the Wabash River.

————. *The Worst Boy in Town* (pub. 1880).

Mark Twain thought about including a selection from this book ("by the ass Habberton") in his *Library of Humor* while planning the anthology in 1881 (NB 19, *N&J,* 2: 428). But when the *Library* appeared in 1888 it contained none of Habberton's writings.

The Habits of Good Society: A Handbook for Ladies and Gentlemen. New York: G. W. Carleton & Co., 1879. 320 pp.

Source: MTLAcc, entry #2145, volume donated from Clemens' library by Clara Clemens Gabrilowitsch in 1910.

Hadow, William Henry (1859–1937). *Studies in Modern Music.* London: Seeley & Co., 1893.

Inscription: "To Miss Clemens/from A. Mulligan/'Musik is die wahre/allgemeine Menschensprache'/June, 1896/Durban, Natal."

Marginalia: pencil marks on pp. 241; cynical comments in an unidentifiable hand on pp. 257–258 about Hadow's interpretation of Wagner. Apparently no marginalia by Clemens.

Location: Mark Twain Library, Redding, Conn.

Copy examined: Clara Clemens' copy, presumably.

Haeckel, Ernst Heinrich (1834–1919). *The Wonders of Life: A Popular Study of Biological Philosophy.* Trans. by Joseph McCabe. New York: Harper & Brothers, 1905.

Hyatt Howe Waggoner reported that Clara Clemens Gabrilowitsch recalled her father's reading this book ("Science" [1937], p. 362), but Clemens' copy has never appeared. Haeckel intended *Wonders* as a supplement to his *Riddle of the Universe* (1899).

Haggard, (Sir) Henry Rider (1856–1925). *Allan's Wife.* New York: J. S. Ogilvie, n.d. 180 pp.

Source: MTLAcc, entry #2257, volume donated from Clemens' library by Clara Clemens Gabrilowitsch in 1910.

On 5 August 1892 Clemens mentioned Haggard's name in a letter to William Walter Phelps (Huntington), but he gives no indication whether he read any of Haggard's romantic novels set in South Africa, such as *King Solomon's Mines* (1885) and *She* (1887).

————. *The Brethren.* Illus. New York: McClure, Phillips & Co., 1904. 411 pp.

Source: MTLAcc, entry #1278, volume donated by Clemens.

Ha! Ha! Ha!: 72 Pages of Fun by Leading Humorists. New York: J. S. Ogilvie & Co., 1882.

On 19 September 1882 Clemens wrote Charles L. Webster to demand copies of a book that he had learned was using the name "Mark Twain": "Get & send me this 'Ha-ha-ha' " (*MTBus,* p. 197).

Haines, John Thomas. *The French Spy; or, The Siege of Constantina. A Military Drama in Three Acts* (melodrama, prod. 1830).

Clemens saw Adah Menken play the title role in this play in San Francisco; she was "a frisky Frenchman, and as dumb as an oyster" (13 September 1863, *MTEnt*, p. 80).

Hale, Edward Everett (1822–1909) and Susan Hale. *A Family Flight*. Boston: D. Lothrop & Co., 1884.

Catalog: C1951, #D36, listed among volumes signed by Clemens.

————. "The Man Without a Country" (short story, pub. 1863).

Mark Twain listed Hale to receive a complimentary copy of *The Prince and the Pauper* in 1881 (NB 19, *N&J*, 2: 385), his first reference to this clergyman-author. In chapter 33 of *Life on the Mississippi* (1883) Mark Twain calls the man who owns a mid-river island in the Mississippi "the man without a country"; similarly in chapter 8 of *Following the Equator* he refers to two natives who mysteriously appear in a canoe in mid-Pacific as "those Men Without a Country." Following Olivia Clemens' death, Clemens announced to Charley Langdon: "I am a man without a country. Wherever Livy was, that was my country" (Florence, 19 June 1904, MTM). Edward Everett Hale was third on Mark Twain's list of ten nominees for the American Academy of Arts and Letters in 1905 (SLC to Robert Underwood Johnson, 28 April 1905, American Academy). In "Adam's Soliloquy" (1905) the mother in the park exclaims: "You must be the Man Without a Country—the one the story tells about. You don't seem to have any nationality at all." Hale wrote to Clemens in 1906 to reveal that the copyright on his famous story "expires this year" (IVL Journal, 10 April 1906, TS p. 155, MTP). In his Autobiographical Dictation of 4 February 1907 Mark Twain spoke of the "great and pathetic sensation" Hale's story made "when it issued from the press in the lurid days when the Civil War was about to break out [*sic*]" (*MTE*, p. 286).

————. *Susan's Escort, and Others*. New York: Harper & Brothers, 1898. 416 pp.

Source: MTLAcc, entry #1559, volume donated by Clemens.

Hale, Lucretia Peabody (1820–1900). *The Peterkin Papers*. Boston: Ticknor & Company, 1880.

Mark Twain included "The Peterkins Decide to Learn the Languages" in *Mark Twain's Library of Humor* (1888).

Halévy, Ludovic (1834–1908). *L'abbé Constantin, par Ludovic Halévy. With English Notes by Frederick C. Sumichrast*. New York: W. R. Jenkins; Boston: C. Schoenhof, 1888. 203 pp.

Clemens entered the title of this book in Notebook 30 (TS p. 15) in December 1890. The work was first published in Paris in 1882; W. R. Jenkins brought out editions in New York in 1883, 1885, 1886, and 1888. The edition listed above was the most recent when the book came to Clemens' attention.

————. *Parisian Points of View*. Trans. by Edith Virginia Brander Matthews. Intro. by Brander Matthews (1852–1929). New York: Harper & Brothers, 1894. 195 pp.

Livy Clemens wrote to her husband from Paris on 27 April 1894, reporting, "I have read the book that Edith Matthews translated. I find it extremely charming. The stories are bright and delightful and the translating is perfect; you could not believe that it was a translation it is so easy flowing" (ALS, Mark Twain Research Foundation, Perry, Mo.; quoted in *The Twainian*, 37 [May-June 1978], 4).

Haliburton, Thomas Chandler (1796–1865), pseud. "Sam Slick." *The Clockmaker, or Sayings and Doings of Sam Slick* (1837, 1838, 1840).

Cyril Clemens reported in 1941 that during "a long talk" with Laura Hawkins Frazer (1837–1928) of Hannibal she told him an anecdote about Sam Clemens' early reading. Supposedly young Clemens haggled with a Yankee pack-peddler before buying a copy of Haliburton's *Clockmaker*, "which had a bright yellow cover." Sam Clemens then carried the book about with him everywhere he went, even chuckling over it in church ("Unpublished Recollections of Original Becky Thatcher," p. 20). Cyril Clemens repeats this story in *Young Sam Clemens* (Portland, Maine: Leon Tebbetts Editions, 1942), pp. 37–38. Mark Twain listed "Sam Slick" among the humorists he was considering for possible inclusion in an anthology in 1880 (NB 19, *N&J*, 2: 363); in 1881 he included "Haliburton" in another compilation of American humorists' names (NB 19, *N&J*, 2: 429).

Hall, Basil (1788–1844). *Travels in North America, in the Years 1827 and 1828.* 3 vols. Edinburgh: Cadell and Co., 1829.
 Marginalia: some passages marked by Clemens.
 Catalog: A1911, #215, $1.25.
 Mark Twain alluded to this work as "the starter of the *real* swarm" of British travelers to the United States in the manuscript for an unused portion of *Life on the Mississippi.* In chapter 15 of vol. 3 Hall gives a description of "deck-fare" passengers on a river steamboat, a lively account of a pause at a "wooding" station, a detailed picture of a backwoodsman's farm, and an explanation—complete with map—of how steamboat pilots steer while going upstream and downstream (pp. 348–368).

Hall, Florence Marion (Howe) (1845–1922). *Social Usages at Washington.* New York: Harper & Brothers, 1906. 166 pp.
 Source: MTLAcc, entry #394, volume donated by Clemens.

————. [Another identical copy.]
 Source: MTLAcc, entry #1356, volume donated by Clemens.

Hall, Herbert Byng. *The Bric-à-Brac Hunter; or, Chapters on Chinamania.* London, 1875.
 In chapter 20 of *A Tramp Abroad* (1880) Mark Twain pretends to champion "that elegant Englishman, Byng [*sic*], who wrote a book called 'The Bric-à-Brac Hunter,' " against ignorant people who ridicule Byng for " 'gushing' over these trifles; and for exhibiting his 'deep infantile delight' in what they call his 'tupenny collection of beggarly trivialities'; and for beginning his book with a picture of himself, seated, in a 'sappy, self-complacent attitude, in the midst of his poor little ridiculous bric-à-brac junk shop.' " See also the entry for William Prime, *Pottery and Porcelain.*

Hallam, Henry (1777–1859). *Introduction to the Literature of Europe,* 2 vols.; *Constitutional History of England from Henry VII's Accession to the Death of George II,* 2 vols. New York, 1880.
 Catalog: A1911, #216, 4 vols., $3.25 total.

Halm, Friedrich, pseud. of Eligius von Münch Bellinghausen (1806–1871). *Ingomar, the Barbarian* (melodrama).
 From St. Louis, Missouri, young Samuel Clemens wrote to his brother's Muscatine, Iowa *Journal* on 5 March 1855: "[George W.] Jameison, the tragedian, is playing an engagement at the People's Theatre. He appears as Ingomar tonight" (*MTLMusc*, p. 27). Clemens later saw *Ingomar* performed in Virginia City in November 1863; he then wrote a burlesque, " 'Ingomar' Over the Mountains," which was published in the San Francisco *Golden Era* and the *Territorial Enterprise* (*WG*, pp. 58–60). In 1881 he parodied the closing lines of

Ingomar in Notebook 19, altering "Two souls with but a single thought,/Two hearts that beat as one" into "Two tramps with but a single shirt,/Two beats that bilk as one" *(N&J,* 2: 412). Sydney J. Krause reports that Halm originally wrote the play as *Der Sohn der Wildness* (1843), that it was translated into English by William H. Charlton, and that as *Ingomar* it was first performed in English around 1850 *(MTC,* pp. 47–50).
LAMT, pp. 35, 90–92, p. 288 n. 96.

———. *Wildfeuer.* Wien: Carl Gerolds Sohn, 1896.
Inscription: flyleaf missing.
Location: Mark Twain Library, Redding, Conn.
Copy examined: presumably Clemens' copy.
Hemminghaus, "Mark Twain's German Provenience," p. 472.

Hamerton, Philip Gilbert (1834–1894). *Chapters on Animals.* Illus. Boston: Roberts Brothers, 1881. 253 pp.
Source: MTLAcc, entry #539, volume donated by Clemens.

———. *French and English, A Comparison.* Boston: Roberts Brothers, 1889. 480 pp.
In November 1889 Clemens noted: "P Gilbert Hamerton 'French & English.' Roberts Bros. Boston" (NB 29, TS p. 31). Hamerton's book studies national characteristics; it was based on seven articles that appeared in the *Atlantic Monthly* in 1886 and 1887.

———. *Wenderholme. A Story of Lancashire and Yorkshire.* Boston: Roberts Brothers, 1876. 433 pp.
Source: MTLAcc, entry #2258, volume donated from Clemens' library by Clara Clemens Gabrilowitsch in 1910.

Hamilton, Anna E. "We long to see Jesus" (hymn).
In "Captain Stormfield's Visit to Heaven" (1909), "The prodigious choir struck up—/We long to hear thy voice,/To see thee face to face." Stormfield calls it "noble music, but the uneducated chipped in and spoilt it, just as the congregations used to do down on earth." Shortly thereafter "the choir struck up —/The whole wide heaven groans,/And waits to hear that voice" *(RP,* pp. 82, 83).

Hamilton, Anthony (1646?–1720). *Mémoires du Comte de Gramont.* Two vols. in one. Paris, 1850.
Catalog: A1911, #217, $1.
Hamilton wrote the memoirs of his brother-in-law, Comte de Gramont.

Hamilton, Thomas (1789–1842). *Men and Manners in America. By the Author of "Cyril Thornton,"* &c. Philadelphia: Carey, Lea & Blanchard, 1833.
Marginalia: on page 61 Clemens wrote: "There are several of these fellows who give you a slap, and then turn immediately and kick a member of their family, stupidly imagining that the kick heals the slap. If they had stopped with either the kick or the slap, they wouldn't have offended both parties." Clemens also made other marginal notations.
Catalog: A1911, #218, $2.
In a chapter deleted from the published version of *Life on the Mississippi* Mark Twain quotes and ridicules "a countryman" of Mrs. Trollope, " 'Author of Cyril Thornton, Etc.,' (no other brand given)," whose book about America "differs from the books of most of the other foreign tourists of that day, in this— that it is not dignified, not brave, and not tolerant." A little farther on, listing the parade of visitors to the United States, Mark Twain again refers to " 'Author

of Cyril Thornton, etc.,' a now forgotten literary celebrity, 1833–4" (Limited Editions Club [1944], pp. 394–395). Hamilton published *The Youth and Manhood of Cyril Thornton* in 1827. He had served as an English officer in warfare against the American nation between 1812 and 1815.

Ganzel, "Twain, Travel Books," p. 41 n. 4.

Hammond, Edward Payson. *Sketches of Palestine Descriptive of the Visit of the Rev. Edward Payson Hammond, M.A., to the Holy Land.* Intro. by the Reverend Robert Knox. Boston: Henry Hoyt, n.d. [Introduction is dated 8 February 1868.]

Inscription: Clemens wrote in pencil on the front free endpaper: "This book belongs to S. L. Clemens's Library of Literary 'Hogwash.' Hartford 1876." The front pastedown endpaper is signed by Edward P. Judd.

Marginalia: Prolific annotations in pencil by Clemens, uniformly derisive. Choice passages have been scissored from many pages, leaving the volume much mutilated. On page 148 Clemens refers to Hammond as a "putrid . . . humbug." Alan Gribben reproduces pages 142 and 153 in facsimile, illustrating how adeptly Clemens mimicked Hammond's verse with marginal quatrains of his own invention (" 'I Kind of Love Small Game': Mark Twain's Library of Literary Hogwash" [1976]).

Location: Mark Twain Papers, Berkeley, California. A typed page of description accompanying the volume explains that it was formerly in the collection of Professor James Westfall Thompson, who acquired it from a New Haven book dealer. A note on a loose index card indicates that the book was donated to the Mark Twain Papers by Miss Cornelia Beall of Berkeley.

Copy examined: Clemens' copy.

Hammond wrote these "sketches" in the form of poems. On 27 October 1879 Clemens notified an unnamed correspondent that he had written a review of this "admirable singer" (ALS in Newberry Library, Chicago). Philip B. Eppard— "Mark Twain Dissects an Overrated Book" (1977)—has established the fact that Twain published his humorous essay as an anonymous contribution to the June 1877 issue of the *Atlantic Monthly*.

Hammond, (Mrs.) Natalie (Harris). *A Woman's Part in a Revolution.* New York and Bombay: Longmans, Green, and Co., 1897.

Inscription: "To Dear Mark Twain who cheered many a weary heart before he reached mine, From the Author, April 1897."

Marginalia: contains marginal notes and underlinings by Clemens. His comments are generally favorable. See *The Twainian*, May-June 1954; January-February 1958.

Catalog: C1951, #D69, listed among books signed by Clemens.

Location: collection of Chester Davis, Mark Twain Research Foundation, Perry, Missouri.

Copy examined: this volume was unavailable for inspection when I visited Perry, Missouri in 1970.

Twice in Notebook 38 Clemens alluded to Mrs. Hammond's serious illness in 1896 (TS pp. 22, 33). In chapter 65 of *Following the Equator* (1897) Mark Twain refers to the recently published book "by Mrs. John Hays Hammond, a vigorous and vivid diarist, partial to the Reformers"; in chapter 66 he reports her criticism of Doctor Jameson; in chapter 67 he summarizes her sympathetic view of the Reform Committee. Mrs. Hammond's husband had been imprisoned after Jameson's raid in Johannesburg, South Africa.

Madigan, "Mark Twain's Passage to India," p. 359.

Hancock, Almira (Russell). *Reminiscences of Winfield Scott Hancock. By His Wife.* New York: Charles L. Webster & Co., 1887. 340 pp.

Issued by Clemens' publishing firm.

142   LINES.

'Twas in that olive press I felt
    That Thou didst bleed for me ;—
Alas ! how great I saw my guilt
    While in Gethsemane.

I thought of how Thy heart did throb,
    While 'all' Thine own did flee,
And left Thee with the cruel mob
    In sad Gethsemane.

How earnestly with tears we pled
    For friends across the sea,
That they might cling to Thee who bled
    In lone Gethsemane.

'Twas there I felt my guilt and shame
    In oft forsaking Thee ;
How precious was Thy very name
    In dear Gethsemane.

Should e'er our love to Thee grow cold,
    And we forgetful be,
We 'll call to mind Thy love untold
    While in Gethsemane.

And now I've thought out all the rot
    That rhymes with vowel ε ;
Let not this service be forgot —
    Ta-ta, Gethsemane.

Plate 7:   Marginalia written in pencil in Edward P. Hammond's *Sketches of Palestine*. Clemens was impressed with Hammond's verse prayer to Christ during Hammond's visit to the Garden of Gethsemane. (Copyright © 1980, Trustees Under the Will of Clara Clemens Samossoud.) *(Courtesy of Mark Twain Papers, University of California, Berkeley.)*

290

FAREWELL TO PALESTINE. 153

Thou Holy Land, adieu!
  Farewell ye Bible scenes ;
Soon thou wilt vanish from our view,
  Thou Land of Palestine.

From thee the Saviour rose
  Victorious o'er the grave,
Thus triumphing o'er all His foes,
  That He the lost might save.

'Twas from thine Olive Mount
  He left the sight of men,
And on that mount His feet shal' stand
  When He shall come again.

We thank our blessed Lord
  That we have seen thy face,
With more of love we'll read His Word,
  And thus its beauty trace.

We've climbed thy rugged hills,
  And scaled thy mountains high ;
We've rested by thy sparkling rills,
  But now a long good-bye !

After forty hours of sailing
O'er the classic Mediterranean,
It was on a Lord's-day morning
That they landed in the city
Built by the great Alexander.
  With the help of Captain Layard
They passed thro' the ranks of Arabs,

Plate 8: Clemens' penciled annotation beside Edward P. Hammond's lyrical leave-taking of Palestine. (Copyright © 1980, Trustees Under the Will of Clara Clemens Samossoud.)
(Courtesy of Mark Twain Papers, University of California, Berkeley.)

Handbook for Travellers in Ireland. Maps. London, 1871.
   Catalog: A1911, #261, $4.25.

Handbook of Florence. Illus. N.p.: M. Contrucci & Co., n.d. 152 pp.
   Source: MTLAcc, entry #549, volume donated by Clemens.

Hanna, Septimus James (1844–1921). *Christian Science History.* Boston: Christian
   Science Publishing Society, 1899.
      In *Christian Science* Mark Twain quotes from page 16 of Hanna's book
   (WIM?, pp. 319, 570).

Hapgood, Hutchins. *The Spirit of the Ghetto. Studies of the Jewish Quarter in New
   York.* New York, 1902.
      Inscription: signed "S. L. Clemens, 1902."
      Catalog: A1911, #220, $3.50.

Harben, William Nathaniel (1858–1919).
      Evidently Clemens castigated Harben in a letter to William Dean Howells, for
   on 11 February 1910 Howells replied from New York City: "You seem to
   require a novelist to be true to the facts and if the facts are not pleasant, to be
   pleasant himself. That seems rather difficult. . . . But I believe you will end by
   liking poor old Harben as much as I do. He didn't make North Georgia; he only
   made a likeness of it. Don't shoot the artist" *(MTHL,* p. 852). Howells published
   a review, "Mr. Harben's Georgia Fiction," in the March 1910 issue of *North
   American Review.* During the last months of his life Clemens entered both cen-
   sure and praise for Harben in Notebook 49, sometimes writing in German (TS
   pp. 1–3, 10); generally he seems to concur with Harben's philosophy but objects
   to his narrative techniques. Howells recalled in *My Mark Twain* (1910): "In the
   very last weeks of his life he burst forth, and, though too weak himself to write,
   he dictated his rage with me for recommending to him a certain author whose
   truthfulness he could not deny, but whom he hated for his truthfulness to sordid
   and ugly conditions. At heart Clemens was romantic" (p. 42).

————. *Abner Daniel. A Novel.* New York: Harper & Brothers, 1905. 312 pp.
   Source: MTLAcc, entry #1037, volume donated by Clemens.

————. *Ann Boyd; A Novel.* New York: Harper & Brothers, 1906. 390 pp.
   Source: MTLAcc, entry #1008, volume donated by Clemens.

————. [Another identical copy.]
   Source: MTLAcc, entry #1434, volume donated by Clemens.

————. *The Georgians. A Novel.* New York: Harper & Brothers, 1904. 338 pp.
   Source: MTLAcc, entry #158, volume donated by Clemens.

————. [Another identical copy.]
   Source: MTLAcc, entry #1562, volume donated by Clemens.

————. *Gilbert Neal; A Novel.* New York: Harper & Brothers, 1908. 362 pp.
   Source: MTLAcc, entry #1560, volume donated by Clemens.

————. *Mam' Linda; A Novel.* Illus. New York: Harper & Brothers, 1907. 388 pp.
   Source: MTLAcc, entry #1561, volume donated by Clemens.

————. *Pole Baker; A Novel.* New York: Harper & Brothers, 1905. 358 pp.
   Source: MTLAcc, entry #1010, volume donated by Clemens.

————. [Another identical copy.]
> *Source:* MTLAcc, entry #1258, volume donated by Clemens.

————. *The Redemption of Kenneth Galt.* New York: Harper & Brothers, 1909. 351 pp.
> *Source:* MTLAcc, entry #1421, volume donated by Clemens.

————. *The Substitute.* New York: Harper & Brothers, 1903. 330 pp.
> *Source:* MTLAcc, entry #1009, volume donated by Clemens.

Hardy, Arthur Sherburne (1847–1930). *But Yet A Woman; A Novel.* Boston: Houghton, Mifflin & Co., 1883. 348 pp.
> *Source:* MTLAcc, entry #2259, volume donated from Clemens' library by Clara Clemens Gabrilowitsch in 1910.

Hardy, E. R. "The Restoration," *Christian Science Journal,* 16 (October 1898), 456.
> In chapter 6 of "Christian Science" (1907) Mark Twain quoted four excerpts extolling Christian Science (*WIM?*, pp. 238, 242).

Hardy, Mary McDowell Duffus. *A Casual Acquaintance: A Novel Founded on Fact.* London: Low & Co., 1866.
> After Clemens conversed with Lady Hardy in London in July 1873 he recorded the gist of their discussion in Notebook 12 (*N&J*, 1: 557–559). Clemens wrote to Mrs. Fairbanks on 6 July 1873: "Lady Hardy has written a number of novels & is well known here, but I think not in America. She told us the *facts* upon which her <'Chance'> 'Casual Acquaintance' was founded—a thrilling recital & admirably done. Pity people can't always *talk* a book instead of writing it" (*MTMF,* p. 176).

Hardy, Thomas (1840–1928). *Far from the Madding Crowd.* New York, 1874.
> *Inscription:* signed on title page, "Saml. L. Clemens, Hartford, 1875."
> *Catalog:* A1911, #222, $5.
> Clemens labeled Hardy's work "haggard, hideous," but included Hardy in the list of eminent authors he constructed to pass the time while snowbound in New York City in March 1888 (NB 27, TS p. 61). Dr. James Ross Clemens (1866–1918), a distant relative who met Clemens in London in 1897, is responsible for the story that Clemens did not recognize Hardy when they encountered each other one day in a country inn and exchanged literary opinions. Later Clemens was chagrined to learn that he had attacked Hardy's literary reputation to his face. Dr. Clemens states that he heard the anecdote from Clemens himself ("Reminiscences of Mark Twain" [1929], p. 105).

————. *Jude the Obscure.* New York and London: Harper & Brothers, 1895.
> *Inscriptions:* Albert Bigelow Paine noted on the inner front cover: "This book was read by Mark Twain, April 9–10–11–1910 in Bermuda" (quotation supplied by Bigelow Paine Cushman). In a flyleaf inscription Paine recorded: "This is the last book he ever read through. He died April 21. When he finished it, he asked me to read it 'so we can talk about it.' I began it by his bedside and continued it on the ship. We did talk about it—more or less, and never afterwards of any other" (quoted in "A. B. Paine's Part in Boosting Library," Redding, Connecticut *Pilot,* 15 June 1972 [section titled "New Mark Twain Library," p. 18]).
> *Location:* owned by Professor Bigelow Paine Cushman, Department of English, Western Connecticut State College, Danbury, Conn. Professor Cushman supplied the information for this entry.

———. *Poems of the Past and the Present.* New York, 1901.
  Inscription: signed "S. L. Clemens, Riverdale, Dec., 1901."
  Catalog: A1911, #221, $1.50.

Hare, Augustus John Cuthbert (1834–1903). *Walks in London.* 2 vols. Illus. Daldy, Isbister & Co., 1878. [American edition: New York: George Routledge and Sons, 1878. 500 pp.]
  Clemens once recalled how he spent an unspecified period in London: "Nobody in town. Bought [John] Timbs—[Hare's] Walks—[John] Stow—Leigh Hunt, & a lot of other authorities & read about a thing, then went leisurely to see it" (undated MS scrap, DV115, MTP). He may have meant Edward Pugh's *Walks Through London* (London: E. Williams, 1817), but Hare's historical guidebook seems the far more likely referent.

———. *Walks in Rome.* New York, 1874.
  Inscription: signed "Saml. L. Clemens, Bateman's Point, Newport, R. I., Aug., 1875."
  Catalog: A1911, #223, $3.

Harper's Bazar (periodical, pub. 1867–   ).
  On 12 September 1901 Clemens requested Frederick A. Duneka to change his mailing address for *Harper's Bazar* to Riverdale-on-the-Hudson, New York (Berg). In June 1904 Clemens asked Isabel Lyon to change his address for "3 Harpers" (*Weekly, Monthly,* and *Bazar*) when he left the Villa di Quarto (MS note in MTP).

Harper's Guide to Paris and the Exposition of 1900. Illus. New York: Harper & Brothers, 1900. 292 pp.
  Source: MTLAcc, entry #1347, volume donated by Clemens.

Harper's Monthly Magazine (periodical, pub. 1850–   ).
  In a sketch published in the 6 May 1865 issue of *The Californian* Clemens alluded to "a neat remark" about Martin Farquhar Tupper "which the editor of *Harper's Magazine* made three years ago." In 1867 Clemens mentioned the attention to utterances by precocious children shown by the "Editor's Drawer" (NB 10, *N&J*, 1: 472). Clemens reminded himself to "get full Harper Monthly for Sue [Crane]" at a secondhand bookstore in New York City in July 1877 (NB 13, *N&J*, 2: 38). On 10 August 1878 in Baden-Baden Clemens went "to bed early, with the new home magazines [*Harper's* and *Atlantic*], which I had saved all day & wouldn't cut a leaf" (NB 15, *N&J*, 2: 134); a clipping pinned to a leaf in Notebook 14 (*N&J*, 2: 91) was taken from the July 1878 issue of *Harper's.* In chapter 59 of *Life on the Mississippi* (1883) Mark Twain burlesques an anonymous article, "Sketches on the Upper Mississippi," *Harper's Monthly Magazine,* 7 (July 1853), 182 (see *MTBP*, pp. 91–93).
  William Dean Howells took over the "Editor's Study" column for six years beginning in October 1885 (*MTHL*, p. 538 n. 1). In 1888 Clemens wrote of *Harper's* and *Century:* "there is no choice between the two magazines, since they stand equally high" (SLC to Baroness Alexandra Gripenberg, 15 September 1888, quoted by Ernest J. Moyne, "Mark Twain and Baroness Alexandra Gripenberg," *AL,* 45 [November 1973], 373). Clemens jotted a note in September 1889 about "the train-boy who sold me a September Harper" (NB 29, TS p. 26). In May 1891 Clemens made arrangements to receive his *Harper's* subscription in Europe (NB 30, TS p. 40). From Berlin on 9 November 1891 Clemens instructed Franklin G. Whitmore to stop Harper's from sending two copies of the magazine; Whitmore was asked to keep the extra copy himself (MTM). "Mrs. Clemens fears the subscription to Harper's Monthly has run out —& she wants that magazine," Clemens informed Franklin G. Whitmore on 3 August 1894, while Livy was in Paris (MTP). "Of whom do you order the

magazine for us?" Clemens grumbled to Whitmore from Rouen on 7 October 1894. "It is *many months* since either a Harper or a Century has arrived" (MTP). From Paris Clemens again complained on 6 November 1894 that "No Harper has arrived yet," and he instructed Whitmore to "give it up" and renew any *Harper's* subscriptions when they expire; he and Livy were obliged to purchase in Paris the current issue containing a story by Charles Dudley Warner (MTP). In January 1896 Clemens read Edwin Lord Weeks' article on Bombay in the November 1895 issue (NB 36, TS p. 22).

Although Howells left the "Editor's Study" in 1892, his fiction continued to appear in *Harper's;* on 2 April 1899 Clemens reported from Vienna that he was "waiting for the April Harper" which contained an installment of *Their Silver Wedding Journey (MTHL*, p. 689). Clemens mentioned that he was receiving copies of *Harper's* in a letter to Joseph H. Twichell written at Kaltenleutgeben, near Vienna, on 13 September 1898 *(MTL*, p. 666). Charles Dudley Warner conducted the "Editor's Study" after Howells resigned until the column was dropped in 1898; Clemens lamented to Howells on 3 January 1899 from Vienna: "I have never gotten over your abandoning the Study to those pathetic stages—famine, water-logged derelict, unlamented submersion. The family feels the same way" *(MTHL*, p. 686). On 12 September 1901 Clemens asked Frederick A. Duneka to change his subscription address to Riverdale (Berg); on 3 January 1902 he requested Duneka to send another copy of the Christmas 1901 issue, since his was lost (Berg). Clemens referred knowledgeably to several pieces in the December 1903 issue when he wrote to Howells on 4 December 1903 from Florence *(MTHL*, pp. 774–775). In June 1904 Clemens directed Isabel Lyon to change the address for his subscriptions to the "3 Harpers" when he left Florence (MS note in MTP). On 2 October 1905 Mark Twain suggested that "A Horse's Tale" be sold to either the *Ladies' Home Journal* or *Collier's* so that it would reach the audience that "can't afford" *Harper's* (Berg). Miss Lyon wrote to *Harper's* from Dublin, New Hampshire on 29 September 1905 requesting that the mailing department begin sending Clemens' subscription to 21 Fifth Avenue (MTP).

Harper's Pictorial History of the War with Spain, 2 vols.; *History of the War in the Philippines*, 3 vols. New York, 1899--190?.
    Catalog: A1911, #439, $9 total.

Harper's Weekly (periodical, pub. 1857–1916).
    Clemens noticed in 1861 that the houses around Carson City were papered with engravings from *Harper's Weekly* (SLC to Jane Lampton Clemens, 26 October 1861, TS in MTP). The library on the *Quaker City* contained two volumes of *Harper's Weekly,* along with fifteen copies of the *Plymouth Collection of Hymns* (reported by Dr. Abraham R. Jackson, New York *Herald,* 21 November 1867). In November 1872 Clemens congratulated Thomas Nast, the staff artist of the *Weekly,* for his anti-Greeley cartoons during the Grant campaign *(MTL*, p. 202). Clemens mentioned the magazine in a letter to Frank Bliss on 10 May 1879 *(MTLP*, p. 114). From Vienna Clemens wrote to Howells on 3 January 1899: "The Weekly has just come" *(MTHL*, p. 686). On 12 September 1901 Clemens asked Frederick A. Duneka to change his mailing address for the *Weekly* to Riverdale (Berg). "The Weekly is just received," Clemens wrote to Howells on 29 April 1903 *(MTHL*, p. 768). While Olivia Clemens lay ill in 1904 Clemens wrote her an undated note to accompany an issue of *Harper's Weekly* containing "not very interesting" war pictures (MTP). In June 1904 Clemens gave instructions to Miss Lyon about notifying *Harper's Weekly* of his new address in the United States (MS note in MTP).

Harraden, Beatrice (1864–1936). *Ships That Pass in the Night*. New York: J. S. Ogilvie, 1894.
    In New York City in February 1894 Clemens reminded himself: "Ships that Pass in the Night. Get 2—send one to Paris" (NB 33, TS p. 53). Livy was then living in Paris.

Harris, George Washington (1814–1869). *Sut Lovingood: Yarns Spun by a "Nat'ral Born Durn'd Fool."* New York: Dick & Fitzgerald, 1867.

Mark Twain noticed the issuance of this collection of stories in a brief paragraph published in the 14 July 1867 *Alta California;* he referred to the sketches as those "that used to be so popular in the West." Although he thought "the book abounds in humor," he predicted that "the Eastern people will call it coarse and taboo it" *(MTTMB,* p. 221). In 1880 Mark Twain again noted the title and publisher of the edition ("Sut Lovengood [*sic*]—Dick & Fitzgerald") while listing authors for possible inclusion in an anthology of humor (NB 19, *N&J,* 2: 362). He jotted down "Sut Lovengood" [*sic*] for the same purpose in 1881 (NB 19, *N&J,* 2: 429). When Mark Twain made notes in August 1885 for an "Essay on Humor," he decided to quote from "that forgotten Tennessee humorist" (NB 24, TS p. 36). *Mark Twain's Library of Humor* (1888) contained one sketch from *Sut Lovingood: Yarns*—"Sicily Burns's Wedding."

Long, "Sut Lovingood" (1949); *CTMT,* pp. 132–140; *MT&SH,* pp. 134, 138, 139; Hennig Cohen, "Mark Twain's Sut Lovingood" (1962); *MTC,* p. 298; *NAH,* p. 101; Tanner, *Reign of Wonder* (1965), pp. 100–103; *NF,* p. 243; *MT&HF,* pp. 242–243.

Harris, Joel Chandler (1848–1908). *Free Joe and Other Georgian Sketches.* New York, 1887.
Inscription: "With the regards of the author, Joel Chandler Harris."
Catalog: A1911, #225, $10.50.

———. *Nights with Uncle Remus: Myths and Legends of the Old Plantation.* Boston: James R. Osgood and Co., 1883.
Mark Twain's Library of Humor credited "The Tar Baby" and "Mr. Fox Victimized" to this collection, though Mark Twain first encountered both pieces in *Uncle Remus: His Songs and His Sayings* (1880). Harris and Mark Twain had compared versions of one of the tales in *Nights,* "A Ghost Story" (SLC to Harris, 12 December 1881, *MTL,* pp. 403–404); Mark Twain called his variant "The Golden Arm."

———. *On the Wing of Occasions.* Illus. New York: Doubleday, Page & Co., 1900. 310 pp.
Source: MTLAcc, entry #2260, volume donated from Clemens' library by Clara Clemens Gabrilowitsch in 1910.

———. *Uncle Remus: His Songs and His Sayings. The Folk-Lore of the Old Plantation.* New York: D. Appleton & Co., 1890.
Inscription: signed in pencil on the flyleaf: "S. L. Clemens, Hartford, 1890."
Catalogs: C1951, #D21, $32.50; *Zeitlin 1951,* #19, $50.
Clemens probably owned an earlier edition of this book as well. In July 1880 he noted: "<Old Si> (?) Uncle Remus writer of colored yarns" (NB 19, *N&J,* 2: 362). On 28 November 1880 Clemens wrote to Fields, Osgood, & Company from Hartford: "Dr. Sirs: Please send me 'Uncle Remus's Songs & Sayings.' Yrs. truly, S. L. Clemens" (ALS quoted in undated catalog, Maxwell Hunley Rare Books [1958?], item #161).
Clemens praised the narrator of these tales in a letter to Harris written on 10 August 1881: "In reality the stories are only alligator pears—one merely eats them for the sake of the salad-dressing. Uncle Remus is most deftly drawn, and is a lovable and delightful creation; he, and the little boy, and their relations with each other, are high and fine literature, and worthy to live, for their own sakes; and certainly the stories are not to be credited with *them*" *(MTL,* pp. 401–402).
Of the stories in this collection Clemens favored "Brer Rabbit, Brer Fox, and the Tar Baby." On 27 February 1881 he informed William Dean Howells from Hartford: "I read in Twichell's chapel Friday night, & had a most rattling high

time—but the thing that went best of all was Uncle Remus's Tar Baby"
(MTHL, p. 356). He noted the title in 1885 as a possible piece for public
reading (NB 23, TS pp. 41, 42); and in October 1889 he planned to "read Tar-
Baby at tail-end of Author's Reading in Brooklyn Dec. 16, '89, Academy of
Music" (NB 29, TS p. 28). Meanwhile, he selected this tale and another sketch
—"Mr. Fox is Again Victimized"—for inclusion in *Mark Twain's Library of
Humor* (1888). (The latter piece Mark Twain published as an extension of "Mr.
Rabbit Grossly Deceives Mr. Fox.") "The Tar Baby" was the only selection
by another author that Mark Twain planned to read at Bryn Mawr in 1891
(NB 30, TS pp. 23, 25, 32); he also scheduled it for use in his Dresden reading in
December 1891 (NB 31, TS p. 16). Notebook 35 reveals that the tar-baby
story was part of Mark Twain's repertoire when he began his lecture tour around
the world in July 1895 (TS pp. 4, 14). In chapter 49 of *Following the Equator*
(1897) Mark Twain employed a phrase from the tar-baby story: " 'Brer fox he
lay low,' as Uncle Remus says." During Brer Rabbit's monologue with the
silent tar-baby this line is repeated as a refrain: "Tar-Baby stay still, en Brer
Fox, he lay low" *(Uncle Remus: His Songs and His Sayings* [New York:
D. Appleton Co., 1895], pp. 8–10).

Mark Twain first met Harris in May 1882 in New Orleans, where Harris,
Mark Twain, and George Washington Cable read from their writings to neighborhood children at Cable's house; "I read Remus' stories & my own stuff to
them," Clemens wrote to Livy on 2 May 1882 *(LLMT,* p. 212). In chapter 47
of *Life on the Mississippi* (1883) Mark Twain mentioned Harris' extreme shyness
and praised his ability to write Negro dialect ("the only master the country has
produced"). On 5 November 1892 Clemens wrote to Clara Clemens from Florence to describe recent literary readings at Villa Viviani: after laying aside
Browning ("too sombre & difficult") and Tennyson ("too tame & effeminate"), he
and his circle were "bracing up on Uncle Remus, evenings, for a change" (MTP).
From Paris Clemens wrote to Henry H. Rogers on 27 December 1894: "I . . .
went to a masked ball blacked up as Uncle Remus, taking Clara along; and we
had a good time" *(MTHHR,* p. 112). Harris was one of Clemens' nominations for
membership in the American Academy of Arts and Letters in 1905 (SLC to
Robert Underwood Johnson, 28 April 1905, American Academy). "Susy and
Clara . . . knew his book by heart through my nightly declamation of its tales to
them," he once recalled (16 October 1906 AD, *MTE,* p. 136).

Harris, William Torrey (1835–1909). *The First Reader.* Illus. New York: D. Appleton and Co., 1880. 90 pp.
   Source: MTLAcc, entry #447, volume donated by Clemens.

[Harrison, Austin (1873–1928)]. *The Pan-Germanic Doctrine; Being a Study of
German Political Aims and Aspirations.* Maps. New York: Harper & Brothers,
1904. 379 pp.
   Source: MTLAcc, entry #1500, volume donated by Clemens.

Harrison, (Mrs.) Constance (Cary) (1843–1920). *An Edelweiss of the Sierras;
Golden-Rod, and Other Tales.* New York: Harper & Brothers, 1892. 209 pp.
   Source: MTLAcc, entry #1485, volume donated by Clemens.

———. *The Story of Helen Troy.* New York: Harper & Brothers, [cop. 1881].
202 pp.
   Source: MTLAcc, entry #1173, volume donated by Clemens.

Harrison, Frederic (1831–1923). *Theophano, the Crusade of the Tenth Century; A
Novel.* New York: Harper & Brothers, 1904. 484 pp.
   Source: MTLAcc, entry #1104, volume donated by Clemens.

————. [Another identical copy.]
Source: MTLAcc, entry #2261, volume donated from Clemens' library by Clara Clemens Gabrilowitsch in 1910.

Hart, Albert Bushnell (1854–1943) and Blanche E. Hazard, eds. *Colonial Children.* Source Readers in American History, No. 1. New York: Macmillan, 1902.
Clemens joked in a letter to Charles J. Langdon on 25 July 1904 from Lee, Massachusetts: "Ida's 'Colonial Children' are perfectly safe: I only brought it away to hold as security against the return of the [shaving] brush" (MTM).

Hart, Jerome Alfred (1854–1937). *A Levantine Log-Book.* Illus. New York: Longmans, Green and Co., 1905. 404 pp.
Inscription: first flyleaf inscribed "Samuel L. Clemens, Esq., with respects and good wishes from an admirer of many years./Jerome A. Hart/January, 1906."
Location: Mark Twain Library, Redding, Conn. Donated by Clemens (MTLAcc, entry #587).
Copy examined: Clemens' copy, unmarked.

Harte, Bret (1836–1902). *Condensed Novels* (pub. 1867).
In a portion of Mark Twain's letter of 2 February 1867 that was deleted in publication by the *Alta California* he referred to Harte's "capital *Condensed Novels*," a book then in press (*MTTMB*, p. 284, n. 5).

————. *Drift from Two Shores.* Boston: Houghton, Osgood & Co., 1878.
Mark Twain's Library of Humor (1888) included a sketch from this volume, "A Sleeping-Car Experience."

————. *Gabriel Conroy* (novel, pub. 1876).
Clemens discussed the details of Harte's royalties for this novel in letter of 5 July 1875 to Howells (*MTHL*, p. 92). "His long novel, Gabriel Conway, is as much like Dickens as if Dickens had written it himself" (14 June 1906 AD, *MTE*, p. 267).

————. *An Heiress of Red Dog, and Other Tales.* London: Chatto & Windus, 1879. 300 pp.
Source: MTLAcc, entry #2264, volume donated from Clemens' library by Clara Clemens Gabrilowitsch in 1910.
"Chatto sent me Harte's new book of Sketches, the other day," Clemens wrote to Howells on 15 April 1879. "I have read it twice": the first time "through tears of rage over the fellow's inborn hypocrisy & snobbishness, his apprentice-art, his artificialities, his mannerisms, his pet phrases"; but on the second reading Clemens became aware of "a most decided brightness on every page of it—& here & there evidences of genius" (*MTHL*, p. 261). Clemens resolved to write a review of Harte's work (*MTHL*, p. 262); he published such a critique as an anonymous essay in the "Contributors' Club," *Atlantic Monthly*, 45 (June 1880), 850–851.

————. *In the Carquinez Woods.* Boston: Houghton, Mifflin and Co., 1884. 241 pp.
Source: MTLAcc, entry #2262, volume donated from Clemens' library by Clara Clemens Gabrilowitsch in 1910.

————. *The Lectures of Bret Harte, Compiled from Various Sources.* Ed. by Charles Meeker Kozlay. New York: Charles Meeker Kozlay, 1909. 53 pp.
Inscription: "To Samuel L. Clemens with the compliments of Charles Meeker Kozlay/Oct. 21, 1909."
Location: Mark Twain Library, Redding, Conn.
Copy examined: Clemens' copy, unmarked and with several leaves unopened.

————. *The Luck of Roaring Camp, and Other Sketches.* Boston: Fields, Osgood, 1870. 239 pp.

Marginalia: heavily annotated by Clemens, possibly in the course of recommending pieces for *Mark Twain's Library of Humor.* Bradford A. Booth reproduces the marginalia in "Mark Twain's Comments on Bret Harte's Stories" (1954).

Catalog: C1951, #33a, $200. Purchased by Wilbur Smith, Special Collections librarian at U.C.L.A. (Glen Dawson, "Mark Twain Library Auction," *American Book-Prices Current, 1950–51* [New York: R. R. Bowker, 1951], 106).

Location: Mark Twain Papers, Berkeley, California.

Copy examined: Clemens' copy.

Mark Twain believed that the title story of this collection "blasted the Heathen Chinee out of the way and opened the road" to literary acclaim for Harte ("John Hay and the Ballads," *Harper's Weekly,* 21 October 1905). "Luck" was "a loftier grade of literature" than Harte had previously attempted (14 June 1906 AD, *MTE,* p. 266). Clemens thought that one of the sketches in the *Luck* volume, "Boonder," was written "in Bret's best *vein*—it is his 'strongest' suit' " (Booth, "Mark Twain's Comments," p. 495). "The Outcasts of Poker Flat," Clemens noted, "ranks next to 'The Luck' unquestionably" (Booth, "Mark Twain's Comments," p. 493).

MTC, pp. 202–220; Duckett, *MT&BH* (1964); *NAH,* p. 159 n. 3; *MTWY,* p. 157; *LAMT,* pp. 152, 298 n. 86; *MT&HF,* pp. 113–114.

————. *Mrs. Skagg's Husbands, and Other Sketches.* Boston: J. R. Osgood & Co., 1873. 352 pp.

Source: MTLAcc, entry #2263, volume donated from Clemens' library by Clara Clemens Gabrilowitsch in 1910.

————, ed. *Outcroppings.* San Francisco: A. Roman & Co., 1865.

Clemens mentioned this book of western verse in a letter to the Virginia City *Territorial Enterprise* published on 19 December 1865: "I have to be a little severe, now, because I am a friend to 'Outcroppings' " *(MTCor,* p. 22).

————. *Poetical Works.* Boston: Houghton, Mifflin & Co., 1871.

Mark Twain's Library of Humor (1888) attributed two poems to this collection —"Plain Language from Truthful James" and "The Society on the Stanislaus." Clemens felt that "Plain Language from Truthful James," generally known as "The Heathen Chinee," made Harte "the most celebrated man in America today" (SLC to J. H. Riley, 3 March [1871], Berg); but it also "stopped his lofty march" to higher literary attainment ("John Hay and the Ballads," *Harper's Weekly,* 21 October 1905). When published, the poem "created an explosion of delight whose reverberations reached the last confines of Christendom" (14 June 1906 AD, *MTE,* p. 266).

————. *Susy.* London: Chatto & Windus, 1893. 304 pp.

Source: MTLAcc, entry #2265, volume donated from Clemens' library by Clara Clemens Gabrilowitsch in 1910.

————. *Tales of the Argonauts, and Other Sketches.* Boston: James R. Osgood and Co., 1876.

Marginalia: contains depreciatory remarks throughout in Clemens' handwriting. Pages following 272 are torn out; they contain "A Jersey Centenarian" (pp. 274–283).

Location: Mark Twain Papers, Berkeley, California. Donated in 1963 by Mrs. Samuel C. Webster.

Copy examined: Clemens' copy.

Mark Twain's Library of Humor (1888) contained a sketch from this collection, "A Jersey Centenarian."

————. "Tennessee's Partner" (short story).
Mark Twain once referred to "the finer glory of 'The Luck of Roaring Camp,' 'Tennessee's Partner,' and those other felicitous imitations of Dickens" (14 June 1906 AD, *MTE,* p. 266).

————. "Thankful Blossom, A Romance of the Jerseys, 1779" (pub. 1876).
Perhaps because Harte wrote this tale at Clemens' house in Hartford, Clemens was convinced "that it belongs at the very top of Harte's literature" (4 February 1907 AD, *MTE,* p. 277). In 1909, reports Alice Hegan Rice, "discovering my romantic attachment to Bret Harte, he [Clemens] delighted in recalling incidents that did not redound to that author's credit." But Clemens also told her with some pride the story of Harte's producing "Thankful Blossom" during a four-hour early-morning stint while intoxicated at Clemens' home (*The Inky Way,* pp. 78–80).
Duckett, *MT&BH,* pp. 109, 124.

————. *The Twins of Table Mountain.* London: Chatto and Windus, n.d. [Publisher's house list at the back is dated June 1879.]
Inscription: first flyleaf and paper cover are missing.
Marginalia: contains Clemens' penciled marginalia throughout. Sydney J. Krause transcribes Clemens' annotation in *MTC,* pp. 212–220.
Catalog: "Retz Appraisal" (1944), p. 8, valued at $35.
Location: Mark Twain Papers, Berkeley, Ca.
Copy examined: Clemens' copy.

————. *The Twins of Table Mountain, and Other Stories.* Boston: Houghton, Mifflin and Co., 1881.
Marginalia: Clemens' caustic marginalia indicate his reasons for rejecting most of Harte's pieces for inclusion in *Mark Twain's Library of Humor.* "I am at work upon Bret Harte," he notified Howells on 23 March 1882, "but am not enjoying it. . . . He is blind as a bat. He never sees anything correctly, except Californian scenery" (*MTHL,* p. 396).
Location: Mark Twain Papers, Berkeley, Ca. Donated in 1963 by Mrs. Samuel C. Webster.
Copy examined: Clemens' copy.

————. *Two Men of Sandy Bar* (play, prod. 1876).
"The play entertained me hugely, even in its present crude state" (SLC to WDH, 14 September 1876, *MTHL,* p. 152).

Hartford, Connecticut *Courant* (newspaper).
The Mark Twain Papers contain a receipt for Clemens' subscription to the *Courant* from 10 October 1872 until 10 May 1873; a note on the receipt also credits payment through 20 January 1874. On 14 September 1876 Clemens referred to Charles Dudley Warner's "good & appreciative review" of Howells' campaign biography of Hayes (*MTHL,* p. 150). Clemens enclosed a clipping from the *Courant*—a review of Howells' *Yorick's Love*—in his letter of 11 March 1880 to Howells (*MTHL,* p. 292). Clemens received a bill for "Daily Courant from 1 April 1880 to 1 October 1880 $4.00" which he paid on 4 October 1880 (MTP); on 1 January 1881 he paid another bill for the period from 1 October 1880 to 1 January 1881 (MTP); he was billed for a "1 quarter" subscription on 12 June 1885 (MTP). Clemens criticized a *Courant* editorial against Ingersoll in 1887 (NB 27, TS p. 3). On 29 September 1892 Clemens complained to Frank G. Whitmore from Florence: "We have not received a Weekly Courant for several weeks. Please see what the matter is" (MTP). When Clemens wrote to William Walter Phelps' daughter from Florence on 14 February 1893 he referred to a political opinion expressed in the Hartford *Courant* (Huntington). In February or March 1894 Clemens noted: "Stanley's Interpreter's Account of the Meeting between Stanley and Livingston—get it out of the Courant" (NB 33, TS p. 56). Pressed by his creditors, Clemens directed Whitmore on 24 March 1895 to "pay this Courant bill & *stop the paper* for the present" (MTM).

Hartley, Cecil B. *The Gentlemen's Book of Etiquette and Manual of Politeness.* Boston: J. S. Locke & Co., 1873. 332 pp.
> *Source:* MTLAcc, entry #2143, volume donated from Clemens' library by Clara Clemens Gabrilowitsch in 1910.

Harvey, George Brinton McClellan (1864–1928). *Women, Etc. Some Leaves from an Editor's Diary.* New York: Harper & Brothers, 1908.
> *Inscription:* signed in black ink inside the front cover: "SL. Clemens/Stormfield, Jan. 1, 1909."
> *Location:* Antenne-Dorrance Collection, Rice Lake, Wis.
> *Copy examined:* Clemens' copy, unmarked.

Haskell, Charles Courtney. *Perfect Health: How to Get It and How to Keep It, by One Who Has It. True Scientific Living.* Norwich, Conn.: Published by the author, [cop. 1901]. 209 pp.
> *Source:* MTLAcc, entry #899, volume donated by Albert Bigelow Paine, Clemens' designated biographer. Possibly Clemens saw this book, since the men exchanged reading materials.

Haskins, Charles Waldo (1852–1903). *How to Keep Household Accounts: A Manual of Family Finance.* New York: Harper & Brothers, 1903. 116 pp.
> *Source:* MTLAcc, entry #679, volume donated by Clemens.

Hastings, Thomas (1784–1872). "Child of sin and sorrow, filled with dismay" (hymn).
> " 'Child of sin and sorrow,/filled with dismay,/Wait not till to-morrow,/yield thee to-day;/Grieve not that love/Which, from above'—" ("A Curious Experience" [1881]).

Haswell, Charles Haynes (1809–1907). *Mechanics' and Engineers' Pocket-Book of Tables, Rules, and Formulas Pertaining to Mechanics, Mathematics, and Physics.* New York: Harper & Brothers, 1908. Last leaves missing; 1048 pages intact.
> *Source:* MTLAcc, entry #1819, volume donated by Clemens.

Haswell, James M. *The Story of the Life of Napoleon III. And Part II, The Same Story as Told by Popular Caricaturists.* London, [1871].
> *Inscription:* signed in ink on flyleaf: "S. L. Clemens, Hartford, 1875."
> *Catalogs:* C1951, #D46; Zeitlin 1951, #20, $35.

Hatton, John Liptrott (1809–1886), ed. *The Songs of England. A Collection of English Melodies, Including the Most Popular Traditional Ditties, and the Principal Songs and Ballads of the Last Three Centuries.* London: Boosey, n.d. 240 pp.
> *Marginalia:* contains many notes by Clemens; one reads "Key of Go down Moses."
> *Catalog:* A1911, #54, $2.50.
> Clemens purchased a volume on 10 May 1877 titled "Songs of Old England" [*sic*], according to a bill from James R. Osgood & Company of Boston (Scrapbook #10, p. 69, MTP).

Hatton, Joseph (1841–1907). *The Old House at Sandwich. A Novel.* New York: F. M. Lupton Publishing Co., [189–]. 258 pp.
> *Source:* MTLAcc, entry #157, volume donated by Clemens.

Hauptmann, Gerhart (1862–1946). *Einsame Menschen. Drama.* Berlin: G. Fischer, 1903. 136 pp.
> *Inscription:* half-title page signed in black ink "Jean L. Clemens/21 Fifth Ave./New York City./April 1905."
> *Location:* Humanities Research Center, University of Texas at Austin.
> *Copy examined:* Jean Clemens' copy.

Haven, Gilbert (1821–1880). *The Pilgrim's Wallet; or, Scraps of Travel Gathered in England, France, and Germany*. New York: Carlton & Porter, 1866. 492 pp.
Inscription: flyleaf torn out.
Location: Mark Twain Library, Redding, Conn. Donated by Clemens (MTLAcc, entry #553).
Copy examined: Clemens' copy.

Haweis, Mary Joy (d. 1898). *Chaucer for Children: A Golden Key*. London: Chatto & Windus, 1877.
Clemens wrote "Chaucer for Children" in Notebook 18 (1879), *N&J*, 2: 335.

Hawes, Charles Henry (1867–1943). *Crete, The Forerunner of Greece*.
Catalog: C1951, #D16, listed among books signed by Clemens.

Hawkins, (Sir) Anthony Hope (1863–1933), pseud. "Anthony Hope." *The Intrusions of Peggy*. Illus. New York: Harper & Brothers, 1902. 387 pp.
Source: MTLAcc, entry #1565, volume donated by Clemens.

————. *Sophy of Kravonia; A Novel*. New York: Harper & Brothers, 1906. 332 pp.
Source: MTLAcc, entry #1097, volume donated by Clemens.

Hawthorne, Julian (1846–1934). *Hawthorne and His Circle*. Illus. New York: Harper & Brothers, 1903. 372 pp.
Source: MTLAcc, entry #1381, volume donated by Clemens.

————. *Noble Blood*. New York: D. Appleton & Co., 1885. 214 pp.
Source: MTLAcc, entry #2268, volume donated from Clemens' library by Clara Clemens Gabrilowitsch in 1910.

Hawthorne, Nathaniel (1804–1864). "The Christmas Banquet" and "Egotism, or the Bosom Serpent" (short stories).
Clara Clemens discussed both tales in her commonplace book (ca. 1888?) (Paine 150, MTP).

————. *Doctor Grimshawe's Secret; A Romance*. Ed. with preface and notes by Julian Hawthorne. Boston: J. R. Osgood and Co., 1883. 368 pp.
Source: MTLAcc, entry #2267, volume donated from Clemens' library by Clara Clemens Gabrilowitsch in 1910.

————. *The House of the Seven Gables* (pub. 1851).
In "Eddypus" (written 1901–1902) Mark Twain predicted that in the future Charles Frohman would inadvertently be given credit for writing "a book, presumably upon architecture, called 'The House of the Seven Gables' " *(FM,* p. 335).

————. *The Marble Faun, or the Romance of the Monte Beni*. Illus. 2 vols. Boston: Houghton, Mifflin and Co., 1890.
Catalog: A1911, #226, $2.25.
Location: C. Waller Barrett Collection, Alderman Library, University of Virginia, Charlottesville.
Copy examined: Clemens' unmarked copy. Contains *A1911* auction label inside front cover.
Livy Langdon copied passages from this novel into her commonplace book in March and October 1867 (DV161, MTP). Mark Twain commented in 1870 that the average reader, less perceptive than Hawthorne's publisher, might simply have "said the 'Marble Faun' was tiresome" ("A General Reply," *The Galaxy*, November 1870, *CG*, p. 97).

————. *Mosses from an Old Manse*. 2 vols. New edition, rev. Boston: Fields, Osgood & Co., 1871. 297 pp.
   Source: MTLAcc, entry #2266, volume 2 only, donated from Clemens' library by Clara Clemens Gabrilowitsch in 1910.

————. *The Scarlet Letter, A Romance*. Boston: James R. Osgood, 1872.
   Inscription: signed twice by Clemens, who wrote "Clemens" in pencil on the flyleaf and signed the title page in black ink: "SL. Clemens".
   Marginalia: pencil markings on pages 65, 190–191. An undated newspaper clipping of jokes from *Puck* and the Buffalo *Express* is inserted.
   Location: Antenne-Dorrance Collection, Rice Lake, Wis.
   Copy examined: Clemens' copy.
   The narrator of "The Loves of Alonzo Fitz Clarence and Rosannah Ethelton" (1878) notes the presence of books by Hawthorne in Aunt Susan's "private parlor of a refined and sensible lady." When Mark Twain compared American and English accomplishments in 1879, he argued that "nobody writes a finer & purer English than Motley[,] Howells, Hawthorne & Holmes" (NB 18, *N&J*, 2: 348). But later he complimented William Dean Howells by writing: "You make all the motives & feelings perfectly clear without analyzing the guts out of them, the way George Eliot does. I can't stand George Eliot, & Hawthorne & those people; I see what they are at, a hundred years before they get to it, & they just tire me to death" (SLC to WDH, 21 July 1885, *MTHL*, p. 534). In 1895 Mark Twain said: "We in the United States, of course, look up to Nathaniel Hawthorne as possessing that something which marks genius and makes a man live forever. It is always remarkable to me that he should have written such incisive English at a time when that was not the prevailing style of authors" ("Mark Twain in Sydney," Sydney, Australia *Argus*, 17 September 1895, clipping in Scrapbook #26, MTP). Clemens owned a copy of F. O. C. Darley's illustrations of *The Scarlet Letter*; see the Darley entry.

————. *The Scarlet Letter: A Romance*. Philadelphia: Henry Altemus, 1893. 348 pp.
   Source: MTLAcc, entry #156, volume donated by Clemens.

————. *Selections from the Writings of Nathaniel Hawthorne, Arranged Under the Days of the Year*. Boston: Houghton, Mifflin & Co., 1889. [109 pp.]
   Source: MTLAcc, entry #2120a, volume donated from Clemens' library by Clara Clemens Gabrilowitsch in 1910.

Hay, John (1838–1905). *The Bread-Winners: A Social Study*. New York: Harper & Brothers, 1905. 319 pp.
   Source: MTLAcc, entry #340, volume donated by Clemens.
   Hay's novel was serialized anonymously in 1884. Clemens wrote to Edward H. House from Hartford on 14 January 1884 and mentioned that he was reading "the middle portion" (CWB). "*I believe John Hay wrote it, but I don't know,*" Clemens told Mrs. Fairbanks on 30 January 1884 (*MTMF*, p. 256). Clemens mentioned the book and its anonymous authorship again in a letter of 23 May 1884 to Edward H. House (CWB).
   Smith, *Mark Twain's Fable of Progress*, p. 38; Kenton J. Clymer, "John Hay and Mark Twain" (1973), p. 403.

————. *Castilian Days*. Boston: Houghton, Mifflin and Co., 1899.
   Inscription: signed "S. L. Clemens, 1905."
   Marginalia: passages on page 88 marked with small crosses.
   Catalog: A1911, #227, $6.75.
   Isabel Lyon noted on 21 October 1905, while packing to leave Dublin, New Hampshire, that Clemens "is sitting in the living room now reading John Hay's 'Castilian Days' " (IVL Journal, TS p. 109, MTP). In his "Acknowledgments" preceding "A Horse's Tale" (1906) Mark Twain explains that he has never seen a bull-fight, "but I needed a bull-fight in this story, and a trustworthy one will be found in it. I got it out of John Hay's *Castilian Days*."

―――. *Pike County Ballads and Other Pieces*. Boston: Houghton, Mifflin & Co., 1871.

    In 1905 Mark Twain published a letter defending Hay against insinuations that his ballads imitated Bret Harte's ("John Hay and the Ballads," *Harper's Weekly*, 49 [21 October 1905], 1530). By 1910 Howells had "forgotten what piece [of poetry] of John Hay's it was that he liked so much" (*MMT*, p. 16).

Haydn, Joseph Timothy (1786–1856). *Haydn's Dictionary of Dates and Universal Information*. Ed. by Benjamin Vincent (1818?–1899). New York: Harper & Brothers, 1883. 796 pp.
    Source: MTLAcc, entry #731, volume donated by Clemens.

Hays, (Mrs.) Helen (Ashe). *The Adventures of Prince Lazybones, and Other Stories*. Illus. New York: Harper & Brothers, [cop. 1884].
    Source: MTLAcc, entry #434, volume donated by Clemens.

―――. *The Princess Idleways*. Illus. New York: Harper & Brothers, 1905. 124 pp.
    Source: MTLAcc, entry #424, volume donated by Clemens.

Hazlitt, William (1778–1830). *Lectures on the Dramatic Literature of the Reign of Queen Elizabeth*. London, 1882.
    Catalog: A1911, #228, $4.50.

Head, Richard (1637?–1686?) and Francis Kirkman. *The English Rogue* (pub. 1665–1671).
    Mark Twain cites " 'The English Rogue': London, 1665" as his source for a song of the underworld used in chapter 17 of *The Prince and the Pauper* (1882). Chapters 18 and 20 also give evidence of this book's influence. A history of vagabonds and criminals, *The English Rogue* contains slang, songs, and escapades of London lowlife.
    Dickinson, "Sources of *The Prince and the Pauper*" (1949); *IE*, p. 113; *MT&JB*, pp. 52–53, 331 n. 14.

Headley, Joel Tyler (1813–1897). *The Great Rebellion*. Chicago, 1866.
    In 1885 Clemens mentioned that " 'Headley's History of the War' " sold 200,000 copies in America (NB 24, TS p. 25).

―――, ed. *Mountain Adventures in Various Parts of the World. Selected from the Narratives of Celebrated Travellers*. Illus. New York: Charles Scribner & Co., 1872. 356 pp.
    Source: MTLAcc, entry #2003, volume donated from Clemens' library by Clara Clemens Gabrilowitsch in 1910.

――― and Willis Fletcher Johnson (b. 1857). *Stanley's Adventures in the Wilds of Africa*. Illus. [Philadelphia:] Edgewood Publishing Co., [cop. 1889]. 687 pp.
    Source: MTLAcc, entry #552, volume donated by Albert Bigelow Paine, Clemens' designated biographer. Possibly Clemens saw this book, since the men exchanged reading materials.

Heard, Albert F. *The Russian Church and Russian Dissent*. New York: Harper & Brothers, 1887. 310 pp.
    Source: MTLAcc, entry #1238, volume donated by Clemens.

Hearn, Lafcadio (1850–1904). *Stray Leaves from Strange Literature; Stories Reconstructed from the Anvari-Soheili, Baitál-Pachísí, Mahabharata, Pantchatantra-Gulistan, Talmud, Kalewala, Etc*. Boston: J. R. Osgood and Co., 1884. 225 pp.
    On 18 October 1886 Clemens urged Edward H. House to obtain this "little book" and read "the Buddhist tale called 'Yamarajah' " to find proof that Charles Warren Stoddard had not plagiarized one of House's stories (CWB).

————. *Two Years in the French West Indies.* New York: Harper & Brothers, 1890.
Catalog: C1951, #31c, $20, listed among books signed by Clemens.

————. *Youma, Story of a West Indian Slave.* New York: Harper & Brothers, 1890.
Catalog: C1951, #05, listed among books containing Livy Clemens' signature.

Heaton, Mrs. Charles. *Masterpieces of Flemish Art, Including Examples of the Early German and the Dutch Schools, with Memoirs of the Artists.* Twenty-six photographs. London, 1869.
Catalog: A1911, #230, $1.50.

Heber, Reginald (1783–1826). *Poetical Works.* Illus. New York, n.d.
Catalog: A1911, #231, $1.25.
Clemens vastly enjoyed Heber's surging "Missionary Hymn" (1829), generally known as "From Greenland's Icy Mountains," though he disagreed with its message. (Lowell Mason [1792–1872] composed the tune.) The title of this hymn appears amid German sentences in Notebook 27 (September 1887), TS p. 1. In chapter 1 of "Those Extraordinary Twins" (1894) Angelo Capello attempts to sing Heber's hymn but Luigi maliciously drowns out the sound "with a rude and rollicking song." On 5 January 1896 Clemens copied the first eight lines into Notebook 36; below the final ones—"They ask us to deliver/Their land from error's chain"—he wrote "NO" (TS p. 17); at the time Clemens was sailing toward Ceylon. On 15 February 1896 Clemens passed the time aboard a train from Calcutta to Darjeeling by constructing an attack on "that most self-complacent of all poems, Greenland's Icy Mountains." Concerning the supposed "call" by native peoples "to deliver their land from Error's chain," wrote Clemens, "The call was never made, never has been made" (NB 36, TS p. 45). Mark Twain quoted from the hymn in chapter 37 of *Following the Equator:* " 'What though the spicy breezes blow soft o'er Ceylon's isle'—an eloquent line, an incomparable line; it says little, but conveys whole libraries of sentiment, and Oriental charm and mystery, and tropic deliciousness." He refers to Heber's hymn in chapter 55 as "my favorite poem" and quotes the first eight lines that he copied in Notebook 36 in 1896. "Those are beautiful verses," he adds, "and they have remained in my memory all my life"; however, he proceeds to criticize the implied notion that Westerners have an obligation to preach their religion to inhabitants of the Eastern hemisphere. He quoted a line from the hymn ("Where every prospect pleases & only man is vile") in Notebook 44 in 1901 (TS p. 21). Two lines from the hymn appear in chapter 11 of "A Horse's Tale" (1906). In Letter VII of Mark Twain's "Letters from the Earth," evidently written in 1909, the microbes within Noah's intestines gleefully sang: "Constipation, O constipation,/The joyful sound proclaim/Till man's remotest entrail /Shall praise its Maker's name" (*LE,* p. 31). The third stanza of Heber's hymn concludes: "Salvation! O salvation!/The joyful sound proclaim,/Till earth's remotest nation/Has learned Messiah's name."

Hector, (Mrs.) Annie (French) (1825–1902), pseud. "Mrs. Alexander." *The Wooing o' T; A Novel.* New York: Henry Holt and Co., 1874. 483 pp.
Source: MTLAcc, entry #1832, volume donated from Clemens' library by Clara Clemens Gabrilowitsch in 1910.

Hedge, Frederic Henry (1805–1890). *Prose Writers of Germany.* Fourth edition. New York: James Miller, 1863.
Edgar Hemminghaus reported seeing Clemens' copy of this volume of translations at the Mark Twain Library in Redding, Conn. ("Mark Twain's German Provenience" [1945], pp. 467–469). Albert E. Stone did not include it in his checklist of Clemens' books that he compiled in Redding in 1955, and I was unable to find the book in 1970.

Heine, Heinrich (1797–1856). "Du Bist wie eine Blume!" (poem, song).

Mark Twain quoted four lines from this poem in "Meisterschaft: In Three Acts" (1888).

————. *Heinrich Heine's Buch der Lieder.* Diamat-Ausgabe. Illus. by Philipp Grot Johann (1841–1892). Berlin: G. Grote'sche Verlagsbuchhandlung, 1889. 270 pp.

Inscription: "Clara L. Clemens/June 8th 1894/Paris/Mrs. Willard".

Location: Mark Twain Library, Redding, Conn.

Copy examined: Clara Clemens' copy, unmarked.

Clemens himself owned or borrowed several other copies of *Buch der Lieder,* first published in 1827. In 1883 Clemens copied lines or verses from six poems in this collection (NB 22, TS pp. 25–26). He made a memorandum in 1884: "Heine's Works" (NB 22, TS p. 34). Henry Fisher remembered hearing Clemens say in London in 1891 that "Heine's songs will make the world happier as long as it stands"; Clemens also told Fisher: "Howells introduced me to Heine. . . . I am glad he did. . . . I read Heine only for his glittering wit, the scintillating glow of his fancy" *(AMT,* pp. 75, 160–161). Clemens also spoke of "that nimbleness of language," that "airy, fairy lightness" in Heine's verse *(AMT,* p. 138). Howells loaned Clemens at least one volume of Heine's writings, for on 25 July 1903, explaining the loss of another book that Howells lent him, Clemens remarked: "Oh, that volume of Heine! the worrying nights it cost me" *(MTHL,* p. 773).

————. "Ich wollt' meine Lieb' ergösse sich" ("I would that my love") (song). Melody by Felix Mendelssohn-Bartholdy.

Clemens made a favorable reference to this song in Notebook 16 (1878), *N&J,* 2: 212); he also jotted down its German title and Mendelssohn's name in Notebook 17 (1878), *N&J,* 2:220), possibly as a selection for his music box.

————. "Die Lorelei" (song). Melody by Friedrich Silcher (1789–1860).

Clemens first heard this song in April 1878, when Bayard Taylor introduced it to the Clemenses and Clara Spaulding on board the *Holsatia* as they sailed for Germany *(MTB,* p. 618). In June 1878 Clemens copied its lyrics into Notebook 14 in German and English *(N&J,* 2: 100). He made use of a phrase from its first verse *"Gipfel des Berges"* ("peak of the mountain") in July 1878 in Notebook 15 *(N&J,* 2: 118); and he copied the first line into Notebook 15 on 1 August 1878, noting: "Very popular in Germany. 30 years old, but the bands all play it" *(N&J,* 2: 125). "Lorelei" was one of the ten tunes Clemens finally selected for the $400 music box he purchased in Geneva in 1878 (SLC to Susan Warner, 20 November 1878, Yale; NB 16, *N&J,* 2: 212). Clemens recalled in January 1879 that Bayard Taylor "repeated the Lorelei & a German sang it on ship—first time I heard it" (NB 17, *N&J,* 2: 268). In chapter 16 of *A Tramp Abroad* (1880) Mark Twain quotes and discusses "Die Lorelei," reproducing the musical notes as well as the lyrics. "I could not endure it at first, but by and by it began to take hold of me, and now there is no tune which I like so well," he added. "Lorelei" appears in a list of what appear to be Clemens' favorite songs in August 1889 (NB 29, TS p. 21). Isabel Lyon recorded on 6 March 1906: "Tonight after Jean played it, Mr. Clemens said: 'The dearest and sweetest lie I ever heard is the Lorelei.' And then he chuckled" (IVL Journal, TS p. 142, MTP).

OPMT, p. 21.

————. "The two grenadiers" (song, 1840). Original German title: "Die beiden Grenadiere." Melody by Robert Schumann.

"I'll claim The Grenadiers for sure, dear heart!" Clemens wrote to Clara Clemens from Dublin, New Hampshire on 8 June 1905. "Thank you for remembering" (TS in MTP). Evidently Clara had offered to sing one of Clemens' favorite pieces at a concert, for on 29 June 1905 Clemens wrote to her: "I am very sorry you are not going to be able to sing the Two Grenadiers" (MTP). Clara quoted Heine's verse in her commonplace book with obvious admiration (Paine 150, MTP, ca. 1888?).

Helm, W. H. *Studies in Style*. London, 1900.
   Catalog: A1911, #232, $3.

Hemans, Felicia Dorothea (1793–1835). "Bird at sea" (song). Melody by C. Meineke.
   When Mark Twain saw a land bird hovering over the becalmed *Smyrniote* in 1866, he noted: "he is a long way from home—thought of the old song—'Bird at Sea'" (NB 5, *N&J*, 1: 138). He also mentioned this song in chapter 38 of *Lon-Miss* (1883) and "About All Kinds of Ships" (1893).

————. "Casabianca" (poem).
   Clemens employed two slightly misquoted lines from this poem in his 5 December 1863 dispatch from Carson City that parodied L. O. Stern's oratorical style (*MTEnt*, pp. 92–95). He quotes "let the flames that shook the battle's wreck, shine round it o'er the dead"; Hemans wrote "The flame that lit the battle's wreck/ Shone round him o'er the dead." In his letter of 14 January 1864 Clemens chuckles over the "old-fashioned *impressive* style" of oratorical inflection imposed on school pupils "ever since Mrs. Hemans wrote that verse" (*MTEnt*, p. 135). He also quotes a drunk's rendition of the piece in a column for the 23 August 1864 issue of the San Francisco *Call* (*CofC*, p. 134). He joked about "what became of the boy that stood on the burning deck" (since "no inquest" was held) in Notebook 7 on board the *San Francisco* in January 1867 (*N&J*, 2: 292). Very likely it was Mark Twain who organized the "Country School Exhibition" aboard the *Montana* on 10 July 1868. Part of the evening's entertainment, according to Mark Twain's "Programme," was a "Recitation—The Boy Stood on the Burning Deck, with his Baggage checked for Troy," performed by "Mr. M." (*Alta California*, 6 September 1868; reprinted in *The Twainian*, 7 [November-December 1948], 5). In chapter 44 of *Innocents Abroad* Mark Twain describes his trek through Syria by invoking a line from the poem: "Tired? Ask of the winds that far away with fragments strewed the sea." Mark Twain claimed that "Casabianca" served him as copy for exercises on the first typewriter he purchased in 1873: "At home I played with the toy, repeating and repeating and repeating 'The Boy stood on the Burning Deck,' until I could turn that boy's adventure out at the rate of twelve words a minute" ("The First Writing-Machines" [1905]).
   These rehearsals of Mrs. Heman's declamatory piece preceded Mark Twain's best-known reference to it in chapter 21 of *Tom Sawyer* (1876), where a wooden execution of "The Boy Stood on the Burning Deck" is an unavoidable feature of the Examination Evening program at the village schoolhouse. Mr. Dobbins the schoolmaster also listens absent-mindedly to a recitation of the poem in Act 3 of "Tom Sawyer: A Play," written 1875–1884 (*HH&T*, p. 303). In chapter 31 of *Following the Equator* Mark Twain quotes a fellow passenger's opinion of Australian railroads: "Goodness knows! Ask of the winds that far away with fragments strewed the sea, as the boy that stood on the burning deck used to say." In June 1898 Mark Twain had the idea of adding the boy in Heman's poem to Huck, Tom, and other "Creatures of Fiction" he planned to assemble in a tale; later Mark Twain added: "Make Casabianca sing 'All in the Downs the Ship lay moored' & dance hornpipe" (NB 40, TS p. 27). In "Mrs. Eddy in Error" (written 1903), Book 2 of *Christian Science*, Mark Twain again wrote: "As the ballad says: 'Ask of the winds that far away [around]/ With fragments strewed the sea'" (*WIM?*, p. 390). No. 44 calls it "The Boy Stood on the Burning Deck" and says "It's a poem. It hasn't been written yet, but it's very pretty and stirring. It's English" (chapter 26, "No. 44, The Mysterious Stranger," written 1902–1908, *MSM*, p. 362). In chapter 28 of "No. 44" August Feldner intones two lines from this poem (*MSM*, p. 373).

————. *The Forest Sanctuary.*
   Clara Clemens listed this work in her commonplace book sometime between 1888 and 1904 (Paine 150, MTP).

————. *Select Poetical Works of Felicia Hemans.* Collection of British Authors Series. Leipzig: B. Tauchnitz, 1865. 342 pp.
  Catalog: C1951, #D1, $8, listed among the books signed by Clemens.

Henderson, Archibald (1877–1963).
  Clemens read an article that this professor of mathematics at the University of North Carolina had written about the works of Mark Twain, and liked it (IVL to Henderson, February 1909, PH in MTP). Henderson hoped to write Clemens' biography, but Clemens decided to confine his authorization to Paine's project. "Your article in the Deutsche Revue pleases Mr. Clemens very much indeed," Paine wrote to Henderson from Redding on 15 November 1909 (PH in MTP).

Henderson, Mary Newton (Foote) (1842–1931). *The Aristocracy of Health.* New York: Harper & Brothers, 1906. 772 pp.
  Source: MTLAcc, entry #401, volume donated by Clemens.

Henderson, Peter (1822–1890). *Practical Floriculture; A Guide to the Successful Cultivation of Florists' Plants, for the Amateur and Professional Florist.* Third edition. New York: Orange Judd Co., 1882.
  Inscription: signed in ink on the front flyleaf: "Olivia L. Clemens/Hartford/4 June 1883." Below this someone else (not Clemens) has added in black ink, written over in brown ink, in a ragged hand: "Presented to/Mr. Dnl Maloy/4 June 1883/Gardner [*sic*]/to S L Clemens/Mark Twain/Farmington Avenue/Hartford /Conn/USA." Photocopy of flyleaf is in MTP.
  Marginalia: pencil marks throughout.
  Location: Mark Twain Memorial, Hartford, Conn. Donated by Harry Hinkleman in 1958.
  Copy examined: Livy Clemens' copy, given to the family's gardener.

Hendrik, Hans. *Memoirs of Hans Hendrik, The Arctic Traveller, Serving Under Kane, Hayes, Hall and Nares, 1853–1876. Written by Himself.* Trans. from the Eskimo language by Henry Rink. Ed. by George Stephens. London: Trübner & Co., 1878. 100 pp.
  Inscription: signed and inscribed in pencil on the second flyleaf: "S. L. Clemens/Munich, Bavaria,/January, 1879./A very valuable book/—& unique."
  Marginalia: approximately five penciled comments are scattered through the small volume. On page 24 Clemens noted about a brief exchange of simple questions and answers, "An Ollendorfian conversation." On page 68 he wrote vertically: "Afloat in mid-ocean for near 6 months in the darkness of the long arctic night." Many pencil markings throughout.
  Location: Mark Twain Library, Redding, Conn.
  Copy examined: Clemens' copy.
  From Hendrik's narrative Mark Twain probably obtained the facts about Eskimo hunting techniques that he employed in "The Esquimau Maiden's Romance" (1893).

Heness, Gottlieb. *Der Leitfaden für den unterricht in der deütschen sprache.* New York: H. Holt & Co., [1884?]. 253 pp.
  Source: MTLAcc, entry #367, volume donated by Clemens.

Henkle, John Fletcher (b. 1837). *The National Peacemaker; A Treatise on Present Conditions in the United States.* Chicago: Privately printed, 1904. 140 pp.
  Source: MTLAcc, entry #528, volume donated by Clemens.

Henley, William Ernest (1849–1903). *A Book of Verses*. Second edition. London: David Nutt, 1889.

> *Inscription:* inscribed on flyleaf: "To Samuel L. Clemens, in admiration of his happy gift of making his fellow creatures happy. From W. E. H. Glasgow, Sept. 30, '89."
>
> *Location:* Carrie Estelle Doheny Collection, St. John's Seminary, Camarillo, California. Donated by Mrs. Doheny in 1940 after its purchase from Maxwell Hunley Rare Books of Beverly Hills for $12.20.
>
> *Copy examined:* Clemens' copy, with leaves opened.

————. *Hawthorn and Lavender, with Other Verses*. New York: Harper & Brothers, 1901. 113 pp.

> *Inscription:* inscribed by Clemens on inner front cover: "To/Mrs. Olivia L. Clemens—Nov. 27, 1871 or 2—Upon the occasion & celebration of one of her early birth-days, when she did not mind them so much./from/SLC./Riverdale-on-Hudson/Nov. 1901."
>
> *Catalog: C1951,* #54a, $40.
>
> *Location:* Carrie Estelle Doheny Collection, St. John's Seminary, Camarillo, California. Donated by Mrs. Doheny in 1953 after its purchase from Aubrey Davidson on 8 August 1952 for $175.
>
> *Copy examined:* Livy Clemens' copy, unmarked.

————. [An identical (or same?) copy.]

> *Source:* MTLAcc, entry #1343, volume donated by Clemens.

Henry VII, King of England. *The Statutes of Henry VII in Exact Facsimile from the Rare Original, Printed by [William] Caxton in 1489*. Ed., with notes and introduction, by John Rae. London: J. C. Hotten, 1869.

> *Catalog: A1911,* #73, $8.

Henry of Huntingdon (1084?–1155). *The Chronicle of Henry of Huntingdon, Comprising the History of England, from the Invasion of Julius Caesar to the Accession of Henry II. Also, The Acts of Stephen, King of England and Duke of Normandy*. Trans. and ed. by Thomas Forester. London: Henry G. Bohn, 1853. 430 pp.

> *Inscription:* first flyleaf signed in pencil: "S L Clemens/Hartford 1877".
>
> *Marginalia:* heavily annotated. Black ink markings and notes begin on page 48 and continue throughout, concentrated especially at Henry's credulity about omens. The corners of many pages are folded down for reference. Clemens also read and annotated in ink "The Acts of Stephen, King of England and Duke of Normandy, by an Unknown But Contemporaneous Author" (pp. 321–430).
>
> *Catalog: A1911,* #256, $2.50.
>
> *Location:* Henry E. Huntington Library, San Marino, Ca.
>
> *Copy examined:* Clemens' copy.

In November 1877 James R. Osgood & Company of Boston billed Clemens for a copy of "Huntingdon's Hist. England," purchased on 24 October 1877 (Scrapbook #10, p. 69, MTP). In his early notes for *CY* Mark Twain made plans to include "remnants of monkish legends. Get them from Wm [*sic*] of Huntingdon" (NB 25 [December 1885], TS p. 33). In "As Concerns Interpreting the Deity" (written 1905) Twain pokes fun at Henry's notions of divine providence: "Whenever God punishes a man, Henry of Huntingdon knows why it was done, and tells us; and his pen is eloquent with admiration; but when a man has earned punishment, and escapes, he does not explain." In the same piece Mark Twain also quotes from *The Acts of Stephen*.

> *WIM?,* pp. 114–117.

Henschel, George (1850–1934). *Personal Recollections of Johannes Brahms: Some of His Letters to and Pages from a Journal Kept by George Henschel.* Boston: R. G. Badger, 1907. 95 pp.
    Catalog: A1911, #47, $3.75.

Hensel, Sebastian (1830–1898). *The Mendelssohn Family (1729–1847) from Letters and Journals.* Eight portraits by Wilhelm Hensel (1794–1861). Trans. by Carl Klingemann and an American collaborator, with a notice by George Grove. 2 vols. New York: Harper & Brothers, 1881.
    Catalogs: A1911, #234, $1.25; *Lexington 1912,* #15, $5.
    Before leaving for Boston and New York City in April 1882, Clemens wrote the title of this book in Notebook 20 (*N&J,* 2: 460), probably intending to purchase a copy. Among a group of book titles he listed in September 1887 he included "Mendellsohn's [*sic*] Letters 2 vols." (NB 27, TS p. 13). The letters in *The Mendelssohn Family* are for the most part those exchanged by Felix Mendelssohn-Bartholdy and his sister, Fanny Mendelssohn-Bartholdy Hensel.

Hensman, Howard. *Cecil Rhodes: A Study of a Career.* Portraits. Illus. New York, 1902.
    Inscription: on one flyleaf Clemens wrote: "All about the Empire Builder and Pirate . . . S. L. Clemens, Riverdale, Feb., 1902."
    Catalog: A1911, #235, $4.

Henty, George Alfred (1832–1902). *In the Hands of the Cave-Dwellers.* New York: Harper & Brothers, 1904. 205 pp.
    Source: MTLAcc, entry #426, volume donated by Clemens.

———. *St. George for England: A Tale of Cressy and Poitiers.* Illus. by Gordon Browne. New York: Scribner and Welford, [188–]. 352 pp.
    Source: MTLAcc, entry #1889, volume donated from Clemens' library by Clara Clemens Gabrilowitsch in 1910.

Hepburn, Thomas Nicoll (1861–1930), pseud. "Gabriel Setoun." *Sunshine and Haar; Some Further Glimpses of Life at Barncraig.* New York: Harper & Brothers, 1896. 257 pp.
    Source: MTLAcc, entry #1444, volume donated by Clemens.

Herbert, Edward, first Baron Herbert of Cherbury (1583–1648). *Autobiography* (pub. 1764).
    Mark Twain intended to cite this work in his proposed appendix to *A Connecticut Yankee* (Baetzhold, "Course of Composition," p. 200). Lord Herbert's work was available in the "Choice Autobiographies" series edited by William Dean Howells for James R. Osgood & Company of Boston.

Herbert, George (1593–1633).
    Clemens at least knew of Herbert's writings, for in 1887 he identified him as the "Country Parson," the alternative title for Herbert's *A Priest to the Temple* (1652) (NB 27, TS p. 11).

Herford, Oliver (1863–1935). *Artful Anticks.* Illus. by the author. New York: The Century Co., 1897.
    Inscription: inscribed on inside front cover: "To that from this/in memory of Dec. 25th, 1901." Herford drew a picture of a cat on the half-title page, with the notation: "Not a good cat but my own. By me, Oliver Herford."
    Location: Carrie Estelle Doheny Collection, St. John's Seminary, Camarillo, California. Donated by Mrs. Doheny in 1940 after its purchase from Maxwell Hunley Rare Books of Beverly Hills for $12.20.
    Copy examined: Clemens' copy, unmarked.

————. *A Child's Primer of Natural History.* Illus. by the author. New York: C. Scribner's Sons, 1901. 95 pp.
   Source: MTLAcc, entry #1890, volume donated from Clemens' library by Clara Clemens Gabrilowitsch in 1910.

————. *The Rubáiyát of a Persian Kitten.* Illus. by the author. New York: Charles Scribner's Sons, 1904.
   Inscription: inscribed by Clemens inside the front cover: "Clara—from Bambino/1904."
   Location: Carrie Estelle Doheny Collection, St. John's Seminary, Camarillo, California. Donated by Mrs. Doheny in 1940 after its purchase from Maxwell Hunley Rare Books of Beverly Hills for $12.20.
   Copy examined: Clemens' copy, unmarked.

Herndon, William Lewis and Lardner Gibbon. *Exploration of the Valley of the Amazon, Made Under the Direction of the Navy Department.* 2 vols. Washington, D. C.: Robert Armstrong, 1853–1854.
   Clemens wrote to his brother Henry on 5 August 1856 that Jane and Orion Clemens "have Herndon's Report now," and he hopes they can be persuaded of the feasibility of his projected trip to the Amazon *(MTL,* pp. 34–35). (Herndon wrote only vol. 1 of the work.) In "The Turning-Point of My Life" (1910) Mark Twain described the allurements he found in Herndon's account, especially his "astonishing tale about *coca,* a vegetable product of miraculous powers [it is the source for cocaine!]. . . . I was fired with a longing to ascend the Amazon. Also with a longing to open up a trade in coca with all the world" *(WIM?,* p. 459). Herndon discusses the "coca" crop on pages 88–89 of vol. 1. See also the entry for W. G. Mortimer, *Peru.*

Herodotus (5th century B.C.). *The History of Herodotus. A New English Version.* Trans. by George Rawlinson and others. Maps and illus. 4 vols. New York, 1875.
   Marginalia: a few passages marked by Clemens.
   Catalogs: A1911, #237, $2.25; *Lexington 1912,* #16, $7.50.
   Mark Twain attributes a (fictitious) quotation to Herodotus at the beginning of the Appendix to *A Tramp Abroad* (1880). In January 1894 Mark Twain made plans to include Herodotus' writings in the projected "Back Number" magazine (NB 33, TS p. 46). "Just like the case recorded by Herodotus," Clemens noted alongside a Maori oracle's ambiguous prophecy in F. E. Maning's *Old New Zealand* (1887), presented to Clemens in Dunedin in November 1895. In "Eddypus" (written 1901–1902) Mark Twain assigned to himself the appellation by which Herodotus is generally known, "Father of History."

————. *The Life and Travels of Herodotus in the Fifth Century Before Christ.* Trans. by J. Talboys Wheeler. 2 vols. New York: Harper & Brothers, 1856.
   Location: Mark Twain Library, Redding, Conn.
   Copy examined: Clemens' copy, unsigned and unmarked.

————. *Stories of the East from Herodotus.* Trans. and ed. by Alfred John Church (1829–1912). Illus. New York: Dodd, Mead & Co., n.d. 299 pp.
   Source: MTLAcc, entry #1878, volume donated from Clemens' library by Clara Clemens Gabrilowitsch in 1910.

Herrick, (Mrs.) Christine (Terhune) (1859–1944). *The Expert Maid-Servant.* New York: Harper & Brothers, 1904. 139 pp.
   Source: MTLAcc, entry #675, volume donated by Clemens.

Herrick, Robert (1591–1674). "Greeting to the Violets" (poem).
Olivia Langdon copied this poem on an undated sheet of paper laid in her commonplace book (DV161, MTP).

————. *Selections from the Poetry of Robert Herrick*. Preface by Austin Dobson (1840–1911). Illus. by Edwin A. Abbey (1852–1911). New York: Harper & Brothers, 1882. 188 pp.
Inscription: front flyleaf inscribed by Clemens in blue ink: "Livy L. Clemens/ from/S. L. Clemens/Xmas 1882."
Location: collection of Professor Bigelow Paine Cushman, Danbury, Conn.
Copy examined: Livy Clemens' gift copy, unmarked.

Herrick, Sophia Bledsoe. *The Earth in Past Ages*. Illus. New York, 1888.
Inscription: signed on flyleaf "S. L. Clemens 1889."
Catalog: A1911, #238, $1.25.

Hertz, Henrik (1798–1870). *King René's Daughter; A Danish Lyrical Drama.*
Trans. by Theodore Martin. New York: H. Holt and Co., 1880. 100 pp.
Source: MTLAcc, entry #2033, volume donated from Clemens' library by Clara Clemens Gabrilowitsch in 1910.
In Bavaria in August 1893 Mark Twain mentioned seeing this play (NB 33, TS p. 25).

Hervey, George Winfred. *A System of Christian Rhetoric, for the Use of Preachers and Other Speakers*. New York: Harper & Brothers, 1873. 632 pp.
Source: MTLAcc, entry #1393, volume donated by Clemens.

Hervey, Maurice H. *Amyas Egerton, Cavalier*. Illus. by J. Skelton. New York: Harper & Brothers, 1896. 354 pp.
Source: MTLAcc, entry #1563, volume donated by Clemens.

Herzl, Theodor (1860–1904). *Der Judenstaat* (pub. 1896).
Mark Twain mentions Herzl's "clear insight" regarding a plan to gather Jews of the world together in Palestine ("Concerning the Jews" [1889]).
TS p. 25).

Hesse-Wartegg, Ernst von (1851–1918). *Mississippi-fahrten: Reisebilder aus dem amerikanischen Suden (1879–1880)*. Leipzig: C. Reissner, 1881. 354 pp.
Mark Twain quoted this German tourist's description of a yellow fever epidemic in Memphis in chapter 29 of *LonMiss* (1883). Apparently Mark Twain translated the passage himself.
Ganzel, "Twain, Travel Books," p. 42 n. 9.

Hewlett, Maurice Henry (1861–1923). *Fond Adventures: Tales of the Youth of the World*. New York: Harper & Brothers, 1905.
Inscription: signed inside the front cover: "SL. Clemens/21—5th Ave./1905."
Marginalia: two words underlined in text.
Catalog: C1951, #D57.
Location: Mark Twain Papers, Berkeley, Ca. Donated in 1974 by Professor Robert Falk of the University of California at Los Angeles. Professor Falk purchased the volume at the *C1951* auction.
Copy examined: Clemens' copy.
Sometime in 1903 (probably in December) Clemens wrote to E. B. Caulfield, asking for Hewlett's winter address in Florence (CWB).

————. *The Ruinous Face*. New York: Harper & Brothers, 1909.
Catalog: C1951, #D68, listed among the books signed by Clemens.

Hey, Wilhelm (1789–1854). *Fünfzig Fabeln für Kinder. In Bildern gezeichnet von Otto Speckter*. Neue Ausgabe. Gotha: Friedrich Andreas Perthes, n.d. [1878]. 70 pp.
Inscription: inscribed on first flyleaf: "Susie Clemens/Christmas 1878/ Fraulein Vanlweiner/Munich, Bavaria".
Location: Mark Twain Library, Redding, Conn.
Copy examined: Susy Clemens' copy, unmarked.
Hemminghaus, "Mark Twain's German Provenience," p. 472.

Heyse, Paul von (1830–1914). *Im Paradiese. Roman in Sieben Büchern*. Fourth edition. 3 vols. Berlin: Verlag von Wilhelm Herz, 1876.
Inscription: all three vols. inscribed on the title pages by Livy Clemens: "Saml. L. Clemens/Feb. 2nd 1879/Munich/Bavaria". The vols. were rebound (and the title pages cropped) after she inscribed them. A sticker on the inside back cover of vol. 2 identifies the bookbinder as the Case, Lockwood & Brainard Company of Hartford, Connecticut.
Catalog: Zeitlin 1951, #21, $15.
Location: Mark Twain Papers, Berkeley, Ca. Gift of Jake Zeitlin.
Copy examined: Clemens' copy, unmarked. Each vol. contains a *C1951* sale label.

————. *Kinder der Welt. Roman in Sechs Büchern*. Fifth edition. 3 vols. Berlin: Berlag von Wilhelm Herz, 1875.
Inscriptions: all three vols. inscribed by Livy Clemens on title pages: "Saml. L. Clemens/Feb. 2nd 1879/Munich". The books were rebound (with title pages cropped) after they were inscribed.
Catalog: Zeitlin 1951, #22, $10, vols. 2 and 3 only.
Locations: Humanities Research Center, University of Texas at Austin (vol. 1 only); vols. 2 and 3 in the Mark Twain Papers, Berkeley, Ca., gift of Jake Zeitlin.
Copies examined: Clemens' copies, unmarked. Vols. 2 and 3 contain *C1951* sale labels.

————. *Novellen*. 3 vols. Berlin, n.d.
Inscription: vol. 1 signed "Jean L. Clemens."
Catalogs: A1911, #239, $10 (sold to the Mark Twain Company); resold at *C1951,* #J18, listed among books belonging to Jean and Clara Clemens.

Hézecques, Comte de. *Recollections of a Page to the Court of Louis XVI*. Trans. by Charlotte M. Yonge. London: Hurst & Blackett, 1873.
In July 1873 Clemens noted the title, translator, and publisher of this book (NB 12, *N&J,* 1: 559).

Hichens, Robert Smythe (1864–1950). *Barbary Sheep; A Novel*. New York: Harper & Brothers, 1907. 253 pp.
Source: MTLAcc, entry #1564, volume donated by Clemens.

————. *The Call of the Blood* (pub. 1906).
While Hickens' novel was running serially in *Harper's Bazar,* Clemens wrote to Mary Benjamin Rogers on 19 November 1906 to suggest another (unnamed) book: "It is virile and rugged and will make a pleasant change for you after the polished diction of The Call of the Blood" *(MTLM,* p. 89).

————. *The Garden of Allah*. New York: F. A. Stokes Co., [cop. 1904]. 482 pp.
Source: MTLAcc, entry #2270, volume donated from Clemens' library by Clara Clemens Gabrilowitsch in 1910.

————. *A Spirit in Prison.* Illus. by Cyrus Cuneo. New York: Harper & Brothers, 1908. 664 pp.
Source: MTLAcc, entry #2269, volume donated from Clemens' library by Clara Clemens Gabrilowitsch in 1910.

Higginson, Thomas Wentworth Storrow (1823–1911). *Atlantic Essays.* Boston, 1871.
Inscription: signed "S. L. Clemens, Hartford, 1876."
Marginalia: a few passages marked.
Catalog: A1911, #240, $3.

————. *Cheerful Yesterdays* (pub. 1898).
On two small sheets of manuscript sold as item #344 at the *A1911* sale, Clemens commented: "Higginson's Cheerful Yesterdays is one long record of disagreeable services which he had to perform to content his spirit. He was always doing the fine and beautiful and brave and disagreeable thing that others shrank from and were afraid of—and his was a happy life."

————. "Emily Dickinson's Letters," *Atlantic Monthly,* 68 (October 1891), 444–456.
In October 1891 Clemens copied Higginson's description of the Dickinson house in Amherst: "one of those large, square, brick mansions so familiar in our older New England towns, surrounded by trees and blossoming shrubs" (NB 31, TS pp. 8–9).

———— and William MacDonald. *History of the United States from 986 to 1905.* Rev. edition. New York: Harper & Brothers, 1905. 632 pp.
Inscription: front pastedown endpaper signed in ink "S. L. Clemens/21—5th ave. 1905."
Marginalia: two penciled notes in Clemens' holograph on pages 548 ("13th") and 568 ("re/Secy/of/State/Fish."). Several hundred vertical lines, marginal dots (an uncharacteristic notation for Clemens, but apparently his), and underscorings. Clemens' penciled marginalia begin on page 160 and end on page 610, centering on slavery, the Civil War, Reconstruction politics, and statistical data.
Catalog: C1951, #D26, listed among books signed by Clemens.
Location: private collection of Kevin Mac Donnell, Austin, Texas. Purchased in 1976. I am grateful to Mr. Mac Donnell for supplying the information reported here.

————. *Malbone: An Oldport Romance.* Boston: Fields, Osgood & Co., 1869. 244 pp.
Source: MTLAcc, entry #2271, volume donated from Clemens' library by Clara Clemens Gabrilowitsch in 1910.

————. *Travellers and Outlaws, Episodes in American History.* Boston: Lee and Shepard, [c. 1888]. 340 pp.
Clemens noted the title in Notebook 28 (TS p. 37) in December 1888. Higginson's book includes an account of Nat Turner's insurrection.

————. *Young Folks' History of the United States.* Boston: Lee and Shepard; New York: C. T. Dillingham, 1875. 382 pp. Repr. 1876, 1877, 1879.
On 13 December 1880 a member of Clemens' household purchased "1 Higginson U. S." for $1.20, according to a bill sent on 1 January 1881 by Brown & Gross, Hartford booksellers (MTP).

Hildreth, Richard (1807–1865). *The History of the United States of America*. 6 vols. New York: Harper & Brothers, 1877–1880.
 Source: MTLAcc, entries #1288–#1293, complete set donated by Clemens (vols. 1, 2, and 3, pub. 1877; vols. 4 and 5, 1879; vol. 6, 1880).

Hill, Frederick Trevor (1866–1930). *The Accomplice*. New York: Harper & Brothers, 1905. 326 pp.
 Source: MTLAcc, entry #2272, volume donated from Clemens' library by Clara Clemens Gabrilowitsch in 1910.
 Isabel Lyon recorded on 6 July 1905: "Mr. Clemens took a novel to bed with him last night. It was 'The Accomplice' by Frederic Trevor Hill, and he didn't go to sleep until past 2 o'clock" (IVL Journal, TS p. 74, MTP).

————. *Decisive Battles of the Law; Narrative Studies of Eight Legal Contests . . . Between the Years 1800 and 1886*. New York: Harper & Brothers, 1907. 268 pp.
 Source: MTLAcc, entry #1803, volume donated by Clemens.

————. *The Story of a Street; A Narrative History of Wall Street*. New York: Harper & Brothers, 1908. Illus. 171 pp.
 Source: MTLAcc, entry #1719, volume donated by Clemens.

Hillern, Wilhelmine (Birch) von (1836–1916). *Am kreuz; ein passionsroman aus Oberammergau*. Stuttgart: Union deutsche verlagsgesellschaft, 1890. 383 pp.
 Source: MTLAcc, entry #377, volume donated by Clemens.
 Edgar Hemminghaus saw Clemens' copy of this religious romance in the Mark Twain Library at Redding in 1945 ("Mark Twain's German Provenience," p. 473), but it has since disappeared.

————. *Geier-Wally: A Tale of the Tyrol*. New York: D. Appleton and Co., 1876. 237 pp. [Originally pub. in German: *Die Geier-Wally; eine geschichte aus den Tyroler Alpen*. 2 vols. (Berlin, 1875).]
 In August 1893, at Krankenheil-Tölz, Mark Twain inscribed a copy of *The £1,000,000 Bank-Note*: "To Frau von Hillern—from one who has read with pleasure & profoundly admires 'Geier-Wally' " (volume in the collection of Ronald von Klaussen, New York City).

Hinchliff, Thomas Woodbine. *Summer Months Among the Alps; With the Ascent of Monte Rosa*. London: Longman, Brown, Green, Longmans & Roberts, 1857.
 Marginalia: pages 18–32 removed; a penciled note by Clemens on the remaining illustration (a map) explains: "See one of my later books of travel for the missing pages./Paris, Apl/1879." Numerous notes and markings in pencil throughout; pages 130–135 are marked in brown ink. On page 60, concerning Frutizen, Clemens penciled: "Where we saw the German family." On page 87 he wrote: "Where we saw the girl fall over the precipice" (near the village of Täsch). Opposite page 90 at the top of an illustration of the Matterhorn he noted: "Copy this". At the top of page 128 he observed in pencil: "From the Rizi the lakes & country look like a highly colored 'raised' map."
 Location: Carrie Estelle Doheny Collection, St. John's Seminary, Camarillo, Ca. Donated by Mrs. Doheny in 1951 after its purchase from Zeitlin & Ver Brugge Booksellers for $45.
 Copy examined: Clemens' copy. A note on the half-title page records that Zeitlin & Ver Brugge Booksellers purchased the volume at the *C1951* auction.
 In September 1878 Clemens made references in Notebook 16 to pages 255–256 and 306 of Hinchliff's book (*N&J*, 2: 194). Chapter 34 of *TA* (1880) contains a lengthy extract from Hinchliff's account of his ascent of Monte Rosa. Mark Twain pretends that this narrative is what discourages him from attempting a similar climb.

Hindley, Charles, ed. *The Old Book Collector's Miscellany; or, a Collection of Readable Reprints of Literary Rarities . . . during the Sixteenth and Seventeenth Centuries.* Facsimile title-pages and woodcuts. 3 vols. London, 1871–1873.
  Catalog: A1911, #241, $5.

————, ed. *The Roxburghe Ballads. Collection of Ancient Songs and Ballads, Written on Various Subjects and Printed between the Year MDLX and MDCC.* Woodcuts. 2 vols. London, 1873.
  Catalog: A1911, #413, $5.50.

Hinman, Russell (1853–1912). *Eclectic Physical Geography.* Illus. New York: American Book Co., [1888]. 382 pp.
  Hinman sent Jean Clemens a copy of his book on 18 September 1893. The next day Clemens explained to Livy from New York City that he had met "Hinman the great authority on physical geography" and had told him that the Clemens family—"particularly Jean"—were all interested in geography. "That is how he comes to send her his book" (TS in MTP).

Hislop, Alexander (1807–1865), comp. *The Proverbs of Scotland; with Explanatory and Illustrative Notes, and a Glossary.* First American edition, from the third Edinburgh edition. New York: L. D. Robertson, 187?.
  On 14 July 1880 Estes & Lauriat of Boston billed Clemens for twenty-one books, including "1 Scot Proverbs"; he paid on 20 July 1880 (receipt in MTP).

Historical Records of New South Wales. . . . 1762–1811. Seven vols. in nine. Vol. 1 edited by A. Britton; vols. 2–7 ed. by F. M. Bladen. Illus. Sydney: Government Printing, 1892–1901.
  At the top of page 112 in Clemens' copy of *The Selected Works of Marcus Clarke,* the first page of "The Seizure of the 'Cyprus,'" Clemens wrote: "Copy this, separately, but so mark it as to show that it follows immediately after the 'appendix' account of the trial of Capt. Dennott, from 'Historical Records of New South Wales.' SLC" (MTP).

The History of a Slave.
  Clemens discovered this unidentified book in the London Library on 22 October 1896 (NB 39, TS p. 12). Possibly he was referring to the same narrative in December 1896 when he wrote: "The mulatto's terrible fate—322 vol. 2 quarto" (NB 39, TS p. 32).

The History of the Most Remarkable Tryals in Great Britain and Ireland, in Capital Cases, viz. Heresy, Treason, Felony, Incest, Poisoning, Adultery, Rapes, Sodomy, Witchcraft, Pyracy, Murder, Robbery, Etc., Both by the Unusual Methods of Ordeal, Combat, and Attainder, and by the Ecclesiastical, Civil and Common Laws of These Realms. Faithfully Extracted from Records, and Other Authentick Authorities, as Well [as] Manuscript Printed. 2 vols. London: Printed for A. Bell [, etc.], 1715–1716.
  Catalog: A1911, #146, $6, vol. 1 only.

Hitchcock, Ripley (1857–1918), ed. *Decisive Battles of America, by Albert Bushnell, Thomas Wentworth Higginson, et al.* Illus. New York: Harper & Brothers, 1909. 396 pp.
  Inscription: signed inside front cover "SL. Clemens/1909."
  Location: Antenne-Dorrance Collection, Rice Lake, Wis.
  Copy examined: Clemens' copy, unmarked.

Hoffman, Charles Fenno (1806–1884). "Sparkling and Bright" (poem, song, 1830). Melody by James B. Taylor.

Mark Twain borrowed this title for a limerick he wrote in praise of cigars (NB 5 [1866], *N&J*, 1: 157). See also entry for F. M. Finch.

OPMT, p. 7 n. 27.

Hoffmann, Heinrich (1809–1894). *Der Struwwelpeter* (pub. 1847).

In Berlin in October 1891 Mark Twain translated Hoffmann's verses for children into English, explaining in an introduction that "Struwwelpeter is the best known book in Germany, & has the largest sale known to the book trade, & the widest circulation" (MS in Yale University Library). Mark Twain's translation was not published until 1935, when it was issued by Harper & Brothers. On 16 October 1893 (or 1898?) Clemens reported to Clara Clemens that Fred J. Hall had told him the translation "is in the hands of these publishers of baby-books—just lying there—nothing being done about it" (TS in MTP). Clara recalled that her father "frequently . . . brought the old German nonsense rhymes called Struwelpeter [*sic*] to the lunch table and read them aloud with great emphasis" for his daughters' enjoyment *(MFMT*, p. 56). In 1906 Mark Twain said of *Struwwelpeter* that "crude as the pictures were, and unconventional and fearfully original as the poetry was, they were smart and witty and humorous, and to children they were limitlessly captivating" (22 November 1906 AD, MTP).

Dixon Wecter, "MT as Translator from the German" (1941); *OPMT*, p. 27; Gisela M. Cloud, "MT's Translation of *Der Struwwelpeter* and *Die Schrecken der Deutschen Spreche*," Master's thesis, University of Georgia, 1966.

Hofmann, Karl (1836–1916). *A Practical Treatise on the Manufacture of Paper in All Its Branches*. Illus. Philadelphia: H. C. Baird; London: S. Low, Marston, Low & Searle, 1873. 422 pp.

Inscription: shaky signature in black ink on front free endpaper: "Mark Twain." Obviously forged. Book label of Robert Beall, Bookseller and Stationer, Washington, D. C.

Location: Humanities Research Center, Univ. of Texas at Austin. (Not part of the Frank C. Willson collection.)

Copy examined: copy displaying a crude counterfeit signature of Clemens' pseudonym.

Holcombe, Return Ira. *History of Marion County, Missouri*. Saint Louis, Missouri: E. F. Perkins, 1884.

Location: Mark Twain Papers, Berkeley, Ca.

Copy examined: Clemens' copy, unsigned but containing a pencil mark on page 902.

Holcombe wrote to Clemens on 29 August 1883 from Palmyra, Missouri, enclosing a prospectus for the volume and asking for Clemens' assistance in preparing a sketch of John Marshall Clemens (MTP). Clemens sent the letter to Orion Clemens, who contributed to the book.

HH&T, pp. 152–153.

Holder, Charles Frederick (1851–1915). *Marvels of Animal Life*. Illus. New York: Charles Scribner's Sons, 1885. 240 pp.

Inscription: inscribed by Olivia Clemens in brown ink on the first flyleaf: "Clara L. Clemens/Xmas 1888".

Location: Mark Twain Library, Redding, Conn. Donated from Clemens' library by Clara Clemens Gabrilowitsch in 1910 (MTLAcc, entry #1951).

Copy examined: Clara Clemens' copy.

Holden, Edward Singleton ((1846–1914). *Real Things in Nature; A Reading Book of Science for American Boys and Girls.* New York: Macmillan Co., 1903. 443 pp.
   Source: MTLAcc, entry #1952, volume donated from Clemens' library by Clara Clemens Gabrilowitsch in 1910.

Holland, Josiah Gilbert (1819–1881). *Bitter-Sweet: A Poem.* New York: C. Scribner, 1862. 220 pp.
   Source: MTLAcc, entry #636, volume donated by Clemens.

———, pseud. "Timothy Titcomb." *Plain Talks on Familiar Subjects.* New York, 1866.
   Inscription: flyleaf signed "S. L. Clemens".
   Catalog: A1911, #244, $1.50.
   Mark Twain informed James Redpath on 18 July 1872 that he planned to criticize "Timothy Titcomb" in a magazine piece (New York Public Library). The essay was written but not published; see *MTDW*, p. 191 n. 5.20.

Holley, Marietta (1836–1926), pseud. "Josiah Allen's Wife." *Josiah Allen's Wife.* Hartford: American Publishing Company, 1877. 580 pp.
   In 1880 Mark Twain included "Josiah Allen's Wife" in his list of humorists to be considered for inclusion in an anthology (NB 19, *N&J*, 2: 364). *Mark Twain's Library of Humor* (1888) contained "A Pleasure Exertion" from the *Josiah Allen's Wife* volume.

Hollingshead, John (1827–1904). *Under Bow Bell; A City Book for All Readers.* London: Groombridge and Sons, 1860. 312 pp. Twenty-five stories and sketches of London.
   Source: MTLAcc, entry #155, volume donated by Clemens.

Holmes, (Mrs.) Mary Jane (Hawes) (1825–1907). *The Homestead on the Hillside.* New York: Hurst & Co., 1900. 273 pp.
   Source: MTLAcc, entry #2273, volume donated from Clemens' library by Clara Clemens Gabrilowitsch in 1910.

Holmes, Oliver Wendell (1809–1894). *The Autocrat of the Breakfast-Table.* Boston: Phillips, Sampson and Company, 1858.
   Inscription: first two flyleaves are missing.
   Marginalia: Bradford A. Booth reproduces the marginalia in the copy Clemens marked for Olivia Langdon's amusement in 1869 ("MT's Comments on Holmes's *Autocrat*" [1950]). Clemens apparently read the book first, then gave it to Olivia. Booth notes that seemingly "the game was unpremeditated," since the early chapters in the first hundred pages contain only scanty annotation. Clemens' penciled comments run the gamut from modest admissions of ignorance ("Did you ever read a single paragraph of Aristotle, Livy?—I never did" [p. 302]) to playful literary allusions: "We that have free souls, it touches us not.—(Hamlet" (p. 354).
   Provenance: contains bookstamps of the Mark Twain Library at Redding. Possibly Clara Clemens retrieved the volume from that collection and then later sold it in California. Mrs. Carrie Estelle Doheny purchased the book from Maxwell Hunley Rare Books of Beverly Hills for $12.20 in 1940.
   Location: Carrie Estelle Doheny Collection, St. John's Seminary, Camarillo, Ca. Donated by Mrs. Doheny in 1940.
   Copy examined: Clemens' copy.
   Around 1869 Livy Langdon filled four and a half pages of her commonplace book with prose quotations from *The Autocrat* (DV161, MS pp. 90–94, MTP). Dixon Wecter reported (but did not publish) Clemens' reference to Holmes'

book in a letter to Olivia Langdon on 8 March 1869 in the calendar of letters in *LLMT*. On 30 September 1869 Mark Twain wrote to Holmes from Buffalo, stating that he had already read *The Autocrat* twice when "a superior young lady" asked him to "marginal-note" a copy for her; he did so, he told Holmes, and then read the book again for his own enjoyment (Library of Congress). In chapter 36 of *GA* (1873) Laura Hawkins requests a copy of *The Autocrat of the Breakfast-Table* while shopping in a bookstore, but the uneducated clerk replies that his shop does not sell cookbooks. Clemens punned on Holmes'— famous line from chapter six—"Good Americans, when they die, go to Paris"— in Notebook 18 *(N&J*, 2: 320): "Trivial Americans go to Paris when they die." (Holmes was quoting Thomas Appleton.) In the same notebook Clemens observed: "Nobody writes a finer & purer English than Motley Howells, Hawthorne & Holmes" (p. 348). On 25 January 1894 Clemens wrote to Livy from Boston about his having told Holmes how "you & I used the Autocrat as a courting book & marked it all through, & that you keep it in the sacred green box with the love letters" (MTP).

Sherwood Cummings, *"What Is Man?: The Scientific Sources"* (1964), 110–111.

———. "The Chambered Nautilus" (poem).
Mark Twain quoted this poem at the Whittier Birthday dinner on 17 December 1877 in his burlesque of highbrow American poets.
MTB, p. 1644; Smith, " 'That Hideous Mistake' " (1955).

———. "The Deacon's Masterpiece" (poem).
Clemens wrote in pencil above this poem in chapter 11 of his copy of *The Autocrat* (p. 295): "This is *all* good" (quoted by Booth, "MT's Comments," p. 462). "The Deacon's Masterpiece" was one of the pieces Mark Twain included in his *Library of Humor* (1888). In 1899 Mark Twain referred to "the principle of the 'one-hoss shay' " in a manuscript sketch of the Kellgren treatment (DV13, MTP).

———. *Elsie Venner* (novel, pub. 1861).
Clemens informed Holmes on 30 September 1869 that the young lady for whom Clemens had recently annotated a copy of *The Autocrat* would shortly receive from him a similarly marked copy of *Elsie Venner* (ALS in Library of Congress).

———. "A Good Time Going!" (poem).
Clemens underscored the three concluding lines in the second stanza, noting "This figure is good." Stanza five he also declared "good" in his 1869 marginalia in *The Autocrat*, reproduced in Booth's "MT's Comments" (1950), p. 462.

———. "Grandmother's Story of Bunker Hill Battle" (poem, 1875).
In a letter to Howells of 5 July 1875 Clemens commented on the publication of this poem in the New York *Tribune* without the permission of Holmes or Holmes' publisher *(MTHL*, p. 92).

———. *The Guardian Angel* (novel, pub. 1867).
Clemens mentioned the title of Holmes' novel in January 1888 (NB 27, TS p. 48).

———. *The Last Leaf. Poem.* Illus. by George Wharton Edwards and F. Hopkinson Smith. Cambridge: Riverside Press, 1886.
Inscription: inner front cover signed "S. L. Clemens".
Catalog: A1911, #245, $4.
"The Last Leaf" might qualify as Clemens' favorite lyric poem. The lines he quoted in his 30 April 1867 letter from New York City echoed through his

writings thereafter: "The mossy marbles rest/On the lips that he had pressed/In their bloom;/And the names he loved to hear,/Have been carved for many a year/On the tomb" (*MTTMB,* pp. 164–165). Into Olivia Langdon's common-place book Clemens himself copied these same lines sometime between 1868 and 1870 (DV161, MTP). Clemens remarked of his boyhood friend Pet McMurray, whom he saw for the first time in many years in 1885: "Well, see O W Holmes' 'The Last Leaf' for what he is now" (SLC to OLC, 23 January 1885, *LLMT,* p. 233). At an Authors' Reading in 1888 Mark Twain heard Holmes recite "The Last Leaf" so poignantly that the house delivered a standing ovation (26 February 1906 AD, MTP). Clemens returned from Hannibal and St. Louis, Missouri in 1902 with a sense of how rapidly death was winnowing his early friends; amid notes he made then for reassembling Tom Sawyer's gang fifty years after their youth, he twice copied passages he recalled from "The Last Leaf" (NB 45 [May–June 1902], TS pp. 14, 18). In his tribute to a friend's writings, "William Dean Howells" (1906), Mark Twain quoted these lines as an example of "the quality of certain scraps of verse which take hold of us and stay in our memories, we do not understand why." Albert Bigelow Paine remembered Clemens' quoting these lines in December 1909; they "put in compact form the thing which we have all vaguely felt," Clemens told Paine (*MTB,* pp. 1555–56).

————. "Mare Rubrum" (poem).
Mark Twain employed lines from this poem in his unfortunate Whittier Birthday Dinner speech in 1877 (*MTB,* p. 1645).
Smith, " 'That Hideous Mistake' " (1955).

————. "Ode for a Social Meeting, with Slight Alterations by a Teetotaler" (poem).
Mark Twain alludes to this piece in Notebook 22 (1884), TS p. 33.

————. *Poems of Oliver Wendell Holmes.* New Revised Edition. Illus. Boston: Houghton, Mifflin and Co., 1881.
Inscription: first flyleaf inscribed by Clemens in blue ink: "Livy L. Clemens/ from S.L.C./December, 1885".
Catalog: C1951, #21c, $17.50.
Location: Carrie Estelle Doheny Collection, St. John's Seminary, Camarillo, Ca. Donated by Mrs. Doheny in 1951 after she purchased the volume from Maxwell Hunley Rare Books of Beverly Hills for $32.
Copy examined: Livy Clemens' copy, unmarked.

————. *Selections from the Writings of Oliver Wendell Holmes, Arranged Under the Days of the Year.* New York: Houghton, Mifflin & Co., 1889.
Source: MTLAcc, entry #2126, volume donated from Clemens' library by Clara Clemens Gabrilowitsch in 1910.

————. *Songs in Many Keys.* Boston: Ticknor and Fields, 1862.
Songs gathers poems that Holmes wrote between 1849 and 1861; it does not contain "The Last Leaf," but it contains other pieces that Clemens enjoyed —"The Deacon's Masterpiece," "Mare Rubrum," and "The Chambered Nautilus." The edition brought out by Ticknor and Fields was bound in blue morocco leather embossed with gold lettering. In June 1861, bed-ridden in Honolulu, Clemens passed time by reading the only book in his hotel—"the first volume of Doctor Holmes's blue-and-gold series. I read the book to rags, and was infinitely grateful to the hand that wrote it" (April 1904 AD, *MTA,* 1:240). Mark Twain felt that this prolonged perusal of Holmes' book resulted in accidental plagiarism; the dedication to *Innocents Abroad* (1869), Mark Twain was convinced, was virtually identical to Holmes' tribute in *Songs.* The

resemblance is not as obvious as Twain supposed. Holmes inscribed his work "To/The Most Indulgent of Readers,/The Kindest of Critics,/My Beloved Mother,/All That Is Least Unworthy of Her/in This Volume/Is Dedicated/By Her Affectionate Son." Mark Twain's book is prefaced by the statement: "To/My Most Patient Reader/and/Most Charitable Critic,/My Aged Mother,/This Volume Is Affectionately/Inscribed." Mark Twain used this similarity as an example of "unconscious plagiarism" in a speech at the *Atlantic Monthly* breakfast to Holmes on 3 December 1879, when he related the circumstances about the Honolulu hotel in which he "read and reread Doctor Holmes's poems till my mental reservoir was filled up with them to the brim" *(MTSpk,* p. 135). See also *MTB,* p. 288 and *MTL,* p. 732.

————. *Soundings from the Atlantic.* Boston: Ticknor, 1884. 468 pp. [First pub. 1864.]
A selection from this volume, "A Visit to the Asylum for Aged and Decayed Punsters," appeared in *Mark Twain's Library of Humor* (1888). Mark Twain had included Holmes' name in several lists of humorists he compiled in preparation for editing the anthology (NB 19 [1880], *N&J,* 2: 363; [1881], p. 429).

————. "Two Armies" (poem).
Clemens recorded his admiration for this poem in 1869 in his copy of *The Autocrat:* several lines in "Two Armies" (p. 260) are labeled as "fine," and the last stanza is marked "very fine" (Booth, "MT's Comments" [1950], p. 462).

————. "The Voiceless" (poem).
Clemens' annotation in his copy of *The Autocrat* in 1869 declared that "The Voiceless" is "incomparable" (Booth, "MT's Comments" [1950], p. 461).

Holwell, John Zephaniah. *A Genuine Narrative of the Deplorable Deaths of the English Gentlemen, and Others, Who Were Suffocated in the Black Hole in Fort William, at Calcutta . . . in . . . June, 1756.* London, 1758.
"Mr. Holwell's long account of the awful episode was familiar to the world a hundred years ago, but one seldom sees in print even an extract from it in our day. . . . From the middle of Mr. Holwell's narrative I will make a brief excerpt" (ch. 54, *FE* [1897]).
Mutalik, *MT in India,* p. 114.

Home, Daniel Dunglas (1833–1886). *Incidents in My Life.* New York, 1863.
Catalog: A1911, #246, $1.25.
Home was a Scottish spiritualist medium who came to the United States as a boy in 1842 and moved to England in 1855.

Homer. *The Iliad of Homer.* Trans. by Alexander Pope (1688–1744). 2 vols. New York: W. Borradaile, 1825.
Inscription: "Olivia Langdon, Salina, June 8, 1833." (This was Livy Clemens' mother, Olivia Lewis Langdon [1810–1890], who married Jervis Langdon on 23 July 1832.)
Catalog: A1911, #247, $1.75, vol. 2 only.
Provenance: MTLAcc, entry #2079, volume 1 only (284 pp.) donated from Clemens' library by Clara Clemens Gabrilowitsch in 1910.

————. *The Iliad of Homer. Translated by Alexander Pope* (1688–1744). 2 vols. New York: A. S. Barnes & Co., 1858.
Source: MTLAcc, entry #2078, volume 1 only (274 pp.) donated from Clemens' library by Clara Clemens Gabrilowitsch in 1910.
See also the entry for Alexander Pope.

————. *The Iliad of Homer. Translated into English Blank Verse by William Cullen Bryant*. 2 vols. Boston: Houghton, Mifflin and Co., n.d. [cop. 1870].
> *Inscription:* front flyleaves of both vols. inscribed in black ink by Livy Clemens: "Susy Clemens/Hartford/March 19th 1884/Mamma".
> *Catalog:* Hunley 1958, #23, $7.50.
> *Location:* Humanities Research Center, University of Texas at Austin.
> *Copy examined:* Susy Clemens' copy, unmarked.

Homer, Mark Twain advised those who would be literary "connoisseurs" in 1865, is accountable for "all the heroic poetry, about the impossible deeds done before Troy" (*Californian,* 17 June 1865, *LAMT,* p. 142). In 1867 Clemens was impressed at seeing "the harbor whence Agamemnon's fleet sailed to the siege of Troy" (NB 9, *N&J,* 1: 392), as well as the site of ancient Troy itself. Mark Twain referred to "imperial Homer, in the ninth book of the Iliad" in "Political Economy" (1870), quoting Latin verse. "Aeneas" is P. Dusenheimer's nickname in *GA* (1873) because his hotel is located in Ilium, Pennsylvania. The second book of Homer's *Iliad* is mentioned facetiously in "Some Thoughts on the Science of Onanism" (DV200 no. 3, MTP). Clemens wrote to Karl and Hattie Gerhardt on 31 July 1881 to help them find a copy of the *Iliad* in Paris; if Galignani's did not have one, he advised, they should write to Chatto & Windus in London (Boston Public Library). In a letter written to Andrew Lang around 1890 Mark Twain objected to the common notion that Homer is more valuable to a civilization than "the little everybody's-poet whose rhymes are in all mouths to-day and will be in nobody's mouth next generation" (*MTL,* p. 526).

————. *The Iliad of Homer, Rendered into English Blank Verse. To Which Are Appended Translations of Poems Ancient and Modern*. Trans. from Greek by Edward George Geoffrey Smith Stanley (1799–1869), 14th Earl of Derby. 2 vols. London: John Murray, 1894.
> *Source:* MTLAcc, entry #2053, volume 1 only (339 pp.) donated from Clemens' library by Clara Clemens Gabrilowitsch in 1910.

————. *The Odyssey of Homer, Translated into English Blank Verse by William Cullen Bryant* (pub. 1871–1872).
> *Catalog:* C1951, #09, listed as containing only Livy Clemens' signature.

Early in 1887 Clemens made a memorandum in Notebook 26: "Get Bryant's Homer (no—only Odyssey)" (TS p. 33). He had previously (in 1875) urged Howells to "build an article upon A Boy's Comments Upon Homer" (*MTHL,* p. 105). In September 1880 he copied into Notebook 19 John Sheffield's famous praise—"Read Homer once . . . and Homer will be all the books you need" (*N&J,* 2: 371). The Mark Twain Papers contain a fragmentary twenty-five-page (AMS) burlesque review of *The Odyssey* (dated 1883) in which Mark Twain satirizes journalistic "book notices" (Paine 8). The review begins by faulting Homer's decision to write in verse, criticizes his concentration upon "a vanished race," and complains about a surplus of details. Homer obviously exaggerates the facts. Moreover, he ruins his narrative by filching names such as Ithaca and Troy from a New York state map. Mark Twain follows Ulysses into the cave of Polyphemus, but the review breaks off during a discussion of Greek gods. Homer is mentioned with veneration twice in Mark Twain's "A Cure for the Blues" (1893). In "Which Was the Dream?" (written 1897) a California gold mine is named the "Golden Fleece" (*WWD?,* pp. 55, 61). Homer is mentioned favorably in "Sold to Satan" (written 1904), "From an English Notebook" (*LE,* p. 172), and a letter from Clemens to Colonel W. D. Mann, 3 January 1906 (MTP). Mark Twain also refers to Homer in Part 6 of "What Is Man?" (1906). In "Captain Stormfield's Visit to Heaven" (1909) Homer is one of the "prophets" ranked with Shakespeare; nevertheless Homer stands behind the chair of an unknown tailor from Tennessee (*RP,* pp. 67, 73).
> Tony Tanner, *Reign of Wonder,* p. 152.

Hood, Thomas (1799–1845). *The Poetical Works of Thomas Hood.* Boston: Crosby, Nichols, Lee & Co., 1860. 480 pp.
   Source: MTLAcc, entry #2036, volume donated from Clemens' library by Clara Clemens Gabrilowitsch in 1910.

————. "Those Evening Bells" (poem).
   S. B. Liljegren shows how Mark Twain's "Those Annual Bills" (1875) was influenced by Hood's parody of Thomas Moore's sentimental poem, "Those Evening Bells" ("Revolt" [1945], pp. 28–30).

————. *Up the Rhine* (pub. 1839).
   Minnie M. Brashear (*MTSM,* pp. 218–222) suggests the letters in this volume as the ones with which Clemens compared Orion's style of letter-writing: "It reminds me strongly of Tom Hood's letters to his family (which I have been reading lately)" (18 March 1860, *MTL,* p. 45).

Hood, Thomas (1835–1874), known as Tom Hood.
   "Gone" is "Tom Hood," Clemens noted in July 1899 in London (NB 40, TS p. 60). Mark Twain published "How I Escaped Being Killed in a Duel" in *Tom Hood's Comic Annual for 1873* (London, 1873); another story, "Jim Wolfe and the Cats," appeared in *Tom Hood's Comic Annual for 1874* (London, 1874).

Hooker, Mary Ann (Brown) (1796–1838). *Memoir of Mary Anne Hooker.* Philadelphia: American Sunday-School Union, [cop. 1840]. 177 pp.
   Source: MTLAcc, entry #928, volume donated by Clemens.

Hooker, Worthington (1806–1867). *The Child's Book of Nature.* New York: Harper & Brothers, 1874. 179 pp.
   Source: MTLAcc, entry #1953, volume donated from Clemens' library by Clara Clemens Gabrilowitsch in 1910.

Hooper, Johnson Jones (1815–1862). *Some Adventures of Captain Simon Suggs, Late of the Tallapoosa Volunteers* (pub. 1845).
   "Simon Suggs," wrote Clemens in his list of humorists for an anthology in July 1880 (NB 19, *N&J,* 2: 361, 363); but in 1881 he temporarily forgot Suggs' name and wrote "Captain Jones of Alabama" in a similar list (NB 19, p. 428). *Mark Twain's Library of Humor* (1888) contains "Simon Suggs Gets a 'Soft Snap' on His Daddy." Several scholarly commentaries have examined similarities between chapter 10 of *Simon Suggs,* "The Captain Attends a Camp-Meeting," and chapter 20 of Mark Twain's *Huckleberry Finn* (1885), in which the King invades a Pokeville religious gathering. Mark Twain alluded to Hooper's sketch—"the man who 'went in on nary pair' (at camp meeting.)"—in a list of humorists and their writings he compiled in 1880 for an anthology (NB 19, *N&J,* 2: 363).
   Meine, *Tall Tales* (1930), p. 425; *MTAm* (1932), p. 255; *MT&SH,* pp. 81–86; *MT&HF,* pp. 279–281, 326–327, 329; chapter 10 of *Simon Suggs* is reprinted with commentary in Hill and Blair, eds., *Art of HF,* pp. 453–469; Lynn, ed., *HF,* pp. 144–149; Bradley, Beatty, and Long, eds., *Adventures of HF,* pp. 237–243.

Hoover, Bessie Ray (b. 1874). *Pa Flickinger's Folks.* Illus. New York: Harper & Brothers, 1909. 274 pp.
   Source: MTLAcc, entry #1443, volume donated by Clemens.

Hopkins, John Henry (1820–1891). *Three Kings of Orient. A Christmas Carol.* Illus. New York: Hurd & Houghton, [cop. 1865].
   Source: MTLAcc, entry #1218, volume donated by Clemens.

Hopkins, Manley. *Hawaii: The Past, Present, and Future of Its Island-Kingdom.* London: Longman, Green, Longman, and Roberts, 1862.

Mark Twain quoted from this book on the front endpaper of Notebook 5 (1866) and he also quoted a sentence and summarized Hopkins' comments in Notebook 6 (1866, *N&J*, 1: 227).

Hopkins, (Mrs.) Margaret Sutton (Briscoe) (b. 1864). *The Change of Heart; Six Love Stories.* New York: Harper & Brothers, 1903. 172 pp.

Source: MTLAcc, entry #1431, volume donated by Clemens.

————. *The Sixth Sense, and Other Stories.* Illus. New York: Harper & Brothers, 1899. 274 pp.

Source: MTLAcc, entry #1108, volume donated by Clemens.

[Hopkins, Samuel]. *The Life and Character of . . . Jonathan Edwards, Together with Extracts from His Private Writings and Diary and Also Seventeen [sic] Select Sermons on Various Important Subjects.* Northampton, Mass.: Andrew Wright, 1804.

Marginalia: a few pencil marks.
Location: Mark Twain Papers, Berkeley, Ca.
Copy examined: Clemens' copy.

In June 1882 Clemens wrote in his pocket notebook: "Life of Jon. Edwards about 1820 Northampton Mass" (NB 20, *N&J*, 2: 484). There was no edition published in Northampton in 1820, as he may have learned, so he purchased the 1804 edition instead. This book did not credit Hopkins' authorship of the brief biographical sketch, which forms a headnote for eighteen of Edwards' sermons, a few miscellaneous writings, and extracts from his diary.

Hopkinson, Joseph (1770–1842). "Hail, Columbia" (patriotic song, 1789).

Mark Twain mentioned this song in Notebook 5 (1866), *N&J*, 1: 121. The ship's choir "assaulted Hail Columbia" to celebrate the Fourth of July on the *Quaker City* (ch. 10, *IA* [1869]). "Brass bands bray 'Hail Columbia' " as steamboats depart in a race (ch. 16, *LonMiss* [1883]). "The pride of country rose in his [Alfred Parrish's] heart, Hail Columbia boomed up in his breast" in "The Belated Russian Passport" (1902).

Hoppin, Augustus (1828–1896). *Ups and Downs on Land and Water.* Boston: James R. Osgood & Co., 1871.

On 22 December 1873 Olivia Clemens was billed by Brown & Gross, Hartford booksellers, for "1 Ups & Downs $10.00" (MTP). Hoppin's book was the only volume with this title which cost as much as $10.

Horace. *Odes.*

Mark Twain seemed to know of Horace's line, "dulce et decorum est" (Bk III, ii, 13) when he wrote in 1869: "It is sweet to die for one's native land" ("Ye Cuban Patriot: A Calm Inspection of Him," Buffalo *Express*, 25 December 1869). The cholera germ in chapter 6 of "Three Thousand Years Among the Microbes" (written 1905) quotes the *Odes*, Book I, ode 2 (*WWD?*, p. 455). The narrator adds a note containing a translation of the Latin: "It means, 'Be thou wise: take a drink whilst the chance offers; none but the gods know when the jug will come around again.' "

————. *Q Horatii Flacci Opera omnia.* Ed. by Johann Gottfried Stallbaum (1793–1861). Leipzig: B. Tauchnitz, 1854. 256 pp.

Source: MTLAcc, entry #372, volume donated by Clemens.

Hornaday, William Temple (1854–1937). *Popular Official Guide to the New York Zoological Park, by William T. Hornaday, Director and General Curator.* Ninth ed. Illus. New York: New York Zoological Society, 1907. 171 pp.
    Source: MTLAcc, entry #1982, volume donated from Clemens' library by Clara Clemens Gabrilowitsch in 1910.

Horne, Charles Francis (1870–1942), ed. *Great Men and Famous Women.* 4[?] vols. Illus. New York, 1894.
    Catalog: A1911, #202, vols. 1 and 2 only, $1.75.

————. *The Technique of the Novel: The Elements of the Art, Their Evolution and Present Use.* New York: Harper & Brothers, 1908. 285 pp.
    Source: MTLAcc, entry #860, volume donated by Clemens.

Horner, Susan and Joanna Horner. *Walks in Florence and Its Environs.* 2 vols. London: Smith, Elder & Co., 1884.
    Inscriptions: two flyleaves torn from vol. 1; second flyeaf in vol. 2 signed: "Olivia Langdon Clemens/Florence 1892."
    Marginalia: Clemens made two corrections on page 79; in one of them he drew brackets around a sentence beginning "A long procession . . ." and re-marked in the margin: "Of course a procession moves in procession." The first volume also contains Clemens' pencil markings on pages 233, 242, and 244. Someone, possibly Clemens, marked pages 2, 3, 5, 6, 7, 8, 9, 11, 12, 15, 16, and 17 in the second volume.
    Location: Mark Twain Library, Redding, Conn.
    Copies examined: Livy Clemens' copies, annotated by Clemens.

Hornung, Ernest William (1866–1921). *A Bride from the Bush.*
    In the appendix to *AC* (1892) containing "Weather for Use in This Book" Mark Twain employed a passage depicting a dust-storm from Hornung's novel about Australia. But see also the entry for Susannah Moodie.

————. *The Rogue's March, A Romance.* New York: C. Scribner's Sons, 1903. 403 pp.
    Source: MTLAcc, entry #1013, volume donated by Clemens.

————. *The Shadow of the Rope.* New York: Charles Scribner's Sons, 1904. 328 pp.
    Source: MTLAcc, entry #162, volume donated by Clemens.

Horse-Car Poetry. Republished from the New Monthly Magazine "Record of the Year." New York: G. W. Carleton & Co., 1876. 14 pp.
    Inscription: paper cover inscribed in pencil by Clemens: "A Centennial gift—from my beloved nephew, W. H. Marsh [W. A. Warck?], July 4th 1876." Clemens also wrote the name "Mary O. Hayes" vertically on the paper wrapper.
    Location: Carrie Estelle Doheny Collection, St. John's Seminary, Camarillo, Ca. Donated by Mrs. Doheny in 1953 after its purchase from Aubrey Davidson of Pasadena.
    Copy examined: Clemens' copy.
    Contains Mark Twain's jingle, "Punch, Brothers, Punch!"

Hough, Emerson (1857–1923). *The Young Alaskans.* Illus. New York: Harper & Brothers, 1908. 292 pp.
    Source: MTLAcc, entry #1194, volume donated by Clemens.

House, Edward Howard (1836–1901). *Japanese Episodes.* Boston: James R.
  Osgood & Co., 1881. 247 pp.
    Source: MTLAcc, entry #572, volume donated by Clemens.
    In a postscript to a letter written to James R. Osgood & Company on 6
January 1883 Clemens requested a copy of "Japanese Legends" [*sic*] (*MTLP*,
pp. 161–162). House's volume contains four brief sketches intended to portray
"the inner life of the Japanese, of their domestic relations, their pleasures, or
the gentler romance of their nature" (p. 3). "Little Fountain of Sakanoshita"
describes the narrator's vacation in the scenic Sakanoshita region; "A Japanese
Statesman at Home" recounts House's visit with an esteemed official, Hirosawa
Hiosuké, who was later assassinated; "To Fuziyama and Back" promotes a
scenic tour; and "A Day in a Japanese Theatre" explains how a favorite
Japanese fable is presented on the stage.

House, Edward John (b. 1879). *A Hunter's Camp-Fires.* Illus. from photographs
  by the author. New York: Harper & Brothers, 1909. 402 pp.
    Source: MTLAcc, entry #1983, volume donated from Clemens' library by
Clara Clemens Gabrilowitsch in 1910.

Housman, Alfred Edward (1859–1936). *A Shropshire Lad.* Illus. New York:
  Mitchell Kennerley, 1908. 126 pp.
    Source: MTLAcc, entry #2034, volume donated from Clemens' library by
Clara Clemens Gabrilowitsch in 1910.

Howard, Bronson Crocker (1842–1908).
    Mark Twain dined with Howard and conversed with him at the Savile Club
in London in July 1900 (SLC to Brander Matthews, 11 July 1900, Columbia;
NB 43, TS p. 22). In 1905 Mark Twain nominated Howard for membership
in the American Academy of Arts and Letters (SLC to Robert Underwood
Johnson, 28 April 1905, American Academy).

Howard, George Elliott (1849–1928). *The American Nation: A History. Pre-*
  liminaries of the Revolution, 1763–1775. Portrait and maps. New York, 1905.
    Inscription: inner cover signed "S. L. Clemens, Sept. 1905."
    Catalog: A1911, #248, $3.50.

Howard, (Mrs.) Hattie. *Poems.* Hartford, Conn.: [Press of the Case, Lockwood &
  Brainard Co.,], [cop. 1886]. 108 pp.
    Source: MTLAcc, entry #627, volume donated by Clemens.

Howard, H. R., comp. *The History of Virgil A. Stewart, and His Adventures in*
  Capturing and Exposing the Great "Western Land Pirate" and His Gang. New
  York: Harper & Brothers, 1836.
    In chapter 29 of *LonMiss* (1883) Mark Twain quotes extensively from
Stewart's narrative of John A. Murrell's life, which he introduces as "a now
forgotten book which was published half a century ago." Howard's edition is
one of several possible sources for the extract; see also Augustus O. Walton.

Howard, Leland Ossian (1857–1950). *Mosquitoes: How They Live; How They*
  Carry Disease; How They Are Classified; How They May Be Destroyed. Illus.
  New York: McClure, Phillips & Co., 1901. 241 pp.
    Source: MTLAcc, entry #1954, volume donated from Clemens' library by
Clara Clemens Gabrilowitsch in 1910.

Howe, Edgar Watson (1853–1937). *A Moonlight Boy.* Boston: Ticknor and Co.,
  1886. 342 pp.
    Source: MTLAcc, entry #488, volume donated by Clemens.

———. *The Story of a Country Town.* Illus. by W. L. Wells. Atchison, Kansas: Howe & Co., 1883. 226 pp.

Inscription: flyleaf inscribed: "S. L. Clemens, Hartford, March 1884, Sent by the Author".

Marginalia: only one note on page 3 reported in *The Twainian* issues of January-February and March-April 1968.

Location: collection of Chester Davis, Mark Twain Research Foundation, Perry, Mo.

Copy examined: this volume was not available for inspection when I visited Perry, Missouri in 1970.

Soon after Mark Twain read the complimentary copy of *Story* that Howe sent from Atchison, Kansas, he responded on 13 February 1884 with a well-known letter that mixed praise and disapproval (published by C. E. Schorer in "MT's Criticism of *The Story of a Country Town*" [1955]). Mark Twain congratulated Howe on his simple, direct style of writing, but picked a few faults with his grammar, dismissed the preface, suggested more appearances for Big Adam and fewer speeches by Biggs, and rebuked the blatant sentimentality.

MTC, pp. 262–271; Claude M. Simpson, "Introduction," *The Story of a Country Town* (Cambridge, Mass.: Harvard University Press [Belknap Press], 1961), ix–xviii.

———. *The Story of a Country Town.* Boston: James R. Osgood & Co., 1885. 413 pp.

Source: MTLAcc, entry #154, volume donated by Clemens.

Howe, Julia (Ward) (1819–1910). "The Battle Hymn of the Republic" (hymn, 1862).

Mark Twain recalled that his children enjoyed this hymn greatly (7 June 1907 AD, MTP). In 1901 he wrote a mordant parody of the hymn, "The Battle Hymn of the Republic (Brought down to date)" (DV74, MTP, pub. in *OPMT*, p. 128). See *MTHL*, pp. 462–463.

Howells, Mildred (b. 1872). "At the Wind's Will" (poem), *Harper's Monthly*, 112 (March 1906), 576.

Isabel Lyon "came across a beautiful little poem by Mildred Howells" on 25 February 1906 and she "took it to Mr. Clemens this morning, he read it aloud to me and then cut it out of the magazine" (IVL Journal, TS p. 138, MTP). She recorded that later the same day he read it to Witter Bynner, "saying that he had wasted a whole chapter to say what she had said in a few lines." In a letter to William Dean Howells written that same evening Clemens complimented the "depth, & dignity, & pathos, & compression, & fluent grace & beauty" of the poem. All day long it had "sung in the ears of my spirit like a strain of solemn music" *(MTHL,* p. 800).

Howells, William Dean (1837–1920). "After the Wedding" (poem), *Harper's Monthly*, 114 (December 1906), 64–69.

"I read 'After the Wedding' aloud to Jean & Miss Lyon, & we felt all the pain of it & the truth. It was very moving & very beautiful." The pauses in the poem "furnished me time to brace up my voice, & get a new start" (SLC to WDH, 26 June 1906, *MTHL*, p. 814). Howells had sent Clemens a manuscript copy of the poem in advance of its publication. Albert Bigelow Paine remembered that Clemens read "After the Wedding" and "The Mother" *(MTB,* p. 1313).

———. *Annie Kilburn, A Novel.* New York: Harper & Brothers, 1891. 331 pp.

Source: MTLAcc, entry #1569, volume donated by Clemens.

————. *Between the Dark and the Daylight*. New York: Harper & Brothers, 1907.
Inscription: signed in black ink on inside front cover: "SL. Clemens/1908."
Marginalia: markings on page 61 (beside last three lines) and page 65 (lines 20–21).
Location: Antenne-Dorrance Collection, Rice Lake, Wis.
Copy examined: Clemens' copy.

————. *Boy Life; Stories and Readings Selected from the Works of William Dean Howells*. Ed. by Percival Chubb (b. 1860). Illus. New York: Harper & Brothers, 1909. 189 pp.
Catalog: C1951, #D71, listed with books signed by Clemens, $15.

————. *A Boy's Town, Described for "Harper's Young People."* New York: Harper & Brothers, 1890. 247 pp.
Clemens entered the title of Howells' autobiographical reminiscences in Notebook 30 (1890), TS p. 8. To Howells he wrote: " 'A Boy's Town' is perfect —perfect as the perfectest photograph the sun ever made" (27 November 1890, *MTHL,* p. 633).
IE, pp. 70–71; Hunter, "MT and the Boy-Book," p. 435.

————. *A Chance Acquaintance*. Boston: James R. Osgood and Co., 1873.
Inscription: inscribed on verso of first flyleaf: "To S. L. Clemens with ever so much friendship, W. D. Howells. Cambridge, May 16, 1873."
Catalog: C1951, #81c, $25, listed among books signed by Clemens.
Location: Carrie Estelle Doheny Collection, St. John's Seminary, Camarillo, Ca. Donated by Mrs. Doheny in 1951 after its purchase from Maxwell Hunley Rare Books of Beverly Hills for $32.
Copy examined: Clemens' copy, unmarked.
Mark Twain included Howells' name among two lists of humorists he made up in anticipation of editing an anthology of humor (NB 19 [1880], *N&J,* 2: 363; [1881], p. 429). *Mark Twain's Library of Humor* (1888) included two selections from *A Chance Acquaintance,* "Kitty Answers" and "Love's Young Dream."

————. *A Chance Acquaintance*. Boston: Houghton, Mifflin and Co., 1882. 271 pp.
Source: MTLAcc, entry #2274, volume donated from Clemens' library by Clara Clemens Gabrilowitsch in 1910.

————. *Christmas Every Day and Other Stories Told for Children*. Illus. New York: Harper & Brothers, [cop. 1892]. 150 pp.
Source: MTLAcc, entry #1596, volume donated by Clemens.

————. "The Christmas Spirit" (poem), *Harper's Weekly,* 46 (6 December 1902), 24–25.
"I read to people—& praised— . . . the Santa Claus poem" (SLC to WDH, 24 December 1902, *MTHL,* p. 756).

————. *The Coast of Bohemia*. Illus. New York: Harper & Brothers, 1893. 340 pp.
Source: MTLAcc, entry #1566, volume donated by Clemens.

————. *A Counterfeit Presentment. Comedy*. Boston: J. R. Osgood & Co., 1885. 199 pp. [Play, prod. 1877.]

Source: MTLAcc, entry #2276, volume donated from Clemens' library by Clara Clemens Gabrilowitsch in 1910.

"When does [Lawrence] Barrett open in your piece in N.Y. (or Boston). I calculate to be there" (SLC to WDH, 27 June 1877, *MTHL*, p. 184). Clemens saw it played in Hartford and he wrote to Howells: "The play is enchanting. I laughed & cried all the way through it. The dialogue is intolerably brilliant. . . . I cannot remember when I have spent so delightful an evening in a theatre" (4 January 1878, *MTHL*, p. 216).

————. "The Country Printer," *Scribner's Monthly*, 13 (May 1893), 539–558.

On 12 May 1893 Clemens wrote from New York: "I forgot to tell you how thoroughly I enjoyed your account of the country printing office, & how true it all was & how intimately recognizable in all its details" (*MTHL*, p. 652). See the entry for Howells' *Impressions and Experiences* (1896).

————. "A Difficult Case," *Atlantic Monthly*, 86 (July 1900), 24–36; (August 1900), 205–217.

"I read the Difficult Situation [*sic*] night before last, & got a world of evil joy out of it" (SLC to WDH, London, ca. 1 August 1900, *MTHL*, p. 719).

————. *Dr. Breen's Practice* (novel, pub. 1881).

In "Mental Telegraphy" (1891) Mark Twain cites the case of a woman who submitted a similar story to the *Atlantic Monthly* after Howells' novel was already set in type for serialization. "I had read portions of Mr. Howells' story, both in MS. and in proof," Mark Twain adds. In a letter of 14 April 1903 to Howells, he again referred to the coincidence, attributing it to "mental telegraphy" (*MTHL*, p. 767).

————. "Edgar Allan Poe," *Harper's Weekly*, 53 (16 January 1909), 12–13.

"I have to write a line, lazy as I am, to say how your Poe article delights me & charms me; & to add that I am in agreement with substantially all you say about his literature" (SLC to WDH, Redding, 18 January 1909, *MTHL*, p. 841, corrected from PH of ALS, MTP).

————. "The Father," chapter one of *The Whole Family* (a composite novel by twelve authors), *Harper's Bazar*, 41 (December 1907), 1161–70.

In the summer of 1906 the editor of *Harper's Bazar* tried to entice Mark Twain to contribute to *The Whole Family,* a novel narrated by a dozen different characters created by twelve eminent authors, by showing him the first two chapters. "Mr Howells began the composite tale," Twain noted in an auto- biographical dictation of 29 August 1906. "He held the pen and through it the father delivered his chapter—therefore it was well done" (*MTE*, pp. 243–244). Twain was less favorably impressed by the second chapter, written by Mary Wilkins Freeman. Uninspired, Twain declined the invitation. *The Whole Family* appeared as twelve monthly installments in *Harper's Bazar* between December 1907 and November 1908. Harper & Brothers issued a book edition in 1908.

————. *A Fearful Responsibility and Other Stories*. Boston, 1881.

Inscription: "Mrs. Clemens/With the regards of W. D. Howells. Belmont, July 26, 1881."

Catalog: Zeitlin 1951, #23, $10.

Clemens noted "July Scribner" in Notebook 19 (1881), *N&J*, 2: 396, probably intending to obtain the second installment of Howells' story while the Clemenses were spending their summer at Branford, Connecticut.

————. *Fennel and Rue; A Novel.* Illus. by Charlotte Harding. New York: Harper & Brothers, 1908. 130 pp.
Source: MTLAcc, entry #2279, volume donated from Clemens' library by Clara Clemens Gabrilowitsch in 1910.

————. *The Flight of Pony Baker; A Boy's Town Story.* Illus. New York: Harper & Brothers, 1902. 223 pp.
Inscription: on first flyleaf: "To S. L. Clemens/Author of 'Huck Finn' and other/Outcast literature/W. D. Howells."
Catalog: C1951, #65c, $32.50.
Location: Clifton Waller Barrett Collection, Alderman Library, University of Virginia, Charlottesville.
Copy examined: Clemens' copy, unmarked.
"It is a charming book, & perfectly true" (SLC to WDH, York Harbor, Maine, 3 October 1902, *MTHL,* p. 746).
IE, p. 71.

————. [Another identical (or the same?) copy.]
Source: MTLAcc, entry #2278, volume donated from Clemens' library by Clara Clemens Gabrilowitsch in 1910.

————. *A Foregone Conclusion.* Boston: James R. Osgood and Co., 1875.
Inscription: "Mrs. S. L. Clemens with the best regards of W. D. Howells, Cambridge, Dec. 4, 1874."
Marginalia: two penciled corrections by Clemens on pages 9 and 172. Leaves opened throughout.
Catalog: "The Fine Library of the Late Ingle Barr," Sotheby Parke-Bernet, Los Angeles, Sale No. 68 (18–19 February 1973), item #291, sold for $125; offered for sale by John Howell Books, San Francisco, 24 February 1973, $150.
Copy examined: (in 1973) Livy Clemens' copy, read by Clemens.
From Elmira on 21 June 1874 Clemens declared the first installment in the *Atlantic,* upon a "re-reading," to be "such absolute perfection of character-drawing & withal so moving in the matter of <tears> pathos <now, & laughter then> now, humor then, & both at once, occasionally, that Mrs. Clemens wanted me to defer my smoke & drop you our thanks—& in truth I was nothing loath" *(MTHL,* pp. 17–18). On 22 August 1874, having read the third installment to Livy, Clemens reported: "We think you have even outdone yourself. I should think that this must be the daintiest, truest, most admirable workmanship that was ever put on a story. The creatures of God do not act out their natures more unerringly than yours do" *(MTHL,* p. 21).
Livy Clemens thanked Howells on 6 December 1874 for the copy of *A Foregone Conclusion* "which reached me yesterday." She reiterated how "thoroughly" she and her husband "enjoyed the story each month as it came to us in the Atlantic" *(MTHL,* pp. 48–49). In Florence in October 1878 Clemens noted "preserved rose leaves at the Arminian convent" (NB 17, *N&J,* 2: 225)—apparently a reference to the "jar of that conserve of rose-leaves" described in chapter 2 of Howells' novel. Clemens saw a dramatic adaptation of *A Foregone Conclusion* on 12 November 1889 at the Tremont Theatre in Boston *(MTHL,* pp. 620–621).

————. "Frank Norris," *North American Review,* 175 (December 1902), 769–778.
"But I *did* read it. And moreover, I found in it . . . a chemist's mastery of analysis & proportion" (SLC to WDH, Riverdale, N.Y., 24 December 1902, *MTHL,* p. 756).

————. *A Hazard of New Fortunes* (pub. 1890).
"It is a great book; but of course what I prefer in it is the high art by which it is made to preach its great sermon without seeming to take sides or preach at all" (SLC to WDH, Hartford, 11 February 1890, *MTHL*, p. 630).
Smith, *MT's Fable of Progress*, pp. 20–25.

————. *Heroines of Fiction*. 2 vols. New York, 1901.
Inscription: title page signed "Olivia L. Clemens. Riverdale, Oct. 1901."
Catalogs: C1951, #01 and #013, the 2 vols. mistakenly listed separately, both grouped with books signed by Livy Clemens; *Zeitlin 1951*, #24, 2 vols. listed together, $6.

————. *An Imperative Duty. A Novel.* New York: Harper & Brothers, 1893.
150 pp.
Source: MTLAcc, entry #1567, volume donated by Clemens.

————. *Impressions and Experiences* (pub. 1896).
In 1893 Clemens had praised one of the pieces collected in this volume, "The Country Printer." On 30 December 1898 he confessed to Howells from Vienna that "the last chance I had at a bound book of yours was in London nearly two years ago—the last volume of your short things by the Harpers. I read the whole book twice through & some of the chapters several times" and then "lent it to another admirer of yours & he is admiring it yet" *(MTHL*, pp. 684–685).

————. *Indian Summer* (novel), in *Harper's Monthly*, vols. 71–72, pub. serially between July 1885 and February 1886.
Indian Summer elicited Clemens' most fervent praise for Howells' novels: "You are really my only author; I am restricted to you; I wouldn't give a damn for the rest." Having read the second part twice ("to my mind there isn't a waste-line in it"), Clemens awaited part one, which the mails had delayed. "I am going to read both parts aloud to the family." He especially appreciated the manner in which "you make all the motives & feelings perfectly clear without analyzing the guts out of them" (SLC to WDH, Elmira, 21 July 1885, *MTHL*, p. 533).

————. "John Hay in Literature," *North American Review*, 181 (September 1905), 343–351.
In "John Hay and the Ballads," *Harper's Weekly* (21 October 1905), Mark Twain quoted from Howells' article and tried to correct the impression that Hay's *Pike County Ballads* were indebted to Bret Harte's examples.

————. *The Lady of the Aroostook* (novel), in *Atlantic Monthly*, vols. 42–43, published serially November 1878–March 1879.
From Munich Clemens reported on 17 November 1878: "We gathered around the lamp, after supper, . . . & tackled the new magazines. I read your new story aloud, amid thunders of applause." Clemens facetiously recommended future plot developments for the novel, which was running in the *Atlantic Monthly (MTHL*, pp. 240–241). On 21 January 1879 Clemens added: "Well, I have read-up, now, as far [as] you have got,—that is, to where there's a storm at sea approaching,—& we three think you are clear out-Howellsing Howells. If your literature has not struck perfection now we are not able to see what is lacking.—It is all such truth—truth to the life; everywhere your pen falls it leaves a photograph" *(MTHL*, p. 245). On 30 January 1879 Clemens chaffed in Munich: "Consound that February number. I wish it would fetch along the Lady of the Aroostook" *(MTHL*, p. 250). Nearly a decade later Clemens amused himself by listing the chief characteristics of prominent authors; for Howells he wrote "truth" (NB 27 [March 1888], TS p. 61).

————. *The Landlord at Lion's Head* (pub. 1897).

The first version of Mark Twain's "The Turning-Point of My Life," probably written in December 1909, expressed a critical opinion omitted in its final form: he called Howells' *Landlord* ("his latest book," Mark Twain mistakenly wrote) "his masterpiece, as I think," and quoted a sentence from it *(WIM?,* p. 527).

————. *Letters Home.* New York: Harper & Brothers, 1903. 299 pp.
Source: MTLAcc, entry #1571, volume donated by Clemens.

———— and Thomas Sergeant Perry (1845–1928), eds. *Library of Universal Adventure by Sea and Land.* New York: Harper & Brothers, 1888.
Location: Mark Twain Library, Redding, Conn.
Copy examined: Clemens' copy, unmarked.

————. *Life of Rutherford B. Hayes.* Boston: Hurd & Houghton, 1876.
Howells informed Clemens on 8 September 1876: "I finished the book yesterday. . . . Of course I'll send you a copy at once" *(MTHL,* p. 149). On 14 September 1876 Clemens wrote: "I am reading & enjoying the biography. It is a marvelous thing that you read for it & wrote it in such a little bit of a time" *(MTHL,* p. 150).

————. *Literary Friends and Acquaintances.* Illus. New York: Harper & Brothers, 1900.
Inscriptions: front free endpaper inscribed "Herr Gabrilowitsch's friend, with the hope of his continued acquaintance, W. D. Howells, April 27, 1901" *(Hunley 1958).* Flyleaf inscribed: "Wishing Herr Gabrilowitsch a safe journey back to Russia, a pleasant stay there & a speedy return to his friends in America. Olivia L. Clemens/April 24th 1901."
Catalogs: C1951, #029, listed among books signed by Livy Clemens; *Hunley 1958,* #56, $22.50.
Location: Mark Twain Research Foundation, Perry, Mo. Described in *The Twainian,* 34 (May-June 1975), 3–4.
Copy examined: gift copy from Livy Clemens.

————. *Literature and Life; Studies.* Illus. New York: Harper & Brothers, 1902. 323 pp.
Source: MTLAcc, entry #1798, volume donated by Clemens.

————, ed. *A Little Girl Among the Old Masters.* Intro. and Commentary by William Dean Howells. Boston: James R. Osgood and Co., 1884.
Inscription: flyleaf inscribed by Howells: "Susy and Clara Clemens, from Pilla's Papa. Hartford, Nov. 13, 1883."
Location: Carrie Estelle Doheny Collection, St. John's Seminary, Camarillo, Ca. Donated by Mrs. Doheny in 1940 after the volume was purchased from Maxwell Hunley Rare Books of Beverly Hills for $12.20.
Copy examined: Susy and Clara Clemens' copy. A photograph of Mildred Howells is inserted.
Howells compiled this book from the drawings that ten-year-old Mildred ("Pilla") Howells made during a tour of Italy in 1882. Clemens was familiar with the volume (see *MTHL,* p. 490).

————. *London Films* (pub. 1905).
Catalog: C1951, #58c, $12.

————. ["Machiavelli,"] *Harper's Monthly,* 110 (April 1905), 803–806.
In "William Dean Howells" (1906) Mark Twain selected an excerpt from Howells' "Easy Chair" column, a paragraph concerned with Louis Dyer's *Machiavelli and the Modern State* (1904), to illustrate "how clear, how limpid, how understandable" is Howells' prose.

―――. *Miss Bellard's Inspiration; A Novel.* New York: Harper & Brothers, 1905. 224 pp.
Source: MTLAcc, entry #1476, volume donated by Clemens.

―――. [Another identical copy.]
Source: MTLAcc, entry #2277, volume donated from Clemens' library by Clara Clemens Gabrilowitsch in 1910.

―――. *A Modern Instance,* in *Century Magazine,* vols. 23–24, pub. serially December 1881–October 1882.
When Clemens saw the March 1882 installment in *Century Magazine,* in which Bartley Hubbard angrily departs from Equity, Maine, is met at the train station by Marcia Gaylord, and elopes with her to Boston, Clemens made a memorandum in his Notebook 20: "Howells, your new book is fine." Clemens crossed out the entry after he told Howells this opinion. Subsequently his admiration increased; on 22 June 1882 he wrote from Hartford: "I am in a state of wild enthusiasm over this July instalment of your story. It's perfectly dazzling—it's masterly— incomparable." Howells' humor was "so very subtle, & elusive" *(MTHL,* p. 407). On 24 July 1882 Clemens confessed to a feeling that he himself resembled Bartley Hubbard, "& I enjoy him to the uttermost, & without a pang" *(MTHL,* p. 412). On 30 October 1882 he acclaimed the concluding chapters; they were "prodigious" *(MTHL,* p. 417).

―――. "The Mother" (poem), *Harper's Monthly,* 106 (December 1902), 21–26.
"I read 'The Mother' aloud [to Jean Clemens and Miss Lyon] & sounded its human deeps with your deep-sea lead. I had not read it before, since it was first published" (SLC to WDH, New York City, 26 June 1906, *MTHL,* p. 814). Howells had written four years earlier, on 29 July 1902, to say that he was "glad" Clemens liked the poem and to promise that he would soon send a copy to Olivia Clemens *(MTHL,* p. 743). But evidently Clemens was too concerned about his wife's ill health to permit her to read the piece. He wrote to Howells from Riverdale on 24 December 1902: "I read to people—& praised—. . . the deep & moving one which you wrote at York, & which I wanted Mrs. Clemens to see, there, & which I hide from her now—because we guard her against feelings & thinkings all we can" *(MTHL,* p. 756). See also *MTB,* p. 1313.

―――. *The Mother and the Father. Dramatic Passages.* New York: Harper & Brothers, 1909.
Inscription: first flyleaf inscribed "S. L. Clemens/from W. D. Howells./May 22, 1909."
Location: Antenne-Dorrance Collection, Rice Lake, Wis.
Copy examined: Clemens' copy, unmarked.

―――. *The Mouse-Trap* (farce), pub. in *Harper's Monthly* in 1886; reprinted in England by David Douglas in 1897.
Clemens wrote to Howells from Vienna on 30 December 1898: "At the house of an English friend, on Christmas Eve, we saw the Mouse-Trap played & *well* played. I thought the house would kill itself with laughter" *(MTHL,* p. 684).

―――. *An Open-Eyed Conspiracy; An Idyl of Saratoga.* New York: Harper & Brothers, 1897. 181 pp.
Source: MTLAcc, entry #1568, volume donated by Clemens.

————. "Our Spanish Prisoners at Portsmouth," *Harper's Weekly,* 42 (20 August 1898), 826–827.
"This morning I read to Mrs. Clemens from your visit to the Spanish prisoners, & have just finished reading it to her again—& lord, how fine it is & beautiful, & how gracious & moving" (SLC to WDH, Kaltenleutgeben, 30 August 1898, *MTHL,* p. 679).

————. *Out of the Question.* Boston, 1885.
Catalog: A1911, #249, $2.75.
When the play was appearing serially in the *Atlantic Monthly* (between February and April 1877) Clemens addressed an undated letter to Howells: "Been reading Out of the ? aloud to the family & have just finished it. All hands bewitched with it. It is wonderful dialogue" (*MTHL,* p. 173).

————. *A Pair of Patient Lovers.* New York: Harper & Brothers, 1901. 368 pp.
Inscription: presented to Clemens by the author.
Catalog: C1951, #48c, $27.50, listed among the books signed by Clemens.
A collection of short stories.

————. *A Parlor Car. Farce.* Boston: Houghton, Mifflin & Co., 1883. 74 pp.
Source: MTLAcc, entry #2275, volume donated from Clemens' library by Clara Clemens Gabrilowitsch in 1910.

————. *The Parlor Car. Farce.* Boston: Ticknor and Co., 1886. 74 pp.
Location: Mark Twain Papers, Berkeley, Ca.
Copy examined: Clemens' copy, unmarked.
Howells' play was published in the September 1876 issue of *Atlantic Monthly.* On 23 August 1876 Clemens wrote to him from Elmira: "The farce is wonderfully bright & delicious, & *must* make a hit. . . . I read it aloud to the household this morning & it was better than ever" (*MTHL,* p. 147). Clemens added on 14 September 1876 from Hartford: "You may well know that Mrs. Clemens liked the Parlor Car—enjoyed it ever so much." Clemens suggested adding an "odious train-boy" who would sell "foul literature" and candy, and urged Howells to expand the play to full-length (*MTHL,* p. 152). In an undated letter probably written in March 1877 Clemens reminded Howells that "The Parlor Car was as much as 25 times better, in print, than it was when you read it to me" (*MTHL,* p. 173). Mark Twain often felt strong impulses to burlesque what he admired in literature. A brief MS playlet that survives in the Mark Twain Papers (DV322) is titled "Love on the Rail—A REHEARSAL." The two characters in Mark Twain's undated piece discuss the stage problems involved in dramatizing scenes of Love at First Sight, the Bridal Trip, and Three Months After the Marriage. The playlet ends when they realize that "Three Months After" would require more than one parlor car, since by then the husband would more likely be found in the smoker.

————. *A Parting and a Meeting* (novel), pub. serially in the issues of *Cosmopolitan* between December 1894 and February 1895.
In a letter written from Paris to Henry H. Rogers on 23 January 1895 Clemens showed an awareness that Howells' "story" was then appearing (*MTHHR,* pp. 122–123).

————. *Private Theatricals* (novel), in *Atlantic Monthly,* vols. 36–37, appeared serially between November 1875 and May 1876. Not published as a book under this title (issued in 1921 as *Mrs. Farrell, A Novel*).
"Company interfered last night, & so 'Private Theatricals' goes over till this evening, to be read aloud" (*MTHL,* p. 113).

————. *Ragged Lady* (novel), pub. serially in the issues of *Harper's Bazar* between July and November 1898.

Clemens wrote to Howells from Vienna on 30 December 1898 that he "saved up your last story," but that another Howells admirer had carried away the magazine before he could begin *(MTHL*, p. 684).

————. *The Register: Farce*. Boston: James R. Osgood and Co., 1884.
Location: Mark Twain Papers, Berkeley, Ca.
Copy examined: Clemens' copy, unmarked.

————. *The Rise of Silas Lapham* (novel), in *Century Magazine*, vols. 29–30, pub. serially November 1884–August 1885.

"I was glad & more than glad to meet young Hubbard again . . . ; the story starts most acceptably" (SLC to WDH, 20? October 1884, *MTHL*, p. 512). "I & madam are clear behind with Silas Lapham, but Clara Spaulding is booming with it" (SLC to WDH, 26 March 1885, *MTHL*, p. 524). "I read the June instalment in bed a while ago this morning, & found it as great & fine & strong & beautiful as Mrs. Clemens had already proclaimed it to be. You are always writing your best story, & as usual this one is also your best" (SLC to WDH, 5 June 1885, *MTHL*, p. 531). At Quarry Farm, Livy Clemens noted in her diary on 1 July 1885 that an Elmira acquaintance "read to us . . . the part of Mr Howells['] Silas Lapham in the July Century that we found also unusual, it seems as if it showed more the moral struggles of mortals than any thing Mr Howells has ever done before. The characters are all so well drawn. You are compelled to like 'Silas' and 'Persis' in spite of their commonness—particularly Silas" (DV161, MTP).

————. *Roman Holidays and Others* (pub. 1908).
Catalog: C1951, #D44, listed with books signed by Clemens.

————. *Seven English Cities*. New York: Harper & Brothers, 1909.
Location: Antenne-Dorrance Collection, Rice Lake, Wis.
Copy examined: Clemens' copy, unmarked.

————. *The Shadow of a Dream* (short novel), in *Harper's Monthly*, 80 (March 1890), 510–529; (April 1890), 766–782; (May 1890), 865–881.

Howells apparently read the first portion of *The Shadow of a Dream* to the Clemenses in Hartford on 2 and 3 November 1889 *(MTHL*, p. 625).

————. *The Shadow of a Dream; A Story*. New York: Harper & Brothers, 1890. 218 pp.
Source: MTLAcc, entry #1570, volume donated by Clemens.

————. "A Shaker Village," *Atlantic Monthly*, 37 (June 1876), 699–710.

"We have just finished the Shaker article. . . . so full of pathos" (SLC to WDH, Hartford, May [?] 1876, *MTHL*, p. 139).

————. *Sketch of the Life and Character of Rutherford B. Hayes. . . . Also a Biographical Sketch of William A. Wheeler*. New York: Hurd and Houghton, 1876. 226 pp.
Source: MTLAcc, entry #830, volume donated by Clemens.

————. *The Son of Royal Langbrith* (novel), in *North American Review*, vols. 178–179, pub. serially January-August 1904.

"Last night I read your 27 pages in the N.A.R. with vast interest. It stimulated me out of a couple of hours of sleep" (SLC to WDH, Florence, 16 January 1904, *MTHL*, p. 779).

————. *The Son of Royal Langbrith, A Novel.* New York: Harper & Brothers, 1905. 369 pp.
   Source: MTLAcc, entry #1307, volume donated by Clemens.

————. "Sorrow, My Sorrow" (poem), *Harper's Monthly,* 108 (December 1903), 147.
   Clemens praised "your moving & beautiful poem. How many it comes home to; how many have felt it" (SLC to WDH, Florence, 4 December 1903, *MTHL,* p. 774).

————. *Suburban Sketches.* New York: Hurd and Houghton, 1871.
   Inscription: flyleaf inscribed (in pencil) "S. L. Clemens/1871." The handwriting appears to be that of Livy Clemens.
   Location: Carrie Estelle Doheny Collection, St. John's Seminary, Camarillo, Ca. Donated in 1940 after Mrs. Doheny purchased the volume from Maxwell Hunley Rare Books of Beverly Hills for $12.20.
   Copy examined: Clemens' copy, unmarked.

———— and Henry Mills Alden, eds. *Their Husbands' Wives.* Harper's Novelettes Series. New York: Harper & Brothers, 1906.
   Inscription: signed inside front cover: "S. L. Clemens/1906."
   Location: Carrie Estelle Doheny Collection, St. John's Seminary, Camarillo, Ca. Donated in 1940 after Mrs. Doheny purchased the volume from Maxwell Hunley Rare Books of Beverly Hills for $12.20.
   Copy examined: Clemens' copy, unmarked.
   Contains "Eve's Diary" (1905) by Mark Twain on pages 1–27. Mark Twain had readily consented to Howells' request to include this piece (WDH to SLC, 19 December 1905, *MTHL,* pp. 799–800).

————. *Their Silver Wedding Journey* (novel), in *Harper's Monthly,* vols. 98–100, pub. serially January–December 1899.
   At Howells' urging, Clemens promised from Vienna to read this novel when it would begin to appear (SLC to WDH, 30 December 1898, *MTHL,* p. 684). "I am waiting for the April Harper, which is about due now; waiting, & strongly interested," Clemens wrote on 2 April 1899 (*MTHL,* p. 689). After the issue arrived, Clemens informed Howells that he detected in the characters "the weariness & indolence of age; indifference to sights & things once brisk with interest" (5 April 1899, *MTHL,* pp. 689–690). "Day before yesterday the Harper came, & in the evening I hunted it up & was lying on the sofa, & kept interrupting the family's repose with laughter & chuckles" because Clemens recognized Livy in Mrs. March (SLC to WDH, 12 May 1899, *MTHL,* p. 695). "Your September instalment was delicious—every word of it. You haven't lost *any* of your splendid art" (SLC to WDH, Sanna, Sweden, 26 September 1899, *MTHL,* p. 706).

————. *Their Wedding Journey.* Illus. by Augustus Hoppin. Boston: James R. Osgood and Co., 1872.
   Inscription: flyleaf inscribed "To Mr. Samuel L. Clemens with the regards of W. D. Howells. Cambridge, March 15, 1872."
   Marginalia: a few underlinings and notes, not in Clemens' hand.
   Location: Carrie Estelle Doheny Collection, St. John's Seminary, Camarillo, Ca. Donated by Mrs. Doheny in 1940 after she purchased the volume for $12.20 from Maxwell Hunley Rare Books of Beverly Hills.
   Copy examined: Clemens' copy.
   Olivia Clemens mentioned this book to her husband in a letter of 30 December 1871 (MTP). On 18 March 1872 Clemens thanked Howells for a complimentary copy of the novel: "We bought it & read it some time ago, but we prize this copy most on account of the autograph" (*MTHL,* p. 10). *Mark Twain's Library*

of Humor (1888) contained four selections from *Their Wedding Journey:* "Trying to Understand a Woman," "At Niagara," "Their First Quarrel," and "Custom House Morals."

————. "Thomas Bailey Aldrich."
On 27 March 1907 Isabel Lyon, rummaging through cases of books and papers from Charles L. Webster & Company, "ran upon a sketch of Mr. Aldrich's life in ms. written by Mr. Howells which I brought home" (IVL Journal, TS p. 236, MTP).

————. *Tuscan Cities* (pub. 1886).
"Lately I was once more reading your incomparable Tuscan Cities—a book whose details I love to forget, so that I can read them again with the pristine relish. If I had a memory I should know the book by heart by this time" (SLC to WDH, Redding, 24 September 1908, *MTHL*, p. 835).

———— and Henry Mills Alden (1836–1919), ed. *Under the Sunset.* New York: Harper & Brothers, 1906. 264 pp.
Source: MTLAcc, entry #2280, volume donated from Clemens' library by Clara Clemens Gabrilowitsch in 1910.

————. *The Undiscovered Country.* Boston: Houghton, Mifflin and Co., 1880.
Inscription: first flyleaf inscribed on verso in purple ink: "S. L. Clemens/with ever so much affection,/W. D. Howells./Belmont,/June 18, 1880."
Marginalia: light pencil marks, possibly not Clemens', throughout pages 1–65. On page 2 Clemens made a revision in black ink, crossing out "Oh, I don't know that I prefer. . . . the business," marking the rest of the paragraph, and writing in the margin: "from here down to here." On the verso of a flyleaf at the back, someone, perhaps Miss Lyon, made a note in pencil: " 'Bambino makes music more than what it is'—when he sings a chorus to the Wedding March—".
Catalog: C1951, #D56.
Location: Clifton Waller Barrett Collection, Alderman Library, Charlottesville, Virginia.
Copy examined: Clemens' copy.
This novel began to appear serially in the *Atlantic Monthly* in January 1880. Clemens wrote to Howells from Hartford on 8 January 1880: "The Undiscovered starts off delightfully—I have read it aloud to Mrs. C. & we vastly enjoyed it" (*MTHL*, p. 287). "I've read the Feb. Undiscovered, & it is perfectly wrote—as Susy says.—What a master hand you are to jabber the nauseating professional slang of spiritism" (SLC to WDH, Elmira, 24 January 1880, *MTHL*, p. 288). Mark Twain quoted a passage from this novel (see marginalia above) in "William Dean Howells" (1906) to illustrate Howells' gift for description.

————. *Venetian Life* (pub. 1866).
Sometime before 1870 Clemens copied a passage from *Venetian Life* (describing "the ghost of dead Venice") into Livy Langdon's commonplace book (DV161, MTP). In chapter 36 of *GA* (1873) Laura Hawkins reads "a familiar passage" in Howells' book while browsing in a Washington, D.C. bookstore. In "William Dean Howells' (1906) Mark Twain quoted excerpts from the book and recalled: "I read his *Venetian Days* [sic] about forty years ago. . . . For forty years his English has been to me a continued delight and astonishment." Afterwards Howells wrote to Clemens good-naturedly about the mistaken title that *Venetian Life* was given in the essay: "You are the only person in the world who may do this and not be destroyed" (1 August 1906, *MTHL*, p. 816).
MT&GA, pp. 51, 292 n. 50.

————. "The White Mr. Longfellow," *Harper's Monthly*, 93 (August 1896), 327–343.

"Certainly your White Longfellow is perfect—wholly flawless" (SLC to WDH, Southampton, England, 5 August 1896, *MTHL*, p. 660).

————. *A Woman's Reason* (novel), in *Century Magazine*, vols. 25–26, pub. serially February-October 1883.

"We have read your two opening numbers in the Century, and consider them almost beyond praise. I hear no dissent from this verdict" (SLC to WDH, Hartford, 1 March 1883, p. 427). "We are enjoying your story with our usual unspeakableness; & I'm right glad you threw in the shipwreck & the mystery—I *like* it" (SLC to WDH, Elmira, 22 August 1883, *MTHL*, p. 439).

————, adapt. *Yorick's Love* (play, prod. 1878). Adapted from *Un Drama Nuevo* by Manuel Tamayo y Baus.

"Last night, for the first time in ages, we went to the theatre—to see Yorick's Love [in Hartford]. The magnificence of it is beyond praise. The language is so beautiful, the passion so fine, the plot so ingenious, the whole thing so stirring, so charming, so pathetic!" (SLC to WDH, Hartford, 11 March 1880, *MTHL*, p. 292).

Howells, William Hooper. *The Rescue of Desdemona, and Other Verse*. No. 188 of 1,000 copies. Illus. Philadelphia: Butterfly Press, 1908. 106 pp.
Source: MTLAcc, entry #2035, volume donated from Clemens' library by Clara Clemens Gabrilowitsch in 1910.

Howitt, Mary (Botham) (1799–1888). *Birds and Flowers; or, Lays and Lyrics of Rural Life*. Illus. London, 1873.
Catalog: A1911, #250, $2.25.

————. *Our Four-Footed Friends*. London: S. W. Partridge & Co., [1862?]. 168 pp.
Source: MTLAcc, entry #1891, volume donated from Clemens' library by Clara Clemens Gabrilowitsch in 1910.

[Hoyos, Camilla.] *The "Lettre de Cachet" and Other Stories*. By C. H. London: Digby, Long & Co., 1900.
Inscription: flyleaf inscribed: "To/Mr. Clemens in the hopes of receiving very much more than I have to offer/from Camilla Hoyos. May 24th, 1900."
Location: Carrie Estelle Doheny Collection, St. John's Seminary, Camarillo, Ca. Donated by Mrs. Doheny in 1940 after she purchased the volume for $12.20 from Maxwell Hunley Rare Books of Beverly Hills.
Copy examined: Clemens' copy, unmarked.

Hoyt, Charles Hale (1860–1900). *A Rag Baby* (play, prod. 1884).
"There is a young fellow, playing here [in Boston] in a thing called The Rag Baby, who c'd do Sellers perfectly well. . . . He does an amateur pugilist and walkist, named Sport" (SLC to Charles L. Webster, 10 May 1884, *MTBus*, p. 253).

Hubbard, Elbert Green (1856–1915). *Health and Wealth*. East Aurora, N.Y.: The Roycrofters, 1908.
Location: Mark Twain Library, Redding, Conn.
Copy examined: Clemens' copy, unmarked.

Hubbard's Newspaper and Bank Directory.
"I have 'Hubbard's Newspaper & Bank Directory of the World,' 3 bulky volumes, which you can have for your office" (SLC to Charles L. Webster, n.d., TS in MTP).

Huber, François (1750–1831). *New Observations on the Natural History of Bees* (pub. 1806).

In "The Bee" (written 1902?) Mark Twain mentions this Swiss naturalist as one of "the great authorities" on honeybees (Box 1, no. 1, MTP).

Huc, Évariste Régis (1813–1860). *Recollections of a Journey Through Tartary, Thibet, and China, During the Years 1844, 1845, and 1846.* New York: D. Appleton & Co., 1852. [Title varies in subsequent editions.]

In November 1889 Clemens made a note concerning the narrative of this French Roman Catholic priest and missionary: "M. Huc's Thibet, Mongolia & China" (NB 29, TS p. 32).

Huch, Ricarda Octavia (1864–1947). *Fra Celeste.* Leipzig: H. Haessel, 1899. 273 pp.

Source: MTLAcc, entry #386, volume donated by Clemens.

Hughes, Rupert (1872–1956). *Zal, An International Romance.* New York: Century Co., 1905. 346 pp.

Source: MTLAcc, entry #2281, volume donated from Clemens' library by Clara Clemens Gabrilowitsch in 1910.

[Hughes, Thomas (1822–1896).] *The Scouring of the White Horse; or, the Long Vacation Ramble of a London Clerk.* By the author of "Tom Brown's School Days." Illus. by Richard Doyle. Cambridge, England and London: Macmillan and Co., 1859. 244 pp.

Inscription: first flyleaf inscribed by Livy Clemens in blue ink: "Clara L. Clemens/Hartford/June 8th 1883".

Provenance: contains bookstamps of Mark Twain Library at Redding. Donated from Clemens' library by Clara Clemens Gabrilowitsch in 1910 (MTLAcc, entry #1922).

Catalog: Mott 1952, #61, $10.

Location: Mark Twain Memorial, Hartford, Conn. Gift of anonymous donor in 1960.

Copy examined: Clara Clemens' copy, unmarked.

———. *Tom Brown at Oxford.* London: Macmillan & Co., 1882. 546 pp.

Source: MTLAcc, entry #2282, volume donated from Clemens' library by Clara Clemens Gabrilowitsch in 1910.

———. *Tom Brown's School Days.* New York: Hurst & Co., n.d. 233 pp.

Source: MTLAcc, entry #427, volume donated by Clemens.

Mark Twain mentioned Tom Hughes in chapter 15 of *FE,* but inadvertently conflated the titles of his novels by referring to him as "the author of 'Tom Brown at Rugby.' " Hughes' first novel—*Tom Brown's School Days* (1857)—depicted a pupil's life at Rugby; its inferior sequel, *Tom Brown at Oxford* (1861), caused Mark Twain's confusion.

Hugo, Adele (Foucher) (1806–1868). *Victor Hugo, by a Witness of His Life.* Trans. by Charles Edwin Wilbour. New York: Carleton, 1863. 175 pp. First published in Paris in 1863.

"I have read half of Les Miserables, two or three minor works of Victor Hugo, & also that marvelous being's biography by his wife" (SLC to Mollie Fairbanks, Elmira, 6 August 1877, *MTMF,* p. 207).

Hugo, Victor Marie, Comte (1802–1885). *Angelo* (play, prod. 1835).
    Franklin R. Rogers argues that the second half of Mark Twain's "Legend of Count Luigi" (ch. 21, *IA* [1869]) is a burlesque of Hugo's *Angelo* and *Lucrezia Borgia* (*MTBP*, pp. 48–49). Clara Clemens summarized the plot of *Angelo* ("full of satisfactory scenes for the divine Sarah") in her commonplace book, probably in the 1890's (Paine 150, MTP). Clara also listed the title of Hugo's *Hernani* (play, 1830) and *Ruy Blas* (play, 1838).

—————. *The Destroyer of the Second Republic, Being Napoleon the Little*. Trans. by a clergyman of the Protestant Episcopal Church, from the sixteenth French edition. New York: Sheldon & Co., 1870.
    Location: Mark Twain Library, Redding, Conn.
    Copy examined: Clemens' copy, unmarked.

—————. *Fantine, or the Felon and the Fallen*. [*Les misérables*]. New York: W. L. Allison Co., 1893. 195 pp.
    Source: MTLAcc, entry #151, volume donated by Clemens.

—————. *The Man Who Laughs*. Trans. by William Young. New York: D. Appleton and Co., 1869.
    Mark Twain based a burlesque, "L'Homme Qui Rit" (written 1869), on Young's translation. Portions of Mark Twain's manuscript consist of pages from the book. In *MTBP* (pp. 40–48, 114–127) Franklin R. Rogers discusses Mark Twain's burlesque and demonstrates how the pattern of Gwynplaine's life parallels that of Mark Twain's *P&P* (1882).

—————. *Marius; or, The Son of the Revolution* [*Les misérables*]. Trans. from the author's latest Paris "Definitive" edition. New York: W. L. Allison Co., [cop. 1893]. 192 pp.
    Source: MTLAcc, entry #152, volume donated by Clemens.

—————. *Les Misérables* (novel, pub. 1862).
    "I have read half of Les Miserables, two or three minor works of Victor Hugo, & also that marvelous being's biography by his wife" (SLC to Mollie Fairbanks, 6 August 1877, *MTMF*, p. 207). This admiration was mixed with scorn: in 1885 Mark Twain listed Hugo among the names of Carlyle, Napoleon, Mirabeau, Washington, Emerson, Grant, and others in whom "was allied the infinitely grand & the infinitely little" (NB 23, TS p. 37).

—————. *Ninety-Three*. [Trans. from French by Helen B. Dole.] Chicago: M. A. Donohue & Co., n.d. 372 pp
    Source: MTLAcc, entry #150, volume donated by Clemens.

—————. *Ruy Blas* (play).
    Clemens' letter to the Keokuk *Saturday Post* on 18 October 1856 mentions *Don Caesar de Bazan* (*TJS*, p. 14), a possible reference. Franklin R. Rogers feels that MT's *P&P* (1882) "owes a substantial debt" to Hugo's play or to another play based upon it, *Don Caesar de Bazan* (*MTBP*, pp. 173–174 n. 29). MT describes Miles Hendon as "a sort of Don Caesar de Bazan in dress, aspect, and bearing." Rogers sees parallels in Miles' protecting Edward from the threatening crowd, Miles' receiving Edward's whipping for him, and—possibly—Mark Twain's using exchanged identities in the novel. Clara Clemens listed *Ruy Blas* in her commonplace book sometime between 1888 and 1904 (Paine 150, MTP).

—————. *Story of the Candlesticks* [*Les misérables*]. New York: Harper & Brothers, n.d. 158 pp.
    Source: MTLAcc, entry #1333, volume donated by Clemens.

————. *Things Seen (Choses Vues.)* Portrait. New York, 1887.
   Inscription: flyleaf signed "S. L. Clemens, 1887."
   Catalogs: A1911, #253, $1.25; *Lexington 1912,* #18, $2.50.

————. *The Toilers of the Sea.* New York: Harper & Brothers, 1866.
   Mark Twain spoofed this novel in January 1867 with "Who Was He?," a
burlesque written on board the *San Francisco.* Perhaps he found a copy of Hugo's
novel in the ship's library. "In an insane moment I ventured to read the opening
chapters of the Toilers of the Sea & now I am entangled. My brain is in hope-
less disorder." In Mark Twain's satire the novelist pauses repeatedly to define
and discuss ordinary phenomena and objects—a storm, a man, a windowsill. At
every possible juncture he ruminates upon human existence. "Who Was He?"
was written in Notebook 7 *(N&J,* 1: 280–284); it is published in *S&B,* pp. 25–48.
In a letter published in the *Alta California* (19 April 1867) Mark Twain claimed
that the porter of the Heming House [actually the Deming House] in Keokuk
brought him a copy of a "romance" entitled *The Toilers of the Sea (MTTMB,*
p. 153), which so amused him that he repeated the story in chapter 57 of *IA*
(1869). In chapter 47 of *IA* Mark Twain recounted the way in which his pilgrim-
companions hailed a boat on the Sea of Galilee and "the toilers of the sea ran
in and beached their barque."
   MTBP, p. 44.

Huish, Robert. *The Celebrated Huish "Memoirs." Private and Public Life of George
   IV and His Court.* Portraits. New York: Adams, Victor & Co., [1875].
   Inscription: front paper cover signed in brown ink: "Saml. L. Clemens."
Beneath, faintly penciled: "Hartford, 1875."
   Catalogs: A1911, #254, $4.25; "First and Other Editions of Samuel L.
Clemens," List No. 3, Seven Gables Bookshop, New York City (August 1972),
item #139, $100.
   Location: Mark Twain Memorial, Hartford, Conn. Gift of anonymous donor
in 1973, according to *Mark Twain Memorial Newsletter,* 7 (August 1973), 5.
   Copy examined: Clemens' copy.

Hulbert, William Davenport (1868–1913). *Forest Neighbors; Life Stories of Wild
   Animals.* Illus. New York: McClure, Phillips & Co., 1902. 241 pp.
   Source: MTLAcc, entry #1955, volume donated from Clemens' library by
Clara Clemens Gabrilowitsch in 1910.

Hume, David (1711–1776). *The History of England, from the Invasion of Julius
   Caesar to the Revolution of 1688.* 6 vols. New York: Harper & Brothers, 1854.
   Inscriptions: three vols. signed by Clemens.
   Marginalia: passages marked throughout.
   Catalog: A1911, #255, $15.50, edition erroneously reported as 1864.
   "Bring Hume's Henry VIII & Henry VII," Clemens reminded himself while
traveling toward Hartford from New York City in July 1877 (NB 13, *N&J,* 2:
39). Another note refers to Froude's *History of England,* so he evidently intended
to take materials from his home library to Quarry Farm for background study
preparatory to writing *P&P* (1882). Mark Twain's working notes cite the page
numbers on which historical events and characters of special interest to him are
described—pp. 303, 307, 314, 317, 319, 320, 424 (DV115, MTP). These appear
to relate most logically to the court intrigues during the reign of Henry VIII,
recounted in the third volume. Five notes in *P&P* quote from this third volume.
On 30 September 1896 Clemens again (in London this time) made a memorandum to obtain a copy of "Hume—Henry VIII" (NB 39, TS p. 6).
   TIH, pp. 151–152.

———. "Of Miracles," section 10 of *An Enquiry Concerning Human Understanding* (pub. 1748).

In 1878 Clemens noted "Hume's Essay on Miracles, and Paley's Evidences of Christianity" (NB 17, *N&J*, 2: 219).

Humperdinck, Engelbert (1854–1921). *Hänsel und Gretel* (opera, prod. 1893).

Humperdinck's opera, based on Grimm's fairy tale, was performed in German at the Metropolitan Opera House in 1905, with Alfred Hertz conducting. Clemens attended "a part of Hansel and Gretel" on 6 December 1905 in New York City, but at Colonel Harvey's insistence left early so that he would not become overtired (IVL Journal, TS p. 112, MTP). Miss Lyon recorded that he enjoyed the opera. On 15 March 1906 he endorsed a benefit performance of the work by the Metropolitan Opera Company; the chorus of "that lovely masterpiece," he wrote, is "deep and satisfying" (SLC to Legal Aid Society, *The Twainian* [November 1942], 3).

Huneker, James Gibbons (1860–1921). *Iconoclasts* (pub. 1905).

Clara Clemens listed the title of this book in her commonplace book (Paine 150, MTP).

Hunt, Leigh (1784–1859). "Abou Ben Adhem" (poem).

Mark Twain employed a phrase from the first line of the poem—"may his tribe increase!"—in chapter 9 of *IA* (1869). He attempted a parody—"Abou Ben Butler"—in Notebook 19 (1880), *N&J*, 2: 372–373. In June 1885 he noted: "Perfect: About ben Adhem & the Rubiyât" (NB 24, TS p. 25).

———. *A Day by the Fire and Other Papers*,
Roberts Brothers, 1870.
Inscription: signed in black ink: "Livy L. Clemens".
Location: Mark Twain Library, Redding, Conn.
Copy examined: Livy Clemens' copy.

———. *The Town* (pub. 1848).

An undated scrap of paper in the Mark Twain Papers contains a note by Clemens: "Nobody in town.—Bought Timbs—Walks—Stow<e>—Leigh Hunt, & a lot of other authorities & read about a thing, then went leisurely to see it" (DV 115). Mark Twain's working notes for *P&P* (1882) include references to "Drunken habits of James I & his court—Hunt—413" and "Tom dines in greater state, asking (see Lee [*sic*] Hunt" DV115, MTP). In a footnote to chapter 16 of *P&P* Mark Twain cites Hunt's *The Town* as his source for a "quotation from an early tourist" that describes preparations for the king's meal.

Hunt, Thornton. "Shelley. By One Who Knew Him," *Atlantic Monthly*, 11 (February 1863), 197.

Mark Twain's "In Defence of Harriet Shelley" (1894) quotes the admission by Leigh Hunt's son that "there is not a trace of evidence or a whisper of scandal against her."

Hunter, Peter Hay (1854–1910). *James Inwick, Ploughman and Elder*. New York: Harper & Brothers, 1896. 194 pp.
Source: MTLAcc, entry #1572, volume donated by Clemens.

Hunter, William Wilson (1840–1900). *The Indian Empire: Its History, People, and Products*. London: Trübner & Co., 1882. [Second ed. pub. 1886; new rev. ed. 1893.]

In chapter 59 of *FE* (1897) Mark Twain quotes from Hunter's description of the Taj Mahal to show the "fairy structure" that is often "built by excitable literary people."

Madigan, "MT's Passage to India," p. 360.

Hurst, John Fletcher (1834–1903). *Indika. The Country and the People of India and Ceylon.* New York: Harper & Brothers, 1891. 794 pp.
   Source: MTLAcc, entry #1720, volume donated by Clemens.

———. *Short History of the Reformation.* Illus. New York: Harper & Brothers, 1885. 125 pp.
   Source: MTLAcc, entry #1382, volume donated by Clemens.

Hutton, Laurence (1843–1904). *A Boy I Knew and Four Dogs.* Illus. New York: Harper & Brothers, 1898. 87 pp.
   Source: MTLAcc, entry #1927, volume donated from Clemens' library by Clara Clemens Gabrilowitsch in 1910.

———. *A Boy I Knew, Four Dogs, and Some More Dogs.* Illus. New York: Harper & Brothers, [cop. 1900]. 116 pp.
   Source: MTLAcc, entry #1597, volume donated by Clemens.

———. *Curiosities of the American Stage.* New York: Harper & Brothers, 1891.
   On 3 February 1891 Clemens addressed a letter to "Dear Eddard," quite possibly a nickname for Hutton, to thank him for a book "which could not have come more timely, shut up as I am this rainy morning." He declares that the night before he had felt "a longing for a sight of this very book" (Princeton University Library).

———. *Edwin Booth.* Illus. New York: Harper & Brothers, 1893. 59 pp.
   Source: MTLAcc, entry #1767, volume donated by Clemens.

——— and Eleanor Hutton. *Laurence and Eleanor Hutton: Their Books of Association.* Compiled by Mary Ellen Wood. New York: privately printed (The DeVinne Press), 1905. 208 pp.
   Catalog: C1951, #93c, listed among books signed by Clemens.

———. *Literary Landmarks of Florence.* Illus. New York: Harper & Brothers, [cop. 1897]. 81 pp.
   Source: MTLAcc, entry #1793, volume donated by Clemens.

———. *Literary Landmarks of Rome.* Illus. New York: Harper & Brothers, [cop. 1897]. 75 pp.
   Source: MTLAcc, entry #1794, volume donated by Clemens.

———. *Literary Landmarks of Venice.* Illus. New York: Harper & Brothers, 1905. 71 pp.
   Source: MTLAcc, entry #1795, volume donated by Clemens.

Huxley, Thomas Henry (1825–1895). *Evolution and Ethics* (pub. 1893).
   Clara Clemens Gabrilowitsch informed Hyatt H. Waggoner that her father read this book ("Science in the Thought of MT" [1937], p. 362), but his copy has evidently not survived.
   Waggoner, "Science," pp. 364–367; Cummings, *"What Is Man?:* The Scientific Sources" (1964), p. 114.

———. *Hume.* English Men of Letters series. Ed. by John Morley. New York: Harper & Brothers, 1879.
   In Notebook 20 (1882) Clemens simply wrote, "Huxley's Hume" (*N&J*, 2: 463).

————. *Life and Letters of Thomas Henry Huxley, by His Son Leonard Huxley.* 2 vols. New York: Appleton and Co., 1900.

Isabel Lyon noted on 17 October 1905 in Dublin, New Hampshire that she had "sent back to Library" one volume of Huxley's correspondence (IVL Journal, Antenne-Dorrance Collection, Rice Lake, Wis.).

Hyde, John, Jr. *Mormonism: Its Leaders and Designs.* New York: W. P. Fetridge & Co., 1857.

Hyde's book was one of Mark Twain's sources for details about the Mormons used in *Roughing It* (1872), according to Franklin R. Rogers *(RI, p. 563).*

Hyde, William De Witt (1858–1917). *The Art of Optimism as Taught by Robert Browning.* New York: T. Y. Crowell & Co., [cop. 1900]. 35 pp.

Source: MTLAcc, entry #870, volume donated by Mrs. Ralph W. Ashcroft (formerly Isabel Lyon), Clemens' secretary.

Ibsen, Henrik (1828–1906). *Hedda Gabler* and *The Master Builder.* Vol. 10 of Ibsen's *Works.* Trans. by Edmund Gosse and William Archer. Intro. by William Archer. New York, 1907.

Inscription: signed "S. L. Clemens, 1906" [sic], according to *A1911.*
Catalog: A1911, #257, $4.50.

In Berlin around 1891 Henry Fisher understood Clemens to say that Strindberg sought "to out-Ibsen the Norwegian" in harsh portrayals of women *(AMT,* p. 79). Mark Twain mentioned Ibsen noncommittally in "Ancients in Modern Dress" *(FM,* p. 436), written 1896–1897. In an Autobiographical Dictation of 4 September 1907 Twain insisted: "I have not read Nietzsche or Ibsen, nor any other philosopher" (quoted in *WIM?,* p. 17).

"I had an old horse whose name was Methusalem" (song).
See *MTB,* pp. 295–296 and *MTEnt,* pp. 52, 219 n. 5.

"I know that my Redeemer lives" (Negro spiritual). Also known as: "Sinner, please don't let this harvest pass."
Mentioned in Notebook 30 (1890), TS p. 14.

Iles, George (1852–1942). *Flame, Electricity and the Camera; Man's Progress.* Illus. New York: Doubleday & McClure Co., 1901. 398 pp.

Source: MTLAcc, entry #666, volume donated by Clemens.

Clemens wrote to Iles on 28 October 1900 to thank him for an unspecified book which was "just the kind of reading I enjoy the most. There'll not be any skipping done, you may be sure of that" (McGill University Library).

————. *Inventors at Work, with Chapters on Discovery.* New York: Doubleday, Page & Co., 1906. 503 pp.

Catalog: C1951, #88c, presentation copy, $10, listed among books signed by Clemens.

The Independent (periodical, New York, pub. 1848–1928).

On 1 January 1874 Geer & Pond, Hartford booksellers, billed Clemens for "Inde from Nov. 1/73 to Jan. 1/74"; on 28 January 1874 they billed him for five additional copies (MTP). In a letter dated only "3 May" Clemens requested the editor to send him a copy of a poem by Caroline Mason "which appeared in the Independent about last August or September" (TS in MTP).

Ingelow, Jean (1820–1897). *Off the Skelligs. A Novel.* Boston: Roberts Brothers, 1873. 666 pp.

Source: MTLAcc, entry #2283, volume donated from Clemens' library by Clara Clemens Gabrilowitsch in 1910.

————. *Poems.*
    Catalog: C1951, #O10, edition not supplied, listed among books signed by
Livy Clemens.

————. *The Poetical Works of Jean Ingelow, Including the Shepherd Lady and
Other Poems.* New York: T. Y. Crowell & Co., [cop. 1863]. 520 pp.
    Source: MTLAcc, entry #2037, volume donated from Clemens' library by
Clara Clemens Gabrilowitsch in 1910.

————. "We Two" (poem).
    In the month of her wedding—February 1870—Livy Langdon copied this
poem, a romantic love pledge, into her commonplace book (DV161, MTP).

Ingersoll, Ernest (1852–1946). *The Ice Queen.* Illus. New York: Harper &
    Brothers, [cop. 1884]. 256 pp.
    Source: MTLAcc, entry #431, volume donated by Clemens.

————. *Wild Life of Orchard and Field; Papers on American Animal Life.* Illus.
New York: Harper & Brothers, [cop. 1880]. 347 pp.
    Inscription: "Jean L. Clemens/Riverdale on the Hudson/March 1902".
    Location: Mark Twain Library, Redding, Conn. Donated from Clemens' library
by Clara Clemens Gabrilowitsch in 1910 (MTLAcc, entry #1957).
    Copy examined: Jean Clemens' copy.

————. *Wild Neighbors; Out-Door Studies in the United States.* Illus. New York:
Macmillan Co., 1902. 301 pp.
    Source: MTLAcc, entry #1956, volume donated from Clemens' library by
Clara Clemens Gabrilowitsch in 1910.

Ingersoll, Robert Green (1833–1899). *The Ghosts and Other Lectures.* Washington,
    D. C.: C. P. Farrell, 1879.
    Inscription: "Saml Clemens Esq/from his friend/R. G. Ingersoll/Dec 11, 79".
    Marginalia: contains Clemens' pencil marks.
    Catalog: "Retz Appraisal" (1944), p. 9, valued at $10.
    Location: Mark Twain Papers, Berkeley, Ca.
    Copy examined: Clemens' copy.
    When Clemens returned from the Chicago reunion of the Army of the Ten-
nessee in 1879 he called Ingersoll "the most beautiful human creature that ever
lived" and declared of the speech he heard Ingersoll deliver: "Its music will sing
through my memory always as the divinest that ever enchanted my ears" (SLC
to WDH, Hartford, 17 November 1879, *MTHL,* p. 279). He had listened to
Ingersoll raise the twelfth toast at the banquet, a tribute to "The Volunteer
Soldiers of the Union." On 9 December 1879 Clemens wrote to Ingersoll from
Hartford to request "a perfect copy of your peerless Chicago speech" (TS in
MTP). In response Ingersoll sent Clemens copies of *Ghosts* and other volumes.
Clemens thanked him on 14 December 1879 "for the books—I am devouring
them—they have found a hungry place, and they content it & satisfy it to a
miracle. I wish I could hear you *speak* these splendid chapters before a great
audience" *(MTL,* p. 373). Howells remembered how much "he greatly admired
Robert Ingersoll, whom he called an angelic orator, and regarded as an evangel of
a new gospel" *(MMT* [1910], p. 27). Grace King noted that "strength always
inspires him. He admires Ingersoll. He loves to see Ingersoll knock down his
opponents" (undated MS, ca. 1888, "Mark Twain, Second Impression," quoted
by Robert Bush, "Grace King and MT," p. 40). Clemens owned other books by
Ingersoll, but they have disappeared. On 20 December 1900 Clemens assured
a Mr. Griswold: "I shall be very glad indeed to have the Dresden Edition of my
old friend's books in my library in this house [at 14 West 10th Street, New
York City]. I knew him twenty years, and was fond of him, and held [him] in as
high honor as I have held any man living or dead" (TS in MTP).

MTSP, p. 116; Raymond A. Hall, "MT's Relation to Robert G. Ingersoll's Program of Frontier Free Thought," Master's thesis (University of Washington, Seattle, 1951); Thomas D. Schwartz, "MT and Robert Ingersoll" (1976).

Inglis, Julia (Selina). *The Siege of Lucknow. A Diary*. London: Osgood & McIlvaine; Leipzig: Bernhard Tauchnitz, 1892.
 Lady Inglis' husband, John E. W. Inglis, commanded the defense of Lucknow during the Sepoy Mutiny (1857). In chapters 58 and 59 of *FE* (1897) Mark Twain quoted from her account of events within the besieged garrison.

Ingraham, Joseph Holt (1809–1860). *The Prince of the House of David* (1855).
 Mark Twain listed the title of Ingraham's book among those which *Quaker City* passengers were instructed to bring with them *(Alta California*, 5 April 1868, *TIA*, p. 303).

Ingulf, Abbot of Crowland (d. 1109). *Ingulph's Chronicle of the Abbey of Croyland, with the Continuations by Peter of Blois and Anonymous Writers*. Trans. from Latin by Henry T. Riley. London: H. G. Bohn, 1854. 546 pp.
 Inscription: half-title page signed in pencil: "S. L. Clemens, Hartford, 1877".
 Marginalia: several penciled notes and markings by Clemens.
 Catalogs: A1911, #259, $3.25; "The Collection of Alan N. Mendleson," Parke-Bernet Galleries, Sale No. 1719 (December 1956), item #95; sold for $55, according to *American Book-Prices Current Index 1955–1960* (New York: Bowker, 1961), p. 258.
 Clemens purchased this volume on 24 October 1877, according to a bill he received in November 1877 from Osgood and Company of Boston (Scrapbook #10, p. 69, MTP).

[Institoris, Henricus (d. 1508) and Jakob Sprenger (fl. 1494)]. *Malleus Maleficarum, or Hexenhammer ("Hammer of Witches")* (pub. 1489).
 Henry Fisher reports that Clemens was eager in 1891 to see whether the Imperial Library of Berlin had an edition of *The Witch Hammer*, which was published in German and Latin editions between 1489 and 1669. Fisher wrote: "I forget now which edition of that murderous book we examined, but I do remember some of the figures we jotted down at the librarian's suggestion. The Witch Hammer, that is, a voluminous 'treatise for discovering, torturing, maiming and burning witches,' was first published, we learned, in 1487" *(AMT*, p. 179). Fisher further recalled that "some years later Mark related the story of our search for the Witch Hammer before a motley crowd of litterateurs at Brown's Hotel" in London. On that occasion Clemens gave Bram Stoker, the author of *Dracula*, a recipe for witch salve—hemlock, mandragora, henbane, belladonna— which Clemens said "Fisher and I dug . . . up at the Berlin Royal Library" *(AMT*, pp. 180–181).

Investigations of M. Shawtinback. San Francisco, Calif.: J. Winterburn & Co., 1879. 263 pp.
 Source: MTLAcc, entry #556, volume donated by Clemens.

Ireland, Alleyne. *The Far Eastern Tropics: Studies in the Administration of Tropical Dependencies: Hong-Kong, British North Borneo, Sarawak, Burma, Etc*. Boston: Houghton Mifflin, 1905.
 Inscription: signed in black ink on inside front cover: "SL. Clemens/1906." Inscribed on the first flyleaf: "To Samuel L. Clemens Esq. with the author's sincere regards./Alleyne Ireland,/1906."
 Catalog: A1911, #260, $3.25.
 Provenance: library bookplate of Jerome Kern on inside front cover.
 Location: Mark Twain Memorial, Hartford, Conn.
 Copy examined: Clemens' copy, unmarked.

Ireland, (Mrs.) Annie Elizabeth (Nicholson) (d. 1893). *Life of Jane Welsh Carlyle, by Mrs. Alexander Ireland*. New York: Charles L. Webster & Co., 1891. 329 pp.
Clemens' publishing firm brought out this biography of Thomas Carlyle's wife.

Irving, Washington (1783–1859). *The Adventures of Captain Bonneville*. Lovell's Library Series, No. 311. New York: John W. Lovell Co., n.d.
Marginalia: on the front paper wrapper Clemens penciled: "A narrative poorly & wordily told." He made several other annotations in pencil as well.
Catalog: "Retz Appraisal" (1944), p. 9, valued at $15.
Location: Mark Twain Papers, Berkeley, Ca.
Copy examined: Clemens' copy.
In a 6 July 1884 letter Clemens started to ask Charles L. Webster for a work by Washington Irving, but changed his mind and deleted the request. The same letter instructed Webster to send him *"personal narratives of life & adventure out yonder on the Plains & in the Mountains" (MTBus*, p. 265). The copy of *Captain Bonneville* that Clemens read and annotated was a paperbound edition that cost 20¢.

————. *The Alhambra: A Series of Tales and Sketches of the Moors and Spaniards* (pub. 1832).
Before leaving on the *Quaker City* in 1867, Clemens noted: "Irving's Spain/ Moors" (NB 8, *N&J*, 1: 328). In chapter 59 of *IA* (1869) he mentions his disappointment at not being able "to visit the Alhambra at Granada" because of a cholera quarantine.

————. *Astoria* (novel, pub. 1836).
Clemens wrote "Astoria" among a list of miscellaneous entries in Notebook 22 (TS p. 42) in 1884, possibly hoping to derive historical details about the Far West for use in "Huck Finn and Tom Sawyer Among the Indians."

————. *The Life of Oliver Goldsmith* (pub. 1849).
Paul Fatout constructs a strong case for believing that Irving's account of the first-night performance of *She Stoops to Conquer* (1773) materially influenced Mark Twain's description of his first San Francisco lecture (1866) included in chapter 78 of *RI* (1872). See "MT's First Lecture" (1956).

————. "Rip Van Winkle" (short story, pub. in *The Sketch-Book* [1819–1820]).
Under a column headed "Rip Van Winkle" Mark Twain related in a letter published in the 29 September 1867 issue of the *Daily Alta California* how a train whistle at Pompeii "woke me up and reminded me that I belonged to the nineteenth century, and wasn't a rusty mummy, caked with ashes and cinders, eighteen hundred years old" *(TIA*, p. 82). Mark Twain included Irving in two lists of humorists from whom he intended to select representative pieces for an anthology (NB 19 [1880], NB 19 [1881], *N&J*, 2: 364, 429). *Mark Twain's Library of Humor* (1888) contained "Rip Van Winkle" and cited an edition of Irving's *Sketch-Book* published by G. P. Putnam's Sons of New York. Mark Twain was perennially amused by Joseph Jefferson's performances in the stage adaptation of Irving's story (see Dion Boucicault); on 6 October 1896 Twain confided to Henry H. Rogers that until Frank Mayo's death he had entertained notions of similarly establishing *Pudd'nhead Wilson* as a popular favorite: "I had begun to think it possible that Mayo would succeed in making the play a permanency, like Rip Van Winkle" *(MTHHR*, p. 239). When "Bkshp-Huck" of "Three Thousand Years Among the Microbes" (written 1905) assigns new literary names to his microbe friends, he calls one of them Rip Van Winkle *(WWD?*, p. 471).

————. *The Sketch-Book of Geoffrey Crayon, Gent.* Illus. New York: G. P. Putnam, 1860. 465 pp.
    Source: MTLAcc, entry #1016, volume donated by Clemens.

————. *Works of Washington Irving.* Author's Revised Edition. Illus. 28 vols. New York: G. P. Putnam's Sons, 1881.
    Catalog: A1911, #262, "Author's Revised Edition," 12 vols. only, $3.75 total. On 15 October 1881 Clemens wrote to an unnamed publishing house: "Irving for $13.34 is satisfactory—send her along" (TS in MTP, courtesy of The Scriptorium, Beverly Hills, Ca.).
    MTBP, p. 67; *MTDW,* p. 53.

Irwin, Wallace (1875–1959), pseud. "Hashimiro Togo." "Letters of a Japanese Schoolboy," pub. in *Collier's Weekly* (1908–1909).
    On 6 July 1908 Mark Twain wrote *Collier's* to commend Togo and to request an early copy of his "Letters" when they issued as a book (published in 1909). "That Boy is the dearest & sweetest & frankest & wisest & funniest & delightfulest & loveablest creation that has been added to our literature for a long time. I think he is a permanency & I hope so, too" (ALS in Yale University Library; see "Letter about the Japanese Schoolboy," *Collier's Weekly,* 41 [8 August 1908], 22). A few months later Mark Twain complimented Irwin's schoolboy English ("how hard it hits, how straight to the mark it goes") because it allows Irwin's character (like Huck Finn) to be "innocently unconscious" of its effects (22 December 1908 AD, MTP).
    Aspiz, "MT's Reading," pp. 110–111 n. 107.

Irwin, William Henry (1873–1948). *The City That Was; A Requiem of Old San Francisco.* New York: B. W. Huebsch, 1906. 47 pp.
    Source: MTLAcc, entry #574, volume donated by Clemens.

Isaacs, Abram Samuel (1851–1920). *Stories from the Rabbis.* New York: Charles L. Webster & Co., 1893. 201 pp.
    Brought out by Clemens' publishing firm, which advertised the book as "entertaining tales in popular style from legends of the Talmud and Midrash" (*Publishers' Trade List Annual for 1893*).

Jackson, Edward Payson (1840–1905). *A Demigod; A Novel.* New York: Harper & Brothers, 1887. 337 pp.
    Source: MTLAcc, entry #1315, volume donated by Clemens.

Jackson, (Mrs.) Gabrielle Emilie (Snow) (b. 1861). *Wee Winkles & Her Friends.* Illus. by Rachel Robinson. New York: Harper & Brothers, 1907. 155 pp.
    Source: MTLAcc, entry #1598, volume donated by Clemens.

————. *Wee Winkles & Snowball.* Illus. by Mary Theresa Hart. New York: Harper & Brothers, 1906. 147 pp.
    Source: MTLAcc, entry #520, volume donated by Clemens.

————. *Wee Winkles & Wideawake.* Illus. by Mary Theresa Hart. New York: Harper & Brothers, 1905. 153 pp.
    Source: MTLAcc, entry #1192, damaged copy donated by Clemens.

————. *Wee Winkles at the Mountains.* Illus. by Rachael Robinson. New York: Harper & Brothers, 1908. 138 pp.
    Source: MTLAcc, entry #1599, volume donated by Clemens.

Jackson, Helen Maria (Fiske) Hunt (1831–1885), pseud. "H. H." *Cat Stories*. 3
vols. in 1. Illus. Boston: Roberts Bros., 1886.
    Source: MTLAcc, entry #511, volume donated by Clemens.

———. *Mercy Philbrick's Choice*. Boston: Roberts Bros., 1876. 296 pp.
    Source: MTLAcc, entry #1850, volume donated from Clemens' library by
Clara Clemens Gabrilowitsch in 1910.

———. *Verses. By H. H*. Boston: Roberts Bros., 1888. 135 pp.
    Source: MTLAcc, entry #2038, volume donated from Clemens' library by
Clara Clemens Gabrilowitsch in 1910.

Jackson, Julia Newell. *A Winter Holiday in Summer Lands*. Chicago: A. C.
McClurg and Co., 1890. 221 pp.
    Inscription: inscribed in black ink inside front cover: "To Mark Twain:/
With the kind regards of his old shipmate and friend,/ A. Reeves Jackson/
Chicago, April 16, 1890."
    Location: Antenne-Dorrance Collection, Rice Lake, Wis.
    Copy examined: Clemens' copy, unmarked.
    Jackson's travel book mainly describes Cuba and Mexico.

Jacobs, William Wymark (1863–1943). *Dialstone Lane*. New York: Charles
Scribner's Sons, 1904. 337 pp.
    Mark Twain informed Mary Benjamin Rogers on 27 August 1906 from
Dublin, New Hampshire that he had just finished dictating an autobiographical
chapter which contained "a word about W. W. Jacobs's delightful 'Dialstone
Lane'" *(MTLM*, p. 48). In a letter of 28 October 1908 to Jacobs Mark Twain
declared: "It is my conviction that Dialstone Lane holds the supremacy over
all purely humorous books in our language," and he mentioned that he had kept
his copy "moving" among his friends *(MTL*, p. 823).

———. *Sailors' Knots*. London: Methuen & Co., 1909.
    Inscription: inscribed on first flyleaf: "To Samuel L. Clemens/With compli-
ments/W. W. Jacobs/Oct 1909".
    Catalog: "Retz Appraisal" (1944), p. 9, valued at $40.
    Location: Mark Twain Papers, Berkeley, Ca.
    Copy examined: Clemens' copy, unmarked. A few pages opened by tearing.

———. *Salthaven*. New York: Charles Scribner's Sons, 1908. 316 pp.
    Catalog: C1951, #21a, $65, listed among books containing Clemens'
marginal notes.
    Clemens wrote to Jacobs from Redding on 28 October 1908: "I place Salthaven
close up next to Dialstone [Lane] because I think it has a fair and honest right
to that high position. I have kept the other book moving; I shall begin to hand
this one around now. And many thanks to you for remembering me" *(MTL*,
p. 823). Notebook 49 contains a reference to Jacobs' *Salthaven* (TS p. 1), entered
in January 1910. The same notebook entry observes that while another author
"paints with whitewash brush, Jacobs [paints] with camelhair pencil." During
the last year of his life Clemens read from "that brilliant book" to a young girl,
Helen Allen (MS notes owned by Professor Bigelow Paine Cushman, Danbury,
Connecticut).

Jacobsen, Jens Peter (1847–1885). *Niels Lyhne*. Illus. Leipzig: Eugen Diederichs,
1898. 302 pp.
    Source: MTLAcc, entry #374, volume donated by Clemens.

James, (Mrs.) Alice Archer (Sewall) (b. 1870). *An Ode to Girlhood and Other Poems.* New York: Harper & Brothers, 1899. 73 pp.
  Source: MTLAcc, entry #1457, volume donated by Clemens.

James, Edmund James (1855–1925). *The Immigrant Jew in America, by Edmund J. James . . . Oscar R. Flynn . . . Dr. J. R. Paulding, Mrs. Simon N. Patton (Charlotte Kimball) . . . Walter Scott Andrews.* Issued by the [National] Liberal Immigration League. Illus. New York: B. F. Buck & Co., 1907.
  Inscription: "S. L. Clemens, Tuxedo Park, Sept. 1907."
  Catalog: A1911, #258, $1.25.

James, George Payne Rainsford (1799–1860). *Heidelberg* (novel, pub. 1846).
  On 2 August 1878, shortly after Clemens left Heidelberg for Baden-Baden, he jotted down a pithy opinion of James' melodramatic novel set in the seventeenth century: "G P R James's 'Heidelberg' is rot" (NB 15, *N&J*, 2: 126).

James, (Sir) Henry (1803–1877). *Facsimiles of National Manuscripts from William the Conqueror to Queen Anne, Selected [by Sir Thomas Duffus Hardy] under the Direction of the Master of the Rolls and Photozincographed . . . by . . . Sir H. James.* With Translations and Notes by W. B. Sanders. Four parts. Southampton, 1865–1868.
  Inscription: in Clemens' handwriting: "Presented to S. L. Clemens, 1874 by Sir Thomas Duffus Hardy."
  Marginalia: two remarks by Clemens.
  Catalog: A1911, #22, $8, part 2 only.

James, Henry (1843–1916). *The Ambassadors; A Novel.* New York: Harper & Brothers, 1904. 432 pp.
  Source: MTLAcc, entry #1573, volume donated by Clemens.

————. *The American Scene.* New York, 1907.
  Inscription: inner front cover signed "S. L. Clemens, 1907."
  Catalog: A1911, #264, $5.50.

————. *The American Scene.* New York: Harper & Brothers, 1907. 443 pp.
  Source: MTLAcc, entry #1300, volume donated by Clemens.

————. *The Awkward Age, A Novel.* New York: Harper & Brothers, 1904. 457 pp.
  Source: MTLAcc, entry #1106, volume donated by Clemens.

————. *The Bostonians* (novel, pub. serially in the *Century Magazine,* 1885).
  From Chicago Clemens reported to his wife on 3 February 1885, during his platform tour with George Washington Cable: "Yes, I tried to read the Bostonians, but couldn't. To me it was unspeakably dreary. I dragged along half-way through it & gave it up in despair" (MTP). He was similarly unequivocal in censuring the novel in a letter of 21 July 1885 to Howells from Elmira: "And as for the Bostonians, I would rather be damned to John Bunyan's heaven than read that" (*MTHL*, p. 534). But Clemens' attitude toward James was variable; in a letter to T. Douglas Murray written on 31 January 1900 he referred to James as "a master" (MTP).
  MTHL, pp. 160, 161 n. 2.

————. *Daisy Miller: A Study. An International Episode. Four Meetings.* Collection of British Authors Series. Leipzig: B. Tauchnitz, 1879. 288 pp.
  Source: MTLAcc, entry #2284, volume donated from Clemens' library by Clara Clemens Gabrilowitsch in 1910.

————. *The Golden Bowl.* 2 vols. New York: C. Scribner's Sons, 1905.
   Source: MTLAcc, entries #2286 and #2287, volumes donated from Clemens' library by Clara Clemens Gabrilowitsch in 1910.
   On 27 July 1907 Isabel Lyon noted that she was surprised to observe Clemens "stealing quietly up to my study after I was about to get into bed, to get a paper knife to cut the leaves of 'The Golden Bowl' with" (IVL Journal, TS p. 264).

————. *An International Episode.* New York: Harper & Brothers, [cop. 1878]. 136 pp.
   Source: MTLAcc, entry #2285, volume donated from Clemens' library by Clara Clemens Gabrilowitsch in 1910.

————. *An International Episode.* Illus. by Harry W. McVickar. New York, 1892.
   Inscription: inside front cover inscribed in Clemens' hand: "Olivia L. Clemens, 1903".
   Catalog: Zeitlin 1951, #25, $10.

————. *A Little Tour in France.* Boston: James R. Osgood and Co., 1885. Also issued by Bernhard Tauchnitz of Leipzig.
   "Henry James's Summer trip through Provence," Clemens wrote in Notebook 31 in September 1891 while he was in France (TS p. 5). He noted the correct title of James' travel sketches on the endpaper of Notebook 44 in 1901. Houghton, Mifflin and Company of Boston brought out a new edition in 1900 illustrated by Joseph Pennell.

————. *Nathaniel Hawthorne.* New York: Harper & Brothers, n.d. 177 pp.
   Source: MTLAcc, entry #1282, volume donated by Clemens.

————. *Washington Square.* Illus. by George Du Maurier. New York: Harper & Brothers, 1901. 264 pp.
   Source: MTLAcc, entry #1433, volume donated by Clemens.

James, Robert (1705–1776). *A Medical Dictionary* (pub. 1743).
   An undated sheet of manuscript contains Mark Twain's notation: "A medicinal Dic. by R. James, M.D. London, 1743" *(A1911,* #290a). Twice in 1888 Mark Twain considered using the book in *CY:* "Dose of Medicine—Dr James Dict—y" (NB 27, TS p. 63); "The leech gives him recipes from James's medical Dictionary. Result bedrids him 2 months" (NB 28, TS p. 17). Twain devoted an entire sketch, "A Majestic Literary Fossil" (1890), to examining this "literary relic. It is a *Dictionary of Medicine,* by Dr. James, of London, assisted by Mr. Boswell's Doctor Samuel Johnson, and is a hundred and fifty years old. . . . For three generations and a half it had been going quietly along, enriching the earth with its slain." Mark Twain quotes extensively from James' textbook to illustrate the ancient/modern contrast he had recently emphasized in *CY* (1889), ridiculing the antiquated remedies and antidotes. In chapter 7 of "Those Extraordinary Twins" (1894) Twain again turned to this source for a ludicrous prescription ("Galen's favorite") recommended for Angelo by Dr. Claypool. Mark Twain summarized James' "ancient treatment" again in "Bible Teaching and Religious Practice" (written 1890), for the book had become to him a comforting emblem of man's undeniable scientific progress during the past century. Presumably James' *Dictionary* furnished the primitive medical treatments which the befuddled physician administers to George Harrison of Indiantown in chapter 12 of "Which Was It?" (written 1899–1903, *WWD?,* pp. 285–286). Likewise Mark Twain seemed to be repeating James' medical practices in the outline of early nineteen-century procedures he supplied in an Autobiographical Dictation of 22 November 1906 (MTP): bleeding accompanied by doses of fat, toad livers, ipecac, calomel, spiders, and other "odious mixtures."

James, William (1842–1910). *The Principles of Psychology.* Authorized Edition. 2 vols. New York: Henry Holt & Co., 1890.

In Florence in December 1892 Clemens made a series of notes which seem to indicate that he had purchased an unspecified book by William James (NB 32, TS pp. 51, 53). Clemens stated in a letter to Livy written on 27 January 1894 that Elinor Howells "convinced *me,* before she got through, that she and William James are right—hypnotism & mind-cure are the same thing" (*MTHL,* p. 659). On 30 September 1896 in London Clemens included "Prof. Wm. James's psychological book among works he wished to obtain (NB 39, TS p. 6). Probably he borrowed a copy at the London Library, which he mentions in his notebook; late in October 1896 he referred to a juggler's ability to perform his feats despite a lapse of thirty years in practicing, "so powerful is a habit once acquired. Quoted by Prof. Wm James in his 'Principles of Psychology' " (NB 39, TS p. 11). Clemens and James corresponded in 1900 about the efficacy of Jonas Kellgren's treatments (SLC to William James, 17, 23 April 1900, Houghton Library, Harvard).

WWD?, p. 17; *MTSatan,* p. 27; John S. Tuckey, "MT's Later Dialogue: The 'Me' and the Machine," *AL,* 41 (January 1970), 536.

————. *The Varieties of Religious Experience; A Study in Human Nature.* London: Longmans, Green, and Co., 1902. 534 pp.
Inscription: signed "S. L. Clemens/ 1903."
Marginalia: notations by Clemens.
Location: collection of Judge Harry Pregerson, Los Angeles, Calif. (1977). Information for this entry derives from a memorandum in the Mark Twain Papers at Berkeley.

Jameson, (Mrs.) Anna Brownell (Murphy) (1794–1860). *Sketches of Art, Literature, and Character.* Boston: J. R. Osgood & Co., 1875. 502 pp.
Source: MTLAcc, entry #665, volume donated by Clemens.

"Jan and Dan" (song).
George Washington Cable inquired, in a speech at a celebration of Clemens' seventieth birthday in New York City in 1905, "Do you remember, Mark, how [during their reading tour of 1884–85] we sang almost nightly that old Mississippi ditty, 'Jan and Dan'?" ("Mark Twain's 70th Birthday," *Harper's Weekly,* 49 [23 December 1905], 1889; reprinted in Arlin Turner's *MT&GWC* [1960], p. 127).

Jane, Frederick Thomas (1865–1916). *All the World's Fighting Ships.* New York: Harper & Brothers, 1901. 375 pp.
Source: MTLAcc, entry #1367, volume donated by Clemens.

Janvier, (Mrs.) Catherine Ann (Drinker) (1841–1923). *London Mews.* Illus. New York: Harper & Brothers, 1904. [37 pp.]
Source: MTLAcc, entry #1371, volume donated by Clemens.

Janvier, Thomas Allibone (1849–1913). *The Aztec Treasure-House; A Romance of Contemporaneous Antiquity.* Illus. New York: Harper & Brothers, [cop. 1890]. 446 pp.
Source: MTLAcc, entry #1574, volume donated by Clemens.

————. *The Christmas Kalends of Provence.* New York: Harper & Brothers, 1902.
Inscription: signed in black ink on front pastedown endpaper: "SL. Clemens/ 1902".
Location: Antenne-Dorrance Collection, Rice Lake, Wis.
Copy examined: Clemens' copy, unmarked.

————. *An Embassy to Provence.* New York: The Century Co., 1893.
In 1901 Clemens wrote "Embassy to Provence (Janvier)" among a list of books on the rear flyleaf of Notebook 44.

————. *Henry Hudson, A Brief Statement of His Aims and His Achievements.* Illus. New York, 1909.
Inscription: "S. L. Clemens, 1909."
Catalog: A1911, #266, $3.25.
In "Official Report to the I.I.A.S." (written 1909) Mark Twain employs an extract from Hudson's log taken from Janvier's book *(LE,* p. 150).

————. *In Great Waters: Four Stories.* Illus. New York, 1901.
Inscription: flyleaf signed "S. L. Clemens, Riverdale, Nov. 1901."
Catalog: A1911, #265, $5.75.

————. *In the Sargasso Sea, A Novel.* Harper & Brothers, 1898. 293 pp.
Source: MTLAcc, entry #186, volume donated by Clemens.

Japanese Colored Picture Book. [Title, publisher, date unknown.]
Catalog: A1911, #267, no bibliographical information supplied, $2.

Jardine, David. *Lives and Criminal Trials of Celebrated Men.* Philadelphia, 1835.
Catalog: A1911, #269, .75¢.

Jarves, James Jackson (1818–1888). *History of the Hawaiian or Sandwich Islands.* Second edition. Boston: James Munroe and Co., 1844.
Marginalia: Clemens penciled a note on the first flyleaf scoffing at the type of education given Hawaiian youths ("translating Greek, &c") when the islands were forced to import mechanics. The back cover of this paperback book contains references to four books related to the Sandwich Islands. Clemens made a few pencil marks in the text.
Catalog: "Retz Appraisal" (1944), p. 9, valued at $20.
Location: Mark Twain Papers, Berkeley, Ca.
Copy examined: Clemens' copy.
Mark Twain quoted from Jarves' book in a letter published in the Sacramento *Weekly Union* (21 July 1866) to show that "the natives have been improved by missionary labor" *(LSI,* p. 103). He credited Jarves for his information about Captain Cook *(LSI,* p. 157). In Mark Twain's letter of 2 March 1867 from New York City he confessed that he "stole a book" from "Father" Damon, pastor of the Seaman's Mission in Honolulu. He seems to mean Jarves' *History.* On 20 May 1867 he announced that he had mailed the book back to Damon *(MTTMB,* p. 213). Mark Twain used "Mr. Jarves' excellent history" to correct Hawaiian legends in chapters 65 and 68 of *RI* (1872). See the Iowa-California Edition of *RI,* pp. 415, 437–441, 601.

Jarvis, Edward. "The Increase of Human Life," *Atlantic Monthly,* 24 (October 1869), 495–506; (November 1869), 581–598; (December 1869), 711–718.
On the basis of two entries Clemens made in a notebook, James D. Williams ("Use of History") deduced Mark Twain's extensive borrowing from Jarvis' article for chapter 23 of *CY* (1889), "Sixth-Century Political Economy." Jarvis discussed sixteenth-century (and later) statistics, so Mark Twain's figures were speculative.

Jay, Edith Katharine Spicer, pseud. "E. Livingston Prescott." *The Apotheosis of Mr. Tyrawley.* New York: Harper & Brothers, 1896. 248 pp.
Source: MTLAcc, entry #1643, volume donated by Clemens.

Jayne's Medical Almanac and Guide to Health (1854[?] edition).
One of two books that Clemens found on 16 July 1855 in the "reading room" of the only hotel in Paris, Missouri was "Jayne's Med. Almanac" (NB 1, 1: 37). David Jayne (1799–1866), a Philadelphia drug manufacturer, published his almanac annually as an advertising circular.

Jefferson, [First name not supplied]. *A Book About Doctors*. 2 vols. Leipzig: B. Tauchnitz, [date not supplied].
Catalog: C1951, #D1, $8 ea. vol., listed among books signed by Clemens.
Neither the *British Museum Catalogue* nor the *National Union Catalog* contains such a work by an author named Jefferson.

Jefferson, Joseph (1829–1905). *The Autobiography of Joseph Jefferson*. New York: The Century Co., 1890. 501 pp.
Clemens wrote Charles L. Webster from Hartford on 11 May 1887: "Joe Jefferson has written his Autobiography! . . . I will read the MS for 'literary quality,' . . . & meantime you can be thinking of the terms to offer him" *(MTBus, p. 382)*. On 28 May 1887 Clemens informed Webster: "Joe Jefferson's MS is delightful reading, & I see that it has this additional great advantage: it is quite largely a book of *foreign travel*, & the illustrations can be made to show up that feature prominently" *(MTBus, p. 383)*. But on 20 October 1887 Jefferson notified Webster that on account of Clemens' "long silence" negotiations were underway with another publisher (TS in MTP). As Clemens later recalled the series of events, "Joe Jefferson wrote me and said he had written his autobiography and he would like me to be the publisher. Of course I wanted the book. . . . Webster did not decline the book. He simply ignored it" (2 June 1906 AD, *MTE*, pp. 187–188).

Jenkins, Edward (1838–1910). *Ginx's Baby: His Birth and Other Misfortunes. A Satire*. Toronto: The Canadian News and Publishing Co., 1871. 168 pp. [The paper wrapper was imprinted by a different publisher—Baltimore: The Baltimore News Co., 1871.]
Inscription: title page is inscribed in brown ink: "Life is no joke/When I am broke!/Mark Twain". Beneath the inscription, also in brown ink, is a drawing labeled "Tear-Jug" that resembles the illustration in chapter 20 of *TA*.
Catalog: the volume contains a tipped-in entry from an unidentified bookshop catalog advertising the book as #118, "Mark Twain the optimist in a sad moment." A price is marked in red pencil—$15.
Location: Special Collections, University Research Library, University of California at Los Angeles.
Copy examined: a copy supposedly signed by Clemens.
Robert Regan turned up evidence that Clemens definitely was familiar with Jenkins' book. In a column entitled "British Benevolence" that appeared in the 27 January 1873 issue of the New York *Daily Tribune*, Mark Twain wrote: "I coud reel off instances of prodigal charity conferred by stealth in that city [London] till even THE TRIBUNE'S broad columns would cry for quarter. 'Ginx's Baby' could not satirize the national disposition toward free-handed benevolence —it could only satirize instances of foolish and stupid methods in the application of the funds by some of the charitable organizations. But in most cases the great benevolent societies of England manage their affairs admirably" (Regan to Gribben, 22 July, 4 November 1972). In *Ginx's Baby* Jenkins reveals that only a fraction of the funds collected for a foundling baby are left for the baby's keep after the collection committee deducts its expenses. Jenkins moralizes: "In an age of luxury we are grown so luxurious as to be content to pay agents to do our good deeds for us; but they charge us three hundred per cent. for the privilege" (p. 103).
The copy of *Ginx's Baby* at U.C.L.A. may contain a forgery, however. Clemens rarely signed the title pages of volumes (generally preferring the flyleaves), and

virtually never used his *nom de plume*—even when the book was intended for someone else. A "Mark Twain" signature could easily have been traced from one of the volumes in his "Authorized Edition" of works. The sophomoric rhyming couplet is scarcely worthy of the writer who would later devise the Pudd'nhead Wilson maxims, and the "f," "k," and "b" are not characteristic of Clemens' handwriting. The tear-jug sketch is an anachronism, since it would not appear in chapter 20 of *A Tramp Abroad* until 1880.

On the other hand, it admittedly seems improbable that (a) anyone except a scholar would have guessed that Clemens read and referred to *Ginx's Baby*, and that (b) anyone would take the trouble to make the forgeries for the slight association value they lent this obscure paperback book. Wilbur Smith, former Special Collections Librarian at U.C.L.A., reportedly purchased the volume because it was priced cheaply since the bookseller could not guarantee the authenticity of Clemens' signature. Evidence suggests a spurious provenance and the book ought to be treated skeptically. Stranger and even less profitable forgeries have been perpetrated.

————. *Ginx's Baby: His Birth and Other Misfortunes. A Satire*. Boston: J. R. Osgood & Co., 1871. 125 pp.
      Source: MTLAcc, entry #533, volume donated by Clemens.

Jericho and the Jordan.
      Mark Twain listed this unidentified book among those the pilgrims were instructed to obtain for the *Quaker City* voyage, but he supplied no author's name (*Daily Alta California*, 5 April 1868; *TIA*, p. 303).

Jerome, Irene Elizabeth (b. 1858). *One Year's Sketch-Book*. Illus. by the author. Boston: Lee & Shepard, 1886. 6 pp.
      Source: MTLAcc, entry #1223, volume donated by Clemens.

Jerome, Jerome Klapka (1859–1927). *Three Men in a Boat (To Say Nothing of the Dog)*. Illus. by A. Frederics. New York: H. Holt & Co., 1890. 298 pp.
      Source: MTLAcc, entry #2288, volume donated from Clemens' library by Clara Clemens Gabrilowitsch in 1910.

Jesse, John Heneage (1815–1874). *London: Its Celebrated Characters and Remarkable Places*. 3 vols. London: Richard Bentley, 1871.
      Inscription: flyleaf of vol. 1 signed in brown ink: "Saml L. Clemens/London 1873".
      Marginalia: vol. 1 contains penciled corrections and markings on pages 150, 215, 216, with many leaves cut and torn open; vol. 2 is heavily annotated in pencil, with a few notes in purple ink concerning London Bridge and its houses and accidents (pp. 278–283), and pencil markings and notes in the Table of Contents as well as on pages 88 and 215 (Horace Walpole's criticisms of Garrick's acting "were perfectly just, at the time, for he was really in his apprenticeship then"); vol. 3 contains a purple ink mark beside a description of the founding of Christ's Hospital, but many other pages are unopened.
      Catalog: C1951, #D17, 3 vols.
      Location: Huntington Library, San Marino, Ca. The volumes were purchased from Zeitlin & Ver Brugge of Los Angeles in 1951.
      Copies examined: Clemens' copies, much worn from repeated use.
      In chapter 33 of *P&P* (1882) Mark Twain cites Jesse's *London* as the source from which he obtained information about Christ's Hospital.
      MT&JB, p. 52.

La Jeunesse de l'Impératrice Josephine.
Jean Clemens read aloud to Isabel Lyon from this book (in French) on one occasion while Clemens was away visiting Clara (IVL Journal, 16 August 1905, TS p. 89, MTP). My efforts to identify the author have not been successful.

Jewett, John Howard (1843–1925), pseud. "Hannah Warner." *The Easter Story.* Illus. New York: Harper & Brothers, 1904. 20 pp.
Source: MTLAcc, entry #450, volume donated by Clemens.

————. [Another identical copy.]
Source: MTLAcc, entry #1705, volume donated by Clemens.

Jewett, Sarah Orne (1849–1909). *The Queen's Twin, and Other Stories.* Boston: Houghton, Mifflin & Co., 1900. 232 pp.
Source: MTLAcc, entry #2289, volume donated from Clemens' library by Clara Clemens Gabrilowitsch in 1910.

————. *Tales of New England.* Boston: Houghton, Mifflin & Co., 1890. 276 pp.
Source: MTLAcc, entry #2290, volume donated from Clemens' library by Clara Clemens Gabrilowitsch in 1910.
Clemens was acquainted socially with this local colorist. In May 1892 in Venice he recalled trying to explain his "driveway-loop" puzzle (concerning the side of a carriage from which a passenger would alight) to Jewett and Mrs. James T. Fields (NB 31, TS p. 47); on 25 January 1894 Jewett and her sister attended a dinner for Oliver Wendell Holmes—at Mrs. Fields' house—where Clemens was present (SLC to OLC, Boston, 25 January 1894, *MTL,* p. 602; ALS in MTP).

————. *York Garrison—1640.* [Unidentified edition.]
Source: MTLAcc, entry #1892, volume donated from Clemens' library by Clara Clemens Gabrilowitsch in 1910. Listed as "destroyed in circulation."

Jeypore Portfolios of Architectural Details. Ed. by Colonel Jacobs. Seven portfolios.
In a letter to Richard Watson Gilder written on 12 March 1896 Clemens lauded these "intricate and exquisite forms and patterns invented by the artists of the great days of the Mogul Empire." Gilder published the letter in "A Gift from India," *The Critic,* 28 (25 April 1896), 285. Neither the editor nor the title is listed in the *British Museum Catalogue.*

"Jinny git de hoecake done" (song).
Jim the slave sings this folk song in jail after he becomes more cheerful in chapter 9 of "Tom Sawyer's Conspiracy" *(HH&T,* p. 234).

Job, Herbert Keightley (1864–1933). *Among the Water-Fowl: Observation, Adventure, Photography.* Illus. New York: Doubleday, Page & Co., 1902. 224 pp.
Source: MTLAcc, entry #1958, volume donated from Clemens' library by Clara Clemens Gabrilowitsch in 1910.

————. *Wild Wings: Adventures of a Camera-Hunter Among the Larger Wild Birds of North America.* Intro. by Theodore Roosevelt. Illus. with photographs by the author. Boston: Houghton, Mifflin & Co., 1905. 341 pp.
Inscription: "Jean L. Clemens/with the love of her/Father./21 Fifth Avenue/November 27, 1904."
Location: Mark Twain Library, Redding, Conn. Donated from Clemens' library by Clara Clemens Gabrilowitsch in 1910 (MTLAcc, entry #1959).
Copy examined: Jean Clemens' unmarked copy.

"John Brown's body" (song, 1861). Lyrics attributed variously; tune is "Glory, glory, hallelujah."

"With a brass band at his heels playing 'John Brown' " (letter from Virginia City, 16 May 1864, *MTEnt*, p. 187). Mark Twain heard the muleteers in the Azores singing this song (NB 8[1867], TS p. 30). He included "Chorus—Old John Brown had One little Injun" in a burlesque "Country School Exhibition" he organized aboard the *Montana* on 10 July 1868 (*Alta California*, 6 September 1868, reprinted in *The Twainian*, 7 [November-December 1948], 5). In chapter 6 of *IA* (1869) Mark Twain reported hearing "the irrepressible muleteers" of Fayal sing " 'John Brown's Body' in ruinous English." In November 1887 Clemens simply jotted "John Brown" in Notebook 27 (TS p. 7).

John, Eugenie (1825–1887), pseud. "E. Marlitt." *Das Geheimniss der Alten Mamsell. Roman von E. Marlitt*. Die Deutsche Library. New York: G. Munroe, 1881. First published in 1868 in Leipzig.

In May 1878 Mark Twain quoted in German a sentence from this novel (NB 14, *N&J*, 2: 83), a work from which he would translate in Appendix D of *TA* (1880). When he listed his current reading for Edward H. House on 14 January 1884, he included "in German . . . the concluding chapters of Das Geheimniss der Alten Mamsell" (CWB).

Johnson, Clifton (1865–1940). *Highways and Byways of the Mississippi Valley*. Illus. by the author. New York: Macmillan Co., 1906. 287 pp.
Source: MTLAcc, entry #603, volume donated by Clemens.

Johnson, Owen McMahon (1878–1952). *In the Name of Liberty; A Story of Terror*. New York: Century Co., 1905. 406 pp.
Source: MTLAcc, entry #187, volume donated by Clemens.

Johnson, Robert Underwood (1853–1937) and Clarence C. Buel, eds. *Battles and Leaders of the Civil War*. New York: The Century Co., 1887.

Clemens attempted to secure publication rights for the magazine series that formed this book, but failed (Charles L. Webster to SLC, 16 March 1885, *MTBus*, p. 307). Nevertheless Clemens became friends with Johnson, a member of the *Century Magazine* staff, and in March 1888 Johnson's name appeared in Clemens' list of authors whose works he generally liked (NB 27, TS p. 61).

Johnson, Samuel (1709–1784). *Letters of Samuel Johnson*. Ed. by George Birbeck Hill. 2 vols. New York: Harper & Brothers, 1892.
Inscription: inner front cover of vol. 1 signed "S. L. Clemens, 1909"; vol. 2 unsigned.
Marginalia: Clemens corrected one of Johnson's sentences on page 184 of vol. 1.
Catalog: A1911, #270, vol. 1 only, $2.25.
Location: vol. 2 only in Mark Twain Library, Redding, Conn.
Copy examined: Clemens' unmarked copy of vol. 2 only.
Possibly Clemens had read Johnson's *Letters* by March 1894, when he noted in his copy of Sarah Grand's *The Heavenly Twins* that Grand's chief characters "talk like Dr. Samuel Johnson" (p. 270). Around 1896, however, Clemens supposedly denied to Bram Stoker and Henry Fisher that he had ever read "a written word" of Johnson's; instead, Clemens reportedly said in a London restaurant, "I gauge Johnson's character by his talks with that sot Bozzy" (*AMT*, p. 151). Whether this is true or not, when Clemens temporarily edited the Hannibal, Missouri *Journal* in May 1853 he employed the pseudonym "Rambler" —presumably in homage to Johnson's bi-weekly *Rambler* that appeared between 1750 and 1752.

————. *The Lives of the Most Eminent English Poets* (1779).

Johnson's was one of the "biogs of Milton" that Clemens listed in Notebook 27 (TS p. 22) in September 1887.

Johnston, Alexander (1849–1889). *Connecticut: A Study of a Commonwealth Democracy.* American Commonwealths Series. Boston: Houghton, Mifflin Co., 1887. 409 pp.

In April 1887 Clemens noted the author, title, and publisher in Notebook 26 (TS p. 44).

Johnston, Alexander W. *Strikes, Labour Questions, and Other Economic Difficulties.* London: Bliss, Sands, and Foster, 1895. 128 pp.

Source: MTLAcc, entry #529, volume donated by Clemens.

Johnston, Mary (1870–1936). *Prisoners of Hope. A Tale of Colonial Virginia.* Boston: Houghton, Mifflin & Co., 1900. 378 pp.

Source: MTLAcc, entry #188, volume donated by Clemens.

————. *Sir Mortimer. A Novel.* Illus. New York: Harper & Brothers, 1904. 350 pp.

Source: MTLAcc, entry #189, volume donated by Clemens.

Johnston, Richard Malcolm (1822–1898). *Dukesborough Tales.* New York: Harper & Brothers, 1883.

On 29 November 1884 Clemens wrote to Livy from Baltimore: "R. M. Johnston, author of The Dukesboro Tales has called—I will see him presently" (MTP). In April 1888 Clemens jotted down " 'Dukesboro' Tales" in Notebook 27 (TS p. 63). He included a story from *Dukesborough Tales*, "The Expensive Treat of Colonel Moses Grice" (which first appeared in *Scribner's Monthly*, 21 [January 1881], 370–376) in *Mark Twain's Library of Humor* (1888); Johnston's tale is widely believed to have influenced the drunk's bareback riding act that so astonishes Huckleberry Finn in chapter 21 (1885). When Clemens heard that Johnston would visit the Warners in Hartford in 1888, Clemens wrote on 9 November to invite him to stay over two additional days at the Clemenses' (Enoch Pratt Free Library). In a letter written from Hartford on 4 January 1889 Mark Twain planned a benefit reading with Johnston to help "poor" Thomas Nelson Page (Enoch Pratt Free Library). Henry P. Goddard—in *Harper's Weekly* (1906)—reports authoritatively that Mark Twain turned over to Johnston the $700 that was Twain's share for their joint reading in Baltimore; Mark Twain had replaced Thomas Nelson Page on the program, and he wished to assist the financially needy Johnston. Goddard was present at a dinner after the reading at the University Club of Baltimore when Mark Twain, upon being toasted, "paid a loving tribute to Colonel Johnston" (p. 280).

NAH, p. 154; *MT&HF*, pp. 315–316; Kenneth S. Lynn, ed., *Huckleberry Finn* (1961), pp. 149–156; Hamlin Hill and Walter Blair, eds., *The Art of Huckleberry Finn* (1962), pp. 471–483; Dewey Ganzel, "Twain, Travel Books" (1962), p. 53.

————. *Mr. Absalom Billingslea, and Other Georgia Folk.* New York: Harper & Brothers, 1888. 414 pp.

Source: MTLAcc, entry #2291, volume donated from Clemens' library by Clara Clemens Gabrilowitsch in 1910.

————. [Another identical copy.]

Source: MTLAcc, entry #2293, volume donated from Clemens' library by Clara Clemens Gabrilowitsch in 1910.

————. *Mr. Billy Downs and His Likes.* New York: Charles L. Webster & Co., 1892. 232 pp.
Clemens' publishing firm issued this collection of six stories, but earlier it had declined another work by Johnston. On 5 April 1887 Clemens wrote Johnston to explain how "our wheels are now clogged with existing contracts" (Enoch Pratt Free Library).

————. *Old Mark Langstan; A Tale of Duke's Creek.* New York: Harper & Brothers, 1883. 338 pp.
Source: MTLAcc, entry #2292, volume donated from Clemens' library by Clara Clemens Gabrilowitsch in 1910.

John Van Buren, Politician; A Novel of To-day. New York: Harper & Brothers, 1904. 289 pp.
Source: MTLAcc, entry #15, volume donated by Isabel V. Lyon, Clemens' secretary.

John Van Buren, Politician; A Novel of To-day. New York: Harper & Brothers, 1905. 289 pp.
Source: MTLAcc, entry #1503, volume donated by Clemens.

Joline, Adrian Hoffman (1850–1912). *The Diversions of a Book-Lover.* New York: Harper & Brothers, 1903. 323 pp.
Source: MTLAcc, entry #848, volume donated by Clemens.

————. *Meditations of an Autograph Collector.* Illus. New York: Harper & Brothers, 1902. 315 pp.
Inscription: front flyleaf signed in a large scrawl: "Clemens/1902".
Location: Mark Twain Library, Redding, Conn. Donated by Clemens (MTLAcc, entry #849).
Copy examined: Clemens' unmarked copy.
On page 101 Joline compliments Mark Twain for his immense popularity.

————. [Another identical copy.]
Source: MTLAcc, entry #1701, volume donated by Clemens.

"The jolly raftsman" (minstrel song).
In chapter 3 of *Life on the Mississippi* (1883) Huck Finn relates: "They sung 'Jolly, Jolly Raftsman's the Life for Me,' with a rousing chorus."

Jomini, Henri (1779–1869). *Jomini's Handbook of Military Etiquette.* West Point Edition. 1905.
Mark Twain listed this work as one of his sources of "knowledge about military minutiae" in "A Horse's Tale" (1906).

Jonas, (Miss). [Unidentified poem.]
Isabel Lyon reported that on 17 January 1906 "a Miss Jonas, a southerner, came with a letter of introduction from E. C. Stedman. She had a little poem she had written, a negro mother's tragic cry over the lynching of her son." Clemens read the piece aloud to Miss Lyon to test its oral effect: "He sat up in bed and reached out his arms with all the tragic feeling of the negro mother, and he was wonderful to behold" (IVL Journal, TS p. 124).

Jones, C. P. and A. L. Sykes. *Quick, My Rifle.* New York: J. J. Little & Co., 1907. 313 pp.
Source: MTLAcc, entry #190, volume donated by Isabel V. Lyon, Clemens' secretary.

Jones, Charles Colock (1831–1893). *Negro Myths from the Georgia Coast, Told in the Vernacular.* Boston: Houghton, Mifflin and Co., 1888. 171 pp.

"I read the 'Negro Myths' several years ago, & they have vanished out of my memory, leaving nothing but an impression—the impression that they were of small value" (SLC to "Dear Sir," 27 November 1891, ALS in MTP).

Jones, Dora Duty. *The Technique of Speech: A Guide to the Study of Diction According to the Principles of Resonance.* New York: Harper & Brothers, 1909. 330 pp.

Inscription: by Clemens in black ink: "Clara/1909".
Location: Mark Twain Library, Redding, Conn.
Copy examined: Clara Clemens' copy.

Clemens wrote to Clara Clemens from Bermuda on 6 March 1910, referring to a book Clara had championed: "Oh, by George I *am* glad to know of the success of Miss Jones's book" (CWB).

Jones, Hamilton C. (b. 1798). "Cousin Sally Dilliard" (burlesque sketch).

Jones' brief, well-constructed yarn originally appeared in a North Carolina newspaper in the 1830's; thereafter it appeared in numerous other newspapers and magazines, including (in 1844) William Trotter Porter's *The Spirit of the Times.* Henry Watterson published the piece in *Oddities in Southern Life and Character* (Boston: Houghton, Mifflin, 1882), pp. 474–478. More recently Franklin J. Meine reprinted Jones' sketch in *Tall Tales of the Southwest* (New York: Alfred A. Knopf, 1930), pp. 41–43. I am grateful to Walter Blair for assistance in identifying Jones as the author of "Cousin Sally Dilliard." The sketch recounts the courtroom testimony of Mr. Harris, "a fat, shuffy old man, a 'leetle' corned," who is questioned about a fight he supposedly witnessed by a stuffy attorney, Mr. Chops. (Jones himself was reputedly a North Carolina lawyer.) Like Mark Twain's Simon Wheeler, Mr. Harris is prone to circumlocution; after lengthy and often-interrupted testimony he turns out not to know anything whatever about the fight. The exasperated Mr. Chops has succeeded only in establishing the irrelevant fact that Cousin Sally Dilliard came by Harris' home to ask whether his wife could go to a nearby party. In a letter to Orion written on 13 April 1862 from Esmeralda, Clemens quipped: "And, as Cousin Sally Dillard [*sic*] says, this is all that I know about the fight" (TS in MTP). Later Mark Twain considered including the piece in his anthology of humor: in 1880 the name "Cousin Sally Dillard" [*sic*] appeared in a list of possible selections (NB 19, *N&J*, 2: 363), and the same title appeared as an entry in Notebook 27 (TS p. 23) in 1887. *Mark Twain's Library of Humor* (1888), however, did not contain Jones' sketch.

Jones, Henry Arthur (1851–1929).

In 1906 Clemens "had a stag dinner party (Howells, Aldrich, [George] Harvey, & Andrew Carnegie) to meet the English dramatist Henry Arthur Jones" (SLC to Jean Clemens, New York City, 13 November 1906, TS in MTP). Clemens does not indicate which plays by Jones—who wrote *The Liars* (1897) and many other comedies—he had seen.

Jones, Joseph Stevens (1809–1877). *The People's Lawyer, A Comedy* (play, perf. 1839). Also known as *Solon Shingle.*

Mark Twain hoped his *Colonel Sellers* play might "run twenty years, in this country, like Jo Jefferson's 'Rip Van Winkle' & John E. Owens's 'Solon Shingle'" (SLC to Mr. Watt, Hartford, 26 January 1875, Berg Collection). John Edmond Owens (1823–1886) first played Solon Shingle in 1856; he came to be identified with this character, performing the role for many years.

Jonson, Ben (1572–1637).

Though Mark Twain alluded to Jonson several times in print, it was not until 1908 that he mentioned seeing and enjoying one of Jonson's dramatic works—a masque performed at the New York Plaza Hotel (19 February 1908 AD). Jonson's praise for Shakespeare is one piece of evidence that Mark Twain must overcome in proving the thesis of "Is Shakespeare Dead?" (1909): in Part 3 he notes that Jonson "waited seven years" before he penned his encomium; in Part 5 he reiterates that it was only in 1623 that "Ben Jonson awoke out of his long indifference and sang a song of praise and put it in the front of the book" of Shakespeare's plays; in Part 10 Mark Twain quotes from *Timber* (1641) Jonson's laudatory remarks about Francis Bacon's oratorical speech.

Jónsson, Jón (1829–1868). "Jón Jónsonn's Saga: The Genuine Autobiography of a Modern Icelander," ed. by George Ralph Fitz-Roy Cole, *Littell's Living Age,* 132 (10 February 1877), 407–430. Reprinted from *Fraser's Magazine* (London, 1877).

Casting about in January 1894 for materials to use in a proposed (never-founded) magazine to be called "Back Number," Clemens noted: "John Johnson (Iceland) in old Littell. Susy Crane has it" (NB 33, TS p. 47). Clemens refers to an autobiographical sketch by an Icelandic farmer who taught himself English after a fashion. Jónsson's diction is simple and his words frequently misspelled, but his earnestness and his sincere enjoyment of small pleasures breathe life into the account. He describes his childhood, his efforts to educate himself, his reading, his farm labors, his fishing, his residence for a time in Copenhagen, his violin-playing ("I am the sole person in the shire Thingosissel in Icland, that can have the name of a musical, for the people on the northward Icland have not the least understanding of music . . . and one cannot gain a farthing by playing" [p. 412]). Jónsson supported himself by haymaking, farming, and painting churches. His life is arduous: a volcano threatens his town; his animals starve for want of winter provender; he tries with some success to cultivate potatoes and cabbage despite the cold; he fishes often for trout. In 1858 he observes: "So this year passed away, so monotonously as the others, in our farms on Icland. We have very few pleasures or divertisements" (p. 420). He visits with English travelers whenever possible.

Jónsson's tale is fascinating partly because he holds nothing back. He is admittedly ashamed when he drinks too much in a strange village and allows himself to be robbed by a fellow traveler whom he knows only as "Jack"; but he doggedly tracks the culprit and finally recovers his ring and most of his money where Jack buried it in the snow. At the conclusion of Jónsson's journal its editor adds that Jónsson died shortly after finishing "this quaint, simple record of a man's life, a genuine modern saga, simple and true" (p. 430).

Albert Bigelow Paine recorded the fact that "a story of an Iceland farmer, a human document, . . . had an unfading interest" for Clemens and Theodore Crane during the pleasant summer of 1874 at Quarry Farm (*MTB*, p. 510). In May 1887 Clemens jotted a memorandum: "Novel about the Esquimaux nabob who owned 5 flints. Told by John in that old Icelander's English" (NB 26, TS p. 48). This suggests that Jónsson's narrative contributed something to Twain's "The Esquimau Maiden's Romance" (1893), but even though Lasca the Eskimo girl leads a Spartan existence, Twain's tale is of an altogether different order.

Jordan, David Starr (1851–1931) and Barton Warren Evermann (1853–1932). *American Food and Game Fishes. A Popular Account.* Illus. New York: Doubleday, Page & Co., 1905. 572 pp.
   Source: MTLAcc, entry #743, volume donated by Clemens.

Jordan, Elizabeth Garver (1867–1947). *May Iverson—Her Book.* Illus. New York: Harper & Brothers, 1905. 282 pp.
   Source: MTLAcc, entry #1600, volume donated by Clemens.

————. *Tales of the Cloister.* New York: Harper & Brothers, 1901.
  Location: Antenne-Dorrance Collection, Rice Lake, Wis.
  Copy examined: Clemens' unmarked copy.

Josephus, Flavius (37?–100). *The Genuine Works of Josephus.* Trans. by William
  Whiston (1667–1752). 2 vols. Philadelphia, 1829.
  Catalog: A1911, #271, $1.75.
  In 1878 Clemens made a one-word entry in Notebook 17: "Josephus" *(N&J,*
  2: 219). Clara Clemens listed Flavius Josephus' *Antiquities of the Jews* in her
  commonplace book sometime between 1888 and 1904 (Paine 150, MTP).

Journal of American Folklore (1888).
  Robert Regan noticed that Clemens was among the 245 members of the
  American Folklore Society who were listed in the first volume of the *Journal
  of American Folklore* in 1888 *(UH,* p. viii).

Joyce, John A. *Edgar Allan Poe.* New York and London: F. Tennyson Neely
  Co., n.d. [cop. 1901].
  Inscription: in black ink inside front cover: "Catharine Leary."
  Marginalia: Clemens made sarcastic notes in pencil throughout the entire
  volume, ridiculing Joyce's grammar and prose style as well as his opinions. Joyce
  states as a "Preface": "In boiling down the life of Poe into one handy volume,
  I blow off the foam and scum of encomiums, and endeavor to get to the bed-
  rock of a character that may be misunderstood through the coming ages";
  Clemens underlined "boiling down" and added at the top of the page: "A new
  way to boil down—that is, in literature. We use his method with dried apples;
  we boil down a pint of them & they swell to a bushel." Clemens' comments
  became still more scornful: at the top of one page in the "Introduction" he
  observed: "It is a shame that this sentimental hyena should be allowed to disinter
  Poe's remains & paw them over" (p. x); on the next page Clemens added:
  "This book is an impertinence—an affront," and called its contents "old tenth-
  rate thoughts, triumphs of commonplace—hashed up & warmed over" (p. xi).
  At the bottom of another page Clemens was reminded of a favorite foe: Joyce
  possesses "the style of Mrs. Baker G. Eddy before her polisher has been over
  her MS" (p. xii). (This remark suggests that Clemens annotated the book during
  or shortly after his intensive reading in Christian Science publications in 1902
  and 1903.) Clemens fixed his view of Joyce at the top of the first page of the
  text: "If he *had* an idea he couldn't word it./The most remarkable animal that
  ever cavorted around a poet's grave." Similarly belittling notes, brief ejaculations
  ("rot!" "bow-wow!"), and underlinings abound throughout the volume.
  Location: Antenne-Dorrance Collection, Rice Lake, Wis.
  Copy examined: Clemens' copy.

Joyce, Robert Dwyer (1836–1883). *Deirdrè.* [*A Poem.*] Boston: Roberts Bros.,
  1877. 262 pp.
  Source: MTLAcc, entry #2006, volume donated from Clemens' library by
  Clara Clemens Gabrilowitsch in 1910.

Judd, Sylvester (1813–1853). *Margaret. A Tale of the Real and the Ideal, Blight
  and Bloom.* Boston: Roberts Bros., 1871. 401 pp.
  Source: MTLAcc, entry #191, volume donated by Clemens.
  From Hartford on 28 February 1874 Clemens notified Dr. John Brown of
  Edinburgh: "I shipped the novel ('Margaret') to you from here a *week* ago";
  in the same letter he informed Brown that he "shipped to you, from Liverpool,
  Darley's Illustrations of Judd's 'Margaret' " *(MTL,* p. 215). (See entry for
  Felix Octavious Carr Darley.) In the January 1905 issue of *North American
  Review* Clemens mentioned Judd in a catalogue of prominent authors that
  included Cooper, Irving, Poe, and Hawthorne ("Concerning Copyright").

Judson, Edward Zane Carroll (1823–1886), pseud. "Ned Buntline." *The Black Avenger of the Spanish Main; or, The Fiend of Blood* (1847).

A youthful Sam Clemens referred condescendingly to this dime novel in an undated (1856?) character sketch, "Jul'us Caesar" (TS in MTP, DV400). Such "instructive and entertaining books" were "food and drink" to a fellow lodger in his boardinghouse, Clemens wrote. Walter Blair observed that Tom Sawyer's creator borrowed his buccaneer's sobriquet in chapters 8 and 13 of *Tom Sawyer* (1876) from the title of Ned Buntline's book ("On the Structure of *TS*" [1939], p. 77). Clemens conceivably might have seen Judson himself before leaving Hannibal: in the autumn of 1851 Orion Clemens' Hannibal *Journal* announced the arrival of Ned Buntline to lecture on Cuban filibustering, a cause he espoused *(SCH*, p. 195).

MT&HF, p. 64; *IE*, p. 65.

————. *The Convict; or, The Conspirator's Victim.* New York: W. F. Burgess, 1851.

In Notebook 4 Clemens jotted down an idea for a "d–d girl always reading novels like [']The Convict, Or The Conspirator's Daughter,' & going into ecstasies about them to her friends" *(N&J*, 1: 76).

Judson, (Mrs.) Emily (Chubbuck) (1817–1854). *An Olio of Domestic Verses.* New York: Lewis Colby, 1852. 235 pp.

Source: MTLAcc, entry #612, volume donated by Clemens.

Junius (pseud.). *Letters of Junius* (pub. serially 1768–1772).

In "The Wild Man Interviewed," a column for the 18 September 1869 issue of the Buffalo *Express*, Mark Twain's wild man claims that he "wrote those crazy Junius letters." The "implacable Junius" is mentioned in "Letter from the Under-World" (Paine 260, MTP), a manuscript letter concerning Byron which Mark Twain penned in 1869. Mark Twain's autobiographical dictation for 30 January 1907 paraphrased a sentence from the dedication of Junius' *Letters* ("The liberty of the press is the *Palladium* of all the civil, political, and religious rights of an Englishman") and remarked that "it was a true saying."

Jusserand, Jean Adrien Antoine Jules (1855–1932). *English Wayfaring Life in the Middle Ages (XIVth Century).* Trans. by Lucy T. Smith. Illus. from illuminated manuscripts. New York: G. P. Putnam's Sons, 1889. 451 pp.

Inscription: "S. L. Clemens, 1889."

Catalog: A1911, #272, $11.50.

The French writer and diplomat Jusserand published *Les Anglais au Moyen Âge* in 1884.

Kalakaua, David (1836–1891), king of Hawaii. *The Legends and Myths of Hawaii: The Fables and Folk-Lore of a Strange People.* Ed. and with an intro. by Rollin Mallory Daggett. New York: Charles L. Webster & Company, 1888.

Clemens reminded himself to discuss Kalakaua's book with Charles L. Webster in October 1886 (NB 26, TS p. 25), perhaps because Clemens had known its editor. Albert Bigelow Paine mentions that the book "barely paid for the cost of manufacture" after Clemens' firm published it *(MTB*, p. 856).

Kaler, James Otis (1848–1912), pseud. "James Otis." *Ezra Jordan's Escape from the Massacre at Fort Loyall.* Illus. Boston: Dana Estes & Co., [cop. 1895]. 109 pp.

Source: MTLAcc, entry #874, volume donated by Mrs. Ralph W. Ashcroft (formerly Isabel Lyon), Clemens' secretary.

————. *Left Behind; or, Ten Days a Newsboy.* Illus. New York: Harper & Brothers, [cop. 1884]. 205 pp.
Source: MTLAcc, entry #1613, volume donated by Clemens.

————. *Mr. Stubb's Brother.* Illus. by W. A. Rogers. New York: Harper & Brothers, [cop. 1882]. 283 pp.
Source: MTLAcc, entry #505, volume donated by Clemens.

————. *Silent Pete; or, The Stowaways.* Illus. New York: Harper & Brothers, [cop. 1886]. 192 pp.
Source: MTLAcc, entry #425, volume donated by Clemens.

————. *Toby Tyler; or, Ten Weeks with a Circus.* Illus. New York: Harper & Brothers, [cop. 1881]. 265 pp.
Source: MTLAcc, entry #1171, volume donated by Clemens.

Kalfus, Berthold. *Aus zwei Welten. Gedichte.* N.p., n.d. 115 pp.
Source: MTLAcc, entry #392, volume donated by Clemens.

Kane, Elisha Kent (1820–1857). *Arctic Explorations: The Second Grinnell Expedition in Search of Sir John Franklin, 1853, '54, '55.* Illus. 2 vols. Philadelphia: Childs & Peterson, 1856. Reprinted in 1857 and 1858.
In describing to Orion Clemens (on 9 March 1858) the struggle by the steamboat *Pennsylvania* to pass through ice on the Mississippi River, Clemens finally wrote: "But in order to understand our situation you will have to read Dr. Kane" (*MTL,* p. 37). Perhaps Kane's account inspired Clemens' depiction of the men in the yawl as looking "like rock-candy statuary." In chapter 7 of volume 1 Kane tells about the narrow escape of his group when a gale lashed their brig as it lay among ice-floes.

Kant, Immanuel. *Critique of Pure Reason. In Commemoration of the Centenary of Its First Publication.* Trans. by F. Max Müller. 2 vols. New York: Macmillan, 1881.
In April 1882 Clemens made this entry in Notebook 20: "Kant's Critique of Pure Reason—Max Müller's translation. Macmillan, N. Y." (*N&J,* 2: 455).

Kathrens, R. D. *Side Lights on Mary Baker Eddy-Glover-Science Church Trustees Controversy. "Next Friends" Suit.* Kansas City, Missouri: Frank T. Riley Publishing Co., 1907. 88 pp.
Marginalia: broad blue pencil marks that are uncharacteristic of Clemens.
Provenance: contains a catalog label #90, with red borders. These labels appear in other volumes that once belonged to Clemens and formed part of the original Mark Twain Papers.
Location: Mark Twain Papers, Berkeley, California.
Copy examined: Clemens' copy, unmarked by him.
Kathrens reviews the legal suit by Mrs. Eddy's son against the Christian Science Church over her properties and financial affairs. Much of the text consists of letters to Kathrens, and the volume is not very enlightening.

Kaulbach, Wilhelm von (1805–1874). *Female Characters of Goethe, from the Original Drawings of William Kaulbach.* Explanatory Text by G. H. Lewes. New York: T. Stroefer; Munich: F. Bruckman, [1868]. 98 pp.
Catalog: C1951, #O8.
Lewes' accompanying text contains quotations from Goethe's works. In November 1878 Clemens noted in Munich that "the old masters never dreamed of women as beautiful as those of Kaulbach" (NB 17, *N&J,* 2: 251).

Keary, Annie (1825–1879). *Castle Daly: The Story of an Irish Home Thirty Years Ago*. New Edition. London: Macmillan and Co., 1876. 576 pp. Reprinted in 1886.
Clemens misspelled the names of the author, title, and publisher in a notebook entry of September 1887 (NB 27, TS p. 13).

————. *Janet's Home*. New York: Macmillan Co., 1882. 426 pp.
Source: MTLAcc, entry #2294, volume donated from Clemens' library by Clara Clemens Gabrilowitsch in 1910.
"Anna Keary novels/Jennette's Home [*sic*], Castle Bailey [*sic*], & others. Mc Millan," Clemens noted to himself in September 1887 (NB 27, TS p. 13).

Keats, John (1795–1821). *Endymion* (poem).
"And so you think a baby is a thing of beauty and a joy forever?" Clemens wrote around 1865 in "Answers to Correspondents" *(SN&O)*.

————. *The Poetical Works of John Keats*. Ed. by John Turner Palgrave. Golden Treasury Series. London: Macmillan and Co., 1889. 284 pp.
Source: MTLAcc, entry #2082, volume donated from Clemens' library by Clara Clemens Gabrilowitsch in 1910.

[Keddie, Henrietta (1827–1914)]. *Honor Ormthwaite; A Novel*. New York: Harper & Brothers, 1896. 253 pp.
Source: MTLAcc, entry #1505, volume donated by Clemens.

————, pseud. "Sarah Tytler." *Noblesse Oblige*. New York: H. Holt & Co., 1876. 386 pp.
Source: MTLAcc, entry #1852, volume donated from Clemens' library by Clara Clemens Gabrilowitsch in 1910.

Keeler, Ralph (1840–1873). *Gloverson and His Silent Partners*. Boston: Lee and Shepard, 1869. 372 pp.
Clemens instructed Elisha Bliss to send Keeler a complimentary copy of *IA* (12 November 1871, ALS in MTP, *MTHL*, p. 8). In a futuristic spoof which Clemens sent to Livy on 16 November 1874 he announced that "the monument to the author of 'Gloverson & His Silent Partners' is finished" and referred to the novel as a "noble classic" which would, by 1935, be "adored by all nations & known to all creatures" *(MTHL*, p. 40). But according to Clemens' designated biographer, poor Keeler was delighted simply to find a copy of his novel about California mines and stocks in a public library near Boston *(MTB*, pp. 449–450). Evidently Clemens was remembering this pathetic incident when he noted Keeler's name and his novel in December 1897, adding "librarian had a copy" (NB 42, TS p. 50). Mark Twain mentioned Keeler familiarly in "My Boyhood Dreams" (1900). Keeler's name also appears in a list of writers Clemens compiled from those he had known personally on 16 January 1903 (NB 46, TS p. 6). Still another reference to *Gloverson* occurs among anecdotes Clemens recalled in 1904 (NB 46, TS p. 34).
Anyone interested in the biography of Keeler, who vanished from the steamer *Cienfuegos* off the coast of Cuba in December 1873, might wish to consult Philip Graham's "Ralph Keeler, Journalism's Mystery," *Journalism Quarterly*, 40 (Winter 1963), 45–52. Graham reports that *Gloverson* "failed almost before it came from the presses"; he could locate only one copy—that of the Library of Congress.

Keightley, (Sir) Samuel Robert (1859–1940?). *The Last Recruit of Clare's; Being Passages from the Memoirs of Anthony Dillon . . . Late Colonel of Clare's Regiment in the Service of France*. New York: Harper & Brothers, 1901. 299 pp.
Source: MTLAcc, entry #1018, volume donated by Clemens.

Keightley, Thomas (1789–1872). *An Account of the Life, Opinions, and Writings of John Milton.* London: Chapman and Hall, 1855. 484 pp.

Keightley's was one of the "biogs of Milton" Clemens listed in Notebook 27 (TS p. 22) in September 1887.

Keim, DeBenneville Randolph. *Sheridan's Troopers on the Borders: A Winter Campaign on the Plains.* Philadelphia: Claxton, Remsen & Haffelfinger, 1870. 308 pp.

Mark Twain was always grateful to discover material that seemed to disprove the existence of the Indians drawn by James Fenimore Cooper. In "The Noble Red Man," a *Galaxy* sketch that appeared in the September 1870 issue, Mark Twain cited "Dr. Keim's excellent book" as his source for Indian atrocities committed during 1868 and 1869 against unoffending whites. "These facts and figures are official," Mark Twain declared, "and they exhibit the misunderstood Son of the Forest in his true character—as a creature devoid of brave or generous qualities, but cruel, treacherous, and brutal" *(CG,* p. 72; also reprinted in *MT: Life as I Find It,* pp. 107–108).

HH&T, pp. 82 n. 1, 331; McNutt, "MT and the American Indian."

Keller, Gottfried. *Die Leute von Seldwyla. Erzählungen von Gottfried Keller.* 3 vols. Dritte Auflage [Third ed.] Stuttgart: G. J. Göschen'sche Verlagshandlung, 1876.

Inscriptions: "Sam¹ L. Clemens/Feb. 2ⁿᵈ 1879/Munich" written in both volumes in brown ink by Olivia Clemens. Inscriptions slightly cropped when books were rebound.

Marginalia: Clemens wrote the words "I feel" on page 15 of vol. 1; he also made a few pencil markings in this volume, particularly on page 105.

Provenance: C1951 sale labels in both volumes. Bookplates of the University of California at Berkeley identify the books as gifts from Jake Zeitlin.

Catalog: Zeitlin 1951, p. 4, item #26. Price $10.

Location: Mark Twain Papers, Berkeley, California.

Copies examined: Clemens' copies.

Keller, Helen Adams (1880–1968). *Helen Keller Souvenir No. 2 (1892–1899), Commemorating the Harvard Final Examination for Admission to Radcliffe College, June 29–30, 1899.* Washington, D. C.: Volta Bureau for the Increase and Diffusion of Knowledge Relating to the Deaf, 1900.

Inscription: "Olivia L. Clemens" in Clemens' hand on the front flyleaf.

Catalog: "Retz Appraisal" (1944), p. 9, valued at $5.

Location: Mark Twain Papers, Berkeley, California.

Copy examined: Clemens' copy.

Souvenir contains essays about Miss Keller's academic studies written by Anne M. Sullivan and other teachers and supervisors, and by Miss Keller herself. It concludes with a facsimile certificate of her college admission.

Clemens was aware of Helen Keller's achievements before he received this book. He had written to her on 12 September 1890 to thank her for sending a gift (ALS in Stowe-Day Library, Hartford, Connecticut), and he had mentioned and praised her accomplishments in *FE* (1897, chapter 61).

———. *The Story of My Life.* New York: Doubleday, Page & Co., 1903.

Inscription: (not actually in Braille, but the letters are raised rather than printed): "To Mr. Clemens/If my book finds favor in thy sight dear Friend I shall count my darkness light and each loss a privilege./Helen Keller/March Tenth/1903."

Location: Antenne-Dorrance Collection, Rice Lake, Wis.

Copy examined: Clemens' unmarked copy.

Clemens wrote to Miss Keller on St. Patrick's Day, 1903, from Riverdale: "I am charmed with your book—enchanted." He complimented Anne M. Sullivan, whose "brilliancy, penetration, originality, wisdom, character, & the fine literary competencies of her pen" were apparent in her own letters (*MTB*, pp. 1198–99; *MTL*, p. 731).

————. *The Story of My Life.* [Another copy.]
    Catalog: C1951, #D25, $27.50, listed among the volumes signed by Clemens.

————. *The World I Live In.* New York: The Century Co., 1908.
    Inscription: Miss Keller wrote in pencil on the front flyleaf: "Dear Mr. Clemens, come live in my world a little while/Helen Keller". On the inside front cover Clemens noted in black ink: "It is a lovely book—& Helen is herself another lovely book./SLC/1908."
    Location: Antenne-Dorrance Collection, Rice Lake, Wis.
    Copy examined: Clemens' copy, unmarked.
    Elizabeth Wallace reported that Clemens read aloud from Miss Keller's articles in *Harper's Magazine* in Bermuda in March and April 1908; he and Henry H. Rogers were impressed with her phrasing (*MT&HI*, p. 94). Probably Miss Wallace meant *Century Magazine,* which published several Helen Keller poems and articles in 1908.

Kelley, James Douglas Jerrold (1847–1922). *The Ship's Company and Other Sea People.* Illus. New York: Harper & Brothers, 1897. 222 pp.
    Source: MTLAcc, entry #1368, volume donated by Clemens.

Kellogg, Robert H. *Life and Death in Rebel Prisons: Giving a Complete History of the Inhuman and Barbarous Treatment . . . at Andersonville, Ga., and Florence, S. C., Describing Plans of Escape, Arrival of Prisoners, with . . . Anecdotes of Prison Life. By Robert H. Kellogg, Sergeant-Major 16th Regiment Connecticut Volunteers. Prepared from His Daily Journal.* Illus. Sold by Subscription Agents Only. Hartford, Conn.: L. Stebbins, 1865.
    Clemens made a memorandum in February 1882: "Get Kellogg's Andersonville experiences through short-hand reporter" (Notebook 20, *N&J,* 2: 446). His next notebook entry mentions the sinking of the *Hornet* and the ordeal of her crew in an open boat, which Mark Twain wrote up from a survivor's journal and published in 1866. Possibly he had something similar in mind for Kellogg's journal; he might have considered incorporating these experiences in the sections of *LonMiss* (1883) that discuss the Civil War. In 1882 Kellogg was a general agent for the Connecticut Mutual Life Insurance Company in Hartford. Perhaps he or his former publisher still owned the original journals.

Kelly, Fanny (Wiggins). *Narrative of My Captivity Among the Sioux Indians.* Hartford, Conn.: Mutual Publishing Co., 1871. 285 pp. Reprinted in 1873.
    On 17 February 1876 Clemens requested Elisha Bliss to send this book and several others to a disabled soldiers' home in Virginia (CWB).

Kelly, Michael (1764?–1826). *Reminiscences of Michael Kelly, of the King's Theatre, and Theatre Royal Drury Lane.* 2 vols. London: H. Colburn, 1826.
    Clara Clemens listed this book title in her commonplace book (Paine 150, MTP).

Kelly, (Mrs. Tom). *A Leddy in Her Ain Richt. A Brief Romance.* London: Hurst & Blackett, 1897. 291 pp.
    Source: MTLAcc, entry #192, volume donated by Clemens. Inscribed to Mark Twain by author.

Kelvin, William Thomson (1824–1907). "The Age of Earth as an Abode Fitted for Life," *Science,* 9 (12 and 19 May 1899), 665–674, 704–711.

Sherwood Cummings—"Mark Twain and Science" (1950), pp. 21–22—suggests this two-part article as the most likely source for Mark Twain's knowledge that Kelvin favored a shorter span of time for the earth's formation than his scientific colleagues theorized. (Kelvin believed it to be one hundred million years, with man inhabiting it for 30,000 years.) Albert Bigelow Paine quoted Clemens on this subject in *Mark Twain: A Biography,* page 1358.

H. H. Waggoner, "Science" (1937), p. 362.

Ken, Thomas (1637–1711). "Praise God, from whom all blessings flow" ("The doxology") (hymn, pub. 1695).

This four-line stanza is often sung at the conclusion of "Old Hundred," and its identity has merged with that of William Kethe's longer hymn. In chapter 17 of *TS* (1876) the minister exhorts the overjoyed congregation to celebrate the three boys' safe deliverance by wholeheartedly singing "Praise God from whom all blessings flow" and "Old Hundred"; they shook the rafters of the village church. "The Doxology" formed the text of a telegram celebrating the election returns that Clemens sent to William Dean Howells from Hartford (9 November 1876, *MTHL,* p. 163). In chapter 25 of *HF* (1885) "somebody over in the crowd struck up the doxolojer, and everybody joined in with all their might."

Kendall, Henry Clarence (1841–1882). *Poems of Henry Clarence Kendall.* Ed. by Alexander Sutherland. Melbourne: George Robertson and Co., 1890.

Inscription: (on second flyleaf) "Miss Clemens,/with the best wishes of/S. Talbot Smith/Adelaide, 15th October, 1895".

Marginalia: pencil marks in Table of Contents beside various poem titles. They do not resemble Clemens' customary markings.

Location: Antenne-Dorrance Collection, Rice Lake, Wis.

Copy examined: Clara Clemens' copy.

Mark Twain mentions Kendall in *FE* (1897, ch. 22) among the Australian authors who have built "a brilliant and vigorous literature."

Madigan, "Mark Twain's Passage to India," p. 360.

Kendall, W. A. *The Voice My Soul Heard.* San Francisco: privately printed, 1868. 16 pp.

Whether or not Clemens saw this volume of poetry, he knew Kendall in the 1860's as a fellow contributor to the *Golden Era* and the *Californian.* On 7 January 1872 Clemens vouched for Kendall's character ("a good fellow") when enlisting William Dean Howells' assistance for this victim of "hard luck" (*MTHL,* p. 9).

Kennan, George (1845–1924). *Siberia and the Exile System.* 2 vols. New York: The Century Co., 1891.

These articles appeared as a series in *Century Magazine* between 1887 and 1891. Howard G. Baetzhold convincingly proves Mark Twain's familiarity with Kennan's allegations of Russian atrocities and banishment ("The Course of Composition of *CY* [1961], 207–211; *MT&JB,* p. 349 n. 32). Kennan's sympathies led Clemens to suppose in 1901 that Kennan might collaborate on a book about Southern lynchings (Clemens to Frank Bliss, 8 September 1901, ALS in Humanities Research Center, Univ. of Texas at Austin).

Louis J. Budd, "Twain, Howells, and the Boston Nihilists" (1959); *MTSP,* pp. 146–147.

————. *Tent Life in Siberia, and Adventures among the Koraks and Other Tribes.* New York: G. P. Putnam & Sons, 1870. 425 pp.

Inscription: upper portion of second flyleaf torn out.

Location: Mark Twain Library, Redding, Conn. Donated by Clemens (MTLAcc, entry #597).

Copy examined: unmarked copy, shelved with Clemens' library books when Albert Stone, Jr. catalogued the collection in 1955 (and when I examined the same copy in 1970).

Kennedy, Charles Rann (1871–1950). *The Servant in the House* (play, perf. 1908, New York City).

Clemens saw a performance on 6 June 1908 and declared it to be "a noble play"; he dined with its author ("whom I very much wish to know") the next evening (Clemens to Dorothy Quick, 7 June 1908, ALS at Columbia Univ.). A week later it still seemed "a wonderful play" (Clemens to Dorothy Quick, 14 June 1908, ALS at Columbia Univ.). In Dorothy Sturgis Harding's reminiscences about her 1908 visit to Clemens' Stormfield, she recalled the nickname of his business manager, Ralph W. Ashcroft: "Also there was Mr. Ashcroft, known as 'Benares,' because of *The Servant in the House,* a very popular current play" ("Mark Twain Lands an Angel-Fish," *Columbia Library Columns,* 16 [February 1967], 8).

————. *The Winterfeast.* Illus. New York: Harper & Brothers, 1908. 159 pp.

Source: MTLAcc, entry #1575, volume donated by Clemens.

Kennedy, Harry. "Cradle's empty, baby's gone" (song, cop. 1880).

Clemens heard two Negro cabin hands on the *City of Baton Rouge* sing this song to banjo accompaniment in 1882 (NB 21, *N&J,* 2: 562).

Kennedy, James Mackintosh (1848–1922). *The Scottish and American Poems of James Kennedy.* Edinburgh: Oliphant, Anderson & Ferrier, [cop. 1907]. 228 pp.

Source: MTLAcc, entry #2134, volume donated from Clemens' library by Clara Clemens Gabrilowitsch in 1910.

Kennedy, John Pendleton. *Swallow Barn* (novel, pub. 1832).

During the autumn of 1851 Orion Clemens published extracts from *Swallow Barn* in the Hannibal *Journal* (*SCH,* p. 240).

Kennedy, Kate. *Doctor Paley's Foolish Pigeons, and Short Sermons to Workingmen.* San Francisco: Cubery & Co., 1906. 272 pp.

Source: MTLAcc, entry #676, volume donated by Isabel V. Lyon, Clemens' secretary.

Kennedy, William. "The pirate's serenade" (song, ca. 1838). Melody by John Thompson.

Mark Twain associated two lines from this poem with the tropical scenery he first viewed in the Sandwich Islands. In 1866 he copied the lines into Notebook 6: "Oh, islands there are/on the face of [the] deep/Where the leaves never fade/ & the skies never weep" (*N&J,* 1: 200). Previously he had adapted the second line ("& skies weep") in copying them into Notebook 5 (*N&J,* 1: 163), and he explained in a fragmentary sketch about the Sandwich Islands—begun in 1884 (DV111, MTP)—that "the skies do weep, there, but the leaves never fade." Mark Twain included "The Captive Pirate's Lament" [*sic*] among the songs that display "soft sentimentality about the sea" in "About All Kinds of Ships" (1893). He quoted his favorite lines again in chapter 15, Book II, of "Christian Science" (1907); there he claimed that Mary Baker Eddy led her followers "to a tropical paradise like that of which the poet sings: 'O, islands there are on the face of the deep/Where the leaves never fade and the skies never weep' " (*WIM?,* pp. 358, 574).

Kenney, James (1780–1849). *Raising the Wind* (farce, 1803).

In a letter of 27 June 1878 to William Dean Howells, Clemens called Bret Harte "a swindler, a snob, a sot, a sponge, a coward, a Jeremy Diddler" (*MTHL*, p. 235). Reaching for these insults, Clemens seems to have known that Kenney created Jeremy Diddler as a character who was continually "raising the wind" by borrowing small sums which he never repaid.

Keokuk Directory and Business Mirror for the Year 1857. Ed. by Orion Clemens. Keokuk, Iowa: Ben Franklin Book and Job Office, 1857.

Provenance: formerly owned by W. C. Stripe of Keokuk. It is unlikely that Samuel L. Clemens ever owned this particular copy, which was once part of Frank C. Willson's book collection.

Location: Humanities Research Center, University of Texas at Austin. Acquired in 1965 along with other books that definitely belonged to Clemens.

Copy examined: copy belonging to a resident of Keokuk, Iowa.

Sam Clemens helped his brother Orion prepare the 1856 edition of this publication, but the younger Clemens left Keokuk before the 1857 book was issued.

Keppel, (Lady) Caroline. "Robin Adair" (song, ca. 1750).

In Mark Twain's "A Dog's Tale" (1903) Robin Adair is a "very handsome and courteous and graceful" Irish setter who belongs to the Scotch minister. Isabel V. Lyon recorded "Robin Adair" as one of the Scottish airs Clemens requested her to play on 14 February 1906 (IVL Journals, TS p. 135, MTP).

Ker, David (1842–1914). "From the Sea to the Desert," *Cosmopolitan,* 6 (March 1889), 466–470.

In March 1889 Clemens expressed an abhorrence for Ker's "travel-papers in the Cosmopolitan." (Ker had previously published "Over the Cossack Steppes," *Cosmopolitan,* 6 [February 1889], 343–348.) "Pity to put that flatulence between the same leaves with that charming Chinese story [by Chin Foo Wong]," Clemens wrote (NB 28, TS p. 49). Ker's essay in the March number describes North Africa, the Sahara Desert, and the city of Constantine. He writes with much assurance but little dexterity; his prose is everywhere overfreighted with adjectives. For instance, this is how Ker pictures some "jutting crags": "The gaunt, distorted, skeleton trees that cling to them with clawed, twisted roots, might well pass for demons breaking forth from the regions of eternal night" (p. 466). Ker especially enjoys jokes of the international variety, such as his anecdote about an English tourist with poor vision who mistook a silently praying Mohammedan "for the stump of a tree" beside the Ganges, and carved his name on this "ill-starred Brahmin. . . . As it would have been a deadly sin to move before the prayer was finished, it was 'rough' on that Brahmin!" (p. 468).

Kerr, (Lady) Amabel. *Blessed Joan of Arc (1412–1431).* Third Edition with Postscript. London: Catholic Truth Society, 1909.

Inscription: a penciled note appears on the first flyleaf in a script that does not resemble Clemens': "It's getting to be a habit with me!"

Provenance: contains *C1951* auction label.

Catalog: Zeitlin 1951, item #27, price $15.

Location: Mark Twain Papers, Berkeley, California. Gift of Jake Zeitlin, Los Angeles.

Copy examined: Clemens' copy, unmarked.

Kester, Paul (1870–1933). *When Knighthood Was in Flower* (play, perf. 1901, New York City). Adapted from Charles Major's novel (pub. 1898).

"This family—by special request of Mr. Major, author of the play [*sic*]—are booked for the Criterion Theatre to-morrow night," Clemens wrote to Henry H. Rogers on 22 January 1901 *(MTHHR,* p. 458). Clemens had listed Kester's New York City address in a notebook for 1898 (NB 42, TS p. 66). Kester, incidentally, would publish a four-act dramatization of *Tom Sawyer* in 1932.

Kethe, William. "Old hundred," also known as "Old hundreth" (hymn, pub. 1561). Melody attributed to Louis Bourgeois or Guillaume Franc.

This hymn—beginning "All people that on earth do dwell"— is usually followed in church services by Thomas Ken's "Doxology" ("Praise God, from whom all blessings flow"). The congregation sings both hymns when Tom and his friends return to life in chapter 17 of *TS* (1876): "Old Hundred swelled up with a triumphant burst, and . . . it shook the rafters." The minister exhorts the people to "put your hearts in it!" Earlier, in Mark Twain's "Private Habits of Horace Greeley" *(The Spirit of the Times,* 7 November 1868), Greeley shaves while humming: "He knows part of a tune and takes an innocent delight in regarding it as the first half of Old Hundred."

PMT, p. 395; Arthur M. Kompass, "Twain's Use of Music," p. 617 n. 2.

Key, Francis Scott (1799–1843). "The star-spangled banner" (anthem, pub. 1814).

Mark Twain and Charles Dudley Warner mentioned "this stirring song" in chapter 16 of *GA* (1873). In August 1895 Mark Twain alluded to Negro soldiers who sang the song (NB 35, TS p. 23). In chapter 13 of "A Horse's Tale" (1907) the military band plays Key's anthem "in a way to make a body's heart swell and thump and his hair rise!" Mark Twain also refers to "The Star-Spangled Banner" in an Autobiographical Dictation of 28 January 1907 *(MTE,* p. 76).

Kiefer, F. J. *The Legends of the Rhine from Basle to Rotterdam.* Second Edition. Trans. by L. W. Garnham. Mayence: David Kapp, 1870. 313 pp.

Inscription: original title page missing; Clemens has supplied a handwritten title page on the blank recto of the frontispiece.

Marginalia: Clemens' annotations in pencil occur throughout.

Provenance: inside the back cover is the sticker of a Leipzig bookseller. The volume was listed in "Retz Appraisal" (1944), p. 9, valued at $20.

Location: Mark Twain Papers, Berkeley, California.

Copy examined: Clemens' copy.

Kiefer's legends were the literary source for some of the stories Mark Twain told in *A Tramp Abroad* (1880). One legend, "The Converted Sceptic," Mark Twain reworked into the legend of Dilsberg Castle, giving a Rip Van Winkle theme to the narrative of a raft captain (chapter 19). But Garnham's translation from the German tickled Mark Twain immensely. In chapter one of *TA* he introduces Garnham's "toothsome" book to his readers, describing the translator's "quaint fashion of building English sentences on the German plan," and quoting a legend called "The Knave of Bergen" as an example. In chapter 16 he quotes Garnham's sorry attempt to translate the song titled "The Lorelei" into English: "I believe this poet is wholly unknown in America and England; I take peculiar pleasure in bringing him forward because I consider that I discovered him."

———. [An identical (or the same?) copy.]

Source: MTLAcc, entry #1866, volume donated from Clemens' library by Clara Clemens Gabrilowitsch in 1910.

King, Basil (1859–1928). *The Inner Shrine; A Novel of Today.* Illus. New York: Harper & Brothers, 1909. 356 pp.

Source: MTLAcc, entry #1420, volume donated by Clemens.

————. *In the Garden of Charity.* New York: Harper & Brothers, 1903. 320 pp.
  Source: MTLAcc, entry #1017, volume donated by Clemens.

[————]. *The Wild Olive; A Novel.* Illus. by Lucius Hitchcock. New York: Harper
  & Brothers, 1910. 347 pp.
  Source: MTLAcc, entry #1842, volume donated from Clemens' library by
  Clara Clemens Gabrilowitsch in 1910.

King, Charles (1844–1933). *Between the Lines, A Story of the War.* Illus. New
  York: Harper & Brothers, [cop. 1888]. 312 pp.
  Source: MTLAcc, entry #1576, volume donated by Clemens.

————. *Between the Lines, A Story of the War.* Illus. New York: Harper &
  Brothers, 1898. 312 pp.
  Source: MTLAcc, entry #1019, volume donated by Albert Bigelow Paine,
  Clemens' designated biographer. Possibly Clemens saw this book, since the men
  exchanged reading materials.

————. *Cadet Days, A Story of West Point.* Illus. New York: Harper & Brothers,
  [cop. 1894]. 293 pp.
  Source: MTLAcc, entry #1601, volume donated by Clemens.

————. *To the Front; A Sequel to Cadet Days.* Illus. New York: Harper &
  Brothers, 1902. 261 pp.
  Source: MTLAcc, entry #522, volume donated by Clemens.

————. *To the Front; A Sequel to Cadet Days.* Illus. New York: Harper &
  Brothers, 1908. 261 pp.
  Source: MTLAcc, entry #201, volume donated by Clemens.

————. *A War-Time Wooing; A Story.* New York: Harper & Brothers, 1888.
  195 pp.
  Source: MTLAcc, entry #2295, volume donated from Clemens' library by
  Clara Clemens Gabrilowitsch in 1910.

King, Clarence (1842–1901). *Mountaineering in the Sierra Nevada.* Boston: J. R.
  Osgood, 1872. 292 pp.
  Inscription: signed "S. L. Clemens."
  Catalog: A1911, #273, $5.50.
  "I wish Clarence King would put his Pike County people on [the stage],"
  Clemens commented in a now-incomplete letter written to William Dean Howells
  on 7 May 1875 (*MTHL*, p. 82). In 1888 Clemens passed the time while
  snowbound in the Murray Hill Hotel of New York City by listing authors with
  whom he was familiar; Clarence King's name appears in the generally
  "favorable" list that Clemens constructed (Notebook 27).

King, Edmund Fillingham, ed. *Ten Thousand Wonderful Things; Comprising the
  Marvelous and Rare, Odd, Curious, Quaint, Eccentric, and Extraordinary in
  All Ages and Nations.* Illus. London and New York: G. Routledge and Sons,
  186-[?]. 684 pp. Originally pub. in New York by Dick & Fitzgerald, 1859[?].
  [The edition purchased by Clemens has not been established.]
  On 14 July 1880 Estes & Lauriat of Boston billed Clemens for "1 10,000
  Wond Things $1"; he paid on 20 July 1880 (receipts file, MTP).

King, Grace Elizabeth (1852–1932). "Earthlings" (novella, pub. 1888).
  After Clemens read this story in the November 1888 issue of *Lippincott's
  Magazine,* he wrote to the authoress on 16 November: "I do suppose you

struck twelve on Earthlings. It does not seem possible that you or any one else can overmatch that masterpiece. I cannot find a flaw in the art of it—I mean the art which the intellect put there—nor in the nobler & richer art which the heart put in it. I *felt* the story, just as if I were living it; whereas with me a story is usually a procession & I am an outsider watching it go by—& always with a dubious, & generally with a perishing interest. If I could have stories like this one to read, my prejudice against stories would die a swift death & I should be grateful" (quoted by Robert Bush, "Grace King and Mark Twain," *AL*, 44 [March 1972], 41–42).

————. *Monsieur Motte*. New York: A. C. Armstrong and Son, 1888. 327 pp.
    On 17 June 1888 Olivia Clemens wrote to Grace King (in a letter not sent until 7 August 1888): "Mr. Clemens and I are sitting on the Ombra this hot Sunday afternoon. . . . I have just finished Monsieur Motte, . . . a copy of which Mr. Warner gave me. It is simply charming—every line in the book delighted me. I had never before read the last two sketches in the book. Of course now I read it right through together. I don't believe you can know how fine it all is" (ALS in Louisiana State Univ. Library, Baton Rouge). When Grace King dramatized the novel, Clemens introduced her to playwright-producer Augustin Daly in November 1888 to see whether he might produce it. Daly declined the play on 24 November 1888.
    Robert Bush, "Grace King and Mark Twain" (1972), 42–45.

————. *Tales of a Time and Place*. New York: Harper & Brothers, 1892. 303 pp.
    Source: MTLAcc, entry #2296, volume donated from Clemens' library by Clara Clemens Gabrilowitsch in 1910.

Kinglake, Alexander William (1809–1891). *Eōthen*. Edinburgh: A. W. Blackwood & Sons, 1892. 371 pp.
    Source: MTLAcc, entry #2297, volume donated from Clemens' library by Clara Clemens Gabrilowitsch in 1910.
    Henry Nash Smith quotes Kinglake's "historical sublime" treatment of the Sphinx (chapter 20), showing how Mark Twain's description in *IA* (1869) was modeled on Kinglake's rhapsodic inventory of scenes witnessed by the Sphinx (*MTDW*, p. 29). In chapter 42 of *FE* (1897) Mark Twain notes: "Kinglake was in Cairo many years ago during an epidemic of the Black Death, and he has imagined the terrors that creep into a man's heart at such a time." Twain then quotes a lengthy extract from chapter 18, which Kinglake titled "Cairo and the Plague."
    Madigan, "Mark Twain's Passage to India," pp. 360–361.

————. *The Invasion of the Crimea*. Illus. and maps. 6 vols. New York: Harper, 1863–1888. [Only vol. 1 of Clemens' copy is known to exist.]
    Catalog: A1911, #274, $1.25, vol. 1 only.
    In February 1888 Clemens jotted an entry in Notebook 27: "Get Kinglake's Crimean War—v small vols—Harper" (TS p. 58). Leon Dickinson reasons in his explanatory notes for a forthcoming edition of *Innocents Abroad* (1869) that Mark Twain used Kinglake's history to visualize (in chapter 35 of *IA*) the Siege of Sebastopol during the Crimean War (TS in MTP).

Kingsley, Charles (1819–1875). *Charles Kingsley: His Letters and Memories of His Wife*. Ed. by Frances Eliza Kingsley. New York: Scribner, Armstrong & Co., 1877. 502 pp.
    Olivia Clemens mentioned to her sister-in-law Mollie Clemens on 29 July 1877 that she and Susan Crane "are reading together this summer the Life and Letters of Charles Kingsley" (ALS in MTP). Clemens was probably reading the volume when he noted in July 1877: "The Deity filled with humor. Kingsley. God's laughter" (NB 13, *N&J*, 2: 37).
    MT&JB, p. 200.

————. *Favorite Poems, by Charles Kingsley, Owen Meredith [pseud. of E. R. Bulwer Lytton], and Edmund Clarence Stedman.* Illus. Boston: J. R. Osgood and Co., 1877.

Scrapbook #10 in the Mark Twain Papers at Berkeley contains a bill from J. R. Osgood & Company of Boston for this book, purchased by Clemens on 6 August 1877 (p. 69).

————. *The Heroes, or Greek Fairy Tales for My Children.* Illus. Chicago: Donohue, Henneberry & Co., [1900?]. 181 pp.

Inscription: Kingsley dedicated his book "To my children/Rose, Maurice, and Mary." On the dedication page Clemens noted in black ink: "(I knew Rose & Mary.)/SLC./And the papa."

Marginalia: Clemens wrote in black ink inside the front cover: "Of course I shall not deny that a fellow endowed with such overweening self-conceit, when he comes to write about himself[,] will set down much which cannot be taken entirely on trust.—(Remark of John Addington Symons concerning Benvenuto Cellini./S. L. Clemens/1906." On page 31 Clemens made a correction, first in ink and then in pencil.

Location: Carrie Estelle Doheny Collection, St. John's Seminary, Camarillo, California. Mrs. Doheny donated the volume in 1940 after she purchased it from Maxwell Hunley Rare Books of Beverly Hills.

Copy examined: Clemens' copy.

Albert Bigelow Paine reported that Kingsley called on Clemens in London in the summer of 1873 *(MTL,* p. 207).

————. *Hypatia; or New Foes with an Old Face.* Boston: Crosby and Nichols, 1862. 487 pp.

Source: MTLAcc, entry #2300, volume donated from Clemens' library by Clara Clemens Gabrilowitsch in 1910.

Clemens wrote to Olivia Langdon from Boston on 28 November 1869: "Twichell gave me one of Kingsley's most tiresomest books— 'Hypatia'—& I have tried to read it & can't. I'll try no more" *(LLMT,* p. 126).

————. *Hypatia; or, New Foes with an Old Face.* 2 vols. Illus. by William Martin Johnson. New York: Harper & Brothers, 1895.

Source: MTLAcc, entries #1130 and #1131, volumes donated by Clemens.

————. *Madame How and Lady Why; or, First Lessons in Earth Lore for Children.* New York: Macmillan & Co., 1888. 321 pp.

Inscription: second flyleaf inscribed by Livy Clemens: "Jean Clemens/July 26th 1890/Onteora/Mamma".

Location: Mark Twain Library, Redding, Conn. Donated from Clemens' library by Clara Clemens Gabrilowitsch in 1910 (MTLAcc, entry #1960).

Copy examined: Jean Clemens' unmarked copy.

————. *Song of the River.* Illus. Boston: Estes and Lauriat, 1887. 19 leaves.

Inscription: (on half-title page) "Clara Clemens/From her Friend/F. C. H. [?]/Xmas 1889".

Location: Paine 150 in Mark Twain Papers, Berkeley, California.

Copy examined: Clara Clemens' copy, unmarked.

This small volume consists of line etchings with captions from Kingsley's three-stanza poem.

————. *Two Years Ago.* Boston: Ticknor and Fields, 1864. 540 pp.

Source: MTLAcc, entry #2299, volume donated from Clemens' library by Clara Clemens Gabrilowitsch in 1910.

————. *The Water-Babies. A Fairy Tale for a Land-Baby*. Illus. by Joseph Noël Paton. Boston: T. O. H. P. Burnham, 1870. 310 pp.
>   *Inscription:* second flyleaf signed "Livy L. Clemens/Aug. 1871/Quarry Farm".
>   *Marginalia:* pencil markings at poetry on pages 42 and 76–77.
>   *Provenance:* sticker inside rear cover reads "Preswick Morse & Co./Booksellers/114 Water St./Elmira, N. Y."
>   *Location:* Mark Twain Library, Redding, Conn. Donated from Clemens' library by Clara Clemens Gabrilowitsch in 1910 (MTLAcc, entry #1893).
>   *Copy examined:* Livy Clemens' copy.

————. *Westward Ho!* New York: Macmillan and Co., 1874. 519 pp.
>   *Source:* MTLAcc, entry #2298, volume donated from Clemens' library by Clara Clemens Gabrilowitsch in 1910.

Kingsley, Henry (1830–1876). *Ravenshoe*. 2 vols. New York: Charles Scribner's Sons, 1905.
>   *Inscriptions:* first flyleaf of vol. 1 signed "Clara Clemens/S. S. 'Rosaluck'/June 29 1907." First flyleaf of vol. 2 signed "Clara Clemens".
>   *Marginalia:* extensive revisions in vol. 2 signal a reader's dissatisfaction with Kingsley's prose style.
>   *Location:* Mark Twain Library, Redding, Conn. Donated from Clemens' library by Clara Clemens Gabrilowitsch in 1910 (MTLAcc, entries #2301 and #2302).
>   *Copies examined:* Clara Clemens' copies.

————. *The Recollections of Geoffry Hamlyn*. Melbourne, Australia: E. W. Cole, n.d. 433 pp.
>   *Source:* MTLAcc, entry #193, volume donated by Clemens.
>   On 8 January 1896, sailing in the Indian Ocean, Clemens found time to expound discursively on this portrait of Australian life: "Henry Kingsley's book, Geoffry Hamlin[,] is a curiosity. In places, & for a little while at a time, it strongly interested me, but the cause lay in the action of the story, not in the story's people. All the people are offensive. Some of them might be well enough if they could be protected from the author's intolerable admiration of them. . . . The reader is lost in wonder that any man can be so piteously bewitched & derationalized by his own creations. The book's grammar is bad, its English poor & slovenly, its art of the crudest. There is one very interesting feature: the author is never able to make the reader believe in the things that happen in the tale. It is not that the things are extraordinary, it is merely that the author lacks the knack of making them look natural. . . . And how misty, vague, unreal, artificial the characters are" (NB 37, TS pp. 3–4). Probably Mark Twain was preparing a criticism for *FE* (1897); at any rate he reminded himself on 1 December 1896: "Slam at Geoffrey Hamlyn" (NB 39, TS p. 29). He did not carry through this intention into print.
>   *MTC*, p. 235 n. 10.

Kingsley, Mary Henrietta (1862–1900). *The Story of West Africa*. London: Horace Marshall & Son, [1899]. 169 pp.
>   *Inscription:* "Mark Twain, with M. H. Kingsley's respect and thanks."
>   *Location:* Mark Twain Library, Redding, Conn.
>   *Copy examined:* Clemens' unmarked copy.

Kinkaid, (Mrs.) Mary Holland (McNeish) (b. 1861). *Walda; A Novel*. New York: Harper & Brothers, 1903. 312 pp.
>   *Source:* MTLAcc, entry #1577, volume donated by Clemens.

Kinkel, Johanna (Mockel) (1810–1858). *Hans Ibeles in London. Ein familienbild aus dem flüchtlingeleben.* 2 vols. Stuttgart: J. G. Cotta, 1860.
    Inscriptions: title-pages of both volumes inscribed by Livy Clemens: "S. L. Clemens/Feb 2nd 1879/Munich". Afterwards the books were rebound and their title-pages were cropped.
    Provenance: both volumes contain *C1951* sale labels.
    Catalog: Zeitlin 1951, item #28, $20.
    Location: Mark Twain Papers, Berkeley, California. Donated by Jake Zeitlin of Los Angeles.
    Copies examined: Clemens' unmarked copies.

[Kipling, Alice (Macdonald) (1837–1910) and Alice Macdonald (Kipling) Fleming (b. 1868)]. *Hand in Hand; Verses by a Mother and Daughter.* New York: Doubleday, Page & Co., 1902. 122 pp.
    Inscription: inside front cover inscribed by Clemens with black ink: "From Doubleday/to/SL. Clemens/New York, August 1904/Poems by Kipling's/ mother & sister."
    Location: Mark Twain Library, Redding, Conn. Donated from Clemens' library by Clara Clemens Gabrilowitsch in 1910 (MTLAcc, entry #2017).
    Copy examined: Clemens' copy, unmarked.

Kipling, Rudyard (1865–1936). "The Absent-Minded Beggar" (poem).
    Astonished that Kipling would support conscription for the Boer War in 1902, Mark Twain wrote a parody of this poem (Clemens to F. H. Skrine, 7 January 1902, ALS in National Library of Scotland; a fuller draft of the burlesque exists in MTP, DV152).
    D. M. McKeithan, "A Letter to Francis Henry Skrine in London," *MLN,* 63 (February 1948), 134–135; *MT&JB,* p. 359 n. 35; *MTAL,* p. 228.

———. "Back to the Army Again" (poem).
    The literary tastes of Clemens and his financial advisor, Henry H. Rogers, agreed on only a few writers—of whom Kipling was the most notable. When Rogers offered to send Clemens a new Kipling poem, Clemens responded on 9 December 1894: "Kipling *can't* pad. He's always got a line or two at least that saves each piece that he writes. Remember the 'lousy ulster' line in the poem we read in the 'L' [in Chicago]? All by itself it made a good poem out of an indifferent one" *(MTHHR,* p. 102). As first published in the *Pall Mall Magazine,* 3 (August 1894), 589–594, the poem began: "I'm 'ere in a lousy ulster an' a broken billycock 'at,/A-layin' on to the Sergeant I don't know a gun from a bat." Kipling changed the phrase that Clemens applauded to "ticky ulster," however, when the poem was collected in *The Seven Seas* (1896).

———. "The Ballad of the *Bolivar*" (poem).
    On 29 February 1908 Clemens read aloud this poem and others by Kipling to Henry H. Rogers, Isabel Lyon, and a small group gathered in his hotel in Bermuda. "We went from shouting joys to tears over the beauties, the perfections," wrote Miss Lyon (IVL Journals, TS p. 306, MTP). Elizabeth Wallace was present at another informal Kipling reading in Bermuda, and she remembered that "we laughed delightedly" at the comic *Bolivar* ballad *(MT&HI,* pp. 97–99).

———. *Barrack-Room Ballads and Other Verses.* Leipzig: Heinemann and Balestier, 1892. 245 pp.
    Source: MTLAcc, entry #2040, volume donated from Clemens' library by Clara Clemens Gabrilowitsch in 1910.

————. "The Bell Buoy" (poem).

On 12 October 1903 Clemens thanked Frank N. Doubleday for sending some books; evidently one of these volumes contained "The Bell Buoy," which Clemens said he had been reading "over and over again—my custom with Kipling's work." Clemens added that during nights aboard Henry H. Rogers' yacht, the *Kanawha*, he had listened to the voice of this bell buoy speaking "in his pathetic and melancholy way . . . and I got his meaning—now I have his words! . . . Some day I hope to hear the poem chanted or sung—with the bell-buoy break-ing in, out of the distance" *(MTL,* p. 746).

MT&JB, pp. 189–190.

————. *The Brushwood Boy* (novelette, pub. 1895).

In a letter that Clemens wrote to Dorothy Sturgis (later Harding) on 30 September 1908 he alluded to "the Brushwood Boy's seat" at Stormfield (ALS at Columbia Univ.). Dorothy Sturgis Harding would recall that when she visited Stormfield in 1908 she and Clemens "sat on a rock and read aloud to each other, especially Kipling, and we agreed that our favorite story was 'The Brushwood Boy.' From then on we called each other the 'Major' [Georgie Cottar, the Brushwood Boy] and 'Annie-an-Louise' [the girl in Georgie's dreams]" ("Mark Twain Lands an Angel-fish," *Columbia Library Columns,* 16 [February 1967], 8–9).

————. *Collected Verse of Rudyard Kipling.* New York: Doubleday, Page & Co., 1907. 367 pp.

Inscription: inside front cover signed in black ink: "SL. Clemens/Feb. '08/ from Doubleday".

Marginalia: Clemens marked with ink the titles of poems in the table of con-tents that appear on pages 19, 24, 34, 45, 53, 55, 65, 70 ("The Song of Diego Valdez," a title he marked twice for emphasis), 75, 76, 78, 80 ("The Long Trail," marked emphatically), 131, 136, 159, 176, 194, 208, 219, 220, 241, 252, 261 (both poems), 265, 270, 271, 274, 281, 285, 305, 333, 339 ("Chant-Pagan," which Clemens identified by its refrain—the word "ME"), and 341. In the text Clemens merely marked a phrase on page 4: "A whisper in the Void."

Location: Antenne-Dorrance Collection, Rice Lake, Wis.

Copy examined: Clemens' copy.

It seems reasonable to believe that this is the volume of Kipling's verse from which Clemens repeatedly read aloud to groups of vacationing Americans in Bermuda in 1908. "These people had never, never heard anything of the real Kipling before," an admiring Isabel Lyon commented in her journal. Following a reading on March 27th Miss Lyon heard one of the fifteen people present, a Mr. Chamberlain, declare that "there isn't anyone else in the world who could read between the lines as the King can" (IVL Journals, TS p. 313, MTP). Another account of these Kipling readings appears in Elizabeth Wallace's valu-able if saccharine memoir, *Mark Twain and the Happy Island* (1913), pp. 93–100. Miss Wallace, the dean of women at the University of Chicago, heard Clemens entertain Henry H. Rogers and other friends in his hotel room in Hamilton on several occasions in March and April 1908. She remembered that Clemens held his pipe in one hand and gesticulated with it during highly dramatic passages. Rogers urged his friend Clemens not to read "too slowly." One of the poems Clemens marked in the table of contents, "The Long Trail," was among the favorites that Miss Wallace later heard Clemens read at Stormfield in 1909, along with the poem titled "The Three-Decker."

————. "The Courting of Dinah Shadd" (short story).

Clemens used this work to compare the costs of typesetting by the Paige machine ($6.50) and those of ordinary printing compositors ($72.50) in January 1891 (NB 30, TS p. 20).

————. "Danny Deever" (poem). Set to music by Walter Damrosch (cop. 1897).
On 7 [or 8?] February 1894 Clemens reported to Livy that he had heard Richard Harding Davis sing "the hanging of Johnny Deever [*sic*], which was of course good" (ALS in MTP). At a benefit for the Mark Twain Library of Redding on 21 September 1909, David Bispham sang this ballad at Clemens' request (Clemens to Elizabeth Wallace, 22 September 1909, *MT&HI*, pp. 131–133). Clemens also liked to read the piece aloud; he listed "Files on Parade" (one voice in the poem) as a tentative addition to his program for a reading at Bryn Mawr in 1891 (NB 30, TS p. 23).

————. *The Day's Work* (short stories, collected in 1898).
Catalog: C1951, #D45, listed among the volumes signed by Clemens.

————. *Departmental Ditties, Barrack-Room Ballads, and Other Verses.* New York: United States Book Co. (successors to John W. Lovell Co.), [cop. 1890]. 270 pp.
Marginalia: Clemens employed pencil to mark several poems for oral interpretation. He underscored words in the third, fourth, and fifth stanzas of "Tommy" (pp. 61–62): "Then," "aren't," "food," "wait," "rations," "treat," "rational." On page 249 he twice altered the word "heaved" to read "hove" in the fourth stanza of "The Galley-Slave."
Location: Mark Twain Library, Redding, Conn. Donated from Clemens' library by Clara Clemens Gabrilowitsch in 1910 (MTLAcc, entry #2039).
Copy examined: Clemens' copy. I discovered this book on the circulating shelves in the Mark Twain Library in September 1970, and I asked the librarian to add it to their collection of volumes from Clemens' personal library.

————. *The Five Nations.* New York: Doubleday, Page & Co., 1903. 215 pp.
Inscription: inscribed to Livy Clemens on 10 October 1903.
Catalogs: C1951, #59c, $25, listed among the books signed by Clemens; *American Book-Prices Current Index 1960–1965* (New York, 1968), p. 368, item #64, $80.
Isabel Lyon reported in a diary entry for 28 July 1904 that Richard Watson Gilder visited the Clemens cottage while Clemens, Jean, and Miss Lyon were playing euchre. "We kept on with our game, and Mr. Gilder read bits of 'Ponka-pog Papers' and Kipling's 'Five Seas' " (IVL Journals, TS p. 25, MTP). She may have meant either collection of Kipling's verse, *The Five Nations* (1903) or *The Seven Seas* (1896). When Clemens became irritated on 4 January 1908, Miss Lyon recorded, "he reached for Kipling's 'Five Seas' [*sic*] and he read aloud, 'The Bell Buoy' [a poem in *Five Nations*]. Gradually his mood changed to his sweet naturalness again" (IVL Journals, TS p. 291, MTP).

————. *The Five Nations.* New York: Doubleday, Page & Co., 1907. 215 pp.
Source: MTLAcc, entry #197, volume donated by Clemens.

————. "For to Admire" (poem).
In London in 1896 Mark Twain copied down the opening lines from this poem (NB 39, TS p. 26), and he used them in chapter 62 of *FE* (1897): "One of Kipling's ballads has delivered the aspect and sentiment of this bewitching sea correctly: 'The Injian Ocean sets an' smiles/So sof', so bright, so bloomin' blue;/There aren't a wave for miles and miles/Excep' the jiggle from the screw.' " Mark Twain also included a phrase from this poem ("a time-expired man") in his 5 December 1905 speech thanking those who attended his seventieth birthday dinner at Delmonico's restaurant *(MTSpk,* p. 466).
MT&JB, p. 359 n. 29.

―――. *From Sea to Sea: Letters of Travel.* 2 vols. London: Macmillan and Co., 1900. Only vol. 2 has been located.

Location: Antenne-Dorrance Collection, Rice Lake, Wis. (vol. 2 only).

Copy examined: Clemens' unmarked copy of vol. 2.

In 1906 Clemens said that Kipling "came over and traveled about America, maintaining himself by correspondence with Indian journals. He wrote dashing, free-handed, brilliant letters but no one outside of India knew about it" (11 August 1906 AD, published in *MTE*, p. 309). Clemens was familiar with the portion of vol. 2, "An Interview with Mark Twain," that described their first meeting in Elmira in 1890. On 15 August 1906 Clemens wrote to Isabel Lyon from Dublin, New Hampshire: "Please look at Kipling's account of his visit to me at Susy Crane's farm, & see if *Mrs. Clemens* as well as Susy Clemens was present" (ALS in MTP).

―――. *From Sea to Sea: Letters of Travel.* 2 vols. in 1. New York: Doubleday, Page & Co., 1907.

Source: MTLAcc, entry #196, volume donated by Clemens.

―――. "Gunga Din" (poem).

This replaced the usual Robert Browning poem in Mark Twain's program for a public reading at Bryn Mawr in 1891 (NB 30, TS p. 23). In chapter 46 of *FE* (1897) Mark Twain refers to an Indian Thuggee chieftain "who soils a great name borne by a better man—Kipling's deathless 'Gungadin.'"

―――. *The Jungle Book* (pub. 1894); *The Second Jungle Book* (pub. 1895).

Planning a tale of child "Creatures of Fiction" in June 1898, Mark Twain noted that "last comes Mogli [*sic*] on elephant with his menagerie & they all rode away with him" (NB 40, TS p. 27). Isabel Lyon's journal for 17 March 1905 reveals that Clemens had written a new story about an Admiral with a cat named Bagheera (TS p. 44, MTP). This tale became Mark Twain's long-unpublished "The Refuge of the Derelicts" (DV309a, MTP). In chapter 2 of "Refuge" the Admiral takes down a volume from his book shelves (a book with a "brown back") and quotes Kipling's description of Bagheera the black panther from volume 7 of Kipling's *Collected Works.* The Admiral declares that *The Jungle Books* are "immortal" and will "outlast the rocks" *(FM,* pp. 173–174). On 30 May 1906 Clemens read aloud to his household "from the first Jungle book" before going to bed (IVL Journal, TS p. 161, MTP). Isabel Lyon noted again on 7 June 1906, also in Dublin, New Hampshire: "Evenings Mr. Clemens reads aloud to us. The Jungle Books now" (TS p. 163, MTP). "The incomparable Jungle Books must remain unfellowed permanently," Clemens said in an Autobiographical Dictation of 13 August 1906 *(MTE,* p. 312).

The Mark Twain Papers at Berkeley contain a bill addressed to Clemens from G. P. Putnam's Sons, New York City, for a purchase Clemens made on 4 March 1909: "1 Jungle Book" and "1 Second Jungle Book"; Clemens paid the bill on 10 April 1909. Subsequently Mark Twain utilized Baloo the bear and Hathi the elephant in his "A Fable," published in the December 1909 issue of *Harper's Magazine.* At some point Mark Twain scrawled the word "bandar-log" in his copy of Saint-Simon's *Memoires* (vol. 2, chapter 32) to express his disdain for the Duc d'Orleans' stupidity.

MT&JB, pp. 191–192.

―――. *Just So Stories for Little Children.* New York: Doubleday, Page & Co., 1902.

Inscription: Clemens wrote in black ink on the front pastedown endpaper (the first word only is in pencil): "For/Olivia L. Clemens/1902/from SLC".

Catalog: C1951, #D38, listed among books signed by Clemens, $27.50.

Location: Humanities Research Center, University of Texas at Austin.

Copy examined: Livy Clemens' unmarked copy. Contains *C1951* sale label.

————. *Kim*. Illus. New York: Doubleday, Page & Co., 1901. 463 pp.
Source: MTLAcc, entry #194, volume donated by Clemens.

————. *Kim*. New York: Doubleday, Page & Co., 1908. 463 pp. Half title: The Pocket Kipling.
Inscription: front cover of soft red leather is signed in black ink, "SL. Clemens/1908." Front pastedown endpaper signed in black ink, "SL. Clemens/1908/from Doubleday."
Marginalia: in chapter 4 (p. 112) Clemens revised with black ink the phrase "I should have rendered thee some service" so that it reads "I render thee some service." On page 197 of chapter 7 he corrected "herd-hunters" to "head-hunters," also with black ink.
Provenance: C1951, item #D13; resold by Glen Dawson's Bookshop of Los Angeles in 1952.
Location: Humanities Research Center, University of Texas at Austin. Donated by Ed W. Owen of San Antonio, Texas, who acquired it from Dawson's Bookshop.
Copy examined: Clemens' copy.
"I think it was worth the journey to India to qualify myself to read *Kim* understandingly and to realize how great a book it is," Clemens announced in an Autobiographical Dictation of 13 August 1906. "The deep and subtle and fascinating charm of India pervades no other book as it pervades Kim. . . . I read the book every year" (*MTE*, p. 312).

————. *The Light That Failed*. New York: National Publishing Co., 1890. 186 pp.
Source: MTLAcc, entry #981, volume donated by Albert Bigelow Paine, Clemens' designated biographer. Possibly Clemens saw this book, since the men exchanged reading materials.

————. *The Light That Failed*. London: Macmillan and Co., 1899.
Inscription: "Jean Lampton Clemens/14 West 10th St./New York City./Christmas, 1900,/from Julie."
Location: Antenne-Dorrance Collection, Rice Lake, Wis.
Copy examined: Jean Clemens' unmarked copy.
After Susy's death, Clemens wrote to Livy from Guildford on 26 August 1896: "I am alone with my memories of the Light that Failed" (*LLMT*, p. 325). For a biography of Susy, Clemens thought of beginning: "This is the history of a promise—a Light that Failed" (NB39 [London, January 1897], TS p. 58).

————. "Mandalay" (poem).
On 7 [or 8?] February 1894 Clemens wrote from New York City to Livy, then in Paris, telling her he heard Richard Harding Davis sing "that most fascinating (for what reason I don't know) of all Kipling's poems, 'On the Road to Mandalay,' sang it tenderly, & it searched me deeper & charmed me more than the [Danny] Deever" (ALS in MTP). In a newspaper interview of 1895 Mark Twain singled out "Mandalay" as a "poem of mingled pathos and humour [which] had the aroma of the Orient, the sound of the sea on the sand and the breezes among the palms in it" (undated clipping, "Mark Twain Put to the Question," [15 October?] 1895 issue of Adelaide *South Australian Register*, Scrapbook #26, p. 121, MTP).

————. *Many Inventions*. New York: D. Appleton & Co., 1893. 427 pp.
Source: MTLAcc, entry #2303, volume donated from Clemens' library by Clara Clemens Gabrilowitsch in 1910.

————. *Many Inventions.* New York: Doubleday, Page & Co., 1908. 427 pp.
Location: Mark Twain Library, Redding, Conn. Donated by Clemens
(MTLAcc, entry #198).
Copy examined: Clemens' copy, unmarked.

————. "The *Mary Gloster"* (poem).
Elizabeth Wallace, who witnessed one of Clemens' informal Kipling readings
in Bermuda in 1908, recalled that even the hard-boiled Henry H. Rogers "blinked
hard" to suppress tears when Clemens read the most successful poem, "The
Mary Gloster."

————. *Mine Own People.* Intro. by Henry James. New York: George Munro's
Sons, 1896. 108 pp. Paperbound.
Source: MTLAcc, entry #200, volume donated by Albert Bigelow Paine,
Clemens' designated biographer. Possibly Clemens saw this book, since the men
exchanged reading materials.

————. "The Naulahka" (poem), one of the group titled "Chapter Headings."
Albert Bigelow Paine describes how Clemens picked out this verse heading in
the *Saturday Times Review.* "I could stand any amount of that," he said, referring to the lines that begin "Now it is not good for the Christian's health to
hustle the Aryan brown,/For the Christian riles, and the Aryan smiles and he
weareth the Christian down" *(MTB,* p. 1502).

————. *The Naulahka, A Story of West and East. Written in Collaboration with
Wolcott Balestier.* New York: Doubleday, Page & Co., 1907. 379 pp.
Source: MTLAcc, entry #199, volume donated by Clemens.

————. "The Old Men" (poem, pub. 1902).
On 12 October 1903 Clemens thanked Frank N. Doubleday for some books,
adding, "I have been reading 'The Bell Buoy' and 'The Old Men' over and
over again. . . . 'The Old Men,' delicious, isn't it? And so comically true. I
haven't arrived there yet, but I suppose I am on the way" *(MTL,* p. 746). When
we are aged men, Kipling wrote, "We shall peck out and discuss and dissect, and
evert and extrude to our mind,/The flaccid tissues of long-dead issues offensive
to God and mankind—/. . . . And whatever we do, we shall fold our hands
and suck our gums and think well of it."

————. *The Phantom 'Rickshaw, and Other Tales.* New York: M. J. Ivers & Co.,
1890. 207 pp.
Source: MTLAcc, entry #2306, volume donated from Clemens' library by
Clara Clemens Gabrilowitsch in 1910.

————. *Plain Tales from the Hills.* Unabridged ed. New York: M. J. Ivers & Co.,
1890. 208 pp.
Source: MTLAcc, entry #2305, volume donated from Clemens' library by
Clara Clemens Gabrilowitsch in 1910.
Carlyle Smythe, one of Clemens' companions during his lecture tour of 1895–
96, reported in 1898 that Clemens "reads Kipling as much for style as for
subject" ("The Real 'Mark Twain,'" p. 31). Clemens became convinced that he
did not begin reading Kipling's prose until around September 1890, when he
wrote to Helen Keller: "I have just found out that whereas Kipling's stories are
plenty good enough on a first reading they very much improve on a second"
(12 September 1890, ALS in MTM). At the dinner table on 18 September 1905
Clemens rehearsed the story of George Warner's introducing him to the wonderful *Plain Tales* in 1890 (IVL Journals, TS p. 100a, MTP), an anecdote that he
repeated in an Autobiographical Dictation of 13 August 1906: "The little book was
the *Plain Tales* and he left it for me to read, saying it was charged with a new

and inspiriting fragrance and would blow a refreshing breath around the world that would revive the nations" *(MTE,* pp. 311–312). Albert Bigelow Paine repeated this version of Clemens' encounter with *Plain Tales (MTB,* p. 881). Twice Clemens alluded to Terence Mulvaney, a literary character who first appeared in Kipling's "The Three Muskateers" in *Plain Tales* (though he also figured in other stories)—in a letter of 16 June 1906 to Charlotte Teller (ALS in Berg Collection), and in a notebook entry of 1910 (NB 49, TS p. 5).

————. *Plain Tales from the Hills.* New York: National Publishing Co., [1890?]. 287 pp.
   Source: MTLAcc, entry #982, volume donated by Albert Bigelow Paine, Clemens' designated biographer. Possibly Clemens saw this book, since the men exchanged reading materials.

————. *Puck of Pook's Hill.* Illus. by Arthur Rackham. New York: Doubleday, Page & Co., 1906. 277 pp.
   Source: MTLAcc, entry #195, volume donated by Clemens.
   Isabel Lyon took a copy to Clemens on 1 June 1907, and he fancied he saw in it resemblances to parts of his "Mysterious Stranger" manuscripts (IVL Journals, 2 June 1907, TS p. 248, MTP).

————. "Recessional" (poem).
   On 21 January 1901 Clemens wrote to William Thomas Stead, editor of *Review of Reviews,* to request a copy of a poem that Clemens called "Lest we forget" (ALS in CWB).

————. "Red Dog" (short story).
   On the evening of 11 June 1906 Clemens "read aloud" to his household and a neighbor the short story "Red Dog," and praised Kipling's diction in picturing the python, Kaa ("the light seemed to go out of his eyes and leave them like stale opals" was Kipling's phrase). " 'Stale opals'—*such* a good description, he said" (IVL Journals, TS p. 164, MTP).

————. "Soldier an' Sailor Too" (poem).
   Mark Twain quotes two lines from the poem in his "Was the World Made for Man?" (DV12, MTP), apparently written in 1903; the Pterodacty, he says there, is "a kind of a giddy harumfrodite—soldier an' sailor too!" *(WIM?,* p. 105). He jotted down three words from its text in Notebook 48—"harumfrodite," "cosmopolouse," and "procrastitute" (TS p. 18). Isabel Lyon recorded that on 26 March 1908 Clemens entertained Henry H. Rogers and other friends by reading aloud from Kipling's poetry. "He was never in better spirit—never in a completer understanding," she noted. His rendition of "Soldier an' Sailor Too," Miss Lyon averred, was "a thing never again to be repeated" (IVL Journals, TS p. 313, MTP).

————. *Soldier Stories.* New York: International Book and Publishing Co., 1899. 203 pp.
   Source: MTLAcc, entry #2307, volume donated from Clemens' library by Clara Clemens Gabrilowitsch in 1910.

————. "They" (short story).
   At luncheon on 28 January 1907 Isabel Lyon showed Clemens a copy of "They" in book form. "He read it aloud as we sat at the table," she wrote, "and he was deeply moved by its beauty and by the last part of it especially" (IVL Journals, TS p. 222, MTP).

———. "To Thomas Atkins" (poem).

In February 1891 Mark Twain considered using this poem in his public reading at Bryn Mawr (NB 30, TS p. 23). "Those barrack-room ballads were true to life," he told a newspaper reporter in 1895. "There had been nothing like them written before. For example, that one of Tommy Atkins," and Mark Twain quoted from the poem ("Mark Twain Put to the Question," [15 October?] 1895 Adelaide *South Australian Register,* undated clipping in Scrapbook #26, p. 121, MTP). "Certain of the ballads have a peculiar and satisfying charm for me," Mark Twain said in his Autobiographical Dictation for 13 August 1906 *(MTE,* p. 312)—though he did not name any titles.

———. *Traffics and Discoveries.* London: Macmillan & Co., 1904. 393 pp.
Source: MTLAcc, entry #2304, volume donated from Clemens' library by Clara Clemens Gabrilowitsch in 1910.

———. *The Works of Rudyard Kipling.* 27 vols. [Edition unspecified.] Includes: *Plain Tales from the Hills; Soldiers Three and Military Tales,* Parts I and II; *In Black and White; The Phantom 'Rickshaw; Under the Deodars and Other Stories; The Jungle Book; The Second Jungle Book; The Light That Failed* (two copies listed); *The Naulahka; Verses; Captains Courageous; The Day's Work,* Parts I and II; *From Sea to Sea,* Parts I and II; *Early Verse; Stalky and Co.; Abaft the Funnel; Puck of Pook's Hill; Many Inventions; Actions and Reactions; Traffics and Discoveries; Life's Handicap; Kim.*
Catalog: C1951, #D2 (18 volumes), #D13 (9 volumes), $72 total, listed among books signed by Clemens.

Of Kipling's writings in general, Clemens once said: "I know them better than I know anybody else's books. They never grow pale to me; they keep their color; they are always fresh" (13 August 1906 AD; *MTE,* p. 312). Indeed, every kind of evidence indicates his unstinting esteem for Kipling. Clemens' house-keeper Katy Leary recalled that "Mr. Clemens used to love to read him; he used to read aloud from Kipling and right up to the end, just before he died, he had a book of Kipling's that he read from" *(LMT,* p. 161). Clemens told Isabel Lyon that he could understand and appreciate Kipling's viewpoint, for Kipling's train-ing "makes him cling to his early beliefs; then he loves power and authority and Kingship—and that has to show itself in his religion" (IVL Journal, 22 January 1907, TS p. 220, MTP).

MTB, pp. 1208, 1440, 1540; *MTE,* pp. 54–55, 309; *MT&JB,* p. 189; *OPMT,* p. 24 (merely mentions Kipling); *FE,* chapter 54; *MT&JB,* pp. 187–195 (a care-ful treatment of the Clemens-Kipling relationship). Louis J. Budd of Duke University has compiled a collection of newspaper clippings relating to Mark Twain's world tour in 1895–96; Professor Budd reports that Mark Twain men-tioned Kipling in the following interviews with reporters: Minneapolis *Times,* 24 July 1895, p. 2; Melbourne *Argus,* 17 September 1895, p. 5; Melbourne *Age,* 27 September 1895, p. 6; Adelaide *South Australian Register,* 15 October 1895; Durban, Republic of South Africa *Weekly Natal Mercury,* 8 May 1896, p. 5989, also called *Natal Mercury* and reprinted in the *Natal Witness,* 9 May 1896, and the *Pretorian Press,* 15 May 1896, p. 3.

Kirby, William (1817–1906). *The Golden Dog (Le chien d'or). A Romance of the Days of Louis Quinze in Quebec.* Illus. Boston: L. C. Page & Co., 1900. 624 pp.
Inscription: signed "Clemens, 1902."
Catalog: A1911, #275, $1.

———. [An identical (or same?) copy.]
Source: MTLAcc, entry #2308, volume donated from Clemens' library by Clara Clemens Gabrilowitsch in 1910.

Kirby, William Egmont (b. 1867). *Insects: Foes and Friends*. Adapted from the German. Preface by W. F. Kirby. Illus. London: S. W. Partridge & Co., 1898. 138 pp.

Source: MTLAcc, entry #1962, volume donated from Clemens' library by Clara Clemens Gabrilowitsch in 1910; subsequently lost, according to the library files.

Kirk, John Foster (1824–1904). *History of Charles the Bold, Duke of Burgundy.* 3 vols. Portraits and map. Philadelphia: J. B. Lippincott & Co., 1864–68.
Catalog: A1911, #276, $3.50.

Mark Twain refers to the "unspeakable atrocities" of Charles the Bold in chapter 27 of *JA* (1896).

Kirkham, Samuel. *English Grammar in Familiar Lectures, Accompanied by a Compendium; Embracing a New Systematick Order of Parsing, a New System of Punctuation, Exercises in False Syntax, and a System of Philosophical Grammar in Notes; . . . Designed for the Use of Schools and Private Learners.* 105th Ed. Baltimore: John Plaskitt, 1835.

Inscriptions: several signatures in pencil and ink, sometimes traced in both. Two on the front free endpaper read "Saml Clemens/Hannibal, Mo." and "Sammy Clemens/Hannibal, Mo." Another appears on the rear pastedown endpaper: "Sam Clemenses/Book".

Marginalia: someone has written other names near the signatures—"John Bowman," "Lucian Gray," and "Lucien Grays Book." A pencil sketch on the front pastedown endpaper depicts the "TEECHER" threatening an angelic "SAMMY" (over whose head a halo hovers) with a rod. Someone has made a pencil note at the top of the front free endpaper: "I promise to pay $[?] Smith & Co".

Provenance: the authenticity and provenance of this volume have been in doubt since its first sale. A notarized letter laid in the volume attests that this copy of Kirkham's *Grammar* was discovered by a construction worker, Charles Lange, during the remodeling of an old printing office storeroom in La Crosse, Wisconsin. Lange's son, Edward Harving Lange, sold the book to the Glen Dawson Bookshop of Los Angeles; the notarized letter, which Charles Lange also signed, was sworn there on 17 March 1923. The younger Lange affirmed in the letter that he had owned the book "for five or six years" and that he had added no notes to it during the time it was in his possession. Lange wrote that the diary of William Yarrington, a printer's apprentice who worked for an employer named Ament in 1875, was found in the same place; an entry in the diary mentions that "Mr. Ament has given me some books on composition which I will make use of if I have time."

Location: Mark Twain Papers, Berkeley, California. Donated in May 1964 by Warren R. Howell of John Howell Books in San Francisco. A letter of 14 May 1964 from Howell to Frederick Anderson, Editor of the Mark Twain Papers, is laid in the book.

Copy examined: the volume seems to merit acceptance as one of young Clemens' school textbooks, though one wishes for additional corroboration of its authenticity. True, Clemens once worked in the Hannibal newspaper office of Joseph P. Ament. In 1875 Ament was the city mayor of Muscatine, Iowa, where he and his brother were in business together (information supplied by Ralph Gregory, author of "Joseph P. Ament—Master Printer to Sam Clemens," *Mark Twain Journal*, 18 [Summer 1976], 1–4). But the sketch of Clemens and the "TEECHER" seems almost too perfect from a twentieth-century perspective—the kind of thing that people would expect him to have drawn as a child. And Clemens was never known to use "Sammy" as a form of his name, though anything is presumably possible in schoolroom doodling. The fact remains that Clemens remembered his youthful struggles with a copy of Kirkham's *Grammar*. Moreover, a motiveless forgery in 1923 (the book very likely brought only a few dollars, despite the notarized letter) seems an improbable deed to perpetrate merely for creating a spurious association copy.

In chapter 23 of *TA* (1880) the character named Harris claims that he recalls "doubled-up have's" and other grammatical lapses in this renowned reference book. Mark Twain referred to Kirkham's *Grammar* as one of the "schoolbooks" popular "fifty or sixty years ago" in his Autobiographical Dictation of 6 January 1907 (MTP).

Kirkman, Marshall Monroe. *The Romance of Gilbert Holmes: An Historical Novel.* Chicago: The World Railway Publishing Co., 1900. 425 pp.
  Inscription: front free endpaper signed in pencil, carelessly: "Clemens/1902".
  Catalog: A1911 #277, $1.70[?].
  Location: Beinecke Rare Book and Manuscript Library, Yale University. Bookplate on the rear flyleaf indicates that Walter Francis Frear and Mary E. Dillingham Frear donated the volume in 1942.
  Copy examined: Clemens' copy, unmarked. Many leaves are unopened. An *A1911* label is pasted on the inside front cover.
  This novel opens on the Mississippi River at New Orleans. Possibly Clemens purchased it to pass the time during his railroad journey to Columbia, Missouri in 1902.

Kirlicks, John A. (d. 1923). *I've Got the Blues Tonight & Other Troubles.* Houston, 1896. 38 pp. Wrappers.
  Kevin B. Mac Donnell of Austin, Texas speculates that Isabel Lyon referred to this publication when she wrote to Kirlicks from New York City on 11 December 1907: "Mr. Clemens asks me to write for him & thank you very much for your pleasant letter & the poem & the little pamphlet. He wishes me also to say that such messages & good wishes as yours are always welcome" (TS copy in collection of Kevin B. Mac Donnell, quoted in a letter to Alan Gribben, 7 June 1977).

Kirtley, James Samuel. *The Young Man and Himself; His Tasks, His Dreams, His Purposes, . . . His Complete Life.* Intro. by Henry Hopkins. Kansas City, Missouri, 1902. 493 pp.
  The Reverend James Kirtley wrote books for the American Baptist Society and the Young People's Union; some of his writings quoted prominent people, such as his *Half-Hour Talks on Character Building by Self-Made Men and Women* (1910). On 13 November 1902 he wrote to Clemens: "I have asked the publishers to send you a copy of the book on 'The Young Man.' " He thanked Clemens for "approving my quotations from your Hannibal 'sermon' in the book" (MTP).

Kirwan, Daniel Joseph. *Palace and Hovel; or, Phases of London Life. Being Personal Observations of an American in London.* Illus. Hartford: Belknap & Bliss, 1870. 662 pp.
  Source: MTLAcc, entry #583, volume donated by Clemens.

Kittredge, George Lyman (1860–1941). *The Old Farmer and His Almanack; Being Some Observations on Life and Manners in New England a Hundred Years Ago.* Illus. Boston: William Ware and Co., 1904. 403 pp.
  Source: MTLAcc, entry #800, volume donated by Clemens.

Klein, Charles (1867–1915). *The Lion and the Mouse* (play, perf. 1905).
  Isabel Lyon noted on 6 January 1906 that she and Clemens attended this play at the Lyceum Theatre in New York City. He called it "a clean little play, but so stupid" (IVL Journals, TS p. 120, MTP).

————. *The Music Master* (play, perf. 1904).

Clemens saw David Warfield perform in a matinee of *The Music Master* on Saturday, 7 April 1906. Warfield had the part of a piano-player in a dime museum in New York City who rediscovers his lost daughter. Isabel Lyon recorded Clemens' opinion: he not only enjoyed the drama but thought it to be a better drama than Boucicault's adaptation of *Rip Van Winkle* (a major tribute coming from Clemens, who envied the popularity of that work); moreover, he believed that David Warfield was a finer actor than Joseph Jefferson in his prime (IVL Journal, Humanities Research Center, University of Texas at Austin). *MTB*, p. 1305.

————. *Two Little Vagrants* (play, perf. 1896). Adapted from Pierre Decourcelle's *Les Deux Gosses*.

Clemens jotted two entries concerning this play (which he mistakenly called *Two Little Vagabonds*) in Notebook 39 (TS pp. 22, 25) while in London in 1896.

Knapp, Adeline (1860–1909). *Upland Pastures, Being Some Out-Door Essays Dealing with the Beautiful Things That the Spring and Summer Bring.* East Aurora, New York: Roycroft Printing Shop, 1897. 62 pp. Number 92 of an edition limited to 600 copies.

Inscription: flyleaf has been torn out; it may have been signed by Clemens, the author, or the publisher (Elbert Hubbard). Initials "E H" appear on the front colophon page.

Location: Mark Twain Library, Redding, Conn.

Copy examined: Clemens' copy, unmarked.

Knife and Fork Club. Kansas City, Missouri. *The Book of the Knife and Fork Club of Kansas City, Covering the Period from December, 1898, to December, 1905.* Compiled by F. N. Tufts, J. M. Lee, J. J. Vineyard. Illus. Printed by the F. P. Burnap Stationery and Printing Co., [1906]. Unpaged. Boxed.

Inscription: inside front cover signed and inscribed in black ink: "SL. Clemens. /1906. The illustrations are bright & cunning & gracefully done. (Preserve the book.)" [The volume contains photographs and pen and ink sketches.]

Provenance: bookplate of W. T. H. Howe library is pasted above inscription on the inside front cover. A note from Isabel Lyon to Howe, dated 12 July 1936, is laid in the book: "I remember so well the winter morning at 21 Fifth Avenue, when I carried this little book to Mr. Clemens, who studied it carefully as he sat propped against his pillows in the wide Italian bed. Then he inscribed it, wrote a personal note to the sender, & handed the book back to me for safe-keeping."

Catalog: A1911, #45, $6.50.

Location: Henry W. and Albert A. Berg Collection, New York Public Library.

Copy examined: Clemens' copy, otherwise unmarked.

On 24 February 1906 Clemens refused an invitation from Govinier Hall to speak at a program of the club, but he thanked Hall for sending the book and praised its illustrations as "bright, graceful, & humorous, & eloquently competent" (ALS in MTP). Most of the speakers listed in this commemorative volume were distinguished men of Kansas and Missouri.

Knight, Charles (1791–1873), ed. *London.* 6 vols. Illus. London: Charles Knight and Co., 1841–44.

Provenance: most vols. contain the sticker of "Marshall, Bookseller & Stationer, 21 Edgware Road" inside the front covers. An *A1911* auction label is pasted on the inside front cover of each volume.

Catalog: A1911, #278, $1.75, "many of the illustrations are marked by slips of paper."

Location: Mark Twain Memorial, Hartford, Conn. Purchased for $37.50 from the Old Mystic Book Shop in 1966.

Copies examined: Clemens' copies, unmarked.
Knight's book employed different contributors for each subject, as many as twenty per volume.

————. *Studies of Shakspeare* (pub. 1849).
Clara Clemens listed this book in her commonplace book (undated entry, Paine 150, MTP).

Knight, Cornelia (1757–1837) and Thomas Raikes (1777–1848). *Personal Reminiscences.* Ed. by Richard Henry Stoddard. New York: Scribner, Armstrong and Co., 1875. 339 pp.
Inscription: endpaper signed "Saml. L. Clemens, Hartford, 1875."
Catalog: A1911, #279, $2.

Knight, Edward Frederick (1852–1925). *Where Three Empires Meet: A Narrative of Recent Travel in Kashmir, Western Tibet, Gilgit, and the Adjoining Countries.* London: Longmans, Green, and Co., 1893. 495 pp. New edition published 1894, 1895 (528 pp.).
While at sea in April [?] 1896 Mark Twain made two references to this book in Notebook 37: he cited page 61 ("for English administration in India") and page 64 ("for what India was before the English occupation") (TS p. 47).

Knight, (Mrs.) Helen (Cross) (1814–1906). *Saw Up and Saw Down; or, the Fruits of Industry and Self-Reliance.* New York: Am. Female Guardian Society, 1852. 32 pp.
Source: MTLAcc, entry #1894, volume donated from Clemens' library by Clara Clemens Gabrilowitsch in 1910.

Knighton, William (1834–1900). *The Private Life of an Eastern King. By a Member of the Household of His Late Majesty, Nussir-u-Deen, King of Oude.* London: Hope and Co., 1855. 330 pp. Revised edition pub. 1856.
Nāsir al-Dīn, King of Oudh, died in 1837. Clemens made a note on 21 January 1896 in Bombay: "Private Life of an Eastern King—Chelsea Library. *Get it"* (NB 36, TS p. 22). On 22 October 1896 he jotted down a memorandum that he had withdrawn this book from the London Library (NB 39, TS p. 12).

Knowles, James Sheridan (1784–1862). *William Tell* (play, perf. 1825).
Mark Twain referred to this perennial favorite in "The Indignity Put Upon the Remains of George Holland by the Rev. Mr. Sabine" (1871): ten preachers cannot "hold their own against any one of five hundred William Tells that can be raised up upon five hundred stages in the land at a day's notice" *(WIM?,* p. 53).

Knox, Isa (Craig) (1831–1903). *The Little Folks' History of England.* Illus. by R. E. Gallindo and others. New York and London: Cassell & Co., n.d. 284 pp.
On 1 January 1881 Brown & Gross, Hartford booksellers, billed Clemens for "1 Craig Knox England" purchased for .80¢ on 24 November 1880. Clemens paid for the book on 17 January 1881 (receipt in MTP).

Knox, Thomas Wallace (1835–1896). *Backsheesh! or, Life and Adventures in the Orient.* Illus. Hartford: A. D. Worthington & Co., 1875. 694 pp.
Source: MTLAcc, entry #584, volume donated by Clemens.

————. *The Boy Travellers in Australasia.* Illus. New York: Harper & Brothers, 1899. 538 pp.
Source: MTLAcc, entry #475, volume donated by Clemens.

————. *The Boy Travellers in Central Europe*. Illus. New York: Harper & Brothers, [cop. 1889]. 532 pp.
Source: MTLAcc, entry #477, volume donated by Clemens.

————. *The Boy Travellers in Mexico*. Illus. New York: Harper & Brothers, 1905. 552 pp.
Source: MTLAcc, entry #478, volume donated by Clemens.

————. *The Boy Travellers in Northern Europe*. Illus. New York: Harper & Brothers, 1905. 531 pp.
Source: MTLAcc, entry #476, volume donated by Clemens.

————. *The Boy Travellers in South America*. Illus. New York: Harper & Brothers, [cop. 1885]. 510 pp.
Source: MTLAcc, entry #473, volume donated by Clemens.

————. *The Boy Travellers in the Far East . . . in a Journey to Japan and China*. Illus. New York: Harper & Brothers, [cop. 1879]. 421 pp.
Source: MTLAcc, entry #468, volume donated by Clemens.

————. *The Boy Travellers in the Far East; Part Second, . . . in a Journey to Siam and Java*. Illus. New York: Harper & Brothers, [cop. 1880]. 446 pp.
Source: MTLAcc, entry #469, volume donated by Clemens.

————. *The Boy Travellers in the Far East; Part Third, . . . in a Journey to Ceylon and India*. Illus. New York: Harper & Brothers, [cop. 1881]. 483 pp.
Source: MTLAcc, entry #470, volume donated by Clemens.

————. *The Boy Travellers in the Far East; Part Fourth, . . . in a Journey to Egypt and the Holy Land*. Illus. New York: Harper & Brothers, 1905. 438 pp.
Source: MTLAcc, entry #471, volume donated by Clemens.

————. *The Boy Travellers in the Far East; Part Fifth, . . . in a Journey Through Africa*. Illus. New York: Harper & Brothers, 1905. 473 pp.
Source: MTLAcc, entry #472, volume donated by Clemens.

————. *The Boy Travellers in the Russian Empire*. Illus. New York: Harper & Brothers, 1905. 505 pp.
Source: MTLAcc, entry #474, volume donated by Clemens.

————. *Overland Through Asia; Pictures of Siberian, Chinese, and Tartar Life*. Hartford, Conn.: American Publishing Co., 1871. 608 pp.
Clemens purchased this volume at the wholesale price of $1.30 on 8 December 1876, according to a bill from the American Publishing Company (Scrapbook #10, p. 77, MTP).

Kock, Charles Paul de (1793–1871).
Kock wrote vaudevilles and stories such as *Le Barbier de Paris* (1829). Henry Fisher recalled that Clemens referred to Kock derogatorily when Clemens was in Europe in the mid-nineties (Fisher dates the conversation as the year William Jennings Bryan was defeated in a contest for the U. S. Senate, an event that occurred in both 1893 and 1895). According to Fisher, Clemens remarked that Kock's books ranked even below French novels *(AMT,* p. 116).

Kock, Rosalie (1810–1880). *Der berggeist im Riesengebirge*. Illus. Berlin: Winckelmann und söhne, [18—?]. 249 pp.
Source: MTLAcc, entry #1679, volume donated by Clemens.

The Koran: Commonly Called the Alkoran of Mohammed. Translated into English from the Original Arabic. With Explanatory Notes. Intro. by George Sale (1697?–1736). London: Frederick Warne and Co., n.d. 470 pp.
   Inscription: pencil note on title page: "S. L. Clemens' signature in book when received—signature now missing".
   Location: Mark Twain Library, Redding, Conn.
   Copy examined: Clemens' copy, unmarked. Accession #2667.

The Koran: Commonly Called the Alkoran of Mohammed. Translated into English from the Original Arabic, by George Sale [1697?–1736]. New York: American Book Exchange, 1880.
   Inscription: "S. L. Clemens/Hartford, Conn./1880." Inscription later reported to be missing.
   Source: card catalog of Mark Twain Library, Redding, Conn. In 1979 the volume could not be found.
   Mark Twain mentions the *Koran* in chapters 9 and 34 of *IA* (1869) and—politely—in Notebook 28 (March 1889), TS p. 49. Huckleberry Finn refers to "the Koran, which they think is a Bible," in chapter 13 of *Tom Sawyer Abroad* (1894). Mark Twain's most extensive comment on this book occurs in "Autobiography of a Damned Fool" (written 1877), where he ascribes to Orion Clemens a brief faith in the Islam religion, along with a conviction that he must assemble a harem. "I had diligently and thoughtfully read the Koran during my sickness," Orion says, "and was now a firm and restful believer in the religion of Mahomet" (*S&B*, p. 145).

Kossuth, Lajos (1820–1894).
   An epigram from Kossuth's speeches or writings heads the preface to Mark Twain's *JA* (1896): "Consider this unique and imposing distinction. Since the writing of human history began, Joan of Arc is the only person, of either sex, who has ever held supreme command of the military forces of a nation *at the age of seventeen.*" On 28 July 1901 Clemens quipped: "Kossuth couldn't raise 30 cents in Congress, now, if he were back with his moving Magyar-Tale" (Clemens to Joseph H. Twichell, *MTL*, p. 711).

Kotzwara, Franz, composer. "The battle of Prague" (piano solo, 1793?).
   This favorite American parlor piece has no words and therefore does not properly belong in a catalog of Clemens' library and reading, but surely an exception can be made for such an important constituent of his musical knowledge. Mark Twain recorded how he endured a rendition of "The Battle of Prague" while he was in Interlaken on 22 August 1878: a young woman "tackled an old rattle trap piano with such vigor & absence of expression . . . that she soon cleaned out the great reading room" (NB 15, *N&J*, 2: 142). Recounting the same incident in chapter 32 of *TA* (1880), Mark Twain related the manner in which she "turned on all the horrors of the 'Battle of Prague,' that venerable shivaree, and waded chin deep in the blood of the slain." This musical score was among those he noted on the piano in "The House Beautiful," chapter 38 of *LonMiss* (1883). Huckleberry Finn heard the girls in the Grangerford household play "The Battle of Prague" on their tinny old piano (ch. 17, *HF* [1885]).
   PMT, p. 326; Joseph Slater, "Music at Col. Grangerford's" (1949), 108–111; Arthur M. Kompass, "Twain's Use of Music" (1964), p. 617 n. 2.

Kraatz, Curt and M. Neal. *The Mountain Climber* (three-act farce, perf. 1906).
   Charles Frohman produced this play on 5 March 1906 at his Criterion Theatre in New York City (*Best Plays of 1899–1909*, 1: 510). Isabel Lyon probably echoed Clemens' opinion by reporting that on 26 March 1906 "after dinner we went up to see Francis Wilson in 'The Mountain Climbers' [sic]. It was a foolish enough play, but the Vorses are lovely and Rodman Gilder was handsome" (IVL Journals, TS p. 152, MTP).

Krauser, Rudolf. *Starters and Regulators.* Illus. New York: Harper & Brothers, 1904. 132 pp.
 Source: MTLAcc, entry #1374, volume donated by Clemens.

Kravchinski, Sergei Mikhailovich (1852–1895), pseud. "Stepniak." *Russia Under the Tsars.* Trans. by William Westall. "Authorized Edition." New York: Charles Scribner's Sons, 1885. 381 pp.
 Catalog: C1951, #O2, listed among books containing Olivia Clemens' signature, no edition specified.

————. *Underground Russia: Revolutionary Profiles and Sketches from Life.* Preface by Petr A. Lavrof. Trans. from the Italian. Second edition. New York: Charles Scribner's Sons, 1885. 272 pp. Reprinted in 1888.
 Inscription: a note to Clemens by the author.
 Catalog: C1951, #53c, $10, listed among the books signed by Clemens, no edition specified.
 William Dean Howells sent Clemens a letter of 11 April 1891 to introduce Kravchinski, a Russian exile who had settled in London *(MTHL,* p. 643). Kravchinski visited the Clemenses in Hartford in April 1891, and Kravchinski's letter of 19 April 1891 to Olivia Clemens mentions that he has sent Clemens a copy of *Underground Russia* (ALS in Samossoud Collection, TS in MTP).
 Louis J. Budd, "Twain, Howells, and the Boston Nihilists" (1959).

[Kremnitz, Fran Marie Charlotte (von Bardeleben) (1852–1916)]. *Reminiscences of the King of Roumania.* Ed. with intro. by Sidney Whitman. Authorized Edition. New York: Harper & Brothers, 1899. 367 pp.
 Source: MTLAcc, entry #1782, volume donated by Clemens.

Krippen Kalender. [Unidentified publication.] 1899. 788 pp.
 Source: MTLAcc, entry #1681, volume donated by Clemens.

Krout, Mary Hannah.
 In chapter 3 of *FE* (1897) Mark Twain quotes from "a sketch by Mrs. Mary H. Krout" which enables him "to perceive what the Honolulu of to-day is, as compared with the Honolulu of my time." Obviously he extracted these quotations before Mrs. Krout issued her *Hawaii and a Revolution: The Personal Experiences of a Newspaper Correspondent* (London and New York, 1898). Francis V. Madigan, Jr.—"Mark Twain's Passage to India" (1974), p. 361—explains that Mark Twain consulted her newspaper columns describing the Hawaiian political turmoil of the 1890's.

Kubinyi, Victor von (b. 1875). *The King of Rome; A Biography.* Illus. New York: Knickerbocker Press, 1907. 116 pp.
 Source: MTLAcc, entry #1214, volume donated by Isabel V. Lyon, Clemens' secretary. Fine binding, boxed.

Kuehn, Herman (1853–1918), pseud. "Evelyn Gladys." *Thoughts of a Fool.* Chicago: E. P. Rosenthal and Co., 1905. 258 pp.
 Source: MTLAcc, entry #794, volume donated by Clemens.
 Kuehn's publisher sent a complimentary copy to Clemens on 7 April 1905, asking his opinion of whether "the fool who thought the thoughts, . . . thought something funny" (E. P. Rosenthal to Clemens, MTP). Rosenthal refers to the author as a woman. Previously Rosenthal's firm had presented Clemens with a copy of Oscar L. Triggs' *Chapters in the History of the Arts and Crafts Movement* (1902).

Kugler, Franz Theodor (1808–1858). *Handbook of Painting: The German, Flemish, and Dutch Schools.* Based on the Handbook of Kugler as Revised by Gustav Friedrich Waagen. A New Edition, Revised by J. A. Crowe. 2 vols. Illus. London: J. Murray, 1874.
 Catalog: A1911, #219, $4.50 total (sold with next entry here).

————. *Handbook of Painting: The Italian Schools.* Based on the Handbook of Kugler as Revised by Charles L. Eastlake. Fourth Edition. Revised by Elizabeth Eastlake. 2 vols. Illus. London: J. Murray, 1874.
 Catalog: A1911, #219, $4.50 total (sold with preceding entry here).

Kuka, Meherjibhai Nosherwanji, compiler and translator. *The Wit and Humour of the Persians.* Illus. Bombay: Printed at the Education Society's Steam Press, 1894. 255 pp.
 Inscription: (on verso of dedication page) "To/Samuel Clemens Esquire/alias 'Mark Twain'/with the respectful compliments/of the author/M. N. Kuka". A letter from Kuka to Clemens, Bombay, 25 January 1896, is mounted on the leaf facing the title-page.
 Marginalia: Clemens' comments and markings register his distaste for some of the Persian humor represented in this volume; "Witless Rubbish," he remarked on page 33. But on page 37 he pronounced "good" a simile that compares a large city to the setting of a ring designed for holding the turquoise stone of the sky. Clemens made penciled markings and notations on pages 32, 33, 35, 36 ("Perhaps was neat in the original," he wrote), 37, 38 ("Untranslatable"), 39, 40.
 Provenance: carries the bookstamps and accession number of the Mark Twain Library, Redding, Connecticut.
 Catalog: Mott 1952, item #62, $37.50.
 Location: Mark Twain Papers, Berkeley, California.
 Copy examined: Clemens' copy.

Labouchère, Henry Du Pre (1831–1912), editor of *Truth* (London periodical, 1877–1957).
 At one time Mark Twain became fascinated by the weekly column titled "Legal Pillory" that Labouchère compiled for *Truth.* In an unpublished essay, "Labouchère's 'Legal Pillory,'" Mark Twain condemns the English game-poaching laws and the courts that enforce them; he bases his remarks on this "most interesting literature—and the most blood-stirring—to be found anywhere in print, it seems to me" (MS in DV72, MTP). From Labouchère he learned that it is better to face a magistrate on charges of wife-beating than to be tried for poaching. Filed with Twain's manuscript is a packet of clippings in an envelope from the Players Club of New York City. Each clipping is marked "A" and details various cases in which the penalties for heinous crimes against persons seem ludicrously lenient. Presumably these were clipped from the "Legal Pillory" column in *Truth.* The only clue to the dating of the manuscript is Mark Twain's remark within it that Labouchère has cited abuses of legal authority "fifty times a year for the past two years or thereabouts."

Laboulaye, Édouard de (1811–1883). *Laboulaye's Fairy Book; Fairy Tales of All Nations.* Trans. by Mary Louise Booth (1831–1889). Illus. New York: Harper & Brothers, [cop. 1866]. 363 pp.
 Source: MTLAcc, entry #1177, volume donated by Clemens.

————. *Last Fairy Tales.* Trans. by Mary Louise Booth (1831–1889). New York: Harper & Brothers, [cop. 1884]. 382 pp.
 Source: MTLAcc, entry #1602, volume donated by Clemens.

————. *Last Fairy Tales*. Trans. by Mary Louise Booth. New York: Harper & Brothers, 1885. 382 pp.

Source: MTLAcc, entry #1895, volume donated from Clemens' library by Clara Clemens Gabrilowitsch in 1910.

Lacombe, Paul (1834–1919). *Arms and Armour in Antiquity and the Middle Ages; Also a Descriptive Note of Modern Weapons*. Trans. from French, and with a preface, notes, and an additional chapter on arms and armour in England, by Charles Boutell (1812–1877). New York: D. Appleton & Co., 1870. 296 pp.

Source: MTLAcc, entry #2002, volume donated from Clemens' library by Clara Clemens Gabrilowitsch in 1910.

Lacroix, Paul (1806–1884). *The Arts in the Middle Ages, and at the Period of the Renaissance*. Illus. by F. Kellerhoven. "Fourth Thousand." New York: D. Appleton and Co., 1875. 520 pp.

Inscription: front free endpaper signed in pencil: "SL. Clemens/Hartford 1876". The number "5c" appears in pencil on the front pastedown endpaper.

Catalog: C1951, #5c.

Location: collection of W. C. Attal, Jr., Austin, Texas. Purchased from R. Harbey of Houston, Texas.

Copy examined: Clemens' copy, unmarked. Spine is broken.

————. *Manners, Customs, and Dress During the Middle Ages, and During the Renaissance Period*. Illus. by F. Kellerhoven. London: Chapman and Hall, 1874. 554 pp.

Inscriptions: front free endpaper signed in black ink: "Saml. L. Clemens/London, Nov. 1873." The number "5c" appears in pencil on the front pastedown endpaper.

Marginalia: "Table of Illustrations" (pp. xiii–xiv) heavily marked in pencil from (alphabetically) "Anne of Brittany" to "Butler at his Duties," also from "Cook, The Sixteenth Century" to "Costume of Emperors at Their Coronation." On page 329 Clemens corrected the figure 24,000 francs to read "2,400 francs," adding a vertical pencil line beside the revision. On page 345 he drew double pencil brackets at the fourth line from the bottom, which reads: "The King was forbidden from granting written orders *(praecepta)* for carrying off rich widows, young virgins, and nuns."

Catalog: C1951, #5c.

Location: collection of W. C. Attal, Jr., Austin Texas. Purchased from R. Harbey of Houston, Texas.

Copy examined: Clemens' copy. Broken spine (half of it is missing).

The Ladies' Home Journal (Philadelphia periodical, pub. 1883–   ).

In April 1891 Clemens mentioned the journal and its founder, Edward W. Bok, in Notebook 30 (TS p. 34). Clemens was embarrassed by an article about himself which appeared in the October 1898 issue (he generally disliked these biographical sketches, arguing that they should be withheld during an author's lifetime); he scoffed at the writer of this essay, James B. Pond, "who emptied that sewage down the back of the Chambermaid's Home Journal" (Clemens to Henry H. Rogers, Vienna, 17 November 1898, *MTHHR*, p. 379).

La Fontaine, Jean de (1621–1695). *Fables*. Paris, 1890. [Edition undetermined; possibly *Fables avec les dessins de Gustave Doré*. Paris: Hachette et cie, 1890. 864 pp.]

Inscription: inscribed by Jean Clemens in Paris on 2 February 1894.

Catalog: Mott 1952, item #63, $3.

————. *Fables de J. De La Fontaine.* Ed. par Décembre Alonzier. Paris: Bernardin-Bechet, 1875.

Inscription: flyleaf signed "Olivia L. Clemens/Hartford/Ct."

Marginalia: corner of page 238 is folded over at "Le rat et l'éléphant."

Location: Carrie Estelle Doheny Collection, St. John's Seminary, Camarillo, Ca. Donated by Mrs. Doheny after she purchased it from Maxwell Hunley Rare Books of Beverly Hills in 1940. Price $12.20.

Copy examined: Livy Clemens' unmarked copy.

Minnie M. Brashear correctly noted that despite Mark Twain's efforts to write fables, "no reference to Aesop or La Fontaine is to be found in his writings" (*MTSM*, p. 233).

Laighton, Albert (1829–1887). *Poems by Albert Laighton.* Boston: Brown, Taggard & Chase; Portsmouth, N.H.: J. H. Foster, 1859. 135 pp.

Inscription: "To Frank Fuller, with the best wishes of his friend, Albert Laighton."

Catalog: A1911, #281, .50¢.

Clemens knew Frank Fuller when he was a prominent political figure in the territories of Utah and Nevada during the Civil War; the men remained friends when Fuller later moved to New York City and operated a soap and health food company.

Lamar, John B. "Polly Peablossom's Wedding" (pub. 1842, collected in Lamar's *Homespun Yarns* in 1851).

Bernard DeVoto points out unmistakable correspondences between Lamar's sketch, which was widely circulated in the frontier press, and Mark Twain's "Ye Sentimental Law Student," a sketch written for the Virginia City *Territorial Enterprise (MTAm,* pp. 157–158).

Lamartine, Alphonse Marie Louis de (1790–1869). "Heloise," *Memoirs of Celebrated Characters.* 3 vols. New York: Harper & Brothers, 1854, 1: 138. [The edition that Clemens consulted is not known.]

"Such is the story of Abelard and Heloise. Such is the history that Lamartine has shed such cataracts of tears over" (*IA* [1869], ch. 15). Livy Langdon's commonplace book contains several quotations attributed to an unidentified work by Lamartine; Livy copied these around 1866 or 1867 (DV161, MTP). See the entry for Orlando W. Wight.

————. *A Pilgrimage to the Holy Land; Comprising Recollections, Sketches, and Reflections Made During a Tour in the East, in 1832–1833* (pub. 1835). Reprinted in New York by Appleton in 1848.

In chapter 55 of *IA* (1869) Mark Twain predicted that the pilgrims will say they were sorry to leave Palestine, for "they do not wish to array themselves against all the Lamartines and Grimeses in the world."

Lamb, Charles (1775–1834). "A Dissertation Upon Roast Pig," *Essays of Elia. First Series* (pub. 1823).

Mark Twain included "Lamb's Origin of Roast Pig" in a list of mostly American humorous writers he was considering for inclusion in an anthology (Notebook 19 [1880], *N&J,* 2: 363).

————. *The Last Essays of Elia.* New York: International Book Co., [1885?]. 163 pp.

Source: MTLAcc, entry #900, volume donated by Clemens.

————. "Specimens from the Writings of Fuller, The Church Historian," collected in *Rosamund Gray, Essays, Letters, and Poems* (pub. 1849).

Clemens referred to this essay in a letter he wrote to Mollie Fairbanks on 9 February 1876: "There is an old book by Thomas Fuller—I have forgotten its name, but I think Charles Lamb devotes a chapter to it. . . . Old Fuller . . . boils an elaborate thought down & compresses it into a single crisp & meaty sentence. It is a wonderful faculty. When I had the book I purposed searching out & jotting down a lot of these pemmican sentences, . . . but I neglected it, of course. . . . I remember that to express pompous & empty show, old Fuller uses a figure something like this: 'They that are many stories high, are usually found to be but indifferently furnished in the cockloft' " *(MTMF,* pp. 195–196). Clemens' version compares well with the sentence Lamb actually quotes regarding *"Intellect in a very Tall One.*—'Oftimes such who are built four stories high, are observed to have little in their cockloft.' " Lamb offers numerous pithy observations by Fuller because "his works are now scarcely perused but by antiquaries" *(Works of Charles Lamb,* 5 vols. [New York: W. J. Widdleton, 1870], 4: 128).

————and Mary Ann Lamb (1764–1849). *Tales from Shakespeare.* Illus. by John Moyr Smith. London: Chatto and Windus, 1879. 270 pp.
   Source: MTLAcc, entry #1929, volume donated from Clemens' library by Clara Clemens Gabrilowitsch in 1910.

————. *The Works of Charles Lamb.* 5 vols. New York: H. W. Derby, 1859–61. Each volume contains an individual title-page: (vol. 1) *The Life and Letters of Charles Lamb,* ed. by Thomas Noon Talfourd [1795–1854]; (vol. 2) *The Essays of Elia. A New Edition;* (vol. 3) *Rosamund Gray, Essays, Letters, and Poems;* (vol. 4) *Specimens of the English Dramatic Poets. A New Edition;* (vol. 5) *The Final Memorials of Charles Lamb,* ed. by Thomas Noon Talfourd.
   Inscriptions: flyleaves torn out of vols. 1–4.
   Location: vols. 1–4 are in the Mark Twain Library, Redding, Conn.; vol. 5 is missing. I discovered these four volumes on the circulation shelves when I visited the Mark Twain Library in September 1970. Because the flyleaves were torn out in the same manner as those from other volumes definitely belonging to Clemens' library, and since Clemens' copies of Lamb's works have never been located, I asked the librarian at Redding to place these volumes in the special bookcase with Clemens' library books, as a precautionary measure.
   Copies examined: possibly Clemens' copies. They lack inscriptions or marginalia that might reveal the identities of previous owners.
   Clemens' references to Lamb are mostly unfavorable in tone. "No, I detest Lamb," Clemens insisted on 25 November 1874 in reply to William Dean Howells' suggestion that the style of Clemens' earlier (16 November 1874) letter resembled Lamb's. Howells jokingly contended that Clemens' real initials might be "C. L. Clemens," but Clemens responded: "I am named after more obscure but nobler beings" *(MTHL,* pp. 42, 44), Clemens mentioned Lamb in a letter written to Mrs. Fairbanks on 31 October 1877, merely referring to Lamb's being a famous author *(MTMF,* p. 212). Rereading Bret Harte's writings on 23 March 1882, Clemens complained to Howells that Harte seemed "as slovenly as Thackeray, and as dull as Charles Lamb" *(MTHL,* p. 396.) In June 1882 Clemens made a stern memorandum for his Mississippi River travel book: "Make no end of Chas. Lamb, & people who have been educated to think him readable, & really *do* think him so. The same prejudice of education in favor of some other passè authors" (NB 20, *N&J,* 2: 489). Lamb is mentioned in a cryptic but adverse connection with Sydney Smith and Thomas Bailey Aldrich (NB 24 [June 1885], TS p. 28). Paradoxically, Mark Twain alluded to Lamb with seeming esteem in a newspaper interview a decade later: "Look at Lamb, getting the quaintest, most spirit-moving effects with the tears just trembling on the verge of every jest" ("Visit of Mark Twain," Sydney [Australia] *Morning Herald,* 17 September 1895, pp. 5–6). The next year, however, the Reverend Joseph H. Twichell testified otherwise: "He does not much enjoy Charles Lamb," wrote Twichell, who considered this a "surprising" literary aversion ("Mark Twain," p. 822).

Lambert, B. *The History and Survey of London and Its Environs from the Earliest Period to the Present Time.* 4 vols. Plates, portraits, maps. London: Printed for T. Hughes and M. Jones by Dewick and Clarke, 1806.
    Catalog: A1911, #282, $1.50.

Lamon, Ward Hill (1828–1893).
    In Berlin in 1891 Clemens and Henry Fisher met Lamon, author of *The Life of Abraham Lincoln* (1872). Lamon told Clemens some anecdotes about Lincoln (*AMT,* pp. xviii, 118).

La Motte-Fouqué, Friedrich Heinrich Karl (1777–1843). *Undine.* Edition unknown (title-page missing).
    Inscriptions: signed in black ink, "Livy L. Clemens/Munich/1879," to which has been added (in pencil): "To/Susy Clemens/Hartford/April 1882."
    Location: Mark Twain Library, Redding, Conn.
    Copy examined: Livy Clemens' copy, later Susy Clemens'.

————. *Undine.* [Another copy.]
    Catalog: C1951, #J2, listed among the books of Jean and Clara Clemens. Was this the same copy offered for sale at the 1911 auction?

————. *Undine: A Romance, and Sintram and His Companions.* Illus. by Heywood Sumner. New York: G. P. Putnam's Sons, [1888]. 384 pp.
    Inscription: presented to Miss Clemens by Charles Dudley Warner.
    Catalog: A1911, #171, $3.50.

Lampman, Archibald (1861–1899).
    In the summer of 1889 Clemens made a note of "Lampman's Poems" (NB 29, TS p. 18), evidently referring to the Canadian poet. Perhaps Clemens had heard about Lampman's *Among the Millet, and Other Poems* (1888).

Lampton, William James (d. 1917). *Yawps, and Other Things.* Philadelphia: Henry Altemus Co., [cop. 1900]. 196 pp.
    Source: MTLAcc, entry #645, volume donated by Clemens.

————. [Another identical copy.]
    Source: MTLAcc, entry #1268, volume donated by Clemens.
    Mark Twain scoffed at the sentiments in a poem from this collection—"Ready If Needed"—as they reflected the American invasion of the Philippines (letter from Clemens to Lampton, published in *Army and Navy Journal,* 28 (23 March 1901], TS in MTP). He mentioned and quoted Lampton's poem titled "The Twentieth Century" *(Pearson's Magazine* [1 January 1901], 1) in an unpublished piece, "The Stupendous International Procession."

The Land of the Morning Calm [unidentified publication].
    In March 1888 Clemens noted "The Land of the Morning Calm, Ticknor" (NB 27, TS p. 60), possibly a book title.

Landon, Melville De Lancey (1839–1910), pseud. "Eli Perkins." *Saratoga in 1901. Fun, Love, Society and Satire.* Illus. by Arthur Lumley. New York: Sheldon & Co., 1872. 249 pp.
    Inscription: on the flyleaf Clemens wrote in pencil (large, bold script): "Saratoga in 1891/or,/The Droolings of an Idiot."
    Marginalia: in penciled comments throughout the book Clemens calls Perkins a "humbug," "sham" (p. 104), "cur" (p. 129), and "little-minded person" (p. 186), whose jokes and sketches are the "Wailings of an Idiot" (p. 152). On page 124 Clemens accuses him of repeating an "Ancient Californian Joke from John Phoenix"; on pages 131, 134, 135, and 145 Clemens charges him with using material from Artemus Ward ("Stolen—& poorly stolen at that," Clemens sneers

on page 134); and on page 187 Clemens notices that Perkins is "stealing [Josh] Billings's style." Additional claims of theft appear on pages 94, 132, 180, 189, and 190. Clemens wrote and underscored the word *"lie"* beside Perkins' reference to "my old friend, Artemus Ward (whose biography I have written to be published by Carleton)" (p. 98). At the bottom of page 99 Clemens observed smugly: "Evidently there were some people there with brains enough to estimate this foetus at his correct value." Clemens' vicious marginal notes qualify this book for inclusion in his hypothetical "Library of Literary Hogwash." The Mark Twain Papers at Berkeley contain photocopies of twenty-seven pages of Clemens' marginalia.

Location: Mark Twain Library, Redding, Conn. Donated by Clemens (MTLAcc, entry #362).

Copy examined: Clemens' copy.

In an Autobiographical Dictation of 31 July 1906, Mark Twain mentioned Eli Perkins among the American humorists whose fame passed within a few years (*MTE*, p. 201).

Landor, Arnold Henry Savage (1865–1924). *The Gems of the East; Sixteen Thousand Miles of Research Travel Among . . . Enchanting Islands.* Illus. New York: Harper & Brothers, 1904. 567 pp.

Source: MTLAcc, entry #1721, volume donated by Clemens.

Landor, Walter Savage (1775–1864).

Clemens knew that Professor Willard Fisk's villa "is the one which Walter Savage Landor lived in so many years" (NB 32 [May 1892], TS p. 8).

Lane, (Mrs.) Elinor (Macartney) (d. 1909). *Katrine, A Novel.* New York: Harper & Brothers, 1909. 315 pp.

Source: MTLAcc, entry #1441, volume donated by Clemens.

Lang, Andrew (1844–1912). *The Maid of France, Being the Story of the Life and Death of Jeanne d'Arc.* Portraits. London: Longmans, Green and Co., 1908. 379 pp. Reprinted in 1909.

Catalog: C1951, #90c, $15, listed among the books signed by Clemens.

———. *A Monk of Fife: A Romance of the Days of Jeanne d'Arc, Done into English from the Manuscript in the Scots College of Ratisbon.* London: Longmans, Green and Co., 1895.

Having "just finished" reading this book in Pretoria, South Africa on 25 May 1896, Clemens wrote to Livy to say that he was sending it along to her. On 7 June 1896 he mentioned the book in another letter, this one written in King Williams Town, Cape Colony, adding, "Hope you got it" (both ALS in Samossoud Collection, TS in MTP).

———. *Old Friends: Essays in Epistolary Parody.* London: Longmans, Green and Co., 1890. 205 pp. Edition limited to 150 copies.

Catalog: A1911, #283, $3.

Langland, William (1332?–1400?).

In "Captain Stormfield's Visit to Heaven" (1909) Sandy McWilliams reports having "had some talk with one Langland and a man by the name of Chaucer—old-time poets—but it was no use, I couldn't quite understand them, and they couldn't quite understand me" (*RP*, p. 78).

Langmann, Philipp (1862–1931). *Bartel Turaser, drama in drei Akten.* Leipzig: R. Friese, 1897. 107 pp.

On 15 March 1898 Clemens informed Henry H. Rogers from Vienna that he planned to translate this "melancholy" play, a "dismal but interesting piece" currently enjoying popularity in three European countries. "It's the quaintest thing—doesn't much resemble a play—but it crowds the houses every time it is billed" *(MTHHR,* p. 326). Clemens sent his adaptation to Rogers on 22 March 1898: "With the right actor for the chief part, it is bound to go, I suppose. . . . If it goes in America I will then try it in England" *(MTHHR,* pp. 333–334). None of Clemens' translation is known to survive.

Lanigan, George Thomas (1846–1886), pseud. "G. Washington Aesop." *Fables by G. Washington Aesop, Taken "Anywhere, Anywhere, Out of the World."* Illus. by F[rederick] S[tuart] Church. New York: The World, 1878.
 Inscription: twice signed "S. L. Clemens, 1877."
 Catalog: A1911, #2, $2.50.

————. *Fables by G. Washington Aesop, Taken "Anywhere, Anywhere, Out of the World."* Illus. by F[rederick] S[tuart] Church. New York: The World, 1878.
 Inscription: inner front cover signed "SL. Clemens's book./Nov. '05." Pasted above the signature is a newspaper clipping of Lanigan's poem titled "A Threnody" ("The Ahkoond [*sic*] of Swat").
 Location: the collection of Professor Bigelow Paine Cushman, Department of English, Western Connecticut State College, Danbury, Conn.
 Copy examined: I am grateful to Professor Cushman for a photocopy of Clemens' inscription and for all of the information supplied here.
 On 14 July 1880 Estes & Lauriat of Boston charged Clemens $1.35 for "1 Aesop"; Clemens paid the bill on 20 July 1880 (receipt in MTP). This presumably referred to Clemens' copy of *Bewick's Select Fables of Aesop,* but it is conceivable that Clemens bought a second copy of *Fables by G. Washington Aesop* at this time. In any event, he repeatedly included Lanigan's book title among lists of materials he intended to evaluate for a proposed anthology of humor; he constructed these lists of humorous works twice in 1880, one of them late in July (NB 19); another in 1881 (NB 19); and one in March 1882 (NB 20, *N&J,* 2: 365, 366, 429, 450). When *Mark Twain's Library of Humor* eventually issued in 1888 it contained eight of Lanigan's fables collected from the New York *World* in his *Fables* (1878): "The Villager and the Snake," "The Grasshopper and the Ant," "The Merchant of Venice," "The Good Samaritan," "The Centipede and the Barbaric Yak," "The Kind-Hearted She-Elephant," "The Fox and the Crow," and "The Ostrich and the Hen."

————. "A Threnody" (humorous poem, pub. 1878).
 Lanigan wrote humorous rhymes as well as prose "fables." His most popular poem was the often-reprinted "A Threnody," which begins: "What, what, what,/ What's the news from Swat?/Sad news,/Bad news/ . . . Your great Akhoond is dead!/That's Swat's the matter!" Lanigan's doggerel was inspired by London newspaper notices of the death on 17 January 1878 of Abdul Ghafur, the aged Akhoond of the territory of Swat on the northwest border of India. Rossiter Johnson soon published Lanigan's jingle in an anthology *(Play-day Poems* [New York: Henry Holt and Co., 1878], pp. 191–192), and it became a great favorite in American newspapers.
 Clemens pasted a newspaper clipping of Lanigan's "Threnody" in the copy of *Fables* signed in 1905; the poem is introduced there by the editor of "Notes and Queries," who writes: "During the last six months I have been several times asked by different correspondents to publish a correct copy of the late G. T. Lanigan's verses. I now reprint them under their original title" ["A Threnody"]. Mark Twain evidently intended to include the piece in his anthology of American humor, for he referred to it four times in his notebooks of 1880 and 1881 (NB

19 and NB 20, *N&J*, 2: 365, 366, 429, 450); yet for some reason it does not appear in *Mark Twain's Library of Humor* (1888). Later Mark Twain mentioned "the Ahkoond [*sic*] of Swat" among a catalogue of "sounding titles" he enjoyed hearing in Bombay (NB 36 [January 1896], TS p. 21), and in Jeypore he reminded himself to quote the poem in his next travel book (NB 36, TS p. 55). Chapter 39 of *FE* (1897) lists "the Ahkoond of Swat's" title among the "sumptuous" names of India.

Lardner, Lena Bogardus (Phillips) (1834–1918). *"This Spray of Western Pine."* New York: Broadway Publishing Co., 1903. 46 pp.

On 23 July 1904 the authoress wrote to Clemens from her home in Niles, Michigan: "As a mark of loving admiration for our country's best author, I have sent—(thru my publisher,) my simple little volumes of prose and verse" (MTP). She also enclosed a small advertising leaflet puffing *"This Spray of Western Pine"* as "a dainty book of dainty verse, daintily produced. Illustrated prettily" (MTP). Clemens wrote on the envelope, "Wait for this book."

Larive et Fleury. *La deuxième anné de grammaire: revision, syntaxe, style, littérature, histoire littéraire, 380 exercises, lezique, 80 redactions nouvelles.* [Sixty-sixth edition.] Paris: Armand Colin et Cie, n.d. 240 pp. Originally pub. 1877.

Inscription: "Jean Clemens/Convent Assomption/Le 10 Janvier 1894/Paris./Convent de l'Assomption".

Location: Mark Twain Library, Redding, Conn.

Copy examined: Jean Clemens' unmarked copy.

[Larkin, George.] *The Visions of John Bunyan, Being His Last Remains; Giving an Account of the Glories of Heaven, the Terrors of Hell, and of the World to Come.* New York: Tiebout, 1806. 126 pp.

Source: Albert E. Stone, Jr.'s catalog of Clemens' books in the Mark Twain Library at Redding, Connecticut in 1955. I could not find this volume when I visited the Mark Twain Library in 1970.

First published in 1711, this work is now attributed to George Larkin. *MT&JB*, p. 374 n. 21.

Larned, Josephus Nelson (1836–1913), ed. *The Literature of American History: A Bibliographical Guide, in Which the Scope, Character, and Comparative Worth of Books in Selected Lists Are Set Forth in Brief Notes by Critics of Authority.* Boston: Houghton Mifflin Co., 1902.

Inscription: (by Clemens) "From George Iles. S. L. Clemens. Riverdale, 1902."

Catalog: A1911, #291, $3.40.

Larousse, Pierre Athanase (1817–1875). *Grammaire supérieure. Troisieme année.* Nouvelle Edition (19e). Paris: Librairie Larousse, n.d. [1880?].

Inscription: flyleaf signed "Jean L. Clemens/21 Fifth Avenue/New York City/December 1904."

Location: Mark Twain Library, Redding, Conn.

Copy examined: Jean Clemens' unmarked copy, which possibly belonged previously to another member of the Clemens family.

————. *Petite grammaire du premier age.* Paris: Librairie Larousse, 1891.

Inscription: title-page signed "Jean Clemens/Florence, Italie/October 1892."

Marginalia: a penciled notation in Clemens' hand appears at the back of the volume: "The following verbs are conjugated with être, also all reflective verbs"; a list of twelve French verbs follows.

Location: Mark Twain Library, Redding, Conn.

Copy examined: Jean Clemens' copy, also used by Clemens.

"De las' sack! De las' sack" (unidentified song).
"And the half-naked crews of perspiring negroes that worked them [the steamboats] were roaring such songs as 'De Las' Sack! De Las' Sack!'—inspired to unimaginable exaltation by the chaos of turmoil and racket" (*LonMiss* [1883], ch. 16).

The Last Act, Being the Funeral Rites of Nations and Individuals (author unidentified).
Catalog: *C1951*, #D20, $15, listed among the books signed by Clemens.

Lathbury, Mary Artemisia (1841–1913). *The Birthday Week; Pictures and Verse.* New York: R. Worthington, [cop. 1884]. [15 pp.]
Source: MTLAcc, entry #1896, volume donated from Clemens' library by Clara Clemens Gabrilowitsch in 1910.

Lathrop, George Parsons (1851–1898). *Would You Kill Him? A Novel.* New York: Harper & Brothers, 1890. 384 pp.
Source: MTLAcc, entry #1578, volume donated by Clemens.

Laurie, James Stuart (1831–1904). *The Story of Australasia: Its Discovery, Colonisation, and Development.* Map. London: Osgood, McIlvaine & Co., 1896. 388 pp.
In chapter 10 of *FE* (1897) Mark Twain quotes briefly from Laurie's account of the heartless treatment received by transported convicts; a much longer extract appears in chapter 29 of *FE*, where Mark Twain employs the words of "the historian Laurie, whose book, 'The Story of Australasia,' is just out," to describe the Derwent estuary near Hobart "with considerable truth and intemperance." (Twain counterpoises Laurie's grandiose flights with his own deflating remarks about the scenery.) Dennis Welland—"Mark Twain's Last Travel Book" (1965), p. 44—reports that the manuscript for chapter 29 of *FE* originally included two entire pages of quotations from Laurie's book; these were deleted by Mark Twain's publisher. In the manuscript version Mark Twain criticized Laurie's style but praised his "eye for scenery."
Madigan, "Mark Twain's Passage to India," pp. 164 ff., 361.

Lavedan, Henri Léon Émile (1859–1940). *The Duel* (three-act play, perf. 1906). Translated by Louis N. Parker.
On 7 May 1906 Clemens praised and defended Mary Lawton's performance as the Duchess de Chailles in *The Duel* (Clemens to Otis Skinner, PH in MTP). Charles Frohman produced this play at the Hudson Theatre in New York City in February 1906; it contained only two female roles.

Lawrence, George Alfred (1827–1876). *Silverland.* London: Chapman and Hall, 1873. 259 pp.
Clemens made a memorandum on the rear flyleaf of Notebook 17 in November 1878: "Return 'Silverland.' " He may have borrowed this book from his fellow tourists, Mr. and Mrs. August Chamberlaine. Lawrence's novel is set in the Pacific Coast region of the United States. See *N&J*, 2: 281.

Lawrence, Henry Montgomery (1806–1857).
In chapter 58 of *FE* (1897) Mark Twain writes that the chief cause of the Great Mutiny in India was "the annexation of the kingdom of Oudh by the East India Company—characterized by Sir Henry Lawrence as 'the most unrighteous act that was ever committed.' " Lawrence wrote *Adventures of an Officer in the Service of Runjeet Singh* (1845) and *Adventures of an Officer in the Punjaub* (1846). But Francis V. Madigan, Jr.—"Mark Twain's Passage to India" (1974) —points out that Mark Twain took the Lawrence quotation from Julia Inglis' *The Siege of Lucknow. A Diary.*

Laws of Tennessee. Nashville, Tenn., 1860. 708 pp.
   Source: MTLAcc, entry #888, volume donated by Clemens.

Lawson, Thomas William (1857–1925). *Frenzied Finance*. New York: The Ridgway-Thayer Co., 1905. 559 pp. First part, "The Story of Amalgamated," pub. separately in 1904.
   Clemens and Henry H. Rogers exchanged derogatory remarks about the serialized publication of Lawson's exposé, "Frenzied Finance: The Story of Amalgamated," which commenced in the July 1904 issue of *Everybody's Magazine* and ran through 1905. The earliest installments assailed Rogers as "the big brain, the big body, the Master of 'Standard Oil' " (vol. 9 [August 1904], 158). Rogers joked somewhat prematurely about Lawson's being "played out" in a letter to Clemens of 11 July 1905 (*MTHHR*, pp. 589; 590); Clemens predicted that "it is Lawson's turn, now" on 7 August 1905 (*MTHHR*, pp. 595–596).

Layard, Austin Henry (1817–1894). *Early Adventures in Persia, Susiana, and Babylonia . . . Before the Discovery of Nineveh*. 2 vols. London: John Murray, 1887.
   On 9 June 1893 Clemens wrote from Florence to Joseph H. Twichell about meeting this English archaeologist and diplomat and reading Layard's narrative of his adventures as a young man (ALS in Yale). Clemens quotes a footnote from Layard's book that might be expected to interest Twichell. This same footnote is entered in the notebook that Clemens kept for this period (NB 33, TS p. 15); Clemens found it on page 357 in the second volume of Layard's *Early Adventures*. Describing Mr. Lucas, the plain-spoken old quartermaster of the *Assyria*, Layard adds there: "This same quartermaster was celebrated among the English in Mesopotamia for an entry in the log-book. The 'Assyria' had been left under his care near Basra, when there arose one of those violent tornadoes which occasionally sweep over this part of Arabia. The vessel was in great danger. After the storm was over Mr. Lucas thus recorded the event: 'The windy and watery elements raged. Tears and prayers was had recourse to, but was of no manner of use. So we hauled up the anchor and got round the point.' " Clemens was also impressed by the coincidence of Layard's unexpected appearance in Florence just as Clemens was reading his *Early Adventures*. Twice—on a slip of paper inserted into Notebook 33 and in an entry jotted down on 28 May 1896 (NB 38, TS p. 22)—Clemens recorded his astonishment at being called away from reading this book to go to dinner and then finding Layard himself present there.

Lea, Henry Charles (1825–1909). *An Historical Sketch of Sacerdotal Celibacy in the Christian Church*. Second edition, enlarged. Boston: Houghton, Mifflin and Co., 1884. 682 pp.
   In February 1888, after making a note regarding the issuance of the first two volumes of Lea's *Inquisition*, Clemens added: "Also, his 'Sacerdotal Celibacy' " (NB 27, TS p. 59).

————. *A History of the Inquisition of the Middle Ages*. 3 vols. New York: Harper & Brothers, 1888.
   "History of the Inquisition—2 vols. ready. (Harper.) Henry C. Lea," Clemens noted in February 1888 (NB 27, TS p. 58).
   MTAL, p. 146.

Lear, Edward (1812–1888). *Letters of Edward Lear, Author of "The Book of Nonsense," to Chichester Fortescue, Lord Carlingford, and Frances, Countess Waldegrave*. Ed. by Constance (Braham) Strachie (Lady Strachey). Second edition. London: T. Fisher Unwin, 1907. 327 pp.
   Inscription: "To Mr. S. L. Clemens/with the compliments of/'the Editor'/Aug. 1908."
   Location: Mark Twain Library, Redding, Conn.
   Copy examined: Clemens' copy, unmarked.

Leavitt, Lydia. *Bohemian Society*. Brockville [Ontario] Times Printing and Publishing Co., 188–. 65 pp.
> *Inscription:* (on flyleaf) "To 'Mark Twain,' with the compliments of the author/ Toronto Dec. 9th 1884".
> *Location:* Mark Twain Library, Redding, Conn.
> *Copy examined:* Clemens' copy, unmarked.

Lebert, Siegmund (1822–1884) and Louis Stark (1831–1884). *Grand Theoretical and Practical Piano-School for Systematic Instruction*. Trans. by C. E. R. Müller. Four parts.
> "1 Leibert [*sic*] & Stark's Piano School Book I. 4.00" reads a bill to Clemens of 1 December 1880 from M. L. Bartlett, Hartford (MTP).

Leblanc, Maurice (1864–1941). *The Exploits of Arsène Lupin*. Trans. by Alexander Louis Teixeira de Mattos (1865–1921). New York: Harper & Brothers, 1907. 314 pp.
> *Source:* MTLAcc, entry #1114, volume donated by Clemens.

Lecky, William Edward Hartpole (1838–1903). *A History of England in the Eighteenth Century*. 8 vols. New York: D. Appleton and Co., 1887–1890.
> *Inscription:* flyleaf of vol. 6 signed "S. L. Clemens."
> *Catalog:* A1911, #285, $3.50, 6 vols. only (these six published 1887–1888).
> Notebook 28 (September 1888) contains Clemens' reference to "impressment of sailors & soldiers, Vol 3, last pages" (TS p. 19); another entry mentions "584 vol 3—18th Cent." (TS p. 19). Lecky's book also appears in Mark Twain's tentative appendix for *CY* (1889), credited for details about "the woman burnt" and the "mansion house" (NB 29 [1889], TS pp. 13, 15).
> Coleman O. Parsons, "Background" (1960), 67 n. 32; James D. Williams, "The Use of History" (1965), 103, 104; Howard G. Baetzhold, *MT&JB*, pp. 152–153, 230, 344 n. 48; William M. Gibson, *MSM*, pp. 21, 151–152; Paul Baender, *WIM?*, pp. 540–541.

———. *History of European Morals from Augustus to Charlemagne*. 2 vols. New York: D. Appleton and Co., 1874.
> *Inscriptions:* vol. 1 flyleaf signed "T. W. Crane/1874 New York" in pencil. (Theodore W. Crane was Clemens' brother-in-law.) Clemens also signed the same flyleaf in black ink with a shaky hand: "SL. Clemens/1906." The flyleaf of vol. 2 is signed "T. W. Crane 1877" in pencil; Clemens also signed his name ("SL. Clemens") in black ink.
> *Marginalia:* Albert Bigelow Paine quoted a few of Clemens' remarks (*MTB*, pp. 511–512), which Paine tantalizingly described as "notes not always quotable in the family circle." Paine attributed these marginalia to "two volumes of Lecky, much worn" (*MTB*, p. 1539). Chester L. Davis continued this chaste tradition when he reported Clemens' notations in issues of *The Twainian* between May and December 1955 (also the issue of November-December 1962); Davis' transcription omitted "those things which . . . are too rough for the eyes of some of our young people," as well as Clemens' "many short corrections of language . . . or short exclamations" (November-December 1955 issue, p. 4). The brevity of Paine's quotations and the unreliability of Davis' transcript have created a problem for Mark Twain scholars. Walter Blair—*MT&HF*, pp. 134–135, 401 n. 6—points out that the few comments quoted by Paine do not match up with any of the marginalia appearing in *The Twainian*. This leads Blair to speculate that Clemens may have owned another copy of Lecky's book which did not survive after Paine consulted it in writing *Mark Twain: A Biography* (1912). Blair's theory has resulted in additional confusion, since some commentators therefore have mistakenly inferred that Clemens annotated one copy around 1874 (when Paine dates the marginalia) and then wrote in another copy in 1906, the date Davis erroneously supposed Clemens both inscribed and marked

his copy. But it seems more likely that Clemens owned and annotated only one copy, which (presumably because it already contained the signature of his brother-in-law) he never bothered to inscribe until 1906. My examination of the volumes at Chester Davis' home in August 1970 revealed that Clemens re-read them numerous times; his profuse marginalia record different readings in various shades of brown, black, and blue ink—together with many markings and notes in pencil. Clemens' writing instruments sometimes alternate from page to page. The first volume, for instance, displays annotation in brown ink on page 192, pencil marks on page 193, and a note and brackets in blue ink on page 194. Unfortunately there are virtually no dates or topical references among Clemens' marginalia, although he does allude (in pencil) to the "Canadian Indians" of Francis Parkman on page 191 of the second volume.

In the short time at my disposal I inspected Clemens' notes and marks on the following pages of volume 1: 5 (note in brown ink, a late hand), 6, 115, 175, 176, 191, 192 (grammatical correction), 193, 194, 195–197, 210, 214 (a comment in blue ink concerning recent theories that death is not actually painful), 215–220 (blue ink markings), 221 (pencil marks), 222 (a lengthy marginal comment in pencil pokes fun at Christ's release from Purgatory, suggesting that Purgatory merely functions to produce revenue), 235 (a brown-ink note laments that money has replaced liberty as the god of the American republic), 262, 267, 269, 293 (sentence beginning "but they" and concluding "to reveal" is underscored and marked with brown ink; Clemens comments that this satisfactorily explains for him why actors employ exaggerations of style), 299 (a penciled note disputes the notion that 80,000 voices could be heard any better than a single voice), 308, 310–334 (pencil marks), 322 (penciled annotation regarding slavery in the American South), 325, 326, 328, 329 (both pencil marks and notations), 359 (a minor alteration of diction in black ink).

Catalog: *C1951,* #36a and #43a (evidently the two volumes were listed separately among books containing Clemens' marginal notes), sold for $50.

Location: Mark Twain Research Foundation, Perry, Missouri.

Copies examined: Clemens' copies, briefly.

Clemens' notebooks contain only a single explicit reference to *European Morals,* possibly because Clemens used the margins of Lecky's book as a repository of his own reflections. In a tentative appendix for *CY* in Notebook 29 (1889) Mark Twain acknowledged Lecky as his source for "Hermits & Stylites" and "Roman Laws" (TS p. 15). An allusion to Lecky himself ("This was at Mr. Lecky's [dinner party]. He is Irish, you know") occurs in a letter Clemens wrote to Joseph H. Twichell from London on 4 March 1900 *(MTL,* p. 697). These mentions hardly suggest the true significance of Lecky in Clemens' intellectual development. No serious student of Mark Twain's works should neglect reading at least a few chapters of Lecky's historical survey. (The most readily available edition is usually the facsimile reprint containing C. Wright Mills' introduction [New York: George Braziller, 1955], which is used here.) The first part of volume one is devoted to historical categorizations of moral philosophies; Lecky quickly takes issue with Utilitarianism, pointing out the inconsistencies in its doctrines and disputing Bentham and other Utilitarian advocates. In the course of Lecky's analysis he comments upon the reasons and motivations for good (right) or pernicious (wrong) behavior. The problem centers upon the question of whether man really possesses a moral faculty, an innate sense of right and wrong. While inductive Utilitarians answered "no," Lecky took the position that mankind *does* have a natural moral perception (Lecky once studied for the Church of England), and his opening chapter attempts to prove this thesis. Lecky's arguments remind us that Utilitarianism still possessed considerable intellectual force in the mid-1860's; Mill published his important essay by that name in 1861, the same decade in which Lecky's *European Morals* first issued (1869).

Clemens no doubt appreciated Lecky's habit of periodically summing up his points for convenient memorizing. Probably Clemens saw in these pages what one part of him wished to write—anti-Catholic, anti-slavery, pro-military-discipline history, buttressed by hundreds of pages of facts drawn from all periods of human life. Lecky's numerous quotations in lengthy footnotes form a kind of anthology of readings in intellectual history and philosophy. To Lecky's way of thinking, events like the victory of Christianity or the conversion of Rome did not simply "happen"; one can find rational, discernible causes for their occurrence.

But Clemens' ambivalent attitudes toward Lecky are more complex than is sometimes supposed. The student interested in Lecky's influence should approach the problem under the tutelage of helpful commentaries written by Walter Blair, Roger B. Salomon, and Howard G. Baetzhold. Blair provides a full explication of Lecky's impact on Mark Twain's thought and examines his use of Lecky in writing *HF* (*MT&HF*, pp. 135–144, 338, 401 n. 6). Salomon's elucidating remarks about the reflections of Lecky's Whig-Liberal bias against the Roman Church which are apparent in *CY* (*TIH*, pp. 98–102) is another good place to begin understanding the Lecky/Clemens relationship. Baetzhold's study communicates the importance and complexity of the intermingling of Lecky's theories with Clemens' reasoning, and the discussion of Lecky's influence on "What Is Man?" is a lucid analysis of Mark Twain's tedious and murky dialogue (*MT&JB*, pp. 59, 218–228). In fact, Baetzhold succeeds in proving that "What Is Man?" simply must be read in conjunction with Lecky's *European Morals*, and this finding, more than anything else, demonstrates the failings of Mark Twain's philosophical treatise.

Even these and other excellent treatments of this topic have not yet explored all of the reverberations of Lecky in Mark Twain's later writings. Lecky's diatribe against the doctrine of infant damnation (1:96), for example, seems related to Mark Twain's notebook draft for "The Mysterious Stranger" contained in Notebook 42 (11 November 1898). An alter ego whom Mark Twain created in "Which Was It?," Sol Bailey (known to the Indiantown villagers as "Ham-fat Bailey the Idiot Philosopher"), is a freethinker whose dogma is "that all motives are selfish"; consequently one need only choose between "high" and "low" selfish motives (*WWD?*, p. 302). In formulating Bailey's "Gospel of Self," a denial of the existence of any but selfish impulses, Mark Twain resumed his debate with Lecky (*WWD?*, p. 379; written 1899–1903). In "The International Lightning Trust" (written 1909) Jasper Hackett credits Lecky's *European Morals* with giving him the original scheme upon which the story hinges (*FM*, pp. 79, 85). In chapter two Jasper quotes from chapter three of volume 1 (p. 367) of *European Morals* to provide examples of superstitious fears held by early pagans—Augustus, Tiberius, Caligula. "I'll read you a sentence or two out of Mr. Lecky's History of European Morals. . . . That's the passage that gave me my splendid idea" (*FM*, p. 85).

We can also credit Lecky with bringing the phrenological term "temperament" to Clemens' recollection (see Alan Gribben, "Mark Twain, Phrenology and the 'Temperaments'" [1972]). Mark Twain constructed much of the dialogue in "What Is Man?" around the concept of "temperament," which he defines there as "the disposition you were born with." This piece of phraseology clung to his thought and expression to the end of his life, though he had not used the word much after he copied passages from George Sumner Weaver's *Lectures on Mental Science* into Notebook 1 in 1855. Repeated exposures to Lecky's writing, however, awakened his memories of this early classification of physical and mental characteristics. Lecky's discussions of human character in *History of European Morals* contain numerous references to "temperaments," "dispositions," "faculty," "organ," "cultivation" of "moral types," and other catchwords of phrenology (see 1: 3, 60–61, 88, 156, 157, 172, 187–188, *et passim;* also 2: 192–194). Besides using these terms prevalently, Lecky also divides mankind into two loosely-defined "temperaments"—one of which (the temperament Lecky identifies with the Protestant nature) closely fits the sanguine temperament (2: 124). As a youth of nineteen Clemens believed that the description of the sanguine temperament accorded with his own disposition and appearance.

Lecky does not specifically mention phrenology in his book, since the currency of its distinctive terminology was outliving its main hypothesis of detectable mental traits. But the presence of these classifications in *European Morals* (1869) demonstrates the pervasive residual influence of the jargon popularized by this pseudoscience. The texts of other books by Lecky that Clemens is not known to have read—*The Map of Life: Conduct and Character* (1899; revised edition 1900) and *Historical and Political Essays* (1908)—employ still more explicit phrenological vocabulary terms: "bilious temperament," "lymphatic temperament," the "buoyant temperament" of a "sanguine and cheerful spirit," "a singularly equable, happy, and sanguine temperament" *(Map,* rev. ed., p. 11, 66, 238–239; *Essays,* p. 245). Like Lecky, Mark Twain became accustomed at an early date to this convenient method of categorizing character types, much as we today are wont to rely upon terms available to us from current psycho-analytical theories. In rereading Lecky after 1895, Clemens was reminded (whether consciously or not) of this previous article of his belief, and he incorporated it into a psychological framework suitable for his late treatises on human character. Clemens emphasizes the overwhelming determinism of "temperament" in Autobiographical Dictations of 25 June 1906 and 4 February 1907 (MTP); in the latter instance he says it accounts for the plight of Bret Harte's daughter, who reportedly had been committed to a home for the indigent and friendless in Portland, Maine.

MTB, pp. 511–512, 743, 1539; Olin H. Moore, "MT and Don Quixote" (1922), pp. 341–343; Henry A. Pochmann, "Mind of MT" (1924), pp. 21, 176; *MTSM,* p. 244; Harold Aspiz, "MT's Reading" (1949), pp. 340–347, and "Lecky's Influence on MT" (1962), an especially valid analysis; *MT&HF,* pp. 134–135, 338, 401 n. 6; Hamlin Hill and Walter Blair, eds., *The Art of HF* (1962), pp. 484–491; Sherwood Cummings, *"WIM?:* The Scientific Sources" (1964), p. 113; Coleman Parsons, "Background of *The MS,"* (1960), pp. 63, 70; James D. Williams, "The Use of History in MT's *A CY"* (1965), 103 n. 20, 104; Philip Y. Coleman, "MT's Desperate Naturalism" (1964), pp. 26–30; Rodney O. Rogers, "Twain, Taine, and Lecky" (1973), 436–447; Roger B. Salomon, *TIH* (1961), pp. 98–102; Howard G. Baetzhold, *MT&JB* (1970), pp. 54, 57, 59, 134–143, 331 n. 16, 343 n. 39, 363 n. 13; Paul Baender, *WIM?,* pp. 98–100, 544.

————. *History of the Rise and Influence of the Spirit of Rationalism in Europe* (pub. 1865).

William M. Gibson proposes this work as the source for Mark Twain's assertion in "The Chronicle of Young Satan" (written 1897–1900) that the rules for dealing with witchcraft were "all written down by the Pope" *(MSM,* p. 79).

Lee, Albert (b. 1868). *He, She & They.* Illus. by H. B. Eddy. New York: Harper & Brothers, 1899. 141 pp.

Source: MTLAcc, entry #202, volume donated by Clemens.

Lee, Henry (1826–1888). *The Octopus; or, The "Devil-Fish" of Fiction and of Fact. By Henry Lee, Naturalist of the Brighton Aquarium.* Illus. London: Chapman and Hall, 1875. 114 pp.

Inscription: (on flyleaf) "To Saml. L. Clemens Esq/from his friend/The Author./Henry Lee/ Augt. 13th 1879".

Location: Special Collections, University Library, University of Nevada, Reno. Purchased in 1963 from Mrs. Lewis A. (Haydee U.) Zeitlin of Santa Monica, California.

Copy examined: Clemens' copy, unmarked but worn by usage.

In a letter written to Elisha Bliss on 5 November 1873, Clemens stipulated that Henry Lee was to receive a "very early" copy of *GA* (ALS in CWB). Clemens noted that Lee was among those "gone" when he returned to London in July 1899 (NB 40, TS p. 60).

Lee, Jennette Barbour (Perry). *Uncle William, The Man Who Was Shif'less.* New York: The Century Co., 1906. 298 pp. Reprinted in 1907.
     On 13 February 1908 Isabel V. Lyon noted that "Mrs. Riggs [Kate Douglas Wiggin] recommended a book for the King, 'Uncle William' by Jeanette Lee" (IVL Journals, TS p. 302, MTP).

Lee, Robert Edward (1843–1914). *Recollections and Letters of General Robert E. Lee [1807–1870], by His Son, Captain Robert E. Lee.* New York: Doubleday, Page & Co., 1904. 461 pp. Reprinted in 1905.
     Clemens requested Isabel Lyon to search his library for this book on Friday, 6 January 1905, but she noted in her journal that in sorting his books since the move to 21 Fifth Avenue she had not seen this volume (IVL Journals, TS p. 36, MTP).

Lee, Sidney (1859–1926).
     Clemens met Lee twice in March 1903 (Clemens to Laurence Hutton, 18 March 1903, ALS at Princeton; Notebook 46, TS p. 13). Lee entertained Clemens in England in 1907 *(MTE,* p. 332).

Leech, John (1817–1864). *Pictures of Life & Character, by John Leech. From the Collection of Mr. Punch.* London: Bradbury and Evans, n.d. [Originally pub. 1854–1863 as four volumes.]
     Inscription: to the Clemens family from the [Theodore W.] Crane family, Christmas 1871.
     Catalog: Mott 1952, item #64, oblong folio, $7.50.

[Le Feuvre, Amy.] *"Probable Sons."* Chicago: F. H. Revell Co., [cop. 1896]. 120 pp.
     Source: MTLAcc, entry #872, volume donated by Mrs. Ralph W. Ashcroft (formerly Isabel Lyon), Clemens' secretary.

Lefevre, Edwin (1871–1943). *Sampson Rock, of Wall Street. A Novel.* Illus. New York: Harper & Brothers, 1907. 394 pp.
     Source: MTLAcc, entry #1579, volume donated by Clemens.

————. *Sampson Rock, of Wall Street. A Novel.* Illus. New York: Harper & Brothers, 1908. 394 pp.
     Source: MTLAcc, entry #1020, volume donated by Clemens.

Le Gallienne, Richard (1866–1947), trans. *Odes from the Divan of Hafiz.* Boston: L. C. Page Co., [cop. 1903]. 194 pp.
     Source: Clara Clemens listed the title and translator in her undated commonplace book (Paine 150, MTP).

————. *An Old Country House.* Illus. by Elizabeth Shippen Green. New York: Harper & Brothers, 1905. 143 pp.
     Inscription: Clemens inscribed an illustration pasted on the front cover: "S. L. Clemens, 1905, to I. V. Lyon, 1908."
     Catalog: Swann Galleries, Inc., New York City, 11 June 1970, item #314.

————. *Painted Shadows.* Boston: Little, Brown and Co., 1904. 339 pp.
     Isabel Lyon seemingly referred to this book when she recorded on 6 January 1905: "Mrs. Whitmore has sent me Richard Le Gallienne's last book. This morning I took it in to Mr. Clemens and he was glad to see it, saying 'an able

cuss and writes deliciously' " (IVL Journals, TS p. 36, MTP). In writing to thank Mrs. Whitmore for the Christmas present on 8 January 1905 (the letter is misdated "1904"), Miss Lyon reported that Clemens, who had been ill for three weeks at 21 Fifth Avenue, "took the book from me—saying of its author— 'An able cuss who writes deliciously'—and today he remarked that the book is 'ever so charming' " (ALS in MTM). The book title is confirmed in a journal entry for 9 July 1905, when Miss Lyon herself got around to reading the volume; she recalled then how she "carried my new 'Painted Shadows' " into Clemens' room and heard him pronounce Le Gallienne to be "an able cuss who writes deliciously" (IVL Journals, TS p. 77, MTP).

Leibniz, Gottfried Wilhelm von (1646–1716).
   At Heidelberg University on 2 July 1878 Clemens heard Professor Kuno Fischer lecture on Leibniz' life and writings (NB 14, *N&J,* 2: 105).

Leighton, Robert Fowler. *Latin Lessons Adapted to Allen and Greenough's Latin Grammar.* Boston: Ginn Brothers, 1872. 252 pp. [Reprinted frequently between 1873 and 1887.]
   Catalog: C1951, #J30, edition unspecified, listed among books belonging to Jean and Clara Clemens.

Leland, Charles Godfrey (1824–1903). *Hans Breitmann's Party, with Other Ballads.* New and enlarged edition. Philadelphia: T. B. Peterson & Brothers, 1869. 48 pp.
   On 6 July 1873 Clemens wrote to Mrs. Fairbanks from London to tell her he had met "Hans Breitman" [*sic*] among other "pleasant people" (*MTMF,* p. 173). *Mark Twain's Library of Humor* (1888) would include two of Leland's verses, "Hans Breitmann's Party" and "Ballad of the Rhine."

————. *The Hundred Riddles of the Fairy Bellaria.* Illus. London: T. Fisher Unwin, 1892.
   Inscription: flyleaf inscribed "A hundred riddles to one who has raised a hundred million peals of laughter all over the world, i e Mark Twain. From/ Charles G. Leland/Florence Jan. 26 1893".
   Location: Carrie Estelle Doheny Collection, St. John's Seminary, Camarillo, California. Mrs. Doheny purchased the volume in 1940 from Maxwell Hunley Rare Books of Beverly Hills.
   Copy examined: Clemens' copy, unmarked.

———— and John Dyneley Prince (b. 1868), trans. *Kulóskap the Master, and Other Algonkin Poems; Translated Metrically.* Illus. New York: Funk & Wagnalls Co., 1902. 370 pp.
   Inscription: inside front cover signed in black ink "Clemens/1902".
   Location: Mark Twain Library, Redding, Conn. Donated by Clemens (MTLAcc, entry #614).
   Copy examined: Clemens' copy, unmarked.

————. *Legends of Florence; Collected from the People and Re-Told by . . . (Hans Breitmann).* First Series. Second edition, revised and enlarged. London: David Nutt, 1896. 280 pp.
   Inscription: flyleaf signed "SL. Clemens/Villa di Quarto/Florence/Xmas/ 1903/Given to me by Livy."
   Catalogs: C1951, #43c, $17.50 (purchased by Hollywood director Samuel Fuller and his wife); *Fleming 1972.*
   Source: I am grateful to the late Frederick Anderson, former Editor of the Mark Twain Papers, for transcribing Clemens' inscription. Mr. Anderson inspected the volume at the New York City firm of John F. Fleming, Inc. in April 1972.

————. *Legends of the Birds.* New York: H. Holt & Co., 1874. 16 pp.
   Source: MTLAcc, entry #2136, volume donated from Clemens' library by
Clara Clemens Gabrilowitsch in 1910.

Leland, Henry Perry (1828–1868). "Frogs Shot Without Powder," *Spirit of the
   Times,* 26 May 1855.
   Bernard DeVoto calls this source the "likeliest" printed variant of the folk tale
for Clemens to have known. DeVoto publishes this variant and lists several of
its reprintings (*MTAm,* p. 174, 340–342).
   Blair, *NAH,* p. 156.

Le Nordez, (Mgr.) Albert-Léon-Marie, évêque de Dijon. *Jeanne d'Arc racontée
   par l'image, d'après les sculpteurs, les graveurs et les peintres.* Paris: Hachette,
   1898. 395 pp.
   Inscription: half-title signed "SL. Clemens/London, 1899."
   Marginalia: Clemens' notes on pages 2, 116, 215, 231, 249, and 267 compare
the illustrations of Joan ("caricatures") with those that appear in his own
version. Most comments are derogatory.
   Catalogs: C1951, #3c, listed among books signed by Clemens; *Fleming 1972.*
   Source: I am indebted to the late Frederick Anderson, former Editor of the
Mark Twain Papers, for a transcription of Clemens' marginalia. Mr. Anderson
looked at the book in April 1972 at the offices of John F. Fleming, Inc., New
York City.

Leonard, William Ellery (1876–1944). *Sonnets and Poems.* Boston: [F. H. Gilson
   Co.,] 1906. 67 pp.
   Source: MTLAcc, entry #2135, volume donated from Clemens' library by
Clara Clemens Gabrilowitsch in 1910.

Leonowens, Anna Harriette. *English Governess at the Siamese Court; Being
   Recollections of Six Years in the Royal Palace at Bankok.* Illus. Boston: James
   R. Osgood & Co., 1871.
   Inscription: signed "Saml L. Clemens/1871."
   Source: card catalog of Mark Twain Library, Redding, Conn. The book was
missing in 1979.

Le Pileur, Auguste (b. 1810). *Wonders of the Human Body. From the French.*
   Illus. New York: Scribner, Armstrong & Co., 1873. 256 pp.
   Source: MTLAcc, entry #1996, volume donated from Clemens' library by
Clara Clemens Gabrilowitsch in 1910.

Le Row, Caroline Bigelow, comp. *English As She Is Taught. Genuine Answers to
   Examination Questions in Our Public Schools.* New York: Cassell & Co., 1887.
   109 pp.
   Inscription: (on front free endpaper) " 'Mark Twain,' with the gratitude and
admiration of the compiler,/Caroline B. Le Row,/April, 1887."
   Catalog: "Retz Appraisal" (1944), p. 9, valued at $5.
   Location: Mark Twain Papers, Berkeley, Ca.
   Copy examined: Clemens' copy, unmarked and with some leaves unopened.

————. *English As She Is Taught.* [Another copy.]
   Inscription: front endpaper signed in pencil "S. L. Clemens/Riverdale/Oct.
1901."
   Catalogs: C1951, #37c, listed among the books signed by Clemens; *Fleming
1972.*
   Source: Frederick Anderson, then Editor of the Mark Twain Papers at Berk-
eley, examined this copy in April 1972 at the New York City offices of John F.
Fleming, Inc. I appreciate the use of Mr. Anderson's notes.

Mark Twain offered Le Row the use of his name to protect her teaching position, but she declined. He did encourage the publication of her book, however, and he helped publicize it. Her disclosures furnished Mark Twain with examples in his own essay for the April 1887 issue of *Century Magazine*, also titled "English As She Is Taught." (This duplication of titles has caused confusion about whether "Caroline Le Row" was really another pseudonym for Samuel L. Clemens.) Mark Twain turned over to her the $250 check he received from the *Century*. In a letter to Miss Le Row written on 4 November 1888 Clemens urged her to continue her crusade in behalf of the "mishandled" pupils (ALS in collection of Mrs. Robin Craven, New York City, PH in MTP). Mark Twain returned to *English As She Is Taught*, "a collection of American examinations made in the public schools of Brooklyn," in chapter 61 of *FE* (1897); there he quotes an excerpt, ostensibly to defend the grammatical errors committed by natives of India.

MTB, p. 841; *MTHL*, p. 587 n. 2; Madigan, "MT's Passage to India," p. 361.

Le Sage, Alain René (1668–1747). *The Adventures of Gil Blas of Santillane* (pub. 1715–1735).

"I am now reading Gil Blas," Clemens wrote to Olivia Langdon on 27 December 1869 from New Haven, "but am not marking it. If you have not read it you need not. It would sadly offend your delicacy" (*LLMT*, p. 132). He was most likely reading Tobias Smollett's translation, published in 1868 by D. Appleton Company of New York City (764 pages) and J. B. Lippincott & Company of Philadelphia (531 pages). Clemens' copy apparently does not survive. On 5 July 1875 Clemens remarked in a letter to William Dean Howells that he had decided not to take Tom Sawyer's adventures beyond Tom's childhood because "it would be fatal to do it in any shape but autobiographically—like Gil Blas" (*MTHL*, p. 91). Yet when Brander Matthews pointed out similarities between *Gil Blas* and *Huckleberry Finn* ("an unheroic hero . . . who is often little more than a recording spectator"), Matthews "was not at all surprised when Mark promptly assured me that he had never read 'Gil Blas'; I knew he was not a bookish man" (essay dated 1919, collected in *Tocsin of Revolt* [1921], p. 267). Clara Clemens listed Le Sage's *Gil Blas* among mostly undated entries in her commonplace book (Paine 150, MTP).

MTB, p. 132; *MT&HF*, p. 98.

Leslie, Eliza (1787–1858). *The American Girls' Book; or, Occupation for Play Hours.* New York: R. Worthington, 1879. 383 pp.
Source: MTLAcc, entry #1897, volume donated from Clemens' library by Clara Clemens Gabrilowitsch in 1910.

Lessing, Gotthold Ephraim (1729–1781). *Fabeln. Drei Bücher. Nebst Abhandlungen mit dieser Dichtungsart verwandten Inhalts.* Stuttgart: G. J. Göschen, 1876. 125 pp. [Bound with a copy of Lessing's *Laokoon*.]
Marginalia: the number "4853" in black ink on the blank verso of page 125.
Location: see entry for Lessing's *Laokoon*.

————. *Hamburgische Briefe; Hamburgische Dramaturgie.*
Clara Clemens entered these titles in her largely undated commonplace book (Paine 150, MTP).

————. *Laokoon, oder über die Grenzen der Mahlerey und Poesie . . . Mit beyläufigen Erläuterungen verschiedener Punkte der alten Kunstgeschichte.* Stuttgart: G. J. Göschen, 1881. 224 pp. [Bound with a copy of Lessing's *Fabeln*.]
Inscription: on first flyleaf in blue ink "Olivia L. Clemens/May 1885/ Hartford".
Catalog: Zeitlin 1951, item #30, $7.50.
Location: Mark Twain Papers, Berkeley, Ca. Contains *C1951* label pasted on

inner front cover. A University of California bookplate acknowledges Jake Zeitlin as the donor.
  Copy examined: Olivia Clemens' unmarked copy.

Lester, Charles Edwards (1815–1890). *The Life of Sam Houston, The Hunter, Patriot, and Statesman of Texas. (The Only Authentic Memoir of Him Ever Published).* Illus. New York: J. C. Derby; Boston: Phillips, Sampson & Co., 1855. 402 pp.
  Inscription: flyleaf torn out.
  Location: Mark Twain Library, Redding, Conn.
  Copy examined: presumably Clemens' copy, unmarked.

"Let each now choose" (unidentified song).
  In "Mock Marriage" (written in the early 1900's), "the music struck up 'Let each now choose,' etc." *(FM,* p. 292).

Lewis, Alfred Henry (1857–1914). *Wolfville Days.* Frontispiece by Frederic Remington. New York: F. A. Stokes Co., [cop. 1902]. 311 pp.
  Source: MTLAcc, entry #203, volume donated by Clemens.

————. *Wolfville Nights.* New York, n.d. [Pub. in 1902 and 1905 by Grosset & Dunlap; also pub. in 1902 by F. A. Stokes Co.]
  Inscription: inside front cover signed in ink "S. L. Clemens, 1905".
  Catalogs: C1951, #D24, $17.50, listed among the books signed by Clemens; *Zeitlin 1951,* item #31, $25, edition unspecified.

Lewis, Charles Bertrand (1842–1924), pseud. "M. Quad." "The Demon and the Fury" (sketch).
  In the "Weather" appendix to *AC* (1892) Mark Twain quotes a passage in which Lewis describes a thunderstorm.
  Blair, "On the Structure of *TS,*" p. 79.

Lewis, George Edward. *Heart Echoes.* Illus. by Marie Jewell Clark. Grand Rapids, Michigan: Press of Tradesman Co., [1899]. 181 pp.
  Catalog: C1951, #58a, $17.50, listed among the books containing marginalia by Clemens.
  When relocated, this volume of poetry may prove to belong in Mark Twain's hypothetical "Library of Literary Hogwash."

Lewis, Henry Taliaferro. "The Harp of a Thousand Strings" (mock sermon).
  Still considering material for *Mark Twain's Library of Humor* in the autumn of 1887, Clemens wrote "Harp of 1000 Strings" in Notebook 27, TS p. 23.
  Walter Blair reprints Lewis' piece in *Native American Humor,* pp. 388–389.

Leypoldt, Frederick (1835–1884), pseud. "L. Pylodet." *New Guide to German Conversation.* New York: H. Holt & Co., [cop. 1868]. 279 pp.
  Source: MTLAcc, entry #381, volume donated by Clemens.

Lichtenberg, Georg Christoph (1742–1799).
  John S. Tuckey cites Lichtenberg's writing on dream experiences as part of the background for Mark Twain's "The Great Dark" (written 1898). Professor Tuckey points out that "in his working notes Mark Twain planned to have his narrator quote Lichtenberg to convince his wife of the possibility of confusing dream and reality" *(WWD?,* p. 17). Mark Twain's "The Mad Passenger" *(WWD?,* pp. 560–567) might also be indebted to Lichtenberg's ideas. But Lichtenberg's works were only available in German in the 1890's, so Mark Twain's source is unknown.

Liechtenstein, (Princess) Marie Henriette Norberte. *Holland House*. Third edition. London: Macmillan and Co., 1875. 370 pp. [Other editions were two vols.]
    Catalog: C1951, #85c, listed among books signed by Clemens, apparently one vol. only.

Life Magazine (New York weekly, pub. 1883–1936).
    In June 1905 Clemens praised the "very cunning portraits" of Petrarch, Dante, Shakespeare, and Emerson that appeared in *Life* (SLC to Clara Clemens, 19 or 20 June 1905, MTP).

The Life Within. Boston: Lothrop Pub. Co., [cop. 1903]. 385 pp.
    Source: MTLAcc, entry #14, volume donated by Clemens.

————. [Another identical copy.]
    Source: MTLAcc, entry #1257, volume donated by Clemens.
    Mark Twain referred readers of his "Christian Science" (1907) to this anonymous work: "For a clear understanding of the two claims of Christian Science [healing the body and healing the spirit], read the novel *The Life Within*, published by Lothrops, Boston" (Book 2, chapter 15, footnote, *WIM?*, pp. 358, 575).

Liljencrantz, Ottilia Adelina (1876–1910). *Randvar the Songsmith; A Romance of Norumbega*. New York: Harper & Brothers, 1906. 314 pp.
    Source: MTLAcc, entry #1580, volume donated by Clemens.

Lillie, (Mrs.) Lucy Cecil (White) (b. 1855). *The Colonel's Money*. Illus. New York: Harper & Brothers, 1900. 393 pp.
    Source: MTLAcc, entry #423, volume donated by Clemens.

————. *The Household of Glen Holly*. Illus. New York: Harper & Brothers, [cop. 1888]. 368 pp.
    Source: MTLAcc, entry #415, volume donated by Clemens.

————. *Phil and the Baby*. Illus. New York: Harper & Brothers, 1906. 123 pp.
    Source: MTLAcc, entry #445, volume donated by Clemens.

————. *The Story of Music and Musicians for Young Readers*. Illus. New York: Harper & Brothers, [cop. 1886]. 245 pp.
    Source: MTLAcc, entry #1460, volume donated by Clemens.

Lincoln, A. H. *Familiar Lectures on Botany*. 1838.
    Source: Albert E. Stone, Jr. included this volume in his catalog of Clemens' library books in the Mark Twain Library at Redding in 1955, but he questioned whether it really belonged in the bookcase containing Clemens' volumes. I could not find the book when I visited Redding in 1970.

Lincoln, Abraham (1809–1865). *An Address Delivered Before the Springfield Washingtonian Temperance Society at the Second Presbyterian Church, on the Twenty-second Day of February, 1842*. Springfield, Ill.: T. J. Crowder, Illinois State Register Press, 1906. 12 pp.
    Inscription: blank verso of front cover signed in black ink, "Mark Twain." Clemens almost never signed his pseudonym in books belonging to his personal library. Although the signature is authentic-looking, faint outlines of what could be trace marks are visible here and there among the letters and in the flourish beneath the name. The signature may well be counterfeit.
    Marginalia: someone made a correction in dark brown ink on page 11, changing "poisons" to "passions"; the hand is not Clemens'. A bookseller has priced the pamphlet at $20 on the back cover.
    Location: Humanities Research Center, University of Texas at Austin.
    Copy examined: possibly spurious association copy.

———. "Gettysburg Address" (speech delivered 1863).

"Mr. Lincoln's words are simple, tender, beautiful, elevated; they flow as smoothly as a poem. This is probably the finest prose passage that exists in the English language" ("Comments on English Diction," written around 1876, quoted by Jervis Langdon in *Some Reminiscences* [1935], p. 21). In June 1885 Clemens characterized Lincoln's speech as "perfect" (NB 24, TS p. 25). He parodied the address ("government of the grafter, by the grafter, for the grafter") in an observation published in *More Maxims of Mark Twain* (privately printed, 1927), p. 14.

MTC, p. 113.

———. "Second Inaugural Address" (delivered 1865).

Clemens quoted and paraphrased a passage from this speech in Notebook 5 (1866, *N&J*, 1: 143), declaring it "very simple & beautiful." In 1880 Clemens hoped to find "a yarn or two" about Lincoln that would be suitable for inclusion in an anthology of humor (NB 19, *N&J*, 2: 364). Clemens referred to Lincoln as "that great American" in a speech titled "The Day We Celebrate" which Clemens delivered to the American Society in London on 4 July 1907 (*MTSpk*, p. 570).

Lincoln, Joseph C. *Cape Cod Ballads and Other Verse, by Joe Lincoln.* Illus. by Edward W. Kemble. Trenton, New Jersey: Albert A. Brandt, 1902. 198 pp.

Clemens was especially fond of the poem titled "The Village Oracle," consisting of Old Dan'l Hanks' narrow-minded opinions on travel, education, and religion. "Says I, 'how d'yer know you're right?'/'How do I *know?*' says he;/'Well, now, I vum! I know, by gum!/I'm right because I *be!*'" Clemens kiddingly adopted the nickname "Dan'l Hanks" for Harry Rogers, the son of his friend Henry H. Rogers (SLC to Henry H. Rogers, Florence, 18 December 1903, *MTHHR*, pp. 545, 546 n. 2). In August 1904 Clemens copied the title of Lincoln's book and a stanza from this poem into Notebook 46 (TS p. 33). In 1906 Clemens alluded to the "limitless knowledge and daring and placid self-confidence" of "the late Simon Hanks [*sic*], of Cape Cod" and quoted (or, rather, paraphrased) a stanza from the poem in "Introducing Doctor Henry Van Dyke" (*MTS*[1923], p. 298). Again, on 28 October 1908, in a letter to W. W. Jacobs, Clemens misquoted his favorite stanza; evidently he depended on memory, for three of the four lines contain errors and he mistakenly calls the title character "Simon Hanks" (*MTL*, p. 823). The lines Clemens liked so much are these: "The Lord knows all things, great or small,/With doubt He's never vexed;/He, in his wisdom, knows it all,—/But Dan'l Hanks comes next."

Lindau, Rudolf (1829–1910).

Was Clemens referring to a work by this German writer of fiction when he urged Lindau to "send us that book" in a letter of 24 April 1901 (CWB)?

Lindh, E. I. (unidentified article).

In chapter 7, Book 2 of "Christian Science" (1907), Mark Twain refers to Lindh's "hopeful article on the solution of the problem of the 'divided church'" that appeared in an issue of the Boston *Transcript* in February 1903.

Lindsay, (Mrs.) Anna Robertson (Brown) (1864–1948). *What Is Worth While?* New York: T. Y. Crowell & Co., [cop. 1893]. 32 pp.

Source: MTLAcc, entry #869, volume donated by Mrs. Ralph W. Ashcroft (formerly Isabel Lyon), Clemens' secretary.

Lindsay, (Lady) Caroline Blanche Elizabeth (Fitzroy). *From a Venetian Balcony and Other Poems of Venice and the Near Lands.* Illus. by Clara Montalba. Second edition. London: Kegan Paul, Trench, Trübner & Co.; Venice: Rosen, 1904. 68 pp.

Inscription: front pastedown endpaper signed in black ink "SL. Clemens/June, 1907./London./From Lady Lindsay."

Catalogs: A1911, #289, $1.75; *Hunley 1958,* item #72, $6.50.

Location: Humanities Research Center, University of Texas at Austin. Contains *A1911* sale label. Another label has been removed from the front free endpaper. Priced in pencil on rear endpaper: $12.50.

Copy examined: Clemens' copy, unmarked.

————. *Godfrey's Quest: A Fantastic Poem.* London: Kegan Paul, Trench, Trübner & Co., 1905. 128 pp.

Inscription: inside front cover signed in brown ink: "SL. Clemens/London, June 1907./From Lady Lindsay."

Marginalia: one pencil scrawl on final page.

Location: Antenne-Dorrance Collection, Rice Lake, Wis.

Copy examined: Clemens' copy.

Lingard, John (1771–1851). *A History of England from the First Invasion by Romans.* Fifth edition. 8 vols. Paris: Baudry's European Library, 1840. Half-title: Collection of Ancient and Modern British Authors.

Catalog: A1911, #290a, .50¢, vol. 2 only.

The whereabouts of Clemens' set of Lingard is unknown. Isabel Lyon testified that Clemens kept these books "near at hand" while writing *CY,* and she recalled with indignation how Albert Bigelow Paine "broke up that priceless 20 volume [*sic*] Lingard in order to include in the first sale . . . two or three odd volumes rich with Mr. Clemens's notes jotted along the margins" ("Notes Re. *A Connecticut Yankee,*" Henry W. and Albert A. Berg Collection, New York Public Library). The *A1911* catalog listed only the second volume of Clemens' copy, however.

James D. Williams, "Genesis, Composition, Publication" (1961), p. 95; "Use of History" (1965), p. 104.

Linley, George (1798–1865). "Ever of thee" (song, pub. 1852). Melody composed by Foley Hall.

Clemens' letter of 6 February 1863 from Carson City mentions a baritone's singing "Ever of thee I'm fondly dreaming" (*MTEnt,* p. 59).

Linton, (Mrs.) Elizabeth (Lynn) (1822–1898). *The True History of Joshua Davidson.* Philadelphia: J. B. Lippincott & Co., 1873. 279 pp.

Inscription: flyleaf signed "S. L. Clemens, Hartford, 1882."

Catalogs: A1911, #290b, $1.25; *American Book-Prices Current Index 1960–1965* (New York, 1968), p. 368, item #64, $27, listed (probably erroneously) as an 1883 edition.

In March 1882 Clemens wrote the book title and the author's name in Notebook 20 (*N&J,* 2: 452). Perhaps its unusual combination of religion and politics piqued his interest. *Joshua Davidson* is the fictional biography of a young Cornwall carpenter whose religious beliefs determine him to practice Christ's precepts totally. (This theme of seriously applying the teachings of Christ to contemporary society would recur in Rose Terry Cooke's sketch titled "The Deacon's Week" [collected in *Root-Bound* in 1885] and in Charles M. Sheldon's *In His Steps* [1896].) There are explicit parallels between Davidson's life and Christ's, as when the modern man sharply questions his parish clergyman about pious hypocrisy (pp. 4–12). The crude narrative, purportedly written by Davidson's friend and disciple named John, is more of a tract than a novel. Joshua becomes the avowed enemy of "Ecclesiastical Christianity" and "Society"; he moves to London and attempts to bring Christ to the working men. Eventually he concludes that Christ would have taken different actions in nineteenth-century England: "The modern Christ would be a politician." Davidson pledges himself to an organization having "the equalization of classes as its end. It is Communism" (p. 83). He labors to achieve "Christian Communism."

In London, Davidson befriends a prostitute, Mary Prinsep, recognizing her "natural virtue" (p. 106). He denounces the reformatory as "a place of humiliation and penitent degradation" (pp. 122–123). He helps to establish the International Working Men's Association. An aristocrat attempts to cooperate with Davidson's movement, but Lord X's efforts are feeble and short-lived. Around 1871 Davidson goes to Paris to assist the Commune during the war between France and Russia. Mary Prinsep is killed there, and French politicians hostile to Communism ultimately triumph ("for the present, God help this poor sorrowful world of ours!" [p. 247]).

Joshua Davidson and the narrator return to England, where Davidson—now branded a Communist who is "wilfully and willingly guilty of every crime under heaven" (p. 262)—begins a series of lectures to "show how Christ and his apostles were Communists, and how they preached the same doctrines which the Commune of Paris strove to embody" (p. 267). At Lowbridge, where he is denounced by his former clergyman, an incited crowd beats and kicks Davidson to death. The narrator ponders: "Is the Christian world all wrong, or is practical Christianity impossible?" (p. 276).

Lippard, George (1822–1854). *Legends of the American Revolution; or, Washington and His Generals. With a Biography of the Author's Life by C. Chauncey Burr.* Philadelphia: T. B. Peterson, [1847]. 538 pp.

Evidence regarding Clemens' early reading is so scanty that even the knowledge that he was familiar with this patriotic book is immensely welcome. Clemens wrote to his brother Orion on 26 October 1853 from Philadelphia, describing a recent sight-seeing excursion: "Geo. Lippard, in his 'Legends of Washington and his Generals,' has rendered the Wissahickon [River] sacred in my eyes" *(MTB, p. 100; MTL, p. 27; TS in MTP).*

George Washington's reputation for veracity became a touchstone for Mark Twain. Judge Thatcher alludes to "Washington's lauded Truth about the hatchet" in chapter 35 of *Tom Sawyer* (1876). Clemens referred to the "little hatchet" in a letter of 16 March 1876 to the Chairman of the Knights of St. Patrick *(DE,* 20: 437). A letter to William Dean Howells, written on 11 October 1876, jokingly refers to Washington's probity as a "fault" *(MTHL, p. 158).* Act 4 of *Ah Sin* (produced in 1877) mentions Washington. In chapter 5 of *Huckleberry Finn* (1885), Huck "took up a book and began something about General Washington and the wars" to prove to Pap Finn that he could read. "The deeds of Washington, the patriot, are the essential thing," Twain emphasized in "Switzerland, the Cradle of Liberty" (1892); "the cherry-tree incident is of no consequence." Huck refers admiringly to Washington in chapter 10 of *Tom Sawyer Abroad* (1894). In "The Secret History of Eddypus" (written 1901–1902), however, Washington is barely remembered as "George Wishington" who "drowned at Waterloo" *(FM,* pp. 329–330). Twain dated his savage polemic, "A Defence of General Funston," on February 22nd, "the great Birth-Day," and compared Funston to Washington throughout the essay *(North American Review,* May 1902). He also referred to Washington in Notebook 45 (1902), TS p. 38; chapter 5 of "A Horse's Tale" (1906); Part 6 of "What Is Man?," published in 1906 *(WIM?, p. 200);* "Mighty Mark Twain Overawes Marines," New York *Times,* 12 May 1907; and an Autobiographical Dictation of 3 July 1908 *(MTE,* p. 294).

Literary Digest (weekly periodical, pub. 1890–1938). New York: Funk & Wagnalls.
In Book 2 of "Christian Science" (chapters 7 and 8), Mark Twain quoted from the *Literary Digest* issues of 25 January 1902 and 14 February 1903 *(WIM?,* pp. 311–312, 335–336, 572). Twain's clipping of an article from the issue of 6 December 1902, "Mrs. Eddy and Contagious Disease," survives in the Mark Twain Papers at Berkeley (DV102b, Box 30, no. 6), with his caustic remarks in its margins. In "Was the World Made for Man?" *(LE,* p. 211), Twain used a quotation from this journal as an epigraph; the excerpt concerned Alfred Russel Wallace's theory about the earth as the only habitable globe.

Literature (New York weekly magazine, began publication in February 1888).
Clemens' friend William Dean Howells started writing regularly for *Literature* in 1898, when Harper & Brothers took control of the magazine *(MTHL,* p. 687 n. 9). Presumably Clemens had a special interest in its contents after this development. In a letter of 1 and 2 March 1899 written from Vienna, Clemens thanked John Kendrick Bangs and "Mr. Harper" for a complimentary subscription to *Literature;* he also mentioned an article on copyright that appeared in the 10 February 1899 issue (ALS in Berg Collection). Jean Clemens employed this subscription to watch the results of Bangs' poll of his readers' choices for ten favorite living authors, as reported in *Literature* between February and April 1899 (SLC to WDH, 5 April 1899, *MTHL,* p. 691).

Littell's Living Age (American weekly journal, pub. 1844–1941).
On 1 April 1874 the Hartford magazine and newspaper firm Geer & Pond billed Clemens for "Mar 21 Age Dec. 6/73 to Mar. 21/74 $2.45"; he paid on 3 April 1874 (receipt in MTP). In January 1894 Clemens recollected an article he had read "in old Littell. Susy Crane has it" (NB 33, TS p. 47). He was referring to "Jón Jónsonn's Saga: The Genuine Autobiography of a Modern Icelander," *Littell's Living Age,* 132 (10 February 1877), 407–430. But Clemens did not find these reprinted British materials uniformly interesting. On 2 June 1906 Isabel Lyon noted while he was summering in Dublin, New Hampshire: "There are a lot of old bound volumes of Littell's Living Age in the house and Mr. Clemens has taken them as his reading, but [is] finding about one readable article in a volume. It's a pretty dull collection, and . . . as Mr. Clemens opened one of them he said it was 'like looking at an asphalt pavement' for dull monotony" (IVL Journals, TS p. 161, MTP; repeated in IVL Journal, Humanities Research Center, Univ. of Texas at Austin).

Litteratur-Institut. Vienna: L. and A. Last, 1896. 474 pp.
Source: MTLAcc, entry #560, volume donated by Clemens.

The Little Flower Girl, and Other Stories in Verse, by "Robin." London: W. S. Sonnenschein, 1884. 111 pp.
Source: MTLAcc, entry #626, volume donated by Clemens.

Little Folks. Vol. 1. Illus. New York: American News Co., n.d. 416 pp.
Source: MTLAcc, entry #466, volume donated by Clemens.

Little French Masterpieces. Ed. by Alexander Jessup. Trans. by George Burnham Ives *et al.* 6 vols. New York: G. P. Putnam's Sons, 1903–1905.
Inscription: one volume signed "Jean L. Clemens, 1909."
Catalogs: A1911, #292, 6 vols., listed as 1909 edition, $3, purchased by J. O. L. representing the Mark Twain Company; *C1951,* #D15, listed among books signed by Clemens, erroneously listed as "8 vols."
The set collects fiction by Flaubert, Daudet, Mérimée, Maupassant, Gautier, Balzac, and others.

Liveing, Henry George Downing. *Records of Romsey Abbey: An Account of the Benedictine House of Nuns, with Notes on the Parish Church and Town (A. D. 907–1558). Compiled from Manuscript and Printed Records.* Illus. Winchester: Warren and Son, 1906. 342 pp.
   Inscription: signed "S. L. Clemens, 1906."
   Catalog: A1911, #293, $2.50.

Livingston, (Mrs.) Margaret Vere (Farrington) (b. 1863). *Tales of King Arthur and His Knights of the Round Table.* Illus. by Alfred Fredericks and others. New York: G. P. Putnam's Sons, 1888. 276 pp.
   Source: MTLAcc, entry #1883, Jean Clemens' copy, volume donated by Clara Clemens Gabrilowitsch in 1910.

Livingstone, David (1813–1873) and Charles Livingstone (1821–1873). *Narrative of an Expedition to the Zambesi and Its Tributaries. . . . 1858–1864.* Illus. New York: Harper & Brothers, 1886. 638 pp.
   Source: MTLAcc, entry #1722, volume donated by Clemens.

Lloyd, Henry Demarest (1847–1903). *Man, the Social Creator.* New York: Doubleday, Page & Co., 1906. 279 pp.
   Source: MTLAcc, entry #799, volume donated by Clemens.

————. *Wealth against Commonwealth.* New York: Harper & Brothers, 1903. 563 pp.
   Source: MTLAcc, entry #1700, volume donated by Clemens.

Lloyd, John William (b. 1857). *Dawn-Thought on the Reconciliation; A Volume of Pantheistic Impressions and Glimpses of Larger Religion.* Wellesley Hills, Mass.: Maugus Press, [cop. 1900]. 197 pp.
   Source: MTLAcc, entry #909, volume donated by Clemens.

Lloyd's Weekly (London weekly newspaper, pub. 1843–1918).
   In "To the Person Sitting in Darkness" (1901), Mark Twain refers to, and quotes from, an issue of *Lloyd's Weekly* that appeared "some days before the affair of Magersfontein" during the Boer War. A British private speaks there of serving the Boers some mercy *"with the long spoon."*

"Loch Lomond" ("The bonnie banks of Loch Lomond") (Scottish air).
   "When I came away she was singing, 'Loch Lomond.' The pathos of it! It always moves me so when she sings that" ("Was It Heaven? Or Hell?," ch. 5 [1902]). Isabel Lyon played this song at Clemens' request on 14 February 1906 (IVL Journal, Humanities Research Center, Univ. of Texas at Austin).

Locke, David Ross (1833–1888), pseud. "Petroleum V. Nasby."
   Clemens was well acquainted with Locke and his writings, yet (curiously) no copies of Locke's books survived in Clemens' library and Locke was the major omission from *Mark Twain's Library of Humor* (1888). On 23 January 1869 Clemens gloated over his own lecturing triumph in the city where Locke edited the Toledo *Blade* (SLC to Joseph H. Twichell, ALS in Samossoud Collection, TS in MTP). Clemens met Locke on 9 March 1869 and sat up to converse with him until six o'clock in the morning (SLC to Susan Crane, 9, 31 March 1869, ALS in MTP). In 1877 Locke proposed to Clemens that they write a play together, but the collaboration never took place (SLC to F. D. Millet, 7 August 1877, Harvard Library). Clemens noted Locke's name and address in Notebook 13 (1877), *N&J,* 2: 11. He mentioned Locke complimentarily in a speech in Quebec on 31 January 1882, "On After-Dinner Speaking" *(MTSpk,* p. 167). Locke's name appears prominently among Clemens' lists of literary comedians to be considered for inclusion in an anthology of American humor (NB 19

[1880], *N&J*, 2: 362; NB 19 [1881], p. 429). Clemens also meant to "refer to & quote from Nasby" in a proposed "Essay on Humor" (NB 24 [August 1885], TS p. 36). Thereafter Clemens recalled Locke's name and anecdotes in 1887 (NB 27, TS p. 6), April 1891 (NB 30, TS p. 33), January 1903 (NB 46, TS p. 6), and 1906 (NB 48, TS p. 10). In an Autobiographical Dictation of 31 July 1906 Mark Twain alluded to Locke as one of the American humorists "whose writings and sayings were once in everybody's mouth" but whose renown depended wholly on "an odd trick of speech and of spelling. . . . Presently the fashion passes and the fame along with it" *(MTE, pp. 201–202).*
　　MTAm, p. 219; *MT&GWC*, p. 73.

Locke, John (1632–1704).
　　"(Shall I confess it?) I have never read Locke nor any other of the many philosophers quoted by you. . . . So, all these months I have been thinking the thoughts of illustrious philosophers, and didn't know it" (Clemens to Sir John Adams, Vienna, 5 December 1898, in Lawrence Clark Powell's "An Unpublished Mark Twain Letter," *AL,* 13 [March 1942], 405–407).

Locke, William John (1863–1930). *The Morals of Marcus Ordeyne. A Novel.* New York: John Lane, 1905. 303 pp.
　　Source: MTLAcc, entry #204, volume donated by Albert Bigelow Paine, Clemens' designated biographer. Possibly Clemens saw this book, since the men exchanged reading materials.

Locker-Lampson, Frederick (1821–1895). *London Lyrics.* London: Strahan & Co., 1872. 200 pp.
　　Source: MTLAcc, entry #2061, volume donated from Clemens' library by Clara Clemens Gabrilowitsch in 1910.

Lockyer, Joseph Norman (1836–1920). *Elementary Lessons In Astronomy.* New Edition. Illus. London: Macmillan and Co., 1877. 348 pp.
　　Inscription: signed "S. L. Clemens, Munich, Dec. 1878".
　　Marginalia: a few passages marked and a note ("A body could buy one") written in reference to a planet.
　　Catalog: A1911, #295, $4.
　　On 7 July 1907 Clemens dined with this astronomer (AD, 30 August 1907, MTP).

Lodge, Henry Cabot (1850–1924). *The War with Spain.* New York: Harper & Brothers, [cop. 1899]. 288 pp.
　　Source: MTLAcc, entry #1723, volume donated by Clemens.

Lodge, (Sir) Oliver Joseph (1851–1940). *The Ether of Space.* Illus. New York and London: Harper & Brothers, 1909. 167 pp.
　　Inscription: inside front cover signed "S. L. Clemens, 1909."
　　Catalog: A1911, #296, $2; *L1912,* item #19, $4.

————. *The Substance of Faith Allied with Science; A Catechism for Parents and Teachers.* New York: Harper & Brothers, 1907. 144 pp.
　　Inscription: inside front cover signed in black ink "SL. Clemens/1907".
　　Location: Mark Twain Library, Redding, Conn. Donated by Clemens (MTLAcc, entry #917).
　　Copy examined: Clemens' copy, unmarked.
　　The subject matter of this book certainly was Clemens' meat: "Ascent of Man," "Development of Conscience," "Nature of Evil," "The Meaning of Sin," just to name a few chapter titles. Each chapter opens with a question, followed by an answer which harmonizes science and religion. Clemens must have been terribly weary the day he looked through this volume and decided against marking it.

————. *The Substance of Faith Allied with Science; A Catechism for Parents and Teachers*. New York: Harper & Brothers, [cop. 1907]. 144 pp.
   Source: MTLAcc, entry #1391, volume donated by Clemens.

————. "What Is Life," *North American Review*, 180 (May 1905), 661–669.
   Sherwood Cummings traces Mark Twain's quotation of Lodge in "Three Thousand Years Among the Microbes" (written 1905) to page 663 of this article, which illustrates the minute size of atoms (Cummings, "Mark Twain and Science" [1950], p. 32). In "Three Thousand Years" the narrator remarks, "Take a man like Sir Oliver Lodge, and what secrets of Nature can be hidden from him? *(WWD?,* p. 447).
   MTB, pp. 1663–70.

Loew, William Noah (1847–1922), trans. *Magyar Songs. Selections from Hungarian Poets*. New York: Samisch & Goldmann, 1887. 248 pp.
   Source: MTLAcc, entry #2058, volume donated from Clemens' library by Clara Clemens Gabrilowitsch in 1910.

Logan, Olive (1839–1909).
   Mark Twain derided Logan—the author of fiction and writings on theatre and homelife—in an Autobiographical Dictation of 11 April 1906 (MTP).

Loisette, Alphonse. *Physiological Memory; or, The Instantaneous Art of Never Forgetting. Part IV*. New York: Alphonse Loisette, 1886. 32 pp.
   Inscription: Albert Bigelow Paine wrote the words "Loisette Memory" in pencil on a leaflet that accompanies this pamphlet.
   Location: Mark Twain Papers, Berkeley, Ca.
   Copy examined: Clemens' copy, presumably. No marks.
   In 1887 Clemens sent a published broadside which quoted himself to the Reverend John Davis of Hannibal, Missouri; in it he testified that an hour of personal counsel from Loisette gave him confidence worth ten thousand dollars (CWB). Page 2 in the Appendix of Loisette's 1887 edition of *The Loisettian School of Physiological Memory. The Instantaneous Art of Never Forgetting* reprints a letter Clemens wrote on 4 March 1887 stating that "Prof. Loisette. . . . proved to me that I already *had* a memory, a thing which I was not aware of till then. . . . The information cost me but little, yet I value it at a prodigious figure" (TS in MTP; also published in *Harper's Weekly,* 2 April 1887). On 9 July 1887 Clemens sent Franklin G. Whitmore a new draft of his testimonial for "that Loisette circular" (ALS in MTP). Beset by complications with the Paige typesetter and the details of publishing *A Connecticut Yankee,* however, on 23 November 1889 Clemens instructed Whitmore to answer inquiries by saying that whereas Clemens formerly believed the Loisette method to be worthwhile, he had changed his opinion "long ago" (ALS in MTP).

London. *Forty-One Colored Views of London, Designed and Engraved by [Augustus Charles] Pugin [1762–1832] and [Thomas] Rowlandson [1756–1827] and Printed in Aquatint by [Joseph Constantine] Stadler, from "Historic Anecdotes and Secret Memoirs of the Legislative Union Between Great Britain and Ireland."* London, n.d.
   Catalog: A1911, #297, $5.95, publisher unidentified.

London *Daily Chronicle*.
   Clemens quibbled with some grammar he noticed in an October 1896 issue (NB 39, TS p. 14). On 12 October 1898 he requested Chatto & Windus to change his subscription address to Vienna (ALS in Berg Collection). He instructed Percy Spalding of Chatto & Windus to stop the mailing of his London *Chronicle* to Vienna on 24 May 1899 (ALS in CWB).

London *Daily Mail.*

Clemens was impressed by Alfred C. Harmsworth's success with the London *Daily Mail* (SLC to Henry H. Rogers, London, 5 February 1900, *MTHHR,* p. 431).

London *Daily News.*

In Paris in 1879, following a note about Josh Billings, Robert Burdette, and the Danbury News Man, Clemens made a memorandum to "see scrap book for Am & English humor" *(N&J,* 2: 301). In his 1878/1879 scrapbook is a clipping from the London *Daily News* which comments on the "boldness" American humorists exhibit in treating religious ideas and biblical topics, and their overall "astounding coolness and freedom of manners" (MTP). In a letter to Chatto & Windus written on 5 August 1893 from Krankenheil-Tölz, Bavaria, Clemens complained that his issues of the *Daily News* were not arriving as he had requested. He claimed that on 30 July 1893 he had asked Chatto & Windus to take out a six-month subscription in his name (ALS in Lilly Collection, PH in MTP).

London *Illustrated News.*

On 28 April 1902 Henry H. Rogers sent Clemens a clipping which retold "A Riddle of the Sea," the disappearance in the 1860's of the brig *Marie Celeste,* bound from Boston to Mediterranean ports. Clemens jotted his opinion on the envelope: "Wonderful sea-tale" *(MTHHR,* pp. 485–486).

London, Jack (1876–1916). *The Call of the Wild.* Illus. by Philip R. Goodwin and Charles Livingston Bull. New York: Macmillan Co., 1903. 231 pp.
   Source: MTLAcc, entry #1963, volume donated from Clemens' library by Clara Clemens Gabrilowitsch in 1910.

London *Morning Post.*

Clemens placed advertisements in this newspaper while cook-hunting in October 1896 (NB 39, TS p. 7).

London. National Gallery. *A Complete Illustrated Catalogue to the National Gallery.* Ed. by Henry Blackburn (1830–1897). 242 illus. London, 1879.
   Inscription: flyleaf signed "S. L. Clemens/London, Aug. 6 '79".
   Marginalia: several illustrations marked with an "X."
   Catalog: A1911, #44, $1, no publisher specified.

London *Saturday Review.*

On 28 January 1885 Clemens urged Charles L. Webster to "see fine notice [of *HF*] in London Saturday Review—get it at Brentano's for your scrapbook" *(MTBus,* p. 298).

London *Standard.*

Clemens wrote an undated letter (presumably in 1873) to Charles W. Stoddard, instructing him to sift through the "huge bundle" of *Standard* issues Clemens left behind, and also asking Stoddard to subscribe for all issues dating back to 17 October. Clemens wished to "scrap-book" all reports on the Tichborne Claimant trial for a future sketch he planned to write (ALS in MTP). In 1888 Clemens cited an unrelated fact which he attributed to the London *Standard* (NB 28, TS p. 60).
   AMT, p. 194.

London *Times*.
    The sheer volume of its articles impressed Clemens most about this news-
paper. He noted the number of words in an average issue in Notebook 17 (25
January 1879), *N&J*, 2: 262, and on the front endpaper of Notebook 18 (1879).
Subsequently he referred to the *Times* as "the bulkiest daily newspaper in the
world" and reported that it "often contains 100,000 words of reading matter"
(*TA*, Appendix F, "German Journals"). He also mentioned this "grim journal"
in chapter 42 of *TA* (1880). In September and November 1888 Clemens
examined its column space for possible applications of the Paige typesetting
machine (NB 28, TS pp. 28, 34). The epigraph to "The Czar's Soliloquy"
(1905) consists of a quotation Mark Twain took from the London *Times*. In an
Autobiographical Dictation of 24 November 1908 Mark Twain spoke of the
Times as Lord Northcliffe's journal which for a century had wielded political
power with world rulers (MTP).
    MT&JB, pp. 35–36.

London *World*.
    Clemens mentions that George Warner once showed him a copy of the London
World containing a sketch of Rudyard Kipling; this formed part of his introduction to the important British writer (13 August 1906 AD, *MTE*, p. 312).

Long, Gabrielle Margaret Vere (Campbell) (1888–1952), pseud. "Marjorie Bowen."
    The Master of the Stair. New York: McClure, Phillips & Co., 1907.
    On 25 March 1907 Clemens thanked "Miss Marjorie" for her wish to dedicate
The Master of the Stair to him (*MTLW*, p. 127). In May 1907 Clemens recommended the novel to Mary Benjamin Rogers, but he couldn't recall the title
and he mistakenly supposed it to be the author's only published work. Clemens at
least remembered that Marjorie Bowen had dedicated it to him, adding that
this made it difficult for him to read the novel "without prejudice or predilec-
tion. . . . It is based on the Massacre of Glencoe, but it mercifully leaves out
(or very gently touches) the main horrors. I think that it is greatly to the girl's
credit, for there would naturally be a strong temptation to do the other thing"
(*MTLM*, pp. 99–100).

————. *The Viper of Milan: A Romance of Lombardy*. New York: McClure,
    Phillips & Co., 1906. 362 pp.
    Catalog: C1951, #20a, $20, listed among the books containing Clemens'
marginal notes, no edition specified.
    Sometime in 1906 Clemens wrote a letter from Fifth Avenue addressed to
"Dear Sirs" (probably the publishers) in which he expressed appreciation for a
copy of this novel. He also registered disbelief that a mere girl, whether fifteen
or even nineteen years old, could write such a work; clearly she must be at
least twenty-five, he insisted: such craftsmanship requires lengthy training.
Clemens gives his assent to the laudatory notice of *The Viper* that appeared in the
Times Saturday Review (PH of ALS in MTP). Since Clemens thought so highly
of the novel, he must have meant *The Viper* when writing of a "remarkable
book . . . by a child of fifteen" to which he referred Mary Benjamin Rogers on
19 November 1906. He praised that unidentified book as "virile and rugged"
(*MTLM*, p. 89).

Long, John Luther (1861–1927). *Madame Butterfly*. Illus. by C. Yarnall Abbott.
    Japanese Edition. New York: The Century Co., 1903. 152 pp. [Edition conjec-
    tured. Originally published as a short story in 1898; later adapted for the stage
    as an operetta.]
    When Isabel Lyon noticed on 10 October 1906 that Clemens was looking
about aimlessly for a book to read, she gave him a copy of Long's story.
"Tonight at dinner," she reported, "the King said he had read 'that beautiful,
beautiful story, and it is perfect. There is no flaw in it. There is no word to be

changed. He makes you see a country you are a stranger to, and he makes you suffer as if you had been in the story yourself' " (IVL Journals, TS p. 194, MTP). When Clemens was attempting to demonstrate in 1909 how the Shakespeare/Bacon identity might have been mistaken, he reminded Albert Bigelow Paine that "even in this day John Luther Long's 'Madame Butterfly' is sometimes called Belasco's play, though it is doubtful if Belasco ever wrote a line of it" (*MTB,* p. 1480).

————. "Purple Eyes," *Century Magazine,* 56 (July 1898), 354–363. Collected in *Madame Butterfly; Purple Eyes; A Gentleman of Japan and a Lady; Kito; Glory.* New York: The Century Co., 1898. 224 pp.
   Pained and moved by *Madame Butterfly,* Clemens told Isabel Lyon on 10 October 1906 "that he hadn't read 'Purple Eyes' yet and that he wouldn't read it for anything" (IVL Journals, TS p. 194, MTP).

Long, Thomas (1621–1707). *An Exercitation Concerning the Frequent Use of Our Lord's Prayer in the Publick Worship of God. And a View of What Hath Been Said by Dr. Owen Concerning That Subject.* London: Printed by J. G. for R. Marriot, 1658. 166 pp.
   Clemens copied the title of this book into his notebook in 1873, maybe because he found it amusing (NB 12, *N&J,* 1: 554).

Long, William Joseph (1867–1952). *Beasts of the Field.* Illus. by Charles Copeland. New York: Ginn & Co., [cop. 1901]. 332 pp.
   Source: MTLAcc, entry #1966, volume donated from Clemens' library by Clara Clemens Gabrilowitsch in 1910.
   In 1907 Clemens became extremely interested in a dispute between Theodore Roosevelt and this Congregational clergyman who wrote on animal life. Clemens thought Long to be a "pleasant and entertaining" naturalist whose books were mainly popular with children. Although Long's works do not measure up to John Burroughs', Clemens said, at least Long writes from his own observations. His only fault is that he may sometimes overestimate the intelligence of the wild creatures he describes (AD, 29 May 1907, MTP; *MTE,* p. 20). On 2 June 1907 Clemens told Isabel Lyon that he wished to write something about the Roosevelt-Long clash over Long's nature books (IVL Journals, TS p. 248, MTP). Later Clemens alluded to Long as the "nature fakir" (possibly Roosevelt's term for Long) in an Autobiographical Dictation of 18 October 1907 (*MTE,* p. 8) and in Notebook 48 (TS p. 9).

————. *Fowls of the Air.* Illus. by Charles Copeland. New York: Ginn & Co., 1902. 310 pp.
   Source: MTLAcc, entry #1964, volume donated from Clemens' library by Clara Clemens Gabrilowitsch in 1910.

————. *School of the Woods; Some Life Studies of Animal Instincts and Animal Training.* Illus. by Charles Copeland. New York: Ginn & Co., [cop. 1902]. 361 pp.
   Source: MTLAcc, entry #1965, volume donated from Clemens' library by Clara Clemens Gabrilowitsch in 1910.

Longfellow, Henry Wadsworth (1807–1882). "The Day Is Done" (poem, pub. 1844).
   Clemens particularly liked the closing stanza of this poem: "The night shall be filled with music,/And the cares that infest the day/Shall fold their tents, like the Arabs,/And as silently steal away." He quoted from these lines in a letter to the *Alta California* written from the Holy Land in September 1867 (*TIA,* p. 183); twice in chapter 42 of *IA* (1869); once in chapter 45 of *GA* (1873); and again in a letter to Francis H. Skrine ("gone silently away like Longfellow's Arab") written in Vienna on 3 November 1897 (CWB).

————. *The Divine Tragedy.* Boston: James R. Osgood and Co., 1871. 150 pp.
Inscription: front flyleaf inscribed by Livy Clemens in ink, "S. L. Clemens/
1872".
Provenance: formerly in the Mark Twain Library, Redding, Conn. Donated
from Clemens' library by Clara Clemens Gabrilowitsch in 1910 (MTLAcc, entry
#2056).
Location: Elihu Burritt Library, Central Connecticut State College, New
Britain, Conn.
Copy examined: photocopies of inscription and title page, supplied by Francis
J. Gagliardi, Assistant Director, Library Services.

————. *Evangeline: A Tale of Arcadie* (play). Adapter unidentified.
In July 1888 Clemens noted that George Knight had joined E. E. Rice in
presenting *Evangeline* on the stage (NB 28, TS p. 8).

————. *The Golden Legend.* Boston: Ticknor and Fields, 1862. 326 pp.
Source: MTLAcc, entry #2046, volume donated from Clemens' library by
Clara Clemens Gabrilowitsch in 1910.
"I have read & sent home The Golden Legend," Clemens informed Livy on
9 January 1872 in a letter written during his lecture tour in Ohio (ALS in MTP).
She replied on 7 January 1872: "I think the Golden Legend is beautiful. I
wonder you did not mark it still more than you have" (ALS in MTP). Subse-
quently Clemens sent his wife another, unnamed poem by Longfellow (based
on a "beautiful old legend"), though Clemens indicated that he preferred a
different version produced by an unidentified woman poet (20 January 1872,
Harrisburg, Pennsylvania, ALS in MTP). In chapter 36 of *GA* (1873) Laura
Hawkins would rank Longfellow with Hawthorne and Tennyson, "favorites of
her idle hours."
LLMT, p. 173 n. 10.

————. *The Hanging of the Crane* (pub. 1874).
Catalog: C1951, #95c, $30, listed among books signed by Clemens, no edition
specified.

————. "The Hemlock Tree" (poem).
On 13 February 1884 George Washington Cable reported from Hartford that
Clemens "went to the piano & sang a German song—one that Longfellow has
translated—'O hemlock tree, O hemlock tree,/How faithful are thy branches'"
(MT&GWC, pp. 31–32).

————. "The Legend of Rabbi Ben Levi," poem in *Tales of a Wayside Inn* ("The
Spanish Jew's Tale," Part 1) (pub. 1863).
Livy Langdon copied this poem into her commonplace book around 1868;
only two pages farther on, Clemens himself wrote in the same book (DV161,
MTP).

————. *The New England Tragedies. (I.) John Endicott; (II.) Giles Corey of the
Salem Farms.* Boston: Ticknor and Fields, 1868. 179 pp.
Source: MTLAcc, entry #2055, volume donated from Clemens' library by
Clara Clemens Gabrilowitsch in 1910.
"I have read & sent home . . . The New England Tragedies," Clemens wrote
to Livy on 9 January 1872 from Steubenville, Ohio (ALS in MTP, *LLMT,* p.
172). In "Sociable Jimmy" (New York *Times,* 29 November 1874; *The Twainian,*
2 [February 1943], 5), probably written in 1872 or 1873, Mark Twain states
that he kept notes of his conversation with a young Negro boy on the flyleaf of
a copy of *New England Tragedies.*

————. *Nuremberg; A Poem.* Illus. Nuremberg: J. L. Schrag, n.d. 15 pp.
  Source: MTLAcc, entry #2057, volume donated from Clemens' library by
Clara Clemens Gabrilowitsch in 1910.

————. *Poems of Henry Wadsworth Longfellow.* Boston: Houghton, Mifflin and
Co., 1882.
  Marginalia: both the text and the index at the rear are marked, but apparently
not by Clemens.
  Location: Antenne-Dorrance Collection, Rice Lake, Wis.
  Copy examined: evidently a copy belonging to a member of Clemens' family.
  Possibly Clemens intended to buy this edition when he made a memorandum
in Notebook 20 in April 1882: "Osgood get a Longfellow for Clara's birthday."
Longfellow had died on 24 March 1882, and many eulogies were appearing in
the press. Clemens planned to meet publisher James R. Osgood in Boston on
14 April (WDH to SLC, 7 April 1882, *MTHL*, p. 399). Clara's eighth birthday
was to be on 8 June 1882.

————. *Poets and Poetry of Europe.* New York: James Miller, 1863.
  Source: Edgar H. Hemminghaus—"Mark Twain's German Provenience"
(1945), pp. 467–468—reported seeing Clemens' copy of these translations,
biographies, and critical notices in the Mark Twain Library at Redding, Connecticut, in 1945. Albert E. Stone, Jr. did not find the volume there in 1955, however; and I was unable to locate *Poets and Poetry of Europe* when I visited
Redding in 1970.

————. "A Psalm of Life" (poem).
  Clemens concluded a letter of 20 November 1860 to his brother Orion by
quoting the fifth stanza: "In the world's great [*sic*] field of battle,/ . . . Be a *hero*
in the strife" (quoted by Allan C. Bates in "Mark Twain and the Mississippi
River," unpublished doctoral dissertation [Univ. of Chicago, 1968], p. 158). In
chapter 50 of *IA* (1869) Mark Twain alluded to the first stanza: "The poet has
said, 'Things are not what they seem.' " He employed the seventh stanza of the
poem in his ill-fated Whittier Birthday Dinner speech on 17 December 1877
(MTB, p. 1646). "Ask me not, in mournful numbers," Mark Twain quipped in
chapter 28 of *LonMiss* (1883), paraphrasing the opening line of "A Psalm of
Life." "This is art, and art is long, as the poet says," he wrote in chapter 6 of
FE (1897); Longfellow's fourth stanza observed that "Art is long, and Time is
fleeting."

————. *Selections from the Writings of Henry Wadsworth Longfellow, Arranged
Under the Days of the Year.* Boston: Houghton, Mifflin & Co., 1889. [128 pp.]
  Source: MTLAcc, entry #2125, volume donated from Clemens' library by
Clara Clemens Gabrilowitsch in 1910.

————. *The Song of Hiawatha* (pub. 1855).
  In Mark Twain's sketch titled "A Memory" (August 1870 *Galaxy),* he pretended that as a boy he wrote a parody of *Hiawatha*—substituting language from
a warranty deed of property for the words of his father's favorite poem. Twain
quotes six lines of the resulting burlesque *(CG,* p. 66; also reprinted in *Mark
Twain: Life As I Find It,* pp. 100–103). The story is sheer nonsense, of course;
Clemens' father, John Marshall Clemens, died in 1847 before *Hiawatha* was even
published. "Honor be to Mudjeheewis!/You shall hear how Pau-Puk-Keewis—"
intones the imposter in Mark Twain's address at the Whittier Birthday Dinner
on 17 December 1877 *(MTB,* p. 1644). Mark Twain informs the readers of his
Life on the Mississippi (1883) that "the tales in 'Hiawatha' . . . came from
[Henry R.] Schoolcraft's book." In chapter 59 Twain publishes Schoolcraft's version of "Peboan and Seegwun, an Allegory of the Seasons," noting that the tale
"is used in 'Hiawatha'; but it is worth reading in the original form, if only that

one may see how effective a genuine poem can be without the helps and graces of poetic measure and rhythm."

Aspiz, "MT's Reading" (1949), pp. 116–117; Smith, " 'That Hideous Mistake' " (1955).

————. "The Village Blacksmith" (poem).

Mark Twain's speech at the Whittier Birthday Dinner on 17 December 1877 included the lines "Thanks, thanks to thee, my worthy friend,/For the lesson thou hast taught" *(MTB,* p. 1646).

Smith, " 'That Hideous Mistake' " (1955).

Longstreet, (Mrs.) Abby Buchanan. *Social Etiquette of New York.* New York: D. Appleton & Co., 1879. 187 pp. Revised, enlarged edition pub. 1881.

In Mark Twain's unfinished "Burlesque of Books on Etiquette" (written 1881) he quotes from and cites Mrs. Longstreet's book as "one of the ablest of our recent works on Deportment" *(LE,* p. 200); he is especially concerned with her dictum on calling cards. The dating of Mark Twain's composition of the manuscript (DV68, MTP) derives from his letter to James R. Osgood of 7 March 1881 ("Yes, send me a collection of etiquette books") and William Dean Howells' letter to Clemens, written on 17 April 1881 ("Why don't you go on with the Etiquette Book?") (both letters quoted in *MTHL,* pp. 360 n. 2, 362). Mrs. Longstreet also wrote separate manuals on wedding ceremonies, general manners, health care, debutantes, and calling cards.

Longstreet, Augustus Baldwin (1790–1870). *Georgia Scenes, Characters, Incidents, &c., in the First Half Century of The Republic. By a Native Georgian.* Second ed. Illus. New York: Harper & Brothers, 1845.

Inscription: front free endpaper is signed "James W. Hunt"; below this signature Clemens added his own in pencil: "S. L. Clemens/Hartford, 1876." An *A1911* sale label and the bookplate of W. T. H. Howe are pasted on the inside front cover. A note to Howe from Isabel V. Lyon, Clemens' one-time secretary (dated 26 August 1938), authenticates Clemens' ownership of the volume; Lyon's note is laid in the book.

Marginalia: Clemens made blue ink marks on pages 9 and 11 of "Georgia Theatrics" and on pages 23 and 31 of "the Horse-Swap." In the same ink he also jotted a few instructions: for the illustration of an imaginary fight captioned "A Lincoln [County] Rehearsal" (opposite page 10) he wrote, "Reproduce & use this picture. SLC"; on pages 23 and 24 of "The Horse-Swap" he changed several italicized words to "Rom." in the margins; near the illustration of a horseback rider opposite page 24 he directed, "Make fac-simile of this picture & use it. SLC"; and on page 25 he deleted the words "or hawked" in the sentence reading "If a stick cracked, or if any one moved suddenly about him, or coughed, or hawked, or spoke a little louder than common, up went Bullet's tail like lightning."

Catalog: A1911, #298, $5, quotes marginalia.

Location: Henry W. and Albert A. Berg Collection, New York Public Library.

Copy examined: Clemens' copy.

Mark Twain clearly intended to include material from *Georgia Scenes* in *Mark Twain's Library of Humor,* published in 1888. The title of Longstreet's book appears in a list of humorists and their works which Mark Twain began in 1880 (NB 19, *N&J,* 2: 362). Shortly thereafter he wrote "Hall (Georgia Scenes" (NB 19, p. 362), an allusion to one of the pseudonyms Longstreet signed to his sketches in *Georgia Scenes;* its title page does not name the author, and Longstreet alternates the names "Hall" and "Baldwin" in crediting his tales. In 1881 Mark Twain reminded himself of "Georgia Sketches" (NB 19, *N&J,* 2: 429). The two stories Mark Twain annotated in his own copy of *Georgia Scenes* were both ascribed by Longstreet to "Hall." One of them, "Georgia Theatrics," is the first piece in Longstreet's collection (pp. 9–11); it describes a ploughboy's pretended thrashing of a detested opponent. The other, "The Horse-Swap" (pp. 23–31), relates how the boastful Yellow Blossom from Jasper ("I'm a *leetle*, jist a *leetle*, of the best man at a horse-swap that ever trod shoe-leather") trades an ornery swayback called Bullet for the gentle sorrel, Kit, owned by a local farmer named Peter Ketch. "I'm for short talk in a horse-swap," declares the seemingly gullible Ketch, and the inequitable exchange takes place hurriedly. A few minutes later Blossom learns to his dismay that he has acquired an animal both blind and deaf. Longstreet's stories were worthy of inclusion in Mark Twain's anthology, and Twain's marginal notes display his intention to use their illustrations as well, yet for some reason Longstreet's work was excluded from the final version of *Mark Twain's Library of Humor*. Possibly Charles L. Webster & Company, Mark Twain's publishing firm, encountered difficulties in negotiations with Harper & Brothers, which had reprinted *Georgia Scenes* as recently as 1884.

NAH, pp. 153, 287–289; *MT&HF*, p. 62; *LAMT*, p. 9; *MT&SH*, p. 69; Gribben, "Mark Twain Reads Longstreet's *Georgia Scenes*" (1978).

Lonsdale, Margaret. *Sister Dora. A Biography.* Boston: Roberts Brothers, 1880. 290 pp.
   Source: MTLAcc, entry #840, volume donated by Clemens.

Lord, John (1810–1894). *Beacon Lights of History.* 8 vols. New York: Fords, Howard, and Hulburt, 1884–1896. [Only Clemens' copy of vol. 1 is known to survive.]
   Inscription: front free endpaper of vol. 1 inscribed in purple pencil: "2 vols subscribed for—& the same taken & *paid for,* June 17 '85./S. L. Clemens".
   Catalogs: C1951, #97c, $8, listed among books signed by Clemens; *Fleming 1972,* vol. 1 only.
   Source: I am grateful to the late Frederick Anderson, former Editor of the Mark Twain Papers at Berkeley, for the information supplied here. In 1972 Mr. Anderson examined Clemens' copy of volume 1 at the New York City firm of John Fleming, Inc.
   The first volume of Lord's work treats "Antiquity": Moses, Socrates, Phidias, Julius Caesar, Chrysostom, Saint Ambrose, Saint Augustine, Theodosius the Great, Leo the Great. Albert E. Stone, Jr. has suggested that Clemens was also familiar with the fifth volume, which treats great women in history ("Mark Twain's *Joan of Arc:* The Child as Goddess," p. 4). On 28 August 1907 Clemens spoke to Isabel Lyon about "Dr. Lord's Lectures on Roman History—etc. took 200 subscriptions in Hartford in 12 days. Canvassed that book for 26 yrs." (IVL Notebook #3, TS p. 3, MTP). Clemens again mentioned "Dr. Lord's Lectures and the great subscription sales they had in '79 or so" in discussing copyright profits with Isabel Lyon on 31 August 1907 (IVL Journals, TS p. 274, MTP).

Lord, John Chase (1805–1877). *Occasional Poems.* Buffalo: Breed & Lent, 1869. 141 pp.
   Source: MTLAcc, entry #2042, volume donated from Clemens' library by Clara Clemens Gabrilowitsch in 1910.

Lords and Commons (London journal, published 11 February–20 May 1899).
   Clemens was elated when he placed an essay in this "swell new London political periodical" (SLC to Henry H. Rogers, Vienna, 19 February 1899, *MTHHR*, p. 390). His "The 'Austrian Parliamentary System'? Government by Article 14" appeared in the 25 February 1899 issue of this short-lived journal.

"The Lord's Prayer" (Matthew 6: 9–13, from the biblical Sermon on the Mount).
    "The average clergyman, in all countries and of all denominations, is a very bad reader. One would think he would at least learn how to read the Lord's Prayer, by and by, but it is not so. He races through it as if he thought the quicker he got it in, the sooner it would be answered. A person who does not appreciate the exceeding value of pauses, and does not know how to measure their duration judiciously, cannot render the grand simplicity and dignity of a composition like that effectively" *(TA* [1880], ch. 36).

Lossing, Benson John (1813–1891). *The Empire State: A Compendious History of the Commonwealth of New York.* Illus. with facsimiles of 335 pen-and-ink drawings by H. Ross. Hartford, Conn.: American Publishing Co., 1888. 618 pp.
    Catalog: A1911, #300, $1, "back torn."

————. *Harper's Popular Cyclopaedia of United States History.* 2 vols. Illus. New York: Harper & Brothers, 1899.
    Source: MTLAcc, entries #1230 and #1231, volumes donated by Clemens.

————. *The Pictorial Field-Book of the War of 1812.* Illus. New York: Harper & Brothers, 1869. 1084 pp.
    Source: MTLAcc, entry #1725, volume donated by Clemens.

————. *The Story of the United States Navy; for Boys.* Illus. New York: Harper & Brothers, [cop. 1880]. 418 pp.
    Source: MTLAcc, entry #1189, volume donated by Clemens.

"Lost child" (song?).
    On 20 April 1900 Clemens noted: " 'Lost Child'! Heard it only in Hannibal. Was it never in England or elsewhere?" (NB 43, TS p. 7).

Loughran, Edward Booth (b. 1850). *'Neath Austral Skies. Poems.* Melbourne: Melville, Mullen & Slade, 1894. 204 pp.
    Inscription: presented to Clemens by the author, Melbourne, 28 October 1894.
    Catalog: Mott 1952, item #66, $12.50.
    Provenance: MTLAcc, entry #2060, volume donated from Clemens' library by Clara Clemens Gabrilowitsch in 1910.

Louisville, Kentucky *Evening Post.*
    In a portion of manuscript deleted from the final version of *LonMiss* (1883), Mark Twain quotes "a recent article in the Evening Post" that decried lawless behavior in Kentucky (Heritage Edition, p. 415).

Lounsbury, Thomas Raynesford (1838–1915). *James Fenimore Cooper.* Boston and New York: Houghton, Mifflin and Co., 1882. 306 pp. Fifth edition pub. 1885.
    Mark Twain quotes Lounsbury's laudatory assessment of *The Pathfinder* and *The Deerslayer* at the beginning of "Fenimore Cooper's Literary Offences" (1895). He intended for the same quotation to head a second comic lecture, "Cooper's Prose Style" *(LE,* pp. 137–145).

————. *The Standard of Usage in English.* New York: Harper & Brothers, 1908.
    Source: MTLAcc, entry #854, volume donated by Clemens.

Louvet de Couvrai, Jean Baptiste (1760–1797). *Aventures du Chevalier de Faublas* (pub. 1787–1789).
    In the autumn of 1885 Clemens noted the author and title of this erotic novel (NB 25, TS p. 26).

Love, Robertus (1867–1930). *Poems All the Way from Pike.* St. Louis, Missouri: Pan-American Press, 1904. 126 pp.
   Inscription: (on title-page) "To Mark Twain,/The First Missourian,/from Robertus Love,/one of the latest./Arcadia, Mo.,/May 3, 1906."
   Location: Mark Twain Library, Redding, Conn. Donated from Clemens' library by Clara Clemens Gabrilowitsch in 1910 (MTLAcc, entry #2041).
   Copy examined: Clemens' copy, unmarked.

Lovejoy, Joseph Cammet and Owen Lovejoy. *Memoir of the Rev. Elijah P. Lovejoy, Who Was Murdered in Defence of the Liberty of the Press at Alton, Illinois, November 7, 1837.* Intro. by John Quincy Adams. New York: J. S. Taylor, 1838. 382 pp.
   In the course of planning a book on American lynchings, Mark Twain wrote to Frank Bliss about a historical account that the research assistant whom Bliss was supposed to hire "must be sure to get. . . . Let him examine the life of Owen Lovejoy [*sic*] in the Hartford library or the Boston Public—better still, let him *buy* the book, if he can, by advertising through a second-hand book dealer" (ALS in Humanities Research Center, Univ. of Texas at Austin). Surely Mark Twain meant the martyred abolitionist Elijah P. Lovejoy (1802–1837), whose brother Owen (1811–1864) was present when a mob killed Elijah. Owen Lovejoy did not publish an autobiography, and no biography existed for this Congregational clergyman and loyal Lincoln supporter until Edward Magdol wrote *Owen Lovejoy: Abolitionist in Congress* (New Brunswick, N. J.: Rutgers Univ. Press, 1967).

Low, (Sir) Alfred Maurice (1860–1929). *The Supreme Surrender: A Novel.* New York: Harper & Brothers, 1901. 230 pp.
   Source: MTLAcc, entry #1581, volume donated by Clemens.

Lowell, James Russell (1819–1891). *The Biglow Papers.* Philadelphia: H. Altemus, n.d. 221 pp.
   Source: MTLAcc, entry #2137, volume donated from Clemens' library by Clara Clemens Gabrilowitsch in 1910.
   Clemens exultantly reported to his family in St. Louis that "James Russell Lowell ('Hosea Biglow') says the Jumping Frog is the finest piece of humorous writing ever produced in America" (19 April 1867, ALS in MTP). A Longfellow imposter improperly claimed credit for *The Biglow Papers* in Mark Twain's speech at the Whittier Birthday Dinner on 17 December 1877 *(MTB,* p. 1646). In 1880 and 1881 Mark Twain listed Lowell among the humorists he wished to consider for inclusion in an anthology (NB 19, *N&J,* 2: 363, 429), and *Mark Twain's Library of Humor* (1888) contained three pieces from Lowell's *Biglow Papers:* "The Courtin'," "Birdofredom Sawin as a Volunteer," and "Birdofredum Sawin After the War."
   NAH, p. 160; *OPMT,* pp. 11, 81–92.

————. "The First Snowfall" (poem).
   In 1867 Livy Langdon copied Lowell's poem into her commonplace book (DV161, MTP).

————. *Letters of James Russell Lowell.* Ed. by Charles Eliot Norton. 2 vols. New York: Harper & Brothers, 1893.
   Inscription: signed "SL. Clemens/1909."
   Marginalia: both volumes are profusely annotated. Clemens canceled many "that's" and other words whose usage he found excessive; he also made grammatical corrections. Clemens observed at one point: "He is much too 'thatful' for me—it annoys a body." Several notes in the first volume (on pages 126 and 305) are dated April 1909. On page 375 of volume one, Clemens discussed his own suicidal impulse in 1866, defending the bravery of those who actually commit the act; he dated this note 21 April 1909. Lowell had written: "I

suppose scarce a young man of sensibility ever grew his shell who didn't, during the process, meditate suicide a great many times. I remember in '39 putting a cocked pistol to my forehead—and being afraid to pull the trigger, of which I was heartily ashamed, and am still whenever I think of it. . . . I am glad now that I was too healthy, for it is only your feeble Jerusalems that fairly carry the thing out and rid the world of what would have been mere nuisances." Clemens responded in the margin: "3 a.m., Apl. 21/09. Down to 'trigger' I am with him, but no further. It is odd that I should stumble upon this now, for it is only two days ago since something called to my mind *my* experience of 1866 & I told it at dinner. I put the pistol to my head but wasn't man enough to pull the trigger. Many times I have been sorry I did not succeed, but I was never ashamed of having tried. Suicide is the only really sane thing the young or old ever do in this life. 'Feeble Jerusalems' never kill themselves; they survive the attempt. Lowell & I are instances" (quoted in "Note Bares Twain Attempt at Suicide," Los Angeles *Times,* 15 April 1951, Part 1, p. 40; text corrected against notes taken by Frederick Anderson when he examined the volumes in 1972).

Catalogs: C1951, $14a, $35, 2 vols., listed among books containing Clemens' marginal notations (purchased by Hollywood director Samuel Fuller and his wife); *Fleming 1972,* 2 vols.

Source: The late Frederick Anderson, former Editor of the Mark Twain Papers at Berkeley, inspected these volumes in 1972 at the New York City office of John Fleming, Inc.

On 12 April 1909 Clemens wrote to Frederick A. Duneka of Harper & Brothers (publishers of Lowell's *Letters)* to request a copy of page 31 in volume two; the page contained Lowell's letter to E. L. Godkin in 1869, and Clemens desired to read from it at a political banquet for William T. Jerome (ALS in collection of R. J. Friedman, TS in MTP). On 17 April 1909, at 3 o'clock in the morning (four days before he dated his note about suicide on page 375 of volume one), Clemens wrote to William Dean Howells: "I am reading Lowell's letters, & smoking. I woke an hour ago & am reading to keep from wasting the time." Clemens was amused to run across Lowell's reference (on page 305 of the first volume) to "young" Howells in a note written to Hawthorne in 1860. "I have just margined a note," Clemens joshed his slightly junior friend: " '*Young* friend! I like *that!* You ought to see him *now'* " (*MTHL,* p. 843). Frederick Anderson reported that these exact words appear in the margin of Clemens' copy of the volume. In April 1909 Clemens recorded a criticism of Lowell's letter-copy-writing while rereading his own letters of 1878: "If it was worth mentioning, it was worth quoting. I am reading Lowell's Letters, & in them he commits that irritating crime all the time, & the compiler of the Letters makes himself an accessory after the fact by not inserting the thing mentioned" (*MTHL,* p. 244).

MTB, p. 1540.

————. "Longing" (poem).

Livy Langdon copied this poem into her commonplace book on 19 February 1865 (DV161, MTP).

————. *My Study Windows* (essays, pub. 1871).

In March 1889 Clemens noted the author and title of these miscellaneous essays (NB 28, TS p. 44), which treat Thoreau, Lincoln, Chaucer, Emerson, Carlyle, and other subjects.

————. *The Poetical Works of James Russell Lowell.* Complete Edition. Boston: James R. Osgood & Co., 1871. 453 pp.

Inscription: signed "S. L. Clemens."

Catalog: A1911, #302, $5.

Clemens remembered Lowell as one of the eminent authors who declined Orion Clemens' invitation in 1853 to write something for the Hannibal *Journal*

(10 September 1906 AD, *MTE*, p. 236). On 15 November 1871 Clemens assured Livy that he intended to annotate a copy of Lowell's writings for her enjoyment, though he regretted marking "such dainty pages" (ALS in MTP); perhaps he referred to the volume described here.

————. *Selections from the Writings of James Russell Lowell. Arranged Under the Days of the Year.* Boston: Houghton, Mifflin & Co., 1889. [109 pp.]
  Source: MTLAcc, entry #2129, volume donated from Clemens' library by Clara Clemens Gabrilowitsch in 1910.

————. *The Vision of Sir Launfal.* Boston: Ticknor and Fields, 1861. 33 pp.
  Source: MTLAcc, entry #2059, volume donated from Clemens' library by Clara Clemens Gabrilowitsch in 1910.
  " 'What is so rare as a day in June?' " Clemens quoted (from Part One, "Prelude") under the heading for 22 December 1903 in Notebook 46. "That is this day, exactly," Clemens added—a sunny, balmy respite from winter (TS p. 31).

Lowrie, John Marshall (1817–1867). *Adam and His Times.* Philadelphia: Presbyterian Board of Publication, [cop. 1861]. 291 pp.
  Source: MTLAcc, entry #916, volume donated by Clemens.

Lowry, Henry Dawson (1869–1906). *Make Believe.* Illus. by Charles Robinson. London: John Lane, 1896. 177 pp.
  Source: MTLAcc, entry #1928, volume donated from Clemens' library by Clara Clemens Gabrilowitsch in 1910.

Lubbock, Alfred Basil (1876–1944). *Round the Horn Before the Mast.* Illus. New York: E. P. Dutton & Co., 1902. 375 pp.
  Inscription: signed "S. L. Clemens, Jan., 1903."
  Catalog: A1911, #303, $3.75.

Lubbock, (Sir) John (Baron Avebury) (1834–1913). *Ants, Bees, and Wasps: A Record of Observations on the Habits of the Social Hymenoptera.* The International Scientific Series. New York: D. Appleton and Co., 1901. [First pub. in 1882.]
  Inscription: signed "S. L. Clemens, 1902."
  Marginalia: "A bee has 7,000 eyes; what it needs is 14,000," Clemens wrote in chapter ten. There he also commented on the poor hearing ability Lubbock noted in certain bees: "But these were from the asylum," Clemens quipped.
  Catalog: A1911, #23, $8, quotes a few annotations.
  Clemens' admiration for this book is understandable even from Lubbock's first sentence on page 1 of the Introduction, which begins: "The Anthropoid apes no doubt approach nearer to man in bodily structure than do any other animals; but when we consider the habits of Ants, their social organisation, their large communities, and elaborate habitations, their roadways, their possession of domestic animals, and even, in some cases, of slaves, it must be admitted that they have a fair claim to rank next to man in the scale of intelligence." The implicit anthropomorphism attracted Clemens to this book in the year of its original publication and held his interest throughout his lifetime. In the autumn of 1882 Clemens commented: "Lubbock shows that ants are warriors, statesmen, &c. which led me to think they might have religion," and he suggested how an ant-Bible might read (NB 20, *N&J*, 2: 507). Clemens had the notion of quoting a "slave-making ant" in 1888 (NB 28, TS p. 2).
  Between 28 and 31 March 1896, sailing aboard the *Wardha* from Calcutta to Ceylon, Clemens concocted in Notebook 37 a burlesque of missionaries that parodied Lubbock's method of scientific investigations. In this brief essay Clemens claims that in Jeypore he painted forty-five ants different hues and

loosed them among "four miniature houses of worship—a Mohammedan mosque, a Hindu temple, a Jewish synagogue & a Xn cathedral." To his professed disappointment the ants always preferred whatever type of church in which he had placed a cube of sugar; he facetiously deduces that this behavior demonstrates how the ant is "the opposite of man" in religious matters. In one canceled passage Clemens wonders why Lubbock respected the ant so highly, since Lubbock's experiments seem to show that man overestimates the ant's intelligence (TS pp. 11–13). Mark Twain's decision not to include this amusing spoof in *FE* (1897) was unfortunate, but as he wrote to Richard Watson Gilder (who wanted the essay for *Century Magazine*) on 13 January 1897, he feared that a digression on ants might unduly interrupt the travel-narrative structure of *FE,* and he removed this passage from the manuscript (ALS at U.C.L.A., PH in MTP).

During Clemens' Indian Ocean voyage he also produced—between 11 and 23 April 1896—profuse notes that index his thoughts while "reading Sir John Lubbock" (NB 37, TS pp. 38–44). He begins by remarking that "this is a good time to read up on scientific matters & improve the mind": the ship required twenty-eight days to make its voyage. "To-day I have been storing up knowledge from Sir John Lubbock about the ant." Clemens quotes from the first and third sentences of Lubbock's chapter 6 *(Ants,* p. 119). He is especially interested in Lubbock's findings regarding the ant's ability to recognize members of his own nest, sometimes from a population of 500,000; and he quotes an entire paragraph out of chapter 6 *(Ants,* pp. 122–123) about an ant's capability of recognizing his friends after a separation of twenty-one months. As Clemens reads of the ants' accomplishments, they begin to appear nearly human-size: "We seem to be reading about our own race—some stirring old episode of a field day in heretic time." He is gratified when Lubbock concludes that ants know their brethren "just by vision alone." At one point Clemens adduces various similarities between ants and men: armies, farms, governments, houses, thieves. He praises the ants' disregard for "the overestimated male."

In January 1897 Clemens constructed a burlesque anatomy of the ant; though he does not mention Lubbock, his book is obviously the inspiration (NB 39, TS p. 40). Clemens looked forward to meeting Lubbock in London on 5 April 1900, when he was scheduled to breakfast at Lubbock's London address on St. James Square (NB 43, TS p. 6a). In a piece titled "The Bee" (written around 1902), Mark Twain alluded to Lubbock as one of "the great authorities" on that insect (MS in Box 1, No. 1, MTP). Another of Mark Twain's manuscripts from the period of 1901 and 1902, "The Secret History of Eddypus," refers to Lubbock as one of the "extraordinary men" of the nineteenth century *(FM,* p. 357).

Either Mark Twain's notes from 1896 or a deleted portion of *FE* (1897) served as his source for the example in Part Six of "What Is Man?"—ants who rescue their comrades but reject strangers when performing life-saving measures. The Old Man cites John Lubbock's experiments and argues that the ant's abilities at memory and recognition cannot be dismissed as mere instinct *(WIM?,* pp. 196–198). From Lubbock's *Ants, Bees, and Wasps,* Mark Twain may also have learned about the wasps' habit of catching live spiders to feed their young— which figures in chapter one of "Little Bessie," written in 1908 or 1909 *(FM,* p. 36).

Cummings, *"WIM?: The Scientific Sources"* (1964), 113–114.

Lübke, Wilhelm (1826–1893). *Ecclesiastical Art in Germany During the Middle Ages.* Trans. by L. A. Wheatley. Illus. Edinburgh: Thomas C. Jack, 1877.
    Catalog: A1911, #304, $2.25, 184 illustrations.

————. *Outlines of the History of Art.* Ed. by Clarence Cook. 2 vols. Illus. New York: Dodd, Mead, and Co., 1881.

Inscriptions: flyleaves in both volumes inscribed by Clemens in brown ink: "Olivia L. Clemens/1886."

Marginalia: the second volume is marked in pencil; except for a marking on page 359, these annotations do not appear to be Clemens'. They occur on pages 115, 204, 208, 210, 217, 224, 234, 252, 354, 362, 367, 379, and 380 (where someone has written "Look for the Tintoretto's Dresden Gallery").

Location: Mark Twain Library, Redding, Conn.

Copies examined: Livy Clemens' copies.

Lucas, Daniel Bedinger (1836–1909) and J. Fairfax McLaughlin, eds. *Hour Glass Series.* New York: Charles L. Webster & Co., 1891. 241 pp.

Source: Clemens' firm advertised this curious volume in the *Publishers' Trade List Annual for 1893* as "historical epitomes of national interest." It contains sketches on Fisher Ames, Henry Clay, Daniel O'Connell, Benjamin Robbins Curtis, John Randolph of Roanoke, Thomas Jefferson's first election, and the origin of "The Star-Spangled Banner."

Luckie, David Mitchell. *The Raid of the Russian Cruiser "Kaskowiski": An Old Story of Auckland. With an Introduction and Appendix on Colonial Defence, Etc.* Wellington, New Zealand: New Zealand Times Co., 1894.

Inscription: title page inscribed in red ink: "To Samuel L. Clemens—/Better Known as 'Mark Twain'—/with respectful compliments/From D. M. Luckie/21.11.95."

Location: Mark Twain Library, Redding, Conn.

Copy examined: Clemens' copy, unmarked.

In chapter 17 of *FE* (1897) Mark Twain credits Luckie for figures concerning Australasian production and exports, but he mentions no book title.

Ludlow, James Meeker (1841–1932). *The Captain of the Janizaries, A Story of the Times of Scanderbery and the Fall of Constantinople.* New York: Harper & Brothers, [cop. 1890]. 404 pp.

Source: MTLAcc, entry #205, volume donated by Clemens.

Lukens, Henry Clay (1838–1900?), pseud. "Erratic Enrique." *Jets and Flashes.* Illus. by René Bache. New York: John W. Lovell Co., [1883]. 200 pp.

Inscription: (in red ink on front free endpaper) "To Samuel L. Clemens/of Hartford, Conn.,/with the sincere esteem of/Henry Clay Lukens/Oct. 5, 1883./ An humble effort, dear Mark Twain,/This volume brief,/To cheer the homes where love doth reign/And Mirth is chief."

Location: Mark Twain Library, Redding, Conn.

Copy examined: Clemens' copy, unmarked.

Lumley, Benjamin (1812–1875). *Reminiscences of the Opera.* London: Hurst and Blackett, 1864. 448 pp.

Clara Clemens listed the author and title of this book among undated entries in her commonplace book (Paine 150, MTP).

Lutfullah (b. 1802). *Autobiography of Lutfullah, A Mohamedan Gentleman.* Ed. by Edward B. Eastwick. Copyright Edition. Collection of British Authors Series. Leipzig: Bernhard Tauchnitz, 1857. 342 pp.

Catalog: C1951, #D1, $8, listed among volumes signed by Clemens.

Luther, Martin (1483–1546).

Mark Twain favorably mentioned "Luther's Chorale" in 1878 (NB 16, *N&J,* 2: 213). In Appendix B to *TA* (1880), Twain states that "Luther's wedding ring was shown me" in Heidelberg Castle. Twain also alludes to Luther in "English

As She Is Taught" (1887). In "Which Was It?" (written 1899–1903), Mark Twain referred to Luther as a member of "the world's master-minds" who never examined his belief in witches (*WWD?*, p. 306). Luther and Joan of Arc were "that splendid pair equipped with temperaments not made of butter, but of asbestos," Twain wrote in "The Turning-Point of My Life" (1910).

Lyall, (Sir) Alfred Comyn (1835–1911). *Verses Written In India*. London: Kegan Paul, Trench & Co., 1889. 138 pp.
  Catalog: A1911, #305, $1.
  En route to Ceylon on 4 January 1896, Mark Twain quoted "Sir Alfred Lyall" concerning the religious divisions of Asia (NB 36, TS p. 15).

Lyell, (Sir) Charles (1797–1875). *Principles of Geology* (3 vols., pub. 1830–1833).
  There is evidence that the young Sam Clemens knew about Lyell's geological theories. For instance, Clemens drew pencil marks around Lyell's works in the list of "Authorities" at the front of his copy of J. L. Comstock's *Elements of Geology* (1851), which Clemens signed in 1856. Clemens remembered "Lyell's Geology" as the "whole library" of "old Davis," the mate on the Mississippi steamboat *John J. Roe* (31 August 1906 AD, MTP). Lyell, declared Mark Twain in "The Secret History of Eddypus" (written 1901–1902), was one of the "wonderful men" of the nineteenth century. "Lyell contributed Geology and spread the six days of Creation into shoreless aeons of time comparable to Herschel's limitless oceans of space" *(FM,* pp. 357, 379).

Lyle, Eugene Percy (b. 1873). *The Lone Star*. Illus. by Philip R. Goodwin. New York: Doubleday, Page & Co., 1907. 431 pp.
  Source: MTLAcc, entry #206, volume donated by Clemens.
  Historical fiction about Texas.

Lyly, John (1554?–1606). *Euphues, the Anatomy of Wit* (pub. 1579); *Euphues and His England* (pub. 1580).
  The narrator of Mark Twain's *1601* (1880) overhears "fine words and dainty-wrought phrases from the ladies now, one or two being, in other days, pupils of that poor ass, Lille[*sic*], himself." Jonson and Shakespeare are restless at listening to these affected speeches, but they constrain their remarks from knowledge that the Queen was "ye very flower of ye Euphuists herself" (Franklin J. Meine's edition, privately printed for the Mark Twain Society [Chicago, 1939], pp. 38–39).

Lynch, George (b. 1868). *The War of Civilisations, Being the Record of a "Foreign Devil's" Experiences with the Allies in China*. Illus. London: Longmans, Green, and Co., 1901. 319 pp.
  Inscription: half-title page signed and inscribed in black ink by Clemens: "SL. Clemens/Riverdale, Nov. 1, 1901,/from George Lynch."
  Marginalia: Clemens made stylistic revisions in pencil on page 19, correcting the text to read: "but it certainly would have been next to impossible to <have> construct<ed> a railway across this stretch of land so as to <have> avoid<ed> them." He made penciled markings on page 20.
  Catalog: A1911, #306, $4.25.
  Location: Humanities Research Center, University of Texas at Austin.
  Copy examined: Clemens' copy.

Lyte, E[liphalet] O[ram]. "Even me" (hymn).
  On 31 March 1869 Clemens wrote to Susan Crane from Hartford: "We play euchre every night, & sing 'Geer' [John Cawood's "Hark! what mean those holy voices," melody composed by George Jarvis Geer], which is Livy's favorite, & 'Even Me,' which is mine, & a dozen other hymns" (ALS in MTP). This explains why Clemens made a note for Livy Langdon—dated midnight, 25 March 1869

—in the margin of his copy of Oliver Wendell Holmes' *Autocrat of the Breakfast-Table* (at page 251): "I wish 'Even Me' to be sung at my funeral" (quoted by Bradford A. Booth, "Mark Twain's Comments on Holmes's *Autocrat*," *AL*, 21 [January 1950], 461). "Even Me" can be found in the *Franklin Square Song Collection, No. 1*, comp. J. P. McCaskey (New York: Harper & Brothers, 1881), p. 114. The first stanza is: "Pass me not, O God, my Father,/Sinful though my heart may be;/Thou might'st leave me, but the rather/Let Thy mercy fall on me./[Refrain:] Even me, Even me,/Let Thy mercy fall on me."

Lytton, Edward George Earle Lytton Bulwer-Lytton, 1st Baron (1803–1873). *The Coming Race; or, the New Utopia*. Repr. from the English edition. New York: F. B. Felt & Co., 1871. 209 pp.
    Source: MTLAcc, entry #37, volume donated by Clemens.

————. *Eugene Aram* (pub. 1832).
    "Read Eugene Aram all day—found it tedious—skipped 4 pages out of 5. Skipped the corporal *all* the time. He don't amount to *any*thing" (Clemens to Livy Clemens, Milford, Mass., 31 October 1871, *LLMT*, p. 162). In chapter 55 of *RI* (1872) Mark Twain mentions Lytton's reputation for literary productivity.

————. *Harold, the Last of the Saxon Kings* (pub. 1848).
    Catalog: C1951, #D8, listed among volumes signed by Clemens.

————. *Kenelm Chillingly: His Adventures and Opinions. A Novel*. Harper's Library Edition. New York: Harper & Brothers, 1873. 511 pp.
    Inscription: flyleaf signed in pencil "Saml. L. Clemens/Hartford, Conn."
    Marginalia: considerable penciled annotations by Clemens—mainly brackets, vertical lines, and underscorings. These markings are most frequent in the first half of the volume, but they continue at intervals as far as page 424. None of Clemens' notations indicate displeasure with either style or content. In the margin of page 140 Clemens discusses a joke from *Punch* that he also jotted down in Notebook 20 in 1882: "Advice to persons about to marry—don't." Clemens employed the half-title page as a temporary substitute for his notebooks, recording there a joke, a criticism of New York City police, an adventure undergone by one of Captain [Charles Francis] Hall's men in the Arctic (Clemens dated this entry 30 April 1872), and other random entries. Someone placed pencil marks in the house list of Harper & Brothers at the rear of this book beside Boswell's *Johnson* and Motley's *Dutch Republic* and *United Netherlands* (books Clemens owned and read). The verso of the rear flyleaf contains a penciled sketch of a house floorplan; it resembles the first floor of the residence which Clemens built in Hartford in 1874.
    Catalog: C1951, #24a, $35, listed among volumes containing Clemens' notations.
    Location: Mark Twain Papers, Berkeley, California. Purchased from Maxwell Hunley Rare Books of Beverly Hills, California.
    Copy examined: Clemens' copy.
    Clemens' extensive marginalia contradict Albert Bigelow Paine's assertion that "Clemens had not read Bulwer—never *could* read him at any length" (*MTB*, p. 428).

————. *The Lady of Lyons, or Love and Pride* (play, perf. 1838).
    Mark Twain alludes to this popular romantic play in chapter 12 of *IA* (1869); there he says that in France he "saw the Lady of Lyons and thought little of her comeliness."
    McKeithan, *TIA*, pp. 54–55, 59 n.

————. *The Last Days of Pompeii* (pub. 1834).
   Catalog: C1951, #D8, listed among volumes signed by Clemens.
   Chapter 31 of *IA* (1869), "The Buried City of Pompeii," very likely was influenced by Lytton's celebrated work.

————. *The Last Days of Pompeii.* Boston: Little, Brown & Co., [cop. 1893].
561 pp.
   Source: MTLAcc, entry #4, volume donated by Clemens.

————. *The Last of the Barons* (pub. 1843).
   Catalog: C1951, #D8, listed among volumes signed by Clemens.

————. *"My Novel."* 2 vols. New York: Harper & Brothers, 1860.
   Source: MTLAcc, entry #1146, volume 2 only, donated by Clemens.

————. *Richelieu, or the Conspiracy* (play, perf. 1839).
   Clemens condensed lines from this blank-verse play in a letter written from Carson City on 8 February 1862 to his mother and sister: "In the bright lexicon of youth,/There's *no such word* as Fail" (*MTL*, p. 65).

————. *Rienzi, the Last of the Roman Tribunes* (pub. 1835).
   Catalog: C1951, #D8, listed among volumes signed by Clemens.

————, pseud. "Pisistratus Caxton." *What Will He Do with It?* New York, n.d.
   Inscription: signed "Livy L. Langdon. Elmira, New York, 1866."
   Catalog: Mott 1952, #67, $2.50.

————. *Zanoni* (pub. 1842).
   Clara Clemens copied a quotation from this novel into her mostly undated commonplace book (Paine 150, MTP).

Lytton, Edward Robert Bulwer-Lytton, 1st Earl (1831–1891), pseud. "Owen Meredith." *Chronicles and Characters.* 2 vols. Boston: Ticknor and Fields, 1868.
   Source: MTLAcc, entries #2065 and #2066, volumes donated from Clemens' library by Clara Clemens Gabrilowitsch in 1910.

————. *Leila; or, the Siege of Granada.* Philadelphia: J. B. Lippincott & Co., 1872. 351 pp.
   Source: MTLAcc, entry #2176, volume donated from Clemens' library by Clara Clemens Gabrilowitsch in 1910.

————. *Lucile.* Author's Edition. Boston: Ticknor and Fields, 1866. 352 pp.
   Source: MTLAcc, entry #2067, volume donated from Clemens' library by Clara Clemens Gabrilowitsch in 1910.

Mabie, Hamilton Wright (1846–1916), ed. *Fairy Tales Every Child Should Know.* New York: Doubleday, Page & Co., 1907. 370 pp.
   Source: MTLAcc, entry #484, volume donated by Clemens.

————, ed. *Famous Stories Every Child Should Know.* New York: Doubleday, Page & Co., 1907. 300 pp.
   Source: MTLAcc, entry #485, volume donated by Clemens.

————, ed. *Heroes Every Child Should Know.* New York: Doubleday, Page & Co., 1908. 332 pp.
   Source: MTLAcc, entries #482–485, volumes donated by Clemens.

————, ed. *Heroines That Every Child Should Know*. New York: Doubleday, Page & Co., 1908. [281 pp.]
Source: MTLAcc, entry #483, volume donated by Clemens.

————. *Nature and Culture*. New York: Dodd, Mead & Co., 1904. 325 pp.
Clara Clemens discussed this work in her mostly undated commonplace book (Paine 150, MTP).

————. *Under the Trees and Elsewhere*. New York: Dodd, Mead and Co., 1900. 298 pp.
Inscription: front free endpaper inscribed by an unidentified hand in ink: " 'I remember the first time I saw Rosalind I saw the light of the Arden sky in her eyes, the buoyancy of the Arden air in her step, the purity and freedom of the Arden life in her nature.' June 8th 1901".
Marginalia: vertical pencil markings on pages 2, 3, 15, 22, 23, 55, 86, 87, 202, 203. These marks are not characteristic of Clemens' mode of annotation.
Provenance: contains the bookstamps and charge slip of the Mark Twain Library, Redding, Conn. However, the original accession number (#2899) does not match any of those assigned to the books that Clemens and his daughter Clara are known to have donated (which only go up to #2315 in the accession list that has been discovered).
Location: Elihu Burritt Library, Central Connecticut State College, New Britain, Conn.
Copy examined: photocopies of title page, marked passages, and rear endpapers of volume possibly belonging to someone in the Clemens household.

————. *William Shakespeare: Poet, Dramatist, and Man*. Illus. New York: Macmillan Co., 1902. 345 pp.
Inscription: Clemens inscribed the inner front cover in black ink: "<SL.> Clara Clemens/1902."
Location: Antenne-Dorrance Collection, Rice Lake, Wis.
Copy examined: Clara Clemens' unmarked copy.
On 29 April 1901 Clemens noted that Mabie had finished his Shakespeare book and had assumed the Trumbull lectureship at Johns Hopkins (NB 44, TS p. 9).

Mabinogion. *The Boy's Mabinogion; Being the Earliest Welsh Tales of King Arthur in the Famous Red Book of Hergest*. Ed., with an intro., by Sidney Lanier (1842–1881). Illus. by Alfred Fredericks. New York: Charles Scribner's Sons, 1881. 361 pp.
Source: MTLAcc, entry #1868, volume donated from Clemens' library by Clara Clemens Gabrilowitsch in 1910.

McAdoo, William (1853–1930). *Guarding a Great City, by William McAdoo, Police Commissioner, New York City, 1904–1906*. New York: Harper & Brothers, 1906. 349 pp.
Inscription: signed "S. L. Clemens, 1906."
Catalog: A1911, #322, $3.50.

————. [Another identical copy.]
Source: MTLAcc, entry #1361, volume donated by Clemens.

McAllister, [Samuel] Ward (1827–1895). *Society As I Have Found It*. New York: Cassell Publishing Co., [cop. 1890].

Marginalia: Clemens wrote in pencil on the front flyleaf: "There is here nothing but the vulgarity of good society—just that and not another specialty. Unchastity, the bar sinister, greed, swinishness, insolence, arrogance, and many other absolute essentials of a real Aristocracy are wanting" (quoted in *Zeitlin 1951*).

Catalog: C1951, #19a, $75, listed among books containing Clemens' marginal notes; *Zeitlin 1951,* item #32, $115.

"The 400. Ward McAlister" [*sic*] wrote Clemens in a notebook entry on 12 April 1900 (NB 43, TS p. 7). In an undated manuscript, "The Curse of Mc-Allister . . . A Defence" (DV313, MTP), Mark Twain sought to prove that McAllister "doesn't know what an Aristocracy is." The American "aristocracy," lacking a monarchy, long descent, and hereditary title and privilege, cannot truly qualify for the term. Mark Twain quotes from pages 212–213 and 229–231 of McAllister's *Society*. He intended to disprove McAllister's methods of analysis, but Twain's enthusiasm flagged and he ended the unfinished piece on the first manuscript page of chapter 3. Dan Beard reported that Mark Twain told him: "I spent three months writing a satire on that book of Ward McAllister's, and when I got through, I again read McAllister's book, and then my satire, and then tore the blamed thing up. Some things are complete in themselves and cannot be improved upon, and I take off my hat to Mr. McAllister" (quoted by Merle Johnson, comp., *A Bibliography of the Works of Mark Twain* [New York: Harper & Brothers, 1910], p. 159).

"Macallum" (unidentified author).

Evidently Mark Twain invented—or at least modified—a description of the system of reparation meted out by the Pawnee Indians (retribution on any whites for damages inflicted by a single white person) quoted in "To the Person Sitting in Darkness" (1901), where he attributes the words to Macallum's *History*. In "To My Missionary Critics" (1901) he refers to his previous quotation "from Macallum's (imaginary) 'History.'"

Macaulay, Thomas Babington Macaulay, 1st Baron (1800–1859). "The Battle of Naseby" (poem).

Clemens' nephew Jervis Langdon remembered that when Clemens conducted fireside poetry readings, his family and friends often requested, as the climax, " 'The Battle of Naseby,' which he delivered with supreme eloquence and emotion" (*Reminiscences*, p. 15).

————. *Critical, Historical, and Miscellaneous Essays*. 7 vols. New York: D. Appleton and Co., 1859–1861. Reprinted repeatedly. [Title and edition are

Catalog: C1951, #60a, "Macaulay's Miscellaneous Essays [*sic*], Vol. I. conjectured.]

through Vol. VII, incl.," listed among books containing Clemens' annotations, $160.

On January 1887 Clemens instructed "friend Gross" (Brown & Gross were Hartford booksellers): "As I understand it, you already have [John R.] Green in $\frac{1}{2}$ calf, & can get a $\frac{1}{2}$ calf Macaulay from Estes [& Lauriat of Boston] at $11.50. That'll do—send 'em along" (CWB). In Mark Twain's undated and unpublished essay, "Walt Whitman Controversy," Mark Twain remarks that Boccaccio "is praised by Macaulay" (DV36, MTP).

————. "Essay on Bacon."

In Part 9 of *Is Shakespeare Dead?* (1909) Mark Twain cites Macaulay's essay for the light it throws on Bacon's "horizonless magnitude" of talent. In Part 10 Twain quotes at length several passages from "Essay on Bacon" to show that Bacon "was competent to write the Plays and Poems."

MT&JB, pp. 186, 262.

————. "Essay on Lord Clive."

The names of Clive and Macaulay were intertwined for Mark Twain. He mentioned Robert Clive (1725–1774) in 1892 as a historical personage (NB 32, TS p. 40). "The famine in India in 1770. See Macaulay's Lord Clive," Clemens wrote in Notebook 34 (TS p. 44) on 30 November 1895. Farther on in the same notebook he added another comment about the natives of India and reminded himself to "see close of Clive." Clemens was surprised to discover that Calcutta had no statues or monuments to Clive or Warren Hastings, though "there's a street or two named for Clive" (NB 36, 13 February 1896, TS p. 43). At sea in April 1896, Mark Twain alluded to Browning's poem titled "Clive" and then launched into an idealizing essay about the "romance" lived by "the great Clive," who governed Bengal (NB 37, TS 37–38). Mark Twain said that Clive was "a sufficiently crooked person sometimes, but straight as a yardstick when compared with . . . Warren Hastings" ("Edmund Burke on Croker and Tammany," speech at the Waldorf-Astoria in New York City, 17 October 1901). Clemens told Albert Bigelow Paine that he wrote a poem called "The Derelicts" after reading about Lord Clive and Hastings in Macaulay's writings—"how great they were and how far they fell"; Clemens guessed that this was "in '93, I think" (*MTB*, p. 1499).

OPMT, pp. 105–107; *MT&JB*, p. 186.

————. "Essay on Warren Hastings."

"Macaulay has a light-throwing passage upon this matter [criminal behavior by Indian natives] in his great historical sketch of Warren Hastings," writes Mark Twain in chapter 43 of *FE* (1897), and he quotes from Macaulay's essay. "Wherever that extraordinary man [Hastings] set his foot, he left his mark," Mark Twain declares in chapter 52 of the same work. "Some of his acts have left stains upon his name which can never be washed away, but he saved to England the Indian Empire." In a speech delivered to the Order of the Acorns in New York City on 17 October 1901 ("Edmund Burke on Croker and Tammany"), Twain called Hastings a "fiendish" usurper who governed worse than Richard Croker. "The most of us know no Hastings but Macaulay's," said Twain, "and there is good reason for that: when we try to read the impeachment-charges—merely those—against him we find we cannot endure the pain of the details" (MS in Box 3, No. 1, MTP).

MTC, p. 237; *MT&JB*, p. 357 n. 16; Madigan, "MT's Passage to India," p. 361.

————. *The History of England from the Accession of James II*. 4 vols. Illus. Boston: Phillips, Sampson & Co., 1856.

Source: MTLAcc, entries #605–608, volumes donated by Clemens.

————. *The History of England from the Accession of James II*. Ed. by Hannah More (Macaulay) Trevelyan. 5 vols. Philadelphia: J. B. Lippincott & Co., 1869.

Inscription: flyleaf of vol. 5 inscribed with ornate printed letters: "Livy L. Langdon/Elmira 1869."

Catalog: C1951, #021, 2 vols. only, listed among books containing Livy Clemens' signature.

Location: vol. 5 only is in the Mark Twain Papers, Berkeley, Ca.

Copy examined: Livy Clemens' copy of vol. 5 only, unmarked.

In chapter 47 of *IA* (1869) Mark Twain referred to "the march of his

[Macaulay's] stately sentences," and in 1870 he began a hoax "review" of *IA* with a tribute to Lord Macaulay *(MTB,* p. 428). "Macaulay lies here" in the Poets' Corner of Westminster Abbey, Mark Twain noted in "A Memorable Midnight Experience" (1874). The character called "Harris" in *TA* (1880) criticizes Macaulay for sometimes using "doubled-up have's" (chapter 23). In May 1885, when Clemens wished to compare the sale of Grant's *Memoirs* with other publishing successes, he wondered whether "Macaulay's great check was . . . for the whole 5 vols?" (NB 24, TS p. 15).

Clemens wrote to Hartford booksellers Brown & Gross on 15 January 1887, requesting Macaulay's *History of England* (ALS sold by Alta California Bookstore, April 1976; purchased by C. A. Valverde, Wahrenbrock's Book House, San Diego, Calif.). On 16 July 1889 Clemens wrote to Susy Clemens: "For forty years Macaulay's England has been a fascinator of mine, from the stately opening sentence to the massacre at Glencoe. I am glad you are reading it. And I hope it is aloud, to Mamma" (TS in MTP). When one dined with Macaulay, Clemens speculated on 10 May 1892, "Macaulay would give you the spectacle of a Vesuvius in eruption, & you would be glad to listen to the explosions & look at the fire-spouts" (NB 32, TS p. 9).

Mark Twain was reading Macaulay's *History* during an Indian Ocean voyage on 8 and 9 April 1896, for he made notes about Titus Oates, executions, and the Tower of London—details based on incidents described in chapters 4 and 5 of the first volume (NB 37, TS pp. 32–33). Twain's most extensive comments about Macaulay's *History* appear in a portion of manuscript deleted from the final version of *FE* (1897): "A library can not justly be called dull which has that in it. In our day people say its style is too studied, too precise, too trim, ornate, dress-paradish; but how do they find that out? For the moment one opens any volume of the five, at any place in the volume, he sinks into a profound unconsciousness of everything this worldly—flights of time, & waiting duties, the pains of disease, of hunger, burdens of life, the encroachments, the insults of age,—everything vanishes out of his consciousness except the sense of being pervasively content, satisfied, happy. I have read that History a number of times, & I believe <it has no dull places in it.>" (MS in Henry W. and Albert A. Berg Collection, New York Public Library; quoted in *MTC,* p. 235). Clemens listed Macaulay's *History* under the heading of *"For Cheap Books"* in July 1899 (NB 40, TS p. 58). Earlier, Clemens had admitted that one good argument for loopholes in the copyright legislation was that "I can buy Macaulay's *History,* 3 vols., bound, for $1.25." If Americans were to read such easily available works, he reasoned, "a generation of this sort of thing ought to make this the most intelligent & the best-read nation in the world" (SLC to WDH, 30 October 1880, *MTHL,* p. 334). See also the catalog entry for Otto Trevelyan's *The Life and Letters of Lord Macaulay.*

Sydney J. Krause, *MTC,* pp. 7, 229, 235; *MT&JB,* p. 186.

————. *The History of England from the Accession of James the Second.* 5 vols. New York: Harper & Brothers, 1898–1899.

Source: MTLAcc, entries #1726–1728, volumes 1 (1898), 2 (1898), and 5 (n.d.) only, donated by Clemens.

————. *Lays of Ancient Rome* (poems, pub. 1842).

Mark Twain included this collection among a list headed *"For Cheap Books"* in Notebook 40 (July 1899), TS p. 58. The poem titled "Horatius" figures in chapter 26 of *IA* ("the bridge which Horatius kept 'in the brave days of old' ") and in chapter 34 of *CY* ("the king ordered me to play Horatius and keep the bridge"). Mark Twain quotes from the poem titled "Ivry: A Song of the Huguenots" in describing the "glimpses of Paradise" he saw in France *(IA* [1869], ch. 12): "We knew, then, what the poet meant, when he sang of—'thy corn-fields green, and sunny vines,/O pleasant land of France!' "

MT&JB, p. 186.

Macbean, Lachlan (1853–1931). *Marjorie Fleming: The Story of Pet Marjorie, Together with Her Journals and Her Letters, by L. Macbean. To Which Is Added, Marjorie Fleming; A Story of Child-Life Fifty Years Ago, by John Brown, M.D.* Illus. New York: G. P. Putnam's Sons, 1904. 203 pp.

Inscription: inside front cover inscribed in black ink: "To Clara/1904./This enlargement will properly go with the first 'Marjorie Fleming' which Dr. John Brown gave to your mother in Edinburg [*sic*] in 1873./S.L.C."

Marginalia: heavily marked and annotated in pencil and black ink. Clemens also folded down the corners of many pages. On the front free endpaper Clemens noted in pencil: "travels/8—sea/3—land/No journal after 6½? lost?" Pages 8, 10, 12, and 16 are folded down and marked in both pen and pencil. Pages 22–24 contain numerous marks for extracts. Pages 26–29 are marked for sequential renumbering of paragraphs. On page 36 Clemens wrote in black ink in the margin: "Just passed 6 yr." Beside Macbean's observation on page 72 that in Marjorie's second journal "the landscape is ashen grey," Clemens wrote: "in her Presbyterian heaven". Clemens also made other notes on pages 85, 90, 119, 129, and 148; and he bent down the corners of pages 90 and 99. There are many markings throughout the text of Dr. Brown's sketch as well. Clemens made numerous notations on the rear endpapers of the volume; these mainly concern Marjorie's journals and their correspondences to her age. On the paste-down endpaper Clemens listed a column of page numbers from both men's sketches, one labeled "MacB." and the other headed "Dr. B." Clemens also experimented there with variant spellings of the girl's name: "Madgie/jory/jorie".

Location: Carrie Estelle Doheny Collection, St. John's Seminary, Camarillo. Donated by Mrs. Doheny in 1940 after she purchased the volume from Maxwell Hunley Rare Books of Beverly Hills. Price $12.20.

Copy examined: Clemens' copy.

In an undated note that Clemens sent to Livy's sickroom around 1904, he quotes a poem and a diary passage written by "that quaint darling, Marjorie Fleming" (CWB). Because Mark Twain's "Marjorie Fleming, the Wonder-Child" (1909) employed quotations from her journals that appeared in Macbean's book, Mark Twain asked his own publisher (Harper & Brothers) to seek permission from Putnam's to quote these passages (SLC to Miss Jordan, undated ALS, NYPL). A footnote in Mark Twain's published essay credited "Mr. L. Macbean's new and enlarged and charming biography . . . published five years ago" as the source of extracts from Marjorie Fleming's journals. He unquestionably gained factual information from Macbean's book as well (TS in MTP, Box 27, No. 17b).

————. *The Story of Pet Marjorie (Marjory Fleming).* Illus. London: Simpkin, Marshall, Hamilton, Kent & Co., 1904. 119 pp.

Inscription: inside front cover signed in brown ink: "SL. Clemens/1909."

Marginalia: a pencil mark in the Table of Illustrations.

Location: Carrie Estelle Doheny Collection, St. John's Seminary, Camarillo, California. Donated in 1940 after Mrs. Doheny purchased the volume from Maxwell Hunley Rare Books of Beverly Hills. Price $12.20.

Copy examined: Clemens' copy.

McCarthy, Justin (1830–1912). *A History of Our Own Times, from the Accession of Queen Victoria to the General Election of 1880.* 2 vols. New York: Harper & Brothers, 1880. [Edition conjectured.]

Inscription: flyleaf signed "S. L. Clemens, Hartford, 1880."

Catalog: A1911, #323, vol. 1 only, $1.

————. *A History of Our Own Times.* 5 vols. Illus. New York: Harper & Brothers, 1901–1905.
Source: MTLAcc, entries #1731 and #1732, volumes 2 (n.d.) and 5 (1905), donated by Clemens.

————. *A History of the Four Georges.* 4 vols. [Edition unidentified; possibly: New York: Harper & Brothers, 1893—reprinted in 1901.]
Catalog: C1951, #022, "The Four Georges, Vol. I & II; and the Four Georges and William IV, Vol. III & IV," listed among volumes signed by Livy Clemens.
"Human Glory. Laugh at it," wrote Clemens in his notebook for 1901. "Quote the death-beds of the renowned. See George I, Prince Charlie, Robert Walpole, Swift, &c in McCarthy" (NB 44, TS p. 12, entry made under heading of 10 June 1901).

————. *Portraits of the Sixties.* Illus. New York: Harper & Brothers, 1903. 340 pp.
Source: MTLAcc, entry #1770, volume donated by Clemens.

————. *The Reign of Queen Anne.* 2 vols. New York: Harper & Brothers, 1902.
Inscriptions: inside front covers of both volumes signed in black ink "S. L. Clemens/ 1902".
Catalogs: A1911, #324, $4.25; *Hunley 1958,* item #132, $7.50.
Location: Clifton Waller Barrett Collection, Alderman Library, University of Virginia, Charlottesville.
Copies examined: Clemens' copies.

————. *Reminiscences.* New York: Harper & Brothers, 1899. 424 pp.
Source: MTLAcc, entry #1362, volume donated by Clemens.

McCarthy, Justin Huntly (1860–1936). *The Dryad; A Novel.* New York: Harper & Brothers, 1905. 314 pp.
Source: MTLAcc, entry #1622, volume donated by Clemens.

————. *The Duke's Motto; A Melodrama.* New York: Harper & Brothers, 1908. 303 pp.
Source: MTLAcc, entry #209, volume donated by Clemens (erroneously listed as donated by Mrs. Julian Hawthorne).

————. *Marjorie.* Illus. New York: R. H. Russell, 1903. 292 pp.
Source: MTLAcc, entry #1425, volume donated by Clemens.

————. *Needles and Pins; A Novel.* New York: Harper & Brothers, 1907. 371 pp.
Source: MTLAcc, entry #208, volume donated by Clemens.
Fiction about François Villon.

————. [Another identical copy.]
Source: MTLAcc, entry #1450, volume donated by Clemens.

————. *The Proud Prince.* Illus. New York: R. H. Russell, 1903. 276 pp.
Source: MTLAcc, entry #211, volume donated by Clemens.

————. *Seraphica; A Romance.* New York: Harper & Brothers, 1908. 304 pp.
Source: MTLAcc, entry #210, volume donated by Clemens.

————. [Another identical copy.]
Source: MTLAcc, entry #1623, volume donated by Clemens.

————. *The Wife of Socrates* (play). Adapted from the French of Théodore de Banville.

Apparently Clemens was alluding to this one-act play when he assured Augustin Daly in the autumn of 1888: "I'll take them [the Clemens family] to The Wife, tonight" (ALS in Houghton Library, Harvard). Daly's theater used *The Wife of Socrates* as a curtain-raiser to precede Daly's *The Lottery of Love* (Joseph Francis Daly, *The Life of Augustin Daly* [New York: Macmillan, 1917], p. 482).

McCaskey, John Piersol, comp. *Franklin Square Song Collection. Songs and Hymns for Schools and Homes, Nursery and Fireside.* Franklin Square Library. 8 vols. New York: Harper & Brothers, 1881–1892. Subtitle varies.

Clemens noted "Franklin Square Song Collection" in 1883 (NB 22, TS p. 16). The series contained a great many of Clemens' favorite songs and hymns, including Eliphalet O. Lyte's "Even Me" (1: 114).

McClellan, George Brinton (1826–1885). *McClellan's Own Story: The War for the Union, the Soldiers Who Fought It, the Civilians Who Directed It, and His Relations to It and to Them.* New York: Charles L. Webster & Co., 1887. 678 pp.

Catalog: A1911, #325, $1.50.

Rather surprisingly for a book issued by Clemens' publishing firm, *McClellan's Own Story* contains a biographical sketch written by William C. Prime (1825–1905), the detested "William C. Grimes" whom the narrator belittles in *IA* (1869). In a letter to Livy written on 26 July 1887, Clemens compared McClellan's memoirs unfavorably with those by Metternich: "This difference between him & Gen. McClellan is conspicuous. Metternich's book removes the obloquy from his name; but McClellan's deepens that upon *his*, & justifies it" (*LLMT*, p. 249).

McClelland, Mary Greenway (1853–1895). *St. John's Wooing, A Story.* Illus. New York: Harper & Brothers, 1895. 175 pp.

Source: MTLAcc, entry #1323, volume donated by Clemens.

McClure, Alexander Kelly (1828–1909). *Our Presidents, and How We Make Them.* Portraits. New York: Harper & Brothers, 1902. 481 pp.

Inscription: endpaper signed "S. L. Clemens, Riverdale, Feb. 1902."
Catalog: A1911, #326, $3.25.

————. *Our Presidents and How We Make Them.* Illus. New York: Harper & Brothers, [cop. 1905]. 509 pp.

Source: MTLAcc, entry #1733, volume donated by Clemens.

McClure's Magazine (monthly periodical, New York City, pub. 1893–1929).

From Vienna, Clemens explained to Richard Watson Gilder on 13 January 1897: "A week ago I subscribed for McClure's Magazine for Jean; two or three copies arrived from London last night"; he was furious upon finding that Frank Bliss was excerpting passages from *FE* into *McClure's* (ALS in U.C.L.A. Library). On 13 September 1898 Clemens informed Joseph H. Twichell that copies of *McClure's* were reaching his present address in Kaltenleutgeben, Austria (*MTL*, pp. 666). "I have been waiting and waiting for that McClure [containing Ida Tarbell's history of the Standard Oil Company]—and yesterday I found it in one of the daughters' rooms; it had been there a fortnight, I judge. They carry off anything that is addressed to me, if it looks interesting" (SLC to Henry H. Rogers, Florence, Italy, 21 March 1904, *MTHHR*, p. 559). Clemens praised a story by Inez Haynes Gillmore that he found in the June 1905 issue (Inez Haynes Gillmore to SLC, Scituate, Mass., 3 June 1905, MTP).

McCook, Henry Christopher (1837–1911). *Ant Communities, and How They Are Governed.* Illus. New York: Harper & Brothers, 1909. 321 pp.
 Location: Mark Twain Library, Redding, Conn. Donated from Clemens' library by Clara Clemens Gabrilowitsch in 1910 (MTLAcc, entry #1967).
 Copy examined: Clemens' copy, unmarked.

———. *Nature's Craftsmen: Popular Studies of Ants and Other Insects.* Illus. New York: Harper & Brothers, 1907. 317 pp.
 Inscription: front pastedown endpaper signed and dated by Clemens in black ink; subsequently Clemens added an inscription above the signature in darker ink to read: "To Miss Lyon/from/SL. Clemens/1907."
 Marginalia: a note or clipping, once pinned to the front free endpaper, has been removed. There are pencil marks in the text on page 118 (word underlined), page 119 (word underlined), and page 160 (a grammatical correction, changing "owe them" to "owe to them"). Isabel Lyon recorded a conversation in notes on the rear pastedown endpaper: "[abbreviated name, underlined]/'You'd know this man was a/parson for he drivels/psalmody all through the/book.'/[abbreviated name, underlined/Well somebody must do it—/July 18–15."
 Catalog: George Robert Minkoff Rare Books, Catalog #37 (1977), item #34, $225.
 Location: collection of Kevin Mac Donnell, Austin, Texas. Acquired in 1977. I am grateful to Mr. Mac Donnell for supplying the facts reported here.

———. *Nature's Craftsmen: Popular Studies of Ants and Other Insects.* Illus. New York: Harper & Brothers, 1907. 317 pp.
 Source: MTLAcc, entry #1800, volume donated by Clemens.

McCracken, William Denison (1864–1923), "Mrs. Eddy's Relation to Christian Science," *North American Review,* 176 (March 1903), 349–364.
 McCrackan was an exponent of Christian Science. "He believes Mrs. Eddy's word," Mark Twain scoffed in "Mrs. Eddy in Error" (pub. 1903, later appended to *CS* [1907], collected in *WIM?,* p. 395). Clemens had written a cordial letter to McCrackan on 15 December 1902, thanking him for sending "your N. A. Review articles" and stating that he had read them the previous night "with admiration & with profit" (PH in MTP, courtesy of Charles W. Sachs, The Scriptorium, Beverly Hills, California).
 Robert Peel, *Mary Baker Eddy,* pp. 196–205.

McCutcheon, John Tinney (1870–1949). *The Mysterious Stranger and Other Cartoons.* New York: McClure, Phillips & Co., 1905. 161 plates.
 Source: MTLAcc, entry #1226, volume donated by Clemens.

MacDonald, Donald (1857–1932). *Gum Boughs and Wattle Bloom, Gathered on Australian Hills and Plains.* London and New York: Cassell & Co., [1887?]. 256 pp.
 Inscription: "To Mark Twain/with the author's compliments/26/11/95."
 Location: Mark Twain Library, Redding, Conn.
 Copy examined: Clemens' copy, unmarked.

MacDonald, George (1824–1905). *At the Back of the North Wind.* Illus. by Arthur Hughes. New York: George Routledge and Sons, 1871. Reprinted in 1882. 378 pp. [First edition pub. in London, 1871].
 Clemens and Livy attended a garden party at MacDonald's home on 16 July 1873 (NB 12), and in 1881 Clemens designated MacDonald to receive a complimentary copy of *P&P* (NB 19, *N&J,* 2: 386). MacDonald's tale for children, *At the Back of the North Wind,* constituted a common vocabulary for Clemens and his young daughters, particularly Susy. At their urging, Clemens would invent additional stories about little Diamond, the coachman's son whom the benevolent

North Wind carried among the stars *(MFMT,* p. 25). In an undated letter Clemens posed as Santa Claus, explaining to Susy: "Our last lot of kitchen-furniture for dolls has just gone to a very poor little child in the North Star away up in the cold country above the Big Dipper" *(MFMT,* p. 37).

On 19 September 1882 Mark Twain wrote to MacDonald from Elmira: "I'll send you the book [*Life on the Mississippi*], with names in it, sure, as soon as it issues from the press. . . . Since I may choose, I will take the *Back of the North Wind* in return, for our children's sake; they have read and re-read their own copy so many times that it looks as if it had been through the wars" (quoted by Greville MacDonald, *George MacDonald and His Wife* [London: George Allen & Unwin, 1924], p. 458). In a letter to MacDonald written from Hartford on 9 March 1883, Clemens thanked him "in advance for the North Wind which is coming," and then added a postscript to report that "The North Wind has arrived; & Susy lost not a moment, but went to work & ravenously devoured the whole of it once more, at a single sitting" (ALS in MTP). After Susy's death Clemens wrote: "I have been moved to-night by the thought of a little old copy in the nursery of *At the Back of the North Wind*. Oh, what happy days they were when that book was read, and how Susy loved it! . . . Death is so kind, benignant, to whom he loves" *(MTB,* p. 1074). (In the final chapter of MacDonald's book, an omniscient, feminine form of the North Wind reappears to the ailing Diamond and takes the little boy on a final journey to "the country at the back of the north wind"; he fails to recognize her as a pleasant image of Death.)

Considering Clemens' associations of this work with Susy, who died in 1896; MacDonald, who died in 1905; childhood innocence; blessed death; and visitations of supernatural figures (the North Wind takes different shapes in visionary conversations with the boy named Diamond), *At the Back of the North Wind* should be viewed as an inspirational source for his "No. 44, the Mysterious Stranger," written between 1902 and 1908. Mark Twain's Satan, called "Forty-four" in this version of *The Mysterious Stranger,* represents a bitter and perverse transmogrification of MacDonald's kindly North Wind, who performs good deeds for an ungrateful human populace and eventually imparts the greatest favor of all—swift and painless death. She possesses the same power as Mark Twain's Satan to render earthlings capable of seeing their existence from the horizonless perspective of distance and time (MacDonald alludes to Herodotus' history on several occasions). Coleman O. Parsons has already suggested that Mark Twain derived from this book the mode of airborne conveyance employed by Satan to transport himself and Theodore Fischer in "The Chronicle of Young Satan" ("Background" [1960], p. 64).

But MacDonald's book has even more significant affinities with Satan's explanation of our "dream existence" to August Feldner at the conclusion of "No. 44, The Mysterious Stranger." One need only consider the following excerpts from chapters thirty-six and thirty-seven of *North Wind* to recognize correspondences between MacDonald's story and Mark Twain's ending: " 'Please, dear North Wind,' he said, 'I am so happy that I'm afraid it's a dream. How am I to know that it's not a dream? 'What does it matter?' returned North Wind. . . . 'The dream, if it is a dream, is a pleasant one—is it not?' " (chapter 36). " 'I can't bear to find it a dream, because then I should lose you. You would be nobody then, and I could not bear that. You ain't a dream, are you, dear North Wind? Do say *No,* else I shall cry, and come awake, and you'll be gone for ever.' . . . 'I'm either not a dream, or there's something better that's not a dream, Diamond,' said the North Wind" (chapter 36). " 'I don't think you could dream anything that hadn't something real like it somewhere' " (chapter 36). " 'Yes,' said North Wind. 'The people who think lies, and do lies, are very likely to dream lies. But the people who love what is true will surely now and then dream true things' " (chapter 37). " ' I suppose it's only the people in it that make you like a place, and when they're gone, it's dead, and you don't care a bit about it' " (chapter 37). " 'I thought that would be it,' said North Wind. 'Everything, dream and all, has got a soul in it, or else it's worth nothing, and we don't care a bit about it' " (chapter 37).

The fact that we know Clemens to have frequently read these passages to his own children and the indication that they were linked closely in his mind with Susy and her untimely death give the words special significance. Clemens did not borrow any language directly, but the poignant ending of *At the Back of the North Wind* contributed fully as much to the composition of the last-written version of *The Mysterious Stranger* as another source, Anatole France's *Le Crime de Sylvestre Bonnard*.

————. *Robert Falconer* (pub. 1868).

In a lengthy criticism of the novel which forms part of Clemens' letter to Mrs. Fairbanks of 2 September 1870, he declared: "My! but the first half of it is superb! We just kept our pencils going, marking brilliant & beautiful things—but there was nothing to mark, after the middle. Up to the middle of the book we did so admire & like Robert—& after that we began to dislike & finally ended by despising him for a self-righteous humbug, devoured with egotism. . . . Shargar was the only character in the book <worthy to live & worthy of> who was *always* welcome, & of him the author gave us just as little as possible, & filled his empty pages with the added emptiness of that tiresome Ericson & his dismal 'poetry'—hogwash, *I* call it. . . . Mind you, we are not through yet—two or three chapters still to read—& that idiot is still hunting for his father." In a postscript Livy apologized for her husband's intemperate mood, but confirmed that "the last part of the book we have not enjoyed as much as the first part, but the first we did enjoy intensely" *(MTMF,* pp. 134–137).

MT&GA, p. 33.

————. *A Rough Shaking.* Illus. by W. Parkinson. New York: George Routledge and Sons, [1890]. 384 pp.

Inscription: a Christmas present to Jean Clemens from "her loving uncle." *Catalog: Mott 1952,* item #68, $5.

————. *Sir Gibbie.* Seaside Library Edition. New York: G. Munro, 1879. 75 pp. (paperbound).

In July 1880 J. R. Barlow, Hartford booksellers, billed Clemens for "1 Sir Gibbie .20¢" purchased on 10 May 1880; Clemens paid on 5 July 1880 (receipt in MTP). Munro's paperbound edition cost .20¢.

————. *Thomas Wingfold, Curate.* New York: George Routledge and Sons, 1876. 666 pp.

Inscription: "S. L. Clemens, Hartford, 1874 [*sic*]," quoted in *A1911* catalog. *Catalog: A1911,* #307, $1.25.

Macdonough, August Rodney, trans. *The Lovers of Provence, Aucassin and Nicolette: A MS. Song-Story of the Twelfth Century Rendered into Modern French by Alexander Bida. Translated into English Verse and Prose by A. Rodney Macdonough.* Illus. New York: Fords, Howard & Hulbert, [cop. 1880].

Brown & Gross, booksellers in Hartford, billed Clemens on 1 January 1881 for "1 Lovers of Provence" purchased for $2.50 on 20 December 1880; Clemens paid his account on 17 January 1881 (receipt in MTP).

MacFall, Haldane (1860–1928). *The Masterfolk.* New York: Harper & Brothers, 1903. 440 pp.

Source: MTLAcc, entry #1110, volume donated by Clemens; subsequently withdrawn from circulation.

MacGahan, Januarius Aloysius (1844–1878). *Campaigning on the Oxus, and the Fall of Khiva. By J. A. MacGahan, Correspondent of the "New York Herald."* Illus., maps. New York: Harper & Brothers, 1874. 438 pp.
  Inscription: signed "S. L. Clemens, Hartford, 1876."
  Catalog: A1911, #308, $1.25.

————. [An identical copy.]
  Source: MTLAcc, entry #1729, volume donated by Clemens.

McGovern, John (1850–1917). *The Golden Censer; or, the Duties of To-Day and the Hopes of the Future.* Sold by Subscription Only. Chicago: Union Publishing House, 1884. 448 pp.
  Location: collection of Ralph Gregory, former curator, Mark Twain Birthplace Memorial Shrine in Florida, Mo. Gift of Mrs. Mary Gertrude (Stotts) Shotwell, Graybull, Wyoming, in 1965. Mr. Gregory now lives in Marthasville, Mo.
  Copy examined: Orion Clemens' copy.

McGuffey, William Holmes (1800–1873). *McGuffey's Eclectic Readers.*
  Sydney J. Krause *(MTC,* pp. 92, 112) has suggested that Mark Twain was referring to *McGuffey's Readers* when he wrote that "considering the 'Standard School Readers' and other popular and unspeakably execrable models, the real wonder is . . . that they [the pupils] write at all without bringing upon themselves suspicions of imbecility" ("Report to the Buffalo Female Academy," Buffalo *Express,* 18 June 1870).

Mackay, Alexander (1808–1852). *The Western World; or, Travels in the United States in 1846–47 . . . Including a Chapter on California.* 3 vols. London: R. Bentley, 1849. [Second edition also pub. 1849; third and fourth editions pub. 1850; American edition pub. in Philadelphia from second London edition: Lea & Blanchard, 1849.]
  Mark Twain quotes from volume 3 of Mackay's book in chapter 27 of *LonMiss* (1883) and mentions him in a portion of manuscript omitted from the book. Presumably *The Western World* was among the twenty-five "books relating to travels in the U. S. by English people in the first half of the century" which James R. Osgood and Company sent to Mark Twain on 22 July 1882 (W. Rowland to SLC, ALS in MTP). Mark Twain did not specify which edition of Mackay's work he used.
  Dewey Ganzel, "Twain, Travel Books," pp. 41 n. 4, 42 n. 8, 47, 52; *MT&HF,* pp. 298–299.

Mackay, Charles (1814–1889). *Memoirs of Extraordinary Popular Delusions and the Madness of Crowds* (London, 1841).
  Clemens may have known Mackay's account of the Children's Crusade to Palestine, a cynical scheme to sell youths into slavery in North Africa. The words "The Children's Crusade to Palestine" appear in Notebook 24 (July 1885), TS p. 32; Clemens repeated them in the same notebook in August 1885 (TS p. 37).

Mackay, (Mrs.) Katherine. *The Stone of Destiny.* New York: Harper & Brothers, 1904. 112 pp.
  Source: MTLAcc, entry #1442, volume donated by Clemens.

Mackaye, James (1872–1935). *The Economy of Happiness.* Boston: Little, Brown and Co., 1906. 533 pp.
  Source: MTLAcc, entry #851, volume donated by Clemens.

Mackenzie, (Sir) George (1636–1691). *The Laws and Customes of Scotland, in Matters Criminal* (Edinburgh, 1678).

In a fragmentary manuscript, "The Great Witchcraft Madness" (DV129[4], Box 37, MTP), Mark Twain quotes Sir George Mackenzie's description of a woman who confessed to witchcraft because, "being defamed for a witch, she knew she would starve"—no villager thereafter would show her any charity or have any intercourse whatever with her. Albert Bigelow Paine dated this manuscript in the 1890's or later. Obviously Mark Twain consulted this fragment in writing about Grandmother Narr's confession and her execution in chapter four of "The Chronicle of Young Satan," written between 1897 and 1900 (*MSM*, pp. 79–80). Without being aware of Mark Twain's earlier fragment, Coleman O. Parsons has showed how Twain based the Grandmother Narr episode on Sir Walter Scott's account of the burning of two Scottish witches in *Letters on Demonology and Witchcraft* (1830), Letter 9. Parsons also revealed that Scott in turn was relying on Mackenzie's book ("Background," pp. 67–68).

MacKinnon, Alexander. *Prince Charles Edward; or, the Rebellion of 1745–46.* Charlestown, P.E.I., 1873.
> *Inscription:* front cover signed "Clemens."
> *Catalog: A1911,* #309, $1.

MacLane, Mary (1881–1929). *The Story of Mary MacLane, by Herself.* Chicago: H. S. Stone and Co., 1902. 322 pp.

"I subscribe for a weekly paper which gets here [York Harbor, Maine] every two weeks, and I learn from that that Mary MacLane is exploring the East for The World," Clemens told a newspaper reporter in 1902. " 'Is the young woman a genie,' he asked, 'or is her book a composite of thoughts that had been written before?' " Clemens was reluctant to accept her own word about her writings. " 'I can't,' he said, 'in view of her frank declarations about her own mendacity' " ("My First Vacation and My Last—Mark Twain," New York *World*, 7 September 1902).

McLaren, Elizabeth T. *Dr. John Brown and His Sister Isabella: Outlines.* Edinburgh: David Douglas, 1889. 62 pp.
> *Inscription:* front free endpaper signed "Olivia L. Clemens/Hartford/1890."
> *Location:* Mark Twain Papers, Berkeley, Ca.
> *Copy examined:* Livy Clemens' unmarked copy.

John ("Jock") Brown, Dr. Brown's son, wrote to Clemens on 28 December 1889 from Edinburgh: "I think you will like the small book I have sent you. It is written by a Miss McLaren who knew my father very well and understood him" (ALS in MTP). Then on 25 January 1890 he wrote again: "I think it as well to send you by letter post another copy of the little book as you may not get the first. . . . If I do not hear from you I will know you have got one or [the] other copy" (ALS in MTP). Clemens wrote from Hartford to thank Jock Brown on 11 February 1890: "Both copies came, and we are reading and re-reading the one, and lending the other. . . . It is an exquisite book, the perfection of literary workmanship. . . . In this book the doctor lives and moves just as he was" (*MTL*, p. 529; also quoted in John Brown and D. W. Forrest, *Letters of John Brown* [London, 1907], p. 361). In March 1898 Clemens noted "Recollections of Dr. John Brown" (NB 42, TS p. 61).

McLellan, Charles Morton Stewart (1865–1916), pseud. "Hugh Morton." *The Belle of New York, A Musical Comedy in Two Acts* (perf. 1897). Music by Gustave Adolph Kerker (1857–1923).

Henry W. Fisher mentioned that he and Clemens saw *The Belle of New York* while it was playing in London (*AMT*, p. xx).

McLennan, William (1856–1914). *Songs of Old Canada.* Montreal: Dawson Brothers, 1886. 83 pp.

Source: MTLAcc, entry #2063, volume donated from Clemens' library by Clara Clemens Gabrilowitsch in 1910.

————. *Spanish John; Being a Memoir . . . of the Early Life and Adventures of Colonel John McDonell [1728–1810] . . . in the Service of the King of Spain Operating in Italy.* Illus. by F. de Myrbach. New York: Harper & Brothers, 1898. 270 pp.

Inscription: front free endpaper inscribed "S. L. Clemens/from G H[?]/N. Y. Feb. 21, 1902".

Location: Mark Twain Library, Redding, Conn.

Copy examined: Clemens' copy, unmarked.

MacManus, Anna (Johnston) (1866–1902), pseud. "Ethna Carbery." *The Four Winds of Eirinn. Poems by Ethna Carbery.* Ed. by Seumas MacManus. New Enlarged Edition. Dublin: M. H. Gill, 1906. 154 pp. [First pub. 1902.]

On 30 March 1907 Isabel Lyon noted in her diary that "Seumas MacManus has written a sweet note to say he is sending books, 1 for the King [Clemens], 1 for C. C. [Clara] and 1 for me—his late wife's poems" (IVL Journals, TS p. 236, MTP).

MacManus, Seumas (1869–1960). *A Lad of the O'Friel's.* Dublin: M. H. Gill & Son, 1906. 318 pp.

Inscription: flyleaf inscribed: "To Mark Twain, with admiration—/Seumas MacManus/of Donegal/29.3.'07." A clipping or letter, now missing, was formerly pinned to the half-title page.

Marginalia: brown ink underlinings, brackets, and a note quoting Robert Browning (" 'And did you once see Shelley—plain?' "), all on page 70.

Provenance: bookstamps, accession number, other markings of Mark Twain Library, Redding, Conn.

Catalog: "Retz Appraisal" (1944), p. 10, valued at $5.

Location: Mark Twain Papers, Berkeley, Ca.

Copy examined: Clemens' copy.

McNaughton, John Hugh (1829–1891). "Belle Mahone" (song). Melody also by McNaughton.

In a letter to Hattie Lewis, written on 10 January 1869 from Galesburg, Illinois, Clemens referred to "Sweet Belle Mahone" in mentioning "ghastly old sea-sickening sentimental songs" *(LLMT,* p. 48).

Macpherson, James (1736–1796). *The Poems of Ossian, the Son of Fingal. Translated from the Original Gaelic* (Edinburgh, 1762).

Mark Twain included books by Ossian in "The House Beautiful" *(LonMiss* [1883], ch. 38). The abortive but often reattempted novel, "Simon Wheeler, Detective" (written 1877–1898?), is set in the "sleepy little Missouri village" of Guilford, where "Ossian and [Jane Porter's] Thaddeus of Warsaw were still read, fire and brimstone still preached" *(S&B,* p. 312). In chapter three of this uncompleted novel, when Judge Griswold rehearsed "the grisly theme" of the Dexter-Burnside feud, "he pictured one after another its valorous encounters and their varying fortunes in all their chivalrous and bloody splendor, his fervor grew, the light of battle was in his eye, and it was as if the spirit of some old Gaelic bard had entered into him and he chanted the glories of a great past and of a mighty race that had departed and left not their like behind them" *(S&B,* p. 336).

MacPhilpin, John. *The Apparitions and Miracles at Knock. Also the Official Depositions of the Eye-Witnesses. Prepared and Edited by John MacPhilpin, Nephew of the Archbishop of Tuam.* New York: P. J. Kenedy, 1898. 142 pp. [Bound with Mary Francis Cusack's *Three Visits to Knock.* New York: P. J. Kenedy, 1898].

>   *Location:* Antenne-Dorrance Collection, Rice Lake, Wis.
>   *Copy examined:* Clemens' copy, unmarked.

>   In 1882 Clemens jotted down the title and publisher of MacPhilpin's book and intended to "compare one of these with a miracle from the Bible—& make a devout old Presbyterian fool contend that the ancient miracle proves the modern one" (NB 20, *N&J,* 2: 475–476). See also the catalog entry for Mary Francis Cusack.

Macready, William Charles (1793–1873). *Macready's Reminiscences, and Selections from His Diaries and Letters.* Ed. by Sir William Frederick Pollock. Portraits. New York: Harper & Brothers, 1875. 721 pp.

>   *Inscription:* flyleaf signed "Saml. L. Clemens, Hartford, 1875."
>   *Catalog: A1911,* #310, $3.50.

McWilliam, Robert. *Longmans' Handbook of English Literature. Pt. III. From Ben Jonson to Locke.* London: Longmans, Green & Co., 1889. 116 pp.

>   *Source:* MTLAcc, entry #806, volume donated by Clemens.

Maeterlinck, Maurice (1862–1949). *The Life of the Bee.* Trans. by Alfred Sutro. New York: Dodd, Mead and Co., 1901. 427 pp.

>   *Catalog: C1951,* #25a, $30, listed among volumes containing Clemens' marginal notes.

>   "It was Maeterlinck who introduced me to the bee. I mean, in the psychical & scientific way, & in the poetical way" ("The Bee," written around 1902, MS in Box #1, no. 1, MTP; *DE,* 26: 280). Farther on in this essay, which discusses the bee's habits in a comical but informed manner, Mark Twain alludes to Huber, Lubbock, and Maeterlinck as "the great authorities."

>   *MTB,* p. 1162.

————. *Monna Vanna, A Play in Three Acts.* Trans. by Alexis Irénée DuPont Coleman. New York: Harper & Brothers, 1903. 143 pp. [Also pub. in Paris in 1902.]

>   Isabel Lyon recorded in her journal that she and the Clemenses went "to the theatre to see a play by Maeterlinck, acted by his wife" on an unspecified date (probably in February 1904) while the Clemenses resided near Florence (IVL Journals, 28 February 1904, TS p. 14, MTP). O. Luchini, who acted on Clemens' behalf in the lawsuit against the Countess Massiglia, added a postscript to his letter to Clemens of 14 February 1905: "P. S. My daughter wishes to know your exact address, in order to send you back *Maeterlinck's book Monna Vanna*" (ALS in MTP).

————. *Thoughts from Maeterlinck, Chosen and Arranged by E. S. S. [Esther Stella Sutro, comp.].* New York: Dodd, Mead and Co., 1903. 283 pp.

>   *Inscription:* "To Miss Jean L. Clemens. Dec. 25, 1907."
>   *Catalog: Mott 1952,* item #69, $2.

Mahan, Alfred Thayer (1840–1914).

>   One of Clemens' ten nominations for the American Academy of Arts and Letters was "A. T. MAHAN (if he is the naval historian)" (SLC to Robert Underwood Johnson, 28 April 1905, ALS in the collection of the American Academy of Arts and Letters). Mahan was the author of *The Influence of Sea Power Upon History, 1660–1783* (Boston: Little, Brown and Co., 1890), and similar works.

Mahony, Francis Sylvester (1804–1866). *The Reliques of Father Prout.* Illus. by Daniel Maclise. New edition, rev. and enlarged. London: Bell & Daldy, 1866. 578 pp.

Inscription: engraved title-page signed "Saml. L. Clemens, Hartford, 1875"; frontispiece signed "Saml."

Catalog: A1911, #311, $3.50.

Maile Quarterly (Honolulu, monthly magazine, pub. 1865–   ). Also issued as *Maile Wreath.*

In Notebooks 5 and 6 (1865) Mark Twain alluded to an article from this journal of the Hawaiian Mission Children's Society, "The Legend of Ai Kanaka."

Major, Charles (1856–1913), pseud. "Edward Caskoden." *When Knighthood Was in Flower; or, The Love Story of Charles Brandon and Mary Tudor.* Indianapolis: Bowen-Merrill Co., 1898. 249 pp.

Clemens knew in advance that he would meet "Mr. Major, author of 'When Knighthood was in Flower' " at a London dinner on 29 March 1900 (NB 43, TS p. 6a). On 22 January 1901 Clemens informed Henry H. Rogers from New York City: "The family—by special request of Mr. Major, author of the play—are booked for the Criterion Theatre to-morrow night" *(MTHHR,* p. 458). Actually Paul Kester made the dramatization.

Malleson, George Bruce (1825–1898). *Dupleix.* Maps. Oxford: Clarendon Press, 1890. 188 pp. Reprinted 1892, 1895.

In January 1896 Clemens noted the author, title, and publisher of this "beautiful book" about Joseph François Dupleix (1697–1763) (NB 37, TS p. 1). Dupleix revealed the "supreme characteristic" of the French, Clemens noted on 10 April 1896—"treachery"; the next day Clemens contemplated an essay about whether the human race should even be allowed to continue, and planned to cite Dupleix as a central example (NB 37, TS pp. 35, 36).

———. *The Indian Mutiny of 1857.* London: Seely and Co., 1891. 421 pp. Reprinted repeatedly.

While approaching Bombay on 18 January 1896, Mark Twain resolved: " 'The Indian Mutiny'—Col. G. B. Malleson, C. S. I. Review it. Abuse his spelling of Kahnpur, &c" (NB 36, TS p. 19).

Mallock, William Hurrell (1849–1923). *A Critical Examination of Socialism.* New York: Harper & Brothers, 1907. 303 pp.

Source: MTLAcc, entry #1359, volume donated by Clemens.

———. *The Reconstruction of Religious Belief.* New York: Harper & Brothers, 1905. 302 pp.

Inscription: (on front free endpaper) "S. L. Clemens/on his seventieth birthday /with the highest regard and esteem of/G. Hes. [?]"

Location: Mark Twain Library, Redding, Conn. Donated by Clemens (MTLAcc, entry #923).

Copy examined: Clemens' copy, unmarked.

———. [Another identical copy.]

Source: MTLAcc, entry #1702, volume donated by Clemens.

Malory, (Sir) Thomas (15th century). *The Boy's King Arthur; Being Sir Thomas Malory's History of King Arthur and the Knights of the Round Table.* Ed. by Sidney Lanier. Illus. by Alfred Kappes. New York: Charles Scribner's Sons, 1880. 403 pp.

Clemens' introduction to Malory's heroes of the Round Table seemingly took place with this children's book, a previously overlooked source for *A Connecticut Yankee* (1889). On 18 November 1880 someone in the Clemens household purchased "1 Boys King Arthur" for $2.40, according to a bill sent on 1 January 1881 by Brown & Gross, Hartford booksellers. The same statement also records another purchase on 13 December 1880 of "1 Boys King Arthur," also for $2.40. Perhaps the latter was intended as a Christmas gift. Clemens paid up his account with the bookstore on 17 January 1881.

————. *Le Morte D'Arthur.* The Globe Edition. Ed. by Sir Edward Strachey. London and New York: Macmillan and Co., 1868; Philadelphia: J. B. Lippincott and Co., 1868. 496 pp. Reprinted 1870, 1876, 1879, 1883, 1884.

Edition: Robert H. Wilson—"Malory in the *Connecticut Yankee*" (1948), 185–196—establishes Strachey's Globe Edition as the text Mark Twain employed in *CY* (1889). The exact printing has not yet been determined. Albert Bigelow Paine refers to the "little green, cloth-bound book" *(MTB,* p. 790), but no copy owned by Clemens survives. Perhaps he cannibalized the pages of his original copy for the lengthy extracts that appear in *CY.*

The commonly held assumption that George Washington Cable first introduced Clemens to Malory's *Morte d'Arthur* in a Rochester bookstore during the winter of 1884—a story set down by Clemens in 1889 (NB 23, TS p. 11) and repeated by Cable in 1910 *(MT&GWC,* pp. 135–136)—cannot withstand scrutiny. For one thing, there are the copies of *The Boy's King Arthur* purchased by the Clemenses in 1880 (see preceding entry). Equally significant, however, is the letter Clemens wrote to Mrs. Cincinnatus A. Taft on 14 August 1883 when her physician-husband was ill. From Elmira, Clemens urged that no one else be allowed to take up Dr. Taft's practice in Hartford: "For what is Sir Kay in Sir Launcelot's armor, but only Sir Kay, after all, & not Sir Launcelot?" (ALS in MTM; quoted in *S&MT,* p. 170, where the letter is misdated as 17 August). Clemens and Cable would not begin their reading tour until more than a year after Clemens wrote, dated, and signed this letter.

Clemens made many references to Malory's book. In 1892, for instance, he mentioned the "intrepid deeds of Launcelot (shut up in his safety-suit)" (NB 32, TS p. 40). When expressing doubts about the authenticity of Archdeacon Wilberforce's Holy Grail (August [?] 1907 AD, *MTE,* pp. 343–344), Mark Twain alluded to Arthur, Galahad, Bors de Ganis, and Launcelot. In an article titled " 'The Master Hand of Old Malory': Mark Twain's Acquaintance with *Le Morte D'Arthur*" (1978) I trace several patterns of his allusions. See also the entry for Tennyson's *Idylls of the King.*

MTB, pp. 790, 891, 1320, 1455, 1540; Olin H. Moore, "MT and Don Quixote" (1922), pp. 340–341; Henry Pochmann, "The Mind of MT" (1924), pp. 19, 179; John B. Hoben, "MT's *A Connecticut Yankee*" (1946), pp. 200–201—an especially lucid essay; Robert H. Wilson, "Malory in the *CY*" (1948), pp. 186–199; Harold Aspiz, "MT's Reading" (1949), pp. 338–358; James D. Williams, "The Use of History" (1965), p. 103; Robert Regan, *UH* (1966), p. 175; Howard G. Baetzhold, *MT&JB* (1970), pp. 102, 132–133.

Mandeville, (Sir) John (pseudonym of unknown compiler, 14th century).

Clemens' copy of *Early Travels in Palestine* (1848) contains Mandeville's lengthy account of his putative journey to the Holy Land (see entry for Thomas Wright, editor). This was one of the chapters Clemens annotated in Wright's book. On page 229 Clemens alluded to Hubert Howe Bancroft, which seems to suggest a post-1874 reading; the mixture of pen and pencil markings, however, indicate that he read the chapter attributed to Mandeville (pp. 127–282) several different times. In an Autobiographical Dictation on 30 May 1907, Mark Twain mentioned Sir John Mandeville and other ancient naturalists *(MTE,* pp. 22–23).

Maning, Frederick Edward (1812–1885), pseud. "A Pakeha Maori." *Old New Zealand, A Tale of the Good Old Times; and a History of the War in the North Against the Chief Heke, in the Year 1845. Told by an Old Chief of the Ngapuhi Tribe.* Intro. by George Robert Charles Herbert, 13th Earl of Pembroke. London: R. Bentley and Son, 1887. 278 pp.

Inscription: (in black ink) "To Mr. Clemens, with Malcolm Ross' comps., Dunedin, 7 Nov. 1895."

Marginalia: a few marks and notes in pencil by Clemens, including those on pages 43 (he lines through the words "Be careful not to read *rations*"), 102 and 103 ("This" written in margins), 107, 109 (marginal scoring), 125, 126 ("Begin here" noted in margin), 129 ("India again" noted at the top), 131 (marginal scoring), 150 ("This"), 158 ("Just like the case recorded by Herodotus," Clemens wrote alongside a Maori oracle's ambiguous prophecy).

Catalog: Hunley 1958, item #78, $18.50.

Location: Mark Twain Research Foundation, Perry, Mo.

Source: Chester Davis reported on this volume and its marginalia in *The Twainian,* 37 (July-August 1978), 2–4.

On 6 November 1895 Clemens noted in Dunedin, New Zealand: "Very valuable books given me by Malcom [*sic*] Ross—among them Old New Zealand" (NB 34, TS p. 32). In chapter 35 of *FE* (1897), Mark Twain cites Maning's account of internecine native wars, explaining that Maning was among the "highest class of white men who lived among the Maoris in the earliest time [and who] had a high opinion of them and a strong affection for them." Madigan, "MT's Passage to India," pp. 361–362.

Mann, (Mrs.) Mary Tyler (Peabody) (1806–1887), "Mrs. Horace Mann." *Moral Culture of Infancy, and Kindergarten Guide.* New York: J. W. Schemerhorn & Co., 1874. 206 pp.

Source: MTLAcc, entry #811, volume donated by Clemens.

Manning, Anne (1807–1879). *Deborah's Diary. A Fragment. By the Author of Mary Powell.* London: Arthur Hall, Virtue & Co., 1860. 192 pp.

Location: Mark Twain Library, Redding, Conn.

Copy examined: unmarked copy that presumably belonged to a member of the Clemens family. Shelved with other volumes donated by Clemens. Binding is loose; some leaves may be missing.

Miss Manning's historical tale purports to be a journal kept between 1665 and 1680 by John Milton's daughter, Deborah. The diction and spelling are deliberately archaic.

———. *The Household of Sir Thos. More.* New ed., with appendix. New York: Dodd, Mead & Co., [18–?]. 257 pp.

Source: MTLAcc, entry #569a, volume donated by Clemens.

Manning, Marie. *Judith of the Plains; A Novel.* New York: Harper & Brothers, 1904. 331 pp.

Source: MTLAcc, entry #1023, volume donated by Clemens.

Manning, William (d. 1905), comp. *The Year-Boke of the Odd Volumes: An Annual Record of the Transactions of the Sette. Seventh Year 1894–95.* Limited Edition: Number 136 of 149 copies. London: Privately printed, 1897.

Inscription: "To Mr. Samuel L. Clemens/with the best regards/of the compiler, /W. Manning/O. V. Seer./21 Radcliffe Gardens/London S. W./July 4, 1899."

Location: Mark Twain Library, Redding, Conn.

Copy examined: Clemens' copy, unmarked.

On 1 July 1899 Clemens attended one of the regular dinner meetings held by the Sette of Odd Volumes at Limmer's Hotel in London (NB 40, TS p. 57). The gift volume which Manning presented to Clemens contains the inaugural address of Francis Elgar, fifteenth president, delivered on 4 May 1894.

"The Man o'Airlie (Scottish song).
  Clemens noted this title among the songs he heard played in 1873 by a
military band in London (NB 12, *N&J*, 1: 544).

Manzoni, Alessandro (1785–1873). *I promessi sposi. The Betrothed.* London: G.
  Bell and Sons, 1876. 723 pp.
    Inscription: half-title page signed in pencil "S. L. Clemens, Hartford, 1876".
    Catalogs: C1951, #D55, listed with volumes signed by Clemens; *Zeitlin 1951,*
  item #33, $17.50.

Mapes, Victor (b. 1870).
    On 8 November 1900 Clemens noted his intention to attend a "Victor Mapes
  play" at the Empire Theatre in New York City (NB 43, TS p. 28). Mapes'
  dramatic works of this period included *Don Caesar's Return, A Romantic Play
  in Four Acts* (published 1900) and *Montriveau, A Play in Four Acts* (published
  1901).

*Maps and Views to Accompany a Message from the President of the United States
  to the . . . First Session Thirty-third Congress, Dec. 6, 1853.* Washington, D. C.,
  1853–54.
    Catalog: A1911, #313, sold for .25¢. A note by William Stotts, surveyor of
  the port of Keokuk, Iowa, is laid in the small folio volume; the note is dated
  May 1861. Stotts was Orion Clemens' father-in-law.

Marcet, (Mrs.) Jane (Haldimand) (1769–1858). *Conversations on Natural Philosophy, in Which the Elements of That Science Are Familiarly Explained, and
  Adapted to the Comprehension of Young Pupils.* Ed. by John Lauris Blake. Illus.
  1826.
    Source: Albert E. Stone's checklist of Clemens' books in the Mark Twain
  Library at Redding in 1955. Stone supplies the date (1826), but provides neither
  the place of publication nor publisher. The book was issued by Lincoln & Ed-
  mands of Boston and by J. Grigg of Philadelphia. Stone mentions that various
  names appear in pencil on the flyleaf. I was unable to locate the volume when
  I visited Redding in 1970.

Marchand, Charles M. *New Method of French Conversation.* Boston: Carl Schoenhof, [1887?]. 257 pp.
    Source: MTLAcc, entry #1682, volume donated by Clemens.

Marcy, Randolph Barnes (1812–1887). *Thirty Years of Army Life on the Border,
  Comprising Descriptions of the Indian Nomads of the Plains, Explorations of
  New Territory, a Trip Across the Rocky Mountains in the Winter.* Illus. New
  York: Harper & Brothers, 1866. 442 pp.
    On the verso of Clemens' letter of 24 July 1884 requesting a book by Richard
  Irving Dodge whose title "contains the words 'twenty-five years,' " Charles L.
  Webster noted a book Clemens might want: "Thirty Years of Army Life on the
  Border/Harper Bros./1866" (Webster Collection, TS in MTP).

Marguérite d'Angoulême, Queen of Navarre (1492–1549). *The Heptameron of
  Margaret, Queen of Navarre.* Trans. from the French by Walter K. Kelly. Portrait. London: Henry G. Bohn, 1864. 427 pp.
    Inscription: verso of portrait is signed "Saml. L. Clemens, Hartford, 1875."
    Marginalia: several passages marked.
    Catalog: A1911, #236, sold for $10.25.
    In Mark Twain's *1601* (1880), Sir Walter Raleigh relates a bawdy tale of at-
  tempted rape which he attributes to "ye ingenious Margrette of Navarre" (Franklin
  J. Meine's edition, p. 39). In "The Walt Whitman Controversy" (DV36, MTP),

an unpublished manuscript possibly written in 1880, Clemens says that he owns a copy of Marguérite's collection of tales; he begins to quote ("at random—it is all alike") from Tale 46 to demonstrate its unsuitability for young readers. Clemens also mentions—but does not name—a story from *The Heptameron* which excels even Rabelais in "filthiness." Chapter one of *LonMiss* (1883) mentions that "when DeSoto took his glimpse of the river. . . . Margaret of Navarre was writing the 'Heptameron' and some religious books—the first survives, the others are forgotten, wit and indelicacy being sometimes better literature-preservers than holiness." Hank Morgan recorded that in Arthur's court: "Ladies answered back with historiettes that would almost have made Queen Margaret of Navarre or even the great Elizabeth of England hide behind a handkerchief" (*CY* [1889], ch. 17).

    MT&JB, pp. 82, 83, 337 n. 31.

————. *The Mirror of the Sinful Soul. A Prose Translation from the French of a Poem by Queen Margaret of Navarre, Made in 1544 by the Princess (Afterwards Queen) Elizabeth, Then Eleven Years of Age. Reproduced in Fac-Simile, with Portrait, for the Royal Society of Literature of the United Kingdom.* Ed. by Percy W. Ames. London: Asher and Co., 1897. 65 pp.

    Catalog: A1911, #335, sold for $9.

    Location: Henry E. Huntington Library, San Marino, Ca.

    Copy examined: Clemens' copy, unmarked. Entry #335 from an unidentified rare book catalog (advertising this volume) is pasted on the inside front cover. Two newspaper clippings about Mark Twain—both dated 25 May 1899—are inserted loose in the book.

Marion, Fulgence. *Wonderful Balloon Ascents; or, the Conquest of the Skies. A History of Balloons and Balloon Voyages. From the French of F. Marion.* Illus. New York: Charles Scribner & Co., 1871. 218 pp.

    Location: Mark Twain Library, Redding, Conn. Donated by Clemens (MTLAcc, entry #575).

    Copy examined: Clemens' copy, unmarked.

————. *The Wonders of Optics.* Trans. from French by Charles William Quin. Illus. New York: Scribner, Armstrong & Co., 1872. 276 pp.

    Source: MTLAcc, entry #1986, volume donated from Clemens' library by Clara Clemens Gabrilowitsch in 1910.

Mariot de Beauvoisin, Auguste. *A Summary of the French Verbs, Embracing an Entirely New System of Conjugation, by Which the Forms of Any French Verb Can Be Ascertained at a Glance.* First pub. under this title in 1862; often reprinted thereafter in London.

    In Mark Twain's "Playing Courier" (1891), the narrator expects his charges to fetch their *French Verbs at a Glance*.

Marks, Jeannette Augustus (b. 1875) and Julia Eleanor Moody (b. 1869). *Little Busybodies; The Life of Crickets, Ants, Bees, Beetles, and Other Busybodies.* Illus. New York: Harper & Brothers, 1909. 182 pp.

    Source: MTLAcc, entry #1185, volume donated by Clemens.

Marlowe, Christopher (1564–1593). *Hero and Leander* (1598).

    "In the Hellespont we saw where Leander and Lord Byron swam across, the one to see her upon whom his soul's affections were fixed with a devotion that only death could impair, and the other merely for a flyer" (*IA* [1869], ch. 33). Clemens once wore a bathing-suit when enacting a parlor-game charade of Leander's separation from Hero (*MFMT*, p. 58).

Marriott, Crittenden (1867–1932). *Uncle Sam's Business Told for Young Americans.*
New York: Harper & Brothers, 1908. 321 pp.
  Source: MTLAcc, entry #1603, volume donated by Clemens.

Marryat, Frederick (1792–1848). *The Children of the New Forest* (pub. 1847).
  This was a favorite book of the Clemens girls; apparently Clemens read it
aloud to them (*MFMT,* p. 25).

————. *A Diary in America, with Remarks on Its Institutions.* New York: William
H. Colyer, 1839.
  Inscription: title page signed "S. L. Clemens."
  Marginalia: many passages bear Clemens' markings; he made brief pencil
notations on pages 5 (regarding Harriet Martineau); 25 (noting a humorous remark about military life); 34 (correcting the size of the Van Rensselaer estate
in New York); 67 (concerning the Yankee propensity for whittling); 71 (the Blue
Laws); 118 (favorably commenting on a description); 124 (referring to the martyred abolitionist Elijah P. Lovejoy, killed in 1837); 124 (another note, specifying
"20,000 in St. L[ouis]," and underlining a passage which appears in chapter 22
of *LonMiss);* 129 (querying a date).
  Catalog: A1911, #314, $4.50, label damaged; Edward Morrill & Son Rare
and Scholarly Books and Prints, Catalogue No. 132 (Boston, 1967), page 36, item
#791, $275, "covers almost loose, lacks most of label," quotes marginalia;
described more fully in a letter from Edward Morrill & Son to Theodore H.
Koundakjian, 2 February 1967, PH in MTP.
  Dewey Ganzel, "Twain, Travel Books," p. 41 n. 4.

————. *The Pacha of Many Tales.* [Author's Edition.] London: George Routledge
& Sons, [1874?]. 155 pp. Paperbound.
  Source: MTLAcc, entry #221, volume donated by Clemens.
  Ensconced in a gondola being rowed near Venice, "a steady, heavy rain"
falling outside, Clemens lit a cigar, propped up his feet, and—"wonderfully snug
& cosy"—"got out Marryatt's [*sic*] Pacha of Many Tales & read" (13 October
1878, NB 16, *N&J,* 2: 209). (Clemens often misspelled Marryat's name.) In
"Villagers of 1840–3" (written 1897), Clemens listed "Marryatt" among the
favorite authors of early-day Hannibal residents (*HH&T*), p. 34).

————. *Second Series of a Diary in America.* Philadelphia, 1840.
  Marginalia: satirical remarks in pencil in Clemens' handwriting; at one point
he refers to manners in New York City, noting: "Conductors, and even hotel
clerks, are almost civil now" (quoted in *A1911).*
  Catalog: A1911, #315, $4, "worn and loose."
  Dewey Ganzel's valuable article, "Samuel Clemens and Captain Marryat"
(1962), shows that in *LonMiss* Mark Twain took his uncredited account of the
outlaw John Murrell (the quotation from "a now-forgotten book") out of Marryat's *Second Series,* pp. 89–92. Moreover, the religious camp meeting in chapter
20 of *HF* (1885) draws upon Marryat's description of a revival meeting he
attended near Cincinnati (Ganzel, pp. 407–410). But Ganzel fails in his attempts
to demonstrate a Colonel Sherburn-Captain Marryat connection (Ganzel, pp.
411–414). See also the entry for A. Walton's *History.*
  Ganzel, "Twain, Travel Books," p. 41 n. 4; Albert E. Stone, Jr., *IE,* p. 177
n. 13.

Marsh, Othniel Charles (1831–1899).
  In "A Horse's Tale" (1906), Soldier Boy discusses the American discoveries of
this Yale paleontologist (chapter 1).

Marshall, Edward (1870–1933). *Lizette: A Story of the Latin Quarter.* Illus. by C. D. Williams and J. C. Fireman. New York: Lewis, Scribner & Co., 1902. 295 pp.
Source: MTLAcc, entry #215, volume donated by Clemens.

Marshall, (Mrs.) Frances (Bridges), pseud. "Alan St. Aubyn." *Fortune's Gate.* London: Chatto & Windus, 1898. 306 pp.
Source: MTLAcc, entry #252, volume donated by Clemens.

Marshall, John (1818–1891). *Anatomy for Artists.* Illus. by J. S. Cuthbert. New York: Macmillan and Co., 1878. 436 pp.
Inscription: inscribed by Clemens to Karl Gerhardt, the young Hartford sculptor whose Paris studies Clemens supported. Flyleaf inscription is dated February 1881.
Catalog: unidentified; a memorandum in the Mark Twain Papers at Berkeley merely notes that this volume was advertised for sale in 1977.

Marshall, Nina Lovering (b. 1861). *The Mushroom Book. A Popular Guide.* Illus. New York: Doubleday, Page & Co., 1901. 167 pp.
Source: MTLAcc, entry #1222, volume donated by Albert Bigelow Paine, Clemens' designated biographer. Possibly Clemens saw this book, since the men exchanged reading materials.

———. *The Mushroom Book. A Popular Guide.* Illus. New York: Doubleday, Page, & Co., 1902. 167 pp.
Source: MTLAcc, entry #741, volume donated by Clemens.

Marston, Ellis. *Of the House of Chloe; A Tale of the Times.* London: Simpkin, Marshall, Hamilton, Kent & Co., 1900. 262 pp.
Source: MTLAcc, entry #216, volume donated by Clemens.

Martel de Janville, Sibylle Gabrielle Marie Antoinette (de Riguetti de Mirabeau), comtesse de (1849–1932), pseud. "Gyp."
Henry Fisher reports that Clemens called this French novelist "warm, yet not torrid" *(AMT,* p. 198).

Martialis, Marcus Valerius. *The Epigrams of Martial. Translated into English Prose. Each Accompanied by One or More Verse Translations from the Works of English Poets, and Various Other Sources.* Half-title: Bohn's Classical Library. Preface signed by Henry G. Bohn. London: Bell & Daldy, 1865. 660 pp.
Inscription: signed "S. L. Clemens, Hartford, 1875."
Catalog: A1911, #316, $6.25.

Martin, Edward Sandford (1856–1939). *The Courtship of a Careful Man.* Illus. New York: Harper & Brothers, 1905. 185 pp.
Source: MTLAcc, entry #1437, volume donated by Clemens.

———. *Lucid Intervals.* Illus. New York: Harper & Brothers, 1900. 263 pp.
Source: MTLAcc, entry #667, volume donated by Clemens.

———. *Poems & Verses.* New York: Harper & Brothers, 1902. 125 pp.
Inscription: inside front cover signed "Clemens, 1902."
Catalog: A1911, #317, $2.

———. [An identical copy.]
Source: MTLAcc, entry #2062, volume donated from Clemens' library by Clara Clemens Gabrilowitsch in 1910.

Martin, Henri (1810–1883). *A Popular History of France, from the First Revolution to the Present Time.* Trans. by Mary L. Booth and A. L. Alger. Illus. 3 vols. Boston: D. Estes and C. E. Lauriat, 1877–1882.
> *Inscription:* each volume signed "S. L. Clemens."
> *Catalog: A1911,* #318, $9 total.

Martin, John (1846–1876). *A Legacy, Being the Life and Remains of John Martin, Schoolmaster and Poet.* Ed. by Mrs. Dinah Maria (Mulock) Craik (1826–1887). New York: Harper & Brothers, 1878. 294 pp.
> *Source:* MTLAcc, entry #1137, volume donated by Clemens.

Martin, (Mrs.) Martha (Evans) (d. 1925). *The Friendly Stars.* Intro. by Harold Jacoby. Illus. New York: Harper & Brothers, 1907. 264 pp.
> *Catalog: C1951,* #D59, listed among volumes signed by Clemens.

————. [An identical copy.]
> *Source:* MTLAcc, entry #1620, volume donated by Clemens.

Martin, Thomas Commerford (1856–1924). "Nikola Tesla." *Century Magazine,* 47 (February 1894), 582–585.
> In February 1894 Clemens wrote to Livy about his meeting "Nikola Tesla, the world-wide illustrious electrician; see article about him in Jan. or Feb. Century" *(MTL,* p. 609).

Martine, Arthur. *Martine's Sensible Letter-Writer.* New York: Dick & Fitzgerald, [cop. 1866]. 206 pp.
> *Source:* MTLAcc, entry #2146, volume donated from Clemens' library by Clara Clemens Gabrilowitsch in 1910.

Martineau, Harriet (1802–1876). *Autobiography.* Ed. by Maria Weston Chapman. 2 vols. Boston: James R. Osgood & Co., 1877.
> Clemens may have been alluding to Martineau's anecdote on page 278 (about the "feminine oaths of a hundred years ago" sworn by Mary and Agnes Berry) when he wrote in Notebook 14 *(N&J,* 2: 101) in June 1878: "English swore (Misses Berry?) up to end of last century."

————. *The Peasant and the Prince: A Story of the French Revolution.* New York: D. Appleton and Co., 1841. 180 pp. Repr. 1848.
> Howard G. Baetzhold—"Mark Twain's *The Prince and the Pauper*" (1954)—finds it interesting that Martineau wrote a historical novel by this title and that Mark Twain reminded himself while writing *P&P* (1882): "Miss Martineau describes a coronation. See 'Little Duke' " (DV115, MTP). Actually Mark Twain was confused: Martineau never published a book with such a title; Charlotte M. Yonge published *The Little Duke.* But the similarity of titles between Mark Twain's novel and Martineau's is intriguing.

————. *Retrospect of Western Travel.* 2 vols. London: Saunders and Otley; New York: Harper & Brothers, 1838.
> *Inscription:* vol. 1 signed in ink by Clemens in 1875; inside front cover of vol. 2 inscribed in pencil in Clemens' hand: "T. W. Crane/to/S. L. Clemens/ Xmas 77."
> *Marginalia:* in volume 1 Clemens noted that "no matter whence a man comes, slavery brutalizes him. The hardest overseers were Northerners and Negroes." Clemens heavily annotated (in pencil) pages 5–17 of volume 2, the chapter entitled "Mississippi Voyage." Samples: "Think of this weary slow travel!" (p. 9); "Not like mate of St. Nicholas & man in Va City theatre" (cf. *N&J,* 2: 536) and "Snagged & not *know* it!" (p. 12). There are no marks in volume 2 beyond page 17.
> *Catalogs: A1911,* #319, $6 (though both volumes were advertised, apparently only the first was sold); vol. 2 only listed in "Retz Appraisal" (1944), p. 10, valued at $15.

Location: volume 2 only is in the Mark Twain Papers, Berkeley, Ca. The number "49" appears in blue pencil on the title page and also on a red label pasted to the title page.

Copy examined: Clemens' copy of volume 2.

Clemens wrote delightedly to Mrs. Jervis Langdon on 25 December 1877 to thank the Langdon family for their Christmas gifts: "Theodore could hardly have sent me a book more to my liking than Miss Martineau's Western Travels—I am charmed with the calm way she sharpens the hob-nails in her No. 13s & walks over our late fellow citizens" (ALS in MTP, gift of Mrs. Eugene Lada-Mocarski in 1972).

Ganzel, "Twain, Travel Books," p. 41 n. 4.

————. *Society in America.* 2 vols. Third edition. New York: Saunders and Otley, 1837. [First American edition.]

Marginalia: vol. 1 contains pencil marks on pages 109 (a vertical line beside her comments on "depravity" of American newspapers), 111 (ditto), 115 (where Clemens draws a vertical pencil line and writes the word "citizenship" in the margin near Martineau's comments on American political activities). The only chapters annotated in the first volume are those titled "Newspapers" and "Apathy in Citizenship." Clemens commented more extensively in volume 2, noting "Horrible" at the top of page 116, a discussion titled "Morals of Slavery" which describes the use of slave women as mistresses and casual sex partners, and mentions the quadroon women kept in New Orleans; writing "Rebuke of England" in pencil at the top of page 168, where Martineau remarks upon "the English insolence of class to class" (Americans manifest class disdain only toward blacks, whereas the English aristocracy scorn everyone below them); exclaiming "Good heavens!" in pencil at the top of page 209, in which Martineau treats American peculiarities of language, especially the reluctance to use the word "woman"; marking (with pencil) pages 209 and 210, which concern the Americans' preference for the terms "females" or "ladies" instead of "women"; drawing a line and commenting in pencil ("Murderer of Helen Jewett") on page 288, where Martineau tells about a criminal case in which a young man, though guilty, was acquitted because the jury did not wish to have any more hangings; adding pencil marks and writing "Literature" at the top of page 300, in which Martineau discusses popular books in America and quotes the *Edinburgh Review* concerning the unfortunate results for any country that lacks an esteemed national literature. Yale University has reproduced eighteen pages of Clemens' marginalia on microfilm, and the Mark Twain Papers at Berkeley contains a copy of this microfilm (Box #36) as well as a larger, more usable copy made by the Xerox Copyflo process.

Location: Mark Twain Library, Redding, Conn. (both volumes).

Copies examined: Clemens' copies. The cover of vol. 2 is worn and its spine is broken. Ganzel, "Twain, Travel Books," p. 41 n. 4.

Marvin, Charles Thomas (1854–1890). *The Russians at the Gates of Herat.* Illus. Maps. Harper's Franklin Square Library, No. 463. New York: Harper & Brothers, [1885]. 46 pp.

First published in England, this book describes Russian expansion in the 1870's in the direction of India. Clemens wrote "The Russians at the Gates of Herat (Franklin Square)" in Notebook 24 (1885), TS p. 18.

"Mary Had a Little Lamb" (nursery rhyme).

If (as seems likely) Clemens arranged the "Country School Exhibition," amateur theatricals presented on board the *Montana* between San Francisco and Panama on 10 July 1868, then it was he who chose this piece as part of the programme: "Poem—Mary had a little Lamb—Mr. O. G." (*Alta California,* 6 September 1868; reprinted in *The Twainian,* 7 [Nov.-Dec. 1948], 5). In chapter

22 of *IA* (1869) Mark Twain refers to St. Mark's "tame lion" which "used to travel with him—and everywhere St. Mark went, the lion was sure to go." In the course of the graduation declamations in chapter 21 of *TS* (1876), "a little shamefaced girl lisped 'Mary had a little lamb,' etc., performed a compassion-inspiring curtsy, got her meed of applause, and sat down flushed and happy." John D. Rockefeller, Jr. "thinks Joseph was Mary's little lamb; this is an error," quipped Mark Twain in an Autobiographical Dictation of 20 March 1906 (*MTE*, p. 87). In the last year of Clemens' life he composed in Notebook 49 a variation of the rhyme in German, which translates as "Mary had a little lamb,/and wanted to get another one—/The lamb has fallen down" (TS p. 2).

"Mary's gone away wid de coon" (song).
    Clemens heard two black cabin hands sing this racially derogatory folk song on the *City of Baton Rouge* in 1882 (NB 21, *N&J*, 2: 562).

Mascagni, Pietro (1863–1945), composer. *Cavalleria Rusticana* (one act opera, perf. 1890). Libretto by Guido Menasci and Giovanni Targioni-Tozzetti.
    From the Villa Viviani Clemens wrote to Clara on 5 November 1892: "Susy & the Kings are down at the Opera—Cavalleria. Next Thursday they are going down to see its author fetch out his new opera" (ALS in MTP). On 2 November 1903 Clemens noted that "the band (on the ship) played the Cavalleria Rusticana which is forever associated in my mind with Susy. I love it better than any other, but it breaks my heart" (NB 46, TS p. 29; *MTN*, p. 384). Isabel Lyon recorded how Clemens referred to the "Intermezzo" from this work as "the Susie one" in asking Miss Lyon to play it on 2 March 1906. He told Miss Lyon that he could "fit the words" to this piece. "Susy calls to me in the Intermezzo, & her mother in the Largo," he said (IVL Journal, Humanities Research Center, Univ. of Texas at Austin).

Mason, Alfred Edward Woodley (1865–1948). *The Broken Road*. New York: Charles Scribner's Sons, 1907. 419 pp.
    Source: MTLAcc, entry #1036, volume donated by Clemens.

Mason, (Mrs.) Caroline Atherton (Briggs) (1823–1890). [Unidentified poem.]
    Clemens wrote to *The Independent* sometime in the 1870's (his letter is dated 3 May) to request a copy of Caroline Mason's poem "which appeared in the Independent about last August or September. I can't recal the title of it: I only remember that a mother calls, 'Is that you, Pet?' & is answered, not by the favorite, but by another of her children, 'It isn't Pet, mamma, it's only me.' There are only 4 stanzas." He explained that he wished to use the verses in a platform performance: "I hate to make a reading entirely out of my own pathos" (TS in MTP).

Mason, Fanny Witherspoon, pseud. "Mary Frances." *Daddy Dave*. New York: Funk & Wagnalls, 1887. 116 pp.
    Source: MTLAcc, entry #1848, volume donated from Clemens' library by Clara Clemens Gabrilowitsch in 1910.

Massett, Stephen C. (1820–1898). *"Drifting About"; or, What "Jeems Pipes, of Pipesville," Saw-and-Did. An Autobiography*. New York: Carleton, 1863. 371 pp.
    In a letter written to Mrs. Fairbanks from San Francisco on 17 June 1868, Clemens enclosed a clipping by "this good-natured, well-meaning ass, 'Pipes,'" whom Clemens accused of using his and Artemus Ward's material for readings in Calcutta and Hong Kong (*MTMF*, p. 32).

Masson, David (1822–1907). *The Life of John Milton, Narrated in Connexion with the Political, Ecclesiastical, and Literary History of His Time.* 7 vols. Index. Cambridge, London: Macmillan & Co., 1859–1894.

"Mason's [*sic*] London '59 '71 (lit hist of the time)" was one of the "biogs of Milton" that Clemens listed in September 1887 (NB 27, TS p. 22).

Masters in Art: A Series of Illustrated Monographs, Issued Monthly. Part 4. Illus. Boston: Bates & Guild Co., 1900. 36 pp. Paperbound.

Source: MTLAcc, entry #403, volume donated by Clemens.

Mather, Cotton (1663–1728). *Magnalia Christi Americana; or, the Ecclesiastical History of New-England from Its First Planting . . . unto . . . 1698.* 2 vols. Hartford, Conn.: Silas Andrus; Roberts & Burr, Printers, 1820. [First American edition; London edition pub. in 1702.]

Inscriptions: both volumes signed "S. L. Clemens/Hartford, Nov. 1881."

Marginalia: on page 41 of the first volume Clemens marked a passage and wrote: "The wise man of one age is the idiot of the next." Beside another passage, where Mather describes how a man recovered from illness, "but about half a year after this he fell into another sickness, whereof he dy'd," Clemens gibed: "But why didn't they rip out some more prayers and get him up again?" Clemens underscored Mather's account of a fire which killed a man's three children and destroyed his home, noting "The miserable injustice of it."

Catalog: A1911, #320, $37.50, quotes marginalia.

Location: Special Collections, Case Western Reserve University Libraries, Cleveland, Ohio. Donated in 1958 by Willis Thornton. Maureen Neff, Special Collections Librarian supplied information about these volumes.

Clemens underlined a reference to Mather's *Magnalia* on page 22 of J. Hammond Trumbull's *The True-Blue Laws of Connecticut and New Haven* (1876), a volume Clemens inscribed in 1877. Trumbull states that Dr. Henry More's *Antidote to Atheism* "abounds in marvels, some of which are unsurpassed, as tests of credulity, by any in Mather's *Magnalia*" (Detroit Public Library, PH in MTP). As a facetious demonstration of the infallibility of Providence, Mark Twain cited Mather's *Magnalia* in an Autobiographical Dictation of 13 June 1906: "I remembered that in the *Magnalia* a man who went home swearing from a prayer meeting one night got his reminder within the next nine months. He had a wife and seven children, and all at once they were attacked by a terrible disease, and one by one they died in agony till at the end of a week there was nothing left but the man himself. I knew that the idea was to punish the man, and I knew that if he had any intelligence he recognized that that intention had been carried out, although mainly at the expense of other people" (*MTE*, p. 261).

Coleman O. Parsons, "Background," p. 65.

———. *The Wonders of the Invisible World* (pub. 1693 in Boston).

In "Bible Teaching and Religious Practice" (1890), Mark Twain refers derisively to "the parson" at Salem who "clung pathetically to his witch-text after the laity had abandoned it in remorse and tears" (*WIM?*, p. 75). The Eskimos in Mark Twain's "The Esquimau Maiden's Romance" (1893) adopt the Puritans' "trial by water" method of determining guilt. Chapter four of "The Chronicle of Young Satan," written between 1897 and 1900, relates the burning of Gottfried Narr's grandmother as a witch, together with another, similar story about eleven girls in a school (*MSM*, pp. 78–80). Frau Brandt is burned as a witch in chapter seven of the same work; she defies the villagers, refuses to confess or recant, and dies forgiving them for the sake of their innocent childhoods (*MSM*, p. 133). Mark Twain mentions "the Witch Madness" in "The Secret History of Eddypus" (*FM*, p. 367), written 1901–1902, and reviles the witch burnings in "Three Thousand Years among the Microbes" (*WWD?*, pp. 529–530), written in 1905. See also the entry for Samuel P. Fowler's *Salem Witchcraft* (1865), which reprints Mather's *Wonders of the Invisible World.*

William M. Gibson, *MSM*, p. 21.

Mathews, Frances Aymar. *The Undefiled, A Novel of To-day*. New York: Harper & Brothers, 1906. 278 pp.
    Source: MTLAcc, entry #1022, volume donated by Clemens.

Matson, Nehemiah (1816–1883). *Pioneers of Illinois, Containing a Series of Sketches Relating to Events That Occurred Previous to 1813, . . . Drawn from History, Tradition, and Personal Reminiscences*. Chicago: Knight & Leonard, 1882. 306 pp.
    Inscription: "Samuel L. Clemens/Compliments of the author" (not in Clemens' hand).
    Marginalia: black ink marks characteristic of Clemens appear on pages 186 (beginning of the first paragraph), 187 (beside references to the town of Cahokia in the first and second paragraphs), 188 (mid-page), and 189 (top).
    Location: Mark Twain Library, Redding, Conn.
    Copy examined: Clemens' copy.

Matthewman, Lisle de Vaux. *Crankisms, by Lisle de Vaux Matthewman. Pictured by Clare Victor Dwiggins*. Illus. Philadelphia: Henry T. Coates & Co., 1901. 100 pp.
    Inscription: Clemens inscribed the front free endpaper in black ink: "From the artist./ SL. Clemens/Riverdale-on-Hudson/Feb. 1902".
    Catalog: A1911, #127, $2.
    Location: Humanities Research Center, University of Texas at Austin.
    Copy examined: Clemens' unmarked copy. Matthewman's *Crankisms* are brief witticisms reminiscent of Mark Twain's Pudd'nhead Wilson maxims, illustrated with drawings of languid women and Gibson girls.

Matthews, Brander (1852–1929). "American Authors and British Pirates," *New Princeton Review*, 4 (September 1887), 201.
    Mark Twain penned a querulous, antagonistic reply to Matthews' article and published the retort in the January 1888 issue of the *New Princeton Review*.

————. *Americanisms and Briticisms, with Other Essays on Other Isms*. New York: Harper & Brothers, 1892. 190 pp.
    Inscription: flyleaf inscribed in pencil by Matthews: "Col. Mark Twain from his friend/B M/Nov 1893/The Players".
    Marginalia: Clemens penciled the table of contents at the essay on Mark Twain; he also placed pencil marks on pages 5, 12, 14 (folded down), 150 (turned down—the essay titled "Of Mark Twain's Best Story" begins on the facing page), 151 (Clemens noted "1884–5" above the title of Matthews' essay), 152 (turned down), 152–153 (brackets penciled around a passage in which Matthews describes the moment in the cave in *TS* when the hand bearing a light turns out to be Injun Joe's as "one of the very finest things in the literature of adventure since Robinson Crusoe first saw a single footprint in the sand of the sea-shore"). There are no further marks, though other pages are turned down.
    Location: Carrie Estelle Doheny Collection, St. John's Seminary, Camarillo, Ca. Purchased from Maxwell Hunley Rare Books of Beverly Hills in 1940.
    Copy examined: Clemens' copy.
    This collection contains Matthews' essay on "The Centenary of Fenimore Cooper."

————. [An identical copy.]
    Source: MTLAcc, entry #658, volume donated by Clemens.

————. *Aspects of Fiction and Other Ventures in Criticism*. New York: Harper & Brothers, 1896. 234 pp.
    Location: Antenne-Dorrance Collection, Rice Lake, Wis.
    Copy examined: Clemens' copy, unmarked.
    Chapter three of Matthews' book is titled "The Penalty of Humor."

————. *Aspects of Fiction and Other Ventures in Criticism.* New York: Harper & Brothers, 1900. 234 pp.

Source: MTLAcc, entry #859, volume donated by Clemens.

————. *The Historical Novel and Other Essays.* New York: Charles Scribner's Sons, 1901. 321 pp.

Inscription: the book is dedicated to Mark Twain; on the dedication page Matthews added in pencil: "Witness my hand: Brander Matthews Feb. 20th 1901." On the front flyleaf Matthews wrote: "By a recent decision of the Supreme Court the man to whom a book is dedicated is personally responsible for all the opinions in it./B. M./Feb. 20th 1901."

Catalog: C1951, #41c, $32.50.

Location: Carrie Estelle Doheny Collection, St. John's Seminary, Camarillo, Ca. Purchased from Maxwell Hunley Rare Books in 1951 for $44.50.

Copy examined: Clemens' copy, unmarked. A few leaves in the essay on Daudet are unopened.

In November 1900 Clemens gave his consent ("glad & proud") for Matthews to dedicate this book to him (SLC to Matthews, ALS at Columbia Univ.). Matthews' dedication page is fulsome: "To/Mark Twain/In Testimony of My Regard for the Man and of My Respect for the Literary Artist."

Krause, *MTC*, p. 153.

————. *An Introduction to the Study of American Literature.* New York: American Book Company, 1896. 256 pp.

Matthews designed this as a school textbook. He mentions Mark Twain in the chronology at the rear and includes his portrait on page 233. The book was Mark Twain's source for the quotations from "the Professor of English Literature in Columbia" which appear as epigraphs at the head of "Fenimore Cooper's Literary Offences" (July 1895). Not only does Twain quote the three sentences out of order (they actually appear on pages 63, 62, and 58), but he seems unfair in removing them from the context. In fact, Mark Twain implies their endorsement of the very thesis they reject. In his Cooper chapter, Matthews compares Cooper to Scott, since "he was an optimist, an idealizer"; he notes that Cooper did not tell the whole truth about American Indians (p. 67); and he closes by acknowledging that "novelists have a more finished art nowadays" (p. 68).

————. "New Trials for Old Favorites," *Forum,* 25 (August 1898), 749–760.

Matthews defends Goldsmith's *The Vicar of Wakefield* against Mark Twain's disparagements in *FE* (1897), which Matthews terms "the glad exaggeration of the wanton humorist" (p. 749). Clemens wrote to Joseph H. Twichell on 13 September 1898 from Kaltenleutgeben, a village near Vienna: "I thank you very much for sending me Brander's article. . . . His article is as sound as a nut. Brander knows literature, and loves it; . . . and he can discover and praise such merits as a book has, even when they are half a dozen diamonds scattered through an acre of mud. And so he has a right to be a critic" *(MTL,* pp. 666–667).

————. *Parts of Speech: Essays on English.* New York: Charles Scribner's Sons, 1901. 350 pp.

Catalog: C1951, #79c, $10, listed among the books signed by Clemens.

————. *The Story of a Story, and Other Stories.* Illus. New York: Harper & Brothers, 1893. 234 pp.

Source: MTLAcc, entry #1482, volume donated by Clemens.

————. *Studies of the Stage*. New York: Harper & Brothers, 1894. 214 pp.
  Location: Mark Twain Library, Redding, Conn. Donated by Clemens
(MTLAcc, entry #662).
  Copy examined: Clemens' copy, unmarked.

————. *Tales of Fantasy and Fact*. New York: Harper & Brothers, 1896. 216 pp.
  Source: MTLAcc, entry #1621, volume donated by Clemens.

Matthews, Franklin (1858–1917). *The New-Born Cuba*. New York: Harper &
Brothers, 1899. 389 pp.
  Source: MTLAcc, entry #1730, volume donated by Clemens.

Maudsley. [Unidentified author and work.]
  Clara Clemens discussed and summarized "Professor Maudsley's" beliefs about
plants in her commonplace book (undated entry, Paine 150, MTP). Possibly she
meant Henry Maudsley, M. D. (1835–1918), who published many works on
psychology but none on plants.

Mauris, Maurice (Marchese di Calenzano). *French Men of Letters*. New York: D.
Appleton & Co., 1880. 263 pp.
  Source: MTLAcc, entry #831, volume donated by Clemens.

Maxwell, (Mrs.) Mary Elizabeth (Braddon) (1837–1915). *An Ishmaelite*. New York:
George Munro, [1884]. 338 pp.
  Source: MTLAcc, entry #2182, volume donated from Clemens' library by
Clara Clemens Gabrilowitsch in 1910.

————. *Phantom Fortune*. Chicago: Belford, Clarke & Co., [188–?]. 408 pp.
  Source: MTLAcc, entry #31, volume donated by Clemens.

————. *The Venetians; A Novel*. New York: Harper & Brothers, 1892. 442 pp.
  Source: MTLAcc, entry #1090, volume donated by Clemens.

Maxwell, William Hamilton (1792–1850). *Life of Field-Marshal His Grace the
Duke of Wellington*. Portraits, illus. 3 vols. London, n.d. [Three-volume editions
were published by A. H. Baily & Co., 1839–41; H. G. Bohn, 1845–46 and
(fifth edition) 1852; and Bickers and Son, (sixth edition) 1862(?). Clemens'
edition is undetermined.]
  Catalog: A1911, #321, .50¢, title page of vol. 1 missing.

May, (Mrs.) Georgiana Marion (Craik) (1831–1895). *Only a Butterfly, and Other
Stories*. Copyright Edition. Leipzig: B. Tauchnitz, 1874. 288 pp.
  Source: MTLAcc, entry #2187, volume donated from Clemens' library by
Clara Clemens Gabrilowitsch in 1910.

May, Samuel Joseph (1797–1871). *Some Recollections of Our Antislavery Conflict*.
Boston: Fields, Osgood & Co., 1869. 408 pp.
  Location: Mark Twain Library, Redding, Conn. Donated by Clemens
(MTLAcc, entry #567).
  Copy examined: presumably Clemens' copy, unmarked.

Mayhew, Henry (1812–1887). *London Labour and the London Poor; A Cyclopaedia
of the Condition and Earnings of Those That Will Work, Those That Cannot
Work, and Those That Will Not Work*. 2 vols. London: G. Woodfall and Son,
1851.
  An entry in Clemens' notebook for 1866 reads: "They need Bishop Staley's
Missionary labors more in England than they do in H. I.—See London Labor
& London Poor" (NB 5, *N&J*, 1: 164).

———. *The Wonders of Science; or, Young Humphry Davy (The Cornish Apothecary's Boy, Who Taught Himself Natural Philosophy, and Eventually Became President of the Royal Society). The Life of a Wonderful Boy, Written for Boys.* Illus. New York: Harper & Brothers, n.d. [Preface is dated 1854; Harper & Brothers pub. first American edition in 1856.] 452 pp.
> *Location:* Mark Twain Library, Redding, Conn. Donated by Clemens (MTLAcc, entry #690).
> *Copy examined:* Clemens' copy. Binding is loose; flyleaf may be missing.

Mayo, William Starbuck (1812–1895). *Kaloolah: Adventures of Jonathan Romer of Nantucket.* New York: G. P. Putnam's Sons, 1872. 514 pp. Repr. 1873, 1878. [Originally pub. in 1849 as *Kaloolah; or, Journeyings to the Djébel Kumri: An Autobiography of Jonathan Romer.*]
> Estes & Lauriat of Boston billed Clemens for twenty-one books on 14 July 1880, including "1 Kaloolah $1"; Clemens paid the bill on 20 July 1880 (receipt in MTP).

Means, James (1853–1920). *Oppressive Tariff Taxation.* Rev. ed. Illus. Boston: Massachusetts Tariff Reform League, 1888. 30 pp. Paper wrappers.
> A political cartoon on the front cover depicts a worker carrying a manufacturer and a heavy load of "Tariff Taxes." In 1889 or 1890 James Means of Boston sent Clemens the pamphlet and an undated letter which requested a document "that our Reform League can circulate throughout the country. Let it appeal to the workingmen." Means wrote because he "read between the lines in your 'Yankee.'" Clemens noted in pencil at the top of Means' letter: "Brer [Whitmore], preserve letter & pamphlet, & write him I am too desperately hard-worked these months, but I will keep his letter & pamphlet to remind me & at a future day will see if I really can write anything worth printing" (letter and pamphlet in MTP).

Mechnikov, Iĺ iȃ Iĺ ich (1845–1916). *The Nature of Man; Studies in Optimistic Philosophy, by Élie Metchnikoff.* English trans., ed. by Peter Chalmers Mitchell. New York: G. P. Putnam's Sons, 1903. 309 pp.
> Isabel Lyon's journal refers to a conversation about "Metchnikoff's Book" between Clemens and William Dean Howells which took place on 25 March 1906 (TS p. 152, MTP). It was Howells who brought up this topic, one which was "always interesting to Mr. Clemens" (IVL Journal, Humanities Research Center, Univ. of Texas at Austin). Mechnikov was the Russian zoologist and bacteriologist, associated with Pasteur, who made microscopic studies of diseases of the blood.

Mee, Huan (pseud.). *A Diplomatic Woman.* New York: Harper & Brothers, 1900. 174 pp.
> *Source:* MTLAcc, entry #1625, volume donated by Clemens.

Meiners, Christoph (1747–1810). *Lebensbeschreibungen berühmter Männer aus den Zeiten der Wiederherstellung der Wissenschaften.* 3 vols. Zurich, 1795–1797.
> Clara Clemens alluded to "Meiners' lines of Mirandula and Politian" in her mostly undated commonplace book, begun about 1888 (Paine 150, MTP). Meiners' book included stories of Johann Picus von Mirandula and Angelus Politianus.

Méjan, Maurice (1765–1823). *Recueil des causes célèbres, et des arrêts qui les ont décidées*. Seconde éd. 21 vols. Paris: Garnery, 1808–1814.

   Inscription: front pastedown endpaper of vol. 1 signed with blue-black ink, "SL. Clemens".

   Marginalia: vol. 1 contains penciled markings on pages 52, 214; penciled notes by Clemens on pages 54, 105, 117, 195, and rear pastedown endpaper. Chester Davis began to publish Professor Louis J. Budd's report on the marginalia in *The Twainian*, 38 (March–April 1979), 3–4.

   Catalog: A1911, #328, vol. 8 only (pub. 1810), .50¢.

   Location: vol. 1 only in collection of Chester Davis, Executive-Secretary, Mark Twain Research Foundation, Perry, Mo.

   Copy examined: photocopies of annotated pages in vol. 1; Professor Louis J. Budd kindly provided these in September 1978.

   Isabel Lyon, Clemens' secretary, recorded on Sunday, 10 March 1907: "Tonight at dinner . . . he told me one or 2 stories which he has been reading from 'Causes Celèbres' [*sic*], one of a set of queer and battered little volumes that he ran across in the library" (IVL Journal, TS p. 230, MTP). Clemens' signature in volume one of Méjan's work looks as though it could belong to 1907, but his marginalia has the appearance of handwriting from an earlier period.

   Cf. a possibly related entry under the title *Causes célèbres*.

Melbourne *Age* (newspaper).
   "Mr. Edmund Barton called. He is going to get me a full file of the Age containing the Dean case" (NB 35, 10 October 1895, TS p. 58).

Melbourne *Punch* (journal).
   "Punch (Melbourne) & Bulletin (Sydney) good papers. Good & bright cartoons in both" (October 1895, NB 34, TS p. 14).

Meller, Henry James. *Nicotiana; or, the Smoker's and Snuff-Taker's Companion; Containing the History of Tobacco, . . . with an Essay in Its Defence. . . . Interspersed with Original Poetry and Anecdotes*. Third ed. London: Effingham Wilson, 1833. 128 pp.

   Catalog: A1911, #329, contains bookplate of Alfred Buckland, $5.50.

Memorial Concerning Conditions in the Independent State of the Kongo. April 19, 1904. Committee on Foreign Relations. U. S. Senate. 58th Congress, 2d Session. Document No. 282.

   Marginalia: Clemens annotated the paper wrapper and the text with black ink. On the front he noted: "Splendid Progress of our Xn Civilization. Too Cold an Interest taken in it by pulpit & press & public." He belittles Leopold II, "a person of brutal history & infamous character." Of the native soldiers he wrote on page 126: "It is like employing the red Indians of 200 yrs ago—*if* they could have been hired to harry their own people." He made other notes and markings.

   Catalog: "Retz Appraisal" (1944), p. 10, valued at $15.

   Location: Mark Twain Papers, Berkeley, Ca.

   Copy examined: Clemens' copy.

   On 16 October 1904 E. D. Morel wrote to Clemens from the Murray Hill Hotel in New York City: "I send you by an express messenger a packet of Congo literature"; among other publications, "it includes . . . a special copy of the Memorial, which I would like you to keep and show to any friends as a document of perhaps unique historical interest (together with a rough copy enclosed)" (ALS in MTP). Clemens replied from the Hotel Grosvenor in New York City on the same day: "The Senate Memorial reached me early this a.m., & I have remained in bed to read it." He requested an additional copy of the publication (ALS in British Library of Political and Economic Science, London).

Memories of Westminster Hall; A Collection of Interesting Incidents, Anecdotes, and Historical Sketches Relating to Westminster Hall, Its Famous Judges and Lawyers and Its Great Trials. Historical intro. by Edward Foss (1787–1870). 2 vols. Boston: Estes & Lauriat, 1874. [Only vol. 2 of Clemens' copy has been found.]

Inscription: front flyleaf of vol. 2 signed in pencil, "Saml L. Clemens/Hartford 1874."

Marginalia: in vol. 2 Clemens changed the words "would have lived" to read simply "lived" (p. 14); corrected the name "Gates" to read "Oates" (p. 37); altered the phrase "years past" to form "years passed"; drew marginal brackets to set off passages on pages 7, 9, 41, 42, and 43; and made a few other grammatical revisions. There are no markings beyond page 43. All of Clemens' annotations are in pencil.

Catalogs: A1911, #64, vol. 2 only, sold with fourteen other vols. for $8.50 total; offered for sale in 1963 by John Swingle, Alta California Rare Books, Berkeley, Calif.

Location: Mark Twain Memorial, Hartford, Conn. Gift of an anonymous donor in 1965.

Source: Diana Royce, Librarian of the Stowe-Day Library, supplied the facts presented in this entry.

Memories of Westminster Hall includes a chapter on "The Great Tichborne Case," the trial in 1873 of a claimant to the Tichborne estate whose allegations fascinated Clemens.

Menault, Ernest (1830–1903). *The Intelligence of Animals, with Illustrative Anecdotes.* Trans. from French. Illus. New York: Scribner, Armstrong & Co., 1872. 368 pp.

Source: MTLAcc, entry #1988, volume donated from Clemens' library by Clara Clemens Gabrilowitsch in 1910.

Mendel, Hermann (1834–1876). *Musikalisches Conversations-lexicon. Eine encyklopädie.* 11 vols. Berlin: R. Oppenheim, 1880–1882. [Also pub. in Leipzig: List & Francke, 1884, repr. 1890–1891.]

Clara Clemens listed the author and title in her commonplace book (undated entry, Paine 150, MTP).

Mendes, Henry Pereira (1852–1937). *The Earl of Beaconsfield, K. G. Keys to the Famous Characters Delineated in His Historical Romances.* Ed. by Robert Arnot. Portraits. New York and London: M. Walter Dunne, [cop. 1904].

Inscription: presented by the publisher to "Herbert S. 'Burt,' Esq." Bookplate of Herbert Seymour Barnes pasted on front inner cover.

Location: Mark Twain Library, Redding, Conn.

Copy examined: a possibly spurious addition to Clemens' library. Though Albert E. Stone, Jr. included this title in his catalog of Clemens' books in 1955, and though it was shelved with Clemens' library when I visited Redding in 1970, I could see no reason to presume that this unmarked volume belonged to him.

Men of the Time: A Dictionary of Contemporaries. Eighth ed. Edited by Thompson Cooper (1837–1904). London: George Routledge and Sons, 1872.

Inscription: written vertically in pencil across the title page, by Clemens: "Saml. L. Clemens,/London/1874."

Marginalia: Beside the entry for his own name, Clemens noted in black ink: "From Routledge's 'Men of the Time' ". On the other side of the page, in the right margin, Clemens crossed out the lines beginning "He has continued his labours as a lecturer. . . ." through the end of the entry and wrote in black ink: "Add the MS., here, in place of the lines stricken out. S.L.C." There is no other annotation, even in Bret Harte's entry. Some pages remain unopened, but others—such as those concerning Henry Ward Beecher—have been cut apart.

Location: Mark Twain Library, Redding, Conn. Donated by Clemens (MTLAcc, entry #895).

Copy examined: Clemens' copy.

Men of the Time: A Dictionary of Contemporaries. Tenth ed. Edited by Thompson Cooper (1837–1904). London: George Routledge and Sons, 1879.

> *Location:* catalogued by Albert E. Stone in 1955 as one of Clemens' library volumes in the Mark Twain Library at Redding, Connecticut. I was unable to locate this volume at Redding in 1970. Clemens donated the book (MTLAcc, entry #894).

> This is the version Clemens reprinted for general distribution, as he informed William Dean Howells from Hartford on 19 October 1880: "The idea of that printed biography is a noble good one: saves me time, rage, excuses, declinations, disgust, humiliation; . . . & besides, it at the same time furnishes to the inquiring idiot connected with the literary society exactly what he has ASKED for" (*MTHL,* pp. 331, 332 n. 2). In May 1889 Clemens reminded himself: "Send Charley Clark [of the Hartford *Courant*] Men of the Time Biog slip" (NB 28, TS p. 57).

Men of the Time: A Dictionary of Contemporaries. Eleventh ed. Edited by Thompson Cooper (1837–1904). London: George Routledge and Sons, 1884.

> *Location:* Mark Twain Library, Redding, Conn. Donated by Clemens (MTLAcc, entry #893).

> *Copy examined:* Clemens' copy, virtually unopened.

Meredith, George (1828–1909). *Diana of the Crossroads* (novel, 1885).

> In September 1886 Clemens made a memorandum of the title and author (NB 26, TS p. 20). Clara Clemens remembered that when Livy read aloud to the family at Quarry Farm, Clemens often expressed his opinion that Meredith was too wordy (*MFMT,* p. 61). Albert Bigelow Paine reports that Livy and her friends read Meredith's novels "with reverential appreciation." Clemens, however, "found his characters artificialities—ingeniously contrived puppets rather than human beings." When *Diana of the Crossways* was read aloud in 1887 (the date Paine supplies), Clemens remarked: "It doesn't seem to me that Diana lives up to her reputation. The author keeps telling us how smart she is, how brilliant, but I never seem to hear her say anything smart or brilliant. Read me some of Diana's smart utterances" (*MTB,* p. 847). Carlyle Smythe declared in 1898 that "Meredith, perhaps not unnaturally, provokes him to laughter" ("The Real 'Mark Twain,' " *Pall Mall Magazine,* 16 [September 1898], 31). Affecting literary ignorance in June 1909, Clemens told his biographer, Paine: "I never could stand Meredith and most of the other celebrities" (*MTB,* p. 1501).

————. *The Egoist: A Comedy in Narrative* (London, 1879).

> Clemens made a note of this novel and its author in April 1888 (NB 27, TS p. 63).

Merezhkovskiĭ, Dmitriĭ Sergeevich (1865–1941). *The Romance of Leonardo da Vinci, the Forerunner. . . . Exclusively Authorized Translation from the Russian* of *"The Resurrection of the Gods."* Trans. Herbert Trench. New York: G. P. Putnam's Sons, 1902. 463 pp.

> Livy Clemens noted the title of this translation on the verso of a "sick-room" note which Clemens sent to her around 1902 or 1903 (MTP).

Mérimée, Prosper (1803–1870). *Prosper Mérimée's Letters to an Incognita; with Recollections by Lamartine and George Sand.* Ed. by Richard Henry Stoddard (1825–1903). New York: Scribner, Armstrong & Co., 1874. 350 pp.

> *Source:* MTLAcc, entry #686, volume donated by Clemens.

Merivale, Charles (1808–1893). *History of the Romans Under the Empire.* 7 vols. (pub. 1840–1862).

> Anxious to compare Ulysses S. Grant with Caesar, Clemens made a note in June 1885: "Merivale's History of the Romans—first 2 vols (Caesar)" (NB 24, TS p. 26).

"The mermaid" (folk song); also known as "The stormy winds do blow" and "On Friday morn."

On 4 February [1903] Clemens wrote to Livy: "And now the stormy winds do blow, as the sailor-ballad says" (MTP).

Merriam, George Spring (1843–1914). *A Living Faith*. Boston: Lockwood, Brooks and Co., 1876. 282 pp.

James R. Osgood & Company of Boston listed this title on a bill for books Clemens purchased between 21 January and 24 October 1877 (Scrapbook #10, p. 69, MTP).

Merrick, George Byron (1841–1931). *Old Times on the Upper Mississippi; The Recollections of a Steamboat Pilot from 1854 to 1863*. Portraits and illus. Cleveland: A. H. Clark Co., 1909 [cop. 1908]. 323 pp.

Inscription: "Saml. L. Clemens, Pilot, with compliments of the author, Geo. B. Merrick, Madison, Wis., Nov. 30, 1908." Also signed "S. L. Clemens, 1908." *Catalog: A1911,* #330, $6.

Merritt, Ernest George (1865–1948). "The New Element Radium," *Century Magazine,* 67 (January 1904), 451–460.

In "Sold to Satan" (written 1904), Satan lauds the untapped powers of radium, citing its properties and peculiarities.

Sherwood Cummings, "Science" (1961).

Merwin, Samuel (1874–1936).

Merwin, the author of such novels as *Calumet "K"* (1901) and *Comrade John* (1907), sent Mark Twain a handsome commendation on 4 August 1903; he wrote that Mark Twain's books "brought something really new into our literature" (*MTL,* pp. 743–744; *IE,* pp. 275–276). Did Clemens ever reciprocate by looking into Merwin's books?

Metternich-Winneburg, Clemens Lothar Wenzel von (1773–1859). *Memoirs of Prince Metternich*. Ed. by Prince Richard Metternich. Comp. by M. A. de Klinkowström. Trans. by Mrs. Alexander Napier. 5 vols. New York: Charles Scribner's Sons, 1880–1882. [Also pub. by Harper & Brothers, 1881.]

Clemens wrote to Livy on 26 July 1887 from the St. James Hotel in New York City: "I read the 4th volume of Metternich's memoirs all the way down in the cars yesterday—& last night. Apparently no narrative that tells the facts of a man's life, in the man's own words, can be uninteresting. Even this man's State papers are after a fashion interesting, when read by the light of his private remarks & comments. And this difference between him & Gen. McClellan is conspicuous. Metternich's book removes the obloquy from his name; but McClellan's deepens that upon *his,* & justifies it" (*LLMT,* p. 249; ALS in MTP).

James D. Williams, "Genesis" (1961), p. 105.

Meunier, Victor (1817–1903). *Adventures on the Great Hunting Grounds of the World*. Illus. New York: Scribner, Armstrong & Co., 1873. 297 pp.

Source: MTLAcc, entry #1989, volume donated from Clemens' library by Clara Clemens Gabrilowitsch in 1910.

Michelet, Jules (1798–1874). *The Bird*. Illus. by Hector Giacomelli. London: T. Nelson and Sons, 1869. 340 pp.

Source: MTLAcc, entry #1968, volume donated from Clemens' library by Clara Clemens Gabrilowitsch in 1910.

————. *Historical View of the French Revolution.* Trans. by Charles Cocks. London: H. G. Bohn, 1848. 606 pp.

Henry W. Fisher recalled how Clemens told him (in Vienna, in the late 1890's) that the Clemens family used Michelet's book in Paris to locate "all the places of horror, made odious during the White Terror" *(AMT,* p. 59).

Blair, "French Revolution," p. 24.

————. *Jeanne d'Arc (1412–1432).* Paris: Librairie Hachette et Cie., 1873. 152 pp. [A separate printing of the fifth volume of Michelet's *Histoire de France,* 17 vols., pub. 1833–1867.]

Marginalia: annotated throughout by Clemens in pencil and brown ink. Albert E. Stone *(IE,* pp. 209, 211–212) and Roger Salomon *(TIH,* pp. 170–173) have quoted and discussed a few of Clemens' marginal comments.

Catalog: "Retz Appraisal" (1944), p. 10, valued at $20.

Location: Mark Twain Papers, Berkeley, Ca.

Copy examined: Clemens' copy. Paper wrappers; pages loose.

Albert E. Stone—"Mark Twain's *Joan of Arc*" (1959), p. 3; *The Innocent Eye* (1961), p. 212—proposes an American edition of Michelet's fifth volume of *Histoire de France* as the book from which young Clemens purportedly found a stray leaf in Hannibal in 1849 *(MTB,* pp. 81–82; *SCH,* p. 211). Grace King claimed that it was she who, while Mark Twain was writing *JA* in Florence, told him about Michelet's *Histoire de France* "and he promised to get it and read it" *(Memories,* p. 174). On the page preceding Mark Twain's "Translator's Preface" to *JA* (1896), he listed Michelet's *Jeanne d'Arc* among the "authorities examined" in preparation for the book. Mark Twain mentions Michelet in footnotes to chapters 12 and 30 of *JA.* Afterward he recalled Michelet as one of his three main sources for the novel *(MTB,* p. 958).

Stone, "Mark Twain's *JA*" (1959), pp. 8–9.

————. *La Sorcière: The Witch of the Middle Ages* (pub. 1862 in Paris).

Source: Coleman O. Parsons, "Background," pp. 60, 67—speculation about Mark Twain's *MS* (1916).

Michie, Alexander (1833–1902). *Missionaries in China.* London: E. Stanford, 1891. 107 pp.

Inscription: signed "S. L. Clemens, Riverdale, Nov. 1901, from Alexander Michie."

Marginalia: several passages marked in pencil.

Catalog: A1911, #331, $1.

Mighels, Philip Verrill (1869–1911). *Bruvver Jim's Baby.* New York: Harper & Brothers, 1905. 265 pp.

Source: MTLAcc, entry #1605, volume donated by Clemens.

Theodore Dreiser (whose comments about Clemens cannot be trusted) recalled meeting Clemens and "several acquaintances, if not cronies," in the back parlor of a New York saloon in 1907 or 1908; on that occasion "a forty-year-old dynamic and very positive and argumentative writer whose name I have forgotten, but who had written a book entitled *Bruvver Jim's Baby,*" sat on one hand of Clemens ("Three Contacts," p. 162A).

————. *Chatwit, the Man-Talk Bird.* Illus. New York: Harper & Brothers, 1906. 265 pp.

Source: MTLAcc, entry #1607, volume donated by Clemens.

————. [Another identical copy.]

Source: MTLAcc, entry #1969, volume donated from Clemens' library by Clara Clemens Gabrilowitsch in 1910.

————. *The Crystal Sceptre; A Story of Adventure*. New York: Harper & Brothers, 1906. 346 pp.
   Source: MTLAcc, entry #1604, volume donated by Clemens.

————. *Dunny, A Mountain Romance*. New York: Harper & Brothers, 1906. 264 pp.
   Source: MTLAcc, entry #1606, volume donated by Clemens.

Mill, John Stuart (1806–1873). *Autobiography*. New York: Henry Holt & Co., n.d.
   Inscription: signed and dated in 1908 by Clemens.
   Catalogs: C1951, #D42, listed among books signed by Clemens; *American Book-Prices Current Index 1960–1965* (New York, 1968), p. 368, entry #64, $110.

————. *A System of Logic; Ratiocinative and Inductive*. New York: Harper & Brothers, n.d. 659 pp.
   Source: MTLAcc, entry #1804, volume donated by Clemens.

Millais, John Guille (1865–1931). *The Life and Letters of Sir John Everett Millais, President of the Royal Academy, by His Son, John Guille Millais*. Illus. 2 vols. London: Methuen Co., 1899.
   In London, on 10 November 1899, Mark Twain inserted a quotation from page 316 of volume 2 (copied by an unknown assistant) into a manuscript titled "Postscript—Osteopathy" (DV13, MTP). Mark Twain took the quotation from Lord Leighton's letter of 19 May 1895 to Sir John Millais, which recommended Jonas Henrik Kellgren's therapy of Swedish massage. (Clemens strenuously advocated Kellgren's treatments to anyone who would listen in 1899; see, for instance, *MTHHR*, pp. 403–408, 740). Clemens' manuscript refers to "the recently published Life & Letters of Sir John Millais" (MS p. 36) and adds: "I think it a pity that Sir John Millais [a victim of throat cancer] did not follow that advice" (MS p. 38). On 24 November 1899 Clemens wrote to J. Y. W. Mac-Alister, quoting the passage from Lord Leighton's letter to Millais, and asking whether Lord Leighton had actually used the Kellgren system himself (ALS in CWB).

Miller, (Mrs.) Annie (Jenness) (b. 1859). *Physical Beauty: How to Obtain and How to Preserve It*. New York: Charles L. Webster & Co., 1892. 246 pp.
   Clemens' publishing firm advertised this book for women—a handbook on hygiene, food, sleep, skin, eyes, hair, dress, and "cultivation of Individuality"—in the *Publishers' Trade List Annual for 1893*.

Miller, Elizabeth Jane (b. 1878). *The Yoke: A Romance of the Days When the Lord Redeemed the Children of Israel*. Indianapolis, Ind.: Bobbs-Merrill Co., [cop. 1904]. 616 pp.
   Source: MTLAcc, entry #220, volume donated by Clemens.

Miller, George Ernest (b. 1855). *Luxilla: A Romance*. [Mobile, Alabama], n.d. [cop. 1885]. 54 pp.
   According to a notebook Clemens kept during the summer of 1886, he planned to "review 'Luxilla' that hogwash novel from the South" (NB 26, TS p. 9a).

Miller, (Mrs.) Harriet (Mann) (1831–1918), pseud. "Olive Thorne Miller." *Little Folks in Feathers and Fur, and Others in Neither*. New York: E. P. Dutton & Co., 1880. 368 pp.
   Source: MTLAcc, entry #1970, volume donated from Clemens' library by Clara Clemens Gabrilowitsch in 1910. "Susie and Clara Clemens' copy," binding worn.

Shortly after Annie Moffett Webster moved from Fredonia to New York City, she wrote to her brother Samuel E. Moffett about her Christmas-gift buying excursion: "We meant to go to Leggat's but I was thankful to stop at Dutton's on Broadway and buy all the books we wanted there. We bought . . . 'Little Folks in feathers and fur' for Susie [Clemens]" (19 December 1881, ALS in MTP).

————. *Little People of Asia.* New York: E. P. Dutton & Co., 1883. 405 pp.
Source: MTLAcc, entry #1898, volume donated from Clemens' library by Clara Clemens Gabrilowitsch in 1910.

————. *True Bird Stories.* Illus. New York: Houghton, Mifflin & Co., 1903. 156 pp.
Source: MTLAcc, entry #1971, volume donated from Clemens' library by Clara Clemens Gabrilowitsch in 1910.

Miller, Hugh (1802–1856). *The Cruise of the Betsey; or, A Summer Ramble Among the Fossiliferous Deposits of the Hebrides.* Ed. by W. S. Symonds. Boston: Gould and Lincoln, 1858. 524 pp.
Inscription: flyleaf signed "S. L. Clemens, 1908." On the flyleaf Clemens drew a diagram which contrasts the age of the world and the period of man's existence.
Catalog: A1911, #332, "a few leaves loose, part of back broken," $5.50.

————. *The Foot-Prints of the Creator.* From the third London edition. Biographical memoir by Louis Agassiz. Illus. Boston: Gould and Lincoln, 1866. 337 pp.
Source: MTLAcc, entry #537, volume donated by Clemens.

————. *The Testimony of the Rocks; or, Geology in Its Bearings on the Two Theologies, Natural and Revealed. . . . With Memorials of the Death and Character of the Author.* Boston: Gould and Lincoln, 1857. 502 pp.
On Saturday, 5 December 1908, Isabel Lyon noted that "at dinner the King talked a lot about Geology, a never failing topic full of interest for him. Just now he is reading Hugh Miller on the Rocks. . . . The wonders and mystery of the earth never lose their mysteries for him" (IVL Journals, TS p. 344, MTP). Clemens made a notation on the inside front cover of his copy of Alexander Winchell's *Sketches of Creation* (1903): "I had been re-reading Hugh Miller (ed. 1857), & wanted to contrast the geology of to-day with the geology of his day. I discovered no contrast" (MTP). See also Mark Twain's "No Poets in Pittsfield" (MS in Paine 246, MTP).
Cummings, "Science" (1961).

Miller, Joaquin, i.e. Cincinnatus Heine Miller (1841–1913). *Songs of the Sierras.* Boston: Roberts Brothers, 1871. 299 pp.
Inscription: front flyleaf inscribed (by Livy Clemens) "S L Clemens/1871".
Location: Mark Twain Library, Redding, Conn. Donated from Clemens' library by Clara Clemens Gabrilowitsch in 1910 (MTLAcc, entry #2064).
Copy examined: Clemens' copy.

————. *Unwritten History: Life Amongst the Modocs.* Hartford: American Publishing Co., 1874. 445 pp.
Marginalia: one note by Clemens in pencil—on page 438 he refers humorously to Miller's illegible handwriting.
Catalog: A1911, #333, $2.50.
Location: California Historical Society Library, San Francisco, California.
Copy examined: Clemens' copy (inspected in 1971). Contains bookplate of Laurance Irving Scott.
Miller was a literary lion in London when the Clemens family arrived there to spend the summer in 1873. (Clemens had known Miller in the 1860's in San Francisco.) On 1 July 1873 Clemens wrote cordially to Miller (CWB), and on 6

July 1873 Clemens informed Mrs. Fairbanks: "We see Miller every day or two, & like him better & better all the time. He is just getting out his Modoc book here & I have made him go to my publishers in America with it (by letter) & they will make some money for him" (*MTMF*, p. 174). Clemens mentioned Miller's forthcoming book in a letter to Elisha Bliss written on 16 July 1873 (NB 12, *N&J*, 1: 567). In 1873, incidentally, Susy Clemens acquired the nickname "Modoc" because of the cut of her hair (*S&MT*, p. 20). Clemens ordered a copy of Miller's book (and four written by himself, along with three others) to be shipped to a disabled soldiers' home in Elizabeth, Virginia, on 17 February 1876 (SLC to Elisha Bliss, ALS in CWB). In 1907 Clemens would remember attending a dinner in England in honor of Joaquin Miller: "He was affecting the picturesque and untamed costume of the wild Sierras at the time, to the charmed astonishment of conventional London, and was helping out the effects with the breezy and independent and aggressive manners of that faraway and romantic region." Now, Clemens added in 1907, "Joaquin Miller is white-headed and mute and quiet in his dear mountains" (August? 1907 AD, *MTE*, pp. 332–333).

Miller, Mary Farrand (Rogers) (b. 1868). *The Brook Book; A First Acquaintance with the Brook and Its Inhabitants*. New York: Doubleday, Page & Co., 1902. 241 pp.
   Source: MTLAcc, entry #1972, volume donated from Clemens' library by Clara Clemens Gabrilowitsch in 1910.

Miller, Samuel (1769–1850). *An Essay on the Warrant, Nature, and Duties of the Office of the Ruling Elder, in the Presbyterian Church*. Philadelphia: Presbyterian Board of Publication, [cop. 1832]. 339 pp.
   Inscription: (in a hand resembling Clemens') in brown ink: "Orion Clemens/ Christmas Tree/ 1865". Bookplate of Orion Clemens pasted on inside front cover.
   Location: Mark Twain Library, Redding, Conn. Donated by Clemens (MTLAcc, entry #931).
   Copy examined: Orion Clemens' copy.

Miller, Francis Davis (1846–1912). *The Expedition to the Philippines*. New York: Harper & Brothers, 1899. 275 pp.
   Source: MTLAcc, entry #1734, volume donated by Clemens.

Millet, Pierre (1635–1709). *Captivity Among the Oneidas in 1690–91 of Father Pierre Milet of the Society of Jesus*. Ed. by John D. G. Shea. Trans., annotated by Mrs. Emma Augusta Ayer. Chicago: Blakely Printing Co., 1897. 72 pp. Number 54 of 75 copies printed.
   Inscription: a questionable "Mark Twain" autograph.
   Location: Rare Books Room, University Library, University of Illinois at Urbana-Champaign.
   Copy examined: none. Information compiled from PH copy of library card supplied by respondent, Mrs. Mary Ceibert. The book was not available for inspection in 1974.

Millhouse, John and Ferdinando Bracciforti. *New English and Italian Pronouncing and Explanatory Dictionary*. Eighth edition. 2 vols. Milan: Ferdinando Bracciforti, 1900.
   Inscription: front free endpaper inscribed "To dear Miss Lyon,/with much love/and best wishes for a Merry Christmas./Jean L. Clemens./Firenze, Dec. 25th 1903."
   Marginalia: second volume contains pencil marks and a note by Miss Lyon at the top of page 512; there are a few grammar notes at the back of the volume.
   Location: Mark Twain Memorial, Hartford, Conn. Donated by Professor Norman Holmes Pearson in 1966.
   Copy examined: Isabel Lyon's copy, a gift from Jean Clemens. Miss Lyon was Clemens' secretary-factotum after the death of Livy Clemens in 1904.

Mills, S. M. *Palm Branches*. Sandusky, Ohio: Register Steam Press, 1878. 128 pp.
    Marginalia: on the recto of the blank page opposite the copyright notice
Clemens speculated that the writer must be about fifteen years old. He jotted
derogatory remarks throughout the volume, first in black ink, then purple ink,
and finally (in the latter half) in pencil. On page 65 he penciled his opinion that
"puberty will do much for this authoress." Later, on page 120, he noted that
when the character named Daisy remained the same "simple, beautiful maiden"
despite Mr. Russell's lavishing every luxury upon her (including "pearls and
precious gems that a princess might have coveted"), it was "a school-girl's idea
of triumph." There are numerous other sarcastic comments.
    Catalog: "Retz Appraisal" (1944), p. 10, valued at $15.
    Location: Mark Twain Papers, Berkeley, Ca.
    Copy examined: Clemens' copy.

Mills, Weymer Jay (b. 1880). *Caroline of Courtlandt Street*. Illus. by Anna Whelan
Betts. New York: Harper & Brothers, 1905. 291 pp.
    Source: MTLAcc, entry #1047, volume donated by Clemens.

Milne, James (b. 1865). *The Romance of a Pro-Consul; Being the Personal Life
and Memoirs of the Right Hon. Sir George Grey, K. C. B.* London: Chatto &
Windus, 1899. 214 pp.
    Inscription: on front free endpaper (not in Clemens' hand): "R. W. G. from
C L. C."
    Marginalia: first eleven pages (but none beyond those) contain voluminous
notes in pencil by Clemens, mainly derogatory. He labeled various passages
"meaningless," "unnecessary—& juvenile," and "not simple enough—too
affected." Beside the third paragraph on page 11, a passage Milne set off by
quotation marks, Clemens noted: "This was taken down short-hand or it would
have been bitched." He added: "*This* is *English,* & plain, simple, respectable."
At numerous points Clemens corrected the text as though he were its editor. On
a blank leaf at the front of the volume, Clemens made this assessment: "The
book is affected, artificial, vulgar, airy, trivial, a mess of wandering & aimless
twaddle, a literary puke. Its empty, noisy, assiduous imitation of Carlyle is a
comical thing—Carlyle's batteries firing blank cartridges. It is a foolish poor
book, & nothing to say & has accomplished its mission." Clemens concluded
this evaluation by explaining how he had "struck out a part of the lavish surplusage," marking with the symbol ⊗ those "passages which had no discoverable
meaning—& no purpose, except to be 'fine,' " and designating as *"c. 1."* ("cow
literature") the prose "which is intelligible but lumbering & clumsy."
    Catalog: C1951, #23a, $17.50, listed among books containing Clemens' mar-
ginal notations.
    Location: Humanities Research Center, University of Texas at Austin.
    Copy examined: Clemens' copy.

Milner, Henry M. *Mazeppa; or, The Wild Horse of Tartary. A Romantic Drama,
in Three Acts. Dramatized from Lord Byron's Poem* (pub. London, 1850).
    Clemens saw Adah Isaacs Menken play this role in San Francisco (13 Sep-
tember 1863 letter, *MTEnt,* pp. 78-80), but her script might have been the one
written by Henry James Byron *(q. v.).*

Milnes, Richard Monckton, Lord Houghton 1st Baron (1809–1855).
    Clemens met this poet and statesman in London in 1873 (NB 12, *N&J,* 1: 519,
532–535).

The ———— book is affected,
artificial, vulgar,
airy, trivial, a mess of
wandering & aimless ~~tos~~
twaddle, a literary puke. ~~
Its empty, noisy, assiduous imitation of Carlyle is a
comical thing—Carlyle's
batteries firing blank cartridges. It is a foolish
poor book, & had nothing to
say & has ~~accomplished~~ its
mission.

I have struck out a part
of the lavish surplusage; & now
& then irrelevancies; also ~~~~
passages which had no discoverable meaning—& no purpose,
except to be "fine."

Plate 9: Clemens' evaluation on blank verso of page ix in James Milne's
Romance of a Pro-Consul (1899).
(Courtesy of Humanities Research Center, University of Texas, Austin.)

II

HOME ~~IS THE WARRIOR~~

THINGS call to each other after the great silence has fallen, scenes come together, and that is how it seems here.

A ship, bound on a far voyage, lay in Plymouth waters the day that the Queen succeeded to the throne. It was laden with an expedition for the new wonderland of the Australias, whither it duly sailed. As leader, the expedition had a young lieutenant of the 83rd Foot Regiment, George Grey.

On a spring afternoon, fifty-seven years later, there landed at the same port, from a New Zealand liner, an aged man who received marked attention. He was as a gnarled oak of the wide-ranged British forest, and the younger trees bent in salute to him. It was Sir George Grey, returned finally to the Motherland, which had sent him forth to build nations.

He had gone in a tubby wooden craft, the winds his carrier, across oceans that were pathless, except to the venturer. He returned by steam, through seas which it had tamed to the churn and rumble of the

4

Plates 10 A, B: Pages 4 and 5 of Milne's *Romance of a Pro-Consul,* containing Clemens' symbol ⊗ for empty rhetoric and a passage he labeled "c. 1." ("cow literature").
(Courtesy of Humanities Research Center, University of Texas, Austin.)

THE QUEEN'S COMMANDS

screw. What thought in the contrasting pictures of the world! The two Englands might have met each other in the street, and passed, strangers.

'From the windows of my hotel at Plymouth,' Sir George ~~recalled~~, 'I watched the citizens proclaim the young Queen. Who among them could have imagined the glorious reign hers was to be? It was to surpass in bounty of achievement all foretelling.' said

Now, he would meet, for the last time, the Sovereign who, like himself, had tended the rise of Oceana. This was at Windsor, to which he had summons soon after he reached England. He had been exalted a member of the Privy Council, and must be sworn in by the Queen. The tribute was cheerful (gratifying?) to him, since the very nature of it set seal upon his services to the Empire. The longing for some word of England's remembrance had assuredly been in his heart, which had often been left desolate. It was all rapture to England, like a child's to its mother. c. l.

'For mere honours themselves,' ~~was his broad attitude thereon~~ he said, 'I entertain no special regard. A title to one's name, a red ribbon, or something else, what are they but baubles, unless ~~there is more~~? ~~What more? Why~~, they hand down a record of the public work that a person may have endeavoured to perform. In that respect they should have esteem, being the recognition of efforts to serve Queen and people.

'Nothing could be more unfortunate than that a country should neglect services rendered to it. The

5

(as it clearly did in his case)

Plate 10B:

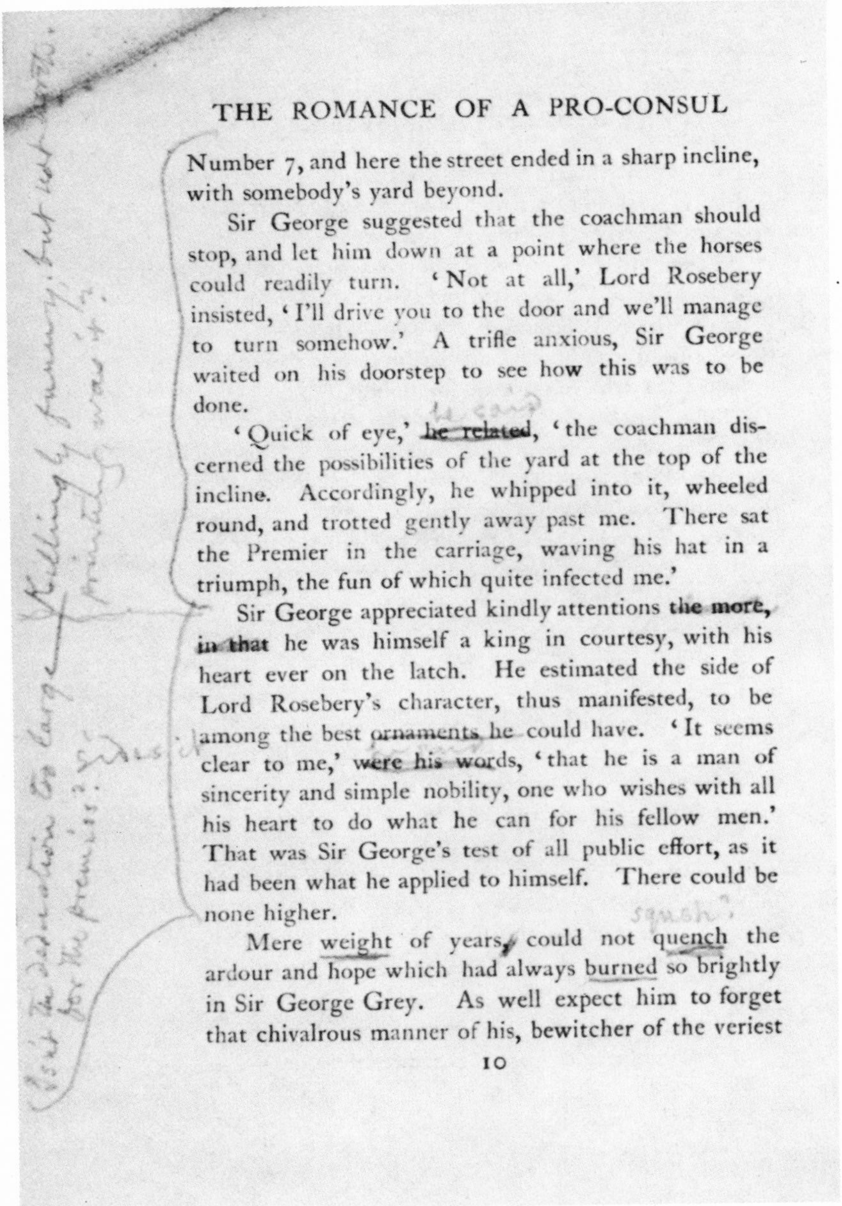

THE ROMANCE OF A PRO-CONSUL

Number 7, and here the street ended in a sharp incline, with somebody's yard beyond.

Sir George suggested that the coachman should stop, and let him down at a point where the horses could readily turn. 'Not at all,' Lord Rosebery insisted, 'I'll drive you to the door and we'll manage to turn somehow.' A trifle anxious, Sir George waited on his doorstep to see how this was to be done.

'Quick of eye,' ~~he related~~, 'the coachman discerned the possibilities of the yard at the top of the incline. Accordingly, he whipped into it, wheeled round, and trotted gently away past me. There sat the Premier in the carriage, waving his hat in a triumph, the fun of which quite infected me.'

Sir George appreciated kindly attentions ~~the more, in that~~ he was himself a king in courtesy, with his heart ever on the latch. He estimated the side of Lord Rosebery's character, thus manifested, to be among the best ~~ornaments~~ he could have. 'It seems clear to me,' ~~were his words~~, 'that he is a man of sincerity and simple nobility, one who wishes with all his heart to do what he can for his fellow men.' That was Sir George's test of all public effort, as it had been what he applied to himself. There could be none higher.

Mere weight of years, could not quench the ardour and hope which had always burned so brightly in Sir George Grey. As well expect him to forget that chivalrous manner of his, bewitcher of the veriest

10

Plates 11 A, B: Pages 10 and 11 in Milne's *Romance of a Pro-Consul*, annotated in pencil.
(Courtesy of Humanities Research Center, University of Texas, Austin.)

FAREWELL TO FROUDE

stranger. He would find his tall hat, search out his staunch umbrella, and convoy the visitor forth, when the hour of parting had arrived. Nothing less would suffice him, and as to his company, it was a delight for ever. Another veteran might have been lonely with a younger generation knocking at the door, indeed in full possession. He was not ; he strode in the van with the youngest.

Yet he felt, perhaps, the void time had wrought in the circle of his friends. He held the fort silently, while the long scythe cut another swathe very near him. He heard that his friend, James Anthony Froude, who had been lying ill in Devonshire, was steadily losing strength.

' I have made inquiries about him, poor fellow,' he murmured, ' but now I must telegraph for the latest particulars. He and I are old companions, and I have liking and admiration for him. When he visited me at my island of Kawau, off the New Zealand coast, we had a capital while together. He wanted to ask me, if I approved the manner in which he had written Carlyle's life, a subject that brought him a good deal of criticism. My reply was that I believed Carlyle would have wished to be presented just as he was ; not a half picture, but complete, for that would ultimately make him appear all the greater.'

Somewhat before his illness, Froude published a book, and the London daily paper which Sir George Grey took in, had a handsome review of it. ' I'll send the cutting to Froude,' he declared ; ' it will do him

11

Plate 11 B

Milton, John (1608–1674). *Milton's Paradise Lost*. Illus. by Gustave Doré. Ed. and Intro. by Robert Vaughn, D. D. New York: Cassell Publishing Co., [1866]. 311 pp. 50 plates.

Clemens wrote to Livy Langdon from Utica on 15 January 1870: "I am so glad the Milton pleases my idol—I am delighted. Oh, we'll read, & look at pictures when we are married!" (ALS in MTP). Presumably this was the Gustave Doré book Clemens mentioned sending Livy on 6 and 10 January 1870 (MTP). He alluded to *Paradise Lost* frequently. While piloting on the river around 1858, he wrote to Orion: "What is the grandest thing in 'Paradise Lost'—the Arch-Fiend's terrible energy!" *(MTB, p. 146)*. On 20 March 1862 Clemens informed his mother from Carson City: "There are no prairies, Ma, because sage-brush deserts don't come under that head, in this portion of Paradise Lost" *(PRI,* p. 36). In a 10 September 1866 letter from Honolulu to the Sacramento *Weekly Union,* Mark Twain congratulated Hawaii and California on their futures: "We have found the true and only direct route to the bursting coffers of 'Ormus and of Ind' " (*LH,* p. 56; cf. *Paradise Lost,* 2: 2). "If it had been left to you [the reader], you would have said . . . that even 'Paradise Lost' lacked cheerfulness" ("A General Reply," November 1870 *Galaxy, CG,* p. 97). Clemens mentioned *Paradise Lost* to Mrs. Fairbanks on 31 October 1877 *(MTMF,* p. 212). In Mark Twain's speech to the Nineteenth Century Club on 20 November 1900, he quipped: "I don't believe any of you have ever read 'Paradise Lost,' and you don't want to. That's something that you just want to take on trust. It's a classic, just as Professor Winchester says, and it meets his definition of a classic—something that everybody wants to have read and nobody wants to read" ("Disappearance of Literature," *MTS1923,* p. 210; *MTB,* p. 1120).

Parsons, "Background" (1960), p. 62; Baetzhold, *MT&JB,* pp. 262–264; Gibson, *MSM,* p. 32 n. 77.

————. *Milton's Poetical Works . . . Together with the Life of the Author.* New York: Charles Wells, [183?]. 321 pp.

Marginalia: someone totted up figures (totals of 4.38, 39, and 4.96) on the verso of the flyleaf opposite the title page; the hand might be young Clemens'. A large, ornate letter "C" has been drawn in brown ink. There are small penciled "x's" beside some stanzas of "The Hymn" (pp. 162–166). A rear flyleaf contains figures which total 1.97. No other marks.

Location: Mark Twain Library, Redding, Conn.

Copy examined: possibly a copy that belonged to Clemens as a youth.

Mark Twain advised aspiring newspaper critics of literature to assign "all the grand ponderous [verse], with a solemn lustre as of holiness about it, to Milton" *(Californian,* 17 June 1865; *LAMT,* p. 141). Milton's remains are buried in Westminster Abbey, Mark Twain noted in "A Memorable Midnight Experience" (1872). A footnote to chapter 16 of *RI* (1872) credits Milton with coining the word "smouched." In September 1887, inspired by Ignatius Donnelly's *The Great Cryptogram,* Mark Twain constructed an elaborate argument "proving" that John Milton rather than John Bunyan actually wrote *The Pilgrim's Progress.* Twain listed every major event in Milton's life, sometimes referring to page numbers of a biography, and demonstrated that Milton's experiences adequately prepared him to write the work for which Bunyan received credit. In the course of Mark Twain's argument, he alludes to most of Milton's major poems. Although Twain is joshing here (he also claims that Bunyan must have written *Paradise Lost),* Twain's pro-Bacon treatise of 1909 ("Is Shakespeare Dead?") will follow the same logic: Milton traveled more, knew more famous people, possessed a greater reputation among his contemporaries, was a finer scholar, and therefore must have written the "immortal *Dream"* of *Pilgrim's Progress* (NB 27, TS pp. 19–22). Clemens listed Milton among the famous personages "materialized" by charlatan spiritualists in *AC* (ch. 3, 1892). In December 1892 Clemens referred to "Milton, Sonnet" when devising literary japes in Notebook 32 (TS p. 47). Mark Twain jocularly attributes the author-ship of *The Lay of the Last Minstrel* to Milton in "My First Lie, and How I Got Out of It" (1899). Twain seems momentarily sincere in "About Cities in the Sun" (written 1901?, DV357, MTP) when he acknowledges what "a wonder-ful experience" it would be to stand in the New Jerusalem "& hear Shakspeare & Milton & Bunyan read from their noble works" (MS p. 19). On 9 December 1908 Clemens wrote regretfully to decline an invitation to a ceremony in New York City honoring John Milton; had Clemens attended, he wrote, he might have "lifted some of that cloud" from the "solemn & sombre function" and "let in the sunshine" (SLC to Frances Nunnally, ALS in collection of Mrs. John Goodrich, TS in MTP).

————. *Paradise Lost*. New York: J. W. Lovell Co., 1881. 291 pp.
Source: MTLAcc, entry #2072, volume donated from Clemens' library by Clara Clemens Gabrilowitsch in 1910.

————. *Paradise Lost*. Portrait. London, n.d.
Inscription: (in pencil on flyleaf) "Olivia Langdon presented by her father Edward Lewis."
Catalog: A1911, #334, "24mo, sheep, not returnable," sold for $3 to the Mark Twain Company.

————. *Il Penseroso*.
Mark Twain uses the phrase "dim religious light" in chapter 23 of *IA* (1869); the phrase occurs again in Clemens' dictation of June 1873 concerning the Athenaeum Club in London (NB 12, *N&J*, 1: 533). Lines 159–160 of Milton's poem refer to "Storied windows richly dight,/Casting a dim religious light."

————. *The Poetical Works of John Milton*. Ed. by Sir Samuel Egerton Brydges. Illus. by John Martin and J. W. M. Turner. Boston: Crosby, Nichols, Lee & Co., 1861. 858 pp.
Source: MTLAcc, entry #2121a, donated from Clemens' library by Clara Clemens Gabrilowitsch in 1910. "Cover broken."

Mines, John Flavel (1835–1891). *A Tour Around New York*. Illus. New York: Harper & Brothers, 1893. 518 pp.
Source: MTLAcc, entry #1735, volume donated by Clemens.

Mining Life in Wales. [Unidentified book.]
Mark Twain intended to include this book in the projected series he planned to title "Royalty & Nobility Exposed" (NB 26, May 1887, TS p. 49). Unfor-tunately he did not supply the author's name.

The Missionary Herald at Home and Abroad (Congregational Church periodical, Worcester, Mass., 1805–   ).
Mark Twain recalled that "bound copies of The Missionary Herald" were generally observable in homes of Honolulu in the 1860's *(FE*, ch. 3, 1897). Old Mrs. Richards of "The Man That Corrupted Hadleyburg" (1900) is "reading the *Missionary Herald* by the lamp" when the malevolent stranger deposits a sack of gold with her (ch. 1).

Mitchell, Donald Grant (1822–1908), pseud. "Ik Marvel." *About Old Story-Tellers; Of How and When They Lived, and What Stories They Told*. Illus. New York: Scribner, Armstrong, and Co., 1878. 237 pp.
Source: MTLAcc, entry #1899, volume donated from Clemens' library by Clara Clemens Gabrilowitsch in 1910.

————. *Dream-Life*. New York: H. M. Caldwell Co., [190?]. 265 pp.
Location: Antenne-Dorrance Collection, Rice Lake, Wis.
Copy examined: a copy shelved with Clemens' library books. Its provenance is uncertain.

————. *Dream Life*. New York: Optimus Printing Co., n.d. 234 pp.
Source: MTLAcc, entry #692, volume donated by Albert Bigelow Paine, Clemens' designated biographer. Possibly Clemens saw this book, since the men exchanged reading materials.

————. *Reveries of a Bachelor; or, a Book of the Heart. A New Edition*. New York: Charles Scribner and Co., 1866. 280 pp.
Inscription: signed in pencil "SL Clemens". The style of the signature is similar to Clemens' of the 1860's.
Location: Mark Twain Library, Redding, Conn.
Copy examined: Clemens' copy, unmarked but worn.
On Christmas morning in 1877 Clemens kidded Mrs. Jervis Langdon in a thank-you letter: "I have taken Ida's House Beautiful & Baby Days & Ik Marvel's book, & shall give Livy & the children copies of my works in place of them" (ALS in MTP, gift of Mrs. Eugene Lada-Mocarski in 1972). Henry P. Goddard recalled giving a dinner for Mitchell in Hartford around 1879, which Clemens attended as a guest *(Harper's Weekly,* 1906).

Mitchell, Edward Cushing (1829–1900). *The Critical Handbook of the Greek New Testament*. New and enl. edition. New York: Harper & Brothers, 1896. 270 pp.
Source: MTLAcc, entry #1469, volume donated by Clemens.

Mitchell, Isaac (1759?–1812). *The Asylum; or, Alonzo and Melissa* (pub. 1811). More widely known as *Alonzo and Melissa; or, the Unfeeling Father. An American Tale*. Authorship claimed by Daniel Jackson.
In a letter of 24 March 1869, Mark Twain jocularly proposed the name of this Gothic romance as a title for the book that became *IA (MTMF,* p. 87). "The House Beautiful" in chapter 38 of *LonMiss* (1883) contained a copy of "Alonzo and Melissa."
MTSM, p. 204 n. 22.

Mitchell, Josiah Angier (1812–1876). *The Diary of Captain Josiah A. Mitchell*. N.p., 1866. 110 pp.
In 1898 Mark Twain recalled how he relied on Mitchell's manuscript log— and the diaries kept by the Ferguson brothers—in reconstructing their harrowing "Forty-three Days in an Open Boat" (1866) after the burning of the clipper ship *Hornet* ("My Début as a Literary Person").

Mitford, Algernon Bertram Freeman-Mitford (1837–1916). *Tales of Old Japan* (pub. 1871).
In the margin of another book—Shiuichiro Saito and Edward Greey's *Japanese Romance* (New York, 1880)—Clemens opined: "Mitford's translation of the Ronin story is better literature than this one. S. L. C." (quoted in *A1911,* #268).

Mitford, John (1781–1859). *The Life of Milton*. Published in *The Poetical Works of John Milton, with a Life of the Author*. London: W. Pickering, 1851.
Mitford's was one of the "biogs of Milton" that Clemens listed in September 1887 (NB 27, TS p. 22).

Mitford, Mary Russell (1787–1855). *The Friendships of Mary Russell Mitford as Recorded in Letters from Her Literary Correspondents*. Ed. by Alfred Guy Kingan L'Estrange (b. 1832). New York: Harper & Brothers, 1882. 460 pp.
Source: MTLAcc, entry #1296, volume donated by Clemens.

Mocasson. [Unidentified author and article.]

On 5 April 1905 Clemens read the manuscript of an article by Mocasson about Henry H. Rogers; the next day Clemens conferred with Rogers; and on 6 and 7 April Clemens discussed the article with Mocasson (Isabel V. Lyon's Journal, Antenne-Dorrance Collection, Rice Lake, Wis.).

Modi, (Sir) Jivanji Jamshedji (1854–1933).

"The model of the Towers [of Silence, a Parsee shrine,] shown & explained by Mr. Modi. See his book," noted Clemens on 26 January 1896 in Bombay (NB 36, TS p. 26). Modi published numerous books in Bombay about the ceremonies and religion of the Parsees.

Moffett, Samuel Erasmus (1860–1908). "Captains of Industry: Henry Huttleston Rogers," *Cosmopolitan,* 33 (September 1902), 532–534.

Reference: Henry H. Rogers to SLC, 24 February 1903, *MTHHR*, p. 519.

————. *Suggestions on Government.* Chicago and New York: Rand, McNally & Co., 1894. 200 pp.

On 21 September 1893 Clemens wrote to Pamela Moffett and Annie Webster from New York City: "I will ask Mr. Hall for Sam's book; I shall be very glad to read it" (Webster Collection, TS in MTP). Moffett also published *The Tariff. What It Is and What It Does.* Washington: Potomac Publishing Co., 1892. 112 pp.

Mogridge, George (1787–1854). *Learning to Think.* Philadelphia: Presbyterian Board of Publications, 1846. 197 pp. This book and two other volumes in the series, *Learning to Act* and *Learning to Feel,* were also published in Philadelphia by the American Sunday-School Union.

In November 1877 James R. Osgood & Company of Boston billed Clemens for "1 set Learning to Think" (Scrapbook #10, p. 69, MTP).

"The Mohamedan's Prayer" (unidentified poem).

In 1870 Livy Clemens copied this poem into her commonplace book (DV161, MS pp. 99–100, MTP).

Moltke, Helmuth Karl Bernhard von (1800–1891). *Essays, Speeches and Memoirs.* Trans. by Charles Flint McClumpha, Charles St. Leger Barter, and Mary Herms. 2 vols. New York: Harper & Brothers, 1893.

Source: MTLAcc, entries #1778 and #1779, volumes donated by Clemens.

————. *Letters of Field-Marshall Count Helmuth von Moltke to His Mother and His Brothers.* Trans. by Clara Bell and Henry W. H. Fischer. Illus. New York: Harper & Brothers, 1893. 309 pp.

Source: MTLAcc, entry #1780, volume donated by Clemens.

Fisher's *Abroad with Mark Twain* (1922) mentions his sending Clemens "my translation of Field Marshal Count Moltke's Letters" (p. 120).

Monahan, Michael (1865–1933). "Saint Mark," *The Papyrus* (December 1904).

Clemens wrote to Monahan from New York City on 28 January 1905: "It is strong & eloquent & beautiful & I thank you very much for giving me an opportunity to read it. The inspiration which tipped your pen with fire is from the Maid" (ALS in MTP). Monahan eventually would publish *My Jeanne d'Arc: Her Wonderful Story in the Light of Recent Researches; with Notes from a Pilgrimage in France.* New York and London: The Century Co., [cop. 1928]. 298 pp.

See entry for *The Papyrus.*

Le Moniteur (serial publication of the French Revolutionary period).

Clemens supposedly told Henry Fisher in the late 1890's that while in Paris "I was particularly interested in the 'Official Gazette' of the guillotine, 'The Moniteur,' and my girls helped me read and digest many tell-tale pages yellow with age and tattered by usage" (*AMT*, p. 59).

Blair, "French Revolution," p. 22; *MT&HF*, p. 312.

Monnier, Marc (1827–1885). *The Wonders of Pompeii. Translated from the Original French.* Illus. New York: Scribner, Armstrong & Co., 1872. 250 pp.

Inscription: front free endpaper signed (in pencil) "Saml. L. Clemens./Hartford, 1874."

Marginalia: a penciled note in the margin of page 51: "2712–913 377—Mon".

Provenance: Mark Twain Library at Redding, Conn. Donated from Clemens' library by Clara Clemens Gabrilowitsch in 1910 (MTLAcc, entry #1991).

Catalog: Mott 1952, item #70, $10.

Location: Mark Twain Memorial, Hartford, Conn. Donated anonymously in 1963.

Copy examined: Clemens' copy. Spine is missing. Contains bookstamps and charge slip of the Mark Twain Library at Redding, Conn.

Montaigne, Michel Eyquem de (1533–1592). *Works of Michael de Montaigne, Comprising His Essays, Journey into Italy, and Letters, with Notes from All the Commentators, Biographical and Bibliographical Notices, Etc.* Ed. by William Hazlitt. New, revised ed. prepared by O. W. Wight. 4 vols. New York: Hurd and Houghton, 1866.

Inscription: vol. 1 signed "Saml. L. Clemens, Hartford, 1873"; the other vols. signed "S. L. Clemens."

Marginalia: a few remarks by Clemens in pencil.

Catalog: A1911, #336, $15 total.

In Mark Twain's *1601* (1880), Shakespeare recalls feats of sexual prowess as well as other matters of sex discussed by Montaigne (Meine edition, p. 36).

MT&HF, p. 94.

[Monteith, John.] *Parson Brooks: A Plumb Powerful Hard Shell. A Story of Humble Southern Life.* St. Louis: O. H. P. Applegate, 1884. 115 pp.

Source: MTLAcc, entry #1849, volume donated from Clemens' library by Clara Clemens Gabrilowitsch in 1910.

Montgomery, Lucy Maud (1874–1942). *Anne of Avonlea.* Boston: L. C. Page & Co., 1909. 367 pp.

Source: MTLAcc, entry #1484, volume donated by Clemens.

————. *Anne of Green Gables.* Boston: L. C. Page & Co., 1908. 429 pp.

On 10 October 1908 Clemens wrote to Frances Nunnally from Redding: "I'll send you a book—'Anne of Green Gables.' It came two days after you went away, & I was to read it & give it to Frances Wilson; but I was at once so taken with it that I thought I would send it to you & get another copy for him. I think Anne is a very pleasant child to know, & that the literary quality of the book is fine" (ALS in collection of Mrs. John Goodrich, TS in MTP). An advertisement in the house list of publications at the rear of the "59th impression, 1926" quotes a letter from Mark Twain to Francis Wilson: "In 'Anne of Green Gables' you will find the dearest and most delightful child since the immortal Alice."

Monti, Luigi (1830–1914), pseud. "Samuel Sampleton." *Adventures of a Consul Abroad*. Boston: Lee and Shepard, 1878. 270 pp.

Clemens noted the title and publisher in Notebook 20 in March 1882 (*N&J*, 2: 450), around the time he was consulting with Ulysses S. Grant about President Arthur's intention to replace William Dean Howells' father as the U. S. consul at Toronto. Monti's *Adventures* narrates the problems that beset a Cape Cod schoolmaster who obtains a consular appointment to the mythical Mediterranean city of Verdecuerno. The inexperienced and underpaid functionary blunders through unfamiliar European formalities and bungles his official responsibilities. Monti's book satirizes the American spoils system, which changed appointees after every shift of political power in Washington. (The death of President Garfield had jeopardized the elder Howells' consular post.) Monti laments: "Our government sends men abroad, who, after hard labor and long experience, learn a complicated, delicate, and responsible profession; and no sooner have they learned it, and are able to perform creditably . . ., than they are recalled, and replaced by inexperienced men, who have to go through the same ordeal, and never stay long enough to be of real service to their country" (p. 270).

Moodie, (Mrs.) Susannah (Strickland) (1803–1885).

Harold Aspiz—"Mark Twain's Reading" (1949), p. 224—cites a book by Mrs. Moodie titled *A Bride from the Bush* as the source of one of the weather descriptions appended to *AC* (1892), but she published none by this name. She did write a narrative called *Roughing It in the Bush,* however. (Mark Twain simply credited a book titled "A Bride from the Bush.")

See the entry for E. W. Hornung.

Moody, Dwight Lyman (1837–1899).

In Mark Twain's "The Loves of Alonzo Fitz Clarence and Rosannah Ethelton" (1878), books by Moody and evangelist Ira David Sankey are noticeable in the "private parlor of a refined and sensible lady," Aunt Susan. Mark Twain mentions the prayer requests of Moody and Sankey in "The Shakspeare Mulberry" (DV383, MS in MTM). "This bartender got converted at a Moody and Sankey meeting in New York," wrote Mark Twain in chapter 2 of "Extract from Captain Stormfield's Visit" (1909). Christian Science "is calculated to strikingly impress a person accustomed to Moody and Sankey and Sam Jones revivals" ("Christian Science" [1907], Book 2, ch. 7).

Mookerjee, Mohindonauth. *Onoocool Chunder Mookerjee [1829–1871]; A Memoir. Fifth Edition. Printed Verbatim from the First Edition.* Calcutta: Thacker, Spink and Co., 1895. 72 pp. [First edition pub. 1873.]

In chapter 61 of *FE* (1897) Mark Twain quotes "from a little book which is famous in India—the biography of a distinguished Hindoo judge, Onoocool Chunder Mookerjee; it was written by his nephew, and is unintentionally funny— in fact, exceedingly so."

Moon, George Washington (1823–1909). *Learned Men's English: The Grammarians. A Series of Criticisms on the English of Dean [Henry] Alford, Lindley Murray, and Other Writers on the Language. Being the Twelfth Edition of "The Dean's English," and "Bad English Exposed."* London: George Routledge & Sons, 1892. Two parts: 215 and 227 pp.

Inscription: (on endpaper) "Clara L. Clemens, from an Arrogant Autocrat."

Marginalia: several marginal notes and underscorings in pencil by Clemens, including one on page 195 which reads: "There is no such thing as 'the Queen's English.' The property has passed into the hands of a joint stock company, and we own the bulk of the shares." A note on page 192 is dated 1897. See "Mark Twain's Marginal Notes on 'The Queen's English,' " *The Twainian*, 25 (March-April 1966), 1–4.

Catalog: Hunley 1958, item #107, price $35.
Location: Mark Twain Research Foundation, Perry, Missouri.
Copy examined: none. This volume was not available when I visited Perry in 1970.

Moore, Clement Clarke (1779–1863). "The Night Before Christmas" (ballad, pub. 1822). Also known as "A Visit from St. Nicholas."
On Christmas Eve, Livy Clemens always recited this poem, and Clemens sometimes impersonated Santa Claus afterwards *(MFMT,* p. 36).

Moore, George (1852–1933).
Henry Fisher reported that Clemens "was visibly tickled" when Fisher told him about a compliment Moore paid to his writing—praising Mark Twain's power of presenting pathetic situations without "slush" *(AMT,* p. 194).

Moore, H. B. *Queen Bee.* Illus. Melbourne: Melville & Mullen, [cop. 1905]. 118 pp.
Source: MTLAcc, entry #441, volume donated by Clemens.

Moore, John Howard (1862–1916). *The Universal Kinship.* Chicago: Charles H. Kerr & Co., 1906. 329 pp.
Late in 1906 or early in 1907 Clemens wrote to Moore: "The book has furnished me several days of deep pleasure & satisfaction; it has compelled my gratitude at the same time, since it saves me the labor of stating my own long-cherished opinions & reflections & resentments [about human instincts and morals] by doing it lucidly & fervently & irascibly for me" (quoted in *MTB,* p. 1363; also quoted in *MTL,* p. 804).

Moore, (Mrs.) Julia A. (Davis) (1847–1920). *Original Poems.* Grand Rapids, Mich.: C. M. Loomis, 1878. 56 pp.
Source: MTLAcc, entry #2071, volume donated from Clemens' library by Clara Clemens Gabrilowitsch in 1910.

————. *The Sentimental Song Book.* Grand Rapids, Mich.: C. M. Loomis, 1877. 60 pp. [First edition pub. 1876.]
"The Sweet Singer of Michigan, Queen & Empress of the Hogwash Guild" is how Clemens described this poetess to a correspondent in 1906 (SLC to John Horner, 12 January 1906, dictation copy by SLC's secretary, Isabel V. Lyon, MTP). It is generally agreed that the didactic doggerel of this farmer's wife inspired Emmeline Grangerford's lugubrious elegies in *HF* (1885). In *FE* (1897) Mark Twain returned to *The Sentimental Song Book* ("forgotten by the world in general, but not by me," he declared), and quoted from different poems in chapters 8 ("Frank Dutton"), 36 ("William Upson"), and 44 ("The Author's Early Life"). Moore, he wrote, had that ineffable and "subtle touch" necessary for genuine hogwash—"the touch that makes an intentionally humorous episode pathetic and an intentionally pathetic one funny" (ch. 36). Clemens may also have seen Moore's *"The Sweet Singer of Michigan": Later Poems.* Grand Rapids, Mich.: Eaton, Lyon & Co., 1878. 90 pp.
MT&HF, pp. 209–213, 406 n. 13; *The Art of HF* (1962), eds. Hamlin Hill and Walter Blair, pp. 445–451; *HF* (1962), eds. Sculley Bradley, Richmond Croom Beatty, and E. Hudson Long, pp. 253–254; *HF* (1961), ed. Kenneth S. Lynn, pp. 156–160; *The Sweet Singer of Michigan,* ed. Walter Blair (Chicago: P. Covici, 1928); Madigan, "MT's Passage to India" (1974), p. 362.

Moore, Thomas (1779–1852). *The Epicurean, a Tale.* New York: J. Miller, 1875. 176 pp.
Inscription: "Saml. L. Clemens, Hartford, 1875."
Catalog: A1911, #337, $2.50.

————. "Hours there were" (song). Melody composed by J. Wade.
This piece was among the music on the piano in "The House Beautiful" (*LonMiss* [1883], ch. 38). In a piece written for the 17 June 1865 issue of the *Californian*, Mark Twain advised the would-be literary "connoisseur" to attribute "all the tender, broken-hearted song-verses to Moore" (quoted in *LAMT*, p. 141).

————. *Lalla Rookh, An Oriental Romance* (pub. in London, 1817).
In a forthcoming edition of *IA* (1869), Leon Dickinson traces Mark Twain's reference to "gazelles, of 'soft-eyed' notoriety" (ch. 55) to Part 5, "The Fire-Worshippers." In chapter 32 of *HF* (1885) Aunt Sally is reminded of the steamboat explosion of "the old Lally Rook."

————. "The last rose of summer" (song, pub. 1813).
Clemens named this title among songs that "tended to regrets for bygone days and vanished joys," favorites among early-day Hannibal residents ("Villagers of 1840–3," written 1897, *HH&T*, p. 34). In "Answers to Correspondents" (1865) Mark Twain mentioned "that exquisite melody, 'The Last Rose of Summer.' " On 11 August 1878 Clemens observed: "When they play Martha, the liars applaud all along—but when The Last Rose of Summer drops in, they forget & the applause is something tremendous" (NB 15, *N&J*, 2: 140). Clemens referred to the song favorably in Notebook 16 (1878), *N&J*, 2: 212). In "Simon Wheeler, Detective," a novel written between 1877 and 1898, Hugh Burnside "detected the long-drawn, wheezy agony of 'The Last Rose of Summer' on a hand-organ" (*S&B*, p. 398). On 1 June 1902 Mark Twain expressed his intention to use the song in his next work about Huck and Tom (NB 45, TS p. 15). "I am that rose, the last rose of my summer, I suppose. I shall not be here any more, I imagine" (speech at University of Missouri Commencement, 4 June 1902, *MTSpk*, p. 436). Isabel Lyon noted on 1 December 1904 that this piece was one of Clemens' favorite songs for the orchestrelle (IVL Journals, TS p. 29, MTP).

————. "Oft in the stilly night" (song, pub. 1818). Music from a Scotch air, arranged by Sir John Stevenson.
Susy Clemens' death reminded Clemens in January 1897 of lines 5–10 from the first stanza of Moore's song: "The smiles the tears of childhood [Moore wrote "boyhood's"] years/The words of love then spoken,/The eyes that shone now dim'd & gone/The happy [Moore wrote "cheerful"] hearts now broken" (NB 39, London, TS p. 58). In 1897 Clemens included the song in his list of those popular during his childhood in Hannibal ("Villagers of 1840–3," *HH&T*, p. 34). On 1 June 1902 Clemens made plans to use this song in a future piece about Huck and Tom (NB 45, TS p. 15).

———— and William Jerdan (1782–1869). *Personal Reminiscences by Moore and Jerdan*. Ed. by Richard Henry Stoddard. Portraits. Bric-a-brac Series. New York: Scribner, Armstrong and Co., 1875. 293 pp.
Inscription: flyleaf signed "Saml. L. Clemens, Hartford, 1875."
Catalog: A1911, #338, $2.75.
In "Rambling Notes of an Idle Excursion" (1877) Mark Twain jokingly refers to Moore's sojourn in Bermuda "more than seventy years ago." In January 1894 Mark Twain wanted to include "Tom Moore's Auto" in the projected "Back Number" magazine (NB 33, TS p. 46).

————. "Those Evening Bells" (poem).
Mark Twain penned a parody titled "Those Annual Bills," which he published with Moore's poem ("Two Poems: By Moore and Twain") in 1865.
S. B. Liljegren, "Revolt Against Romanticism" (1945), pp. 28–30.

————. "The World Is All a Fleeting Show" (poem).
References: title quoted in "On Linden, Etc." (7 April 1866 *Californian; Ssix,* p. 209); quoted again in "Some Rambling Notes of An Idle Excursion" (1877).

More, Hannah (1745–1833). *Letters.* [Unidentified book.]
Listed in Clara Clemens' commonplace book (undated entry, Paine 150, MTP).

————. *Moses in the Bulrushes: A Sacred Drama* (verse).
More's four-part, twenty-five-page version of the Biblical story from the Book of Exodus was well-known in the early nineteenth century. Lines 34–36 of Part One convey her tone: "Did not God/Sometimes withhold in mercy what we ask,/We should be ruined at our own request." The first edition of Mark Twain's *TA* (1880) gave "Titian's Moses" as a burlesque caption for the frontispiece sketch of a tearful infant among bulrushes. In chapter one of *HF* (1885), the Widow Douglas "got out her book and learned me about Moses and the Bulrushers, and I was in a sweat to find out all about him." In chapter 8 of Mark Twain's "Tom Sawyer's Conspiracy," written between 1897 and 1902, Huck Finn mentions "the pillar of cloud that led Moses out of the bulrushers" (*HH&T*, p. 226). Mark Twain made up a joke about Moses in the bulrushes in August 1898 (NB 40, TS p. 30). More's poem may be related to these allusions.

————. *The Shepherd of Salisbury Plain* (pub. 1795).
This was one of the books the *Quaker City* voyagers were expected to bring with them, Mark Twain reported (5 April 1868 *Daily Alta California; TIA,* p. 303). Mark Twain's unfinished play, "The *Quaker City* Holy Land Excursion" (MS in MTP) suggests that More's tract was in the ship library (Act 2, Scene 1). "The House Beautiful" in chapter 38 of *LonMiss* (1883) contains "two or three goody-goody works—'Shepherd of Salisbury Plain,' etc." In "Christian Science" (1907), Mark Twain scoffs at Mary Baker Eddy for explaining the identity of someone as well known as Hannah More (Book 2, chapter 1).

Morel, Edmund Dene (1873–1924). *King Leopold's Rule in Africa.* Illus. London: W. Heinemann, 1904. 466 pp.
Inscription: "S. L. Clemens, 1904."
Catalog: A1911, #339, $1.75.
On 16 October 1904 Morel wrote to Clemens to "thank you once again for the privilege and pleasure given me to-night, and . . . for the warm way in which you have taken up this question." He informed Clemens: "I send you by an express messenger a packet of Congo literature—all I have got left here. . . . When I get home, I will send you much other matter, including my book" (ALS in MTP). Mark Twain's King Leopold describes Morel as "a Congo reformer. That sizes *him* up. He publishes a sheet in Liverpool called 'The West African Mail' " ("King Leopold's Soliloquy" [1905]). On 8 January 1906 Clemens praised Morel's "splendid equipment of energy, brains, diligence, concentration, persistence" (SLC to Dr. Barbour, ALS in Berg Collection, New York Public Library, Astor, Lennox and Tilden Foundations). But Isabel Lyon recorded how Clemens, declaring that "Morel is a[n auto]mobile, I'm a wheel-barrow." sought on 10 January 1906 to extricate himself from the role of spokesman on Belgian Congo affairs (IVL Journals, TS p. 121, MTP).

————. *Red Rubber; The Story of the Rubber Slave Trade Flourishing on the Congo in the Year of Grace 1906.* Intro. by Sir Harry H. Johnston. Maps. London: T. F. Unwin, 1906. 213 pp.
Morel mentioned this book in a letter to Clemens written on 18 January 1907 (ALS in MTP).

Morgan, Emily Malbone (1862–1937). *A Poppy Garden*. Hartford: Belknap &
Warfield, 1892. 54 pp.
   Inscription: front free endpaper inscribed "Livy L. Clemens/from S. R. D./
December 25th/92". The handwriting is neither Livy's nor Clemens'.
   Catalog: Mott 1952, item #71, $6.
   Location: Mark Twain Memorial, Hartford, Conn. Donated anonymously in
1963.
   Copy examined: Livy Clemens' copy. Contains bookstamps of the Mark Twain
Library, Redding, Conn.

Morgan, Forrest (1852–1924).
   Mark Twain's "Stirring Times in Austria" (1898) quotes from the "intelligent
sketch" on Austrian affairs written by "Mr. Forrest Morgan, of Hartford."
Morgan's essay appeared in the *Traveler's Record*.

Morgan, Sallie B. *Tahoe; or, Life in California. A Romance*. Atlanta, Ga.: J. P.
Harrison & Co., 1881. 245 pp.
   Source: MTLAcc, entry #222, volume donated by Clemens.

Morgan, Sydney (Owenson), Lady (1783?–1859). *Lady Morgan's Memoirs: Auto-
biography, Diaries and Correspondence*. Copyright Edition. Collection of British
Authors Series. 3 vols. Leipzig: B. Tauchnitz, 1863.
   Catalog: C1951, #D1, $8 per vol., listed among books signed by Clemens.

Morier, James Justinian (1780?–1849). *The Adventures of Hajji Baba, of Ispahan*.
First edition. 3 vols. London: John Murray, 1824.
   Inscription: each vol. signed "S. L. Clemens."
   Catalog: A1911, #340, $14 total.

————. *The Adventures of Hajji Baba of Ispahan*. London, n.d.
   Inscription: verso of title page signed "S. L. Clemens."
   Catalog: A1911, #341, "16mo, boards, back torn off and covers detached,"
$1.25.
   Clemens dictated a notebook entry to a stenographer in June 1873: "Work
upon Persia by a representative of Great Britain at the court of Teheran. Title
something like *Ali Baba* in Arabian Nights" (NB 12, *N&J*, 2: 534). Nasr-Ed-Din,
the Shah of Persia, was coming to visit London; Mark Twain would write five
letters concerning this event for the New York *Herald* during July 1873. By
1881 Mark Twain still had not mastered Morier's name; casting about for
humorists to include in an anthology, Twain referred to " 'Hajji Something'—
written by Morton" (NB 19, *N&J*, 2: 428).

Morley, John Morley, Viscount (1838–1923). *Burke*. English Men of Letters Series.
New York: Harper & Brothers, [1879?]. 214 pp.
   Source: MTLAcc, entry #1281, volume donated by Clemens.

Morley, Margaret Warner (1858–1923). *Wasps and Their Ways*. New York: Dodd
Mead and Co., 1900. 316 pp.
   Inscription: front inside cover signed "Clemens/1902".
   Location: Carrie Estelle Doheny Collection, St. John's Seminary, Camarillo,
Ca. Purchased from Maxwell Hunley Rare Books of Beverly Hills in 1940.
   Copy examined: Clemens' copy, unmarked.
   Perhaps it was Morley's book that taught Clemens how wasps leave live spiders
as food for young wasps, a practice Clemens cites in "The Refuge of the Derelicts" (written 1905–1906) to illustrate the absurdity of believing in the benevolence of Nature (*FM*, p. 247). In "Little Bessie" (written 1908–1909), the title
character is appalled that "the wasps catch spiders and cram them down their
nests in the ground—*alive*, mamma!—and there they live and suffer days and
days and days" while young wasps devour them (*FM*, p. 36).

Morris, Clara (1849–1925). *A Pasteboard Crown: A Story of the New York Stage.* New York: Charles Scribner's Sons, 1902. 370 pp.

    Catalog: C1951, #35c, $10, listed among the books signed by Clemens, "given to Mark Twain by the author."

    "Clara Morris—at Wallack's," Clemens noted on 20 April 1902 (NB 45, TS p. 10). On that day the Clemenses "went into town (NYC) to hear Clara Morris lecture. . . . Mr. Clemens introduced her," Livy Clemens recorded in her diary (DV161, MTP).

————. *A Pasteboard Crown: A Story of the New York Stage.* New York: Charles Scribner's Sons, 1903. 370 pp.

    Source: MTLAcc, entry #224, volume donated by Clemens.

Morris, George Pope (1802–1864). "The Oak" (poem and song). Better known as "Woodman, Spare That Tree." Melody composed by Henry Russell (1812–1900).

    In 1881 Clemens claimed that he stopped Franklin Chamberlin from chopping trees on a lot adjoining Clemens' by calling out: "Woodman spare that tree,/ Forego, forego thy hacks,/ And list, oh list, to me,/ Lay down thy gory axe" *(S&MT,* p. 136).

Morris, Gouverneur (b. 1876). *Aladdin O'Brien.* New York: The Century Co., 1902. 298 pp.

    Inscription: signed "S. L. Clemens, Riverdale, Dec. 1902."

    Catalog: A1911, #342, $2.

    On 10 December 1902 Isabel Lyon wrote to Richard Watson Gilder at Clemens' behest, reporting that her employer "finds Gouverneur Morris's book 'a charming story and beautifully told' " (ALS in collection of Rosamond Gilder, PH in MTP).

Morris, William (1834–1896). *The Earthly Paradise, A Poem.* 4 vols. in 3. Boston: Roberts Brothers, 1871.

    Source: MTLAcc, entries #2068–2070, volumes donated from Clemens' library by Clara Clemens Gabrilowitsch in 1910.

————. *Pygmalion and the Image.* Illus. by Sir Edward Burne-Jones. New York: R. H. Russell, 1903. 35 pp.

    Location: Mark Twain Library, Redding, Conn. Donated by Clemens (MTLAcc, entry #1685).

    Copy examined: Clemens' copy, unmarked, mint condition.

————. *Pygmalion and the Image.* Illus. by Sir Edward Burne-Jones. New York: R. H. Russell, 1903. 35 pp.

    Location: Mark Twain Library, Redding, Conn. Donated from Clemens' library by Clara Clemens Gabrilowitsch in 1910 (MTLAcc, entry #2138).

    Copy examined: Clemens' copy, unmarked, waterstained and damaged.

————. "Shameful Death" (poem), collected in *The Defence of Guenevere, and Other Poems* (1858).

    Shortly after Clemens' death in 1910, William Dean Howells recalled that his friend "had favorite poems which he liked to read to you," and "remembered how he fiercely revelled in the vengefulness of William Morris's *Sir Guy of the Dolorous Blast,* and how he especially exulted in the lines which tell of the supposed speaker's joy in slaying the murderer of his brother: 'I am threescore years and ten,/ And my hair is nigh turned gray,/ But I am glad to think of the moment when/ I took his life away' " *(MMT,* p. 16).

    Howells refers to one of the villains in the poem, rather than its title. Sir Guy of the Dolorous Blast and Sir John the knight of the Fen ambushed and hanged the newly married Lord Hugh; the speaker, Lord Hugh's brother, tells of his revenge on the cowardly murderers: "I am threescore and ten,/And my hair is all turn'd grey,/But I met Sir John of the Fen/Long ago on a summer day,/And am glad to think of the moment when/I took his life away." In the next, penultimate stanza, the narrator adds: "I am threescore and ten,/And my strength is mostly pass'd,/But long ago I and my men/When the sky was overcast,/And the smoke roll'd over the reeds of the fen,/Slew Guy of the Dolorous Blast" (*A Choice of William Morris's Verse*, ed. Geoffrey Grigson [London: Faber and Faber, 1969], p. 64).

William Dean Howells, *Literary Friends and Acquaintances,* ed. David F. Hiatt and Edwin H. Cady (Bloomington: Indiana Univ. Press, 1968), pp. 265, 332.

————. *The Story of Sigurd the Volsung and the Fall of the Niblungs.* Boston: Roberts Brothers, 1877. 392 pp.

James R. Osgood & Company of Boston billed Clemens in November 1877 for a volume he purchased on 22 March 1877, "1 Sigurd &c $3.00 discounted to $2.40 plus postage" (receipt in Scrapbook #10, MTP). In 1945 Edgar H. Hemminghaus ("Mark Twain's German Provenience," p. 468) reported seeing this book in the Mark Twain Library at Redding, but Albert E. Stone, Jr. did not include it in his checklist in 1955 and I was unable to locate Clemens' copy when I visited Redding in 1970.

George Bernard Shaw "regretted" that Clemens "had not known Morris" (23 August 1907 AD, MTP).

Morrison, Arthur (1863–1945). *Martin Hewitt, Investigator.* Illus. New York: Harper & Brothers, 1907. 216 pp.

Source: MTLAcc, entry #226, volume donated by Clemens.

————. [Another identical copy.]

Source: MTLAcc, entry #1255, volume donated by Clemens.

Morrison, Daniel H., comp. *The Treasury of Song for the Home Circle: The Richest, Best-Loved Gems, Sacred and Secular.* Philadelphia: Hubbard Brothers, [cop. 1882]. 548 pp.

Inscription: (printed in brown ink on half-title page) "Susie O. Clemens/ Hartford, Conn./1883./Uncle Theodore."

Marginalia: on a front flyleaf Clemens penciled the lyrics to one of his favorite songs, a nonsensical version of a hymn by Andrew Young: "There is a happy land/Far far away,/Where they have ham & eggs,/Three times a day./ O how those boarders yell,/When they hear that dinner bell,/They *give* that landlord *rats*/Three times a day." Clemens' penciled notes throughout the volume supply the proper musical key for various songs. He drew pencil marks beside the titles of several songs, including Thomas Moore's "The Last Rose of Summer" (p. 61) and "Oft in the Stilly Night" (p. 541). Above the title of "Larboard Watch" (p. 22) Clemens wrote "There is a happy land." In the index at the rear of the book Clemens marked with pencil the titles of fifty-five songs that were evidently his favorites.

Catalog: "Retz Appraisal" (1944), p. 11, valued at $20.

Location: Mark Twain Papers, Berkeley, Ca.

Copy examined: Clemens' copy, worn from usage.

Morrison, George Ernest (1862–1920). *An Australian in China, Being the Narrative of a Quiet Journey Across China to British Burma.* London: H. Cox, 1895. 299 pp.

Mark Twain added a footnote to "The United States of Lyncherdom" (written in 1901) to substantiate the futility of Christian efforts toward converting the vast population of China: "These figures are not fanciful; all of them are genuine and authentic. . . . See Doctor Morrison's book on his pedestrian journey across China; he quotes them and gives his authorities. For several years he has been the London *Times's* representative in Peking."

Morrison, William McCutchan (1867–1918). "Report by W. M. Morrison, American Missionary in the Congo Free State." [Unidentified publication.]

King Leopold reads this report of atrocities "with evil joy" in "King Leopold's Soliloquy" (1905). The American Presbyterian Congo Mission published several books by Morrison.

Morse, Edward Sylvester (1838–1925). *Japanese Homes and Their Surroundings.* Illus. by the author. Boston: Ticknor and Co., 1886. 372 pp.
Catalog: A1911, #343, $4.

Morse, Harriet Clara. *A Cowboy Cavalier.* Illus. by Samuel F. B. Morse. Boston: C. M. Clark Publishing Co., 1908. 294 pp.
Source: MTLAcc, entry #1056, volume donated by Clemens.

Morse, Livingston Burrill. *The Road to Nowhere. A Story for Children.* Illus. by Edna Morse. New York: Harper & Brothers, 1906. 236 pp.
Source: MTLAcc, entry #420, volume donated by Clemens.

Mortimer, James (1833–1911). *The White Fawn; or, the Loves of Prince Buttercup and the Princess Daisy* (extravaganza, perf. 1868).

In a letter written on 1 February 1868, Mark Twain advised his readers: "I have been to New York . . . and on the 21st of January I went with some newspaper men to see the new spectacle at Niblo's [Garden], the 'White Fawn,' the splendid successor of the splendid 'Black Crook.' Everybody agrees that it is much more magnificent than the Crook. . . . I think these hundreds of princely costumes are changed every fifteen minutes during half the night. . . America has not seen anything before that can equal the 'White Fawn.' " But Mark Twain goes on to denounce the "appalling" influence these extravaganzas have wrought on young minds, breeding "a species of infamous pictorial literature" (3 March 1868 *Alta California).*

Mortimer, William Golden. *Peru: History of Coca, "the Divine Plant" of the Incas; with an Introductory Account of the Incas, and of the Andean Indians of To-Day.* New York: J. H. Vail & Co., 1901. 576 pp.
Source: MTLAcc, entry #604, volume donated by Clemens.

"I beg to fulfill a deferred privilege, that of presenting to you a copy of my book—Peru: History of Coca—a story of those children of the sun, phenomenal socialists of long ago who enjoyed life and chewed Coca until routed from their dreams by the Spanish [mur?]ders. . . . [I] do not recall that you have ever written of the Incas nor of that marvelous plant which they termed 'divine,' each of which affords an endless fund for solace and romance. Will you be good enough to accept this book from an admirer" (William Golden Mortimer to SLC, New York, 6 December 1905, ALS in MTP). It hardly seems coincidental that Clemens mentioned the coca plant in his AD of 29 March 1906 (MTP).

Morton, John Maddison (1811–1891). *Box and Cox* (farce, 1847).

In a letter written to a London neighbor on 19 January 1897, Clemens complained about the piano-playing of the man's daughter: "I am sure I do not know what to do. <It is Box & Cox in a new form>" (SLC to J. Woulfe Harragan, ALS in MTP). August Feldner explains in chapter 24 of "No. 44, The Mysterious Stranger," written between 1902 and 1908: "All our lives we have been what 44 called Box and Cox lodgers in the one chamber . . . never encountering each other save for a dim and hazy and sleepy half-moment on the threshold" *(MSM,* p. 343).

Mother Goose. *Mother Goose; or, the Old Nursery Rhymes.* Illus. by Kate Green-away (1846–1901). New York: G. Routledge and Sons, [1881?]. 48 pp.
 Inscription: in pencil, "Clara Clemens/Hartford, Conn. 1881. Mama."
 Provenance: Mark Twain Library, Redding, Conn. Donated from Clemens' library by Clara Clemens Gabrilowitsch in 1910 (MTLAcc, entry #1884).
 Catalog: Mott 1952, #58, $7.50.

———. [Another identical copy.]
 Source: MTLAcc, entry #1885, volume donated from Clemens' library by Clara Clemens Gabrilowitsch in 1910.

Motley, John Lothrop (1814–1877). *The Correspondence of John Lothrop Motley.* Ed. by George William Curtis (1824–1892). 2 vols. New York: Harper & Brothers, 1889.
 Catalog: A1911, #344, $7.50.

———. *The Correspondence of John Lothrop Motley.* Ed. by George William Curtis. 2 vols. New York: Harper & Brothers, [cop. 1889].
 Source: MTLAcc, entries #1773 and #1774, volumes donated by Clemens.

———. *History of the United Netherlands from the Death of William the Silent to the Twelve Years' Truce—1609.* 4 vols. New York: Harper & Brothers, 1860–1868. Repr. frequently.
 Catalog: C1951, #J21, 2 vols., listed among books belonging to Jean and Clara Clemens, edition unspecified.

———. *Motley's Dutch Nation, Being the Rise of the Dutch Republic (1555–1584) . . . Condensed, with Introduction, Notes, and a Brief History of the Dutch People to 1908, by William Elliot Griffis.* New Edition. Illus. New York: Harper & Brothers, 1908. 960 pp. [Originally pub. 1856.]
 Catalog: A1911, #345.
 Clemens knew that Motley was in London when Clemens visited England in 1873 (SLC to "Dear Sir," 31 July 1873, ALS in Massachusetts Historical Society). On 17 May 1877 Clemens "had a lantern hung at my head & read self to sleep with Motley's Netherlands" while aboard the S. S. *Bermuda.* The next evening, however, he "said to myself presently, 'Come it's a recreation trip—*why* should I torture myself to store up knowledge about people dead 300 yrs ago?" (Notebook 13, *N&J,* 2: 16–17). On 6 August 1877 Clemens remarked to Mollie Fairbanks, in a letter inveighing against "all shades & forms of republican government," that "I read as much of Motley's Dutch Republic as I could stand, on my way to Bermuda, & would have thrown the book into the sea if I had owned it, it did make me so cordially despise those pitiful Dutchmen & their execrable Republic" (*MTMF,* p. 208). In July 1879 Clemens visited the place near the Hague where Motley had stayed for a time (NB 18, *N&J,* 2: 331); "good portraits of him there," Clemens noted. Later in 1879 Clemens expressed the opinion that Americans need not accede to English notions of superiority in prose: "nobody writes a finer & purer English than Motley, Howells, Hawthorne & Holmes" (NB 18, *N&J,* 2: 348).

Mott, Edward Harold (1845–1920). "The Old Settler" (sketch, pub. in New York *Sun).*
 This piece appeared in *Mark Twain's Library of Humor* (1888). The next year Mott published *The Old Settler and His Tales of the Sugar Swamp* (Chicago: Belford, Clarke & Co., 1889).

Mott, Lawrence (1881–1931). *To the Credit of the Sea.* Illus. New York: Harper & Brothers, 1907. 296 pp.
    Inscription: signed "S. L. Clemens, 1909."
    Catalog: A1911, #346, $1.50.

————. An identical copy.]
    Source: MTLAcc, entry #227, volume donated by Clemens.

Mottelay, Paul Fleury and Thomas Campbell-Copeland, eds. *The Soldier in Our Civil War: A Pictorial History of the Conflict, 1861–65. . . . Illustrated from Sketches Drawn by Forbes, Waud, Taylor, Hillen, Becker, Louie, Schell, Crane, and Other Eye-Witnesses.* Intro. by Robert B. Beath. 2 vols. Hartford, 1886.
    Catalog: A1911, #82, $2.75.

Moulton, Louise (Chandler) (1835–1908). *In the Garden of Dreams: Lyrics and Sonnets.* Boston: Roberts Brothers, 1890. 170 pp.
    Catalog: C1951, #018, listed among books containing Livy Clemens' signature.

————. *Some Women's Hearts.* Boston: Roberts Brothers, 1874. 364 pp.
    Source: MTLAcc, entry #213, volume donated by Clemens.

Mozart, Johann Chrysostom Wolfgang Amadeus (1756–1791). *Le Nozze de Figaro (The Marriage of Figaro)* (opera, 1786). Libretto by Lorenzo Da Ponte.
    In Rome in April 1892 Clemens noted: "Monday eve, Marriage of Figaro" (NB 31, TS p. 37).

Muhlenberg, William Augustus (1796–1877). "I would not live alway" (song, pub. 1860). Melody composed by George Kingsley.
    Mark Twain remembered this song of "love and sentiment" as one likely to be on music stands in parlors in Honolulu in the 1860's *(FE* [1897], ch. 3).

Mukerji, Satya Chandra. [Unidentified guidebook.]
    In chapter 59 of *FE* (1897) Mark Twain quotes a description of the Taj Mahal from "the excellent little guide-book of Mr. Satya Chandra Mukerji."

Mulford, Prentice (1834–1891).
    On 7 August 1877 Clemens mentioned that "I never hear of Prentice Mulford now-a-days" (SLC to Millet, Elmira, ALS at Harvard). Clemens included Mulford in a list of humorists he compiled in July 1880 for a projected anthology (NB 19, *N&J,* 2: 366). He mentioned Mulford again on 17 January 1903 (NB 46, TS p. 7). On page 138 of the second volume of Moncure Conway's *Auto-biography* (1904) Clemens wrote, probably in October 1905 when he signed the front pastedown endpaper: "(imitator of Harte's condensed novels—perished in a canoe. *(Now* I recal his name—Prentice Mulford."

Müller, Friedrich Max (1823–1900). *India: What Can It Teach Us?* New York, London, 1883.
    Catalog: C1951, #32c, listed among books signed by Clemens, no edition specified.
    In January 1879 Clemens alluded to Müller as an eminent philologist (NB 17, *N&J,* 2: 266).

Munchausen. *The Adventures of Baron Munchausen. A New and Revised Edition.* Intro. by T. Teignmouth Shore. Illus. by Gustave Doré. London: Cassell, n.d. 216 pp.
    Inscription: "To/Jean L. Clemens./With the love of her sister,/Susy Clemens./Elmira, N. Y. /July 26/'89."

Catalog: C1951, #92c, listed (erroneously) among books signed by Clemens, $17.50; *Fleming 1972*.

Source: Frederick Anderson, then Editor of the Mark Twain Papers at Berkeley, inspected this volume in 1972 at the New York City office of John Fleming, Inc. I am grateful to Mr. Anderson for the information supplied in this entry.

References: Baron de Munchausen, "the world-famed liar" (6 February 1866 letter, Virginia City *Territorial Enterprise; MTCor*, p. 44); "flights of fancy lying that make the inventions of Munchausen seem poor and trifling" (27 October 1866 Sacramento *Weekly Union; LSI*, p. 202); "Ananias Twain, alias Baron Munchausen" ("Mark Twain's Burlesque Autobiography" [1871]); "complete and unquestioning belief in Munchausens, and in all other conceivable extravagances" (August? 1907 AD, *MTE*, p. 341).

Mundt, Klara (Müller) (1814–1873), pseud. "Louise Mühlbach." *Henry VIII. and His Court; or, Catharine Parr. An Historical Novel.* New York: D. Appleton and Co., 1899. 418 pp.
   Location: Antenne-Dorrance Collection, Rice Lake, Wis.
   Copy examined: Clemens' copy, unmarked.

Mungen, William (1821–1887). "To an Absent One" (poem, pub. 1868).
   Mungen was a Congressman from Ohio. When he published this poem in the Washington *National Intelligencer,* Clemens ridiculed it as "bosh" and "Mungenical poetry" *(Washington in 1868,* ed. Cyril Clemens [Webster Groves, Mo.: International Mark Twain Society, 1943], pp. 11–14).

Munich. *Münchener Tages-Anzeiger* (newspaper).
   Clemens "counted the reading-matter" in the issue of 25 January 1879 (less than that in United States newspapers, he found), and logged it in Notebook 17 *(N&J,* 2: 262–263). He analyzed the same issue in "Appendix F" of *TA* (1880).

Munich. Pinakothek, Alte. *Catalogue of the Paintings in the Old Pinakothek, Munich.* Intro. by Franz von Reber. Trans. by Joseph Thacher Clarke. "Unabridged Official Edition." Illus. Munich: Verlagsanstalt für Kunst und Wissenschaft, n.d. 303 pp.
   In chapter 16 of *TA* (1880), Mark Twain declares: "Even Garnham has a rival [as a translator]. Mr. X. had a small pamphlet with him which he had bought while on a visit to Munich. It was entitled 'A Catalogue of Pictures in the Old Pinacotek,' and was written in a peculiar kind of English." Mark Twain quotes nearly two pages of these clumsy attempts at producing idiomatic English prose.

Munkittrick, Richard Kendall (1853–1911). *The Moon Prince, and Other Nabobs.* Illus. New York: Harper & Brothers, 1893. 340 pp.
   Source: MTLAcc, entry #1187, volume donated by Clemens.

Munn, Charles Allen (1859–1924). *Three Types of Washington Portraits: John Trumbull, Charles Wilson Peale, Gilbert Stuart.* New York: Privately printed, 1908. 66 pp.
   Inscription: " 'Mark Twain'/with the compliments of/Charles A. Munn."
   Location: Mark Twain Library, Redding, Conn.
   Copy examined: Clemens' copy, unmarked.

Munro, Bruce Weston (1860–1900?). *Groans and Grins of One Who Survived.* [*Short Stories and Poems*]. Toronto, Canada: Warwick & Sons, 1889. 385 pp.
   Source: MTLAcc, entry #361, volume donated by Clemens.

Munro, Neil (1864–1930). *Bud; A Novel.* New York: Harper & Brothers, 1907. 315 pp.
   Source: MTLAcc, entry #1345, volume donated by Clemens.

————. *Bud; A Novel.* New York: Harper & Brothers, 1908. 315 pp.
   Source: MTLAcc, entry #1057, volume donated by Clemens.

Munroe, George H.
   Clemens included "Templeton," the pseudonym under which Munroe wrote weekly letters from Boston for the Hartford *Courant,* among those designated to receive complimentary copies of *P&P* (NB 19 [1881], *N&J,* 2: 386).

Munroe, Kirk (1850–1930). *The Blue Dragon, A Tale of Recent Adventure in China.* Illus. New York: Harper & Brothers, 1905. 268 pp.
   Source: MTLAcc, entry #1608, volume donated by Clemens.

————. *Campmates; A Story of the Plains.* Illus. New York: Harper & Brothers, [cop. 1891]. 333 pp.
   Source: MTLAcc, entry #1176, volume donated by Clemens.

————. *Chrystal, Jack, & Co., and Delta Bixby; Two Stories.* Illus. New York: Harper & Brothers, [cop. 1888]. 221 pp.
   Source: MTLAcc, entry #1170, volume donated by Clemens.

————. *Derrick Sterling; A Story of the Mines.* New York: Harper & Brothers, [cop. 1888]. 256 pp.
   Source: MTLAcc, entry #410, volume donated by Clemens.

————. *The Flamingo Feather.* Illus. New York: Harper & Brothers, [cop. 1887]. 255 pp.
   Source: MTLAcc, entry #467, volume donated by Clemens. Reported as "missing" shortly thereafter.

————. *For the Mikado; or, A Japanese Middy in Action.* Illus. New York: Harper & Brothers, 1905. 270 pp.
   Source: MTLAcc, entry #1609, volume donated by Clemens.

————. *The Painted Desert; A Story of Northern Arizona.* Illus. New York: Harper & Brothers, [cop. 1897]. 274 pp.
   Source: MTLAcc, entry #1199, volume donated by Clemens.

————. *Snow-Shoes and Sledges.* Illus. New York: Harper & Brothers, [cop. 1895]. 271 pp.
   Source: MTLAcc, entry #1610, volume donated by Clemens.

————. *Wakulla; A Story of Adventure in Florida.* Illus. New York: Harper & Brothers, [cop. 1885]. 255 pp.
   Source: MTLAcc, entry #444, volume donated by Clemens.

Munsey's Magazine (New York periodical, pub. 1889–1929).
   Walter Besant praised Mark Twain and *Huckleberry Finn* in the February 1898 issue (p. 660). Clemens wrote to Besant on 22 February 1898 from Vienna: "I have just read it in Munsey for February" (ALS in Berg Collection, New York Public Library).

Murai, Gensai (1863–1927). *Hana, A Daughter of Japan.* Illus. Tokyo: The Hochi Shimbun, 1904. 298 pp.
   Catalog: C1951, #94c, $15, listed among the books signed by Clemens.

Murfree, Fanny Noailles Dickinson. *Felicia; A Novel.* Boston: Houghton, Mifflin and Co., The Riverside Press, 1891. 358 pp. [Serialized in the *Atlantic Monthly* in 1890–1891.]

Mark Twain's "Weather" appendix to *AC* (1892) quotes two sentences about a snowfall from Murfree's *Felicia.*

Murfree, Mary Noailles (1850–1922), pseud. "Charles Egbert Craddock." *Down the Ravine.* [*A Story.*] Boston: Houghton, Mifflin and Co., 1885. 196 pp.

Source: MTLAcc, entry #2203, volume donated from Clemens' library by Clara Clemens Gabrilowitsch in 1910.

————. *In the "Stranger People's Country: A Novel.* Illus. New York: Harper & Brothers, 1891. 360 pp.

Mark Twain quotes a purple passage from this local-color novel (citing Murfree's pseudonym) in the "Weather" appendix to *AC* (1892).

————. *In the Tennessee Mountains.* Boston: Houghton, Mifflin and Co., 1884. 322 pp. [These stories first appeared in the *Atlantic Monthly.*]

In 1884 Clemens noted "Tennessee Mountain Tales, by Craddock. (Houghton.)" (NB 22, TS p. 36).

————. *The Prophet of the Great Smoky Mountains.* Boston: Houghton, Mifflin and Co., 1885. 308 pp.

On 1 July 1885 Livy Clemens recorded in her journal a visit to Quarry Farm by Ella Corey and Grace Collin: "Ella read to us from the July Atlantic the last installment of Charles Egbert Craddock's 'Prophet of The Great Smoky.' It was wonderfully fine—I think perhaps the strongest [and] best number that we have yet read although it is all strong and fine" (OLC Diary, DV161, MTP). Livy surely knew the actual name of "Charles Egbert Craddock"; on 5 June 1885 Clemens had written to William Dean Howells from Hartford to ask the Howellses to visit them on 10 June: "Miss Murfree & her sister are coming that day to stay 24 hours" (*MTHL*, p. 531).

Murphy, John Mortimer. *Sporting Adventures in the Far West.* Illus. New York: Harper & Brothers, 1880. 469 pp.

Source: MTLAcc, entry #1612, volume donated by Clemens.

Murray, (Sir) Charles Augustus (1806–1895). *Travels in North America During the Years 1834, 1835 & 1836, Including a Summer Residence with the Pawnee Tribe of Indians, in the Remote Prairies of the Missouri, and a Visit to Cuba and the Azore Islands.* 2 vols. London: R. Bentley, 1839.

Marginalia: penciled notes, marks, and underscorings in vol. 2.

Catalog: A1911, #350, vol. 2 only, $2.25.

Mark Twain quotes this "unimaginative Scotchman" in chapter 22 of *LonMiss* (1883).

Ganzel, "Twain, Travel Books," p. 41 n. 4.

Murray, David Christie (1847–1907). *The Martyred Fool; A Novel.* New York: Harper & Brothers, 1895. 265 pp.

Source: MTLAcc, entry #1636, volume donated by Clemens.

Murray, Eustace Clare Grenville (1824–1881), pseud. "Trois-Étoiles." *The Member for Paris: A Tale of the Second Empire.* Boston: James R. Osgood and Co., 1871. 206 pp.

On 9 January 1872 Clemens wrote to Livy from Steubenville, Ohio: "I am reading 'The Member from Paris' [*sic*] a very bright, sharp, able French political novel, very happily translated. It is all so good & Frenchy that I don't know where to mark!" (ALS in MTP).

————. *Strange Tales.* Collection of British Authors Series. Leipzig: B. Tauchnitz, 1878. 272 pp.
>   *Catalog: C1951,* #D1, Tauchnitz Edition specified, listed among books signed by Clemens, $8.

————. *That Artful Vicar.* Collection of British Authors Series. 2 vols. Leipzig: B. Tauchnitz, 1879. Paperbound.
>   *Source:* MTLAcc, entry #229, volume 2 only (288 pp.), donated by Clemens.

Murray, John, publisher in London. *Handbook for North Germany, from the Baltic to the Black Forest, and the Rhine, from Holland to Basle.* Nineteenth edition. Maps. London: John Murray, 1877. 448 pp.
>   Clemens seems to be referring to page 422 of this guidebook in comments he made in July 1878 (NB 15, *N&J,* 2: 118).

————. *A Handbook for Travellers in Spain.* Fourth edition. London: John Murray, 1869.
>   Clemens may have used this guidebook on his visit to Gibraltar (cf. NB 8).

————. *A Handbook for Travellers in Switzerland, and the Alps of Savoy and Piedmont.* Fourteenth edition. London: John Murray, 1871. 557 pp.
>   Clemens may have used this guidebook in the Swiss Alps, though he remarks that Baedeker "has run Murray out of Europe" (NB 16, *N&J,* 2: 193).

————. *A Handbook for Travellers in Syria and Palestine.* Ed. by Josias Leslie Porter. 2 vols. London: John Murray, 1858. [New and Revised Edition, 1868.]
>   Clemens' entries in Notebook 9 (1867) suggest his familiarity with the first edition of this work. As a matter of fact, Clemens probably consulted Murray's *Handbooks* regarding most of the countries through which the *Quaker City* pilgrims traveled.

Murray, John O'Kane (1847–1885). *Little Lives of the Great Saints.* Illus. New York: P. J. Kenedy, 1889. 513 pp.
>   *Inscription:* signed "Clemens."
>   *Catalog: A1911,* #51, $1.

Murray, Ross, comp. *The Modern Householder: A Manual of Domestic Economy in All Its Branches.* Illus. London: F. Warne and Co.; New York: Scribner, Welford, and Armstrong, [1872]. 722 pp.
>   A bill listing twenty-one books from Estes & Lauriat of Boston (14 July 1880) begins with a copy of "Mod Householder" for $1.25; Clemens paid the bill on 20 July 1880 (receipt in MTP).

Murray, T. Douglas (1841–1911), ed. *Jeanne d'Arc, Maid of Orleans, Deliverer of France; Being the Story of Her Life, Her Achievements, and Her Death, as Attested on Oath and Set Forth in Original Documents.* Illus., Map. London: W. Heinemann, 1902. 396 pp.
>   *Inscription:* flyleaf signed "S. L. Clemens, September, 1902." Publisher's presentation slip pasted on front endpaper. Bookplate of W. H. Arnold.
>   *Catalog: A1911,* #352, "frontispiece loose," $6.50; Anderson Auction Catalogue No. 3911 (1931), item #111.
>   In September 1899 Mark Twain read the book in manuscript after he consented to write an introduction (*MTHHR,* pp. 409–411). Although this arrangement fell through, Heinemann the publisher nevertheless sent Mark Twain a complimentary copy of Murray's book in advance of its issuance, requesting that no public reference be made before 10 September 1902 (Heinemann's note is summarized in *A1911).*

Musset, Paul Edme de (1804–1880). *Mr. Wind and Madame Rain.* Trans. by Emily Makepeace. Illus. by Charles Bennett. New York: Harper & Brothers, n.d. 126 pp.
    Source: MTLAcc, entry #1911, volume donated from Clemens' library by Clara Clemens Gabrilowitsch in 1910.

Myers, Cortland (1864–1941). *Would Christ Belong to a Labor Union? or, Henry Fielding's Dream.* New York: Street & Street, [cop. 1900]. 216 pp.
    Source: MTLAcc, entry #1058, volume donated by Albert Bigelow Paine, Clemens' designated biographer. Possibly Clemens saw this book, since the men exchanged reading materials.

Myers, Frederic William Henry (1843–1901). *Human Personality and Its Survival of Bodily Death.* [Ed. by Richard Hodgson and Alice Johnson after Myers' death.] 2 vols. London: Longmans, Green, and Co., 1903.
    In 1907 Mark Twain identified Myers as "the late president of the British Psychical Society" and referred to "Mrs. Myers (widow of the author of *Human Personality and Its Survival of Bodily Death)"* (August? 1907 AD, *MTE*, pp. 339, 342).

————. *Wordsworth.* English Men of Letters Series. New York: Harper & Brothers, 1899. 182 pp.
    Source: MTLAcc, entry #1284, volume donated by Clemens.

Myers, Louisa Palmier. *An Idyl of the Rhine.* Illus. New York: F. T. Neely Co., [1901]. 41 pp.
    Inscription: (on title page) "To Mark Twain with regards of F. T. Neely, Sept. 25." Signed "S. L. Clemens, Riverdale, Nov., '01."
    Catalog: A1911, #356, $1.50.